Joan C. Chrisler · Donald R. McCreary
Editors

Handbook of Gender Research in Psychology

Volume 2: Gender Research in Social and Applied Psychology

Editors
Joan C. Chrisler
Department of Psychology
Connecticut College
270 Mohegan Avenue
New London CT 06320
USA
jcchr@conncoll.edu

Donald R. McCreary
Department of Psychology
Brock University
St. Catharines ON Canada York University
Toronto ON
Canada
mccreary@yorku.ca

ISBN 978-1-4419-1466-8   e-ISBN 978-1-4419-1467-5
DOI 10.1007/978-1-4419-1467-5
Springer New York Dordrecht Heidelberg London

Library of Congress Control Number: 2009941984

© Springer Science+Business Media, LLC 2010
Chapter 28 is published under Crown right: © Angela R. Febbraro & Ritu M. Gill, Defence R&D Canada

All rights reserved. This work may not be translated or copied in whole or in part without the written permission of the publisher (Springer Science+Business Media, LLC, 233 Spring Street, New York, NY 10013, USA), except for brief excerpts in connection with reviews or scholarly analysis. Use in connection with any form of information storage and retrieval, electronic adaptation, computer software, or by similar or dissimilar methodology now known or hereafter developed is forbidden.
The use in this publication of trade names, trademarks, service marks, and similar terms, even if they are not identified as such, is not to be taken as an expression of opinion as to whether or not they are subject to proprietary rights.

Printed on acid-free paper

Springer is part of Springer Science+Business Media (www.springer.com)

Contents

1 **Introduction** 1
   Donald R. McCreary and Joan C. Chrisler

Part VIII   Personality Psychology

2 **Gender and Personality** 19
   Jayne E. Stake and Heather Eisele

3 **Gender and Motivation for Achievement, Affiliation–Intimacy, and Power** 41
   Lauren E. Duncan and Bill E. Peterson

4 **Gender Issues in Psychological Testing of Personality
   and Abilities** 63
   Nancy Lynn Baker and Janelle L. Mason

Part IX   Abnormal and Clinical Psychology

5 **Gender Stereotypes in Diagnostic Criteria** 91
   Alisha Ali, Paula J. Caplan, and Rachel Fagnant

6 **Gender Identity Disorder: Concerns and Controversies** 111
   Kate Richmond, Kate Carroll, and Kristoffer Denboske

7 **Gender, Sexual Orientation, and Vulnerability to Depression** 133
   Mark L. Hatzenbuehler, Lori M. Hilt, and Susan Nolen-Hoeksema

8 **Gender and Body Image** 153
   Rachel M. Calogero and J. Kevin Thompson

Part X   Psychotherapy

9 **Feminist Psychotherapies: Theory, Research, and Practice** 187
   Cynthia M. Bruns and Ellyn Kaschak

10 **Psychotherapy with Men** 221
    Matt Englar-Carlson, Mark A. Stevens, and Robert Scholz

11 **Gender Issues in Family Therapy and Couples Counseling** 253
    Louise B. Silverstein and Gary R. Brooks

v

Part XI   Social Psychology

12 **Gender, Peer Relations, and Intimate Romantic Relationships** 281
    Tara C. Marshall

13 **Gender, Aggression, and Prosocial Behavior** 311
    Irene Hanson Frieze and Man Yu Li

14 **Gender and Group Behavior** 337
    Linda L. Carli

15 **Sexual and Gender Prejudice** 359
    Ritch C. Savin-Williams, Seth T. Pardo, Zhana Vrangalova, Ryan S. Mitchell, and Kenneth M. Cohen

Part XII   Industrial-Organizational Psychology

16 **Gender and Occupational Choice** 379
    Helen M.G. Watt

17 **Gender and the Division of Labor** 401
    Scott Coltrane and Kristy Y. Shih

18 **The Gendered Nature of Workplace Mistreatment** 423
    Vicki J. Magley, Jessica A. Gallus, and Jennifer A. Bunk

19 **Gender and Leadership: Negotiating the Labyrinth** 443
    Ronit Kark and Alice H. Eagly

Part XIII   Health Psychology

20 **Gender, Health, and Health Behaviors** 471
    Christina Lee

21 **Gender, Stress, and Coping** 495
    Amy Zwicker and Anita DeLongis

22 **Gender and Health-Care Utilization** 517
    Cheryl Brown Travis, Andrea L. Meltzer, and Dawn M. Howerton

23 **Gender Issues in the Diagnosis and Treatment of Chronic Illness** 541
    Vivian S. Hwang and Sharon Danoff-Burg

Part XIV   Special Topics in Applied Psychology

24 **Gender in Sport and Exercise Psychology** 563
    Diane L. Gill and Cindra S. Kamphoff

25 **Ethical and Methodological Considerations for Gender Researchers in Forensic Psychology** 587
    Kenneth V. Heard

26 **The Treatment of Gender in Community Psychology Research** 613
    Sharon M. Wasco and Meg A. Bond

Mängelexemplar

Handbook of Gender Research in Psychology

27	**Gender and Media: Content, Uses, and Impact**	643
	Dara N. Greenwood and Julia R. Lippman	
28	**Gender and Military Psychology**	671
	Angela R. Febbraro and Ritu M. Gill	
Author Index		697
Subject Index		777

Contributors

Alisha Ali New York University, New York, NY, USA

Nancy Lynn Baker Fielding Graduate University, Santa Barbara, CA, USA

Susan A. Basow Lafayette College, Easton, PA, USA

Uli Boehmer Boston University, Boston, MA, USA

Meg A. Bond University of Massachusetts Lowell, University Avenue Lowell, MA, USA

Deborah J. Bowen Boston University, Boston, MA, USA

Leslie R. Brody Boston University, Boston, MA, USA

Gary R. Brooks Baylor University, Waco, TX, USA

Jeanne Brooks-Gunn Columbia University, New York, NY, USA

Cynthia M. Bruns Central Washington University, Ellensburg, WA, USA

Jennifer A. Bunk West Chester University, West Chester, PA, USA

Rachel M. Calogero University of Kent, Kent, UK

Paula J. Caplan Harvard University, Cambridge, MA, USA

Linda L. Carli Wellesley College, Wellesley, MA, USA

Kate Carroll Big Brothers Big Sisters, Southeastern PA, USA

Joan C. Chrisler Connecticut College, New London, CT, USA

Katherine H. Clemans University of Florida, Gainesville, FL, USA

Sam V. Cochran University of Iowa, Iowa City, IA, USA

Kenneth M. Cohen Cornell University, Ithaca, NY, USA

Scott Coltrane University of Oregon, Eugene, OR, USA

Bonnie Cramond University of Georgia, Athens, GA, USA

Sharon Danoff-Burg University at Albany, State University of New York, Albany, NY, USA

Anita DeLongis University of British Columbia, BC, Canada

Kristoffer Denboske John Jay College of Criminal Justice, New York, NY, USA

Laura M. DeRose Adelphi University, Garden City, NY, USA

Lauren E. Duncan Smith College, Northampton, MA, USA

Alice H. Eagly Northwestern University, Chicago, IL, USA

Crystal Ehresman University of Lethbridge, Lethbridge, AB, Canada

Heather Eisele University of Missouri, St. Louis, MO, USA

Matt Englar-Carlson California State University, Fullerton, CA, USA

Marina Epstein University of Michigan, Ann Arbor, MI, USA

Rachel Fagnant Metropolitan Council on Jewish Poverty, New York City, NY, USA

Angela R. Febbraro Defence R&D Canada, Toronto, ON, Canada

Gordon B. Forbes Millikin University, Decatur, IL, USA

Irene Hanson Frieze University of Pittsburgh, Pittsburgh, PA, USA

Jessica A. Gallus University of Connecticut, Storrs-Mansfield, CT, USA

Mary M. Gergen Pennsylvania State University, Media, PA, USA

Diane L. Gill University of North Carolina, Greensboro, NC, USA

Ritu M. Gill Defence R&D Canada, Toronto, ON, Canada

Julia A. Graber University of Florida, Gainesville, FL, USA

Leeat Granek Princess Margaret Hospital and Sunnybrook Odette Cancer Centre, Toronto, ON, Canada

Karen Greenspan John F. Kennedy University, Pleasant Hill, CA, USA

Dara N. Greenwood University of Michigan, Ann Arbor, MI, USA

Chanita Hughes Halbert University of Pennsylvania, Philadelphia, PA, USA

May Ling Halim New York University, New York, NY, USA

Judith A. Hall Northeastern University, Boston, MA, USA

Jennifer Hambaugh Indiana University of Pennsylvania, Indiana, PA, USA

Kristin A. Hancock John F. Kennedy University, Pleasant Hill, CA, USA

Mark L. Hatzenbuehler Yale University, New Haven, CT, USA

Kenneth V. Heard University of Rhode Island, Kingston, RI, USA

Peter Hegarty University of Surrey, Guildford, England, UK

C. Peter Herman University of Toronto, Toronto, ON, Canada

Lori M. Hilt Yale University, New Haven, CT, USA

Dawn M. Howerton University of Tennessee, Knoxville, TN, USA

Vivian S. Hwang University at Albany, State University of New York, Albany, NY, USA

Janet Shibley Hyde University of Wisconsin, Madison, WI, USA

Ingrid Johnston-Robledo State University of New York, Fredonia, NY, USA

Cindra S. Kamphoff Minnesota State University, Mankato, MN, USA

Ronit Kark Bar-Ilan University, Ramat Gan, Israel

Ellyn Kaschak Department of Psychology, San Jose State University, San Jose, CA, USA

Carol A. Lawton Indiana University-Purdue University, Fort Wayne, IN, USA

Christina Lee University of Queensland, Brisbane, QLD, Australia

Man Yu Li Chinese University, Hong Kong, China

Julia R. Lippman University of Michigan, Ann Arbor, MI, USA

Vicki J. Magley University of Connecticut, Storrs-Mansfield, CT, USA

Tara C. Marshall Brunel University, Kingston Ln, Uxbridge, UK

Janelle L. Mason Fielding Graduate University, Santa Barbara, CA, USA

Marianne Schmid Mast University of Neuchatel, Neuchâtel, Switzerland

Donald R. McCreary Brock University, St. Catharines, ON, Canada; York University, Toronto, ON, Canada

Maureen C. McHugh Indiana University of Pennsylvania, Indiana, PA, USA

Andrea L. Meltzer University of Tennessee, Knoxville, TN, USA

Ryan S. Mitchell Cornell University, Ithaca, New York, USA

Sarah K. Murnen Kenyon College, Gambier, OH, USA

Nora S. Newcombe Temple University, Philadelphia, PA, USA

Nicky J. Newton University of Michigan, Ann Arbor, MI, USA

Susan Nolen-Hoeksema Department of Psychology, Yale University, New Haven, CT, USA

Alexander R. Pagnani University of Georgia, Athens, GA, USA

Seth T. Pardo Cornell University, Ithaca, New York, USA

Jennifer Petersen University of Wisconsin, Madison, WI, USA

Bill E. Peterson Smith College, Northampton, MA, USA

Janet Polivy University of Toronto, Toronto, ON, Canada

Felicia Pratto University of Connecticut, Storrs, CT, USA

Heather A. Priess University of Wisconsin, Madison, WI, USA

Kate Richmond Muhlenberg College, Allentown, PA, USA

Alecia Robinson Boston University, Boston, MA, USA

Diane Ruble New York University, New York, NY, USA

Mark A. Runco University of Georgia, Athens, GA, USA

Alexandra Rutherford York University, Toronto, ON, Canada

Deborah Saucier University of Lethbridge, Lethbridge, AB, Canada

Ritch C. Savin-Williams Cornell University, Ithaca, New York, USA

Robert Scholz Pepperdine University, Malibu, CA, USA

Joseph A. Schroeder Connecticut College, New London, CT, USA

Sabine Sczesny University of Bern, Bern, Switzerland

Kristy Y. Shih Department of Sociology, University of California, Riverside, CA, USA

Louise B. Silverstein Yeshiva University, Brooklyn, NY, USA

Andrew P. Smiler Wake Forest University, Winston-Salem, NC, USA

Christine A. Smith University of Wisconsin, Green Bay, WI, USA

Linda Smolak Kenyon College, Gambier, OH, USA

Jayne E. Stake University of Missouri-St. Louis, St. Louis, MO, USA

Mark A. Stevens California State University, Northridge, CA, USA

Abigail J. Stewart University of Michigan, Ann Arbor, MI, USA

J. Kevin Thompson Department of Psychology, University of South Florida, Tampa, FL, USA

Cheryl Brown Travis University of Tennessee, Knoxville, TN, USA

Zhana Vrangalova Cornell University, Ithaca, New York, USA

Sharon M. Wasco University of Massachusetts Lowell, Lowell, MA, USA

Helen M.G. Watt Monash University, Melbourne, VIC, Australia

Amy Zwicker University of British Columbia, Vancouver, BC, Canada

About the Editors

Joan C. Chrisler is Class of 1943 Professor of Psychology at Connecticut College. She has published extensively on gender roles, attitudes toward menstruation and menopause, women's health and embodiment, and other topics. She has edited seven previous books, most recently *Lectures on the Psychology of Women* (4th ed., 2008, McGraw-Hill) and *Women over 50: Psychological Perspectives* (2007, Springer). She has served as editor of *Sex Roles* and on the Editorial Boards of *Psychology of Women Quarterly*, *Sex Roles*, *Psychology of Men & Masculinity*, and *Teaching of Psychology*. Dr. Chrisler is a fellow of the Association for Psychological Science and the American Psychological Association (Divisions 1, 2, 9, 35, 38, 46, 52).

Donald R. McCreary is an adjunct professor of Psychology at Brock University and York University. He has published extensively on gender roles, the psychology of men, and other topics. He has co-edited one previous book, *Applied Social Psychology* (1997, Prentice Hall). He has served as associate editor of *Psychology of Men & Masculinity* and of the *International Journal of Men's Health* and is a member of the Editorial Boards of *Sex Roles*, *Journal of Men's Studies*, and *Body Image*. Dr. McCreary is a fellow of the American Psychological Association (Division 51).

About the Contributors

Alisha Ali, Ph.D., is associate professor of Applied Psychology at New York University. She conducts research on women's mental health with a particular focus on the effects of poverty, abuse, and self-silencing on women's depression. Her work has been published widely, and her research funding includes grants from the National Institute of Mental Health, Eli Lilly, and the Allstate Foundation.

Nancy L. Baker, Ph.D., ABPP, is director of the Forensic Concentration at Fielding Graduate University. She has served as chairperson of the APA Committee on Women in Psychology and as president of the Society for the Psychology of Women (APA Division 35). Her work focuses on the interplay of those things generally called gender, ethnicity, sexual orientation, and social class.

Susan A. Basow, Ph.D., is Charles A. Dana Professor of Psychology at Lafayette College. She is a social/counseling psychologist who specializes in gender issues. She is the author of the textbook *Gender: Stereotypes and Roles,* and has published many research articles on women's body issues and on how gender issues affect student ratings of professors. Dr. Basow is a fellow of four divisions of the American Psychological Association and has been an officer of the Society for the Psychology of Women (Div. 35).

Uli Boehmer, Ph.D., is assistant professor of Social and Behavioral Sciences at Boston University School of Public Health. Her research focuses on cancer survivorship and disparities, with a particular emphasis on disparities linked to sexual orientation. Currently she is the PI of three funded studies that focus on sexual orientation and breast cancer survivorship.

Meg A. Bond, Ph.D., is professor of Psychology, director of the Center for Women and Work at the University of Massachusetts Lowell and a resident scholar at the Brandeis University Women's Studies Research Center. She is a community psychologist whose work focuses on the dynamics of gender and race/ethnicity in the workplace, sexual harassment, and collaboration among diverse constituencies in community settings; she is particularly interested in the articulation of a feminist community psychology.

Deborah J. Bowen, Ph.D., is professor of Social and Behavioral Sciences in the School of Public Health at Boston University and an investigator in the regional Cancer Prevention Network. She has been PI of several intervention projects on breast and ovarian cancer risk feedback and communications, on a web-based melanoma prevention study, and community wide studies of smoking cessation and dietary change. She is currently conducting community-based research to improve the health of Native people in the Pacific Northwest, Alaska, and the Northeastern US.

Leslie R. Brody, Ph.D., is professor of Psychology at Boston University. She has served as director of the Boston University Clinical Psychology Ph.D. program and was the Marion Cabot Putnam fellow at the Radcliffe Bunting Institute (1994–1995). Her research interests include gender and ethnic differences in coping and emotion and the use of autobiographical narratives as a therapeutic tool. She has published widely about these issues, and she is well-known for her book *Gender, Emotion, and the Family* (1999, Harvard University Press).

Gary R. Brooks, Ph.D., is professor of Psychology at Baylor University; he worked for 28 years as a psychologist with the Central Texas VA Health Care System. He is a fellow of the American Psychological Association and has been president of two APA divisions (Family Psychology, Men and Masculinity). He has authored or co-authored five books, including *The Centerfold Syndrome* (1995), *A New Psychotherapy for Traditional Men* (1998), and *The New Handbook of Counseling and Psychotherapy for Men* (2001; 2005).

Jeanne Brooks-Gunn, Ph.D., is the Virginia and Leonard Marx Professor of Child Development and Education at Teachers College and the College of Physicians and Surgeons at Columbia University and director of the National Center for Children and Families (www.policyforchildren.org). Her research concerns factors that contribute to both positive and negative outcomes across childhood, adolescence, and adulthood, with a particular focus on key social and biological transitions over the life course; she is also interested in the design and evaluation of intervention programs for children and parents.

Cynthia M. Bruns, Ph.D., is coordinator of Training for the APA internship program at the Central Washington University Counseling Center. She received her doctorate in clinical psychology from the California School of Professional Psychology, where she specialized in women's issues and feminist therapy. She has published articles in *Women & Therapy* and *Lesbian Studies*. She is an ad hoc reviewer for *Women & Therapy* and *Sex Roles*.

Jennifer A. Bunk, Ph.D., is assistant professor of Psychology at West Chester University of Pennsylvania. She is an industrial/organizational psychologist with a specialization in occupational health psychology. Her research interests include workplace stress, work–family conflict, and the experience and enactment of workplace incivility with particular focuses on cognitive appraisal and individual differences.

Rachel M. Calogero, Ph.D., is a postdoctoral fellow at the University of Kent in Canterbury, UK. She has worked in the area of body image and eating disorders for 10 years, with particular interests in the role of self- and social objectification. Her research also focuses on broader social psychological processes, such as the role of open-mindedness vs. closed-mindedness in support for the status quo and specific health practices, such as the role of mindful exercise in the prevention of eating disorders.

Paula J. Caplan, Ph.D., is a clinical and research psychologist. She has been a research associate at Harvard University's DuBois Institute and professor of Applied Psychology and head of the Centre for Women's Studies in Education at the Ontario Institute for Studies in Education. Dr. Caplan is the author or editor of 11 books, dozens of book chapters and articles in scholarly journals, and numerous articles and essays in popular publications.

Linda L. Carli, Ph.D., is a social psychologist and has been a faculty member at Wellesley College since 1991. An authority on gender discrimination and the challenges faced by professional women, she is the author (with Alice Eagly) of the recent book *Through the Labyrinth: The Truth About How Women Become Leaders* (Harvard Business School Press, 2007), published in conjunction with the Center for Public Leadership of the Kennedy School of Government; the book received the 2008 Distinguished Publication Award from the Association for Women in Psychology.

About the Contributors

Kate Carroll completed her undergraduate degree in Psychology and Sociology at Muhlenberg College in Allentown, PA. She currently lives in Philadelphia and works for the non-profit mentoring organization Big Brothers Big Sisters of Southeastern PA.

Katherine H. Clemans, MS, is a doctoral candidate in developmental psychology at the University of Florida. Her research focuses on emotional factors related to moral development and aggression during adolescence.

Sam V. Cochran, Ph.D., is director of the University Counseling Service and Clinical Professor of Counseling Psychology at the University of Iowa in Iowa City, Iowa. He recently served as editor of *Psychology of Men & Masculinity*. His current research and practice interests include mood disorders in men and mental health issues in higher education.

Kenneth M. Cohen, Ph.D., is a licensed clinical psychologist at Cornell University's Counseling and Psychological Services, where he specializes in gay, lesbian, and bisexual issues. He is also a lecturer in Cornell's Feminist, Gender, & Sexuality Studies program and co-editor of *The Lives of Lesbians, Gays, and Bisexuals: Children to Adults*. As a consultant for the Human Rights Campaign's *FamilyNet*, he offers advice to sexual minorities and their families regarding gay youth development.

Scott Coltrane, Ph.D., is dean of the College of Arts and Sciences at the University of Oregon and a sociologist whose research focuses on fathers and families. He is the author of several books, including *Family Man*, *Gender and Families*, *Families and Society*, and *Sociology of Marriage and the Family*, and has published numerous scholarly journal articles and essays. His most recent funded research projects investigate the impact of economic stress and the meaning of fatherhood in Mexican American and European American families.

Bonnie Cramond, Ph.D., is professor of Educational Psychology and Instructional Technology at the University of Georgia. She has been a member of the board of directors of the National Association for Gifted Children, director of the Torrance Center for Creativity and Talent Development, and editor of the *Journal of Secondary Gifted Education*. She is particularly interested in the identification and nurturance of creativity, especially among students considered at risk because of their different way of thinking, such as those misdiagnosed with ADHD, emotional problems, or those who drop out.

Sharon Danoff-Burg, Ph.D., is associate professor of Psychology and director of Graduate Studies in Psychology at the State University of New York at Albany. Much of her research focuses on coping with chronic illness. As a clinical psychologist and a health psychologist, she is interested not only in pathology and vulnerability but also in resilience and positive adaptation.

Anita DeLongis, Ph.D., is associate professor of Psychology at the University of British Columbia, Canada. Her primary research interest lies in dyadic coping and the interpersonal dynamics of stress and coping.

Kristoffer Denboske graduated from Muhlenberg College in 2008 with a bachelor's degree in Psychology. He is currently working on his master's degree in criminal justice at John Jay College.

Laura M. DeRose, Ph.D., is an assistant professor of Psychology at Adelphi University, where she teaches courses in developmental psychology to undergraduate and graduate students. She is the current chair of Adelphi University's Institute for Parenting. Her research focuses on pubertal development and adjustment during adolescence.

Lauren E. Duncan, Ph.D., is associate professor of Psychology at Smith College. She teaches courses in the psychology of women, social psychology, and personality, including seminars on women's lives in context and the psychology of social movement participation. Her research interests include understanding how social events shape people's life outcomes and how individuals become motivated to change or maintain society.

Alice H. Eagly, Ph.D., is chair of the Department of Psychology, James Padilla Professor of Arts and Sciences, faculty fellow in the Institute for Policy Research, and professor of Management and Organizations at Northwestern University. She has published numerous journal articles on gender, attitudes, prejudice, cultural stereotypes, and leadership and is the author of three books, *Sex Differences in Social Behavior: A Social Role Interpretation* (1987), (with Shelly Chaiken) *The Psychology of Attitudes* (1993), and (with Linda Carli) *Through the Labyrinth: The Truth About How Women Become Leaders* (2007). She has been honored for her research, most recently with the Distinguished Scientific Contribution Award of the American Psychological Association.

Crystal Ehresman is a graduate student at the University of Lethbridge. Her research concerns the role of the hippocampus and neurogenesis in producing sex differences in object location memory.

Heather Eisele is a graduate student in Clinical Psychology at the University of Missouri-St. Louis. Her research interests are in women's mental health, self-esteem, and feminism. Her clinical interests include psycho-oncology and the intersection of physical and mental health.

Matt Englar-Carlson, Ph.D., is associate professor of Counseling at California State University, Fullerton. He co-edited the books *In the Room with Men: A Casebook of Therapeutic Change* (2006), *Counseling Troubled Boys* (2008), and the upcoming book series *Theories of Psychotherapy* to be published by APA Books, and he developed the APA DVD *Engaging Men in Psychotherapy* (2009). He has counseled boys, men, and families in community, school, and university settings.

Marina Epstein, Ph.D., is a postdoctoral fellow at the University of Michigan Substance Abuse Research Center. Her research interests include the socialization of gender roles and the negotiation of competing and conflicting gender expectations and gender beliefs. She is currently exploring the enactment of, as well as the costs to men, of adhering to traditional masculine roles, in particular with regard to sexual risk taking and substance abuse.

Rachel Fagnant, MA, is a psychotherapist and career counselor at the Metropolitan Council on Jewish Poverty in New York City, where she works primarily with victims of domestic violence during the transition to self-sufficiency.

Angela R. Febbraro earned her Ph.D. in Applied Social Psychology and her MA in Industrial/Organizational Psychology at the University of Guelph, Canada, and is currently a research scientist at Defence Research & Development Canada (DRDC) – Toronto, and an adjunct instructor at York University and Wilfred Laurier University. She has published a number of research articles on women, leadership, and gender integration in the Canadian military, and her current research concerns cultural diversity and intergroup relations in the military and broader context.

Gordon B. Forbes, Ph.D., is a licensed clinical psychologist, professor emeritus of Psychology at Millikin University, and the director and cofounder of the Millikin Project on Social Perceptions. His research interests include cross-cultural, ethnic, gender, and generational differences in body image; cross-cultural and gender differences in interpersonal aggression; and sexism.

About the Contributors

Irene Hanson Frieze, Ph.D., is professor of Psychology and Women's Studies at the University of Pittsburgh. She has published widely on topics related to motivation and aggression, as well as to interpersonal relations. She is the editor of *Sex Roles*.

Jessica A. Gallus is a doctoral candidate in I/O Psychology at the University of Connecticut and a senior consultant at Booz Allen Hamilton. Her research concerns individuals' assertive responses to workplace incivility and sexual harassment. Her most recent work examines the stimulus, contextual, and individual predictors that prompt targets to blow the whistle on experiences of sexual harassment.

Mary M. Gergen, Ph.D., is professor emerita of Psychology at Pennsylvania State University, Brandywine. She has published widely on gender issues, aging, narrative psychology, and philosophical psychology. She is the author of *Feminist Reconstructions in Psychology: Narrative, Gender and Performance* (Sage, 2001) and co-author of *Social Construction: Entering the Dialogue* (Taos Institute Publication, 2004).

Diane L. Gill, Ph.D., is professor of Exercise and Sport Science at the University of North Carolina at Greensboro. Her research concerns social psychological aspects of physical activity. Her scholarly publications include the textbook *Psychological Dynamics of Sport and Exercise*, several book chapters, and over 100 journal articles. Current projects emphasize gender and cultural diversity and the relationship between physical activity and quality of life.

Ritu M. Gill earned her MA and Ph.D. in Social Psychology at Carleton University and is currently a research scientist at Defence R&D Canada – Toronto. Her area of research includes gender discrimination against women, with a focus on psychological factors that may facilitate the perception of discrimination, and factors that may empower women to challenge discrimination.

Julia A. Graber, Ph.D., is associate professor of Psychology at the University of Florida and associate chair of the Developmental Area. Her research focuses on the development of psychopathology and health-compromising and health-promoting behaviors during adolescence. Much of this work has been on the experience of puberty with particular attention to bio-psychosocial processes, pubertal timing, and individual differences in navigating developmental transitions during adolescence.

Leeat Granek, Ph.D., earned her doctorate in History and Theory of Psychology at York University in Toronto, Canada. Dr. Granek's research areas include psycho-oncology, grief and mourning, and women's health. She works at Princess Margaret Hospital and Sunnybrook Odette Cancer Centre, and she is currently writing a book on grief, death, and dying.

Karen Greenspan is a doctoral student in Clinical Psychology at John F. Kennedy University's Graduate School of Professional Psychology and is an intern at Santa Rosa Junior College's Student Psychological Services. She is the membership committee co-chair for APA Division 44 (Society for the Psychological Study of Lesbian, Gay, Bisexual and Transgender Issues).

Dara N. Greenwood, Ph.D., is assistant professor of Communication Studies at the University of Michigan. She is a social psychologist who studies emotional and interpersonal motivations for engaging with entertainment media. Her research also examines the role that idealized female media icons play in young women's self and body image concerns.

Chanita Hughes Halbert, Ph.D., is associate professor of Psychiatry and a researcher at the Abramson Cancer Center at the University of Pennsylvania. Her research focuses on the effects of sociocultural and psychological factors on cancer disparities among medically underserved populations and factors that influence minority participation in cancer prevention and control research.

May Ling Halim is a doctoral candidate in Psychology at New York University. Her research interests concern the cross-section of identity and stereotyping and how they affect health, academic achievement, adjustment, and work-related outcomes.

Judith A. Hall, Ph.D., is professor of Psychology at Northeastern University. She is a social psychologist and previously was on the faculty at Johns Hopkins University. Her research is on communication processes, with emphasis on nonverbal communication in relation to gender and to physician–patient relationships.

Jennifer Hambaugh is a doctoral candidate in the clinical psychology program at Indiana University of Pennsylvania, where she is conducting her dissertation research on gossip. Previously she studied psychology and women' studies at the University of Illinois.

Kristin A. Hancock, Ph.D., is professor of Psychology at John F. Kennedy University's Graduate School of Professional Psychology. Dr. Hancock is a fellow of the American Psychological Association, and she has been active for many years in APA governance. She served as president of APA Division 44 (Society for the Psychological Study of Lesbian, Gay, Bisexual, and Transgender Issues), and she has served on the Board for the Advancement of Psychology in the Public Interest, Board of Professional Affairs, Committee on Professional Practice and Standards, Committee on Women in Psychology, and Committee on Lesbian, Gay, and Bisexual Concerns. She co-authored the APA *Guidelines for Psychotherapy with Lesbian, Gay, and Bisexual Clients*.

Mark L. Hatzenbuehler, MS, M.Phil., is a doctoral candidate in Clinical Psychology at Yale University. His research focuses on the mechanisms that link stigma-related stress to psychopathology, particularly among sexual minorities. His research has been funded by the National Institutes of Health (National Research Service Award), the American Psychological Association (Division 44 Maylon-Smith Award), and the Williams Institute at the UCLA School of Law (Small Grant Research Award).

Kenneth V. Heard, Ph.D., recently defended his dissertation in Clinical Psychology at the University of Rhode Island. He teaches at several colleges and universities in Rhode Island, Massachusetts, and Connecticut. His research interests are in psychology and law, decision-making and clinical judgment, and the evaluation of scientific evidence. He has published and presented on diverse topics and is founder and past chair of the Science Committee of the Society of American Baseball Researchers.

Peter Hegarty, Ph.D., is senior lecturer in Psychology at the University of Surrey. He researches social cognition, intergroup relations, and the history of psychology. He enjoys dividing his time between London and County Dublin with his partner, Andrew Penman.

C. Peter Herman, Ph.D., is professor of Psychology at the University of Toronto, where he has taught since 1976. His research focuses on eating, self-regulation, and social influence. He is co-executive editor of the journal *Appetite*.

Lori M. Hilt, Ph.D., recently earned her doctorate in Clinical Psychology from Yale University. She is currently an NIMH postdoctoral fellow in emotion research. Her research focuses on the development of depression and non-suicidal self-injury in adolescent girls.

Dawn M. Howerton, MA, is a doctoral student in Social Psychology program at the University of Tennessee, where she is also working toward a graduate certificate in Women's Studies. Her interests include social justice and equity. She has co-authored papers on same-sex sexual harassment and acquaintance rape.

Vivian S. Hwang is a doctoral student in Clinical Psychology at the State University of New York at Albany. Her research interests include psycho-oncology, posttraumatic growth, and psychosocial factors of coping with chronic illness.

Janet Shibley Hyde, Ph.D., is Helen Thompson Woolley Professor of Psychology and Gender and Women's Studies at the University of Wisconsin–Madison. Her specialty is the psychology of women and gender development, and she has conducted numerous meta-analyses of research on psychological gender differences. This work led her to propose the gender similarities hypothesis. Dr. Hyde is a former editor of *Psychology of Women Quarterly*.

Ingrid Johnston-Robledo, Ph D., is associate professor of Psychology and director of Women's Studies at the State University of New York at Fredonia. She teaches courses on the psychology of women, women's health, and human sexuality. Her research interests are women's health, reproductive health education, and women's experiences with pregnancy, childbirth, breastfeeding, postpartum adjustment, and motherhood.

Cindra S. Kamphoff, Ph.D., is assistant professor of Human Performance at Minnesota State University, Mankato. Her research focuses on gender and cultural diversity, including projects on male and female athletes' interest in the coaching profession, cultural competence in physical activity settings, and former women coaches' experiences.

Ronit Kark, Ph.D., is senior lecturer in Psychology at Bar-Ilan University, Israel, and currently heads the Social–Organizational Section (Department of Psychology) and the "Gender in The Field" Program (Graduate Program for Gender Studies). Her research interests include leadership, identity and identification processes, emotions, and gender in organizations. She is a member of the editorial boards of *Academy of Management Review*, *Leadership Quarterly*, and *International Journal of Management Review*.

Ellyn Kaschak, Ph.D., is professor of Psychology at San Jose State University, where she has also been chair of the graduate program in Marriage, Family, and Child Counseling and director of the University's Family Counseling Service. She is one of the founders of the field of feminist psychology, which she has practiced since its inception some 35 years ago. Dr. Kaschak has published numerous articles and chapters on feminist psychology and therapy, as well as the award-winning book *Engendered Lives: A New Psychology of Women's Experience*. She is editor of *Women & Therapy*.

Carol A. Lawton, Ph.D., is professor of Psychology at Indiana University-Purdue University in Fort Wayne. She has conducted research on gender differences in spatial cognition and wayfinding for 25 years, and she has published extensively on these topics and on the psychology of women and gender more generally.

Christina Lee, Ph.D., is professor of Health Psychology at the University of Queensland, Australia, and director of the Queensland Centre for Mothers & Babies, a research centre focused on strategies for providing integrated consumer-focused maternity care. She was previously the national coordinator of the Australian Longitudinal Study on Women's Health, a cohort study involving over 40,000 women across the life span. She is the author of *Women's Health: Psychological and Social Perspectives* (Sage, 1998) and co-author of *The Psychology of Men's Health* (Open University Press, 2002).

Man Yu Li graduated from the Chinese University of Hong Kong with a bachelor's degree and will be starting her doctoral study shortly. She has designed and conducted studies related to intimate partner violence and peer sexual harassment.

Julia R. Lippman is a doctoral student in the Communication Studies at the University of Michigan. Her research is focused on cultural representations of stalking and the effects of these representations on the public's understanding of stalking. Other research interests include media representations of gender and psychological predictors of media use.

Vicki J. Magley, Ph.D., is associate professor of Psychology at the University of Connecticut. The main focus of her research is occupational health psychology, and she combines organizational and feminist perspectives in the study of workplace mistreatment. She has published her work on the effects of self-labeling experiences as sexual harassment, outcomes that are associated with experiencing sexual harassment – for both men and women, the effectiveness of sexual harassment training programs, the buffering impact of an intolerant climate for sexual harassment on outcomes, coping with sexual harassment, and the incidence and effects of non-sexualized, yet uncivil, work experiences.

Tara C. Marshall, Ph.D., is lecturer in Psychology at Brunel University in London. She recently conducted postdoctoral research at the University of Tokyo and the University of Western Ontario. Her research examines the influence of gender, culture, and attachment styles in close relationships.

Janelle L. Mason, MA, is a doctoral student in Clinical Psychology at Fielding Graduate University. Her research interests include violence in intimate partner relationships and gender issues in assessment.

Marianne Schmid Mast is professor of Work and Organizational Psychology at the University of Neuchatel in Switzerland. Her research focuses on the observation and analysis of social interactions with an emphasis on questions of (1) power, leadership, and hierarchies, (2) social perception and interpersonal judgment, (3) behavioral observation and analysis of verbal and nonverbal behavior, and (4) effects of gender in the realm of the aforementioned areas of expertise.

Maureen C. McHugh, Ph.D., is professor of Psychology at Indiana University of Pennsylvania, where she teaches graduate and undergraduate courses in gender and in diversity. She has published extensively on the psychology of women, human sexuality, violence against women, and research methods. One of the special issues of *Psychology of Women Quarterly* that she co-edited with Irene Frieze received the Distinguished Publication Award from the Association for Women in Psychology (AWP). Dr. McHugh has also been honored by feminist organizations for her leadership and mentoring.

Andrea L. Meltzer, MA, is a doctoral candidate in Social Psychology at the University of Tennessee. She recently co-authored a chapter on women's health and is currently studying gender and racial disparity among heart bypass surgery patients. Her research interests include women's issues, objectification and its effects on relationship satisfaction, gender stereotyping, and gender discrimination.

Ryan S. Mitchell is a doctoral student in Human Development at Cornell University. His main areas of study include same-sex-attracted youth and young adults, adolescents' friendships and romantic relationships, and adolescents' use of the Internet for socialization.

Sarah K. Murnen, Ph.D., is professor of Psychology and chair of the Department of Psychology at Kenyon College. She has published extensively on the social construction of gender as it relates to body image and to sexual attitudes and behaviors.

Nora S. Newcombe, Ph.D., is professor of Psychology and James H. Glackin fellow at Temple University. Her research focuses on spatial development and the development of episodic memory. Dr. Newcombe is the author of numerous chapters, articles, and books, including *Making Space* (with Janellen Huttenlocher). Her work has been recognized by awards including the George A. Miller Award and the G. Stanley Hall Award. She has served as editor of the *Journal of Experimental Psychology: General* and associate editor of *Psychological Bulletin*. She is currently PI of the NSF-funded Spatial Intelligence and Learning Center.

Nicky J. Newton is a doctoral candidate in Psychology at the University of Michigan and a student fellow of the International Max Planck Research School "The Life Course: Evolutionary and Ontogenetic Dynamics (LIFE)." Her research interests include the antecedents and outcomes of life span personality development, with a particular focus on women in midlife.

Susan Nolen-Hoeksema, Ph.D., is professor of Psychology at Yale University. She has written numerous empirical and theoretical articles about women's mental health and three books for the popular press on the topic. Her research focuses on the role of cognitive processes, particularly rumination, in depression and related mental health problems.

Alexander R. Pagnani is a doctoral student in Educational Psychology at the University of Georgia, where he is specializing in gifted and talented education. His research interests include residential gifted acceleration programs, college early entrance programs, the social and emotional needs of gifted boys, and the reading interests and patterns of gifted boys.

Seth T. Pardo, MA, is a doctoral candidate in Human Development at Cornell University. He uses an ecological approach to focus on the conceptualizations, meanings, and expressions of transgender identities in late adolescence and adulthood. His experimental work uses a fuzzy-trace approach to explore the intersections of identity, risk perception, and behavior.

Jennifer L. Petersen is a doctoral candidate at the University of Wisconsin-Madison. Her primary research interests include gender studies, the development of sexuality, and peer sexual harassment victimization.

Bill E. Peterson, Ph.D., is professor of Psychology at Smith College. His research interests are in the areas of adult personality development and political psychology, with specific interests in psychosocial generativity and the psychology of authoritarianism and gender. Most recently he has served as an associate editor for the *Journal of Personality*.

Janet Polivy, Ph.D., is professor of Psychology at the University of Toronto, where she has taught since 1976. Her research focuses on eating, dieting, and self-regulation. She serves on the editorial board of several journals, has a clinical practice in the field of eating disorders, and is a fellow of the Royal Society of Canada.

Felicia Pratto, Ph.D., is a professor of Psychology at the University of Connecticut. She researches intergroup power and social cognition, and has served as vice president of the International Society for Political Psychology. She enjoys travel, opera, jazz, her three children, her many students and fantastic former students, and the humor and cooking of her husband, Tom Wood.

Heather A. Priess, MS, MPA, is a doctoral student in Developmental Psychology at the University of Wisconsin-Madison. Her research concerns the gendered nature of development in adolescence, including the emergence of the gender difference in depression and gender similarities and differences in academic achievement motivation and academic performance. She is also interested in the development and application of novel quantitative techniques to developmental research questions.

Kate Richmond, Ph.D., is assistant professor of Psychology at Muhlenberg College. She recently completed her internship and postdoctoral residency at the University of Pennsylvania. Dr. Richmond has a private practice in Philadelphia, where she specializes in trauma-related disorders. She is active is APA governance and has served on the executive committees of Division 35 (Psychology of Women) and 52 (International Psychology).

Alecia Robinson is a doctoral student at the Boston University School of Public Health. Prior to entering her current program at BU, she was project administrator for a subsidiary of the California Medical Association. She has interests in mental health disparities research and disparities-based health-care policy.

Diane Ruble, Ph.D., is professor emerita of Psychology at New York University. She previously taught at Princeton University and the University of Toronto. Her interests are in the field of social and developmental psychology, particularly the development of children's knowledge about and identification with social categories, such as gender and ethnicity, and she has published extensively in those areas.

Mark A. Runco, Ph.D., is the E. Paul Torrance Professor of Creative Studies and Gifted Education at the University of Georgia. He is editor of the *Creativity Research Journal*, co-editor of the *Encyclopedia of Creativity,* and has served as president of the APA Division 10 (Aesthetics, Creativity, and the Arts).

Alexandra Rutherford, Ph.D., is associate Professor of Psychology at York University in Toronto, where she teaches in history and theory of psychology, women's studies, and science and technology studies programs. Her research interests include the history of feminist psychology, and, more generally, the history of the science/politics or objectivity/advocacy nexus in psychology. Her books include *Beyond the Box: B. F. Skinner's Technology of Behavior from Laboratory to Life, 1950s–1970s* and the forthcoming *Handbook of International Perspectives on Feminism*.

Deborah Saucier, Ph.D., holds a Canada Research chair in Behavioral Neuroscience and is professor of neuroscience at the University of Lethbridge. Her research focuses on individual differences in spatial ability in human and non-human animals, with particular interest in how hormonal variation affects these abilities.

Ritch C. Savin-Williams, Ph.D., is professor of Human Development and chair of the Department of Human Development at Cornell University. His several books on the development of sexual minorities include *The New Gay Teenager* (2005, Harvard University Press) and *"Mom, Dad, I'm Gay": How Families Negotiate Coming Out* (2001, American Psychological Association). He is currently researching the spectrum of sexual attractions, fantasies, and behavior among straight-identified, sexually fluid, and same-sex-attracted young men.

Robert Scholz, a licensed professional counselor and marriage and family therapist, serves in Pepperdine University's Counseling Center as a staff counselor and Alcohol and Other Drugs Program coordinator, and teaches courses on substance abuse and forensic psychology. He is co-author of *Engaging Resistance: Creating Partnerships for Change in Sex Offender Treatment,* which draws from his 15 years of clinical expertise in the fields of sexual violence, addictive behaviors, and men's issues.

Joseph A. Schroeder holds a BA in Psychology from Franklin and Marshall College and a Ph.D. in Cell Biology and Pathology from Thomas Jefferson University. He is assistant professor of Psychology at Connecticut College, where he teaches courses in neuroscience, sensation and perception, comparative psychology, and neuroimaging. Dr. Schroeder's research interests include the neurobiology of drug addiction, neurodegeneration, and spatial navigation and cognitive map formation.

Sabine Sczesny, Ph.D., is associate professor of Social Psychology at the University of Bern, Switzerland. In her research, she focuses on basic and applied aspects of stereotyping, such as automatic and controlled processes of stereotyping; the validity of the social role theory; the interplay of language, cognition, and gender on gender stereotypes over the course of time; and age stereotyping in organizations.

Kristy Y. Shih is a doctoral candidate in Sociology at the University of California, Riverside. Her research interests focus on immigrant, transnational, and racial/ethnic families; gender and power dynamics; and intergenerational family relations. Her dissertation research examines family politics and constructed meanings among mothers, sons, and daughters-in-law in Taiwanese, ethnic Chinese-American, and Mexican American families.

Louise Bordeaux Silverstein, Ph.D., is professor of Psychology at the Ferkauf Graduate School of Psychology at Yeshiva University, where she teaches courses in family therapy and integrating gender and race/ethnicity. She is a past president of the APA Division on Family Psychology and is a former chair of the APA Committee on Women in Psychology. Dr. Silverstein is co-author of *Qualitative Data: An Introduction to Coding and Analysis* (2003) and *Feminist Family Therapy: Empowerment and Social Location* (2003). Her work focuses on fathering, family therapy, feminist theory, and the use of qualitative research to bridge the gap between research and practice in psychotherapy.

Andrew P. Smiler, Ph.D., is visiting assistant professor of Psychology at University Wake Forest. In addition to measurement issues in gender research, he is interested in the ways that men and women define and enact masculinity. He also studies adolescent sexual behavior, with a focus on normative patterns and individual differences.

Christine A. Smith, Ph.D., is assistant professor of Psychology at the University of Wisconsin-Green Bay. She is a social psychologist who has been researching gender-related issues for over 15 years. She currently coordinates the Teaching Psychology of Women Workshop for APA Division 35.

Linda Smolak, Ph.D., is Samuel B. Cummings Jr. Professor of Psychology at Kenyon College. She has published many articles on body image and eating disorders in children and adolescents. She co-edited (with J.K. Thompson) *Body Image, Eating Disorders* and *Obesity in Youth: Assessment, Prevention, and Treatment* (2nd ed., American Psychological Association, 2009).

Jayne E. Stake, Ph.D., is professor emerita of Psychology at the University of Missouri-St. Louis. She has published widely in the area of gender issues in personality. She is a fellow of the American Psychological Association and has served as editor of *Psychology of Women Quarterly*.

Mark A. Stevens, Ph.D., is director of the University Counseling Services at California State University-Northridge. He co-edited with Matt Englar-Carlson the book *In the Room With Men: A Casebook of Therapeutic Change* (2006), and he is the featured therapist in an APA-produced video (2003) on *Counseling and Psychotherapy with Men*. He is a past president of APA Division 51: The Society for the Psychological Study of Men and Masculinity.

Abigail J. Stewart, Ph.D., is Sandra Schwartz Tangri Professor of Psychology and Women's Studies at the University of Michigan and director of the UM ADVANCE project. She has received the Henry Murray Award (in personality psychology) and the Carolyn Wood Sherif Award (in psychology of women) from the American Psychological Association. Dr. Stewart has published many scholarly articles and several books on the psychology of women's lives, personality, adaptation to personal and social changes, and women's experiences in science and technology.

J. Kevin Thompson, Ph.D., is professor of Psychology at the University of South Florida. He has published extensively in the area of body image and eating disorders for 25 years. He has been on the editorial board of the *International Journal of Eating Disorders* since 1990 and is currently an associate editor of *Body Image*.

Cheryl B. Travis, Ph.D., is professor of Psychology and chair of the Women's Studies Program at the University of Tennessee-Knoxville. Her recent work on women and health-care issues has focused on gender and race disparities in the treatment of heart disease. She recently has co-authored chapters on women's health, and her latest books include an edited volume on *Evolution, Gender, and Rape* and a co-edited volume on *Sexuality, Society, and Feminism*.

Zhana Vrangalova is a doctoral student in Human Development at Cornell University. She is interested in exploring non-traditional sexual expressions and identities and their relationship to psychological, social, and sexual well-being.

Sharon M. Wasco, Ph.D., is assistant professor of Psychology at the University of Massachusetts Lowell. She is a community psychologist, and her program of collaborative research and action aims to understand and improve the way communities reduce the harm done by gender-based violence, with a focus on sexual assault in adulthood. Dr. Wasco is the co-author of *Evaluating Services for Survivors of Domestic Violence and Sexual Assault* (2002, Sage).

Helen M.G. Watt, Ph.D., is a faculty member at Monash University, Melbourne, Australia, and has previously served on the faculties of the University of Michigan, the University of Western Sydney, the University of Sydney, and Macquarie University. She has received several national and international early career awards. Her research interests include motivation, mathematics education, gendered educational and occupational choices, motivations for teaching, and teacher self-efficacy.

Amy Zwicker, MA, is a doctoral student in Clinical Psychology at the University of British Columbia. Her research focuses on the role of interpersonal relationships in well-being.

Chapter 1
Introduction

Donald R. McCreary and Joan C. Chrisler

The Development of Gender Studies in Psychology

Studies of sex differences are as old as the field of psychology, and they have been conducted in every subfield of the discipline. There are probably many reasons for the popularity of these studies, but three reasons seem to be most prominent. First, social psychological studies of person perception show that sex is especially salient in social groups. It is the first thing people notice about others, and it is one of the things we remember best (Fiske, Haslam, & Fiske, 1991; Stangor, Lynch, Duan, & Glass, 1992). For example, people may not remember who uttered a witty remark, but they are likely to remember whether the quip came from a woman or a man. Second, many people hold firm beliefs that aspects of physiology suit men and women for particular social roles. Men's greater upper body strength makes them better candidates for manual labor, and their greater height gives the impression that they would make good leaders (i.e., people we look up to). Women's reproductive capacity and the caretaking tasks (e.g., breastfeeding, baby minding) that accompany it make them seem suitable for other roles that require gentleness and nurturance. Third, the logic that underlies hypothesis testing in the sciences is focused on difference. Researchers design their studies with the hope that they can reject the null hypothesis that experimental groups do not differ. Even though similarities between women and men can tell us as much about human behavior as differences between them can do, researchers often are disappointed by, and reviewers and editors uninterested in, studies that require acceptance of the null hypothesis.

If we accept the founding of Wundt's laboratory in 1879 as the beginning of formal psychology, then we can say that, for almost the first 100 years of its history, psychological research and theory was focused on "sex" (i.e., universal, biologically based causes of behavior). Although some psychoanalytic theorists (e.g., Deutch, Horney, Jung) wrote about ideas we now understand as "gender," the idea that human behavior is multiply determined (i.e., has biopsychosocial determinants) was not acknowledged until recent decades. Feminist psychologists, influenced by the Women's Liberation Movement of the 1960s and 1970s, began to write about sociocultural influences on the psychology of women. They used the word "gender" to describe psychological and social aspects of behavior and social roles. Gradually the term "gender roles" came to replace the older term "sex roles," as psychologists realized the extent to which social and cultural influences operated to move people into particular roles (e.g., breadwinner, bread baker). The notion that gender is performed (i.e., something we "do" rather than something we "have"; West & Zimmerman, 1987) also makes "gender" a better modifier for the active performance of role-related activities.

D.R. McCreary (✉)
Brock University, St. Catharines, ON Canada; York University, Toronto, ON, Canada

The formal study of gender in psychology can be dated to the early 1970s. The first psychology of women textbooks for undergraduate and graduate courses were published in 1971 (Unger, 1998). The founding of Division 35 (Psychology of Women) of the American Psychological Association in 1974 is another important marker, as a subfield can certainly be said to have coalesced when it is large enough to earn a place as an APA division. The journal *Sex Roles* published its first issue in 1975; *Psychology of Women Quarterly* came next in 1977, followed by *Women & Therapy* in 1982. The first issue of *Feminism & Psychology* appeared in 1991. In the early days of gender studies, and even today—at least among the general public (Pryzgoda & Chrisler, 2000)—the word "gender" has often been synonymous with women. We hope that this idea seems ridiculous to our readers. However, psychologists who believed that "man" is the norm and "woman" is the "other" were slow to come to the realization that the psychology of men is as influenced as the psychology of women by the society and the culture in which people live, as well as by the social interactions of everyday life. Although feminist men authored books about the stresses associated with masculinity as early as the 1970s, it was not until 1997 that APA Division 51 (Psychology of Men and Masculinity) was founded. The first issue of its journal *Psychology of Men & Masculinity* was published in 2000.

Early studies of sex and gender differences were often atheoretical and sometimes simplistic (e.g., only one independent and one dependent variable, small and homogeneous samples). Researchers were so focused on looking for gender differences that they looked anywhere and everywhere with little or no rationale other than their personal interest in the particular phenomenon or ability. Studies were conducted on such varied topics as reaction time, auditory acuity, social conformity, eating behavior, extroversion, problem solving, creativity, criminality, and cognitive development. The scattershot nature of many of these early studies, as well as the low status associated with studies of women's issues, led many journal editors, tenure and promotion committees, and other establishment entities to think of the psychology of gender as a fringe area and the journals that published it as low quality. Today things look very different. The psychology of gender is a well-established area, and researchers have many strong theories to guide them in their work. The journals mentioned above have developed good reputations (e.g., high rejection rates, impressive impact factors), and studies of gender can be found in most mainstream journals these days. Nevertheless, some research is still being done atheoretically, especially in countries whose work in this area is still in an early stage of development, and many psychologists are unfamiliar with the terminology of gender research (e.g., they frequently conflate "sex" and "gender"), the current questions under study, and the wide variety of methods used to answer those questions. We hope that the *Handbook of Gender Research in Psychology* will be helpful in clarifying that confusion and setting an agenda for future research.

We recently looked through the first few volumes of *Sex Roles* (*SR*) and *Psychology of Women Quarterly* (*PWQ*) to see what was of interest to researchers in those early days. Most of the articles described gender comparative studies, some described studies of the psychology of women, and only one (an article on fathering) concerned the psychology of men. The most popular topic across both journals was work and career. Both journals contained multiple articles about gender differences in achievement motivation. *PWQ* published articles on women in male-dominated occupations, re-entry women workers and students, and assertiveness training. Early articles in *SR* concerned gender stereotypes (especially in the media), children's attitudes toward gender roles, and differences between feminists and nonfeminists. Examples of the scattershot work we derided above are one article each on gender and handedness, gender roles and criminality, and gender and conformity. *PWQ* also published an article on the empty nest syndrome, which is rarely even discussed these days. Of course, all of the articles referred to "sex roles"; there was no mention of gender, and the majority of the samples were all (or predominantly) White and heterosexual (when explicit sample descriptions were provided and probably when they were not).

Recent issues of *SR*, *PWQ*, and *Psychology of Men & Masculinity* (*PMM*) tell a different story. The journals continue to publish articles on a wide variety of topics, especially *SR*, which is interdisciplinary, and, as a monthly journal, publishes many more pages and articles than the other two do. Gender comparative studies are still common, especially in *SR*, but most are designed to test theories, and so the results are of more than passing interest. Some of the studies are specifically designed to reduce inequalities (e.g., studies of workshops to improve girls' spatial skills), and articles on recurring topics (e.g., gender stereotypes in the media) allow readers to understand changes over time. Topics of current interest in both *PMM* and *PWQ* concern body image, aggression and violence, homophobia and heterosexism, physical and mental health, and social cognition (e.g., studies of discrimination and stereotyping). All three journals have published a number of new measures that can be applied in gender research. All three journals also require authors to use the words "gender" and "gender roles," even *SR*, which, ironically, has decided to keep its original name even though the only place the term "sex roles" is used is on the cover (Chrisler, 2007). All three journals prefer to publish studies with diverse samples, and all three have published special issues, special sections, and articles focused on ethnic and sexual minorities. Much progress has been made in gender studies thanks to the leadership of these journals' editorial boards, and our psychological science, theory, and practice are richer as a result.

Methodological Issues

In its publication manual, the APA urges researchers to include both women and men in their studies and to explore possible gender differences. But the APA provides no guidance on how to interpret those gender differences (or similarities) when they emerge. As there is no over-arching theory of gender that researchers can use to interpret their results, many (especially those not particularly interested in gender research) are left not quite knowing what their findings mean. As a result, gender is often considered a nuisance variable and its variance tends to be partialled out of the main analyses. In other words, gender is often used only as a statistical control variable. Other researchers report gender differences in their Results section, but then ignore the findings in the Discussion.

Fortunately, there have been a series of recent methodological and statistical changes that either have had, or presently are having, an important influence on the way researchers study the psychology of gender. On the methodological side, Hesse-Biber and Leavy (2008) described several new methodological approaches in their recent *Handbook of Emergent Methods*. These include a variety of grounded theory, interview, discourse analytic, and ethnographic approaches. For many researchers who study the psychology of gender, some of these emerging methods are not really new. However, for those just beginning to study the area or those who have noticed that their statistical control variable is explaining a lot more variance than they would expect—and want to know why—these new methods provide some powerful tools to help researchers to understand the role that gender plays in any field of interest.

On the statistical side, the increased use of moderating variable analyses (Baron & Kenny, 1986) has allowed researchers to go from focusing on mean differences between men and women (or boys and girls) on a single variable of interest to examining the extent to which the associations between two or more variables differ as a function of gender or gender role. It is true that researchers have been examining gender-based interactions in ANOVA models for decades, but regression-based interactions allow researchers to gain more power when working with multiple independent variables. Furthermore, the extension of regression to structural equation modeling (i.e., assessing multiple group comparisons or conducting tests of measurement or structural invariance) allows for more complex model testing and multivariate tests of gender differences. For instance, structural modeling allows researchers to incorporate multiple dependent, as well as independent, variables into their conceptualizations.

However, the change that has had the largest impact on how researchers study gender is meta-analysis. In conjunction with the APA Task Force on Statistical Inference (Wilkinson and the Task Force for Statistical Inference, 1999), meta-analysis has helped to promote an increased focus on effect size (as opposed to a sole focus on statistical significance testing). In the past, researchers would test for differences between women and men or girls and boys, and, if the mean differences reached the threshold for statistical significance (i.e., $p < .05$), it was said only that the two groups differed. Rarely was there a mention of whether the magnitudes associated with those significant differences were trivial, moderate, or large. However, the introduction of meta-analysis allowed researchers to go back to those studies, compute the effect sizes, and then to determine how strong the effects were overall, to group similar studies together in order to explore the stability of the effect sizes across time, and to study the role that mediators and moderators played in influencing the size of those effects. In addition, the APA Task Force on Statistical Inference encouraged researchers to report effect sizes in all of their published research so that readers do not have to wait for a meta-analysis to be conducted. As a result, even though many researchers include gender as a variable in their research, they are now somewhat better equipped to interpret the findings within the context of their theories, models, or hypotheses.

Purpose and Goals of this Handbook

Given psychology's long history of studying gender, combined with the changes in both content and methodology, we thought it was time to bring together the ideas, theories, and research from as much of the discipline as possible. Our hope was that such an undertaking would provide a critical overview of the current state of affairs in psychological research on gender and help to provide concrete direction for graduate students and early career professionals who wish to work in gender studies. A handbook of this nature also serves to inform all psychologists of the gender-related research being conducted throughout the entire range of the discipline. Most psychologists who study gender tend to work in the social, clinical, and developmental areas. As a result, most consumers of gender research, especially psychology instructors, are probably more familiar with work in those areas than they are with work in other subfields (e.g., neuroscience). In other words, most of us know less about how gender is studied and the findings that have emerged in the domains outside of the social–clinical–developmental core.

To determine the breadth of topics to cover in this handbook, we surveyed a variety of current Introduction to Psychology textbooks and identified the most common chapter titles and themes. This gave us 14 potential sections for the handbook, which we used to create a preliminary list of the most commonly studied topics within each. Discussions with colleagues helped us identify which topics had enough material to be covered in their own chapters and which topics might be best combined with related matter.

Next came the most difficult part of the process: recruiting authors. It was our plan to enlist a mixture of established and emerging researchers. Established researchers bring a combination of breadth and depth gained from a career spent working in their respective fields. Emerging researchers (those with recently awarded doctorates and current graduate students) can bring fresh insight to their fields, and they also represent the psychologists of the future, those who are most likely to move their areas forward. Emerging authors were recruited in two ways. First, some early career psychologists were recruited based on their work or reputation. Second, we invited all established authors to collaborate with graduate students, post-docs, or junior colleagues.

Once we knew what topic areas we wanted covered and who we would like to author each of the chapters, we charged the authors with four tasks. First, we asked them to think broadly about gender. As we mentioned earlier, too often in the field, the word "gender" is assumed to be a code word for women. We did not want the authors to assume that a handbook designed to describe the gender research in psychology would really focus only on the psychology of women. We asked them specifically to consider men, boys, women, and girls. But we also asked the authors to explore the intersection of racial, ethnic, and sexual minority status (including transgender) whenever possible. Some authors went beyond that and also addressed the role of social class and other demographic influences. Second, we asked authors not just to summarize the research that shows significant gender differences, but to explore critically the areas in their subfields where gender is studied, to discuss where the differences are and where they are not, and then to offer some form of interpretation of those effects or noneffects (e.g., effect sizes from meta-analyses). Third, we asked the authors to consider international research whenever possible. We recognized that this would be easier for some topics than others. In some areas, the focus would have to be on North American research findings (or even those specific to the United States) because the wide variety of legal or cultural factors would preclude a thorough analysis of cross-cultural issues. Other chapters would more easily allow for these comparisons. However, in most chapters, authors were able to provide at least some focus on research conducted outside the United States. Finally, because all authors are experts in their respective subfields, we asked them to conclude their chapters with a section that describes what they think researchers should do next (i.e., future directions). This could be theory development, new research methodologies or statistical approaches, or topics that need attention; whatever the authors thought would help to propel their area forward was appropriate.

Handbook Overview

Our survey of the most common topical areas within psychology led us to create 14 sections for this handbook, each with multiple chapters. The sheer number of chapters resulted in the decision that the handbook would have to be produced in two volumes. This meant ordering those sections into two sets of conceptual wholes. This was not an easy task, but we came to the following compromise. *Volume I* would begin with a section on the history of gender research in psychology and with a consideration research methods. We decided that this was the right way to begin because these are the important basics that psychologists must learn before going on to other topics. The remaining sections in Volume I are Brain and Behavior; Learning, Education, and Cognitive Processes; Communication; Emotion and Motivation; and Lifespan Development. In total, these seven sections represent the areas of general and experimental psychology. *Volume II*, on the other hand, contains the sections that address the social and applied aspects of psychology. This volume contains sections on personality psychology, abnormal and clinical psychology, psychotherapy, social psychology, industrial–organizational psychology, health psychology, and special topics in applied psychology. A brief description of these sections, and the chapters in them, is provided next.

Volume I: Gender Research in General and Experimental Psychology

History of Psychology

Volume I begins with a three-chapter section on the history of gender research in psychology. First, Alexandra Rutherford and Leeat Granek describe the emergence of the study of the psychology of women in the late 1800s as it was studied by the first generation of women who became psychologists. They situate the development of the field in the historical context of events and movements (e.g., World War II, the Women's Liberation Movement, multiculturalism) that drove psychologists to organized activism and affected what they saw as important topics of study. Next, Sam V. Cochran dates the emergence of the study of men and masculinity to the Women's Liberation Movement of the 1960s, which spurred men, as well as women, to consider how their lives had been shaped and limited by gender-role socialization. He traces the growth of the field and introduces readers to the major topics, theories, and measures that have preoccupied researchers thus far. Then, Kristin A. Hancock and Karen Greenspan discuss the emergence and development of the psychological study of lesbian, gay, bisexual, and transgender issues. They use a generational framework to show how the field has changed from first generation work on "male homosexuals" at a time when gay men and lesbians were thought to be mentally ill to second generation work that challenged that position and showed that lesbians and gay men could be happy and healthy in the absence of social stigmatization and discrimination. Third generation researchers have broadened the base to include bisexual and trans people, to include ethnic and racial diversity, and to study aspects beyond mental health and illness, including family life.

Research Methods

This section contains six chapters that provide an overview of some of the major topics related to research methods in the psychological study of gender. The first two chapters explore the two main approaches for conducting gender-based research: quantitative and qualitative methods. In the first of these, Sarah K. Murnen and Linda Smolak discuss experimental and quasi-experimental research methodologies; they describe these methods' advantages, disadvantages, and the various ways that researchers can offset the effects of some of those disadvantages. Throughout their chapter, they use examples from the recent research literature to highlight their points. Next, Mary Gergen describes the wide range of qualitative research methods available to study the psychology of gender. Her chapter describes the basic characteristics of qualitative research in general and then provides descriptions of the many different approaches for conducting qualitative research and illustrates them with examples from current literature.

The remaining four chapters examine specific methodological limitations that researchers face. First, Andrew P. Smiler and Marina Epstein address the complex issue of assessment. They organized their chapter around various types of measures of gender: measures of support for, and adherence to, cultural gender norms; measures of gender-role conflict and gender-role stress; and measures related to the relative position of men and women in society. Within each of these sections, Smiler and Epstein describe the reliability and validity of some of the most commonly used measures. In the next chapter, Gordon Forbes describes the various approaches to the cross-cultural study of gender. This chapter provides an excellent overview for those who are not familiar with conducting research across cultural boundaries. It discusses the differences between various social groups, the elements of culture, approaches to the psychological study of culture, and the measurement problems researchers can expect to face. Then, Deborah J. Bowen, Chanita Hughes Halbert, Alecia Robinson, and Uli Boehmer discuss the importance of sample diversity in gender research. They describe various procedures researchers can use to maximize the recruitment of a wide variety of minority groups (e.g., social, ethnic, and sexual minorities) into their studies. This section concludes with a chapter by Peter Hegarty and Felicia Pratto, who write about the important issue of how researchers interpret and communicate findings from gender-related research. They compare and contrast "sex differences" and "gender differences," and they note the important influence of social and political climates, as well as scientific metaphors and social norms, in framing how differences are interpreted by authors and their readers.

Brain and Behavior

The three chapters in this section focus on current research and theory in neuroscience and evolutionary theory. First, Deborah Saucier and Crystal Ehresman discuss the physiology of sex differences. They summarize the current knowledge about genetic and hormonal effects on human development and behavior, including menstrual cycle effects and physiological differences related to sexual orientation. In the next chapter, Joseph A. Schroeder examines the evidence for sex-related differences in sensation and perception. He examines the sensory systems one by one to show what evidence, if any, there is that men and women have different thresholds and acuities, and he shows how modern brain imaging techniques are making it possible to study subtle, and gender-related, differences in these important functions. Then, Nora S. Newcombe casts a critical eye on evolutionary psychology theory. She examines the research on spatial cognition to show how an interactionist model can better account for the data at hand.

Learning, Education, and Cognitive Processes

This section contains four chapters that address gender-related issues associated with how and what we learn. In the first chapter, Susan A. Basow describes the many ways that gender influences find their way into classrooms. She describes a wide variety of issues from the gendered nature of the teaching profession and the curriculum to the students themselves. She also describes gender differences in educational attainment and provides an overview of the most frequently studied factors that are presumed to influence this outcome. Next, Heather A. Priess and Janet Shibley Hyde examine gender differences in academic abilities and preferences. After providing readers with an overview of some methodological issues, they present a critical review of the research in a number of areas, including intelligence, mathematical and verbal abilities, and academic preferences. Their findings suggest that, although gender similarities are more frequent than gender differences, the questions are complex and require more than a simple difference approach to understand the issues. Third, Carol A. Lawton explores factors that influence gender differences in spatial abilities and wayfinding. Spatial abilities, especially mental rotation, represent one of the more robust findings in the gender difference literature, but Lawton discusses how the underlying biological, cognitive, and social factors that influence these differences are complex and muddy the proverbial waters. The fourth chapter in this section explores gender differences in creativity. After providing an historical overview, Mark A. Runco, Bonnie Cramond, and Alexander R. Pagnani discuss the criteria for assessing creativity, describe how those criteria are applied in scientific research, and review the role of gendered personality and cognitive factors in creative thinking and productivity.

Communication

The three chapters in this section explore the importance of communication—written, oral, and nonverbal. In the first chapter, Christine A. Smith, Ingrid Johnston-Robledo, Maureen C. McHugh, and Joan C. Chrisler discuss the impact that gendered language use has on readers and listeners, describe the history of the development of the APA's guidelines for avoiding bias, and provide some definitions and suggestions for the use of gender-related terminology in speech and writing. Next, Maureen C. McHugh and Jennifer Hambaugh critique the "difference as deficit" model of gendered speech, summarize which hypothesized gender differences the research supports and which it does not, examine sexism in the "naming" of some speech acts (e.g., nagging, gossip), and advocate for a postmodern approach to future research in this area. In the third chapter, Marianne Schmid Mast and Sabine Sczesny interrogate the long-standing theory that gender differences in nonverbal behavior are due to status and power differentials. After their careful review of the literature, they conclude that men's and women's nonverbal behavior differs in a number of ways, and high- and low-status people's nonverbal behavior differs in some ways, but status and gender differences do not map onto each other consistently. They call for more complex studies that allow researchers to examine interaction effects between gender and status, given the important effect nonverbal behaviors can have on impressions of women and men, especially in the workplace and in leadership positions.

Emotion and Motivation

There are three chapters in this section, and each explores a different area in which gender influences the way we feel and express our feelings or our motivation to act in a given way. The first chapter, written by Leslie R. Brody and Judith A. Hall, explores gender and emotion. They examine topics such as gender stereotypes about emotional display rules and emotional regulation, gender-related issues associated with the nonverbal expression of emotion, and emotional competence. In the next chapter, C. Peter Herman and Janet Polivy discuss gender-related issues in eating behavior. For example, why is it that, even after we control for men's typically greater body size, men tend to eat more than women, and the food they eat is not as healthy as what women eat? Herman and Polivy explore the main biological, psychological, and social factors that influence this important aspect of human behavior. Next, Jennifer Petersen and Janet Shibley Hyde review the research on gender differences in sexuality. After exploring the many theories that address this issue, Petersen and Hyde review the empirical data on sexual behavior and attitudes, as well as the biological, psychological, and social factors that influence them.

Lifespan Development

The three chapters in this section explore gender-related developmental influences across the lifespan. The first chapter examines the development of gender identity, gender roles, and gender stereotypes in children. May Ling Halim and Diane Ruble also explore the many aspects that influence these factors, including the roles of cognitive development, parents, and sociocultural factors, and they discuss the behavioral consequences of gender-role socialization in this age group. In the second chapter, Katherine H. Clemans, Laura M. DeRose, Julia A. Graber, and Jeanne Brooks-Gunn describe how adolescent gender roles are influenced by an increasing degree of interactions with an expanding social network. Changes in adolescents' bodies influence the ways girls and boys see themselves, how others see them, and how they interact with the world. For a minority of adolescents, this can be a problematic time, thus, the authors also discuss some of the more common intra- and interpersonal problems associated with adolescence. Abigail J. Stewart and Nicky J. Newton conclude this section with their exploration gender-related development across adulthood. They offer a review and critical analysis of theory and research on changes in personality, with a focus on Erikson's theory of psychosocial development. Stewart and Newton also discuss the role of the aging body and how changes in social roles can influence adults' gender enactment.

Volume II: Gender Research in Social and Applied Psychology

Personality Psychology

In the first chapter in this section Jayne E. Stake and Heather Eisele review the research on gender similarities and differences in important aspects of personality, such as agency and communion, the Big Five personality traits, and self-concept. They emphasize the importance of social context on the expression of personality traits and introduce readers to some new directions in the study of well-being and healthy personalities. Next, Lauren E. Duncan and Bill E. Peterson review the research on gender and motivation for achievement, power, and affiliation. They discuss traditional and contemporary methods of studying social motives and show how expression of these motives may differ across cohorts due to historical events and cultural contexts. The chapter concludes with a call for future research that includes diverse samples and the potential to evaluate the impact of mediating and moderating variables. In the third chapter in this section Nancy Lynn Baker and Janelle L. Mason discuss the ways that gender bias (and other forms of prejudice) complicate researchers' and clinicians' attempts to measure personality and abilities. Among the topics the authors examine are assumptions about tests and test takers, the influence of context and experience on test scores, and problems with how norms for test scores are constructed and which norms assessors should use. Issues with particular tests are also reviewed.

Abnormal and Clinical Psychology

The chapters in this section discuss gender (and other) stereotypes in the conceptualization of psychiatric diagnoses and gender differences in two psychological problems for which people often seek psychotherapy. First, Alisha Ali, Paula J. Caplan, and Rachel Fagant discuss the social construction of the diagnostic categories in the American Psychiatric Association's *Diagnostic and Statistical Manual of Mental Disorders (DSM)*. They show how androcentric, heterosexist, and racist ideas can shape expectations for how people "should" behave and what type of "treatment" is required to maintain the status quo. Special attention is paid to issues in the diagnoses of personality, anxiety, and mood disorders. Next, Kate Richmond, Kate Carroll, and Kristoffer Denboske interrogate the social construction of gender identity disorder. Is deviance in gender performance necessarily a mental illness? Whose interests does this diagnosis serve? Is it possible to reform the "diagnosis" to meet the needs of trans people without pathologizing gender nonconformity? These are some of the provocative questions the authors raise. In the next chapter, Mark L. Hatzenbuehler, Lori M. Hilt, and Susan Nolen-Hoeksema review the literature on gender differences and sexual orientation differences in depression rates. They examine the evidence for biopsychosocial causes of depression and then propose a new model they call the "stress-mediation model of vulnerability to depression" that accounts for the evidence to date. In the fourth and last chapter in this section, Rachel M. Calogero and J. Kevin Thompson discuss gendered aspects of negative body image, such as appearance anxiety, drive for muscularity, and drive for thinness. The relationship of these body image concerns to eating disorders, anabolic steroid abuse, body dysmorphic disorder, and elective cosmetic surgery is discussed in light of explanations such as objectification theory and the tripartite model of social influence.

Psychotherapy

The three chapters in this section concern gender issues in the process of psychotherapy and the issues that bring people to a therapist. First, Cynthia Bruns and Ellyn Kaschak recount the history of the development of feminist therapy and the impact of the Women's Liberation Movement's consciousness-raising technique on our understanding of women's mental health and "dis-order." The authors review the research that supports the utility of a gender and power analysis in therapy, critique the evidence-based treatment movement, and consider issues such as whether men can be feminist therapists. Next, Matt Englar-Carlson, Mark A. Stevens, and Robert Scholz discuss gender issues in psychotherapy with men. As masculinity is currently constructed, it works against men's willingness to admit vulnerability, to seek psychotherapy when they need it, and to feel comfortable "sharing" in the therapy setting. The authors examine the types of problems that typically bring men to therapy, provide advice on how to engage and support men during therapy sessions, and discuss the ways that male clients benefit from a gender analysis of their stresses and problems. In the last chapter in this section Louise B. Silverstein and Gary Brooks examine gender issues in family and couples counseling with lesbian, gay, and heterosexual couples. They critique gender stereotypes in family systems therapy, encourage therapists to adopt a social justice and multicultural perspective in family and couples therapy, and critique the absence of intersectionality in evidence-based treatment models.

Social Psychology

Social psychology is one of the areas where gender research has flourished. Four of the main areas are summarized here. In the first chapter in this section, Tara C. Marshall provides an overview of the theories and research associated with gender, peer relationships, and intimate relationships. She reviews a wide variety of topics, including factors that influence the development and maintenance of same-sex and cross-sex friendships, as well as potential romantic partners. Marshall concludes with a discussion of gender-related factors associated with the ending of romantic relationships. The second chapter, written by Irene Hanson Frieze and Man Yu Li, explores gender-related factors in aggression and prosocial behavior. They provide a review of the gender stereotypes associated with aggression, as well as an overview of the findings from a wide variety of experimental and quasi-experimental research on gender and aggression. Frieze and Li also discuss gender differences in various types of prosocial behavior, including empathy, nurturance, personal disclosure, and helping behavior. The third chapter explores gender issues in group behavior. Linda Carli describes the many ways in which a group's gender composition can influence people's behaviors in that group, as well as how gender composition affects the group's performance on a variety of tasks. Carli highlights the importance of the gender stereotypes we bring to our group interactions. In the fourth chapter, Ritch C. Savin-Williams, Seth T. Pardo, Zhana Vrangalova, Ryan S. Mitchell, and Kenneth

M. Cohen provide an overview of the research associated with sex and gender prejudice. After discussing the prevalence and correlates of prejudice against gay, lesbian, and bisexual individuals, the authors address prejudice against transgendered individuals. They conclude their chapter on a positive note by describing research that suggests that attitudes toward sexual minorities might be improving.

Industrial–Organizational Psychology

This section includes chapters that focus on different aspects of work, including social interactions in the workplace and work–life balance. Helen M.G.Watt starts off the section with a review of the literature on gender and occupational choice, with a special focus on how gender-role socialization affects people's interest in STEM (science, technology, engineering, mathematics) fields. She examines the myriad ways that gender stereotypes, peers, teachers, parents, and popular culture impact boys' and girls' perceived abilities and motivation. Next, Scott Coltrane and Kristy Y. Shih review the literature on gender and the division of labor, with a focus on household labor and childcare. They examine theories that purport to explain why, despite the massive increase in the number of women in the formal workplace, women still do much more household labor than men do. Coltrane and Shih also compare and contrast lesbian and gay couples' division of labor with that of heterosexual couples, and they discuss the negative and positive effects of work-to-family and family-to-work spillover. Vicki J. Magley, Jessica A. Gallus, and Jennifer A. Bunk examine gendered aspects of workplace mistreatment, including incivility, bullying, and sexual harassment. They consider the causes and consequences of mistreatment and suggest ways that institutions can reduce mistreatment in their workplaces. Finally, Ronit Karik and Alice H. Eagly review the literature on gender and leadership, which traditionally has been associated with men and masculinity. They discuss the role of gender stereotypes, social capital, leadership style, and barriers to advancement in the relative rates of advancement up the corporate ladder and the political hierarchy.

Health Psychology

This section contains four chapters that describe the main types of gender-related research conducted in health psychology. In the first chapter, Christina Lee reviews the area of gender, health, and health behaviors. Her chapter begins by exploring gender differences in life expectancy and then describes the ways in which gender differences in health-promoting behaviors can impact longevity. She notes the complex nature of the factors that influence health and discusses ways in which factors such as socioeconomic and cultural context influence these types of gender differences. The second chapter, written by Amy Zwicker and Anita DeLongis, discusses gender differences in stress and coping. After providing a general overview of the main models, Zwicker and DeLongis discuss research on two gender-related, stressful contexts: interpersonal relationships and the workplace. In addition to their examination of the role of coping, the authors describe the importance of social support in mitigating the adverse effects of stress. The third chapter explores gender issues in health-care access and utilization. Cheryl B. Travis, Andrea L. Meltzer, and Dawn M. Howerton begin by describing gender differences in health-care utilization, including access to ambulatory care and medications. They then discuss the main gender-related factors that can influence whether and when people seek health care, including gender stereotypes, differences in symptom-reporting style, and communication with medical professionals. The authors then apply these issues to health utilization practices in three areas: cancer, diabetes, and sexual and reproductive health. In the final chapter of this section, Vivian S. Hwang and Sharon Danoff-Burg summarize and discuss research on gender differences in the diagnosis and treatment of chronic illness. For example, the importance of early disease diagnosis often is important for treatment success, but early diagnosis can be complicated by gender stereotypes. Hwang and Danoff-Burg also focus on gender differences in adjustment to chronic illnesses, such as cancer and HIV.

Special Topics in Applied Psychology

The last section of the handbook contains five chapters on special topics within gender research. In the first of these, Diane L. Gill and Cindra S. Kamphoff review gender research in sports psychology. Although trained in psychology, sports psychologists work primarily with physiologists, biomechanists, and motor behavior researchers, and this affects the way they approach topics such as gender. Gill and Kamphoff discuss a number of important areas, including the history of women in college sports and the role of governmental legislation on access to sport participation, as well as gender differences in sport participation and the barriers that influence access to and interest in sport. The second chapter provides an overview of some of the important methodological issues encountered by those who study gender-related issues in forensic psychology. Kenneth V. Heard discusses the importance of doing forensic research that can stand up to court scrutiny, the differences between being a forensic researcher and a psychotherapist who works in a forensic environment, and a myriad of ethical and methodological issues faced by forensic researchers. In the third chapter, Sharon M. Wasco and Meg A. Bond describe how gender is treated within community psychology. After describing the goals of community psychology and how gender is typically conceptualized in that field, Wasco and Bond summarize gender-related findings from the main journals on the topic. They note that gender in this area tends to be treated either as a grouping, process, or contextual variable. They describe examples of all of these types to help illustrate their use. The fourth chapter, written by Dara Greenwood and Julia Lippman, explores gender in the media. They review research that explores how often, and in what capacity, women and men are presented in traditional media (especially television and video games), as well as gender differences in the use of so-called new media (e.g., internet, cell phones). Greenwood and Lippman also explore gender differences in the influences these media have on boys, girls, men, and women. The final chapter in this section, and the handbook and a whole, is Angela R. Febbraro and Ritu M. Gill's examination of gender in military psychology. The chapter is focused mostly on women in the male-dominated and hypermasculine military, and the authors examine issues related to career progression, leadership, harassment, and work–life balance. Febbraro and Gill conclude with a discussion of sexual orientation and military service in various countries.

Observations and Gaps

Reading through each of the chapters gave us an appreciation for how far psychology has come in understanding gender's multi-faceted influence on people's lives. However, we also began to realize how much farther psychology, as a discipline, has yet to go. In other words, we began to identify some gaps in the research.

Where are the Men and Boys in Gender Research? One of the first things we noticed when we started reading the initial chapter submissions was the absence of men and boys in gender research. There is a myth within psychology that all of the knowledge that came before the arrival of second wave feminism was based solely on men, and, as such, there is an abundance of knowledge about men, but an absence of knowledge about women. The reality, however, is quite different. Although men were used most often as participants in psychological research, diversity among men was rarely studied. Most of the men who participated in this early psychological research were White and upper middle class or upper class; differences based on economic, cultural, racial, ethnic, and sexual orientation were rarely studied. Feminist scholars were correct to say that the results of that work might not be generalizable to women, but it has only recently become apparent that they are not always generalizable to all men either.

The relative absence of men and boys in gender research in psychology was evident in almost all chapters. For example, when Kark and Eagly discussed gender issues in leadership, they rarely mentioned studies of the barriers that men face in becoming leaders, perhaps because no such studies have yet been done. The false assumption is that all men have an equal chance to become leaders. Similarly, Gill and Kamphoff's overview shows that gender research in sport psychology rarely addresses the barriers that boys and men face in accessing, excelling in, or ignoring sports (e.g., Are boys who do not want to participate in sports marginalized?). And Travis, Meltzer, and Howerton's chapter emphasizes how researchers have focused on barriers to women's health-care utilization but have rarely studied how gender-role socialization has influenced men's greater risk for early mortality.

There has been a growth in the study of the psychology of men and masculinity, but some areas of gender research have been at the forefront of discussions of men's and boys' issues and an integration of those issues into theories and research. For example, there is a growing discussion of men's and boys' gender-related problems in counseling (e.g., Silverstein and Brooks) and health psychology (e.g., Lee). Research in the body image area is an excellent example of this, and it was addressed in several chapters. That is, whereas past research has shown that men and boys display fewer weight-related body image concerns than women and girls do, when researchers began asking men and boys about their muscularity concern, they found it was associated with a wide variety of adverse outcomes, including poor self-esteem and higher levels of both anxiety and depression (McCreary & Sasse, 2000). Thus, men's and women's body images are focused on different ideals (i.e., the thin ideal versus the muscular ideal), but both ideals can result in serious consequences (e.g., eating disorders, anabolic steroid abuse). The research in this area has grown substantially since this differentiation became salient in the literature.

Differences in Doing Gender Research Across Fields. A second thing we noticed was that gender is studied differently in some fields of psychology (e.g., neuroscience and sports psychology vs. social and clinical psychology), as these researchers use different techniques, theories, models, measures, or terminology. In many ways, these differences are a reflection of the point we raised earlier in this Introduction that gender research tends to be situated more often in the social, clinical, and developmental areas of psychology. As a result, there is a critical mass of gender researchers in some fields, but not others. In areas where there are many gender researchers, people get to know one another. They meet regularly at conferences and collaborate in a wide range of research endeavors. This leads to the development of a wider range of topical expertise within the study of gender. That became obvious to us as we were recruiting authors for this handbook. Many authors easily could have written two or more chapters (and two did!) because they are regarded as experts in more than one aspect of the psychology of gender. But, based on our observations, this does not appear to be the same for those who study gender outside of the core gender research areas.

There are many pitfalls for this type of segregated gender research. The first potential concern is that it could lead to miscommunication among gender researchers. For example, we noted, during the process of putting this handbook together, that those who do research from within the core areas tend to use different terminology than those who work in the noncore areas. Those in the core, for example, tended to make a distinction between "gender differences" and "sex differences," as well as "gender roles" and "sex roles." This can be a frustrating experience for many and leads to the question of how gender researchers in all areas of psychology can work effectively together, even though these barriers such as this exist. In other words, do these differences prevent collaborations between the two groups? Also, are there any exclusional factors operating among gender researchers that impede communication and make collaboration difficult? It is important for gender researchers to ask themselves these questions.

Overstating the Magnitude of Differences. A third issue we noticed is that, when there is no focus on interpreting effect sizes, many people (researchers included) tend to overemphasize the magnitude of gender differences. That is, even though women and men, or boys and girls, appear to be more similar than different, many researchers overemphasize statistical differences without interpreting effect sizes. This often leads to the use of language that suggests all men do X, or are Y, whereas all women do A, or are B. There is no qualifying the findings, such as noting that men "tend to" act or be a certain way, whereas women "tend to" act or be the same way somewhat less or more. Similarly, even gender researchers frequently use the colloquial phrase "opposite sex" when we all know that women and men are more alike than different. The term "other sex" is more appropriate, even though that phrase still suggests a dichotomy that does not include those who are intersex.

But how do psychologists pursue a desire not to overstate differences when the professional and popular presses emphasize significant differences and make it almost impossible to publish research findings of similarities or nonsignificant differences? How do theories get developed and described in a way that does not overly magnify gender differences, but accurately reflects potential similarities and differences as a function of various psychological or cultural factors? These are considerations that researchers and their professional organizations need to consider in depth.

Measurement. A fourth issue that became apparent is that our measures of psychological gender are woefully inadequate. Many instruments are based on gender stereotypes that may be dated (e.g., Bem Sex Role Inventory [Bem, 1974]; Personal Attributes Questionnaire [Spence, Helmreich, & Stapp, 1975]). The use of outdated items on gender-related questionnaires can lead to a wide variety of problems with both validity and reliability. For example, the failure to adopt current and relevant content reduces the construct validity of the instrument, that is, it no longer measures the construct it was designed to measure or it does not measure it as accurately as it once did. Similarly, the attempt to measure gender-related content using dated instruments could become obvious to participants and lead to potential response biases.

A related problem is that some researchers, especially those who base their work on Sandra Bem's (1974) theory of androgyny, use gender-role measures inappropriately. Bem's androgyny theory suggests that those who are higher than average on both masculinity and femininity are androgynous, whereas those who are higher on either masculinity or femininity are gender-typed (or cross-gender-typed, if they are higher on the nonsex-specific trait component). Assessment of someone's androgyny is dependent upon being able to measure people's global levels of masculinity and femininity. Initially, this is what people thought the Bem Sex Role Inventory and Spence et al.'s Personal Attributes Questionnaire did. Numerous studies were devised and conducted, and many findings seemed to support Bem's theory (Cooke, 1985). However, several problems emerged with these measures, including a realization that the questionnaires measure only two smaller dimensions of masculinity and femininity: agency or instrumentality and communion or expressivity (e.g., Archer, 1989; McCreary, 1990; Spence, 1984). In addition, several studies (e.g., Lubinski,

Tellegen, & Butcher, 1983) showed that the agency or instrumental scales tend to be moderately correlated with self-esteem because of the perceived or actual increased degree of mastery over one's environment these traits can provide. Given these definitional problems, androgyny theory cannot be properly tested, although people continue to try. If this is the case, then what role do the existing studies play in our understanding of the psychology of gender? Should we discount those findings entirely, or even partially? How much credibility do we give the findings? Are those studies useful in other ways? And what should journal editors do when they receive new submissions based on these outdated measurement principles?

The problem with trying to assess global masculinity and femininity that both men and women internalize led some researchers to focus on the development of gender-specific measures. Questionnaires such as the Conformity to Male Norms Scale (Mahalik et al., 2003) and the Adolescent Femininity Ideology Scale (Tolman & Porche, 2000) assess gender-related characteristics in only women/girls or only men/boys. Although questionnaires such as these may be easier to create and represent cleaner constructs (i.e., avoiding the complexity of trying to define measures that are reliable and valid in both male and female participants), they come at a price: Using questionnaires such as these means that researchers can no longer study the degree to which gender-role socialization influences the myriad of gender differences described in this handbook (e.g., risky health behaviors, performance on educational attainment measures, sexual motivation, mental health outcomes). In other words, researchers who use these types of measures can no longer study the extent to which gender role interacts with gender to influence important outcomes.

Conclusion

The 2 years we spent organizing and editing this handbook was an exciting time for us. We learned a lot by reading about subfields in which we do not ourselves work, and we are grateful to the authors because every chapter gave us something new to consider. We hope that our readers will gain as much from the experience of reading the handbook as we did from editing it. And, we hope that you, our readers, will answer some of the questions, solve some of the problems, and fill in some of the gaps we mentioned above. Each chapter ends with suggestions for future research, and there is much to be done. So, let us get to it!

References

Archer, J. (1989). The relationship between gender-role measures: A review. *British Journal of Social Psychology, 28*, 173–184.

Baron, R. M., & Kenny, D. A. (1986). The moderator-mediator variable distinction in social psychological research: Conceptual, strategic, and statistical considerations. *Journal of Personality and Social Psychology, 51*, 1173–1182.

Bem, S. L. (1974). The measurement of psychological androgyny. *Journal of Consulting and Clinical Psychology, 42*, 155–162.

Chrisler, J. C. (2007). The subtleties of meaning: Still arguing after all these years. *Feminism & Psychology, 17*, 442–446.

Cooke, E. P. (1985). *Psychological androgyny*. New York: Pergamon Press.

Fiske, A. P., Haslam, N., & Fiske, S. T. (1991). Confusing one person with another: What errors reveal about the elementary forms of social relations. *Journal of Personality and Social Psychology, 60*, 656–674.

Hesse-Biber, S. N., & Leavy, P. (2008). *Handbook of emergent methods*. New York: Guilford.

Lubinski, D., Tellegen, A., & Butcher, J. N. (1983). Masculinity, femininity, and androgyny viewed and assessed as distinct concepts. *Journal of Personality and Social Psychology, 44*, 428–439.

Mahalik, J. R., Locke, B. D., Ludlow, L. H., Diemer, M. A., Scott, R. P. J., Gottfried, M., et al. (2003). Development of the conformity to masculine norms inventory. *Psychology of Men & Masculinity, 4*, 3–25.

McCreary, D. R. (1990). Multidimensionality and the measurement of gender-role attributes: A comment on Archer. *British Journal of Social Psychology, 29*, 265–272.

McCreary, D. R., & Sasse, D. K. (2000). An exploration of the drive for muscularity in adolescent boys and girls. *Journal of American College Health, 48*, 297–304.

Pryzgoda, J., & Chrisler, J. C. (2000). Definitions of sex and gender: The subtleties of meaning. *Sex Roles, 43*, 553–569.

Spence, J. T. (1984). Masculinity, femininity, and gender-related traits: A conceptual analysis and critique of current research. In B. A. Maher & W. B. Maher (Eds.), *Progress in experimental personality research* (Vol. 13, pp. 1–97). New York: Academic Press.

Spence, J. T., Helmreich, R. L., & Stapp, J. (1975). Ratings of self and peers on sex role attitudes and their relation to self-esteem and conceptions of masculinity and femininity. *Journal of Personality and Social Psychology, 32*, 29–39.

Stangor, C., Lynch, L., Duan, C., & Glass, B. (1992). Categorization of individuals on the basis of multiple social features. *Journal of Personality and Social Psychology, 62*, 207–218.

Tolman, D. L., & Porche, M. V. (2000). The Adolescent Femininity Ideology Scale: Development and validation of a new measure for girls. *Psychology of Women Quarterly, 24*, 365–376.

Unger, R. K. (1998). *Resisting gender: Twenty-five years of feminist psychology*. Thousand Oaks, CA: Sage.

West, C., & Zimmerman, D. H. (1987). Doing gender. *Gender & Society, 1*, 125–151.

Wilkinson, L., & the Task Force on Statistical Inference. (1999). Statistical methods in psychology journals: Guidelines and explanations. *American Psychologist, 54*, 595–604.

Part VIII
Personality Psychology

Chapter 2
Gender and Personality

Jayne E. Stake and Heather Eisele

Personality is the study of individual differences and thus holds promise for a better understanding of how our gendered society shapes and reinforces differences in women's and men's attitudes, emotions, and behaviors. Two strengths of present-day personality research are particularly relevant for the study of gender. First, personality researchers gather data from large samples of normally functioning individuals and emphasize the importance of accurate generalizations of their findings to other normal samples. This methodology allows for the veridical assessment of similarity and difference trends in women's and men's personality characteristics. Second, is the attention personality researchers typically give to the careful measurement of constructs through adequate sampling of concept domains, empirical validation, and reliability checks.

Despite these potential advantages for the study of gender, the personality field has been slow to contribute to gender theory or to provide meaningful, fully validated, gender-related knowledge. Historical and present-day limitations of personality research are responsible for this lack of progress. For the first several decades of personality research, little attention was paid to women or to issues that tend to be particularly important in women's lives. Ethnicity, sexual orientation, and other individual difference variables were similarly ignored. Samples were often exclusively comprised of white men, and hypotheses were generated from a white, androcentric perspective. Nevertheless, researchers typically interpreted their data as having validity for the human personality more generally. When women were included as study participants, gender differences were usually not a focus of study and often were not reported.

A second limitation of personality research, which remains a problem today, is that most personality researchers rely on self-report as their primary source of data, a practice that is particularly problematic when variables are value laden. Although one can argue that only individuals themselves can accurately report on their internal experiences, self-reports are affected by response sets that are shaped by societal expectations relevant to gender. For example, the societal prohibition against the expression of weakness may affect boys' and men's willingness to disclose, or even to recognize within themselves, pangs of anxiety or bouts of depression. In contrast, women and girls experience fewer sanctions for expressing such negative emotions and, therefore, may feel less inhibited from doing so.

Progress in this field is further limited by the essentialist orientation of many personality researchers who have focused largely on what they assume to be inherent traits and have proposed models that include primarily distal causes such as evolutionary forces (e.g., Nettle, 2006) and the heritability of personality (e.g., Bouchard, 2004). Related to this essentialist emphasis, some personality researchers have been interested in linking observed gender differences in behavior to

---

J.E. Stake (✉)
University of Missouri-St. Louis, St. Louis, MO, USA

physiological differences (e.g., Sellers, Mehl, & Josephs, 2006). In this type of explanatory model, physiological variables are presumed to be based on heredity, and a one-way causal effect is assumed between physiological factors and behavior. These models do not recognize that although physiological variables affect personality and behavior, so too can environmental and social factors affect the physiological development and ongoing physiological state of the individual (e.g., Gabbard, 2005).

In this chapter, we review and critique gender-related personality theory and research with an emphasis on current issues. We begin by discussing the central importance of social factors and contexts for the understanding of personality and gender. We then describe how the personality traits traditionally linked in our society with masculinity and femininity have come to be conceptualized and researched over time and report recent research advances in this area. The ways in which these traditional gendered dimensions correspond to the five domains of the currently popular five-factor model of personality and to identified dimensions of self-concept are then reviewed. Methodological problems in five-factor research are discussed, as are methods for measuring self-esteem and self-concept. We conclude with suggestions for expanding the scope of personality theory and research to include a greater emphasis on social and contextual variables and on newly emerging personality constructs that transcend traditional indices of mental health, well-being, and adjustment.

Social Influences on Gender Differences in Personality

Despite the relatively minor role typically attributed in personality theory and research to social and contextual factors, any full comprehension of personality necessitates recognition of these variables. By disregarding them, one is in danger of committing the fundamental attribution error (Ross, 1977) by overattributing behavior to inherent personality traits rather than to variables within the social context. For example, women as a group are assumed to be naturally more nurturing than men and men to be naturally more aggressive than women. Personality researchers seldom recognize or discuss how these gender differences may be influenced by the different social contexts men and women inhabit, which provide gendered reinforcement patterns, role models, and messages about appropriate behavior.

Feminist theorists have explained that all individuals have their own combination of situated social identities and live within complex social contexts that correspond to that set of identities. Eagly (1987) posited in her social role theory that it is these different social roles, rather than biological sex, that provide the primary explanation for gender differences in behavior. According to social role theory, gender roles directly and indirectly create gender differences in behavior. When individuals conform to and act in accordance with their gender roles, they directly confirm stereotypes about what is natural for men and women. In addition, the experiences that men and women gain by enacting their social roles indirectly shape their behaviors by influencing the confidence and values they place on particular occupations, avocations, relationships, and skill development. Thus, the observed traditional gender differences in behaviors, skills, preferences, and aptitudes are directly and indirectly created by men's and women's gender roles. It is not necessary for individuals to internalize these gender norms fully for gender differences in behavior to develop. Social pressure from others and the broader society to conform to these roles, as well as the potential punishment for nonconformity and the rewards for conformity, can induce gender-stereotyped behavior regardless of individuals' personal beliefs and preferences (Eagly, 1987).

Contextual cues influence which social identity will be most salient for an individual at a particular point in time and which behaviors are most appropriate for the setting. Although some contextual cues are obvious, such as whether one is in an organizational setting (making a work identity salient) or a familial setting (making a relational identity salient), other contextual cues are more subtle. For example, when women have been in work groups comprised mostly of men, their task performance has been negatively affected; men's performance, however, has not been affected by the gender composition of their work group (Inzlicht & Ben-Zeev, 2000; Miller, 2001). Eagly (1987) proposed that gender roles are often activated in ambiguous situations in which other role identities are not salient. She suggested that participants in laboratory experiments are in ambiguous situations and may resort to traditional gendered behavior in the absence of other cues for appropriate behavior.

According to social role theory, therefore, gender differences in behavior are tied to traditional social roles for women and men and do not reflect inherent gender differences in personality traits. If this theory is correct, then women's and men's behaviors should change as their social context changes; further, if they are placed in a social context that is more common to individuals of the other gender, their behavior should change accordingly to fit that context. The importance of social context in determining observed gender differences has been strongly supported by recent research on contextual factors and gendered behaviors. For example, women are often assumed to be more empathic than men (Manstead, 1992), yet Ickes, Gesn, and Graham (2000) reported, based on a meta-analysis of 15 studies, that women have been shown to be more empathic than men only when gender-role stereotypes were made salient. When participants were not asked to rate the accuracy of their empathic skills (thereby priming gender-role stereotypes), the gender difference effect size (d) was 0.04, or essentially zero (Ickes et al., 2000). Contextual factors have also influenced the accuracy of men's and women's inferences about others' thoughts and feelings. Men have displayed levels of accuracy similar to those of women in some types of relationships (Thomas & Fletcher, 2003) and when they were paid to be accurate (Klein & Hodges, 2001). Furthermore, meta-analyses on self-disclosure (Dinda & Allen, 1992) and smiling (LaFrance, Hecht, & Paluck, 2003) have indicated that although overall gender differences in these behaviors exist ($d = 0.18$ for self-disclosure, 0.41 for smiling), these differences are moderated by the type of social context. In the case of self-disclosure, men were not less disclosing than were women when participants were engaged in conversations with men or strangers (Dinda & Allen, 1992).

As further evidence for role theory, research has demonstrated that individuals act in accord with their specific power-related roles rather than with their ascribed gender role. For example, Moskowitz, Suh, and Desaulniers (1994) provided evidence that men's and women's agentic behavior in their work settings was not related to their biological sex. Instead, they found that the workers' role in specific situations determined their behavior; individuals behaved least agentically when engaged with a supervisor and most agentically with a supervisee. In addition, both men and women acted equally submissively with an individual of greater authority regardless of the authority figure's gender (Helwig-Larson, Cunningham, Carrico, & Pergram, 2004). Thus, research on empathy, sociability, and power supports the theory that gender differences in behavior are better explained by social roles and status than by inherent personality differences between women and men.

Masculinity and Femininity in Personality Theory

History of the Masculinity and Femininity Constructs

In 1936, Terman and Miles developed the first psychological test to focus on gender differences in personality. This test was designed to document fundamental differences in masculine and feminine traits (Bem, 1993; Lippa, 2001). Masculinity and femininity were conceptualized as personality traits that were inherent, natural, and healthy for men and women, respectively. In this early test, femininity items included liking babies, liking nursing, being careful about one's manner of dress, preferring others to take the lead, and being afraid of the dark. Masculinity items included liking soldiering, liking hunting, being extremely disobedient as a child, and being able to withstand pain (Bem, 1993). Although Terman and Miles were not explicit in stating the source of these differences, they maintained the essentialist position that these differences were fundamental to men and women and represented a core aspect of their personality (Lippa, 2001).

Important critiques of this early conceptualization of masculinity and femininity were provided by feminist theorists. A primary concern with this model was that masculinity and femininity were defined as a unidimensional, bipolar construct, with masculinity at one end and femininity at the other (Bem, 1993; Lippa, 2001). This model did not allow for high levels of masculinity and femininity in the same individual, a perspective that conformed to the prevailing cultural belief at the time that men and women are and should be fundamentally and fully distinct from one another. Furthermore, deviance from accepted gender-role scripts was conflated with sexual orientation (Bem, 1993; Lippa, 2001). Bem and other critics pointed out that Terman and Miles were not measuring inherent personality differences between men and women but, instead, adherence to gendered cultural norms of the time period (Bem, 1993).

The conceptualization of masculinity and femininity as a bipolar construct was generally accepted until the 1970s when feminist theorists began to uncouple the concept of masculinity and femininity from biological sex. Constantinople (1973) published a review article in which she critiqued masculinity/femininity research conducted before 1970. She presented evidence that femininity and masculinity are separate dimensions rather than opposite ends of a single dimension and reported findings that masculinity and femininity scores correlated with such demographic variables as socioeconomic status and level of education (Constantinople, 1973). During this time, Bem (1974) proposed and began conducting research on the concept of psychological androgyny based on the notion that masculinity and femininity are two separate, orthogonal constructs and that people can develop any combination of levels of masculine and feminine traits. Bem designed the Bem Sex Role Inventory (BSRI; Bem, 1974) to assess how closely individuals' self-descriptions adhered to gender-role stereotypes. "Masculinity" items on the BSRI included traits that have typically been associated with the instrumental or agentic aspects of the masculine role, such as athletic, self-reliant, analytical, competitive, and aggressive. "Femininity" items included traits associated with the expressive or communal aspects of the feminine role, such as affectionate, sensitive to other's needs, compassionate, soft spoken, and warm. Bem theorized that exclusive functioning in either the masculine or the feminine domain was related to poor adjustment and mental health problems, whereas a blend of both sets of traits (androgyny) was optimal for mental health in both men and women.

Research conducted with the BSRI (Bem, 1974) and the Personal Attributes Questionnaire (PAQ; Spence, Helmreich, & Stapp, 1975) has provided evidence for the premise that stereotypically masculine and feminine traits are not tied to biological sex. In fact, studies have revealed large within-sex variability on these traits, with considerable overlap between men's and women's scores and relatively small mean gender differences (Bem, 1974; Spence & Helmreich, 1980; Spence et al., 1975). In addition, the finding that gender differences in masculine stereotyped traits have shrunk in recent years (Twenge, 1997) supports the view that these characteristics, once thought to be tied to biological sex, are malleable and can be affected by social context.

Sexual orientation may be one of the factors that explains the intra-sex variation on these scores. Lippa (2005) provided a summary of data from eight studies in which the expressive and instrumental scores of gay men, lesbians, and heterosexual men and women were analyzed. Women who identified as lesbian tended to describe themselves higher on instrumentality than did women who identified as heterosexual ($d = 0.27$), and men who identified as gay reported greater expressivity ($d = 0.37$) than did men who identified as heterosexual. Lippa (2005) suggested the interesting possibility that it may be biological factors other than genetic sex, such as prenatal hormones, that underlie individual differences in instrumentality and expressiveness. It should be noted, however, that these differences between sexual orientation groups are small, and no differences were found between lesbian and heterosexual women for expressiveness or between gay and heterosexual men for instrumentality.

Given that strong relationships were not found between biological sex and the traits originally conceptualized as masculine and feminine, Spence and Helmreich (1980) proposed that these types of scales not be considered global measures of masculinity and femininity. They argued that the BSRI and the PAQ were not assessing femininity and masculinity but, instead, expressiveness (an interpersonal orientation) and instrumentality (a self-assertive orientation), terms originally proposed by Parsons and Bales (1955). This reconceptualization of masculinity and femininity as instrumentality and expressiveness has contributed to the decoupling of biological sex from qualities traditionally associated with masculinity and femininity.

The realm of gender-role traits has also been re-defined and expanded to include the notions of unmitigated agency and unmitigated communion (Spence, Helmreich, & Holahan, 1979). These terms refer to the negative, socially undesirable aspects of gender roles. Unmitigated agency refers to an extreme focus on the self that is untempered by expressiveness or communality, such as dominance, solely for self-gain and self-enhancement. Unmitigated communion refers to an extreme focus on others that is untempered by instrumentality or agency, such as avoidance of overt group conflict at the expense of oneself (Helgeson, 1994). Given these definitions, the unmitigated form of one set of traits should be negatively related to the unmitigated form of the other, and negative and positive aspects of the same set of traits should relate to one another (Helgeson, 1994). Some support has been demonstrated for these expectations: Negative correlations have been reported between unmitigated agency and unmitigated communion (Bozionelos & Bozionelos, 2003; Saragovi, Koestner, Di Dio, & Aube, 1997), and positive correlations have been reported between instrumentality and unmitigated agency and between expressiveness and unmitigated communion (Saragovi et al., 1997).

Instrumentality and Expressiveness as Mediators of Gender Differences

The conceptualization of instrumentality and expressiveness as personality traits distinct from biological sex has led to studies in which these dimensions are tested as potential explanatory mechanisms for the relation between biological sex and psychological variables. In general, these studies provide evidence that instrumentality and expressiveness account for much of what had been attributed to biological sex. Instrumentality and expressiveness mediated gender differences in internalizing symptoms (e.g., depression, perfectionism) and externalizing symptoms (e.g., lying, stealing) in adolescent boys and girls (Hoffman, Powlishta, & White, 2004; Huselid & Cooper, 1994). Individuals with high instrumentality and low expressiveness were more likely to report externalizing symptoms regardless of gender, whereas individuals with low instrumentality, combined with low social attractiveness and self-worth, were more likely to report internalizing symptoms (Hoffman et al., 2004). Thus, levels of instrumentality and expressiveness explained gender differences in symptoms of psychological distress. In another study in which gender-role traits were tested as mediators, expressiveness was demonstrated to mediate gender differences in emotion-focused communication goals (Burleson & Gilstrap, 2002). Those who were high in expressiveness were more likely to utilize communication styles that emphasized addressing, and not avoiding, others' emotions. Thus, it seems that gender-role variables can explain much of what have been reported as biologically based sex differences in personality.

Expressiveness, Instrumentality, and Mental Health

The constructs of expressiveness and instrumentality have been linked to mental health indices in both women and men. Numerous correlational, self-report studies have demonstrated that measures of instrumentality are positively correlated with self-esteem (Allgood-Merton & Stockard, 1991; Stein, Newcomb, & Bentler, 1992). In addition, instrumentality has related positively to well-being (Saragovi et al., 1997; Sharpe, Heppner, & Dixon, 1995) and social confidence (Woodhill & Samuels, 2003; Saragovi et al., 1997) and negatively to depression and anxiety (Bruch, 2002; Hermann & Betz, 2006; Lengua & Stormshak, 2000; Whitley, 1984). Similarly, expressiveness measures have related positively to general self-esteem (Stein et al., 1992; Woodhill & Samuels, 2003), life satisfaction (Hunt, 1993), well-being (Sharpe et al., 1995), social adjustment (Saragovi et al., 1997), and social self-esteem (Allgood-Merton & Stockard, 1991; Jones, Chernovetz, & Hansson, 1978) and negatively to depression and distress (Hermann & Betz, 2006; Saragovi et al., 1997). However, instrumentality has generally been more strongly related to these mental health variables than expressiveness. Only for variables that are very closely tied to expressiveness, such as congeniality and relationship satisfaction, does expressiveness appear to be more advantageous than does instrumentality (Stake, Zand, & Smalley, 1996).

The positive findings for instrumentality have been questioned, however, on methodological grounds. Because researchers have generally relied on self-report measures to test all variables, correlations between mental health variables and instrumentality may have been artificially inflated. It is certainly likely that people who purport to have a very high level of instrumental traits (e.g., assertiveness, self-confidence) would give high self-ratings as well on variables associated with mental health (Baumeister, Campbell, Krueger, & Vohs, 2003). In addition, the content of the items on self-esteem and instrumentality measures overlaps substantially so that there is little conceptual distance between the two types of measures (Whitley, 1984). A third criticism is that self-ratings have been made in the abstract, outside of naturally occurring life settings, despite evidence that situation-specific expectations and pressures can have strong influences on gender-linked variables and can create intra-individual variations in behavior across situations.

As a response to these limitations in past research, the first author developed alternative methods for testing relationships between mental health variables and expressiveness/instrumentality. In one set of studies, participants described how they responded behaviorally to work-related situations that called for a blend of expressiveness and instrumentality. Individuals who chose to respond to such situations in either an androgynous or an expressive mode experienced more positive well-being within the situation than did those who chose an instrumental or indeterminate (i.e., neither instrumental nor expressive) approach (Stake, 1997). In addition, there was no significant difference in global self-esteem between those who chose to respond androgynously, instrumentally, or expressively and those with little social support in the setting experienced less stress if they responded more androgynously (Stake, 2000). These findings suggest that, when responding in real-life settings in which both expressiveness and instrumentality are expected, an instrumental approach is not necessarily the mode of choice for high self-esteem individuals and may not lead to the most satisfactory mental health outcomes.

As another means of circumventing the limitations of previous research, the first author developed a scale to measure perceptions of situation-specific social expectations for instrumentality and expressiveness (Stake et al., 1996). This measure made possible the evaluation of links between the level of expectations within meaningful life settings and measures of mental health. As might be expected from earlier research, the more people perceived that their life setting (home, school or work) required instrumentality, the higher their setting-specific self-ratings of self-esteem, well-being, and giftedness. The more situations required expressiveness, the higher the self-ratings of likeability and satisfaction within the setting. However, these main effects were qualified by interaction effects between expressiveness and instrumentality for each mental health variable: When instrumentality expectations were high, expressiveness expectations did relate to self-esteem, well-being, and self-perceptions of giftedness; when expressiveness expectations were high, instrumentality expectations were related to self-perceptions of likeability and satisfaction (Stake et al., 1996). In a related study, Saragovi et al. (1997) found that self-reported expressive traits were related to better adjustment when participants rated themselves higher in instrumentality but not when they rated themselves low in instrumentality. Although not entirely consistent with Bem's (1974) original expectations about the value of androgyny, these findings suggest that high amounts of both instrumental and expressive functioning yield the best situation-specific adjustment.

Less is known about the mental health outcomes associated with unmitigated agency and unmitigated communion. Research that is available has linked unmitigated agency to increased pathology, delays in help-seeking behavior, poorer adjustment after hospitalization for heart disease, and difficulty in expressing emotions (Helgeson, 1994). Unmitigated communion has also been associated with decreased help-seeking behavior and poorer adjustment after hospitalization for heart disease (Helgeson, 1994). Negative relationships between unmitigated forms of traditional gender roles and mental health are understandable, given the definitions of these variables. Extreme and negative forms of traditional gender traits deserve greater attention because they can broaden our understanding of how gender roles may negatively affect personal development and adjustment.

Understanding Gender Differences Through the Five-Factor Model

The history of the field of personality is replete with models of the structure of personality. The prevailing model at this time is the five-factor model (FFM), a simple five-dimensional schema developed from an atheoretical, factor analytic approach. As the FFM was developed, writers applied various labels for the dimensions (often referred to as the *Big Five*) or suggested additional factors, and the qualities identified for each domain have varied. However, there appears to be a general agreement at this time about the labels and descriptions applied to the FFM domains, as described later (Costa, Terracciano, & McCrae, 2001).

Agreeableness refers to the nature or tone of one's relationships with others. Agreeableness comprises facets of one's interpersonal functioning—degree of altruism, compliance, modesty, straightforwardness, tender-mindedness, and trust of others.

Openness is the willingness and even eagerness to seek out new experiences and is unrelated to level of aptitude. The following aspects of openness to experience are measured: actions, aesthetics, fantasy, emotions, ideas, and values.

Conscientiousness includes elements of self-control and persistence in behavior toward long-range goals. Elements of conscientiousness are achievement striving, competence, deliberation, dutifulness, order, and self-discipline.

Extroversion pertains to the tendency of the individual to seek out relationships with others and with the environment and to prefer social activity to individual pursuits. Specific qualities of extroversion are high degrees of activity, assertiveness, excitement seeking, gregariousness, positive emotions, and warmth.

Neuroticism is the tendency to perceive one's world as threatening and difficult to manage and, therefore, to experience high levels of negative emotions. Included in the neuroticism domain are angry hostility, anxiety, depression, impulsiveness, self-consciousness, and vulnerability.

As can been seen from these descriptions, the Big Five categories are very broad, with seemingly disparate qualities included within a single domain. Some of the traits within domains have a logical relation (order and self-discipline as components of conscientiousness); however, others do not appear to have a close link (straightforwardness and modesty as components of agreeableness). There is evidence that each of the domains includes at least some aspects of instrumentality and some aspects of expressiveness (Ansell & Pincus, 2004). The Big Five are typically measured with the NEO Personality Inventory-Revised (NEO-PI-R) or the NEO Five Factor Inventory (NEO-FFI; Costa & McCrae, 1992).

The five-factor model has received widespread, international acceptance and is considered by some to provide a valid map of universal, endogenous tendencies inherent in the human personality. The NEO-PI-R and NEO-FFI have been translated into many languages and administered to cultural groups around the world to test the robustness of the model (e.g., Chinese: McCrae, Costa, & Yik, 1996; Hebrew: Rubinstein & Strul, 2006; Marathi [India]: Lodhi, Deo, & Belhekar, 2002; Russian: Martin, Oryol, Rukavishnikov, & Senin, 2000). Because some cultures are considered to be more collectivistic and others more individualistic in character (see Markus & Kitayama, 1991), one might expect that people from some cultures would be more likely to endorse traits associated with a more collectivistic orientation (e.g., agreeableness, conscientiousness) and others might endorse traits associated with a more individualistic orientation (e.g., openness, extroversion). McCrae (2001) has reported some limited support for such differences. In particular, measures of extroversion and cultural individualism were related. For example, Americans and Norwegians self-reported higher levels of extroversion than did Chinese and South Koreans. Despite some cultural differences, however, variation in mean levels of traits across cultures has been small, and the structure of the Big Five has shown consistency across cultures (McCrae, 2001). After factor analyzing data from 26 cultures, McCrae concluded that the model replicated well, particularly when the NEO-PI-R was translated into Western languages and for the dimensions of neuroticism and conscientiousness. The openness dimension has not replicated as well, and the model has been less robust in non-Western cultures (Becker, 2006; McCrae, 2001).

Gender Differences in FFM Traits

Gender differences within each of the five domains have been assessed for the NEO measures as well as for other personality scales that measure similar aspects of personality. Because sample sizes have generally been large and data have been gathered across many cultures, this work has some potential for improving our understanding of gender differences in personality. Overall, reported differences for the various components of the measures have been modest; they range in size from zero to close to one-half standard deviation across aspects of the dimensions, and the majority of effect sizes have been less than one-quarter standard deviation (McCrae, 2001). The size and the nature of gender differences have varied somewhat among samples within the United States and across cultures. Reported gender differences have also varied by the specific item content of scales intended to measure the same trait and by the mode of measurement. Added to this complexity, most of the domains include both traits for which men tend to score higher and traits for which women tend to score higher. Despite these problems, a coherent pattern of gender differences has been emerging within each of the five domains. These findings are discussed within the context of the instrumental/expressive dimensions.

The set of traits designated for the agreeableness domain tend to be associated with a prosocial, expressive orientation; they suggest a willingness and perhaps aptitude for developing meaningful, fulfilling, and authentic relationships with others. Although significant gender differences have seldom been found for all agreeableness traits within the same sample or culture, women have tended to endorse them to a greater extent than have men. These gender differences have been reported by Feingold (1994), who performed four meta-analyses across 50 years of US personality research, as well as by researchers in countries outside the United States, such as Finland (Feldt, Metsapelto, Kinnunen, & Pulkkinen, 2007) and India (Lodhi et al., 2002), and by Costa et al. (2001), who evaluated data from 26 cultures, including the United States. These findings are in line with widespread societal expectations that women invest themselves in the development and maintenance of positive, enduring personal relationships.

The domain of openness has also yielded fairly consistent gender differences. One might expect a stance of openness to be relevant to both an expressive and an instrumental orientation and that, given societal pressures, some aspects of openness may be more common among men and others more common among women. In line with these expectations, there is evidence that women tend to report greater openness to feelings, aesthetics, and values (Costa et al., 2001; Feingold, 1994; Feldt et al., 2007; Lodhi et al., 2002). In contrast, men have shown an openness to experience equal to that of women (Feingold, 1994) and greater openness to ideas (Costa et al., 2001).

Conscientiousness may best be considered both an instrumental and expressive dimension because both successful action and cooperative interpersonal functioning are implied in the components of this domain. Thus, gender differences would be expected to be small for this domain. Indeed, reported gender differences in conscientiousness have been small and scattered, with little consistency across studies (Costa et al., 2001; Feingold, 1994). Thus, in at least these aspects of instrumentality, women and men have shown virtually no differences.

The remaining domains, extroversion and neuroticism, also include a balance of instrumental and expressive traits, and they provide a complex pattern of gender differences. Women tend to score higher on extroversion traits that can be described as expressive, such as gregariousness, warmth, and positive emotions (Costa et al., 2001; Feingold, 1994; Lodhi et al., 2002; Rubinstein & Strul, 2006), whereas men tend to score higher on the extroversion traits linked to instrumentality, such as activity, excitement seeking and assertiveness (Costa et al., 2001; Feingold, 1994; Lodhi et al., 2002; Lynn & Martin, 1997). Thus, it appears that people tend to express their extroversion in line with traditional gender expectations. The neuroticism domain comprises a wide variety of mental health variables that may be associated with unmitigated communion (e.g., anxiety, depression, vulnerability) or unmitigated agency (e.g., hostility, impulsiveness). Although gender differences were not found in some samples (e.g., Feldt et al., 2007), most researchers have reported gender differences. Women have tended to report more neurotic symptoms generally (Lynn & Martin, 1997; Rubinstein & Strul, 2006) and particularly more anxiety and depression, at least in Western cultures (Costa et al., 2001; Feingold, 1994), and men have tended to score higher on measures associated with hostility and impulsiveness (Feingold, 1994; Lengua & Stormshak, 2000). Thus, gender differences in self-reported neuroticism are dependent on the nature of the mental health symptoms included under the neuroticism label.

Little FFM research has focused on differences associated with sexual orientation. However, we might expect that, because gay men have reported greater expressiveness than have heterosexual men and lesbians have reported greater instrumentality than have heterosexual women (Pillard, 1991; Haslam, 1997), sexual orientation groups may tend to show FFM differences that parallel those found between men and women. Lippa (2005) has provided partial support for this possibility. He found large correlations between sex differences on the FFM (and on masculinity/femininity measures) and sexual orientation differences on the same measures. However, only some of the gender difference findings described earlier, which were drawn from very large and diverse data sets, were replicated in Lippa's work, which has been confined primarily to college samples. More research is clearly needed to determine the value of the FFM model as a tool for better understanding personality differences between sexual orientation groups.

Evaluation of FFM Research and Directions for Future Study of Gender Issues

One would expect that gender differences in the FFM personality traits would be attenuated in cultures that hold more gender egalitarian values and in which women have more opportunities for education. However, Costa et al. (2001) found that gender differences were significantly greater in the more egalitarian countries studied. In explaining their surprising findings, Costa et al. (2001) suggested that people in more traditional cultures may use a different frame of reference in making their self-ratings than do people in more egalitarian cultures. Those in traditional cultures may be more likely to compare themselves to same-sex others or to attribute their actions more to societal demands than to their own inherent personality traits.

These explanations highlight one of the significant limitations of FFM research: Virtually all data have been derived from self-report, with very little validation from other sources of measurement. It is possible, then, that response sets may account for many of the gender and cultural differences reported. The issue of response sets appears to be particularly relevant to the interpretation of gender differences. If women are more open to their feelings and more straightforward than are men, as it appears from self-reports, it follows that women would report more negative feelings than would men because women would be both more aware of their feelings and more willing to admit to them. Men may, therefore, tend to underreport their anxiety, depression, and perhaps other neuroticism variables. Consistent with this possibility, when Costa et al. (2001) controlled for reports of openness to feelings and straightforwardness, women were no longer higher on some of the neuroticism variables, and gender differences on the other related scales were reduced. Furthermore, the measures of openness to feelings and straightforwardness are themselves derived from self-reports, and men may be less willing to admit that they are not open to their feelings or that they are not straightforward. If so, then more veridical indices of openness to feelings and straightforwardness are needed to determine whether even more of the observed gender differences on the FFM measures may be explained by these variables.

Another limitation of the FFM in understanding possible gender differences is that many variables associated with social roles were not included in model development, and gender-role variables do not fit well into the FFM. Saucier and Goldberg (1998) identified a set of adjectives to represent masculinity/femininity and other characteristics that might be "outside the Big Five." They derived two clusters from the set that they identified as relevant to gender roles. Although they concluded that the two masculinity/femininity clusters were not outliers from the FFM, only one FFM domain, agreeableness, was correlated with either gender cluster. As would be expected, the agreeableness domain was correlated with femininity and not with masculinity. These findings help to explain why agreeableness is the only FFM domain to show a consistent gender difference both across all domain-designated traits and across studies. Connections between FFM variables and gender and other social roles clearly deserve more attention from FFM researchers.

The coherence of the FFM factor structure poses another challenge for FFM researchers. The meaning of the constructs purported to underlie each factor is brought into question by the wide variety of traits subsumed within each domain. Factor analysis of a large sample of FFM participants did not reveal the predicted factor structure for all scales from the NEO-PI-R (Costa et al., 2001). For example, in a Procrustes rotation, impulsiveness did not load significantly on its target factor, neuroticism, but did load significantly on extroversion (positive loading) and conscientiousness (negative loading). Moreover, an analysis of gender differences in factor structure on the NEO-FFI revealed several problems at the item and sum-score levels (Becker, 2006). Specifically, Becker reported that analyses of men's and women's openness data supported neither unidimensionality nor equivalency. He suggested that separate scales be developed for men and women to measure openness and perhaps other FFM dimensions as well.

A final criticism of FFM researchers is that they have paid little attention to social and cultural factors that may influence the development and enactment of FFM traits. For example, Brummett et al. (2006) reported a positive relation between body mass index (BMI) and the FFM domain of neuroticism for women but not for men and a stronger negative relation between BMI and conscientiousness for women but not for men. Although the authors noted that obesity is a greater social stigma for women, they failed to consider that experiences associated with that stigma could contribute to women's anxiety and depression, core aspects of the neuroticism domain, or that, given the greater pressure on women to be slim, women would be more likely than men to channel their conscientiousness into controlling their weight. Instead, the authors suggested that women who suffer from negative (neurotic) feelings may eat more as a way to cope with those feelings and may be less likely to exercise. Thus, neuroticism was viewed as an endogenous, causal factor rather than as a reaction to the social context within which the neuroticism was expressed.

A second example of the emphasis FFM researchers have given to endogenous explanations is Nettle's (2006) effort to tie the FFM domains to evolutionary mechanisms. Nettle attempted to explain how high and low levels of each set of traits carry benefits as well as costs in biological selection and, hence, why a wide range of levels of the traits continue to be observed in the population. Although he was able to link both ends of the extroversion dimension to physiological correlates and to some survival costs and benefits, he was unable to make a credible case for the other domains. Further, although Nettle did briefly mention that other explanatory mechanisms are possible, he failed to consider the powerful social forces, such as modeling and reinforcement, that may contribute to the development and expression of FFM traits.

Recent efforts to link behaviors associated with FFM traits to social context provide evidence of the importance of situational variables in understanding how the traits may be expressed (Fleeson, 2007; Sheldon, Ryan, Rawsthorne, & Ilardi, 1997). For example, variations in the characteristics of situations as perceived by the individual, such as friendliness and anonymity, have been linked to intra-individual variations in the expression of the Big Five traits, and the relation between situational characteristics and trait expression has differed reliably between individuals (Fleeson, 2007). For example, those with below-average levels of trait extroversion tended to show less behavioral extroversion (e.g., talkativeness) in more anonymous situations, whereas those with above-average levels of trait extroversion tended to show more behavioral extroversion in more anonymous situations. Single measures of traits taken in laboratory settings are inadequate for capturing such individual differences in variations across settings.

In conclusion, the FFM research tells us something about how men and women describe themselves in structured personality questionnaires in the United States and around the world. In many instances, the observed gender differences in self-reported personality follow from what would be expected from traditional gender roles and are fairly consistent across cultures. Women report traits needed for building and maintaining strong personal relationships, and they report more openness to emotions and aesthetics, whereas men tend to describe themselves as more emotionally stable, assertive, open to ideas, and impulsive. Some recent research indicates that better understanding of the expression of the Big Five traits can come only when research methodology incorporates situational variables. Future researchers should also address how response sets, such as expectancies for appropriate responding and internal comparison norms, affect how people describe themselves on the FFM dimensions, and multi-method approaches to trait measurement should be employed to verify the validity of self-reports.

Gender Differences in Self-evaluations

Global Self-esteem

Self-esteem has long been considered important for the understanding of personality and behavior. Although a number of types of self-esteem have been identified, the most commonly researched is global self-esteem, defined as "the level of global regard that one has for oneself as a person" (Harter, 1993, p. 88). Many studies have suggested that measures of self-esteem are related to mental health benefits, including increased positive and decreased negative affect, more positive adjustment, and greater resilience in stressful situations (see Kling, Hyde, Showers, & Buswell, 1999, for a review). Based on these findings, self-esteem has sometimes been theorized to be essential for positive mental health (Taylor & Brown, 1988).

Given the apparent importance of global self-esteem, any findings of group differences in self-esteem have been met with concern because they suggest that a particular group may have poorer outcomes on a host of psychological factors. This concern has been particularly publicized in the case of girls and women, who have sometimes been found to have lower global self-esteem than have boys and men (Allgood-Merton & Stockard, 1991; Fertman & Chubb, 1992). Any findings of gender differences in global self-esteem have been assumed by the lay public to be large and to reflect a problem for girls and women, whereas boys' and men's higher self-esteem has been considered normative and healthy. These assumptions regarding gender differences in global self-esteem are particularly prevalent in discussions of adolescent girls' self-esteem. Popular books, such as *Reviving Ophelia* (Pipher, 1994), reinforce the idea that girls' self-esteem plunges as they enter adolescence, resulting in a crisis of low self-esteem.

A careful analysis of the research on this topic provides a different and more nuanced picture of gender differences in global self-esteem. Three meta-analyses of gender differences in global self-esteem have aggregated data across hundreds of studies and included responses from thousands of participants. These meta-analyses have demonstrated very small to small effect sizes ($d = 0.10$–0.21) for overall gender differences where men and boys have higher scores (Feingold, 1994; Kling et al., 1999; Major, Barr, Zubek, & Babey, 1999). When African-Americans were analyzed separately, gender difference effect sizes were negligible ($d = -0.04$–0.03; Kling et al., 1999; Major et al., 1999). These meta-analyses have also revealed that gender differences in self-esteem change over time. Effect sizes in gender differences have ranged from 0.01 to 0.16 for preadolescents, 0.12–0.23 for middle school students, and 0.16–0.33 for high school students. After high school, gender differences in global self-esteem appear to decrease throughout the life span. Effects sizes have decreased from 0.13 to 0.18 during college, to 0.10 in mid-adulthood, to –0.03 for samples over 60 years of age (Kling et al., 1999; Major et al., 1999). It should be noted that, although gender differences in global self-esteem vary across the life span, the size of the difference at its largest point is still small. (An effect size of 0.20 represents an 85% overlap in the distribution between two groups and is generally considered undetectable in daily life, though potentially important.) Thus, gender differences in global self-esteem range from negligible to small and clearly do not support the notion popularized in the media that girls experience a precipitous drop in self-esteem during adolescence.

The assumption that gender differences in self-esteem indicate a problem for girls is, in any case, not clearly supported by empirical data and reflects the androcentric bias of always judging what man and boys do to be normative and preferable. Recent research provides evidence that, rather than serving as a universal advantage, high self-esteem may sometimes be related to poor adjustment. Some researchers have reported that people who carry high, but unstable, global self-esteem may, when they perceive their self-esteem is threatened, engage in negative behaviors to bolster their self-image. These behaviors, such as physical aggression, bullying, risky sexual activity, and experimentation with drugs and alcohol, may cause harm to self and others (see Baumeister et al., 2003, for a review). Thus, rather than indicating more positive mental health, higher self-esteem may sometimes reflect a mental health concern. Because high self-esteem has been assumed to be unconditionally positive, and the high self-esteem of men and boys assumed to be normative, few studies have assessed this potential mental health problem. Future researchers should investigate possible negative implications of self-reported high self-esteem, particularly in men and boys.

Multi-dimensional Self-concept

Although the construct of global self-esteem continues to be included in personality studies as a potential explanatory variable, the value of global self-esteem as a predictor of human behavior has been brought into question because measures of the construct have generally failed to relate substantially to intended outcomes (Swann, Chang-Schneider, & McClarty, 2007; Wylie, 1974, 1979). Given that, as discussed earlier, high self-ratings may have differential connotations among respondents, these findings are not surprising. The construct of global self-esteem is so vague and diffuse that it has limited potential to explain individual differences in behavior.

Wylie undertook extensive critical reviews of the extant self-esteem research in 1974 and 1979. Given the limited utility of global self-esteem measures, she called upon researchers to focus on specific measures of self-perceptions that would more reliably predict behavior. Shavelson, Hubner, and Stanton (1976) responded to this need by proposing a model of self-evaluation that was multi-dimensional and hierarchical. With global self-esteem at the top of the hierarchy, multiple subcategories were specified. Shavelson et al. (1976) predicted that these components become increasingly distinct from early childhood to adulthood. Marsh (1988, 1992a, 1992b) developed a set of three measures, the Self-Description Questionnaires I, II, and III (SDQ I, SDQ II, and SDQ III), based on the Shavelson et al.'s model, to measure self-concept in grade school, high school, and college age students, respectively. In an extensive research program that has spanned more than two decades and many cultures, Marsh has found that the SDQ subscales have strong psychometric properties with a well-defined factor structure that is invariant across gender at all three age groups and is generally invariant across cultures (Kaminski, Shafer, Neumann, & Ramos, 2005; Marsh, 2003; Marsh, Parada, & Ayotte, 2004). In regard to differentiation, Marsh (2003) found that, contrary to Shavelson et al. (1976), full differentiation of self-concept components has occurred by late childhood/early adolescence, with a steep drop in correlations among components between Grades 2 and 5.

The SDQ subscales were designed for children and adolescents and, therefore, are specific to self-evaluations in those areas, such as parental relations and school performance, which are appropriate to the child and adolescent stages of development. To measure self-concept in adults, it is important to identify self-concept components at a mid-level of specificity that will be germane to a wide range of adult life contexts and experiences. Measures at this level of specificity have the advantage of providing maximum generalizability across situations with maximum distinctiveness between categories (Rosch, 1978). For this purpose, the first author developed the Six Factor Self-Concept Scale for adults (SFSCS; Stake, 1994). Beginning with components of self-evaluation that had emerged from previous research, six subscales were identified for the SFSCS through a series of exploratory and confirmatory factor analytic techniques. Two components pertain to harmonious interpersonal functioning (i.e., likeability, morality) and four to aspects of agentic functioning [i.e., task accomplishment, giftedness, power, vulnerability (reverse scored)]. These factors are distinct from personality traits in that they are self-evaluative dimensions, with positive and negative poles, rather than merely self-descriptions. The six SFSCS subscales show strong psychometric properties, are invariant across gender, and have replicated with ethnic/racial minority women (African-Americans, Asian-Americans, Latinas, and Native Americans; Stake, 1994; Yanico & Lu, 2000).

Wylie (1979) suggested that global self-esteem measures might mask important gender differences in particular components of self-evaluations. Higher self-evaluations among boys and men in some areas might be balanced by higher self-evaluations among girls and women in other areas. Research with the SDQ and other self-concept measures has confirmed this expectation for students in grade school through college. Across a great many samples in the United States and elsewhere, despite similar levels of general self-esteem, girls have consistently rated themselves higher than boys in academic areas associated with verbal ability, in qualities associated with maintaining friendships, and in moral qualities such as honesty, trustworthiness, and spirituality (Kaminski et al., 2005; Marsh, 2003, 2004; Shapka & Keating; 2005; Wilgenbusch & Merrell, 1999). Boys have consistently rated themselves higher in academic areas associated with mathematical ability, in physical/athletic abilities, in emotional stability, and in appearance (Kaminski et al., 2005; Marsh, 2003, 2004; Shapka & Keating, 2005; Wilgenbusch & Merrell, 1999). Girls and boys show little difference in their self-views pertaining to school in general, parent/family relationships, happiness, and relationships with the other sex (Marsh, 2003; Wilgenbusch & Merrell, 1999). These differences follow, for the most part, the instrumental/expressive distinction discussed earlier and seen in the FFM research.

Findings from the SRSCS have been consistent with the patterns described above for child and adolescent samples. Composite scores on the SFSCS, which represent a type of global self-evaluation index, have been highly similar for women and men. At the same time, gender differences in sources of self-esteem are evident and parallel the instrumental/expressive distinction (Stake, 1992, 1994). Women have evaluated themselves more highly than have men on likeability and moral qualities, whereas men have rated themselves more highly than have women on power, (in)vulnerability, and giftedness. (Men and women described themselves similarly on the task accomplishment subscale.) These findings are consistent with earlier adult self-concept research that shows women to have more positive self-concepts in the areas of interpersonal relationships and moral goodness and men to have more favorable self-concepts in the areas of leadership, persuasiveness, and emotional stability (Stake, 1992).

The multi-dimensional approach to the study of self-evaluation opens many avenues for research on gender and self-concept that are not possible with global scales. A key issue is the development of gender differences in childhood and adolescence. Although self-concept components continue to become more differentiated during the grade school years, Marsh (2003) has found that gender differences on the SDQ subscales appear as early as Grade 1 and persist through the childhood and adolescent years in a similar pattern. A meta-analysis of data from more than 19,000 elementary and high school students revealed consistent gender differences for the majority of self-concept components beginning in the elementary school years (Wilgenbusch & Merrell, 1999). Some interesting exceptions were uncovered in this meta-analysis, however, that suggest developmental changes that should be further researched. For example, boys were found to have a slightly higher academic self-esteem than girls in elementary school, whereas this difference was not seen in high school. Further, boys gave only slightly higher self-ratings of appearance than did girls in elementary school, but this difference was stronger in high school—in the moderate range. These changes over time suggest some fluidity in gender-related self-evaluations from grade school to high school and, therefore, the possibility for effective interventions when low or high self-evaluations may signal potential mental health concerns (Marsh, 2004).

Another self-concept topic that can be better investigated with multi-dimensional scales is the influence of social context on self-evaluations. Eagly (1987) proposed that gender differences are exaggerated when observations and self-ratings are made under abstract laboratory conditions rather than in meaningful life contexts because study participants rely more on gender stereotypes when they have few cues about appropriate responding. To address this possibility, the first author (Stake, 1992) compared the pattern of gender differences in SFSCS self-ratings when made in the abstract to those made within specific, meaningful life contexts from the perspective of target persons and knowledgeable observers. Contrary to Eagly's hypothesis, the gendered patterns for self-evaluations derived from target persons for work, school, and family settings were very similar to those found with abstract ratings. Moreover, the same gendered pattern emerged when observers familiar with the target persons within those life contexts gave their estimates of how the target persons would rate themselves. Thus, the tendency for women and men to draw their positive self-views from different sources appears to be quite stable across life settings and has been corroborated by informed observers. It is important to note, however, that these gender differences accounted for only 3–7% of the variance in self-ratings. This modest amount of explained variance is equivalent to that reported for most variables that have an established relationship to gender.

Directions for Future Research

Social and Situational Contexts

Given the need to understand personality within social contexts, it is important that future personality researchers place greater emphasis on the intersection of personality and situational variables. To do so, a number of methodological issues must be addressed. First, the scope of social contexts should be defined and described. Although there have been attempts to develop a taxonomy of social situations, these efforts have had little success because of the vast numbers of potential situations to be categorized (Yang, Read, & Miller, 2006). Perhaps a more useful way to conceptualize social context is through social roles because this approach provides for a broader view of social context (Roberts, 2007; Stryker, 2007). Social roles have been defined as a "set of behavioral expectations attached to a position in an organized set of social relationships" (Stryker, 2007, p. 1083). Based on this definition, social roles can be conceptualized as "conglomerations of situations that all share a common thread of expectations and behavioral signatures" (Roberts, 2007, p. 1073). For example, leadership can be assessed across a variety of situations and interactions (e.g., work, community activities) in which the individual is expected to take on a leadership role. This conceptualization of social roles and related contexts is particularly useful because it parallels the notion of personality traits as predispositions to engage in similar types of behaviors across situations.

A second issue in conducting this type of research is the method through which situational factors are introduced to study participants. When social context has been included in personality research designs, participants have often been asked directly to imagine themselves in a situation or role and then to respond to questions as though they were in the situation (Heller, Watson, Komar, Min, &

Perunovic, 2007). This method is susceptible to the influence of social desirability bias and stereotypes because participants may answer based on how they think they should feel or behave in these situations, rather than on how they might actually feel or behave (Heller et al., 2007). Researchers should therefore consider alternative methods for studying situational influences, such as the use of diaries or the manipulation of the salience of social context during administration of personality measures (Heller et al., 2007).

Another important point in designing research in this area is to avoid a dualistic approach that creates a false dichotomy between personality traits and social context. A more complex, interactional perspective is needed, one that recognizes that personality traits and social context have a nonrecursive relationship, as each affects the other. Through such an approach, we can come to a better understanding of personality as both stable and variable. One example of a more integrative methodology for personality/context research is the measurement of intra-individual variability or how much individuals vary around their central tendency for a certain trait across situations (Fleeson, 2007). Another example can be found in the Personality and Role Identity Structural Model (PRISM; Wood & Roberts, 2006), which provides a hierarchical framework for nesting individuals' various role identities (how they perceive themselves within certain contexts) within their general identity (how they perceive their general personality). By determining stability in broad personality constructs, we can gain knowledge regarding individual differences, and by addressing intra-person variability, we can increase our knowledge of factors that influence the expression of behavior within settings (Fleeson, 2007).

Personality researchers have devoted their efforts almost entirely to quantitative studies; yet, such studies are limited in their potential to elucidate complex interactions among nets of personality and situational variables. A quite different methodological approach for assessing meaningful situational categories and exploring the influence of social contexts is qualitative research. In contrast to quantitative studies, grounded, ecological approaches do not impose preconceived structures on study participants but rather allow them to explain what is meaningful within their own experience. Qualitative researchers emphasize the importance of gaining the trust of participants so that they are willing to provide veridical, nondefensive accounts of their lived experiences. Such approaches can potentially lead to greater insight into meaningful categorizations of situational variables and their relation to the expression of personality characteristics.

The link between social context and personality constructs is particularly important for the study of gender and personality. Feminist theorists have criticized psychology researchers for accepting findings of gender differences as an endpoint of research, thereby promoting an essentialist view of gender. They argue that gender differences should be seen as a starting point for research to investigate the underlying causes of these differences (Crawford & Unger, 2004; Yoder, 2003). As discussed in this chapter, research on social context suggests that what differences do exist may be better explained by social roles and situational contexts rather than by biological sex. Future researchers should critically examine findings of gender differences in personality research and assess the role of social factors in bringing about those observed differences.

Promising Directions for Studying Wellness and Transcendence

Psychology as a discipline has, in general, tended to focus on problematic and pathological characteristics and behavior. Even in the field of personality, which is by definition focused on normal functioning and normal populations, little research has been directed toward the study of healthy living, resilience, or transcendence from adversity. Three personality constructs have emerged that appear to be promising steps in that direction and are refreshingly free of traditional gender connotations. *Experience of pleasure* is a construct defined as the individual's ability or willingness to experience enjoyment in everyday life events (Gard, Gard, Kring, & John, 2006). Defined as a trait disposition, the experience of pleasure may be consummatory—the resolution of desire—or may be the anticipation of the future fulfillment of a goal. The Temporal Experience of Pleasure Scale (TEPS; Gard et al., 2006) was designed to measure both consummatory pleasure (e.g., "I appreciate the beauty of a fresh snowfall") and anticipatory pleasure (e.g., "Looking forward to a pleasurable experience is in itself pleasurable"). The TEPS appears to have good psychometric qualities: There is evidence for the distinction between consummatory and anticipatory pleasure and for low correlations with social desirability, positive affect, and negative affect. Further attention to this construct is warranted because the ability to experience pleasure, particularly in the types of everyday experiences described in the TEPS, may well lead to higher life satisfaction for both women and men. It is interesting to find preliminary evidence that women have scored higher on both the Consummatory and Anticipatory subscales of the TEPS, with effect sizes in the moderate range ($d = 0.42$ and 0.49, respectively) and on the total TEPS ($d = 0.55$; Gard et al., 2006). If women do tend to draw more pleasure from everyday events, such a finding might help to explain the lower incidence of dangerous risk taking, substance abuse, and anti-social behavior in women.

Sense of Coherence

Sense of coherence (SOC) refers to a world perspective that provides meaning to the individual's experience and that leads to successful coping and resilience under stress (Antonovsky, 1987). This model comprises three themes: (a) comprehensibility—the perspective that one's situation and experiences are understandable and can be explained within a credible belief system; (b) manageability—the assessment that one has the necessary resources to meet life circumstances; and (c) meaningfulness—the belief that life demands are worth one's investment and engagement. Feldt et al. (2007) reported that a measure designed to assess SOC appears to be stable across time, particularly for people over age 30 (stability coefficients = 0.67–0.82). Nevertheless, Feldt et al. (2007) have claimed that SOC develops over time from life experiences and does not, as do personality traits, represent innate tendencies. They have difficulty in making this distinction, however, partly because SOC has been highly related ($r > –0.70$) to neuroticism, which is viewed as a central aspect of personality. The value of the SOC construct is that the focus of study is directed toward understanding characteristics of the individual that promote health and wellness. Little empirical research is available on this topic thus far, but women and men do not appear to be distinctly different in their SOC (Feldt et al., 2007). Future researchers should consider ways in which all individuals may benefit from a strong sense of coherence.

A third new development in personality research is *self-compassion,* which refers to (a) showing kindness and understanding toward oneself in difficult times rather than becoming self-critical and judgmental, (b) understanding that one's hardships and inadequacies are shared by others as part of the human experience rather than being particular to the self, and (c) allowing painful thoughts to be experienced mindfully rather than either suppressing them or becoming overly identified with them (Neff, Kirkpatrick, & Rude, 2007). The Self-Compassion Scale (SCS; Neff, 2003) has been shown to have strong psychometric properties; relates positively to measures of life satisfaction, capacity for intimacy, and regulation of affect; and is negatively related to depression and anxiety (Neff, 2003; Neff et al., 2007). Gilbert (2005) has explained that self-compassionate people enjoy feelings of well-being because they can soothe themselves when faced with adversity and failure, and they experience a continued feeling of being cared for by the self and feeling emotionally connected to others.

Self-compassion has been compared to self-esteem. Both qualities provide the benefits of positive self-affect and self-acceptance; however, unlike self-compassion, the maintenance of high self-esteem may depend on distorted, overly positive evaluations of the self and may be unstable across performance outcomes. Because self-compassion does not require positive evaluations of one's ability and judgments that the self is better than others, it may relate more consistently to mental health. Self-esteem may be viewed as more relevant to the instrumental realm, whereas self-compassion appears to be a more expressive characteristic. Thus, women may be somewhat more capable of and prone to self-compassion than are men. However, because women are typically expected to care for others, giving priority to others over themselves, they may tend to be less self-compassionate in some respects than are men. Given that self-compassion leads to the benefits of self-esteem without the potential costs, further investigation of this construct and of methods for enhancing self-compassion in women and men appears to be a fruitful avenue of research. Indeed, as Neff et al. (2007) have recommended, programs designed to develop self-compassion may be far more effective than self-esteem enhancement programs for the promotion of mental health.

Conclusions

The field of personality continues to hold promise as a means of elucidating how gendered processes and structures in our society influence human behavior. However, to date, much personality research has been designed and interpreted through an essentialist lens, and the field has been slow to consider the interface of personality and contextual factors. More emphasis is needed on capturing the subtle and ongoing interplay of relationships between peoples' personality tendencies and situational cues, opportunities, and pressures, as well as the long-term effects of environments on the individual. Alternate methodological approaches are needed to accomplish this task, and more recent research paradigms are emerging that place more emphasis on person/context connections and that measure intrapersonal as well as interpersonal variation in cognition, affect, and behavior. Although quantitative research methods can harvest a wealth of data to inform our understanding of gender, qualitative methodologies can provide an important means of moving beyond essentialist paradigms to enlighten our understanding of the salient contextual and cultural influences that shape people's gendered behavior.

References

Allgood-Merton, B., & Stockard, J. (1991). Sex role identity and self-esteem: A comparison of children and adolescents. *Sex Roles, 25*, 129–139.

Ansell, E. B., & Pincus, A. L. (2004). Interpersonal perceptions of the five factor model of personality: An examination using the structural summary method for circumplex data. *Multivariate Behavioral Research, 39*, 167–201.

Antonovsky, A. (1987). *Unraveling the mystery of health. How people manage stress and stay well*. San Francisco, CA: Jossey-Bass.

Baumeister, R. F., Campbell, J. D., Krueger, J. I., & Vohs, K. D. (2003). Does high self-esteem cause better performance, interpersonal success, happiness, or healthier lifestyles? *Psychological Science in the Public Interest, 4*, 1–44.

Becker, G. (2006). NEO-FFI scores in college men and women: A view from McDonald's unified treatment of test theory. *Journal of Research in Personality, 40*, 911–941.

Bem, S. L. (1974). The measurement of psychological androgyny. *Journal of Consulting and Clinical Psychology, 42*, 155–162.

Bem, S. L. (1993). *The lenses of gender: Transforming the debate on sexual inequality.* New Haven, CT: Yale University Press.

Bouchard, T. J. (2004). Genetic influence on human psychological traits. *Current Directions in Psychological Science, 13*, 148–151.

Bozionelos, N., & Bozionelos, G. (2003). Instrumental and expressive traits: Their relationship and their association with biological sex. *Social Behavior and Personality, 31*, 423–430.

Bruch, M. A. (2002). The relevance of mitigated and unmitigated agency and communion for depression vulnerabilities and dysphoria. *Journal of Counseling Psychology, 49*, 449–459.

Brummett, B. H., Babyak, M. A., Williams, R. B., Barefoot, J. C., Costa, P. T., & Siegler, I. C. (2006). NEO personality domains and gender predict levels and trends in body mass index over 14 years during midlife. *Journal of Research in Personality, 40*, 222–236.

Burleson, B. R., & Gilstrap, C. M. (2002). Explaining sex differences in interaction goals in support situations: Some mediating effects of expressivity and instrumentality. *Communication Reports, 15*, 43–55.

Constantinople, A. (1973). Masculinity–femininity: An exception to a famous dictum? *Psychological Bulletin, 80*, 389–407.

Costa, P. T., & McCrae, R. R. (1992). *Revised NEO Personality Inventory (NEO PI-R) and NEO Five-Factor Inventory (NEO-FFI).* Odessa, FL: Psychological Assessment Resources.

Costa, P. T., Terracciano, A., & McCrae, R. R. (2001). Gender differences in personality traits across cultures: Robust and surprising findings. *Journal of Personality and Social Psychology, 81*, 322–331.

Crawford, M., & Unger, R. (2004). *Women and gender: A feminist psychology* (4th ed.). Boston, MA: McGraw-Hill.

Dinda, K., & Allen, M. (1992). Sex differences in self-disclosure: A meta analysis. *Psychological Bulletin, 112*, 106–124.

Eagly, A. H. (1987). *Sex differences in social behavior: A social-role interpretation.* Hillsdale, NJ: Erlbaum.

Feingold, J. (1994). Gender differences in personality: A meta-analysis. *Psychological Bulletin, 116*, 429–456.

Feldt, T., Metsapelto, R., Kinnunen, U., & Pulkkinen, L. (2007). Sense of coherence and five-factor approach to personality: Conceptual relationships. *European Psychologist, 12*, 165–172.

Fertman, C. I., & Chubb, N. H. (1992). The effects of a psychoeducational program on adolescents' activity involvement, self-esteem, and locus of control. *Adolescence, 27*, 517–526.

Fleeson, W. (2007). Situation-based contingencies underlying trait-content manifestation in behavior. *Journal of Personality, 75*, 825–861.

Gabbard, G. O. (2005). Mind, brain, and personality disorders. *American Journal of Psychiatry, 162*, 648–655.

Gard, D. E., Gard, M. G., Kring, A. M., & John, O. P. (2006). Anticipatory and consummatory components of the experience of pleasure: A scale development study. *Journal of Research in Personality, 40*, 1086–1102.

Gilbert, P. (2005). Compassion and cruelty: A biopsychosocial approach. In P. Gilbert (Ed.), *Compassion: Conceptualisations, research, and use in psychotherapy* (pp. 9–74). London: Routledge.

Harter, S. (1993). Causes and consequences of low self-esteem in children and adolescents. In R. F. Baumeister (Ed.), *Self-esteem: The puzzle of low self-regard* (pp. 87–116). New York: Plenum Press.

Haslam, N. (1997). Evidence that male sexual orientation is a matter of degree. *Journal of Personality and Social Psychology, 73*, 862–870.

Helgeson, V. S. (1994). Relation of agency and communion to well-being: Evidence and potential explanations. *Psychological Bulletin, 116*, 412–428.

Heller, D., Watson, D., Komar, J., Min, J., & Perunovic, W. Q. E. (2007). Contextualized personality: Traditional and new assessment procedures. *Journal of Personality, 75*, 1229–1253.

Helwig-Larson, M., Cunningham, S. J., Carrico, A., & Pergram, A. M. (2004). To nod or not to nod: An observational study of nonverbal communication and status in female and male college students. *Psychology of Women Quarterly, 28*, 358–361.

Hermann, K. S., & Betz, N. E. (2006). Path models of the relationship of instrumentality and expressiveness, social self-efficacy, and self-esteem to depressive symptoms in college students. *Journal of Social and Clinical Psychology, 25*, 1086–1106.

Hoffman, M. L., Powlishta, K. K., & White, K. J. (2004). An examination of gender differences in adolescent adjustment: The effect of competence on gender role differences in symptoms of psychopathology. *Sex Roles, 50*, 795–810.

Hunt, M. G. (1993). Expressiveness does predict well-being. *Sex Roles, 29*, 147–169.

Huselid, R. F., & Cooper, M. L. (1994). Gender roles as mediators of sex differences in expression of pathology. *Journal of Abnormal Psychology, 103*, 595–603.

Ickes, W., Gesn, P. R., & Graham T. (2000). Gender differences in empathic accuracy: Differential ability or differential motivation? *Personal Relationships, 7*, 95–109.

Inzlicht, M., & Ben-Zeev, T. (2000). A threatening intellectual environment: Why females are susceptible to experiencing problem-solving deficits in the presence of males. *Psychological Science, 11*, 365–371.

Jones, W. H., Chernovetz, M. E., & Hansson, R. O. (1978). The enigma of androgyny: Differential implications for males and females? *Journal of Consulting and Clinical Psychology, 46*, 298–313.

Kaminski, P. L., Shafer, M. E., Neumann, C. S., & Ramos, V. (2005). Self-concept in Mexican American girls and boys: Validating the Self-Description Questionnaire I. *Cultural Diversity and Ethnic Minority Psychology, 11*, 321–338.

Klein, K. J., & Hodges, S. D. (2001). Gender differences, motivation, and empathic accuracy: When it pays to understand. *Personality and Social Psychology Bulletin, 27*, 720–730.

Kling, K. C., Hyde, J. S., Showers, C. J., & Buswell, B. N. (1999). Gender differences in self-esteem: A meta-analysis. *Psychological Bulletin, 125*, 470–500.

LaFrance, M., Hecht, M., & Paluck, E. L. (2003). Contingent smile: Meta-analysis of sex differences in smiling. *Psychological Bulletin, 129*, 305–334.

Lengua, L. J., & Stormshak, E. A. (2000). Gender, gender roles, and personality: Gender differences in the prediction of coping and psychological symptoms. *Sex Roles, 43*, 787–820.

Lippa, R. (2001). On deconstructing and reconstructing masculinity–femininity. *Journal of Research in Personality, 35*, 168–207.

Lippa, R. A. (2005). Sexual orientation and personality. *Annual Review of Sex Research, 16*, 119–153.

Lodhi, P. H., Deo, S., & Belhekar, V. M. (2002). The five-factor model of personality: Measurement and correlates in the Indian context. In R. R. McCrae, & J. Allik (Eds.), *The five-factor model of personality across cultures* (pp. 227–248). New York: Kluwer.

Lynn, R., & Martin, T. (1997). Gender differences in extraversion, neuroticism, and psychoticism in 37 countries. *Journal of Social Psychology, 137*, 369–373.

Major, B., Barr, L., Zubek, J., & Babey, S. H. (1999). Gender and self-esteem: A meta-analysis. In W. B. Swann, J. Langlois, & L. A. Gilbert (Eds.), *Sexism and stereotypes in modern society: The gender science of Janet Taylor Spence* (pp. 223–253). Washington, DC: American Psychological Association.

Manstead, A. (1992). Gender differences in emotion. In A. Gale, & M. W. Eysenck (Eds.), *Handbook of individual differences: Biological perspectives* (pp. 355–387). Chichester, UK: Wiley.

Markus, H. R., & Kitayama, S. (1991). Culture and the self: Implications for cognition, emotion, and motivation. *Psychological Review, 98*, 224–253.

Marsh, H. W. (1988). *Self-Description Questionnaire II: A theoretical and empirical basis for the measurement of multiple dimensions of preadolescent self-concept.* San Antonio, TX: Psychological Corporation.

Marsh, H. W. (1992a). *Self-Description Questionnaire II: Manual.* Macarthur, Australia: Publication Unit, Faculty of Education, University of Western Sydney.

Marsh, H. W. (1992b). *Self-Description Questionnaire III: Manual.* Macarthur, Australia: Publication Unit, Faculty of Education, University of Western Sydney.

Marsh, H. W. (2003). Do multiple dimensions of self-concept become more differentiated with age? The differential distinctiveness hypothesis. *Journal of Educational Psychology, 95*, 687–706.

Marsh, H. W., Parada, R. H., & Ayotte, V. (2004). A multidimensional perspective of relations between self-concept (Self-Description Questionnaire II) and adolescent mental health (Youth Self-Report). *Psychological Assessment, 16*, 27–41.

Martin, T. A., Oryol, V. E., Rukavishnikov, A. A., & Senin, I. G. (2000, July). *Applications of the Russian NEO-PI-R.* Paper presented at the International Congress of Psychology, Stockholm, Sweden.

McCrae, R. R. (2001). Trait psychology and culture: Exploring intercultural comparisons. *Journal of Personality, 69*, 819–846.

McCrae, R. R., Costa, P. T., & Yik, M. S. M. (1996). Universal aspects of Chinese personality structure. In M. H. Bond (Ed.)? *The handbook of Chinese psychology* (pp. 189–207). Hong Kong: Oxford University Press.

Miller, R. J. (2001). Gender differences in illusion response: The influence of spatial strategy and sex ratio. *Sex Roles, 44*, 209–225.

Moskowitz, D. S, Suh, E. J., & Desaulniers, J. (1994). Situational influences on gender differences in agency and communion. *Journal of Personality and Social Psychology, 66*, 753–761.

Neff, K. D. (2003). The development and validation of a scale to measure self-compassion. *Self and Identity, 2*, 233–250.

Neff, K. D., Kirkpatrick, K. L., & Rude, S. S. (2007). Self-compassion and adaptive psychological functioning. *Journal of Research in Personality, 41*, 139–154.

Nettle, D. (2006). The evolution of personality variation in humans and other animals. *American Psychologist, 61,* 622–631.
Parsons, T., & Bales, R. F. (1955). *Family, socialization, and interaction process.* Glencoe, IL: Free Press.
Pillard, R. C. (1991). Masculinity and femininity in homosexuality: "Inversion" revisited. In J. C. Gonsiorek & J. D. Weinrich (Eds.), *Homosexuality: Research implications for public policy* (pp. 32–43). Newbury Park, CA: Sage.
Pipher, M. (1994). *Reviving Ophelia: Saving the selves of adolescent girls.* New York: Ballentine Books.
Roberts, B. W. (2007). Contextualizing personality psychology. *Journal of Personality, 75,* 1071–1082.
Rosch, E. (1978). Principles of categorization. In E. Rosch, & B. B. Lloyd (Eds.), *Cognition and categorization* (pp. 27–48). Hillsdale, NJ: Erlbaum.
Ross, L. (1977). The intuitive psychologist and his shortcomings: Distortions in the attribution process. In L. Berkowitz (Ed.), *Advances in experimental social psychology* (Vol. 10, pp. 173–220). New York: Academic Press.
Rubinstein, G., & Strul, S. (2006). The five factor model (FFM) among four groups of male and female professionals. *Journal of Research in Personality, 41,* 931–937.
Saragovi, C., Koestner, R., Di Dio, L., & Aube, J. (1997). Agency, communion, and well-being: Extending Helgeson's (1994) model. *Journal of Personality and Social Psychology, 73,* 593–609.
Saucier, G., & Goldberg, L. R. (1998). What is beyond the big five? *Journal of Personality, 66,* 495–524.
Sellers, J. G., Mehl, M. R., & Josephs, R. A. (2006). Hormones and personality: Testosterone as a marker of individual differences. *Journal of Research in Personality, 41,* 126–138.
Shapka, J. D., & Keating, D. P. (2005). Structure and change in self-concept during adolescence. *Canadian Journal of Behavioural Science, 37,* 83–96.
Sharpe, M. J., Heppner, P. P., & Dixon, W. A. (1995). Gender role conflict, instrumentality, expressiveness, and well-being in adult men. *Sex Roles, 33,* 1–18.
Shavelson, R. J., Hubner, J. J., & Stanton, G. C. (1976). Self-concept: Validation of construct interpretations. *Review of Educational Research, 46,* 407–441.
Sheldon, K. M., Ryan, R. M., Rawsthorne, L. J., & Ilardi, B. (1997). Trait self and true self: Cross-role variation in the big-five personality traits and its relations with psychological authenticity and subjective well-being. *Journal of Personality and Social Psychology, 73,* 1380–1393.
Spence, J. T., & Helmreich, R. L. (1980). Masculine instrumentality and feminine expressiveness: Their relationships with sex role attitudes and behaviors. *Psychology of Women Quarterly, 5,* 147–163.
Spence, J. T., Helmreich, R. L., & Holahan, C. K. (1979). Negative and positive components of psychological masculinity and femininity and their relationships to self-reports of neurotic and acting out behaviors. *Journal of Personality and Social Psychology, 37,* 1673–1682.
Spence, J. T., Helmreich, R. L., & Stapp, J. (1975). Ratings of self and peers in sex-role attributes and their relation to self-esteem and conceptions of masculinity and femininity. *Journal of Personality and Social Psychology, 32,* 29–39.
Stake, J. E. (1992). Gender differences and similarities in self-concept within everyday life contexts. *Psychological of Women Quarterly, 16,* 349–363.
Stake, J. E. (1994). Development and validation of the Six-Factor Self-Concept Scale for Adults. *Educational and Psychological Measurement, 54,* 56–72.
Stake, J. E. (1997). Integrating expressiveness and instrumentality in real-life settings: A new perspective on the benefits of androgyny. *Sex Roles, 37,* 541–564.
Stake, J. E. (2000). When situations call for instrumentality and expressiveness: Resource appraisal, coping strategy choice, and adjustment. *Sex Roles, 42,* 865–885.
Stake, J. E., Zand, D., & Smalley, R. (1996). The relation of instrumentality and expressiveness to self-concept and adjustment: A social context perspective. *Journal of Social and Clinical Psychology, 15,* 167–190.
Stein, J. A., Newcomb, M. D., & Bentler, P. M. (1992). The effect of agency and communality on self-esteem: Gender differences in longitudinal data. *Sex Roles, 26,* 465–483.
Stryker, S. (2007). Identity theory and personality theory: Mutual relevance. *Journal of Personality, 75,* 1083–1102.
Swann, W. B., Chang-Schneider, C., & McClarty, K. L. (2007). Do people's self-views matter? Self-concept and self-esteem in everyday life. *American Psychologist, 62,* 84–94.
Taylor, S. E., & Brown, J. D. (1988). Illusion and well-being: A social psychological perspective on mental health. *Psychological Bulletin, 103,* 193–210.
Thomas, G., & Fletcher, G. J. O., (2003). Mind reading accuracy in intimate relationships: Assessing the roles of the relationship, the target, and the judge. *Journal of Personality and Social Psychology, 58,* 1079–1094.
Twenge, J. M. (1997). Changes in masculine and feminine traits over time: A meta analysis. *Sex Roles, 36,* 305–325.
Whitley, B. E., Jr. (1984). Sex-role orientation and psychological well-being: Two meta-analyses. *Sex Roles, 12,* 207–225.

Wilgenbusch, T., & Merrell, K. W. (1999). Gender differences in self-concept among children and adolescents: A meta-analysis of multidimensional studies. *School Psychology Quarterly, 14*, 101–120.

Wood, D., & Roberts, B. W. (2006). Cross-sectional and longitudinal tests of the personality and role identity structural model (PRISM). *Journal of Personality, 74*, 779–809.

Woodhill, B. M., & Samuels, C. A. (2003). Positive and negative androgyny and their relationship with psychological health and well-being. *Sex Roles, 48*, 555–565.

Wylie, R. C. (1974). *The self-concept* (Vol. 1). Lincoln, NE: University of Nebraska Press.

Wylie, R. C. (1979). *The self-concept* (Vol. 2). Lincoln, NE: University of Nebraska Press.

Yang, Y., Read, S. J., & Miller, L. C. (2006). A taxonomy of situations from Chinese idioms. *Journal of Research in Personality, 40*, 750–778.

Yanico, B. J., & Lu, T. G. C. (2000). A psychometric evaluation of the Six-Factor Self-Concept Scale in a sample of racial/ethnic minority women. *Educational and Psychological Measurement, 60*, 84–97.

Yoder, J. D. (2003). *Women and gender: Transforming psychology* (2nd ed.). Upper Saddle River, NJ: Prentice Hall.

Chapter 3
Gender and Motivation for Achievement, Affiliation–Intimacy, and Power

Lauren E. Duncan and Bill E. Peterson

Research on achievement, affiliation–intimacy, and power motivation is tied intimately to the Thematic Apperception Test (TAT), co-developed by Christiana D. Morgan and Henry A. Murray (1935). In the TAT, respondents are shown pictures of people (often line drawings) and asked to write a story in response to each picture cue. Researchers assume that test takers will tell stories that reflect their own conscious and unconscious motives and impulses. As the methodology evolved, these stories (or thought samples) were content coded by experts for recurring themes that reflect major human motives. The three most studied motives, also referred to as social motives, are achievement, affiliation–intimacy, and power.

Early researchers conducted experiments with samples of college men to derive objective categories that would enable researchers to code stories for motive content (e.g., Atkinson, 1958; McClelland, Atkinson, Clark, & Lowell, 1953). For example, one group of men would be put in an achievement-arousing situation and another would be put in a neutral situation. Differences in the types of stories composed by men in the two groups were assumed to reflect differences in achievement motivation. Decades of research have shown that the resulting scoring definitions for each motive can be applied to written material in a reliable way by different researchers. In order to assess social motives, individuals write stories under neutral arousal conditions. Individuals are hypothesized to tell stories that reveal the motive concerns uppermost in their minds. For example, someone high in achievement motivation is expected to write stories filled with images of unique accomplishments under neutral arousal conditions; someone high in affiliation–intimacy motivation is expected to write stories about maintaining close interpersonal relationships.

This arousal methodology was used to develop and elaborate the constructs of achievement, affiliation–intimacy, and power motivation. Achievement motivation is defined as a concern for standards of excellence and doing well on tasks. According to Winter (1991a), written imagery that indicates the presence of achievement motivation includes adjectives that evaluate positive performance, goals or performances that are described as successes, success in competition with others, unique accomplishments, and negative affect expressed in the face of failure. The affiliation–intimacy motive is a concern for establishing, maintaining, and repairing friendly relationships as well as experiencing warm and close interactions with others. Key imagery includes companionate activities; nurturant acts; expressions of warm, positive, friendly feelings toward other people; and negative affect about the disruption of friendly relationships. Power motivation involves a heightened concern about having impact or influence over other people. Key written images that denote power motivation include strong vigorous actions that necessarily impact others, behaviors that arouse

L.E. Duncan (✉)
Smith College, Northampton, MA, USA

strong emotions in another person, attempts to influence others, mentions of prestige or fame, control or regulation of other people, and giving help that is not explicitly solicited.

Those who conduct research on achievement, affiliation–intimacy, and power motivation are encouraged to use the term picture story exercise (PSE) to denote the systematic administration of picture cues to participants (Schultheiss & Pang, 2007). Older studies of implicit motives, though, may use the term TAT in honor of Morgan and Murray's contributions to understanding human personality. However, the contemporary use of the PSE recognizes the 70 years of experimental work that have gone into the refinement and assessment of achievement, affiliation–intimacy, and power motivation. In order to distinguish PSE motives from other types of motivational constructs (e.g., the hunger motive), the terms "social motives" and "implicit motives" are often used to refer to PSE achievement, affiliation–intimacy, and power as a group. For any given motive, "n X" might be used in place of "X motivation." Thus, "n Power" refers to "power motivation." Some researchers use abbreviations when referring to each motive (i.e., nACH, nAFF, nPOW), but we will not do so here.

In this chapter we examine how gender has been treated by social motive researchers. In our review, we emphasize research published since the early 1980s, when Stewart and Chester (1982) last reviewed research on gender and PSE-based motives in a comprehensive way. First, though, we set the stage by discussing recent trends in motive research, best practices for assessing motives in men and women, and the difference between implicit and explicit motives.

Reemergence of Interest in Social Motives

The peak of social motive research occurred between the 1950s and the 1970s (Atkinson, 1958; Heyns, Veroff, & Atkinson, 1958; McAdams, 1980; McClelland, 1975; McClelland et al., 1953; Winter, 1973; Winter & Stewart, 1978). Probably because of questions about reliability and the time-intensive nature involved in the coding of social motives, psychological research after the 1970s tended to focus more on Likert-scaled questionnaire items that assessed achievement, affiliation, and power as trait-like variables. However, in the past decade, there seems to have been a resurgence of interest in studying implicit social motives. One reason new research has increased in the past decade may be attributable to Winter's (1991a, 1991b) *Manual for Scoring Motive Imagery in Running Text*. This manual consolidated existing scoring systems for achievement, affiliation–intimacy, and power in such a way that investigators can reliably learn to content code all three motives at one time. Furthermore, the coding system can be applied to any kind of written document (including archival materials) that is not purely technical (e.g., PSE stories, letters, novels). Although not all social motive researchers use the running text system, it has opened up new content areas for possible exploration.

For example, in a recent study, Winter (2007) used the running text system to score political documents to examine the role of social motives in international conflict escalation. He coded the diplomatic exchanges, speeches, and media commentary made by key figures of opposing countries locked in potential military disputes and found that the documents related to crises that eventually led to armed conflict (e.g., the US Bay of Pigs Invasion) contained more power imagery by both sides involved, whereas documents related to crises that were resolved peacefully contained more achievement and affiliation–intimacy imagery (e.g., the Cuban Missile Crisis). In addition to studying war and peace (Winter, 1993, 2003, 2005; see also Smith, 2008), Winter and his colleagues have used social motives to predict the behaviors of US presidents at the aggregate (e.g., Winter, 1987) and individual levels (e.g., Winter, 1998, 2005; Winter, Hermann, Weintraub, & Walker, 1991). Because most political documents recorded statements originally uttered or written by men, there is a dearth of research on women's political leadership and social motivation. The 2008 US presidential election, with the prominence of Republican Sarah Palin and Democrat Hillary Clinton, punctuates the fact that this is clearly an area too long neglected but ripe for investigation. Research on women business leaders and politicians is needed and would enhance our understanding of how social motives relate to the behavior of contemporary leaders.

In addition to studying a leader's motivation "at a distance" by coding political (and other) documents, social motive investigators have increased their use of standard experimental and survey research designs. Much of this work has focused on establishing relationships between social motives and other existing constructs. For example, Woike (Woike, Gershkovich, Piorkowski, & Polo, 1999; Woike, Lavezzary, & Barsky, 2001; Woike & Polo, 2001) has focused attention on how implicit motives influence the content and structure of autobiographical memory. In general terms, her work demonstrates that variations in the content, structure, and affect of autobiographical memories are accounted for by individual differences in social motivation. For example, Woike et al. (1999) showed that high intimacy individuals (who were also low on achievement and power) discussed emotional memories in ways that emphasized integration of themes rather than differentiation. Other constructs recently studied in relation to social motives include creativity (Fodor & Carver, 2000), emotions (Fodor, Wick, & Hartsen, 2005; Zurbriggen & Sturman, 2002), agency and communion (Saragovi, Aube, Koestner, & Zuroff, 2002), identity (Hofer, Busch, Chasiotis, & Kiessling, 2006), and life satisfaction (Brunstein, Schultheiss, & Grassmann, 1998; Hofer & Chasiotis, 2003; Hofer, Chasiotis, & Campos, 2006). It is interesting that of the 16 studies conducted in the 11 articles cited in this paragraph, 2 of them sampled men only, 4 sampled women only, and 1 did not report the gender of the participants; only 9 sampled both women and men (women made up 54% of these mixed samples). Given the evidence of unbalanced gender ratios in some of these studies, researchers interested in the meaning of gender for the expression of social motives have much work ahead of them. For most variables the correlates of social motives do not differ for women and men; however, there may be some domains (e.g., types of achievement sanctioned by society and accessible to individuals) where it is important to sample both women and men in comprehensive ways.

Best Practices for Measuring Social Motives in Women and Men

Social motive researchers have spent decades developing reliable and valid coding systems for assessing achievement, affiliation–intimacy, and power (Smith, 1992). As noted earlier, Winter (1991b) adapted these scoring systems into a running text system that allows researchers to code all three types of motives at one time. However, for those doing laboratory research with the PSE, comparable efforts have not yet been made to establish a set of procedures to evoke motive imagery. This means that laboratory researchers have had to use their own intuitions or advice from senior colleagues about the best picture cues to use to assess motives. Because different labs use different picture cues, the comparison of absolute levels of motive scores across (and sometimes within) labs becomes impossible. For example, in an ambitious study, Veroff, Depner, Kulka, and Douvan (1980) and Veroff, Reuman, and Feld (1984) assessed social motives in two US national samples in 1957 and 1976. Unfortunately, in part because no standardized set of cues was available, Veroff and his colleagues made the decision to use different sets of picture cues for men (featuring male protagonists) and women (featuring female protagonists). For example, Card 5 for men depicted seven men grouped around a conference table, whereas Card 5 for women showed two women preparing food in a kitchen. The rationale was that matching the gender of participants with the gender of people portrayed in the cues was necessary to allow respondents to project their own desires onto the characters. However, PSE researchers have noted that different picture cards "pull" for, or evoke, different kinds of motive imagery. For example, the picture of a ship captain tends to elicit more images of power (rather than achievement or affiliation) from both women and men. Thus, when different PSE cards are used with women and men, it becomes difficult to compare absolute levels of motive imagery across gender. In the studies above, for example, it may be that the picture cues used with women (e.g., Card 5) pulled for more affiliation than the picture cues used with men did. The cues that depict men, by contrast, might have evoked more power or achievement imagery than those that depict women.

In order to address the lack of a standardized set of picture cues to use with modern motive scoring systems, Schultheiss and Brunstein (2001) and Pang and Schultheiss (2005) focused their efforts on establishing baseline motive information on "classic" picture cues. They tested six picture cues often used by researchers, three of which depicted both men and women (couple on bench by river, trapeze artists, and nightclub scene). Of the remaining three cues, two featured male protagonists (ship captain, boxer) and one featured female protagonists (two women in lab coats in laboratory). In these two studies the authors addressed issues such as gender differences in motive strength (women wrote longer stories and scored higher than did men on affiliation–intimacy, which is discussed later), cue strength in pulling for the expression of certain motives, and order effects in the presentation of picture cues. It is a good idea for those who want to conduct research on social motives to consult this work, especially Schultheiss and Pang (2007), who provided concrete advice about motive scoring systems, picture cues, test administration, and data management (see also Chusmir, 1983; Lundy, 1988). Schultheiss and Pang (2007) suggested that researchers administer between four and eight picture cues in relaxed conditions, use cues that pull for motives of interest, and use cues that are similar to the situations in which dependent variables are assessed. Schultheiss and Pang's (2007) efforts to standardize PSE administration in this way seem reasonable. Clearly, summarizing future work that examines social motives and gender will be made easier if researchers use the same picture cues for women and men across samples. Right now, fortunately, most researchers routinely use the same PSE cues for male and female study participants. (Note that the scoring definitions for achievement, affiliation–intimacy, and power contained in Winter's running text system are the same for stories written by women and men. Ideally, the identity and gender of the respondent is completely masked before scoring begins.)

Distinction Between Implicit and Explicit Measures

One final topic needs discussion before we consider each social motive more closely. Researchers who use the PSE have agreed for some time that social motives correlate only weakly with self-report scales of similar motives and traits (but see Thrash, Elliot, & Schultheiss, 2007, for recent work that questions this point). For example, in his meta-analysis, Spangler (1992) found that the average correlation between need for achievement and questionnaire measures of achievement was 0.09. Findings like these led McClelland and his colleagues (Koestner, Weinberger, & McClelland, 1991; McClelland, 1980; McClelland, Koestner, & Weinberger, 1989) to argue that the PSE provides an operant measure of implicit motives, whereas questionnaire measures (where items are assessed on Likert scales) provide respondent measures of explicit motives. McClelland argued that PSE-based motives tap into people's nonconscious intrinsic desires to achieve, affiliate, or exercise power; expression of the motive is rewarding in and of itself. The PSE should be best at predicting long-term trends in behavior where people are free to choose their own activities. By contrast, questionnaire-based motives (and traits) assess a person's explicitly articulated (i.e., conscious) image of self;

people high in a self-attributed motive seek to maintain consistency in social situations where motive expression is expected. Thus, people who score high on a questionnaire measure of affiliation may find it important to act sociably at dinner parties with strangers. Because social motives are sometimes out of awareness, people high on need for affiliation–intimacy would desire close relations with other people, but might or might not act sociably in a public setting depending upon how comfortable they felt with the other people at the parties. They value friendships and partnerships but choose them on their own terms rather than acting affiliative to maintain consistency between their behavior and their self-image. This distinction between implicit and explicit measures continues to be refined by contemporary researchers (e.g., Schultheiss, 2007a, 2008).

Researchers have used the fact that PSE and questionnaire motives rarely correlate to study the interactive effects of implicit and explicit traits and motives. For example, in two samples of adult women, Winter, John, Stewart, Klohnen, and Duncan (1998) found that the trait of extraversion tended to facilitate the expression of affiliation and power motivation, whereas the trait of introversion tended to interfere with motive expression. In other work, Woike (2008) introduced a model that stresses the importance of the two-motive systems for understanding the formation of autobiographical memories. In King's (1995) examination of implicit and self-attributed motives, there was no relationship between the two types of measures. However, she found that personal strivings for power correlated with PSE power for men but not for women. Although these results were based on a small sample of men ($N = 28$), King suggested that the relationship of implicit and self-attributed motivation might be an interesting avenue in which to examine the relations between gender and motivation. The relationship of social expectations to the expression and satisfaction of motive-related strivings is an area ripe for future research. For the purposes of this chapter, however, keep in mind that we are reviewing only PSE-based implicit motives that use variations of the PSE for assessment (McClelland et al., 1989; Sheldon, King, Houser-Marko, Osbaldiston, & Gunz, 2007; see Spangler, 1992, for a review of explicit measures of achievement, affiliation, and power motivation).

Achievement Motivation

The need for achievement was defined by McClelland (1985) as a concern with "doing things better, with surpassing standards of excellence" (p. 190). Decades of research have shown n Achievement to be related to moderate risk taking, responsiveness to feedback, future-time-orientation, personal responsibility for performance outcomes, and participation in entrepreneurial activity (see McClelland & Koestner, 1992, for an overview of correlates).

It is not surprising that research on gender and achievement motivation has been influenced by prevailing views about gender differences. Stewart and Chester (1982) focused their review of these differences on two areas—differential responses to achievement arousal and behavioral correlates of achievement. At the time their chapter was published, many researchers believed that it was difficult to arouse achievement motivation in women, most likely because achievement was seen as an exclusively masculine concern. It was also quite likely that because the original arousal studies had only male participants, key imagery to distinguish between high and low achievement-motivated women was left out of the coding categories. Stewart and Chester (1982) reviewed the early research on the arousal of n Achievement, and, after pointing out flaws in research design and missed opportunities to interpret main effects, they concluded that there is no consistent evidence that the motive was difficult or impossible to arouse in women. In particular, they argued that researchers, without realizing it, were finding that expressions of n Achievement for men were restricted to the traditional domains of work and leadership and that this is linked to a rigid masculine gender role. For women, on the other hand, *n* Achievement could be aroused with cues from a wide variety of domains because achievement opportunities in the traditional domain of work were less available to women at that time.

In their review of the behavioral correlates of achievement motivation in women and men, Stewart and Chester (1982) concluded that there were no gender differences in the relationship between achievement and performance on laboratory tasks, behavior outside the laboratory, or scores on personality variables. For both women and men, *n* Achievement was positively related to quick and accurate performance on timed verbal and mathematical tests, career success in people who valued paid employment, and preference for taking academic classes with equally skilled classmates. Later research confirmed these early findings (e.g., McClelland & Franz, 1992; McClelland & Koestner, 1992).

The expression of *n* Achievement, however, does seem sensitive to prevailing gender role norms. For example, Veroff (1982) examined two national data sets collected in 1957 and 1976 and found that, for men, scores on *n* Achievement remained consistent, whereas, for women, achievement motivation scores increased over that time period. Veroff argued that the increase in achievement motivation between 1957 and 1976 was directly attributable to the changes in gender role expectations and norms that resulted from the Women's Movement of the 1960s and the 1970s. Veroff also reported that college-educated women and men scored higher in achievement motivation than did their high school-educated peers, and that, for women, *n* Achievement varied depending on birth cohort. Taken together, these results imply that *n* Achievement is sensitive to the social context.

To bolster this argument, Veroff (1982) reported a variety of positive correlates with achievement motivation and successful traditional gender role socialization in the same sample. For example, for men, high *n* Achievement was positively related to preferring work to leisure, seeing work as fulfilling a major life value, not seeing work as interfering with family but also with strong feelings of efficacy, happiness, marital satisfaction, low drug use, integration into the community, and good health. For women, high *n* Achievement was positively related to being the oldest child in the family, participating in challenging leisure time activities, seeing leisure as fulfilling a major life value, high marital interaction, and reporting many experiences of zest. Veroff argued that these findings show that for many women and men, *n* Achievement is correlated with excellence in traditionally gendered domains—men in achieving at work, women in achieving at home, as wives and mothers. He concluded that *n* Achievement is related for many (but not all) people to successful gender role socialization. Consistent with Veroff's work, Elder and MacInnis (1983) found that high achievement women born in the early 1920s with family orientations tended to focus their adult lives on raising families, whereas high *n* Achievement women with work interests started families at a later age. It seems likely that achievement motivation is often channeled into traditionally gendered outlets but that if there are opportunities that allow excellence in non-traditional domains, some individuals will pursue achievement in those domains (see, e.g., Peterson & Stewart, 1993).

For example, in research conducted in the 1980s, when women managers were relatively rare, Chusmir (1985) found that 62 female managers enrolled in an MBA program had higher achievement and power motivation than did 62 male managers enrolled in the same program (there were no gender differences in affiliation–intimacy). Chusmir argued for a selection effect. That is, women who became managers in the 1970s and the 1980s probably had higher levels of achievement motivation than did men who became managers at the same time because management was a non-traditional occupation for women, and only those women looking for an occupational arena in which to express their *n* Achievement would seek out management positions. On the other hand, because management was a traditional career for men, those men who were motivated to pursue such a career would represent a wider range of *n* Achievement scores than would the women who pursed business careers (whose *n* Achievement scores should have been clustered at the top of the range). It might be worthwhile to note that similar arguments can be made for women entering science and engineering professions today (i.e., research shows that most women who enter those professions have very high standardized math test scores, whereas men who enter those professions have a much wider range of standardized math test scores; Maple & Stage, 1991).

In longitudinal research with women who graduated from college in 1967, Jenkins (1987) argued that in addition to entrepreneurial activity, which was seen as the classic achievement-compatible career in men, teaching could serve the same purpose for women, in that it involved moderate challenges, autonomy, and rapid performance feedback. She further argued that college teaching in particular could be achievement arousing. Consistent with her arguments, Jenkins (1987) found that senior year n Achievement scores were related to employment in teaching 14 years later. In terms of career values, high achievement women working in achievement-compatible positions (i.e., college teaching, supervisory business positions) valued future status mobility and competition with a standard of excellence. On the other hand, high achievement women working in positions incompatible with achievement goals (i.e., non-college teaching, non-supervisory positions) valued other, non-achievement aspects of their jobs such as working with people and wielding power. Women employed in achievement-compatible positions showed an increase in achievement motivation over 14 years compared with women employed in achievement-incompatible professions. Furthermore, Jenkins found that high achievement women working in achievement-incompatible positions were more likely than high achievement women working in achievement-compatible positions to value advancement less, to perceive fewer status mobility routes, to have interrupted careers, and to be more involved in homemaking and mothering than in work. She argued that the high achievement women working in achievement-incompatible professions pursued excellence through their families, hobbies, or volunteer work, rather than through ambitious career goals. Jenkins concluded that life structure interacts with n Achievement to affect life outcomes and life satisfaction in both women and men. One's life structure could act specifically to arouse or suppress achievement motivation or channel it in different directions.

Motive to Avoid Success

Measures of the motive to avoid success (fear of success) were developed in response to early researchers who thought it was difficult to arouse achievement motivation in women. The fear of success had its analogue in early conceptualizations of power motivation, which included both a hope for power and a fear of power (Veroff, 1992). Fear of success was assessed by asking women (and men) to write a story in response to the verbal cue, "After first term finals, Anne (John) finds herself (himself) at the top of her (his) medical school class." Stories were coded for absence of instrumental activity, lack of responsibility for goal attainment, interpersonal engagement, and negative consequences (Fleming, 1982).

> Fear of success is a learned, latent, stable characteristic of the personality acquired early in life in conjunction with the learning of sex role standards and other learned motives; is more prevalent and much more easily aroused in women than in men; is not equally important for all women; is much more strongly aroused in competitive achievement situations reflecting intelligence and leadership ability than in noncompetitive settings; will function, once aroused, as a negative inhibitory tendency acting to reduce the expression of the positive tendency to achieve; and is presumed to interact with other motivational and personality variables as a complex function of motive strength, incentive value, and probability of success (Fleming & Horner, 1992, pp. 179–180).

Horner's (1968) early research showed that the expectation of negative consequences of achievement was related to anxiety in women study participants (Fleming & Horner, 1992). Although the

PSEs of men who participated in these studies also showed evidence of fear of success, the negative effects on performance were far greater for women. The early studies were criticized on methodological grounds, and Horner and her colleagues worked to develop a more reliable coding system for the motive (Fleming, 1982; Fleming & Horner, 1992). The original interpretation of this construct located fear of success as a dispositional characteristic created by gender socialization. Other researchers critiqued the dispositional argument and posited instead that women were simply reflecting in PSEs their knowledge of the very real negative consequences of non-traditional achievement for women (see Fleming, 1982; Fleming & Horner, 1992, for reviews).

In general, it appears that motive researchers have largely abandoned the construct of fear of success as assessed via PSEs (in a search of *PsycINFO* conducted in May 2008, the most recent article found was published in 1998, although Schultheiss and colleagues continue to reference the construct in theoretical models; e.g., Schultheiss & Pang, 2007). However, researchers have not abandoned the construct altogether; rather, the research appears to have transformed in two ways. First, Metzler and Conroy (2004) have attempted to resurrect the construct with a questionnaire measure developed by Zuckerman and Allison (1976) to assess fear of success in sport. Note that this line of research rejects the gendered assessment of fear of success and instead focuses equally on the anxieties male and female athletes experience while seeking success.

Second, a more closely related construct in social psychology, stereotype threat, has captured the imaginations of many researchers. Stereotype threat (Steele, 1997) was developed to explain the underperformance of African Americans (relative to European Americans) on standardized English tests and the underperformance of women (relative to men) on standardized math tests. Defined as the fear of confirming a negative stereotype about a group to which one belongs, stereotype threat can be elicited by simply making salient the group membership that is associated with a negative stereotype. Further, removing that stereotype as a possible explanation for poor performance has the effect of equalizing performance on these tests. Similar to the motive to avoid success, stereotype threat is related to performance decrements for members of subordinate groups. However, unlike fear of success, it is assumed to be a situational variable, not a personality characteristic, and thus fairly malleable.

Relationship of Implicit Measures to Explicit Measures of n Achievement

Contemporary researchers appear to utilize questionnaire, or self-attribution measures, of *n* Achievement more frequently than implicit PSE measures (see Senko, Durik, & Harackiewicz, 2008, for a current review of theory and measurement of explicit achievement motivation). As mentioned earlier, research has established that these two types of measures are usually unrelated and predict different phenomena. In two meta-analyses of the validity of implicit (PSE) versus self-attributed (questionnaire) measures of achievement motivation, Spangler (1992) found that PSE measures of achievement were positively correlated with career success measured in the presence of intrinsic, or task-related, achievement incentives (e.g., farm or industry output). On the other hand, extrinsic questionnaire measures of achievement were positively correlated with outcomes, particularly in the presence of external or social achievement incentives (e.g., school grades; see also Brunstein & Maier, 2005). Spangler also found that, on average, PSE correlations were larger than questionnaire correlations.

More recent research has shown that implicit and explicit measures of achievement motivation may not be as unrelated as they have seemed from previous studies. Thrash et al. (2007) found that when implicit and explicit measures of *n* Achievement were matched on content, there was a small positive correlation ($r = 0.17$). In addition, they found that for people who scored high on private body consciousness (i.e., awareness of their own physiological arousal), low on self-monitoring (i.e., less concerned about how they appeared to others), and high on need for consistency, implicit and explicit achievement motivation were correlated. They concluded that implicit and explicit motives are more closely related than previously thought, but that the relationship between the two is often attenuated by methodological inconsistency and moderated by certain individual difference variables.

In sum, research on gender and achievement motivation has reflected the social-evaluative and competitive aspects of the construct and indicates that people who score high on achievement motivation are interested in living up to their own internal standards and that these standards are influenced by prevailing social values about gender. If the construct were to be reinvented today, researchers would need not only to include women in derivation experiments but also to focus on aspects of excellence relevant to both women and men. That is, the original derivation experiments put men in traditional academically competitive situations and emphasized competition with others. Certainly women have been able to hold their own in academic settings; however, what might achievement motivation look like if the *competitive with others* aspect of the construct was deemphasized and setting a goal for oneself was emphasized? Early studies on fear of success make it clear that women's awareness of the negative consequences of surpassing others means that an achievement motivation defined mostly on competition with others is probably less likely to capture the full spectrum of achievement motivation, especially in groups stigmatized for achieving success.

Affiliation–Intimacy Motivation

As with the need for achievement, the coding categories for the need for affiliation were developed with male participants in the initial derivation studies (Heyns et al., 1958). However, as noted by Stewart and Chester (1982), subsequent research showed that women's and men's need for affiliation could be aroused in the same way and that similar patterns of correlates across gender exist for the affiliation motive. Stewart and Chester (1982) reported that women sometimes scored higher on *n* Affiliation relative to men but that these findings were often confounded by the gender of protagonists in picture cues, and so direct comparisons were not possible. In early studies, women were more likely to be shown PSE picture cues featuring girls and women rather than boys and men. Due to social stereotypes about women's communal interests, the presence of female characters may have led any test taker, man or woman, to express more affiliation imagery.

Koestner and McClelland (1992) provided a general summary of research on affiliation motivation. Classic studies indicate that people high in *n* Affiliation (compared to those low in affiliation) spent more time interacting with people, learned social networks quickly, expressed sympathy toward others (and accommodated them), and had an aversion to interpersonal conflict, although it is interesting that *n* Affiliation seemed to be *negatively* (albeit weakly) correlated with popularity among peers. The latter finding and others like it led researchers to argue that a fear of rejection often underlies the behaviors and actions of people high in affiliation (Boyatzis, 1973). That is, highly affiliative people (especially under stress) may try too hard to establish connections and avoid rejection, which can lead other people to move away from them. Critics of the affiliation motive note that the original derivation studies often involved arousal of the motive by placing people in situations where rejection or acceptance by peers was emphasized. Thus, the coding categories for affiliation motivation may have inadvertently picked up on a fear of rejection embodied by the arousal manipulation. In order to develop a measure of affiliation that tapped more purely the positive aspects of interpersonal exchange, McAdams derived a new PSE measure of intimacy motivation.

McAdams (1992) summarized his validation efforts in the late 1970s and the early 1980s. In the end, his measure seemed to tap a preference for warm, close, and communicative interaction with other people, and it emphasized only the positive aspects of interpersonal communion. As reported by McAdams (1992), scores on affiliation and intimacy tended to correlate positively within samples in the 0.25–0.55 range. Although early studies suggested that men and women were equally likely to express intimacy motivation in PSE stories (e.g., McAdams & Constantian, 1983), later research showed that women tended to score higher than men. In an article devoted to the topic of gender differences, McAdams, Lester, Brand, McNamara, and Lensky (1988) provided evidence from a sample of 1,500 undergraduate students that women scored significantly higher than men on most of the subcategories that define the intimacy coding system. The magnitudes of the effects for each of the coding subcategories were not always large but were reliable. Women seemed to be more likely to express intimacy themes in response to PSE picture cues. This gender difference could reflect women's greater socialization as girls to express intimacy or their training in the maintenance of close relationships.

Regardless of any gender differences in absolute levels of n Intimacy, the correlates of intimacy motivation are generally the same for men and women. Thus, for example, McAdams and Constantian (1983) showed, through the use of experience sampling (using pagers), that individuals high on intimacy motivation were more likely to be "caught" thinking about or interacting with other people than were those low on intimacy. In a later study, McAdams, Hoffman, Mansfield, and Day (1996) found no gender differences in how people high in intimacy motivation reconstructed important autobiographical memories in communal terms. It seems reasonable to conclude that women probably have higher levels of implicit intimacy motivation but that not all studies show a gender difference. Furthermore, the patterns of correlates for n Intimacy are virtually the same for men and women.

Because need for affiliation and need for intimacy tend to overlap, Winter (1991a) simplified and combined the two measures into a single scoring system that assesses "affiliation–intimacy" motivation in running text. Researchers partial to either affiliation or intimacy have not objected strongly. Rather, many PSE researchers seem to recognize the value of such a merging. However, they also recognize the advantage of using the older system if one is interested in the more anxious aspects of affiliative need and of using the new intimacy system if one is interested solely in the positive aspects of interpersonal union. Contemporary research on gender and affiliation–intimacy has focused on relationships and physiological correlates.

Affiliation–Intimacy and Relationships

Although people high on affiliation–intimacy are interested in establishing and maintaining close relationships with others, research has shown that, under conditions of threat, highly affiliative people act "prickly" or defensively (Boyatzis, 1973; Winter & Carlson, 1988). Mason and Blankenship (1987) assessed affiliation motivation, life stress, and activity inhibition (a measure of restraint) in undergraduate students who were married or in dating relationships. They found that highly affiliative women who were low in activity inhibition were more likely than any other group to inflict physical and psychological abuse on their male partners when experiencing high levels of life stress. There were no main effects or interactions with men's affiliation motivation, although the impact of men's power motivation (also measured in the study) on abuse is discussed later.

Similar findings regarding affiliation–intimacy motivation were found in research by Zurbriggen (2000), who studied motives and aggressive sexual behavior. Affiliation–intimacy in men was uncorrelated with self-reports of sexual aggressiveness toward women. For women, however, affiliation–intimacy was correlated positively with using sexual coercion and seduction in their relationships with men. The positive relationship between affiliation and coercion was most prominent for women who made cognitive associations between power and sex. That is, women centrally concerned with maintaining romantic relationships who associated dominance with intimate relationships tended to try to maintain those relationships by using manipulation and coercion.

In interpreting these relationships' results, keep in mind that the PSE measures used involved affiliation–intimacy (or affiliation alone), which includes its defensive aspects. The McAdams' (1992) measure of intimacy motivation has not, to date, been associated with problematic romantic behavior. (In fact, McAdams and Vaillant, 1982, showed in a longitudinal sample of male Harvard graduates that age 30 PSE intimacy predicted marital satisfaction in the mid-40s, $r = 0.38$.) All of the findings discussed about relationships need to be further qualified by the fact that only heterosexual relationships were examined. How affiliation–intimacy motivation might direct the relationship strategies of lesbians and gay men, absent heterosexual power–sex linkages, is a question for future research. Much work remains to be done to clarify for all people how affiliation–intimacy motivation enhances romantic unions and how it might create fractures under some conditions.

Physiological Correlates of Affiliation–Intimacy

As discussed in more detail later, recent work on the physiological correlates of affiliation–intimacy has focused on the gonadal (sex) hormones such as progesterone. However, McClelland's (1987) early work on the biological substrates of affiliation–intimacy examined other types of hormones and cellular activity. To give two brief examples, Jemmott et al. (1990) showed that low stress people high in affiliation had the greatest levels of natural killer cell activity (a major component of the body's immune system). In another study, McClelland, Patel, Stier, and Brown (1987) had people watch films saturated with affiliation images. After participants viewed these films, a positive correlation emerged between levels of dopamine and PSE affiliation motivation. Although both of these studies included both women and men as participants, neither article reported results by gender. It is unclear whether McClelland and his colleagues found no gender differences or whether they did not think participant gender would influence the relationships between affiliation motivation, natural killer cell activity, and the release of dopamine.

More recent work on the relationships between affiliation–intimacy and sex hormones, by contrast, has focused on gender because levels of these hormones differ in the bodies of men and women. For example, Schultheiss, Dargel, and Rohde (2003) examined how implicit motives were related to the presence of gonadal steroid hormones in women. They separated women into two groups—18 women who were using oral contraceptives and 18 with normal menstrual cycles. A group of 18 men was also examined and tested at what would be menstrual, midcycle, and premenstrual phases in normally cycling women. Two findings from this study are illustrative. One, women using oral contraceptives scored higher on affiliation–intimacy than did people in the other two groups. Two, in normally cycling women, levels of progesterone and affiliation–intimacy were positively correlated. With regard to the first finding, the authors suggested that gender differences in levels of affiliation–intimacy that are found in some studies may be due to the numbers of women who were taking birth control pills in these samples. The authors argued that the high level of gestagens (synthetic progesterone) in oral contraceptives presumably induces increased levels of affiliation–intimacy in women. However, it is also quite likely that women high in affiliation–intimacy motivation are more likely than those low in affiliation–intimacy to be involved in committed intimate relationships and using birth control pills as contraception. Also interesting in this study is that progesterone levels in men were negatively related to affiliation–intimacy. The authors explained that progesterone is related to reduced sex drive in men and argued that affiliation–intimacy "reflects to some extent sexual motivation" (p. 300) for both men and women, so low progesterone should be related to high affiliation–intimacy in men. (See also Schultheiss, Wirth, and Stanton, 2004, and Wirth and Schultheiss, 2006, for additional studies of the relations between progesterone, testosterone, cortisol, and affiliation–intimacy arousal.) The implications of Schultheiss' work on the physiological correlates of affiliation–intimacy are not yet clear. Schultheiss and colleagues are working at the level of sex differences and similarities in physiological arousal. Biological sex, however, is not always a good marker of psychological gender. Right now researchers working on the biology of motives seem rather agnostic in their approach to gender. They pay close attention to gender when dealing with sex hormones, but collapse across gender for other physiological variables (e.g., natural killer cell activity).

In sum, researchers have found that women score higher than men in affiliation–intimacy motivation in many studies. However, few gender differences have been found in the correlates of affiliation–intimacy. Why gender differences have been found in absolute motive levels is unclear. Some possible explanations are that women are better socialized at intimacy expression than are men or that greater levels of circulating progesterone increase affiliation–intimacy motivation. A third potential explanation could relate to the particular picture cues used to elicit imagery. A useful avenue of future research might test alternative cues meant to elicit affiliation imagery in men. For example, stories written in response to a picture of a father and a son interacting in an affiliative manner might elicit more affiliation imagery in men. (Other ideas include a picture of a group of men playing a friendly game or a man proposing marriage to a woman.) Another explanation for these consistent gender differences is related to women's lower social status. That is, people in low power positions need, for their own safety and survival, to be attentive to the needs of others and to avoid interpersonal conflict. This is an intriguing possibility, one that could be tested experimentally by manipulating status and subsequently measuring motives. This would be most interesting, of course, if it were tested in both people of color and White women and men. Similar strategies were used successfully to show that status, rather than gender, was implicated in the differential use of influence strategies (Sagrestano, 1992) and indirect aggression (Duncan & Owen-Smith, 2006). Research of this sort may also shed light on why women (but not men) high in affiliation–intimacy are more likely to behave in problematic ways when romantic relationships are under stress.

Power Motivation

Fairly early on, researchers devoted theoretical attention to the question of gender similarities and differences in the expression of power motivation. For this reason, psychologists now have a fairly sophisticated understanding of how need for power operates in the lives of women and men. Two overlapping but distinct types of power motivation were part of the original conceptualization of the construct: fear of weakness and hope for power (Veroff, 1992; Winter, 1992). Over the years, research on power motivation has emphasized the latter, or people's desires to attain and wield personal power. In fact, the scoring definitions for Winter's (1991a) running text system focus on power as impact over others rather than concerns with personal autonomy or weakness in the face of another person's power.

A recent review of key findings in the power motive literature can be found in Winter (in press). The classic correlates indicate that power motivation at the individual level is related to (among other things) gaining formal social influence (e.g., through elected offices), ownership of prestigious possessions (as defined by one's peer group), taking risks to get noticed, a preference for jobs where one controls the behavior of other people, a somewhat negative self-image, aggressiveness, and impulsivity.

With regard to gender, Stewart and Chester (1982) noted that power motivation is aroused in women and men in the same way (e.g., inspirational speeches, watching a hypnotist control another person) and that women and men do not differ on levels of power motivation expressed in the PSE. Based upon our review of research since 1982, the observations of Stewart and Chester seem to hold true as much now as they did then. Furthermore, the behavioral correlates of power motivation also continue to show similarities across women and men. For example, Fodor and Carver (2000) found that negative feedback from a person in power compromised the creativity of power-motivated women and men. Schultheiss and Brunstein (2002) found that when highly power-motivated women and men (who were also high in activity inhibition) were placed in a power-arousing situation, they were more verbally fluent and used heightened gesturing and eyebrow lifts to make their arguments more convincing to others. In both of these studies the authors reported no significant gender differences. However, consistent gender differences are found in the relationship of power motivation to profligate or impulsive behavior, though these relationships are moderated by individual differences in levels of responsibility.

Profligacy and Responsibility Training

As discussed by Winter and Barenbaum (1985), women and men high in power motivation are adept at gaining formal social power and influence. Alongside this socialized form of power, however, evidence also shows a relationship, especially in men, between high power motivation and excessive alcohol use, drug use, gambling, physical and verbal aggression, and the exploitation and repression of women. Given this pattern of findings, it is not surprising that heterosexual men high in power experience significant trouble in their intimate relationships with women (Stewart & Rubin, 1976). Indeed, research has shown that power motivation in men is related to sexual aggressiveness (Yost & Zurbriggen, 2006) and the infliction of physical abuse on women (Mason & Blankenship, 1987). Evidence suggests that these correlates are enhanced in men who have formed cognitive associations between power and sex (Zurbriggen, 2000). Heterosexual women high in power do not have this record of negative relationships with men.

Winter and Barenbaum (1985) found that individual differences in personal responsibility moderated the negative effects of power motivation in both women and men. That is, women and men who were high in responsibility exercised power in prosocial ways, whereas women and men low in responsibility were more likely to engage in profligate behaviors. Winter (1988) also showed that formal responsibility training at home during childhood (e.g., taking care of younger siblings, frequency of household chores) also channeled power motivation away from profligacy for both women and men. Alternatively, the absence of responsibility training led high-powered adults toward profligate expressions of the motive. Winter (1988) argued that high-powered women in general do not behave in profligate ways because girls in contemporary society are given more responsibility training while growing up than are boys: "Thus, the differences between 'responsible' and 'profligate' expressions of the power motive may have to do with variables that reflect socialization rather than sex as such" (Winter, 1988, p. 518). Furthermore, because power is intimately tied to privilege, it may be that individual differences in motive expression reflect individual differences in levels of entitlement in both women and men. Future researchers could examine how social status affects individual differences in the desire to have an impact on others or on the world at large. Much like Jenkins' (1987) research on the effects of achievement-compatible vs. achievement-incompatible occupations, it is likely that experiences with power can act either to increase or decrease future power motivation and channel it in different ways.

Winter (2006) argued that power is like fire; it is very useful if tamed but dangerous when out of control. Other researchers picked up on this theme and examined how power fused with affiliation–intimacy motivation was related to positive outcomes. For example, McAdams (1985) and Peterson and Stewart (1993) showed that PSE measures of power and affiliation–intimacy worked in additive and interactive ways to foster prosocial generative strivings. By contrast, Jemmott et al. (1990) focused on the problematic health outcomes of people high in power and low in affiliation who were under stress (i.e., the stressed power motivation syndrome). Careful examinations of the interactive effects of power and affiliation–intimacy may shed further light on how power can be channeled in positive ways for both women and men. In the meantime, the research reviewed above suggests that socialization and social expectations play a big role in how power motivation gets expressed as profligacy in women and men.

Physiological Correlates of Power

Research on the physiological correlates of power showed that the stressed power motive syndrome is related to sympathetic nervous system activation, release of stress hormones, consequent depression of immune system functioning, and subsequent illness (McClelland, 1989; McClelland, Floor, Davidson, & Saron, 1980). On the other hand, high power motivation coupled with low stress in life seems to lead to particularly low levels of illness. Other researchers, such as Fodor (1985), offered support for McClelland's ideas about the role of frustration in leading to physiological arousal among high-powered individuals. In more recent work, Schultheiss, Campbell, and McClelland (1999) showed that high-powered, impulsive men had elevated levels of testosterone after winning a (rigged) paper and pencil contest against another man, but not after losing. In a variation of this experiment, Schultheiss and Rohde (2002) demonstrated that high levels of power motivation in victorious men enhanced their ability to learn a task if necessary for victory. If men were placed in the loser condition, on the other hand, high power motivation impaired learning of the contest task. The authors suggested that besting an opponent is a rewarding experience for power-motivated men who are low in activity inhibition (highly impulsive), and thus behaviors related to winning are reinforced and learned quickly.

Schultheiss et al. (2005) used this basic paradigm to study both women and men. They replicated key aspects of their earlier work in that men (competing against men) and women (competing against women) high in power motivation learned a task better if placed in the victory condition than in the loser condition. However, a gender difference did emerge in the way testosterone levels changed in women and men. In a replication of their first study, high-powered men who won a contest had increased levels of testosterone over their baseline. High-powered men who lost had decreased levels of testosterone. All high-powered women, however, showed increased levels of testosterone after the contest, and this was especially pronounced among high-powered *losers*. The authors acknowledged that there are very few human or animal models of how testosterone operates in females. Even so, they speculated that the increase in women's testosterone might reflect activity in the biological stress axis (rather than the gonads). Given that testosterone levels are much lower in women than in men, any rise in the pituitary gland's secretion of cortisol (a stress hormone) and testosterone precursors may show up as significant in the bodies of high-powered women (both winners and losers), but not in men (see also Wirth, Welsh, & Schultheiss, 2006).

Schultheiss (2007b) showed that some of the energizing and reward functions of social motives have biological links. In his work he is especially interested in how gonadal hormones influence the arousal and expression of power motivation. Given biological differences in the levels of gonadal hormones that circulate in women and men, gender differences in the precise pathways that link testosterone to power are likely to emerge. However, other biological systems (e.g., the effects of sympathetic catecholamine release in high-powered women and men for dealing with an impending challenge) may show similarities between women and men. It seems right now that personality psychologists with biobehavioral interests know enough about the relationships between need for power and separate biological variables (e.g., gonadal steroids, catecholamines) to develop larger models that integrate several biological systems, at least in men. Such models, understood in conjunction with socialization and social context factors, would represent a big advance in our understanding of how power motivation (and achievement and affiliation–intimacy) develops and manifests within individuals.

In sum, gender differences are not usually found in mean levels of power motivation. Correlates of power motivation tend to be similar in women and men; however, power motivation is more strongly linked to profligate behaviors in men than in women. Responsibility training moderates this relationship such that high-power women and men high in responsibility tend not to engage in profligate behaviors, whereas their high-power counterparts low in responsibility tend to engage in profligacy. In women and men, power motivation is also associated with increased levels of circulating testosterone. It is important to note that no claims to causality are made here. That is, behavior may cause changes in hormone levels just as hormones may direct behavior.

One final point needs to be made about power motivation. Contemporary feminists tend to think about power as entailing both "power over" and "power to" (Yoder & Kahn, 1992). Current power motive scoring systems clearly emphasize power over, or the control of others, rather than power to, or the control over one's own thoughts, feelings, and behaviors, and this is most certainly an artifact of the original derivation studies. For example, Veroff's (1957) arousal experiments compared the PSE stories of 34 college men running for elective office with 34 men taking a psychology course. Winter (1973) aroused power in men enrolled in Harvard Business School's MBA program by having them watch a videotape of the 1961 inauguration oath and speech of President John F. Kennedy. In both of these cases, bureaucratic power (a traditional domain of men) was aroused. On the other hand, if the experimental manipulations had aroused, for example, self-empowerment, rather than attempts to influence others, the coding categories might look different. Furthermore, if women had been included in the original derivation studies for power motivation, the researchers might have found additional coding categories. Again, one might expect to see more concerns with autonomy reflected in the stories written by members of subordinate groups and more concerns with controlling others reflected in the stories written by members of dominant groups. Interested researchers could develop a more comprehensive measure of power motivation by experimentally manipulating status and examining stories written for additional images of power, perhaps refining the categories already developed for fear of weakness (Veroff, 1992).

Social Contextual Factors and Social Motives

Social motives are intimately tied to the social context in which they are measured. This is clearly illustrated in the case of gender and social motives. For example, as described earlier, Veroff and colleagues' (Veroff, Atkinson, Feld, & Gurin, 1960) national studies of US adults in 1957 and 1976 showed changes in motive levels that were consistent with changes in the social roles of women and men. That is, women's achievement motivation increased between the 1950s and the 1970s, presumably reflecting opportunities created by the women's movement. Similarly, men's affiliation motivation dropped and their hope for power increased over that same time period, which was interpreted as reflecting a change in men's work environments away from emphasis on a paternalistic work environment and toward a more competitive one. In addition, both women and men increased in fear of power by 1976. The turbulent 1960s and the early 1970s (e.g., Watergate, protests against the Vietnam War) may have reduced the American public's faith in the good will of large institutions, thus enhancing individual fears of being controlled by others. This study, and related ones (e.g., Veroff et al., 1984), demonstrated that historical and developmental forces affect and channel the expression of social motives.

Psychologists have long theorized that all human beings are motivated by a need to have an impact on their environment (*n* Power) and to form close personal relationships (*n* Affiliation–intimacy; Bakan, 1966; Erikson, 1963; Maslow, 1954; Rogers, 1961), but how these motives are expressed, and relative levels of each, should be affected by culture, ethnicity, sexual orientation, and social class, among other factors. Very little research to date has examined how such variables might impact social motives. For example, with regard to achievement motivation, McClelland and Koestner (1992) argued that research from the 1960s to the 1990s showed that although definitions of what constitutes success differ by culture, age, and gender, the concern with *doing something better* is consistently measured by the *n* Achievement coding system. On the other hand, Salili (1996) argued that the original *n* Achievement coding system was biased toward Western, individualistic cultures and did not consider collectivistic value systems more commonly found in Eastern and immigrant cultures. Salili included an additional 10 achievement themes in the coding to account for more communal achievement goals such as successes that benefited or gained recognition from family members.

In their study of American college students, Pang and Schultheiss (2005) found that women had higher levels of affiliation motivation than did men and argued that this might be due to either hormonal or socialization causes. They also found that Asian Americans had higher affiliation motivation than did European Americans and that these higher scores were consistent with the collectivist values of many Asian cultures. Finally, they found that African Americans had higher levels of achievement motivation than did Asian Americans or European Americans and argued that this might be due to a selection effect; essentially, African Americans attending college might be especially concerned with achievement. In terms of cultural effects, it seems likely that the existing coding systems might be used fruitfully within each culture or group to correlate motives with outcome variables. However, when comparing across groups or cultures, it is essential to consider the social position of each group and recognize that certain groups or cultures may have different values that influence motive expression (see Morling & Kitayama, 2008, for a review of how culture affects motivation).

In addition to social groups and cultures, motives are also affected by life structure factors. Jenkins' (1987) study that shows that women in achievement-compatible positions increased in achievement motivation is a classic example of this. In addition, some researchers have examined the development of social motives, particularly the effects of parenting practices. For example, based on longitudinal data, McClelland and Franz (1992) and McClelland and Pilon (1983) showed that mothers' parenting impacted the later development and expression of children's social motives. Specifically, severity of toilet training and scheduled feedings were correlated across genders with greater levels of achievement when offspring were 31 years old. In addition, mothers who were moderately permissive about sex and aggression produced offspring who were high in socialized power motivation and work accomplishment, *if* those mothers were also warm toward sons and cool toward daughters. McClelland and Franz suggested that mothers who were less close to their daughters steered them away from the traditional 1950s feminine gender role (occupied by the mother) toward a non-traditional focus on work and power motivation. These findings are probably limited to children born during the early years of the baby boom (i.e., the age of children was 5 in the sample in 1951) and reflect common child-rearing practices and gendered social expectations of the time. As shown by this example, though, parenting styles and historical context are intertwined and exert a strong influence on how motives develop and are expressed in individuals.

Some Advice and Promising Areas for Future Research

We have several recommendations for researchers studying gender and social motives. First, try to use the same PSE cues across studies. As noted earlier, previous research has shown that different PSE cues elicit different levels of motives; that some PSE cues "pull" for achievement, for example, whereas others pull for affiliation–intimacy; that cues that show women and men in traditional or non-traditional situations tend to elicit different motive levels in women and men; and that PSE cues are sensitive to prevailing social values, including those about gender. Although Schultheiss and colleagues (Pang & Schultheiss, 2005; Schultheiss & Brunstein, 2001; Schultheiss & Pang, 2007) made a good start in their examination of six widely used PSE cues, future researchers should examine more systematically the validity and reliability of various PSE cues in people of color, non-college-educated participants, gay men and lesbians, and other understudied groups, paying special attention to how the prevailing social stereotypes about each group might affect the motive imagery found in their stories. The use of the same cues across studies would enable researchers to identify the strengths and weaknesses of each cue and the cues most appropriate to elicit motive imagery in each population.

Second, researchers should follow Yoder and Kahn's (2003) advice and look beyond the documentation of simple gender differences to understand the meaning of gender. That is, it is more useful to view gender as a marker for a constellation of experiences that can then be generalized to other groups of people rather than to view gender as an essentialist category. For example, a social status explanation for the gender difference in affiliation–intimacy motivation could be tested easily in samples of people of color and White women and men. If researchers found in such experiments that participants put in positions of low status subsequently wrote PSE stories filled with affiliation imagery, and these results were replicated across groups, we would learn something important about how experiences with dominance affect affiliation–intimacy motivation. Using gender as a starting point to understand how status is related to motivation could help us better understand phenomena universal to humans.

Third, when developing theories or hypotheses, women's and other understudied groups' experiences would help researchers to ask new questions and explore new theoretical models. Some motive researchers have already done this. For example, Winter et al.'s (1998) examination of how traits channel motives was conducted in two samples of college-educated White women. They found, for example, that high-affiliation introverts had more trouble with their intimate relationships than did high-affiliation extroverts. Whether these results are generalizable to men is a question for future research. Research has shown the sensitivity of social motives to the social context; therefore, it makes sense that, for example, people with less than a college education might express their achievement motivation differently than people who are college educated (with whom most of the previous studies were conducted). It would be useful for our derivation studies to capture this diversity in motive expression. Recent research with college students has shown that Asian Americans had higher affiliation motivation scores than did European Americans, and African Americans had higher levels of achievement motivation than did Asian Americans or European Americans (Pang & Schultheiss, 2005). Delving into the reasons for these group differences, and relating them to similar findings about gender differences, will allow us to theorize more completely about the effects of social contextual variables on motives.

Finally, we encourage researchers to continue the current trend toward complicating research on gender and motives by looking at mediating and moderating variables. Recent researchers have examined the moderating effects of gender and cognitions on the relationship of power and affiliation motivation and the use of coercive relationship strategies (Yost & Zurbriggen, 2006; Zurbriggen, 2000), the moderating effects of traits on the relationship between affiliation and power motivation on career and relationship success in women (Winter et al., 1998), and the moderating effects of success and failure on the increase in gonadal hormones in high and low power-motivated women and men (Schultheiss et al., 2005). Other promising avenues for research on moderators include work on how motive-compatible and motive-incompatible life structures contribute to changes in motive levels over time. In addition, paying attention to life stage or interactions with developmental tasks (e.g., identity development, ego integrity; Erikson, 1963) might reveal a great deal about how implicit motives drive behavior that eventually leads to psychologically healthy aging. In sum, considering motives in conjunction with other psychological variables, including social context, physiology, cognitions, and traits, would help us to understand human behavior better.

Summary and Conclusion

Similar to Stewart and Chester's (1982) review, we found very little evidence for consistent gender differences in the absolute levels and correlates of achievement and power motivation. Evidence exists, however, for gender differences in levels of affiliation–intimacy as expressed in the PSE. However, current investigators are complicating the research on gender and social motives by examining how gender might moderate relationships between motives and outcome measures, in most cases, by providing explanations consistent with different social expectations for women and men. In arenas where consistent gender differences are found (e.g., different patterns of relationships between gonadal hormones and power and affiliation motivation), little research has explicated why such differences are found. Indeed, future researchers would benefit from understanding within-gender variability as a way to understand between-gender variability. We see the future of gender research on motives as very promising, and because social motives are so sensitive to changing social mores, we see such research as critical to understanding how social expectations are translated into the very personal experiences of individuals.

References

Atkinson, J. W. (Ed.). (1958). *Motives in fantasy, action, and society*. Princeton, NJ: Van Nostrand.
Bakan, D. (1966). *The duality of human existence*. Chicago: Rand McNally.
Boyatzis, R. (1973). Affiliation motivation. In D. C. McClelland & R. S. Steele (Eds.), *Human motivation* (pp. 252–276). Morristown, NJ: General Learning Press.
Brunstein, J., & Maier, G. (2005). Implicit and self-attributed motives to achieve: Two separate but interacting needs. *Journal of Personality and Social Psychology, 89*, 205–222.
Brunstein, J. C., Schultheiss, O. C., & Grassman, R. (1998). Personal goals and emotional well-being: The moderating role of motive dispositions. *Journal of Personality and Social Psychology, 75*, 494–508.

Chusmir, L. (1983). Male-oriented vs. balanced-as-to-sex Thematic Apperception Tests. *Journal of Personality Assessment, 47*, 29–35.

Chusmir, L. (1985). Motivation of managers: Is gender a factor? *Psychology of Women Quarterly, 9*, 153–159.

Duncan, L. E., & Owen-Smith, A. (2006). Powerlessness and the use of indirect aggression in friendships. *Sex Roles, 55*, 493–502.

Elder, G., & MacInnis, D. (1983). Achievement imagery in women's lives from adolescence to adulthood. *Journal of Personality and Social Psychology, 45*, 394–404.

Erikson, E. H. (1963). *Childhood and society*. New York: Norton.

Fleming, J. (1982). Projective and psychometric approaches to measurement: The case of fear of success. In A. J. Stewart (Ed.), *Motivation and society* (pp. 63–96). San Francisco: Jossey-Bass.

Fleming, J., & Horner, M. S. (1992). The motive to avoid success. In C. P. Smith (Ed.), *Motivation and personality: Handbook of thematic content analysis* (pp. 179–189). New York: Cambridge University Press.

Fodor, E. M. (1985). The power motive, group conflict, and physiological arousal. *Journal of Personality and Social Psychology, 49*, 1408–1415.

Fodor, E. M., & Carver, R. A. (2000). Achievement and power motivation: Performance, feedback, and creativity. *Journal of Personality, 34*, 380–396.

Fodor, E. M., Wick, D. P., & Hartsen, K. M. (2005). The power motive and affective response to assertiveness. *Journal of Research in Personality, 40*, 598–610.

Heyns, R. W., Veroff, J., & Atkinson, J. W. (1958). A scoring manual for the affiliation motive. In J. W. Atkinson (Ed.), *Motives in fantasy, action, and society* (pp. 205–218). Princeton, NJ: Van Nostrand.

Hofer, J., Busch, H. Chasiotis, A., & Kiessling, F. (2006). Motive congruence and interpersonal identity status. *Journal of Personality, 74*, 511–541.

Hofer, J., & Chasiotis, A. (2003). Congruence of life goals and implicit motives as predictors of life satisfaction: Cross-cultural implications of a study of Zambian male adolescents. *Motivation and Emotion, 27*, 251–272.

Hofer, J., Chasiotis, A., & Campos, D. (2006). Congruence between social values and implicit motives: Effects on life satisfaction across three cultures. *European Journal of Personality, 20*, 305–324.

Horner, M. S. (1968). *Sex differences in achievement motivation and performance in competitive and non-competitive situations*. Unpublished doctoral dissertation, University of Michigan, Ann Arbor, MI.

Jemmott, J. B., Hellman, C., McClelland, D. C., Locke, S. E., Krause, L., Williams, R. M., et al. (1990). Motivational syndromes associated with natural killer cell activity. *Journal of Behavioral Medicine, 13*, 53–73.

Jenkins, S. (1987). Need for achievement and women's careers over 14 years: Evidence for occupational structure effects. *Journal of Personality and Social Psychology, 53*, 922–932.

King, L. (1995). Wishes, motives, goals, and personal memories: Relations of measures of human motivation. *Journal of Personality, 63*, 985–1007.

Koestner, R., & McClelland, D. C. (1992). The affiliation motive. In C. P. Smith (Ed.), *Motivation and personality: Handbook of thematic content analysis* (pp. 205–210). New York: Cambridge University Press.

Koestner, R., Weinberger, J., & McClelland, D. C. (1991). Task-intrinsic and social-extrinsic sources of arousal for motives assessed in fantasy and self-report. *Journal of Personality, 59*, 57–82.

Lundy, A. (1988). Instructional set and thematic apperception test validity. *Journal of Personality Assessment, 52*, 309–320.

Maple, S. A., & Stage, F. K. (1991). Influences on the choice of math/science major by gender and ethnicity. *American Educational Research Journal, 28*, 37–60.

Maslow, A. (1954). *Motivation and personality*. New York: Harper & Row.

Mason, A., & Blankenship, V. (1987). Power and affiliation motivation, stress, and abuse in intimate relationships. *Journal of Personality and Social Psychology, 52*, 203–210.

McAdams, D. P. (1980). A thematic coding system for the intimacy motive. *Journal of Research in Personality, 14*, 413–432.

McAdams, D. P. (1985). *Power, intimacy, and the life story: Personological inquiries into identity*. New York: Guilford.

McAdams, D. P. (1992). The intimacy motive. In C. P. Smith (Ed.), *Motivation and personality: Handbook of thematic content analysis* (pp. 224–228). New York: Cambridge University Press.

McAdams, D. P., & Constantian, C. A. (1983). Intimacy and affiliation motives in daily living: An experience sampling analysis. *Journal of Personality and Social Psychology, 45*, 851–861.

McAdams, D. P., Hoffman, B. J., Mansfield, E. D., & Day, R. (1996). Themes of agency and communion in significant autobiographical scenes. *Journal of Personality, 64*, 339–377.

McAdams, D. P., Lester, R., Brand, P., McNamara, W., & Lensky, D. B. (1988). Sex and the TAT: Are women more intimate than men? Do men fear intimacy? *Journal of Personality Assessment, 52*, 397–409.

McAdams, D. P., & Vaillant, G. E. (1982). Intimacy motivation and psychosocial adjustment: A longitudinal study. *Journal of Personality Assessment, 46*, 586–593.

McClelland, D. C. (1975). *Power: The inner experience*. New York: Irvington.

McClelland, D. C. (1980). Motives dispositions: The merits of operant and respondent measures. In L. Wheeler (Ed.), *Review of personality and social psychology* (pp. 87–113). New York: Wiley.

McClelland, D. C. (1985). *Human motivation*. Glenview, IL: Scott, Foresman.

McClelland, D. C. (1987). Biological aspects of human motivation. In F. Halisch & J. Kuhl (Eds.), *Motivation, intention, and volition* (pp. 11–19). Berlin: Springer.

McClelland, D. C. (1989). Motivational factors in health and disease. *American Psychologist, 44*, 576–683.

McClelland, D. C., Atkinson, J. W., Clark, R. A., & Lowell, E. L. (1953). *The achievement motive*. New York: Appleton-Century-Crofts.

McClelland, D. C., Floor, E., Davidson, R. J., & Saron, C. (1980). Stressed power motivation, sympathetic activation, immune function and illness. *Journal of Human Stress, 6*, 11–19.

McClelland, D., & Franz, C. (1992). Motivational and other sources of work accomplishments in mid-life: A longitudinal study. *Journal of Personality, 60*, 679–707.

McClelland, D. C., & Koestner, R. (1992). The achievement motive. In C. P. Smith (Ed.), *Motivation and personality: Handbook of thematic content analysis* (pp. 143–152). New York: Cambridge University Press.

McClelland, D. C., Koestner, R., & Weinberger, J. (1989). How do self-attributed and implicit motives differ? *Psychological Review, 96*, 690–702.

McClelland, D. C., Patel, V., Stier, D., & Brown, D. (1987). The relationship of affiliative arousal to dopamine release. *Motivation and Emotion, 11*, 51–66.

McClelland, D. C., & Pilon, D. A. (1983). Sources of adult motives in patterns of parent behavior in early childhood. *Journal of Personality and Social Psychology, 44*, 564–574.

Metzler, J., & Conroy, D. (2004). Structural validity of the Fear of Success Scale. *Measurement in Physical Education and Exercise Science, 8*, 89–108.

Morgan, C. D., & Murray, H. A. (1935). A method for examining fantasies: The Thematic Appercepition Test. *Archives of Neurology and Psychiatry, 34*, 289–306.

Morling, B., & Kitayama, S. (2008). Culture and motivation. In J. Y. Shah & W. L. Gardner (Eds.), *Handbook of motivation science* (pp. 417–433). New York: Guilford.

Pang, J. S., & Schultheiss, O. C. (2005). Assessing implicit motives in U.S. college students: Effects of picture type and position, gender and ethnicity, and cross-cultural comparisons. *Journal of Personality Assessment, 85*, 280–294.

Peterson, B. E., & Stewart, A. J. (1993). Generativity and social motives in young adults. *Journal of Personality and Social Psychology, 65*, 186–198.

Rogers, C. R. (1961). *On becoming a person*. Boston: Houghton Mifflin

Sagrestano, L. M. (1992). Power strategies in interpersonal relationships. *Psychology of Women Quarterly, 16*, 481–495.

Salili, F. (1996). Achievement motivation: A cross-cultural comparison of British and Chinese students. *Educational Psychology, 16*, 271–279.

Saragovi, C., Aube, J., Koestner, R., & Zuroff, D. (2002). Traits, motives, and depressive styles as reflections of agency and communion. *Personality and Social Psychology Bulletin, 28*, 563–577.

Schultheiss, O. C. (2007a). A memory-system approach to the classification of personality tests: Comment on Meyer and Kurtz (2006). *Journal of Personality Assessment, 89*, 197–201.

Schultheiss, O. C. (2007b). A biobehavioral model of implicit power motivation arousal, reward, and frustration. In E. Harmon-Jones & P. Winkielman (Eds.), *Social neuroscience: Integrating biological and psychological explanations for social behavior* (pp. 176–196). New York: Guilford.

Schultheiss, O. C. (2008). Implicit motives. In O. P. John, R. W. Robins, & L. A. Pervin (Eds.), *Handbook of personality: Theory and research* (3rd ed., pp. 603–663). New York: Guilford.

Schultheiss, O. C., & Brunstein, J. C. (2001). Assessment of implicit motives with a research version of the TAT: Picture profiles, gender differences, and relations to other personality measures. *Journal of Personality Assessment, 77*, 71–86.

Schultheiss, O. C., & Brunstein, J. C. (2002). Inhibited power motivation and persuasive communication: A lens model analysis. *Journal of Personality, 70*, 553–582.

Schultheiss, O. C., Campbell, K. L., & McClelland, D. C. (1999). Implicit power motivation moderates men's testosterone responses to imagined and real dominance success. *Hormones and Behavior, 36*, 234–241.

Schultheiss, O. C., Dargel, A., & Rohde, W. (2003). Implicit motives and gonadal steroid hormones and behavior. *Journal of Research in Personality, 37*, 224–230.

Schultheiss, O. C., & Pang, J. (2007). Measuring implicit motives. In R. W. Robins, R. C. Fraley, & R. F. Krueger (Eds.), *Handbook of research methods in personality psychology* (pp. 322–344). New York: Guilford.

Schultheiss, O. C., & Rohde, W. (2002). Implicit power motivation predicts men's testosterone changes and implicit learning in a contest situation. *Hormones and Behavior, 41*, 195–202.

Schultheiss, O. C., Wirth, M. M., & Stanton, S. J. (2004). Effects of affiliation and power motivation arousal on salivary progesterone and testosterone. *Hormones and Behavior, 46*, 592–599.

Schultheiss, O. C., Wirth, M. M., Torges, C. M., Pang, J. S., Villacorta, M. A., & Welsh, K. M. (2005). Effects of implicit power motivation on men's and women's implicit learning and testosterone changes after social victory or defeat. *Journal of Personality and Social Psychology, 88*, 174–188.

Senko, C., Durik, A., & Harackiewicz, J. (2008). Historical perspectives and new directions in achievement goal theory: Understanding the effects of mastery and performance-approach goals. In J. Y. Shah & W. Gardner (Eds.), *Handbook of motivation science* (pp. 100–113). New York: Guilford.

Sheldon, K. M., King, L. A., Houser-Marko, L., Osbaldiston, R., & Gunz, A. (2007). Comparing IAT and TAT measures of power versus intimacy motivation. *European Journal of Personality, 21*, 263–280.

Smith, A. G. (2008). The implicit motives of terrorist groups: How the needs for affiliation and power translate into death and destruction. *Political Psychology, 29*, 55–75.

Smith, C. P. (Ed.). (1992). *Motivation and personality: Handbook of thematic content analysis*. New York: Cambridge University Press.

Spangler, W. (1992). Validity of questionnaire and TAT measures of need for achievement: Two meta-analyses. *Psychological Bulletin, 112*, 140–154.

Steele, C. M. (1997). A threat in the air: How stereotypes shape intellectual identity and performance. *American Psychologist, 52*, 613–629.

Stewart, A. J., & Chester, N. L. (1982). Sex differences in human social motives: Achievement, affiliation, and power. In A. J. Stewart (Ed.), *Motivation and society* (pp. 172–218). San Francisco: Jossey-Bass.

Stewart, A. J., & Rubin, Z. (1976). The power motive in the dating couple. *Journal of Personality and Social Psychology, 34*, 305–309.

Thrash, T. M., Elliot, A. J., & Schultheiss, O. C. (2007). Methodological and dispositional predictors of congruence between implicit and explicit need for achievement. *Personality and Social Psychology Bulletin, 33*, 961–974.

Veroff, J. (1957). Development and validation of a projective measure of power motivation. *Journal of Abnormal and Social Psychology, 54*, 1–8.

Veroff, J. (1982). Assertive motivations: Achievement versus power. In A. J. Stewart (Ed.), *Motivation and society* (pp. 99–132). San Francisco: Jossey-Bass.

Veroff, J. (1992). Power motivation. In C. P. Smith (Ed.), *Motivation and personality: Handbook of thematic content analysis* (pp. 278–285). New York: Cambridge University Press.

Veroff, J. Atkinson, J. W., Feld, S., & Gurin, G. (1960). The use of thematic apperception to assess motivation in a nationwide interview study. *Psychological Monographs, 74*, Whole No. 499.

Veroff, J., Depner, C., Kulka, R., & Douvan, E. (1980). Comparison of American motives: 1957 versus 1976. *Journal of Personality and Social Psychology, 39*, 1249–1262.

Veroff, J., Reuman, D., & Feld, S. (1984). Motives in American women and men across the adult life span. *Developmental Psychology, 20*, 1142–1158.

Winter, D. G. (1973). *The power motive*. New York: Free Press.

Winter, D. G. (1987). Leader appeal, leader performance, and the motive profiles of leaders and followers: A study of American presidents and elections. *Journal of Personality and Social Psychology, 52*, 196–202.

Winter, D. G. (1988). The power motive in women–and men. *Journal of Personality and Social Psychology, 54*, 510–519.

Winter, D. G. (1991a). Measuring personality at a distance: Development of an integrated system for scoring motives in running text. In A. J. Stewart, J. M. Healy, Jr., & D. Ozer (Eds.), *Perspectives in personality: Approaches in understanding lives* (pp. 59–89). London: Kingsley.

Winter, D. G. (1991b). *Manual for scoring motive imagery in running text* (3rd ed.). Unpublished scoring manual, Department of Psychology, University of Michigan.

Winter, D. G. (1992). Power motivation revisited. In C. P. Smith (Ed.), *Motivation and personality: Handbook of thematic content analysis* (pp. 301–310). New York: Cambridge University Press.

Winter, D. G. (1993). Power, affiliation, and war: Three tests of a motivational model. *Journal of Personality and Social Psychology, 65*, 532–545.

Winter, D. G. (1998). A motivational analysis of the Clinton first term and the 1996 presidential campaign. *Leadership Quarterly, 9*, 367–376.

Winter, D. G. (2003). Asymmetrical perceptions of power in crises: A comparison of 1914 and the Cuban Missile Crisis. *Journal of Peace Research, 40*, 251–270.

Winter, D. G. (2005). Things I've learned about personality from studying political leaders at a distance. *Journal of Personality, 73*, 557–584.

Winter, D. G. (2006). Taming power. In D. L. Rohde (Ed.), *Moral leadership: The theory and practice of power, judgment, and policy* (pp. 159–175). San Francisco: Jossey-Bass.

Winter, D. G. (2007). The role of motivation, responsibility, and integrative complexity in crisis escalation: Comparative studies of war and peace crises. *Journal of Personality and Social Psychology, 92*, 920–937.

Winter, D. G. (in press). Power in the person: Exploring the psychological underground of power. In A. Guinote & T. Vescio (Eds.), *The social psychology of power*. New York: Guilford.

Winter, D. G., & Barenbaum, N. B. (1985). Responsibility and the power motive in women and men. *Journal of Personality, 53*, 335–355.

Winter, D., & Carlson, L. (1988). Using motive scores in the psychobiographical study of an individual: The case of Richard Nixon. *Journal of Personality, 56*, 75–103.

Winter, D. G., Hermann, M. G., Weintraub, W., & Walker, S. G. (1991). The personalities of Bush and Gorbachev at a distance: Follow-up on predictions. *Political Psychology, 12*, 457–464.

Winter, D. G., John, O. P., Stewart, A. J., Klohnen, E. C., & Duncan, L. E. (1998). Traits and motives: Toward an integration of two traditions in personality research. *Psychological Review, 105*, 230–250.

Winter, D. G., & Stewart, A. J. (1978). Power motivation. In H. London & J. Exner (Eds.), *Dimensions of personality* (pp. 391–447). New York: Wiley.

Wirth, M. M., & Schultheiss, O. C. (2006). Effects of affiliation arousal (hope of closeness) and affiliation stress (fear of rejection) on progesterone and cortisol. *Hormones and Behavior, 50*, 786–795.

Wirth, M. M., Welsh, K. M., & Schultheiss, O. C. (2006). Salivary cortisol changes in humans after winning or losing a dominance contest depend on implicit power motivation. *Hormones and Behavior, 49*, 346–352.

Woike, B. A. (2008). A functional framework for the influence of implicit and explicit motives on autobiographical memory. *Personality and Social Psychology Review, 12*, 99–117.

Woike, B., Gershkovich, I., Piorkowski, R., & Polo, M. (1999). The role of motives in the content and structure of autobiographical memory. *Journal of Personality and Social Psychology, 76*, 600–612.

Woike, B., Lavezzary, E., & Barsky, J. (2001). The influence of implicit motives on memory processes. *Journal of Personality and Social Psychology, 81*, 935–945.

Woike, B., & Polo, M. (2001). Motive-related memories: Content, structure, and affect. *Journal of Personality, 69*, 391–415.

Yoder, J. D., & Kahn, A. S. (1992). Toward a feminist understanding of women and power. *Psychology of Women Quarterly, 16*, 381–388.

Yoder, J. D., & Kahn, A. S. (2003). Making gender comparisons more meaningful: A call for more attention to social context. *Psychology of Women Quarterly, 27*, 281–290.

Yost, M. R., & Zurbriggen, E. (2006). Gender differences in the enactment of sociosexuality: An examination of implicit social motives, sexual fantasies, coercive sexual attitudes, and aggressive behavior. *Journal of Sex Research, 43*, 163–173.

Zuckerman, M., & Allison, S. (1976). An objective measure of fear of success: Construction and validation. *Journal of Personality Assessment, 40*, 422–430.

Zurbriggen, E. L. (2000). Social motives and cognitive power-sex associations: Predictors of aggressive sexual behavior. *Journal of Personality and Social Psychology, 78*, 559–581.

Zurbriggen, E. L., & Sturman, T. S. (2002). Linking motives and emotions: A test of McClelland's hypotheses. *Personality and Social Psychology Bulletin, 28*, 521–535.

Chapter 4
Gender Issues in Psychological Testing of Personality and Abilities

Nancy Lynn Baker and Janelle L. Mason

The breadth of material that falls under the category of psychological testing is vast. For that reason, this chapter is an overview of the psychological testing field in which we address various sources of gender bias in psychological testing. We discuss some of the ways in which context influences both test performance and the broader task of psychological assessment. We then focus on the treatment of gender in psychological tests, particularly tests that assess personality. We identify three theoretical challenges or critiques of personality testing as it has historically been practiced; we also identify some of the current directions in personality theory and test development. These new directions create opportunities for assessment research and practice. Because many of the issues involved in gender identity (see Chapter 6) and gender and cognitive abilities (see Volume I, Chapter 15) are covered elsewhere, we do not focus on the assessment of gender identity or intelligence, although intellectual assessment is touched on briefly in the general context of psychological testing.

For the purpose of this chapter, we treat gender as an identity variable and a social construct, not a biological sex category. However, it is important to note that this distinction is neither articulated nor universally followed in the psychological testing literature or practice. Gender is routinely conflated or equated with sex, and the effects on behavior of gender roles and gendered expectations are rarely addressed. In addition, gender identity is often conflated with sexual orientation, despite the lack of any meaningful empirical or theoretical justification for that assumption. In fact, the lack of any nuanced or developed understanding or treatment of gender and gender role is central to the problems with the treatment of gender in psychological testing.

Psychological Assessment and Psychological Testing

The focus of this chapter is on psychological tests and testing. However, psychological testing is generally done in the context of the larger activity of psychological assessment. Psychological assessment is a process of combining information from psychological tests, usually multiple tests, clinical interview, behavioral observations, and other sources of information (Meyer et al., 2001). The purpose of psychological assessment is generally to respond to some specific referral questions raised in the assessment request (Meyer et al.). Psychological tests usually consist of one or more scales developed to measure specific abilities, traits, states, attitudes, beliefs, or dispositional factors (Meyer et al.). The role of psychological testing is to assist in the assessment process by

N.L. Baker (✉)
Fielding Graduate University, Santa Barbara, CA, USA

providing measures of an individual's performance on measures of various traits, dispositional tendencies, abilities, and, in some cases, current symptoms.

Virtually all psychological tests attempt to assess relatively abstract constructs often called "personality," "psychopathology," and "intelligence," as well as their more specific derivations and dimensions (e.g., "extroversion," "depression," and "gifted"). Dimensions of personality and forms of psychopathology are not as easily defined or measured as are dimensions such as height, weight, and age. Thus, the processes of defining the various constructs and developing ways to measure them are complex and open to the effects of social bias. Critiques of the use of men's behavior and activities, usually those of men with social power, as the norm for mental health and the standard against which all behaviors are measured have long been a centerpiece of feminist psychology (Ballou & Brown, 2002; Bohan, 2002; Broverman, Broverman, Clarkson, Rozenkrantz, & Vogel, 1970; Caplan & Cosgrove, 2004; Hare-Mustin & Marecek, 1988; Marecek & Hare-Mustin, 1991; Raitt & Zeedyk, 2000; Unger & Crawford, 1992). It is no surprise that the use of androcentric frameworks has been involved, implicitly and explicitly, in the development of psychological tests.

Any identity variable, including gender, has three components relevant to psychological assessment and bias in psychological assessment. Those components are the following: each individual's personal self-assignment of identity position (e.g., I am a woman), the identity assigned by external observers to an individual (e.g., he is a man), and the standards, both individual and cultural, for what the gender label means and how it influences behavior (i.e., women or men should be or do "x" but not "y" and are rewarded and punished accordingly). Each of these components is a source of both relevant information and bias in the process of psychological assessment. However, only the first (i.e., self-definition) is directly assessed in psychological testing, albeit in an unsophisticated manner without addressing the variability of meaning and the categories subsumed under the simple dichotomous category labels. Often the second two components, if they are considered at all, are simply considered to be sources of bias.

Context and the Assessment Experience

Psychological assessment occurs in a context. That context includes the assessment purpose and setting, the assessor, and the individual being assessed. Psychology borrowed the concept of standardized conditions for testing from the natural sciences. Unfortunately, just because psychological tests are administered and scored in a standard manner does not mean that the experience of all test takers is the same. How people think about things matters (Bandura, 1982). As sentient beings, people come into the testing setting with their own expectations and concerns, about both themselves and other people. Individuals also bring their expectations and prior experiences with psychological testing, the particular setting, and the reasons for which the assessment is being conducted. These varied expectations and experiences guarantee that the testing experience is not standardized even when the test procedures are.

Assessor bias can influence the assessment process (Bowers & Bieschke, 2005). Expectations about what will be found may shape the choice of assessment instruments. For example, a middle-aged, middle-class White woman may not be assessed for alcoholism, and a middle-aged, heterosexual man may not be assessed for an eating disorder. Similarly, information, including test results, that confirms an assessor's biases is more likely to be accepted than is information that does not. Assessor bias can influence the behavior of the individual being assessed through subtle and not-so-subtle cues, including the assessor's body language and verbalizations or the expectations communicated by the way in which questions are framed.

The test taker's performance may also be shaped by prior experience, or the lack of it, with test taking and with mental health professionals. Defensiveness, exaggeration, and other forms of non-cooperation are all subject to the influence of the testing situation (Brener, Billy, & Grady, 2003). Individual performance on ability measures can be influenced by stereotype threat, that is, the decline in performance that occurs when an individual is being tested on something for which stereotypes describe the individual's group as being inferior (Helms, 2005; Steele, 1997; Steele, 2003; Steele, James, & Barnett, 2002). Examples include Blacks' performance on intelligence tests and women's performance on math tests. Furthermore, the nature of stereotype threat is such that context factors can invoke or reduce it. As a result, stereotype threat may increase or decrease for the same potential test taker as a result of assessor or other context factors. For example, a woman taking an ability test for entry into a male-dominated field may experience heightened stereotype threat. This is even more probable if she is the only woman in the room when a group of job seekers are being tested or if the assessor has communicated any subtle or overt bias in favor of male job seekers.

Assumptions in Psychological Testing

As noted previously, psychological testing generally refers to the use of particular psychological scales, or combinations of scales, that are administered for the purpose of generating a score (Meyer et al., 2001). Scores on psychological tests are traditionally based on, or given meaning by, how a given individual's performance compares to the norms established for that test. Those norms are usually the statistically transformed distribution of the test scores generated by a sample, referred to as the normative sample, in the development of the test.

For the most part, psychological testing has grown out of the tradition within psychology that viewed personality as the sum of an individual's stable cross-situational behavioral dispositions and traits (Mischel & Shoda, 1995). Similarly, abilities are viewed as relatively stable, cross-situational, cognitive, or behavioral performance capacities. Within this tradition, gender is generally conflated or equated with sex, then measured or accounted for as a dichotomous cross-situational consistency dimension or a dichotomous demographic fact. What that means in practice is that "gender," defined by a forced choice between the label "male" and the label "female," is usually used either to define the composition of the normative sample or to construct two different sets of norms for the various scales included on a psychological test. Those "gendered" norms become the basis for interpreting or providing meaning to the test results of individual test takers.

Just as most psychological tests assume that personality is made up of stable traits and dispositions, there is also an assumption that gender is a dichotomous and unchanging characteristic. The notion of gender as performance raised by some feminist theorists (e.g., Crawford, 1995) is ignored. Most psychological tests also ignore the issues of people who define their gender differently than their biological sex. There are, for example, no instructions given on how an individual is to determine whether to mark "female" or "male" on the test form. But there is an expectation that people can and will label themselves with one or the other of the two gender choices. Some tests can not even be scored unless the test taker responds to the gender question by marking only one of the two boxes. Transgendered people, especially individuals whose gender identity or public presentation may be inconsistent with their biological sex, have neither guidance nor visibility on standardized psychological tests.

Psychometric Theory

The tradition and practice of psychological testing developed during the early- to mid-twentieth century. Most of the psychological tests currently in use are based on what is referred to as psychological measurement theory or psychometrics. Psychometric theories were well developed by the middle of the twentieth century. Gulliksen's (1950) *Theory of Mental Tests* is considered to be the classic articulation of psychological measurement principles. Although psychometric theory and practice has undergone considerable fine tuning in the 60 intervening years as statistical sophistication has increased, the principles of psychological measurement as defined by psychometric theory remain largely unchanged (Urbana, 2004).

There are psychometric procedures, recommendations, statistical assumptions, and formulas related to how psychological tests should be developed and how the reliability and validity of the tests should be demonstrated. These range from recommendations that items on a scale be equally balanced between or among the various possibilities for endorsement (e.g., true and false) and that items be spread out over the full range of the construct or knowledge domain being assessed. There are also a number of statistical assumptions, including the assumptions that longer tests are better measures of a variable or a construct than are shorter tests and that the statistical parameters obtained from a sufficiently large sample are accurate estimates of the population parameters on whatever variable is being assessed.

Universal Humans or Cultural Beings?

One of the core assumptions for much of psychology during the period in which many psychological tests that are currently in use were developed was that the traits and abilities under study are universal human abilities. Issues of culture, national origin, native language, gender, and racial identity, to the extent that they made a difference, were viewed as differences in people on the dimensions under study rather than as indicators of possible biases in the tests or the constructs on which the tests were based. It was also assumed that standardized administration ensures that all test takers have the same test-taking experience. The notion that culture could alter fundamental issues, such as the nature of perception or important components of intelligence, both of which have since been demonstrated (Hedden, Ketay, Aron, Markus, & Gabrieli, 2008; Maynard & Greenfield, 2003), was incomprehensible to mainstream psychologists during the development of psychological measurement practices.

Feminists and other critical theorists have challenged the core assumption that people can be meaningfully studied or understood separate from the various context factors generally described as identity, such as gender, race, ethnicity, culture, national origin, social class, and ability status (e.g., Bohan, 2002; Greenfield, 1997; Hare-Mustin & Marecek, 1990; Helms, 2006, 2007a, 2007b; Steele, 1997, 2003; Steele et al., 2002). As a result, there is a growing recognition that the relationship between the identity of the person being tested and the composition of the normative sample is important. According to standards established in the current American Psychological Association Ethics Code (American Psychological Association, 2002), psychologists are expected to use tests that have been demonstrated to be reliable and valid for the population being tested. The issue of how that requirement is met by those constructing psychological tests and those using them is discussed in greater detail later.

In addition to the recognition that tests should be reliable and valid for the population under study, there are two theoretical challenges to the classical testing theories that are generally called psychometrics. These challenges come from radically different directions. One is the critique by social constructionist and postmodern theorists (Burman, 1998). These theorists argue that, if psychological tests have any utility, it is because they provide us with useful information to assist in a current decision-making process, not because the tests tell us "truth" about the test taker or about real and universal underlying abilities or traits. As Jeanne Marecek (2002, p. 12) summarized, "The meaning of our psychological constructs…are local, time bound, and matters of social negotiation." The second critique is from quantitative experts and is known as item response theory (IRT; Hambleton & Swaminathan, 1985; Hambleton, Swaminathan, & Rogers, 1991). This critique takes the form of an alternative methodology. Unlike classical test theory (i.e., psychometrics), where items derive their meaning from the performance of the normative sample, in IRT an item's meaning is theoretically generated based on its relationship to the construct under study. Both of these critiques are addressed in later sections of this chapter.

Personality: Traits or Processes?

Another core assumption in psychological testing and assessment is that individuals possess a stable personality and stable abilities that can be described through the assessment process (Segal & Coolidge, 2004). A corollary of that assumption is that individuals can or should be described by the sum or the distribution of scores on measures of various traits, dispositional tendencies, and abilities. The effects of situations on behavior are considered to be measurement "noise," that is, something that interferes with accurate assessment of the stable traits, dispositional tendencies, and abilities.

The previously discussed critiques by postmodernists and IRT theorists apply to this assumption. In addition, Walter Mischel (Mischel, 1968; Mischel & Peake, 1982; Mischel & Shoda, 1995), well known for his critical reviews of the cross-situational consistency model of personality, noted that decades of study have failed to yield evidence for high levels of cross-situational consistency. He summarized the state of the research as indicating that cross-situational consistencies are quite low, but greater than zero, which provides evidence that people do differ on the various traits and behavioral tendencies studied, but not to a degree that allows for much accuracy in behavioral prediction (Mischel & Shoda).

Mischel and his colleagues (Mischel, 2003; Mischel & Shoda, 1995; Mischel, Shoda, & Mendoza-Denton, 2002; Shoda, LeeTiernan, & Mischel, 2002; Shoda & Mischel, 2006) have proposed an alternative view of personality that accounts for both the lack of high-level cross-situational consistency and the general subjective sense that people do, in fact, have stable personalities. This model of personality differs from the classic model of personality as a sum of traits and dispositional factors. Mischel and Shoda (1995) described a process model for personality, supported by data, which indicates that it is possible to identify relatively stable consistencies in the patterns of variability demonstrated by individuals. This process model incorporates earlier theorizing (Bem & Allen, 1974) that people's behavioral consistencies will be found only on those traits or dispositional factors that the individual considers important or consistent. However, in this process model, Mischel (2003) theorized that what we call personality is not found in general cross-situational consistencies but in the stable pattern of what he called "if–then" situation–behavior profiles.

The cognitive-affect personality system (CAPS; Mischel, 2003; Mischel & Shoda, 1995; Mischel et al., 2002; Shoda et al., 2002) includes values and goals, beliefs, an individual's expectations or schemas about self and others, affect, and competencies (Mischel & Shoda). It has been used to develop assessment strategies that successfully predict various health-related behaviors (Shoda & Mischel, 2006) and intervention strategies (Dweck, 2008).

One of the exciting aspects of this process model of personality is that it creates the opportunity for the more nuanced and complex study of gender as a process rather than a dichotomous characteristic. This is something feminist theorists have long suggested (Crawford, 1995; Deaux & Major,

1987; Eagly, 1987; Kroska, 2000). We could also think of gender identity as multi-dimensional, much in the way that Helms (2007b) has conceptualized racial identity. In a multi-dimensional process model of gender, various aspects of gendered behavior and gender identity could vary independently, as could the importance that an individual places on gender identification. A process model also creates opportunities for studying the intersection of gender with other identity issues, something that has also long been identified as an important challenge to psychology (Peplau, DeBro, Veniegas, & Taylor, 1999; Suyemoto, 2002). Assessments based on such a model of gender could provide useful information to incorporate in a process-based model of personality such as the one Mischel (2003) has outlined. For at least some people, gender of the actor and gendered expectations for social behavior are an important source of the if-then consistencies that Mischel identified as important.

The ability to test complex models for understanding personality and the potential assessment strategies and tools that derive from these complex models are, to some extent, relatively new phenomena. These capabilities are the result of the explosion in computing power that occurred in the late twentieth century. Calculations that would have been career consuming 60 years ago can now be accomplished in seconds. It is now relatively easy to evaluate moderators, mediators, and pathways in the prediction of behavior. Whether future researchers will take advantage of these new opportunities for the development of more sophisticated understandings of gender is not yet clear.

Gender and Norms

As we noted previously, scores on psychological tests generally have little or no meaning in their raw score form. Scores are given meaning by comparing them to the norms established for the test during test development. One of the critical issues for any test is how gender is treated in the development of those norms. There are three main strategies, each with strengths and limitations.

Gender Neutral

One strategy, often used in intelligence or cognitive ability tests, is to require that the scales are constructed to be gender neutral (Brody, 1992; Halpern et al., 2007). This means that the scales are constructed (i.e., items are selected for the scale) so that there is no difference in the mean scores obtained by men and women or boys and girls. This strategy generally ensures that the test is free of gender bias for the majority of test takers, particularly those in the middle range of the test score distribution. However, it may create opportunities for gender bias at the extreme upper ends of performance. For example, if performance on the most difficult items in spatial reasoning would benefit from exposure to certain video games that girls are less likely than boys to play, then boys will have an advantage. Gender-based differential familiarity with the most difficult items on a scale is unlikely to result in differences between the scores of women and men at most points in the distribution. This is because mathematically the effect on the mean from scores of the upper one-tenth of 1% of the normative sample is extremely limited. However, at the upper ranges of the distribution, where minimal differences in the number of correct answers can result in considerable differences in the standardized score, even tiny differences in familiarity with the task being assessed may lead to statistically significant performance differences. It is interesting that this pattern of performance (i.e., men and boys doing better at the extreme upper ends of the distribution) is exactly what is generally found on certain tests of cognitive ability (Halpern et al., 2007).

Gender Based

A second strategy is to use the so-called gender-based norms. Depending on whether the test takers in the normative sample identified themselves as "female" or "male" in the boxes marked "gender," their scores are the basis of either the "female" or the "male" norms. This strategy assumes that behaviors and dispositions vary in their probability based on whether an individual is a man or a woman, and it deals with that difference by comparing men to other men and women to other women. As a result, the same endorsement pattern will result in different scores depending on whether the test takers checked the box to identify themselves as men or women. This is the strategy used by the MMPI and the MMPI-2. Some tests, such as the 16 Personality Factor (16PF; Cattell, Cattell, & Cattell, 1993; Russell & Karol, 1994), provide a mix of gendered and non-gendered norms.

One problem with the use of gendered norms or gender-based score adjustments for generating a standardized score on tests of personality or psychopathology is that the test manuals generally do not provide gendered interpretations of those scores. Thus, the same interpretation is provided for different levels of behavior, an obvious source of bias. Most test publishers that provide gendered norms recently have also begun making scores generated from gender-combined norms available because of concerns that the use of gendered norms in employment contexts could constitute discrimination.

Gender Irrelevant

The third strategy is to include roughly equal numbers of men and women in the normative sample but ignore gender in the construction of norms. Proponents of this strategy argue that any differences in the prevalence of behaviors or tendencies between men and women in the population represent differences that should be reflected in different scores. This strategy is free of gender bias only if the constructs themselves and the operationalization of them are free of gender bias, which is an unlikely condition.

The question of whether it is more "fair" to compare women's and men's test scores to aggregate or to gendered norms is, at least on the surface, an interesting one. Is it more informative in evaluating an individual to compare him or her to how other men or women behave or to how other people behave? A long history of extensive research has documented that gendered expectations create different patterns of behaviors for women and men (Deaux & LaFrance, 1998; Skrypnek & Snyder 1982; Snyder, Tanke, & Berscheid, 1977; Stoppard & Gunn-Gruchy, 1993). When compared to other women, a verbally assertive woman might score relatively high on a global measure of aggressiveness; however, if she is compared to an aggregate sample that includes men, she may be closer to the norm. But what does it mean to say that a woman is verbally aggressive? Research indicates that women's behaviors in this area are evaluated more negatively than men's, thus the same act is more likely to be labeled as aggressive if performed by women. For example, in one study by LaFrance (1992), both men and women viewed the act of a woman interrupting a man more negatively than the act of a man interrupting a woman. There is a circularity created by the reciprocal influencing system of gendered expectations, gendered social contexts, individual actor's gender identity, and the actor's behavior. As a result, it becomes difficult to declare any of these strategies as ideal for dealing with gender in the norms of psychological tests. In practice, the issue is probably less about how the tests were constructed and more about how the results are being used. Thus, if scores on "aggressiveness" are being used as limit scores for selection (i.e., applicants above or below a certain percentile are automatically excluded or included), aggregate norms are probably most appropriate. By contrast, when the issue of an individual's general emotional and social functioning is being evaluated, both sets of norms may provide at least somewhat useful information.

The Current Practice of Psychological Testing

Psychological tests typically focus on either cognition and achievement or personality and symptoms. This reflects traditional distinctions within psychology between cognition and emotion and between ability and personality that are increasingly being challenged by our expanding understanding of how people actually function (Bandura, 1982; Dodge 1993; Dweck, Hong, & Chiu, 1993; Fiske & Taylor, 1991). Unfortunately, assessment instruments, many of which have been in use for decades, have not caught up with psychology's increased sophistication. For example, cognitive tests do not generally evaluate an individual's cognitive capacities or judgment in the context of emotional states. Yet, it is easy to imagine that evaluations of judgment under both stressful and non-stressful conditions might be a better predictor than IQ of many performance issues.

Types of Tests

Psychological tests can be divided or categorized in a number of different ways. As noted previously, psychological tests are usually divided into broad categories of cognitive abilities and achievements, on the one hand, and personality and psychopathology, on the other hand. Cognitive ability tests include various intelligence tests, most commonly editions of the Wechsler Adult Intelligence Scales (WAIS; Wechsler, 2008). There are a number of measures designed to assess a broad range of specific aspects of cognitive function including memory, attention, impulse control, and concept formation. As noted previously, cognitive tests are generally constructed to be gender neutral or are presented with gender-based norms (Halpern et al., 2007). Although cognitive tests are generally claimed to be tests of ability, performance on them can be influenced by experience and exposure (Feng, Spence, & Pratt, 2007).

Within the general category of personality and psychopathology, tests can be further divided based on whether they focus on identifying psychopathology (although some information about personality functioning is also generally provided) or on identifying general personality dispositions and traits without reference to specific psychopathology. Examples of tests that focus on identifying psychopathology include the Minnesota Multiphasic Personality Inventory-2 (MMPI-2; Butcher, Graham, Ben-Porath, Tellegen, & Dahlstrom, 2001), the Personality Assessment Inventory (PAI; Morey, 1991), the Millon Clinical Multiaxial Inventory-III (MCMI-III; Millon, Millon, & Davis, 1994), the Rorschach (Exner, 2003), the Beck Depression Inventory (BDI; Beck, Steer, & Brown, 1996), and the Trauma Symptom Inventory (TSI; Briere, 1995), to name only a few of literally hundreds of psychological tests in existence.

Tests of personality and psychopathology can also be divided based on whether they are "objective" or "projective" tests. This distinction refers to both the types of responses test takers are expected to provide and the type of stimuli used in the test. Objective tests present a series of statements (usually written) and require a specific response generally in the form of true/false or a numerical rating. Projective tests use stimuli that are considered ambiguous or abstract and allow for a more free-form response. The prototypical objective test is the MMPI-2, where test takers respond by marking 567 statements as either "true" or "false" as applied to themselves. Items cover a wide range of topics from symptoms of psychological problems to more general preferences. For example, the MMPI-2 items include statements such as "I think I would like the work of a librarian," and "I enjoy a race or a game more when I bet on it." The prototypical projective test is the Rorschach, where test takers respond to the query "What might this be?" as they are handed each of 10 cards with inkblots printed on them (Exner, 2003).

Test Functions

Another way to think about the use of psychological tests is to focus on the assessment functions that are performed in an evaluation where testing is being used. From a functional perspective, assessment is generally undertaken to identify achievement, facilitate selection, generate a diagnosis, facilitate intervention, or some combination of those tasks. In addition to the general cognitive and personality tests described briefly above, the functions of identifying achievement or facilitating selection often include tests specifically designed for those purposes.

Tests of Achievement

Tests of achievement include such things as frequently given elementary school achievement tests, high school graduation tests, and licensing exams. In achievement testing, a competency measure, often called a criterion-based measure, may be used to assess whether the individual can demonstrate knowledge of the required material or possession of the required skill. For example, the ability to make change, balance a checkbook, and read a bus schedule might all be used as basic competency measures for high school graduation. Criterion-based measurement requires that there be an agreed upon knowledge base or skill level that equates with competency. Achievement may also be tested with a comparison measure that assesses how much the individual appears to know compared to others of the same age or educational level. Comparison measures do not establish standards for achievement independent of the performance of the reference group.

Gender bias can enter such achievement tests in a variety of ways that feminists have documented extensively over the years (Deaux & LaFrance, 1998; Rowe, 1981; Unger & Crawford, 1992). These include obvious items such as whether a math problem asks about travel time or cooking time or whether the examples themselves mention a woman or a man. There are also more subtle sources of bias such as the weight given to areas, such as mental rotation of objects with which boys and men historically have had more experience, and whether test material includes content such as facts about wars or facts about historical styles of clothing to which one gender or the other is more likely to have been exposed outside of school (Le, 2000).

Tests for Selection

Assessment for selection usually involves asking either of the following: Does the individual possess the needed skills or traits? or Does the individual "test like" other successful incumbents? Some selection measures are interest inventories; they compare an individual's interests and attitudes to those of a sample of job incumbents. It should be obvious that, to the extent that women, people of color, or any other relevant group has not been a significant part of the incumbent group, any comparison based on the incumbent group has a great risk of containing task-irrelevant bias. Recently, some selection processes have begun using samples of the actual tasks required by the job instead of using the more traditional selection tests. The limited data available suggest that this process, when carefully done, can be relatively effective in encouraging bias-free evaluations (Anderson, Lievens, van Dam, & Born, 2006).

Exams, such as the Scholastic Aptitude Test (SAT) and the Graduate Record Examination (GRE), are used in the selection of students for college and graduate school. The SAT has historically been considered a measure of aptitude, as evidenced by its name, although the exam now emphasizes achievement rather than aptitude and the publishers prefer that it be known simply as the SAT

(Camara, 2009). However, critics have pointed out that the SAT, like many tests developed during the middle of the twentieth century, still has numerous problems. These include that it has no theoretical link to aptitude or college performance (Sternberg, 2008) and that it is influenced by nonindividual social factors (Everson & Millsap, 2004). SAT performance is also affected by stereotype threat for both race and gender (Helms, 2005; Nankervis, 2007). In addition to these documented problems, selection exams, such as the SAT and the GRE, share the avenues for gender bias common to all tests of achievement.

When any test, whether an achievement test, an aptitude or ability test, or a personality test, is used for selection, there is always the issue of whether men and women generally perform the function for which they are being selected in the same way. If they do not, then the skills or knowledge that men and women need to perform the task may also be different. Selection standards and tests based on the way men perform the task will automatically contain hidden gender bias.

The full complexity of this point may be more easily demonstrated with a physical example. Consider the hypothetical selection process for a task that has been performed by moving a moderately heavy box and unpacking it. Most men will use upper body strength to move the box, whereas most women will lift with their legs. A selection test designed for this task based on the way men do the job might test an applicant's upper body strength. Even if the assessor avoids the obvious bias against women and tests ability to lift, rather than upper body strength, there still may be gender bias involved, especially if the task has historically been done by men. It may be that women would organize the task differently, perhaps unpacking the box without moving it or using teams to lift and unpack boxes together. The issues involved here are not strictly gender issues; they are about size and strength, especially upper body strength. But, either because of differences in abilities or differences in social expectations, women and men may approach tasks or roles differently. If those constructing tests or selection processes do not appreciate that possibility, gender bias is the almost certain result.

Diagnosis and Intervention

The list of tests designed to facilitate diagnosis or intervention includes a variety of psychological instruments designed to measure personality or psychopathology. The purpose of the diagnosis is sometimes also related to determination of a medical–legal issue. There are a wide variety of gender-related concerns associated with legal evaluations, including those related to domestic violence (Walker, 1987). Raitt and Zeedyk (2000) provided an interesting overview and social constructionist critique of the problems associated with gender issues in legal evaluations that goes well beyond those concerns related specifically to psychological tests (see also Chapter 25).

Tests used in diagnosis also include measures developed specifically to assess for exaggeration or intentional production of symptoms by the test taker. Cognitive and ability tests are generally based on the assumption that people are trying to do their best, and they do not include any scales to assess for test taker effort. As a result, a number of special tests have been developed to measure the failure to put forward maximum effort in the testing process. Historically, personality or psychopathology tests have included some scales designed to identify inaccurate self-presentation, although some specific measures to identify symptom exaggeration and malingering also exist. These efforts to identify malingering or "faking" use a variety of strategies including the production of improbable symptoms, unusual symptom combinations, and excessively broad numbers and categories of symptoms (Rogers, 1997). Scales designed to identify efforts to present oneself in an unrealistically positive manner often assess tendencies to claim unusual numbers of socially desirable but improbable virtues, for example, being nice to everybody all of the time. All of these scales and tests are subject to the gender-related concerns that apply to tests generally.

Gender Bias and Tests of Personality and Psychopathology

As we noted previously in reference to psychological testing generally, the treatment of gender in tests of personality and psychopathology is neither sophisticated nor nuanced. Gender is rarely addressed specifically in projective tests. Primarily for that reason, this discussion focuses on the so-called objective tests of personality and psychopathology. In objective tests, gender is routinely conflated with biological sex and generally "assessed" by asking the individual test taker to mark either "male" or "female" under the heading of "gender" on the answer sheet. The use the test user makes of that information varies in important ways related to the test's construction. However, there are some issues related to gender and gender bias common to virtually all of these tests.

Gender bias in the personality assessment process has been described as the result of two different processes, which have been labeled assessment bias and criterion bias by several personality and testing theorists (Morey, Warner, & Boggs, 2002; Widiger, 1998; Widiger & Spitzer, 1991). Morey and his colleagues described assessment bias as the same behaviors or symptoms being rated differently based on the gender of the individual who exhibits them. They described criterion bias as problems in the diagnostic system when the construct or the pathology is based on a gender-biased model. A more useful way of thinking about categories of bias may be to separate the issues of bias in the construct on which the test is based: bias in the specific operationalization of the construct and bias in the statistical assumptions and structural aspects of the tests.

Biased Theories

When the construct itself reflects gender bias, even a well-constructed test to assess the construct will also include gender bias. This gender bias at the theory level may be represented by bias in specific traits or diagnostic categories. There is also the larger concern raised by feminists that the components considered to be important dimensions of personality are based on an androcentric understanding of personhood (Bohan, 2002). This form of bias is evidenced not only by what is on the various tests but also by what is omitted from them.

The view that there is gender bias in the diagnostic systems generally used by psychologists and other mental health professionals has been consistently raised from the beginnings of feminist psychology (see, for example, Ballou & Brown, 2002; Chesler, 1972; Unger & Crawford, 1992). Feminists (e.g., Broverman et al., 1970; Caplan, 1995; Caplan & Cosgrove, 2004; Kaplan, 1983; Walker, 1993; see also Chapter 5) have been particularly critical of the gender bias in the American Psychiatric Association's diagnostic system, including the diagnostic manual for the most recent iteration of that system (American Psychiatric Association, 2000). Among the problems feminists have identified in this diagnostic system is a tendency to ignore the social context of behavior and to pathologize behavior that is encouraged by gender roles. For example, the *DSM-IV* (American Psychiatric Association, 2000) diagnostic category of dependant personality disorder is defined as an "excessive need to be taken care of that leads to submissive and clinging behavior and fears of separation" (p. 721). Feminists have long noted that these behaviors are much more strongly encouraged for women than for men (Walker, 1993).

It can be difficult to separate the construct from the operationalization of the construct. The definition of a particular psychological problem can include more of the ways that men or women, but not both, behave in response to their psychological state or emotional feelings. Take, for example, the construct of depression. Women may be more likely to cry when they are upset, whereas men may be more likely to drink excessively, drive recklessly, or be angry and irritable (Romans & Clarkson,

2008). Tearfulness is part of the diagnostic picture for depression, but drinking, reckless driving, and anger are not. The failure to include the ways that men behave in response to "being down," such as increased alcohol consumption, thrill seeking, and heighted aggressiveness, may create a gender bias in the construct of depression that is also reflected in tests to assess depression, although this has not generally been demonstrated (Nolen-Hoeksema, 2008; Nolen-Hoeksema & Jackson, 2001). To the extent that there is a gender bias, it is not clear whether that bias is in the theory of depression or in the way that the theory is operationalized.

Biased Operationalization

Other forms of bias are located more clearly in the application of the theory. The use of gendered norms can be considered a form of biased operationalization. Tests can be constructed based on the way women or men, but not both, engage in a behavior. Other examples of gender bias in the tests occur at the item level.

Biased Test Construction

It is especially important for tests designed to assess psychopathology to evaluate the manner in which the test was developed. Some have argued that the use of items with differential probability of endorsement by women and men does not represent bias if the items relate to symptoms of genuine dysfunction (Morey et al., 2002). However, regardless of the legitimacy of the items as markers of dysfunction, a scale based on the way a problem manifests only or primarily in men versus only or primarily in women has a distinct possibility to be gender biased.

Tests can also be biased because the test is based on the manifestations of a psychological construct in a context that would include more of one group or the other. For example, consider two hypothetical measures developed to assess Post-traumatic Stress Disorder (PTSD). One is based only on the experiences of rape trauma victims, most of whom are women. The other is based only on the experiences of combat veterans, most of whom are men. The results could be two distinctly different tests (Berberich, 1998; Kimerling, Ouimette, & Weitlauf, 2007). The two tests would be likely to generate gendered levels of diagnoses even though all of the items would be legitimate symptoms of PTSD, a diagnostic construct not generally considered to be gender biased.

Almost any test could be constructed based on symptoms that are more prevalent among either men or women. For example, consider the rates of diagnosis that might be generated by a depression scale that emphasizes tearfulness and subjective states of sadness compared to a scale that emphasizes restlessness. Although both tests include only symptoms agreed to be markers of depression (American Psychiatric Association, 2000), the first symptoms are more socially appropriate for women and the second are more socially appropriate for men (Nolen-Hoeksema, 2008). Thus, the first test would be likely to result in more false negatives for men, whereas the second would probably under diagnose women.

Finally, a test could be developed from the study of only women or only men. The development of the Psychopathy Check List – Revised (PCL-R; Hare, 1980, 1985), a widely used measure of psychopathy, used this process. The PCL-R was developed by studying male prisoners diagnosed as psychopathic (Hare, 1980, 1985; Forouzan & Cooke, 2005). Although women can be assigned reasonably reliable scores on the PCL-R (Kennealy, Hicks, & Patrick, 2007), researchers have found differences in the physiological reactions of men and women diagnosed as psychopathic on physiological dimensions (O'Leary, Loney, & Eckel, 2007). Physiological reactivity to emotionally loaded situations is considered core to the construct of psychopathy.

There is also evidence that the model assessed by the PCL-R is less useful for predictions of recidivism in women (Schmidt, McKinnon, Chattha, & Brownlee, 2006). Results of a study of female prisoners stratified by PCL-R scores (Vablais, 2007) suggest that some issues assessed in the measure (e.g., sexual promiscuity and relying on a relationship partner for support) are not particularly useful in assessing psychopathy in women. In the same study, issues concerning connection to one's children, a factor not identified as significant in men, appeared to capture the core of the psychopathic construct for female prisoners better than did their total PCL-R scores. All these suggest that although the construct of psychopathy may or may not reflect a gender bias, the manner in which it is operationalized often does. This gender bias is not trivial. A psychopathy diagnosis can affect eligibility for treatment and parole.

Differential Item Endorsement Probability

In the previous examples, the entire tests contained possible gender bias. However, bias can also occur at the level of individual items. One form of biased operationalization occurs at the item level if the same behavior or symptom is more likely to be endorsed by men or women and either is or is not always considered pathological. For example, endorsement of statements that indicate satisfaction with the self or confidence in the test taker's abilities, both of which are more common for men than women (Morey et al., 2002), can be an indication either of narcissism or of healthy self-esteem. However, this is not the only form of gender-biased operationalization.

Even when the items are legitimate symptoms, if a scale includes items that have gender differences in the likelihood of endorsement, the scale itself may be gender biased. A scale with more items likely to be endorsed by men than by women with a given type of psychological problem has a high probability of resulting in consistently higher scores for men suffering from the problem. The reverse is true if the test assesses more of women's than of men's typical symptoms. Even if only some of the items have a gendered differential probability, the presence of that gender inequity at the item level has a strong probability of resulting in gender bias at the scale level.

Different Item Meaning: Reference Groups

Gender bias can occur if the items on the test are not given the same meaning by a woman and a man taking the test. Objective tests include the assumption that the various statements in them, such as "I am more sensitive than most other people," have an objective meaning common to all of the test takers. For that assumption to be true and unbiased, test takers must not only have a common definition of the words (e.g., what does it mean to be "sensitive") but also agree on the appropriate comparison group. The gender of the actor has been demonstrated to influence the evaluation of a wide range of behaviors in virtually every domain of human behavior (Deaux & LaFrance, 1998). For example, both men and women view it as more appropriate for women to be emotionally expressive and for men to be emotionally composed (Riggio & Friedman, 1986). In our example above, a woman might define sensitivity as awareness of others' needs, a definition drawn from expectations for women's behavior, whereas a man might give the word a different meaning. It is likely that gender influences the meaning given to the de-contextualized statements and self-descriptors found on most psychological tests.

It is also possible that some individual test takers may respond to questions that require a comparison by comparing their behavior to that of same-sex others, whereas other test takers may use an androcentric standard or a gender-aggregated group for their comparison. This means that, for example, the statement "I drink a lot" may be translated by some women to mean "Compared to other women, I drink a lot." Other women may compare themselves to the population generally. Similarly, men considering their level of sensitivity may compare themselves to other men, to women, or to a gender-aggregated group. It may be that the comparison group also changes for at least some test takers based on whether the behavior or the attribute is generally associated with stereotypes for men's behavior (e.g., drinking) or women's behavior (e.g., sensitivity).

Although the test taker's mental reference group may be an issue, to some extent, for any identity or demographic variable, it is likely to be particularly serious with respect to gender. There is a large and well-documented feminist critique of the tendency for behavior to be evaluated based on the actor's gender but against an androcentric standard, where men's stereotypic behavior is defined positively and women's stereotypic behavior is defined negatively (Deaux & LaFrance, 1998). Thus, the question of whether men and women are using the same comparison group for their mental self-evaluations is a possible avenue for gender bias in the assessment process. Some researchers have studied whether women and men differ in how ambiguous they consider the various items on some psychological tests to be (Dahlstrom, Welsh, & Dahlstrom, 1975), but the question of to whom people actually compare themselves when responding to these test items has not, to our knowledge, been studied empirically.

Although the issue of comparison group has not been specifically studied, new statistical methods for assessing the general issue of item bias have been developed. These new methods are based on item response theory (IRT; Embretson & Yang, 2006; Hambleton & Swaminathan, 1985; Thissen, Steinberg, & Gerrard, 1986). IRT-based methods, which are discussed in more detail in a later section of this chapter, make it possible to evaluate whether an item works in the same way for different groups of people. Although identifying differential item functioning based on gender does not tell us why that differential functioning occurred, it does at least identify the need to ask the question.

Gendered Correlates of Item Bias

In some cases, gender bias can be the result of bias against some category that correlates highly with gender. For example, both rape victims and adults molested as children are categories of traumatic experience that include substantially more women than men. This problem has been raised with respect to some scales on the MMPI-2, including the MMPI-2 Infrequency (F) Scale and the Infrequency-Psychopathology (Fp) Scale. In a study of non-litigant adult victims of child sexual abuse, researchers found that measures of dissociation, post-traumatic stress, depression, and family environment correlated significantly with F and accounted for 40% of its variance (Flitter, Elhai, & Gold, 2003). Among the problems identified with the F and Fp Scales was the inclusion of four items about the test taker's evaluation of her or his parents as good people for whom the test taker feels love (e.g., "I love/loved my mother," or "My father is/was a good man."). Although most people would respond to these items affirmatively, an individual seeking treatment to deal with the aftermath of childhood incest might not. Four items is not a trivial number, especially on the Fp Scale where only four scored items places an individual above the interpretable standardized score level (T-Score greater than 65; Butcher et al., 2001). On the surface, this appears to be an issue about sexual abuse, not gender bias, but there is a gender difference in the probability of having experienced childhood sexual abuse. Evidence indicates that more women than men were sexually abused as children (Cappelleri, Eckenrode, & Powers, 1993). As a result, an instrument that unfairly assesses sexual abuse victims should also be considered gender biased. Other researchers have found evidence of bias against women in the MMPI-2 Fake-Bad-Scale (Butcher, Arbisib, Atlisa, & McNulty, 2008), such that women are more likely than men to be falsely diagnosed as malingerers, although the correlates of this bias are less clear.

Gender and Social Appropriateness of Items

Another possibility of bias occurs if an item or a marker is more socially appropriate as a self-description for either men or women, but is not pathological at all, or could be a manifestation of pathology or healthy behavior (Lindsay & Widiger, 1995). Many items on scales of histrionic and narcissistic tendencies are, in moderation, simply signs of being socially comfortable and having a positive self-image. Differential levels of social appropriateness for such items can result in biased scales. Research findings suggest that men may endorse more of the items that indicate positive self-image on scales of narcissism, whereas women may endorse more of the items related to sociability on histrionic scales (Morey et al., 2002). There is also some evidence that men endorse depressive symptoms differently than do women (Sigmon et al., 2005).

Bias in Structural Issues and Statistical Assumptions

Bias, including gender bias, may be present in psychological tests due to issues associated with the statistical assumptions used in the process of test construction. Problems in this area include the previously discussed issues of how gender is dealt with in the construction of norms, but there are other issues related to statistical assumptions and standardized test scores. For example, psychometric theory assumes that the standard error of measurement is the same for all individuals, although it is computed from the data provided by the normative or the standardization sample. Yet, there is empirical evidence that multiple dimensions of identity shape the self-descriptions of individuals (Sinclair, Hardin, & Lowery, 2006). One can easily imagine different levels of variability in endorsement of statements concerning, for example, alcohol consumption, use of profanity, and verbal aggressiveness among a sample of women from New York City as compared to a sample of women from the rural southern United States. Similarly, even if one has normative data for African American women generally, it is unclear how to compare the data from African American women with law degrees to data gathered from a predominately high school-educated group of African American women. Psychological tests, to the extent that they track and account for variability in factors such as education, rural versus urban settings, and region of the country, are unlikely to account for the interactions between these various factors and other identity issues such as gender and race/ethnicity in developing their norms.

In fact, one of the disturbing tendencies in the efforts to develop tests that have been demonstrated to be reliable and valid for the population being tested is to use a normative sample that is said to be comparable in composition to the US census. The argument is that this provides test norms based on the "average American." The problem, of course, is that the majority of the US population is White. To the extent that culture and language matter, how appropriate are scores based on the Personality Assessment Inventory's (PAI; Morey, 1991) normative sample, which was roughly 85% White and 12% Black, for evaluating Asian Americans? In fact, how appropriate are those norms for evaluating Blacks? Similarly, one could ask whether the presence of 77 Native Americans, 73 Hispanic Americans, or 19 Asian Americans in the 2,600 person normative sample for the MMPI-2 (Butcher et al., 2001) provides sufficient support for the use of that test with any of those populations. Even the 214 African Americans included represent only a little more than 8% of the sample. In the above examples, the numbers become even smaller when the various groups are also divided by gender. Yet, cultural differences in gender scripts may be of particular importance when evaluating a person's psychological functioning. It becomes circular to argue that differences in psychological test performance reflect real differences in the prevalence of psychological disorders in the population when some of the diagnoses are justified in part because of scores on the psychological tests. It requires nothing more than high school math to realize that the only way to ensure that a test is reliable and valid for a particular group is to oversample under-represented groups in order to obtain a meaningful sample of that group.

The concerns about the selection of normative samples are magnified further when tests are used with immigrants and when tests developed in Western nations are used in other countries and cultures. Greenfield (1997) has argued that all tests are culture bound. Although a full discussion of this issue is beyond the scope of this chapter, it is important to remember that higher education generally involves participation in a tradition of thinking based in large part on a Western intellectual foundation. Thus, when new normative samples are developed for cross-cultural test use, the educational levels of the normative sample and those of the test-taking population should be similar.

Construction of Personality Tests

One of the major distinctions is between theoretically based and empirically based personality tests. As with many distinctions, this one breaks down in practice, especially in contemporary practice where almost all test developers use some combination of theory and empirical refinement in the construction of their tests. Nonetheless, some review of the distinction may be useful for our discussion of test construction.

Empirical Tests

Heavy reliance on statistical techniques is the hallmark of empirically developed tests. The two main empirical methods employed are known-groups comparisons and factor analysis. The MMPI (Hathaway & McKinley, 1943) was constructed using the known-groups comparison method. Cattell's (1943, 1946) Sixteen Personality Factor Questionnaire (16PF) was developed using factor analysis. Both of these empirical processes start from the assumption that the structure of personality is universal rather than a gendered or culturally defined entity.

MMPI and MMPI-2

This test remains the most commonly used personality test in the world (Butcher, Atlis, & Hahn, 2004). The original construction of the MMPI used a known-groups comparison technique. Items were selected for an MMPI scale if they were answered differently by the non-patient sample than by the patient group the scale sought to identify (Butcher et al., 2001; Greene, 1991, 2000). The relationship of an item's content to any theoretical definition of the diagnostic group was irrelevant. The only standard was that the target or criterion group item responded to the item differently than the people in the comparison or control group. Greene (1991, 2000) reported that the comparison or control group was usually individuals who had not been diagnosed with any mental illness. In addition to this unique construction technique, the original MMPI had a number of problems from the standpoint of psychometric theory. These included the use of the same test item on multiple scales, unequal scale length, and an imbalance between true and false items on the scales. Although these issues create problems in the test, they are not particularly related to gender issues.

The original MMPI did not generally address the social notion of gender and did not place much emphasis on biological sex categories. There was not any rigorous effort to ensure gender balance in the groups selected either as the target-patient group or as the comparison or normal group (Greene, 2000). However, the published version of the MMPI and the re-standardized MMPI-2 (Butcher et al.,

2001) base scores on gendered norms. Although the needed tables are not provided in the *MMPI-2 Manual*, non-gendered scores are available on some of the computer-generated scoring reports. (Problems with gender bias in some of the various specific scales of the MMPI and MMPI-2 were discussed earlier.)

The technique used to develop the original MMPI has been derisively referred to as "dust bowl empiricism" because of the total lack of interest in any relationship between the items' content and the scale's function (Butcher, Atlis, & Hahn, 2004). One problem with the known-groups comparison as a test construction technique is that, in any comparison, the difference in item endorsement for two groups will include some amount of measurement error. That error is related to idiosyncratic factors associated with the particular people in the two groups used for the test development rather than to the distinction between the groups. When items are selected for a scale without any theoretical relationship to the construct the scale is meant to measure, the probability that any item reflects measurement error associated with idiosyncratic factors is increased. This probability becomes even greater when the number of people in the groups is relatively small, as was the case in the construction of the original MMPI. Given the lack of attention to gender balance in the criterion group (Greene, 2000), it is quite probable that at least some of those idiosyncratic measurement errors are related to gender issues.

The developers of the original MMPI explicitly addressed gender issues in only one area other than the use of gendered norms. That was the development for the MMPI of the Masculinity–Femininity (Mf) Scale, which was originally developed to identify members of the then pathological category of "homosexuals" rather than to evaluate gender per se (Butcher et al., 2001; Greene, 2000). Not only is homosexuality no longer considered pathological, today we also recognize that sexual orientation is not synonymous with gender.

It is, perhaps, reflective of the non-pathological nature of sexual orientation that the test's developers, Hathaway and colleagues, were unable to identify any common response patterns on the MMPI for those individuals who had been labeled "homosexuals" (Greene, 1991). Because of that, the target group ultimately selected for the construction of the Mf Scale consisted of 13 men who had been diagnosed as homosexual and who had a very feminine pattern of presentation, which was labeled "sexual inversion" at the time the original test was developed (Butcher & Williams, 1992; Greene, 1991). Greene (1991) also noted that this original group of 13 was selected because, other than their "sexual inversion," the individuals were free from any psychopathology. Greene (1991, p. 155) reported that the test developers used two "normal" (e.g., presumptively heterosexual) comparison groups, 54 male soldiers, and 67 female flight attendants. They sought to identify items that differentiated the target group of 13 gay men from the soldiers and the soldiers from the flight attendants.

Two new gender role scales [i.e., the Gender Role – Masculine Scale (GM) and the Gender Role –Feminine (GF) Scale] were added during the development of the re-standardized MMPI-2. In contrast to the original Mf Scale that treated gender as a unitary bipolar construct, the two additional gender scales were based on the notion that the masculine and the feminine gender roles represent two separate constructs. Some have suggested that these gender scales reflect a caricature of stereotypic gender roles (Greene, 1991), and they have not been found to correlate well with other efforts to define gender identity or gender role-related behavior (Butcher et al., 2001). Consistent with the description of these scales as gender caricatures, for both women and men, the GM Scale correlates positively with well-being, and the GF Scale is associated with "excessive sensitivity" (Butcher et al., 2001, p. 41).

Since the introduction of the MMPI-2, work on revising the test has continued or perhaps accelerated. In 2003, the Revised Clinical (RC) Scales were introduced (Tellegen et al., 2003). These scales are an attempt to assess the core construct associated with each of the eight clinical scales among the MMPI's Basic Scales as well as an overall demoralization factor. The Mf Scale and the Introversion–Extroversion Scale (Scale Si) were omitted because the core construct for those scales is not about psychopathology. The RC Scales use items from the MMPI-2. However, the scales were theoretically constructed and did not reuse items on more than one scale, a methodological problem in the original and re-standardized test. In addition, the RC Scales do not use gendered norms. In 2008, the MMPI-Restructured Form (MMPI-RF; Ben-Porath & Tellegen, 2008) was introduced. Like the RC Scales, the MMPI-RF uses items from the MMPI-2. It is theoretically constructed and does not use gendered norms. However, gendered norms, along with a number of other comparison groups, are available. Because it is theoretically constructed, the MMPI-RF shares the problems with gender issues previously discussed with respect to theoretically constructed tests and tests that use gender aggregate norms.

16PF

The 16PF was also developed empirically (Cattell, 1943, 1946, 1973; Cattell et al., 1993). Cattell started with a list of personality traits developed by Allport and colleagues and supplemented them with items developed from various theories of personality (Anastasi, 1982). A number of factor analyses were conducted on this list based on individuals' ratings of themselves and others. The ratings of others were both subjective and based on direct behavioral observation. Cattell also theorized that the basic traits could be summarized into higher order global factors. Identification of the various clusters was done by the empirical process of the factor analyses. The theoretical contribution was in the labeling of the 16 factors identified and in the selection and labeling of the five higher order factors. The development of the 16PF did not address gender. The fifth edition of the 16PF (Cattell et al., 1993) provides both gendered and gender-aggregated norms, which allow test users to select the norms they prefer.

The 16PF is designed to measure "normal" personality, not psychopathology or psychological disorders. It is prototypic of efforts to measure or assess personality through the use of a sum of traits model. The manual for the most recent revision in 1993 included both theoretical and empirical efforts by the test developers to eliminate gender bias, along with other forms of bias, from the individual test items. However, the issue of gender bias in the construct of personality that the test was designed to identify was not addressed. The predictive validity of the 16PF, like all efforts to identify cross-situational behavioral consistencies, is greater than zero but not exceptionally high. Test–retest reliability for the 16PF basic traits at 2 months ranges from 0.56 to 0.79 (Conn & Rieke, 1994). The failure to address gender issues in the test development process leaves the 16PF vulnerable to all of the critiques of androcentric bias previously discussed.

Theoretically Developed Tests

Virtually all well-known tests developed within the last 30 years have used some combination of theoretical framework and empirical procedures. In practice this means that items are developed to measure theoretically meaningful constructs. These items are then subjected to empirical analysis in the process of developing the final version of the test. Standardized scores are then generally developed for the final version of the test through the use of a normative sample.

Some tests are specifically designed to identify psychopathology, often with a focus on a particular type of pathology. Tests designed to assess particular forms of psychopathology include, for example, the Beck Depression Inventory (BDI-II; Beck et al., 1996) and the TSI (Briere, 1995).

These tests are generally based on some combination of the diagnostic symptoms generally accepted as markers of the particular psychopathology.

Other tests are designed to measure both psychopathology and personality traits. These tests include the PAI (Morey, 1991), the Millon Clinical Multiaxial Inventory- III (MCMI-III; Millon, Millon, Davis, & Grossman, 2006), and the reformatted version of the MMPI-2 (MMPI-RF; Ben-Porath & Tellegen, 2008). Still others are designed to test personality traits, dispositions, and identity issues. These include tests like the NEO-Personality Inventory (Costa & McCrae, 1985, 1992), which was developed based on the five-factor model of personality (McCrae & John, 1992), and a wide variety of more specific tests.

With all theoretically developed tests, the goal is to assess the content of the theoretical construct, usually by measuring the presence or the absence of the various symptoms, behaviors, attitudes, and beliefs that are considered to be manifestations of the pathology, trait, or disposition. Well-designed tests usually include items reflective of symptoms at all levels of severity and across all symptoms categories. Often developers use a combination of expert evaluators and empirical tests to identify and eliminate biased items (Morey, 1991). Most of these tests use gender-aggregated normative samples. None of these personality or trait tests use the gender-neutral approach common in the construction of intelligence tests. Thus, any gender bias in the constructs can be expected to carry over into the tests. Some of the test developers have argued that any gender differences in test results represent "real" differences in the gendered frequency of the specific item or the diagnostic category (Morey).

Perhaps the most problematic of the theoretically derived tests with respect to gender is the MCMI-III. This test is based on Millon's (1990) theory of personality, a theory he described as based in evolutionary theory. His theory includes three over-arching dimensions that Millon referred to as polarities: pleasure–pain, passive–active, and other–self. These became the basis for his categories of personality and personality disorders as well as his other categories of psychopathology. Millon's personality theory is generally subject to the same feminist criticism that has been raised with respect to other diagnostic frameworks and other applications of evolutionary theory to psychology (e.g., Travis, 2003; see also Volume I, Chapter 13). One practice relatively unique to the MCMI-III is that only patients were used in the development of the test. The stated goal of the test is to identify the most likely diagnosis based on the presumption that a diagnosis should be given. In addition, the MCMI-III scoring process adjusts scores for women and men depending on the estimated base rates for the particular diagnostic labels being assigned to women or men. Unfortunately, there is little empirical justification for this built-in bias (Hynan, 2004). As a result, users of the MCMI-III are cautioned to be careful about potential gender bias over and above the general issues of gender bias common to all tests.

Item Response Theory (IRT)

The existence of a theoretical basis for most of the newer tests is important. The theoretical models for these tests allow for the use of a new approach to test construction and test evaluation based on IRT (Embretson & Yang, 2006; Hambleton & Swaminathan, 1985). IRT is another example of a development made possible by advances in the ability to perform complex mathematical calculations as a result of modern computer power. Embretson (1996), an expert on IRT, attributed the origins of IRT to the work of Lord and Novick. Full explanation of the IRT is well beyond the scope of this chapter or the competency of its authors. However, there are some important properties and possibilities associated with IRT that warrant discussion here.

Hambleton and colleagues described IRT as a model-based measurement rather than a population-based measurement (Hambleton & Swaminathan, 1985, Hambleton et al., 1991). What that means is that the value of any item is based on the value assigned to it based on the theoretical construct being tested rather than on the behavior of the normative sample. One of several important differences between IRT and traditional psychometric theory, or classic test theory (CTT), is in the way the standard error of measurement is developed. CTT requires the use of the normative sample to calculate the standard error of measurement, which in turn is used to calculate the standard deviation, and thus the probability of any given score. The standard error is the same for all scores in the distribution. In IRT the standard error of measurement is estimated using the theoretical probability that an item will be endorsed based on a mathematical model of what is being measured. In a dichotomous model, the simplest of IRT models, the standard error will be lowest in the middle range of scores because it is assumed that there will be a normal distribution of scores, with most scores in the middle range.

One of the most important, but statistically complicated, implications of IRT is that unbiased estimates of item properties do not depend on whether or not the sample is representative. As a result, it becomes possible to test the way in which an item functions in two different populations and to identify evidence of item-level bias on the test (Thissen et al., 1986). This allows for a more sophisticated assessment of whether or not the test and the theory on which it was based function in the same manner with different groups. At this point, IRT is being used primarily to develop tests of abilities (Embretson & Yang, 2006). The only difficulty with applying IRT to tests of personality and psychopathology is the requirement that test construction be based on a model that allows items to be assigned a value.

IRT methods make it possible to evaluate gender bias in the function of items on tests that were theoretically constructed. Santor and his colleagues (Santor, Ramsay, & Zuroff, 1994) used an IRT-based analysis to evaluate the Beck Depression Inventory for item-based gender bias. This analysis was particularly important because earlier research had indicated some gender-based differential functioning of the BDI (Hammen & Padesky, 1977). The analysis by Santor and his colleagues demonstrated that the theory of depression on which the BDI is based is generally consistent with the manner in which the BDI items function. In other words, for the most part, seriously depressed people endorse items that suggest more serious levels of depression. However, they did identify several items that demonstrated differential functioning in women and men, which suggests gender bias (Santor et al., 1994). They also found that the differential item functioning was different for a sample of college-aged men and women and a treatment sample of men and women. Their results suggest the need for caution in the use of the published criterion scores when the BDI is used with women, particularly young women (Santor et al., 1994). More recently, Waller and colleagues (Waller, Compas, Hollon, & Beckjord, 2005) evaluated the item functioning of the BDI in women with breast cancer and those without breast cancer, and they reported that the items functioned differently in the two populations.

Both of these examples reflect some of the interesting possibilities of evaluating psychological assessment instruments and practices available to those with a grasp of advanced contemporary statistical techniques. However, it is important to remember that identification of bias in item functioning requires that the individual test takers be rated independently of the test items. This independent rating allows researchers to compare the function of items with comparable individuals between groups. Obtaining unbiased ratings of individuals is difficult if the construct itself is biased with respect to the variable that distinguishes the groups. Nonetheless, the ability to assess for differential item functioning remains an interesting step in exploring bias of various types, including gender bias, in psychological tests.

Conclusion and Future Directions

From this overview of psychological testing, we can conclude that psychological testing and assessment, as it is currently practiced, suffer from most of the problems of gender bias that feminists have identified in the field more broadly. Gender bias affects psychological testing in the definitions of the constructs being assessed and in the operationalization of those constructs. The treatment of gender has been both unsophisticated and haphazard. The role of gender identity and gender role constraints as mediators or moderators of test responses or psychological issues has been virtually unexplored. Despite these limitations, there is reason to be hopeful that future developments in the areas of both personality theory and psychological testing will result in more nuanced and useful treatment of gender and the effects of gender and gender roles in psychological testing.

As a practical matter, our review suggests that clinicians should approach test scores with caution. Before asking what the test scores mean, a clinician should ask a number of questions about the appropriateness of the test for the particular test taker, about context factors, about bias in the underlying construct and the construct's operationalization, and about the manner in which the test was developed and standardized. Those questions about context factors include attention to the role of the assessor and the assessor's biases in the interaction with the test taker and the assessment setting. This suggested that caution reflects the concerns and critiques about psychological constructs and diagnostic frameworks raised by feminist theorists, especially feminist social constructionists and postmodern theorists (e.g., Ballou & Brown, 2002; Hare-Mustin & Marecek, 1990). Nothing in the current practice of test construction or test use obviates the value of these critiques.

For researchers, our review suggests a variety of interesting lines of investigation. The use of a process model of personality, particularly the CAPS model developed by Mischel (2003), suggests new avenues for exploring gendered identity and the relationship of gendered assumptions and people's behaviors. The view of personality as something other than a collection of stable traits and dispositions opens up a variety of exciting research directions with the opportunity to study gender in a more sophisticated way. One can ask about the effects of a person's gendered schemas for others as well as for the individual's own gendered representation of self. The relative importance of gender in the personality process, both for the expectations of self and others, could be explored in this context. It seems possible to connect the feminist research traditions about attitudes toward women and gender with personality and clinical realms. It may be that our psychological tests will need to be quite different: more focused and specific, more explicitly inclusive of what we call attitudes and values.

Similarly, for those willing to invest the time and energy required to develop expertise in new statistical methods, the possibility of exploring and identifying various forms of bias, including gender bias, in tests and measures is exciting. It will be important for critics of the socially embedded gender assumptions to be among those versed in these new statistical methods. Without that expertise, new iterations of biased assumptions may gain a mantle of scientific respectability that those lacking in an understanding of the assumptions underlying the statistical procedures are unable to challenge.

References

American Psychiatric Association. (2000). *Diagnostic and statistical manual of mental disorders-IV-TR.* Washington, DC: American Psychiatric Association.

American Psychological Association. (2002). Ethical principles of psychologists and code of conduct. *American Psychologist,* 57, 1060–1073.

Anastasi, A. (1982). *Psychological testing* (5th ed.). New York: Macmillan.
Anderson, N., Lievens, F., van Dam, K., & Born, M. (2006). A construct-driven investigation of gender differences in a leadership-role assessment center. *Journal of Applied Psychology, 91*, 555–566.
Ballou, M., & Brown, L. S. (Eds.), (2002). *Rethinking mental health and disorder.* New York: Guilford.
Bandura, A. (1982). Self-efficacy mechanisms in human agency. *American Psychologist, 37*, 122–147.
Beck, A. T., Steer, R. A., & Brown, G. K. (1996). *Beck Depression inventory manual* (2nd ed.). San Antonio, TX: Psychological Corporation.
Bem, D. J., & Allen, A. (1974). On predicting some of the people some of the time: The search for cross – situational consistencies in behavior. *Psychological Review, 81*, 506–520.
Ben-Porath, Y. S., & Tellegen, A. (2008). *Minnesota Multiphasic Personality Inventory-2 restructured form.* Minneapolis, MN: Pearson.
Berberich, D. A. (1998). Posttraumatic stress disorder: Gender and cross-cultural clinical issues. *Psychotherapy in Private Practice, 17*(2), 29–41.
Bohan, J. S. (2002). Sex differences and/in the self: Classic themes, feminist variations, postmodern challenges. *Psychology of Women Quarterly, 26*, 74–88.
Bowers, A. M. V., & Bieschke, K. J. (2005). Psychologists' clinical evaluations and attitudes: An examination of the influence of gender and sexual orientation. *Professional Psychology, 36*, 99–103.
Brener, N. D., Billy, J. O. G., & Grady, W. R. (2003). Assessment of factors affecting the validity of self-reported health-risk behavior among adolescents: Evidence from the scientific literature. *Journal of Adolescent Health, 33*, 436–457.
Briere, J. (1995). *Trauma Symptom Inventory professional manual.* Odessa, FL: Psychological Assessment Resources.
Brody, N. (1992). *Intelligence* (2nd ed.). New York: Academic Press.
Broverman, I. K., Broverman, D. M., Clarkson, F. E., Rozenkrantz, P. S., & Vogel, S. R. (1970). Sex role stereotypes and clinical judgments of mental health. *Journal of Consulting and Clinical Psychology, 34*, 1–7.
Burman, E. (Ed.) (1998). *Deconstructing feminist psychology.* London: Sage.
Butcher, J. N., Arbisib, P. A., Atlisa, M. M., & McNulty, J. L. (2008). Construct validity of the Lees-Haley Fake Bad Scale. *Archives of Clinical Neuropsychology, 23*, 855–864.
Butcher, J. N., Atlis, M. M., & Hahn, J. (2004). The Minnesota Multiphasic Personality Inventory – 2 (MMPI-2). In M. J. Hilsenroth & D. L. Segal (Eds.), *Comprehensive handbook of psychological assessment: Personality assessment* (pp. 30–38). Hoboken, NJ: Wiley.
Butcher, J. N., Graham, J. R., Ben-Porath, Y. S., Tellegen, A. & Dahlstrom, W. G. (2001). *MMPI-2 manual for administration, scoring, and interpretation* (rev. ed.). Minneapolis, MN: University of Minnesota Press.
Butcher, J. N., & Williams, C. L. (1992) *Essentials of MMPI-2 and MMPI-A interpretation.* Minneapolis, MN: University of Minnesota Press.
Camara, W. J. (2009). College admission testing: Myths and realities in an age of admissions hype. In R. P. Phelps (Ed.), *Correcting fallacies about educational and psychological testing* (pp. 147–180). Washington, DC: American Psychological Association.
Caplan, P. J. (1995). *They say you're crazy.* Reading, MA: Addison-Wesley.
Caplan, P. J., & Cosgrove, L. (Eds.). (2004). *Bias in psychiatric diagnosis.* Northvale, NJ: Jason Aronson.
Cappelleri, J. C., Eckenrode, J., & Powers, J. L. (1993). The epidemiology of child abuse: Findings from the second national incidence and prevalence study of child abuse and neglect. *American Journal of Public Health, 83*, 1622–1624.
Cattell, R. B. (1943). The description of personality: Basic traits resolved into clusters. *Journal of Abnormal and Social Psychology, 38*, 476–506.
Cattell, R. B. (1946). *The description and measurement of personality.* New York: World Book.
Cattell, R. B. (1973). *Personality and mood by questionnaire.* San Francisco: Jossey-Bass.
Cattell, R. B., Cattell, A. K., & Cattell, H. E. P. (1993). *Sixteen Personality Factor questionnaire* (5th ed). Champaign, IL: Institute for Personality and Ability Testing.
Chesler, P. (1972). *Women and madness.* New York: Doubleday.
Conn, S. R., & Rieke, M. L. (1994). *Sixteen Personality Factor questionnaire, technical manual* (5th ed). Champaign, IL: Institute for Personality and Ability Testing.
Costa, P. T., Jr., & McCrae, R. R. (1985). *The NEO Personality Inventory manual.* Odessa, FL: Psychological Assessment Resources.
Costa, P. T., Jr., & McCrae, R. R. (1992). *NEO PI-R professional manual.* Odessa, FL: Psychological Assessment Resources.
Crawford, M. (1995). *Talking difference: On gender and language.* Thousand Oaks, CA: Sage.

Dahlstrom, W. G., Welsh, G. S., & Dahlstrom, L. E. (1975). *An MMPI handbook: Vol. II. Research applications.* Minneapolis, MN: University of Minnesota Press.
Deaux, K., & LaFrance, M. (1998). Gender. In D. T. Gilbert, S. T. Fiske, & G. Lindsey (Eds.), *The handbook of social psychology* (4th ed., pp. 778–827). New York: Oxford University Press.
Deaux, K., & Major, B. (1987). Putting gender into context: An interactive model of gender-related behavior. *Psychological Review, 94*, 369–389.
Dodge, K.. A. (1993). Social-cognitive mechanisms in the development of conduct disorder and depression. *Annual Review of Psychology, 44*, 559–584.
Dweck, C. S. (2008). Can personality be changed? The role of beliefs in personality and change. *Current Directions in Psychological Science, 17*, 391–394.
Dweck, C. S., Hong, Y., & Chiu, C. (1993). Implicit theories: Individual differences in the likelihood and meaning of dispositional inference. *Personality and Social Psychology Bulletin, 19*, 644–656.
Eagly, A. H. (1987). *Sex differences in social behavior: A social role interpretation.* Hillsdale, NJ: Erlbaum.
Embretson, S. E. (1996). The new rules of measurement. *Psychological Assessment, 8*, 341–349.
Embretson, S., & Yang, X. (2006). Item response theory. In J. L. Green, G. Camilli, & P. B. Elmore (Eds.), *Handbook of complementary methods in education research* (pp. 385–409). Mahwah, NJ: Erlbaum.
Everson, H. T., & Millsap, R. E. (2004). Beyond individual differences: Exploring school effects on SAT scores. *Educational Psychologist, 39*, 157–172.
Exner, J. E., Jr. (2003). *The Rorschach: A comprehensive system.* Hoboken, NJ: Wiley.
Feng, J., Spence, I., & Pratt, J. (2007). Playing an action video game reduces gender differences in spatial cognition. *Psychological Science, 18*, 850–855.
Fiske, S. T., & Taylor, S. E. (1991). *Social cognition* (2nd ed.). New York: McGraw-Hill.
Flitter, J. M. K., Elhai, J. D. & Gold, S. N. (2003). MMPI-2 F scale elevations in adult victims of child sexual abuse. *Journal of Traumatic Stress, 16*, 269–274.
Forouzan, E., & Cooke, D. J. (2005). Figuring out la femme fatale: Conceptual and assessment issues concerning psychopathy in females. *Behavioral Sciences & the Law, 23*, 765–778.
Greene, R. L. (1991). *The MMPI-2/MMPI: An interpretive manual.* Boston, MA: Allyn & Bacon.
Greene, R. L. (2000). *The MMPI-2, an interpretive manual* (2nd ed.). Boston, MA: Allyn & Bacon.
Greenfield, P. M. (1997) You can't take it with you: Why ability assessments don't cross cultures. *American Psychologist, 52*, 1115–1124.
Gulliksen, H. (1950). *Theory of mental tests.* New York: Wiley.
Halpern, D. F., Benbow, C. P., Geary, D. C., Gur, R. C., Hyde, J. S., & Gernsbacher, M. A. (2007). The science of sex differences in science and mathematics. *Psychological Science in the Public Interest, 8*, 1–51.
Hambleton, R. K., & Swaminathan, H. (1985). *Item response theory: Principles and applications.* Boston, MA: Kluwer-Nijhoff.
Hambleton, R. K., Swaminathan, H., & Rogers, H. J. (1991). *Fundamentals of item response theory.* Newbury Park, CA: Sage.
Hammen, C. L., & Padesky, C. A. (1977). Sex differences in the expression of depressive responses on the Beck Depression Inventory. *Journal of Abnormal Psychology, 86*, 609–614.
Hare, R. D. (1980). A research scale for the assessment of psychopathy in criminal populations. *Personality and Individual Differences, 1*, 111–119.
Hare, R. D. (1985). Comparison of procedures for the assessment of psychopathy. *Journal of Consulting and Clinical Psychology, 53*, 7–16.
Hare-Mustin, R. T., & Marecek, J. (1988). The meaning of difference: Gender theory, postmodernism, and psychology. *American Psychologist, 43*, 455–464.
Hare-Mustin, R. T., & Marecek, J. (1990). *Making a difference: Psychology and the construction of gender.* New Haven, CT: Yale University Press.
Hathaway, S. R., & McKinley, J. C. (1943). *The Minnesota Multiphasic Personality Inventory.* New York: Psychological Corporation.
Hedden, T., Ketay, S., Aron, A., Markus, H. R., & Gabrieli, J. D. E. (2008). Cultural influences on neural substrates of attentional control. *Psychological Science, 19*, 12–17.
Helms, J. E. (2005). Stereotype threat might explain the Black–White test-score difference. *American Psychologist, 60*, 269–270.
Helms, J. E. (2006). Fairness is not validity or cultural bias in racial-group assessment: A quantitative perspective. *American Psychologist, 61*, 845–859.
Helms, J. E. (2007a). Implementing fairness in racial-group assessment requires assessment of individuals. *American Psychologist, 62*, 1083–1085.

Helms, J. E. (2007b). Some better practices for measuring racial and ethnic identity constructs. *Journal of Counseling Psychology, 54*, 235–246.

Hynan, D. J. (2004). Unsupported gender differences on some personality disorder scales of the Millon Clinical Multiaxial Inventory-III. *Professional Psychology, 35*, 105–110.

Kaplan, B. J. (1983). A woman's view of *DSM-III*. *American Psychologist, 39*, 786–792.

Kennealy, P. J., Hicks, B. M., & Patrick, C. J. (2007). Validity of factors of the Psychopathy Checklist – Revised in female prisoners: Discriminant relations with antisocial behavior, substance abuse, and personality. *Assessment, 14*, 323–340.

Kimerling, R., Ouimette, P., & Weitlauf, J. C. (2007). Gender issues in PTSD. In M. J. Friedman, T. M. Keane, & P. A. Resick (Eds.), *Handbook of PTSD: Science and practice* (pp. 207–228). New York: Guilford.

Kroska, A. (2000). Conceptualizing and measuring gender ideology as an identity. *Gender & Society, 14*, 368–394.

LaFrance, M. (1992). Gender and interruptions: Individual infraction or violation of the social order. *Psychology of Women Quarterly, 16*, 497–512.

Le, V. N. (2000). *Exploring gender differences on the NELS: 88 History achievement tests*. Unpublished doctoral dissertation, Stanford University.

Lindsay, K., & Widiger, T. (1995). Sex and gender bias in self-report personality disorder inventories: Item analysis of the MCMI-II, MMPI, and PDQ-R. *Journal of Personality Assessment, 65*, 1–20.

Marecek, J. (2002). Unfinished business: Postmodern feminism in personality psychology. In M. Ballou & L. S. Brown (Eds.), *Rethinking mental health and disorder* (pp. 3–28). New York: Guilford.

Marecek, J., & Hare-Mustin, R. T. (1991). A short history of the future: Feminism and clinical psychology. *Psychology of Women Quarterly, 15*, 521–536.

Maynard, A. E., & Greenfield, P. (2003). Implicit cognitive development in cultural tools and children: Lessons from Maya Mexico. *Cognitive Development, 18*, 489–510.

McCrae, R. M., & John, O. P. (1992). An introduction to the five-factor model and its applications. *Journal of Personality, 60*, 175–175.

Meyer, G. J., Finn, S. E., Eyde, L. D., Kay, G. G., Moreland, K. L., Dies, R. R., et al.(2001). Psychological testing and psychological assessment: A review of evidence and issues. *American Psychologist, 56*, 128–165.

Millon, T. M. (1990). *Toward a new personality: An evolutionary model*. New York: Wiley.

Millon, T. M., Millon, C., & Davis, R. (1994). *MCMI-III manual*. Minneapolis, MN: Pearson.

Millon, T. M., Millon, C., Davis, R., & Grossman, S. (2006). *MCMI-III manual* (3rd ed.). Minneapolis, MN: Pearson.

Mischel, W. (1968). *Personality and assessment*. New York: Wiley.

Mischel, W. (2003). Challenging the traditional personality psychology paradigm. In R. J. Sternberg (Ed.), *Psychologists defying the crowd: Stories of those who battled the establishment and won* (pp. 139–156). Washington, DC: American Psychological Association.

Mischel, W. & Peake, P. K. (1982). Beyond déjà vu in the search for cross-situational consistency. *Psychological Reviews, 89*, 730–755.

Mischel, W., & Shoda, Y. (1995) A cognitive-affective system theory of personality: Reconceptualizing situations, dispositions, dynamics, and invariance in personality structure. *Psychological Review, 102*, 246–268.

Mischel, W., Shoda, Y., & Mendoza-Denton, R. (2002). Situation–behavior profiles as a locus of consistency in personality. *Current Directions in Psychological Science, 11*, 50–54.

Morey, L. C. (1991). *The Personality Assessment Inventory professional manual*. Lutz, FL: Psychological Assessment Resources.

Morey, L. C., Warner, M. B., & Boggs, C. D. (2002). Gender bias in the personality disorders criteria: An investigation of five bias indicators. *Journal of Psychopathology and Behavioral Assessment, 24*, 55–65.

Nankervis, B. (2007). Predicting sex differences in performance on the SAT-I quantitative section: How content and stereotype threat affect achievement. *Dissertation Abstracts International Section A: Humanities and Social Sciences, 68*(5-A), p. 1858.

Nolen-Hoeksema, S. (2008). It is not what you have; it is what you do with it: Support for Addis's gendered responding framework. *Clinical Psychology, 15*, 178–181.

Nolen-Hoeksema, S., & Jackson, B. (2001). Mediators of the gender difference in rumination. *Psychology of Women Quarterly, 25*, 37–47.

O'Leary, M. M., Loney, B. R., & Eckel, L. A. (2007). Gender differences in the association between psychopathic personality traits and cortisol response to induced stress. *Psychoneuroendocrinology, 32*, 183–191

Peplau, L. A., DeBro, S. C., Veniegas, R. C., & Taylor, P. L. (1999). *Gender, culture, and ethnicity*. Mountain View, CA: Mayfield.

Raitt, F. E., & Zeedyk, M. S. (2000). *The implicit relation of psychology and law: Women and syndrome evidence*. London: Routledge.

Riggio, R. E., & Friedman, H. (1986). Impression formation: The role of expressive behavior. *Journal of Personality and Social Psychology, 50,* 421–427.

Rogers, R. (Ed.) (1997). *Clinical assessment of malingering and deception* (2nd ed.). New York: Guilford.

Romans, S. E., & Clarkson, R. F. (2008). Crying as a gendered indicator of depression. *Journal of Nervous and Mental Disease, 196,* 237–243.

Rowe, M. (1981). The minutiae of discrimination: The need for support. In B. L. Forisha & B. H. Goldman (Eds.), *Outsiders on the Inside* (pp. 155–171). Englewood Cliffs, NJ: Prentice-Hall.

Russell, M., & Karol, D. (1994). *16PF administrator's manual* (5th ed.). Champaign, IL: Institute for Personality and Ability Testing.

Santor, D. A., Ramsay, J. O., & Zuroff, D. C. (1994). Nonparametric item analyses of the Beck Depression Inventory: Evaluating gender item bias and response option weights. *Psychological Assessment, 6,* 255–270.

Schmidt, F., McKinnon, L., Chattha, H. K., & Brownlee, K. (2006). Concurrent and predictive validity of the Psychopathy Checklist: Youth version across gender and ethnicity. *Psychological Assessment, 18,* 393–401.

Segal, D. L., & Coolidge, F. L. (2004). Objective assessment of personality and psychopathology: An overview. In M. J. Hilsenroth & D. L. Segal (Eds.), *Comprehensive handbook of psychological assessment: Personality assessment* (pp. 3–13). Hoboken, NJ: Wiley.

Shoda, Y., LeeTiernan, S., & Mischel, W. (2002). Personality as a dynamical system: Emergence of stability and distinctiveness from intra-and interpersonal interactions. *Personality and Social Psychology Review, 6,* 316–325.

Shoda, Y., & Mischel, W. (2006). Applying meta-theory to achieve generalisability and precision in personality science: Comment. *Applied Psychology, 55,* 439–452.

Sigmon, S. T., Pells, J. J, Boulard, N. E., Whitcomb-Smith, S., Edenfield, T. M., Hermann, B. A., et al. (2005). Gender differences in self-reports of depression: The response bias hypothesis revisited. *Sex Roles, 53,* 401–411.

Sinclair, S., Hardin, C. D., & Lowery, B. S. (2006). Self-stereotyping in the context of multiple social identities. *Journal of Personality and Social Psychology, 90,* 529–542.

Skrypnek, B. J., & Snyder, M. (1982). On the self-perpetuating nature of stereotypes about men and women. *Journal of Experimental Social Psychology, 18,* 277–291.

Snyder, M., Tanke, E. D., & Berscheid, E. (1977). Social perception and interpersonal behavior: On the self-fulfilling nature of social stereotypes. *Journal of Personality and Social Psychology, 35,* 656–666.

Steele, C. M. (1997). A threat in the air: How stereotypes shape intellectual identity and performance. *American Psychologist, 52,* 613–629.

Steele, J. (2003). Children's gender stereotypes about math: The role of stereotype stratification. *Journal of Applied Social Psychology, 33,* 2587–2606.

Steele, J., James, J. B., & Barnett, R. C. (2002). Learning in a man's world: Examining the perceptions of undergraduate women in male-dominated academic areas. *Psychology of Women Quarterly, 26,* 46–50.

Sternberg, R. J. (2008). Using cognitive theory to reconceptualize college admissions testing. In M. A. Gluck, J. R. Anderson, & S. M. Kosslyn (Eds.), *Memory and mind: A festschrift for Gordon H. Bower* (pp. 159–175). Mahwah, NJ: Erlbaum.

Stoppard, J. M., & Gunn-Gruchy, C. D. (1993). Gender, context, and expression of positive emotion. *Personality and Social Psychology Bulletin, 19,* 143–150.

Suyemoto, K. L. (2002). Constructing identities: A feminist, culturally contextualized alternative to "personality." In M. Ballou & L. S. Brown (Eds.), *Rethinking mental health and disorder* (pp. 99–141). New York: Guilford.

Tellegen, A., Ben-Porath, Y. S., McNulty, J. L., Arbisi, P. A., Graham, J. R., & Kaemmer, B. (2003). *MMPI®-2 restructured clinical (RC) scales.* Minneapolis, MN: University of Minnesota Press.

Thissen, D., Steinberg, L., & Gerrard, M. (1986). Beyond group-mean differences: The concept of item bias. *Psychological Bulletin, 99,* 118–128.

Travis, C. B. (Ed.) (2003). *Evolution, gender, and rape.* Cambridge, MA: MIT Press.

Unger, R., & Crawford, M. (1992). *Women and gender: A feminist psychology* (2nd ed.). New York: McGraw-Hill.

Urbana, S. (2004). *Essentials of psychological testing.* Hoboken, NJ: Wiley.

Vablais C. M. (2007). Toward a new model of psychopathy in women: A qualitative analysis of the Psychopathy Checklist – revised and the construct of psychopathy in female offenders. *Dissertation Abstracts International: Section B: The Sciences and Engineering, 68*(2-B), 1323.

Walker, L. (1993). Are personality disorders gender biases? Yes. In S. A. Kirk & S. D. Einbinder (Eds.), *Controversial issues in mental health* (pp. 21–30). New York: Allyn & Bacon.

Walker, L. E. A. (1987). Assessment and intervention with battered women. In P. A. Keller & S. R. Heyman (Eds.), *Innovations in clinical practice: A sourcebook,* (Vol. 6, pp. 131–142). Sarasota, FL: Professional Resource Exchange.

Waller, N. G., Compas, B. E., Hollon, S. D., & Beckjord, E. (2005). Measurement of depressive symptoms in women with breast cancer and women with clinical depression: A differential item functioning analysis. *Journal of Clinical Psychology in Medical Settings, 12*, 127–141.

Wechsler, D. (2008). *Wechsler Adult Intelligence Scale* (4th ed.). San Antonio, TX: Pearson.

Widiger, T. A. (1998). Sex biases in the diagnosis of personality disorders. *Journal of Personality Disorders, 12*, 95–118.

Widiger, T. A., & Spitzer, R. L. (1991). Sex bias in the diagnosis of personality disorders: Conceptual and methodological issues. *Clinical Psychology Review, 11*, 1–22.

Part IX
Abnormal and Clinical Psychology

Chapter 5
Gender Stereotypes in Diagnostic Criteria

Alisha Ali, Paula J. Caplan, and Rachel Fagnant

The purposes of this chapter are to dispel the myth that psychiatric diagnosis is value free and based on sound scientific evidence and to show how the client's sex and the therapist's biases about gender often fill parts of the vacuum left by the absence of science when therapists attempt to identify, categorize, and label people's emotional suffering. We contend that women and men who experience psychological distress are better served if they are aware that the alleviation of mental suffering is not always achieved, and sometimes has been hindered, by reliance on the *Diagnostic and Statistical Manual of Mental Disorders* (*DSM*; American Psychiatric Association, 2000), the book that has come to dominate psychiatry, psychology, and their allied professions.

In any consideration of gender bias in psychiatric diagnosis, it is essential to keep in mind that the categories described in the *DSM* are not "real." These diagnostic categories are invented, defined, and often re-invented by a relatively small group of people, most of whom are White, American, male psychiatrists who are positioned to describe what is normal and what is abnormal (Caplan, 1995; Cohen & Jacobs, 2007). So, we ask the question: Who is served by this categorization process? First, the existence of the *DSM* provides psychiatry and clinical psychology with the appearance of scientific credibility. Second, the *DSM* is part of an enormously profitable mini-industry that consists of the manual and its various supplements, casebooks, sourcebooks, and software packages. The profits swell the coffers of the *DSM*'s publisher, the American Psychiatric Association, which is a lobby group as well as a professional association. Questions about the validity and scientific basis of the *DSM* put such profits in jeopardy and are, therefore, often unwelcome among mental health professionals closely connected with the handbook itself; many therapists from various disciplines also worry that questioning the diagnostic categories threatens their livelihood. However, questioning is necessary if we are to understand the risks for clients when *DSM* labels – and their attendant stigmata and consequences – are applied.

The most commonly chosen standards of psychiatric diagnoses warrant a critical thinking approach, including a challenge to the very notion of objectivity as it is applied to psychiatric diagnosis. In this chapter, we examine the ways in which stereotypic conceptions of women and men powerfully influence diagnostic decision making and, indeed, the very process through which diagnostic criteria are derived and then put into clusters called diagnostic categories. In our discussion, we use the accepted definition of *gender* as encompassing cultural expectations for women and girls (i.e., femininity) and men and boys (i.e., masculinity) and the term *sex* to denote biological maleness or femaleness (Caplan & Caplan, 2009; Lips, 2001). We discuss stereotypes concerning men and women in relation to psychiatric diagnosis, but for three reasons we focus especially on women. First, women represent the majority of clients who seek psychotherapy and thus are the majority

A. Ali (✉)
New York University, New York, NY, USA

of people to whom the bulk of the most damaging diagnoses are applied (Caplan, 1995; Worell & Remer, 2003). Second, in both society in general and diagnostic and other psychiatric discourse, women in particular are saddled with debasing stereotypes of psychological weakness, theories of hormonal susceptibility to disorders, and strict societal expectations about appropriate and inappropriate behavior (Brown, 1994; Caplan & Cosgrove, 2004). Third, in the creation of many diagnostic categories and criteria, the *DSM* authors historically have shown a marked lack of consideration for the realities of women's lives, life contexts, and experiences of victimization. Of course, men, especially racial, ethnic, and sexual minorities, experience many of the same forms of victimization as women do, including poverty, violence, and discrimination. In this chapter, we examine the ways that gender stereotypes in diagnoses affect men and women differently.

We present a critical framework for the examination of gender bias in selected diagnostic categories. Where we use *DSM* terms and quote specific *DSM* criteria, we do so not because these categories have been proven to be valid, but because it is specifically those categories and labels that we want to critique. We first outline the assumptions that guided our consideration of gender-related biases in the *DSM*; we also describe the fundamentally flawed beliefs that together form the basis from which various gender biases are derived. Next, we systematically consider the groups of diagnostic categories that have been most closely scrutinized by critics of the *DSM* with respect to gender bias: personality disorders, mood disorders, and anxiety disorders. We then consider three key over-arching issues that cut across diagnostic categories and are broadly relevant to gender bias in psychiatric diagnosis: poverty, abuse, racism, and sexual orientation and identity. Last, we consider the future of psychiatric diagnoses and the dangers, both societal and individual, that result from gender bias in diagnosis.

Fundamental Assumptions Concerning Gender Bias in Diagnosis

In this section we present two sets of assumptions: (1) the beliefs that informed us as authors in considering gender and gender-related bias in the *DSM* and (2) the beliefs and stereotypes about women and men that have led to diagnostic bias. We begin with the premise that equality ought to underlie all practices applied to men and women, that both sexes ought to receive equal scientific attention and access to help, and that standards of care should be equal for all. Although this assumption appears to be so fundamental that it might scarcely seem worth stating, we will show that current-day diagnosis is replete with examples characterized by considerable disregard for the best interests of women and, in some instances, of men.

A second assumption is that it is important to acknowledge that a psychiatric label often confers on its recipient a cascade of negative effects that can include personal, interpersonal, and, sometimes, medical and legal consequences. Although therapists often assert that their decision making is objective and untainted by sociocultural influences, diagnostic decisions are made about real people, and they are never fully devoid of social stigma or interpersonal challenges. So, for instance, when a person is labeled mentally ill, we need to ask ourselves how that diagnosis (and by this we mean the therapist's *assignment* of a diagnosis, not the patient's emotional difficulties) came about and how living with that diagnosis will alter the person's life circumstances, the person's self-perception, and the perception of that person by others.

Our final assumption is that not every person who is assigned a psychiatric diagnosis is mentally ill. There are two main reasons for this contention. First, sometimes clients are given a diagnosis so that their therapy will be covered by their health insurance. The second, more sinister reason is, we argue, that certain aspects of human experience, which may actually be *normal* responses to abusive or traumatic situations, are labeled as psychiatric *abnormality* in clients when they seek help. This labeling can place abused women in a vulnerable position by emphasizing their supposed individual, psychological weakness rather than the traumatic nature of the abuse. Moreover, although practitioners who adopt the *DSM* approach generally assume that applying a diagnostic label to a person's suffering is essential to helping that person, this presumption is highly questionable, especially given that the changes that are often needed must take place not in the *mind* of the client but rather in the host of damaging and disempowering forces that can surround traumatized women and men, including not only threats of violence but also harassment and discrimination (Caplan, 1995; Worell & Remer, 2003). By focusing on the minds of traumatized individuals rather than on the traumatic context in which they have had to function, we dismiss the sometimes horrific circumstances of their trauma. Caplan (2006) pointed out that such dismissal often occurs in the experiences of individuals returning from war; she stated that "by pathologizing and privatizing their suffering, we add to their burdens the belief that they should have endured the war emotionally unscathed and that no one other than a therapist wants to listen" to their stories (p. 20).

Having considered the assumptions that guide our analysis in this chapter, we now turn to the main assumptions that lead to gender bias in psychiatric diagnosis. One key assumption is a widely held and long-standing belief in the "natural" (i.e., biological) inferiority of women. Although some would insist that psychiatry and medicine in general have moved beyond such beliefs, we present examples of current biases that clearly reflect this assumption; most – but not all – of these examples pertain to the host of psychiatric "disorders" that involve women's susceptibility to hormonal factors. As we discuss below, those who make treatment decisions based on biased diagnoses frequently discount the role of social factors in women's lives and, instead, emphasize and pathologize women's biology.

A second assumption underlying gender bias is the belief that knowledge and expertise lie solely in the domain of medical professionals. Because the medical profession has historically been dominated by men and by androcentric viewpoints (Willard, 2005), women's knowledge of their own bodies and minds can play a secondary role to medical authority. Psychiatry's overreliance on narrowly defined notions of "normal" behavior can also be seen as symptomatic of the field's aim to broaden the range of problems considered as appropriate targets for medical intervention. Furthermore, as we discuss later, definitions of normalcy are never value free.

A final assumption that informs gender bias in diagnosis is the widely propagated notion that many common emotional and behavioral problems are *endogenous* (i.e., stem from an internal cause) in nature, rather than *reactive* (i.e., a response to an external cause). It is this dichotomy, and the corresponding preference for endogenous explanations for suffering, that bolsters the belief that diagnosis can occur in an ideological vacuum, uninfluenced by cultural stereotypes and social norms, including sexist ones. However, stereotypes are common elements of the derivation and application of diagnostic criteria, and stereotypic ideas about sex and gender can moderately or severely impair clients' emotional well-being.

Diagnostic Categories Replete with Gender Stereotypes

Personality Disorders

We begin our critique of various clusters of *DSM* diagnostic categories with personality disorders. The psychiatric categorization of personality disorders is an attempt to formalize definitions of extreme forms of personality patterns that exist in the general population. These diagnoses are questionable largely because they categorize thoughts and actions as disordered by virtue of their *degree* of deviation from what are assumed to be normal patterns of behavior. We all have personality *traits*, but the question for the practitioner is presumably whether a personality pattern is abnormal enough to be considered a disorder. As Caws (1994) stated, the word *diagnosis* "suggests a process of inference: from symptoms to underlying condition. [However], one difficulty with psychiatric diagnoses is that disorders almost never have unambiguously pathognomonic symptoms" (pp. 205–206). Therefore, if a person is diagnosed as having a personality that is in some way "disordered," the diagnosing clinician must infer from the person's thoughts and actions some abnormality that warrants a psychiatric label. From a perspective of gender bias, the *DSM* categories of personality disorders that have been most criticized are dependent personality disorder (DPD), histrionic personality disorder (HPD), borderline personality disorder (BPD), and antisocial personality disorder (APD).

Numerous critics of the *DSM* have argued for decades that a diagnosis of DPD or a diagnosis of HPD is simply applied to a woman's strict conformity to the stereotypic feminine gender role (e.g., Brown, 1992; Gibson, 2004; Rivera, 2002; Walker, 1993). The diagnostic criteria for DPD mainly involve "a pervasive and excessive need to be taken care of that leads to submissive and clinging behavior and fears of separation" (American Psychiatric Association, 2000, p. 721). The diagnostic criteria for HPD mainly involve "pervasive and excessive emotionality and attention-seeking behavior" (American Psychiatric Association, 2000, p. 711). It is not surprising that these diagnostic labels are far more commonly applied to women than to men (American Psychiatric Association, 2000; Cosgrove & Riddle, 2004). These diagnoses are problematic partly because the determination of whether observed behaviors and needs are "excessive" is left up to the individual practitioner's decision about what is normal and what is abnormal. Research has demonstrated that clinicians' diagnostic impressions are influenced by gender-role stereotypes (Cook, Warnke, & Dupuy, 1993; Cosgrove & Riddle, 2004). In particular, studies have shown that clinicians assign diagnoses differentially depending upon a client's gender, such that different diagnoses are applied to women and men whose symptoms are the same. For example, in a classic study of 65 clinicians, Hamilton, Rothbart, and Dawes (1986) used a series of written case histories that described identical symptoms in male and female clients and found that the diagnosis of HPD was applied significantly more often to the women's case histories than to the men's. It seems that gendered traits, such as dependency and emotionality, not only are stereotypically associated with women but also lead disproportionately to the diagnosis of certain psychiatric disorders among women.

The extension of traditional feminine stereotypes into abnormality can be seen as an overt example of the "double bind" in which women often find themselves. Women are required to fulfill the cultural mandates of femininity through self-sacrifice, passivity, and deference to others, but these same characteristics are regarded as signs of weakness, vulnerability, and even mental illness (Caplan, 1995; Walker, 1993). For example, the diagnostic criteria for DPD include going "to excessive lengths to obtain nurturance and support from others, to the point of volunteering to do things that are unpleasant" (American Psychiatric Association, 2000, p. 725), but the cultural imperative for women to volunteer their time in the service of others is a defining facet of the feminine gender role (Bepko & Krestan, 1990; Jack, 1991; Worell & Remer, 2003). Furthermore, many responsibilities that women are typically expected to perform (e.g., housecleaning, diaper changing) are unpleasant but also necessary.

The diagnostic criteria for HPD include the following: "consistently uses physical appearance to draw attention to self" (American Psychiatric Association, 2000, p. 714). Because girls and women in our society are socialized to use physical appearance as a means of asserting self-worth (Bepko & Krestan, 1990), this criterion too can be seen as an extension of the stereotypical feminine role. Certain sub-groups of men are also socialized to use physical appearance to draw attention to themselves. For example, male bodybuilders are expected to seek such attention, but most lay people and most therapists would not readily consider bodybuilders to be histrionic. Moreover, in her study of gender-related stereotypes in personality disorders, Landrine (1989) found that nearly all study participants reported that a histrionic person was most likely to be a woman.

The diagnosis of BPD, also made far more frequently in women than in men (American Psychiatric Association, 2000; Cosgrove & Riddle, 2004), has been criticized for its lack of specificity and validity and for its use as a pathologizing label applied to women's understandably distraught responses to abuse. The diagnostic criteria for BPD include "a pervasive pattern of instability of interpersonal relationships, self-image, and affects, and a marked impulsivity" (American Psychiatric Association, 2000, p. 706). In their study of gender bias in diagnoses, Becker and Lamb (1994) presented over 1,000 clinicians with descriptions of either a male or a female case with an equal number of symptoms from the criteria for both borderline personality disorder and post-traumatic stress disorder. The study revealed that the clinicians were more likely to diagnose the female clients with borderline personality disorder and the male clients with post-traumatic stress disorder even though the symptoms for the male and female clients were identical. These findings are important for a number of reasons, most notably that they demonstrate a lack of reliability in the diagnosis of these conditions and that they show that the diagnosis that involves a reaction to *external* causes (PTSD) was applied more frequently to male clients, whereas the more de-contextualized diagnosis (BPD) was applied more frequently to female clients. People whose emotions are considered to be reactions to external causes are less likely than others whose emotions are not as clearly linked to external causes to be regarded as qualitatively different from most people. Thus, they are less likely to be pathologized and isolated.

Perhaps the most problematic element of bias in the diagnosis of BPD concerns the extremely high percentage of clients with this label who have a history of physical and/or sexual abuse (Fish, 2004; Paris, 1994; Perry, Herman, van der Kolk, & Hoke, 1990; Westen, Ludolph, Misle, Ruffine, & Block, 1990). Because practitioners often neglect to ask – or choose not to ask – whether clients have ever been abused (Brown, 1991; Gallop, McKeever, Toner, Lancee, & Lueck, 1995), there is a high likelihood that the kinds of behavior used to arrive at a diagnosis of BPD are regarded as *intrinsic* to the client rather than as reactions to abuse. We explore this issue in more depth in a later section in reference to PTSD. Readers should keep in mind that borderline personality disorder is the most commonly diagnosed of all personality disorders (Frances & Widiger, 1987; Kroll, 1988), and it is also one of the most stigmatized (Nehls, 1998; Simmons, 1992). Therefore, there are probably large numbers of abused women who carry this derogatory label and who may be unaware that the problems they are experiencing stem from past and/or current abuse. The damage that biased diagnostic categories can create in women's lives is obvious, as they are deprived of the treatment, support, advice, and empathy they sorely need.

It should be noted that the diagnostic criteria for certain personality disorders are biased against stereotypical masculine characteristics as well. Although less attention has been paid to bias against men, it has been argued that the diagnosis of antisocial personality disorder is an example of this. Just as dependent and histrionic personality disorders are seen by some to be extreme forms of the feminine gender role, antisocial personality disorder (APD) is seen as the extreme form of the masculine gender role. The diagnostic criteria for antisocial personality disorder include "a pervasive pattern of disregard for, and violation of, the rights of others" (American Psychiatric Association, 2000, p. 701). Because women are stereotypically expected to play the role of looking after others, the corresponding expectation for men is that they do not have to attend to others' needs and that they can expect women to attend to their needs (Bepko & Krestan, 1990). In APD, a condition that is more commonly diagnosed in men than in women (American Psychiatric Association, 2000; Cosgrove & Riddle, 2004), we see an exaggeration of that expectation. One of the specific criteria for this condition includes extreme aggressiveness, a hallmark trait of hypermasculinity (Lips, 2001). Because of the apparently gendered nature of this diagnostic category, it is possible that clinicians may be "primed" by their gender stereotypes to expect that simply being male makes some clients likely candidates for the antisocial personality diagnosis. For example, in one study (Belitsky et al., 1996), 96 male and female resident psychiatrists were presented with case descriptions of either male or female clients who reported sets of identical symptoms. The results revealed that significantly more male than female clients were given the diagnosis of APD by both male and female psychiatric residents. In her study of gender stereotypes and personality disorders, Landrine (1989) presented participants with verbatim descriptions of *DSM* disorders without the diagnostic labels and asked them to predict for each disorder the demographic characteristics of the person who would fit that description. Twenty-one of the 23 participants stated that the person with APD was male. Landrine explained that the reason for this finding, and for similar findings of stereotypes in diagnosis, "may be that gender-role categories and personality disorder categories are simply flip sides of the same stereotyped coin" (p. 332). As Cale and Lilienfeld (2002) noted, the gender stereotyped nature of the APD category is also evidenced by the fact that its criteria are more reflective of men's typical criminal behavior, such as rape, robbery, and pedophilia, than of women's typical criminal behavior, such as child abuse, shoplifting, and prostitution. It is clear that gender bias in the diagnosis of personality disorders can affect both male and female clients.

Mood Disorders

The most commonly diagnosed psychiatric disorder is major depressive disorder (MDD). The diagnostic criteria for major depression include "depressed mood or the loss of interest or pleasure in nearly all activities" (American Psychiatric Association, 2000, p. 349). It is estimated that twice as many women as men are diagnosed with depression (Kessler, 2003; Stoppard, 1993; see also Chapter 7), and despite the lack of research evidence to support the notion that women's hormones increase their likelihood of experiencing depressed mood, hormonal factors are very often named among the posited explanations for the higher depression rate in women (Hankin, & Abramson, 2001; Whiffen, 2006). Feminist authors have argued against the medicalization of women's emotional distress through the label of "depression" and, instead, support an approach in which women's distressing experiences and life circumstances are more fully explored and articulated (Gammell & Stoppard, 1999; Jack, 1991). For example, Gammell and Stoppard (1999), in reporting their findings from interviews with women who had been diagnosed with depression and were prescribed anti-depressants, concluded that medical practitioners' pathologizing of the women's reactions to stressful situations served to disempower the women and led them to believe that they had little control over their life circumstances. The authors stated that "a medicalized understanding and treatment of women's depressive experiences cannot readily coexist with personal empowerment" (p. 112). The disempowerment of women whose everyday lives are fraught with stress and trauma is particularly problematic, given that such women need to recognize their own sources of strength and resilience in order to alter their life situations. Therefore, the label of depression not only draws attention away from contextual factors in women's lives but can also compromise their abilities to make positive changes that could support their psychological well-being. Furthermore, as Cohen and Jacobs (2007) pointed out, research on treatments for depression by examining only the symptoms of depression and not clients' own personal histories or life circumstances – which usually focuses on drugs – further disempowers depressed individuals. The authors stated that "in the conventional medical framework of psychiatric drug treatment research, the patient's own voice is either eliminated or relegated to a distinctly inferior position" (p. 46). They further argued that depression researchers should study clients' individual stories rather than reducing their experiences to specific symptom profiles. Many women's stories include histories of abuse and other forms of victimization, as well as social factors, such as poverty and discrimination, all of which can serve as precipitating factors for psychological distress (McGrath, Keita, Strickland, & Russo, 1990). Labeling a woman as "depressed" serves to mask the presence of possible factors in her life that should be the focus of work in psychotherapy.

Depression is also important to any discussion of gender bias because it can be argued that the large number of women in the general public who can potentially be labeled as suffering from depression represents a segment of the population that is fervently targeted by pharmaceutical marketing. In the 1960s, psychotropic drugs were marketed not to consumers but to physicians in the form of print advertisements in medical journals. In these advertisements, the diagnostic criteria for depression were portrayed in part through the visual representations of depressed women. The gender-typed nature of these representations is striking in its exploitation of stereotypes of happy and unhappy women. In his book *Prozac on the Couch*, Metzl (2003) examined these representations and illustrated how, by 1970, the stereotype of the unmarried woman came to portray the typical unhappy person in need of medication. He cited as an example the *35 and Single* advertising campaign for Valium in which "Jan," one of the "unmarrieds with low self-esteem," "realizes…that she may never marry" and comes to her physician for treatment – a treatment that undoubtedly includes Valium. For physicians, the women portrayed in these advertisements served as prototypes of the mentally ill patient and of the benefits of appropriate treatment for mental illness. Drug therapy increasingly became the treatment of choice for depression among psychiatrists and general practitioners alike (Metzl, 2003).

Similar manifestations of the depressed person now appear in direct-to-consumer advertising on television and in magazines. Here the symptoms necessary for the diagnosis of depression are represented as people – most often women – who suffer not only from sadness but also, as is explicit in recent advertising campaigns, from vague physical symptoms, such as pain and fatigue. Consumers are expected to conclude that not only might they be depressed, but the solution to their depression is a pharmaceutical drug. Clients and practitioners, therefore, have become (often unwittingly and unknowingly) complicit in the propagation of drug therapy for treating suspected depression. The emphasis on anti-depressants is a serious concern in light of evidence of the negative effects of the antidepressants currently on the market, effects that include dizziness, headaches, gastrointestinal problems, insomnia, difficulties in sexual functioning, risks during pregnancy, and suicidal ideation (Breggin, 2007; Chrisler & Caplan, 2002; Gartlehner et al., 2008; Healy, 2004).

Depression that occurs during the postpartum period has been the focus of much attention of feminist researchers. The mainstream media and the general public presume a biological cause – namely hormones – for women's experience of depression following the birth of a child (Martinez, Johnston-Robledo, Ulsh, & Chrisler, 2000). However, there has yet to be any consistent evidence of a direct link between postpartum depression and women's hormone levels (Whiffen, 2004, 2006). Moreover, research has demonstrated that new fathers also experience an elevated rate of depression (Ballard, Davis, Cullen, Mohan, & Dean, 1994; Vandell, Hyde, Plant, & Essex, 1997). In light of these findings, Whiffen (2004) suggested that our understanding of depression that occurs after the birth of a child should be informed by an analysis of the social system and relational dynamics of the couple rather than by an assumption of maternal hormonal imbalance.

The diagnosis of premenstrual dysphoric disorder (PMDD) has also been criticized for gender bias. PMDD appears in the appendix section of the *DSM-IV-TR* as a diagnosis listed for further study. However, it is also named in the section "Mood Disorders" as a Depressive Disorder Not Otherwise Specified, despite the fact that the diagnostic criteria for PMDD can be met without the presence of depressed mood. The criteria described for PMDD include marked lability of mood, decreased interest in usual activities, difficulty in concentrating, fatigue, appetite changes, difficulties in sleep, feeling out of control, and physical symptoms, such as breast tenderness, headaches, and bloating sensations, all of which occur premenstrually (American Psychiatric Association, 2000, p. 771). The diagnostic description states that "[t]he presence of the cyclical pattern of symptoms must be confirmed by at least 2 consecutive months of prospective daily symptom ratings" (American Psychiatric Association, 2000, p. 772), which implies that there is a sound, systematic grounding to the derivation of the PMDD criteria. However, very little research exists to support the notion that PMDD is a confirmed clinical entity (Caplan, 1995, 2004; Chrisler & Caplan, 2002; Cosgrove & Caplan, 2004; O'Meara, 2001), and the European Union's Committee for Proprietary Medicinal Products has formally reached the conclusion that it is not a recognized "disorder" (Moynihan, 2004). Furthermore, research calls into question the existence of PMDD. In a study by Gallant and colleagues (Gallant, Popiel, Hoffman, Chakraborty, & Hamilton, 1992), when three groups of research participants (women who reported premenstrual problems, women who did not report such problems, and men) completed a checklist of symptoms for late luteal phase dysphoric disorder (the *DSM-III* term for PMDD), no differences in symptom ratings were found between the three groups. Moreover, the *DSM* authors themselves have stated that "[t]here has been very little systematic study on the course and stability of this condition" (American Psychiatric Association, 2000, p. 772).

The inclusion of PMDD in the current *DSM* (along with the inclusion of late luteal phase dysphoric disorder in an earlier edition) has been much criticized. Critics have pointed not only to the lack of research support for the existence of this condition but also to the influence of the pharmaceutical industry on the invention and development of the PMDD diagnosis (Caplan, 1995, 2004; Chrisler & Caplan, 2002; Cosgrove & Caplan, 2004). These criticisms involve the close connection between the positioning of PMDD as a psychiatric condition and the Food and Drug Administration's 1999 approval of Eli Lilly's drug Sarafem as an appropriate treatment for PMDD. Sarafem is actually Prozac; they are simply two different labels for the identical drug (i.e., fluoxetine hydrochloride). In 1999, Eli Lilly's exclusive patent on Prozac was about to expire; unless the drug company could find a psychiatric condition different from depression for which Prozac could also be approved, the company would face a loss of profits. At that time, Eli Lilly sponsored a roundtable discussion on the topic of PMDD, which was the basis for a journal article entitled *Is Premenstrual Dysphoric Disorder a Distinct Clinical Entity?* (Endicott et al., 1999). The authors of that article reported that very recent evidence showed not only that PMDD is a "real" disorder but also that Prozac is an effective treatment for it. In fact, little of the evidence cited in that report was very recent, and none of the studies in question showed clear support for the existence of PMDD as a clinical entity (Caplan, 2004), let alone a psychiatric disorder that is best treated with an antidepressant medication. Nonetheless, based on the recommendations of the roundtable members – many of whom were also on the *DSM* subcommittee for PMDD and had received research funding from Eli Lilly – the FDA deemed Prozac to be an effective and safe treatment for PMDD.

We can presume that many women who are prescribed Sarafem do not know that it is Prozac, as that fact is not made clear in the direct-to-consumer advertisements that women see; perhaps some would choose not to take the drug if they were aware that it is an antidepressant. Furthermore, labeling and treating these women as though they are mentally ill (by prescribing for them a drug that is identical to Prozac in every way except that Sarafem is packaged in pink and purple) suggests that their bodies and minds – presumably due to the effects of some hormonal abnormality – are defective and that their emotional suffering is not grounded in daily life. However, research has shown that women who report premenstrual problems are significantly more likely than other women to be in upsetting life situations, such as enduring domestic abuse or being mistreated at work (Caplan, 1995; Golding & Taylor, 1996; Golding, Taylor, Menard, & King, 2000; Taylor, 1999). A focus on prescribing a drug can lead therapists to ignore external sources of problems and could put women at risk of remaining in unsafe situations.

Men are also subject to diagnostic labels related to the effects of hormones, especially labels concerning sexual function and dysfunction. The creation of the term *andropause*, the male version of menopause in which men's hormones decrease with age, demonstrates society's discomfort with men who do not fit the hypersexual masculine role. Testosterone treatment is the drug therapy usually recommended for andropause, and the research concerning testosterone has shown mixed results. Although some studies have shown that testosterone is not an important determinant of cognitive, psychological, or sexual functioning, others suggest that many psychiatric symptoms accompany a decrease in testosterone (Caplan, 1995). Furthermore, research on the validity of the andropause diagnosis is lacking, and no studies to date have examined whether men themselves are comfortable with accepting this label.

A similar example of the medicalization of the need for hypermasculinity is the diagnosis of muscle dysmorphia. Muscle dysmorphia does not appear in the *DSM*, but it is considered by some to be a form of body dysmorphic disorder, a *DSM* diagnosis characterized by preoccupation with a perceived defect in physical appearance (Pope, Phillips, & Olivardia, 2000). In muscle dysmorphia, usually seen in men, misperceptions and obsessive thoughts concern the individual's desire for muscularity. Pope et al. (2000) suggested a strong role of culture in the development of these thoughts. "Society and the media preach a disturbing double message: A man's self-esteem should be based heavily on his appearance, yet by the standards of modern supermale images, practically no man measures up" (p. 13). Similarly, Cafri et al. (2005) reported that media influences play a key role in precipitating muscle dysmorphia and also that the adolescent boys most at risk for muscle dysmorphia are those who experience teasing and are striving for increased peer popularity. There are considerable similarities between muscle dysmorphia in men and eating disorders in women. For example, McCreary and Sasse (2000) found, in their study of adolescent boys and girls, that the boys with a high drive for muscularity were also the boys with the lowest self-esteem and highest depression in their sample, a finding that parallels psychological correlates of disordered eating in girls. In his conceptual model of muscle dysmorphia, Grieve (2007) described perfectionism as a contributing psychological factor in the development of this condition; perfectionism has also been found in empirical studies to correlate with symptoms of disordered eating in girls (Hewitt, Flett, & Ediger, 1995). The risks associated with what has been termed muscle dysmorphia, including the use of anabolic steroids and unhealthy eating patterns, can severely compromise an individual's health (Pope & Katz, 1994). However, if muscle dysmorphia is formally added to the *DSM*, it is unclear how helpful its designation as a mental disorder would be. Not only would a psychiatric diagnosis add a stigma to the experiences of the men who meet the diagnostic criteria but there would also be an increased likelihood that some drug therapy would be encouraged for them. As with other conditions, attention should be paid to the broader social and cultural factors at play rather than to a presumed mental defect within individuals.

Anxiety Disorders

Women more often than men receive diagnoses of panic and phobic disorders (American Psychiatric Association, 2000; Cosgrove & Riddle, 2004). The cluster of symptoms labeled "agoraphobia" is one category diagnosed far more frequently in women than in men (American Psychiatric Association, 2000; Cosgrove & Riddle, 2004). The criteria for agoraphobia include "anxiety about being in places or situations from which escape might be difficult…or in which help may not be available" (American Psychiatric Association, 2000, p. 429). In agoraphobia, according to the *DSM*, the afflicted individuals' anxiety causes them to avoid certain situations and to restrict their behavior. Although the focus of this diagnosis in the *DSM* system is the set of symptoms, theorists have argued that the central issue in understanding supposed agoraphobic behavior in women is an analysis of why there are so many fear-inducing spaces and situations confronting women. For instance, Holmes (2008) emphasized the need to normalize the agoraphobic response by considering the avoidance of certain spaces and situations to be self-protective for women who feel unsafe and vulnerable among strangers and away from familiar people who could help them should a threat arise. Such normalization could be a useful re-framing of the responses of women who have been victims of violence and, thereafter, fear being in public on their own. Indeed, research indicates elevated rates of physical and sexual abuse among women who receive the diagnosis of "agoraphobic" (Langeland, Draijer, & van den Brink, 2004; Raskin et al., 1989).

In her critique of dominant conceptualizations of agoraphobia that pathologize women who fear to enter public spaces, Bankey (2004) argued that we should focus instead on "a spectrum or continuum of experiences that connect our anxieties and fears to the external worlds in which we live" (p. 348). She favored an approach that attends to the realities that confront women whose fears of venturing into the outside world alone may be rooted in previous trauma. Similarly, McHugh and Cosgrove (2004) stated that we must consider both history of trauma and women's gender-role socialization. They pointed out that being fearful is part of the stereotypical feminine gender role and that women's socialization to be fearful, along with the real threat of possible victimization, can predispose women to adopt behaviors that match the *DSM* symptoms of agoraphobia. However, as those authors pointed out, labeling such fear as a mental illness is not a productive way to help women who are concerned for their safety because it discounts the seriousness of threats that could confront them in their daily lives.

The diagnosis of post-traumatic stress disorder (PTSD) has also been critiqued for gender bias. The diagnostic criteria for PTSD include "intense fear, helplessness, or horror... and numbing of general responsiveness" following exposure to an extreme traumatic stressor, as well as "persistent reexperiencing of the traumatic event" (American Psychiatric Association, 2000, p. 463). Post-traumatic stress disorder has been a controversial diagnosis since it was introduced prior to its addition to the *DSM* in 1980. The category was first introduced as a means of drawing attention to the suffering of Vietnam War veterans who were experiencing a host of trauma-related problems (Linder, 2004). The diagnosis was later broadened to apply to a large range of traumatic experiences, including violent assault, natural disasters, car accidents, and diagnosis of a life-threatening physical illness.

The main controversy about PTSD concerns its use to label those individuals who have suffered extreme trauma as mentally ill. The psychiatric diagnosis of a traumatized person focuses attention on the supposed weaknesses within the individual rather than on the traumatizing situation itself (Becker, 2004; Caplan, 2006). This critique is often discussed in reference to abused women, but it applies to combat veterans of both sexes as well. Theorists have argued that focusing on the psychopathology of victims of violence not only discounts the potentially adaptive – and indeed fundamentally human – nature of their stress responses (e.g., the diagnostic criteria include such responses as "persistent avoidance of stimuli associated with the trauma," "increased arousal," and "hypervigilance," all of which could adaptively help one to avoid further trauma) but also may be detrimental to their recovery (Caplan 2006; Linder, 2004). One consequence of a label of mental illness is that it may compound a victim's sense of self-blame (e.g., "If I am mentally and emotionally flawed, I may have brought this situation upon myself," "I am not feeling fine right now because I am inadequate or sick"). This self-perception can, in turn, erode people's sense of agency and, thereby, neutralize the inner resources they require to escape continued abuse. Furthermore, when a practitioner labels such responses as mental illness, there is implicit in that label the assumption that, regardless of the severity of the stressor, the client should be able to get "back to normal" and to leave the effects of the trauma in their past. Because mental illness denotes abnormality, a diagnostic label carries with it a judgment that deems the thoughts and behaviors in question to be out of the range of normal responses – even when those thoughts and behaviors were precipitated by extreme trauma. That implicit judgment keeps some male combat veterans from seeking a psychotherapist's assistance because it suggests that they are less masculine or less effective at their work than they should be. After all, a "real man" or a "good soldier" should be able to cope bravely with any war-related experience.

From a broader perspective, an emphasis on labeling trauma victims' responses as psychiatric symptoms rather than the results of trauma can distract clients, practitioners, and society in general from the social injustices of victimization. Such social ills as the brutality of war, torture, and violence against women go unexamined, and, instead, victims' mental and emotional states are scrutinized and discussed. The public is thus excused from the responsibility of rectifying the various forms of oppression and violence that lead to psychological trauma. The internal focus on the mind of the sufferer indicates that treatment of that mind is the necessary remedy, and the need for social and political change remains largely invisible.

Some Issues That Cut Across Diagnostic Categories

In addition to those sources of gender bias that are specific to particular diagnostic categories, there are major problems in the lives of women and men that are relevant to many diagnostic categories and to our consideration of the *DSM* in general. These include poverty, various forms of violence, and issues related to race and racism.

Poverty

Because the *DSM* is written from a mainstream psychiatric vantage point, it presents a medicalized view of experience, thus psychological distress is explained as pathology that originates within the individual rather than in social ills. However, there is consistent evidence that social and economic factors have a tremendous impact on psychological suffering. Living in poverty has been identified as an important factor that can increase an individual's likelihood of emotional distress (Belle & Doucet, 2003; Lorant et al., 2003), and poverty itself disproportionately affects women and children (U.S. Census Bureau, 2002). Because poor women in the United States usually have no health insurance, they are generally not seen in psychiatric settings until their distress is severe (Chalifoux, 1996). Possibly as a consequence of this delay, as well as because many clinicians do not believe that poor clients benefit from talk therapy, poor clients are more likely than clients who are not poor to be given psychoactive drugs to manage their distress (Bullock, 2004; Judd, 1986; Killian & Killian, 1990).

In their encounters with the psychiatric establishment, poor women must also contend with widely held stereotypes of low-income people as lazy, morally weak, and not intelligent enough to benefit from psychotherapy (Bullock, 1995; Lott, 2002; Seccombe, 1999). As Bullock (2004) pointed out, mental health professionals often do not understand the realities of poverty, including the absence of safe living conditions and difficulties associated with transportation and basic survival, such as providing for one's children. Consequently, therapists may be unaware that the anger, hostility, and shame they see in the behavior of poor clients may be directly caused by poverty. The shame associated with being poor may be further compounded by a client's awareness that her therapist comes from a position of privilege. This subtext of shame can further influence the client's behavior and leave her vulnerable to diagnostic labels that pathologize her reactions.

In her book *Poor-Bashing: The Politics of Exclusion*, Swanson (2001) described the insidious ways in which policies and public attitudes concerning the poor perpetuate the myth that poverty is a social ill caused by the poor themselves. This victim blaming on the part of the middle and upper classes contributes to self-blame among low-income individuals and to their heightened awareness of their personal failures and shortcomings. Swanson argued that one of the greatest threats to the well-being of poor individuals is the belief that the poor are somehow less deserving than others of the services commonly associated with privilege; these include preventive services that promote psychological wellness. As long as mental healthcare for the poor is construed only as a means of responding to severe psychiatric crises, the biases against them will persist, and their care will remain oriented to drug treatment rather than to supportive services and the need for social and structural change.

Violence and Abuse

As discussed earlier, one risk of using the *DSM* system involves applying a label of mental illness to those who have been victims of violence. Certainly, if people who have experienced rape, incest, or other forms of abuse were excluded from the number of individuals given a psychiatric diagnosis, the reported prevalence of many psychiatric disorders would drop dramatically. Abused women are at risk of receiving psychiatric diagnoses partly because they tend to express anger more readily than non-abused women do (Jack, 1999). However, psychiatric labels are also applied frequently to women who have experienced abuse even when such women are seeking help solely for the mental suffering that results from having been a target of violence. Their abusers, on the other hand, are often seen in psychiatric settings only if mandated to be there by the courts. Consequently, the supposed mental illnesses of abused women rather than the mental states of their abusers are more commonly discussed. Moreover, because severely distressed women may be institutionalized after having sought help, whereas their abusers are institutionalized only if charges are pressed against them, the individual who is deemed unfit to reside in society might be the victim rather than the perpetrator. We should also bear in mind that a woman who is institutionalized for mental illness is viewed as being defective *as a person*, whereas a man who is imprisoned or paroled for violent abuse is punished because of his particular *actions*. This distinction is all the more damaging when we consider that women are socialized to internalize labels that are assigned to them by others and not to question medical and other authorities (Bepko & Krestan, 1990). Therefore, the application of a psychiatric label to an abused woman can present a risk to the woman's sense of self. In the case of men who are victimized, a psychiatric label is particularly damaging because victimization runs contrary to the masculine gender role and is experienced as especially shameful. There is a need for greater recognition among practitioners that men can also be victims of abuse, and those victims must deal with a constellation of physical and psychological effects in a social climate that requires them to act strong at all times and not express their suffering. Thus, for both women and men, there are risks associated with shame and self-blame when attention is paid to their presumed mental weakness rather than to the effects of trauma itself.

Race and Racial Discrimination

As much as bias in psychiatric diagnosis affects female clients in general, the problems of bias are often even more pronounced for racialized women. Because of the dominance of a White, Western viewpoint in psychiatry, the actions and thoughts that are most likely to be considered normal by the *DSM* authors and others in the mental health establishment are those that are acceptable within mainstream White society (Caplan, 1995; Russell, 1994). Thus, kinds of behavior that may be commonplace among people of color and within non-dominant cultures are often labeled "abnormal" (Ali, 2004). At the same time, there is a risk that real emotional suffering is overlooked by mental health professionals when they attempt to apply psychiatric labels to women of color. For instance, a practitioner who holds a stereotype of Asian women as quiet and passive may miss signs of extreme sadness and emotional suffering if an Asian woman is quiet and withdrawn; quiet behavior may be attributed to cultural norms rather than to suffering. More broadly, the very idea of psychiatric categorization, treatment, and institutionalization runs counter to the traditions and beliefs of cultures that value a holistic and broadly encompassing view of wellness for men and women. However, in psychiatric settings, women of color who resist treatment are at risk of being viewed as difficult patients (Greene, 1995).

We also must consider the interaction between sexism and racism in the construction and use of the *DSM* categories. Examples of this interaction have been found in the *DSM-IV Casebook* (Spitzer, Gibbon, Skodol, & Williams, 2002), a widely used book designed for training in the *DSM* approach. In the *Casebook*, women of color are described in more sexualized terms than are men or White women (Cermele, Daniels, & Anderson, 2001). These representations are evidence not only of racist bias within the *DSM* but also of the potential for the *DSM* to shape trainees' stereotypes of women of color.

Another risk associated with race in the use of the *DSM* system is its lack of consideration of the psychological damage that can be inflicted by racism. As with poverty and abuse, racism encountered by women who are also psychiatric clients can be readily "explained away" by the clients' diagnoses. A client who is deemed mentally ill – especially a female client – is in danger of having her every perception and estimation of her own experience challenged (Caplan, 1995). Therefore, when a person of color describes the emotional distress of racist encounters, the focus is often not on the racism itself but on the underlying pathology that is causing him or her to feel distressed (Ali, 2004; Pauling & Beaver, 1997; Root, 1996). Racist bias, therefore, inflicts on individuals from non-dominant backgrounds an additional threat of harm to their emotional well-being when they seek help within the psychiatric system.

Stereotypes Concerning Sexual Orientation and Identity

There is evidence that bias in the *DSM*'s medicalized approach extends beyond social and racial arenas into sexuality. As in other forms of psychiatric bias, elevated rates of diagnosed conditions are presumed to indicate that greater numbers of individuals in a given group are mentally flawed or psychologically ill. In the case of LGBT individuals, in which researchers have found higher rates of depression, suicide, and substance abuse than in members of the general population (Cochran & Mays, 2006), the presumption of psychological weakness is often a reflection of homophobic bias in the psychiatric system. For example, although in the 1970s the *DSM* authors said that they would remove homosexuality from the next edition (Stein, 1993), in fact, they did not do so. It remained listed as "ego dystonic homosexuality," a diagnosis that pathologized the consequences of a homophobic, intolerant society that made it difficult for gay men and lesbians to be totally comfortable with their sexual orientation (Caplan, 1995). Despite the ultimate removal of the "disorder" from the *DSM*, research on psychological issues of LGBT individuals has been skewed by recruitment practices that often draw research participants from help-seeking samples rather than from community samples (Cochran & Mays, 2006). In addition, the focus on diagnostic categories leads clinicians and researchers to ignore the psychological stress that can stem from the lack of social (and/or familial) support, social isolation from peers, and the social stigmatization of being an oppressed minority. Research has shown that the internalized oppression often experienced in the LGBT population is correlated with depression (Majied, 2003). Furthermore, a study (Jones, 2001) of depression, alcoholism, and substance abuse among older LGBT persons revealed that a primary trigger for these conditions is the devastating effect of the AIDS epidemic that has left many LGBT elders with only small support networks, as they have lost many friends and community members. Therefore, there is a need for research on mental health issues among LGBT individuals to address the realities of social, familial, and societal stressors.

Gender-Role Factors in Seeking Treatment

For men in particular, shame and stigma are associated with seeking help in the form of psychiatric treatment. Men are socialized to keep their emotions to themselves and not to express feelings of sadness, anxiousness, or fear (Bepko & Krestan, 1990; Lips, 2001; see also Chapter 10). For both men and women, seeking a psychotherapist's help is often seen as a sign of mental and emotional weakness and as an indication of an inability to cope with one's problems. Furthermore, mental illness can be under-diagnosed in men because many forms of mental illness are assumed to affect only women. In a classic study of the influence of gender-related stereotypes on ideas about mental illness, Broverman, Broverman, Clarkson, Rosenkrantz, and Vogel (1970) found that mental health professionals' ideal of the mentally healthy person was similar to their ideal of the mentally healthy man, but that their descriptions of what constitutes a mentally healthy woman were quite different from their descriptions of what constitutes a mentally healthy person in general. These findings indicate that it is more challenging for the typical woman to be considered mentally healthy than it is for the typical man, and this remains true today, as Seem and Clark (2006) recently replicated the Broverman et al. study.

More recent studies have indicated that both women and men are more likely to be regarded as mentally ill if they behave in ways that are inconsistent with their respective gender stereotypes (Rosenfield, 1982; Waisberg & Page, 1988). In addition, Landrine (1988) found that participants in her undergraduate sample described depressed people in more feminine terms and non-depressed people in more masculine terms. Because masculine and feminine stereotypes differ in important ways, different types of behavior are considered acceptable for men than for women. For instance, as Doyle (1995) described, aggressive behavior on the part of men is less likely to be considered pathological than is women's aggressive behavior. Women's own affective states may also be influenced by the awareness of certain diagnostic categories that presume emotional vulnerability in women. For example, Nash and Chrisler (1997) found that undergraduate women who read a description of the PMDD diagnostic criteria reported more negative affect after reading the description than did men who read the same description. In terms of help-seeking behavior, we can assume that women's exposure to assumptions of women's psychological weakness (as presented by the media and by the public) leads women to seek psychiatric treatment more readily than do men.

Future Directions

In this chapter we argue that the use of gender-biased psychiatric diagnoses obscures the realities of people's lives. It is important to consider the risks that may be associated with treatment decisions entailed by the *DSM*'s de-contextualized emphasis on an individual's symptoms over the examination of sociocultural factors. The focus on specific psychiatric symptoms in the *DSM* diagnostic system is an attempt to divorce mental illness from the broader contexts of clients' lives on the assumption that, regardless of the particular environments they inhabit, individuals who fall within a particular diagnostic category have in common precisely that: their diagnosis. However, the very belief that individuals can be understood outside of their life contexts is highly questionable. Some observers (Caplan, 1995; Kutchins & Kirk, 1997) of the process by which the *DSM* is created have argued that the *DSM* itself is a formalization of prevailing norms of acceptability as determined by the dominant groups in society (that is, male, White, heterosexual, economically privileged people). We contend that future research should be directed toward uncovering alternate views of understanding and conceptualizing mental and emotional suffering.

One important area of future research is investigation of the effectiveness of community involvement and advocacy in helping individuals to take an active role in changing the circumstances of their lives and the lives of others. Helping others can be personally empowering, can lead to an increased sense of self-efficacy (McWhirter, 1994), and may be, for some, a favorable option over traditional psychotherapy. In addition, researchers should investigate specific effects of psychiatric labeling with respect to the damage to a client's sense of self after having received a label, as well as the effects of community-based alternatives to traditional mental health services that do not rely on diagnostic labels. If psychiatry is positioned to dictate what kinds of behavior are acceptable and unacceptable, as well as what means are most effective for attaining normalcy, then both clients and non-clients must accept that its system of defining and remedying problematic behaviors is superior to any other approaches. However, by locating illness in the individual, mental health professionals neglect to acknowledge the realities of people's lives and the oppression encountered by the disadvantaged. Moreover, when medications are routinely favored over social and community-based interventions and other means of creating personal, interpersonal, and contextual change, clients are taught that their problems lie within them. Thus, no change is needed in the status quo.

Research should also be directed at systematically exploring the influence of social inequality and oppression on psychological well-being. If we shift the focus of research away from diagnostic entities and toward the broad causes of human suffering, we can discover innovative means of alleviating distress. For example, as we consider gender bias in the *DSM*, we must bear in mind that the over-representation of women across numerous diagnostic categories is the result of several interactive forces. It is not solely scientific and diagnostic bias that is responsible for women being deemed mentally ill more often than are men. If, in our society, women's lives disproportionately include suffering and high levels of stress, then it should be expected that women will experience more psychological distress than men do. However, what the creators of the *DSM* ignore is the crucial and necessary consideration of *why* women's lives so often are fraught with emotional anguish. It is true that psychiatric treatment has been of benefit to many who have suffered psychological distress. The dangers of the system arise when scientists, practitioners, clients, and the public become blind to – and, therefore, do not challenge – the unscientific and biased nature through which individuals are labeled and their problems are treated.

References

Ali, A. (2004). The intersection of racism and sexism in psychiatric diagnosis. In P. J. Caplan & L. Cosgrove (Eds.), *Bias in psychiatric diagnosis* (pp. 71–75). Lanham, MD: Jason Aronson.
American Psychiatric Association. (2000). *Diagnostic and statistical manual of mental disorders-IV-TR*. Washington, DC: Author.
Ballard, C. G., Davis, R., Cullen, P. C., Mohan, R. N., & Dean, C. (1994). Prevalence of postnatal psychiatric morbidity in mothers and fathers. *British Journal of Psychiatry*, 164, 782–788.

Bankey, R. (2004). The agoraphobic condition. *Cultural Geographies*, 11, 347–355.

Becker, D. (2004). Post-traumatic stress disorder. In P. J. Caplan & L. Cosgrove (Eds.), *Bias in psychiatric diagnosis* (pp. 205–212). Lanham, MD: Jason Aronson.

Becker, D., & Lamb, S. (1994). Sex bias in the diagnosis of borderline personality disorder and posttraumatic stress disorder. *Professional Psychology*, 25, 55–61.

Belitsky, C. A., Toner, B. B., Ali, A., Yu, B., Osborne, S. L., & deRooy, E. (1996). Sex-role attitudes and clinical appraisal in psychiatry residents. *Canadian Journal of Psychiatry*, 41, 503–508.

Belle, D., & Doucet, J. (2003). Poverty, inequality, and discrimination as sources of depression among U.S. women. *Psychology of Women Quarterly*, 27, 101–113.

Bepko, C., & Krestan, J. A. (1990). *Too good for her own good*. New York: Harper & Row.

Breggin, P. (2007, July 21). Pregnant mothers should not take SSRI ant-depressants. *Huffington Post*. Accessed June 2009 at www.huffingtonpost.com/dr-peter-breggin/pregnant-mothers-should-n_b_57270.html.

Broverman, I. K., Broverman, D. M., Clarkson, F. E., Rosenkrantz, P. S., & Vogel, S. R. (1970). Sex role stereotypes and clinical judgments of mental health. *Journal of Consulting and Clinical Psychology*, 34, 1–7.

Brown, L. S. (1991). Diagnosis and dialog. *Canadian Psychology*, 2, 142–144.

Brown, L. S. (1992). A feminist critique of personality disorders. In L. S. Brown & M. Ballou (Eds.), *Personality and psychopathology: Feminist reappraisals* (pp. 206–228). New York: Guilford.

Brown, L. S. (1994). *Subversive dialogues: Theory in feminist therapy*. New York: Basic Books.

Bullock, H. E. (1995). Class acts: Middle-class responses to the poor. In B. Lott & D. Maluso (Eds.), *The social psychology of interpersonal discrimination* (pp. 118–159). New York: Guilford.

Bullock, H. E. (2004). Diagnosis of low-income women. In P. J. Caplan & L. Cosgrove (Eds.), *Bias in psychiatric diagnosis* (pp. 115–120). Lanham, MD: Jason Aronson.

Cafri, G., Thompson, J. K., Ricciardelli, L., McCabe, M., Smolak, L., & Yesalis, C. (2005). Pursuit of the muscular ideal: Physical and psychological consequences and putative risk factors. *Clinical Psychology Review*, 25, 215–239.

Cale, E. M., & Lilienfeld S. O. (2002). Sex differences in psychopathy and antisocial personality disorder: A review and integration. *Clinical Psychology Review*, 22, 1179–1207.

Caplan, P. J. (1995). *They say you're crazy: How the world's most powerful psychiatrists decide who's normal*. Reading, MA: Addison-Wesley.

Caplan, P. J. (2004). The debate about PMDD and Sarafem: Suggestions for therapists. *Women & Therapy*, 27(3/4), 55–67.

Caplan, P. J. (2006). Ambiguity, powerlessness, and the psychologizing of trauma: How the backlash affects the context of working with trauma. *Journal of Trauma Practice*, 5, 5–24.

Caplan, P. J., & Caplan, J. B. (2009). *Thinking critically about research on sex and gender*. Boston: Allyn & Bacon.

Caplan, P. J., & Cosgrove, L. (2004). Is this really necessary? In P. J. Caplan & L. Cosgrove (Eds.), *Bias in psychiatric diagnosis* (pp. xiii–xv). Lanham, MD: Jason Aronson.

Caws, P. (1994). Subjectivity, self-identity, and self-description: Conceptual and diagnostic problems in autism, schizophrenia, borderline personality disorder, and the dissociative disorders. In J. Z. Sadler, O. P. Wiggins, & M. A. Schwartz (Eds.), *Philosophical perspectives on psychiatric diagnostic classification* (pp. 193–208). Baltimore: Johns Hopkins University Press.

Cermele, J., Daniels, S., & Anderson, K. L. (2001). Defining normal: Constructions of race and gender in the *DSM-IV* casebook. *Feminism & Psychology*, 11, 229–247.

Chalifoux, B. (1996). Speaking-up: White, working-class women in therapy. *Women & Therapy*, 18(3/4), 25–34.

Chrisler, J. C., & Caplan, P. J. (2002). The strange case of Dr. Jekyll and Ms. Hyde: How PMS became a cultural phenomenon and a psychiatric disorder. *Annual Review of Sex Research*, 13, 274–306.

Cochran, S. D., & Mays, V. M. (2006). Estimating prevalence of mental and substance-using disorders among lesbians and gay men from existing national health data. In A. M. Omoto & H. S. Kurtzman (Eds.), *Sexual orientation and mental health* (pp. 143–166). Washington, DC: American Psychological Association.

Cohen, D., & Jacobs, D. H. (2007). Randomized controlled trials of antidepressants: Clinically and scientifically irrelevant. *Debates in Neuroscience*, 1, 44–54.

Cook, E. P., Warnke, M., & Dupuy, P. (1993). Gender bias and the *DSM-III-R*. *Counselor Education and Supervision*, 32, 311–322.

Cosgrove, L., & Caplan, P. J. (2004). Medicalizing menstrual distress. In P. J. Caplan & L. Cosgrove (Eds.), *Bias in psychiatric diagnosis* (pp. 221–230). Lanham, MD: Jason Aronson.

Cosgrove, L., & Riddle, B. (2004). Gender bias and sex distribution of mental disorders in the *DSM-IV-TR*. In P. J. Caplan & L. Cosgrove (Eds.), *Bias in psychiatric diagnosis* (pp. 127–140). Lanham, MD: Jason Aronson.

Doyle, J. A. (1995). *The male experience*. Madison, WI: Brown & Benchmark.

Endicott, J., Amsterdam, J., Erikson, E., Frank, E., Freeman, E., Hirschfield, R., et al. (1999). Is premenstrual dysphoric disorder a distinct clinical entity? *Journal of Women's Health and Gender-Based Medicine*, 8, 663–679.

Fish, V. (2004). Some gender biases in diagnosing traumatized women. In P. J. Caplan & L. Cosgrove (Eds.), *Bias in psychiatric diagnosis* (pp. 312–220). Lanham, MD: Jason Aronson.

Frances, A., & Widiger, T. A. (1987). A critical review of four *DSM-III* personality disorders: Borderline, avoidant, dependent, and passive-aggressive. In G. L. Tischler (Ed.), *Diagnosis and classification in psychiatry: A critical appraisal of DSM-III* (pp. 269–289). New York: Cambridge University Press.

Gammell, D. J., & Stoppard J. (1999). Women's experiences of treatment of depression: Medicalization or empowerment? *Canadian Psychology*, 40, 112–128.

Gallant, S., Popiel, D., Hoffman, D., Chakraborty, P., & Hamilton, J. (1992). Using daily ratings to confirm premenstrual syndrome/late luteal phase dysphoric disorder, Part II: What makes a "real" difference? *Psychosomatic Medicine*, 54, 167–181.

Gallop, R., McKeever, P., Toner, B. B., Lancee, W., & Lueck, M. (1995). Inquiring about childhood sexual abuse as part of the nursing history: Opinions of abused and non-abused nurses. *Archives of Psychiatric Nursing*, 9, 146–151.

Gartlehner, G., Gaynes, B. N., Hansen, R. A., Thieda, P., DeVeaugh-Geiss, A., Krebs, E. E., et al. (2008). Comparative benefits and harms of second-generation antidepressants. *Annals of Internal Medicine*, 149, 734–750.

Gibson, P. R. (2004). Histrionic personality. In P. J. Caplan & L. Cosgrove (Eds.), *Bias in psychiatric diagnosis* (pp. 201–206). Lanham, MD: Jason Aronson.

Golding, J. M., & Taylor, D. L. (1996). Sexual assault history and menstrual distress in two general population samples. *Journal of Women's Health*, 5, 143–152.

Golding, J. M., Taylor, D. L., Menard, L., & King, M. J. (2000). Prevalence of sexual abuse history in a sample of women seeking treatment for premenstrual syndrome. *Journal of Psychosomatic Obstetrics and Gynecology*, 21, 69–80.

Greene, B. (1995). Institutional racism in the mental health professions. In J. Adleman & G. Enguidanos (Eds.), *Racism in the lives of women: Testimony, theory, and guides to antiracist practice* (pp. 113–126). Binghamton, NY: Harrington Park Press.

Grieve, F. G. (2007). A conceptual model of factors contributing to the development of muscle dysmorphia. *Eating Disorders*, 15, 63–80.

Hamilton, S., Rothbart, M., & Dawes, R. M. (1986). Sex bias, diagnosis, and *DSM-III*. *Sex Roles*, 15, 279–284.

Hankin, B. L., & Abramson, L. Y. (2001). Development of gender differences in depression: An elaborated cognitive vulnerability-transactional stress theory. *Psychological Bulletin*, 127, 773–796.

Healy, D. (2004). *Let them eat Prozac: The unhealthy relationship between the pharmaceutical industry and depression*. New York: New York University Press.

Hewitt, P. L., Flett, G. L., & Ediger, E. (1995). Perfectionism traits and perfectionistic self-presentation in eating disorders attitudes, characteristics, and symptoms. *International Journal of Eating Disorders*, 18(4), 7–26.

Holmes J. (2008). Space and the secure base in agoraphobia: A qualitative survey. *Area*, 40, 375–382.

Jack, D. C. (1991). *Silencing the self: Women and depression*. Cambridge, MA: Harvard University Press.

Jack, D. C. (1999). *Behind the mask: Destruction and creativity in women's aggression*. Cambridge, MA: Harvard University Press.

Jones, B. E. (2001). Is having the luck of growing old in the gay, lesbian, bisexual, transgender community good or bad luck? *Journal of Gay & Lesbian Social Services*, 13(4), 13–14.

Judd, P. (1986). The mentally ill poor in America: The anatomy of abuse. *Journal of Applied Social Science*, 10, 40–50.

Kessler, R. C. (2003). Epidemiology of women and depression. *Journal of Affective Disorders*, 74, 5–13.

Killian, T. M., & Killian, L. T. (1990). Sociological investigations of mental illness: A review. *Hospital and Community Psychiatry*, 41, 902–911.

Kroll, J. K. (1988). *The challenge of the borderline patient: Competency in diagnosis and treatment.* New York: Norton.

Kutchins, H., & Kirk, S. A. (1997). *Making us crazy: DSM, the psychiatric bible, and the creating of mental disorders.* New York: Free Press.

Landrine, H. (1988). Depression and stereotypes of women: Preliminary empirical analyses of the gender-role hypothesis. *Sex Roles,* 19, 527–541.

Landrine, H. (1989). The politics of personality disorder. *Psychology of Women Quarterly,* 13, 325–339.

Langeland, W., Draijer, N., & van den Brink, W. (2004). Psychiatric comorbidity in treatment-seeking alcoholics: The role of childhood trauma and perceived parental dysfunction. *Alcoholism,* 28, 441–447.

Linder, M. (2004). Creating post-traumatic stress disorder: A case study of the history, sociology, and politics of psychiatric classification. In P. J. Caplan & L. Cosgrove (Eds.), *Bias in psychiatric diagnosis* (pp. 25–40). Lanham, MD: Jason Aronson.

Lips, H. M. (2001). *Sex and gender.* Mountain View, CA: Mayfield.

Lorant, V., Deliege, D., Eaton, W., Robert, A., Philippot, P., & Annseau, M. (2003). Socioeconomic inequalities in depression: A meta-analysis. *American Journal of Epidemiology,* 157, 98–112.

Lott, B. (2002). Cognitive and behavioral distancing from the poor. *American Psychologist,* 57, 100–110.

Majied, K. (2003). The impact of racism and homophobia on depression. *Dissertation Abstracts International Section A: Humanities and Social Sciences,* 64(5-A), 1849.

Martinez, R., Johnston-Robledo, I., Ulsh, H. M., & Chrisler, J. C. (2000). Singing "the baby blues": A content analysis of popular press articles about postpartum affective disturbances. *Women & Health,* 31(2/3), 37–56.

McCreary, D. R., & Sasse, D. K. (2000). An exploration of the drive for muscularity in adolescent boys and girls. *Journal of American College Health,* 48, 297–304.

McGrath, E., Keita, G. P., Strickland, B. R., & Russo, N. F. (1990). *Women and depression: Risk factors and treatment issues.* [Final report of the American Psychological Association Task Force on Women and Depression.] Washington, DC: American Psychological Association.

McHugh, M., & Cosgrove, L. (2004). Agoraphobia. In P. J. Caplan & L. Cosgrove (Eds.), *Bias in psychiatric diagnosis* (pp. 177–181). Lanham, MD: Jason Aronson.

McWhirter, E. H. (1994). *Counseling for empowerment.* Alexandria, VA: American Counseling Association.

Metzl, J. M. (2003). *Prozac on the couch: Prescribing gender in the era of wonder drugs.* Durham, NC: Duke University Press.

Moynihan, R. (2004). Controversial disease dropped from Prozac product information. *British Medical Journal,* 328, 365.

Nash, H. C., & Chrisler, J. C. (1997). Is a little (psychiatric) knowledge a dangerous thing? *Psychology of Women Quarterly,* 21, 315–322.

Nehls, N. (1998). Borderline personality disorder: Gender stereotypes, stigma, and limited system of care. *Issues in Mental Health Nursing,* 19, 97–112.

O'Meara, K. P. (2001, April 30). Misleading medicine. *Insight on the News* (*Washington Times Magazine*), p. 10.

Paris, J. (1994). The etiology of borderline personality disorder: A biopsychosocial approach. *Psychiatry,* 57, 316–325.

Pauling, M. L., & Beaver, A. S. (1997, November). *Treating racism as traumatic stress.* Paper presented at the meeting of the International Society for Traumatic Stress Studies, Montreal, Canada.

Perry, J., Herman, J., van der Kolk, B., & Hoke, L. (1990). Psychotherapy and psychological trauma in borderline personality disorder. *Psychiatric Annals,* 20, 33–43.

Pope, H. G., & Katz, D. L. (1994). Psychiatric and medical effects of anabolic-androgenic steroid use: A controlled study of 160 athletes. *Archives of General Psychiatry,* 51, 375–382.

Pope, H., Phillips, K., & Olivardia, R. (2000). *The Adonis complex: The secret crisis of male body obsession.* New York: Free Press.

Raskin, M., Nurnberg, G., Prince, R., Fine, J., Levine, P. E., & Seigel, O. (1989). Abuse of the child and anxiety in the adult. *New York State Journal of Medicine,* 89, 138–140.

Rivera, M. (2002). The Chrysalis Program: Feminist treatment community for individuals diagnosed as personality disordered. In M. Ballou & L. S. Brown (Eds.), *Rethinking mental health and disorder: Feminist perspectives* (pp. 231–261). New York: Guilford.

Root, M. P. (1996). Women of color and traumatic stress in "domestic captivity": Gender and race as disempowering statuses. In A. J. Marsella, M. J. Friedman, E. T. Gerrity, & R. M. Scurfield (Eds.), *Ethnocultural aspects of posttraumatic stress disorder* (pp. 363–388). Washington, DC: American Psychological Association.

Rosenfield, S. (1982). Sex roles and societal reactions to mental illness: Labelling of "deviant" deviance. *Journal of Health and Human Behavior,* 23, 18–24.

Russell, D. (1994). Psychiatric diagnosis and the interests of women. In J. Z. Sadler, O. P. Wiggins, & M. A. Schwartz (Eds.), *Philosophical perspectives on psychiatric diagnostic classification* (pp. 246–258). Baltimore: Johns Hopkins University Press.

Seccombe, K. (1999). *So you think I drive a Cadillac? Welfare recipients' perspectives on the system and its reform.* Needham Heights, MA: Allyn & Bacon.

Seem, S. R., & Clark, M. D. (2006). Healthy women, healthy men, and healthy adults: An evaluation of gender role stereotypes in the twenty-first century. *Sex Roles*, 55, 247–258.

Simmons, D. (1992). Gender issues and borderline personality disorder: Why do females dominate the diagnosis? *Archives of Psychiatric Nursing*, 6, 219–223.

Spitzer, R. L., Gibbon, A. E., Skodol, J. B., & Williams, M. B. (2002). *DSM-IV-TR casebook*. Washington, DC: American Psychiatric Association.

Stein, T. S. (1993). Overview of new developments in understanding homosexuality. In J. M. Oldham, M. B. Riba, & A. Tasman (Eds.), *Review of psychiatry* (Vol. 12, pp. 9–40). Washington, DC: American Psychiatric Press.

Stoppard, J. M. (1993). Gender, psychosocial factors, and depression. In P. Cappeliez & R. J. Flynn (Eds.), *Depression and social environment: Research and intervention with neglected populations* (pp. 121–129). Montreal: McGill-Queens University Press.

Swanson, J. (2001). *Poor-bashing: The politics of exclusion*. Toronto: Between the Lines.

Taylor, D. (1999). Effectiveness of professional peer-group treatment: Symptom management for women with PMS. *Research in Nursing & Health*, 22, 496–511.

U.S. Census Bureau. (2002). *Poverty in the United States: 2001*. Washington, DC: U.S. Government Printing Office.

Vandell, D. L., Hyde, J. S., Plant, E. A., & Essex, M. J. (1997). Fathers and "others" as infant-care providers: Predictors of parents' emotional well-being. *Merrill-Palmer Quarterly*, 43, 361–385.

Waisberg, J., & Page, S. (1988). Gender role nonconformity and perception of mental illness. *Women & Health*, 14, 3–16.

Walker, L. (1993). Are personality disorders gender biased? Yes! In S. A. Kirk & S. D. Einbinder (Eds.), *Controversial issues in mental health* (pp. 21–32). New York: Allyn and Bacon.

Westen, D., Ludolph, P., Misle, B., Ruffine, S., & Block, J. (1990). Physical and sexual abuse in adolescent girls with borderline personality disorder. *American Journal of Orthopsychiatry*, 60, 55–66.

Whiffen, V. E. (2004). Myths and mates in childbearing depression. *Women & Therapy*, 27(3/4), 151–164.

Whiffen, V. E. (2006). *A secret sadness*. Oakland, CA: New Harbinger.

Willard, B. (2005). Feminist interventions in biomedical discourse: An analysis of the rhetoric of integrative medicine. *Women's Studies in Communication*, 28, 115–148.

Worell, J., & Remer, P. (2003). *Feminist perspectives in therapy: Empowering diverse women*. Hoboken, NJ: Wiley.

Chapter 6
Gender Identity Disorder: Concerns and Controversies

Kate Richmond, Kate Carroll, and Kristoffer Denboske

Gender identity disorder (GID) remains the focus of considerable debate and, arguably, has divided interested parties (including health providers, transgendered people, transsexual people, and lesbian, gay, bisexual, and questioning community members) into different camps of thought regarding reform of the diagnosis. For example, several researchers and clinicians (Bockting & Ehrbar, 2005; Lev, 2005; Winters, 2007), who believe that gender is socially constructed, have questioned the purpose and necessity of pathologizing unconventional gender practices and have called for elimination of the diagnosis and/or significant reform, whereas other researchers and clinicians (Fink, 2005; Gagne, Tewksbury, & McGaughey, 1997) believe that GID is critical as a diagnostic category because it not only has the potential to assist individuals who report persistent preference for cross-gender roles but also serves as a "gatekeeper" for insurance reimbursement of medications (hormones), surgical procedures, and psychotherapy, which is required prior to sex reassignment surgery (SRS).

Indeed, these are complex and complicated issues. In this chapter we examine several aspects of GID in an attempt to provide a framework for the current controversy regarding reform. We begin by situating the diagnosis in a historical context and providing the current diagnostic criteria. Following this, we explore the prevalence rates and concerns regarding accurate assessment and research with individuals who exhibit symptoms associated with GID. We then provide a review of the etiological explanations of GID and corresponding treatment recommendations. Finally, we outline the current controversies about the diagnosis and end with potential recommendations for future research.

History and Diagnostic Criteria

Though the term transsexualism was introduced to psychiatric nomenclature in 1923 (Hirschfeld, 1923), it was not until 1980 that transsexualism, as well as the related gender identity disorder of childhood (GIDC), first appeared as diagnoses in the *Diagnostic and Statistical Manual of Mental Disorders-III* (*DSM-III*; American Psychiatric Association, 1980). To meet criteria for transsexualism, an individual had to express continuous interest in changing his or her sexual anatomy and corresponding gender-specific role for at least 2 years. Coincidentally, *DSM-III* was the first edition to eliminate homosexuality as a psychiatric disorder (Minter, 1999), which led many to believe that transsexualism provided a new framework for pathologizing homosexuality (Money, 1994a;

K. Richmond (✉)
Muhlenberg College, Allentown, PA, USA

Sedgwick, 1990; Wilson, Griffin, & Wren, 2002). This claim, however, was denied by the contributing subcommittee members of the *DSM-III*, though it remains a contentious issue (Whittle, 2006; Zucker & Spitzer, 2005).

The addition of transsexualism to the *DSM-III* (American Psychiatric Association, 1987) emerged during a shift in psychiatric paradigms, when contributors were motivated to construct diagnostic criteria in a more rigorous scientific process, which meant eliminating other theoretical perspectives in favor of the medical model (Bryant, 2006). The medicalization of sexuality in particular was criticized for its regulation of "normal" sexual practices, and there was considerable concern about its institutionalization in the *DSM* (Bryant, 2006; Foucault, 1990; Tiefer, 1987). Though contributors maintained that the scientific process and the professional consensus were the catalyst for the presence of transsexualism (Zucker & Spitzer, 2005), others asserted that the process instead reflected conflict, considerable negotiations, and political struggles (Bowker & Star, 2000; Bryant, 2006). This assertion exposes the real limitations of all universal diagnostic categories, which, despite widely accepted usage, tend to disguise political and social struggles of representation (Bowker & Star, 2000).

In the *DSM-IV* (American Psychiatric Association, 1994), transsexualism was replaced with gender identity disorder (GID), which was added to a newly introduced section on Sexual and Gender Identity Disorders, along with gender identity disorder of childhood (GIDC) and gender identity disorder not otherwise specified (GIDNOS). (In the *DSM-III*, all of the above-mentioned diagnoses were listed under Disorders First Evident in Infancy, Childhood, or Adolescence.) If individuals met criteria for either GID or GIDNOS, they were to be subclassified according to sexual orientation: attracted to male partners; attracted to female partners; attracted to both; attracted to neither. The authors believed that this classification system would assist clinicians in determining if specific treatment approaches needed to be tailored based on sexual preference (Pfafflin, Bockting, Coleman, Ekins, & King, 1998).

According to the current *DSM-IV-TR* (American Psychiatric Association, 2000), criteria necessary for the diagnosis of GID are the following:

(1) There must be evidence of strong and persistent cross-gender identification, which is the desire to be or the insistence that one is, of the other sex (Criterion A).
(2) There is evidence of persistent discomfort about one's assigned sex or a sense of inappropriateness in the gender role of that sex (Criterion B).

In addition, the individual may not have a concurrent physical intersex condition (e.g., congenital adrenal hyperplasia or partial androgen insensitivity syndrome) (Criterion C), and there must be a significant decline in social and occupational functioning (Criterion D).

According to the *DSM-IV-TR* (American Psychiatric Association, 2000), common signs in young boys include interest in wearing their mother's clothes, jewelry, and shoes and a preoccupation with feminine toys, including the Barbie doll. In young girls, common signs include an intense aversion to wearing feminine clothes, specifically dresses, and an intense anatomic dysphoria (Bradley & Zucker, 1990). Most children with GID also display less overt gender-atypical behavior, which often diminishes with time; however, during adolescence, the gender dysphoria becomes more chronic (Meyenburg, 1999). Thus, in adolescents and adults, there is a stronger preoccupation with actually becoming the other sex; for example, adolescents and adults diagnosed with GID tend to "pass" as the other sex. Also, there is "a preoccupation with getting rid of primary and secondary sex characteristics" (American Psychiatric Association, 2000, p. 577).

Estimated Prevalence

Currently, GID is considered an extremely rare occurrence. The *DSM-IV-TR* (American Psychiatric Association, 2000) reports that the estimated prevalence of GID is 1 in 30,000 adult men and 1 in 100,000 adult women. These statistics are based primarily upon a sampling of referrals to a gender identity clinic in the Netherlands. More recent reviews suggest an incidence rate of approximately 0.15–1.58 per 100,000 people (Olsson & Moller, 2003). Mathy, Schillace, Coleman, and Berquist (2002) reported similar figures among Internet users; they found that 0.2% identified as transgender.

These figures have been widely reported, but researchers acknowledge that there are significant weaknesses to the surveys, and prevalence rates are still being fervently contested and debated (Plante, 2006; Roughgarden, 2004). For example, Conway (2006) observed that rates reported in the *DSM-IV-TR* do not match the number of SRS procedures performed each year. Instead, Conway proposed a process that would account for individuals who seek surgery:

(1) 800–1000 male-to-female transsexuality (MtF) surgeries are performed in the United States each year.
(2) From 1960 to 2000, between 30,000 and 40,000 procedures were performed.
(3) Approximately 32,000 post-op MtF transsexuals are currently living in the United States (Conway based this number on mortality rates and the average age of SRS patients at time of surgery).
(4) 32,000/8,000,000 (number of MtF SRS procedures/number of US men aged 18–60) = 1/2500.

Conway's calculations led to the estimation that 1 of every 2500 men seek out SRS. To generalize the rate to people with GID, Conway included an approximation of transgendered individuals who did not undergo SRS in addition to those who seek SRS abroad. The conclusion was that GID has a prevalence rate of 1:500. It is not clear where Conway acquired the surgical data, but this method holds promise and suggests that the prevalence of GID may be severely underestimated.

An additional notable deficit in the little available research on gender identity disorder is a failure to acknowledge issues of class, race, and ethnicity (Roen, 2006). In an analysis of articles in the *Medline* database that have an LGBT focus, Boehmer (2002) found that 85% of LGBT articles omitted race and ethnicity. The studies that did account for race tended to be reports of research on sexually transmitted diseases.

Also widely criticized is the gender asymmetry in referral rates. Boys are six times more likely than girls to be referred for gender identity disorder (Bradley & Zucker, 1990; Wilson et al., 2002; Zucker & Bradley, 1995). Bradley and Zucker (1997) proposed the "social threshold hypothesis" to account for the difference in referral rates. This theory suggests that society is more tolerant of cross-gender behavior in girls than in boys, which derives from an underlying social devaluation of femininity. Furthermore, the Women's Movement in the United States challenged traditional feminine norms, which resulted in greater acceptance of gender role violations among girls and women (Levant, Richmond, Cook, House, & Aupont, 2007). This has not been true for boys and men (Levant & Richmond, 2007).

The social threshold hypothesis may also provide a possible explanation for the finding that MtF is 1.5–3 times higher than female-to-male transsexuality (FtM) (van Kesteren, Gooren, & Megens, 1996). Feminine men may receive a harsher social reception than do masculine women, which places more pressure on MtF transsexuals to "choose" a sex and successfully "pass" as that chosen sex.

The social threshold hypothesis is also supported by research that shows that participants tend to give more negative evaluations of boys who exhibit cross-gender behavior than they do of girls (Wilson et al., 2002). Because gender identity and sexuality are often intertwined, parents may be more likely to seek treatment for their child if they perceive behavior as indicative of future homosexual tendencies. Indeed, parents are more likely to predict homosexuality outcomes in feminine boys than in masculine girls (Bradley & Zucker, 1990). In addition, the diagnostic criteria themselves may contribute to the differential treatment of boys and girls (Langer & Martin, 2004; Wilson et al., 2002). The criteria require that girls state their desire to be another sex, whereas boys need only to "exhibit" an apparent desire.

The lack of high-quality research on gender identity disorder can be partly attributed to the difficulties researchers face in identifying and recruiting the population (Bowen, Bradford, & Powers, 2006). Central to the problem is that there is no consensus on how to assess participants' sexual and gender identifications accurately (Elze, 2007; Harcourt, 2006). The term "transgender" acts as an umbrella for countless self-labels and definitions (Gagne et al., 1997; Peletz, 2006). In a recent study, Kenagy (2005) attempted to address this issue by allowing participants to choose their identification from a list of 14 terms and also provided an option of "Other (specify)." As transsexual communities continue to produce new and individualized self-labels, classification for research purposes becomes increasingly difficult (Meyerowitz, 2002). For example, if a biological man calls himself a cross-dresser, he may not necessarily identify as transgender, though the research community might be likely to label him as such.

Identification leads to another research obstacle: recruitment. Transgendered populations tend to be even less visible than other minority groups because of (1) the ability to "hide" a transgender lifestyle and (2) the unusually high physical and social risks of being "out" (Lev, 2004; Lombardi, Wilchins, Priesing, & Malouf, 2001). Many researchers are, therefore, limited to non-population-based sampling methods, such as volunteer studies and snowball sampling, which are methods that hinder the generalizability of the results (Bowen et al., 2006; Kenagy, 2005).

Many researchers are turning to the Internet as a means of insuring anonymity and increasing participation rates; however, Internet research has its own unique traps and pitfalls. For example, Internet data collection is prone to both coverage and sampling error. Coverage error refers to excluding portions of the population who do not have Internet access (Riggle, Rostosky, & Reedy, 2005), and sampling error refers to a failure in reaching potential participants, despite the fact that these participants have access to the Internet. Despite these flaws, Internet research holds promise for future directions in transgender studies.

Furthermore, the bulk of current research is limited to a pathological view of gender variance (Vitale, 2001). By drawing participants primarily from treatment clinics, researchers limit their scope to a specific subset of the transgendered population – those who are actively seeking "treatment" – usually in the form of sex reassignment surgery. This has essentially eliminated the representation of people with healthy transgendered identities from the current body of research (Lev, 2004). Also contributing to the disease model is the disproportionate amount of transgender research that focuses on sexually transmitted diseases. In Boehmer's (2002) *Medline* analysis, 61% of the articles were disease-specific, which led Boehmer to conclude that research unrelated to sexually transmitted diseases is limited.

Finally, the available GID prevalence research blatantly omits cultural context. By focusing on gender variance as a disorder, researchers ignore other culture-specific occurrences of transgendered identities. Various transgendered identities have been documented by anthropologists in southeast Asia (Peletz, 2006). For example, the Bissu of South Sulawesi are male-bodied persons who dress in women's clothing and engage in sexual relations with men. Rather than being socially ostracized, the Bissu hold a status similar to nobility. Transgendered identities in other cultures are often heavily involved with sacred rituals and practices, as are the Nat Kadaw of Burma (Peletz, 2006). A more well-known group is the Berdache, otherwise known as "Two-Spirit People" or "third gender," who have been documented in several North American native tribes (Conway, 2006; Peletz, 2006). The

Hirja of India is one of the most visible transgendered social groups, with their own designated caste in Indian society (Conway, 2006). This designation, however, does not prevent stigmatization. Teh (2001) found that although the Mak Nyah (male transsexuals in Malaysia) formed slightly different identities from other transsexual groups based upon culture, they also experience stigmatization similar to other transsexuals in other countries and cultures.

Etiology

Within the psychological literature, explanations for the development of gender identity are complex and have significantly developed within the last few decades (West & Zimmerman, 1998; Zucker & Green, 1992). Earlier research tended to rely heavily on positivism (Torgerson, 1986), but recent articles have represented a variety of scholarly approaches, including feminist and sociological analyses (Hausman, 2000; Lorber, 2000). Because of the unique sociopolitical implications of research in this area, difficulties have emerged in the use of traditional methodologies (Lev, 2004), and, probably due to the transgender movement, research has expanded beyond an exclusive clinical focus (Avery, 2002; Bolin, 1992). In this section, we provide a brief review of the literature with a specific focus on the mechanisms that are suspect in the development of GID. Though not exhaustive, this review provides a summary of the biological, psychosocial, and psychodynamic explanations of GID.

Biological Explanations

Investigations into biological determinants of human psychosexuality have yielded limited results. Many initial findings were later rejected because of an inability to be replicated, and other studies have been criticized for poor methodology (Di Ceglie, 1995; Gooren, 1990; Hoenig & Kenna, 1978; Zucker & Green, 1992). An additional limitation of biological research is that researchers often do not differentiate between transsexuality and homosexuality (Gooren, 2006). Nevertheless, biological investigations continue to be central to conceptualizing transsexuality, and research methods rely on animal studies or "experiments of nature." Researchers examine the occurrence of genetic or endocrine disorders, the exposure to exogenous external hormones, or the use of drugs containing estrogen during pregnancy (Gooren, 1990; Money, 1994b).

Results of animal studies suggest that hormones shape or stimulate a predisposition toward certain sex-dimorphic behavioral patterns, particularly during the critical period of prenatal and/or postnatal development when sexual differentiation of the external genitalia and the brain occurs (Gooren, 2006; Money, 1994a). Sexual differentiation appears to be coordinated by gonadal steroids, and a lack of androgen stimulation in males and an increase of androgens in females may contribute to the development of cross-gender identity (Cohen-Kettenis & Gooren, 1999; Woodson, Balleine, & Gorski, 2002). The primary androgen is testosterone, and in animal studies, more or less testosterone has been shown to influence the main regions of the brain that are involved in sexual differentiation (Gorski, 2002; Migeon & Wisniewski, 2003; Money, 1981). The presence of testosterone also prevents the pituitary's luteinizing hormone (LH) from reacting to an estrogen stimulus (Cohen-Kettenis & Gooren, 1999).

Nevertheless, researchers have qualified the above-mentioned findings because prenatal sex hormones may have a less powerful role in sexual differentiation among humans, particularly because in humans, other factors, such as hormone receptors and postreceptor events, may play a role in a hormone's actual biological effect (Gooren, 2006). Furthermore, the influence of prenatal androgens seems to play a larger role in gender role behavior than in gender identity (Gooren, 2006).

Another link between prenatal sex hormones and GID has been inferred from examination of patients with congenital adrenal hyperplasia (CAH), an inherited recessive disorder in which normal amounts of corticosteroids are not produced by the adrenal gland (Money, 1994a). Women with this disorder show an increase in adrenocorticotropic hormone secretion, which stimulates an increase in testosterone and results in external genitalia that are ambiguous or masculinized (Money, 1994a; Zucker & Green, 1992). Although this can be surgically altered to resemble sex-consistent genitalia, women with this disorder often display more masculine behaviors than do women without CAH (Ehrhardt & Baker, 1974; Zucker & Green, 1992). Nevertheless, few women with CAH actually show symptoms of GID, although incidence of GID may be higher among women with CAH than in the general population (Money, 1968; Zucker & Green, 1992). In general, humans with ambiguous genitalia (as in the case of CAH) or hypogonadism do *not* report symptoms consistent with GID.

As with hormones, research has been done to determine whether chromosome combinations might have some effect on gender identity. However, to date, no evidence has been reported to indicate that any combination of chromosomes contributes to the development of GID (Gooren, 2006).

Although research into the biological factors of transsexualism has not produced concrete causes of the disorder, a difference in the size of the central subdivision of the bed nucleus of the stria terminalis (BSTc), a brain area that is crucial in the development of sexual behavior, has been implicated as a possible explanation for GID (Zhou, Hofman, Gooren, & Swaab, 1995). Generally, the volume of the BSTc is larger in heterosexual men than in heterosexual women. In one study (Zhou et al., 1995), MtF transsexuals showed a BSTc comparable in size to that of a genetic female, and in another study, FtM transsexuals showed BSTc sizes comparable to those of a genetic male (Kruijver et al., 2000). In both studies, these findings were independent of sexual orientation.

The size variations in the BSTc have been attributed to the influence of androgens during prenatal development (Kruijver et al., 2000). Castration in adult animals did not appear to influence the volume of the BSTc, which provides evidence that varied sex hormone levels in adulthood may not play a significant role. Castration of newly born male rats, however, did cause a decrease in the number of BSTc neurons, and the introduction of androgens in newly born female rats caused an increase in neurons in the BSTc area (Zhou et al., 1995). Though these findings support the notion that transsexuality is related to a unique sexual differentiation process during the prenatal stage, more recent research has suggested that the variation in the volume of the BSTc becomes sexually dimorphic in early adulthood (Chung, De Vries, & Swaab, 2002). As noted by Gooren (2006), it is difficult to resolve this finding with the knowledge that children can experience gender dysphoria and that there does not appear to be evidence for prenatal hormonal abnormalities in transsexual humans.

Psychosocial Explanations

Social factors, such as family composition and child rearing, may also contribute to the development of symptoms associated with GID (Bradley & Zucker, 1997; Cohen-Kettenis & Gooren, 1999; Sabalis, Frances, Appenzeller, & Moseley, 1974; Seil, 1996). Individuals with GID tend to come from higher socioeconomic backgrounds, to have higher IQ scores, and to be raised by both biological parents (Zucker, 2001). Boys diagnosed with GID tend to have a higher number of older siblings than control boys do (Blanchard & Sheridan, 1992; Green, 2000). As the number of male offspring increases, mothers tend to have an increased wish for a daughter, which may contribute to differential treatment of the youngest son (Sabalis et al., 1974).

The degree of parental acceptance of initial gender-atypical behavior indeed is related to the continuation of cross-gender behavior (Green, 1987), and there is evidence that a child diagnosed with GID may have been reinforced for gender-atypical behavior (Moebius, 1998). A male child diagnosed with GID, for example, may observe his mother's preference for his female siblings. The child then may mimic his sisters' behavior to receive attention from his mother (Sabalis et al., 1974). Fathers may also reinforce their daughter's cross-gender behavior, particularly if she is seen as the "family tomboy," a desirable role (Seil, 1996). Furthermore, some parents of children diagnosed with GID reported disappointment with the sex of their child and admitted a preference for a child of the other sex (Haldeman, 2000; Sabalis et al., 1974). These parents may have unknowingly shaped their child's behavior to satisfy their own unmet desire. However, these explanations must be held tenuously because no empirical support was found in replication studies (Bradley & Zucker, 1990).

Level of physical attractiveness may also play a role in the development of cross-gender behaviors. Green (1987) found that parents of behaviorally feminine boys recalled that their sons were beautiful and feminine as infants. In addition, college students judged girls diagnosed with GID as less attractive, less beautiful, less pretty, and less cute than girls not diagnosed with GID (Fridell, Zucker, Bradley, & Maing, 1996). Levels of physical attractiveness may contribute to child-rearing practices, such as a tendency for parents to respond to the child as if he/she was the other sex (Bradley, Fridell, Maing, & Zucker, 1996; Stoller, 1975). Furthermore, mothers of feminine boys have been found to dress their sons in stereotypically feminine attire (Green, 1974).

There is some evidence that internalized sexism and a constant devaluing of femininity and overvaluing of masculinity also may influence the development of cross-gender behavior in girls (Bradley & Zucker, 1990, 1997). Feminists have argued that the stereotypical feminine role is *not* healthy for girls and women and that gender roles are set up primarily to benefit the maintenance of patriarchal society (Pleck, 1981; Worell & Johnson, 1997). Among adolescent girls, traditional femininity has been linked to depression, lower self-esteem, eating disorders, and diminished positive sexual health (Mahalik et al., 2005; Tolman, 2002; Tolman, Impett, Tracy, & Michael, 2006). These findings are consistent with a broader body of research that has addressed the negative effects of femininity on women's lives (Chodorow, 1978; Diquinzio, 1999; Fauldi, 1991; Fredrickson & Roberts, 1997; Gilligan, 1982; Hare-Mustin & Marecek, 1990; Johnson, Roberts, & Worell, 1999; Miller, 1976; Pipher, 1994; Richards & Larson, 1989; Tavris, 1992; Tolman et al., 2006). Thus, it is not surprising that a girl would behave in accordance with the more valued role and model the behavior of successful and/or male figures in her life.

There is other evidence to suggest that the binary definition of sex and gender informs children's socialization and ultimately shapes societal decisions about gender roles (Hausman, 2000). In a very compelling challenge to the scientific and medical application of the term "gender," Hausman (2000) introduced the term "coercive femininity" to describe a common theme in most autobiographies of transsexual experiences. Hausman suggested that, in response to coercive gender role conditioning, some individuals react with rebellion. But, because they have already internalized the dichotomous definition of gender, these individuals conclude that if they are not "one," they must be "the other." Hausman described the unconscious thought process as "I *won't* be a girl," therefore "I *must* be a boy."

Psychodynamic Explanations

Psychodynamic explanations tend to focus on the maternal role in the development of gender identity (Stoller, 1975). Maternal depression and personality disorders have been reported in GID cases, and these factors may cause ambivalent mother–child relationships (Bradley & Zucker, 1997). Among FtM transsexuals, fathers seem to protect their children from the mothers' aggression and thus establish a "father–son" relationship with them (Stoller, 1975). This relationship encourages the daughter to identify with her father instead of her mother. According to Stoller (1975) and Seil (1996), the opposite is true of MtF transsexuals. These boys tend to form a symbiotic relationship with their mothers, whereas their fathers are distant and rejecting. Furthermore, severe separation anxiety that results in the fantasy of permanent fusion with the mother is another explanation that has been set forth for GID (Person & Ovesey, 1974).

These early explanations, however, were later criticized for their pathogenic view of motherhood and their polarized view of gendered parenting roles (Hare-Mustin, 1988). Furthermore, feminists have questioned the assumption that early exchanges between parental figures and infants can account for later developmental tasks, such as gender identity (Kagan, 1984).

Treatment

Treatment recommendations for gender-variant children and adolescents have been controversial, and some have argued that treatment may actually be harmful (Burke, 1996; Lev, 2004). Opponents have claimed that some interventions, particularly with children, resemble conversion therapies (deemed unethical by the American Psychological Association in 1997 and by the American Psychiatric Association in 1998) and that the diagnosis and eventual treatment may be misused to "cure" children who display early signs of homosexuality (Menvielle, 1998). Defendants refute such claims (Zucker, 1999) and state that treatment is justified because a transgendered lifestyle represents a mental health concern and that the distress of their clients is notable (Zucker, 1999, 2006).

With children, the goal of treatment is to reduce the social ostracism that clients experience, to treat underlying pathologies, and to reduce distress (Zucker, 2006). Behavioral interventions have been identified in the literature as a favored approach to reducing cross-gender behavior (Zucker, 2003). For example, one treatment, known as differential social attention, teaches parents to ignore the child's cross-gender behavior and to reinforce play that mimics gender-stereotypical play. A limitation of this approach is that changes in behavior do not generalize to other environments where the parent is absent (Rekers, 1975). Other interventions have included modeling (Bradley & Zucker, 1990), token economies (Rekers & Kilgus, 1998), inpatient hospitalization (Burke, 1996), and play dates with same-sex peers (Meyer-Bahlburg, 1993).

In addition, some treatment models aim to enhance self-image; for example, the therapist actively informs the client that he is valued as a boy or that she is valued as a girl (Zucker, 1999). This self-validation reportedly encourages self-esteem and a sense of comfort with the "appropriate" sex-specific gender role. Reducing social isolation and providing education is another mode of treatment used with children (Rosenberg, 2002). Though this treatment approach allows for some cross-gender behaviors, success can be claimed only when the child adds "gender-syntonic interests" (p. 621). Thus, the "cure" for GID is the adoption of conformist, gender-typical behaviors.

Overall, therapeutic interventions are deemed more successful with younger children than with adolescents and adults; the prognosis is relatively poor for reducing gender-atypical behavior after puberty (Bradley & Zucker, 1990). Although the above treatments actively work to eliminate gender-atypical behavior, some contemporary psychologists are more sensitive to helping people integrate gender-atypical behaviors into their identity. This type of therapy, however, is primarily employed with adults and adolescents who are considering sex reassignment surgeries; it is rarely used with children (Pleak, 1999). Because of the focus on changing gender-variant behaviors, there has been considerable concern about the use of any treatment with children, particularly because outcome studies rarely examine the child's experience of the treatment protocol (Langer & Martin, 2004). Furthermore, the diagnosis could lead to long-lasting feelings of stigmatization that stem from experiences of discrimination and devaluation (Langer & Martin, 2004). These concerns have led some researchers and clinicians to call for significant reform and even removal of the diagnosis as it applies to children (Langer & Martin, 2004; Vitale, 2005; Winters, 1998).

Adults diagnosed with GID, on the other hand, often seek out psychological evaluation and treatment in order to begin the process of sex reassignment surgery (SRS), and many view treatment as a positive beginning directed toward a life change (Minter, 1999). According to the Standards of Care for the Hormonal and Surgical Sex Reassignment of Gender Dysphoric Persons, outlined by the Harry Benjamin International Gender Dysphoria Association (Meyer et al., 2001), a diagnosis of GID is required for SRS. Unless a client can convince a physician to proceed without following the guidelines, that client must meet the criteria of GID in order to receive medical services (Lev, 2004; Meyer et al., 2001).

There is concern that using the diagnosis as a gateway to SRS compromises the therapeutic relationship (Lev, 2004; Walworth, 1997). Many clients who seek therapy as a means to surgery are aware of the requirements (Denny & Roberts, 1997). The integrity of therapy and the client's ability to be genuine and honest are threatened by the additional role the therapist plays as "gatekeeper" to SRS (Walworth, 1997). Rachlin (2002) concluded that gatekeeping is not necessarily harmful to the therapeutic alliance because individuals who are "there for a letter" are completely satisfied after having received that letter. Rachlin's study did, however, indicate that a sizeable number of clients were also seeking help with transitioning and other personal problems. As we discuss later, there remains considerable debate as to whether the diagnosis as an entry point for SRS is appropriate.

SRS also has its opponents. For example, McHugh (2004) has accused proponents of surgical treatment as "cooperating with a mental illness" (p. 36). McHugh argued that "we psychiatrists would do better to concentrate on trying to fix their minds and not their genitalia" (p. 36). Rather than helping his clients to accept and adjust healthily to a different gender identity, McHugh's therapeutic goals include eliminating gender-variant behaviors and preventing them in the future. Yet, because less than 1% of post-surgical clients report gender dysphoria and because personal satisfaction rates are high, SRS is widely accepted as successful in alleviating GID symptoms (Kuiper & Cohen-Kettinis, 1998; Pfafflin, 1992). Certain characteristics are likely to predict poor SRS outcome however, and these include substance abuse, marriage, older age, limited social support, and psychosocial instability (Pfafflin, 1992).

There is some evidence in the literature that psychotherapy can be used to address transgender concerns; however, there is disagreement about the purpose of therapeutic outcomes. Meyenburg (1999, p. 306), for example, defined success as clients' return to their "innate" gender, as dictated by genetic sex. He recounted the largely "successful" story of Holger, who after psychoanalytic treatment "had abandoned all desire to be female, his fetishistic interests had disappeared, and he was developing a clearly heterosexual identity" (p. 312). Meyenberg's language often reveals an extremely rigid, homophobic conception of what a "healthy" gender identity is according to his conceptualization. Although he supports SRS as a last resort, Meyenberg has cautioned against starting hormonal treatment or scheduling surgery "too soon."

Lev (2004), however, argued for a more affirming therapy that transforms the gatekeeping model into one that is rooted in advocacy, education, and support. From this perspective, the therapist actively encourages empowerment and "permits" flexibility in gender expression, which ultimately supports the client in making decisions about SRS. Furthermore, there is a focus on dealing with the loss and isolation that is often associated with transition (Kuiper & Cohen-Kettinis, 1998; Lev, 2004). A number of clinicians and researchers have noted that there are challenges for relatives of transgendered people, and some form of therapeutic attention should be focused on helping the client and the family together to deal with the process of accepting gender variance and possible transitioning (Cooper, 1999; Lev, 2004).

Transgender Health Concerns

In the United States, health care has emerged as a focal point of debate because it is one of the most pressing needs in transgender life. Regardless of whether the treatment being sought is trans-related, providers often refuse any medical treatment to transgendered patients (Hong, 2002). Krieger (2000) described health-care discrimination as occurring simultaneously on several levels, including overt/covert, institutional, and interpersonal. Overt discrimination emerges mainly with regard to SRS-related services: specific clauses that outright deny any coverage for transition-related procedures (e.g., hormone therapy, psychological treatment, breast implants, phalloplasty, vaginoplasty). Covert discrimination occurs when transgendered patients are denied coverage based on loose interpretations of trans-services exclusion clauses (Hong, 2002). Hong cited the example of an insurer who denied a transgendered patient coverage for liver damage because it *may* have resulted from hormone therapy. Other instances of excluding services unrelated to SRS are denying an FtM patient gynecological services or a non-transsexual transgender-related medical coverage, refusing to reimburse anti-depression medication, or refusing to test an MtF patient for prostate cancer (Transgender Law Center, 2004; Hong, 2002).

Discrimination is present in daily provider–patient interactions (Lind, 2004). Such discrimination can be as simple as refusing to refer to a patient by the preferred pronoun or name, invasive and inappropriate questioning about a patient's genitalia, and denying access to gender-specific restrooms or changing facilities (Transgender Law Center, 2004; Krieger, 2000; Hong, 2002). Lombardi (2001) found that providers' attitudes and lack of sensitivity toward transgendered clients do influence an individual's decision to seek treatment and to remain in treatment. Hong wrote about the worst-possible case of a Washington, DC, woman who was struck by a car. Once ambulance workers realized that she was transgender, administration of care was stopped and replaced with joking and insults. The woman (Maria Elena Fernandez) died, and a jury awarded $2.9 million to her family in a wrongful death suit (Hong, 2002).

Unfortunately, the current research paints a bleak picture of transgender health and safety. Transgendered populations appear to be particularly vulnerable to HIV infection, possibly even more so than bisexual and homosexual men (Lombardi, 2001). According to a San Francisco study (Clements-Nolle, Wilkinson, Kitano, & Marx, 2001), 27% of transgendered participants were HIV positive. A Washington, DC, study (Xavier, 2000) yielded similar results; 25% of transgender participants tested positive for HIV.

Harassment and physical violence are other urgent health concerns for transgendered people. The San Francisco assessment (Clements-Nolle, Wilkinson, et al., 2001) also showed that 68% of MtFs and 55% of FtMs had been forced into having sex at least once in their life. Lombardi et al. (2001) sampled 402 transgendered participants, and nearly 60% reported that they had been a victim of violence or harassment over the course of their life. Twenty-six percent said that they had experienced violence, and 37.1% reported having experienced economic discrimination.

Focus groups of transgendered youth (ages 15–21) revealed that their greatest concerns were safety issues related to their transgender status (Grossman & D'Augelli, 2006). It is not surprising that as many as 61% of high school students reported having seen a gender-variant classmate verbally harassed; 21% reported having seen a gender-variant classmate physically abused (Wilchins & Taylor, 2006). In their recent report, GenderPAC (Wilchins & Taylor, 2006) documented 50 transgendered people under the age of 30 who were murdered because of gender variance. Most of the victims were biologically male, economically disadvantaged, and/or ethnic minorities (91%); most were killed by other boys/men of their same age.

In addition to the above concerns, and perhaps because of them, transgendered populations exhibit high rates of suicide. Research indicates that approximately one-third of transgendered individuals have attempted suicide (Clements-Nolle, Marx, & Katz, 2006; Kenagy, 2005). Furthermore, transgendered populations are at higher risks for homelessness, poverty, drug and alcohol addiction, prostitution, and AIDS (Seil, 1996). Clements-Nolle and colleagues (2006) demonstrated that gender discrimination and physical victimization are strong factors in some of the psychosocial difficulties among transgendered people. They concluded that social discrimination and rejection may have more negative effects on transgendered individuals than on LGB individuals because transgender status challenges sexuality norms as well as gender norms. Despite the numerous health problems and risks that plague the transgender community, their access to health care remains severely limited.

Current Controversies

Much of the psychological literature published about GID seems to be limited by an "either/or" perspective and a very polarized nature/nurture debate. This either/or nature/nurture perspective limits current conceptualizations of GID (and, for that matter, other gender/sexuality "disorders") because the nature/nurture perspective is so loosely based on a gender binary (Hausman, 2000). Clearly, this binary notion of gender is limited because, in using it to conceptualize psychological research, scholars attempt to cast a wide net in determining normative gender behavior and identity, which almost always ignores ways in which race, class, and other demographics interact with gender in highly personal and complex ways (Roen, 2006). Furthermore, because of the important political implications of GID, the diagnosis and the identity itself have been used as catalysts for building activism, which, as Wilchins (2004) acknowledged, splinters various groups of people into different camps about the role of the diagnosis in gaining access to health care and civil liberties. In this section we discuss the major arguments currently debated by scholars and activists.

Does GID Qualify as a Mental Disorder?

One issue of controversy concerning GID is whether the criteria actually meet the standards for a mental disorder classification. According to the *DSM-IV-TR* (American Psychiatric Association, 2000), mental disorders are "associated with present distress or disability or with a significantly increased risk of suffering..." (American Psychiatric Association, 2000, p. XXXI). The condition must also "be considered a manifestation of a behavioral, psychological, or biological dysfunction in the individual" (American Psychiatric Association, 2000, p. XXX). With regard to "distress," the *DSM* authors fail to specify whether stress need be inherent, or could be socially imposed, to be a symptom of a mental disorder (Langer & Martin 2004). It is generally agreed that distress associated with GID results from others' reactions to the gender variance, rather than from the cross-gender behaviors themselves. Whether or not this type of indirect stress qualifies the condition for a mental disorder remains contested (Wilson et al., 2002).

Wilson (1998) compared the GID debate to the arguments presented during the movement to eliminate homosexuality from the *DSM*. Wilson argued that the American Psychiatric Association rejected inherent distress as a qualifier for mental disorders by removing homosexuality from the *DSM*. She cited a brief filed by the American Psychiatric Association in 1994:

> The harmful effects of prejudice, discrimination, and violence, however, are not limited to such bodily or pecuniary consequences...The effects can include depression...and efforts to rationalize the experience by viewing one's victimization as just punishment. Gay people, like members of other groups that are subject to social prejudice, also frequently come to internalize society's negative stereotypes. (p. 7)

There is an apparent inconsistency between the American Psychiatric Association's position on distress as a symptom of GID but not of homosexuality. The American Psychiatric Association refused to "blame the victim" in the case of stress associated with homosexuality, but the opposite stance is taken with transgendered individuals who suffer from negative social reactions (Wilson, 1998).

In response to the "present distress" criterion (American Psychiatric Association, 2000, XXXI), researchers have offered high comorbidity rates in individuals with GID as proof of pathology (Rekers & Moray, 1989; Zucker & Bradley, 1995). Data suggest that transgendered people do have higher rates of substance abuse and depression than is found in the general population and that, among children with GID, levels of general psychopathology are equal to those of other children with various mental disorders (Clements-Nolle, Marx, Guzman, & Katz, 2001; Zucker & Bradley, 1995). Again, it is difficult to ascertain if mental health concerns, such as depression and anxiety, are brought on by social stigmatization and discrimination or were already present when the gender-variant behavior began. Wilson et al. (2002) have claimed that harassment is without question a point of distress for people who are gender variant and that, without such harassment, the behavior might not be distressing to the person at all.

The criteria for GID, as stated in the *DSM-IV-TR* (American Psychiatric Association, 2000), are also under fire for lack of transparency. A popular accusation is that the *DSM-IV-TR* fails to differentiate between sex, a biological category, and gender, a social construction. Bartlett, Vasey, and Bukowski (2000) argued that discomfort with one's biological sex is completely separate and different from discomfort with one's gender assignment. They raised the question of why the *DSM-IV-TR* equates an individual who finds her or his genitals revolting with an individual who enjoys cross-gender clothing and activities. There is particular opposition to the fact that the diagnosis may be given without documentation that the individual is uncomfortable with her or his biological sex. This leaves patients vulnerable to changing social definitions of what is feminine and what is masculine (Wilson & Hammond, 1996).

In addition to critiques of the diagnostic criteria, Langer and Martin (2004) challenged the lack of reliability and validity of diagnosis. The extent to which parts of the diagnosis are open to interpretation affects its reliability, as clinicians may be more influenced by personal standards here than they are in diagnosing other disorders (Langer & Martin, 2004; Winters, 2007). For example, the *DSM* states that "To varying degrees, they adopt the behavior, dress and mannerisms of the other sex" (p. 577). It is left to the clinician to decide where the line is drawn along these "varying degrees" between disordered and healthy. There is minimal empirical evidence of diagnostic reliability for boys and none for girls (Langer & Martin, 2004). With regard to validity, researchers will be able to accomplish little until the debates about the definition of a mental disorder are resolved.

Furthermore, the exact language of the *DSM-IV-TR* is vague in that it does not provide guidelines for nonconformity to traditional gender behaviors and intrapsychic illness (Lev, 2004). For example, the current diagnostic criteria for GID include (a) a strong or persistent *cross-gender identification* and (b) persistent discomfort with one's sex or a sense of inappropriateness in the *gender role associated with one's sex*. Implicit in the phrases "cross-gender identification" and "gender role associated with one's sex" is an assumption that notions of femininity and masculinity are clearly definable standards for all people. However, endorsements of traditional feminine and masculine norms do vary among racial and ethnic groups, nationalities, life stages, genders, and sexual orientations (Kimmel, 2004; Levant & Richmond, 2007), and, within multicultural settings, there are differences in the degree of tolerance and acceptance of gender variance (Newman, 2002). In addition, as mentioned earlier, the feminist movement in the United States challenged traditional feminine norms, which has resulted in highly variable role expectations for girls and women. Attempts to satisfy such expectations have become an increasingly difficult process as role expectations and behaviors vary by social context (Gillespie & Eisler, 1992; O'Neil, Good, & Holmes, 1995).

The Insurance Debate

An argument that remains at the forefront of debates on GID involves the psychotherapist's involvement in health care for transgendered people. One camp states that having a diagnostic label of mental disorder benefits the transgender community by securing legal rights and health benefits (Gagne et al., 1997). Others maintain that systems already discriminate against gender-variant people and that the diagnosis benefits only a specific subset of the transgender population (Bornstein, 1994; Wilchins, 1997). Again, notably absent from these arguments are issues of class and race and how they interact with gender identity in a system of inequality (Lorber, 2000).

Several arguments have been made that the GID diagnosis is liberating for transgendered people seeking sex reassignment surgery because it provides a gateway to insurance reimbursements. The logic is that having a certified illness justifies financing treatment, particularly because most insurance companies (that are willing to cover SRS) will do so only if the patient has been officially diagnosed with GID. Many of the debates about the utility of GID for health-care access are exclusive dialogues that ignore two populations within the transgender community: those who are not seeking SRS and those who have no health-care insurance (Lev, 2004). These individuals do not benefit from the GID gateway and may suffer from additional stigmatization because of the diagnosis. As it stands, the GID diagnosis prevents a space for healthy transgendered living because its very presence legitimizes discriminatory policies and attitudes toward transgendered people and steers them toward a "medical makeover" (Winters, 2007).

Others fear for the future of academic debates should GID be removed from future editions of the *DSM* (Bryant, 2006). The concern is that its removal would lead to the absence of any attention and discussion about transgendered populations. Along the same lines, proponents of the diagnosis argue that the label can help to secure legal and social rights, such as protecting children who wish to cross-dress in school (Bryant, 2006; Newman, 2002).

In response to the health-care defense, opponents of the diagnosis are wary of playing into an already discriminatory and hierarchical system. The current discourse on GID and health care fails to acknowledge larger societal issues at play. To argue that GID provides access to insurance reimbursements is to endorse the false impression that the current US health-care system offers equal access. In reality, 15.8% of the US population did not have health insurance coverage in 2006 (DeNavas-Walt, Proctor, & Smith, 2007). Race and class have undeniable influence over who gets health coverage. Rates of uninsured individuals increase as household income decreases, and minority populations have higher percentages of uninsured people (DeNavas-Walt et al., 2007). Kenagy's

(2005) assessment of transgender health needs revealed that economically disadvantaged participants were less likely than others to seek health services.

There is also questionable success in using the diagnosis to access insurance reimbursements (Winters, 2007). Transgendered people are often denied coverage, regardless of whether the medical request applies to a gender transition (Human Rights Commission, 2006). Regarding SRS, many insurance companies exclude coverage or offer it only as a group purchase option. The determining factor is whether a provider considers the procedure to be cosmetic or "medically necessary." Dasti (2002) criticized this rigid and narrow conceptualization of medical necessity. He argued that the definition should be expanded "to account for alleviation of socio-legal burdens imposed upon transgendered patients by the binary sex-classification system" (p. 1743). Such a definition pushes the concept of health beyond immediate physical state and takes into consideration factors such as mental, social, and financial health.

Recommendations to Ensure Insurance Coverage for SRS

In order to address the differential coverage for SRS, several attempts have been made to modify existing health-care plans. In 2001, San Francisco became the first US jurisdiction and employer to remove transgender health access exclusion from their health-care policy plan (Human Rights Commission, 2006). Despite fears that the surgery would be over-utilized, the transgender health benefit program has not added any additional costs and has been deemed more affordable than other more routine procedures. Because of this, 78 companies have agreed to remove the exclusion clause from their health benefits, thus allowing their employees access to transgender-related health treatment. Furthermore, some countries that offer universal health care, such as Brazil and Cuba, have agreed to cover all medical costs for SRS (Associated Press, 2007). Federal prosecutors in Brazil argued that "sexual reassignment surgery is covered under a constitutional clause guaranteeing medical care as a basic right" (p. 4). If the US government adopted a similar position, SRS could be offered to all people who qualify for it, regardless of the ability to pay.

Recommendations for Reform

Several recommendations for reform of GID have been made in the literature (Drummond, 2008; Vitale, 2005; Winters, 2007). In order to reduce harm, new titles have been set forth, including gender expression deprivation anxiety disorder (GEDAD; Vitale, 2001) and incongruent gender dysphoria (IGD; Drummond, 2008). Advocates believe that a change in terminology is essential in reducing stigmatization and discrimination because the wording of the current title implies that any gender-variant identification or behavior is disordered (Winters, 2007).

In addition, Winters (2007) suggested a change in the "maligning terminology" (p. 2). This refers to a lack of sensitivity often found in the language of transgender researchers, including misuse of pronouns and terms such as "the opposite sex." The *DSM* demonstrates this by repeatedly referring to transsexual women as "males" and "he." Such language completely disregards the individual's self-identification as a woman, hence undermining and invalidating that identity. In the 7th edition of its *Media Reference Guide*, the Gay and Lesbian Alliance Against Defamation (GLAAD; 2006) provided a glossary of terminology and guidelines for respectful discussion of transgendered people, in which the reader is encouraged to address transgendered people by the names and pronouns they have chosen for themselves.

Finally, advocates believe that the criteria of the diagnosis should be reworded to focus on distress, rather than on the actual cross-gender behaviors themselves (Vitale, 2005; Winters, 2007). This would be in line with the current World Professional Association for Transgender Health (WPATH) Standards of Care, and it would limit the risk of over-inclusion and pathologizing of all transgendered people (Winters, 2007; WPATH, 2001).

Some researchers and clinicians have called for the removal of GID as a diagnostic criteria altogether, particularly for children (Langer & Martin, 2004; Pleak, 1999). There is deep concern that the diagnosis does little to differentiate children who are distressed from children who are not distressed by their gender variance (Bartlett et al., 2000). Because of this, opponents believe that the diagnosis serves a particular political agenda, and therefore, a neutral stance should be taken with children who are referred for treatment (Di Ceglie, 1998). Otherwise, clinicians risk social policing and marginalizing gender-variant children (Langer & Martin, 2004; Szasz, 1974).

Future Directions

Many exploratory questions remain unanswered by the current psychological research (Riggle, et al., 2005). The research driven by the GID diagnosis has resulted in an incomplete representation of transgendered identities and behaviors, and future researchers should work to enhance the extent of transgender studies (Harcourt, 2006). Developing and researching new models of mental health support for transgendered people may actually be a promising step toward addressing some of the concerns associated with the GID diagnosis (Bryant, 2006). By focusing particularly on discrimination and stigmatization, researchers' work could be a catalyst for reform and could shift the discourse away from a pathological perspective about gender-variant people.

The research community needs to establish a clearer understanding of who transgendered individuals are and how to recruit participation in research. The Internet is a promising avenue for reaching a stigmatized subpopulation, though the web contains unique challenges and pitfalls for researchers. As the population becomes more visible, researchers should strive to produce more trans-positive literature and should highlight personal narratives that focus on the lived experience of transgendered people (Elze, 2007; Raj, 2002).

In addition, more attention should be paid to within-group diversity, and future researchers should identify the unique needs of trans-identified subgroups (Raj, 2002). Such groups include youth and seniors, parents and children, racial minorities, people without health insurance, people living with HIV/AIDS, people with disabilities, and people with substance abuse concerns. Researchers also should address the needs of the families of transgendered people. Such research should stem from a supportive and systemic conceptual framework (Lev, 2004).

Because many graduate programs do not offer courses in sexual or gender identity development, researchers should examine best practices for clinical training and supervision (Lev, 2004; Raj, 2002). Training guidelines should be expanded and assessed for quality assurance. Clinical assessment tools that eliminate a pathological focus should be developed and validated. Following the initiatives of GenderPAC (Wilchins & Taylor, 2006), psychoeducational workshops should continue to be developed and assessed to help parents and educators create safe schools for transgendered children. Additional workshops and seminars should be created for medical and legal enforcement personnel.

Clearly, the GID debate is quite complex and should be approached with sensitivity and respect. Scholarly exchanges must account for the larger sociopolitical context that exists and should include the voices of underrepresented communities, particularly as the American Psychiatric Association updates the *DSM* for the new edition scheduled to be published in 2012.

References

American Psychiatric Association. (1980). *Diagnostic and statistical manual of mental disorders* (3rd ed.). Washington DC: Author.
American Psychiatric Association. (1987). *Diagnostic and statistical manual of mental disorders* (3rd ed. text rev.). Washington DC: Author.
American Psychiatric Association. (1994). *Diagnostic and statistical manual of mental disorders* (4th ed.). Washington DC: Author.
American Psychiatric Association. (2000). *Diagnostic and statistical manual of mental disorders* (4th ed. text rev.). Washington DC: Author.
Associated Press. (2007, August 17). Brazil to offer free sex-change operations: Court rules the surgery is a constitutional right for residents. Retrieved June 15, 2008 from: http://www.msnbc.msn.com/id/20323334
Avery, P. G. (2002). Political socialization, tolerance, and sexual identity. *Theory and Research in Social Education, 30*, 190–197.
Bartlett, N. H., Vasey, P. L., & Bukowski, W. M. (2000). Is gender identity disorder in children a mental disorder? *Sex Roles, 43*, 753–785.
Blanchard, R., & Sheridan, P. M. (1992). Sibship size, sibling sex ratio, birth order, and parental age in homosexual and nonhomosexual gender dysphorics. *Journal of Nervous and Mental Disease, 180*, 40–47.
Bockting, W. O., & Ehrbar, R. D. (2005). Commentary: Gender variance, dissonance, or identity disorder? *Journal of Psychology & Human Sexuality, 17*(3–4), 125–134.
Boehmer, U. (2002). Twenty years of public health research: Inclusion of lesbian, gay, bisexual, and transgender populations. *American Journal of Public Health, 92*, 1125–1130.
Bolin, A. (1992). Coming of age among transsexuals. In T. L. Whitehead & B. V. Reid (Eds.), *Gender constructs and social issues* (pp. 13–39). Champaign, IL: University of Illinois Press.
Bornstein, K. (1994). *Gender outlaw: On men, women, and the rest of us.* New York: Routledge.
Bowen, D. J., Bradford, J., & Powers, D. (2006). Comparing sexual minority status across sampling methods and populations. *Women & Health, 44*(2), 121–134.
Bowker, G. C., & Star, S. L. (2000). *Sorting things out: Classification and its consequences.* Cambridge, MA: MIT Press.
Bradley, S. J., Fridell, S. R., Maing, D. M., & Zucker, K. (1996). Physical attractiveness of girls with gender identity disorder. *Archives of Sexual Behavior, 25*, 17–32.
Bradley S. J., & Zucker, K. J. (1990). Gender identity disorder and psychosexual problems in children and adolescents. *Canadian Journal of Psychiatry, 35*, 477–484.
Bradley, S. J., & Zucker, K. J. (1997). Gender identity disorder: A review of the past 10 years. *Journal of the American Academy of Child and Adolescent Psychiatry, 36*, 872–880.
Bryant, K. (2006). Making gender identity disorder of childhood: Historical lessons for contemporary debates. *Sexuality Research & Social Policy, 3*(3), 23–39.
Burke, P. (1996). *Gender shock: Exploding the myths of male and female.* New York: Anchor Books.
Chodorow, N. (1978). Mothering, object-relations, and the female Oedipal configuration. *Feminist Studies, 4*, 137–158.
Chung, W. C. J., De Vries, G. J., & Swaab, D. F. (2002). Sexual differentiation of the bed nucleus of the stria terminalis in humans may extend into adulthood. *Journal of Neuroscience, 22*, 1027–1033.
Clements-Nolle, K., Marx, R., Guzman, R., & Katz, M. (2001). HIV prevalence, risk behaviors, health care use, and mental health status of transgender persons: Implications for public health intervention. *American Journal of Public Health, 91*, 915–921.
Clements-Nolle, K., Marx, R., & Katz, M. (2006). Attempted suicide among transgender persons: The influence of gender-based discrimination and victimization. *Journal of Homosexuality, 51*(3), 53–69.
Clements-Nolle, K., Wilkinson, W., Kitano, K., & Marx, R. (2001). HIV prevention and health service needs of the transgender community in San Francisco. In W. Bockington & S. Kirk (Eds.), *Transgender and HIV: Risk preventions and care* (pp. 69–89). Binghampton, NY: Haworth.
Cohen-Kettenis, P. T., & Gooren, L. J. G. (1999). Transsexualism: A review of etiology, diagnosis, and treatment. *Journal of Psychosomatic Research, 46*, 315–333.
Conway, L. (2006). *Basic TG/TS/IS information.* Retrieved June 6, 2008, from http://ai.eecs.umich.edu/people/conway/conway.html

Cooper, K. (1999). Practice with transgendered youth and their families. In G. P. Mallon (Ed.), *Social services with transgendered youth* (pp. 111–130). Binghamton, NY: Haworth.

Dasti, J. (2002). Advocating a broader understanding of the necessity of sex-reassignment surgery under Medicaid. *New York University Law Review, 77,* 1738–1775.

DeNavas-Walt, C., Proctor, B., & Smith, J. (2007). *Income, poverty, and health insurance coverage in the United States: 2006.* Retrieved June 18, 2008, from U.S. Census Bureau, Housing and Household Economic Statistics Division: http://www.census.gov/prod/2007pubs/p60-233.pdf

Denny, D., & Roberts, J. (1997). Results of a questionnaire on the standards of care of the Harry Benjamin International Dysphoria Association. In B. Bullough, V. L. Bullough, & J. Elias (Eds.), *Gender blending* (pp. 320–336). Amherst, NY: Prometheus Books.

Di Ceglie, D. (1995). Gender identity disorders in children and adolescents. *British Journal of Hospital Medicine, 53,* 251–261.

Di Ceglie, D. (1998). *A stranger in my own body: Atypical gender identity development and mental health.* London: Karnac Books.

Diquinzio, P. (1999). *The impossibility of motherhood.* New York: Routledge.

Drummond, M. (2008, August 21). *GID reform advocates.* Retrieved August 21, 2008, from www.gidreform.org/advocate.html#drummond

Ehrhardt, A. A., & Baker, S. W. (1974). Fetal androgens, human central nervous system differentiation, and behavior sex differences. In R. C. Friedman, R. M. Richart, & R. L. Vande Wiele (Eds.), *Sex differences in behavior* (pp. 33–51). New York: Wiley.

Elze, D. E. (2007). Research with sexual minority youths: Where do we go from here? *Journal of Gay & Lesbian Social Services, 18*(2), 73–99.

Fauldi, S. (1991). *Backlash: The undeclared war against American women.* New York: Doubleday.

Fink, P. J. (2005). Sexual and gender identity disorders: Discussion of questions for *DSM-V*. *Journal of Psychology & Human Sexuality, 17*(3–4), 117–123.

Foucault, M. (1990). *The use of pleasure.* New York: Random House.

Fredrickson, B. L., & Roberts, T-A. (1997). Objectification theory. *Psychology of Women Quarterly, 21,* 173–206.

Fridell, S. R., Zucker, K. J., Bradley, S. J., & Maing, D. M. (1996). Physical attractiveness of girls with gender identity disorder. *Archives of Sexual Behavior, 25,* 17–31.

Gagne, P., Tewksbury, R., & McGaughey, D. (1997). Coming out and crossing over: Identity formation and proclamation in a transgender community. *Gender & Society, 11,* 479–503.

Gay and Lesbian Alliance Against Defamation (GLAAD). (2006). *Media reference guide* (7th ed.). Retrieved June 17, 2008, from: http://www.glaad.org/media/guide/GLAAD_MediaRefGuide_7thEdition.pdf

Gillespie, B. L., & Eisler, R. M. (1992). Development of the feminine gender role stress scale: A cognitive–behavioral measure of stress, appraisal, and coping for women. *Behavior Modification, 16,* 426–438.

Gilligan, C. (1982). *In a different voice: Psychological theory and women's development.* Cambridge, MA: Harvard University Press.

Gooren, L. (1990). The endocrinology of transsexualism: A review and commentary. *Psychoneuroendocrinology, 15,* 3–14.

Gooren, L. (2006). The biology of human psychosexual differentiation. *Hormones and Behavior, 50,* 589–601.

Gorski, R. A. (2002). Hypothalamic imprinting by gonadal steroid hormones. *Advances in Experimental Medicine and Biology, 511,* 57–70.

Green, R. (1974). *Sexual identity conflict in children and adults.* New York: Basic Books.

Green, R. (1987). *The sissy boy syndrome and the development of sexuality.* New Haven, CT: Yale University Press.

Green, R. (2000). Birth order and ratio of brothers to sisters in transsexuals. *Psychological Medicine, 30,* 789–795.

Grossman, A. H., & D'Augelli, A. R. (2006). Transgender youth: Invisible and vulnerable. *Journal of Homosexuality, 51,* 111–128.

Haldeman, D. (2000). Gender atypical youth: Clinical and social issues. *School Psychology Review, 29,* 192–200.

Harcourt, J. (2006). Current issues in lesbian, gay, bisexual, and transgender (LGBT) health: Introduction. *Journal of Homosexuality, 51,* 1–11.

Hare-Mustin, R. T. (1988). Family change and gender differences: Implications for theory and practice. *Family Process, 37,* 36–41.

Hare-Mustin, R., & Marecek, J. (1990). *Psychology and the construction of gender.* New Haven, CT: Yale University Press.

Hausman, B. L. (2000). Do boys have to be boys? Gender, narrativity, and the John/Joan case. *NWSA Journal, 12,* 114–138.

Hirschfeld, M. (1923). Die intersexuelle konstitution. *Jahrbuch Fuer Sexuelle Zwischenstufen, 23*, 3–27.
Hoenig, J., & Kenna, J. C. (1978). Verbal characteristics of male and female transsexuals. *Psychiatria Clinica, 11*, 233–236.
Hong, K. E. (2002). Categorical exclusions: Exploring legal responses to health care discrimination against trans. *Columbia Journal of Gender & Law, 11*, 88–126.
Human Rights Commission. (2006). *San Francisco city and county transgender health benefit* [Letter from Human Rights Commission]. Retrieved June 17, 2008, from: http://www.hrc.org/issues/transgender/7782.htm
Johnson, N. G., Roberts, M. C., & Worell, J. (1999). *Beyond appearance: A new look at adolescent girls.* Washington, DC: American Psychological Association.
Kagan, D. M. (1984). Acquisition and significance of sex-typing and sex-role identity. In M. L. Hoffman & I. W. Hoffman (Eds.), *Review of child development research* (Vol. 1, pp. 137–168). New York: Russell Sage Foundation.
Kenagy, G. P. (2005). Transgender health: Findings from two needs assessment studies in Philadelphia. *Health and Social Work, 30*, 19–26.
Kimmel, A. J. (2004). Ethical issues in social psychology research. In C. Sansone, C. C. Morf, & A. T. Panter (Eds.), *The Sage handbook of methods in social psychology* (pp. 45–70). Thousand Oaks, CA: Sage.
Krieger, N. (2000). Discrimination and health. In L. Berkman & I. Kawachi (Eds.), *Social epidemiology* (pp. 36–75). Oxford: Oxford University Press.
Kruijver, F., Zhou, J., Pool, C., Hofman, M., Gooren, L., & Swaab, D. (2000). Male to female transsexuals have female neuron numbers in a limbic nucleus. *Journal of Clinical Endocrinology Metabolism, 85*, 818–827.
Kuiper, A. J., & Cohen-Kettenis, P. T. (1998). Gender role reversal among postoperative transsexuals. *International Journal of Transgenderism, 2*. Available at http://www.symposion.com/ijt/ijtc0502.htm
Langer, S. J., & Martin, J. I. (2004). How dresses can make you mentally ill: Examining gender identity disorder in children. *Child and Adolescent Social Work Journal, 21*, 5–23.
Lev, A. I. (2004).*Transgender emergence.* Binghamton, NY: Haworth.
Lev, A. I. (2005). Disordering gender identity: Gender identity disorder in the *DSM-IV-TR*. *Journal of Psychology and Human Sexuality, 17*(3/4), 35–69.
Levant, R. F., & Richmond, K. (2007). A review of research on masculinity ideologies using the male role norms inventory. *Journal of Men's Studies, 15*, 130–146.
Levant, R., Richmond, K., Cook, S., House, A. T., & Aupont, M. (2007). The Femininity Ideology Scale: Factor structure, reliability, convergent and discriminant validity, and social contextual variation. *Sex Roles, 57*, 373–383.
Lind, A. (2004). Legislating the family: Heterosexist bias in social welfare policy frameworks. *Journal of Sociology & Social Welfare, 31*, 21–35.
Lombardi, E. (2001). Enhancing transgender health care. *American Journal of Public Health, 91*, 869–872.
Lombardi, E., Wilchins, R. A., Priesing, D., & Malouf, D. (2001). Gender violence: Transgender experiences with violence and discrimination. *Journal of Homosexuality, 42*, 89–101.
Lorber, J. (2000). Using gender to undo gender: A feminist degendering movement. *Feminist Theory, 79*, 79–95.
Mahalik, J., Morray, E., Coonerty-Femiano, A., Ludlow, L., Slattery, S., & Smiler, A. (2005). Development of the conformity to feminine norms inventory. *Sex Roles, 52*, 417–435.
Mathy, R. M., Schillace, M., Coleman, S. M., & Berquist, B. E. (2002). Methodological rigor with internet samples: New ways to reach underrepresented populations. *CyberPsychology & Behavior, 5*, 253–266.
McHugh, P. (2004). Surgical sex. *First Things, 147*, 34–38.
Menvielle, E. J. (1998). Gender identity disorder. *Journal of the American Academy of Child & Adolescent Psychiatry, 37*, 243–244.
Meyenburg, B. (1999). Gender identity disorder in adolescents: Outcomes of psychotherapy. *Adolescence, 34*, 305–313.
Meyer, W., Bockting, W., Cohen-Kettenis, P., Coleman, E., DiCeglie, D., Devor, H. et al. (2001). *Standards of care for gender identity disorders* (6th ed.). Düsseldorf: Symposium Publications.
Meyer-Bahlburg, H. F. (1993, October). *Gender identity disorder in young boys: A treatment protocol.* Paper presented at the XIII International Symposium on Gender Dysphoria, New York, NY.
Meyerowitz, J. (2002). *How sex changed.* Cambridge, MA: Harvard University Press.
Migeon, C. J. & Wisniewski, A. B. (2003). Human sex differentiation and its abnormalities. *Best Practice and Research in Clinical Obstetrics and Gynecology, 17*, 1–18.
Miller, J. B. (1976). *Toward a new psychology of women.* Boston, MA: Beacon Press.
Minter, S. (1999). Diagnosis and treatment of gender identity disorder in children. In M. Rottnek (Ed.), *Sissies and tomboys* (pp. 9–32). New York: New York University Press.
Moebius, M. M. (1998). Gender identity disorder and psychosexual problems in children and adults. *Journal of the American Academy of Child and Adolescent Psychiatry, 37*, 337–338.

Money, J. (1968). *Sex errors of the body*. Baltimore: Johns Hopkins University Press.
Money, J. (1981). The development of sexuality and eroticism in human kind. *Quarterly Review of Biology, 56*, 379–404.
Money, J. (1994a).*Sex errors of the body and related syndromes*. Baltimore, MD: Brookes.
Money, J. (1994b). The concept of gender identity disorder in childhood and adolescence after 39 years. *Journal of Sex and Marital Therapy, 20*, 163–176.
Newman, L. K. (2002). Sex, gender, and culture: Issues in the definition, assessment, and treatment of gender identity disorder. *Clinical Child Psychology and Psychiatry, 7*, 1359–1045.
O'Neil, J. M., Good, G. E., & Holmes, S. (1995). Fifteen years of theory and research on men's gender role conflict: New paradigms for empirical research. In R. F. Levant & W. S. Pollack (Eds.), *A new psychology of men* (pp. 164–206). New York: Basic Books.
Olsson, E. S., & Moller, A. R. (2003). On the incidence and sex ratio of transsexualism in Sweden: 1972–2002. *Archives of Sexual Behavior, 32*, 381–386.
Peletz, M. G. (2006). Transgenderism and gender pluralism in Southeast Asia since early modern times. *Current Anthropology, 47*, 309–325.
Person, E., & Ovesey, L. (1974). The transsexual syndrome in males II: Primary transsexualism. *American Journal of Psychotherapy, 28*, 4–20.
Pfafflin, F. (1992). Regrets after sexual reassignment surgery. In W. O. Bockting & E. Coleman (Eds.), *Interdisciplinary approaches in clinical management* (pp. 65–89). New York: Haworth.
Pfafflin, F., Bockting, W. O., Coleman, E., Ekins, R., & King, D. (1998). Part three: The full text of the standards of care.*International Journal of Transgenderism, 2*(2). Available at http://www.symposion.com/ijt/ijtc0405.htm
Pipher, M. (1994). *Reviving Ophelia: Saving the selves of adolescent girls*. New York: Ballantine.
Plante, R. F. (2006). *Sexualities in context: A social perspective*. Boulder, CO: Westview.
Pleak, R. (1999). Ethical issues in diagnosing and treating gender-dysphoric children. In M. Rottnek (Ed.), *Sissies and tomboys* (pp. 34–51). New York: New York University Press.
Pleck, J. H. (1981). *The myth of masculinity*. Cambridge, MA: MIT Press.
Rachlin, K. (2002). Transgender individuals' experiences of psychotherapy. *International Journal of Transgenderism, 6*. Retrieved on June 17, 2008, from: http://www.symposion.com/ijt/ijtvo06no01_03.htm
Raj, R. (2002). Toward a transpositive therapeutic model: Developing clinical sensitivity and cultural competence in the effective support of transsexual and transgender clients. *International Journal of Transgenderism, 6*. Retrieved June 17, 2008, from: http://www.symposion.com/ijt/ijtvo06no02_04.htm
Rekers, G. A. (1975). Stimulus control over sex-typed play in cross-gender identified boys. *Journal of Experimental Child Psychology, 20*, 136–148.
Rekers, G. A., & Kilgus, M. D. (1998). Diagnosis and treatment of gender identity disorders in children and adolescents. In L. VandeCreek & S. Knapp (Eds.), *Innovations in clinical practice: A sourcebook* (Vol. 16, pp. 127–141). Sarasota, FL: Professional Resources Press.
Rekers, G. A., & Moray, S. M. (1989). Personality problems associated with childhood gender disturbance. *Italian Journal of Clinical and Cultural Psychology, 1*, 85–90.
Richards, M. H., & Larson, R. (1989). The life space and socialization of the self: Sex differences in the young adolescent. *Journal of Youth and Adolescence, 18*, 617–626.
Riggle, E. D. B., Rostosky, S. S., & Reedy, C. S. (2005). Online surveys for BGLT research: Issues and techniques. *Journal of Homosexuality, 49*, 1–21.
Roen, K. (2006). Transgender theory and embodiment: The risk of racial marginalization. In S. Stryker & S. Whittle (Eds.), *The transgender studies reader* (pp. 656–665). New York: Routledge.
Rosenberg, M. (2002). Children with gender identity issues and their parents in individual and group treatment. *Journal of the American Academy of Child & Adolescent, 41*, 619–621.
Roughgarden, J. (2004). *Evolution's rainbow: Diversity, gender, and sexuality in nature and people*. Berkeley, CA: University of California Press.
Sabalis, R. F., Frances, A., Appenzeller, S. N., & Moseley, W. (1974). The three sisters: Transsexual male siblings. *American Journal of Psychiatry, 131*, 907–909.
Sedgwick, E. K. (1990). How to bring your kids up gay. *Social Text, 29*, 18–27.
Seil, D. (1996). Transsexuals: The boundaries of sexual identity and gender. In R. P. Cabaj & T. S. Stein (Eds.), *Textbook of homosexuality and mental health* (pp. 743–762). Washington, DC: American Psychiatric Press.
Stoller, R. J. (1975). *Sex and gender: Vol. 2. The transsexual experiment*. London: Hogarth.
Szasz, T. (1974). *The myth of mental illness*. New York: Harper and Row.
Tavris, C. (1992). *Mismeasure of woman*. New York: Simon & Shuster.

Teh, K. (2001). Mak nyahs (male transsexuals) in Malaysia: The influence of culture and religion on their identity. *International Journal of Transgenderism, 5*(3). Available at http://www.symposion.com/ijt/ijtvo05no03_04.htm

Tiefer, L. (1987). Social constructionism and the study of human sexuality. In P. Shaver & C. Hendrick (Eds.), *Sex and gender* (pp. 70–94). Thousand Oaks, CA: Sage.

Tolman, D. L. (2002). *Dilemmas of desire: Teenage girls talk about sexuality*. Cambridge, MA: Harvard University Press.

Tolman, D. L., Impett, E. A., Tracy, A. J., & Michael, A. (2006). Looking good, sounding good: Femininity ideology and adolescent girls' mental health. *Psychology of Women Quarterly, 30*, 85–95.

Torgerson, D. (1986). Between knowledge and politics: Three faces of policy analysis. *Policy Sciences, 19*(1), 33–59.

Transgender Law Center. (2004). *Transgender health and the law: Identifying and fighting health care discrimination* [Pamphlet]. San Francisco, CA: Author.

van Kesteren, P. J., Gooren, L. G. J., & Megens, J. A. (1996). An epidemiological and demographic study of transsexuals in the Netherlands. *Archives of Sexual Behavior, 25*, 598–200.

Vitale, A. M. (2001) Implications of being gender dysphoric: A developmental review. *Gender and Psychoanalysis, 6*, 121–141.

Vitale, A. M. (2005). Rethinking the gender identity disorder terminology in the *diagnostic and statistical manual of mental disorders IV*. Retrieved on June 18, 2008, from: http://www.avitale.com/hbigdatalkplus2005.htm

Walworth, J. (1997). Sex reassignment surgery in male-to-female transsexuals: Client satisfaction in relation to selection criteria. In B. Bullough, V. L. Bullough, & J. Elias (Eds.), *Gender blending* (pp. 352–369). Amherst, NY: Prometheus.

West, C., & Zimmerman, D. H. (1998) Doing gender. In K. A. Myers, C. D. Anderson, & B. J. Risman (Eds.), *Feminist foundations: Toward transforming sociology* (pp. 167–190). Thousand Oaks, CA: Sage.

Whittle, S. (2006). The opposite of sex is politics – The UK Gender Recognition Act and why it is not perfect, just like you and me. *Journal of Gender Studies, 15*, 267–271.

Wilchins, R. (1997). The GID controversy: Gender identity disorder diagnosis harms transsexuals. *Transgender Tapestry, 79*(31), 44–45.

Wilchins, R. (2004). *Queer theory, gender theory*. Los Angeles: Alyson Books.

Wilchins, R., & Taylor, T. (2006). *Fifty under 30: Masculinity and the war on America's youth, a human rights report*. Available at http://www.gpac.org/50under30/50u30.pdf

Wilson, K. (1998, June). *The disparate classification of gender and sexual orientation in American psychiatry*. Paper presented at the meeting of the American Psychiatric Association. Retrieved online June 17, 2008, from: http://www.gidreform.org/kwapa98.html

Wilson, K., & Hammond, B. (1996, March). *Myth, stereotype, and cross-gender identity in the DSM-IV*. Paper presented at the meeting of the Association of Women in Psychology, Portland, OR. Retrieved online June 17, 2008, from: http://www.gidreform.org/kwawp96.html

Wilson, I., Griffin, C., & Wren, B. (2002). The validity of the diagnosis of gender identity disorder. *Clinical Child Psychology and Psychiatry, 7*, 335–351.

Winters, K. K. (1998, June). *The disparate classification of gender and sexual orientation in American psychiatry*. Paper presented at the meeting of the American Psychiatric Association, Toronto, Canada.

Winters, K. (2007). *Issues of GID diagnosis for transsexual women and men*. Retrieved online June 17, 2008, from GID Reform Advocates: http://www.gidreform.org/GID30285a.pdf

Woodson, J. C., Balleine, B. W., & Gorski, R. A. (2002). Sexual experience interacts with steroid exposure to shape the partner preference of rats. *Hormones and Behavior, 42*, 148–157.

World Professional Association for Transgender Health (WPATH). (2001). *Standards of care for the hormonal and surgical sex reassignment of gender dysphoric persons*. Stanford, CA: Author. Available at http://wpath.org/Documents2/socv.pdf

Worell, J., & Johnson, N. G. (1997). *Shaping the future of feminist psychology: Education, research, and practice*. Washington, DC: American Psychological Association.

Xavier, J. M. (2000). *The Washington transgender needs assessment survey*. Retrieved June 17, 2008, from: http://www.gender.org/vaults/wmas.html

Zhou, J., Hoffman, M. A., Gooren, L. J., & Swaab, D. (1995). A sex difference in the human brain and its relationship to transsexuality. *Nature, 378*, 68–70.

Zucker, K. J. (1999). Gender identity disorder in the *DSM-IV*. *Journal of Sex and Marital Therapy, 25*, 5–9.

Zucker, K. (2001). Biological influences on psychosexual differentiation. In R. K. Unger (Ed.), *Handbook of the psychology of women and gender* (pp. 101–115). New York: Wiley.

Zucker, K. J. (2003). The politics and science of reparative therapy. *Archives of Sexual Behavior, 32*, 399–402.

Zucker, K. J. (2006). Gender identity disorder. In D. A. Wolfe & E. J. Mash (Eds.), *Behavioral and emotional disorders in adolescents: Nature, assessment, and treatment* (pp. 535–562). New York: Guilford.

Zucker, K. J., & Bradley, S. J. (1995). *Gender identity disorder and psychosexual problems in children and adolescents*. New York: Guilford.

Zucker, K. J., & Green, R. (1992). Psychosexual disorders in children and adolescents. *Child Psychology and Psychiatry, 33*, 107–151.

Zucker, K. J., & Spitzer, R. L. (2005). Was the gender identity disorder of childhood diagnosis introduced into *DSM-III* as a backdoor maneuver to replace homosexuality? A historical note. *Journal of Sex & Marital Therapy, 31*(1), 31–42.

Chapter 7
Gender, Sexual Orientation, and Vulnerability to Depression

Mark L. Hatzenbuehler, Lori M. Hilt, and Susan Nolen-Hoeksema

According to the World Health Organization (WHO, 2008), depression is the leading cause of disability among all diseases or illnesses. Depression differentially affects certain groups, however. In particular, women (Nolen-Hoeksema & Hilt, 2009) and sexual minorities[1] (Meyer, 2003) are twice as likely to suffer depression as men and heterosexuals, respectively. Previous research has identified several factors that confer risk for depression within these groups, but few attempts have been made to identify common vulnerabilities across groups. In this chapter, we examine shared correlates of risk for depression among both women and sexual minorities, and suggest a novel theoretical framework for integrating these risk factors. This necessarily selective approach overlooks factors that are particularly relevant to one group (e.g., estrogen; Angold, Costello, Erkanli, & Worthman, 1999) as well as factors that have not yet been adequately studied (e.g., potential dysregulation of the HPA axis in sexual minorities due to stress exposure). Nevertheless, we believe that developing a process model that incorporates established risk factors across women and sexual minorities can illuminate common pathways that increase vulnerability to depression for these groups.

In this chapter we describe the epidemiology of depression, and we compare women to men and sexual minorities to heterosexuals. Then we review explanations that attribute group differences in rates of depression to group differences in stress, in interpersonal factors, and in cognitive factors. We summarize common vulnerabilities to depression in women and sexual minorities. Then we provide a theoretical model of how factors associated with being a woman, and/or being in a sexual minority group, can increase vulnerability to depression. We conclude with directions for future research, including specific aspects of the model that require further evidence.

Epidemiology

Fortunately, there now exist a number of epidemiological studies of depression conducted in large, representative samples of the United States and some other countries (e.g., Cochran, Mayes, & Sullivan, 2003; Hasin, Goodwin, Stinson, & Grant, 2005; Kessler et al., 2003). More of these studies

---

M.L. Hatzenbuehler (✉)
Yale University, New Haven, CT, USA

[1] We use the commonly accepted term "sexual minority" to refer to gay, lesbian, and bisexual (LGB) individuals in recognition of the various operationalizations of sexual orientation (e.g., self-identification, sexual behavior, romantic attraction) that exist in the literature. The term "LGB" is used in those instances where specific studies have chosen this term.

have focused on comparisons of women and men than on comparisons of sexual minorities and heterosexuals.

Comparisons of Women and Men

One of the most striking descriptive features of depression is the 2:1 gender difference in prevalence; women are diagnosed with depression at twice the rate of men in adulthood (Kessler et al., 2003). Although actual rates of depression vary cross-culturally, women exhibit higher rates of depression than men do across cultures and sociodemographic groups within cultures (Andrade et al., 2003; Weissman et al., 1996).

Epidemiological studies suggest that major depression will affect one of four women and one of eight men in their lifetimes. For example, the National Comorbidity Study, a nationally representative mental health survey conducted in the United States, reported a lifetime prevalence of major depressive disorder as 21.3% for women and 12.7% for men (Kessler, McGonagle, Swartz, Blazer, & Nelson, 1993; Kessler et al., 2003). The National Epidemiologic Survey on Alcohol and Related Disorders reported slightly lower, but similar, lifetime prevalence rates: 17.1% for women and 9.01% for men (Hasin et al., 2005). Although the 2:1 gender difference in depression has remained constant over many years, the lifetime prevalence of major depression has increased in both men and women in more recent cohorts (Kessler, McGonagle, Hughes, Swartz, & Blazer, 1994).

Developmental Trends

Studies of children show that boys and girls have similar rates of depression and depressive symptom levels until mid-adolescence. Starting around age 13, rates of depressive symptoms and depression diagnoses of girls increase, whereas those of boys stay relatively stable (Galambos, Leadbeater, & Barker, 2004; Hankin et al., 1998; Twenge & Nolen-Hoeksema, 2002). By age 18, the 2:1 gender difference is apparent and remains stable throughout adulthood (Eaton et al., 1997). For further discussion of the emergence of gender differences in depression during adolescence, please see Hilt and Nolen-Hoeksema (2008).

First Onsets Versus Duration of Depression

Women could have a greater prevalence of depression than men do because they experience a greater number of first onsets, longer depressive episodes, a greater recurrence of depression, or all of these. Data from several studies of adults (Eaton et al., 1997; Keller & Shapiro, 1981; Kessler et al., 1993) and children or adolescents (Hankin et al., 1998; Kovacs, 2001) show that the gender difference in depression is due to more first onsets in girls and women than in boys and men, and not to longer durations or more recurrence.

Nolen-Hoeksema and Hilt (2009) suggested that factors associated with gender may contribute to more women than men "crossing the line" from dysphoria into a major depressive episode, but once individuals are in an episode, factors unrelated to gender determine the duration of episodes. For example, major stressors may trigger first onsets of depression, but once a man or a woman is depressed, biological changes may occur, such as changes in neurotransmitter regulation or in metabolism in certain brain regions, which create autonomous processes that maintain depression and trigger recurrences (Post, 1992). In addition, once they are depressed, men and women experience more "dependent" stressors of their own making, such as choosing less satisfying mates, failing to meet educational or career goals, and creating more interpersonal conflict (see Hammen, 2003, for a review). These, in turn, could perpetuate depression. Unfortunately, very few studies have examined predictors of first onset of depression and predictors of the duration or the recurrence of depression separately in men or in women. This is an important area for future research.

Symptom Differences and Treatment Seeking

Depression is a heterogeneous disorder, and many different symptom profiles qualify for the diagnosis. Major epidemiological studies have shown no gender differences in the types of symptoms endorsed by women and men (e.g., Kessler et al., 1993). Some researchers have argued, however, that men may express a more externalizing form of depression characterized by irritability and angry outbursts (see Cochran & Rabinowitz, 2000). This is consistent with comorbidity patterns that suggest that men are more likely to experience comorbid drug or alcohol dependence with mood disorders (e.g., Addis, 2008; Grant, 1995; Kessler et al., 1997).

Magovcevic and Addis (2008) developed a Masculine Depression Scale that includes "internalizing" depressive symptoms (e.g., anhedonia, somatic symptoms) and "externalizing" depressive symptoms (e.g., withdrawal, blunting of affect, inability to experience or express soft emotions). They found that men who endorsed more hegemonic masculine norms scored higher on the externalizing depression symptoms than on the internalizing depression symptoms and prototypic depressive symptoms (e.g., sadness, guilt).

Men who adhere to traditional gender norms are also less likely to seek treatment when they do experience prototypic depressive symptoms, due to stigma against treatment seeking (Addis & Mahalik, 2003). These men thus may be in "double jeopardy:" They do not seek treatment for prototypic symptoms, and if they do see a treatment provider, their externalizing expression of depression might be misunderstood by the provider (Addis, 2008; Good & Wood, 1995).

Comparisons of Sexual Minorities and Heterosexuals

Recent epidemiological research has indicated that sexual minorities are at increased risk for psychiatric morbidity across a wide spectrum of outcomes, including depression (Cochran & Mays, 1994, 2000a, 2000b; Cochran et al., 2003; Fergusson, Horwood, & Beautrais, 1999; Fergusson, Horwood, Ridder, & Beautrais, 2005; Gilman, Cochran, Mays, Ostrow, & Kessler, 2001; Sandfort, de Graaf, Bijl, & Schnabel, 2001). Indeed, a recent meta-analysis showed that sexual minority individuals are twice as likely as heterosexuals to have a lifetime mood disorder and almost three times as likely to have a current (i.e., prior 12 months) mood disorder (Meyer, 2003).

These disparities appear to be most pronounced among gay men, who generally have a higher prevalence of depressive symptoms (Cochran & Mays, 1994), *DSM*-diagnosed major depression (Cochran & Mays, 2000a; Cochran et al., 2003; Fergusson et al., 2005; Gilman et al., 2001; Sandfort et al., 2001), and recurrent major depressive episodes (Cochran & Mays, 2000b) than heterosexual men do. Although some studies have shown differences in rates of depression between heterosexual and sexual minority women (e.g., Gilman et al., 2001), these results have not been entirely consistent; other studies have shown no group differences (e.g., Cochran et al., 2003). In contrast to research on birth cohort effects with respect to depression in heterosexuals, there are currently no such published data with sexual minorities, an important avenue for future study.

Developmental Trends

Sexual minority adolescents also appear to be at increased risk for depression, although research on the mental health of sexual minority youth is lacking relative to research on adults. Recent studies with comparison groups and nationally representative or community samples have documented that sexual minority adolescents are at higher risk for depressive symptoms and major depression than are their heterosexual peers (D'Augelli, 2002; Fergusson et al., 1999; Fergusson et al., 2005; Hatzenbuehler, McLaughlin, & Nolen-Hoeksema, 2008; Russell & Joyner, 2001; Safren & Heimberg, 1999).

Summary

Beginning in middle adolescence, girls and women are more likely than boys and men to experience depression, particularly first onsets of depression, and this gender difference continues throughout the adult life span. Some theorists have argued that men express depression differently than women do, with more irritability and aggression, but this has not been definitively supported. Members of sexual minority groups, especially gay men, also appear to be at greater risk for depression than are heterosexuals. This increased risk appears to begin in adolescence, although more research is needed. In addition, few, if any, population-based surveys have included questions on transgendered identity (Mayer et al., 2008). Consequently, there is a paucity of research on depression in transgendered individuals, which remains an important subgroup to study in future research.

Explanations of Group Differences in Depression

Many different explanations of the group differences in depression have been proposed, and it is beyond the scope of this chapter to review all of them. We refer the reader to more comprehensive reviews of the literature on depression in women and men (Hyde, Mezulis, & Abramson, 2008; Nolen-Hoeksema & Hilt, 2009) and on depression in sexual minorities and heterosexuals (Meyer, 2003; Radkowsky & Siegel, 1997) for more thorough discussions of different explanations. In this chapter, we focus on three types of factors that may play a role in the greater rate of depression in both women and sexual minorities. These three were chosen both because they are the most frequently hypothesized risk factors for elevated depression among these groups and because they have received the most empirical support to date.

Stress Explanations

Stress is clearly common in the lives of depressed people (Hammen, 2005). In a review of the literature on stress, Mazure (1998) estimated that 80% of cases of depression were preceded by major stressful events. Although there is great debate about the operationalization and measurement of stress (see Hammen, 2005; Monroe, 2008), even studies that focused only on "independent" or fateful events that could not have been due to the individual's depression or other characteristics have shown a link between stress and depression (see review in Mazure, 1998; Monroe & Hadjiyannakis, 2002). In turn, the differences in depression both between women and men and between sexual minorities and heterosexuals have been attributed to differences in the experience of stress.

Stress and Women's Greater Vulnerability to Depression

One explanation for women's relatively higher rate of depression involves greater exposure to stress due to their lower social status and power. Women are more likely than men to be victimized through sexual abuse, rape, and sexual harassment (Costello, Erkanli, Fairbank, & Angold, 2002; Koss & Kilpatrick, 2001). Women may also experience more chronic strain as a result of their gender role (Nolen-Hoeksema, Larson, & Grayson, 1999).

Victimization

Having been the victim of rape more than doubles one's chances of developing depression (Burnam et al., 1988), and it is estimated that at least 15% of women have been victims of rape during their lifetime (Koss, Gidycz, & Wisniewski, 1987). In addition to rape, victimization through other types of physical and sexual abuse also confers risk for developing depression (see reviews by Weiss, Longhurst, & Mazure, 1999; Widom, DuMont, & Czaja, 2007). One form of victimization that affects many adult women is domestic violence. It is estimated that over one-third of women's visits to hospital emergency departments are the result of abuse by their partners (Massey, 1999).

Although boys and men are also victims of physical and sexual abuse, girls and women are more frequently victimized, and this may partially explain their higher rates of depression. For example, one review estimated that about one-third of the gender difference in adult depression could be attributed to higher rates of child sexual abuse of girls (Cutler & Nolen-Hoeksema, 1991).

Chronic Strain of Gender Role

Women report experiencing more chronic strain than men do, and this strain seems to be related to women's social status and gender roles. Whether women experience gender prejudice as the result of hostile sexism (e.g., sexual harassment at work) or more benevolent forms of sexism (e.g., a boss assuming a woman does not want to take on a new project because of childcare responsibilities), these behaviors reinforce women's subordinate social status (Glick & Fiske, 1996). In addition, women's family roles (e.g., wife, mother) are also associated with chronic strain, which may contribute to depression. Research indicates that women report more chronic strain related to the family, finances, parenting, and workload inequalities within marriages (Nolen-Hoeksema et al., 1999; Simon, 1992; Wu & DeMaris, 1996). These chronic strains partially explained the gender difference in depression in multiple studies (e.g., Nolen-Hoeksema et al., 1999; Wu & DeMaris, 1996).

Although men have traditionally had greater social power and status than do women, those men who lack social power and status may be at increased risk for depression (Cochran & Rabinowitz, 2000). Men who do not believe that they live up to traditional gender expectations of success, competitiveness, and restrictive emotionality tend to score higher on depression questionnaires (Cournoyer & Mahalik, 1995; Good & Wood, 1995; Magovcevic & Addis, 2005; Mahalik & Cournoyer, 2000).

Stress and Sexual Minorities' Greater Vulnerability to Depression

Recently, researchers interested in mental health disparities among sexual minorities have drawn upon the extensive literature on stress and psychopathology (e.g., Dohrenwend, 1998; Kessler, 1997) in order to examine whether stressors that are unique to sexual minority status, which we call sexual minority stress, are associated with greater psychiatric morbidity. Stress in general is believed to over-burden individuals and exceed their capacity and ability to cope with a stressor (Dohrenwend, 1998). Sexual minority stress might be especially taxing because it creates several unique demands on the stigmatized individual, including vicarious stress responses that can result from insults to the individual's collective identity (Miller & Kaiser, 2001). Moreover, because sexual minority stress is considered to be additive to general stressors that are experienced by all individuals, irrespective of their identity, sexual minorities require an "adaptational effort" above and beyond that of non-stigmatized individuals (Meyer, 2003). These additional stressors are therefore hypothesized to account for the increased rates of psychopathology in general, and depression in particular, among the LGB population.

Several stress processes have been hypothesized to lead to adverse mental health outcomes among sexual minorities, including objective discrimination events, expectations of rejection, and the internalization of negative societal attitudes (Meyer, 2003). There is a small, but growing, body of empirical research from community and general population samples that suggests a relationship between these stressors and deleterious mental health outcomes among sexual minorities, including depression (for a review, see Meyer, 2003). Examples of these specific sexual minority stressors are reviewed below.

Victimization

One recent study (Balsam, Rothblum, & Beauchaine, 2005) with a novel research methodology (the comparison sample was heterosexual siblings of the LGB participants) revealed that LGB individuals experienced more forms of victimization over the life course than their heterosexual siblings did. In particular, LGB participants reported more childhood psychological and physical abuse by parents and caretakers, more childhood sexual abuse, more partner psychological and physical abuse in adulthood, and more sexual assault experiences in adulthood. This study also showed significant gender differences in sexual victimization; gay and bisexual men reported more sexual victimization than lesbians and bisexual women did.

Although several studies have shown the adverse consequences of peer victimization among sexual minority adolescents (e.g., Hershberger & D'Augelli, 1995), only a few researchers have examined group differences in peer victimization. Their studies have indicated that LGB adolescents are more likely than their heterosexual peers to be victims of peer violence (e.g., Russell, Franz, & Driscoll, 2001). Studies with representative samples of youth have demonstrated that these group differences in peer victimization partially account for the association between sexual orientation and suicide risk (Russell & Joyner, 2001), although only one study showed this effect for girls (Garofalo, Wolf, Wissow, Woods, & Goodman, 1999). It is important that future researchers determine whether victimization can account for specific disparities in depressive symptoms among sexual minority youth.

Discrimination

Research with probability samples has documented that sexual minorities experience discrimination with greater frequency than heterosexuals do and that this increased stress exposure is associated with greater rates of psychological distress and psychopathology (including major depression) after controlling for relevant sociodemographic covariates (Mays & Cochran, 2001). Research has documented sexual minority discrimination across a variety of domains, including the workplace. For example, gay men earn 10–32% less than similarly qualified heterosexual men with the same job

(Badgett, Lau, Sears, & Ho, 2007). Moreover, seven of eight experiments with controlled scenarios related to employment and public accommodation have revealed evidence of employment discrimination based on sexual orientation (Badgett et al., 2007).

Hate Crimes

Few studies have examined group differences in experiences of hate crimes, although recent research with a national probability sample of sexual minorities has demonstrated that hate crimes are a common experience for this group (Herek, 2009). Herek found that almost one-quarter of participants reported a person or a property crime, and over one-half had experienced verbal harassment. These results also showed gender differences in exposure to sexual minority stressors; gay men were significantly more likely than lesbians and bisexuals to experience hate crimes and to report higher levels of harassment and verbal abuse, which is consistent with the results of prior research (Herek & Garnets, 2007). The greater exposure to some sexual minority stressors among gay men—including hate crimes (Herek, 2009) and victimization (Balsam et al., 2005)—may contribute to the higher rates of depression among gay men relative to lesbians, a reversal of the gender differences evidenced in heterosexuals. Previous researchers who have recruited representative samples of sexual minorities did not simultaneously assess both stress exposure and gender disparities in depression, however. Consequently, this hypothesis warrants testing in future studies.

Interpersonal Factors

Interpersonal theories of depression focus on certain behaviors that contribute to and maintain depressive symptoms, including excessive reassurance seeking, negative feedback seeking, and basing one's self-worth on the opinions of others (see Coyne, 1976; Joiner & Coyne, 1999). These behaviors may drive others away and thus make the depressed individual feel rejected and more depressed.

Interpersonal Factors and Women's Greater Vulnerability to Depression

Women tend to have a much stronger interpersonal orientation than men do (Feingold, 1994). Women's tendency to seek support and form strong interpersonal networks has often been cited as a protective factor for women's health. However, it seems that this protective factor may also function as a vulnerability factor when it comes to psychological distress (Kawachi & Berkman, 2001).

Social Support and Interpersonal Stress

Because women place a high value on interpersonal relationships, if things are going wrong in their relationships, women may become much more distressed than men do (see Nolen-Hoeksema & Hilt, 2009, for further discussion). In fact, research has shown that women identify significantly more interpersonal stressors in their lives than men do (Hammen, 2003).

In addition to experiencing more interpersonal stress, women seem to be more sensitive to the effects of interpersonal stress than men do. For example, in studies of children, interpersonal stress predicts depressive symptoms in girls but not in boys (e.g., Ge, Lorenz, Conger, Elder, & Simons, 1994; Rudolph & Flynn, 2007). Adolescent girls also report that interpersonal stressors impact their well-being more than adolescent boys do (e.g., Leadbeater, Blatt, & Quinlan, 1995). Studies of adults and adolescents also show that women tend to generate more interpersonal stress in their lives than men do (see Hammen, 1991).

Rejection Sensitivity

Many studies have demonstrated that certain behaviors (e.g., excessive reassurance seeking, negative feedback seeking) contribute to depression, but few researchers have examined differences between men and women in these behaviors. One study showed gender differences in the relationships of people with rejection sensitivity, the tendency to "anxiously expect, readily perceive, and overreact to rejection" (Downey, Freitas, Michaelis, & Khouri, 1998, p. 545). In this study, Downey and colleagues found that women who were high in rejection sensitivity were more likely to elicit negative feedback from their partners that eventually led to the breakup of the relationship, thus demonstrating a self-fulfilling prophecy. In the study, couples completed daily diary entries. Results showed that the romantic partners of women high in rejection sensitivity were more likely to experience relationship dissatisfaction when conflict arose; these rejection-sensitive women also perceived their partners to be more withdrawn. This finding was not true of romantic partners of men high in rejection sensitivity, which suggests that the fulfillment of women's rejection expectations may have a greater impact on their interpersonal relationships than is the case for men. This study did not examine depression, but it points to a potential mechanism that may contribute to women's higher rates of depression.

Interpersonal Factors and Sexual Minorities' Vulnerability to Depression

Although stress exposure is the most frequently hypothesized risk factor for mental health disparities among sexual minorities, researchers are increasingly interested in understanding the role of normative psychological processes that have been shown to predict mental health problems in general samples of heterosexuals (Diamond, 2003; Savin-Williams, 2001). Rather than assessing characteristics that distinguish sexual minorities from their heterosexual peers (i.e., sexual minority stress), the researchers examine the numerous psychological processes that these groups share. In this section, we briefly review some evidence for group differences in normative interpersonal processes, which in turn are associated with symptoms of depression and psychological distress in sexual minorities.

Social Support

Perceptions of low social support have been shown to be predictive of depression (Kessler, Price, & Wortman, 1985) as well as delayed recovery from major depressive episodes (McLeod, Kessler, & Landis, 1992). Research with sexual minorities has demonstrated the importance of both parental/family (Goldfried & Goldfried, 2001) and peer (Radkowsky & Siegel, 1997) support in protecting against adverse mental health outcomes. However, only a few researchers have examined group differences in social support between heterosexuals and sexual minorities. Their studies tend to reveal that sexual minorities perceive less social support than do heterosexuals (e.g., Eisenberg & Resnick, 2006) and that this difference accounts for mental health disparities, including depressive symptoms (e.g., Safren & Heimberg, 1999).

Rejection Sensitivity

Experimental research has shown that expectations of rejection can lead to increased psychological distress (including anxiety and depression) following ambiguous cues of peer rejection (e.g.,

Downey, Lebolt, Rinćon, & Freitas, 1998). This research on rejection sensitivity in interpersonal contexts such as intimate relationships has been extended to sensitivity to status-based rejection. For example, research with African American college students has shown that expectations of rejection impair functioning across a variety of domains, including academic performance (Steele, 1997) and affiliation and trust within institutional settings (Mendoza-Denton, Downey, Purdie, Davis, & Pietrzak, 2002). With rare exceptions (Cole, Kemeny & Taylor, 1997; Pachankis, Goldfried, & Ramrattan, 2008), few researchers have examined rejection sensitivity among sexual minorities. However, a recent prospective study of bereaved gay men showed that expectations of status-based rejection were predictive of depressive symptoms (Hatzenbuehler, Nolen-Hoeksema, & Erickson, 2008).

Cognitive Factors

A large literature implicates cognitive factors in the etiology and maintenance of depression (see Dobson & Dozois, 2008). In turn, a few studies have explored whether women and men, or sexual minorities and heterosexuals, differ in their rates of cognitive vulnerabilities and, in turn, whether this contributes to the group differences in depression.

Cognitive Factors and Women's Vulnerability to Depression

Many cognitive factors predict depression both concurrently and prospectively (e.g., dysfunctional attitudes, low self-worth, negative cognitive style, hopelessness), but few have been extensively studied in relation to the gender difference in depression. In this section, we review literature on cognitive factors that seem to contribute to the gender difference in depression.

Rumination

A robust cognitive predictor of depression and of gender differences in depression is rumination, the tendency to dwell passively on and brood about negative thoughts and feelings in a repetitive manner (Nolen-Hoeksema, 1991). There are individual differences in people's tendency to ruminate, and higher levels of rumination predict the onset of major depressive episodes (for a review, see Nolen-Hoeksema, Wisco, & Lybomirsky, 2008). It is interesting that, although both men and women report ruminating, women ruminate significantly more than men do, and this gender difference in rumination has been shown to account statistically for the gender difference in depression in multiple studies (Hilt, McLaughlin, & Nolen-Hoeksema, in press; Nolen-Hoeksema et al., 1999; Roberts, Gilboa, & Gotlib, 1998).

There are many possible reasons why women ruminate more than men do. One is that girls are socialized to cope in emotion-focused ways, whereas boys are socialized to cope in a more direct manner (e.g., problem solving). There is some evidence for this in observational and empirical work with child–parent interactions (e.g., Adams, Kuebli, Boyle, & Fivush, 1995). Very little research has examined reasons for women's higher rates of rumination. One study of young adolescents tested potential mediators of the gender difference in rumination and showed that girls reported having poorer emotional understanding (i.e., not knowing how to deal with intense and labile emotions) and more intense peer relationships (i.e., both talking more about problems with their friends and feeling alienated more from their friends). These factors statistically accounted for girls' higher level of rumination (Hilt et al., in press). It is important for future researchers to conduct studies to illuminate the factors that lead to rumination in order to help prevent depression.

Other Cognitive Factors

A recent review of gender differences in depression discussed two other cognitive factors that may contribute to the gender difference in depression (Hyde et al., 2008). One of these factors is negative attributional style, the tendency to attribute negative events to internal, global, stable causes (e.g., *I was not asked out for a second date because I am a bad person*). Negative attributional style is highly correlated with depressive symptoms, and it interacts with stress to predict increases in depression over time (e.g., Alloy et al., 2000). There is some evidence that adolescent girls may have a more negative attributional style than boys do (Hankin & Abramson, 2002) and that the relationship between a negative attributional style and depressive symptoms is stronger for adolescent girls than for boys (Gladstone, Kaslow, Seeley, & Lewinsohn, 1997), which may contribute to women's greater depression levels.

In addition to rumination and negative attributional style, Hyde and colleagues (2008) suggested that women's greater tendency to attend to their bodies and to have lower body esteem may represent an important cognitive factor in their greater depression level. For example, one study showed that objectified body consciousness predicted increases in depression during adolescence for girls but not for boys (Grabe, Hyde, & Lindberg, 2007).

Cognitive Factors and Sexual Minorities' Vulnerability to Depression

Research has also addressed the extent to which group differences in cognitive risk factors might account for the higher rates of depression among sexual minorities. These studies have focused on two normative cognitive processes that are well-documented risk factors for depression in heterosexuals: hopelessness (Abramson, Metalsky, & Alloy, 1989) and rumination (Nolen-Hoeksema, 1991, 2000).

Hopelessness

Hopelessness is defined as the belief that negative events will occur (or, conversely, that desired events will not occur) and that there is nothing the individual can do to change the situation (Abramson et al., 1989). Studies have indicated that sexual minority adolescents are more likely than their heterosexual peers to feel hopeless (e.g., Safren & Heimberg, 1999), although the results of one study suggested that these differences might be more pronounced among girls than among boys with same-sex attractions (Russell & Joyner, 2001). Group differences in hopelessness have also predicted higher rates of depressive symptoms among sexual minority adolescents (Safren & Heimberg, 1999).

Rumination

As noted, rumination is the tendency to focus passively and repetitively on one's symptoms of distress and the circumstances surrounding these symptoms (Nolen-Hoeksema, 1991). It has been hypothesized that rumination may be an especially salient risk factor for individuals with stigmatized identities, such as sexual minorities (Miller & Kaiser, 2001). Preliminary evidence from a longitudinal study of sexual minority adolescents substantiates this claim (Hatzenbuehler, McLaughlin et al., 2008). Results indicate that sexual minorities were more likely than heterosexuals to ruminate, and group differences in rumination accounted for the higher levels of depressive symptoms among sexual minority youth. Sexual minorities might be more likely than their heterosexual peers to ruminate as a means of coping with stressors created by their inferior status, similar to other socially disempowered groups such as heterosexual women (Nolen-Hoeksema et al., 1999).

A Stress-Mediation Model of Vulnerability to Depression

Our review has documented several common risk factors for depression across gender and sexual orientation groups. Stress exposure has received much attention in both literatures. Evidence from this line of research has indicated that women and sexual minorities experience both acute (e.g., sexual abuse, hate crimes) and chronic (e.g., discrimination) status-related stressors, which have been associated with their greater vulnerability to depression. In addition to stress exposure, there is a prolific line of evidence that normative psychological processes are important in explaining the higher rates of depression among women and sexual minorities. Interpersonal factors, such as rejection sensitivity and social support, as well as cognitive factors, including rumination, hopelessness, and attribution style, have all been shown to contribute to the gender and sexual orientation disparities in depression.

The myriad commonalities in vulnerability to depression between women and sexual minorities suggest shared pathways across these two groups. The field therefore requires an integrative theoretical model that moves beyond correlates to understanding the interplay between established risk factors in the development of depression in women and sexual minorities. We believe that a stress-mediation model offers a promising unified framework because it takes into account group differences both in exposure to status-related stressors and in normative psychological processes that confer risk for depression.

Although there are no current theoretical models that explicate the social stress–depression link specifically among women and sexual minorities, two general stress models identify putative mediators of the relationship between stress and mental health (Pearlin, Lieberman, Menaghan, & Mullan, 1981; Repetti, Taylor, & Seeman, 2002). Although these models focus on somewhat different stressors, they both contend that stress initiates a cascade of responses that directly and indirectly lead to mental health problems. We have adapted these general models to our populations of interest, and we argue that stressors related to social status (e.g., discrimination, victimization/abuse) render women and sexual minorities more vulnerable to psychological processes that confer risk for psychopathology (e.g., rumination). These processes, in turn, are expected to mediate the relationship between status-related stressors and depression (see Fig. 7.1). This stress-mediation model is theoretically grounded in transactional definitions of stress (Monroe, 2008), which posit that both environmental and response (e.g., appraisals, ruminative self-focus) components of stress are important in determining mental health outcomes, including depression. In the remaining section, we review evidence for this model, with particular attention to cognitive (rumination) and interpersonal (social isolation and rejection sensitivity) processes as potential mediators of the social stress–depression relationship in women and sexual minorities.

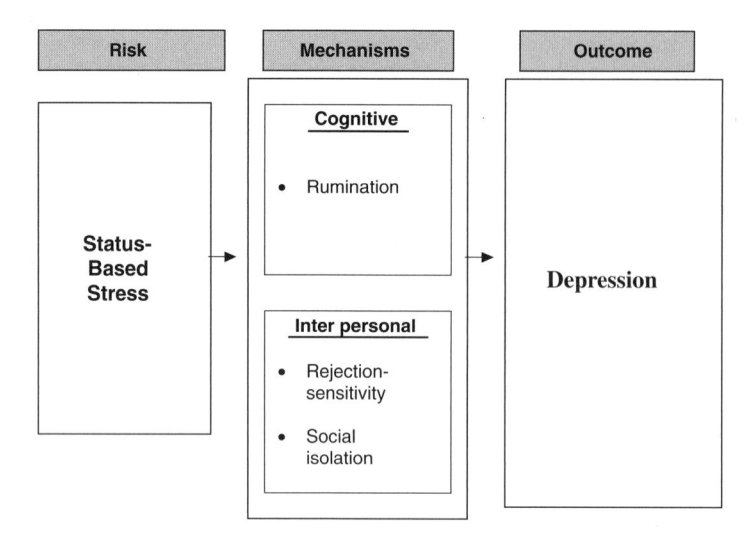

Fig. 7.1 A stress-mediation model of vulnerability to depression in women and sexual minorities

Cognitive Mechanisms

Several lines of evidence suggest that rumination may be a consequence of stress, including status-based stressors. Two prospective studies with adults (Nolen-Hoeksema et al., 1999) and adolescents (McLaughlin & Hatzenbuehler, 2009) have shown that general life stressors are determinants of ruminative self-focus and that rumination mediates the relationship between stress and symptoms of depression. In addition to these general stressors, certain life events or circumstances and the distress they create may be particularly difficult to understand or explain and thus may lead to a tendency to ruminate. Perhaps chief among these is the experience of abuse and neglect as a child. At least three studies have shown that individuals with a history of child sexual abuse are more likely to ruminate as adults than are those without a history of child sexual abuse (Conway, Mendelson, Giannopoulos, Csank, & Holm, 2004; Nolen-Hoeksema, 1998; Spasojevic & Alloy, 2002), even after controlling for group differences in depression. As noted earlier, women are more likely than men to be victims of childhood sexual abuse (Costello et al., 2002); this may contribute to more women than men developing a tendency to ruminate in an attempt to understand the victimization that they have experienced.

There is also evidence that the status-based stressors confronted by sexual minorities contribute to the development of rumination. Sexual minority stress may be particularly likely to contribute to rumination because it engenders hypervigilance (Mays, Cochran, & Barnes, 2007), an element of ruminative self-focus (Lyubomirsky, Tucker, Caldwell, & Berg, 1999). Two longitudinal studies with sexual minorities have substantiated this idea. The first study comes from our own research on bereaved gay men. In the study, 74 bereaved gay male caregivers of loved ones who died from AIDS were assessed before the partner or a close friend died and then at 1, 6, 13, and 18 months post-loss. (Further information on the sample and study design can be found in Hatzenbuehler, Nolen-Hoeksema et al., 2008.) The results demonstrated that those who experienced minority stress (operationalized as perceived danger due to being gay) showed increased tendencies to ruminate and, in turn, increases in depressive symptoms over time. In addition, a longitudinal, community-based study of LGB and heterosexual adolescents showed that rumination mediated the relationship between sexual minority status and depressive symptoms (Hatzenbuehler, McLaughlin et al., 2008).

Interpersonal Mechanisms

In addition to contributing to cognitive processes conferring risk for depression, status-based stress is also a determinant of interpersonal mechanisms that increase vulnerability to depression. Support for the hypothesis that status-based stress leads to low social support comes from two studies of sexual minorities. A cross-sectional study showed that social isolation mediated the relationship between discrimination and psychological distress (Diaz, Ayala, Bein, Henne, & Marin, 2001). Whereas this study adopted an inter-individual approach to modeling the relationships between status-based stress, social isolation, and psychological distress, social stress models (e.g., Pearlin et al., 1981) suggest that variations in social context may also cause intra-individual changes in psychosocial factors that confer risk for psychological problems. In accordance with these models, our prospective study of bereaved gay men mentioned above demonstrated that a specific status-based stressor (i.e., perceived danger due to being gay) created intra-individual variability in social responses (i.e., less social support) that led to increases in depressive symptoms over time.

These results raise the important question of why status-based stress might lead to social isolation, at least among sexual minorities. Whereas many turn to others for support in times of stress (Kawachi & Berkman, 2001), sexual minority stress could actually diminish social support among sexual minorities because it may lead them to isolate themselves from family and friends (both gay and straight). This would be expected in instances where family and friends are perpetrators of the rejection, but isolation might also occur, even from potentially supportive social networks, because sexual minority stress may cause sexual minorities to withdraw from social interactions in order to avoid future rejection (Link, Struening, Rahav, Phelan, & Nuttbrock, 1997). In turn, this lower social support should predict higher levels of depressive symptoms, as demonstrated in the above studies.

Rejection sensitivity represents another potential mediator of status-based stress and depression. Although many researchers have hypothesized that chronic experiences of status-based stressors may contribute to the development of rejection sensitivity among sexual minorities, only one study (Pachankis et al., 2008) has tested this link empirically. The results of the study indicated that reports of parental rejection of participants' sexual orientation were associated with rejection sensitivity, but the relationship between rejection sensitivity and current depression was not assessed. As previously mentioned, rejection sensitivity among gay men has been shown to predict depressive symptoms prospectively (Hatzenbuehler, Nolen-Hoeksema et al., 2008); however, Hatzenbuehler and colleagues did not examine sexual minority stress as a determinant of rejection sensitivity. Thus, there is evidence for both paths of the mediation model, but no researchers have simultaneously assessed relationships between stress, rejection sensitivity, and depression. This remains an important direction for future research on the stress-mediation model of vulnerability to depression.

Conclusion and Future Directions

In this chapter, we reviewed epidemiological evidence for the significantly higher rates of depression among both women and sexual minorities. Two broad risk factors have been shown to account for the higher rates of depression in these groups: (1) stress exposure (e.g., discrimination, victimization/abuse) and (2) normative psychological processes, including cognitive and interpersonal risk factors. We have suggested an integrative model that combines these two classes of correlates to reveal common pathways of vulnerability to depression across gender and sexual orientation groups. Several studies have shown that status-based stressors render women and sexual minorities more vulnerable to established psychological processes (e.g., rumination, social isolation/rejection sensitivity) and that these processes, in turn, account for the relationship between stress and depression (e.g., Diaz et al., 2001; Hatzenbuehler, Nolen-Hoeksema et al., 2008; Nolen-Hoeksema et al., 1999).

Although preliminary evidence exists for this model, important questions remain. For instance, future researchers ought to focus on identifying additional psychosocial sequelae of status-based stressors that can explain higher rates of depression among women and sexual minorities. Although we focused on rumination in this chapter, it is likely that status-based stress initiates a cascade of other cognitions that, in turn, render women and sexual minorities more vulnerable to the development of depression. For example, pessimism is a robust cognitive predictor of depression (Peterson & Seligman, 1984), and studies have shown that the experience of negative life events (Mezulis, Hyde, & Abramson, 2006) and chronic stress in the form of peer victimization (Gibb, Abramson, & Alloy, 2004) predicts the development of hopelessness, a construct similar to pessimism. It is reasonable to consider that individuals who are exposed to status-based stressors might develop negative expectancies about the future, particularly when the stress is recurrent and seems uncontrollable. However, we know of no studies that have tested the hypothesis that status-based stress predicts the development of pessimism, an important avenue for future study of this stress-mediation model.

In addition to identifying other psychological mechanisms that link status-related stress to depression, it will be important to determine which of these mechanisms have greater predictive utility in explaining the development of depression in women and sexual minorities. This will require adequately powered longitudinal studies that assess multiple psychological processes in addition to status-based stressors. Such research can also reveal whether specific status-based stressors are more predictive of certain psychological mechanisms and whether these differ by gender or sexual orientation status. For example, victimization experiences may lead to more rumination, whereas discrimination events may lead to greater hopelessness. Given that prior research on sexual minority stress suggests differential relationships between status-based stressors and psychological mechanisms (Hatzenbuehler, Nolen-Hoeksema et al., 2008), this will be an important avenue for future study.

Although the research evidence reviewed suggests stress mediation, there may be instances in which the psychosocial processes we identified are more likely to moderate the association between stress and depression. For example, whereas status-related stress appears to contribute to social isolation and rejection sensitivity among sexual minorities (Diaz et al., 2001), it seems less probable that similar stressors would contribute to rejection sensitivity among women. Instead, it may be that status-based stress only leads to depression among those women high (versus low) in rejection sensitivity. Future research is therefore needed to clarify the extent to which the relationships between status-based stress, common psychosocial processes, and depression are better explained by mediation or moderation hypotheses.

Improved measurement of status-based stress is an important step in answering these aforementioned questions. Although existing measures of status-related stressors typically rely on subjective appraisals of stress, these may be confounded with depression status (Monroe, 2008). Thus, alternative measures of status-based stress that relies on more objective indices of these stressors, such as state-level employment discrimination and incidents of hate crimes, are warranted (Hatzenbuehler, Keyes, & Hasin, 2009).

The model proposed in this chapter suggests several important avenues for intervention research that targets depression among women and sexual minorities. First, social/structural-level interventions are needed that reduce discrimination and other status-based stressors that confront women and sexual minorities and maintain their elevated levels of depression. Examples of such interventions include recent hate crimes legislation that specifies sexual orientation as a protected category. Because such policies often involve protracted changes over time (Dovidio, Kawakami, & Gaertner, 2000; Link & Phelan, 2001), however, it is essential that the field provides clinical interventions for women and sexual minorities who are currently experiencing depression related to status-based stress. The integrative model advanced in this chapter highlights several psychological processes, including cognitive and interpersonal sequelae of stigma, that are modifiable through existing evidence-based treatments. Further clarification of the processes through which status-based stressors ultimately lead to depression will assist in the development of preventive interventions to decrease rates of depression in these vulnerable groups.

Acknowledgments The authors acknowledge Sarah J. Erickson, Ph.D., and Peter Goldblum, Ph.D., MPH, for their contributions to the bereavement study on bereaved gay men that is discussed in this chapter.

References

Abramson, L. Y., Metalsky, G. I., & Alloy, L. B. (1989). Hopelessness depression: A theory-based subtype of depression. *Psychological Review*, 96, 358–372.

Adams, S., Kuebli, J., Boyle, P. A., & Fivush, R. (1995). Gender differences in parent–child conversations about past emotions: A longitudinal investigation. *Sex Roles*, 33, 309–323.

Addis, M. E. (2008). Gender and depression in men. *Clinical Psychology*, 15, 153–168.

Addis, M. E., & Mahalik, J. R. (2003). Men, masculinity and the contexts of help-seeking. *American Psychologist*, 58, 5–14.

Alloy, L., Abramson, L., Hogan, M., Whitehouse, W., Rose, D., Robinson, M., et al. (2000). The Temple-Wisconsin Cognitive Vulnerability to Depression (CVD) Project: Lifetime history of Axis I psychopathology in individuals at high and low cognitive risk for depression. *Journal of Abnormal Psychology*, 109, 403–418.

Andrade, L., Caraveo-Anduaga, J. J., Berglund, P., Bijl, R. V., DeGraaf, R., Volbergh, W., et al. (2003). The epidemiology of major depressive episodes: Results from the International Consortium of Psychiatric Epidemiology (ICPE) Surveys. *International Journal of Methods in Psychiatric Research*, 12, 3–21.

Angold, A., Costello, E. J., Erkanli, A., & Worthman, C. M. (1999). Pubertal changes in hormone levels and depression in girls. *Psychological Medicine*, 29, 1043–1053.

Badgett, M. V. L., Lau, H., Sears, B., & Ho, D. (2007). Bias in the workplace: Consistent evidence of sexual orientation and gender identity discrimination. *Williams Institute*. Downloaded on September 8, 2008 from http://www.law.ucla.edu/williamsinstitute/publications/Bias%20in%20the%20Workplace.pdf

Balsam, K. F., Rothblum, E. D., & Beauchaine, T. P. (2005). Victimization over the life span: A comparison of lesbian, gay, bisexual, and heterosexual siblings. *Journal of Consulting and Clinical Psychology*, 73, 477–487.

Burnam, M. A., Stein, J. A., Golding, J. M., Siegel, J. M., Sorensen, S. B., Forsythe, A. B., et al. (1988). Sexual assault and mental disorders in a community population. *Journal of Consulting and Clinical Psychology*, 56, 843–850.

Cochran, S. D., & Mays, V. M. (1994). Depressive distress among homosexually active African American men and women. *American Journal of Psychiatry*, 151, 524–529.

Cochran, S. D., & Mays, V. M. (2000a). Relation between psychiatric syndromes and behaviorally defined sexual orientation in a sample of the U.S. population. *American Journal of Epidemiology*, 151, 516–523.

Cochran, S. D., & Mays, V. M. (2000b). Lifetime prevalence of suicide symptoms and affective disorders among men reporting same-sex sexual partners: Results from NHANES III. *American Journal of Public Health*, 90, 573–578.

Cochran, S. D., Mays, V. M., & Sullivan, J. G. (2003). Prevalence of mental disorders, psychological distress, and mental health services use among lesbian, gay, and bisexual adults in the United States. *Journal of Consulting and Clinical Psychology*, 71, 53–61.

Cochran, S. V., & Rabinowitz, F. E. (2000). *Men and depression: Clinical and empirical perspectives*. New York: Academic Press.

Cole, S. W., Kemeny, M. E., & Taylor, S. E. (1997). Social identity and physical health: Accelerated HIV progression in rejection-sensitive gay men. *Journal of Personality and Social Psychology, 72*, 320–335.

Conway, M., Mendelson, M., Giannopoulos, C., Csank, P. A. R., & Holm, S. L. (2004). Childhood and adult sexual abuse, rumination on sadness, and dysphoria. *Child Abuse and Neglect, 28*, 393–410.

Cournoyer, R. J., & Mahalik, J. R. (1995). Cross-sectional study of gender role conflict examining college-aged and middle-aged men. *Journal of Counseling Psychology, 42*, 11–19.

Costello, E. J., Erkanli, A., Fairbank, J. A., & Angold, A. (2002). The prevalence of potentially traumatic events in childhood and adolescence. *Journal of Traumatic Stress, 15*, 99–112.

Coyne, J. C. (1976). Toward an interactional description of depression. *Psychiatry, 39*, 28–40.

Cutler, S. E., & Nolen-Hoeksema, S. (1991). Accounting for sex differences in depression through female victimization: Childhood sexual abuse. *Sex Roles, 24*, 425–438.

D'Augelli, A. R. (2002). Mental health problems among lesbian, gay, and bisexual youths ages 14–21. *Clinical Child Psychology and Psychiatry, 7*, 433–456.

Diamond, L. M. (2003). New paradigms for research on heterosexual and sexual-minority development. *Journal of Clinical Child and Adolescent Psychology, 32*, 490–498.

Diaz, R. M., Ayala, G., Bein, E., Henne, J., & Marin, B. V. (2001). The impact of homophobia, poverty, and racism on the mental health of gay and bisexual Latino men: Findings from 3 US cities. *American Journal of Public Health, 91*, 927–932.

Dobson, K. S., & Dozois, D. J. (2008). *Risk factors for depression*. Oxford: Elsevier.

Dohrenwend, B. P. (1998). *Adversity, stress, and psychopathology*. New York: Oxford University Press.

Dovidio, J. F., Kawakami, K., & Gaertner, S. L. (2000). Reducing contemporary prejudice: Combating explicit and implicit bias at the individual and intergroup level. In S. Oskamp (Ed.), *Reducing prejudice and discrimination* (pp. 137–163). Hillsdale, NJ: Erlbaum.

Downey, G., Freitas, A. L., Michaelis, B., & Khouri, H. (1998). The self-fulfilling prophecy in close relationships: Rejection sensitivity and rejection by romantic partners. *Journal of Personality and Social Psychology, 75*, 545–560.

Downey, G., Lebolt, A., Rinćon, C., & Freitas, A. L. (1998). Rejection sensitivity and children's interpersonal difficulties. *Child Development, 69*, 1074–1091.

Eaton, W., Anthony, J., Gallo, J., Cai, G., Tien, A., Romanoski, A., et al. (1997). Natural history of diagnostic interview schedule/*DSM-IV* major depression. *Archives of General Psychiatry, 54*, 993–999.

Eisenberg, M. E., & Resnick, M. D. (2006). Suicidality among gay, lesbian, and bisexual youth: The role of protective factors. *Journal of Adolescent Health, 39*, 662–668.

Feingold, A. (1994). Gender differences in personality: A meta-analysis. *Psychological Bulletin, 116*, 429–456.

Fergusson, D. M., Horwood, L. J., & Beautrais, A. L. (1999). Is sexual orientation related to mental health problems and suicidality in young people? *Archives of General Psychiatry, 56*, 876–880.

Fergusson, D. M., Horwood, L. J., Ridder, E. M., & Beautrais, A. L. (2005). Sexual orientation and mental health in a birth cohort of young adults. *Psychological Medicine, 35*, 971–981.

Galambos, N. L., Leadbeater, B. J., & Barker, E. T. (2004). Gender differences in and risk factors for depression in adolescents: A 4-year longitudinal study. *International Journal of Behavior Development, 28*, 16–25.

Garofalo, R., Wolf, R. C., Wissow, L. S., Woods, E. R., & Goodman, E. (1999). Sexual orientation and risk of suicide attempts among a representative sample of youth. *Archives of Pediatrics and Adolescent Medicine, 153*, 487–493.

Ge, X., Lorenz, F. O., Conger, R. D., Elder, G. H., & Simons, R. L. (1994). Trajectories of stressful life events and depressive symptoms during adolescence. *Developmental Psychology, 30*, 467–483.

Gibb, B. E., Abramson, L. Y., & Alloy, L. B. (2004). Emotional maltreatment from parents, verbal peer victimization, and cognitive vulnerability to depression. *Cognitive Therapy and Research, 28*, 1–21.

Gilman, S. E., Cochran, S. D., Mays, V. M., Ostrow, D., & Kessler, R. C. (2001). Risk of psychiatric disorders among individuals reporting same-sex sexual partners in the National Comorbidity Survey. *American Journal of Public Health, 91*, 933–939.

Gladstone, T., Kaslow, N., Seeley, J., & Lewinsohn, P. (1997). Sex differences, attributional style, and depressive symptoms among adolescents. *Journal of Abnormal Child Psychology, 25*, 297–305.

Glick, P., & Fiske, S. T. (1996). The Ambivalent Sexism Inventory: Differentiating hostile and benevolent sexism. *Journal of Personality and Social Psychology, 70*, 491–512.

Goldfried, M. R., & Goldfried, A. P. (2001). The importance of parental support in the lives of gay, lesbian, and bisexual individuals. *Journal of Clinical Psychology, 57*, 681–693.

Good, G. E., & Wood, P. K. (1995). Male gender role conflict, depression, and help-seeking: Do college men face double jeopardy? *Journal of Counseling and Development, 74*, 70–75.

Grabe, S., Hyde, J. S., & Lindberg, S. M. (2007). Body objectification and depression in adolescents: The role of gender, shame, and rumination. *Psychology of Women Quarterly*, 31, 164–175.

Grant, B. (1995). Comorbidity between *DSM-IV* drug use disorders and major depression: Results of a national survey of adults. *Journal of Substance Abuse*, 7, 481–497.

Hammen, C. (1991). Generation of stress in the course of unipolar depression. *Journal of Abnormal Psychology*, 100, 555–561.

Hammen, C. (2003). Social stress and women's risk for recurrent depression. *Archives of Women's Mental Health*, 6, 9–13.

Hammen, C. (2005). Stress and depression. *Annual Review of Clinical Psychology*, 1, 293–319.

Hankin, B. L., & Abramson, L. Y. (2002). Measuring cognitive vulnerability to depression in adolescence: Reliability, validity, and gender differences. *Journal of Clinical Child and Adolescent Psychology*, 31, 491–504.

Hankin, B. L., Abramson, L. Y., Moffitt, T. E., McGee, R., Silva, P., & Angell, K. E. (1998). Development of depression from preadolescence to young adulthood: Emerging gender differences in a 10-year longitudinal study. *Journal of Abnormal Psychology*, 107, 128–140.

Hasin, D. S., Goodwin, R. D., Stinson, F. S., & Grant, B. F. (2005). Epidemiology of major depressive disorder: Results from the National Epidemiologic Survey on Alcohol and Related Conditions. *Archives of General Psychiatry*, 62, 1097–1106.

Hatzenbuehler, M. L., Keyes, K. M., & Hasin, D. S. (2009). *State-level discrimination policies and hate crimes: Environmental risk factors for psychiatric morbidity in LGB populations*. American Journal of Public Health, 99, 2275–2281.

Hatzenbuehler, M. L., McLaughlin, K. A., & Nolen-Hoeksema, S. (2008). Emotion regulation and internalizing symptoms in a longitudinal study of sexual minority and heterosexual adolescents. *Journal of Child Psychology and Psychiatry*, 49, 1270–1278.

Hatzenbuehler, M. L., Nolen-Hoeksema, S., & Erickson, S. J. (2008). Minority stress predictors of HIV risk behavior, substance use, and depressive symptoms: Results from a prospective study of bereaved gay men. *Health Psychology*, 27, 455–462.

Herek, G. (2009). Hate crimes and stigma-related experiences among sexual minority adults in the United States: Prevalence estimates from a national probability sample. *Journal of Interpersonal Violence*, 24, 54–74.

Herek, G. M., & Garnets, L. (2007). Sexual orientation and mental health. *Annual Review of Clinical Psychology*, 3, 353–375.

Hershberger, S. L., & D'Augelli, A. R. (1995). The impact of victimization on mental health and suicidality of lesbian, gay, and bisexual youths. *Developmental Psychology*, 31, 65–74.

Hilt, L. M., McLaughlin, K. A., & Nolen-Hoeksema, S. (in press). *Rumination in young adolescents: Predicting depression and understanding the gender difference*. Journal of Abnormal Child Psychology.

Hilt, L. M., & Nolen-Hoeksema, S. (2008). The emergence of gender differences in depression in adolescence. In S. Nolen-Hoeksema & L. Hilt (Eds.), *Handbook of depression in adolescents* (pp. 111–136). New York: Routledge.

Hyde, J. S., Mezulis, A. H., & Abramson, L.Y. (2008). The ABCs of depression: Integrating affective, biological, and cognitive models to explain the emergence of the gender difference in depression. *Psychological Review*, 115, 291–313.

Joiner, T., & Coyne, J. C. (1999). *The interactional nature of depression: Advances in interpersonal approaches*. Washington, DC: American Psychological Association.

Kawachi, I., & Berkman, L. F. (2001). Social ties and mental health. *Journal of Urban Health*, 78, 458–467.

Keller, M., & Shapiro, R. (1981). Major depressive disorder: Initial results from a 1-year prospective naturalistic follow-up study. *Journal of Nervous and Mental Disorders*, 169, 761–768.

Kessler, R. C. (1997). The effects of stressful life events on depression. *Annual Review of Psychology*, 48, 191–214.

Kessler, R. C., Berglund, P., Demler, O., Jin, R., Koretz, D., Merikangas, K. R., et al. (2003). The epidemiology of major depressive disorder: Results from the national comorbidity survey replication (NCS-R). *Journal of the American Medical Association*, 289, 3095–3105.

Kessler, R. C., Crum, R. M., Warner, L. A., Nelson, C. B., Schulenberg, J., & Anthony, J. C. (1997). Lifetime co-occurrence of *DSM-III-R* alcohol abuse and dependence with other psychiatric disorders in the National Comorbidity Survey. *Archives of General Psychiatry*, 54, 313–321.

Kessler, R. C., McGonagle, K. A., Hughes, M., Swartz, M. & Blazer, D. G. (1994). Sex and depression in the National Comorbidity Survey II: Cohort effects. *Journal of Affective Disorders*, 30, 15–26.

Kessler, R. C., McGonagle, K. A., Swartz, M., Blazer, D. G., & Nelson, C. B. (1993). Sex and depression in the National Comorbidity Survey I: Lifetime prevalence, chronicity, and recurrence. *Journal of Affective Disorders*, 29, 85–96.

Kessler, R. C., Price, R. H., & Wortman, C. B. (1985). Social factors in psychopathology: Stress, social support, and coping processes. *Annual Review of Psychology, 36*, 531–572.

Koss, M. P., Gidycz, C. A., & Wisniewski, N. (1987). The scope of rape: Incidence and prevalence of sexual aggression and victimization in a national sample of higher education students. *Journal of Consulting and Clinical Psychology, 55*, 162–170.

Koss, M. P., & Kilpatrick, D. G. (2001). Rape and sexual assault. In E. Gerrity, T. M. Keane, & F. Tuma (Eds.), *The mental health consequences of torture* (pp. 177–194). Dordrecht: Kluwer.

Kovacs, M. (2001). Gender and the course of major depressive disorder through adolescence in clinically referred youngsters. *Journal of the American Academy of Child & Adolescent Psychiatry, 40*, 1079–1085.

Leadbeater, B. J., Blatt, S. J., & Quinlan, D. M. (1995). Gender-linked vulnerabilities to depressive symptoms, stress, and problem behaviors in adolescents. *Journal of Research on Adolescence, 5*, 1–29.

Link, B. G., & Phelan, J. C. (2001). Conceptualizing stigma. *Annual Review of Sociology, 27*, 363–385.

Link, B. G., Struening, E. L., Rahav, M., Phelan, J. C., & Nuttbrock, L. (1997). On stigma and its consequences: Evidence from a longitudinal study of men with dual diagnoses of mental illness and substance abuse. *Journal of Health and Social Behavior, 38*, 177–190.

Lyubomirsky, S., Tucker, K. L., Caldwell, N. D., & Berg, K. (1999). Why ruminators are poor problem solvers: Clues from the phenomenology of dysphoric rumination. *Journal of Personality and Social Psychology, 77*, 1041–1060.

Magovcevic, M., & Addis, M. E. (2005). Linking gender role conflict to non-normative and self-stigmatizing perceptions of alcohol abuse and depression. *Psychology of Men & Masculinity, 6*, 127–136.

Magovcevic, M., & Addis, M. E. (2008). The Masculine Depression Scale: Development and psychometric evaluation. *Psychology of Men & Masculinity, 9*, 117–132.

Mahalik, J., R., & Cournoyer, R. J. (2000). Identifying gender role conflict messages that distinguish mildly depressed from nondepressed men. *Psychology of Men and Masculinity, 1*, 109–115.

Massey, J. (1999). Domestic violence in neurologic practice. *Archives in Neurology, 56*, 659–660.

Mayer, K. H., Brandford, J. B., Makadon, H. J., Stall, R., Goldhammer, H., & Landers, S. (2008). Sexual and gender minority health: What we know and what needs to be done. *American Journal of Public Health, 98*, 989–995.

Mays, V. M., & Cochran, S. D. (2001). Mental health correlates of perceived discrimination among lesbian, gay, and bisexual adults in the United States. *American Journal of Public Health, 91*, 1869–1876.

Mays, V. M., Cochran, S. D., & Barnes, N. W. (2007). Race, race-based discrimination, and health outcomes among African Americans. *Annual Review of Psychology, 58*, 201–225.

Mazure, C. M. (1998). Life stressors as risk factors in depression. *Clinical Psychology, 5*, 291–313.

McLaughlin, K. A., & Hatzenbuehler, M. L. (2009). Mechanisms linking stressful life events and mental health problems in a prospective, community-based study of adolescents. *Journal of Adolescent Health, 44*, 153–160.

McLeod, J. D., Kessler, R. C., & Landis, K. R. (1992). Speed of recovery from major depressive episodes in a community sample of married men and women. *Journal of Abnormal Psychology, 101*, 277–286.

Mendoza-Denton, R., Downey, G., Purdie, V., Davis, A., & Pietrzak, J. (2002). Sensitivity to status-based rejection: Implications for African-American students' college experience. *Journal of Personality and Social Psychology, 83*, 896–918.

Meyer, I. H. (2003). Prejudice, social stress, and mental health in lesbian, gay, and bisexual populations: Conceptual issues and research evidence. *Psychological Bulletin, 129*, 674–697.

Mezulis, A. H., Hyde, J. S., & Abramson, L. Y. (2006). The developmental origins of cognitive vulnerability to depression: Temperament, parenting, and negative life events in childhood as contributors to negative cognitive style. *Developmental Psychology, 42*, 1012–1025.

Miller, C. T., & Kaiser, C. R. (2001). A theoretical perspective on coping with stigma. *Journal of Social Issues, 57*, 73–92.

Monroe, S. M. (2008). Modern approaches to conceptualizing and measuring human life stress. *Annual Review of Clinical Psychology, 4*, 33–52.

Monroe, S. M., & Hadjiyannakis, K. (2002). The social environment and depression: Focusing on severe life stress. In I. H. Gotlib & C. L. Hammen (Eds.), *Handbook of depression* (pp. 314–340). New York: Guilford.

Nolen-Hoeksema, S. (1991). Responses to depression and their effects on the duration of depressive episodes. *Journal of Abnormal Psychology, 100*, 569–582.

Nolen-Hoeksema, S. (1998). The other end of the continuum: The costs of rumination. *Psychological Inquiry, 9*, 216–219.

Nolen-Hoeksema, S. (2000). The role of rumination in depressive disorders and mixed anxiety/depressive symptoms. *Journal of Abnormal Psychology, 109*, 504–511.

Nolen-Hoeksema, S., & Hilt, L. M. (2009). Gender differences in depression. In I. Gotlib & C. Hammen (Eds.), *Handbook of depression* (2nd ed., pp. 386–404). New York: Guilford.

Nolen-Hoeksema, S., Larson, J., & Grayson, C. (1999). Explaining the gender difference in depressive symptoms. *Journal of Personality and Social Psychology*, 77, 1061–1072.

Nolen-Hoeksema, S., Wisco, B. E., & Lybomirsky, S. (2008). Rethinking rumination. *Perspectives on Psychological Science*, 3, 400–424.

Pachankis, J. E., Goldfried, M. R., & Ramrattan, M. E. (2008). Extension of the rejection sensitivity construct to the interpersonal functioning of gay men. *Journal of Consulting and Clinical Psychology*, 76, 306–317.

Pearlin, L. I., Lieberman, M. A., Menaghan, E. G., & Mullan, J. T. (1981). The stress process. *Journal of Health and Social Behavior*, 22, 337–356.

Peterson, C., & Seligman, M. E. P. (1984). Causal explanations as a risk factor for depression: Theory and evidence. *Psychological Review*, 91, 347–374.

Post, R. M. (1992). Transduction of psychosocial stress into the neurobiology of recurrent affective disorder. *American Journal of Psychiatry*, 149, 999–1010.

Radkowsky, M., & Siegel, L. J. (1997). The gay adolescent: Stressors, adaptations, and psychosocial interventions. *Clinical Psychology Review*, 17, 191–216.

Repetti, R. L., Taylor, S. E., & Seeman, T. E. (2002). Risky families: Family social environments and the mental and physical health of offspring. *Psychological Bulletin*, 128, 330–366.

Roberts, J. E., Gilboa, E., & Gotlib, I. H. (1998). Ruminative response style and vulnerability to episodes of dysphoria: Gender, neuroticism, and episode duration. *Cognitive Therapy and Research*, 22, 401–423.

Rudolph, K. D., & Flynn, M. (2007). Childhood adversity and youth depression: Influence of gender and pubertal status. *Development and Psychopathology*, 19, 497–521.

Russell, S. T., Franz, B. T., & Driscoll, A. K. (2001). Same-sex romantic attraction and experiences of violence in adolescence. *American Journal of Public Health*, 91, 903–906.

Russell, S. T., & Joyner, K. (2001). Adolescent sexual orientation and suicide risk: Evidence from a national study. *American Journal of Public Health*, 91, 1276–1281.

Safren, S. A., & Heimberg, R. G. (1999). Depression, hopelessness, suicidality, and related factors in sexual minority and heterosexual adolescents. *Journal of Consulting and Clinical Psychology*, 67, 859–866.

Sandfort, T. G., de Graaf, R., Bijl, R. V., & Schnabel, P. (2001). Same-sex sexual behavior and psychiatric disorders: Findings from the Netherlands Mental Health Survey and Incidence Study (NEMESIS). *Archives of General Psychiatry*, 58, 85–91.

Savin-Williams, R. C. (2001). A critique of research on sexual-minority youths. *Journal of Adolescence*, 24, 5–13.

Simon, R. V. (1992). Parental role strains, salience of parental identity, and gender differences in psychological distress. *Journal of Health and Social Behavior*, 33, 25–35.

Spasojevic, J., & Alloy, L. B. (2002). Who becomes a depressive ruminator? Developmental antecedents of ruminative response style. *Journal of Cognitive Psychotherapy*, 16, 405–419.

Steele, C. M. (1997). A threat in the air: How stereotypes shape intellectual identity and performance. *American Psychologist*, 52, 613–629.

Twenge, J. M., & Nolen-Hoeksema, S. (2002). Age, gender, race, socioeconomic status, and birth cohort differences on the Children's Depression Inventory: A meta-analysis. *Journal of Abnormal Psychology*, 111, 578–588.

Weiss, E. L., Longhurst, J. G., & Mazure, C. M. (1999). Childhood sexual abuse as a risk factor for depression in women: Psychosocial and neurobiological correlates. *American Journal of Psychiatry*, 156, 816–828.

Weissman, M. M., Bland, R. C., Canino, G. J., Faravelli, C., Greenwald, S., Hwu, H. G., et al. (1996). Cross-national epidemiology of major depression and bipolar disorder. *Journal of the American Medical Association*, 276, 293–299.

Widom, C. S., DuMont, K., & Czaja, S. J. (2007). A prospective investigation of major depressive disorder and comorbidity in abused and neglected children grown up. *Archives of General Psychiatry*, 64, 49–56.

World Health Organization (WHO). (2008). Depression. Downloaded on May 12, 2008 from http://www.who.int/mental_health/management/depression/definition/en/

Wu, X., & DeMaris, A. (1996). Gender and marital status differences in depression: The effects of chronic strains. *Sex Roles*, 34, 299–319.

Chapter 8
Gender and Body Image

Rachel M. Calogero and J. Kevin Thompson

That gender has a considerable impact on people's body image may seem obvious based on the considerable attention paid to women's and men's bodies in popular culture (Thompson, Heinberg, Altabe, & Tantleff-Dunn, 1999; Wolf, 1991). Indeed, the different portrayals of women's and men's bodies underscore the different lived experiences of women and men. Gender differences in body image are among the most robust findings in the psychological literature: Women and men feel, think, and behave differently with regard to their bodies (Serdula et al., 1993; Thompson, 1996). Gender differences in body image should not be taken lightly as they have been shown to account for a variety of psychological distresses and disturbances in the lives of women and men (e.g., Thompson & Cafri, 2007; Thompson et al., 1999). This is evident from research that indicates that body image significantly contributes to adolescent suicidal ideation; it is a stronger predictor than other known risk factors such as depression, hopelessness, and past suicidal behavior (Brausch & Muehlenkamp, 2007).

In order to understand gender differences in body image, it is first necessary to consider what the differences actually are and how they manifest themselves in men and women. Therefore, this chapter begins with a selective overview of the most robust gender differences in the body image literature in relation to body perceptions, body feelings, body cognitions, and body behaviors. Then, several different theoretical perspectives are offered to explain these gender differences in body image: the tripartite model of sociocultural influence (Keery, van den Berg, & Thompson, 2004), gender socialization (Eagly, 1987), and objectification theory (Fredrickson & Roberts, 1997). An integration of these perspectives provides a comprehensive social psychological framework for understanding the multiple pathways by which people's body images are shaped. Finally, we identify gaps in the literature on gender and body image as well as potential future research directions for scholars interested in the study of gender and body image.

What Is Body Image?

Body image is a multi-faceted construct that consists of self-perceptions, attitudes, beliefs, feelings, and behaviors related to one's body (Cash & Pruzinsky, 1990; Grogan, 1999; Thompson et al., 1999). Body image is often viewed as a fixed property that is rooted in the minds of individual

R.M. Calogero (✉)
University of Kent, Kent, UK

persons, but it is not fixed. Instead, a person's body image constitutes a dynamic relationship between the individual, the body, and the social environment. Recognition of the multiple facets of body image has led to the development of multidimensional assessments over the last several decades (Cash, 2004; Grogan, 1999; Shroff, Calogero, & Thompson, 2009; Thompson et al., 1999), some of which include body size estimation, body dissatisfaction, appearance investment, body objectification, body-ideal internalization, body image-related quality of life, body appreciation, body responsiveness, drive for thinness, and drive for muscularity.

Our review of gender differences in body image relies on the extant terminology and measurement tools to label the various dimensions that have been studied; however, it is important to note that these variables are not definitive or exhaustive of the body image construct. In addition, body image has been conceptualized and assessed almost exclusively in terms of its negative dimensions, and, therefore, most of the gender differences described in the following sections refer to those dimensions.

Gender and Body Perceptions

Body perceptions refer to what is seen or recognized about the body on a conscious level (Thompson et al., 1999). Gender differences in the way that people perceive their bodies are well documented. In particular, there are three distinct ways of viewing the body that are especially illustrative of the differences between women's and men's body images.

Fragmented vs. Functional

There is evidence to indicate that men and women differ in how they evaluate and talk about their bodies (Halliwell & Dittmar, 2003). A clear pattern has been documented whereby men tend to evaluate and talk about their bodies as whole and functional entities (e.g., Look how fast I can run), whereas women tend to evaluate and talk about their bodies as a collection of different and distinct parts (e.g., I hate the size of my thighs). These different conceptualizations of the body reflect a difference in the nature of women's and men's body awareness and the target of their body focus (Franzoi, 1995; Franzoi, Kessenich, & Sugrue, 1989; Fredrickson & Roberts, 1997; McKinley & Hyde, 1996). In general, it appears that girls and women come to take more fragmented, compartmentalized views of their bodies, whereas boys come to take more functional, holistic views of their bodies.

Third Person vs. First Person

In a similar vein, there is evidence to indicate that men and women differ in the degree to which they view their bodies from a third-person (i.e., her or his body) vs. first-person (i.e., my body) perspective (Eck, 2003; McKinley & Hyde, 1996). Research indicates that women take an external observational standpoint on their bodies more often than men do (Calogero & Watson, 2009; Miller, Murphy, & Buss, 1981). A recent study demonstrated that adolescent girls (aged 11–13) report significantly more third-person perspective taking on their bodies than adolescent boys do, and these gender differences appear at an earlier age than do gender differences in rumination and depression (Grabe, Hyde, & Lindberg, 2007).

Overestimate vs. Underestimate

There is fairly good consensus that in Westernized societies, women overestimate the size of their bodies to a significantly greater degree than men do (Thompson et al., 1999), whereas men underestimate the size of their bodies to a significantly greater degree than women do (Betz, Mintz, & Speakmon, 1994). Grover, Keel, and Mitchell (2003) found that normal weight women were more likely than normal weight men to be critical about their weights and to report being heavier than their actual weight even though the actual weights [based on body mass index (BMI)] between the men and women were not significantly different. Indeed, McCreary (2002) found that almost one-third of women aged 20–64 years perceived themselves to be heavier than they really were, whereas almost 50% of overweight men perceived themselves to be average weight, and 19% of average weight men perceived themselves to be underweight. In other reports, between 28 and 68% of average weight adolescent boys and men believed that they were underweight and desired to gain weight and muscle mass (McCreary & Sasse, 2000). Moreover, Tiggemann (2005) found that adolescent girls who were not overweight, but perceived themselves as overweight or felt dissatisfied with their current weight, reported lower self-esteem than other girls did over a 2-year period.

Some research with non-Western cultures also demonstrates these effects. For example, Japanese women show a greater overestimation of their body relative to their actual measured values and a significantly greater desire to lose weight than Japanese men do (Kagawa et al., 2007). A sample of young Samoan men living on a remote island in the South Pacific were able to estimate their body size accurately, but they chose an ideal body size that was approximately 6.5–11 lbs (3–5 kg) leaner and approximately 17–24 lbs (8–11 kg) more muscular than their actual body size, which is similar to the pattern of body image disparities found for American and European men (Lipinski & Pope, 2002). Other research has shown that, on average, college-aged Nigerian students report being more satisfied than dissatisfied with their body parts, although weight and muscle development were still the primary sites of dissatisfaction. In addition, compared to Nigerian men, Nigerian women reported greater satisfaction with most body parts including their ears, body weight, chest size, size and appearance of sex organs, and even muscularity (Balogun, Okonofua, & Balogun, 1992).

Gender and Body Feelings

Body feelings refer to how people feel about their bodies (i.e., the affective dimension of body image; Thompson et al., 1999). Gender differences in body feelings are also well documented. In particular, three types of body-related feelings are highlighted here: body dissatisfaction, body shame, and appearance anxiety.

Body Dissatisfaction

Body dissatisfaction represents the most important global measure of distress because it captures the essence of one's subjective evaluation of the body on a continuum from satisfaction to dissatisfaction (Thompson et al., 1999). One of the most consistent findings in the body image literature is that women are significantly more dissatisfied with their bodies than men are from adolescence through adulthood (Grogan, 1999; Paxton et al., 1991; Thompson et al., 1999), and this satisfaction gap has increased over time (Feingold & Mazella, 1998; Phares, Steinberg, & Thompson, 2004). Reports indicate that approximately one-half of all American girls and college women make global negative evaluations of their bodies (Bearman, Presnell, Martinez, & Stice, 2006; Thompson et al., 1999).

These gender differences in body dissatisfaction have been observed in young children as well. For example, girls aged 7–11 years reported significantly more body dissatisfaction than did boys aged 11–18 years (Vincent & McCabe, 2000). In fact, boys are more likely than girls to show a decrease in body dissatisfaction during early adolescence (Bearman et al., 2006). This phenomenon is not confined to the United States. A cross-cultural comparison of Argentinean and Swedish adolescents revealed no significant differences in body satisfaction between the two countries; however, the girls from both countries displayed more body dissatisfaction than the boys did (Holmqvist, Lunde, & Frisen, 2007). According to a recent survey of 3,300 girls and women across 10 countries, 90% of women aged 15–64 are dissatisfied with at least one aspect of their physical appearance; body weight ranked the highest (Etcoff, Orbach, Scott, & D'Agostino, 2006).

Despite these noted gender differences, body dissatisfaction among men has been on the rise over the past three decades (Thompson & Cafri, 2007). Some researchers have reported that a remarkable 95% of men experience some degree of body dissatisfaction (Mishkind, Rodin, Silberstein, & Striegle-Moore, 1986). In addition, given the emphasis on appearance within the gay subculture, considerable research has shown that gay boys/men constitute a group particularly vulnerable to body dissatisfaction; they report higher levels of body dissatisfaction than heterosexual men do (Beren, Hayden, Wifley, & Grilo, 1996; Boroughs & Thompson, 2002; French, Story, Remafedi, Resnick, & Blum, 1996; Martins, Tiggemann, & Kirkbride, 2007; Morrison, Morrison, & Sager, 2004; Smolak, Murnen, & Thompson, 2005; Yelland & Tiggemann, 2003). Contrary to the findings for women, men's body dissatisfaction involves both ends of the weight continuum. Researchers have found that men who are above or below an acceptable range in their BMI scores tend to be especially dissatisfied with their physical appearance (Drewnowski & Yee, 1987; Muth & Cash, 1997). In addition, it is important to note that a recent cross-sectional study of children between ages 8 and 11 demonstrated no gender differences in body dissatisfaction, importance placed on weight, strategies to lose weight, or the perceived pressure associated with losing weight (Ricciardelli, McCabe, Holt, & Finemore, 2003). However, boys were more likely than girls to desire a larger body size, place a greater importance on muscles, utilize muscle gain strategies, and perceive a greater pressure to increase their muscles.

Body Shame

Body shame refers to the negative feelings that occur when people evaluate themselves against internalized cultural ideals for appearance and find that they fall short of these ideals (Lewis, 1992; McKinley & Hyde, 1996; Silberstein, Striegel-Moore, & Rodin, 1987). According to Bartky (1990, p. 86):

> Shame is the distressed apprehension of the self as inadequate or diminished: it requires if not an actual audience before whom my deficiencies are paraded, then an internalized audience with the capacity to judge me, hence internalized standards of judgment. Further, shame requires the recognition that I am, in some important sense, as I am seen to be.

Considerable evidence indicates that women feel significantly more shame about their bodies than men do (Calogero, Boroughs, & Thompson, 2007; Groesz, Levine, & Murnen, 2002; McKinley, 1998). In particular, research with North American, British, and Australian women has consistently demonstrated that women who highly value attributes such as weight and physical attractiveness report more body shame than do women who do not highly value these attributes (Calogero & Thompson, 2009; Noll & Fredrickson, 1998; Tiggemann & Kuring, 2004; Tiggemann & Slater, 2001; Tylka & Hill, 2004). Researchers have shown that when appearance is made especially salient (e.g., trying on a swimsuit in front of a mirror), women report significantly more body shame than men do (Fredrickson, Roberts, Noll, Quinn, & Twenge, 1998). Although both men and women reported feeling more self-conscious in situations where their bodies were on display, men reported feeling more "shy" and "silly," whereas women reported feeling more "disgust" and "anger" (Frederick, Peplau, & Lever, 2006; Fredrickson et al., 1998). In a similar situation, Hebl, King, and Lin (2004) also found that women reported more body shame than men did, although this did not vary as a function of type of clothing. Moreover, there were no differences in body shame between Asian American, European American, and Hispanic individuals; however, African American individuals reported lower levels of body shame compared to participants from other ethnic backgrounds, and African American women and men reported similar levels of body shame.

However, as with body dissatisfaction, men's body shame appears to be on the rise. Recent research with Australian (Tiggemann & Kuring, 2004) and British (Calogero, 2009) men indicates that those who highly value attributes such as strength and physical coordination report more body shame than do those who do not highly value these attributes. These findings are consistent with an increased focus on muscularity as the cultural appearance ideal for men (Cafri et al., 2005; McCreary & Sasse, 2000; Thompson & Cafri, 2007), which may render "strength" an important and observable appearance attribute with which to compare themselves.

Also, as with body dissatisfaction, sexual orientation is a critical factor to consider in the study of men's body shame. Given the emphasis on appearance within the gay subculture, gay men may be more likely than heterosexual men to experience body shame in their day-to-day experience. For example, compared to heterosexual men, gay men report feeling markedly more shame about their bodies when their bodies are on display (i.e., wearing a swimsuit vs. a sweater), although it should be noted that heterosexual men are not immune to the experience of body shame (Martins et al., 2007). It is important to note that these differences were found in measures of body shame that are frequently employed in the study of women's body shame, which typically highlight the role of weight/shape in women's body shame. Thus, even weight/shape-based measures have been shown to illuminate differences in men's experiences of body shame.

Appearance Anxiety

Appearance anxiety refers to the worry and concern people express about their bodies being on display and available for evaluation by others (Dion, Dion, & Keelan, 1990). Again, as noted with body shame, the narrow and unrealistic nature of feminine beauty ideals may produce more anxiety for women than for men about how their actual appearance matches these ideals. In addition, the normative evaluation and scrutiny of women's bodies across social contexts is out of women's control, which may increase appearance anxiety. Indeed, there is evidence that women experience significantly more anxiety about the appearance of their bodies than men do (Dion et al., 1990; Tiggemann & Kuring, 2004).

It is particularly important to point out that women's appearance anxiety not only is about "vanity" but also includes concerns about safety and threats to the self because of the greater potential for women to experience sexual victimization and sexually motivated bodily harm (Brownmiller, 1975). When asked to describe what they do on any given day to maintain their personal safety, women list multiple strategies (e.g., checking backseat of car, keeping keys between fingers, pretending to talk on cell phone), whereas men list very few strategies for ensuring their personal safety on a daily basis (Fredrickson & Roberts, 1997). Thus, maintaining a chronic vigilance about both physical appearance and physical safety creates many more opportunities for women than men to experience anxiety. In this way, women's subjective experience of their bodies is markedly different from men's.

However, there is variability in men's appearance anxiety as well, especially when they report negative evaluations of their upper body strength and muscularity (Davis, Brewer, & Weinstein, 1993). Indeed, although girls reported higher social physique anxiety than did boys, drive for muscularity was directly related to social physique anxiety only for boys, whereas these variables, via body comparisons, were only indirectly related for girls (McCreary & Saucier, 2009). This association between high drive for muscularity and high social physique anxiety has been demonstrated in both heterosexual and gay men (Duggan & McCreary, 2004). In addition, men who suffer from muscle dysmorphia, a subtype of body dysmorphic disorder that specifically involves one's physique, report feeling constant anxiety about their appearance (Olivardia, Pope, & Hudson, 2000; Pope, Gruber, Choi, Olivardia, & Phillips, 1997).

Gender and Body Cognitions

Body cognitions refer to the beliefs and attitudes people have about their bodies, which affect how appearance-related information is processed. Until recently, the general consensus was that girls and women have more negative thoughts and beliefs about their bodies than boys and men do (Thompson et al., 1999); however, these patterns appear to be changing such that boys and men are now reporting negative beliefs and thoughts about their bodies.

Body Schematicity

Schemas are cognitive frameworks that organize our knowledge about people, places, things, and ourselves, which in turn help us to process and interpret new information (Markus, Hamill, & Sentis, 1987). Body schemas, then, represent the particular knowledge people have developed about their physical bodies, which in turn affects the way they process information about their appearance. For example, the more often a person has been labeled as "fat," the more likely it is that the person will automatically and quickly think of herself or himself as fat in response to a variety of situations. In this case, the person would be described as schematic for "fatness" or "weight schematic," whereas a person without these characteristics would be described as aschematic for "fatness" or "weight aschematic." Markus et al. (1987) found that weight-schematic individuals were faster to associate heavy rather than thin silhouettes with the self, whereas weight-aschematic individuals showed no difference in judgment time between the two types of silhouettes. However, the weight-schematic and weight-aschematic groups did not differ in how quickly they responded to the words "fat" and "thin," which suggests that, at least among American college women, it may not be possible to be completely aschematic for body weight.

On the one hand, although both men and women can be weight schematic, some research suggests that weight is more often a defining quality of women's than of men's identity (Grover et al., 2003), and women tend to be more psychologically invested in their appearance than men are (e.g., Cash & Hicks, 1990; Muth & Cash, 1997). For example, Grover et al. found that women's explicit and implicit weight identities were consistent such that the heavier they reported themselves to be in their explicit self-reports, the more likely they were to associate themselves with being "heavy" in their implicit self-reports, where implicit measures represent a person's nonconscious beliefs about themselves and others. In contrast, men's explicit and implicit weight identities were not consistent such that men were more likely to associate themselves with being "light" in their implicit self-reports, regardless of whether they identified themselves as "light" or "heavy" in their explicit self-reports.

On the other hand, some research suggests that muscularity is a defining quality of identity more often for men than for women (Gray & Ginsburg, 2007; McCreary & Sasse, 2000; Pope, Phillips, & Olivardia, 2000); one study indicates that 91% of college men desired a more muscular frame, and none of the men wanted to be less muscular (Jacobi & Cash, 1994). Thus, instead of a focus on weight, it is a focus on muscles that may lead boys and men to view themselves as smaller and lighter, which would foster a desire to gain weight and add muscle mass to increase their body size. Moreover, the fact that a small body size has been linked to suicidal ideation and attempted suicide among men (Carpenter, Hasin, Allison, & Faith, 2000) suggests that women are not necessarily more psychologically invested in their appearance than men are.

Body-Ideal Internalization

Beauty ideals represent culturally prescribed attributes of the human face and body that define the standards for physical attractiveness within a culture. According to Zones (2000), at any given time and place, there are fairly "uniform and widely understood models of how particular groups of individuals 'should' look" (p. 87). These ideals represent accepted, yet virtually unattainable, goals of bodily perfection that people strive to achieve. The cultural beauty ideals prescribed for women and men emphasize the importance of pursuing distinctly different appearance attributes: thinness or muscularity. The internalization of these cultural standards for appearance indicates that the person is aware of the standard and believes that meeting the standard is important.

Westernized feminine beauty ideals have almost always promoted the attainment of physically incompatible body attributes. In the late 20th century, women have tried to have a thin waist but large hips, to be full-figured but thin, to have small breasts but curvy hips and waist, and, in the early 21st century, to have sizable breasts and muscle, but no obvious body fat (Calogero et al., 2007). Indeed, the current beauty ideal may represent the ultimate in unrealistic and unnatural attributes for feminine beauty: ultra thinness and large breasts (Thompson & Tantleff, 1992). This "curvaceously thin" ideal for women is virtually impossible to achieve without some form of surgical modification (Harrison, 2003), which makes the current standards of beauty particularly dangerous and women's body images particularly vulnerable.

The most consistent appearance ideal prescribed for women since the 1960s is thinness. Researchers have demonstrated that girls as young as 5 and 6 years report a desire for a thinner body (Flannery-Schroeder & Chrisler, 1996; Lowes & Tiggemann, 2003). This culture of thinness promotes the personal acceptance or the internalization of a thin body as the beauty ideal, at least for women in Westernized societies (Heinberg, Thompson, & Stormer, 1995). *Thin-ideal internalization* refers to the extent to which individuals accept the thin cultural standard of attractiveness as their own personal standard and engage in behaviors designed to help them meet that standard (Thompson et al., 1999). Women who have internalized the thin ideal, and thereby experience a *drive for thinness*, are more vulnerable to the negative outcomes associated with exposure to thin images than are women who have not internalized these ideals (Groesz et al., 2002; Thompson et al., 1999).

Although thin-ideal internalization dominates women's appearance concerns, the pursuit of a muscular ideal is present in some women (Gruber, 2007). Surveys have documented an increasing shift toward a more muscular female body ideal over the last three decades (Garner, 1997). Women's dissatisfaction with their muscle tone has increased over time, from 30% of women in 1972, to 45% in 1985, and to 57% in 1997. In the 1997 survey, 43% of the entire sample, and 67% of the women in the sample with pre-existing body dissatisfaction, reported that "very thin or muscular models" made them feel insecure. Recent research indicates a discrepancy between women's actual and ideal level of muscularity; women now wish to be more muscular than they actually are (Cafri & Thompson, 2004).

There are several notable ethnic differences in women's thin-ideal internalization. Some research has indicated that Latinas born in the United States endorse an even thinner ideal body size than European American women do, whereas Latinas who immigrated to the United States endorse a larger body ideal (Lopez, Blix, & Blix, 1995). This is consistent with research that demonstrates that children of immigrants in the United States may utilize the media as a "cultural guide" for assimilation (Suarez-Orozco & Suarez-Orozco, 2001). Other research has indicated that some ethnic groups do not endorse the thin ideal. For example, it has been found that Black women have more flexible conceptions of beauty and reject White (thin) ideals for beauty; these flexible conceptions have been linked to more positive body image, higher self-esteem, and less guilt about body size, despite Black women's objectively higher average body weights (Bond & Cash, 1992; Lovejoy, 2001; Makkar & Strube, 1995; Molloy & Herzberger, 1998; Parker et al., 1995; Stevens, Kumanyika, & Keil, 1994).

Other research has demonstrated a less straightforward adoption of the thin ideal. For example, Casanova (2004) reported that adolescent girls in Ecuador claim to endorse the White (thin) beauty ideals espoused by White American girls, but they do tend to be less rigid in their judgments of beauty in everyday life, to examine more critically implicit messages about beauty, and to engage in supportive peer interaction about appearance. Yet, the majority of girls reported that it is compulsory to look good because it affects job and romantic opportunities: "You always have to think about what others will think of you" (Casanova, 2004, p. 300).

Some research with non-Western cultures demonstrates the endorsement of an entirely different appearance ideal: *fatness*. A sample of 249 Moroccan Sahraoui women rated their desired body size on a figural rating scale as significantly *larger* than their rating of a healthy body size (Rguibi & Belahsen, 2006). In this sample, the desire to lose weight was very low, even among the majority of large women, and educational level did not affect desire to lose weight. Women who reported dissatisfaction with their body size were more likely to report trying to *gain* weight. Consistent with the literature on thin-ideal internalization, the internalization of a fat ideal is implicated in the body dissatisfaction of these women. Similar results have been reported in samples of Samoans (Brewis, McGarvey, Jones, & Swinburn, 1998), Malaysians (Swami & Tovee, 2005), and women in African societies (Tovée, Swami, Furnham, & Mangalparsad, 2006; Treloar et al., 1999).

Whereas the socially prescribed body size and shape for Western girls and women is small and thin, the socially prescribed body size and shape for Western boys and men is big and muscular (Thompson & Cafri, 2007). Indeed, since the 19th century, the most consistent appearance ideal prescribed for men has been muscularity (Luciano, 2007). Although at the beginning of the 20th century, men with bulging muscles were located at the fringes of society, confined to the bodybuilding subculture and Mr. America contests, the end of the 20th century saw a rapid development in the culture of muscularity in mainstream society, which continues today. Indeed, the current masculine beauty ideal emphasizes a muscular V-shape with a well-developed upper body, flat stomach, and narrow hips (Leit, Pope, & Gray, 2001).

This culture of muscularity promotes the personal acceptance or internalization of a hypermuscular body as the masculine body ideal (Cafri et al., 2005; Grogan & Richards, 2002; McCreary & Sasse, 2000; Thompson & Cafri, 2007). *Muscular-ideal internalization* refers to the extent to which individuals accept the muscular cultural standard of attractiveness as their own personal standard and engage in behaviors designed to help them meet that standard (Thompson & Cafri, 2007). Men who have internalized the muscular ideal, and thereby pursue a muscular body, are more vulnerable to the negative outcomes associated with exposure to muscular images than are men who have not internalized these ideals. In particular, muscular-ideal internalization is associated with a *drive for muscularity* among men in Westernized societies (McCreary & Sasse, 2000), which in turn has been linked to men's body dissatisfaction (Cafri, Blevins, & Thompson, 2006), dieting to gain weight (McCreary & Sasse, 2000), overtraining (Klein, 2007), steroid use (Ricciardelli & McCabe, 2004), muscle dysmorphia (Pope et al., 2005), and body dysmorphic disorder (Phillips & Castle, 2001).

When a desire to be thinner has been documented among boys, it appears to reflect a desire for less body fat or more leanness as opposed to a smaller frame (Cafri, Strauss, & Thompson, 2002). However, research conducted by Yelland and Tiggemann (2003) revealed several interesting patterns with regard to the body image of gay men. First, they found that the gay ideal body shape involves being both thin and muscular; gay men's drive for thinness is on par with women's drive for thinness, and gay men's drive for muscularity is higher than that of heterosexual men. They also found that gay men engage in behaviors to try to achieve this ideal, such as disordered eating, muscle-building exercise, and food supplementation. However, with regard to body dissatisfaction in general, gay men reported being more satisfied than women and just as satisfied as heterosexual men, although gay men did report less satisfaction than did heterosexual men with their current level of muscularity.

The evidence for lesbians is more mixed. Traditional lesbian ideology rejects the culture of thinness and sexist ideologies that persist in Westernized societies (Cogan, 1999), and, therefore, lesbians should be less susceptible to thin-ideal internalization. These notions have been supported to some extent: Lesbians report less body monitoring, less thin-ideal internalization, and less disordered eating than heterosexual women do (Guille & Chrisler, 1999; Schneider, O'Leary, & Jenkins, 1995). However, these effects are quite modest (Owens, Hughes, & Owens-Nicholson, 2003) and suggest that a lesbian subculture may counteract some of the sociocultural pressures for women's appearance but may not be able to protect against the broader sociocultural preference for thin women (Cogan, 1999; Dworkin, 1989). For example, recent research has shown that lesbians and heterosexual women experience similar levels of interpersonal sexual objectification and body shame, but lesbians report even higher body surveillance than heterosexual women do (Kozee & Tylka, 2006). It is important to note that, in that study, interpersonal experiences of sexual objectification were directly linked to lesbians' body shame and disordered eating, whereas it was not the case for heterosexual women.

Gender and Body Behaviors

Body behaviors refer to how people behave toward, and in relation to, their bodies. Often conceptualized as the "outcome" variables in empirical studies, a consideration of the actual behaviors that men and women engage in as a result of their body image-related experiences serves as a grave reminder of the significance of these phenomena in people's lives. As Harrison (2003) noted, to meet the current "curvaceously thin" ideal, women are at risk for doing "double damage" to themselves as they try to reduce and reshape the lower body through disordered eating and exercise practices and to enlarge and reshape the upper body through surgery and drug use (e.g., herbal supplements). Similarly, in order to meet the "masculine ideal of lean muscularity" (Leon, Fulkerson, Perry, Keel, & Klump, 1999), boys and men may simultaneously engage in strategies to gain muscle and strategies to lose weight (Cafri et al., 2005), which may also place them at increased risk for doing "double damage" to their bodies.

Eating Disorders

It has been well documented that eating disorders are gendered phenomena. Indeed, 90% of those affected with anorexia nervosa and bulimia nervosa are girls and women (American Psychiatric Association, 1994), although other eating disorders, such as binge-eating disorder, show fewer gender differences (Johnson & Torgrud, 1996). Body dissatisfaction is the most consistent predictor of the onset of eating disturbances (Cattarin & Thompson, 1994; Thompson et al., 1999), thus it may be no wonder that eating disorders occur at substantially higher rates in girls and women than in boys and men. The behavioral hallmark of these disorders is the pursuit of weight loss by chronic dieting, fasting, binging, purging, and a variety of other methods. Eating disorders have the highest mortality rate of all psychiatric disorders (American Psychiatric Association, 1994); therefore, because of the much higher prevalence rate of eating disturbances for women, it is clear that their risk of death from eating disorders is much higher than that for men.

Body Dysmorphic Disorder (BDD)

BDD refers to an excessive preoccupation with an imagined or slight defect in appearance that brings about emotional suffering and significant disruptions in daily functioning (American Psychiatric Association, 2000; Crerand, Phillips, Menard, & Fay, 2005). Although any body part can become the focus of concern, BDD is typically characterized by intrusive thoughts about one's skin, hair, or facial features. BDD occurs with relatively similar frequency in men and women; however, some of the clinical features may vary. For example, women with BDD tend to be more preoccupied with their hips and weight, pick at pimples on their skin, use makeup to cover imagined defects, and suffer from bulimia nervosa, whereas men with BDD tend to be more preoccupied with bodybuilding, genitals, thinning hair, and using a hat to cover imagined defects, and to be unmarried and have alcohol abuse or dependence (Phillips & Diaz, 1997). The course of BDD tends to be chronic, and the level of impairment can be quite severe, including attempted and completed suicides (Phillips et al., 2005).

The trend toward cultural representations of hypermuscular men parallels a rise in the prevalence of muscle dysmorphia among men, which is described as a type of BDD with an obsessive focus on becoming muscular (Olivardia et al., 2000). Men with BDD and muscle dysmorphia (MD) have a particularly high risk of attempted suicide, poor quality of life, substance use disorder, and anabolic steroid use (Cafri, Olivardia, & Thompson, 2008; Pope et al., 2005). Although there have been documented cases of MD in women, the data to date suggest that men are much more likely to have this type of BDD. However, well-designed prevalence studies are lacking and, to date, no study has specifically compared men and women on MD characteristics and associated features.

Anabolic Steroid Use

Although once restricted to bodybuilders and weight lifters, the use of anabolic-androgenic steroids (AAS) is filtering into the mainstream as men, and increasingly women, strive for a more muscular look (Bahrke, 2007; Thompson & Cafri, 2007). The use of AAS to achieve a more muscular and lean body is associated with many serious negative side effects, such as cardiovascular disease, liver failure, kidney tumors, aggressiveness, mood changes, and substance dependence (Cafri et al., 2005). Most of the research on AAS describes samples of adolescent boys and men because increased muscularity is a body change goal predominant among them; however, AAS may not be a problem only among boys as there is increasing pressure for women to look muscular and toned as well as thin and slim (Harrison, 2003). Estimates suggest that between 1 and 12% of boys and between 0.2 and 9% of girls have used AAS sometime in their life (Ricciardelli & McCabe, 2004).

Cosmetic Surgery

Over the last decade, the rate of cosmetic surgical and nonsurgical procedures has exploded in the United States: There has been a 457% increase in all cosmetic procedures since 1997; nearly 11.7 million procedures were performed in 2007 (American Society for Aesthetic Plastic Surgery, 2008). It is important to emphasize that all forms of cosmetic surgery have become normalized for both women and men. This is most clearly evident in mainstream American television shows, such as *Extreme Makeover* and *The Swan,* which have large prime-time audiences. People on these shows compete to undergo surgical procedures to modify their appearance to make it more acceptable and closer to appearance ideals. Viewership of these types of shows was recently found to be related to positive attitudes toward cosmetic surgery, body dissatisfaction, and eating disturbances (Sperry, Thompson, Sarwer, & Cash, 2009). This normalized practice of surgically modifying the body to meet beauty standards has caused deadly infections, gangrene, nerve damage, loss of sensation, loss of body parts, mutilated body parts, and death (Haiken, 1997): These deleterious effects of cosmetic surgery on physical health and psychological well-being have been reported for decades but do not seem to have harmed its popularity.

In 2007, the top five surgical procedures included liposuction, breast augmentation, eyelid surgery, abdominoplasty, and breast reduction and the top five nonsurgical procedures included botox injection, hyaluronic acid, laser hair removal, microdermabrasion, and laser skin resurfacing (ASAPS, 2008). Both women and men express approval for body-altering surgical procedures to achieve their ideals of bodily perfection (Henderson-King & Henderson-King, 2005), but approximately 10.6 million of these procedures were performed on women (91%), whereas 1.1 million of these procedures were performed on men (9%) in 2007. Although the percentage of men undergoing cosmetic surgery is minimal relative to women, a 44% increase in cosmetic surgery among men was documented between the years 2000 and 2004 (American Society of Plastic Surgeons, 2005); the most common surgical procedures among men included rhinoplasty, hair transplantation, and liposuction.

A recent development in men's body image is the recognition that some men engage in body depilation (Boroughs, Cafri & Thompson, 2005; Boroughs & Thompson, 2002), which is the removal of hair in non-traditional places for men (e.g., arms, legs, genital area). Body depilation is a standard practice among competitive bodybuilders in order to show off the highest possible muscle definition during competitions (Klein, 2007). Yet the practice of body depilation has been extended to men outside this particular athletic subculture. Indeed, the media have coined the term "metrosexual" to characterize a fashion-conscious urban heterosexual man with a strong aesthetic sense who spends a great deal of time and money on his appearance and lifestyle (e.g., clothing, manicures, facials). The cultural idea of the metrosexual might be one contributing factor to explain the emergence of male body depilation and other body enhancing or modification strategies such as cosmetic surgery.

Avoidance

Although seemingly less harmful than cosmetic surgery and steroid use, the actual avoidance of social situations and interactions where the body may be on display can bring its own set of negative consequences to people's lives. There is evidence to indicate that women choose to avoid situations significantly more often than men do because of their appearance. For example, a stunning report by Etcoff and colleagues (2006) revealed that 67% of women aged 15–64 across 10 countries actually withdraw from life-engaging, life-sustaining activities due to feeling badly about their looks. These activities include giving an opinion, meeting friends, exercising, going to work, going to school, dating, and going to the doctor. In a recent study of 52,677 heterosexual adult readers of *Elle* magazine aged 18–65, women reported greater dissatisfaction with their appearance and were more likely than men to avoid situations where their bodies were on display, such as wearing a swimsuit in public (Frederick et al., 2006). In addition, negative body image concerns are linked to the avoidance of sexual intimacy and sexual activity with a partner, at least among some women (Faith & Schare, 1993; Wiederman, 2000).

Theoretical Explanations

The evidence presented above supports the idea that gender has a profound impact on multiple dimensions of body image. Indeed, although some similarities exist, numerous gender differences have been documented with regard to how men and women perceive, feel about, think about, and treat their bodies. In the following sections we turn our attention toward potential explanations for these gender differences. In particular, we describe three theoretical frameworks to help us understand how broader social psychological, sociocultural, and sociostructural mechanisms may contribute to differences in the body images of women and men.

Tripartite Model of Social Influence

According to the tripartite influence model, parents, peers, and media represent three formative influences on body image (Keery et al., 2004; Shroff & Thompson, 2006). The gender differences in body perceptions, body cognitions, body feelings, and body behaviors can be explained partially by the distinctly different messages that boys/men and girls/women receive about their bodies. In particular, considerable evidence indicates that these sociocultural sources consistently promote striving toward the thin ideal among women and the muscular ideal among men.

Parents

Perceptions by both young girls and boys that their parents are concerned about their child's weight predict higher levels of body dissatisfaction in these young children (Gardner, Sorter, & Friedman, 1997); however, the majority of studies indicate that parents exert a stronger influence on the appearance concerns of girls than of boys (Barker & Galambos, 2003; Thompson et al., 1999). For young girls, the desire to be thinner is correlated with actual encouragement to lose weight from both mothers and fathers (Thelen & Cormier, 1995). One study showed that the body esteem of girls was related to mothers' comments about daughters' weight, mothers' complaints about their own weight, mothers' weight loss attempts, and fathers' complaints about their own weight (Smolak,

Levine, & Schermer, 1999). McKinley (1999) provided further evidence that mothers' experiences with their bodies influence daughters' experiences with their bodies. In a sample of 151 undergraduate women and their middle-aged mothers, McKinley demonstrated significant, positive relationships between mothers' and daughters' body esteem and body monitoring. In addition, higher body shame in mothers was associated with lower body esteem in daughters, and daughters' perceptions that the family approved of their appearance significantly predicted their body esteem. Phares et al. (2004) found that, compared to boys, girls exhibited greater body image concern, received more information regarding weight and dieting from their parents, and tried more actively to stay thin.

In contrast, for young boys, the desire to be thinner was not related to perceived or actual encouragement to lose weight from either mother or father (Thelen & Cormier, 1995). Perhaps this is because parents are less likely to encourage boys to lose weight, as this strategy would move boys further away from the muscular ideal. Instead, perceived pressure to increase muscle size may influence weight and/or body dissatisfaction among boys. Recent evidence supports this possibility. McCabe and Ricciardelli (2005) found that pressure from mothers to increase muscularity predicted weight dissatisfaction 8 months later and muscle dissatisfaction more than 1 year later in their sons. In a longitudinal investigation of 237 boys aged 8–11 years, the sole predictor of boys' body dissatisfaction was BMI, and the main predictors of body change strategies were BMI and the perceived pressure to modify weight and muscularity from parents, peers, and media (Ricciardelli, McCabe, Lillis, & Thomas, 2006). Other research has shown that mothers' messages and mothers' own body dissatisfaction predict the degree of body dissatisfaction in boys, whereas the role of fathers appears to be less influential (Lowes & Tiggemann, 2003).

Peers

Appearance-related teasing and commentary from peers is associated with negative body image in girls and women (Murray, Touyz, & Beaumont, 1995; Oliver & Thelan, 1996; Paxton, Schultz, Wertheim, & Muir, 1999). In a nationally representative cohort of middle-aged British women, experiences of appearance-related commentary in childhood continued to exert negative effects on body esteem in later life (McLaren, Kuh, Hardy, & Gauvin, 2004). However, body image concerns may occur in the context of peer relationships for both boys and girls. For example, adolescent boys and girls who reported engaging in frequent conversations about appearance with friends endorsed greater internalization of appearance ideals, which in turn predicted greater body dissatisfaction (Jones, 2001; Jones & Crawford, 2005; Jones, Vigfusdottir, & Lee, 2004). However, among boys, social comparisons appear to be more closely related to body change strategies than to body dissatisfaction per se (Holt & Ricciardelli, 2007).

Other gender differences have been noted as well. In a 3-year prospective study, Lunde, Frisen, and Hwang (2007) evaluated peer victimization and teasing (among other variables) as predictors of body esteem in 10-year-old girls ($n = 474$) and boys ($n = 400$). Their findings indicate that peer victimization had long-term association with girls' weight esteem, but teasing related to appearance was associated with boys' more negative beliefs regarding how others viewed their appearance. Furthermore, in a sample of college-aged men and women, childhood teasing about weight, but not teasing about general appearance or competence, predicted negative body image in men, whereas childhood teasing about weight, general appearance, and competence predicted negative body image in women (Gleason, Alexander, & Somers, 2000). In addition, teasing about competence predicted lower general self-esteem in men, whereas teasing about appearance and competence predicted lower general self-esteem in women. That men's body image was influenced by fewer forms of teasing than was women's body image suggests that women's sense of competence is more intricately tied to their appearance than is men's and, moreover, that men's self-esteem is more likely than women's to develop independently from body image. It should be noted that, whereas some of the questions about teasing in that study referred to "other kids" or "peers" explicitly as the perpetrators of the teasing, other questions referred to "people" more generally as the perpetrators; therefore, it is not clear to what extent the source of the teasing, as opposed to the mere occurrence of teasing, is the critical factor in the development of body image concerns.

Peer effects extend to intimate partners as well. A 1995 survey by *Glamour* magazine showed that men hold unrealistic views of women's bodies and support methods that might bring their partners' bodies more in line with unrealistic cultural standards (Haiken, 1997). *Glamour* asked men: "If it were painless, safe, and free, would you encourage your wife or girlfriend to get breast implants?" More than one-half (55%) of the men sampled answered "yes."

Media

Virtually every form of media communicates the idea that thinness is desirable for women (Levine & Harrison, 2004), including magazines (Englis, Solomon, & Ashmore, 1994), television shows (Harrison & Cantor, 1997), television commercials (Richins, 1991), music videos (Tiggemann & Slater, 2003), films (Silverstein, Perdue, Peterson, & Kelly, 1986), books (Baker-Sperry & Grauerholz, 2003), and children's videos (Herbozo, Tantleff-Dunn, Gokee-Larose, & Thompson, 2004). These images of women consistently portrayed in the media are not realistic as the body proportions are virtually unattainable for most women (Tiggemann & Pickering, 1996). The negative impact of these sources still seems virtually unavoidable even for individuals who do not purposely expose themselves to media sources of these beauty ideals. For example, exposure to ideal body television images was associated with preferences for thinness and approval of cosmetic surgery even for individuals who expressed no interest in viewing television shows with topics such as dieting, nutrition, fitness, and exercise (Harrison, 2003). This finding may be explained, in part, by research that shows that more exposure to thin-ideal media is associated with a greater tendency among women to idealize thinness (Harrison & Cantor, 1997). Indeed, women expect that their lives will change in important and positive ways if they look like the ideal portrayals of women in the media (Engeln-Maddox, 2006; Evans, 2003); that is, women expect that they would be happier, better adjusted, more socially competent, more romantically successful, and have more job opportunities.

Although much of the research on media exposure to unrealistic body ideals has focused on women, there is increasing evidence that men are also targeted and affected. For example, when exposed to pictures of attractive same-sex models, both men and women reported lower body esteem (Grogan, Williams, & Conner, 1996). Boys and men are exposed to hypermuscular male bodies through television, movies, magazines, and other media (Pope et al., 2000). The muscular ideal is the preferred body size and shape among boys and men (Jones, 2001; Pope et al., 2000), and this is the masculine body ideal that is increasingly promoted in the mass media (Luciano, 2007). Researchers have documented the sociocultural shift in portrayals of the muscular male ideal. Leit et al. (2001) found that *Playgirl* centerfolds have become increasingly muscular over the past 25 years by losing 12 lbs (5.4 kg) of fat and gaining 27 lbs (12.25 kg) of muscle. In one study, measurements of the waist, chest, and bicep circumference of male action figures (e.g., GI Joes, wrestlers) indicated increasingly muscular physiques over the past 30 years (Pope, Olivardia, Gruber, & Borowiecki, 1999); some of the measurements far exceed the muscularity of even the largest human bodybuilders. Although research is lacking on how playing with these action figures affects the body image concerns of young boys, one study showed that young adult men report lower body esteem after touching and manipulating hypermuscular action figures (Bartlett, Harris, Smith, & Bonds-Raacke, 2005). Even male mannequins in store windows have become more muscular (Olivardia, 2002). Studies have consistently shown that exposure to muscular images is associated with body image concerns in adolescent boys (Botta, 2003) and adult men (Agliata & Tantleff-Dunn, 2004; Grogan et al., 1996; Leit, Gray, & Pope, 2002).

The idea that the particular content of the media can inform and mold people's views of themselves and the world around them is the basis of cultivation theory (Gerbner, Gross, Morgan, & Signorielli, 1994). In particular, it is the *television* exposure that "cultivates" people's beliefs, attitudes, and behaviors about their bodies such that the more frequently the people are exposed to certain themes and images, the more they view those images as both desirable and realistic; the boundaries between fictitious and real bodies become blurred (Freedman, 1984; Holstrom, 2004). The consistent portrayal of idealized bodies on television has been implicated in the early development of body image. In a study of preadolescents 8–11 years old, patterns of media use were associated with a greater attraction to muscular appearances and athletic ability among boys and a greater attraction to beauty among girls (Jung & Peterson, 2007). McCreary and Sadava (1999) demonstrated a significant positive association between television viewing and both women's and men's beliefs that they were overweight, independent of their actual weight. In a study of children's animated cartoons that appeared on television and movie screens between the 1930s and the 1990s (e.g., Bugs Bunny, Popeye), the researchers concluded that the cartoon characters communicated positive messages about being attractive and negative messages about being unattractive (Klein & Shiffman, 2006). In an investigation of actual eating behavior, researchers found that a "diet of ideal media" predicted smaller amounts of food consumed by women and larger amounts of food consumed by men (Harrison, Taylor, & Marske, 2006), which is consistent with the gendered body ideals of thinness and muscularity "cultivated" by the media.

The cross-cultural work of Ann Becker and her colleagues demonstrates the impact of Westernized media imagery on adolescent girls in Fiji. Since the introduction of television in 1995, young Fijian girls have expressed an increased desire to be thin. Between 1995 and 1998, a cross-sectional, two-wave cohort study revealed increased eating disorder attitudes and behaviors among ethnic Fijian adolescents (Becker, Burwell, Gilman, Herzog, & Hamburg, 2002). This is remarkable considering that the traditionally revered body in Fiji is large and robust; yet, there is no corresponding preoccupation with attaining this robust ideal (Becker, 1995). The narrative responses of adolescent Fijian girls reveal that young girls admire and accept Western ideals of beauty portrayed in the media, and they associate thinness with success and social mobility (Becker, 2004). In addition, these girls reported increased identification with television characters as role models, preoccupation with weight loss, greater motivation to reshape their bodies through dieting and exercise, and disordered eating behaviors. According to Becker (2004, p. 553), "Fijian self-presentation has absorbed new dimensions related to buying into Western styles of appearance and the ethos of work on the body."

Perhaps even more important, the portrayal of thinness and muscularity as good is contrasted with the portrayal of fatness as bad, which prescribes anti-fat attitudes as normative in Westernized societies (Allon, 1982; Bessenoff & Sherman, 2000; Crandall, 1994; Hebl & Mannix, 2003; Puhl & Brownell, 2003; Vartanian, Herman, & Polivy, 2005). The media cultivate fat prejudice and weight stigma by showing a very narrow range of acceptable bodies, especially for women; almost two-thirds of the women portrayed on television weigh 15% less than the average American woman (Spitzer, Henderson, & Zivian, 1999). The media also cultivate fat prejudice by showing derogatory depictions of fat characters such that fat people are portrayed as less active, intelligent, hardworking, attractive, popular, romantically desirable, successful, and athletic than people of average weight; again, this is especially true for depictions of fat women (Fouts & Burggraf, 1999; Greenberg, Eastin, Hofshire, Lachlan, & Brownell, 2003; Hebl & Heatherton, 1997).

This stigmatization of fatness is apparent early in childhood (Goldfield & Chrisler, 1995) and communicated in children's media (Herbozo et al., 2004), and thus affects the perceptions of both boys and girls. However, the biological reality is that the female body has more fat than does the male body; therefore, women will more often naturally deviate from the idealized image of a "fat-free" body (Fallon, 1990). This sets women up to be targeted more often as bad and unacceptable because of their bodies' natural attributes (Chrisler, 1996), and this targeting begins at a very young age. Thus, it may not be the constant media exposure to idealized bodies alone, but also the constant media exposure to the associations between attractive physical appearance and clear rewards or punishments, that leads to the cultivation of women's and men's body images.

In sum, although some research indicates that girls receive and detect more messages than boys do about their bodies from sociocultural sources (McCabe, Ricciardelli, & Ridge, 2006; Smolak, Levine, & Thompson, 2001; Tiggemann, Gardiner, & Slater, 2000; Wertheim, Paxton, Schultz, & Muir, 1997), it is the distinctly different content of the messages that may contribute to the gender differences in body image. Most messages transmitted to boys focus on the importance of the functionality and strength of their bodies, whereas most messages transmitted to girls focus on the importance of the appearance and weight of their bodies (Grogan & Richards, 2002; McCabe et al., 2006), which in turn map onto men's and women's respective pursuits of muscularity and thinness. Thus, the tripartite model of social influence may explain why men and women come to take different perspectives on their bodies and may help to explain the more drastic behavioral measures, such as cosmetic surgery and steroid use, that people may take to try to attain appearance ideals.

Gender Socialization

Both the social construction of what it means to be a boy or a girl and the distinct biology of being male or female contribute to gender socialization (Eagly, Beall, & Sternberg, 2004). From an early age, girls are socialized to focus on their external appearance and on their interpersonal qualities and relationships, whereas boys are socialized to focus on their agentic qualities and abilities (Eagly, 1987; Rodin, Silberstein, & Striegel-Moore, 1984), which contribute to the development of girls' and boys' self-concepts (Wood, Christensen, Hebl, & Rothgerber, 1997). These gender socialization practices, which teach girls to value being communal and boys to value being agentic, extend to the ways in which girls and boys learn to view, experience, and treat their bodies. In particular, it has been documented that the traditional gender roles associated with women (e.g., caregiver, nurturing, relational) are in direct conflict with the values of individualism, independence, and competitiveness promoted in Westernized societies (Brown & Jasper, 1993), whereas the traditional gender roles associated with men are largely in line with societal values. Moreover, women's bodies have often functioned as their primary social and economic currency (Henley, 1977; Hesse-Biber, Leavy, Quinn, & Zoino, 2006; Unger & Crawford, 1996). Because the body serves as an instrument through which social and cultural forces are communicated, "it is hardly surprising that the body is often the arena within which women unconsciously choose to express conflict which they feel in their lives" (Dana & Lawrence, 1988, p. 35). Thus, the disproportionate rate of negative body image typically observed in women relative to men may actually reflect their discontent and unhappiness about their inferior social status; however, it is their appearance, and not their social status, that they might more quickly and directly improve to feel better (Brown & Jasper, 1993).

In conjunction with learning these traditional gender roles, girls experience specific developmental changes that contribute to the gender socialization process. Indeed, women's bodies change more substantially than men's across the life span. There is evidence that physical changes during puberty, menstruation, pregnancy, the postpartum period, and menopause are very often associated with increased difficulties in girls' and women's relationships with their bodies (Ussher, 1989).

Because the physical changes that accompany puberty push girls further away from the thin ideal, whereas their pubertal changes bring boys closer to the muscular ideal, adolescence becomes a critical window for markedly increased negative body image in girls and decreased negative body image in boys. As Ussher (1989, p. 18) wrote, "It is during adolescence that the young woman first experiences a split between her body and her self: between her own experience and the archetype she is expected to emulate."

However, it is not only weight and shape that cause distress about the body for adolescent girls. The social construction of the sexual organs affects girls' body images during this critical developmental period. As Ussher (1989, p. 19) explained it, "...whilst boys learn to perceive their genitals as a source of pride and pleasure, girls mainly develop a sense of shame, disgust, and humiliation about theirs. In this way then, social stereotypes which define women's genitals as unpleasant, odorous and unattractive, are internalized by the female child." Thus, the sexual and reproductive functions of the female body are framed and constrained to fit very narrow standards for acceptable, feminine bodies. In support of these ideas, a longitudinal investigation (Yuan, 2007) of 9,011 girls and 8,781 boys showed that adolescent girls experience more depressive symptoms after than before puberty due to their self-perceptions of being overweight and more physically developed than their peers. In contrast, boys experience more depressive symptoms during than after puberty due to their self-perceptions of not being as large and developed as their peers, whereas pre- and post-pubertal boys did not differ in depressive symptoms.

Part of the problem has been that men's bodies have served as the gold standard for what is good and normal about the human body, and, therefore, by comparison, women's bodies have often been perceived as inferior and deviant from this biological baseline (McNay, 1992). Women's bodily functions, particularly menstruation, have been historically reviled and associated with disgust (Delaney, Lupton, & Toth, 1988), and these negative perceptions remain largely intact in contemporary Westernized societies (Buckley & Gottlieb, 1988; Roberts, 2000; Rozin, Haidt, McCauley, Dunlop, & Ashmore, 1999; Ussher, 1989). In the late 19th century, the *British Medical Journal* published letters from doctors suggesting that women should not prepare hams if it was their "time of the month," and, until recently, withering fruit trees and sour wine were believed to be caused by the contamination of menstrual blood or menstruating women (Einon, 2007; Knight, 1995). In particular, menstruation, pregnancy, and lactation seem to tie women more closely to nature, which in turn has been used to devalue women and judge them as inferior (Tauna, 1993). Evidence from a recent study of American university students indicates that the mere presence of a tampon led both women and men to rate a peer as less competent and likable and to distance themselves physically from her (Roberts, Goldenberg, Power, & Pyszczynski, 2002). According to Roberts et al. (2002, p. 138), "...norms of secrecy and concealment surrounding menstruation nevertheless serve the function of keeping women's corporeal bodies out of the public eye. Thus, the sanitized, deodorized, and idealized images of women's bodies become the only ones we encounter and accept."

The process of gender socialization and the adoption of traditional gender roles may also explain the development of men's body image and the rising trends in men's body image concerns. Boys and young men report feeling a social imperative to be more muscular in order to obtain social power, to avoid ostracism (Drummond, 2002), and to manage the stress associated with deviating from masculine ideals and gender roles (Mussap, 2008). Indeed, the attainment of muscle is indicative of masculinity and having reached the status of "being a man" because muscles convey the masculine qualities of strength, dominance, and power. In contrast, men who are small in stature and not muscular convey weakness, which is inconsistent with masculinity and may leave boys and men more open to ridicule. Men who can achieve a muscular body are simultaneously meeting the ideals for masculinity promoted in Western societies (Connell, 2005; Luciano, 2007). It is not surprising that researchers have demonstrated positive relationships between a drive for muscularity and the endorsement of masculine personality traits and men's traditional social roles (Kimmel & Mahilik, 2004; McCreary, Saucier, & Courtenay, 2005).

Perhaps the most widely accepted criterion for masculinity is the absence of feminine qualities and traits (Holbrook, Andersen, & Cohn, 2000; McCreary, 1994). Indeed, it has been suggested that men's increased concerns with muscularity may reflect their uneasiness with women's improved economic and social status (Luciano, 2007). Some interesting statistics provided by Shellenbarger (2005) explain why men might feel threatened. Since 1990, the proportion of women earning more than $100,000 per year has tripled (whereas men's earnings have declined over the same period), and roughly one-third of wives earn more than their husbands do. Moreover, women hold 58% of all bachelor's degrees and 59% of all master's degrees. If we consider that economic power has long been a critical indicator of masculinity and that higher education and higher-paying occupations have remained almost exclusively in men's domain, it may not be surprising that men are looking for other ways to display their masculinity (Drummond, 2003; Pope et al., 2000). Muscularity remains one area in which women will not be able to surpass or easily match men, and, therefore, the attainment of a muscular physique conveys the message that men are still more powerful than, and physically superior to, women.

In sum, gender differences in body image may be explained by the distinctly different socialization practices and developmental changes that occur in girls and boys. The long-standing and well-documented higher rates of body dissatisfaction among women compared to men may stem, in part, from socialization practices that align women's physically smaller bodies with inferior and devalued social roles (Eagly et al., 2004) and sanction the expression of disgust toward women's naturally changing bodies (Martin, 1992; Roberts et al., 2002). These same socialization practices align men's physically larger bodies with superior and valued social roles, but the improvements in women's social position and gains in freedom have threatened these roles. In order to maintain a superordinate position in the hierarchy, it may seem necessary to bulk up; hence, the increased rates of body dissatisfaction and the importance of appearance in men.

Objectification Theory

A common theme shared by the perspectives described above is that women are defined and treated more often as bodies than men are. What girls and women, and boys and men, come to learn about women's bodies from sociocultural agents and gender socialization is that women's bodies are open to and available for sexual objectification. Being sexually objectified is a pervasive aspect of girls'/women's, but not boys'/men's, social lives in Westernized societies (Bartky, 1990; Calogero et al., 2007; Eck, 2003; Huebner & Fredrickson, 1999; Krassas, Blauwkamp, & Wesselink, 2003; Piran & Cormier, 2005; Plous & Neptune, 1997; Reichert, 2003; Swim, Hyers, Cohen, & Ferguson, 2001; Thompson et al., 1999). Experiences of sexual objectification occur at a very young age; a disturbing 75% of American elementary school girls report experiences of sexual harassment (Murnen & Smolak, 2000). Although both boys and girls may be victims of sexual harassment, girls are more frequently targeted and suffer more devastating effects (Bryant, 1993; Murnen, Smolak, Mills, & Good, 2003). As documented in a well-known study of adolescents supported by the American Association of University Women, after experiences of sexual harassment, girls were nearly five times more likely than boys to be afraid at school and three times less self-confident (Bryant, 1993). Because of the sexual harassment, one-third of the girls did not want to attend school, and nearly one-third did not want to speak up in class.

Particularly insidious is the exposure to sexualized media environments, which have been linked to the development of adolescent girls' and boys' notions of women as sex objects (American Psychological Association Task Force on the Sexualization of Girls, 2007; Busby & Leichty, 1993; Grogan & Wainwright, 1996; Harper & Tiggemann, 2008; Peter & Valkenburg, 2007; Reichert & Carpenter, 2004; Ward & Friedman, 2006). Research has revealed the dominant presence of depictions of women in the role of sex object across virtually every medium, including prime-time television programs (e.g., Grauerholz & King, 1997; Ward, 1995), television commercials (e.g., Lin, 1997), music videos (e.g., Gow, 1995; Vincent 1989), and magazines (e.g., Krassas et al., 2003; Plous & Neptune, 1997). Such sexually objectifying images of women have been increasing over time (e.g., Busby & Leichty, 1993; Reichert & Carpenter, 2004): One report indicates a 60% increase in the portrayal of women in "decorative" roles from 1970 to the mid-1980s (Sullivan & O'Connor, 1988). Moreover, the sexual objectification of women in the media affects men's beliefs about women's bodies. Ward, Merriwether, and Caruthers (2006) demonstrated that heavier media usage by men is linked to greater acceptance of traditional gender ideologies that construct women as sex objects and to positive views of women's bodies and body parts when they serve a sexual function but not when they serve a reproductive function.

Over a decade ago, Fredrickson and Roberts (1997) offered Objectification Theory as a formal framework for understanding how exposure to chronic sexual objectification negatively and disproportionately affects multiple dimensions of women's lives. According to this theory, daily encounters with sexual objectification across multiple interpersonal and social contexts lead girls and women to view themselves as objects. Girls and women come to adopt an objectifying observers' perspective on their bodies such that "they treat *themselves* as objects to be looked at and evaluated" (p. 177, emphasis in original). According to Bartky (1990, p. 72),

> In contemporary patriarchal culture, a panoptical male connoisseur resides within the consciousness of most women: They stand perpetually before his gaze and under his judgment. Woman lives her body as seen by another, by an anonymous patriarchal Other.

This self-perspective, referred to as self-objectification, does not merely reflect social comparison with others, or the fact that women simply do not like the size or the shape of their bodies, but actually reflects a view of the body as belonging "less to them and more to others" (Fredrickson & Roberts, 1997, p. 193) because women learn that it is normative for their bodies to be looked at, commented on, evaluated, and sexually harassed. Despite the heterogeneity among women with regard to ethnicity, class, sexuality, and age, "having a reproductively mature body may create a shared social experience, a vulnerability to sexual objectification, which in turn may create a shared set of psychological experiences" (Fredrickson & Roberts, 1997, p. 3).

Self-objectification has been associated with significant costs to women's emotional well-being (e.g., body shame, appearance anxiety, diminished internal bodily awareness) and cognitive performance (e.g., decreased motivational states, poorer math performance), and disproportionately higher rate of mental health risks (i.e., depression, sexual dysfunction, and disordered eating). In particular, the pervasive sexual objectification of women, and the resultant self-objectification, is one explanation for the disproportionate rate of eating disorders among women in Westernized societies (Calogero, Davis, & Thompson, 2005; Fredrickson & Roberts, 1997; McKinley & Hyde, 1996; Striegel-Moore & Smolak, 2001; Thompson et al., 1999). Thus, the objectified way in which women's bodies are evaluated and treated at both the cultural and the individual level has direct implications for women's quality of life and well-being.

This focus on the negative consequences of the objectification of women is consistent with the aims of objectification theory, but there is evidence to suggest that men's bodies are also becoming objectified (Pope, Olivardia, Borowiecki, & Cochrane, 2001; Thompson & Cafri, 2007). For example, in recent decades, there has been widespread exposure of the nearly nude male body to sell products such as underwear and shaving gel (Luciano, 2007), and fitness magazines expose men to idealized images of the male body, with particular emphasis on extremely muscular and lean bodies that show off the "six-pack abs" (Botta, 2003). In fact, the percentage of nearly nude men portrayed in women's magazines such as *Glamour* and *Cosmopolitan* approximates that of nearly nude images of women (Luciano, 2007). Thus, sexualized depictions of men are becoming more common.

Although women self-objectify to a greater degree than men do (Strelan & Hargreaves, 2005), the nature and patterns of men's self-objectification should be clarified because some men do self-objectify, and those who do also report more body shame and restrained eating (Hebl et al., 2004; Martins et al., 2007; Tiggemann & Kuring, 2004). The degree to which men have internalized this objectified view of their bodies needs further investigation, but there are several indications that men feel pressure to meet body ideals and to invest more effort in their appearance. In a recent cross-cultural study of college-aged men from Austria, France, and the United States, the men, on average, chose an ideal body shape that was approximately 28 lbs (12.70 kg) more muscular than their actual body shape (Pope et al., 2000). As noted earlier, men are increasingly electing to engage in body change strategies, usually to increase their muscle size with steroids or different types of implants (Luciano, 2007). The severity of these trends was underscored by Leit, Gray, and Pope (2002, p. 334), who wrote that "…the cultural ideal of hypermesomorphy may be just as dangerous to men as is the anorexic ideal to women." Of course, the numerous risks to men's health as a result of these body change strategies and procedures are the same as for women and, perhaps ironically, serve to impair performance and function, thus undermining the very attributes traditionally associated with the masculine gender role and bringing men into an arena once reserved for women: the "decorative role."

Although more research is needed to understand the objectification of men, it is still the case that men are allowed much greater variability than are women when it comes to body size and shape (Andersen & DiDomenico, 1992), and men's bodies are still deemed more acceptable in their natural form. Moreover, men's natural bodies are not sexually objectified by women to the same extent as women's bodies are sexually objectified by men (Strelan & Hargeaves, 2005). Thus, objectification theory explains the extreme and pervasive tendency to equate women with their bodies and why this can have such negative consequences for women's body image and beyond. The sexually objectifying male gaze serves as a particularly potent way to limit women's social roles and behaviors by keeping them in a restricted and devalued societal position, which they come to self-monitor and police on their own.

That being said, as mentioned above, the gay men's subculture places an extreme emphasis on appearance and contains a high level of sexual objectification (Siever, 1994). Similar to heterosexual women, gay men try to attract the attention of men who typically place greater value than women do on the appearance of their partners (Siever, 1994). Indeed, researchers have documented higher levels of self-objectification in gay men than in heterosexual men (Martins et al., 2007). We do not submit that these experiences of sexual objectification for straight women and gay men are experientially the same because of the obvious differences in the physicality and relational qualities of the surveyors and their targets. In addition, the nature of the sexual objectification of heterosexual men, or the lack thereof, represents an equally important way in which men experience their own bodies within a patriarchical system. Thus, variability in the presence or the absence of sexual objectification, and the attendant self-objectification, may explain why men and women come to take different perspectives on their bodies.

Future Directions

The conceptualization and measurement of body image are critical for understanding the body image of women and men. Body image has been most often measured as a cross-situational, individual disposition or trait. Although the scope of this research has been invaluable for understanding the nature, meaning, and consequences of body image in people's lives, there are other directions that need to be taken to widen the scope of research on gender and body image. This section identifies several gaps in the literature on women's and men's body images and offers some suggestions for future research directions on this topic.

Body image is not static but can vary across situational contexts, and thus more research is needed on the nature and consequences of body image states (Cash, 2004; Cash, Fleming, Alindogan, Steadman, & Whitehead, 2002; Tiggemann, 2001) and how these states may differ for men and women (e.g., Duncombe, Wertheim, Skouteris, Paxton, & Kelly, 2008). Moreover, most individual difference measures in body image experiences cannot capture the broader societal and cultural forces that operate on people's body image; thus, more qualitative and archival research is needed to investigate these processes, and the development of measurements that are more sensitive to the operation of these processes among women and men with different ethnic backgrounds and sexualities is needed.

An additional point must be considered when evaluating this research. As described above, a focus on muscularity and larger size typifies the body concerns of boys and men, whereas a focus on weight and smaller size typifies the body concerns of girls and women. Most measures of body dissatisfaction focus on evaluations of weight and shape and do not assess evaluations of muscularity; therefore, most measures of body dissatisfaction do not represent key targets of men's appearance evaluations. Although it is clear that girls and women are more dissatisfied with their weight than boys and men are (Gardner et al., 1997; Ricciardelli & McCabe, 2001), we cannot draw firm conclusions about gender differences in body dissatisfaction until we fully consider the distinct dimensions of body image under evaluation by men and women.

Body image has been conceptualized and assessed almost exclusively in negative terms, and therefore there is a dearth of research on positive body image. Important practical and empirical questions that have yet to be answered are the following: What is positive body image? What are the gender similarities and differences in positive body image? How do we promote positive body image at both macro- and micro-levels of society? Some researchers have begun to address this gap in the literature. For example, Avalos, Tylka, and Wood-Barcalow (2005) developed and evaluated a measure of body appreciation, which is characterized by (a) favorable evaluations of the body regardless of perceived discrepancy from the cultural appearance standards; (b) body acceptance regardless of weight, body shape, and imperfections; (c) respect for the body as demonstrated by responding to body's needs and engaging in healthy behaviors; and (d) protection of the body by rejecting unrealistic idealized images portrayed in media. In their acceptance model of intuitive eating, Avalos and Tylka (2006) demonstrated that more perceived body acceptance by others (e.g., family, peers, partners) predicted greater importance of body function (i.e., focus on how the body functions and feels vs. how the body looks), which predicted greater body appreciation, which in turn predicted more intuitive, healthy eating.

We have discussed how the lack of acceptance of women's natural bodies is communicated from a variety of sociocultural sources. The findings described above indicate that by changing the messages transmitted by these same sociocultural sources to convey body acceptance, women may learn to appreciate their bodies more for what they can do than for how they look. Indeed, the idea that body function is linked to body appreciation may explain why many men are less vulnerable to negative body image because the focus on their bodies is more likely to be functionality and agency. Further research on the development and cultivation of positive body image, particularly in women, is sorely needed.

There is also little research available on the role of school environments in the development of girls'/women's and boys'/men's body images. Peer interactions as well as teachers' and coaches' comments play a significant role in the gender socialization process, and we know that experiences of sexual harassment occur early in the lives of children (Murnen & Smolak, 2000). There is also evidence to indicate that teachers' perceptions of students' competence are influenced by aspects of the students' physiques. Specifically, larger sized boys are more likely to be perceived as competent, and they (especially older boys) receive higher grades on achievement test scores (Villimez, Eisenberg, & Carroll, 1986). In contrast, larger sized girls are less likely to be perceived as competent, especially with regard to athletic competence in older girls.

Little systematic research has examined how older individuals respond to contemporary beauty ideals and the effects of aging on their body image (Chrisler, 2007). Clarke (2002) assessed perceptions of body weight in a sample of women aged 61–92 and reported that weight and appearance are still central to women's identity and their perceived social value. The majority of women reported some degree of body dissatisfaction, a desire to lose weight for appearance reasons, and varied degrees of dieting behavior. Because of the social construction of women's bodies and their biological processes, the experience of a changing, menopausal body could be important to women's body image as women's natural bodies diverge more substantially from what they used to look like as well as from cultural appearance ideals (Chrisler & Ghiz, 1993; Dillaway, 2005). Some recent research suggests that the body esteem of older men warrants more consideration as well. In a study of 95 adults aged 60–91 years, it was men, not women, who became more disparaging of the appearance and function of their bodies during the last decades of their life (Kaminiski & Hayslip, 2006).

Conclusions

The frameworks provided by theories of social influence, gender socialization, and objectification converge on the point that women's, and increasingly men's, bodies are not wholly acceptable in their natural form. The extent to which this cultural dissatisfaction becomes internalized introduces a new set of consequences for individual women and men, but it seems clear that people's bodies are systematically subjected to negative scrutiny and objective evaluation, regardless of whether they like their own bodies or not. In addition, it is evident that social and political conflicts and norms are often translated into how the body can be manipulated, controlled, and experienced. As Lee (2003, p. 82) stated, the external body is a "text of culture; it is a symbolic form upon which the norms and practices of a society are inscribed." The critical point is that gender is inscribed on people's bodies. Gender informs body image through the different *fictions* about women's and men's bodies communicated by the media, the different *fashions* for women's and men's bodies encouraged by formative sociocultural agents, and the different biological and social *functions* of women's and men's bodies that define their respective social roles and social value.

References

Agliata, D., & Tantleff-Dunn, S. (2004). The impact of media exposure on males' body image. *Journal of Social and Clinical Psychology, 23*, 7–22.

Allon, N. (1982). The stigma of overweight in everyday life. In B. Wolman (Ed.), *Psychological aspects of obesity: A handbook* (pp. 130–174). New York: Van Nostrand Reinhold.

American Psychiatric Association. (1994). Diagnostic and statistical manual of mental disorders (4th ed). Washington, DC: Author.
American Psychiatric Association. (2000). *Diagnostic and statistical manual of mental disorders* (text rev.; *DSM-IV TR*). Washington, DC: Author.
American Psychological Association Task Force on the Sexualization of Girls. (2007). *Report of the APA Task Force on the Sexualization of Girls*. Washington, DC: American Psychological Association. Retrieved June 10, 2008, from http://www.apa.org/pi/wpo/sexualization_report_summary.pdf
American Society for Aesthetic Plastic Surgery for Statistical Data: Cosmetic Surgery National Data Bank Statistics 2007. Retrieved November 14, 2008, from http://www.surgery.org/download/2007stats.pdf
American Society of Plastic Surgeons (ASPS). (2005). *National Clearinghouse of Plastic Surgery Statistics: 2005 report of the 2004 patient statistics*. Arlington Heights, IL: Author.
Andersen, A. E., & DiDomenico, L. (1992). Diet vs. shape contents of popular male and female magazines: A dose–response relationship to the incidence of eating disorders? *International Journal of Eating Disorders, 11*, 283–287.
Avalos, L., & Tylka, T. L. (2006). Exploring a model of intuitive eating with college women. *Journal of Counseling Psychology, 53*, 486–497.
Avalos, L., Tylka, T. L., & Wood-Barcalow, N. (2005). The Body Appreciation Scale: Development and psychometric evaluation. *Body Image, 2*, 285–297.
Bahrke, M. S. (2007). Muscle enhancement substances and strategies. In J. K. Thompson & G. Cafri (Eds.), *The muscular ideal: Psychological, social, and medical perspectives* (pp. 141–160). Washington, DC: American Psychological Association.
Baker-Sperry, L., & Grauerholz, L. (2003). The pervasiveness and persistence of the feminine beauty ideal in children's fairy tales. *Gender & Society, 15*, 711–726.
Balogun, J. A., Okonofua, F. E., & Balogun, A. O. (1992). An appraisal of body image among Nigerian university students. *Perceptual & Motor Skills, 75*, 832–834.
Barker, E. T., & Galambos, N. L. (2003). Body dissatisfaction of adolescent girls and boys: Risk and resource factors. *Journal of Early Adolescence, 23*, 141–165.
Bartky, S. (1990). *Femininity and domination*. New York: Routledge.
Bartlett, C., Harris, R., Smith, S., & Bonds-Raacke, J. (2005). Action figures and men. *Sex Roles, 53*, 877–885.
Bearman, S. K., Presnell, K., Martinez, E., & Stice, E. (2006). The skinny on body dissatisfaction: A longitudinal study of adolescent girls and boys. *Journal of Youth and Adolescence, 35*, 229–241.
Becker, A. E. (1995). *Body, self, society: The view from Fiji*. Philadelphia, PA: University of Pennsylvania Press.
Becker, A. E. (2004). Television, disordered eating, and young women in Fiji: Negotiating body image and identity during rapid social change. *Culture, Medicine, and Psychiatry, 28*, 533–559.
Becker, A. E., Burwell, R. A., Gilman, S. E., Herzog, D. B., & Hamburg, P. (2002). Eating behaviors and attitudes following prolonged television exposure among ethnic Fijian adolescent girls. *British Journal of Psychiatry, 180*, 509–514.
Beren, S. E., Hayden, H. A., Wilfley, D. E., & Grilo, C. M. (1996). The influence of sexual orientation on body dissatisfaction in adult men and women. *International Journal of Eating Disorders, 20*, 135–141.
Bessenoff, G. R., & Sherman, J. W. (2000). Automatic and controlled components of prejudice toward fat people: Evaluation versus stereotype activation. *Social Cognition, 18*, 329–353.
Betz, N. E., Mintz, L., & Speakmon, G. (1994). Gender differences in the accuracy of self-reported weight. *Sex Roles, 30*, 543–552.
Bond, S., & Cash, T. (1992). Black beauty: Skin color and body images among African American college women. *Journal of Applied Social Psychology, 22*, 874–888.
Boroughs, M., Cafri, G., & Thompson, J. K. (2005). Male body depilation: Prevalence and associated features of body hair removal. *Sex Roles, 52*, 637–644.
Boroughs, M., & Thompson, J. K. (2002). Body depilation in males: A new body image concern? *International Journal of Men's Health, 1*, 247–257.
Botta, R. (2003). For your health? The relationship between magazine reading and adolescents' body image and eating disturbances. *Sex Roles, 48*, 389–399.
Brausch, A. M., & Muehlenkamp, J. J. (2007). Body image and suicidal ideation in adolescents. *Body Image, 4*, 207–212.
Brewis, A. A., McGarvey, S. T., Jones, J., & Swinburn, B. A. (1998). Perceptions of body size in Pacific Islanders. *International Journal of Obesity and Related Metabolic Disorders, 22*, 185–189.
Bryant, A. (1993). Hostile hallways: The AAUW survey on sexual harassment in America's schools. *Journal of School Health, 63*, 355–357.

Brown, C., & Jasper, K. (1993). *Consuming passions: Feminist approaches to weight preoccupation and eating disorders.* Toronto, ON: Second Story Press.

Brownmiller, S. (1975). *Against our will: Men, women, and rape.* New York: Simon & Schuster.

Buckley, T., & Gottlieb, A. (1988). *Blood magic: The anthropology of menstruation.* Berkeley, CA: University of California Press.

Busby, L., & Leichty, G. (1993). Feminism and advertising in traditional and nontraditional women's magazines, 1950 s–1980 s. *Journalism Quarterly, 70,* 247–264.

Cafri, G., Blevins, N., & Thompson, J. K. (2006). The drive for muscle leanness: A complex case with features of muscle dysmorphia and eating disorder not otherwise specified. *Eating and Weight Disorders, 11,* 117–118.

Cafri, G., Olivardia, R., & Thompson, J. K. (2008). Muscle dysmorphia: Prevalence, characteristics, and associated features. *Comprehensive Psychiatry, 49,* 374–379.

Cafri, G., Strauss, J., & Thompson, J. K. (2002). Male body image: Satisfaction and its relationship to well-being using the Somatomorphic Matrix. *International Journal of Men's Health, 1,* 215–231.

Cafri, G., & Thompson, J. K. (2004). Evaluating the convergence of muscle appearance attitude measures. *Assessment, 11,* 224–229.

Cafri, G., Thompson, J. K., Ricciardelli, L. A., McCabe, M. P., Smolak, L., & Yesalis, C. (2005). Pursuit of the muscular ideal: Physical and psychological consequences and putative risk factors. *Clinical Psychology Review, 25,* 215–239.

Calogero, R. M. (2009). Objectification processes and disordered eating in British women and men. *Journal of Health Psychology, 14,* 394–402.

Calogero, R. M., Boroughs, M., & Thompson, J. K. (2007). The impact of Western beauty ideals on the lives of women and men: A sociocultural perspective. In V. Swami & A. Furnham (Eds.), *Body beautiful: Evolutionary and sociocultural perspectives* (pp. 259–298). New York: Palgrave Macmillan.

Calogero, R. M., Davis, W. N., & Thompson, J. K. (2005). The role of self-objectification in the experience of women with eating disorders. *Sex Roles, 52,* 43–50.

Calogero, R. M., & Thompson, J. K. (2009). Sexual self-esteem in American and British college women: Relations with self-objectification and eating problems. *Sex Roles, 60,* 160–173.

Calogero, R. M., & Watson, N. (2009). Self-discrepancy and chronic social self-consciousness: Unique and interactive effects of gender and real-ought discrepancy. *Personality and Individual Differences, 46,* 642–647.

Carpenter, K., Hasin, D., Allison, D., & Faith, M. (2000). Relationships between obesity and *DSM-IV* major depressive disorder, suicide ideation, and suicide attempts. *American Journal of Public Health, 90,* 251–257.

Casanova, E. M. (2004). 'No ugly women': Concepts of race and beauty among adolescent women in Ecuador. *Gender & Society, 18,* 287–308.

Cash, T. F. (2004). Body image: Past, present, and future. *Body Image, 1,* 1–5.

Cash, T. F., Fleming, E. C., Alindogan, J., Steadman, L., & Whitehead, A. (2002). Beyond body image as a trait: The development and validation of the Body Images States Scale. *Eating Disorders, 10,* 103–113.

Cash, T. F., & Hicks, K. L. (1990). Being fat versus thinking fat: Relationships with body image, eating behaviors, and well-being. *Cognitive Therapy and Research, 14,* 237–341.

Cash, T. F., & Pruzinsky, T. (Eds.). (1990). *Body images: Development, deviance, and change.* New York: Guilford Press.

Cattarin, J. A., & Thompson, J. K. (1994). A three-year longitudinal study of body image, eating disturbance, and general psychological functioning in adolescent females. *Eating Disorders, 2,* 114–125.

Chrisler, J. C. (1996). Politics and women's weight. In S. Wilkinson & C. Kitzinger (Eds.), *Representing the other: A Feminism & Psychology reader* (pp. 94–96). Thousand Oaks, CA: Sage.

Chrisler, J. C. (2007). Body image issues of women over 50. In V. Muhlbauer & J. C. Chrisler (Eds.), *Women over 50: Psychological perspectives* (pp. 6–25). New York: Springer.

Chrisler, J. C., & Ghiz, L. (1993). Body image issues of older women. *Women & Therapy, 14* (1/2), 67–75.

Clarke, L. H. (2002). Older women's perceptions of ideal body weights: The tensions between health and appearance motivations for weight loss. *Ageing & Society, 22,* 751–773.

Cogan, J. C. (1999). Lesbians walk the tightrope of beauty: Thin is in but femme is out. *Journal of Lesbian Studies, 3,* 77–89.

Connell, R. W. (2005). *Masculinities* (2nd ed.). Crows' Nest, Australia: Allen & Unwin.

Crandall, C. S. (1994). Prejudice against fat people: Ideology and self-interest. *Journal of Personality and Social Psychology, 66,* 882–894.

Crerand, C. E., Phillips, K. A., Menard, W., & Fay, C. (2005). Nonpsychiatric medical treatment of body dysmorphic disorder. *Psychosomatics, 46,* 549–555.

Dana, M., & Lawrence, M. (1988). *Women's secret disorder: A new understanding of bulimia.* London: Grafton Books.

Davis, C., Brewer, H., & Weinstein, M. (1993). A study of appearance anxiety in young men. *Social Behavior and Personality, 21*, 63–74.

Delaney, J., Lupton, M. J., & Toth, E. (1988). *The curse: A cultural history of menstruation*. Urbana, IL: University of Illinois Press.

Dillaway, H. (2005). (Un)changing menopausal bodies: How women think and act in the face of a reproductive transition and gendered beauty ideals. *Sex Roles, 53*, 1–17.

Dion, K. L., Dion, K. K., & Keelan, J. P. (1990). Appearance anxiety as a dimension of social-evaluative anxiety: Exploring the ugly duckling syndrome. *Contemporary Social Psychology, 14*, 220–224.

Drewnowski, A., & Yee, D. K. (1987). Men and body image: Are males satisfied with their body weight? *Multivariate Behavioral Research, 18*, 197–218.

Drummond, M. J. N. (2002). Men, body image, and eating disorders. *International Journal of Men's Health, 1*, 89–103.

Drummond, M. J. N. (2003). Retired men, retired bodies. *International Journal of Men's Health, 2*, 183–199.

Duggan, S. J., & McCreary, D. R. (2004). Body image, eating disorders, and the drive for muscularity in gay and heterosexual men: The influence of media images. *Journal of Homosexuality, 47*, 45–58.

Duncombe, D., Wertheim, E. H., Skouteris, H., Paxton, S. J., & Kelly, L. (2008). How well do women adapt to changes in their body size and shape across the course of pregnancy? *Journal of Health Psychology, 13*, 503–515.

Dworkin, S. H. (1989). Not in man's image: Lesbians and cultural oppression of body image. *Women & Therapy, 8*, 27–39.

Eagly, A. H. (1987). *Sex differences in social behavior: A social-role interpretation*. Hillsdale, NJ: Erlbaum.

Eagly, A. H., Beall, A. E., & Sternberg, R. J. (2004). *The psychology of gender*. New York: Guilford.

Eck, B. A. (2003). Men are much harder: Gendered viewing of nude images. *Gender & Society, 17*, 691–710.

Einon, D. (2007). The shaping of women's bodies: Men's choice of fertility or heat stress avoidance? In V. Swami & A. Furnham (Eds.), *Body beautiful: Evolutionary and sociocultural perspectives* (pp. 131–158). New York: Palgrave Macmillan.

Engeln-Maddox, R. (2006). Buying a beauty standard or dreaming of a new life? Expectations associated with media ideals. *Psychology of Women Quarterly, 30*, 258–266.

Englis, B. G., Solomon, M. R., & Ashmore, R. D. (1994). Beauty before the eyes of the beholder: The cultural encoding of beauty types in magazine advertising and music television. *Journal of Advertising, 23*, 49–64.

Etcoff, N., Orbach, S., Scott, J., & D'Agostino, H. (2006). *Beyond stereotypes: Rebuilding the foundation of beauty beliefs* [Findings of the 2005 Dove Global Study]. Retrieved November 16, 2008 from http://www.campaignforrealbeauty.com/DoveBeyondStereotypesWhitePaper.pdf

Evans, P. C. (2003). 'If only I were thin like her, maybe I could be happy like her': The self-implications of associating a thin female ideal with life success. *Psychology of Women Quarterly, 27*, 209–214.

Faith, M. S., & Schare, M. L. (1993). The role of body image in sexually avoidant behavior. *Archives of Sexual Behavior, 22*, 345–356.

Fallon, A. (1990). Culture in the mirror: Sociocultural determinants of body image. In T. F. Cash & T. Pruzinsky (Eds.), *Body images: Development, deviance, and change* (pp. 80–109). New York: Guilford.

Feingold, A., & Mazzella, R. (1998). Gender differences in body image are increasing. *Psychological Science, 9*, 190–195.

Flannery-Schroeder, E., & Chrisler, J. C. (1996). Body esteem, eating attitudes, and gender-role orientation in three age groups of children. *Current Psychology: Developmental, Learning, Personality, Social, 15*, 235–248.

Fouts, G., & Burggraf, K. (1999). Television situation comedies: Female body images and verbal reinforcements. *Sex Roles, 40*, 473–481.

Franzoi, S. (1995). The body-as-object versus the body-as-process: Gender differences and gender considerations. *Sex Roles, 33*, 417–437.

Franzoi, S. L., Kessenich, J. J., & Sugrue, P. A. (1989). Gender differences in the experience of body awareness: An experiential sampling study. *Sex Roles, 21*, 499–515.

Frederick, D. A., Peplau, L. A., & Lever, J. (2006). The swimsuit issue: Correlates of body image in a sample of 52, 677 heterosexual adults. *Body Image, 3*, 413–419.

Fredrickson, B. L., & Roberts, T.-A. (1997). Objectification theory: Toward understanding women's lived experience and mental health risks. *Psychology of Women Quarterly, 21*, 173–206.

Fredrickson, B. L., Roberts, T-A., Noll, S. M., Quinn, D. M., & Twenge, J. M. (1998). That swimsuit becomes you: Sex differences in self-objectification, restrained eating, and math performance. *Journal of Personality and Social Psychology, 75*, 269–284.

Freedman, R. (1984). Reflections on beauty as it relates to health in adolescent females. *Women & Health, 9*, 29–45.

French, S. A., Story, M., Remafedi, G., Resnick, M. D., & Blum, R. W. (1996). Sexual orientation and prevalence of body dissatisfaction and eating disordered behaviors: A population-based study of adolescents. *International Journal of Eating Disorders, 19*, 119–126.
Gardner, R. M., Sorter, R. G., & Friedman, B. N. (1997). Developmental changes in children's body images. *Journal of Social Behavior and Personality, 12*, 1019–1036.
Garner, D. M. (1997, February). Survey says: Body image poll results. *Psychology Today*. Retrieved September 21, 2006, from http://www.psychologytoday.com/articles/pto-19970201-000023.html
Gerbner, G., Gross, L., Morgan, M., & Signorielli, N. (1994). Growing up with television: The cultivation perspective. In J. Bryant & D. Zillman (Eds.), *Media effects: Advances in theory and research* (pp. 17–42). Hillsdale, NJ: Erlbaum.
Gleason, J. H., Alexander, A. M., & Somers, C. L. (2000). Later adolescents' reactions to three types of childhood teasing: Relations with self-esteem and body image. *Social Behavior and Personality, 28*, 471–480.
Goldfield, A., & Chrisler, J. C. (1995). Body stereotyping and stigmatization of obese persons by first graders. *Perceptual and Motor Skills, 81*, 909–910.
Gow, J. (1995). Reconsidering gender roles on MTV: Depictions in the most popular music videos in the early 1990 s. *Communication Reports, 9*, 151–161.
Grabe, S., Hyde, J. S., & Lindberg, S. M. (2007). Body objectification and depression in adolescents: The role of gender, shame, and rumination. *Psychology of Women Quarterly, 31*, 164–175.
Grauerholz, E., & King, A. (1997). Primetime sexual harassment. *Violence Against Women, 3*, 129–148.
Gray, J. L., & Ginsberg, R. L. (2007). Muscle dissatisfaction: An overview of psychological and cultural research and theory. In J. K. Thompson & G. Cafri (Eds.), *The muscular ideal: Psychological, social, and medical perspectives* (pp. 14–42). Washington, DC: American Psychological Association.
Greenberg, B. S., Eastin, M., Hofschire, L., Lachlan, K., & Brownell, K. D. (2003). Portrayals of overweight and obese individuals on commercial television. *American Journal of Public Health, 93*, 1342–1348.
Groesz, L. M., Levine, M. P., & Murnen, S. K. (2002). The effect of experimental presentation of thin media images on body satisfaction: A meta-analytic review. *International Journal of Eating Disorders, 31*, 1–16.
Grogan, S. (1999). *Body image: Understanding body dissatisfaction in men, women, and children*. London: Routledge.
Grogan, S., & Richards, H. (2002). Body image: Focus groups with boys and men. *Men and Masculinities, 4*, 219–232.
Grogan, S., & Wainwright, N. (1996). Growing up in the culture of slenderness: Girls' experiences of body dissatisfaction. *Women's Studies International Forum, 19*, 665–673.
Grogan, S., Williams, C., & Connor, M. (1996). The effects of viewing same-gender photographic models on body esteem. *Psychology of Women Quarterly, 20*, 569–575.
Grover, V. P., Keel, P. K., & Mitchell, J. P. (2003). Gender differences in implicit weight identity. *International Journal of Eating Disorders, 34*, 125–135.
Gruber, A. (2007). A more muscular female body ideal. In J. K. Thompson & G. Cafri (Eds.), *The muscular ideal: Psychological, social, and medical perspectives* (pp. 217–234). Washington, DC: American Psychological Association.
Guille, C., & Chrisler, J. C. (1999). Does feminism serve a protective function against eating disorders? *Journal of Lesbian Studies, 3*, 141–148.
Haiken, E. (1997). *Venus envy: A history of cosmetic surgery*. Baltimore, MD: Johns Hopkins University Press.
Halliwell, E., & Dittmar, H. (2003). A qualitative investigation of women's and men's body image concerns and their attitudes toward aging. *Sex Roles, 49*, 675–684.
Harper, B., & Tiggemann, M. (2008). The effect of thin ideal images on women's self-objectification, mood, and body image. *Sex Roles, 58*, 649–657.
Harrison, K. (2003). Television viewers' ideal body proportions: The case of the curvaceously thin woman. *Sex Roles, 48*, 255–264.
Harrison, K., & Cantor, J. (1997). The relationship between media consumption and eating disorders. *Journal of Communication, 47*, 40–67.
Harrison, K., Taylor, L. D., & Marske, A. L. (2006). Women's and men's eating behavior following exposure to ideal-body images and text. *Communication Research, 33*, 1–23.
Hebl, M. R., & Heatherton, T. F. (1997). The stigma of obesity in women: The difference is Black and White. *Personality and Social Psychology Bulletin, 24*, 417–426.
Hebl, M. R., King, E. B., & Lin, J. (2004). The swimsuit becomes us all: Ethnicity, gender, and vulnerability to self-objectification. *Personality and Social Psychology Bulletin, 30*, 1322–1331.
Hebl, M. R., & Mannix, L. M. (2003). The weight of obesity in evaluating others: A mere proximity effect. *Personality and Social Psychology Bulletin, 29*, 28–38.

Heinberg, L. J., Thompson, J. K., & Stormer, S. (1995). Development and validation of the sociocultural attitudes toward appearance questionnaire. *International Journal of Eating Disorders, 17*, 81–89.

Henderson-King, D., & Henderson-King, E. (2005). Acceptance of cosmetic surgery: Scale development and validation. *Body Image, 2*, 137–149.

Henley, N. M. (1977). *Body politics: Power, sex, and nonverbal communication.* Englewood Cliffs, NJ: Prentice-Hall.

Herbozo, S., Tantleff-Dunn, S., Gokee-Larose, J., & Thompson, J. K. (2004). Beauty and thinness messages in children's media: A content analysis. *Eating Disorders, 12*, 21–34.

Hesse-Biber, S., Leavy, P., Quinn, C. E., & Zoino, J. (2006). The mass marketing of disordered eating and eating disorders: The social psychology of women, thinness, and culture. *Women's Studies International Forum, 29*, 208–224.

Holbrook, T. M., Andersen, A. E., & Cohn, L. (2000). *Making weight: Men's conflicts with food, weight, shape, & appearance.* Carlsbad, CA: Gurze Books.

Holmqvist, K., Lunde, C., & Frisen, A. (2007). Dieting behaviors, body shape perceptions, and body satisfaction: Cross-cultural differences in Argentinean and Swedish 13-year-olds. *Body Image, 4*, 191–200.

Holstrom, A. J. (2004). The effects of the media on body image: A meta-analysis. *Journal of Broadcasting and Electronic Media, 48*, 196–218.

Holt, K., & Ricciardelli, L. A. (2007). Social comparisons and negative affect as indicators of problem eating and muscle preoccupation among children. *Journal of Applied Developmental Psychology, 23*, 285–304.

Huebner, D. M., & Fredrickson, B. L. (1999). Gender differences in memory perspectives: Evidence for self-objectification in women. *Sex Roles, 41*, 459–467.

Jacobi, L., & Cash, T. F. (1994). In pursuit of the perfect appearance: Discrepancies among self- and ideal-percepts of multiple physical attributes. *Journal of Applied Social Psychology, 24*, 379–396.

Johnson, W., & Torgrud, L. (1996). Assessment and treatment of binge eating disorder. In J. K. Thompson (Ed.), *Body image, eating disorders, and obesity: An integrative guide for assessment and treatment* (pp. 321–344). Washington, DC: American Psychological Association.

Jones, D. C. (2001). Social comparison and body image: Attractiveness comparison to models and peers among adolescent girls and boys. *Sex Roles, 45*, 645–664.

Jones, D. C., & Crawford, J. K. (2005). Adolescent boys and body image: Weight and muscularity concerns as dual pathways to body dissatisfaction. *Journal of Youth and Adolescence, 26*, 203–216.

Jones, D. C., Vigfusdottir, T. H., & Lee, Y. (2004). Body image and the appearance culture among adolescent girls and boys. *Journal of Adolescent Research, 19*, 323–339.

Jung, J., & Peterson, M. (2007). Body dissatisfaction and patterns of media use among preadolescent children. *Family & Consumer Sciences Research, 36*, 40–54.

Kagawa, M., Kuroiwa, C., Uenishi, K., Mori, M., Dhliwal, S., Hills, A. P., et al. (2007). A comparison of body perceptions in relation to measured body composition in young Japanese males and females. *Body Image, 4*, 372–380.

Kaminiski, P. L., & Hayslip, B., Jr. (2006). Gender differences in body esteem among older adults. *Journal of Women & Aging, 18*, 19–35.

Keery, H., van den Berg, P., & Thompson, J. K. (2004). An evaluation of the tripartite influence model of body dissatisfaction and eating disturbance with adolescent girls. *Body Image, 1*, 237–251.

Kimmel, S. B., & Mahalik, J. R. (2004). Measuring masculine body ideal distress: Development of a measure. *International Journal of Men's Health, 3*, 1–10.

Klein, A. (2007). Size matters: Connecting subculture to culture in bodybuilding. In J. K. Thompson & G. Cafri (Eds.), *The muscular ideal: Psychological, social, and medical perspectives* (pp. 67–83). Washington, DC: American Psychological Association.

Klein, H., & Shiffman, K. S. (2006). Messages about physical attractiveness in animated cartoons. *Body Image, 3*, 353–363.

Knight, C. (1995). *Blood relations: Menstruation and the origins of culture.* New Haven, CT: Yale University Press.

Kozee, H. B., & Tylka, T. L. (2006). A test of objectification theory with lesbian women. *Psychology of Women Quarterly, 30*, 348–357.

Krassas, N. R., Blauwkamp, J. M., & Wesselink, P. (2003). "Master your Johnson": Sexual rhetoric in *Maxim* and *Stuff* magazines. *Sexuality and Culture, 7*, 98–119.

Lee, J. (2003). Menarche and the (hetero)sexualization of the female body. In R. Weitz (Ed.), *The politics of female bodies: Sexuality, appearance, and behavior* (pp. 82–99). New York: Oxford University Press.

Leit, R. A., Gray, J. J., & Pope, H. G. (2002). The media's representation of the ideal male body: A cause for muscle dysmorphia? *International Journal of Eating Disorders, 31*, 334–338.

Leit, R. A., Pope, H. G., & Gray, J. J. (2001). Cultural expectations of muscularity in men: The evolution of *Playgirl* centerfolds. *International Journal of Eating Disorders, 29*, 90–93.

Leon, G. R., Fulkerson, J. A., Perry, C. L., Keel, P. K., & Klump, K. L. (1999). Three to four year prospective evaluation of personality and behavioral risk factors for later disordered eating in adolescent girls and boys. *Journal of Youth and Adolescence, 28*, 181–196.

Levine, M. P., & Harrison, K. (2004). Media's role in the perpetuation and prevention of negative body image and disordered eating. In J. K. Thompson (Ed.), *Handbook of eating disorders and obesity* (pp. 695–717). New York: Wiley.

Lewis, M. (1992). *Shame: The exposed self*. New York: Free Press.

Lipinski, J. P., & Pope, H. G. (2002). Body ideals in young Samoan men: A comparison with men in North American and Europe. *International Journal of Men's Health, 1*, 163–171.

Lopez, E., Blix, G. G., & Blix, A. G. (1995). Body image of Latinas compared to body image of non-Latina white women. *Health Values, 19*, 3–10.

Lovejoy, M. (2001). Disturbances in the social body: Differences in body image and eating problems among African American and white women. *Gender & Society, 15*, 239–261.

Lowes, J., & Tiggemann, M. (2003). Body dissatisfaction, dieting awareness, and the impact of parental influence on young children. *British Journal of Health Psychology, 8*, 135–147.

Luciano, L. (2007). Muscularity and masculinity in the United States: A historical overview. In J. K. Thompson & G. Cafri (Eds.), *The muscular ideal: Psychological, social, and medical perspectives* (pp. 41–65). Washington, DC: American Psychological Association.

Lunde, C., Frisen, A., & Hwang, C. P. (2007). Ten-year-old girls' and boys' composition and peer victimization experiences: Prospective associations with body satisfaction. *Body Image, 4*, 11–28.

Makkar, J. K., & Strube, M. J. (1995). Black women's self-perceptions of attractiveness following exposure to White versus Black beauty standards: The moderating role of racial identity and self-esteem. *Journal of Applied Social Psychology, 25*, 1547–1566.

Markus, H., Hamill, R., & Sentis, K. P. (1987). Thinking fat: Self-schemas for body weight and the processing of weight relevant information. *Journal of Applied Social Psychology, 17*, 60–71.

Martin, E. (1992). *The woman in the body: A cultural analysis of reproduction*. Boston, MA: Beacon Press.

Martins, Y., Tiggemann, M., & Kirkbride, A. (2007). Those speedos become them: The role of self-objectification in gay and heterosexual men's body image. *Personality and Social Psychology Bulletin, 33*, 634–647.

McCabe, M., & Ricciardelli, L. (2005). A prospective study of pressures from parents, peers, and the media on extreme weight change behaviors among adolescent boys and girls. *Behaviour Research and Therapy, 43*, 653–668.

McCabe, M. P., Ricciardelli, L. A., & Ridge, D. (2006). "Who thinks I need a perfect body?" Perceptions and internal dialogue among adolescents about their bodies. *Sex Roles, 55*, 409–419.

McCreary, D. R. (1994). The male role and avoiding femininity. *Sex Roles, 31*, 517–531.

McCreary, D. R. (2002). Gender and age differences in the relationship between body mass index and perceived weight: Exploring the paradox. *International Journal of Men's Health, 1*, 31–42.

McCreary, D. R., & Sadava, S. W. (1999). Television viewing and self-perceived health, weight, and physical fitness: Evidence for the cultivation hypothesis. *Journal of Applied Social Psychology, 29*, 2342–2361.

McCreary, D. R., & Sasse, D. K. (2000). Exploring the drive for muscularity in adolescent boys and girls. *Journal of American College Health, 48*, 297–304.

McCreary, D. R., & Saucier, D. M. (2009). Drive for muscularity, body comparison, and social physique anxiety in men and women. *Body Image, 6*, 24–30.

McCreary, D. R., Saucier, D. M., & Courtenay, W. H. (2005). The drive for muscularity and masculinity: Testing the associations among gender-role traits, behaviors, attitudes, and conflict. *Psychology of Men and Masculinity, 6*, 83–94.

McLaren, L., Kuh, D., Hardy, R., & Gauvin, L. (2004). Positive and negative body-related comments and their relationship with body dissatisfaction in middle-aged women. *Psychology and Health, 19*, 261–272.

McKinley, N. M. (1998). Gender differences in undergraduate body esteem: The mediating effects of objectified body consciousness and actual/ideal weight discrepancy. *Sex Roles, 39*, 113–123.

McKinley, N. M. (1999). Women and objectified body consciousness: Mothers' and daughters' body experience in cultural, developmental, and familial context. *Developmental Psychology, 35*, 760–769.

McKinley, N. M., & Hyde, J. S. (1996). The Objectified Body Consciousness Scale: Development and validation. *Psychology of Women Quarterly, 20*, 181–215.

McNay, L. (1992). *Foucault and feminism: Power, gender, and the self*. Cambridge: Polity Press.

Miller, L. C., Murphy, R., & Buss, A. H. (1981). Consciousness of body: Private and public. *Journal of Personality and Social Psychology, 41*, 397–406.

Mishkind, M. E., Rodin, J., Silberstein, L. R., & Striegel-Moore, R. H. (1986). The embodiment of masculinity: Cultural, psychological, and behavioral dimensions. *American Behavioral Scientist, 29*, 545–562.

Molloy, B. L., & Herzberger, S. D. (1998). Body image and self-esteem: A comparison of African-American and Caucasian women. *Sex Roles, 38*, 631–644.

Morrison, M. A., Morrison, T. G., & Sager, C. (2004). Does body satisfaction differ between gay men and lesbian women and heterosexual men and women? *Body Image, 1*, 127–138.

Murnen, S. K., & Smolak, L. (2000). The experience of sexual harassment among grade-school students: Early socialization of female subordination? *Sex Roles, 43*, 1–17.

Murnen, S. K., Smolak, L., Mills, J. A., & Good, L. (2003). Thin, sexy women and strong, muscular men: Grade-school responses to objectified images of women and men. *Sex Roles, 49*, 427–437.

Murray, S. H., Touyz, S. W., & Beumont, P. J. V. (1995). The influence of personal relationships on women's eating behavior and body satisfaction. *Eating Disorders, 3*, 243–252.

Mussap, A. J. (2008). Masculine gender role stress and the pursuit of muscularity. *International Journal of Men's Health, 7*, 72–89.

Muth, J. L., & Cash, T. F. (1997). Body-image attitudes: What difference does gender make? *Journal of Applied Social Psychology, 27*, 1438–1452.

Noll, S. M., & Fredrickson, B. L. (1998). A mediational model linking self-objectification, body shame, and disordered eating. *Psychology of Women Quarterly, 22*, 623–636.

Olivardia, R. (2002). Body image and muscularity. In J. E. Grant & M. N. Potenza (Eds.), *Textbook of men's mental health* (pp. 307–324). New York: American Psychiatric Press.

Olivardia, R., Pope, H. G., & Hudson, J. (2000). Muscle dysmorphia in male weightlifters: A case–control study. *American Journal of Psychiatry, 157*, 1291–1296.

Oliver, K. K., & Thelan, M. H. (1996). Children's perceptions of peer influence on eating concerns. *Behavior Therapy, 27*, 25–39.

Owens, L. K., Hughes, T. L., & Owens-Nicholson, D. (2003). The effects of sexual orientation on body image and attitudes about eating and weight. *Journal of Lesbian Studies, 7*, 15–33.

Parker, S., Nichter, M., Nichter, M., Vuckovic, N., Sims, C., & Ritenbaugh, C. (1995). Body images and weight concerns among African American and White adolescent females: Differences that make a difference. *Human Organization, 54*, 103–114.

Paxton, S. J., Schultz, H. K., Wertheim, E. H., & Muir, S. L. (1999). Friendship cliques and peer influences on body image attitudes, dietary restraint, extreme weight loss behaviors, and binge eating in adolescent girls. *Journal of Abnormal Psychology, 108*, 255–266.

Paxton, S. J., Wertheim, E. H., Gibbons, K., Szmuckler, G. I., Hillier, L., & Petrovich, J. L. (1991). Body image satisfaction, dieting beliefs, and weight loss behaviors in adolescent boys and girls. *Journal of Youth and Adolescence, 20*, 361–379.

Peter, J., & Valkenburg, P. M. (2007). Adolescents' exposure to a sexualized media environment and their notions of women as sex objects. *Sex Roles, 56*, 381–395.

Phares, V., Steinberg, A., & Thompson, J. (2004). Gender differences in peer and parental influences: Body image disturbance, self-worth, and psychological functioning in preadolescent children. *Journal of Youth and Adolescence, 33*, 421–429.

Phillips, K. A., & Castle, D. J. (2001). Body dysmorphic disorder in men. *British Medical Journal, 323*, 1015–1016.

Phillips, K. A., Coles, M. E., Menard, W., Yen, S., Fay, C., & Weisberg, R. B. (2005). Suicidal ideation and suicide attempts in body dysmorphic disorder. *Journal of Clinical Psychiatry, 66*, 717–725.

Phillips, K. A., & Diaz, S. F. (1997). Gender differences in body dysmorphic disorder. *Journal of Nervous and Mental Disease, 185*, 570–577.

Piran, N., & Cormier, H. (2005). The social construction of women and disordered eating patterns. *Journal of Counselling Psychology, 52*, 549–558.

Plous, S., & Neptune, D. (1997). Racial and gender biases in magazine advertising: A content analytic study. *Psychology of Women Quarterly, 21*, 627–644.

Pope, H. G., Jr., Gruber, A. J., Choi, P., Olivardia, R., & Phillips, K. A. (1997). Muscle dysmorphia: An underrecognized form of body dysmorphic disorder. *Psychosomatics, 38*, 548–557.

Pope, H. G., Gruber, A. J., Mangweth, B., Bureau, B., deCol, C., Jouvent, R., et al. (2000). Body image perception among men in three countries. *American Journal of Psychiatry, 157*, 1297–1301.

Pope, H. G., Olivardia, R., Borowiecki, J. J., & Cochrane, G. H. (2001). The growing commercial value of the male body: A longitudinal survey of advertising in women's magazines. *Psychotherapy and Psychosomatics, 70*, 189–192.

Pope, H. G., Olivardia, R., Gruber, A., & Borowiecki, J. (1999). Evolving ideals of male body image as seen through action toys. *International Journal of Eating Disorders, 26*, 65–72.

Pope, H. G., Phillips, K. A., & Olivardia, R. (2000). *The Adonis complex: The secret crisis of male body obsession.* New York: Free Press.

Pope, C. G., Pope, H. G., Menard, W., Fay, C., Olivardia, R., & Phillips, K. A. (2005). Clinical features of muscle dysmorphia among males with body dysmorphic disorder. *Body Image, 2*, 395–400.

Puhl, R., & Brownell, K. D. (2003). Ways of coping with obesity stigma: Review and conceptual analysis. *Eating Behaviors, 4*, 53–78.

Reichert, T. (2003). The prevalence of sexual imagery in ads targeted to young adults. *Journal of Consumer Affairs, 37*, 403–412.

Reichert, T., & Carpenter, C. (2004). An update on sex in magazine advertising: 1983 to 2003. *Journalism and Mass Communication Quarterly, 81*, 823–837.

Rguibi, M., & Belahsen, R. (2006). Body size preferences and sociocultural influences on attitudes toward obesity among Moroccan Sahraoui women. *Body Image, 3*, 395–400.

Ricciardelli, L. A., & McCabe, M. P. (2001). Self-esteem and negative affect as moderators of sociocultural influences on body dissatisfaction, strategies to decrease weight, and strategies to increase muscle among adolescent boys and girls. *Sex Roles, 44*, 189–207.

Ricciardelli, L., & McCabe, M. (2004). A biopsychosocial model of disordered eating and the pursuit of muscularity in adolescent boys. *Psychological Bulletin, 130*, 179–205.

Ricciardelli, L. A., McCabe, M. P., Holt, K. E., & Finemore, J. (2003). A biopsychosocial model for understanding body image and body change strategies among children. *Journal of Applied Developmental Psychology, 24*, 475–495.

Ricciardelli, L. A., McCabe, M. P., Lillis, J., & Thomas, K. (2006). A longitudinal investigation of the development of weight and muscle concerns among preadolescent boys. *Journal of Youth and Adolescence, 2*, 177–187.

Richins, M. L. (1991). Social comparison and the idealized images of advertising. *Journal of Consumer Research, 18*, 71–83.

Roberts, T.-A. (2000). The woman in the body. *Feminism & Psychology, 12*, 324–329.

Roberts, T.-A., Goldenberg, J. L., Power, C., & Pyszczynski, T. (2002). "Feminine protection": The effects of menstruation on attitudes toward women. *Psychology of Women Quarterly, 26*, 131–139.

Rodin, J., Silberstein, L., & Striegel-Moore, R. (1984). Women and weight: A normative discontent. *Nebraska Symposium on Motivation, 32*, 267–308.

Rozin, P., Haidt, J., McCauley, C., Dunlop, L., & Ashmore, M. (1999). Individual differences in disgust sensitivity: Comparisons and evaluations of paper-and-pencil versus behavioral measures. *Journal of Research in Personality, 33*, 330–351.

Schneider, J. A., O'Leary, A., & Jenkins, S. R. (1995). Gender, sexual orientation, and disordered eating. *Psychology and Health, 10*, 113–128.

Serdula, M. K., Collins, M. E., Williamson, D. F., Anda, R. F., Pamuk, E., & Byers, T. E. (1993). Weight control practices of U.S. adolescents and adults. *Annals of Internal Medicine, 119*, 667–671.

Shellenbarger, S. (2005, April 7). The female midlife crisis. *Wall Street Journal*, p. D3.

Shroff, H., Calogero, R. M., & Thompson, J. K. (2009). Assessment of body image. In D. B. Allison & M. Baskin (Eds.), *Handbook of assessment of methods for eating behaviors and weight-related problems* (pp. 115–136). New York: Guilford.

Shroff, K., & Thompson, J. K. (2006). The tripartite influence model of body image and eating disturbance: A replication with adolescent girls. *Body Image, 3*, 17–23.

Siever, M. D. (1994). Sexual orientation and gender as factors in socioculturally acquired vulnerability to body dissatisfaction and eating disorders. *Journal of Consulting and Clinical Psychology, 62*, 252–260.

Silberstein, L. R., Striegel-Moore, R. H., & Rodin, J. (1987). Feeling fat: A woman's shame. In H. B. Lewis (Ed.), *The role of shame in symptom formation* (pp. 98–108). Hillsdale, NJ: Erlbaum.

Silverstein, L. R., Perdue, L., Peterson, B., & Kelly, E. (1986). The role of mass media in promoting a thin standard of bodily attractiveness for women. *Sex Roles, 14*, 519–532.

Smolak, L., Levine, M. P., & Schermer, F. (1999). Parental input and weight concerns among elementary school children. *International Journal of Eating Disorders, 25*, 263–271.

Smolak, L., Levine, M. P., & Thompson, J. K. (2001). The use of the sociocultural attitudes toward appearance questionnaire with middle school boys and girls. *International Journal of Eating Disorders, 29*, 216–223.

Smolak, L., Murnen, S. K., & Thompson, J. K. (2005). Sociocultural influences and muscle building in adolescent boys. *Psychology of Men and Masculinity, 6*, 227–239.

Sperry, S., Thompson, J. K., Sarwer, D., & Cash, T. F. (2009). Viewership of cosmetic reality TV: Associations with cosmetic surgery attitudes, body image, and eating disturbances. *Annals of Plastic Surgery, 62*, 7–11.

Spitzer, B. L., Henderson, K. A., & Zivian, M. T. (1999). Gender differences in population versus media body sizes: A comparison over four decades. *Sex Roles, 40*, 545–565.

Stevens, J., Kumanyika, S. K., & Keil, J. E. (1994). Attitudes toward body size and dieting: Differences between elderly Black and White women. *American Journal of Public Health, 84*, 1322–1325.

Strelan, P., & Hargreaves, D. (2005). Women who objectify other women: The vicious circle of objectification? *Sex Roles, 52*, 707–712.

Striegel-Moore, R. H., & Smolak, L. (2001). *Eating disorders: Innovative directions in research and practice.* Washington, DC: American Psychological Association.

Suarez-Orozco, C., & Suarez-Orozco, M. M. (2001). *Children of immigration.* Cambridge, MA: Harvard University Press.

Sullivan, G., & O'Connor, P. (1988). Women's role portrayals in magazine advertising: 1958-1983. *Sex Roles, 18*, 181–188.

Swami, V., & Tovée, M. J. (2005). Female physical attractiveness in Britain and Malaysia: A cross-cultural study. *Body Image, 2*, 115–128.

Swim, J. K., Hyers, L. L., Cohen, L. L., & Ferguson, M. J. (2001). Everyday sexism: Evidence for its incidence, nature, and psychological impact from three daily diary studies. *Journal of Social Issues, 57*, 31–53.

Tauna, N. (1993). *The less noble sex: Scientific, religious, and philosophical conceptions of women's nature.* Indianapolis, IN: Indiana University Press.

Thelen, M. H., & Cormier, J. F. (1995). Desire to be thinner and weight control among children and their parents. *Behavior Therapy, 26*, 85–99.

Thompson, J. K. (1996). Body image, eating disorders, and obesity: An emerging synthesis. In J. K. Thompson (Ed.), *Body image, eating disorders, and obesity: An integrative guide for assessment and treatment* (pp. 1–20). Washington, DC: American Psychological Association.

Thompson, J. K., & Cafri, G. (2007). *The muscular ideal: Psychological, social, and medical perspectives.* Washington, DC: American Psychological Association.

Thompson, J. K., Heinberg, L. J., Altabe, M. N., & Tantleff-Dunn, S. (1999). *Exacting beauty: Theory, assessment, and treatment of body image disturbance.* Washington, DC: American Psychological Association.

Thompson, J. K., & Tantleff, S. (1992). Female and male ratings of upper torso: Actual, ideal, and stereotypical conceptions. *Journal of Social Behavior and Personality, 7*, 345–354.

Tiggemann, M. (2001). Person x situation interactions in body dissatisfaction. *International Journal of Eating Disorders, 29*, 65–70.

Tiggemann, M. (2005). Body dissatisfaction and adolescent self-esteem: Prospective findings. *Body Image, 2*, 129–135.

Tiggemann, M., Gardiner, M., & Slater, A. (2000). "I would rather be size 10 than have straight A's": A focus group study of adolescent girls' wish to be thinner. *Journal of Adolescence, 23*, 645–659.

Tiggemann, M., & Kuring, J. K. (2004). The role of body objectification in disordered eating and depressed mood. *British Journal of Clinical Psychology, 43*, 299–311.

Tiggemann, M., & Pickering, A. S. (1996). Role of television in adolescent women's body dissatisfaction and drive for thinness. *International Journal of Eating Disorders, 20*, 199–203.

Tiggemann, M., & Slater, A. (2001). A test of objectification theory in former dancers and non-dancers. *Psychology of Women Quarterly, 25*, 57–64.

Tiggemann, M., & Slater, A. (2003). Thin ideals in music television: A source of social comparison and body dissatisfaction. *International Journal of Eating Disorders, 35*, 48–58.

Tovée, M. J., Swami, V., Furnham, A., & Mangalparsad, R. (2006). Changing perceptions of attractiveness as observers are exposed to a different culture. *Evolution and Human Behavior, 27*, 443–456.

Treloar, C., Porteous, J., Hassan, F., Kasniyah, N., Lakshmandu, M., Sama, M., et al. (1999). The cross cultural context of obesity: An INCLEN multicentre collaborative study. *Health and Place, 5*, 279–286.

Tylka, T. L., & Hill, M. S. (2004). Objectification theory as it relates to disordered eating among college women. *Sex Roles, 51*, 719–730.

Unger, R., & Crawford, M. (1996). *Women and gender: A feminist psychology* (2nd ed.). New York: McGraw-Hill.

Ussher, J. (1989). *The psychology of the female body.* London: Routledge.

Vartanian, L. R., Herman, C. P., & Polivy, J. (2005). Implicit and explicit attitudes toward fatness and thinness: The role of internalization of societal standards. *Body Image, 2*, 373–381.

Villimez, C., Eisenberg, N., & Carroll, J. (1986). Sex differences in the relation of children's height and weight to academic performance and others' attributions of competence. *Sex Roles, 15*, 667–681.

Vincent, R. (1989). Clio's consciousness raised? Portrayal of women in rock videos re-examined. *Journalism Quarterly, 66,* 155–160.

Vincent, M. A., & McCabe, M. P. (2000). Gender differences among adolescents in family and peer influences on body dissatisfaction, weight loss, and binge eating behaviors. *Journal of Youth and Adolescence, 29,* 205–221.

Ward, L. M. (1995). Talking about sex: Common themes about sexuality in prime-time television programs children and adolescents view most. *Journal of Youth and Adolescence, 24,* 595–615.

Ward, L. M., & Friedman, K. (2006). Using TV as a guide: Associations between television viewing and adolescents' sexual attitudes and behavior. *Journal of Research on Adolescence, 16,* 133–156.

Ward, L. M., Merriwether, A., & Caruthers, A. (2006). Breasts are for men: Media, masculinity ideologies, and men's beliefs about women's bodies. *Sex Roles, 55,* 703–714.

Wertheim, E. H., Paxton, S. J., Schultz, H. K., & Muir, S. L. (1997). Why do adolescent girls watch their weight? An interview study examining sociocultural pressures to be thin. *Psychosomatic Research, 42,* 345–355.

Wiederman, M.W. (2000). Women's body image self-consciousness during physical intimacy with a partner. *Journal of Sex Research, 37,* 60–79.

Wolf, N. (1991). *The beauty myth.* New York: Morrow.

Wood, W., Christensen, P. N., Hebl, M. R., & Rothgerber, H. (1997). Conformity to sex-types norms, affect, and the self-concept. *Journal of Personality and Social Psychology, 73,* 523–535.

Yelland, C., & Tiggemann, M. (2003). Muscularity and the gay ideal: Body dissatisfaction and disordered eating in homosexual men. *Eating Behaviors, 4,* 107–116.

Yuan, A. S. V. (2007). Gender differences in the relationship of puberty with adolescents' depressive symptoms: Do boys' perceptions matter? *Sex Roles, 57,* 69–80.

Zones, J. S. (2000). Beauty myths and realities and their impacts on women's health. In M. B. Zinn, P. Hondagneu-Sotelo, & M. Messner (Eds.), *Gender through the prism of difference* (2nd ed., pp. 87–103). Boston, MA: Allyn and Bacon.

Part X
Psychotherapy

Chapter 9
Feminist Psychotherapies: Theory, Research, and Practice

Cynthia M. Bruns and Ellyn Kaschak

The introduction and development of feminist psychotherapy was one of the many accomplishments of second wave feminism in the West and very much a product of the social and cultural context of the late 1960s and early 1970s, during which time feminism enjoyed an unparalleled resurgence in Western societies. Within a brief time, it also appeared in various cultural incarnations in many non-Western and developing countries as local and indigenous groups began to realize that women's rights are human rights.

In the United States, the Civil Rights Act of 1964 provided the legal framework for ending the long-standing discrimination in education and employment; it prohibits racial or ethnic discrimination in all federally assisted programs and activities, including public or private educational institutions. The process of compliance would take the better part of two decades, during which time other similar laws would also be passed; together they would come to be known as affirmative action.

One such law was Title IX, which was enacted in 1972. Title IX basically prohibits discrimination on the basis of gender in educational institutions that receive federal financial assistance (Valentin, 1999). With the stroke of a pen, and all the cultural changes that made that single stroke possible, the solitary woman in Ph.D., medicine, and law programs soon was no more. There was instead an entire generation of women about to learn academic traditions that we would find did not apply to us. How could it be otherwise, as we had not participated in their introduction or development? Yet no one could anticipate how much this structural social change would irrevocably alter the disciplines themselves.

The academic and professional disciplines of the time were based on the shaky foundation of discriminatory gendered and racialized assumptions, even as they proclaimed their own neutrality and objectivity. Objectivity was the nineteenth- and twentieth-century belief that the sciences were not and should not be influenced by perspective, by values, or by the very people asking the questions and seeking the answers. Inquiry should be an antiseptic procedure purified of the germs of personal perspective. The hardest of sciences, physics, has ultimately supported the feminist and multicultural positions as quantum and relativity theories (Einstein & Lawson, 2005; Heisenberg, 2007) soon relegated the illusion of objectivity to the history books.

Psychotherapy theory and practice were far from exempt from these concerns. When the post-Title IX generation of women and ethnic minority men entered graduate programs, we were confronted with the traditional androcentric teachings and the traditional dominant culture of White male professors. Stir in feminism and ethnicity and expect a combustible combination as these

---

C.M. Bruns (✉)
Central Washington University, Ellensburg, WA, USA

students began to uncover and question the assumptions about psychology that came in an increasingly urgent and shocked torrent as we began to realize that important aspects of our own lives had either been kept invisible or were pathologized. We had always been seen through officially designated cultural eyes and never through our own.

The contemporary epistemologies and theories of psychotherapy being taught in the universities and training programs ranged from psychodynamic to humanistic to behavioral. Yet all of these seemingly different approaches to psychological change had more in common than had been noticed from inside their own androcentric and masculinist perspectives. As a consequence, girls and women were seen as inferior, abnormal, or immature by definition. These biases translated directly into practice, as was soon demonstrated by the research of Broverman and her colleagues (Broverman, Broverman, Clarkson, Rosenkrantz, & Vogel, 1970), who found that therapists held different standards of mental health for women and men; the latter group closely matched the therapists' idea of the healthy adult. The common practice of diagnosing African American and non-middle class patients more frequently as psychotic was also documented (Blow et al., 2004; Rayburn & Stonecypher, 1996).

As a result, the first task that faced the new generation of feminist students was to excavate the fields for all the hidden and gendered assumptions about human beings. These misconceptions ranged from the firmly held belief that psychological maturity required the possession of a penis to the definition of ethical and moral maturity as the development of abstract reasoning devoid of interpersonal considerations (Kohlberg, 1981; Piaget, 1965). Feminist graduate students and young scholars began to study these time-honored constructs and to raise the simple, yet revolutionary, question of gender (Chesler, 1972; Gilligan, 1982; Miller, 1976). It readily became apparent that gender did not stand alone and untouched by race, ethnicity, class, or sexual orientation. It took a while to put all the pieces together and to understand the complex interaction of culture and individual psychology, of the inner and outer worlds that we were understanding for the first time. And it took a while because the traditional practitioners fought us on every front; this revolution would not be a peaceful one, but it would eventually be a successful one.

Feminist psychotherapies began with a critique of the accepted epistemologies and practices of the time. *Women and Madness* (Chesler, 1972) provided a scathing critique of the traditional institutions of clinical psychology and psychiatry and ignited an entire generation of academics and professionals to question the misogyny built into these professions. Critique of such Freudian mainstays as castration anxiety, penis envy and the Oedipal conflict, and the anatomically determined inferiority of the female soon followed (Kaschak, 1992; Mitchell, 1974).

"Gender" did not yet exist when we entered these graduate programs. We borrowed the terminology from the structure of the romance languages many of us spoke or had studied. The distinction from what had previously been called "sex" was constructed as we became aware that much of what had been considered biological differences that necessitated different treatment were instead "manmade" sociocultural differences. That distinction provided a conceptual basis for our critique: It was gender based. With the concept of gender, all the accepted schools of psychotherapy began to reveal their biases. Even Rogerian therapies, presented at the time as value free, turned out to be based in the values and perspective of its creator. How could it be otherwise? As a rural youngster, and later as a student of agriculture, Carl Rogers developed the idea that people were just like a crop. Given the best growing conditions, the best version of them would develop so that the role of the therapist was to remove the obstacles to growth by providing the optimal conditions of unconditional concern and respect. That is, if the soil is rich, if it rains enough, and the sun shines enough, the crops grow well. A therapist could accomplish all of this inner climate change without changing the climate beyond in the therapy room. Rogers did not invoke larger ecological systems; he stayed in his own "field."

It slowly became apparent that all of our systems of psychotherapy were based in metaphor and perspective rather than what is also metaphorically called "hard science" (Kaschak, 1992). This extended even to behaviorism, touted by its proponents as empirical and, thus, objective. Instead it was as material and reductionist as the American dustbowl, in which cultural context it was developed. The feminist critiques of all these epistemological systems eventually exposed them as social constructions (Kaschak, 1992; Keller, 1982).

With this developing understanding, and at different paces, various feminist academics, professionals, and grassroots activists began to propose alternatives to traditional, unconscious and conscious, sexist practices in psychotherapy. We met an almost overwhelming resistance, as traditionalists attempted not only to resist but often to demonize feminism and feminists as a form of that resistance. It has never been easy to be a feminist in the United States, but we persevered and supported each other and ourselves. Today feminists are still too often demonized or marginalized and deemed irrelevant, but our insights and practices are just as often incorporated seamlessly into mainstream approaches as if they had always been there. By this sleight of hand, feminism is declared irrelevant rather than threatening and dangerous.

It quickly became apparent to early feminist psychologists and mental health practitioners that psychotherapy itself would have to be taken apart and put back together in ways that considered the importance of gender, ethnicity, and sexual orientation, among other acknowledged influences on human psychology. All the assumptions built into assessment and practice had to be questioned in order for the biases inevitably inherent in the isolated dominant perspectives to be revealed. The official perspective was only that and had no claim on "truth."

In short order, feminist psychotherapists, as we would come to be known, began to develop new practices that considered gender as a central issue in psychological development and the psychological distress that brought people to therapy. With this focus, it became immediately apparent that an inequality of power was embedded deeply in gender differences and that part of the task of feminist therapy was the reparative psychological redistribution of power inside and outside the therapy relationship. This had to include respect for diversity and uniqueness and a simultaneous questioning of the proclivity of clinical psychology and psychiatry to pathologize difference.

Within therapy, this concern translated into the introduction of practices such as bartering for services; negotiating fees, location, and scheduling of meeting times; and the judicious use of self-disclosure. The original feminist therapy groups worked as collectives, emphasized the use of groups rather than individual therapy, and attempted in whatever ways seemed possible to create transparency and eliminate power differentials. Assertiveness training became an important part of empowerment goals.

Many of us also became involved in the development of treatment programs for women and girls who had been raped, sexually molested, and otherwise physically abused. The earliest formal treatment venues were the rape crisis centers and domestic violence programs and shelters, which introduced the revolutionary practice of believing what women reported and looking for resolution within a model of justice, of focusing on the actions of the rapist or the abuser rather than on the psychology of the victim. The misogynist questions of prior psychotherapy approaches (e.g., "How was she dressed?" "Was she asking for it?") were slowly removed from credibility, as was the not-so-subtle implication that, for these crimes only, the victim was suspect and instantly implicated in the crime.

Early feminist psychotherapy theory was equally devoted to unearthing the actual causes of the so-called pathologies that were attributed to women and were indeed much more prevalent in women in Western cultures. These included higher rates of depression, anxiety, eating disorders, and self-destructive behaviors (Kaschak, 1992). We were slowly uncovering the shocking amount of sexual abuse that had been believed to be a rare phenomenon before second wave feminism.

In the confluence of feminist psychology and "sexual revolution" in the larger culture, a more accurate picture of women's sexuality began to emerge. The inaptly named "frigidity" was subjected to the scrutiny of laboratory techniques (Masters & Johnson, 1966) and began to reveal itself as a readily modifiable condition. Simple and effective techniques were developed and offered in women's groups, as the field of sex therapy was born. Yet this therapy with women was not an uncomplicated matter when taken in context.

With these advances, it became increasingly apparent that girls and women are subjected to an enormous amount of abuse and trauma. When the new diagnostic category of post-traumatic stress disorder (PTSD) was introduced into the *DSM-III* in 1987, feminist psychologists and psychiatrists insisted that the ordinary traumas of women's lives be included with the battlefield trauma of Vietnam War veterans. This inclusion was only a partial victory for the acknowledgment of women's trauma, as it often does not get to be "post." As a result, Kaschak (1992) proposed that the categories of acute and chronic trauma were more apt, and Herman (1997) offered the idea of simple and complex PTSD.

Outside the therapy room, we called for and participated in social change as an integral part of practicing a therapy that acknowledged "the personal as political." We hoped that our clients would eventually do the same as a means to rebuild their self-respect and sense of agency. We did not demand it but encouraged it openly for those who were willing and able. We saw ourselves and our clients as part of the same force for social change, and we did not place a boundary between ourselves and our clients in that regard.

Although there are various approaches to feminist therapy, gender analysis is the common factor (Kaschak, 1981). Goals have also included increasing self-esteem, reducing discomfort, building personal efficacy, and promoting social justice (Worrell, 2001). Some practitioners strove to be explicitly feminist; others simply became nonsexist and attempted to eliminate sexist bias in traditional approaches (Kaschak, 1981).

Academic critiques developed along with community-based counseling centers, sometimes in tandem and sometimes by the very same professionals and grassroots activists. By the early 1970s, there were Women's Counseling Services in San Francisco, Boston, and New York. The therapy we began to develop involved connecting the smallest details of a client's life with the larger social context, and it soon became apparent that that context included race and ethnicity, sexual orientation, and socioeconomic class and that gender itself has different meanings in different combinations with these and other aspects of the broader societal context.

Feminist therapy has always been about seeing what society demands that we do not, about making the connections, not just between therapist and client but between the personal suffering that our profession categorizes so neatly in the endless series of *DSM*s and the real treatment of categories of people in the larger society. In that way, it has always been about the alleviation of the most personal suffering and, at the same time, about the achievement of social justice. How could they be separated?

From inception then, feminist therapy was about personal and social change, personal and social justice, and was united with the struggles of peoples in such diverse areas as South Africa, China, and the former Yugoslavia (Sharratt & Kaschak, 1999) and with those of girls and women everywhere on the planet who are subjected to such horrors as genital mutilation, rape, sexual slavery, and other forms of gender-based violence and oppression.

Feminist therapy began to dismantle androcentric approaches and to place women's experiences at the center of the discussion. These early tentative steps have led therapists in several directions theoretically and pragmatically. The early techniques and strategies, including assertiveness training and consciousness raising, are no longer used as commonly. The earliest problems (e.g., the many sexual and nonsexual traumas to which women and children are subjected, eating disorders, depression and anxiety, self-destructive behaviors) have continued to retain the focus of feminist therapies, which still focus on how disordered the societies in which we live are. Yet we have not yet developed a systematic diagnostic system that focuses on the social construction of suffering and the disordered societies in which we live.

After the first decade of theoretical development and practice of feminist psychotherapy, Kaschak (1981) introduced a model for organizing the new feminist approaches to diagnosis and treatment, as well as understanding each one's relationship to the others. In essence, the various psychotherapeutic practices subsumed under the more general feminist rubric were categorized according to the feminist perspective itself rather than according to techniques of intervention. This approach resulted in viewing these therapies as radical, liberal, or nonsexist. This idea has been adopted and extended by other feminist writers, most notably Carolyn Zerbe Enns (1997) in her more recent and comprehensive book *Feminist Theories and Feminist Psychotherapies: Origins, Themes, and Variations*. In the years since the introduction of feminist psychotherapy in the early 1970s and in the ensuing decades in which it has been more extensively developed and applied, many writers have suggested that the feminist approach is more a philosophy and a set of values than a specific set of techniques (e.g., Brown, 1994; Brown & Brodsky, 1992; Leupnitz, 1988). Others (e.g., Kaschak, 1976) have considered feminist therapy to be sociotherapy.

In the ensuing years, the group of radical therapies has evolved into social constructionist approaches. This therapeutic orientation includes overlapping and related social constructionist epistemologies, which do not always identify themselves with feminism, such as multicultural and narrative therapies. The second major category is still a liberal group, as it privileges traditionally feminine forms of relationality and is most prominently represented by relational/cultural approaches, such as that of the Stone Center and the Jean Baker Miller Institute. These theorists and practitioners emphasize interpersonal connection, and they have more recently incorporated cultural issues to a significant extent. They have considered the self-in-relation in contrast with the former group's idea of the self-in-context (Kaschak, 1992). Finally, the group of therapies that consider themselves to be explicitly nonsexist, but not feminist, has expanded greatly and might best be represented by certain psychoanalytically based methodologies that focus on relationship and inter-subjectivity. A fourth category might well be included and that would comprise fields that have grown out of our early practices, but separated themselves from their feminist origins. An example is the field of trauma, in which there are both feminist and nonfeminist theorists and practitioners.

Finally it should be noted that feminist thought has had a profound effect on virtually every kind of contemporary practice, all of which strive to be nonsexist, culturally competent, and not to discriminate against marginalized groups. None of these approaches could credibly claim in the twenty-first century to ignore the concepts of gender, ethnicity, or sexual orientation. These are the more invisible effects of feminist practice that should be made visible.

When we began, homosexuality was still listed in the *DSM*, dual relationships were common and unremarkable, and gender had not yet been named. Domestic violence, acquaintance rape, and childhood physical and sexual abuse had not even been identified. Rape victims were treated by therapists much as they were treated by officers of the law and of the court, all of whom conspired to answer the fundamental question: "Was she asking for it?" No ethical practice could include this question anymore, and no ethical practice could be sexist, racist, or homophobic today. This was not the way we found the field, but it is the way we have changed it.

On the other hand, with managed care, the *DSM* has become even more essential to clinical practice, and, although it is somewhat more transparent on issues of gender and ethnicity, it continues to promote the pre-feminist idea that disorders are characteristic of individuals devoid of social context rather than naming many of them what they are: socially transmitted diseases (STDs).

An extensive literature has been amassed concerning theoretical issues and practical application of feminist therapy (e.g., Brown, 1994; Comas-Díaz & Greene, 1994; Lerman & Porter, 1990; Miller & Stiver, 1997; Worell & Remer, 2003), but formal research on the methodologies and their effectiveness is much scarcer. In this chapter, we first review research that supports the general philosophical foundation of feminist therapy and then address what the actual practice entails. A review of studies of various perceptions and critiques of feminist therapy follows. Finally, outcome research is summarized and suggestions for future research directions discussed.

Psychological Distress: Diagnosis, Assessment, and Sociocultural Influences

From its inception, feminist therapy has questioned the appropriateness of diagnosis and traditional forms of psychological assessment. At the most radical end of the continuum, some writers have taken the stance that it is impossible to combine feminism with any sort of psychological practice, let alone diagnosis, because to do so causes women to "privatize, individualize and pathologize our problems as women…rather than to understand these difficulties as shared consequences of oppression" (Kitzinger & Perkins, 1993, pp. 5–6). Others relied on the foundational principle that the personal is political to question whether mental health assessments are free from a plethora of cultural biases regarding what is normal and functional; these assessments result in diagnoses that are social constructions rather than actual disorders (e.g., Brown & Ballou, 1994; Caplan, 1995; Caplan & Cosgrove, 2004). Kaschak (1992) has suggested that diagnoses be renamed "orders" because they are a predictable outcome of the real social demands and experiences of women in society. They are actually STDs – socially transmitted disorders.

Gender and Sexism in Psychotherapy

Beginning with the classic study by Broverman and her colleagues (1970), research has demonstrated that gender-role expectations held by clinicians influence their assessment of clients' mental health and diagnostic classification. In the decades since that study was conducted, additional research has pointed toward some amelioration of gender bias in the characterization of psychological health (Haskell, 2006). Seem and Clark (2006) evaluated gender bias in counselors-in-training to determine if the Broverman study results continued to hold true in the twenty-first century. The results indicate that there continues to be a significant difference in how healthy women and healthy adults are characterized, whereas there is no statistical difference between the healthy adult and the healthy man. However, whereas, in the Broverman et al. (1970) study, the healthy man description did not include any stereotypically feminine behaviors, this was not the case in Seem and Clark's (2006) study. Although many traditionally masculine descriptions were endorsed, the healthy man was also seen as "idealistic, not at all weak, interested in own appearance, loving, and acts on feelings rather than logic" (p. 253). In addition, the healthy woman in this study was viewed as encompassing both traditionally feminine (e.g., understanding, warm, emotional, sensitive, talkative, soft) and traditionally masculine (e.g., strong, enjoys a challenge, direct, adventurous) traits.

After having identified the role of gender socialization and oppression in real or perceived psychological functioning as well as interpersonal style, many second wave feminists pronounced the diagnostic nomenclature specious (see, for example, Caplan, 1995; Chesler, 1972; Kaschak, 1992). Primary targets of these critiques have been the cluster B personality disorders within the *Diagnostic and Statistical Manual*'s various iterations (American Psychiatric Association, 2000). Diagnoses in this cluster include histrionic, borderline, narcissistic, dependent, and antisocial personality disorders. Because these so-called disorders are considered long-standing and based primarily on interpersonal style, the gendered nature of their construction is more easily seen. For example, the diagnoses of histrionic, borderline, and dependent personality disorder all include emotional lability, sensitivity to relational loss, and problems with independence (American Psychiatric Association, 2000). Traditional gender expectations for women have included being emotional, dependent, and focused on relationships (Broverman et al., 1970; Seem & Clark, 2006), which support the idea that these personality disorders are little more than hyper-conformance to gender-role expectation in the face of gender bias and oppression. A similar argument can be made regarding narcissistic and antisocial personality disorders. These diagnoses are based in the rejection of mutual (or dependent) relationships, a hyper-individuality, and a sense of entitlement, hallmarks of the over-socialized man (Broverman et al., 1970, 1994).

Researchers have found gender differences in the diagnosis of histrionic (Erikson, 2002; Hamilton, Rothbart, & Dawes, 1986), borderline (Becker & Lamb, 1994; Boggs et al., 2005), antisocial (Becker & Lamb, 1994), and narcissistic (Erikson, 2002) personality disorders. Although results differ on the influence of the clinician's gender on diagnostic decision making [e.g., Becker & Lamb (1994) found this effect for the borderline diagnosis], the studies cited above are universal in showing an effect of the client's gender.

With respect to antisocial personality disorder, the research is somewhat mixed; Becker and Lamb (1994) found a significant gender difference in the diagnosis, whereas Hamilton and her colleagues (1986) did not. Hamilton et al. (1986) argued that, of all the cluster B categories, antisocial personality disorder contains the most concrete behavioral descriptions (e.g., illegal behaviors), which makes it less susceptible to stereotype effects. Erikson (2002) extended this line of research by investigating the differential effect of the client's *biological sex* versus the client's *gender presentation* on assigned diagnosis. His findings indicate that gender presentation is more influential in the diagnosis of histrionic and narcissistic personality disorders than is sex; sex had a secondary, lesser effect. These results support the theoretical argument that certain gendered behaviors are associated with certain diagnostic categories; however, they also address the question of whether being pathologized is the exclusive purview of women or whether it can be extended to all those who over-conform to or express non-sex-congruent gender stereotypic behaviors.

The Effects of Other "Isms"

Multicultural and feminist theoreticians have extended early critiques to demonstrate the effects of racism, ethnocentrism, heterosexism, able-ism, and classism on diagnosis and mental health (e.g., Comas-Díaz & Greene, 1994; Firestein & Greene, 2007; Greene & Herek, 1994; Olkin, 2001; Rothblum, 1996). Research tends to support these critiques.

One area that highlights the presence of racial bias in diagnosis is the psychosis category. Rayburn and Stonecypher (1996), in a study of male and female patients, 41% of whom were White and 59% Black, found that, among involuntarily committed psychiatric patients, Black patients were more likely to be diagnosed with psychotic disorders with associated poor prognosis and more potent medications, whereas White patients were more likely to receive a diagnosis of affective disorder with a better prognosis and less medication. They did not report gender differences, although they did find an effect of age in that older patients were more often diagnosed with dementia.

Subsequent researchers (Blow et al., 2004) examined the effect of race on the diagnoses of schizophrenia, schizoaffective disorder, and bipolar disorder in a population of 134,523 US veterans (6.7% women) who had sought services at Veterans Affairs Hospitals. Overall, their sample was largely White (69.5%; 6.9% women) followed by Black (23.6%; 7.1% women) and then Hispanic (6.9%; 3.39% women). Of the entire sample, 4% of those diagnosed with schizophrenia, 8.6% with schizoaffective disorder, and 10.1% with bipolar disorder were women. Results indicated that the Black veterans were four times as likely and Hispanic veterans three times as likely to be diagnosed with schizophrenia than with bipolar disorder in comparison with their White counterparts. Both Black and Hispanic veterans had an elevated probability of being diagnosed with schizoaffective disorder rather than with bipolar disorder, although not at the dramatic rates seen for schizophrenia. In a secondary analysis, Blow et al. (2004) investigated the relation of SES to race and assigned diagnosis. They replicated the finding that lower income is negatively correlated with a probability of being diagnosed with schizophrenia, but SES contributed only a small amount of the predictive variance (4% for Blacks and 3% for Hispanics) to the risk model. The authors reported no significant findings related to gender, which may be a reflection of the small number of women in their sample.

The research reviewed thus far focuses on the relationship between racism and diagnostic decision making. It may be somewhat confounded by the effects of racism in life before and outside of diagnosis. That is, it is also probable that living in a racist society leads to more profound forms of psychological distress and disorganization in certain vulnerable individuals.

Other studies have, in fact, focused on the effects of acculturative stress and discrimination on overall mental health. These experiences have been demonstrated to result in negative effects on mental health in nonclinical populations. In their review of the literature, Joiner and Walker (2002) noted that acculturative stress has been empirically implicated in depression, suicidal ideation, bulimia, and general distress in Hispanic Americans; bulimia, substance abuse, and general distress in African Americans; and general distress among Japanese Americans. In their own study, Joiner and Walker (2002) confirmed the relationship between acculturative stress and depression and anxiety in an African American student population. Although they reported that 60% of the sample were women and 40% were men, they appear to have collapsed analyses across gender, as they did not discuss it at all.

Other researchers have begun to examine the role of acculturation and racial identity development in mental health. An interesting finding from a study by Moradi and Risco (2006) is that greater acculturation to the dominant US culture by people of Hispanic descent may have either positive or negative mental health effects. The direct relationship between the two variables suggests that greater acculturation leads to decreased mental health. However, to the extent that acculturation to the dominant culture leads to a greater sense of personal mastery and control of one's environment, acculturation has been shown to have a positive influence on overall mental health. Furthermore, Moradi and Risco (2006) found that retention of traditional Hispanic cultural identity also has a positive influence on mental health through the same variable of personal mastery. These findings may provide support for one of feminist therapy's goals, that of empowerment, particularly for oppressed communities, as integral to mental health – as well as demonstrate that empowerment can and must occur in culturally salient ways. Once again, although the authors reported that 63% of their sample were women and 37% were men, they did not conduct a gender analysis.

Similarly, Lee (2003) found that, among Asian Americans, degree of ethnic identity correlated positively with psychological well-being but did not mediate the negative effects of discrimination on mental health. Pillay (2005) explored the effect of acculturation on mental health in a group of African American students and found that greater identification with the African culture led to greater psychological distress. The author interpreted this finding as possibly related to stages of racial identity development and experiences of racism, although this interaction was not tested statistically. The results indicate that being a woman was significantly predictive of lower levels of psychological health, and this variable remained significant throughout all three steps of the regression analysis. Higher levels of identification with African culture were predictive of lower levels of psychological well-being. In post hoc analyses, the author found that women had lower levels of psychological well-being in general and specifically lower scores in terms of general positive effect and higher scores on loss of behavioral and emotional control. There were no significant differences between female and male participants on levels of acculturation or stage of ethnic identity development.

A universal, and not surprising, finding is that discrimination is detrimental to a person's mental health. Empirical studies have documented the deleterious effect of discrimination and oppression on psychological well-being among African Americans (Waltermaurer, Watson, & McNutt, 2006), Asian Americans (Lee, 2003), and Hispanic Americans (Moradi & Risco, 2006). International studies have demonstrated the same effect among Brazilian adolescents (Santana, Almeida-Filho, Roberts, & Cooper, 2007) and Bangladeshi women (Barn, 2008). In addition, discrimination based on gender (Landrine, Klonoff, Gibbs, Manning, & Lund, 1995), sexual orientation (Waldo, 1999), and physical ability (Timm, 2003) is negatively correlated with psychological well-being, and it is a better predictor of symptoms rather than general stress.

It must be noted here that there is an absence of analysis of multiple interacting variables in a great deal of multicultural literature, as well as in some of the more liberal branches of feminist literature. We hope that these anomalous remains of myopic perspectives will soon yield fully to the corrective lenses of diversity and multiplicity that more accurately represent the real influences upon any individual in context.

Traumatic Experiences

The experience of trauma, particularly interpersonally perpetrated trauma, has continued to be a crucial contextual factor for feminist therapists largely because it exerts such a strong influence in the lives of women and some men. Just as the research is clear in demonstrating that discriminatory experiences compromise well-being, study after study has documented the negative effect of direct trauma upon mental health. Trauma has been linked to depression (Zlotnick, Warshaw, Shea, & Keller, 1997), anxiety (Saunders, Villeponteaux, Liposvsky, Kilpatrick, & Vernon, 1992), somatization (Pribor, Yutzy, Dean, & Wetzel, 1993), dissociation (Putnam, Guroff, Silberman, Barban, & Post, 1986), self-mutilation (van der Kolk, Perry, & Herman, 1991), borderline (Herman, Perry, & van der Kolk, 1989) and passive-aggressive personality disorders (Townsend, 2004), affect dysregulation, and relationship problems (Courtois, 1979). The *insidious trauma* (Root, 1992) perpetrated by the community upon individuals who differ from the norm can interact with direct (i.e., classically categorized) traumatic events and cause great difficulty. One study provided provisional support for the interactive effect of racism and intimate partner violence upon mental health. Waltermaurer and her colleagues (2006) evaluated experiences of perceived racism and emotional, physical, and sexual violence among a group of Black women aged 18–44 years old. Although their sample size was small, they found that participants who had experienced racial discrimination were more likely to have experienced intimate partner violence. Women who reported both experiences endorsed anxiety symptoms and physical health complaints at a significantly higher rate than did women who reported neither experience.

Dragowski (2006) evaluated the effect of insidious (verbal aggression) and direct (physical attack) traumas related to sexual orientation and found that both are predictive of post-traumatic stress symptoms in lesbian, gay, and bisexual adolescents, over and above the effect of childhood gender atypicality, internalized homophobia, and general life stress. The author found that experiences of verbal aggression were more predictive of post-traumatic stress symptoms than were experiences of direct physical violence. Her results also highlight the role of internalized homophobia in psychological functioning. Taken together, the results of the study point to the importance of not only attending to effects of direct trauma on a client's functioning but also considering larger, contextual violence with which a person may live on a daily basis.

The Meaning of Feminist Therapy

Although the above review of research on the effects of gender, culture, and trauma on diagnosis and psychological well-being is by no means exhaustive, taken together the findings support much of feminist therapy's philosophical foundation. First, the personal is political. Feminist therapists have long critiqued the reification of diagnostic categories and pointed out that the creation of a diagnosis is a political rather than a scientific process with very real and often detrimental effects on people's lives (e.g., Brown & Ballou, 1994; Caplan, 1995; Caplan & Cosgrove, 2004; Herman, 1997). The reliability and the validity of diagnostic categories are called into question, given the ease with which differential diagnosis can be manipulated by changing the gender of the person being diagnosed. Further, the significant difference in risk for a particular diagnosis based on one's ethnicity or class highlights the biased nature of diagnosis.

Second, both the importance of cultural and contextual analysis and the role of oppression in distress are supported by the literature. Research clearly demonstrates the negative effects of living with oppression, discrimination, and prejudice. Feminist therapy holds as a value sensitivity and respect for the plethora of cultural backgrounds and experiences that individuals bring to the therapeutic relationship, as well as a commitment to confronting oppression in all its forms. The findings reviewed thus far support the importance of social deconstruction and question the validity of locating psychopathology within the individual rather than in society. As part of the contextual analysis, research supports feminist therapy's focus on the role of trauma, both insidious and direct, in health and well-being, as well as the importance of working to decrease victimization of all oppressed people. Further, the research by Erikson (2002) points to the importance of challenging prescribed gender roles and broadening the concept of what it means to express feminine or masculine traits, irrespective of one's biological sex. An important point to consider in this area, however, is that feminist psychology has developed its own dominant discourse over time. An example of this is highlighted by a qualitative study of feminist therapists working with lesbian partner abuse (Ristock, 2001). The author analyzed the transcripts of eight focus groups conducted across Canada and noted a reliance on "white, feminist heteronormative categories and constructs to think about violence" (p. 63). The exclusive focus on trauma and one-sided power constructions is an example of heteronormative assumptions derived from analyses of relationship violence of men toward women in which the power imbalance is often crucial. This conceptualization ignores the complex interplay of power dynamics within lesbian relationships, and some work has been done in this regard (Kaschak, 2001a).

Perceptions of Feminist Therapy/Therapists

Feminist therapists may be viewed with distrust, particularly as they eschew the traditional framework of therapy as "neutral" in favor of making underlying values explicit. In fact, Lewis, Epperson, and Foley (1989) found that when a therapist communicated *controversial values* (their term for feminist values) in initial written information given to prospective clients, participants responded negatively. Other analogue research suggests that potential clients may be more reluctant to seek help from a feminist therapist for marital or parenting difficulties (Schneider,

1985). These studies, and others like them, can be criticized for relying on written information that describes a hypothetical therapist, which encourages participants to rely upon stereotypes rather than on actual feminist therapy in practice. Research that utilized videotaped sessions that exemplify various types of therapy has demonstrated either a positive or a neutral effect of a feminist therapist making explicit value statements to a client (Enns, 1987; Enns & Hackett, 1993).

Enns' research demonstrates an interesting evolution in the perception of feminist therapy. In her original study (1987) of female participants' reactions to videotaped examples of radical feminist, liberal feminist, and nonsexist therapy, she found that women, regardless of their own feminist orientation, were more willing to seek help from a feminist therapist rather than a nonsexist therapist for career and sexual harassment concerns, and they expressed no preference for the type of therapist for personal or interpersonal concerns. In a later replication (Enns & Hackett, 1993), this preference was no longer present for either female or male participants. It may be that, by the time of the later study, feminist values had been incorporated into mainstream practice sufficiently so that there was no longer a perceived need for a separate feminist approach even for issues of harassment and discrimination.

Other findings from Enns and Hackett's study (1993) indicate that both women and men expected feminist therapists (radical more so than liberal), as compared to nonsexist therapists, to encourage clients to accept feminist values and to change both their beliefs and behaviors. Feminist therapy, by making values explicit, may seem less neutral to the uninformed consumer who expects a so-called value-free intervention. Alternately consumers may very well be aware of the values embedded in any approach, and, thus, they may even prefer the opportunity to make these values explicit and open to discussion rather than simply assumed.

Research findings are mixed regarding whether clients view feminist therapy as helpful. One qualitative study (Chambless & Wenk, 1982) showed that female participants in both traditional and feminist therapy significantly preferred feminist therapy; they described feeling more comfortable, more supported, and provided with greater encouragement and feedback by the feminist therapist. It is not surprising that women and men who identify as feminists tend to view feminist therapists as more helpful than nonfeminist therapists (Enns & Hackett, 1993). This finding supports earlier research by Marecek, Kravetz, and Finn (1979). However, both men and women who do not identify as feminists tend to view both feminist and traditional therapists as helpful. Therapy clients who identify as feminist may be concerned with finding support for their personal philosophy and beliefs as well as receiving help for their difficulties, whereas nonfeminist clients may be focused solely on amelioration of their problems. Perhaps they do not care how the amelioration happens, so the feminist aspect is less salient to them.

Other research suggests that identifying oneself as a feminist does not mean that feminist therapy will be the preferred model of care. Glidden and Tracey (1989) examined female college students' preferences for personal (i.e., individual focus) versus feminist (i.e., sociocultural focus) therapy to address weight and body image concerns and found that women with *nontraditional gender-role attitudes* (who were presumably inclined toward feminist values) favored the personal intervention. Conversely, and contrary to the authors' expectations, participants who endorsed traditional gender-role attitudes preferred the feminist approach to addressing weight concerns. Perhaps each group was drawn toward a missing component.

One difficulty with research on feminist therapy, as discussed further below, is the diversity of approaches encompassed by the term. However, the research also suggests that clients may want and value different approaches at different times or for different issues and that a therapist needs to be flexible enough to adapt to clients' needs without giving up the heart of her or his theoretical orientation.

Praxis – What Do Feminist Therapists Do?

The question that is still crucial involves what actually happens in the therapy room that is different from generic good therapy. Researchers have taken both qualitative and quantitative approaches to examine this question. In this section we examine the research related to general practice and then we discuss specific aspects of the therapy process.

General Practices

Qualitative Research

Qualitative researchers have focused on the experiences and reflections of self-identified feminist therapists in order to identify common practice behaviors and themes. Hill and Ballou (1998) collected written reflections from 35 members of the Feminist Therapy Institute, who were asked to describe examples of the process of feminist therapy and how a specific, traditional therapeutic technique had been adapted in order to be feminist. The therapists reported multiple ways that they incorporate feminist principles into the therapy process. Hill and Ballou organized the therapists' responses into five general categories, in order of how frequently each topic was discussed: (1) attention to power in therapy, (2) recognition of sociocultural causes of distress, (3) valuing women's experience, (4) an integration of analysis of oppression, and (5) maintaining the goal of social change. Power was most frequently addressed via giving initial information to clients regarding the therapeutic process, values the therapist brings to the relationship, how clients can address concerns within the therapy relationship, and any potentially overlapping relationships. Although the authors separated the next three themes, the participants' responses tended to cross categories; they emphasized the importance of accepting clients' experiences as real, not ascribing socially derived distress to internal causes, understanding experiences common to women and other minority groups, and using a variety of cultural lenses to understand the intersection of a wide variety of diversity variables. Finally, in terms of social change, the therapists in the study noted a multitude of ways they attempted to create change, from the magazines found in the waiting room to making nongendered assumptions about relationship responsibilities and expectations. In terms of adapting traditional techniques, most respondents focused on making interventions more collaborative and teaching clients about the biases inherent in psychological theories.

Marecek and Kravetz (1998) analyzed transcripts from interviews with three practicing feminist therapists, who were asked to discuss how they integrate feminism into therapy. Whereas Hill and Ballou (1998) sought descriptions of practice, Maracek and Kravetz highlighted the ways in which feminist therapists struggle against, yet still incorporate, patriarchal assumptions into their work. The narratives demonstrate the variety of ideas regarding power and influence that feminist therapists may bring to their work; one therapist expressed ambivalence about power (by noting it in one breath and minimizing it in the next), another used her ascribed power to bring about social change (e.g., by working with abusive men), and the third hoped to make power moot through the creation of connection and universality. The researchers noted that "A key issue in contemporary feminist theory has been to devise ways to call attention to women's oppression and its debilitating effects without losing sight of their agency" (p. 34). Again, the diversity of practice among feminist therapists was noted in this study. Little universality was found even among three experienced therapists. Moreover, within these narratives, the researchers found traces of patriarchal assumptions such as an emphasis on "health" (as something that can be quantified and agreed upon), the valorization of the feminine ideal (e.g., care, kindness, connection), and even reductionism (e.g., all abuse is caused solely by gender oppression).

In a qualitative analysis of feminist therapy as practiced by south Asian therapists residing in the United States and working with south Asian immigrant women who were survivors of domestic violence, Kallivayalil (2007) examined the interplay between cultural sensitivity (one feminist value) and empowerment (another feminist value). Practitioners clearly articulated their belief that domestic violence is rooted in patriarchal oppression, and they noted that the stresses of immigration and the pressure to acculturate entrenched patriarchal attitudes even more deeply. Therapists reported that they attempted to educate their clients on the rights of women and the effects of gender oppression but also recognized that multiple cultural factors could prevent south Asian women from naming their experiences as abuse or being able to leave an abusive relationship. Although they acknowledged the realities of saving face, close family ties, filial piety, and self-restraint in Asian families (Ho, 1990), the participants discussed their focus on helping women to develop a sense of self, increase their self-esteem, and become empowered. They strove to facilitate the clients' ability to make concrete decisions that are in their best interests, whatever those interests are determined to be by the women themselves. They reported encouraging women to change their own perspective on their role in the family, yet acknowledged the great patience needed to work with this group.

Results of qualitative research characterize feminist therapy praxis as a series of choice points at which the therapist can decide to reduce power differentials, not to make normative assumptions, to value cultural diversity, and to pathologize society rather than the individual. In many ways, these choice points can be subtle and hard to differentiate from "good therapy." For example, all therapists should ensure that informed consent is obtained from clients. The difference between feminist and traditional therapists may be in the breadth and depth of information offered, including information about potential overlapping relationships, how to address conflict within the therapeutic relationship, and risks and benefits of therapy in contrast to a simple description of the limits of confidentiality, the no-show policy, the right to terminate treatment, or the provision of clients with written information about how to file a complaint. Other choice points include choice of magazines (e.g., those that represent diversity versus mainstream publications) and office decoration, aspects that traditional therapists might not consider as directly related to therapy outcomes.

Feminist and traditional therapists may use similar interventions when working with a client (e.g., paradoxical interventions, thought challenging), but whether a therapist does such an intervention *to* a client or creates an intervention *with* a client by providing education and inviting participation through soliciting feedback determines whether the therapy is feminist. As the practice of psychotherapy has become more multiculturally focused, all major ethical codes stress the importance of cultural sensitivity (e.g., American Counseling Association, 2005; American Psychological Association Ethics Committee, 2002; National Association of Social Workers, 1996), which makes cultural sensitivity no longer the exclusive purview of feminist and multicultural practitioners. However, whereas good therapists attend to and respect cultural differences, feminist therapists go a step further to examine critically the effects of oppression and discrimination both on the individual client and the community and actively work toward both levels of change. Further, feminist therapists acknowledge the values they hold, examine how they may conflict with a client's cultural value system, and collaborate with clients to find the right balance of values rather than assuming that the therapist's values are the correct or healthy ones.

Quantitative Research

Despite the great heterogeneity in practice suggested by the qualitative research, some researchers have attempted to develop quantitative instruments that capture general practices. One of the most prominently used is The Feminist Therapy Behavior Checklist (FTB; Juntunen, Atkinson, Reyes, & Gutierrez, 1994). This self-report instrument lists behaviors derived from the theoretical literature as exemplifying feminist therapy and asks respondents to rate how frequently they engage in each behavior.

Other researchers (Moradi, Fischer, Hill, Jome, & Blum, 2000) have revised the FTB to make it inclusive of therapy behaviors with both female and male clients and added items to address multicultural sensitivity. Moradi and her colleagues (2000) criticized previous research with the FTB because feminist therapists are identified through the use of a unidimensional, dichotomous item that inquired if the practitioner is a feminist therapist. In their study, they asked therapists to rate themselves on a five-point scale on three items ("I am a feminist," "I am a feminist therapist," and "I practice feminist therapy;" p. 287). In addition, participants were asked to rank up to three descriptors of their theoretical orientation from a range of choices. How therapists self-label influences which aspects of feminist therapy are expressed through their practice behaviors. In general, self-labeling as a feminist most strongly predicted a therapist's use of empowerment strategies and gender-role analysis/challenge in practice with female and male clients. However, when therapists reported on their practice with women, identification with any variation of feminism did not predict the use of assertiveness training. In other words, both feminist and nonfeminist therapists were just as likely to work on assertiveness skills with their female clients. It is interesting that identification as a feminist in general, and as practicing feminist therapy in particular, predicted small amounts of variance (5 and 4%, respectively) in the use of assertiveness training with male clients. It may be that feminist and traditional therapists value assertiveness for women, but for different reasons: the feminist therapist in order to increase the status of women in society and the traditional therapist as a function of the belief that assertiveness is a characteristic of a healthy adult. For male clients, feminist therapists may view assertiveness training as an antidote to patriarchal power-over methods of expressing needs and desires, and, therefore, an important part of therapy focused on creating social change first within the individual. Nonfeminist therapists may more readily accept aggressive communication styles from male clients and see a need for change only if overt violence is involved.

Moradi et al. (2000) also asked research participants to rank the top five therapy behaviors (from a list of 64) used in their practice, and then they compared the top five ranked behaviors by all feminist therapists to the number of traditional practitioners who endorsed these same items. For feminist therapy clients, the only item that did not reach significance was the use of empathy and unconditional positive regard toward clients. However, feminist therapists were significantly more likely to endorse paying attention to experiences of discrimination, assuming a collaborative stance, reframing clients' understanding of their problems to include sociocultural influences, and focusing on clients' unique and positive qualities. With regard to working with male clients, the therapists did not differ on the use of empathy and positive regard but differed in their rankings of attending to experiences of discrimination, assuming a collaborative stance, supporting clients' efforts to expand beyond traditional gender-role behaviors, and focusing on positive and unique qualities. The similarity in endorsing the use of empathy and positive regard suggests that this is a component of good therapy rather than of specifically feminist therapy. The other behaviors, however, lend support to feminism's professed focus on the personal as political (focus on discrimination, challenging gender roles) and empowerment (collaboration, self-esteem building). That is, feminist psychotherapy is simultaneously sociotherapy.

This innovative study included as participants both men and women who identified as feminist therapists and also considered feminist therapy with both female and male clients. Historically, there has been a theoretical debate regarding whether men can be feminist therapists (e.g., Kaschak, 1992) and whether feminist therapy is an appropriate modality for male therapy clients (e.g., Ganley, 1988). The Moradi et al. study, particularly when taken together with Enns and Hackett's (1993) results, suggests that men can and do identify themselves as feminist therapists, engage in feminist practices, and expect the therapy experience to be helpful to them. Although further research, particularly in the area of men's experience as a client in feminist therapy, is indicated, the results of the research thus far may be taken as encouragement for the greater applicability of feminist practice.

Other research with the FTB has yielded mixed results. Meginnis-Payne (2000) found that therapists' scores on a global index of feminist identity were predictive of the extent to which they reported focusing on gender-role analysis, redistribution of power, and minimizing the power differential in the therapeutic relationship. In another study focused on the client–therapist relationship, Rader and Gilbert (2005) found no difference in the reported use of feminist therapy interventions between therapists who identify as feminist and those who do not. Their study may be limited by the use of a unidimensional measure of feminist therapy identification, which might not have been sensitive enough to discriminate between true feminist therapists and those therapists who have incorporated some feminist values into their therapeutic approach but resist the feminist label. However, participants in the Rader and Gilbert's (2005) study did show significant differences in the experience of power sharing between feminist-identified therapists and therapists with other identifications. Dahms (2003) also found no difference between the scores on the revised FTB for feminist and nonfeminist therapists. That study used the Feminist Identity Scale (Rickard, 1987) to classify therapists as feminist or not in an attempt to avoid problems associated with self-labeling. It seems that, depending on the sample, many of the values associated with feminist therapy have begun to infiltrate mainstream psychology and perhaps to decrease the distance between feminist and good therapy. Alternatively, it may be that even therapists are susceptible to believing uncritically the stereotypes of feminists and are, therefore, reluctant to identify themselves that way, despite how they practice their craft.

The Therapy with Women Scale (TWS; Robinson & Worell, 1991, as cited in Rader & Gilbert, 2005) is another attempt to quantify feminist therapy behaviors, specifically power sharing. The measure focuses exclusively on therapy with women and is theoretically derived from the literature on feminist therapy. Research with the TWS is surprisingly sparse. The two empirical studies in print both point to greater power sharing by feminist therapists than by other therapists (Rader & Gilbert, 2005; Robinson, 1995). In an interesting validation check, Rader and Gilbert (2005) asked clients of the therapists in their study to complete the Client Therapy with Women Scale (CTWS; Worell, Chandler, & Robinson, 1996, as cited in Rader & Gilbert, 2005). This measure asks clients to reflect on the same power sharing statements included in the TWS, but worded to reflect the clients' experience of therapists' behaviors. They found that, indeed, the clients of feminist therapists perceived them as sharing more power than do nonfeminist therapists. Measures such as the CTWS are important for research in this area; therapist self-report is subject to the same biases as any other group, and what is reported may or may not reflect what actually occurs in the therapy room.

In another study of clients' perceptions of feminist therapy, Mcdonagh (2000) evaluated the experiences of a group of women who were survivors of childhood sexual abuse. The participants reported that feminist therapists asked about histories of abuse and acknowledged, discussed, and contextualized the experience and its effects, whereas traditional therapists failed to do these things. When asked to reflect on the process of therapy, the women's responses generally highlighted therapeutic elements described in the feminist therapy literature, including involvement of clients in structuring therapy, attention to the therapeutic relationship, the role of self-disclosure, empowerment of the client, and integration of social and political contexts. Even given these results, every therapist has had the experience of a client perceiving the therapist's behavior or comments in a completely unexpected way. The qualitative portion of Meginnis-Payne's study (2000) highlights a weakness in the use of therapist self-report with only quantitative measures. Although the quantitative measure in her study (the FTB) suggested that feminist therapists were more likely than other therapists to use feminist therapy techniques in their practice, when a subset of participants were asked to discuss a "memorable case," only 2 of 16 feminist therapy tenets appeared regularly in the discourse: expanding girls' and women's alternatives, and attention to the influence of sociocultural factors on women's lives.

A third questionnaire, the Women and Counselling Questionnaire (WCQ), was developed by Chester and Bretherton (2001) as part of their attempt to investigate feminist therapy among Australian therapists. Although they used different labels for their categories, the researchers found similar foci to be important to Australian feminist therapists: knowledge about gender roles and factors that affect women's lives, egalitarian relationships, understanding women's experience, working toward social change, critiquing the patriarchy, and an expectation of equality for women in the future. Respondents tended to place more importance on challenging gender-role stereotyping and the sociocultural causes of distress rather than on the egalitarian relationship, whereas feminist therapists in the United States seem to emphasize reduced power differentials first; sociocultural critiques have a slightly secondary emphasis. As with any movement, how it develops is influenced by the cultural context in which it exists. An essential factor for North American feminists was the rejection of the individual mode of treatment. From the era of consciousness-raising groups to the return of individual therapy, egalitarianism has been an important rallying cry for feminist therapists, even as true equality within the therapeutic relationship can never be achieved. It may be that, as feminism developed in Australia, the effects of sexism were the rallying point in that country, hence the focus of feminist therapists there is slightly different than that in the United States. The study raises the important point that, although overlap certainly exists, just as feminist therapy is not a monolithic entity in any one country, it is certainly diverse across countries and cultures. Nevertheless, it seems apparent that the relationship in feminist therapy plays a crucial role and, thus, demands further elaboration.

Specific Issues in the Therapeutic Relationship

Nature of the Relationship

One of the specific hallmarks of relationships established in feminist therapy is the intentional effort to reduce power differentials and create egalitarian relationships as much as possible. This goal is often achieved by efforts to provide information, solicit feedback, inform clients of their rights and responsibilities, educate clients about the therapy process, and by not assuming an expert role (Chester & Bretherton, 2001; Hill & Ballou, 1998; Meginnis-Payne, 2000; Rader & Gilbert, 2005). Some early research shows that feminist therapists were perceived as more action oriented and as using problem-solving approaches more often than did traditional therapists (Chambless & Wenk, 1982). Although these results probably reflect an early preference, it may no longer be the case, as there is a renewed interest in psychodynamic approaches. Despite feminism's focus on reducing power differentials and considering the client an expert on herself, Enns and Hackett (1993) found that academic women were more likely to ascribe expert status to feminist therapists than to nonsexist therapists. Perhaps being able to speak to the collective historical experience of women in society not only increases feelings of being understood (Chambless & Wenk, 1982) but also increases confidence that the therapist is knowledgeable, particularly among those who deal with knowledge professionally. Undoubtedly the feminist psychologist or therapist is quite knowledgeable in this sense of the word; however, the client is still the best expert on her or his own life and personal issues.

Self-disclosure

Self-disclosure is of central import in most theoretical orientations. Psychoanalytic or psychodynamic therapies tend to discourage it because of concerns about issues of transference (Rothstein, 1997). Other theoretical orientations (e.g., cognitive–behavioral, systems, existential) may take a less extreme position, such as permitting, but perhaps not encouraging, self-disclosure by therapists (Matthews, 1989). Research suggests that most therapists tend to disclose at least to some degree (Simone, McCarthy, & Skay, 1998), but they may differentiate between self-involving statements (e.g., sharing thoughts or feelings in reaction to statements made by a client) and actual self-disclosure (e.g., Hill, Mahalik, & Thompson, 1989).

Simi and Mahalik (1997) created the Feminist Self-Disclosure Inventory (FSDI), an 18-item self-report instrument, in which each item is rated on a seven-point Likert scale. The items were derived from the literature and included specific types of disclosures (e.g., information about the therapist's socioeconomic class, religion, sexual orientation, angry feelings), the rationale behind self-disclosures (e.g., to decrease power differentials, empower clients), and self-involving statements. The items generated were reviewed and rated by experts in feminist therapy, and the inclusion of the final group of items was then based on these ratings. Next the researchers surveyed 149 practicing female therapists with the FSDI. Participants were classified into three groups based on self-reported theoretical orientation: feminist, psychoanalytic/dynamic, and other (including cognitive–behavioral, humanistic, and family systems). Five factors were identified on the FSDI and labeled as Therapist Background, Promotes Liberatory Feelings, Promotes Egalitarianism, Therapist Availability (to be asked questions by the client), and Empower Client. As expected, psychoanalytic/dynamic therapists endorsed the least amount of self-disclosure, although this group did report self-disclosure and had the highest mean value for reasons of *promoting an egalitarian therapy relationship*. Both feminist and other therapists reported self-disclosure to promote liberatory feelings in the client and to promote egalitarian relationships. Feminist therapists were significantly different from both groups in their disclosure of background information, by making themselves explicitly available for clients to request self-disclosure and to facilitate the goal of empowerment.

The Simi and Mahalik study is important for several reasons. First, it operationalized self-disclosure as a multidimensional and multipurpose activity, which permitted finer discrimination of differences between therapeutic orientations. Second, it points to additional ways that feminist principles, such as egalitarianism and the impossibility of therapeutic neutrality, have begun to infiltrate even the most conservative theoretical orientations. Finally, it demonstrates that some differences do exist between "middle of the road" theoretical orientations and feminism, particularly in terms of the more explicit encouragement of clients to seek information, taking the initiative to self-disclose, and, in these and other ways, seeking to empower clients as a central aspect of the therapeutic relationship. It would be interesting to replicate this study in order to determine if these various therapeutic orientations have grown even more similar over time.

Termination

The manner of termination is another important part of the therapeutic process that has been discussed in the empirical literature. Research in this area tends to focus on the reasons for premature termination (e.g., Bartle-Haring, Glebova, & Meyer, 2007; Hopwood, Ambwani, & Morey, 2007; Philips, Wennberg, & Werbart, 2007). One group of studies tends to focus on some deficit or pathology within the client that, in the therapist's opinion, causes premature termination. Other studies have begun to examine the role of cultural barriers in termination (Bein, Torres, & Kurilla, 2000), clients' and therapists' emotional responses to ending therapy (Shulman, 1999), or the mismatch between clients' and therapists' perceptions of reason for termination (Hunsley, Aubry, Verstervelt, & Vito, 1999). None of these studies, however, examined the process of termination from a feminist perspective.

Ehrenfeld (1996) examined seven female feminist therapists' perspectives on the process of termination and identified five major themes in their conceptualization of termination. The themes were largely relationally focused and included mutuality, connection, empowerment, disconnection, and competence. In terms of mutuality, this group of therapists discussed the importance of both parties participating actively in the therapy relationship, including the decision to end the relationship. Mutuality also includes an acknowledgement that both people are changed through, and take something away from, the therapy relationship. Connection was viewed by the participants in contrast to the implied disconnection in the word "termination" and was operationalized by inviting a return to therapy at a later date, discussing the end of a phase of work rather than an end to the relationship, and having an "open door policy." The researcher summarized this concept as "finite therapy, infinite relationship" (p. 229). Empowerment was defined as respect for and encouragement of a client's decision-making capabilities, including the ability to decide when to end therapy, even if the therapist does not agree with the timing. In this study, the participants did not label these "premature terminations" as literature from a traditional perspective contends but saw these decisions as a facet of empowered action. Disconnections were endings that resulted from relational impasses of some sort and were often noted in relation to situations that a therapist wished that she had handled differently and with more authenticity. These situations might be characterized as premature terminations, but rather than blaming the client for leaving, the feminist therapists in this study tended to look at their own part in the process and to hold themselves at least equally responsible for the disruption. Finally, competence referred to a sense that client and therapist had worked well together and that feedback from the client was an important part of the termination process. Nevertheless, the participants in no way endorsed continuing a relationship with the client once active therapy had ended. They tended to argue that allowing the relationship to transform into a friendship would close the door left open as part of the termination process, rather than speaking of the implications of power imbalances or viewing clients as empowered enough to make choices about relational desires and needs.

As with much early research, the research on termination from a feminist perspective is nascent and focused on the therapists' conceptualization of the process without significant concretization of actual behaviors. Therapists from many theoretical orientations have an "open door policy," and clients who have had a positive therapeutic relationship are likely to return to the same therapist if new problems arise.

Men as Feminist Therapists

Within the early movement, there was a clear mandate that feminist therapy was the exclusive purview of women – by women for women. As feminist therapy evolved, there was room to question whether men could be feminist therapists or whether their privileged place in society meant that a male therapist could only aspire to be nonsexist (Enns, 1992, 1997; Kaschak, 1992). In recent years, research has indicated that (1) a number of male therapists identify as feminist therapists (Chester & Bretherton, 2001; Moradi et al., 2000; Robinson, 1995), (2) men are clients of feminist therapists (Moradi et al., 2000), and (3) men have an expectation that feminist therapists can be helpful (Enns & Hackett, 1993).

Little research has been conducted, however, that specifically focuses on the practices of male feminist therapists. Szymanski, Baird, and Kornman (2002) investigated a variety of differences in attitudes and practices between men who identified as feminist therapists and men who reported other theoretical orientations. Participants completed the Attitudes Toward Feminism and the Women's Movement Scale (FWM; Fassinger, 1994), the Gender Role Subscale of the Liberal Feminist Attitude and Ideology Scale (LFAIS; Morgan, 1996), and the TWS (Robinson & Worell, 1991, as cited in Rader & Gilbert, 2005). As predicted, feminist men were found to hold more positive attitudes toward the women's movement, endorse more liberal gender-role attitudes, and use more feminist therapeutic behaviors than did non-feminist male therapists.

In another study, Baird, Szymanski, and Ruebelt (2007) examined feminist identity development in a sample of 12 self-identified male feminist therapists. Participants discussed the importance of personal experiences, relationships, mentoring, and education in developing a feminist identity. They described becoming aware of the oppressive experiences of women, questioning gender-role models for men after having fathered sons, receiving supportive but challenging feedback from mentors and female colleagues, and taking classes in feminist and multicultural therapy as integral to raising their consciousness. In addition, three participants noted that their identity as gay men and their own experience of oppression helped them to identify with women's experiences of discrimination. All but one of the men described a process of becoming aware of, accepting, then attempting to move beyond socially ascribed privilege, and using that awareness to advocate for women. These therapists discussed the creation of a collaborative environment and actively dealing with power issues in the therapeutic relationship. Participants discussed a sense of isolation from their professional peers, and perhaps even in their personal lives, due to their feminist identity; they noted that it was difficult to find other men with whom to relate, and they often felt put in the position of defending their theoretical orientation.

The nascent research on male feminist therapists also reflects the small number of male therapists who choose a feminist orientation. However, the data suggest that men are conducting feminist therapy and, much as early female feminists were, are isolated by virtue of challenging expectations and the status quo. Not only is more research needed in this area, but it appears that more support and mentoring of men by feminists, both male and female, are necessary to nurture this developing group.

Outcome and Evaluation Research

As is the case for individual feminist therapy, there is an extensive theoretical literature devoted to group design for various populations including Latinas (Rodriguez, 2001), African American women (Brown, Lipford-Sanders, & Shaw, 1995), south Asian women (Singh & Hays, 2008), adolescents (Garrick & Ewashen, 2001), women sexually abused as children (Chew, 1998), and disordered eaters (Chrisler, 1991), to name only a few. Outcome and evaluation research on feminist therapy, however, are generally sparse and without a coherent, systematic research agenda. The studies available for review all evaluate group interventions designed for a special population of people. Research projects are included in this section only if they specifically describe the intervention under investigation as feminist and some form of outcome measure (either qualitative or quantitative) is used.

Immigrant and International Women

Hmong Women Living in the United States

Danner, Robinson, Striepe, and Rhodes (2007) developed a short-term (10-week), culturally specific group, which incorporates relational/cultural theory and narrative therapy techniques, for Hmong immigrant women living in Minnesota. The stated goals of the group were to decrease symptoms of depression and somatic complaints, increase coping skills, and facilitate a sense of connection. The authors discussed specific feminist techniques, such as minimizing power differentials by encouraging group members to rely on one another for feedback and suggestions and emphasizing the reciprocal nature of learning through the group. They also provided extensive psycho-education regarding therapy, role expectations, and coping skills. In addition, facilitators explicitly supported traditional healing methods and incorporated traditional occupational activities into group activities. Finally, the group leaders provided resources and facilitated social service connections, activities that are often seen as outside the traditional therapeutic frame.

As a quantitative outcome measure, the researchers utilized the Hmong Adaptation of the Beck Depression Inventory (HABDI). Mean scores on the HABDI did not change at all from pre- to post-test administrations. However, the exceedingly high mean score reported (59.9) with a relatively small standard deviation (5.5 pre-test, 4.74 post-test), combined with a small sample size ($N=14$), may have influenced the sensitivity of statistical tests. The qualitative data mirror the quantitative findings, as the majority of women reported that they had experienced no symptom reduction as a result of their participation in the group. It is interesting that the women reported a number of positive outcome experiences, among which was improved mood limited to the time they were actually in the group sessions. The authors categorized the positive outcomes as follows: (1) ability to escape daily life stresses for a time each week; (2) a sense of connection with other women who shared similar experiences; (3) help with citizenship applications (a significant source of stress for participants); (4) learning relaxation techniques; (5) developing a support network with other women; (6) advice and education about coping skills from experts; and (7) identifying coping skills already in use. Among negative comments about the group were (1) that the positive effect disappeared once the women returned to their daily context; (2) continued feelings of depression and physical complaints; and (3) that the group did not last long enough.

The authors interpreted the findings to suggest that feminist group therapy with Hmong women needs to be long term, given the tremendous trauma experienced by most of these immigrant women. In addition, the women found practical and concrete interventions that included advocacy aspects, as well as educational programs and opportunities for culturally relevant experiences, to be particularly helpful. Readers were cautioned against pathologizing the participants for their difficulty in translating their group experience to daily life and, thereby, into symptom reduction. The authors noted that little changed in the participants' daily lives and that such an overwhelming context was likely to prevent a sense of personal control and efficacy to make changes. This finding is reminiscent of Moradi and Risco's (2006) finding that a sense of personal control over one's environment is important to predict overall psychological well-being for Latinos/as.

Women in Bosnia–Herzegovina

Two outcome studies of feminist interventions with women residing in Bosnia–Herzegovina and coping with the ongoing effects of war have been published. The first article (Scheffler & Müchele, 1999) described what the authors termed a "training program" for female service providers. However, the authors also described the use of modalities such as dream work and group process as part of their educational techniques and reported significant transformation in group members' self-esteem and sense of empowerment. Given these elements, the intervention was considered therapeutic and, therefore, included in this section.

The goal of Scheffler and Müchele's (1999) program was to teach a group of 16 women, comprised of social workers, psychologists, physicians, teachers, and an Islamic theologian, a "woman-centered" approach to healing the trauma inflicted by war. The program lasted 2 years and consisted of six modules delivered over the course of the intervention. Topics included working with war and trauma victims, the social psychology of war, counseling techniques, methods for deconstructing gender roles, and social work needs. The authors reported that they specifically attempted to construct the trainings using feminist principles of egalitarianism, empowerment, modeling, and provided support and positive reinforcement. In evaluating the reactions to their methods, the researchers noted that their participants were initially very uncomfortable and resisted attempts at empowerment. However, by the end of 2 years, they noted a qualitative difference in the women's self-esteem, the ability to assert themselves, and the sense of ownership of the knowledge they developed, along with an ability to learn from one another. They also reported that the women went from describing themselves as "broken, exhausted, muted, [and] scared" (p. 134) to describing themselves as "safe, well, contemplative, comfortable, [and] relaxed" (p. 134).

The second study, conducted by Schei and Dahl (1999), evaluated the effects of a social service program in Zenica and a psychotherapeutic group in Tuzla, both designed to address the needs of refugee women. The goal of the programs was to improve the psychosocial functioning of the women and to decrease post-traumatic stress symptoms. In the Zenica program, a center was developed to house group activities. Occupational endeavors, conversation, and education were offered to approximately 400 women and 250 children and then expanded to include mobile services within refugee camps. A total of 209 women who used the program at the center and 69 women who used the mobile services completed a background questionnaire, the Post-Traumatic Symptoms Scale (PTSS-10), and an evaluation of the helpfulness of the center's activities. The authors classified women into groups based on the severity of their traumatic experiences, with the most severe traumatic experiences being "incarcerated in a concentration camp, detained with other women, and/or been witnesses or victims of rape" (p. 145). Women with less severe post-traumatic symptoms were more likely to report that "being with other women" was very helpful and that their symptoms were "somewhat or much better" as a result of participating in the center's activities.

Because psychosocial services were being provided by other entities in Tuzla, the researchers chose to conduct psychotherapeutic groups, 3–4 months in duration, with women identified by intake workers as the most highly distressed. Group members were invited to speak about their lives, were provided psycho-education regarding trauma and its effects, were taught anxiety reduction strategies, and were helped to cope actively with their current circumstances. One hundred and fifty-eight women participated in this portion of the study; they completed a background questionnaire, the PTSS-10, and a group experiences questionnaire. In contrast to the intervention in Zenica, participants with higher PTSS-10 scores were more likely than those with lower scores to characterize specific aspects of the group therapy as helping "a lot" or "very much." In particular, they reported benefiting from learning they are not the only ones with these problems, learning to take responsibility for living their own lives, helping other group members, and having a sense of a substitute family in the group members. In comparing the PTSS-10 scores of women with children who had and had not completed the entire group sequence, the researchers found that participants who had completed therapy had significantly lower scores than those who were still participating in the therapy. However, because no pre-test measures were administered, it is difficult to attribute this difference to the intervention. The authors noted the different effects found for the psychosocial and psychotherapeutic interventions. More severely traumatized women reported feeling helped by the therapy program, but not by the psychosocial program.

These studies point out the difficulty in conducting interventions and research in war-torn countries, as well as the difficulty in applying feminist interventions cross-culturally, which requires, at a minimum, an appreciation for the different cultural context. They also point to the desperate need for services, particularly services that address the trauma perpetrated upon women as part of war campaigns. Despite these difficulties, the therapy work and the research must be conducted in a way that is collaborative and empowering to those being served. Taken together with the study by Danner and colleagues (2007), this group of studies supports the necessity of long-term therapeutic support for women who have been traumatized and displaced. The studies also suggest the importance of the group process, which provides a vehicle for connection, mutual empathy, and empowerment – all important aspects of healing (Miller & Stiver, 1997).

Adult Survivors of Childhood Sexual Abuse

The detrimental effects of childhood sexual abuse (CSA) are readily recognized within the field of psychology (e.g., Briere & Runtz, 1993; Bruns, 2002; Courtois, 1996), and there have been many efforts to ameliorate this suffering. Feminist group treatment models often incorporate elements set forth in the book *Trauma and Recovery* (Herman, 1997), such as focusing on creating safety, telling the story of the trauma, and then reintegrating into the community. Feminist principles of empowerment, egalitarianism, societal analysis and critique, and social justice are often included as well. Westbury and Tutty (1999) evaluated the efficacy of a therapy group that incorporated these principles, along with body-focused work, for women who were survivors of CSA. Twenty-two women participated in therapy groups that met once a week for 2.5 hours over the course of 10–12 weeks. They were compared to a group of 10 women in a waiting list condition. Each set of participants completed self-report measures of depression, self-esteem, and trauma symptoms pre- and post-test. The depression severity ratings of the women who participated in the group intervention moved from an average range of moderate/severe to the mild range, whereas the control group remained, on average, in the moderate to severe range of scores. The only subscale on the trauma measure to demonstrate change in response to participation in the group was level of anxiety. The treatment group reported significantly reduced anxiety relative to the control group. No statistically significant differences in self-esteem were noted between the two groups at pre- or post-test measurement. The authors interpreted these findings as tentative support for the efficacy of their group treatment model.

In another study, conducted by Hébert and Bergeron (2007), Canadian women who participated in a feminist-based group treatment program reported reduced psychological distress relative to women in a waiting list control group. This study included follow-up data, which demonstrated that women in the treatment group maintained their gains for at least 3 months following the completion of the group. In their exploratory analyses, the authors noted that women who experienced severe relationship violence in addition to their history of sexual abuse made the greatest gains in reducing feelings of self-blame, stigmatization, and anxiety related to engaging in assertive behaviors. This may be, in some way, a function of the heightened level of trauma, an issue that should be considered in future research.

Those two studies were conducted at community agencies with women who applied for services of their own volition. Cole, Sarlund-Heinrich, and Brown (2007) evaluated the efficacy of a treatment group for incarcerated women who were survivors of CSA. Although the four women who completed the treatment group and the six women in the waiting list control group volunteered for the study, all were identified as potential participants through the mandatory intake process that occurs upon entering a correctional institution. All participants were administered the Symptom Checklist-90-Revised (SCL-90-R; Derogatis, 1994), the Trauma Symptom Inventory (TSI; Briere, 1995), and the Rorschach Inkblot Method, from which the revised Trauma Content Index (TC/R; Armstrong & Lowenstein, 1990) was calculated. The group was intensive; it met for 2.5 hours twice a week. But it was short term; the group met for only 8 weeks. Topics moved from self-soothing and safety, to providing participants with psycho-education about abuse and its effects, to encouraging the women to discuss their abuse experiences, and, finally, to preparation for termination. At the conclusion of treatment, the only statistically significant change in the objective measures occurred on the TC/R. Group participants evidenced a reduction in traumatic content projected into their Rorschach protocols in comparison with their own pre-test scores. No differences within groups were demonstrated on the SCL-90-R or the TSI. In addition, no significant between-group differences were found on any measure. However, given such a small sample size, the utility of statistical analysis is questionable. The authors did note, however, that the women in the waiting list condition demonstrated a worsening of their symptoms, whereas the treatment group's scores held fairly constant. They interpreted this result as favoring treatment as prevention of the aggravation of the distress that is common when survivors of CSA are first incarcerated. At termination, the group participants reported that the group was helpful in providing information (particularly handouts), reducing their sense of isolation, and conferring "expert" status on their own experience within a dehumanizing system. Needless to say, these implications require further research to confirm or disconfirm the authors' observations.

Taken together, these studies demonstrate some preliminary support for the efficacy of feminist group therapy for adult women who were sexually abused as children. However, as with immigrant and refugee women, overall symptom reduction in these studies was fairly small and limited to a few specific areas rather than a global reduction in distress. The exception to this is the study by Hébert and Bergeron (2007), in which participants appear to have made long-lasting and more global gains. This result may be a simple function of greater sample size or of their specific treatment modality.

One finding that seems to emerge, however, is the inadequacy of short-term treatment models for addressing traumatic experiences, particularly when a woman's current situation continues to be traumatic or oppressive in some way. Another issue, which we address at greater length later, is the question of what is considered an "effective" outcome of participating in a therapy group. Studies that collect both quantitative and qualitative data seem to mirror one another in finding little quantitative change in symptoms but significant qualitative improvements in connection, empowerment, support, and mutuality. However, the most that can be said at this point is that more empirical research, both quantitative and qualitative, is needed before firm conclusions can be drawn. This issue is particularly problematic due to the different ways that feminist therapies are understood and implemented. Cross-cultural comparisons are also particularly difficult as a function of all the contextual circumstances that cannot be readily compared. Finally, clinical qualitative descriptions are subject to the bias of perspective.

Men Who Abuse Their Partners

Group treatment of men who abuse their partners almost universally subscribes to elements of feminist theory, specifically a focus on men's socialization and privilege as underlying causes of relationship violence (Feldman & Ridley, 1995). However, evaluation studies of treatment groups that are explicitly feminist or actively integrate feminist therapy into a multidimensional model are rare. The one study that meets this criterion (Lawson et al., 2001) examined the effectiveness of an integrated feminist/cognitive–behavioral and psychodynamic group treatment program with a sample of 31 men. The group met once a week for 2.5 hours over the course of 15 weeks and was led by female/male therapist dyads. The first half of each group session focused on feminist psycho-education regarding relationship violence and used cognitive–behavioral interventions to modify thinking patterns and teach new coping strategies. The second half of each group session was focused on family of origin work and process dynamics to address underlying attachment and personality components of abusive behavior. Participants completed the Conflict Tactics Scale 2 (CTS-2; Straus, 1995) and Marital Satisfaction Inventory-Revised (MSI-R; Snyder, 1997) prior to beginning the group and after having completed the group. By the end of the group, only 21 men were still in a relationship with their original partner; only data from those men were included in the final statistical analysis. The researchers reported significant changes in the CTS-2 between pre- and post-group scores. Specifically, the results suggested a significant decrease in the frequency of physically assaultive behaviors, the level of psychological aggression, and incidents of causing physical injury to their partners. In addition, there was a statistically significant decrease in the aggression subscale of the MSI-R. The men's self-reported reduction in violence was confirmed via telephone interviews with 13 partners of study participants. The partners reported a decrease in violence from pre-group to during the group and from pre-group to post-group. This confirmation is especially important, given the tendency for men who commit abuse to minimize or under-report their behaviors. In terms of qualitative feedback, the partners of the participants reported that time-out skills and improved communication skills were the most important aspects for reducing violence in their relationships.

Summary

Despite a large body of theoretical writings to support and guide treatment design, outcome and evaluation research on feminist therapy is still preliminary. The studies reviewed in this section almost universally suffer from small samples sizes, problems with generalizability, and the need for replication. At the same time, they provide some suggestion that feminist therapy can be helpful to people, and they raise questions such as how to define "helpful" and how it should be measured.

Feminism and feminist therapy have struggled through their difficult birth to some ascendancy as women's movements have taken place across the globe over the last 40 years and through times of patriarchal backlash. Now, feminism in psychology finds itself simultaneously transforming as the third wave of feminism grows and becoming hidden as it is subsumed under the rubric of "just good therapy" by practitioners who are likely to utter the words "I'm not a feminist, but...." Perhaps this is part of the reason for feminist therapy's heavy reliance on theory building and practice guidelines: It is a field that must constantly redefine itself to incorporate different and changing contexts as it resists the invisibility that comes with mainstream acceptability. There is a constant struggle within feminism to be seen as a unique philosophy and practice, which, at the same time, seeks respect from, and a voice within, the dominant culture.

Clearly, feminist therapy practices have influenced mainstream therapy. Therapists from a wide variety of theoretical orientations report attending to power dynamics within the client–therapist relationship, valuing a more egalitarian position, using self-disclosure for a variety of therapeutic reasons, focusing on assertiveness – particularly for women, and incorporating diversity and contextual issues. These are all elements of feminist therapy that are now assumed to be part of "just good therapy." What continues to differentiate feminist therapy is its focus on gender and cultural context, the encouragement of social action, the depth of focus on particular practices such as egalitarianism, and the multitude of ways that values are conveyed to clients through the therapeutic process.

Directions for Future Research

Differentiation Between Feminist Therapists

Second and Third Waves

Feminist therapy is not a monolithic entity with specific treatment protocols for particular problems. This makes standardized, quantitative research exceedingly difficult to conduct. In addition, feminist therapy has evolved over time as the third wave of feminism has come into existence. Many theorists and practitioners have examined the differences between third and second wave feminists (see, for example, Kaschak, 2001a). One important area of research for the next generation is the examination of similarities and differences between the two generations of feminist therapists. Instruments such as the FTB (Juntunen et al., 1994) and the TWS (Robinson & Worell, 1991, as cited in Rader & Gilbert, 2005) were developed through research with second wave feminists, and they may not fully represent third wave practices, thus complicating between-group (feminist versus non-feminist) research. It may be that future researchers need not only to ask a range of questions to classify therapists as feminist therapists, as suggested by Moradi and colleagues (2000), but also to inquire about generation of feminism, as third wave feminists now occupy positions of leadership and, thus, more powerfully influence the practice of feminist therapy.

Feminist praxis has always represented the cutting edge. It may be that many second wave practices have finally been recognized, not as radical ideas but as positive, ethical practice, whereas ideas of the third wave have not yet been fully incorporated. Qualitative research can be used to identify similarities and differences in practice and to form a base from which new quantitative measures can be developed or old ones revised (such as the revision of the FTB to include work with men and multicultural practices by Moradi et al., 2000).

Men as Feminist Therapists

The research in this area is just beginning and is in need of continued investigation. Men have only recently begun to identify themselves in this way. Continued research into how men develop a feminist therapy orientation, how they specifically conduct feminist therapy given their ascribed social power, and difficulties in becoming feminist therapists are some areas in need of investigation. Other areas may include clients' perceptions of and experiences with male feminist therapists as compared to female feminist therapists.

Additional Comparisons Between Feminist and Non-feminist Practices

General Practices

As more sensitive measures of feminist practice, including the clinical intentions behind therapeutic choices, such as those on the FSDI (Simi & Mahalik, 1997), are developed, continued research on what differentiates feminist therapists from their more traditional colleagues is needed. This urgent need is based, in part, on the importance of feminist therapy remaining visible and distinct as a theoretical orientation and to combat the notion that feminism is no longer necessary. In addition, in an era of evidence-based treatment and managed-care reimbursements, feminist therapy must be able to distinguish itself from other types of therapy so that efficacy, effectiveness, and outcome studies can be conducted to demonstrate the utility of feminist treatment. Otherwise, feminist providers may be economically marginalized and/or, as a result, relegated to treatment only with the economically advantaged or with grassroots agencies. Because feminist therapy can never be manualized in the way some other therapeutic approaches can be, some quantitative method of differentiating feminist therapy from other types is urgently required for legitimacy within the contemporary reimbursement structure.

Particular Phases and Processes of Therapy

Although broad examination of the therapeutic process is important, additional attention to particular aspects of therapy may help elucidate differences between feminist and traditional therapists. In particular, how issues such as informed consent, confrontation, therapeutic impasse, ethical challenges, and termination are handled is likely to demonstrate differences between theoretical orientations. Taken in combination with the identification of the general practices of feminist therapists, demonstration of how critical phases and issues are handled can help to dispel inaccurate perceptions of what feminist therapists actually do in therapy. The practice of feminist therapy requires careful analysis and consideration of a multitude of factors that influence the client, the therapeutic relationship, and the context in which the client lives her or his daily life. Research can help to identify the theoretical and practical means by which these decisions are made.

Clients' Perceptions and Experiences of Feminist Therapy

Therapy takes place within a relational context, and the experience of both people within the relationship is vital to the successful outcome of therapy. It is one thing for feminist therapists to self-report, or even to be observed practicing certain behaviors, but without the client's experience, an important part of the process is missing. To leave the client out of the research equation is a violation of feminism's focus on equality, relationality, and shared expertise. A few studies have investigated clients' experience of feminist therapy, but much more research is needed in this area. In particular, research that examines therapist–client dyads and their respective experience of the therapeutic process (e.g., Rader & Gilbert, 2005) is needed to discover if clients are receiving what therapists think they are giving. Preliminary results suggest quite the opposite (Kaschak, 1976). Research could be extended to compare client–therapist dyads across theoretical orientations as well. In addition, some research (e.g., Glidden & Tracey, 1989) suggests that different populations of clients may react more positively than others to feminist therapy interventions for specific problems. However, the Glidden and Tracey study and others similar to it tend to be analog studies; participants give their reactions to a videotaped segment of therapy rather than report on a true experience within a therapeutic relationship. Further research to determine if these differences hold in actual practice is important.

Experience of Diverse Groups

Some of the outcome literature reviewed in this chapter explores the application of feminist therapy to specific cultural groups that have value systems traditionally considered at odds with some feminist principles and practices. By and large, these studies reported positive effects, yet the researchers acknowledged some struggles and initial difficulties. However, additional research is needed to explore not only how feminist therapy is conducted in culturally sensitive and appropriate ways with a wide variety of people but also how individuals from those groups perceive their experience of feminist therapy. Research is needed not only with ethnically diverse clients but also with groups whose values may seem at odds with feminist therapy values, such as male clients and clients from conservative religious or political backgrounds. How these relationships are negotiated and differences addressed may provide interesting data about the broad applicability and adaptability of feminist therapy. College counseling centers might prove fruitful venues for this type of research, especially because many centers have feminist therapists on the staff and because the limited choice of therapists increases the odds that a conservative client is matched with a feminist therapist.

Efficacy, Evaluation, and Outcome Research

Judith Worell (2001) has discussed at length a potential agenda for feminist research in these areas. She differentiated between efficacy research (i.e., demonstrating that a treatment is more effective than other treatments or no treatment under scientifically controlled situations), effectiveness research (i.e., showing that a particular program or treatment is effective in producing the desired results in a clinical, not scientific, setting), and community impact research (i.e., demonstrating an effect in the larger community). Worell challenged the notion that symptom reduction, the hallmark of traditional psychological research, should be the sole benchmark for effectiveness. She stated that measuring feminist goals such as empowerment is important in feminist treatment research, and she suggested the use of the Personal Progress Scale (Worell & Chandler, 1996, as cited in Worell, 2001) and the Gender Socialization Scale (Toner, 1999, as cited in Worell, 2001) as appropriate measures of feminist change as a result of psychotherapy interventions. Other important elements to consider include the development of meaningful connections and support and experiences of perceived mutuality (Genero, Miller, & Surry, 1992). Quantitative measures of feminist therapy behaviors could be used, along with measures of clients' perceptions, to confirm an intervention's feminist nature (rather than relying on a description of the literature upon which the program or therapy is based). This area of research is in such beginning stages that future directions are many.

Theoretical Considerations

In any evaluation of research on feminist therapy, whether considering past or future directions, one must raise the question of whether the master's tools will ever dismantle the master's house. In other words, most psychological research takes place within the traditional, scientific discourse that values objectification, group norms, quantifiable measures, and rejecting the null hypothesis. In other words, there is pressure to design research that conforms to the currently acceptable Western scientific model. The use of traditional research methodologies has its place, namely to build credibility and to help feminist therapy practitioners and theoreticians gain access to places of power and influence in order to create change at multiple levels. However, as Audre Lorde (1984) has so aptly noted, the master's tools "[M]ay allow us temporarily to beat him at his own game, but they will never enable us to bring about genuine change" (p. 12). Feminist researchers and therapists need to take care that they do not fall into the trap of privileging the scientific discourse that values symptom reduction over human connection and meaning making (Birrell & Freyd, 2006), quick fixes over witness, and privatization of pain over social change.

Qualitative research designs are one way to resist the dominant discourse. However, in order to be published, every researcher knows there is an expectation that, in the "limitations and future directions" section of the article, there will be a statement regarding the limits of generalizability, given the small sample size and the qualitative nature of the data. Feminist journal editors need to consider whether yielding to traditional expectations diminishes the meaning and power of feminist research and whether this particular tool of the master is still needed.

Quantitative research does not have to be completely at odds with feminist philosophy or to undermine the purpose of feminist therapy. However, it must be undertaken with thoughtfulness and intentionality. It is important to demonstrate, as many of the studies reviewed in this chapter did, that short-term interventions for long-term, complex, and often insidious trauma do not provide enough support to help survivors work through their experiences. However, the tone in which these articles are written is often apologetic, whereas the authors should state that the push for faster, shorter treatments by fast-paced Western societies eager to wipe away the effects of oppression, discrimination, and violence is ineffective – not to mention inhumane.

Symptom reduction may have its place in research on feminist therapy. Most clients who come to therapy do so because they want to feel better; they are bothered by something in their lives that causes them pain, and they seek therapy in order to ameliorate the pain and live more fully. The question for feminist researchers is: What sort of symptoms are therapists trying to alleviate, and how should they be measured? Is a client's score on the Beck Depression Inventory (Beck & Steer, 1987) a true reflection of what has changed via therapy, or is that score a by-product of increased empowerment, mutuality, authenticity, awareness, and assertiveness? Do less severe scores on the TSI (Briere, 1995) represent reduced trauma symptomatology, or are the more important factors a movement from condemned isolation to reconnection with community and self (Herman, 1997; Miller & Stiver, 1997)? These, and others like them, are questions that feminist researchers should ask in their work.

There is always a tension between subversive and dominant discourses. At best, it is a creative tension. Knowing the expectations of the scientific establishment, yet holding the vision of something new and different, can lead researchers to resist expectations and instead to formulate questions in new and different ways. Finally, feminist research is needed not to prove our worth to the establishment, but to keep feminist theoreticians honest in their thinking and grounded in the real experiences of people in context.

Current and Future Practice

Current grassroots feminist intervention is largely confined to cultural contexts outside the United States, where there is a strong focus on such issues as women in war and sexual slavery. In the United States, feminist therapy has been professionalized and, along with other forms of therapy, is increasingly defined and controlled by narrow definitions of financial efficacy. Although there was some representation of socialism in early models, capitalism has won the day, at least in the United States. There has been a return to emphasizing individual therapy, charging substantial fees, and a general professionalizing of the field with the predictable emphasis on liberal rather than radical perspectives. Despite all of our efforts, many maladies of women have worsened over the years. These include eating disorders, objectification of women's bodies, and abuse of female sexuality. The prevalence of same-sex partner violence has highlighted the need for a more complex analysis than gender alone can provide, and this work is being done by practitioners (Kaschak, 2001b) as well as from the radical perspective of queer theory.

The work continues and the necessity for it must be kept visible. In this review, we have taken care to survey over 35 years of writing about, and practice of, feminist therapy. The custom in psychology publications and graduate research is to go back only 5 or 10 years. This common practice is particularly inappropriate in feminist writings, as it obscures and renders invisible earlier contributions, which leads to the needless and endless rediscovery of the same principles or, more perniciously, to the erasure of feminist history and interventions. We call for the immediate modification of this principle. Students who enter the psychotherapy professions often know little more about feminist therapy than the cultural stereotypes of a quaint and irrelevant movement of the 1970s. We owe it to ourselves, our students, and women everywhere to resist and modify a damaging culture and, as feminists have always done, to make a place for pride and respect for girls and women. For what begins as context ends as self (Kaschak, 1992).

References

American Counseling Association. (2005). *American counseling association code of ethics and standards of practice.* Alexandria, VA: Author.
American Psychiatric Association. (2000). *Diagnostic and statistical manual of mental disorders* (4th ed., text rev.) Washington, DC: Author.
American Psychological Association Ethics Committee. (2002). Ethical principles of psychologists and code of conduct. *American Psychologist, 57,* 1060–1073.
Armstrong, J. G., & Lowenstein, R. J. (1990). Characteristics of patients with multiple personality and dissociative disorders on psychological testing. *Journal of Nervous and Mental Disorders, 178,* 448–454.
Baird, M. K., Szymanski, D. M., & Ruebelt, S. G. (2007). Feminist identity development and practice among male therapists. *Psychology of Men & Masculinity, 8,* 67–78.
Barn, R. (2008). Ethnicity, gender, and mental health: Social worker perspectives. *International Journal of Social Psychiatry, 54*(1), 69–82.
Bartle-Haring, S., Glebova, T., & Meyer, K. (2007). Premature termination in marriage and family therapy within a Bowenian perspective. *American Journal of Family Therapy, 35,* 53–68.
Beck, A., & Steer, R. (1987). *Beck depression inventory manual.* San Antonio, TX: Psychological Corporation.
Becker, D., & Lamb, S. (1994). Sex bias in the diagnosis of borderline personality disorder and posttraumatic stress disorder. *Professional Psychology, 25,* 55–61.
Bein, A., Torres, S., & Kurilla, V. (2000). Service delivery issues in early termination of Latino clients. *Journal of Human Behavior in the Social Environment, 3,* 43–59.
Birrell, P., & Freyd, J. (2006). Betrayal trauma: Relational models of harm and healing. *Journal of Trauma Practice, 5*(1), 49–63.
Blow, F. C., Zeber, J. E., McKarthy, J. F., Valenstein, M., Gillon, L., & Bingham, C. R. (2004). Ethnicity and diagnostic patters in veterans with psychoses. *Social Psychiatry & Psychiatric Epidemiology, 39,* 841–851.
Boggs, C. D., Morey, L. C., Skodol, A. E., Shea, M. T., Sanislow, C. A., Grilo, C. M., et al. (2005). Differential impairment as an indicator of sex bias in *DSM-IV* criteria for four personality disorders. *Psychological Assessment, 17,* 492–496.
Briere, J. (1995). *Traumatic symptom inventory: Professional manual.* Odessa, FL: Psychological Assessment Resources.
Briere, J., & Runtz, M. (1993). Childhood sexual abuse: Long-term sequelae and implications for psychological assessment. *Journal of Interpersonal Violence, 8,* 312–330.

Broverman, I. K., Broverman, D. M., Clarkson, F. E., Rosenkrantz, P. S., & Vogel, S. R. (1970). Sex-role stereotypes and clinical judgments of mental health. *Journal of Consulting and Clinical Psychology, 34*, 1–7.

Broverman, I. K., Vogel, S. R., Broverman, D. M., Clarkson, F. E., & Rosenkrantz, P. S. (1994). Sex-role stereotypes: A current reappraisal. In B. Puka (Ed.), *Caring voices and women's moral frames* (pp. 191–211). New York: Garland.

Brown, L. S. (1994). *Subversive dialogues: Theory in feminist therapy.* New York: Basic Books.

Brown, L. S., & Ballou, M. (1994). *Personality and psychopathology: A feminist reappraisal.* New York: Guilford.

Brown, L. S., & Brodsky, A. (1992). The future of feminist therapy. *Psychotherapy, 29*, 51–57.

Brown, S. P., Lipford-Sanders, J., & Shaw, M. (1995). Kujichagulia: Uncovering the secrets of the heart – group work with African American women on predominantly white campuses. *Journal for Specialists in Group Work, 20*, 151–158.

Bruns, C. M. (2002). Perceived mutuality in child–adult relationships and severity of abuse as predictors of complex PTSD symptoms in women who were sexually abused as children. *Dissertation Abstracts International, 63*, 516.

Caplan, P. J. (1995). *They say you're crazy: How the world's most powerful psychiatrists decide who's normal.* Reading, MA: Addison-Wesley.

Caplan, P. J., & Cosgrove, L. (2004). *Bias in psychiatric diagnosis.* New York: Jason Aronson.

Chambless, D. L., & Wenk, N. M. (1982). Feminist vs. nonfeminist therapy: The client's perspective. *Women & Therapy, 1*, 57–65.

Chesler, P. (1972). *Women and madness.* New York: Doubleday.

Chester, A., & Bretherton, D. (2001). What makes feminist counseling feminist? *Feminism & Psychology, 11*, 527–545.

Chew, J. (1998). *Women survivors of childhood sexual abuse: Healing through group work: beyond survival.* Binghamton, NY: Haworth.

Chrisler, J. C. (1991). Out of control and eating disordered. In N. Van Den Bergh (Ed.), *Feminist perspectives on additions* (pp. 139–149). New York: Springer.

Cole, K. L., Sarlund-Heinrich, P., & Brown, L. S. (2007). Developing and assessing effectiveness of a time-limited therapy group for incarcerated women survivors of childhood sexual abuse. *Journal of Trauma & Dissociation, 8*, 97–121.

Comas-Díaz, L., & Greene, B. (1994). *Women of color: Integrating ethnic and gender identities in psychotherapy.* New York: Guilford.

Courtois, C. (1979). The incest experience and its aftermath. *Victimology, 4*, 337–347.

Courtois, C. (1996). Assessment and diagnosis. In C. Classen (Ed.), *Treating women molested in childhood* (pp. 1–34). San Francisco: Jossey-Bass.

Dahms, T. L. (2003). The effects of feminist identity development and self-identification as a feminist therapist on therapy behaviors and diagnostic practices of female therapists. *Dissertation Abstracts International, 64*, 72.

Danner, C. C., Robinson, B. E., Striepe, M. I., & Rodes, P. F. Y. (2007). Running from the demon: Culturally specific group therapy for depressed Hmong women in a family medicine residency clinic. *Women & Therapy, 30*(1/2), 151–176.

Derogatis, L. R. (1994). *Symptom Checklist-90-R: Administration, scoring, and procedures manual* (3rd ed.). Minneapolis, MN: Pearson.

Dragowski, E. A. (2006). Sexual orientation victimization and posttraumatic stress symptoms among lesbian, gay and bisexual youth. *Dissertation Abstracts International, 67*, 2829.

Ehrenfeld, J. (1996). Termination in psychotherapy: An investigation from a feminist therapy perspective. *Dissertation Abstracts International, 56*, 5414.

Einstein, A., & Lawson, R. (2005). *Relativity: The special and general theory.* New York: Pi Press.

Enns, C. Z. (1987). A comparison of nonfeminist and profeminist women's reactions to nonsexist, liberal feminist, and radical feminist counseling and therapy. *Dissertation Abstracts International, 48*, 3051.

Enns, C. Z. (1992). Toward integrating feminist psychotherapy and feminist philosophy. *Professional Psychology, 23*, 453–466.

Enns, C. Z. (1997). *Feminist theories and feminist psychotherapies: Origins, themes, and variations.* New York: Haworth.

Enns, C. Z., & Hackett, G. (1993). A comparison of feminist and nonfeminist women's and men's reactions to nonsexist and feminist counseling: A replication and extension. *Journal of Counseling and Development, 71*, 499–509.

Erikson, K. B. (2002). Psychologist gender and sex bias in diagnosing histrionic and narcissistic personality disorders. *Dissertation Abstracts International, 62*, 4781.

Fassinger, R. E. (1994). Development and testing of the Attitudes toward Feminism and the Women's Movement (FWM) Scale. *Psychology of Women Quarterly, 18*, 389–402.

Feldman, C. M., & Ridley, C. A. (1995). The etiology and treatment of domestic violence between adult partners. *Clinical Psychology, 2*, 317–348.

Firestein, B., & Greene, B. (2007). *Becoming visible: Counseling bisexuals across the lifespan.* New York: Columbia University Press.

Ganley, A. L. (1988). Feminist therapy with male clients. In M. A. Button & L. E. A. Walker (Eds.), *Feminist psychotherapies: Integration of therapeutic and feminist systems* (pp. 186–205). Norwood, NJ: Ablex.

Garrick, D., & Ewashen, C. (2001). An integrated model for adolescent inpatient group therapy. *Journal of Psychiatric and Mental Health Nursing, 8*, 165–172.

Genero, N. P., Miller, J. B., & Surrey, J. (1992). Measuring perceived mutuality in close relationships: Validation of the Mutual Psychological Development Questionnaire. *Journal of Family Psychology, 6*(1), 36–48.

Gilligan, C. (1982). *In a different voice.* Cambridge, MA: Harvard University Press.

Glidden, C. E., & Tracey, T. J. (1989). Women's perceptions of personal versus sociocultural counseling interventions. *Journal of Counseling Psychology, 36*, 54–62.

Greene, B., & Herek, G. M. (1994). *Lesbian and gay psychology: Theory, research, h and clinical applications.* Thousand Oaks, CA: Sage.

Hamilton, S., Rothbart, M., & Dawes, R. M. (1986). Sex bias, diagnosis, and DSM-III. *Sex Roles, 15*, 269–274.

Haskell, S. M. (2006). Sex-role stereotypes and social workers' judgments of mental health. *Dissertation Abstracts International Section, 66*, 2723.

Hébert, M., & Bergeron, M. (2007). Efficacy of a group intervention for adult women survivors of sexual abuse. *Journal of Child Sexual Abuse, 16*(4), 37–61.

Heisenberg, W. (2007). *Physics and philosophy: The revolution in modern science.* New York: Prometheus Books.

Herman, J. L. (1997). *Trauma and recovery.* New York: Basic Books.

Herman, J. L., Perry, J. C., & van der Kolk, B. A. (1989). Childhood trauma in borderline personality disorder. *American Journal of Psychiatry, 146*, 460–465.

Hill, M., & Ballou, M. (1998). Making therapy feminist: A practice survey. *Women & Therapy, 21*(2), 1–16.

Hill, C. E., Mahalik, J. R., & Thompson, B. J. (1989). Therapist self-disclosure. *Psychotherapy, 26*, 290–295.

Ho, C. (1990). An analysis of domestic violence in Asian American communities: A multicultural approach to counseling. In L. S. Brown & M. P. P. Root (Eds.), *Diversity and complexity in feminist therapy* (pp. 129–150). New York: Harrington Park Press.

Hopwood, C., Ambwani, S., & Morey, L. (2007). Predicting nonmutual therapy termination with the Personality Assessment Inventory. *Psychotherapy Research, 17*, 706–712.

Hunsley, J., Aubry, T., Verstervelt, C. M., & Vito, D. (1999). Comparing therapist and client perspectives on reasons for psychotherapy termination. *Psychotherapy, 36*, 380–388.

Joiner, T. E., & Wlker, R. L. (2002). Construct validity of a measure of acculturative stress in African Americans. *Psychological Assessment, 14*, 462–466.

Juntunen, D. L, Atkinson, D. R., Reyes, C., & Gutierrez, M. (1994). Feminist identify and feminist therapy behaviors of women psychotherapists. *Psychotherapy, 31*, 327–333.

Kallivayalil, D. (2007). Feminist therapy: Its use and implications for south Asian immigrant survivors of domestic violence. *Women & Therapy, 30*(3/4), 109–127.

Kaschak, E. (1976). Sociotherapy: An ecological model for psychotherapy with women. *Psychotherapy, 13*, 61–63.

Kaschak, E. (1981). Feminist psychotherapy: The first decade. In S. Cox (Ed.), *Female psychology: The emerging self* (pp. 387–400). New York: St. Martin's Press.

Kaschak, E. (1992). *Engendered lives: A new psychology of women's experience.* New York: Basic Books.

Kaschak, E. (2001a). *The next generation: Third wave feminist therapy.* New York: Haworth.

Kaschak, E. (2001b). *Intimate betrayal: Domestic violence in lesbian relationships.* New York: Haworth.

Keller, E. F. (1982). *Feminism and science.* Chicago: University of Chicago Press.

Kitzinger, C., & Perkins, R. (1993). *Changing our minds: Lesbian feminism and psychology.* New York: New York University Press.

Kohlberg, L. (1981). *The philosophy of moral development*, San Francisco: Harper and Row.

Landrine, H., Klonoff, E. A., Gibbs, J., Manning, V., & Lund, M. (1995). Physical and psychiatric correlates of gender discrimination: An application of the Schedule of Sexist Events. *Psychology of Women Quarterly, 19*, 473–492.

Lawson, D. M., Dawson, T. E., Kieffer, K. M., Perez, L. M., Burke, J., & Kier, F. J. (2001). An integrated feminist/cognitive–behavioral and psychodynamic group treatment model for men who abuse their partners. *Psychology of Men & Masculinity, 2*, 86–99.

Lee, R. M. (2003). Do ethnic identity and other-group orientation protect against discrimination for Asian Americans? *Journal of Counseling Psychology, 50*, 133–141.
Lerman, H., & Porter, N. (1990). *Feminist ethics in psychotherapy*. New York: Springer.
Leupnitz, D. A. (1988). *The family interpreted*. New York: Basic Books.
Lewis, K. N., Epperson, D. L., & Foley, J. (1989). Informed entry into counseling: Clients' perceptions and preferences resulting from different types and amounts of pretherapy information. *Journal of Counseling Psychology, 36*, 279–285.
Lorde, A. (1984). The master's tools will never dismantle the master's house. In A. Lorde (Ed.), *Sister outsider: Essays and speeches* (pp. 110–113). Berkeley, CA: Crossing Press.
Masters, W., & Johnson, V (1966). *Human sexual response*. Boston: Little Brown.
Mathews, B. (1989). The use of therapist self-disclosure and its potential impact on the therapeutic process. *Journal of Human Behavior and Learning, 6*, 25–29.
Marecek, J., & Kravetz, D. (1998). Putting politics into practice: Feminist therapy as feminist praxis. *Women & Therapy, 21*(2), 17–36.
Marecek, J., Kravetz, D., & Finn, S. (1979). Comparison of women who enter feminist therapy and women who enter traditional therapy. *Journal of Consulting and Clinical Psychology, 47*, 734–742.
Mcdonagh, D. (2000). Exploring client perspectives of therapy: Women survivors in feminist therapy. *Dissertation Abstracts International, 61*, 540.
Meginnis-Payne, K. L. (2000). Feminist identification and feminist therapy behavior: What do feminist therapists do with their clients? *Dissertation Abstracts International, 61*, 3285.
Miller, J. B. (1976). *Toward a new psychology of women*. Boston: Beacon Press.
Miller, J. B., & Stiver, I. P. (1997). *The healing connection: How women form relationships in therapy and in life*. Boston: Beacon Press.
Mitchell, J. (1974). *Psychoanalysis and feminism*. New York: Random House.
Moradi, B., Fischer, A. R., Hill, M. S., Jome, L. M, & Blum, S. A. (2000). Does "feminist" plus "therapist" equal "feminist therapist"? An empirical investigation of the link between self-labeling and behaviors. *Psychology of Women Quarterly, 24*, 285–296.
Moradi, B., & Risco, C. (2006). Perceived discrimination experiences and mental health of Latina/o American persons. *Journal of Counseling Psychology, 53*, 411–421.
Morgan, B. L. (1996). Putting the feminism into feminism scales: Introduction of a Liberal Feminist Attitude and Ideology Scale (LFAIS). *Sex Roles, 34*, 359–391.
National Association of Social Workers. (1996). *Code of ethics of the National Association of Social Workers*. Washington, DC: Author.
Olkin, R. (2001). *What psychotherapists should know about disability*. New York: Guilford.
Piaget, J. (1965). *The moral development of the child*. New York: Free Press.
Philips, B., Wennberg, P., & Werbart, A. (2007). Idea of a cure as a predictor of premature termination, early alliance and outcome in psychoanalytic psychotherapy. *Psychology & Psychotherapy, 80*, 229–245.
Pillay, Y. (2005). Racial identity as a predictor of psychological health of African American students at a predominately White university. *Journal of Black Psychology, 31*, 46–44.
Pribor, E. F., Yutzy, S. H., Dean, J. T., & Wetzel, R. D. (1993). Briquet's syndrome, dissociation, and abuse. *American Journal of Psychiatry, 150*, 1507–1511.
Putnam, F. W., Guroff, J. J., Silberman, E. K., Barban, L., & Post, R. M., (1986). The clinical phenomenology of multiple personality disorder: A review of 100 cases. *Journal of Clinical Psychiatry, 47*, 285–293.
Rader, J., & Gilbert, L. A. (2005). The egalitarian relationship in feminist therapy. *Psychology of Women Quarterly, 29*, 427–435.
Rayburn, T. M., & Stonecypher, J. F. (1996). Diagnostic differences related to age and race of involuntarily committed psychiatric patients. *Psychological Reports, 79*, 881–882.
Rickard, K. M. (1987, March). *Feminist identity development: Scale development and initial validation studies*. Paper presented at the annual meeting of the Association of Women in Psychology, Denver, CO.
Ristock, J .L. (2001). Decentering heterosexuality: Responses of feminist counselors to abuse in lesbian relationships. *Women & Therapy, 23*(3), 59–72.
Robinson, D. A. (1995). Therapy with women: Empirical validation of a clinical expertise. *Dissertation Abstracts International, 56*, 1119.
Rodriguez, G .M. (2001). De almas Latinas (The souls of Latina women): A psychospiritual culturally relevant group process. *Women & Therapy, 24*(3/4), 19–33.
Root, M. P. P. (1992). Reconstructing the impact of trauma on personality. In L. S. Brown & M. Ballow (Eds.), *Personality and Psychopathology: Feminist reappraisals* (pp. 229–265). New York: Guilford.

Rothblum, E. (1996). *Classism and feminist therapy: Counting the costs.* New York: Routledge.
Rothstein, A. (1997). Introduction to symposium on aspects of self-revelation and disclosure: Analyst to patient. *Journal of Clinical Psychoanalysis, 6,* 349–361.
Santana, V., Almeida-Filho, N., Roberts, R., & Cooper, S. P. (2007). Skin color, perception of racism, and depression among adolescents in urban Brazil. *Child and Adolescent Mental Health, 12,* 125–131.
Saunders, B. E., Villeponteaux, L. A., Liposvsky, J. A., Kilpatrick, D. G., & Vernon, L. J. (1992). Child sexual assault as a risk factor for mental disorders among women. *Journal of Interpersonal Violence, 7,* 189–204.
Scheffler, S., & Müchele, A. (1999). War, life crisis, and trauma: Assessing the impact of a women-centered training program in Bosnia. *Women & Therapy, 22*(1), 121–138.
Schei, B., & Dahl, S. (1999). The burden left my heart: Psycho-social services among refugee women in Zenica and Tuzla, Bosnia–Herzegovina during the war. *Women & Therapy, 22*(1), 139–151.
Schneider, L. J. (1985). Feminist values in announcements of professional services. *Journal of Counseling Psychology, 32,* 637–640.
Seem, S. R., & Clark, M. D. (2006). Healthy women, healthy men, and healthy adults: An evaluation of gender role stereotypes in the twenty-first century. *Sex Roles, 55,* 247–258.
Sharratt, S., & Kaschak, E. (Eds.) (1999). *Assault on the soul: women in the former Yugoslavia.* New York: Haworth.
Shulman, S. R. (1999). Termination of short-term and long-term psychotherapy: Patients' and therapists' affective reactions and therapists' technical management. *Dissertation Abstracts International, 66,* 2961.
Singh, A. A., & Hays, D. G. (2008). Feminist group counseling with south Asian women who have survived intimate partner violence. *Journal for Specialists in Group Work, 33,* 84–102.
Simi, N. L., & Mahalik, J. R. (1997). Comparison of feminist versus psychoanalytic/dynamic and other therapists on self-disclosure. *Psychology of Women Quarterly, 21,* 465–483.
Simone, D. H., McCarthy, P., & Skay, C .L. (1998). An investigation of client and counselor variables that influence the likelihood of counselor self-disclosure. *Journal of Counseling and Development, 76,* 174–182.
Snyder, D. K. (1997). *Marital satisfaction inventory – revised manual.* Los Angeles: Western.
Straus, M. A. (1995). *Manual for the conflict tactics scales.* Durham, NH: Family Research Laboratory, University of New Hampshire.
Szymanski, D. M., Baird, M. K., & Kornman, C. L. (2002). The feminist male therapist: Attitudes and practices for the 21st century. *Psychology of Men & Masculinity, 3,* 22–27.
Timm, R. (2003). Disability-specific hassles: The effects of oppression on people with disabilities. *Dissertation Abstracts International, 63,* 5540.
Townsend, A. L. (2004). QEEG and MMPI-2 Profiles of adults reporting childhood sexual abuse: Determining differences and predictor models. *Dissertation Abstracts International, 64,* 6344.
Valentin, I. (1999, August). Title IX: A brief history. women's educational equity act (WEEA) resource center newsletter, pp. 1–3.
van der Kolk, B. A., Perry, J. C., & Herman, J .L. (1991). Childhood origins of self-destructive behavior. *American Journal of Psychiatry, 148,* 1665–1671.
Waldo, C. R. (1999). Working in a majority context: A structural model of heterosexism as minority stress in the workplace. *Journal of Counseling Psychology, 46,* 218–232.
Waltermaurer, E., Watson, C., & McNutt, L. (2006). Black women's health: The effect of perceived racism and intimate partner violence. *Violence Against Women, 12,* 1214–1222.
Westbury, E., & Tutty, L. M. (1999). The efficacy of group treatment for survivors of childhood abuse. *Child Abuse & Neglect, 23*(1), 31–44.
Worell, J. (2001). Feminist interventions: Accountability beyond symptom reduction. *Psychology of Women Quarterly, 25,* 335–343.
Worell, J., & Remer, P. (2003). *Feminist perspectives in therapy: Empowering diverse women* (2nd ed.). New York: Wiley.
Zlotnick, C., Warshaw, M., Shea, M. T., & Keller, M. B. (1997). Trauma and chronic depression among patients with anxiety disorders. *Journal of Consulting and Clinical Psychology, 65,* 333–336.

Chapter 10
Psychotherapy with Men

Matt Englar-Carlson, Mark A. Stevens, and Robert Scholz

Evidence-based practice has become the key focus of evaluation for clinical work. Within the field of psychology there is no consensus on what constitutes good evidence for a practice (Norcross, Beutler, & Levant, 2006). Some suggest that only treatments supported by randomized controlled trials or replicated single-participant designs can be considered to be supported by evidence. Whereas some disorders (e.g., anxiety, panic disorder) and therapies (e.g., CBT) lend themselves more easily to this type of scientific investigation, it can be difficult to find research evidence focused on specific populations or that considers cultural factors. Gender as a dimension of diversity is not adequately addressed in either empirically supported therapies (such as those catalogued by the American Psychological Association [APA] Society of Clinical Psychology's Task Force on Promotion and Dissemination of Psychological Procedures, 1995; Chambless et al., 1996; Chambless & Ollendick, 2001) or psychotherapy as usually practiced.

The APA has adapted the idea of evidence-based practice by defining evidence-based practice in psychology (EBPP) as "the integration of the best available research with clinical expertise in the context of patient characteristics, culture, and preferences" (APA Presidential Task Force on Evidence-Based Practice, 2006). Research evidence includes meta-analyses, random clinical trials, process studies, and other sources of quantitative and qualitative research (Stricker, 2010). Clinical expertise is defined as the ability to identify and integrate the best research data with clinical data to develop effective treatments (APA Presidential Task Force on Evidence-Based Practice, 2006). The emphasis on patient characteristics allows for the inclusion of variables that may create interactions in effects and support efforts at client–treatment matching (Wampold, 2010). Further, APA published a policy that detailed guidelines for psychologists in education, training, research, and practice (APA, 2003) that emphasized three important aspects for culturally competent psychotherapists: knowledge, sensitivity, and skills. Knowledge focuses on knowledge of other cultures as well as knowledge of self, with an emphasis on how the culture of the psychotherapists interacts with that of the client. Sensitivity refers to respect for the client's cultural identity and an understanding of how culture affects the experience of the client. Skills address the ability and competence to intervene appropriately and effectively with clients from many cultures. The intervention or treatment should be compatible with the culture, attitudes, values, and characteristics of the client (Imel & Wampold, 2008). Based on APA's EBPP model and the multicultural guidelines, in this chapter we aim to outline a culturally sensitive EBPP approach tailored to psychotherapy with men.

M. Englar-Carlson (✉)
California State University, Fullerton, CA, USA

Being in psychotherapy is both an obstacle and an opportunity for many male clients. Conversely, many psychotherapists experience male clients as difficult, resistant, or simply not the definition of an ideal client. Some would say that the common element of difficulty is not necessarily that the client is male, but rather that the problem lies with the construction of masculinity and the ways that the field of psychotherapy has, or has not, considered how masculinity influences the enactment of psychotherapy. Masculinity is a focal organizing principle for all aspects of a man's life, and it is an influential contributor not only to why (or why not) a man is in psychotherapy but also to how he "does" psychotherapy and the expectations he has for therapy outcomes. The development of the scholarly discipline of the psychology of men and masculinity has drawn needed attention to the notion that being a man *matters* to the extent that masculinity is a focal organizing principle for all aspects of a man's life (Brooks & Good, 2005; Levant & Pollack, 1995; Pollack & Levant, 1998; Scher, Stevens, Good, & Eichenfield, 1987).

A masculine-sensitive therapeutic style and counseling intervention is critical to the engagement and ultimate success of psychotherapy with male clients. The examination of the differential process of therapy and flexibility of interventions that can be tailored to different types of men is also essential. It is our intention to draw upon the existing research on psychotherapy and on the psychology of men to provide clear guidance about how to create positive, effective therapeutic outcomes with male clients. Some of the points suggested may cause clinicians to pause and question the manner in which they were trained and the way they practice psychotherapy with male clients. We consider such reflection a healthy way to evaluate how the mental health profession can effectively adapt to the needs of men.

The chapter is organized into five sections. We begin with a case example in order to bring the reader into the room with a male client. The next three sections focus on the knowledge, attitudes, beliefs, as well as the therapeutic skills needed to work effectively with male clients. In the final section we revisit the case example and integrate the information presented in this chapter. We end with a discussion of future directions for research on psychotherapy with men.

The Case of David: Finding Strength in Being Vulnerable

David was a 51-year-old man, born in Chicago, the oldest son of Greek immigrant parents. He was college educated and ran his own successful investment company for the better part of the past 10 years. At the age of 21, David married, but got divorced at age 24; they had no children. He remarried at age 39 to Anna, but after 9 years of marriage he separated from his wife about 7 months before the therapy began. They have an 8-year-old son, Peter. Anna moved out of their home 2 months ago, and they made arrangements for Peter to share time between the two homes. David's father died 20 years ago, and his mother lived in another state. He was without close friends or confidants and often relied on business acquaintances as a social outlet. David had a history of alcohol abuse that began when he was in college. After Peter was born, David abstained from alcohol. David also struggled with health problems such as hypertension and diabetes. Anna's individual psychotherapist referred the couple to a male psychotherapist for couples therapy. That was the first time that David had been in counseling, and he went along reluctantly. During therapy Anna complained that he was too controlling in the relationship and did not show her enough affection. David believed he was quite generous and accommodating to Anna's needs, and he wanted her to understand the pressures of his business. In session, David expressed a desire to heal his marriage because he did not want Peter to be from a divorced family. David did not want another failed marriage and he said he had always wanted to have the type of family he did not have as a child. After 2 months of couples therapy, Anna made it clear that she wanted a separation and divorce, and she stopped going to couples therapy. David continued to see the same psychotherapist after the separation.

As readers move through this chapter here are some questions to consider regarding working with David. Toward the end of the chapter we revisit this case example and answer many of these questions.

1. Why did David want to continue therapy after his wife decided to separate? What were his stated goals? What might be his unstated goals?
2. How did David's own rules of masculinity influence the way he "did" therapy?
3. How did David's ambivalence toward being in therapy show up?
4. What kind of feelings was David most comfortable experiencing and sharing?
5. What kind of feelings was David most uncomfortable experiencing and sharing?
6. One of the salient features of this case is unresolved loss. How do men like David tend to deal with issues of loss?
7. How did David deal with his physical health concerns?
8. How did David's paradigm for doing business impact the way he ran his life?
9. How might David adjust to the changing role he would have with his son?
10. What did David appreciate about coming to therapy? Why did he continue to come back?

Knowledge About Working with Male Clients

Over the past 30 years increased awareness and attention has been paid to men as clients in psychotherapy. This focus has raised awareness that there is something unique about being a man (i.e., masculinity) that wholly influences how men experience the world both intrapersonally and interpersonally. Men's socialization into masculine roles contributes to their gender identity and their ways of thinking, feeling, behaving, presenting problems, and attitudes toward and potential fears about psychotherapy. It is the saliency of masculinity for men across all facets of life that has led researchers and clinicians alike to question the influence of masculinity upon mental health, well-being, and psychotherapy itself (Englar-Carlson, 2006; Good, Gilbert, & Scher, 1990).

A Rationale for Masculine-Sensitive Psychotherapy

One of greatest shifts in the practice of mental health care has been the increased sensitivity and awareness given to cultural diversity issues, including the influence of gender roles (Sue & Sue, 2008). Among other identity factors, gender is now recognized as a salient organizing principle of clients' lives and experiences. Addis (2008) pointed out, however, that the term "gender" in most psychological research is synonymous with women, rather than its more appropriate use as a lens to understand the unique experiences of women and men. Understanding the gendered nature of masculinity is an important cultural competency (Levant & Silverstein, 2005; Liu, 2005; Mellinger & Liu, 2006). Guidelines developed for multicultural counseling competency (APA, 2003) and for practice with girls and women (APA, 2007) offer some direction and considerations in regard to psychotherapists' work with men. These guidelines and principles highlight the importance of the sociocultural context in tailoring psychotherapy to embrace the diverse identities of clients. Practice guidelines for boys and men are in development. One of the difficulties in developing practice guidelines for boys and men is the lack of empirical research on the process of psychotherapy with men.

Rather, numerous authors (see Brooks & Good, 2005; Englar-Carlson & Stevens, 2006; Kiselica, Englar-Carlson, & Horne, 2008; Levant & Pollack, 1995; Pollack & Levant, 1998; Rabinowitz & Cochran, 2002) have outlined gender-based cultural adaptations that can be made within the psychotherapy relationship to accommodate male clients of diverse backgrounds.

Despite the fact that most Western societies have historically been dominated by men in powerful positions, the reality is that many individual men do not feel empowered in their lives, and large groups of men (e.g., African American boys and young men; adolescent fathers; blue-collar workers; non-custodial fathers; and men who identify as gay, bisexual, or transgendered; Chin, 2005; Kiselica & Woodford, 2007) are marginalized within the larger society. Further, current and historical legacies of multiple forms of oppression affect men and women alike. Painful and often traumatic early experiences of loss and separation, overlaid by society's expectations of achievement, strength, and toughness, can lead adolescent boys and adult men to feel conflict, anxiety, and confusion about their identity (Robertson & Shepard, 2008). Because the traditional masculine role encourages men to hide more vulnerable emotions, men often have few socially sanctioned outlets for emotional expression. Men seek psychological help at lower rates than women do (Addis & Mahalik, 2003; Vessey & Howard, 1993); have higher rates of substance abuse with greater consequences to themselves and society (Johnston, O'Malley, Bachman, & Schulenberg, 2006; Kessler et al., 1994); die, on average, close to 7 years earlier than women do, and have higher rates of 14 of the 15 leading causes of death (see Courtenay, 2000); are less likely to be diagnosed with anxiety- and depression-related disorders (e.g., Addis, 2008; Sachs-Ericsson & Ciarlo, 2000); are four times more likely to die from suicide attempts (Oquendo et al., 2001); and have significantly less healthy lifestyles than women do (Courtenay, 1998). Higher rates of alcoholism and drug addiction, violence, and successful suicide suggest that many men act out rather than verbally share their emotional pain. Further, epidemiological studies indicate that gay men tend to suffer more depression (Cochran & Mays, 2000), anxiety (Sandfort, de Graaf, Bijl, & Schnabel, 2001), suicide (Cochran & Mays, 2000), substance abuse (Gilman et al., 2001), and panic (Cochran & Mays, 2000) than their heterosexual counterparts do.

It has been argued that almost all of psychology is the psychology of men. After all, most scholars of psychology and psychotherapy research, until recently, were men. Men have traditionally been viewed as representative of humanity; thus, men and their characteristics have been the object of most psychological research (Levant, 1990). However, most research explored men in the aggregate and never considered individual differences. Further, ideas and theories of psychotherapy were created from Western men's view of the world, despite the fact that the majority of clients were, and continue to be, women. However, a gendered approach to understanding human behavior was proposed by feminist scholars in the 1970s as a way to study women's psychological development. The resulting influence from the feminist movement was the understanding that women need to be understood within the context of gendered role restrictions and treated with clinically gender-appropriate models that understood, considered, and adapted to the experience of women. Over time that same understanding has been extended to men. One outcome of the women's movement was the creation of specific therapies and treatments that acknowledged the experience of women and outlined treatment tailored to a woman's way of experiencing the world (Brown, 2010). Building on these advances in conceptualizing both gender and psychotherapy, feminist and men's studies' scholars in the 1980s also began to use a gendered approach to examine masculinity as a complex and multi-layered construct that influenced the experience of men and their experience in psychotherapy (Englar-Carlson, 2006). The feminist and multicultural movements have led to the acknowledgement in current clinical practice that cultural and gender identity and group memberships not only matter but are an integral aspect of ethical and effective clinical practice (Jordan, 2010).

Given the enormous changes in the roles of women in Western societies, men's traditional behaviors can no longer be accepted as a normative standard. When studied from more sophisticated psychological and sociological approaches, men's behavior seems to be guided by socially constructed rules that encourage men to take charge in their relationships, at work, and in their roles as fathers and husbands (Connell & Messerschmidt, 2005). At the same time, situations that call for cooperation, interdependence, or just "being" can create internal conflict for men. The contemporary man is given many mixed messages: Be strong and tough, yet be sensitive to certain social issues, such as violence against women and homosexuality (Nylund, 2007). The crossfire of interpersonal and intrapersonal demands that require response flexibility may result in frustration and confusion in many men who have been shaped by traditional cultural expectations of how a man is supposed to be and act.

For many years an obvious, but historically overlooked, aspect of psychotherapy with men was the fact that male clients were first and foremost men. Male clients often present a unique challenge to clinicians because men are often socialized to fear core components of the therapeutic process: the language of feelings, the disclosure of vulnerability, and the admission of dependency needs (Pollack & Levant, 1998). Male clients' discomfort with the developing intimacy of a psychotherapy relationship can manifest as early termination, anger at the psychotherapist, unproductive intellectualizing, and other forms of resistance (Rabinowitz & Cochran, 2002). Masculine-sensitive psychotherapy draws needed attention to the ways that masculinity influences a man's life and the practice of psychotherapy (see Brooks & Good, 2005; Englar-Carlson & Stevens, 2006; Levant & Pollack, 1995; Pollack & Levant, 1998).

This concerted appreciation of masculinity in terms of mental health and well-being could not come at a better time for men. There have been some changes in societal expectations for men. Scholars have documented men's changing gender roles (Bernard, 1981; Cabrera, Tamis-LeMonda, Bradley, Hofferth, & Lamb, 2000; Kilmartin, 2007) and often highlighted difficulties men have experienced when their own gender role appears "out-dated" or out of line with the demands or behavior of contemporary society. Yet, many of the documented changes in gender role stereotypes, expectations, and norms are associated with women. There is still a great degree of gender role restriction among men (see Davis, Evans, & Lorber, 2006).

Understanding the Cultures of Masculinity

The question "What does it mean to be a man?" has no answer that applies to all men in all contexts. At any given time, there are many forms of masculinity. Masculinity varies between and within cultures (Doss & Hopkins, 1998) with wide variation within cultures when multiple identities are considered (Smiler, 2004). It is common in masculine gender role research to use the word "masculinities" rather than "masculinity" in exploration of the ideologies with which men can identify (Tager & Good, 2005) by sexual orientation and geographic regions (Blazina, 1997); among different racial, ethnic, religious, age, and socioeconomic groups (Gibbons, Hamby, & Dennis, 1997); and across developmental periods (Kimmel & Messner, 2004; O'Neil & Egan, 1992; Robertson & Shepard, 2008). The term masculinities accounts for the different definitions and variations of masculinity that exist among men (e.g., urban African American masculinities may take different forms than those of rural migrant Mexican Americans or White gay men).

Many scholars in this area have adopted a social learning paradigm to understand masculinity (Addis & Cohane, 2005; Smiler, 2004). This paradigm is based on the assumption that men learn gendered attitudes and behaviors from social environments where cultural values, norms, and ideologies about what it means to be a man are reinforced and modeled.

The idea of a social construction of masculinity suggests that masculinity is malleable depending on the dominant social forces in a society during a certain era. Despite the emphasis on multiple masculinities, there is a widespread belief that certain forms of masculinities are more central and associated with greater authority and more social power (Connell & Messerschmidt, 2005). For example, in the USA, depending on the era, the dominant ideal of masculinity has moved from an upper-class aristocratic image to a more rugged and self-sufficient ideal (Kimmel, 2005). Therefore, traditional masculinity can be viewed as the dominant (also referred to as "hegemonic") form of masculinity and, thus, highly influential in what members of a culture take to be normative (e.g., White, middle-class, heterosexual definitions of masculinity).

One of the benchmarks in masculinity ideology theorizing, Brannon's (1976) *blueprint for manhood*, outlined four guidelines for men in the USA. These guidelines describe how a man should act. That is, men are socialized to avoid appearing feminine ("no sissy stuff"), to gain status and respect ("the big wheel"), to appear invulnerable ("the sturdy oak"), and to seek violence and adventure ("give 'em hell"). These guidelines represent the socially determined gender role stereotypes (i.e., what a "man" should do) that many men take as their notion of appropriate masculine behavior and expectations. This socialization supports characteristics such as the restriction and suppression of emotions, the valuing of rationality, the emphasis on independence and achievement, and the avoidance of any characteristics associated with femininity (Mahalik, Good, & Englar-Carlson, 2003). These guidelines support both adaptive and maladaptive behavior, cognitions, and affect in men. For example, Blazina, Eddins, Burridge, and Settle (2007) suggested that adherence to traditional masculinity often results in relational failures in the lives of men. This can lead to the development of a masculine self characterized by emotional distance, avoidance of intimacy, and a defensive style of moving away from others.

Boys learn about gender role expectations from parents, peers, and media, as well as through numerous developmental shaping experiences in which they are called to enact expected gender role norms (Robertson & Shepard, 2008). For example, most young boys get the social message that "big boys don't cry," and they learn that crying is an unacceptable avenue of expression. The other part of that message is that "only girls cry" and so boys learn clear distinctions of gender-"appropriate" behavior that separates boys/men from girls/women (Good, Thomson, & Brathwaite, 2005). For boys, the common experience of injuring themselves, experiencing pain, and then crying is often met with punitive responses from others for their tears. Crying and the expressive of sensitive emotions become indications of weakness and vulnerability that are associated with femininity and/or homosexuality. Men learn that others view repressing and masking emotionality as a sign of strength.

Whereas the blueprint for manhood is a useful tool for conceptualizing masculinity, it does not capture the full range of masculinities. Individual differences in masculinity are associated with a range of responses in regard to different emotion-related processes. Differences in emotional suppression (Wong, Pituch, & Rochlen, 2006), problem-solving appraisal (Good, Heppner, DeBord, & Fischer, 2004), perceptions of stigma associated with depression and alcohol abuse (Magovcevic & Addis, 2005), and negative attitudes toward help seeking (Addis & Mahalik, 2003) are all linked to individual differences in masculinity. In addition, Liu (2002a) suggested that, even though the literature on men and masculinity has grown, the understanding of masculinity among men of color has remained limited. In particular, it is unclear how men of color navigate expectations of hegemonic masculinity. However, recent conceptualizations of masculinities (Arciniega, Anderson, Tovar-Blank, & Tracey, 2008; Hammond & Mattis, 2005; Liu & Chang, 2007) have explored culturally contextualized notions and experiences of manhood.

Subscription to the dominant ideal of masculinity is not linear or without resistance. Most men are socialized to adopt certain masculine ideals, behaviors, and attitudes. Yet this dominant ideology of masculinity often has inherent conflicts. For example, dominant masculinity was predicated historically on the exclusion of men who were not White, upper class, able-bodied, and privileged (i.e., normative masculinity; Liu, 2005). Historically, men who represented any other demographic category were considered to be marginal figures and were not used to define the norm. Therefore, men often find themselves negotiating between dominant masculine ideals that inherently exclude them or deciding not to subscribe to these dominant ideals and thus become marginalized (Connell & Messerschmidt, 2005). Yet marginalized men also create their own communities where they develop their own cultural standards, norms, and values that create an alternative against dominant masculinity. For instance, in racial, ethnic, or gay communities, men may develop forms of resistance in action and attitude that challenge the expectations of dominant masculinity.

Many men of color who grow up outside mainstream European American, heterosexual, middle-class culture are reminded by their experiences of prejudice and oppression on a personal and institutional level that, although they are men, they are less privileged and more vulnerable to forces outside of their control (Caldwell & White, 2001). Questionable stares, increased scrutiny, and automatic suspicion by peers, strangers, and police are regular occurrences for these men who work and live in the mainstream society (Majors & Billson, 1992; Sue, Capodilupo, & Holder, 2008; Sue et al., 2007). Not only are they subjected to the stresses of traditional masculinity, they must also cope with the overlay of subtle and not so subtle racism. A layer of anger related to this cultural predicament is common in many men of color, even those who are trying to live by the rules of mainstream society (Franklin, 1998).

Although not as obvious as skin color, there are other varieties of cultural identity that leave men vulnerable to feelings of alienation. Men who are unemployed or who work in the blue-collar work sector may feel alienated from those in white-collar jobs. Liu (2002a) discussed the social class dimensions of the masculine experience and noted how admonitions to compete and achieve economic success may be particularly salient for men of certain social classes. In particular, Liu suggested that normative masculinity inherently contains class variables such as status ideals and expectations. Hegemonic masculinity in the USA refers to being in control, being a self-made man, and being the "breadwinner" or "good provider," all of which relate to social class and status.

In many places in the world, gay and bisexual men are fearful of expressing aspects of their sexual orientation in the presence of their heterosexual counterparts. The abuse that many gay men and boys suffer at the hands of heterosexual boys and men is well documented (Pascoe, 2003; Plummer, 2001). The fear of heterosexual men, or heterophobia, may manifest as avoidance of situations in which heterosexual men are present, heightened stress responses when obliged to interact with heterosexual men and boys, especially in groups, and self-devaluation and shame. In addition, heterophobia may be expressed as a gay man's wholesale devaluation of heterosexual men and heterosexuality in general (Haldeman, 2001, 2006).

It is crucial for psychotherapists who work with men to note that existing models of masculinity do not account for all men in terms of who they are and how they behave. Traditional and rigid models do not speak to, or necessarily account for, invisible populations and groups of men. For example, transgendered men may not associate any aspects of masculine ideology with their identity. Furthermore, remaining myopically fixed upon traditional notions of masculinity can lead us to overlook the emotionally strong and available, involved and connected, compassionate and nurturing man who exists, but is often ignored and marginalized, not only among groups of men but within society as a whole. When psychotherapists are considering how to work with men from marginalized groups other than their own, they need to pay attention to how their masculinity intersects with those individual cultural, familial, and unique psychological aspects to create their gender identity.

Seeking Psychological Help

Men are less likely than women to seek help for both mental and physical health concerns (Addis & Mahalik, 2003; Andrews, Issakidis, & Carter, 2001; Möller-Leimkuehler, 2002; Sandman, Simantov, & An, 2000). The discrepancy in help seeking even exists when men and women exhibit comparable levels of distress (Pederson & Vogel, 2007). Reports also consistently indicate that men seek professional help less frequently than women do, regardless of age (Husaini, Moore, & Cain, 1994), nationality (D'Arcy & Schmitz, 1979), and ethnic and racial backgrounds (Neighbors & Howard, 1987; Sheu & Sedlacek, 2004). Men tend to hold more restrictive views of mental illness than women do, and they have less confidence in mental health counselors. Yet Galdas, Cheater, and Marshall (2005) suggested that men's tendency to seek help less often is a complex question that cannot be answered merely by looking at differences between women and men. Economic, cultural, and masculine socialization factors intersect to influence men's help-seeking behavior.

Men's relative reluctance to seek professional help stands in stark contrast to the range and severity of the problems that affect them. For example, it has been estimated that over six million men in the USA suffer from depression every year (National Institute of Mental Health [NIMH], 2003). In terms of physical health, men are more likely than women to have gone at least 2 years without seeing a physician, even though men die, on average, close to 6 years earlier than do women, and men have higher rates of 14 of the leading 15 causes of death (Arias, Anderson, Kung, Murphy, & Kochanek, 2003), higher levels of stress, higher rates of completed suicides (four times more than women; Pollack & Levant, 1998), and higher rates of heart disease, cancer, chronic obstructive pulmonary disease, and alcoholism than do women (Anderson, Kochanek, & Murphey, 1997; Courtenay, 2000). Health-care studies report that men fail to get routine checkups, preventive care, and health counseling, and they often ignore symptoms or delay getting medical attention when in need (Commonwealth Fund, 1998; Neighbors & Howard, 1987; Sandman et al., 2000; Van Wuk, Kolk, Van Den Bosch, & Van Den Hoogen, 1992). Rather than seek help, men often explain away medical problems (Galdas et al., 2005).

Men with more traditional conceptions of masculinity also hold more negative attitudes toward the use of both mental health (Addis & Mahalik, 2003; Good & Wood, 1995; Robertson & Fitzgerald, 1992) and career-related counseling services (Rochlen & O'Brien, 2002). African American men have been found to be less receptive to help seeking than European American men are (Neighbors, Musick, & Williams, 1998), working class and poor men are less likely to seek psychological help than middle- and upper-class men are (Hodgetts & Chamberlain, 2002), and a resistance to seeking help has been found in Asian immigrants (Shin, 2002) and Asian American men (Chang & Subramaniam, 2008; Solberg, Ritsma, Davis, Tata, & Jolly, 1994). O'Brien, Hunt, and Hart (2005) found that younger men who had not yet experienced medical problems were most resistant to seeking help, whereas older men who had been through a major illness had more open views. Conditions that directly challenge masculine identity, such as prostate disease or testicular cancer, also seemed positively to affect a man's willingness to seek help.

In the case of the decision to seek psychotherapy, people often weigh the possible benefits, consequences, and social norms related to psychotherapy and arrive at a decision based on a variety of factors. Violating gender role expectations, feeling embarrassed about sharing personal information, and general vulnerabilities in relation to self-disclosing private information might be too much for a man to risk seeking help (Vogel, Wade, Wester, Larson, & Hackler, 2007). Men may also perceive a greater public stigma associated with seeking help than women do (Timlin-Scalera, Ponterotto, Blumberg, & Jackson, 2003). In college settings, men have been found to experience more self-stigma than women do regarding help seeking (Vogel, Wade, & Haake, 2006), and some men perceive that they will be stigmatized for discussing certain concerns with a psychotherapist

(Martin, Wrisberg, Beitel, & Lounsbury, 1997). Other evidence indicates that men are more likely to seek help if they are prompted by someone or if they know someone who has received help in the past. Social network influence appears to be critical in terms of men's expectancies, positive or negative, about the psychotherapy process (Vogel, Wade, et al., 2007).

Another factor that may restrict men's mental health service utilization is the lack of fit between conceptualizations of masculinity and the popular perception of psychotherapy and mental health services (Mahalik et al., 2003). Traditional models of psychotherapy that emphasize the language of feelings, disclosing vulnerability, and admitting dependency needs can create difficulties for men socialized to adopt traditional masculine roles (Rabinowitz & Cochran, 2002). Further, depictions of mental health services on television can overemphasize the risks of psychotherapy over the benefits and further influence a man's unwillingness to seek psychological help (Vogel, Gentile, & Kaplan, 2008). To address this, psychotherapists can tailor the initial clinical encounter to identify the expectations male clients have of the psychotherapist and psychotherapy and to correct those that are erroneous or to change the structure of psychotherapy to be more congruent with a given male client's needs. To address the needs of men, Addis and Mahalik (2003) recommended enacting changes to clinical environments such as providing greater opportunities for reciprocity for men (e.g., with other group members or the community), increasing the perception of normativeness for particular problems, training psychotherapists to recognize the ego-centrality of certain problems (e.g., Is this problem part of me?) in order to be more sensitive to how a man may perceive the relevance of the concern, reduce the stigma of seeking help and of experiencing mental health problems, and create alternative non-traditional forms of assistance more congruent with masculine socialization (e.g., psychoeducational classes in work settings). All of these changes could help men feel more comfortable in seeking help.

Other solutions for increasing psychological help seeking in men have focused on marketing mental health to men (Rochlen & Hoyer, 2005) or offering alternative mental health modalities that may be more appealing to a greater range of men (Brooks & Good, 2005; McKelley & Rochlen, 2007; Rochlen, McKelley, & Pituch, 2006; Rochlen & O'Brien, 2002). Examples from the scholarly literature include support groups (Blazina & Marks, 2001), on-line therapeutic interventions (Hsiung, 2002), professional/executive coaching (McKelley & Rochlen, 2007), and psychoeducational workshops or outreach programs (Blazina & Marks, 2001). McKelley (2007) made the observation that despite efforts to reach populations of men resistant to seeking help for psychological concerns, speculation in the field remains disjointed and there is a need for a stronger theoretical foundation for conceptualizing and addressing men's resistance to seeking professional help. Research in this area of inquiry is in its infancy, and few of the proposed modifications or interventions to reach out to men have been evaluated for their effectiveness (Good et al., 2005).

Presenting Concerns

Many men face unique psychosocial and interpersonal challenges associated with masculine socialization experiences and changing cultural expectations of both masculine behavior and the roles of men (Brooks & Good, 2005). For example, some fathers report social pressure to be the family breadwinner (Doucet, 2004), yet, at the same time, increasingly being expected to assume greater interpersonal involvement as fathers, partners, and coworkers in ways that are often not encouraged through traditional masculine socialization experiences (Cabrera et al., 2000; Good & Sherrod, 1997; Levant & Pollack, 1995; Real, 2002). Further, as men pursue power and privilege in society, they often experience pain, powerlessness, ill health, and isolation (Liu, 2005). Many men do suffer from depression and anxiety-related disorders, but often it is manifested in the forms of addiction, violence, interpersonal conflict, and general irritability. Often men's own psychic pain may not be obvious to them, thus, when they do come for psychotherapy, many male clients are not sure how to behave. They may be confused about how to enter into a relationship with a psychotherapist (or if they really want or need to do so), and they question whether psychotherapy can really make a difference in their life (Englar-Carlson, 2006).

Depression is a serious, yet often undiagnosed, condition in men (Addis, 2008; Cochran, 2005; Cochran & Rabinowitz, 2000; NIMH, 2003; Pollack, 1998; Real, 1997). Cochran and Rabinowitz (2000) noted the influence of gender-role socialization, which encourages stoicism and suppression of emotion, as one of several factors that obscure the expression of depressed mood in many men. Traditional masculine prohibitions against the experience of the mood states of depression (e.g., sadness) and the behavioral expression of those mood states (e.g., crying) make clear and simple descriptions of men's depression difficult. Thus, the true expression of depression for many men creates a conflict. Further, as depression is often "masked," it is difficult for primary care physicians and other health professionals to determine when men are actually experiencing depressive spectrum disorders (Cochran & Rabinowitz, 2000). Many men, after experiencing interpersonal or traumatic loss, react by plunging into a depressive episode (Cochran & Rabinowitz, 1996). It is not uncommon for men to use alcohol or other mood-altering substances or activities to medicate depression (Hanna & Grant, 1997). The extremes of depression include difficulties associated with suicide and homicide. Men are more prone to an aggressive acting out of their depressed mood given their tendency toward action and externalization (Cochran & Rabinowitz, 2000). Despite reporting one-half of the depression rate that women report in epidemiological surveys, men commit suicide three to four times more frequently than women do (NIMH, 2003). This risk rises even higher with age (Kennedy, Metz, & Lowinger, 1995). In addition, homicide is committed more frequently by men than by women (U.S. Department of Justice, 2003).

Although estimates of the sexual abuse of boys vary widely, Baker and King (2004) noted that 16% of adult men report that they were the victims of child sexual abuse. Other researchers have reported that at least 3%, and as many as 20%, of all boys have been the victim of sexual exploitation (Holmes & Slap, 1998). Men who have been verbally, physically, and/or sexually abused as children are likely to have higher rates of all types of mental illness, including affective disorders, substance abuse, and certain personality disorders, and are more likely than other men to come to the attention of clinicians (Lisak, 2001; Weeks & Widon, 1998). Violence, episodes of depression, and suicide rates are also higher among men who have been abused or have witnessed abuse in childhood (Lisak, 1994; Rosenbaum & Leisring, 2003). Because of traditional masculine gender role prohibitions on acknowledging victimization, many men do not willingly reveal the extent of their abuse to others. Homophobia is another factor related to under-reporting. Many boys who have been violated by other boys or by men fear that they will be labeled a homosexual if they reveal the abuse to anyone, so they keep it a secret (Cabe, 1999; Gartner, 1999).

Psychotherapists' Attitudes Toward and Beliefs About Working with Men

An important step in working with men involves taking the time to learn about masculine culture in general and about the specific worldview of individual male clients in particular. Psychotherapists should be willing to examine their assumptions about masculinity in order to avoid shaming men in ways that prevent them from opening up, being vulnerable, examining their views on what it means to be a man, or making desired changes to improve their lives (Robertson & Fitzgerald, 1990; Scher,

2001). Below are some stimulus questions that psychotherapists can use to reflect thoughtfully on their conceptualizations of men and masculinity.

- How have your experiences with men influenced your psychotherapy work with male clients?
- How has your own gender-role journey influenced your psychotherapy work with male clients?
- How has society set and sustained certain expectations of how men should behave?
- What are your stereotypes of how men *do* psychotherapy?
- Is there such a thing as a male identity?
- What is masculine pride?
- How do you see cultural variations of masculinity?
- What might be the potential value for male clients to identify their own masculinity from a cultural perspective?

Negative Biases Against Male Clients

It is possible that psychotherapists themselves hold beliefs about men that restrict men's ability to benefit fully from psychotherapy. Many within the mental health profession see men as reluctant visitors to psychotherapy, coerced by family or legal pressures to attend, and conclude that some men are not good candidates for psychotherapy. It can also be perceived as more difficult to develop therapeutic relationships with male than with female clients (Vogel, Epting, & Wester, 2003). Boysen, Vogel, Madon, and Wester (2006) found that therapist trainees endorsed a stereotype of gay men's mental health that was consistent with five *DSM-IV* disorder categories: mood, anxiety, sexual and gender identity, eating, and personality disorders. One of the factors underlying that perception is that men often exhibit less interpersonal openness and less confidence in the mental health profession (Leong & Zachar, 1999). A question to consider is whether male clients need to adapt their behavior in psychotherapy or whether psychotherapists need to adapt their beliefs and interventions to match the behavior of male clients. We believe that psychotherapists can take proactive steps to overcome any potential discrepancy between the male client and the process and potential benefits of psychotherapy.

To the extent that psychotherapists hold biased views of men that label them as "perpetrators," "resistant," or "difficult," the process of developing empathy for men's struggles is inhibited, and the likelihood of forming effective therapeutic alliances is diminished. Both male and female psychotherapists should have an awareness of the ways in which their own countertransference issues with men might influence their behavior in session (Hayes & Gelso, 2001; Scher, 2001). These reactions may take the more obvious form of negative stereotypes that result from past experiences with men. They can also take the form of blind spots based on shared assumptions that reinforce traditional masculine expectations, such as emotional restrictiveness. Psychotherapists who view emotional awareness and expression as gender inappropriate for men are unlikely to be successful in assisting men in exploring and developing connections to their emotional selves.

Applying the Multicultural Considerations Paradigm to Psychotherapy with Men

Psychotherapists can use Sue, Arredondo, and McDavis' (1992) framework for multicultural competency to understand their own biases about men as clients, to develop an understanding of their client's worldview, and to create culturally congruent clinical interventions, so they may more effectively work with male clients who are both similar and different from their own cultural backgrounds.

Within each of these three domains, psychotherapists need to cultivate the necessary *awareness* (i.e., interpersonal sensitivity), *knowledge* (i.e., facts), and *skills* (i.e., proficiencies). Liu (2005) used this framework to outline different cultural competencies when working with men. In terms of awareness, an important step is the ability to identify and work through one's own negative assumptions, stereotypes, and/or value conflicts pertaining to psychotherapy with men that might result in an inability to understand and empathize with them. For example, a knowledge component in developing culturally congruent interventions might be learning male-centered treatment methods (Brooks, 1998; Rabinowitz & Cochran, 2002), whereas an awareness component in understanding a man's worldview might be to understand how shame and the need to save face influence an Asian American man's expression of emotions or help-seeking behavior (Liu, 2002b; Liu & Chang, 2007; Park, 2006; Zane & Yeh, 2002). In the remaining parts of this section we review some of the common concerns men are likely to present in the therapeutic environment and the special skills and treatment modalities that are most effective in making progress with male clients.

A Strength-Based Perspective

Whereas scholarly inquiry into the psychology of men has clearly raised the level of awareness of mental health professionals about the needs of men, in many ways it may also have presented men and masculinity in more restrictive and binding ways by overly focusing on the deficits and the darker side of men and masculinity. When the topic of men and mental health is considered in the popular press or in a professional forum, it is often focused on the bad things that men do, or about how the masculine socialization process scars boys and men for life, leaving them chronically flawed and in dire need of fixing (Kiselica, 2006). Most of the scholarly literature on men and mental health has overemphasized what is wrong with men and masculinity by focusing on pathology at the expense of highlighting men's strengths and the good things that men do. Over time, this focus on deficits has fostered inaccurate generalizations about boys and men that are linked to potentially harmful biases by psychotherapists working with male clients. These biases include the belief that men are flawed, need to be fixed, and are solely at fault for the problems that bring them to psychotherapy. For example, there is a tendency for mental health professionals to view men as hypo-emotional, even though the existing data on gender differences in emotion challenge the notion that men and women are different emotionally (Wester, Vogel, Pressly, & Heesacker, 2002; see Volume I, Chapter 21). Heesacker and colleagues (1999) found that mental health professionals with stereotypes of men as hypo-emotional were more likely to blame men for the problems they brought to couples therapy. It is rarely stated that most men are reasonably well-adjusted human beings; that most men recognize, experience, and express emotions within the normal range; and that men have long traditions of acting in a pro-social manner (Kiselica, 2006). To meet the needs of men more accurately, psychotherapists must develop a more complex and rich understanding about men's emotional lives, psychological development, and behaviors.

As a way of learning about the healthy aspects of men and masculinity and to incorporate a strength-based framework into psychotherapy, Kiselica, Englar-Carlson, and Fisher (2006) proposed a way of understanding men grounded in positive psychology that includes a recognition of strengths and virtue over disease, weakness, and damage. In line with positive psychology (Seligman & Csikszentmihalyi, 2000), this perspective is focused on building in men what is right rather than fixing in them what is wrong. This perspective includes focusing on and exploring men's relational styles, generative fatherhood, and the ways fathers contribute to their children's development in beneficial ways; the positive contribution that men make to other people's children through the role of being a coach, mentor, teacher, or community leader; men's ways of caring including the tradition of sons caring for elderly parents; their self-reliance; the worker/provider tradition of caring for a man's family and/or partner/spouse; men's daring, courage, and risk-taking; the group orientation of boys and men; and the humanitarian service of fraternal organizations.

It is important to acknowledge that many of the qualities and traits associated with traditional masculinity (e.g., courage, bravery, risk-taking, daring, self-reliance, personal sacrifice, protectiveness) are only useful and positive if men apply them under the right conditions, in appropriate situations, and without uniformity. In that sense, the degree to which these aspects are healthy and optimal depends on the ability of a man to exercise good judgment in knowing when and how to express them (e.g., too much self-reliance can limit a man's ability to ask for help, an over-emphasis on risk-taking can led to dangerous and fatal accidents).

Skills for Working with Men in Psychotherapy

The emphasis on evidence-based practice in psychology has been critiqued by many (Atkinson, Bui, & Mori, 2001; Bernal & Scharron-del-Rio, 2001; Whaley & Davis, 2007) who question whether evidence-based practice appropriately integrates a multicultural perspective. Whaley and Davis urged that practice guidelines for culturally competent services (APA, 2003) be blended with evidence-based practice. They noted that one point of convergence between these two models is the development and use of culturally adapted interventions. Cultural adaptation is focused on modifying existing evidence-based treatments to accommodate the cultural beliefs, expectations, attitudes, and beliefs of the client. Levant and Silverstein (2005) and Cochran (2005) highlighted gender as an aspect of diversity that is often not addressed in evidence-based practice. Levant and Silverstein (2005) noted that no practice, even one grounded in empiricism, is going to be sufficient if it fails to address issues of gender and gender role strain with clients who are in distress.

The scholarly research and writing on the psychology of men has demonstrated an interesting paradox. Even though most of the theoretical work in counseling, psychology, and psychotherapy is predicated on the lived experiences of men's lives, men themselves may not fully benefit from existing and accepted models of clinical treatment (Liu, 2005). Kiselica (2003) noted a fundamental mismatch between the way counseling and psychotherapy tend to be conducted and the relational styles of most men. Kiselica and Englar-Carlson (2008) recalled the work of Bruch (1978), who observed that psychotherapy is a good fit for certain types of individuals, but not others. Based on Holland's (1973) personality theory, Bruch suggested that psychotherapy is tailor-made for people who have a "social" personality type (e.g., those easily able to engage others in an emotionally intimate and engaging manner, those who are comfortable and skilled at talking about their feelings, and those who enjoy self-reflection). Because psychotherapy, as it is traditionally practiced and taught, involves these types of interactions, those who are social personality types can more easily enter the world of psychotherapy and feel at home with some confidence that they are able to complete the tasks associated with the situation. However, other individuals with different personality types feel out of place in traditional psychotherapy. Those with a "conventional" or a "realistic" personality prefer activities that involve manipulation and organization of data and objects. They tend to avoid the less structured, interpersonal, and exploratory activities often employed in psychotherapy. It is not surprising, then, that "conventional" or "realistic" personality types might feel ill-at-ease with psychotherapy as customarily practiced.

Many men, especially those who adhere to traditional notions of masculinity, match these "conventional" or "realistic" types and thus feel out of place in conventional psychotherapy. Masculine-friendly adjustments in the therapy process can be made in order to correct for this mismatch (Kiselica et al., 2008). Below we describe a number of transformations that reflect a masculine-friendly approach to psychotherapy. By masculine-friendly, we mean tapping into the way that men relate to the world and employing a wide range of strategies and activities that appeal to men and that have been shown through research to facilitate therapeutic engagement and the development of effective psychotherapy relationships.

Engaging Men in Psychotherapy

The evidence from clinical trials indicates that clients often drop out before the end of treatment because they do not find the treatment agreeable (Westen & Morrison, 2001). Considering the existing evidence that highlights negative views men hold toward psychological help seeking (see Addis & Mahalik, 2003) and in order to address drop out, initial engagement for men in the therapeutic process is essential. Therapeutic engagement is linked to the client's preference for treatment (Iacoviello et al., 2007) and expectations that improvement will occur (Gibbons et al., 2003). Given the evidence that the strength of the therapeutic alliance is the single best predictor of therapeutic outcome (Messer & Wampold, 2002; Norcross, 2001; Wampold, 2001), psychotherapists would be wise to give additional attention to the therapeutic process with male clients. Gender-based adaptations in service of creating effective psychotherapy relationships are based upon a combination of existing theory and research about the new psychology of men and clinicians' own interpersonal expertise, assessment, judgment, decision-making, and understanding of the contextual differences. Akin to feminist therapy approaches (Brown, 2006), masculine-sensitive psychotherapy aligns with the evidence-based practice movement by focusing on empirically supported therapy relationships (Norcross & Lambert, 2005). Listed below are core adaptations of masculine-sensitive psychotherapy.

Recognize, Acknowledge, and Affirm Gently the Difficulty That Men Have in Entering and Being in Psychotherapy

Men's relative reluctance to seek professional help stands in stark contrast to the range and severity of the problems that afflict them. It is well documented that many men initially experience going to therapy as extremely difficult, as something to avoid at any cost, and usually as the last resort (Rabinowitz & Cochran, 2002). Men often believe that they are coerced into therapy (by a spouse, employer, or the law), and they express a great deal of resentment. Often men experience going to therapy with shame and fear (Levant, 1997; Park, 2006), as asking for help implies weakness and a failure to be self-sufficient. Many men do not want to feel weaker by depending on a therapist. Rather than confronting and possibly confirming a man's fears about being in therapy (and potentially causing the man to flee the situation), we suggest recognizing, acknowledging, and gently affirming the path the client has taken to get to the therapy office; it is important to validate the difficulty he might experience in entering and being in counseling. During this process we suggest reframing thoughts of personal weakness or failure as the courage and "guts" to reach out and work on the issue.

Help the Client Save "Masculine Face"

It is important for psychotherapists to communicate their genuine respect for their male client's decision to begin therapy. It is important to reflect and contextualize that decision as a brave, courageous, and honorable behavior that is congruent with traditional masculine socialization (Liu & Chang, 2007; Park, 2006). For many men, acceptance as a man is needed before they can progress in treatment. Normalizing a man's concerns about therapy can also build therapeutic engagement.

The greater the extent to which men believe a problem is normal, the more likely they are to seek and receive help for that problem (Addis & Mahalik, 2003).

Educate Male Clients Up Front About the Process of Therapy

Many male clients do not know how the therapy process works, and they worry that the psychotherapist will be judgmental or discover their weaknesses (Stevens, 2006). Some male clients have a fear of not being a "good enough" client. They may perceive therapy as a place where they will need to become emotional, and they do not feel ready or equipped to do what they believe they will be asked to do in a traditional therapy setting. Although mystery about and fear of what happens in psychotherapy is potentially present for all clients, it is often a more salient issue for men (Vogel, Wester, & Larson, 2007). It can be useful to check out a man's assumptions of what will be expected of him as a client and to clarify the psychotherapist's role and explain how one practices psychotherapy.

Set Goals That Match the Needs of the Male Client

Find out what goals the client has for the sessions and develop an initial plan to address them. Wester and Lyubelsky (2005) suggested using masculine gender role conflict theory to set up therapeutic goals with male clients. Implied in this discussion is that men appreciate a more explicitly goal-oriented therapy process. Goals such as eliminating stress, increasing happiness, and improving connectedness with others might be more appealing to men than an emphasis on exploring the past, expressing emotions, and sharing problems (Vogel & Wester, 2003). Empirical support for the utility of establishing goals comes from the motivational enhancement literature (e.g., Miller, Rollnick, & Conforti, 2002). Although first used to address alcohol and substance abuse issues, motivational enhancement interventions are focused on resolving ambivalence and increasing commitment to change, and they have recently been expanded to other areas of mental health practice (Burke, Arkowitz, & Dunn, 2001; Miller et al., 2002). Motivational approaches focus on assisting clients to resolve any ambivalence they have about making changes in their lives (Moos, 2007). In addition, motivational enhancement theory assumes that resistant behaviors demonstrated by clients are indications that psychotherapists are not in sync with the clients' readiness to change. Psychotherapists should be able to assess clients effectively and must meet them at the clients' appropriate stage of change at the time they enter therapy.

Be Patient

Male clients often present a unique challenge to the psychotherapist (Englar-Carlson & Stevens, 2006). Male clients' discomfort with the developing intimacy of a psychotherapy relationship can manifest as early termination, anger at the psychotherapist, unproductive intellectualizing, and other forms of resistance. It is important to be patient and understand the walls men have erected before therapists can be let inside. Men may slam their emotional doors and leave therapy if confrontation is used too early (Rabinowitz & Cochran, 2002). Many men need to start therapy slowly, and they resist sharing intimate personal details and feelings up front. Rituals of initial engagement through more traditional masculine means (e.g., small talk, good natured humor, handshakes) are often needed (Englar-Carlson, Smart, Arczynski, Boucher, & Shepard, 2008; Kiselica, 2001). Characteristics, such as dependability, benevolence, and responsiveness, are seen as imperative to the development of a positive therapeutic alliance (Ackerman & Hilsenroth, 2003).

Use a Therapy Language and Approach That Is Congruent with Clients' Gender-Role Identity

It is important for psychotherapists to recognize the relational style of men in contrast to their conception of how therapy should proceed (Kiselica, 2006). Male clients may want to be treated in ways that feel congruent with their masculine socialization. This can be accomplished by listening carefully, projecting warmth without appearing overly sympathetic, and tailoring the clinical work to the male client. This can mean substituting other words for psychotherapy (e.g., consultation, meeting, discussion), using less jargon, being more active and directive as a psychotherapist, and matching one's relational style to the client's need (Englar-Carlson et al., 2008). Some men may be reluctant to label mental health problems as depression or anxiety, but instead may want to call it stress (O'Brien et al., 2005). In addition, communicating an appreciation for a man's style of expression is critical at the beginning of therapy. For example, if a man uses profanity as he discusses his problems, therapists should avoid correcting this type of expression, but rather reflect back the content and emotion of his message with or without using profanity themselves. In an attempt to help the therapeutic process, therapists should understand that many men have had less experience than most women with understanding and expressing their emotions (Good, 1998).

Be Genuine and Real

Modeling self-disclosure is another practice that can strengthen the relationship between the psychotherapist and the male client and assist in revealing personal matters (Kiselica & Englar-Carlson, 2008). When psychotherapists share something about themselves, it can go a long way toward showing clients that they are important. Further, it can model openness and appropriate self-disclosure. Male clients often trust more, and are more engaged in treatment, when they experience their therapist as a "real human being" who is there to help. The Latino concept of *personalismo* (Antshel, 2002; Paniagua, 2005), in which the client expects and values a personal relationship with the mental health-care provider rather than an institutional one, seems to apply here (e.g., socially appropriate physical contact such as handshakes, having brief conversations about sports or other areas of interest that do not have to do with mental health questions or the presenting problem; Englar-Carlson, 2006). Many male clients want to be treated as people first, rather than as problems to be solved or fixed. Cusak, Deane, Wilson, and Ciarrochi (2006) found that the therapeutic bond and perception of treatment helpfulness were more important to whether men would seek help in the future than to whether or not they were comfortable with affect or emotional expression.

Addressing and Assessing Masculine Socialization in Psychotherapy

One of the difficulties associated with psychotherapy with men is that emotional stoicism (Jansz, 2000), the minimizing of painful experiences (Lisak, 2001), irritability (Pollack, 1998), and a reluctance to seek mental health services (Addis & Mahalik, 2003) often create barriers for the appropriate understanding, accurate clinical diagnosis, and effective treatment of male clients. There is no one theoretical orientation that appears to be more effective than others in conceptualizing the distress or treatment of men. Rather scholars and practitioners have tailored existing theoretical views to perspectives on masculine socialization (see Englar-Carlson & Stevens, 2006). Within the existing scholarly literature are treatment suggestions from the psychodynamic (Pollack, 1995; Rabinowitz & Cochran, 2002; Shepard, 2005), cognitive–behavioral (Mahalik, 2001a), interpersonal (Mahalik, 2001b), person-centered (Gillon, 2008), multicultural (Caldwell & White, 2001; Casas, Turner, &

Ruiz de Esparza, 2001), relational–cultural (Jordan, 2010), integrative (Good & Mintz, 2001), and feminist (Brown, 2010; Walker, 2001) perspectives. The consideration of gender-role socialization and a client's "masculinity" in each step of the psychotherapy process is in line with what Good, Gilbert, and Scher (1990) referred to as "gender aware therapy." In this approach, knowledge and understanding of a client's gender-role orientation is placed alongside, and in conjunction with, the psychotherapist's theoretical orientation.

An understanding of masculine socialization provides psychotherapists with keen insight into the inner lives of most male clients. When the influence of masculine socialization is examined and explored by the client and psychotherapist in the open, a potential bridge can be built that links a man's life-long experience with his presenting problem. Talking openly about masculine socialization experiences is a rare event for most men. Masculine socialization is often experienced in silence and not overtly explored or examined. Some male clients may look to see if the psychotherapist will take the first risk and break the silence about socialization. If the psychotherapist is male, talking about masculine socialization can be an opportunity to model openness and appropriate self-disclosure. A male psychotherapist may first disclose some of his own masculine socialization experiences in an effort to make a connection (Englar-Carlson & Shepard, 2005; Kiselica & Englar-Carlson, 2008). This disclosure can show that the psychotherapist is willing to work cooperatively rather than giving all responsibility to reveal and disclose to the client.

Psychotherapists can invite clients to examine their socialization experiences by linking content or process that comes up in psychotherapy (e.g., emotional stoicism, talk about sacrificing, or forgoing his needs for another's) with dictates or messages of masculine socialization (e.g., men are supposed to be tough and support others, boys do not cry), or with specific examples from the past (e.g., What are some experiences you remember that taught you to think and behave this way?). Such questions help a man to gain insight into why he may be experiencing current stressors and often provide an opportunity to examine the restrictive nature of masculine socialization (e.g., role conflicts).

Stevens (2009) developed a model (see Fig. 10.1) that provides psychotherapists with a contextual understanding of some of the symptoms and expressed or unexpressed reasons that bring men to therapy. This model is not meant to be explained to clients, but rather used as a tool to formulate questions that may get to the root of the symptoms that male clients exhibit. At the core level of this model is the understanding that many men are born into the world with a variety of privileges, just because of their sex. For many men this privilege translates into subconscious attitudes and behaviors that contribute to the social institutions that reinforce sexism and heterosexism. On an institutional level sexism and heterosexism are major contributing factors to the formation and reinforcement of homophobia, misogyny, homosexism, and fear of femininity. And, subsequently, men experience and absorb these institutional pressures and lessons in ways that influence how they express their emotions, deal with power/control issues, and define personal success. The outer circle is a consequence of these absorbed lessons, and these are likely to present as the symptoms, complaints, and behaviors that men bring into the therapy setting.

One of the early assessments made in psychotherapy can address a male client's traditionality and rigidity of masculine gender-role beliefs (Englar-Carlson & Shepard, 2005). From the first point of contact, psychotherapists can note and observe whether male clients seem highly competitive and success-oriented and whether they appear reluctant to admit any psychological distress, and psychotherapists can assess clients' level of emotionality (e.g., monitor the use of the words "think" and "feel" and determine if clients are actually matching thoughts with thinking and affect with feeling). For example, *the big wheel* can emerge in a man's complaints about working too much; it can be seen in the pressure a man puts on his children to compete and succeed, and it can emerge in the man's complaints about not being appreciated by his partner or family for how hard he works and how stressed he is by his efforts to succeed. Reluctance to admit psychological distress often is

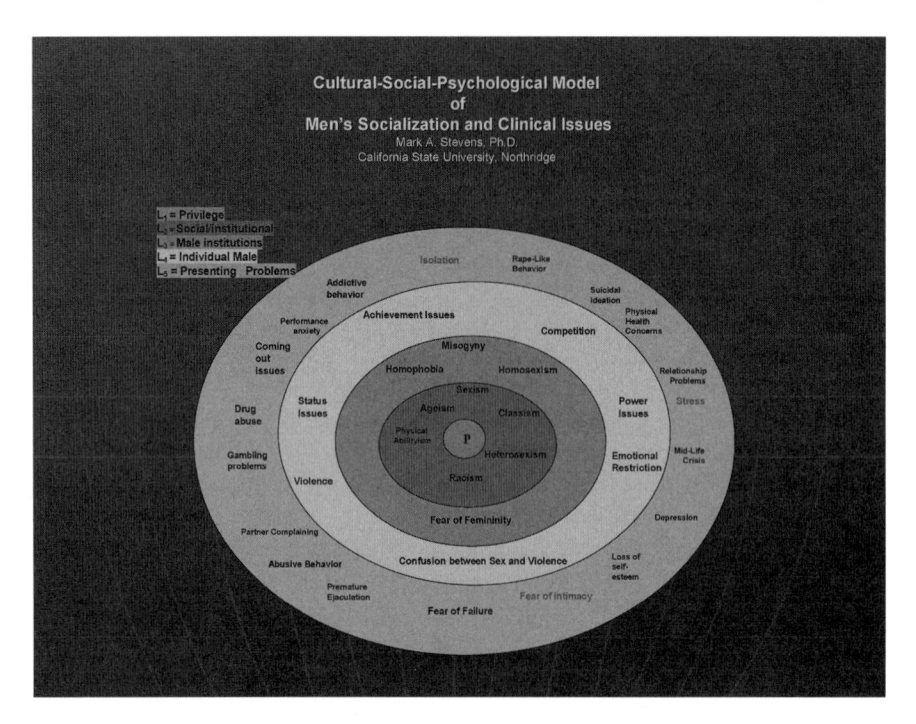

Fig. 10.1 Cultural-social-psychological model of men's socialization and clinical issues

apparent in the man's telling the psychotherapist that there is no real reason to be in psychotherapy, and he is only coming to please someone else (e.g., wife/partner, children, boss).

Psychotherapists assessing boys and men should strive to be aware of traditional masculine gender-role characteristics that may mask underlying psychological states. Traditional masculine gender-role ideology stresses the importance of stoicism in the face of pain, competition in a cross-section of situations, and being in control of one's emotions (see Levant & Pollack, 1995). These traditional norms also suggest that men hide or mask grief, sadness, or depressed mood (Fischer & Good, 1997; Levant et al., 2003; Pollack, 1998; Real, 1997). When a man responds to pain by minimizing or ignoring it, this behavior may appear normative and give the impression that he is coping adequately. Psychotherapists are encouraged to ask questions about mood and affect and to be willing to probe more extensively when met with brief responses to their questions; therapists can also note discrepancies between self-expression and the severity of precipitating factors.

Stevens (2006) suggested a two-component clinical assessment model for use with men. The model consists of classification systems designed to identify both men's strengths (e.g., masculine forms of nurturing) and maladaptive forms of masculinity (e.g., sexism, role conflicts). For example, men are often labeled as unresponsive to the feelings of their partners because they move into a problem-solving mode too quickly. Upon inquiry, men often share that they are quite aware of their partners' feelings and that their attempt to solve the problem is a reflection of the desire to take away some of the pain they perceive their partner to be experiencing. This model encourages more discussion about the development of masculine strengths and virtues in clients and de-emphasizes discussions focused on pathology (Wong, 2006). The first step in the model is to acknowledge a male client's strengths and how these benefit his life. For example, being responsible means that one can be depended upon; clear thinking leads to solutions under pressure; being strong means that others can lean on him; being self-sacrificing lessens the danger for others; physical caring provides security for others; and being practical means that he is time efficient and solution-focused. The second step in the assessment is to recognize that there are often costs associated with his approach to life. For example, the tendency to withhold expressing feelings may contribute to physical health problems; being exclusively fixed in a problem-solving mode may lead to disconnection from others; staying "strong" may limit or eliminate opportunities to grieve; not admitting weakness may limit self-learning and the ability to get assistance for himself; and having a emphasis on "male pride" may lead to unnecessary violence and risk-taking. This model of assessment can help psychotherapists to understand how a male client's enactment of masculinity influences his life and those around him. Further, education about role conflicts can provide some insight for men as to how masculinity influences their well-being.

Revisiting the Case of David

This discussion offers the reader an opportunity to integrate the knowledge, beliefs, and skill aspects presented in this chapter with the case of David. As readers consider this case they should reflect on the questions that were presented at the beginning of the chapter and also consider some of their own questions about how the psychotherapist could approach working with David.

David had a friendly and engaging manner. His main self-indulgent pleasure was reading, and he was a good conversationalist. His success in the business world was a big accomplishment, and he was proud of it. For David, life was measured by taking on many responsibilities at work and at home. During his waking hours he was in the "doing" mode – always taking care of multiple business and family tasks. Since he was a young boy, David had been accustomed to achieving his goals and getting what he wanted. He grew up in a working class household, and, in many respects, he was a self-made man. Through hard work, persistence, and intelligence David thought he had built his dream life. What was his dream? A beautiful wife, an adoring son, a luxurious home, vacations, and future business opportunities. To reach this dream David had avoided alcohol for almost a decade. He attributed this accomplishment to sheer willpower and a desire to be sober for his son. So what happened? How did his dream fall apart, and what emerged inside of David to cause him seek psychotherapy after he was certain his marriage was over?

David wanted desperately to hold onto the marriage. Unbeknownst to David, Anna had made up her mind over a year before that she was never going to be happy in the marriage and wanted to end it. Couples psychotherapy was a way for Anna to break the news to David that their relationship was over. Mistrust, resentment, accusations, and fear had taken over the relationship. From Anna's perspective, starting a family, planning a future, and buying "things" had turned the relationship into a business. The business tasks of the relationship temporarily numbed the feelings of regret and resentment and allowed the relationship to continue without much warmth.

David was good at numbing himself to avoid feeling emotional pain. He used his intelligence to rationalize his unhappy marriage. He ignored his doubts about his wife's intentions even before they got married. David was willing to sacrifice himself and live in a marriage that lacked the reciprocity of true love and caring in order for his son Peter to grow up in a two-parent household. Yet David's bitterness and mistrust were felt by Anna. They attempted to create solutions to getting a divorce such as separate bedrooms and rotating parental living arrangements away from the family home (so that their son would not have to go back and forth). Throughout these attempts David was determined to control the situation so that there would not be a divorce. He was open to financial incentives and to allowing Anna to have other relationships. When Anna finally told him that she needed to move on with her life, David was devastated.

It was this devastation that motivated David to continue therapy after Anna had stopped coming. Like many other men, David had a large capacity to withhold his feelings and absorb relationship discontent. When his dream was shattered, he felt scared, angry, alone, and foolish. He was good at getting what he wanted in business, but his "relationship business" had failed. As hard as he tried, he could not control the outcome of his marriage.

David was afraid of his pain. He sincerely wanted the pain to go away so that he could move on with his life. Initially, David took every opportunity to view an external event as a turning point. This created some temporary relief, yet more disappointment was just around the corner. In sessions, David could vocalize his excitement about pending success, yet it was not uncommon for him to cancel a session when life was not going well. Life going well typically meant that he had a good conversation with his ex-wife or that a business opportunity looked promising. He measured his well-being on a day-to-day basis, usually influenced by an external event. Underneath all of David's attempts to maintain a sense that his life would be okay was a strong fear that he would start to drink alcohol again and lose absolutely everything.

Like many men, David was embarrassed to cry in sessions. In a joking manner, he blamed his therapist for his crying, as he noted that he rarely cried outside of sessions. He tried hard to fight back his tears. When asked what his crying in session meant to him, David responded that it made him feel weak and out of control. Many times he ended sessions when he did not cry by saying, "I must be getting better; I did not cry today." When he did cry, he ended those sessions by stating that he felt better and had let go of some of his pain. Over time, he responded well to the therapist's statements that he respected David for allowing himself to be vulnerable in session and that he understood how important it was for David not to feel weak or out of control. Crying in session became more comfortable for David, particularly when he was able to save face. Often he would save face by making a joke such as, "Here you go again, Doc, making me cry."

Helping David to save face was an important therapeutic consideration. David described his therapist as his friend and being in therapy as a place where he could let down his defenses. Most people did not know the intense pressure and pain David experienced on a day-to-day basis. David was very much like the "sturdy oak." He was a deeply caring and empathic man, who had a difficult time being vulnerable and asking for help. David described himself as someone on whom others could lean. His ability and willingness to lean on the therapist without shame was a large internal shift that eventually transferred outside of the therapy room. David started to open up more about his fear of drinking. He also shared more of his personal struggles with some selected friends and business partners. His connection with others and his willingness to share his vulnerability soothed him in ways similar to drinking. He did not want to be a "weeping willow," but he also did not want to be confined to being only a "sturdy oak." Quite helpful was David's discussions with other men who had had similar experiences. David found it both surprising and reinforcing when other men shared similar tales of fear and anxiety. His sense of shame and isolation was reduced significantly.

Another important aspect of masculine-sensitive psychotherapy that became a focus of treatment was David's transitioning role as a single, divorced father. Woven into this transition were physical health concerns (e.g., high blood pressure and blood sugar) and his relationship with his own father. David's desire to be such an integral part of Peter's life was not congruent with how he physically took care of himself. David's father died when he was an adolescent, and this raised a type of uncomfortable dissonance. Although he worried about his health, he had a very difficult time changing his poor eating and exercise habits. David was quite open to discussing a life-long pattern of soothing with food. What appeared to have the most impact in treatment in terms of creating new patterns was David's willingness to share his vivid dreams about being present with Peter as they both grew older. Sessions slowed down as David described his feelings and images of Peter's college graduation, Peter's wedding, and becoming a grandfather. Tears rolled down his face as he experienced the joy of sharing these images and the fear of not being present at these future celebrations. David also became aware of the anger that he felt toward his father for not taking better care of himself and, subsequently, dying at an early age. This pain and anger opened up his awareness that he did not want Peter to feel the same type of pain and anger. His increased empathy for his son, and his desire to be a "good" father by protecting Peter from future pain, had a great impact on his motivation and ability to change some life-long poor lifestyle habits.

David was dealing with some significant role conflict issues related to parenting and work. He worked long hours, traveled too much, and placed himself in a position where he thought that he was indispensable at work. The custody agreement included equal time for Peter with David and Anna. David showed his advanced ability to solve problems creatively as he re-arranged his life to take care of Peter. His confidence that he could make things happen in business translated into his personal life. He let go of business opportunities that obligated him to out-of-town travel. David let his business associates know of his plans to change some of his work patterns to accommodate his new parenting role. Often in session, David would ask questions about raising a son. His concern for Peter and his anxiety about doing the "wrong thing" as a parent showed a vulnerable and courageous side of David. He shared stories of Peter's successes and struggles with the gleam of an engaged and proud parent. David worked through some of the rejection he felt when Peter was upset about leaving Anna to have an extended stay with him. He came to trust that, over time, the day-to-day interactions would serve as the glue to their relationship for now and the future. David was open to learning about the developmental needs of children Peter's age. Over time, David became more trusting of his abilities as a single father. The opportunities presented by the crisis became more apparent and served as a chance to re-evaluate his priorities and gain a type of nurturing and self-efficacy as a parent that he had never experienced before.

Future Directions for Research on Psychotherapy with Men

There are many useful directions for future research on psychotherapy with men. The foremost question facing the field is essentially the same question that has consumed psychotherapy research for the past 50 years; not does psychotherapy work, but, rather, what works best for the targeted population or presenting problem (Wampold, 2010). Research on effective treatments for masculinity-related problems is extremely limited (Good & Sherrod, 2001). For men, it is clear that there is much more that we do not know than we do know about the process of psychotherapy.

Whereas a sizeable body of scholarly knowledge has been accumulated on topics such as linking aspects of masculinity with negative attitudes toward psychological help seeking (for a review of research, see Addis & Mahalik, 2003) and with a host of mental health concerns (for review of research see Good et al., 2005; Mahalik et al., 2003), there is a need for corresponding treatment development and assessment through clinical trials. Further, studies that explore interventions to improve a man's willingness to seek psychological help would extend the knowledge base. Other potential areas of research are reviewed below.

Helping Men to Seek Psychological Help

More research is needed to bolster effective marketing of mental health services to men. A study that measured the effectiveness of the *Real Men, Real Depression* public health campaign (Rochlen et al., 2006) could serve as good starting point for future mental health market research. The authors recommended that other mental health marketing research campaigns should include input from a diverse group of men throughout the development and implementation of marketing projects. Because a one-size-fits-all marketing approach of any product or service has significant limitations, qualitative research (e.g., focus groups) with culturally diverse men with various degrees of experience (e.g., none to a significant amount) with therapy might provide a richer understanding of the messages that could reach different groups of men.

Although measurements of formal marketing efforts are important, another equally valuable area for future research is work on understanding more about the informal ways men learn about mental health services and how they form their beliefs about these services. Specifically, more research on how men form and maintain their beliefs about help seeking is needed. For example, studies of the role of key relationships in men's lives and their relationship to the development of help-seeking or help-hindering belief structures might yield data about where researchers and prevention specialists need to focus their marketing efforts. Furthermore, studies are needed to examine what types of people are more successful in leading men to receive help and the methods they use to get men started in the professional help-seeking process (Cusack, Deane, Wilson, & Ciarrochi, 2004). Men also receive direct and indirect marketing messages about what it means to seek out mental health services from significant relationships (e.g., friends, coworkers, doctors, coaches, spouses, partners), spiritual institutions, and the media. More studies are needed to investigate how different relational and contextual factors influence men's formation of beliefs about mental health concerns and ways to cope with mental health struggles.

Retaining Men in Psychotherapy

Developing effective interventions and processes to guide psychotherapy services with men will first require more research on the different types of men who receive these services. Although informed suggestions have been offered to guide therapy with diverse groups of male clients, more research on the unique characteristics of men and how they respond to the therapy process is needed. Further, as most existing theories were developed through non-scientific means, studies aimed at understanding the experiences of diverse groups of men in therapy are needed to support or dispel such theories. Both quantitative and qualitative methods could play a role in this empirical theory-testing process. In recent years researchers have become more interested in studying client experiences of the therapy process via qualitative methods (Knox, 2008; Manthei, 2007; Ward, Hogan, Stuart, & Singleton, 2008), although findings specifically related to male clients are lacking.

Given the dearth of psychotherapy process research on men's actual experiences with the counseling process, studies of men's experiences with various stages of the therapy process are needed. One of the few known studies that directly investigated a specific aspect of therapeutic process with male clients is Millar's (2003) examination of 10 British men, who ranged in age from 27 to 61 years, and their experiences with beginning therapy. Further research on men's first impressions of the therapy process and what experiences led them to stay engaged in therapy could provide useful information to therapists who work with men. Research is also needed to understand what factors lead some men to drop out of treatment prematurely and what variables might result in better therapy retention rates.

Effective Treatments and Improving Therapy Outcome

There is a further need to examine therapeutic process variables with male clients. Future researchers could build on the strong evidence that common factors (working alliance, therapist factors, client factors) are important to the process and outcome of psychotherapy (see Wampold, 2010) and explore how men experience, and psychotherapists promote, common factors with men in psychotherapy.

From a positive psychology framework, in-depth studies of men who have made significant gains in their therapy would be useful in better understanding the characteristics of successful clients and the therapists who treated them. Studies of therapists' and their male clients' agreement on key therapeutic factors, such as helpfulness of specific interventions, therapeutic alliance, and recognition of extra-therapeutic factors, would be useful in assessing how well therapists understand and meet the needs of their male clients.

Regarding the helpfulness of specific interventions, outcome research suggests that only a small percentage of successful outcomes can be accounted for by the specific therapeutic model/techniques. Thus, research into what types of interventions appeal to male clients should be conducted, not just for whether they lead to successful outcomes but also for whether the use of certain interventions significantly affects the therapeutic alliance. Studies of the therapeutic alliance could take into account how therapists consider their work with men. Do therapists take specific steps to work differently with their male and female clients? What influences these decisions? How do therapists' personal experiences with men outside of therapy influence their beliefs about men and their behaviors with men in therapy? Each of these questions warrants attention.

Finally, another factor in need of additional research is men's extra-therapeutic relationships. Understanding how individual men and groups of men relate to other men and to women in their friendships, romantic relationships and workplace relationships might provide mental health professionals with insight into factors that enable men to open up, trust others, and stay committed to their relationships. Greif's (2008) study of men's friendships, which he presented in his book, *Buddy System: Understanding Male Friendships*, provides a good starting point for research in this area.

Concluding Thoughts on Psychotherapy with Men

One of the main things that psychotherapists can do is begin to consider and appreciate the unique concerns, needs, and difficulties that men experience in life that are brought to and reenacted in the clinical setting. When psychotherapists are gender-aware, supportive, and affirming in their approach, men can have the opportunity to tell their stories and make sense of what is chaotic, distilling, and conflicting in their lives. For many men, safe spaces such as this are rarely found. The hopes and promises of effective therapy with men are that male clients can learn that asking for help will not kill or weaken them, can understand that their own history has impacted their current life situations, can gain the ability to open up with others, can learn to value the importance of relationships, can learn that vulnerability is a form of strength, and, ultimately, can gain awareness of how to get to know themselves.

References

Ackerman, S. J., & Hilsenroth, M. J. (2003). A review of therapist characteristics and techniques positively impacting the therapeutic alliance. *Clinical Psychology Review*, 23, 1–33.

Addis, M. E. (2008). Gender and depression in men. *Clinical Psychology*, 15, 153–168.

Addis, M. E., & Cohane, G. H. (2005). Social scientific paradigms of masculinity and their implications for research and practice in men's mental health. *Journal of Clinical Psychology*, 6, 633–647.

Addis, M. E., & Mahalik, J. R. (2003). Men, masculinity, and the contexts of help-seeking. *American Psychologist*, 58, 5–14.

American Psychological Association (APA). (2003). Guidelines on multicultural education, training, research, practice, and organizational change for psychologists. *American Psychologist*, 58, 377–402.

American Psychological Association (APA). (2007). Guidelines for psychological practice with girls and women. *American Psychologist, 62*, 949–979.

American Psychological Association (APA) Presidential Task Force on Evidence-based Practice. (2006). Evidence-based practice in psychology. *American Psychologist, 61*, 271–285.

American Psychological Association Task Force on Promotion and Dissemination of Psychological Procedures. (1995). Training in and dissemination of empirically-validated psychological treatment: Report and recommendations. *Clinical Psychologist, 48*, 2–23.

Anderson, R. N., Kochanek, K. D., & Murphy, S. L. (1997). Report of final mortality statistics, 1995. *Monthly Vital Statistics Report, 45*(Suppl. 2).

Andrews, G., Issakidis, C., & Carter, G. (2001). Shortfall in mental health service utilisation. *British Journal of Psychiatry, 179*, 417–425.

Antshel, K. M. (2002). Integrating culture as a means of improving treatment adherence in the Latino population. *Psychology, Health, and Medicine, 7*, 435–449.

Arciniega, G. M., Anderson, C. M., Tovar-Blank, Z. G., & Tracey, T. J. (2008). Toward a fuller conception of machismo: Development of a Traditional Machismo and Caballerismo Scale. *Journal of Counseling Psychology, 55*, 19–33.

Arias, E., Anderson, R. N., Kung, H. C., Murphy, S. L., & Kochanek, K. D. (2003). Deaths: Final data for 2001. *National Vital Statistics Reports, 52*(3), 30–33.

Atkinson, D. R., Bui, U., & Mori, S. (2001). Multiculturally sensitive empirically supported treatments: An oxymoron? In J. G. Ponterotto, J. M. Casas, L. A. Suzuki, & C. M. Alexander (Eds.), *Handbook of multicultural counseling* (2nd ed., pp. 542–574). Thousand Oaks, CA: Sage.

Baker, D., & King, S. E. (2004). Child sexual abuse and incest. In R. T. Francoeur & R. J. Noonan (Eds.), *International encyclopedia of sexuality* (pp. 1233–1237). New York: Continuum.

Bernal, G., & Scharrón-del-Río, M. R. (2001). Are empirically supported treatments valid for ethnic minorities? Toward an alternative approach for treatment research. *Cultural Diversity and Ethnic Minority Psychology, 7*, 328–342.

Bernard, J. (1981). The good-provider role: Its rise and fall. *American Psychologist, 36*, 1–12.

Blazina, C. (1997). Mythos and men: Toward new paradigms of masculinity. *Journal of Men's Studies, 5*, 285–294.

Blazina, C., Eddins, R., Burridge, A., & Settle, A. G. (2007). The relationship between masculinity ideology, loneliness, and separation-individuation difficulties. *Journal of Men's Studies, 15*, 101–109.

Blazina, C., & Marks, L. I. (2001). College men's affective reactions to individual therapy, psychoeducational workshops, and men's support group brochures: The influence of gender-role conflict and power dynamics upon help-seeking attitudes. *Psychotherapy, 38*, 297–305.

Boysen, G. A., Vogel, D. L., Madon, S., & Wester, S. R. (2006). Mental health stereotypes about gay men. *Sex Roles, 54*, 69–82.

Brannon, R. (1976). The male sex-role: Our culture's blueprint of manhood and what it's done for us lately. In D. S. Brannon & R. Brannon (Eds.), *The forty-nine percent majority* (pp. 1–45). Reading, MA: Addison-Wesley.

Brooks, G. R. (1998). *A new psychotherapy for traditional men*. San Francisco, CA: Jossey-Bass.

Brooks, G. R., & Good, G. E. (Eds.). (2005). *The new handbook of psychotherapy & counseling with men: A comprehensive guide to settings, problems, & treatment approaches* (Rev. ed.). San Francisco, CA: Jossey-Bass.

Brown, L. S. (2006). Still subversive after all these years: The relevance of feminist therapy in the age of evidence-based practice. *Psychology of Women Quarterly, 30*, 15–24.

Brown, L. S. (2010). *Feminist therapy*. Washington, DC: American Psychological Association.

Bruch, M. A. (1978). Holland's typology applied to client-counselor interaction: Implications for counseling men. *Counseling Psychologist, 7*, 26–32.

Burke, B. L., Arkowitz, H., & Dunn, C. (2001). The efficacy of motivational interviewing and its adaptations: What we know so far. In W. Miller & S. Rollnick (Eds.), *Motivational interviewing* (2nd ed., pp. 217–250). New York: Guilford.

Cabe, N. (1999). Abused boys and adolescents: Out of the shadows. In A. M. Horne & M. S. Kiselica (Eds.), *Handbook of counseling boys and adolescent males: A practitioner's guide* (pp. 199–218). Thousand Oaks, CA: Sage.

Cabrera, N. J., Tamis-LeMonda, C. S., Bradley, R. H., Hofferth, S., & Lamb, M. E. (2000). Fatherhood in the twenty-first century. *Child Development, 71*, 127–136

Caldwell, L. D., & White, J. L. (2001). African-centered therapeutic and counseling interventions for African American males. In G. R. Brooks & G. E. Good (Eds.), *The handbook of counseling and psychotherapy approaches for men* (pp. 737–753). San Francisco, CA: Jossey-Bass.

Casas, J. M., Turner, J. A., & Ruiz de Esparza, C. A. (2001). Machismo revisited in a time of crisis: Implications for understanding and counseling Hispanic men. In G. Brooks & G. Good (Eds.), *The handbook of counseling and psychotherapy approaches for men* (pp. 754–779). San Francisco, CA: Jossey-Bass.

Chambless, D. C., & Ollendick, T. H. (2001). Empirically supported psychological interventions: Controversies and evidence. *Annual Review of Psychology*, 52, 685–716.

Chambless, D. C., Sanderson, W. C., Shoham, V., Johnson, S. B., Pope, K. S., Crits-Christoph, P., et al. (1996). An update on empirically validated therapies. *Clinical Psychologist*, 49, 5–18.

Chang, T., & Subramaniam, P. R. (2008). Asian and Pacific Islander American men's help-seeking: Cultural values and beliefs, gender roles, and racial stereotypes. *International Journal of Men's Health*, 7, 121–136.

Chin, J. L. (2005). *The psychology of prejudice and discrimination: Bias based on gender and sexual orientation* (Vol. 3). Westport, CT: Praeger.

Cochran, S. D., & Mays, V. M. (2000). Lifetime prevalence of suicide symptoms and affective disorders among men reporting same-sex sexual partners: Results from NHANES III. *American Journal of Public Health*, 90, 573–578

Cochran, S. V. (2005). Assessing and treating depression in men. In G. Brooks & G. Good (Eds.), *The new handbook of psychotherapy and counseling with men* (pp. 121–133). San Francisco, CA: Jossey-Bass.

Cochran, S. V., & Rabinowitz, F. E. (1996). Men, loss, and psychotherapy. *Psychotherapy*, 33, 593–600.

Cochran, S. V., & Rabinowitz, F. E. (2000). *Men and depression: Clinical and empirical perspectives*. San Diego, CA: Academic Press.

Commonwealth Fund. (1998). *Women's and men's health survey, 1998*. Washington, DC: Author.

Connell, R. W., & Messerschmidt, J. W. (2005). Hegemonic masculinity: Rethinking the concept. *Gender & Society*, 19, 829–859.

Courtenay, W. H. (1998). College men's health: An overview and a call to action. *Journal of American College Health*, 46, 279–290.

Courtenay, W. H. (2000). Engendering health: A social constructionist examination of men's health beliefs and behaviors. *Psychology of Men & Masculinity*. 1, 4–15.

Cusack, J., Deane, F. P., Wilson, C. J., & Ciarrochi, J. (2004). Who influences men to go to therapy? Reports from men attending psychological services. *International Journal for the Advancement of Counselling*, 26, 271–283.

Cusak, J., Deane, F. P., Wilson, C. J., & Ciarrochi, J. (2006). Emotional expression, perceptions of therapy, and help-seeking intentions in men attending therapy services. *Psychology of Men & Masculinity*, 7, 69–82.

D'Arcy, C., & Schmitz, J. A. (1979). Sex differences in the utilization of health services for psychiatric problems in Saskatchewan. *Canadian Journal of Psychiatry*, 24, 19–27.

Davis, K., Evans, M., & Lorber, J. (2006). *Handbook of gender and women's studies*. Thousand Oaks, CA: Sage.

Doss, B. D., & Hopkins, J. R. (1998). The Multicultural Masculine Ideology Scale: Validation from three cultural perspectives. *Sex Roles*, 38, 719–741.

Doucet, A. (2004). "It's almost like I have a job, but I don't get paid": Fathers at home reconfiguring work, care, and masculinity. *Fathering*, 2, 277–302.

Englar-Carlson, M. (2006). Masculine norms and the therapy process. In M. Englar-Carlson & M. A. Stevens (Eds.), *In the therapy room with men: A casebook about psychotherapeutic process and change with male clients* (pp. 13–48). Washington, DC: American Psychological Association.

Englar-Carlson, M., & Shepard, D. S. (2005). Engaging men in couples counseling: Strategies for overcoming ambivalence and inexpressiveness. *Family Journal*, 13, 383–391.

Englar-Carlson, M., Smart, R., Arczynski, A., Boucher, M., & Shepard, D. (2008, August). *The process of male sensitive psychotherapy: Qualitative analysis of cases*. Poster presentation at the annual meeting of the American Psychological Association, Boston, MA.

Englar-Carlson, M., & Stevens, M. A. (Eds.). (2006). *In the room with men: A casebook of therapeutic change*. Washington, DC: American Psychological Association.

Fischer, A. R., & Good, G. E. (1997). Men and psychotherapy: An investigation of alexithymia, intimacy, and masculine gender roles. *Psychotherapy*, 34, 160–170.

Franklin, A. J. (1998). Treating anger in African-American men. In W. Pollack & R. Levant (Eds.), *New psychotherapy for men* (pp. 239–258). New York: Wiley.

Galdas, P. M., Cheater, F., & Marshall, P. (2005). Men and health help-seeking behaviour: Literature review. *Journal of Advanced Nursing*, 49, 616–623.

Gartner, R. B. (1999). *Betrayed as boys: Psychodynamic treatment of sexually abused men*. New York: Guilford.

Gibbons, J. L., Hamby, B. A., & Dennis, W. D. (1997). Researching gender-role ideologies internationally and cross-culturally. *Psychology of Women Quarterly*, 21, 151–170.

Gibbons, M. B. C., Crits-Christoph, P., de la Cruz, C., Barber, J. P., Siqueland, L., & Gladis, M. (2003). Pretreatment expectations, interpersonal functioning, and symptoms in the prediction of the therapeutic alliance across supportive-expressive psychotherapy and cognitive therapy. *Psychotherapy Research*, 1, 59–76.

Gillon, E. (2008). Men, masculinity and person-centered therapy. *Person-Centered and Experiential Psychotherapies*, 7, 120–134.

Gilman, S. E., Cochran, S. D., Mays, V. M., Hughes, M., Ostrow, D., & Kessler, R. C. (2001). Risks of psychiatric disorders among individuals reporting same-sex sexual partners in the National Comorbidity Survey. *American Journal of Public Health*, 91, 933–939

Good, G. E. (1998). Missing and underrepresented aspects of men's lives. *SPSMM Bulletin*, 3(2), 1–2.

Good, G. E., Gilbert, L. A., & Scher, M. (1990). Gender aware therapy: A synthesis of feminist therapy and knowledge about gender. *Journal of Counseling and Development*, 68, 376–380.

Good, G. E., Heppner, P. P., DeBord, K. A., & Fischer, A. R. (2004). Understanding men's psychological distress: Contributions of problem solving appraisal and masculine role conflict. *Psychology of Men & Masculinity*, 5, 168–177.

Good, G. E., & Mintz, L. B. (2001). Integrative psychotherapy for men. In G. R. Brooks & G. E. Good (Eds.), *The handbook of counseling and psychotherapy approaches for men* (pp. 582–602). San Francisco, CA: Jossey-Bass.

Good, G. E., & Sherrod, N. (1997). Men's resolution of non-relational sex across the lifespan. In R. Levant & G. R. Brooks (Eds.), *Men and sex: New psychological perspectives* (pp. 182–204). New York: Wiley.

Good, G. E., & Sherrod, N. (2001). The psychology of men and masculinity: Research status and future directions. In R. Unger (Ed.), *Handbook of the psychology of women and gender.* (pp. 201–214). New York: Wiley.

Good, G. E., Thomson, D. A., & Brathwaite, A. (2005). Men and therapy: Critical concepts, theoretical frameworks, and research recommendations. *Journal of Clinical Psychology*, 6, 699–711.

Good, G. E., & Wood, P. K. (1995). Male gender role conflict, depression, and help seeking: Do college men face double jeopardy? *Journal of Counseling and Development*, 74, 70–75.

Greif, G. L. (2008). *Buddy system: Understanding male friendships*. New York: Oxford University Press.

Haldeman, D. C. (2001). Psychotherapy with gay and bisexual men. In G. R. Brooks & G. E. Good (Eds.), *The handbook of counseling and psychotherapy approaches for men* (pp. 796–815). San Francisco, CA: Jossey-Bass.

Haldeman, D. C. (2006). Queer eye on the straight guy: A case of gay male heterophobia. In M. Englar-Carlson & M. A. Stevens (Eds.), *In the room with men: A casebook of therapeutic change* (pp. 301–318). Washington, DC: American Psychological Association.

Hammond, W. P., & Mattis, J. S. (2005). Being a man about it: Manhood meaning among African American men. *Psychology of Men & Masculinity*, 6, 114–126.

Hanna, E., & Grant, B. (1997). Gender differences in *DSM-IV* alcohol use disorders and major depression as distributed in the general population: Clinical implications. *Comprehensive Psychiatry*, 38, 202–212.

Hayes, J. A., & Gelso, C. J. (2001). Clinical implications of research on countertransference: Science informing practice. *Journal of Clinical Psychology*, 57, 1041–1051.

Heesacker, M., Wester, S. R., Vogel, D. L., Wentzel, J. T., Mejia-Millan, C. M., & Goodholm, C. R. (1999). Gender-based emotional stereotyping. *Journal of Counseling Psychology*, 46, 483–495.

Hodgetts, D., & Chamberlain, K. (2002). 'The problem with men': Working class men making sense of men's health on television. *Journal of Health Psychology*, 7, 269–283.

Holland, J. (1973). *Making vocational choices: A theory of careers*. Englewood Cliffs, NJ: Prentice-Hall.

Holmes, W. C., & Slap, G. B. (1998). Sexual abuse of boys: Definition, prevalence, correlates, sequelae, and management. *Journal of the American Medical Association*, 280, 1855–1862.

Hsiung, R. C. (Ed.). (2002). *E-Therapy: Case studies, guiding principles, and the clinical potential of the internet.* New York: W. W. Norton.

Husaini, B. A., Moore, S. T., & Cain, V. A. (1994). Psychiatric symptoms and help seeking behavior among the elderly: An analysis of racial and gender differences. *Journal of Gerontological Social Work, 21*, 77–195.

Iacoviello, B. M., McCarthy, K. S., Barrett, M. S., Rynn, M., Gallop, R., & Barber, J. P. (2007). Treatment preferences affect the therapeutic alliance: Implications for randomized controlled trials. *Journal of Consulting and Clinical Psychology*, 75, 194–198.

Imel, Z. E., & Wampold, B. E. (2008). The common factors of psychotherapy. In S. D. Brown & R. W. Lent (Eds.), *Handbook of counseling psychology* (4th ed., pp. 249–268). New York: Wiley.

Jansz, J. (2000). Masculine identity and restrictive emotionality. In A. H. Fischer (Ed.), *Gender and emotion: Social psychological perspectives* (pp. 166–186). New York: Cambridge University Press.

Johnston, L. D., O'Malley, P. M., Bachman, J. G., & Schulenberg, J. E. (2006). *Monitoring the future – National survey results on drug use, 1975–2005: Volume 1, Secondary school students* [NIH Publication No. 06-5883]. Bethesda, MD: National Institute on Drug Abuse.

Jordan, J. (2010). *Relational-cultural theory.* Washington, DC: American Psychological Association.

Kennedy, G., Metz, H., & Lowinger, R. (1995). Epidemiology and inferences regarding the etiology of late life suicide. In G. Kennedy (Ed.), *Suicide and depression in late life* (pp. 3–22). New York: Wiley.

Kessler, R. C., McGonagle, K. A., Zhao, S., Nelson, C. B., Hughes, M., Eshelman, S., et al. (1994). Lifetime and 12-month prevalence of *DSM–III–R* psychiatric disorders in the United States: Results from the National Comorbidity Survey. *Archives of General Psychiatry*, 51, 8–19.

Kilmartin, C. T. (2007). *The masculine self* (3rd ed.). Cornwall-on-Hudson, NY: Sloan.

Kimmel, M. (2005). *Manhood in America: A cultural history* (2nd ed.). New York: Free Press.

Kimmel, M., & Messner, M. (Eds.). (2004). *Men's lives* (6th ed.). New York: Macmillan.

Kiselica, M. S. (2001). A male-friendly therapeutic process with school-age boys. In G. R. Brooks & G. E. Good (Eds.), *The new handbook of psychotherapy and counseling with men* (Vol. 1, pp. 41–58). San Francisco, CA: Josecy-Bass.

Kiselica, M. S. (2003). Transforming psychotherapy in order to succeed with boys: Male-friendly practices. *Journal of Clinical Psychology*, 59, 1225–1236.

Kiselica, M. S. (2006, August). Contributions and limitations of the deficit model of men. In M. S. Kiselica (Chair), *Toward a positive psychology of boys, men, and masculinity.* Symposium presented at the meeting of the American Psychological Association, New Orleans, LA.

Kiselica, M. S., & Englar-Carlson, M. (2008). Establishing rapport with boys in individual counseling. In M. S. Kiselica, M. Englar-Carlson, & A. Horne (Eds.), *Counseling troubled boys: A guidebook for professionals* (pp. 49–65). New York: Routledge.

Kiselica, M. S., Englar-Carlson, M., & Fisher, M. (2006, August). A positive psychology framework for building upon male strengths. In M. S. Kiselica (Chair), *Toward a positive psychology of boys, men, and masculinity.* Symposium presented at the meeting of the American Psychological Association, New Orleans, LA.

Kiselica, M. S., Englar-Carlson, M., & Horne, A. (2008). A positive psychology perspective on helping boys. In M. S. Kiselica, M. Englar-Carlson, & A. Horne (Eds.), *Counseling troubled boys: A guidebook for professionals* (pp. 31–48). New York: Routledge.

Kiselica, M. S., & Woodford, M. S. (2007). Promoting healthy male development: A social justice perspective. In C. Lee (Ed.), *Counseling for social justice* (pp. 111–135). Alexandria, VA: American Counseling Association.

Knox, R. (2008). Clients' experiences of relational depth in client-centered therapy. *Counseling and Psychotherapy Research*, 8, 182–188.

Leong, F. T. L., & Zachar, P. (1999). Gender and opinions about mental illness as predictors of attitudes towards seeking professional psychological help. *British Journal of Guidance and Counselling*, 27, 123–132.

Levant, R. F. (1990). Introduction to special series on men's roles and psychotherapy. *Psychotherapy*, 27, 307–308.

Levant, R. F. (1997). The masculinity crisis. *Journal of Men's Studies*, 5, 221–231.

Levant, R. F., & Pollack, W. S. (Eds.). (1995). *The new psychology of men.* New York: Basic Books.

Levant, R. F., Richmond, K., Majors, R. G., Inclan, J. E., Rossello, J. M., Heesacker, M., et al. (2003). A multicultural investigation of masculinity ideology and alexithymia. *Psychology of Men & Masculinity*, 4, 91–99.

Levant, R. F., & Silverstein, L. S. (2005). Gender is neglected in both evidence-based practices and "treatment as usual." In J. C. Norcross, L. E. Beutler, & R. F. Levant (Eds.), *Evidence-based practice in mental health: Debate and dialogue on the fundamental questions* (pp. 338–345). Washington, DC: American Psychological Association.

Lisak, D. (1994). The psychological consequences of childhood abuse: Content analysis of interviews with male survivors. *Journal of Traumatic Stress*, 7, 525–548.

Lisak, D. (2001). Male survivors of trauma. In G. R. Brooks & G. E. Good (Eds.), *The new handbook of psychotherapy and counseling with men* (pp. 263–277). San Francisco, CA: Jossey-Bass.

Liu, W. M. (2005). The study of men and masculinity as an important multicultural competency consideration. *Journal of Clinical Psychology*, 6, 685–697.

Liu, W. M. (2002a). Exploring the lives of Asian American men: Racial identity, male role norms, gender role conflict, and prejudicial attitudes. *Psychology of Men & Masculinity*, 3, 107–118.

Liu, W. M. (2002b). The social class-related experiences of men: Integrating theory and practice. *Professional Psychology*, 33, 355–360.

Liu, W. M., & Chang, T. (2007). Asian American masculinities. In F. T. L. Leong, A. Ebero, L. Kinoshita, A. G. Arpana, & L. H. Yang (Eds.), *Handbook of Asian American psychology* (2nd ed., pp. 197–211). Thousand Oaks, CA: Sage.

Majors, R. G., & Billson, J. M. (1992). *Cool pose: The dilemmas of Black manhood in America*. New York: Lexington Books.

Mahalik, J. R. (2001a). Cognitive therapy for men. In G. R. Brooks & G. E. Good (Eds.), *The handbook of counseling and psychotherapy approaches for men* (pp. 544–564). San Francisco, CA: Jossey-Bass

Mahalik, J. R. (2001b). Interpersonal therapy for men. In G. Brooks & G. Good (Eds.), *The handbook of counseling and psychotherapy approaches for men* (pp. 565–581). San Francisco, CA: Jossey-Bass.

Mahalik, J. R., Good, G. E., & Englar-Carlson, M. (2003). Masculinity scripts, presenting concerns, and help-seeking: Implications for practice and training. *Professional Psychology*, 34, 123–131.

Magovcevic, M., & Addis, M. E. (2005). Linking gender role conflict to non-normative and self-stigmatizing perceptions of alcohol abuse and depression. *Psychology of Men & Masculinity*, 6, 127–136.

Manthei, R. J. (2007). Clients talk about their experience of the process of counselling. *Counselling Psychology Quarterly*, 20, 1–26.

Martin, S. B., Wrisberg, C. A., Beitel, P. A., & Lounsbury, J. (1997). NCAA Division I athletes' attitudes toward seeking sport psychology consultation: The development of an objective instrument. *Sport Counselor*, 11, 201–218.

McKelley, R. A. (2007). Men's resistance to seeking help: Using individual psychology to understand counseling-reluctant men. *Journal of Individual Psychology*, 63, 48–58.

McKelley, R. A., & Rochlen, A. B. (2007). The practice of coaching: Exploring alternatives to therapy for counseling-resistant men. *Psychology of Men & Masculinity* 8, 53–65.

Mellinger, T., & Liu, W. M. (2006). Men's issues in doctoral training: A survey of counseling psychology programs. *Professional Psychology*, 37, 196–204.

Messer, S. B., & Wampold, E. B. (2002). Let's face the facts: Common factors are more potent than specific therapy ingredients. *Clinical Psychology*, 9, 21–25.

Millar, A. (2003). Men's experience of considering counseling: "Entering the Unknown." *Counselling and Psychotherapy Research*, 3, 16–24.

Miller, W. R., Rollnick, S., & Conforti, K. (2002). *Motivational interviewing: Preparing people for change* (2nd ed.). New York: Guilford.

Möller-Leimkuehler, A. (2002). Barriers to help-seeking in men: A review of the socio-cultural and clinical literature with particular reference to depression. *Journal of Affective Disorders*, 71, 1–9.

Moos, R. (2007). Theory-based active ingredients of effective treatments for substance use disorders. *Drug and Alcohol Dependence*, 88, 109–121.

National Institute of Mental Health (NIMH). (2003). *Real men. Real depression.* Retrieved October 20, 2008, from http://menanddepression.nimh.nih.gov

Neighbors, H., & Howard, C. (1987). Sex differences in professional help seeking among adult Black Americans. *American Journal of Community Psychology*, 15, 403–417.

Neighbors, H. W., Musick, M. A., & Williams, D. R. (1998). The African American minister as a source of help for serious personal crises: Bridge or barrier to mental health care. *Health Education & Behavior*, 26, 759–777.

Norcross, J. C. (2001). Purposes, processes, and products of the Task Force on Empirically Supported Therapy Relationships. *Psychotherapy*, 38, 345–356.

Norcross, J. C., Beutler, L. E., & Levant, R. F. (2006). *Evidence-based practices in mental health: Debate and dialogue on the fundamental questions*. Washington, DC: American Psychological Association.

Norcross, J. C., & Lambert, M. J. (2005). The therapy relationship. In J. C. Norcross, L. E. Beutler, & R. F. Levant (Eds.), *Evidence-based practices in mental health: Debate and dialogue on the fundamental questions* (pp. 208–218). Washington, DC: American Psychological Association.

Nylund, D. (2007). *Beer, babes, and balls: Masculinity and sports talk radio*. Albany, NY: State University of New York Press.

O'Brien, R., Hunt, K., & Hart, G. (2005). It's caveman stuff, but that is to a certain extent how guys still operate: Men's accounts of masculinity and help seeking. *Social Science & Medicine*, 61, 503–516.

O'Neil, J. M., & Egan, J. (1992). Men's gender role transitions over the lifespan: Transformations and fears of femininity. *Journal of Mental Health Counseling*, 14, 305–324.

Oquendo, M. A., Ellis, S. P., Greenwald, S., Malone, K. M., Weissman, M. M., & Mann, J. J. (2001). Ethnic and sex differences in suicide rates relative to major depression in the United States. *American Journal of Psychiatry*, 158, 1652–1658.

Paniagua, F. A. (2005). *Assessing and treating culturally diverse clients: A practical guide* (2nd ed.). Thousand Oaks, CA: Sage.

Park, S. (2006). Facing fear without losing face: Working with Asian American men. In M. Englar-Carlson & M. A. Stevens (Eds.), *In the room with men: A casebook of therapeutic change* (pp. 151–173). Washington, DC: American Psychological Association.

Pascoe, C. J. (2003). Multiple masculinities? Teenage boys talk about jocks and gender. *American Behavioral Scientist*, 46, 1423–1438.

Pederson, E., & Vogel, D. (2007). Male gender role conflict and willingness to seek counseling: Testing a mediation model on college-aged men. *Journal of Counseling Psychology*, 54, 373–384.

Plummer, D. C. (2001). The quest for modern manhood: Masculine stereotypes, peer culture, and the social significance of homophobia. *Journal of Adolescence*, 24, 15–23.

Pollack, W. S. (1995). No man is an island: Toward a new psychoanalytic psychology of men. In R. F. Levant & W. S. Pollack (Eds.), *A new psychology of men* (pp. 33–67). New York: Basic Books.

Pollack, W. S. (1998). Mourning, melancholia, and masculinity: Recognizing and treating depression in men. In W. S. Pollack & R. F. Levant (Eds.), *New psychotherapy for men* (pp. 147–166). Hoboken, NJ: Wiley.

Pollack, W. S., & Levant, R. F. (1998). *New psychotherapy for men*. New York: Wiley.

Rabinowitz, F. E., & Cochran, S. V. (2002). *Deepening psychotherapy with men*. Washington, DC: American Psychological Association.

Real, T. (1997). *I don't want to talk about it: Overcoming the secret legacy of male depression*. New York: Fireside.

Real, T. (2002). *How can I get through to you? Reconnecting men and women*. New York: Scribner.

Robertson, J. M., & Fitzgerald, L. F. (1990). The (mis)treatment of men: Effects of client gender role and life-style on diagnosis and attribution of pathology. *Journal of Counseling Psychology*, 37, 3–9.

Robertson, J. M., & Fitzgerald, L. F. (1992). Overcoming the masculine mystique: Preferences for alternative forms of assistance among men who avoid counseling. *Journal of Counseling Psychology*, 39, 240–246.

Robertson, J. M., & Shepard, D. S. (2008). The psychological development of boys. In M. Kiselica, M. Englar-Carlson, & A. Horne (Eds.), *Counseling troubled boys* (pp. 3–30). New York: Routledge.

Rochlen, A. B., & Hoyer, W. D. (2005). Marketing mental health to men: Theoretical and practical considerations. *Journal of Clinical Psychology, 67*, 675–684.

Rochlen, A. B., McKelley, R. A., & Pituch, K. A. (2006). A preliminary exploration of the "Real Men. Real Depression" campaign. *Psychology of Men and Masculinity, 7*, 1–13.

Rochlen, A. B., & O'Brien, K. M. (2002). The relation of male gender role conflict and attitudes toward career counseling to interest and preferences for different career counseling styles. *Psychology of Men & Masculinity*, 3, 9–21.

Rosenbaum, A., & Leisring, P. A. (2003). Beyond power and control: Toward an understanding of partner abusive men. *Journal of Comparative Family Studies*, 34, 7–22.

Sachs-Ericsson, N., & Ciarlo, J. A. (2000). Gender, social roles, and mental health: An epidemiological perspective. *Sex Roles*, 43, 605–628.

Sandfort, T. G. M., de Graaf, R., Bijl, R. V., & Schnabel, P. (2001). Same-sex sexual behavior and psychiatric disorders: Findings from the Netherlands Mental Health Survey and Incidence Study (NEMESIS). *Archives of General Psychiatry*, 58, 85–91.

Sandman, D., Simantov, E., & An, C. (2000). *Out of touch: American men and the health care system*. New York: Commonwealth Fund.

Scher, M. (2001). Male therapist, male client: Reflections on critical dynamics. In G. R. Brooks & G. E. Good (Eds.), *The handbook of counseling and psychotherapy approaches for men* (pp. 719–733). San Francisco, CA: Jossey-Bass.

Scher, M., Stevens, M. A., Good, G. E., & Eichenfield, E. (1987). *Handbook of psychotherapy with men*. Thousand Oaks, CA: Sage.

Seligman, M., & Csikszentmihalyi, M. (2000). Positive psychology: An introduction. *American Psychologist*, 55, 5–14.

Shepard, D. S. (2005). Male development and the journey toward disconnection. In D. Comstock (Ed.), *Diversity and development: Critical contexts that shape our lives and relationships* (pp. 133–160). Belmont, CA: Brooks-Cole.

Sheu, H. B., & Sedlacek, W. E. (2004). An exploratory study of help-seeking attitudes and coping strategies among college students by race and gender. *Measurement and Evaluation in Counseling and Development*, 37, 130–143.

Shin, J. K. (2002). Help-seeking behaviors by Korean immigrants for depression. *Issues in Mental Health Nursing*, 23, 461–476.

Solberg, V. S., Ritsma, S., Davis, B. J., Tata, S. P., & Jolly, A. (1994). Asian-American Students' severity of problems and willingness to seek help from university counseling centers: Role of previous counseling experience, gender, and ethnicity. *Journal of Counseling Psychology*, 41, 215–219.

Smiler, A. P. (2004). Thirty years after the discovery of gender: Psychological concepts and measures of masculinity. *Sex Roles*, 50, 15–26.

Stevens, M. A. (2009). *Cultural-social-psychological model of men's socialization and clinical issues*. Unpublished manuscript. California State University, Northridge, CA.

Stevens, M.A. (2006, August). Engaging men in psychotherapy: Respect and challenge. In M. S. Kiselica (Chair), *Toward a positive psychology of boys, men, and masculinity*. Symposium presented at the meeting of the American Psychological Association, New Orleans, LA.

Stricker, G. (2010). *Integrative psychotherapy*. Washington, DC: American Psychological Association.

Sue, D. W., Arredondo, P., & McDavis, R. (1992). Multicultural counseling competencies and standards: A call to the profession. *Journal of Counseling and Development*, 70, 477–484.

Sue, D., Capodilupo, C., & Holder, A. (2008). Racial microaggressions in the life experience of Black Americans. *Professional Psychology*, 39, 329–336.

Sue, D., Capodilupo, C., Torino, G., Bucceri, J., Holder, A., Nadal, K., et al. (2007). Racial microaggressions in everyday life: Implications for clinical practice. *American Psychologist*, 62, 271–286.

Sue, D. S., & Sue, D. (2008). *Counseling the culturally diverse: Theory and practice* (5th ed.). New York: Wiley.

Tager, D., & Good, G. E. (2005). Italian and American masculinities: A comparison of masculine gender role norms. *Psychology of Men & Masculinity*, 6, 264–274.

Timlin-Scalera, R. M., Ponterotto, J. G., Blumberg, F. C., & Jackson, M. A. (2003). A grounded theory study of help-seeking behaviors among White male high school students. *Journal of Counseling Psychology*, 50, 339–350.

U.S. Department of Justice. (2003). *Criminal victimization in the United States, 2002 statistical tables*. Retrieved on October 24, 2008, from http://www.ojp.usdoj.gov/bjs/pub/pdf/cvus0202.pdf.

Van Wuk, C. M. T. G., Kolk, A. M., Van Den Bosch, W. J. H. M., & Van Den Hoogen, H. J. M. (1992). Male and female morbidity in general practice: The nature of sex differences. *Social Science and Medicine*, 35, 665–678.

Vessey, J. T., & Howard, K. I. (1993). Who seeks psychotherapy? *Psychotherapy*, 30, 546–553.

Vogel, D. L., Epting, F., & Wester, S. R. (2003). Counselors' perceptions of female and male clients. *Journal of Counseling and Development*, 81, 131–141.

Vogel, D., Gentile, D., & Kaplan, S. (2008). The influence of television on willingness to seek therapy. *Journal of Clinical Psychology*, 64, 276–295

Vogel, D. L., Wade, N. G., & Haake, S. (2006). Measuring the self-stigma associated with seeking psychological help. *Journal of Counseling Psychology*, 53, 325–337.

Vogel, D. L., Wade, N. G., Wester, S., Larson, L., & Hackler, A. H. (2007). Seeking help from a mental health professional: The influence of one's social network. *Journal of Clinical Psychology*, 63, 233–245.

Vogel, D. L., & Wester, S. R. (2003). To seek help or not to seek help: The risks of self-disclosure. *Journal of Counseling Psychology*, 50, 351–361.

Vogel, D. L., Wester, S. R., & Larson, L. M. (2007). Avoidance of counseling: Psychological factors that inhibit seeking help. *Journal of Counseling and Development*, 85, 410–422.

Walker, L. E. A. (2001). A feminist perspective on men in emotional pain. In G. Brooks & G. Good (Eds.), *The handbook of counseling and psychotherapy approaches for men* (pp. 683–695). San Francisco, CA: Jossey-Bass.

Wampold, B. E. (2001). *The great psychotherapy debate: Models, methods, and findings*. Mahwah, NJ: Erlbaum.

Wampold, B. E. (2010). *The basics of psychotherapy*. Washington, DC: American Psychological Association.

Ward, T., Hogan, K., Stuart, V., & Singleton, E. (2008). The experiences of counselling for persons with ME. *Counselling and Psychotherapy Research*, 8, 73–79.

Weeks, R., & Widon, C. S. (1998). Self-reports of early childhood victimization among incarcerated adult male felons. *Journal of Interpersonal Violence*, 13, 346–361.

Westen, D., & Morrison, K. (2001). A multidimensional meta-analysis of treatments for depression, panic, and generalized anxiety disorders: An examination of the status of empirically supported therapies. *Journal of Consulting and Clinical Psychology*, 69, 875–899.

Wester, S., & Lyubelsky, J. (2005). Supporting the thin blue line: Gender-sensitive therapy with male police officers. *Professional Psychology*, 36(1), 51–58.

Wester, S. R., Vogel, D. L., Pressly, P. K., & Heesacker, M. (2002). Sex differences in emotion: A critical review of the literature and implications for counseling psychology. *Counseling Psychologist*, 30, 629–651.

Whaley, A. L., & Davis, K. E. (2007). Cultural competence and evidence-based practice: A complementary perspective. *American Psychologist*, 62, 563–574.

Wong, Y. J. (2006). Strength-centered therapy: A social constructionist, virtues-based psychotherapy. *Psychotherapy*, 43, 133–146.

Wong, Y. J., Pituch, K. A., & Rochlen, A. B. (2006). Men's restrictive emotionality: An investigation of associations with other emotion-related constructs, anxiety, and underlying dimensions. *Psychology of Men & Masculinity*, 7, 113–126.

Zane, N., & Yeh, M. (2002). The use of culturally-based variables in assessment: Studies on loss of face. In K. S. Kurasaki & S. Okazaki (Eds.), *Asian American mental health: Assessment theories and methods* (pp. 123–138). New York: Kluwer/Plenum.

Chapter 11
Gender Issues in Family Therapy and Couples Counseling

Louise B. Silverstein and Gary R. Brooks

Although this is a handbook on "gender," and a chapter on "gender issues," we believe it is important to focus on feminism. Feminism is a conceptual framework that subsumes gender because it focuses on gendered differences in power and privilege. Scholars who focus on gender often limit their discussion to gender differences in behaviors and ignore differences in power and privilege. This failure to acknowledge power and privilege risks presenting political problems as personal inadequacies and implies that individuals have the power to change aspects of their lives that are beyond their control. Moreover, limiting the discussion to gender differences in behavior is especially problematic because many of these claims have not been substantiated by rigorous empirical research. For example, assertions about gender differences in tolerance for intimacy (Gilligan, 1982), linguistic and communication patterns (Tannen, 1991), adolescent self-esteem (Pipher, 1994), and mating preferences (Buss, 1994) have not been supported by research published in peer-reviewed journals. Authors often fail to report the overlap between the sexes in the phenomena that they study. Unfortunately, despite an emerging body of research that addresses the inaccuracy of these claims (e.g., Hyde, 2005; MacGeorge, Graves, Feng, Gillihan, & Burleson, 2004), these ideas about gender differences remain widely accepted in mainstream psychology.

Within the context of couples therapy, the gender differences discourse has led to the "gender-sensitive" approach. This stance argues that patriarchy oppresses men as well as women and, therefore, that couples therapists should be neutral in terms of addressing power. We discuss this problem in more detail in the section on working with men from a feminist perspective. However, we want to make it clear from the outset that we agree that patriarchy stresses men, but we do not agree that patriarchy oppresses men. Patriarchy is a social and political system that confers power and privilege on men. Therefore, achieving gender equality in couples and families requires men to relinquish their privilege and share their power. Hare-Mustin and Goodrich (1991) have characterized the gender differences and gender-sensitive approaches to couples therapy as "feel-good feminism." By this they mean that one can talk about "feminism" without generating anxiety or anger in men.

There is a similar phenomenon when people talk about race and ethnicity rather than racism. Just as many men tend to get anxious when we talk about male privilege, many White people tend to get anxious when we address White privilege. Thus, we believe that talking about gender differences and sensitivity rather than feminism, and race rather than racism, is a self-protective mechanism used by members of dominant groups to manage their anxiety. In this chapter, we attempt to avoid that defensive stance.

L.B. Silverstein (✉)
Yeshiva University, Brooklyn, NY, USA

We begin with a brief historical overview (1970–2000) of the many ways that the field of family therapy has addressed gender issues. Prior to the 1970s, gender issues were invisible in family therapy. The feminist revision of family therapy began in the late 1970s and continued throughout the 1980s and early 1990s. In the mid-1990s it began to lose momentum, and in the first decade of the 21st century it is practically on life support. The single journal devoted to keeping it alive, the *Journal of Feminist Family Therapy*, remains a vibrant and creative, though marginalized, voice.

We then highlight two areas that have received little attention within family therapy: feminist approaches to working with men and lesbians in couples therapy. In the next section we examine tensions between gender/feminism and race/ethnicity in family and couples therapy, and we argue that the lack of integration of these two domains contributes to the marginalization of both. We conclude with the observation that the future of feminism in family therapy, like the future of feminism in all disciplines, requires a shift from a singular focus on gender toward an examination of the multiple identities and intersectionalities that construct the lives of women and men. As a way of understanding some of the barriers to this shift, we examine the continuing problem of White, heterosexual privilege among feminist family therapists.

Finally, we consider two contrasting contemporary trends in family therapy: the evidence-based treatment (EBT) movement, in which gender and race/ethnicity are either invisible or treated without attention to power and privilege, and the social justice perspective, which expands the goals of therapy beyond the family to include reform of oppressive social institutions. Because we believe that these two sections represent the future, we have included clinical vignettes in order to illustrate these approaches more clearly. The vignettes in the EBT section illustrate the potential negative consequences of ignoring gendered power differences, multiple oppressions, and accountability. The vignettes in the social justice section make salient an intersectionalities approach, but do not address the issue of effectiveness. We conclude our chapter with a recommendation that therapists try to combine the goals of both of these family therapy movements.

The Authors' Social Locations

Our analysis of the state of feminism in family and couples therapy has undoubtedly been influenced (limited) by our social locations. Both of us are White, middle class, and heterosexual. Both of us have two children in the context of long-term marriages. We are experienced family therapists and professors at large universities. Both of us have written on feminist theory and on the psychology of men and masculinity. One of us (LBS) has focused over the past 5 years on integrating gender/feminism and race/ethnicity in family therapy. The other (GB) has focused on developing ways to work with traditional men from a feminist perspective.

Historical Overview of the Feminist Revision of Family Therapy (1970–2000)

In the 1960s gender issues were invisible in family therapy because, with the exception of Virginia Satir, the field was developed by White men, most of whom were psychiatrists with psychoanalytic training (e.g., Ackerman, Bowen, Minuchin). Since that time period, four major reviews of family therapy journals have traced the history of feminism and multiculturalism in family therapy (Goodrich & Silverstein, 2005; Kosutic & McDowell, 2008; Leslie & Morton, 2001; Silverstein, 2003).

In brief (see Silverstein, 2003, for an extended review), the original feminist critique extended from the 1970s through the 1990s. Major articles and books from the late 1970s through the 1980s pointed out that the social construction of gender in terms of both femininity and masculinity constructed and constrained behavior in families. This early revision also called attention to the unequal power relations between men and women in families, and it challenged the construct of mother-blaming that defined much of family therapy practice (see, for example, Ault-Riche, 1986; Braverman, 1988; Goldner, 1985; Hare-Mustin, 1978; Walters, Carter, Papp, & Silverstein, 1988). Beginning in the 1980s, the feminist critique of family therapy also began to address the issues of gay and lesbian couples and families (Krestan & Bepko, 1980; Roth, 1985) and initiated explorations of the ways that differences in race and ethnicity constructed differences in discrimination and oppression (Hall & Greene, 1994; McGoldrick, Pearce, & Giordano, 1982; Pinderhughes, 1986).

Leslie and Morton (2001), in their review of the contents of the two major mainstream journals (i.e., *Journal of Marriage and Family Therapy*, *Family Process*) over the years 1970–2000, identified articles that reflected feminist adaptations of family therapy models (see Gosling & Zangari, 1996; McGoldrick, Anderson, & Walsh, 1989; Prouty & Bermundez, 1999). Other articles presented training guidelines for developing feminist approaches (Avis, 1989; Deinhart & Avis, 1991; Leslie & Clossick, 1992). Still other articles that treated gender as a process variable and focused on issues such as the match between client and therapist (Newberry, Alexander, & Turner, 1991), differences in the experiences of male and female therapists (Shields & McDaniel, 1992), and differences in the experiences of women and men in therapy (Guanipa & Woolley, 2000). More recently, gender has been examined in terms of special kinds of presenting problems, such as medical family therapy (McDaniel & Cole-Kelly, 2003; Prouty-Lyness, 2003) and conflicts in family-run businesses (Nutt, 2003). Other authors have offered feminist revisions of schools of family therapy, for example, Bowen's systems theory (Silverstein, 2005b) and contextual therapy (Dankoski & Deacon, 2000).

Overall, in the 1990s the literature on gay and lesbian couples expanded (e.g., Laird & Green, 1996), as did the focus on race/ethnicity (e.g., Hall & Greene, 1994; Watts-Jones, 1997). In addition, the feminist revision of family therapy began consistently to shift away from examining how gender socialization constructed gender differences in behavior to a recognition that gendered power differences in the wider sociopolitical context structured and maintained male dominance in families (e.g., Goodrich, 1991).

Leslie and Morton (2001) have pointed out that, as the focus on power became more pronounced, the specific clinical problem that received the most attention was violence against intimate partners (Almeida & Bograd, 1991; Bograd, 1984, 1999; Goldner, Penn, Sheinberg, & Walker, 1990; O'Neil & Harway, 1999; Silverstein, 1999). In general, the feminist approach to treating this extremely serious public health issue challenged the traditional family therapy conceptualization of the problem as systemic, that is, that both members of the couples shared equal responsibility for the "cycle of violence." In the traditional approach, the therapist typically worked conjointly with a couple, rather than separating them for the initial phase of treatment.

The feminist approach, in contrast, although acknowledging that both men and women participated in the cycle of abuse, focused on holding men primarily accountable for the violence. Because working with couples in the early phases of therapy often led to an escalation of violence, in this approach the therapist worked separately with each member of the couple until the therapist was confident that the cycle of violence had abated. This emphasis on working with violence in families led to the development of a sub-specialty (i.e., working with men from a feminist perspective) that bridged men's studies and feminist practice.

Working with Men from a Feminist Perspective

The shift in feminist family therapy to an emphasis on men's power and privilege gave rise to a backlash that accused feminists of "male bashing." In response to this backlash, some family therapists developed "gender-sensitive" approaches. For the most part, these models emphasized how gender socialization stressed men as well as women, without acknowledging the gendered power hierarchy. In a "gender-sensitive" approach therapists attempted to address gender differences without acknowledging that achieving equality in relationships, as well as in the broader culture, would require men to relinquish some of their power and privilege. For example, in their effort to "bridge separate gender worlds," Philpot, Brooks, Lusterman, and Nutt (1997) described a process of "gender inquiry," whereby therapists would assist family members to become more attuned to the effects of gender role mandates in their family functioning. These authors also described a process of "gender coevolution," which emphasized the reciprocal influence of female and male family members upon each other. This "coevolution" process was described with only minimal attention to power differentials between male and female family members.

However, not all theorists who used the term "gender sensitive" avoided power issues. Deinhart and Avis (1991) "encouraged men to recognize coercive and illegitimate forms of power and to use alternative ways to express their needs and their caring" (p. 36). Similarly, Brooks (1991) placed great emphasis on the need to neutralize the inappropriate use of power advantages among men by calling for therapists to be alert for "political maneuvers … to covertly undercut their spouse's empowerment" (p. 54). Over time, these therapists abandoned the term "gender sensitive" and became identified with feminist approaches to working with men in family therapy.

In contrast to the popular notion that feminism is "male bashing" and benefits only women, we believe that feminism, especially feminist family therapy, benefits men as well. Bograd (1991) was one of the earliest feminist family therapists to outline the advantages of a feminist approach for working with men. Just as feminist theorists deconstructed beliefs about the "essential nature" of women and freed women to explore many aspects of themselves, the feminist deconstruction of masculinity freed men to do the same. The new psychology of men and masculinity (Levant & Pollack, 1995), based on the gender role strain model (GRS), examines the negative consequences for men of traditional masculinity (O'Neil, 2008; Pleck, 1995). This concept became the framework for deconstructing traditional masculinity and working with men from a feminist perspective.

These models of working with men often include two stages in couples therapy. The first stage is based on a recognition that masculine gender-role socialization discourages men from showing vulnerability and asking for help, which contributes to men's resistance to psychotherapy. Thus these models begin with an initial stage of reaching out to male partners, usually by seeing them alone. After building a firm therapeutic alliance, the subsequent phase focuses on helping men to give up some power and privilege within their relationship. Brooks' mastery model (2003) deals with therapists' countertransference feelings by analyzing a husband's controlling behavior in the context of gender role strain. This helps the therapist to reframe controlling behaviors as reflecting the client's pain and enhances the therapist's ability to express empathy and understanding. A gender role strain perspective also empowers men to change by helping them to reevaluate their values and assumptions about manhood. This reevaluation helps them to adopt more flexible gender roles, which decreases their strain and creating the motivation to relinquish power.

Levant and Silverstein (2001) combined feminist theory and family systems theory to help a husband decrease his tendency to overwork in order to fulfill the traditional gender role of being a good provider. This behavior had been causing his wife to feel emotionally cut off from him after the birth of their first child. Then, using a series of family of origin exercises in which the husband worked on feelings about his own emotionally distant father, the therapist helped him to become aware of his less traditional masculine longing to be emotionally close to his newborn son and wife. Thus feminist family therapy enabled this man to decrease work stress and to establish a nurturing father identity. This approach to working with men helped to give rise to a division in the American Psychological Association, Division 51 – the Society for the Study of Men and Masculinity. Society members have published articles in the division's journal, *Psychology of Men & Masculinity*, that describe research and practice framed in a gender role strain and feminist perspective. However, this approach to men and masculinity remains marginalized in what has come to be known as the new psychology of men. It is rarely seen in mainstream family therapy journals.

Queering the Discussion

Just as working with men from an explicitly feminist perspective has not become mainstream, work with lesbian and gay couples remains similarly marginalized. Between 2002 and 2008, *Family Process* included 260 citations, of which 2 (<0.01%) focused on LGB families. Similarly, the *Journal of Marriage and Family Therapy* included 666 citations, of which 16 (0.024%) focused on LGB families. The *Journal of Feminist Family Therapy* included 127 citations of which 14 (11%) were on LGB families. Seven of those 14 articles were in a single special issue.

In 2005, the *Journal of GLBT Family Studies* was launched. This journal has dramatically increased the number of articles focused on couples and family therapy with LGB families. However, of the 87 originally published from 2005 through 2008, 6 articles (7%) approached therapy or research from an explicitly feminist perspective. During this same time period, only two articles considered the cultural context of their research participants. This specialized journal is an important addition to the literature on gay and lesbian couples and families. Yet the fact that it is not included in mainstream databases, such as *PsycINFO*, illustrates that its status, like its subject matter, is marginalized.

This general marginalization of information on working with LGB couples and families is particularly worrisome because many clinicians have not had the specialized training necessary to ensure that unexamined heteronormativity and homophobia do not color their thinking about LGB families. LGB families experience many external stressors that heterosexual families do not. These families exist in the shadow of the myth of the "normal," married, heterosexual family. They must negotiate the complicated question of whether, when, how, and to whom to come out (Bepko & Johnson, 2000). In most places today they are not accorded either the social validation or the civil rights enjoyed by heterosexual families. The vociferous opposition to same-sex marriage in the first decade of the 21st century reflects the intensity of social stigmatization that these families experience across many social contexts.

Given these additional stressors, when LGB families become symptomatic, it is often difficult to differentiate which symptoms are exogenous and which endogenous to the family's emotional dynamics. For example, the multiple external stressors may tend to generate more fusion in LGB couples as a way of coping with an unsupportive or actively hostile environment. This accumulation of stressors can decrease a family's ability to adapt to, or to recover from, normative stressors such as an illness or death in the extended family. The multiplicative nature of stressors may similarly generate more vulnerability in LGB families and contribute to the termination of relationships.

Although these families defy traditional gender stereotypes by virtue of including same-sex couples, ironically they often suffer from gender stereotypes as well. Green, Bettinger, and Zacks (1996, p. 185) captured this dilemma in their chapter titled "Are Lesbian Couples Fused and Gay Male Couples Disengaged?" The authors addressed the tendency for therapists to utilize the gender stereotypes of women as more emotionally connected, and men as more emotionally distant, in conceptualizing the dynamics of LGB families. In contrast to these stereotypes, Green et al. (1996) reported research conducted in the 1980s that indicated more cohesion in both gay male and lesbian couples than was observed in heterosexual married couples. The authors also examined the assumption that partners in same-sex couples assume stereotypic butch/femme roles. They found evidence that partners in these couples illustrated more gender flexibility and equality than partners in heterosexual couples did. Gay father couples, who could not divide parenting responsibilities based on feminine and masculine gender role norms, have reported similar role flexibility (Schacher, Auerbach, & Silverstein, 2005).

Connolly (2006) pointed out that a gender stereotype that often affects lesbian couples is the assumption that women are less interested in dominance than men are, and, therefore, lesbian partners have more equal power than do heterosexual partners. She pointed out, in contrast, that power struggles arise in all couples and speculated that these struggles might be expressed in a more covert manner in couples that do not include a man. The stereotype of women as less physically violent than men also can lead to denial, in both heterosexual and lesbian communities, that family violence exists in lesbian families. Thus women who suffer from same-sex violence may be reluctant to seek help. Merlis and Linville (2006) reported the findings of a qualitative study of 15 mental health professionals who characterized one Chicago lesbian community's strategies for dealing with domestic violence as (1) protecting the romantic ideal (i.e., maintaining the myth that women are not violent toward each other), (2) shielding the community from harm, and (3) not wanting to add the additional stigma of intimate violence. These responses resulted in denial and silence. The professionals outlined several strategies for dealing with the denial but stated that the community in general had not responded to outreach efforts.

West (2002), in a review of the research on violence in lesbian relationships, reported that 30–40% of lesbians have been involved in at least one physically abusive relationship. She reported that sexual abuse prevalence rates range from 7 to 55%. The most common type of partner abuse, reported in 80% of lesbian couples, was verbal or psychological. Speziale and Ring (2006) pointed out one kind of abuse that is particular to LGB families: forced outing to family, friends, and/or work colleagues. This kind of disclosure can have dramatic negative consequences on psychological well-being. The authors called for professional training to sensitize mental health practitioners and researchers to the special challenges that LGB families face.

West, Speziale, Ring, and others have emphasized the difficulty of effectively addressing intimate violence when LGB relationships are not legally, and sometimes not socially, recognized. Without equal protection under the law, intervention by both law enforcement and social services providers is limited. Within this delimiting context, Istar (1996) suggested including both partners in the initial assessment because seeing the couples together provides an opportunity for the therapist to observe, and then affirm, positive aspects of the relationship. This approach runs counter to the typical feminist approach of assessing each partner in a heterosexual couple separately in order to avoid exacerbating the violence. However, one group of service providers raised questions about whether conceptualizations that had emerged from working with heterosexual couples, even the definition of what constitutes abuse, are appropriate for use with lesbian couples (Ristock, 2003). As Halstead (2003) cautioned, we must continually examine theory and practice for sexist and heterosexist beliefs that are often deeply embedded in "state of the art" theories (p. 49).

In contrast to an emphasis on vulnerability and stress, Connolly (2006) emphasized the resilience that lesbian couples exhibit, despite the amount of societal stress that they experience. In a study of long-term lesbian couples, she observed resilience in the form of (1) mutual dedication to creating the type of relationship they wanted; (2) an us-against-the-world united front against challenges; and (3) an ability to compartmentalize and protect the relationship from external stressors.

Given the extremely limited attention to LGB families in general, it is not surprising that most of the research and practice literature focuses on White, middle-class families. Exceptions to this are the work of Ruth Hall, Beverly Greene, and their colleagues. Greene and Boyd-Franklin (1999) described the experience of African American lesbians as "triple jeopardy," that is, affected by racism, sexism, and homophobia. They pointed out that discrimination occurs at multiple systemic levels: US mainstream culture and society, African American culture and society, nuclear and extended families, and individual intrapsychic dynamics.

Greene and Boyd-Franklin (1999) explored the ways that ethnosexual stereotypes about African American and Caribbean women in general have affected African American lesbians. They argued that stereotypes created by mainstream culture, including images of the "castrating, sexually promiscuous, assertive, matriarchal, and masculinized woman" (p. 254) have been generalized to African American and Caribbean lesbians, who are then seen as women who act like men and are promiscuous. These stereotypes also support the myth that the oppression that Black men experience is caused by strong women rather than by institutionalized racism. By extension, the suggested solution to family problems, as well as to racial discrimination in general, was for African American women to accept male dominance and traditional gender roles. Within this context, lesbians were easily scapegoated and seen as "not normal."

Greene and Boyd-Franklin pointed out that there is great diversity among African American lesbian couples. Important variables are the race of one's partner, the visibility of the relationship, and the resulting acceptance of one's family and community. The gendered racism in the African American community means that many lesbian relationships are unsupported by extended families. Similarly, few African American therapists are trained to work with lesbian couples and families.

Greene and Boyd-Franklin noted further that the external stresses felt by LGB couples and families could be exacerbated if the couple's relationship was interracial. Because of the larger number of White lesbians, lesbians of color often have White partners. They may thus be more identifiable as a couple than two Black lesbians who could more easily "pass" as friends. They might, therefore, experience more homophobia and discrimination. Moreover, a White partner is likely to lose some aspects of White privilege and to experience racism for the first time, which can generate stress within the couple.

Hall and Greene (2002) added still another layer of complexity to the thinking about African American lesbians by focusing on social class. In contrast to the usual focus on the kinds of discrimination African American lesbian couples suffer from outside the relationship, they focused on the problems that class differences between partners can cause within relationships. They pointed out that popular culture assumes that partners who share similar racial, ethnic, and social characteristics can more easily negotiate relationships. However, people with similar attributes such as race, gender, and ethnicity might have different life experiences because of differences in socioeconomic status. Thus the assumption about similarities enhancing intimacy may prove to be false. When this occurs, partners can be so disappointed that the relationship is disrupted. They also pointed out, however, that differences did not always generate problems. Their belief is that differences could be worked through as long as each partner was willing to respond to her partner's concerns.

Frameworks that integrate race/ethnicity and class into models for working with lesbians and gay men reflect the intersectionalities perspective that we discuss below as one of the best practices in couples and family therapy. This trend of looking at the multiple social locations of groups on the margins of mainstream society contributes to moving the family therapy field in a more integrative and progressive direction.

Tensions Between Race/Ethnicity and Gender/Feminism in Family Therapy

In contrast to Hall and Greene's work that integrates multiple perspectives, a number of reviews of the family therapy literature have shown that, as the number of articles on race/ethnicity increased, the number of articles on gender/feminism decreased. In their review of published articles between 1970 and 2000, Leslie and Morton (2001) examined the number of clinical and empirical articles that addressed diversity in families in the two most prominent family therapy journals, the *Journal of Marriage and Family Therapy* and *Family Process*. The authors found that 11% of the total 1,850 articles were devoted to the issue of family diversity. The topic that received the most attention was gender, and the majority of those articles were published in the 1990s. The second largest number of articles addressed race/ethnicity/culture, and, again, most were published in the 1990s. The smallest number of articles (15) addressed sexual orientation, and five of those were published in one special issue. By the first decade of the 21st century, the ratio of articles focused on gender and on diversity had been reversed.

Hall and Greene (1994) were among the first to define multicultural competence in feminist therapy as an ethical mandate. However, several review articles (Arredondo, Psalti, & Cella, 1993; Goodrich & Silverstein, 2005; Reid, 2002; Silverstein, 2005a) have shown that most authors have focused on either multiculturalism or feminism. This splintering of race/ethnicity and gender/feminism has contributed to the marginalization of both. In a review of all articles, books, and chapters on family therapy listed in *PsycINFO*, Silverstein (2005a) found that, from 1990 to 2004, only 2% of articles that focused on race–ethnicity included feminism, and only 6% of articles that focused on gender/feminism included race/ethnicity.

Goodrich and Silverstein (2005) examined trends in feminist training in family therapy and found similar results. They analyzed questionnaires sent to 82 family therapy training programs in the USA and Canada, which were accredited by the American Association of Marriage and Family Therapists (AAMFT), and to 9 postgraduate training institutes. All of the programs reported strong compliance with AAMFT standards that require a curriculum to be infused with content that addresses diversity, power, and privilege. However, the more detailed responses to the questionnaire indicated variations in the way that gender was included in the curriculum. Faculty members varied in the way that they addressed gender issues, from a simple focus on differences to a discussion of power inequalities.

Similarly, Wieling and Rastogi (2003) interviewed 15 therapists of color who were members of AAMFT, 87% of whom had a Masters degree in Family Therapy. Five of the participants reported that their training was positive in terms of diversity issues, whereas 10 reported that their training was inadequate. One participant said, "I felt the curriculum and training are all for the most part geared toward the White population, and we really aren't being prepared for providing services to a variety of cultures" (p. 11). Thus that study replicated the findings of Goodrich and Silverstein (2005); this suggests that family therapy training has not yet made an authentic commitment to integrating gender and multiculturalism in a meaningful way.

To identify the most recent trends, we used *PsycINFO* to search *Family Process* and the *Journal of Marital and Family Therapy* from 2002 to 2008. We found that the total number of articles that included a discussion of gender issues was 12 of 611 (0.02%). Nine articles (0.014%) included race/ethnicity, and only three (0.005%) articles included both. Thus, in mainstream family therapy, both race/ethnicity and gender/feminism are extremely under-represented and continue to be treated as separate, rather than as intersecting, variables. In addition to mainstream journals, we also searched the *Journal of Feminist Family Therapy* for the years 2002–2007. Only 20 (16%) of the 127 articles combined gender/feminism and race/ethnicity. Thus the lack of integration of race/ethnicity and gender/feminism that we have seen in mainstream journals continues even in the most progressive family therapy journal.

In summary, multiple reviews of the state of feminism in mainstream family therapy journals have repeatedly indicated that, although a focus on diversity has increased somewhat over the last two decades, attention to gender and feminism has decreased. Moreover, integration of the multiple aspects of people's lives, in terms of multiple identities or intersubjectivities, has not yet become the *lingua franca* of the family therapy field.

An Intersectionalities Framework

There are several authors whose work stands in sharp contrast to the lack of integration of feminism and race/ethnicity as discussed above. Very early in the feminist revision of family therapy, Pinderhughes (1986) identified the "nodal" position of African American women in terms of oppression by both racism and sexism. She pointed out that, because of the violence routinely suffered by African American men in US society, African American women have traditionally been expected to absorb sexist oppression within their families, including violence against women and sexual abuse. The taboo against confronting sexist oppression within their families emanated from a proscription against exacerbating the plight of African American men who suffer discrimination, violence, and incarceration within the racist mainstream society. In addition to this intrafamily sexism, Lillian Comas-Diaz (1994) called attention to the racism that dark-skinned Latinas (*LatiNegras*) often suffer in their families. Some feminist family therapists of color, sensitive to the intersections of multiple systems of oppression, have struggled with whether and/or when to raise feminist issues with poor ethnic minority women in certain contexts.

Almeida's (2003) cultural context model of family therapy is one model that addresses the tension between culture and sexism by working within culture circles, which are defined as "a therapeutic gathering of diverse individuals and families" (R. V. Almeida, personal communication, February, 16, 2009). These multifamily groups generate a therapeutic community that can provide social support (e.g., advocates, mentors), as well as connections to legal and medical services for families that do not have access to middle-class resources. Within this community context, Almeida has challenged the assumption that in some contexts a feminist approach is culturally insensitive. She has argued that many sexist social practices that are presented as culturally congruent are, in reality, simply rationalizations that sustain male dominance. In her clinical work, she addresses the different trajectory of sexist practices across cultures by allying with culturally relevant role models that reject sexist practices. For example, in response to the myth that submissive behavior on the part of Chinese women is a culturally prescribed norm, she identified movies such as *The Joy Luck Club* and *The Wedding Banquet* that present feminist Chinese women as role models. This kind of deconstruction of the cultural camouflage of male dominance avoids the essentializing of culture, and it can be used to work toward more equitable sharing of power in families from many cultures.

Similarly, Inclan (2003) combined a feminist approach to traditional masculinity ideology with attention to social class differences for working with immigrant Latino/a couples. Inclan described one stratum of middle-class, immigrant couples – small to medium business owners – who were focused on economic advancement. Within this demographic group, despite a division of labor along traditional gender role lines, both members of the couples often become aware of more equitable relationship models within US society. When the wives begin to raise questions about the organization of power within the family, the husbands tend to resist. According to Inclan, "the cultural blanket provides complicity with the husband's point of view" (p. 336). Traditional gender-role socialization within Latin cultures trains women not to question their husbands, and men are socialized to demand respect simply by virtue of being head of the household. As each spouse's position solidifies, the couple tends to become more polarized. Inclan also saw immigration as a powerful catalyst for poor, working class, Latino/a immigrants. The primary goal for poor immigrants is economic survival; all other considerations, including gender-role norms, are sacrificed to this over-arching goal. Women usually enter the labor force, and they may find work before their husbands do, or make more than their husbands earn. Their economic contribution enables their participation in family decision-making in a way that may contrast with pre-immigration cultural norms that prescribe men as in charge. Thus working class immigrants may "walk the walk" of gender equity before their ideology has changed.

Inclan warned that, in each of these contexts, a therapist might begin a discussion of gender ideology or challenge the power distribution in the couple before the husbands are prepared to change. As in other feminist models of working with men in therapy, Inclan argued that these families are not ready for conjoint therapy and that conjoint therapy at this phase in their acculturation process might precipitate termination of therapy. Inclan proposed an initial phase with the husband alone in order to prepare him to renegotiate gender ideology and power sharing. Inclan's interweaving of class, gender, culture, and acculturation is an innovative example of how to work from an intersectionalities perspective.

We have included a description of several family therapists who are moving the field toward an intersectionalities perspective. However, this integrative model is far from the dominant approach in family and couples therapy. There remains much work to be done to integrate this perspective into mainstream family therapy and psychology in general.

The Continuing Problem of White, Heterosexual Privilege

One of the major impediments to moving toward an intersectionalities framework is that the majority of White feminist family therapists have too often been blind to issues of racism and other oppressions in the lives of poor people, men and women of color, immigrants, and sexual minorities. Bograd (1999) pointed out this glaring omission in her own work on domestic violence. She acknowledged her failure to consider how the intersectionalities of multiple oppressions constructed the experience of domestic violence in other-than-White, middle-class families. She recognized that her social location as an upper middle-class, White (heterosexual) woman led her to privilege gender over other aspects of experience. Bograd pointed out the invisibility in the family therapy domestic violence literature of certain populations, such as poor and homeless women, gay and lesbian victims, and ethnic minorities other than African Americans and Latinas. She examined how these intersectionalities affected the probability of seeking treatment. For example, she noted that a Jewish battered woman might hesitate to seek treatment for fear of generating anti-Semitism. Bograd concluded that "It is incumbent on those of us in the field who already have power and prestige to shoulder the responsibility of expanding our models, examining our practices, and giving voice to those who are silenced among us" (p. 285).

Despite this early call to arms, the problem of White heterosexual privilege continues to be a major problem in the field of feminist family therapy. If we examine the authors of articles that do integrate concepts of gender/feminism and race/ethnicity in family therapy, those authors are overwhelmingly women and some men of color (e.g., Almeida, 2003; Comas-Diaz, 1994, 2003; Comas-Diaz & Greene, 1994; Hall & Greene, 2003; Hernandez, Almeida, & Dolan-Del Vecchio, 2005; Inclan, 2003; Pinderhughes, 1986). White feminists are free to ignore race and class in their professional lives because they do not suffer the indignities of racism in their personal lives. A similar phenomenon occurs in the discussion of GLBT family issues. The majority of this literature in family therapy is by GLBT therapists (e.g., Eldridge & Barrett, 2003; Hall & Greene, 1994; Laird & Green, 1996; Perlesz & McNair, 2004). Similarly, the sporadic and uneven efforts to integrate issues of gender, race/ethnicity, and other inequalities of power into the curricula of mainstream family therapy training programs are also reflections of White privilege. As Goodrich and Silverstein (2005) indicated, many training programs and faculty members may "talk the talk" of multiculturalism, but few "walk the walk."

This phenomenon is exceedingly difficult to interrupt. In a recent graduate course, one of us (LBS) encouraged the 21 students to attend a multicultural conference in a nearby town. Two students of color accompanied the professor. None of the 19 White students attended. When this lack of attendance was characterized as an exercise of White privilege, the students were shocked. Some were outraged. Unfortunately, this behavior is not unusual. The vast majority of the attendees at the conference, more than 90%, were professionals of color. Again, the absence of White professionals at these types of conferences is an example of the very exercise of White privilege that many of these conferences are attempting to deconstruct.

However, although many White therapists remain content to ignore multiculturalism and an intersectionalities perspective, others would be open to integrating these viewpoints, but do not have the conceptual framework or content knowledge to do so. For these reasons, multicultural training for both students and professionals is important.

McGoldrick (1994), a White therapist who has shown a commitment to infusing multiculturalism into family therapy (McGoldrick, 1996; McGoldrick et al., 1982), has argued that, because life in the USA is so racially segregated in terms of housing, education, and religious observance, White people feel uncomfortable when they are in a racially mixed situation. This is particularly true when White people are in the minority, rather than in a position of power. It is therefore understandable that White professionals would be reluctant to attend a conference that was organized by, and privileged the perspectives of, professionals of color. Waldegrave (1998) has argued that, because of the worldwide dominance of Western, White societies, White mental health professionals have not had to realize how limited and parochial their ideas about childrearing, family dynamics, diagnoses, etc., actually are.

Pewewardy (2004) proposed that, when the concept "the personal is political" is related only to the personal experiences of White, middle-class, heterosexual feminists, this personal, individualistic perspective results in incomplete theories and practices that reinforce oppression. For example, the White, middle-class feminists' solution for men's violence against intimate partners has typically involved leaving the abusive partner. This strategy may not be realistic for many poor women in both the USA and abroad. Poor women are often dependent on the income of their abusive partners for survival in terms of housing, food, and other life necessities. This is especially true for many women in developing nations. Mittal, a south Asian woman, described feeling conflicted about openly challenging gender roles with poor women in India who did not have the education or income to leave abusive relationships (Mittal & Wieling, 2004). For poor women, developing collectives of supportive women and men who can work and live together is a more effective strategy. Because White, upper middle-class therapists tend to be ignorant of the lived experiences of people from different social locations, they are at risk of responding to their clients with unrealistic goals. If feminism is to be relevant for all women, it must embrace an intersectionalities perspective.

This failure of White feminists remains a major limitation in feminist family therapy. We need to develop strategies to raise the critical consciousness of White, heterosexual feminists. In an attempt to address this problem, Silverstein and Goodrich (2003) required that the authors who contributed to their book include clinical examples with both mainstream and marginalized couples or families. Not every chapter was successful in this regard. However, many of the White feminist authors did address the concerns of both White families and families of color (see, e.g., Mize, 2003; Rice, 2003). Eldridge and Barrett (2003) further complicated the need to acknowledge racial privilege by pointing out that biracial families must examine White privilege within their nuclear as well as extended families. The authors described a lesbian-led family in which the mothers were White and the adopted children were Latino/a. The family ultimately addressed the White privilege that the parents and grandparents enjoyed, but which was not shared by their children.

In addition to insisting on an intersectionalities perspective in publications, another strategy would be to extend this policy to presentations as well. For example, all feminists could refuse to participate in symposia that did not include diverse participants and that did not address topics from an intersectionalities perspective. Finally, in our own racial identity development, personal relationships with mentors, both people of color and White people who have experience confronting their own White privilege, have been essential for personal growth. These types of mentoring relationships should be encouraged for both professionals and students.

Contemporary Trends in Couples and Family Therapy

In this section, we describe two contrasting contemporary trends: evidence-based treatment and the social justice perspective. Evidence-based treatment (EBT) is standardized and manualized in order to provide empirical data as to its efficacy or effectiveness. This body of research has developed independently of feminist and culturally sensitive approaches to couples and family therapy. We begin this section with a review of couples therapy that examines gender differences in response to marital conflict. Although this body of work explicitly considers gender, it does not do so from a feminist perspective. Rather it assumes that gender differences are based in differences in physiological arousal to conflict.

We then review behavioral and emotion-centered couples therapy and argue that these approaches achieve first-order change rather than a deeper reorganization of power and privilege within couples. First-order change, as conceptualized by Watzlawick (1978), refers to superficial changes (e.g., improved communication) without addressing underlying issues of differences in power and privilege. Second-order change, in contrast, is a more transformative alteration in the basic organization of the relationship, and it involves attempts to equalize power and privilege within the couple. Unfortunately, "first-order change" not only leaves a couple vulnerable to relapse when future external stressors occur but it also deprives them of an opportunity to transcend their dysfunctional relationship structure for one that is ultimately more adaptive. We provide clinical vignettes in order to illustrate our perspective. We close by describing beginning efforts to include multicultural sensitivity, but not yet feminism, into this body of work.

Finally, we present the contrasting trend of "just therapy," which is based on a social justice perspective. This trend pushes the boundaries of an intersectionalities approach in that it advocates changing social institutions as well as intrafamily dynamics. Again, we offer vignettes to illustrate this approach to family and couples therapy.

Evidence-Based Treatment in Couples Therapy

Just as tension exists between the challenges of attending to both race/ethnicity and gender/feminism, a parallel tension exists between the need to provide empirical validation for family therapy interventions and the need to conduct research in a fashion that attends to gendered power differences and the multiple sources of oppression. To date, family and couples therapy research has given far greater emphasis to "evidence" than it has to integrating feminist and multicultural awareness (Levant & Silverstein, 2005; Sue, 2005). Efforts that have been made to incorporate these variables into the EBT approaches to couples have focused on either gender or race/ethnicity. To our knowledge, there have not been efforts to incorporate an intersectionalities perspective in models of EBT.

Empirical Research on Couples Interaction: Physiology, Socialization, or Power?

Considerable empirical research has been conducted on the differential reactions that husbands and wives have to marital conflict. One of the most common patterns of marital conflict is the interaction sequence in which one person's request for change is met with a counter-complaint. The original partner then responds with emotional demands, criticism, and complaints that, in turn, are followed by the withdrawal of the second partner. This interaction pattern is commonly known as the demand/withdrawal or pursuer/distancer sequence. Gender differences in this interaction sequence have revealed that women tend to be in the demand role, whereas men tend to be withdrawers. Another way that researchers have characterized this gender difference is that women are conflict confronters, whereas men are conflict avoiders. In a review article, Christenson and Heavey (1990) noted that this pattern of gender differences had been identified as early as 1938 and documented repeatedly by researchers on couples' interactions.

Two major hypotheses about the etiology of these gender differences have emerged. The individual differences model suggests that the observed differences stem from either differences in physiological arousal or gender-role socialization (Gottman & Levenson, 1998; Napier, 1978). The social structural model (Heavey, Lane, & Christenson, 1993; Jacobson, 1983) has pointed to differences in power and privilege as the sources of these contrasting interaction styles.

Gottman and Levenson (1988) noted that men are much more physiologically reactive to stress than are women. They argued that the discomfort that accompanies this arousal leads men to withdraw from conflict. Correspondingly, because women are less physiologically reactive to negative affect, they are more likely to initiate discussion of conflictual issues. Gottman (1994) described the highly damaging interpersonal strategy of "stonewalling," in which a partner withdraws from a problematic interaction, thereby making constructive resolution impossible. Gottman has reported that this negative behavior is more prevalent in men and has argued that this response is largely a product of men's heightened level of physiological arousal and emotional flooding. Gottman, Ryan, Carrere, and Erly (2002) noted that "In marriages that were destined to become happy and stable the wife did not perceive her husband's anger negatively; instead she saw it as neutral" (p. 158). The researchers also found that, among newlywed couples, "positive de-escalation was associated with physiological soothing of the husband by the wife and self-soothing by the husband" (p. 160). Within this theoretical perspective, successful therapy would depend upon the woman altering her reaction to her husband's "unavoidable" behavior and working harder to help him to calm himself enough for interaction to continue.

This perspective perpetuates the common practice of delegating nurturing functions to women and unfairly distributing to them the responsibility for the emotional well-being of all family members. In addition, there appears to be some evidence that certain "positive" behaviors in women can become self-defeating. For example, Epstein and Baucom (2002) found that "overall, the women who showed an increase in positive communication [toward their husbands] ... were more likely to experience marital distress several years later" (p. 60). They further noted that "Instead of perpetuating this differential role for the two genders, the therapist might serve the couple well by ensuring that both partners assume [this] responsibility" (p. 61). In further contrast to Gottman's claims, Julien, Arrellano, and Turgeon (1997) contended that the empirical evidence does not support biological explanations of physiological arousal differences. Rather they argued that the level of relationship distress was actually more predictive of physiological arousal. They also noted that Turgeon (1995) found that when wives had more power than their husbands, the husbands withdrew. They suggested that "pronounced gender roles" increase communication problems within couples, whether the couples are heterosexual, gay, or lesbian. They found better communication when couples engaged in role flexibility.

In another version of the individual differences hypothesis, Napier (1978) and Gilligan (1982) theorized that differential arousal was related to differences in gender-role socialization that train women to be affiliative and emotionally expressive and men to deny vulnerability and strive to be independent. Christenson (1988) similarly argued that these contrasting socialization experiences generate gender differences in tolerance for emotional intimacy, such that women seek more closeness and men seek more distance.

In contrast to the individual differences hypothesis, Jacobson (1983) espoused the social structural model. He pointed out that women bear an unequal burden of responsibility for housework and childcare, even when they are employed full-time. Thus, men are more likely to want to preserve the status quo, whereas women tend to want change. Women who desire change make demands; men withdraw to avoid a confrontation that might force them to change. Christenson and Heavey (1990) further refined this model through an experiment with two conditions: one in which the father wanted change and one in which the mother wanted change. Findings indicated that, overall, mother demandingness was greater than father demandingness. The authors concluded that mothers' lower power status in the social structure leads to greater demandingness overall. Fathers' more privileged status, in contrast, leads to less demandingness, even on issues they wanted changed because they are more satisfied overall with the status quo. Although the authors did not name the context as male dominance, from our perspective, they made an important theoretical advance by recognizing issues of power and privilege within their social structural hypothesis.

In addition to the lack of focus on gendered power differences, we believe that evidence-based couples therapy suffers from the lack of a conceptual model of gender role strain and conflict in men (O'Neil, 2008; Pleck, 1995). Therefore, it does not recognize the need to counter men's negative attitudes toward seeking help, especially in terms of psychotherapy. Many men are thus unlikely to enter therapy without special outreach efforts to engage them. Moreover, many men are also unlikely to realize possible benefits from broadening and redefining their traditionally limited roles. Unfortunately, EBT is completely devoid of such efforts in its theoretical framework and ultimate execution.

Problems with First-Order Change

Baucom, Shoham, Mueser, Daiuto, and Stickle (1998) provided a thorough review of the efficacy of marital behavior therapy. Based upon this accumulation of research evidence, there can be little doubt that such interventions generally produce substantial improvements in the lives of couples that enter and complete treatment. However, from a feminist perspective, there are elements of these approaches that must be critiqued as insufficiently attentive to certain critical gender differences and, thus, are potentially harmful to some persons in marital distress.

We present several clinical vignettes[1] to illustrate some of the primary positive and problematic features of the dominant models of empirically supported treatments for couples.

> Vanessa and Mark, a recently married couple experiencing marital distress, sought help from a counselor with expertise in marital behavior therapy. Vanessa, a pharmaceutical representative, was unhappy with Mark's level of participation in household responsibilities and the decreasing amount of time spent together. Mark, a stockbroker, admitted avoiding Vanessa because he saw her as unappreciative of all that he contributes. Over the next several weeks of active participation in therapy, they developed facility in contracting for reciprocal behavior changes regarding household labor and increased time spent together. These behavioral changes were augmented by therapeutic efforts to improve their communication and problem solving skills. At the conclusion of their therapy, each felt less distressed and more satisfied with their relationship.
>
> Several years later, and in a new location, they again presented for help. This time they reported mutual concerns about emotional distance and feelings of "deadness" in the marriage. Over the next 2 months they engaged actively in "emotion-focused therapy," which helped them to recognize the ways that their early life attachment issues had interfered with their ability to expose vulnerabilities and share intimacy. Once again, they exited marital therapy feeling great satisfaction with their marriage and their emotional connection.

This therapeutic outcome for Vanessa and Mark would certainly be considered successful by most realistic standards. However, as positive as this scenario is, it is far from the only possible one for couples experiencing marital distress. Let us consider two different, and, we would argue, far more common ones.

> Neither Kevin nor Cathy felt that their marriage had been particularly fulfilling. Kevin was employed as a warehouse foreman and spent more than 60 hours each week working at his primary job and doing some part-time work remodeling houses. Cathy, an elementary school teacher, felt overwhelmed trying to manage her job, homemaking duties, and primary parenting of their three teen-age children. As the pressures mounted and she became worried about Kevin's prolonged evening absences from the home, she pleaded with him to accompany her to an appointment with her therapist. Kevin reacted poorly to her request, enraged that she seemed to have such poor appreciation of the already-excessive demands on his time. As she became more desperate and accelerated pressure on Kevin to join her in couples treatment, he shut down his communication with her and subsequently spent far more time away from the home. In the end, they never saw a marital counselor or entered any form of conjoint treatment.

Obviously, marital therapy that never begins cannot have a successful outcome. Moreover, couple intervention will not be helpful if one partner comes reluctantly, participates minimally, and, ultimately, abandons the process. The literature on empirically supported treatment is limited because it draws evidence only from those couples that enter into treatment (or research programs) and do not drop out. Given the commonly reported reluctance of men to enter psychotherapy (e.g., Addis & Mahalik, 2003; Brooks, 1998) and the well-established findings that women are socialized to take greater responsibility for their relationships, it seems quite likely that many more female partners than male partners seek help for their relationships. The typical difference in earnings and power between men and women in most relationships (Christenson, 1988; Jacobson, 1983; Murphy & Meyer, 1991) further limits women's capacity to persuade their male partners to address couple issues. Given these difficulties in attracting many men to psychotherapy, we assume that the literature on empirically supported interventions does not draw its evidence from the broadest population of couples and, therefore, lacks applicability for many real-world situations.

In the next vignette we describe a couple that did come to therapy and did achieve short-term therapeutic success. However, this short-term, first-order change set the stage for longer-term problems.

---

[1]The clinical vignettes in the evidence-based treatment section were created based on the second author's clinical experience, case consultation, and supervision of graduate students. The clinical vignettes in the social justice section are paraphrases from other authors' articles and chapters, as referenced in the text.

Brian and Meredith's marital relationship had been relatively stormy for almost all of its 8 years. Brian was a corporate attorney with excellent prospects for partnership in a large urban consulting firm. Meredith, also an attorney, had restricted herself to a smaller private practice to achieve a better balance between her professional life and what she viewed as "her" domestic responsibilities. Recognizing the declining state of their marriage, they began therapy with a renowned marital therapist who had published extensively regarding the successful outcome of empirically validated treatment.

In therapy, the couple benefited immediately from activities to enhance their communication skills, not only in conflict management, but also in terms of increasing their overall positive communication. Meredith, in particular, learned to "soften" her approach to Brian and to replace her usual challenges to his emotional withdrawal with more statements of appreciation of his stresses. In turn, Brian became more emotionally available to Meredith and accepted the need to provide more time for emotional intimacy. Later in the course of therapy, they explored their childhood experiences with primary attachment figures and speculated upon the role of those experiences in their problems with emotional intimacy. Once again, they reported improvement in their relationship and felt prepared to end treatment.

Fourteen years later Meredith contacted the therapist seeking individual therapy related to the dissolution of the marriage. Brian had shocked her by announcing that he had found another woman and wanted out of the marriage. Although he agreed to provide child support for their older daughter, he insisted that he be granted custody of their 8-year old son. Recognizing that the majority of the couple's financial assets were in Brian's name, Meredith had resigned herself to this arrangement. As the date of the divorce approached, she experienced the onset of anxiety attacks and a profound sense of hopelessness.

Like the therapy described for Meredith and Brian, most empirically supported couples treatments are quite narrow in the choice of goals for relationship improvement. Treatment manuals explicitly identify their objectives as decreasing negative behaviors and increasing positive behaviors in relationships, and researchers have provided impressive evidence that this can be accomplished. In brief, there have been consistent findings that distressed couples engage in many fewer positive behaviors, and many more negative behaviors, toward each other (Epstein & Baucom, 2002; Gottman, 1994; Halford, Kelly, & Markman, 1997; Weiss & Heyman, 1997). Thus, decreasing negative and increasing positive behaviors make sense as a therapeutic goal. However, this limited focus has a number of significant problems rooted in the failure to consider the positive and negative behaviors within a broader cultural context.

In brief, these researchers focused on first-order change but paid no attention to the need for "second-order" change. They did not focus on a possible need to reposition the couple within the larger culture of gender-based disparities in power and opportunity. Meredith's complaints about Brian's emotional unavailability, the discrepancy in their incomes, and Brian's feelings of being unfairly attacked by Meredith are typical problems that are linked to gendered differences in power and entitlement. The therapy addressed the *content* of these issues, but not the gendered power dynamics that constructed them. From our perspective, this failure contributed to their subsequent distress. Both Meredith and Brian changed their behavior as a result of therapy. However, the therapist's failure to address the implications of the imbalance of power rooted in their different career trajectories and earning power contributed to Meredith's vulnerability 14 years later to losing custody of her son.

In summary, it is clear that empirically supported marital therapies frequently are quite beneficial in producing first-order changes in those marital couples who are able and willing to engage in the various behavioral and emotion-based interventions. However, this literature often has neglected the larger organizing role of gender-based differences in access to power and influence, as well as the need to consider second-order change for long-term relationship benefits.

Cultural Competence and EBT

Finally, until very recently, the models of cultural competence in family and couples therapy have developed independently from EBT models (Sue, 2005). In their review of the status of couples therapy (CT) research, Sexton, Alexander, and Mease (2004) noted that "... most participants in CT research were White, middle class, heterosexual, and came from mainstream cultures and ethnic groups ... this is clearly not a random sample... it is currently unclear whether successful CT interventions can be expected to offer the same benefits to clients with other cultural backgrounds" (p. 637). When EBT researchers have tried to address race or ethnicity, these have too often been reduced to categorical variables, such as specific strategies for working with Latino/a or Irish families. This theoretical simplification equates culture with racial or ethnic group membership and does not tap into complex cultural or racial processes. Another attempt to achieve cultural competence has been to match the ethnicity and language of therapist and client. Although this is a positive effort, again it does not address the nuances of differences in class, nationality, and cultural norms that may exist between client and therapist, even when they are members of the same ethnic group. A recent exception to the absence of culture in EBT is a collection of articles (see Leong & Lopez, 2006) that integrates cultural factors into psychotherapy. In general, these articles address culture in a more sophisticated and comprehensive manner. However, none of the articles was focused on couples or family therapy, and none combined a focus on gender or feminism.

The Social Justice Perspective

A social justice perspective is a commitment to identifying and dismantling the social systems that marginalize some groups (e.g., women, people of color, poor people, immigrants) and privilege others (e.g., heterosexuals, able-bodied people). Critical consciousness (Almeida, 2003) and critical multiculturalism (Kosutic & McDowell, 2008) are other terms that have been used to describe this stance. These approaches demand accountability for the misuse of power within families and expand the boundaries of therapy beyond individual families to include communities. The "just therapy" movement challenges family members to engage in social action that holds both family members and social institutions accountable to standards of social justice.

Rhea Almeida (2003) and her colleagues (Almeida, Dolan-Del Vecchio, & Parker, 2008; Hernandez et al., 2005; Waldegrave, 1998) have been at the forefront of this paradigm shift. Their cultural context model (CCM) stands at the intersections of multiple systems: individual, family, and community. CCM begins with 8 weeks of social education in which members of families are separated into same-sex groups (culture circles) and assigned a same-sex mentor. The culture circles help clients to develop a critical consciousness regarding cultural messages about gender, race, class, sexual orientation, and power.

Female sponsors help to empower women to begin demanding more equity in their marriages. The following vignette from Almeida et al. (2008, p. 117) illustrates the model.

> Gina and Tom came into therapy after many unsuccessful attempts at couples therapy. Gina's culture circle helped her to write a letter to her husband, and to read it to him in the safe space of the broader community circle. In the letter, she talked about the ways that he had infantilized and controlled her during pregnancy, made all the important decisions in the family without consulting her, and undermined her authority with the children.

Gina also acknowledged her role in accepting Tom's assertion of power and control.

Male sponsors (men who have completed several phases of the therapy program) mentor men as they struggle to accept responsibility for their behavior. Sponsors often come from a client's cultural background, and they provide emotional support at the same time as they challenge men to abandon male dominance. John, one of Tom's sponsors, spoke in response to Tom's complaint that he did not want to be separated from his wife in a male culture circle.

At first I too was confused and angry that my wife and I were separated. I thought we were coming to therapy to get together, and then they ask us to be in separate circles. But now, having been here for 6 months, I realize that as a couple, we were unable to get enough distance from our problems to see that power and control was destroying our relationship...what's hard is we men like our marriages to be a private thing...We like it the way it is, and we don't want to change (Almeida et al., 2008, p. 116).

Tom eventually asked the men in his culture circle for help. He realized that he had adopted many of the worst of his father's power and control tactics. He eventually wrote three letters: one to his mother expressing compassion for her experiences in a difficult marriage, one to his father that included both the ways that he admired him and the negative impact of his father's controlling behaviors, and, finally, Tom wrote his accountability letter to his wife. In addition to writing letters in which they accept responsibility for their abusive behaviors, husbands are asked to make reparations to their wives. For example, a middle-class husband might cook and shop for his wife, rather than leaving these "second-shift" chores for her to shoulder alone.

The culture circles also raise the clients' consciousness about their different experiences with societal institutions. For example, culture circles might discuss the fact that White, middle-class women are more likely than are working class women of color to be able to leave their jobs early to attend school conferences (Almeida et al., 2008). Through these kinds of discussions, the CCM encourages White clients to become aware of their White privilege and their participation in perpetuating oppression in larger societal institutions. They are challenged to act on this new level of consciousness by holding the institutions accountable. Hernandez et al. (2005) described the example of an African American student who had had his car impounded as part of a university police's profiling policy. As a consequence of this discussion, a group of White men from his culture circle provided a loan that allowed him to sue the police department.

Another frame of reference for the social justice paradigm is a focus on colonialism. This term has come to have two different, but related, meanings within family therapy. Waldegrave (1998) used "colonialism" to refer to Western therapists who are not respectful of cultural practices that contrast with the individualistic, secular, and consumer-oriented norms typical of Western cultures. These therapists, ignorant or disrespectful of cultural differences, impose their own values on individuals from other cultures, which often causes harm rather than being helpful. Waldegrave characterized these practices as colonial domination of the "hearts, spirits, and minds" (p. 412) of people in need of help. Such practices make just therapy impossible.

Dolan-Del Vecchio and Lockard (2004), used a broader, more global frame of reference to define colonialism as "...an inter-group dynamic in which one group, the colonizers, holds political and economic control over another group" (p. 45). They argued that, within this context, differences are not treated respectfully, but rather are used to construct cultural myths that rationalize domination by casting the colonized groups as incompetent and, therefore, in need of domination. Dolan-Del Vecchio and Lockhard argued that most approaches to therapy support the status quo of colonialism, both by providing a diagnosis of pathology and also by failing to question the ways in which aspects of larger social systems are harmful to families. Even when the negative consequences of larger social systems are acknowledged (e.g., the feminist principle that the personal is political), most therapists do not encourage their clients to participate in social action. Dolan-Del Vecchio and Lockhard, in contrast, encourage their clients to become involved in community organizations as an integral part of their therapeutic plan.

These authors believe that therapists often misconstrue as pathology individual and family attempts to conform to dehumanizing social norms and institutions. In an innovative article, Dolan-Del Vecchio and Lockhard (2004) presented an imaginary dialogue between therapists who used a social justice perspective and a family therapy colleague who was skeptical of this approach. A brief synopsis of one clinical case that they described is presented below.

Daniel, a Korean American man, came to therapy because of increasing exhaustion and consequent isolation from his wife, Amy, caused by overwork. His company, a major U.S. corporation, had undergone repeated downsizing, so that the remaining workers were drastically overworked. Fearing that they were both clinically depressed, the couple complained of feeling hopeless and irritable toward each other. The therapist referred the couple to George, a community organizer, who had experienced many of the same challenges in his own workplace. This allowed the couple to make connections to others who could serve as social supports, and also aided them in achieving a collective, rather than an individual, understanding of the problem. The therapist suggested readings and websites that educated them about the negative consequences of corporate globalization (e.g. causing workers to accept increasingly stressful work conditions and lower wages).

George encouraged Daniel to set limits on his job in order to spend more time with his wife. Certain that this would anger his boss, Daniel updated his resume and began networking. These positive actions energized Daniel and confirmed his decision to resist the unreasonable demands of his job. He encouraged his coworkers to do the same, and developed a support group of men determined to take back their life from corporate America. After only 6 months, Daniel and his wife felt more connected to each other and were embedded in a community resistance group. The question of anti-depressant mediation that had been raised at the first session was no longer an issue. Daniel was not downsized, but rather was praised by his manager as performing effectively.

Rather than encouraging individuals and families to change in order to accommodate to toxic systems, the just therapy model, like feminist therapy, challenges individuals to change the destructive systems within which they are embedded. This approach dramatically contradicts the myth of therapeutic neutrality that feminism and postmodernism began to deconstruct. As an antidote to the myth of neutrality, Dolan-Del Vecchio and Lockhard (2004) placed accountability at the center of their therapeutic approach. McGeorge, Carlson, Erickson, and Guttormson (2006), who use a similar theoretical paradigm, have invited students in their training program to participate in social justice projects in their local community. Just as it is important for therapists to understand the subjective experiences of clients from social locations different from their own, attempts to address power and privilege in the real world provided the students with a personalized understanding of what it means to put social justice at the center of therapy. This experience increased their effectiveness as therapists.

In our view, the "just therapy" approach integrates feminism and multiculturalism in a creative manner that moves both of these perspectives from the margins to the center of family therapy. It has the most potential for dealing with the multiple oppressions that the intersectionalities perspective challenges us to address.

Conclusion and Future Directions

Although the social justice perspective in contemporary psychotherapy practice is not widespread, Aldarondo (2007) has reminded us that every major discipline in mental health (i.e., social work, psychoanalysis, counseling psychology, psychiatry, and family therapy) was founded by pioneers with a strong commitment to social justice. Over time as each discipline grew, concerns about social action gave way to issues of professional identity (e.g., profit, status, and competition with other mental health providers). The current focus on evidence-based practice has similarly been fueled by professional concerns about becoming health-care providers eligible for insurance reimbursement. Much of psychotherapy theory and practice is now based on a medical model of pathology. Consequently, social justice concerns have become virtually invisible in the mental health professions. This shift toward a concern with professional identities has resulted in a corresponding failure to integrate social justice theory and practice into our training programs.

Yet, as Aldarondo (2007) has pointed out, the social problems that inspired the mental health pioneers continue to plague US society. The gap between rich and poor is greater than it has been for 50 years; more than one-third of Americans do not have health-care insurance; poor men of color are overrepresented in prisons; women continue to earn less than men for comparable work and are overrepresented in low paying jobs; our public school system continues to fail poor children and the majority of children of color, etc. (US Department of Health and Human Services, 2001; Wilkinson, 2005). These social realities continue to be important sources of stress for individuals, families, and communities. If we are serious about promoting the mental and physical health of our clients, can we afford to continue to ignore these realities? Or must we hold ourselves accountable for our failure to address the "power differentials that are central to the production of mental dysfunction..." (Prilleltensky, Dokecki, Frieden, & Wang, 2007, p. 37)?

The movement to produce evidence as to the effectiveness of our clinical interventions is a beginning effort toward holding ourselves accountable. We have discussed the importance of including feminist and multicultural competencies in models of evidence-based practice (EBP). Qualitative research is one approach that can provide information about the subjective experiences of clients that could improve the multicultural sensitivity of therapeutic approaches. For example, the Yeshiva Fatherhood Project is a large-scale qualitative research project that has interviewed more than 500 fathers from multiple subcultures within the USA. Many of the early studies in the project were focus group interviews of Haitian American fathers, Latino fathers, and gay fathers. This bottom-up approach to research allowed many themes to emerge about the fathering identities of these groups that would not have been visible in researcher-designed, top-down, survey and interview questionnaires (Silverstein, Auerbach, & Levant, 2006). Infusing EBP research with qualitative inquiry would result in better models that address culture in its complexity.

We must also expand EBP research to address the processes that define successful psychotherapy outcomes. For example, Crane (2008) provided dramatic evidence as to the cost-effectiveness of family therapy from multiple real-world settings, such as a health maintenance organization with 180,000 users and the Medicaid system of the entire state of Kansas. He showed that even one session of family therapy decreases the number of health-care visits, especially by high utilizers. Yet, his quantitative data do not provide any suggestions as to how or why family therapy is so much more cost-effective than individual therapy. Silverstein et al. (2006) have argued that EBP research must begin to include qualitative data in order to illuminate the process variables that contribute to therapeutic change. In addition to generating interventions that are multiculturally relevant, qualitative data can illuminate which aspects of therapy were helpful for a particular client and which were not. This information has the potential to enhance the therapeutic alliance and to decrease resistance.

Finally, as Prilleltensky et al. (2007) have suggested, EBP must be expanded to include evidence that addressing social justice issues in therapy has beneficial mental health effects. From Prilleltensky's perspective, the individualistic, intrapsychic stance of cognitive and psychodynamic therapies implicitly blames the victim by decontextualizing the client's experiences. These authors have argued that "psychopolitical training" (p. 27) and consciousness raising about social injustice are equally, if not more, important than exploring a client's intrapsychic dynamics and interpersonal conflicts. Participatory action research, a model based on a collectivist approach and critical consciousness, addresses Prilleltensky's concerns. This form of qualitative research focuses specifically on empowering participants/clients to change institutions as well as themselves and their relationships (see, for example, Cammarota & Fine, 2008; Davidson, Stayner, Lambert, Smith, & Sledge, 2001; Ditrano & Silverstein, 2006). In this approach, the "action" provides the evidence that the intervention has been effective.

Thus, we join Aldarondo (2007) and his colleagues who are attempting to "rekindle the reformist spirit" (p. 5) in mental health practice. The election of Barack Obama, a biracial man, raised by White grandparents in the multicultural context of Hawaii, heralds a new phase in US history. His identities reflect an intersectionalities framework, and his campaign promises emphasized social justice. We hope that his election will change cultural norms so that future directions will integrate the intersectionalities and social justice perspectives into mainstream family therapy and psychology in the USA and beyond.

Acknowledgments Many people have been helpful to us as we prepared this chapter. We want to acknowledge Rhea Almeida and Beverly Greene who read an earlier version of the manuscript. In addition, Guillermo Bernal was helpful in addressing the state of the literature in terms of cultural competence and couples and family therapy.

References

Addis, M. E., & Mahalik, J. R. (2003). Men, masculinity, and the contexts of help-seeking. *American Psychologist, 58*, 5–14.

Aldarondo, E. (2007). Rekindling the reformist spirit in mental health professions. In E. Aldaronda (Ed.), *Advancing social justice through clinical practice* (pp. 3–18). Mahwah, NJ: Erlbaum.

Almeida, R. V. (2003). Creating collectives of liberation. In L. B. Silverstein & T. J. Goodrich (Eds.), *Feminist family therapy: Empowerment and social context* (pp. 293–306). Washington, DC: American Psychological Association.

Almeida, R. V., & Bograd, M. (1991). Sponsorship: Holding men accountable for domestic violence. *Journal of Feminist Family Therapy, 2*, 243–259.

Almeida, R. V., Dolan-Del Vecchio, K., & Parker, L. (2008). *Transformative family therapy: Just families in a just society*. New York: Pearson.

Arredondo, P., Psalti, A., & Cella, K. (1993). The woman factor in multicultural counseling. *Counseling and Human Development, 25*, 1–8.

Ault-Riche, M. (Ed.). (1986). *Women and family therapy*. Rockville, MD: AspersSystems.

Avis, J. M. (1989). Integrating gender into the family therapy curriculum. *Journal of Feminist Family Therapy, 1*, 3–26.

Baucom, D.H., Shoham, V., Mueser, K.T., Daiuto, A. D., & Stickle, T.R. (1998). Empirically supported couple and family interventions for adult mental health problems. *Journal of Consulting and Clinical Psychology, 66*, 53–88.

Bepko, C., & Johnson, T. (2000). Gay and lesbian couples in therapy: Perspectives for the contemporary family therapist. *Journal of Marital and Family Therapy, 26*, 409–419.

Bograd, M. (1984). Family systems approaches to wife battering: A feminist critique. *American Journal of Orthopsychiatry, 54*, 558–568.

Bograd, M. (Ed.). (1991). *Feminist approaches for men in family therapy*. New York: Haworth.

Bograd, M. (1999), Strengthening domestic violence theories: Intersections of race, class, sexual orientation, and gender. *Journal of Marital and Family Therapy, 25*, 275–289.

Braverman, L. (Ed.). (1988). *A guide to feminist family therapy*. New York: Harrington Park Press.

Brooks, G. R. (1991). Traditional men in marital and family therapy. In M. Bograd (Ed.), *Feminist approaches for men in family therapy* (pp. 51–74). New York: Haworth.

Brooks, G. R. (1998). *A new psychotherapy for traditional men*. San Francisco, CA: Jossey-Bass.

Brooks, G. R. (2003). Helping men embrace equality. In L. B. Silverstein & T. J. Goodrich (Eds.), *Feminist family therapy: Empowerment in social context* (pp. 163–176). Washington, DC: American Psychological Association.

Buss, D. M. (1994). *The evolution of desire*. New York: Basic Books.

Cammarota, J., & Fine, M. (Eds.). (2008). *Revolutionizing education: Youth participatory action research in motion*. New York: Routledge.

Christenson, A. (1988). Dysfunctional interaction patterns in couples. In P. Noller & M. A. Fitzpatrick (Eds.), *Perspectives on marital interaction* (pp. 31–52). Clevedon, UK: Multilingual Matters.

Christenson, A., & Heavey, C. L. (1990). Gender and social structure in the demand/withdraw pattern of marital conflict. *Journal of Personality and Social Psychology, 59*, 72–81.

Comas-Diaz, L. (1994). Latinegra: Mental health issues of African Latinas. *Journal of Feminist Family Therapy, 5*, 35–74.

Comas-Diaz, L. (2003). The Black Madonna: The psychospiritual feminism of Guadaloupe, Kali, and Monserrat. In L. B. Silverstein & T. J. Goodrich (Eds.), *Feminist family therapy: Empowerment and social context* (pp. 147–160). Washington, DC: American Psychological Association.

Comas-Diaz, L., & Greene, B. (1994). *Women of color: Integrating ethnic and gender identities in psychotherapy*. New York: Guilford.

Connolly, C. M. (2006). A feminist perspective of resilience in lesbian couples. *Journal of Feminist Family Therapy, 18*, 137–162.
Crane, D. R. (2008). The cost-effectiveness of family therapy: A summary and progress report. *Journal of family Therapy, 30*, 399–410.
Dankoski, M. E., & Deacon, S. A. (2000). Using a feminist lens in contextual therapy. *Family Process, 39*, 51–66.
Davidson, L., Stayner, D. A., Lambert, S., Smith, P., & Sledge, W. H. (2001). Phenomenological and participatory research on schizophrenia. In D. L. Tolman & M. Brydon-Miller (Eds.), *From subjects to subjectivities: A handbook of interpretive and participatory methods* (pp. 163–179). New York: NYU Press.
Deinhart, A., & Avis, J. M. (1991). Men in therapy: Exploring feminist-informed alternatives. In M. Bograd (Ed.), *Feminist approaches for men in family therapy* (pp. 25–50). New York: Haworth.
Ditrano, C., & Silverstein, L. B. (2006). Listening to parents' voices: Action research in the schools. *Professional Psychology, 37*, 359–366.
Dolan-Del Vecchio, K., & Lockard, J. (2004). Resistance to colonialism as the heart of family therapy practice. *Journal of Feminist Family Therapy, 16*, 43–66.
Eldridge, N. S., & Barrett, S. E. (2003). Biracial lesbian-led adoptive families. In L. B. Silverstein & T. J. Goodrich (Eds.), *Feminist family therapy: Empowerment and social context* (pp. 307–218). Washington, DC: American Psychological Association.
Epstein, N. B., & Baucom, D. H. (2002). *Enhanced cognitive-behavioral therapy for couples: A contextual approach.* Washington, DC: American Psychological Association.
Gilligan, C. (1982). *In a different voice: Psychological theory and women's development.* Cambridge, MA: Harvard University Press.
Goldner, V. (1985). Feminism and family therapy. *Family Process, 24*, 31–74.
Goldner, V., Penn, P., Sheinberg, M., & Walker, G. (1990). Love and violence: Gender paradoxes in volatile attachments. *Family Process, 29*, 343–364.
Goodrich, T. J. (Ed.). (1991). *Women and power: Perspectives for family therapy.* New York: Norton.
Goodrich, T. J., & Silverstein, L. B. (2005). Now you see it, now you don't: Feminist training in family therapy. *Family Process, 44*, 267–281.
Gosling, A. L., & Zangari, M. (1996). Feminist family therapy and the narrative approach: Dovetailing two frameworks. *Journal of Feminist Family Therapy, 8*, 47–65.
Gottman, J. M. (1994). *Why marriages succeed or fail.* New York: Simon & Schuster.
Gottman, J. M., & Levenson, R. W. (1988). The social psychophysiology of marriage. In P. Noller & M. A. Fitzgerald (Eds.), *Perspectives on marital interaction* (pp. 182–202). Clevedon, UK: Multilingual Matters.
Gottman, J. M., Ryan, K. D., Carrere, S., & Erly, A. M. (2002). Toward a scientifically based marital therapy. In H. A. Liddle, D. A. Santisteban, R. F. Levant, & J. H. Bray (Eds.), *Family psychology: Science-based interventions* (pp. 147–174). Washington, DC: American Psychological Association.
Green, R. J., Bettinger, M., & Zacks, E. (1996). Are lesbian couples fused and gay male couples disengaged? Questioning gender straightjackets. In J. Laird & R-J. Green (Eds.), *Lesbians and gays in couples and families* (pp. 185–230). San Francisco, CA: Jossey-Bass.
Greene, B., & Boyd-Franklin, N. (1999). African American lesbians: Issues in couples therapy. In J. Laird & R-J. Green (Eds.), *Lesbians and gays in couples and families* (pp. 251–271). San Francisco, CA: Jossey-Bass.
Guanipa, C., & Woolley, S. R. (2000). Gender biases and therapists' conceptualization of couple difficulties. *American Journal of Family Therapy, 28*, 181–192.
Halford, W. K., Kelly, A., & Markman, H. J. (1997). The concept of a healthy marriage. In W. K. Halford & H. J. Markman (Eds.), *Clinical handbook of marriage and couples interventions* (pp. 3–12). Hoboken, NJ: Wiley.
Hall, R. L., & Greene, B. (1994) Cultural competence in feminist family therapy: An ethical mandate. *Journal of Feminist Family Therapy, 6*(3), 5–28.
Hall, R. L., & Greene, B. (2002). Not any one thing: The complex legacy of social class on African American lesbian relationships. *Journal of Lesbian Studies, 6*, 65–74.
Hall, R. L., & Greene, B. (2003). Contemporary African American families. In L. B. Silverstein & T. G. Goodrich (Eds.), *Feminist family therapy: Empowerment in social context* (pp. 107–120). Washington, DC: American Psychological Association.
Halstead, K. (2003). Over the rainbow: The lesbian family. In L. B. Silverstein & T. G. Goodrich (Eds.), *Feminist family therapy: Empowerment in social context* (pp. 39–50). Washington, DC: American Psychological Association.
Hare-Mustin, R. (1978). A feminist approach to family therapy. *Family Process, 17*, 181–194.
Hare-Mustin, R., & Goodrick, T. J. (1991, March). *Feel-good feminism.* Paper presented at the annual meeting of the family therapy network, Washington, DC.

Heavey, C. L., Layne, C., & Christenson, A. (1993). Gender and conflict structure in marital interaction: A replication and extension. *Journal of Consulting and Clinical Psychology, 61*, 16–27.

Hernandez, P., Almeida, R., & Dolan-DelVecchio, K. (2005). Critical consciousness, accountability, and empowerment: Key processes for helping families heal. *Family Process, 44*, 104–119.

Hyde, J. S. (2005). The gender similarities hypothesis. *American Psychologist, 60*, 581–592.

Inclan, J. (2003). Class, culture, and gender in immigrant families. In L. B. Silverstein & T. J. Goodrich (Eds.), *Feminist family therapy: Empowerment in social context* (pp. 333–347). Washington, DC: American Psychological Association.

Istar, A. (1996). Couples assessment: Identifying and intervening in domestic violence in lesbian relationships. *Journal of Gay & Lesbian Social Services, 4*(1), 93–106.

Jacobson, N. S. (1983). Beyond empiricism: The politics of marital therapy. *American Journal of Family Therapy, 11*, 11–24.

Julien, D., Arellano, C., & Turgeon, L. (1997). Gender issues in heterosexual, gay, and lesbian couples. In W. K. Halford & H. J. Markman (Eds.), *Clinical handbook of marriage and couples interventions* (pp. 107–127). Hoboken, NJ: Wiley.

Kosutic, I., & McDowell, T. (2008). Diversity and social justice issues in family therapy literature: A decade review. *Journal of Feminist Family Therapy, 20*, 142–165.

Krestan, J. A., & Bepko, C. S. (1980). The problem of fusion in the lesbian relationship. *Family Process, 19*, 277–389.

Laird, J., & Green, R-J. (Eds.). (1996). *Lesbian and gays in couples and families*. San Francisco, CA: Jossey-Bass.

Leong, F. T. L., & Lopez, S. (2006). Introduction [to the special issue]. *Psychotherapy, 43*, 278–379.

Leslie, L. A., & Clossick, M. L. (1992). Changing set: Teaching family therapy from a feminist perspective. *Family Relations, 41*, 256–263.

Leslie, L. A., & Morton, G. (2001). Family therapy's response to family diversity: Looking back, looking forward. *Journal of Family Issues, 22*, 904–921.

Levant, R. F., & Pollack, W. S. (Eds.). (1995) *A new psychology of men*. New York: Basic Books.

Levant, R. F., & Silverstein, L. B. (2001). Integrating gender and family systems theories: The both/and approach to treating a post-modern couples. In S. H. McDaniel, D-D. Lusterman, & C. L. Philpot (Eds.), *Casebook for integrating family therapy: An ecosystemic approach* (pp. 245–252). Washington, DC: American Psychological Association.

Levant, R. F., & Silverstein, L. B. (2005). How well do empirically supported therapies and "treatment as usual" address gender as a dimension of diversity? In J. C. Norcross, L. E. Beutler, & R. F. Levant (Eds.), *Evidence-based practices in mental health: Debate and dialogue on the fundamental questions* (pp. 338–345). Washington, DC: American Psychological Association.

MacGeorge, E. L., Graves, A. R., Feng, B., Gillihan, S. J., & Burleson, B. R. (2004). The myth of gender cultures: Similarities outweigh differences in men's and women's provision of and responses to supportive communication. *Sex Roles, A Journal of Research, 50*, 143–175.

McDaniel, S. H., & Cole-Kelly, K. (2003). Gender, couples, and illness: A feminist analysis of medical family therapy. In L. B. Silverstein & T. J. Goodrich (Eds.), *Feminist family therapy: Empowerment in social context* (pp. 267–280). Washington, DC: American Psychological Association.

McGeorge, C. R., Carlson, T. S., Erickson, M. J., & Guttormson, H. E. (2006). Creating and evaluating a feminist-informed social justice couples and family therapy training model. *Journal of Feminist Family Therapy, 18*(3), 1–36.

McGoldrick, M. (1994). Culture, class, race, and gender. *Human Systems: The Journal of Systemic Consultation and Management, 5*, 131–153.

McGoldrick, M. (Ed.). (1996). *Revisioning family therapy: Race, culture, and gender in clinical practice* (2nd ed.). New York: Norton.

McGoldrick, M., Anderson, C., & Walsh, F. (Eds.). (1989). *Women in families: A framework for family therapy*. New York: Norton.

McGoldrick, M., Pearce, J. K., & Giordano, J. (Eds.). (1982). *Ethnicity and family therapy*. New York: Guilford.

Merlis, S. R., & Linville, D. (2006). Exploring a community's response to lesbian domestic violence through the voices of providers: A qualitative study. *Journal of Feminist Family Therapy, 18*(1/2), 97–136.

Mittal, M., & Wieling, E. (2004). The influence of therapists' ethnicity on the practice of feminist family therapy: A pilot study. *Journal of Feminist Family Therapy, 16*, 1–24.

Mize, L. K. (2003). Relationships between women in families: Voices of chivalry. In L. B. Silverstein & T. J. Goodrich (Eds.), *Feminist family therapy: Empowerment in social context* (pp. 121–134). Washington, DC: American Psychological Association.

Murphy, C. M., & Meyer, S. L. (1991). Gender, power, and violence in marriage. *Behavior Therapist, 14*, 95–100.

Napier, A. Y. (1978). The rejection-intrusion pattern: A central family dynamic. *Journal of Marriage and Family Counseling, 4*, 5–12.

Newberry, A. M., Alexander, J. F., & Turner, C. W. (1991). Gender as a process variable in family therapy. *Journal of Family Psychology, 5*, 158–175.

Nutt, R. L. (2003). Loyalty to family of origin. In L. B. Silverstein & T. J. Goodrich (Eds.), *Feminist family therapy: Empowerment in social context* (pp. 79–90). Washington, DC: American Psychological Association.

O'Neil, J. M. (2008). Summarizing 25 years of research on men's gender-role conflict using the Gender-Role Conflict Scale: New research paradigms and clinical implications. *Counseling Psychologist, 36*, 358–455.

O'Neil, J. M., & Harway, M. (Eds.). (1999). *New perspectives on men's violence against women.* Newbury Park, CA: Sage.

Perlesz, A., & McNair, R. (2004). Lesbian parenting: Insiders' voices. *Australian and New Zealand Journal of Family Therapy, 25*, 129–140.

Pewewardy, N. (2004). The political is personal: The essential obligation of White feminist family therapists to deconstruct White privilege. *Journal of Feminist Family Therapy, 16*, 53–67.

Philpot, C. L., Brooks, G. R., Lusterman, D. D., & Nutt, R. L. (Eds.). (1997). *Bridging separate gender worlds: Why men and women clash and how therapists can bring them together.* Washington, DC: American Psychological Association.

Pinderhughes, E. (1986). Minority women: A nodal position in the functioning of the social system. In M. Ault-Riche (Ed.), *Women and family therapy* (pp. 51–63). Rockville, MD: Aspen Systems.

Pipher, M. (1994). *Revising Ophelia.* New York: Putnam.

Pleck, J. H. (1995). The gender role strain paradigm: An update. In R. F. Levant & W. S. Pollack (Eds.), *The new psychology of men* (pp. 11–32). New York: Basic Books.

Prilleltensky, I., Dokecki, P., Frieden, G., & Wang, V. O. (2007). Counseling for wellness and justice: Foundations and ethical dilemmas. In E. Aldarondo (Ed.), *Advancing social justice through clinical practice* (pp. 19–42). Mahwah, NJ: Erlbaum.

Prouty, A. M., & Bermudez, J. M. (1999). Experiencing multiconsciousness: A feminist model for therapy. *Journal of Feminist Family Therapy, 11*, 19–39.

Prouty-Lyness, A. M. (Ed.). (2003). *Feminist perspectives in medical family therapy.* New York: Haworth.

Reid, P. T. (2002). Multicultural psychology: Bringing together gender and ethnicity. *Cultural Diversity and Ethnic Minority Psychology, 8*, 103–114.

Rice, J. K. (2003). "I can't go back": Divorce as adaptive resistance. In L. B. Silverstein & T. J. Goodrich (Eds.), *Feminist family therapy: Empowerment and social context* (pp. 51–64). Washington, DC: American Psychological Association.

Ristock, J. L. (2003). Exploring the dynamics of abusive lesbian relationships: Preliminary analysis of a multisite qualitative study. *American Journal of Community Psychology, 31*, 329–341.

Roth, S. A. (1985). Psychotherapy with lesbian couples: Individual issues, female socialization, and the social context. *Journal of Marital and Family Therapy, 11*, 273–286.

Schacher, S., Auerbach, C. F., & Silverstein, L. B. (2005). Gay fathers: Expanding the possibilities for all of us. *Journal of GLBT Family Studies, 1*(3), 31–52.

Sexton, T. L., Alexander, J. F., & Mease, A. L. (2004). Levels of evidence for the models and mechanisms of therapeutic change in family and couple therapy. In M. J. Lambert (Ed.), *Bergin and Garfield's handbook of psychotherapy and behavior change* (pp. 590–646). New York: Wiley.

Shields, C. G., & McDaniel, S. (1992). Process differences between male and female therapists in a first family interview. *Journal of Marital and Family Therapy, 18*, 143–151.

Silverstein, L. B. (1999). The evolutionary origins of male violence. In J. M. O'Neil & M. Harway (Eds.), *New perspectives on men's violence against women* (pp. 61–84). Newbury Park, CA: Sage.

Silverstein, L. B. (2003). Classic texts and early critiques. In L. B. Silverstein & T. J. Goodrich (Eds.), *Feminist family therapy: Empowerment and social context* (pp. 17–36). Washington, DC: American Psychological Association.

Silverstein, L. B. (2005a). Integrating feminism and multiculturalism: Scientific fact or science fiction? *Professional Psychology, 36*, 21–28.

Silverstein, L. B. (2005b). Bowen family systems theory as family therapy. In M. Harway (Ed.), *Handbook of couples therapy* (pp. 103–118). New York: Wiley.

Silverstein, L. B., Auerbach, C. F., & Levant, R. F. (2006). Using qualitative research to enhance clinical practice. *Professional Psychology, 37*, 351–358.

Silverstein, L. B., & Goodrich, T. G. (Eds.). (2003). *Feminist family therapy: Empowerment and social context.* Washington, DC: American Psychological Association.

Speziale, B., & Ring, C. (2006). Intimate violence among lesbian couples: Emerging data and critical needs. *Journal of Feminist Family Therapy, 18*(1/2), 85–96.

Sue, D. W. (2005). Ethnic minority populations have been neglected by evidence-based practices. In J. C. Norcross, L. E. Beutler, & R. F. Levant (Eds.), *Evidence-based practices in mental health: Debate and dialogue on the fundamental questions* (pp. 329–337). Washington, DC: American Psychological Association.

Tannen, D. (1991.) *You just don't understand: Women and men in conversation.* New York: Ballantine Books.

Turgeon, L. (1995). *Marital power, demand/withdrawal pattern, and marital adjustment.* Unpublished doctoral dissertation, University of Laval, Canada, QC.

U.S. Department of Health and Human Services. (2001). *Mental health: Culture, race, and ethnicity [A supplement to mental health: A report of the Surgeon General].* Rockville, MD: U.S. Department of Health and Human Services, Substance Abuse and Mental Health Services Administration, Center for Mental Health Services.

Waldegrave, C. (1998). The challenges of culture to psychology and postmodern thinking. In M. McGoldrick (Ed.), *Revisioning family therapy: Race, culture, and gender in clinical practice* (2nd ed., pp. 404–413). New York: Norton.

Walters, M., Carter, B., Papp, P., & Silverstein, O. (1988). *The invisible web: Gender patterns in family relationships.* New York: Guilford.

Watts-Jones, D. (1997). Toward an African American genogram. *Family Process, 36*, 375–383.

Watzlawick, P. (1978). *The language of change.* New York: Basic Books.

Weiss, R. L., & Heyman, R. E. (1997). A clinical-research overview of couples interactions. In W. K. Halford & H. J. Markman (Eds.), *Clinical handbook of marriage and couples interventions* (pp. 13–42). Hoboken, NJ: Wiley.

West, C. M. (2002). Lesbian intimate partner violence: Prevalence and dynamics. *Journal of Lesbian Studies, 6*, 121–127.

Wieling, E., & Rastogi, M. (2003). Voices of marriage and family therapists of color: An exploratory survey. *Journal of Feminist Family Therapy, 15*, 1–20.

Wilkinson, R. G. (2005). *The impact of inequality: How to make sicker societies healthier.* New York: New Press.

Part XI
Social Psychology

Chapter 12
Gender, Peer Relations, and Intimate Romantic Relationships

Tara C. Marshall

It is popularly believed, by researchers and laypersons alike, that men are from Mars and women are from Venus. When it comes to relationships, however, men and women are more similar than they are different (Burn, 1996; Hyde, 2005). Both sexes develop attachments to close others throughout the life span (Bowlby, 1980; Hazan & Shaver, 1987), and both are largely dependent on relationships for their psychological well-being (Berscheid & Reis, 1998). Nonetheless, researchers and the media tend to focus on gender differences, however small, at the expense of similarities.

In this chapter, I explore the ways that social contexts influence the degree of gender difference and similarity in the experience of close relationships. A basic assumption herein is that gender is a social construction – enacted through interaction with peers and romantic partners and reinforced by the larger sociocultural context. As such, I examine gender influences in relationships by referring to socio-ecological theories or those that focus on the social contexts in which people develop and live, with particular emphasis on social role theory, social structural theory, script theory, and ecological developmental theory. These theories are contrasted with evolutionary accounts, which often widen the gulf between the sexes by emphasizing innate differences rather than the ways that such differences may be socially constructed and culturally transmitted. I first examine the influence of gender within same-sex and cross-sex friendships, then shift the focus to the different phases of a romantic relationship – coming together, relational maintenance, and coming apart. Finally, I discuss the relational and sexual consequences of gender-role traditionalism and end with avenues for future research.

Gender and Peer Relations

Same-Sex Friendships

There tend to be larger differences within than between the sexes in their friendships (Nardi, 1992; O'Connor, 1992), yet it is commonly observed that male friends interact side-by-side and female friends face-to-face (Buss & Malamuth, 1996; Ridgeway & Smith-Lovis, 1999; Wellman & Frank, 2001). For one, men usually have a larger number of same-sex friends, but they tend to experience less emotional intimacy in their friendships than women do in theirs (Claes, 1992). This can be traced, at least in part, to the influence of the traditional masculine role, which encourages activity-based friendships (Pleck, 1976), disparages feminine traits (Thompson & Pleck, 1986), and

T.C. Marshall (✉)
Brunel University, Kingston Ln, Uxbridge, UK

enforces masculinity and heterosexuality through pervasive homophobia (Kimmel, 1997). In particular, the masculine gender role may inhibit two fundamental aspects of intimacy: self-disclosure and responsiveness.

Intimacy is conceptualized by Reis and Shaver (1988) as a reciprocal process of partners' self-disclosures and responsiveness that results in each individual feeling understood, validated, and cared for. Self-disclosure refers to the sharing of personal information (Parks & Floyd, 1996), whereas responsiveness refers to the support, warmth, interest, and attention displayed by others (Reis, Clark, & Holmes, 2004). As such, one reason why women may be more intimate with same-sex friends than men are is because women tend to be more self-disclosing (Dindia & Allen, 1992; Reis, Senchak, & Solomon, 1985) and responsive (Hargie, Tourish, & Curtis, 2001). Female friends are more likely to share feelings and to talk about other people (Boneva, Kraut, & Frohlich, 2001), whereas male friends are more likely to engage in shared activities (Caldwell & Peplau, 1982) and to discuss relatively impersonal topics such as sports, politics, or business (Clark, 1998). Youniss and Smollar (1985) found that adolescent girls preferred "just talking" with same-sex friends more than did boys; in fact, 66% of girls reported having same-sex friendships that involved intimate self-disclosure, whereas 60% of boys reported that they did not have any friendships that involved intimate self-disclosure. Men also tend to be instrumental and goal-oriented in their friendships; women, on the other hand, tend to be expressive (Fox, Gibbs, & Auerbach, 1985) and to offer emotional support to friends in distress (Clark, 1998). Women's expressive and sensitive behavior is characteristic of the behavior of lower status individuals (Snodgrass, 1985). That women's friendships are more likely to exchange emotional support, and men's the exchange of goods and services (Perlman & Fehr, 1987), may thus reflect an accommodation to roles that differ in power and status (Eagly & Wood, 1999).

Women's lesser access to power and resources may also constrain the contexts available for developing friendships (O'Connor, 1992). Traditionally, women's housework and childcare responsibilities meant that they had less time and money to pursue friendships through shared activities outside the home, and, as such, women's conversation with same-sex friends tended to focus on domestic issues, especially those involving personal relationships. Along these lines, Walker (1994) found that working class men, who also lack resources, tend to socialize at home and, in turn, often discuss people and relationships. Furthermore, women who work in white-collar, male-dominated professions report less emotional intimacy in their friendships, similar to middle-class men.

Social learning theories suggest that boys are rewarded for pursuing competitive relationships with other boys, whereas girls are rewarded for pursuing cooperative, intimate friendships. According to Maccoby (1990), for example, male peer groups in early development promote constricting interactive styles based on one-upmanship and establishing dominance hierarchies that inhibit emotional closeness. Female peer groups, on the other hand, promote enabling interactive styles based on cooperation and mutual support. Other perspectives that emphasize context suggest that boys may internalize the homophobic message, still prevalent at the sociocultural level, that excessive closeness with another boy threatens their masculinity (Holland, Ramazanoglu, Sharpe, & Thomson, 1994; Wong & Csikszentmihalyi, 1991).

From an evolutionary perspective, men who successfully compete with other men increase their social dominance and, in turn, are more likely to be chosen by women as sexual partners (Fischer & Mosquera, 2001). Through this process of sexual selection over the course of human history, men have evolved to be competitive and non-intimate with other men. Furthermore, polygynous or extended family arrangements, which compelled women to work together while men procured goods for the family, meant that it was in women's best interests to develop cooperative and intimate relationships with each other.

Whether based on evolutionary or socio-ecological perspectives, research in this area has been criticized for trading on gender stereotypes – casting intimacy as feminine and action as masculine – and overlooking that some of the gender differences in friendships are actually quite small (Ridgeway & Smith-Lovis, 1999) or an artifact of research design. For example, Walker (1994) found that when people were asked global questions about their friendships, they tended to respond in a gender-stereotypical way, but when asked questions about specific friendships, gender differences were small. In fact, both men and women reported engaging in self-disclosure and shared activities with specific friends. Moreover, in Dindia and Allen's (1992) meta-analysis, gender differences in self-disclosure were small ($d = 0.18$). The effect size differed according to the gender composition of the interactants; it ranged from $d = 0.31$ for same-sex interactions to $d = 0.08$ for mixed-sex interactions. That the magnitude of the gender difference varied according to context lends support to social constructivist accounts of the role of gender in close relationships. A final criticism of research in this area is that some studies might be considered "gynocentric," that is, conceptualizations of same-sex intimacy may be based on feminine norms, such that intimacy is conflated with self-disclosure. Men's activity-based friendships arguably may be as intimate in their own way as women's (Wood & Inman, 1993).

Cross-Sex Friendships

This type of relationship is often ignored by researchers, perhaps because cross-sex friendship scripts tend to be less defined than those for heterosexual romantic relationships and are often complicated by sexual tension (O'Meara, 1989). In one study, 58% of participants reported feeling at least some degree of attraction to a cross-sex friend (Kaplan & Keys, 1997). Although some people report feeling uncomfortable with this sexual tension (Bell, 1981; Sapadin, 1988), others think that it adds excitement to the friendship (Rubin, 1985). Cross-sex friends often engage in flirtatious behavior (Egland, Spitzberg, & Zormeier, 1996; Fuiman, Yarab, & Sensibaugh, 1997), but some may also strive to keep the relationship platonic to safeguard it against complications from sexual involvement (Messman, Canary, & Hause, 2000). Nonetheless, Afifi and Faulkner (2000) found that 51% of heterosexual college students reported having engaged in sexual activity with an otherwise platonic cross-sex friend. More than one-half of these participants reported that the friendship did not develop into a romantic relationship, and 67% indicated that sexual activity actually increased the quality of the cross-sex friendship. These results, then, do not support the commonly held belief that sexual activity is injurious for cross-sex friendships; if anything, they point to one of the advantages of cross-sex friends. In a study of undergraduates involved in "friends with benefits" relationships, Puentes, Knox, and Zusman (2008) showed that men were more likely to emphasize the sexual benefits and women were more likely to emphasize the friendship. Future researchers should clarify whether these findings generalize to the same-sex friendships of lesbians and gay men.

One of the reasons why sexual tension may figure prominently in cross-sex friendships is because people tend to misperceive sexual interest in cross-sex interactions. Abbey (1982) found that when women and men surreptitiously observed the interactions of a cross-sex pair in a laboratory, men tended to overestimate the sexual interest of the female actor, whereas women underestimated the sexual interest of the male actor. These findings have been replicated by others (Edmondson & Conger, 1995; Harnish, Abbey, & DeBono, 1990). Note that when a cross-sex friend arouses a strong degree of sexual interest, men and women are equally prone to overestimating the friend's sexual (but not romantic) interest (Koenig, Kirkpatrick, & Ketelaar, 2007). Thus, women and men may both project their own level of interest onto a highly desirable cross-sex friend, which suggests that women may only underperceive the sexual interest of men whom they do not find sexually attractive.

Koenig et al. (2007) argued from an evolutionary perspective that it is functional for both men and women to overperceive interest in an attractive target so as to maximize valuable mating opportunities. Yet misperception of sexual interest may damage a cross-sex friendship, or worse: 15% of sexual assaults take place within cross-sex friendships (Abbey, McAuslan, & Ross, 1998), and misperception is a contributing factor to sexual harassment (Johnson, Stockdale, & Saal, 1991). Furthermore, men who are higher in hostile masculinity, are more likely to engage in impersonal sex, and drink more heavily in dating and sexual situations are more prone to misinterpreting a woman's friendliness as sexual interest (Jacques-Tiura, Abbey, Parkhill, & Zawacki, 2007). Clearly, then, misperception may have negative consequences.

Finally, sexual tension tends to be less present in cross-sex friendships in later life (Rawlins, 1992), and cross-sex friendships are less common in older adults than in younger adults (Fox et al., 1985). Young adults report having, on average, three close friends of the other sex (Buhrke & Fuqua, 1987), whereas older adults have fewer or none. Cross-sex friendships were not encouraged in older generations; moreover, marriage may make it more difficult to pursue and maintain these friendships (Monsour, 2002). From an evolutionary perspective, interest in cross-sex friendships may decline once women and men are past their peak reproductive years. In sum, cross-sex friendships offer many of the expressive and instrumental benefits of same-sex friendships, but are also often overlaid with sexual tension.

Gender and Intimate Romantic Relationships

Despite social movements in the 20th century that led to increased gender equality, gender roles continue to be strongly differentiated in intimate romantic relationships. In patriarchal systems, heterosexual roles tend to be complementary: Men are expected to be agentic, lustful, and sexually active, whereas women are expected to be passive, low in desire, and sexually restricted (Tolman, Striepe, & Harmon, 2003). These roles, usually viewed as normative and often justified by biological imperatives, tend to reinforce the gender imbalance in sexual power. In the following sections, I examine these issues in light of Knapp's (1984) three phases of a romantic relationship (i.e., coming together, maintenance, and coming apart) and interpret the body of findings in terms of evolutionary and socio-ecological perspectives.

Phase I: Coming Together

Mate Preferences

Small but reliable gender differences in mate preferences emerge across studies and samples. In one of the most well-known studies in this area, Buss (1989) found that, across 37 cultures, men were more likely to value physical attractiveness in female partners, whereas women were more likely to value status and earning capacity in male partners. Other studies have revealed similar findings: American men across ethnic groups tend to be less flexible than women are in their desire for an attractive mate (South, 1991), whereas women tend to be less flexible than men are when it comes to a partner's status, resources, warmth, and trustworthiness (Fletcher, Tither, O'Loughlin, Friesen, & Overall, 2004). Women tend to marry up to gain social status, whereas men tend to marry down in terms of a partner's education or income, but not their attractiveness (South, 1991). In polygynous societies, women usually prefer to be the co-wife of a man with resources and status rather than the only wife of a lower status man (Mulder, 1990). Even in societies where polygyny is prohibited, women prefer to engage in sexual activity with higher status men (Kanazawa, 2003; Lalumiere, Seto, & Quinsey, 1995). Women place more emphasis than both gay and straight men do on a partner's age, education, and income (Kurdek & Schmitt, 1987) and less emphasis on physical appearance. A study of personal ads placed by gay and straight women and men showed that gay men emphasized a mate's physical attractiveness the most and lesbians emphasized it the least (Gonzales & Meyers, 1993). The neuroscience of men's preference for attractive mates was investigated in a recent fMRI study (Cloutier, Heatherton, Whalen, & Kelley, 2008), which revealed that men, but not women, showed greater activation in the orbitofrontal cortex (a brain area involved in processing the reward value of a stimulus) when viewing attractive rather than unattractive faces of the other sex. Another study showed that men expended more effort to view beautiful female than male faces, whereas women spent an equal amount of effort to view beautiful male and female faces (Levy et al., 2008), findings that suggest that the female faces are particularly rewarding for men. Men's preference for physically attractive women and women's preference for high-status men have been explained by both evolutionary and socio-ecological theories.

Mate Preferences: Evolutionary Theory

From an evolutionary perspective, gender differences in mate preferences evolved to maximize reproduction and the survival of humanity. Pivotal to this perspective is the concept of parental investment – the amount of time and energy that parents invest in reproduction and child care (Trivers, 1972). Although many men do invest heavily in their offspring, their minimum level of parental investment is much lower than that of women (Symons, 1979). Men need only contribute sperm, whereas women must invest 9 months of pregnancy and usually a period of lactation. During this time, men may potentially produce children with other partners, whereas women can typically produce only one child. Because women invest so heavily in the few infants they are capable of bearing, making a mistake in mate choice is costly; thus, it is adaptive for women to be particularly discriminating about the quality of their partners. For men, on the other hand, it is adaptive to be less choosy when selecting a short-term partner so that they may reproduce with as many women as possible (Kenrick, Sadalla, Groth, & Trost, 1990).

Mate preferences not only vary between the sexes but also within each sex. Sexual strategies theory (SST) was introduced by Buss and Schmitt (1993) to account for men's and women's repertoire of short- and long-term mating strategies. Short-term mating tends to be brief and non-exclusive (e.g., a one-night stand or an extramarital fling), whereas long-term mating involves pairbonding and the investment of emotion and resources over an extended period of time (Schmitt, 2005). Short-term strategies can have evolutionary advantages for both sexes under certain conditions (Buss & Schmitt, 1993). It is adaptive for women to pursue short-term strategies insofar as they seek high genetic fitness in men (as indexed by such markers as physical attractiveness and masculinity) that they may not be able to obtain from a long-term partner. Women with short-term strategies are mostly concerned with the quality rather than with the quantity of men with whom they mate (Gangestad & Thornhill, 1997). Conversely, women with long-term strategies are more likely to look for markers of earning capacity (e.g., high income) and emotional commitment because these signify that a man will be able and willing to provide for her and her offspring over the long term (Kruger, Fisher, & Jobling, 2003).

Men pursuing short-term mating, on the other hand, tend to seek greater sexual variety (Schmitt, Shackelford, Duntley, Tooke, & Buss, 2001) and prefer mates who will quickly engage in sexual activity (Buss & Schmitt, 1993) to ensure maximal reproduction. Because of men's lower parental investment, they tend to be, on average, more disposed than women toward short-term mating

(Schmitt, 2005). Indeed, Schmitt et al. (2001) found that men indicated a greater preference than women did for briefer relationships, sexual variety, a larger number of partners, and less time to elapse before sexual activity. As for men's long-term strategies, they tend to emphasize a partner's appearance, age, and fidelity more so than do women's long-term strategies (Buss, 1989). Overall, mating strategies and choices tend to reflect a trade-off between two types of evolutionary benefits: a partner with genetic fitness or a partner with high parental investment (Gangestad & Simpson, 2000).

The predictions of SST have been supported across diverse cultural samples (Schmitt et al., 2003) and with different research methodologies. For example, some studies have presented women with descriptions of "nice guys" and "jerks" and observed which type of man they prefer. "Nice guys" are described as men whose stereotypic feminine or androgynous traits (e.g., agreeable, attentive, gentle, altruistic) suggest that they would be good long-term partners, and "jerks" are described as men whose stereotypic masculine traits (e.g., strong, confident, outgoing, sexual, dominant) suggest that they would be effective short-term partners (Herold & Milhausen, 1999; McDaniel, 2005). In support of SST, Herold and Milhausen (1999) found that more than one-half of women said that they would rather date a nice guy than a jerk. This was particularly true for women who placed less emphasis on sex, had fewer sexual partners, and were less tolerant of men who had had many partners – women who, presumably, were more oriented toward long-term mating. Similarly, McDaniel (2005) found that women only preferred jerks for low-commitment, short-term dating; women who wanted a committed relationship preferred "nice guys." In line with these findings, Kruger (2006) found that, when women were presented with male faces that had been masculinized or feminized, 66% indicated that they preferred the masculinized face for short-term, extra-pair copulations and 63% chose the feminized face for marriage.

Sexual strategies theory has also received support from research on changes in women's mate preferences across the ovulatory cycle. When women with natural menstrual cycles are most fertile (in the late follicular phase, just before ovulation; Regan, 1996) they tend to report greater sexual desire (Pawlowski, 1999; Wood, 1994), sexual activity (Gangestad, Thornhill, & Carve, 2002), and short-term mating behavior, such as extra-pair flirtation (Haselton & Gangestad, 2006). They also prefer men who possess more masculine traits, which may be considered proxies for higher levels of circulating testosterone (Penton-Voak & Chen, 2004). For example, women at peak fertility tend to prefer men with more masculine faces and bodies (Fink & Penton-Voak, 2002; Gangestad, Garver-Apgar, Simpson, & Cousins, 2007; Little, Jones, & Burriss, 2007), men with deeper voices (Feinberg et al., 2006), and the smell of men with more symmetrical faces (Thornhill et al., 2003). Collectively, these findings suggest that women are more short-term-oriented when conception risk is highest and are most attracted to men whose physical characteristics signal virility and good genetic quality to pass on to offspring (Thornhill & Gangestad, 2006). Although it would seem more adaptive for women to seek long-term partners during peak fertility (i.e., men who would invest in the child should pregnancy occur), women are more likely to favor a long-term strategy during menstruation. At this time, when pregnancy is least likely to occur, women tend to prefer more feminine-looking men (Fink & Penton-Voak, 2002) who are perceived to possess traits associated with fidelity, trustworthiness, and willingness to invest in partners and children. That women may seek masculine men to maximize the genetic fitness of their offspring and feminine men for parental investment may mean that cuckoldry is more common than many people would like to believe. Indeed, some researchers argue that women have engaged in extra-pair copulation throughout evolutionary history and, in response, men's sperm evolved to compete effectively with other men's sperm to fertilize a woman's ova (Shackelford & Goetz, 2007).

Not all of the findings that link mate preferences to ovulatory shifts support sexual strategies theory, however. Although regularly ovulating heterosexual women are indeed faster at categorizing male than female faces at ovulation than at menstruation, women on the birth control pill, who are not fertile, perform similarly to the regularly ovulating women (Johnston, Arden, Macrae, & Grace, 2003). That sexual desire tends to be highest at ovulation (Burleson, Trevathan, & Gregory, 2002; Regan, 1996) suggests that sexual relevance, rather than conception risk alone, may orient women at mid-cycle to indicators of masculinity. To examine this possibility, Brinsmead-Stockham, Johnston, Miles, and Macrae (2008) examined sensitivity to faces in ovulating lesbians, who report the same increase in sexual desire at this point in the menstrual cycle as do heterosexual women. Consistent with a sexual desire rather than conception risk explanation, lesbians were faster to identify female faces than male faces at high fertility than at low fertility. In fact, their identification of male faces did not fluctuate across the menstrual cycle. Contrary to evolutionary arguments, then, women at peak fertility were more sensitive to information that was sexually relevant but not reproductively relevant.

The methods and results of conventional mate preference research were recently challenged by Eastwick and Finkel (2008). They argued that gender differences in mate preferences tend to be found in controlled studies where people explicitly state their mate preferences on questionnaires or look at photos, but not in real-life settings. Indeed, they found that when participants engaged in a speed dating paradigm, ideal mate preferences, stated before the speed dating event, did not predict real-life partner preferences after the event. Thus, even though men stressed physical attractiveness in their ideal preferences, and women stressed earning capacity, they did not report heightened interest in partners who fulfilled these ideals in their post-speed dating evaluations. The authors argued that this disconnect between explicit and implicit mate preferences raises a serious limitation of conventional mate preference research, which tends to focus on explicit mate preferences. Along these lines, the real-life paradigm used in the classic study by Walster, Aronson, Abrahams, and Rottman (1966) – in which female and male college students were randomly paired in the laboratory and then rated how much they liked each other – did not show any gender differences in mate preferences post-event. For women and men alike, the only thing that predicted how much participants liked each other was physical attractiveness.

As a final caveat, in many studies that test hypotheses derived from evolutionary theory, biological sex is conflated with gender. For example, Schmitt et al. (2001) did not include any measures of gender traits in their studies, such as the Bem Sex Role Inventory (Bem, 1974), so it is not possible to establish whether simply being male or possessing stereotypically masculine gender traits was most responsible for men's increased desire for sexual variety. It cannot be ruled out that women who possess stereotypically masculine gender traits also desire greater sexual variety. These limitations suggest the importance of considering alternative accounts of gender differences in mate preferences.

Mate Preferences: Socio-ecological Theories

In contrast to evolutionary perspectives, socio-ecological theories maintain that mate preferences are not innate, but are learned at early ages through influences from the media, family, peers, school, or other important figures (Downs & Harrison, 1985; Trepanier & Romatowski, 1985) and may change in response to contextual stimuli. One way to conceptualize these influential contexts is with ecological developmental theory (Bronfenbrenner, 1979), which places the individual at the center of several concentric circles that represent increasingly distal social influences. Following the basic framework of Tolman et al. (2003), who examined the development of girls' healthy sexuality from this ecological viewpoint, the first, inner circle represents the individual's own self, the second circle represents influences from romantic relationships, the third circle refers to social relationships (peers and family), and the fourth, outermost circle represents the sociocultural–sociopolitical context. In the following sections I examine mate preferences in light of the sociocultural context, and in a later section I discuss the dyadic and social context of relationship initiation.

From a sociocultural perspective, the robust gender differences in mate preferences that have emerged across studies and cultures better reflect the internalization of sociocultural ideals than the expression of evolved, innate preferences. It is particularly noteworthy that, in Buss's study (1989), gender differences in mate preferences – though statistically significant in almost all cultures – were still smaller than were the cultural differences. This variability in the magnitude of the gender differences (larger in traditional cultures and smaller in modern/egalitarian cultures) suggests that mate preferences must be at least somewhat shaped by the sociocultural context.

Accordingly, Eagly and Wood (1999) reinterpreted Buss's (1989) findings in terms of social structural theory. This theory claims that gender differences derive not from evolved dispositions but rather from the division of labor by sex, which creates different role expectations for men and women. Psychological differences between the sexes, then, simply reflect accommodations to the different opportunities and restrictions afforded by traditional gender roles. Thus, men may prefer younger women as mates because having a (presumably) less experienced partner allows men to maintain the more powerful role to which they have accommodated. Women, on the other hand, may prefer men with economic resources because women's less powerful roles mean that they are dependent on a wealthier mate to provide for themselves and their children. In support of this theory, Eagly and Wood (1999) found that, as gender equality increased in a society, the tendency for women to emphasize a mate's earning capacity decreased, as did men's emphasis on a mate's youth and domestic skills.

Cultural variability in mate preferences itself speaks to the influence of the sociocultural context. For example, in cultures where arranged marriage is normative, an individual's mate preferences may be overridden by the wishes of one's parents and family – a point that is often overlooked by evolutionary approaches (Buunk, Park, & Dubbs, 2008). In fact, free choice in mate selection is historically recent and uncommon in most cultures. Even when marriages are not strictly arranged, family approval continues to exert influence in mate selection and relationship termination in many cultures (Chang & Chan, 2007; MacDonald & Jessica, 2006). In south Asian cultures, where arranged marriage is commonly practiced, parents and kin try to choose a mate for their offspring who fulfills traditional criteria, such as good family reputation, dowry, and chastity (Lalonde, Hynie, Pannu, & Tatla, 2004). Approximately 25% of second-generation south Asians living in North America expect to have an arranged marriage (Talbani & Hasanali, 2000). South Asian Canadians who strongly identify with their heritage culture are more traditional in their mate preferences than are those who identify less strongly (Hynie, Lalonde, & Lee, 2006; Lalonde et al., 2004). That cultural identification and acculturation are able to influence mate preferences provides further evidence for the importance of sociocultural contexts.

From a socio-ecological perspective, then, individuals implicitly internalize expectations about what sort of mate they should desire within particular sociocultural milieus (Eastwick & Finkel, 2008). These expectations develop at least in part as a function of family pressure and of social structural affordances and constraints that determine the gendered division of labor and gender equality (Eagly & Wood, 1999).

Relationship Initiation and Dating

In Western societies, heterosexual partners tend to initiate relationships through dating (later I discuss relationship initiation in non-Western societies and same-sex couples). Courtship, a broader but more traditional term than dating, typically refers to the period before marriage when one partner (usually a man) publicly woos a potential spouse with the approval of both families. Dating is also considered an opportunity for two people to spend time together to explore their relationship potential (Rose & Zand, 2002), but, unlike courtship, in which intimacy usually comes after commitment, it is common for dating couples to be intimate with little commitment. Because Western-style dating tends to be limited in many parts of the world, courtship is the more inclusive term. Nonetheless, the bulk of research has examined relationship initiation in terms of dating and, therefore, this chapter reflects that focus.

Contrary to stereotypes of romantic women, some research suggests that it is actually men who tend to fall in love more quickly during the initial stages of a relationship (Huston & Ashmore, 1986). Men also tend to report being in love more often than women do, even though women are more likely to report being currently in love and more deeply in love (Hendrick & Hendrick, 1995). In Western cultures, men tend to be more ludic (game-playing) than women in their love styles, whereas women tend to be more pragmatic, manic (infatuated), and friendship oriented (Hendrick & Hendrick, 1995). One study showed that American and Chinese men's love styles were more agapic (altruistic) than women's, but Chinese men placed more emphasis than did Chinese women on romantic love and sex as important for marriage (Sprecher & Toro-Morn, 2002). Evolutionary psychologists might argue that men are more susceptible to romantic love because of their emphasis on the external attractiveness of mates and men's putatively higher sex drive (Baumeister, Catanese, & Vohs, 2001). Conversely, women's preference for mates with high earning potential, along with women's putatively lower sex drive, might explain why women are more susceptible to pragmatic and companionate love (Hong & Bartley, 1986).

From a social structural perspective, on the other hand, men's greater access to power and resources affords the luxury of emphasizing romantic love and sexual attraction during courtship, whereas women's less powerful social and economic position necessitates pragmatism. It is no coincidence that women who live in economically developing societies – where gender inequality is ubiquitous – tend to be particularly pragmatic during courtship. They tend to show a greater willingness to marry someone who has all the qualities they look for in a mate, but whom they do not love (Levine, Suguru, Hashimoto, & Verma, 1995). Social structural theory, with its emphasis on sociocultural barriers and affordances that shape gendered behavior, is also compatible with ecological developmental theory. As the following sections show, the circles of social influence – sociocultural, social, and dyadic – encourage the learning of traditional roles and behaviors for each sex during courtship and dating.

Sociocultural Contexts: Dating Scripts

According to sexual script theory, culturally derived rules and norms guide courtship and sexual behavior (Greene & Faulkner, 2005; Simon & Gagnon, 1986). These scripts, familiar to individuals socialized within the sociocultural setting from which they derive – most North Americans, for example, are aware of narratives for first dates or one-night stands – operate at cultural, interpersonal, and intrapsychic levels (Simon & Gagnon, 1986). Cultural-level scripts, learned from schools, religious institutions, sex educators, and the mass media, address shared expectations about the who, what, when, where, and how of sexual behavior (Gagnon, 1990; Greene & Faulkner, 2005). In the ambiguous world of dating, adherence to these scripts can help to reduce uncertainty, anxiety, and awkwardness (Laner & Ventrone, 1998). Often, however, these scripts reinforce traditional gender-role behavior, such that men are encouraged to be dominant and women to be submissive. Even people who endorse egalitarian gender-role ideologies tend to follow traditional scripts at the beginning of a relationship (Ganong, Coleman, Thompson, & Goodwin-Watkins, 1996).

Children learn romantic scripts early in life, and rehearsal of these scripts in the media, in social relationships, and eventually in dating relationships may explain their persistence into adulthood. Indeed, these scripts may be so well rehearsed that they operate implicitly (Serewicz & Gale, 2008). For example, children are regularly exposed to movies, television, and fairy tales that suggest that women are beautiful but helpless, whereas men are strong, agentic rescuers of "damsels in distress" (Davis, 1984; Mayes & Valentine, 1979). Such cultural messages of benevolent sexism – the expectation that men should provide for and protect women (Glick & Fiske, 1996) – may be internalized throughout development and influence adult gender-role behavior. For instance, Rudman and Heppen (2003) found that women with implicit romantic beliefs (e.g., automatic association of men with heroism and chivalry) reported less interest in education, work achievement, and power. Along these lines, Tolman (1999) argued that adolescent girls who ascribe to ideologies of traditional femininity are more likely to adhere to romantic ideals that weaken their sense of agency and authenticity in relationships.

In adulthood, a similar message tends to be transmitted by the sociocultural context – that it is acceptable for men to be sexually active, whereas women should be passive and sexually restricted in relationships (MacCorquodale, 1989). These messages are conveyed by popular dating guides such as *He's Just Not That Into You* (Behrendt & Tuccillo, 2004), *The Rules* (Fein & Schneider, 2005), or *Men are from Mars, Women are from Venus* (Gray, 1992), which claim that, because of purportedly fundamental differences between the sexes, men and women should behave in gender-traditional ways to ensure success in attracting and retaining mates (Laner & Ventrone, 2000). In *He's Just Not That Into You*, for example, it is presented as a fact that men evolved to pursue women, and not vice versa. Because of this supposedly innate difference, then, women are exhorted to let men take the control and initiative in dating situations – a script that reinforces and perpetuates men's agency and women's passivity. This theme is particularly ubiquitous in first-date scripts.

The consensus across studies on the actions that comprise a first date, and the actions that are more commonly performed by each sex, suggest that these scripts are well-known cultural products (Laner & Ventrone, 2000; Rose & Frieze, 1989, 1993). In Western cultures, first dates are often considered a rite of courtship that may fundamentally influence the course of a relationship (McDaniel, 2005). To clarify these scripts, Rose and Frieze (1989) asked heterosexual college students to list the sequential actions that typically take place on a first date and then examined whether actions were differentially assigned to men and women. If 25% of the participants mentioned a particular action, it was included in the "script." They found that the participants' scripts reflected patriarchal constructions that emphasized men's agency and control in the public sphere (such as planning, paying, and orchestrating the date) and women's passivity and self-regulation in the private sphere (such as concern with appearance, maintaining conversation, and restraining sexuality). Other studies have confirmed that first-date scripts tend to emphasize men's active, dominant role and women's reactive, passive role (Laner & Ventrone, 2000). For example, it is considered normative for men to initiate first dates (Pryor & Merluzzi, 1985), and, although it is becoming increasingly common for women to initiate dates, especially first ones (Mongeau, Hale, Johnson, & Hillis, 1993), men tend to have greater expectations of sexual involvement for female-initiated dates than for male-initiated dates (Mongeau & Carey, 1996). Similarly, Serewicz and Gale (2008) found that men's first-date scripts were more likely than women's to include sexual involvement, especially if the date was female-initiated, whereas women's scripts involved more romantic elements (e.g., a good-night kiss, without further physical intimacy). They also found, like others, that men tend to be assigned more agentic behaviors than women, which reflects the tendency toward gender-role traditionalism in American college students' first-date scripts. Whether or not these scripts have resonance in other cultural groups remains to be seen, not least because dating tends to be a Western cultural construction (Goodwin, 1999).

Social and Dyadic Contexts: Role of Peers and Romantic Partners

People may initially learn gendered dating behavior by internalizing cultural scripts for first dates. Once set in motion by the first date, traditional role behavior may crystallize throughout dating if it is sustained by the expectations of peers and romantic partners (two circles of influence in the ecological developmental model). Holland (1992) examined the role of the peer group in mediating between the sociocultural milieu and college women's individual attitudes toward heterosexual romance. She found that women who identified as a "romantic" type of personality, for whom romance was more salient to their lives, tended to have greater expertise in negotiating heterosexual relationships. Social interaction with other women tended to enhance identification, salience, and, in turn, expertise, which suggests that women socialized each other into the world of dating at least in part by encouraging greater internalization of cultural models of romance. In this connection, it is noteworthy that Serewicz and Gale (2008) found that women's first-date scripts contained less redundant information than men's did, in line with evidence that women have greater cognitive complexity in their knowledge and memory structures for first dates and relationship escalation (Honeycutt, Cantrill, & Greene, 1989). This may be because women, whose role prescribes that they be "relationship experts," also tend to talk more with friends about the date before and after the date, rehearsing details that become more deeply encoded in their memories.

Dating partners also socialize each other into the world of romance. In Rose and Frieze's (1989) study, for example, experienced daters endorsed greater traditionalism in first-date scripts than did inexperienced daters, which suggests that one's romantic partner may reinforce gendered roles that continue to resonate in adulthood. Through dating experience, people learn that compliance with these scripts may be rewarded and deviations punished. Indeed, Rose and Frieze (1993) found that relationships were less likely to continue in the face of deviations from the traditional first-date script. Morgan and Zurbriggen (2007) also argued that dating scripts may function to inaugurate young adults into the world of dating and, in so doing, reinforce the traditional status quo that mandates men's agency and women's passivity. In their study, heterosexual college students were interviewed about their first significant dating relationship. An emergent theme was the negotiation of sexual activity with one's partner: Women recounted more pressure to engage in sexual activity, whereas men often described their partner as the sexual "gatekeeper" and responded with frustration and acceptance. Along these lines, Kimmel (1997) argued that the predominant script for young men emphasizes hyper-heterosexuality, both as a means of reinforcing masculine identity and of denying homosexuality. Through initial dating experiences, then, young adults may learn that the masculine role is active and sexual, whereas the feminine role is reactive and chaste.

It seems, then, that, despite the growing popularity of egalitarian ideals over the last half-century (Schwartz, 1994), traditional dating scripts continue to be influential. Faced with competing ideologies, young adults may adopt a combination of liberal and traditional attitudes toward relationships and expectations for the future. For instance, Ganong et al. (1996) found that, even though college students generally held egalitarian expectations for their future relationships, women still expected male partners to attain greater commercial success than they themselves would, and men still expected female partners to perform a greater proportion of parenting. It may be the case that individuals endorse egalitarianism on an explicit level, but their behavior continues to be influenced by deeply rehearsed traditional scripts that are automatically activated on an implicit level. Ganong et al. (1996) surmised that the gap between students' egalitarian expectations and their actual, traditional behavior may grow larger as relationships develop throughout adulthood – a disparity that may lead to disappointment and eventual decrease in relationship satisfaction. Sociocultural, social, and dyadic influences that together socialize men's sexual agency and women's passivity, then, may be detrimental to both partners in the long run (Kiefer & Sanchez, 2007).

Relationship Initiation in Gay Men and Lesbians

The gradual progression in conventional heterosexual dating scripts from casual dating between relatively unacquainted partners to more intense physical intimacy and commitment may have less relevance for gay men and lesbians. For example, gay men often include sexual activity in their first-date scripts (Klinkenberg & Rose, 1994), and a number of gay men who pursue new partners are already involved in an open relationship with a regular partner (Hickson et al., 1992). The casual dating phase for many lesbians tends to be shorter or skipped entirely, with rapid escalation to more serious commitment (Cini & Malafi, 1991; Rose, Zand, & Cini, 1993). Lesbians commonly follow a friendship script during their relationship initiation, in which emotional intimacy between friends grows into a committed romantic relationship (Rose & Zand, 2002).

Gay and lesbian relationship initiation scripts are also less likely to be characterized by differentiated gender roles: There is unlikely to be a sexual "gatekeeper" role in men's scripts or a sexual initiator role in women's (Klinkenberg & Rose, 1994). Lesbians tend to reject traditional gender roles that mandate that one partner is active and the other passive; instead, they tend to share roles and to treat their partner as equally as they would a best friend (Rose & Roades, 1987; Rose & Zand, 2002). However, freedom from gender roles that endorse men's initiative may also mean that lesbians are sometimes indirect or cautious in initiating romantic involvement with other women (DeLaria, 1995). As suggested by Huston and Schwartz (2002), similar gender-role socialization for both partners in gay and lesbian couples may mean that they lack some of the traits and behaviors that are usually displayed by the other sex (i.e., expressiveness in women, instrumentality in men). Yet the rejection of gender roles may also result in greater egalitarianism during relationship initiation, such as in initiating physical contact or paying for dates. Some lesbians have indicated that they tend to wait to be asked out on a date, in keeping with women's traditionally passive role, but they are often not shy about indicating sexual interest in nonverbal ways (Rose & Zand, 2002). More experienced lesbians are especially likely to initiate physical intimacy with a new partner, whereas the opposite tends to be true for heterosexual women: With more experience, they are less likely to be sexually assertive and more likely to limit their sexuality (Rose & Frieze, 1989). Gay men report roughly equal frequency in the likelihood that they or their partner initiate sexual activity (Blumstein & Schwartz, 1983).

Relationship Initiation Across Cultures

The experience of romantic love is a cultural universal (Jankowiak & Fischer, 1992), yet dating behavior is culture-specific. Dating, although prominent in the West, tends to be proscribed in cultures where arranged marriage is the norm, such as in south Asian cultures (Goodwin, 1999). It follows that immigrants to the West may experience intergenerational clashes over dating, which are often undergirded by different attitudes toward the changing role of women. Insofar as some immigrant south Asian parents conflate dating with premarital sex, they may oppose dating in an attempt to maintain their children's chastity before marriage (Dasgupta, 1998). This may be especially true for second-generation daughters; the dating activities and sexuality of sons are not nearly as constrained (Mani, 1992). Traditionally, a "good Indian girl" is shy, chaste, and willing to allow her parents to choose a man for her to marry (Agarwal, 1991). Second-generation south Asian women often report that their parents transport their traditional gender ideology to the new host culture, even as the prevailing ideology continues to evolve in the home country (Dasgupta, 1998). The gender difference in parental treatment of sons and daughters stems not only from traditional attitudes toward women but also from the responsibility parents give to second-generation daughters rather than to sons for maintaining Indian culture and traditions in the new host country (Dion & Dion,

2004). As a result, parents may monitor a daughter's behavior more closely, especially her dating behavior. For example, a daughter's exogamy (marriage outside the group) may particularly increase the likelihood that cultural traditions will be neglected in the next generation. One study showed that second-generation south Asian sons were more accepting of dating than were second-generation daughters, which suggests that the latter may have internalized parental strictures against dating (Dasgupta, 1998). This study also found that second-generation women were more egalitarian than were the second-generation men, which hints at the potential for conflicts in heterosexual relationships.

In east Asia, couples commonly date before marriage, but often with more restraint than in the West. In the People's Republic of China, for instance, young adults tend to be very interested in romantic affairs, but conduct themselves with caution and privacy (Moore, 1998). Similar to gender roles elsewhere, men are expected to take the initiative in courtship, and women tend to be subtle in showing interest. Dating partners also tend to be pragmatic and long-term oriented; those who date multiple partners, are flirtatious, or are indiscreet may receive the pejorative label *qingfu*, or "frivolous." Women are more vulnerable to this label than men are and, therefore, risk greater damage to their reputations. In Taiwan, men tend to be more optimistic about the eventual probability of marriage in the early stages of relationship development, similar to the initial romanticism of Western men, whereas women tend to be more sensitive to changes that signal a downturn during courtship (Chang & Chan, 2007). This brief review provides only a glimpse of the wide-ranging cultural variation in dating and courtship and highlights the need for research devoted to understanding the ways that this variation may be explained by cultural differences in gender-role attitudes and behavior.

Phase II: Relational Maintenance

Once a dating relationship is established, partners tend to display relational maintenance behaviors that help to sustain the key components of relationship quality–commitment, intimacy, satisfaction, trust, passion, and love (Fletcher, Simpson, & Thomas, 2000). In general, maintenance behaviors are more likely to be performed by women than by men in conventional heterosexual relationships (Canary & Stafford, 1992; Dainton & Stafford, 1993; Huston & Ashmore, 1986; Ragsdale, 1996). This gender difference has remained stable over the last few decades, even as gender differences have decreased in other domains, such as employment, housework, and parenting (Walzer, 2008). Relational maintenance can be behavioral (such as routine or strategic behaviors) or cognitive (such as having positive illusions about one's partner). Routine maintenance refers to the everyday behaviors that unintentionally reinforce relationships, such as making dinner or listening attentively as a partner describes his or her workday; strategic maintenance behaviors, on the other hand, refer to deliberate attempts to maintain relationship quality, such as complimenting one's partner or trying to improve a problem area in the relationship (Aylor & Dainton, 2004). Some studies suggest that gender differences only emerge for routine maintenance behaviors (Dainton & Aylor, 2002); women, for example, are more likely than men to show routine openness (Aylor & Dainton, 2004). Research has also shown that psychological femininity is a better predictor of routine maintenance behaviors, and masculinity of strategic maintenance behaviors, than is biological sex (Aylor & Dainton, 2004), which suggests that it is simplistic to reduce relational maintenance into "women's work" and "men's work." Relational maintenance affects, and is affected by, three components of relationship quality: commitment, intimacy, and relationship satisfaction.

Commitment

Relationships that are strongly committed, interdependent, and intimate are particularly high in relational maintenance (Rusbult, Arriaga, & Agnew, 2001). Commitment affects the way that men and women differentially perform a cognitive type of routine maintenance – holding positive illusions about one's partner, such that partners are viewed more positively than the self (Murray, Holmes, & Griffin, 1996). Women's relational self-construal tends to encourage greater identification with the relationship (Cross & Madson, 1997), which, in turn, encourages positive illusions that motivate routine relationship maintenance behavior. Thus, women tend to report positive illusions regardless of their level of commitment, but only men who are more committed to their partner, and therefore identify more strongly with the relationship, report positive illusions (Gagné & Lydon, 2003).

Another way of maintaining commitment is to shield a relationship from attractive alternative partners (Rusbult, Drigotas, & Verette, 1994). Women and men who are involved in satisfying close relationships tend to downplay the attractiveness of alternative partners (Lydon, Fitzsimmons, & Naidoo, 2003), pay less attention to them (Miller, 1997), and refrain from behaviors that may signal interest or increase attraction. For example, unconscious mimicry of an interaction partner tends to increase liking between partners. Karremans and Verwijmeren (2008) showed that people involved in a close romantic relationship unconsciously inhibited mimicry of an attractive stranger in the laboratory. This was true for men and women alike; men were not any more prone to mimicry, which suggests that they did not unconsciously behave in such a way that might encourage short-term mating behaviors, such as extra-pair copulation. Unconscious inhibition of mimicry, then, is a cognitive mechanism that serves to protect a relationship and maintain commitment.

Intimacy

The maintenance of intimacy in a romantic relationship, conceptualized here as a process of reciprocal self-disclosure and responsiveness between partners (Reis & Shaver, 1988), further illustrates the role of gendered traits and attitudes in pro-relationship behavior. To the extent that psychological gender affects the maintenance of self-disclosure and responsiveness, intimacy may likewise be experienced differently by women and men.

Self-disclosure

Adherence to traditional gender roles may reduce intimacy in relationships by inhibiting self-disclosure (Marshall, 2008; Neff & Suizzo, 2006; Rubin, Hill, Peplau, & Dunkel-Schetter, 1980). More specifically, the traditional masculine role does not encourage self-disclosure (Thompson & Pleck, 1986), and stereotypically masculine traits such as dominance and independence (Bem, 1974) may inhibit rather than facilitate open communication. Although men tend to disclose factual information (Davidson & Duberman, 1982; Wood & Inman, 1993), it is the disclosure of feelings that facilitates intimacy in relationships (Laurenceau, Barrett, & Pietromonaco, 1998; Morton, 1978). Gender-typed men may fear that expressing feelings might make them appear stereotypically feminine; indeed, Derlega and Chaikin (1976) found that high self-disclosers, especially men, were perceived as more feminine than were low self-disclosers. Even though men who have difficulty self-disclosing are more prone to depression, low disclosure in men and high disclosure in women are commonly perceived as normative and psychologically healthy (Derlega & Chaikin, 1975).

Women, free from such masculinity concerns, tend to be more self-disclosing on average (Dindia & Allen, 1992), but it also depends on the target of disclosure: Women tend to disclose more to a close same-sex friend than men do, whereas the opposite is true when disclosing to a stranger of the other sex (Colwill & Perlman, 1977; Derlega, Winstead, Wong, & Hunter, 1985). Stereotypically feminine traits, such as kindness, selflessness, and sensitivity to others (Bem, 1974; Spence, Helmreich, & Stapp, 1975), are positively associated with self-disclosure within women's social interactions (Schaffer, Pegalis, & Cornell, 1991), and, accordingly, both women and men who are higher in stereotypical femininity are more likely to voice concerns within a relationship (Rusbult, 1987) and to broach emotional topics (Clark & Taraban, 1991). Moreover, stereotypic feminine traits are positively associated with dispositional empathy (Thomas & Reznikoff, 1984), which, in turn, predicts open communication and relationship satisfaction (Davis & Oathout, 1987). Finally, gay men's self-disclosures tend to be more intimate than heterosexual men's are (Bliss, 2000).

On the other hand, extreme stereotypic femininity, known as unmitigated communion (Helgeson, 1993), may actually inhibit, rather than promote, women's self-disclosure. Because traditional women's self-construals are heavily contingent on important relationships (Cross & Madsen, 1997), women may self-silence rather than self-disclose private thoughts or concerns in order to maintain relational harmony and a coherent sense of self (Jack, 1991). A traditional woman partnered with a traditional man may therefore experience particularly inhibited communication; indeed, observational research has shown that traditional women and men talked, laughed, and smiled less when interacting in a laboratory than did non-traditional couples (Ickes & Barnes, 1978). Similarly, Rubin et al. (1980) found that self-disclosure was higher in couples when both members possessed egalitarian gender-role attitudes. The authors reasoned that greater egalitarianism should encourage an "ethic of openness" in romantic relationships, hence more intimacy. Thus, self-disclosure may be low if both partners are traditional, or even if only one partner is traditional. Because self-disclosure is reciprocal (Cozby, 1972), one partner's reluctance to self-disclose may mean that the other partner may be less disclosing. On the other hand, this also suggests that a non-traditional partner's self-disclosure may encourage a traditional partner's disclosure and bring the mean level of intimacy up rather than down.

Responsiveness

Some evidence suggests that women tend to be more responsive and emotionally supportive to partners than men are, a difference that can be attributed to women's greater communion (Fritz, Nagurney, & Helgeson, 2003). In social interactions, women are more likely to provide backchannel support by making minimal verbal utterances (e.g., "mm-hmm") (McLaughlin, Cody, Kane, & Robey, 1981), by asking more questions (Fishman, 1978), and by agreeing with or asking for a partner's opinion (Eakins & Eakins, 1978). All of these verbal devices help to draw out one's conversational partner. It is not surprising, then, that people tend to self-disclose more to women than to men (Dailey & Claus, 2001; Garcia & Geisler, 1988; Hargie et al., 2001). In fact, disclosure tends to be highest in female–female pairings, lowest in male–male pairings, and in between for cross-sex pairings (Hill & Stull, 1987). Whereas interruptions are relatively infrequent in same-sex conversations, men commonly interrupt women in mixed-sex interactions (Zimmerman & West, 1975), which inhibits women's self-disclosure. Fishman (1978) found that, because women are more likely to use a supportive conversational style, topics introduced by men in cross-sex interactions "succeeded" (were further discussed) 96% of the time, whereas women's topics succeeded only 36% of the time.

Gender differences in responsiveness may reflect a learned adaptation to contextual demands. For example, men who work in occupations that require the display of sensitivity and emotional support tend to be just as good as women at decoding emotions (Rosenthal, Archer, DiMatteo, Kowumaki,

& Rogers, 1974). Like self-disclosure, responsiveness may be more a function of psychological femininity than of biological sex, as others are more likely to disclose to more stereotypically feminine men. Similar to associations with self-disclosure, dispositional empathy may mediate between stereotypic femininity and responsiveness (Thomas & Reznikoff, 1984). As such, individuals who are high in stereotypic femininity tend to feel more empathy for a friend with a problem and, in turn, show greater responsiveness, whereas individuals who are high in stereotypic masculinity are more likely to change the topic (Basow & Rubenfeld, 2003). To sum up, a stereotypically feminine communication style, in terms of both self-disclosure and responsiveness, appears to maintain intimacy in relationships.

Relationship Satisfaction

More generally, the finding across studies that psychological femininity tends to promote relational quality has led some to suggest a "femininity effect" in relationships (Steiner-Pappalardo & Gurung, 2002; Stafford, Dainton, & Haas, 2000). For instance, perceiving one's partner as possessing stereotypically feminine traits is related to the relationship satisfaction of both men and women (Lamke, Sollie, Durbin, & Fitzpatrick, 1994). Some evidence suggests that relationship satisfaction is most enhanced when partners are high in stereotypic femininity *and* masculinity (i.e., psychological androgyny). For example, to the extent that stereotypic femininity promotes routine maintenance behaviors, and stereotypic masculinity promotes strategic maintenance behaviors, then androgynous individuals may be effective at both expressive and instrumental communication (Aylor & Dainton, 2004). Furthermore, gender-typing may be particularly toxic for satisfaction in heterosexual relationships. One study showed that the combination of gender-typed wives with extremely gender-typed husbands predicted the poorest marital quality of any type of coupling across a 3-year time span (Helms, Proulx, Klute, McHale, & Crouter, 2006). This combination produces the largest discrepancy in expressivity by pairing expressive wives with extremely non-expressive husbands, and it may be this gap, rather than absolute levels of expressivity per se, that is responsible for poorer relationship quality.

Overall, these findings and others suggest that gender differences in relational maintenance and communication may owe less to biological sex and more to differences that arise through gender-role socialization (Aylor & Dainton, 2004; Stafford et al., 2000). In fact, a meta-analysis of 1,200 studies showed that biological sex only accounted for 1% of the variance in communication behavior (Canary & Hause, 1993). Unless a distinction is made between variance owing to biological sex and psychological gender, research on differences in communication behavior may exaggerate and reinforce gender stereotypes. Even more, to the extent that lay people are led to believe the stereotype that men are from Mars and women are from Venus, they are more likely to internalize and enact these stereotypes in their relationships (Deaux & Major, 1987), which could lead to even greater misunderstanding between the sexes.

Phase III: Coming Apart

Similar to the establishment and maintenance of relationships, gender also contributes to the ways that people cope with the end of a relationship. Several studies suggest that men experience poorer psychological health following the death of a spouse than do women (Carr, 2004; Sonnenberg,

Beekman, Deeg, & van Tilberg, 2000; Williams, 2003). Moreover, research suggests that, after a break-up, men are more likely than women to be upset (Helgeson, 1994; Nolen-Hoeksema & Girgus, 1994), to have greater sexual arousal for their ex-partner (Davis, Shaver, & Vernon, 2003), and to suffer more from break-up-related mental and physical health problems (Bloom, Asher, & White, 1978).

There are several reasons why men might experience greater distress after the loss of a relationship. First, men are less likely than women to initiate break-ups (Helgeson, 1994; Hill, Rubin, & Peplau, 1976), and noninitiators of a break-up are more likely than initiators to experience distress (Sprecher, Felmlee, Metts, Fehr, & Vanni, 1998). Men's greater distress may, therefore, stem from feelings of rejection or from a decrease in feelings of power and control that are emphasized by the masculine gender role (Thompson & Pleck, 1986). Second, because men's self-construal tends to be less relational than women's (Cross & Madsen, 1997), they may be less aware of their partner's thoughts, feelings, and perspective and feel blindsided if their partner ends the relationship (Rubin, Peplau, & Hill, 1981). Finally, that men tend to be particularly dependent on their romantic partner for emotional support (Helgeson, 1994; Pleck, 1976) because they have smaller social support networks than women do (Fischer & Phillips, 1982) may mean that they have fewer people to turn to for solace after the break-up. Whereas women tend to mitigate post-break-up distress by relying on friends and family for support, men are more likely to cope by turning to alcohol and drugs (Davis, Shaver, & Vernon, 2003).

How do women cope with break-ups that are initiated by men? Davis et al. (2003) found that women who did not initiate the break-up reported more anger, hostility, and violence directed at their partner than did men. On the other hand, women also tend to report more positive growth as a result of the break-up than men do (Helgeson, 1994). Regardless of who initiated the break-up, women tend to experience more positive emotions, such as joy and relief (Choo, Levine, & Hatfield, 1996; Sprecher, 1994), and more stress-related growth (Tashiro & Frazier, 2003). The reasons for this difference are not yet clear, but women tend to report more stress-related growth than men do across different domains (Tedeschi & Calhoun, 1996), and, because women are better able to predict break-ups than men are (Hill et al., 1976), their stress-related growth may begin earlier and facilitate preparation for the break-up (Tashiro & Frazier, 2003).

Some findings suggest that gender-role differentiation in relationships may hasten their termination. In contrast to companionate marriages, where husbands and wives are each other's closest companions, there is greater gender differentiation in non-companionate marriages, where men are responsible for instrumental tasks and women for expressive tasks (Riessman, 1990). Such role differentiation may put these couples at higher risk for divorce insofar as each partner's fundamental needs for autonomy and relatedness are not fulfilled (Deci & Ryan, 1985). Along these lines, Walzer (2008) proposed that, if marriage represents the "doing" of gender (i.e., enacting traditional roles), then divorce represents the "redoing" of gender (i.e., reassessing masculine and feminine gender roles). Interviews with divorced women and men revealed that gender differentiation in breadwinning, housework, parenting, and emotional expression was often reassessed post-divorce. For example, some women indicated that, after the divorce, their primary role shifted from housekeeping to economic provision, whereas some men shifted their emphasis from being a provider to being more emotionally expressive. Overall, many people reported that they did not even notice until after their divorce the extent to which gender played a role in their marriage or the ways in which the gendered division of work and love in marriages tends to generate conflict. Indeed, marriages in which women partake in paid work and men in more unpaid work are less likely to end in divorce than are those in which men play a more traditional role (Sigle-Rushton, 2007).

Costs of Gender-Role Traditionalism for Intimate Romantic Relationships

As we have seen, constructions of gender exert considerable influence on the initiation, maintenance, and termination of relationships. Although it has been suggested throughout this chapter that this influence often undermines relationship functioning, the specific relational and sexual costs of gender-role-related behavior are more fully illustrated in this section.

Relational Costs

Do people harm their relationships when they adhere to gendered scripts? Tolman and her colleagues (2003) contend that constructions of masculinity and femininity detract from the human potential to have satisfying romantic and sexual relationships. Indeed, the research reviewed thus far suggested that gender-role-related behavior tends to exert a negative influence on relationship initiation, maintenance, and termination. For example, to the extent that traditionally feminine or masculine first-date behaviors are aimed at "capturing" a partner for a long-term relationship, such behavior may persist as the relationship progresses. This gender-typed behavior may ultimately result in reduced gender equality, openness, and authenticity (Laner & Ventrone, 2000) – qualities that contribute to self-disclosure, intimacy, and relationship satisfaction (Neff & Suizzo, 2006; Rubin et al., 1980). In a recent study (Marshall, 2008), gender-role traditionalism was negatively related to intimacy at least in part because of reduced self-disclosure.

In addition to the effects of gender-typed behavior, relational quality is also influenced by partners' attitudes toward gender equality. Several studies have shown that anti-feminist attitudes, in both women and men, are linked to lower relational and sexual satisfaction. For instance, Rudman and Fairchild (2007) found that, among heterosexuals, feminism and romance were still largely believed to be incompatible. In particular, individuals who endorsed the stereotype of feminist women as lesbian and sexually unattractive were more likely to see feminism as conflictual for heterosexual romance and sexuality and were less likely to support a feminist orientation or women's rights. Women may distance themselves from these feminist stereotypes in an attempt to increase their attractiveness in the eyes of men, which suggests that one consequence of heterosexual romance is that it may undermine feminism and thus reinforce women's subordinate positions in society.

Ironically, there is little truth to the stereotype that feminism is incompatible with heterosexual romance. Rudman and Phelan (2007) showed that heterosexuals who identified as feminist did not report poorer relationship health, as the stereotype implies. In fact, women paired with feminist men reported greater relationship quality, and men paired with feminist women reported greater relationship stability and sexual satisfaction – findings that suggest that both women and men benefit from having a feminist partner. Feminism, then, appears to enhance rather than detract from heterosexual relationships.

Constructions of gender also have consequences for long-term heterosexual relationships and marriage. Despite advances toward gender equality in the past few decades, the division of labor by gender continues to be reflected in these relationships. By and large, women are still more likely to inhabit the private, domestic sphere and men the public sphere. This may at least partially explain why gender differences tend to be found in marital satisfaction. That men tend to report greater marital satisfaction than women (Rhyne, 1981) may be at least partly related to societal devaluation of domestic work, women's boredom with domestic work, or women's stress from juggling work and family concerns. Many partners strive toward egalitarian marriages (Schwartz, 1994), even though they may be more challenging to achieve after a traditional courtship. There is also much variability both across and within cultures in the extent to which partners actually achieve this egalitarian end;

for example, African Americans tend to have more egalitarian heterosexual relationships than other ethnic groups in the USA (Ganong et al., 1996). Deutsch, Kokot, and Binder (2007) found that many college women largely rejected traditional family models, ones in which women sacrifice paid work to tend to the needs of their family. They also rejected "Supermom" models in which women work full time and assume greater domestic responsibility than their husbands do. Instead, college women preferred egalitarian family models that prescribed equal sharing of domestic responsibilities for both parents, particularly when both parents cut back on paid work to spend more time with the family, or when both parents try to balance home/work life. Across studies, then, findings suggest that traditional couple interactions and family structures are not optimal for relationship functioning, and yet people often implicitly enact traditional scripts.

Sexual Costs

Gendered scripts are also consequential for sexual satisfaction. Healthy sexuality consists of self-knowledge, empowerment, and access to birth control and condoms – all of which are circumscribed for women in conventional heterosexual scripts (Tolman et al., 2003). Typically, heterosexual sexual scripts involve an aggressive, lustful, initiating man, and a coy, passive, sexually limiting woman (Byers, 1996). The well-documented double standard refers to the expectation that men can be sexual in various types of relationships, whereas women should restrict sexual behavior to committed relationships (Greene & Faulkner, 2005). Explicitly and/or implicitly, heterosexual men and women have internalized this standard; indeed, women report a preference for sex within committed relationships, whereas men report more permissive attitudes toward casual sex (Hendrick & Hendrick, 1995; Oliver & Hyde, 1993). Men also report a greater number of sexual partners and a more game-playing love style than women do (Hendrick & Hendrick, 1986, 1995). Although the double standard has become less overt in recent years (Sprecher & McKinney, 1993) – one study showed that relative to past generations, college students today are less likely to endorse the double standard and report fewer gender differences in sexual behavior, such as age at first intercourse (Greene & Faulkner, 2005) – it may still take subtle forms. For example, women are expected to have fewer partners in their lifetime than men are (Sprecher, 1989), and so they often underreport their sexual behavior (Rubin, 1990). Gender differences in sexual behavior, then, may represent learned accommodations to social structures such as the sexual double standard.

Because the double standard only encourages men's initiative, it is often difficult for women to express agency and desire in sexual relationships (O'Sullivan & Byers, 1995). Cultural messages about women's sexual passivity are so ubiquitous that many women have internalized these messages on an unconscious level and implicitly associate sex with submission (Kiefer, Sanchez, Kalinka, & Ybarra, 2006). Indeed, women's endorsement of traditional gender roles has been linked with greater sexual passivity and, in turn, decreased sexual satisfaction, whereas men's traditionalism has been linked with *less* sexual passivity and, in turn, greater sexual satisfaction (Kiefer & Sanchez, 2007). Furthermore, contraceptive use, which requires a certain amount of sexual agency to implement, is poorer among people with more traditional gender-role attitudes (Pleck, Sonenstein, & Ku, 1993).

Conversely, men and women who perceive their partners as endorsing feminist beliefs tend to report *greater* sexual satisfaction (Rudman & Phelan, 2007). For men, being paired with a feminist partner may have benefits: Feminist women tend to reject traditional sexual scripts that mandate their passivity, and are thus more likely to express their sexual agency. Furthermore, gender-role nonconformity has been linked to sexual agency for women and men alike and, in turn, greater sexual arousability, facility in achieving orgasm, and overall sexual satisfaction (Kiefer & Sanchez, 2007).

Along these lines, Greene and Faulkner (2005) found that heterosexual dating partners who were less traditional in their gender-role attitudes (i.e., they were less likely to endorse a sexual double standard) reported greater dyadic sexual communication, which, in turn, was related to more satisfying relationships. Collectively, these studies suggest that women and men who reject traditional roles may experience greater sexual and relational satisfaction.

Summary and Future Directions

Despite popular claims that men and women are fundamentally different, meta-analyses reveal that, for most psychological variables, these differences tend to be small or non-existent (Hyde, 2005). In this chapter, I examined gender differences and similarities in friendships and in the initiation, maintenance, and end of intimate romantic relationships. A recurring theme throughout has been the power of context – dyadic, social, and sociocultural – in reproducing, attenuating, or eliminating traditional gendered behavior. That the magnitude of gender difference tends to fluctuate across the life span means that gender differences are not stable or inevitable (Hyde, 2005). Numerous examples from the close relationships literature further underscore that women and men are more similar than popularly believed: Both sexes focus on relational rather than recreational aspects of sexuality when recounting the story of their relationship development (Hendrick & Hendrick, 1995); gender differences in communication behavior tend to be small (Canary & Hause, 1993; Dindia & Allen, 1992); and gender differences are often smaller than cultural differences in terms of mate preferences, love styles, and relationship attitudes (Buss, 1989; Sprecher & Toro-Morn, 2002). Nonetheless, it cannot be disputed that gender roles continue to influence close relationships.

Future researchers could harness new methods and technology to advance our understanding of the role of gender in relationships. Speed dating paradigms, for example, could shed light on how stereotypic gender traits and traditional ideologies might affect impressions and attraction during relationship initiation. One would expect more traditional people to follow conventional scripts (e.g., a man may be more aggressive in pursuing a woman than vice versa) and show less tolerance for gender-role violations. Even people who generally reject gender-role prescriptions might be more likely to fall back on traditional scripts in this potentially anxiety-provoking situation. Collecting data on further contact between partners after the speed dating event could help to determine whether participants who adhered to traditional dating scripts were more or less "successful" than participants who were more egalitarian.

Online dating web sites, too, may provide new research opportunities. A sample of online dating profiles could be content-analyzed for the presence of stereotypic gender traits in self-descriptions and in the description of what people desire in a mate. To the extent that the daters in this sample provide data on their online dating experiences over a period of time (e.g., the number of messages, dates, sexual experiences, or relationships experienced, after researchers control for other factors such as physical attractiveness, wealth, and education), researchers may learn more about the prevalence of traditional role behavior and attitudes in modern dating situations and whether they help or hinder relationship development. Along these lines, daily diary methods can be utilized to examine adherence to traditional scripts at different stages of relationship development and the potential costs and benefits of gender-role-related behavior. Researchers might also investigate how women and men utilize new technologies in their relationships (such as text messaging, instant messaging, and online social networking) and how these technologies influence relationship outcomes.

Much future research needs to be devoted to the role of gender in the relationships of gay men and lesbians, especially during relationship initiation and termination. Likewise, the relationship scripts of people from diverse cultural backgrounds require further exploration. In particular, how does the content of scripts vary in cultures where arranged marriage is normative? And what cultural factors influence the likelihood that people adhere to normative scripts? In cultures where the prevailing gender ideology tends to be traditional, individuals will be particularly likely to follow scripts. This may be especially true for women, who tend to face harsher sanctions than men do if they violate from the script. Other cultural factors may influence compliance with relationship scripts, particularly individualism-collectivism and cultural tightness-looseness (i.e., the strength of social norms and the extent to which they are sanctioned within societies; Gelfand, Nishii, & Raver, 2006).

In light of the shifting migration patterns around the globe, research should also be directed at the ways that acculturation processes influence gender traits and attitudes among immigrants, sojourners, and bicultural individuals. Much as debate about dating, relationships, and the changing role of women can lead to intergenerational conflict in immigrant families, it can also lead to conflict between romantic partners (Flores, Tschann, Marin, & Pantoja, 2004). Women transitioning to Western, industrialized societies tend to embrace the norm of egalitarianism to a greater extent than do their male partners (Tang & Dion, 1999). Researchers could also profitably explore same-sex relationships within acculturative contexts – how changing constructions of gender and sexuality influence same-sex partners' self-perceptions and relational quality.

In sum, much work remains to be done to further our understanding of the influence of gender in close relationships. Although gender continues to play an important role in friendships and intimate romantic relationships, women and men are not as different as we are often led to believe. Locating the source of gender difference and similarity within our dyadic, social, and sociocultural contexts instead of within our genetic codes may do much to debunk the myth that men are from Mars and women are from Venus.

References

Abbey, A. (1982). Sex differences in attributions for friendly behaviour: Do males misperceive females' friendliness? *Journal of Personality and Social Psychology, 42*, 830–838.
Abbey, A., McAuslan, P., & Ross, L. T. (1998). Sexual assault perpetration by college men: The role of alcohol, misperception of sexual intent, and sexual beliefs and experiences. *Journal of Social and Clinical Psychology, 17*, 167–195.
Afifi, W. A., & Faulkner, S. L. (2000). On being "just friends": The frequency and impact of sexual activity in cross-sex friendships. *Journal of Social and Personal Relationships, 17*, 205–222.
Agarwal, P. (1991). *Passage from India: Post 1965 Indian immigrants and their children – conflicts, concerns, and solutions*. Palos Verdes, CA: Yuvati Publications.
Aylor, B., & Dainton, M. (2004). Biological sex and psychological gender as predictors of routine and strategic relational maintenance. *Sex Roles, 50*, 689–697.
Basow, S. A., & Rubenfeld, K. (2003). "Troubles talk": Effects of gender and gender-typing. *Sex Roles, 48*, 183–187.
Baumeister, R. F., Catanese, K. R., & Vohs, K. D. (2001). Is there a gender difference in strength of sex drive? Theoretical views, conceptual distinctions, and a review of relevant evidence. *Personality and Social Psychology Review, 5*, 242–273.
Behrendt, G., & Tuccillo, L. (2004). *He's just not that into you*. New York: Simon Spotlight Entertainment.
Bell, R. R. (1981). Friendships of women and of men. *Psychology of Women Quarterly, 5*, 402–417.
Bem, S. L. (1974). The measurement of psychological androgyny. *Journal of Consulting and Clinical Psychology, 42*, 155–162.
Berscheid, E., & Reis, H. T. (1998). Attraction and close relationships. In D. T. Gilbert, S. T. Fiske, & G. Lindzey (Eds.), *The handbook of social psychology* (4th ed., pp. 193–281). New York: McGraw-Hill.

Bliss, G. K. (2000). Self-disclosure and friendship patterns: Gender and sexual orientation differences in same-sex and opposite-sex friendships. *Dissertation Abstracts International Section A: Humanities and Social Sciences, 61* (5-A), 1749.

Bloom, B. L., Asher, S. J., & White, S. W. (1978). Marital disruption as a stressor: A review and analysis. *Psychological Bulletin, 85,* 867–894.

Blumstein, P., & Schwartz, P. (1983). *American couples*. New York: Morrow.

Boneva, B., Kraut, R., & Frohlich, D. (2001). Using e-mail for personal relationships: The difference gender makes. *American Behavioral Scientist, 45,* 530–549.

Bowlby, J. (1980). *Attachment and loss*. New York: Basic Books.

Brinsmead-Stockham, K., Johnston, L., Miles, L., & Macrae, C. N. (2008). Female sexual orientation and menstrual influences on person perception. *Journal of Experimental Social Psychology, 44,* 729–734.

Bronfenbrenner, U. (1979). Contexts of child rearing: Problems and prospects. *American Psychologist, 34,* 844–850.

Buhrke, R. A., & Fuqua, D. R. (1987). Sex differences in same- and cross-sex supportive relationships. *Sex Roles, 17,* 339–352.

Burleson, M. H., Trevathan, W. R., & Gregory, W. L. (2002). Sex behavior in lesbian and heterosexual women: Relations with menstrual cycle phase and partner. *Psychoneuroendocrinology, 27,* 489–504.

Burn, S. M. (1996). *The social psychology of gender*. New York: McGraw-Hill.

Buss, D. M. (1989). Sex differences in human mate preferences: Evolutionary hypotheses tested in 37 cultures. *Behavioral and Brain Sciences, 12,* 1–49.

Buss, D. M., & Malamuth, N. M. (1996). *Sex, power, conflict: Evolutionary and feminist perspectives*. New York: Oxford University Press.

Buss, D. M., & Schmitt, D. P. (1993). Sexual strategies theory: An evolutionary perspective on human mating. *Psychological Review, 100,* 204–232.

Buunk, A. P., Park, J. H., & Dubbs, S. L. (2008). Parent-offspring conflict in mate preferences. *Review of General Psychology, 12,* 47–62.

Byers, E. S. (1996). How well does the traditional sexual script explain sexual coercion? Review of a program of research. *Journal of Psychology and Human Sexuality, 8,* 7–25.

Caldwell, M. A., & Peplau, L. A. (1982). Sex differences in same-sex friendship. *Sex Roles, 8,* 721–732.

Canary, D. J., & Hause, K. S. (1993). Is there any reason to research sex differences in communication? *Communication Quarterly, 41,* 129–144.

Canary, D. J., & Stafford, L. (1992). Relational maintenance strategies and equity in marriage. *Communication Monographs, 59,* 243–267.

Carr, D. S. (2004). Gender, preloss marital dependence, and older adults' adjustment to widowhood. *Journal of Marriage and Family, 66,* 220–35.

Chang, S., & Chan, C. (2007). Perceptions of commitment change during mate selection: The case of Taiwanese newlyweds. *Journal of Social and Personal Relationships, 24,* 55–68.

Choo, P., Levine, T., & Hatfield, E. (1996). Gender, love schemas, and reactions to romantic break-ups. *Journal of Social Behavior and Personality, 11,* 143–160.

Cini, M. A., & Malafi, T. N. (1991, March). *Paths to intimacy: Lesbian and heterosexual women's scripts of early relationship development*. Paper presented at the meeting of the Association for Women in Psychology, Hartford, CT.

Claes, M. E. (1992). Friendship and personal adjustment during adolescence. *Journal of Adolescence, 15,* 39–55.

Clark, M. S., & Taraban, C. (1991). Reactions to and willingness to express emotion in communal and exchange relationships. *Journal of Experimental Social Psychology, 27,* 324–336.

Clark, R. A. (1998). A comparison of topics and objectives in a cross section of young men's and women's everyday conversations. In D. J. Canary & K. Dindia (Eds.), *Sex differences and similarities in communication: Critical essays and empirical investigations of sex and gender in interaction* (pp. 303–319). Mahwah, NJ: Erlbaum.

Cloutier, J., Heatherton, T. F., Whalen, P. J., & Kelley, W. M. (2008). Are attractive people rewarding? Sex differences in the neural substrates of facial attractiveness. *Journal of Cognitive Neuroscience, 20,* 941–951.

Colwill, N., & Perlman, D. (1977). Effects of sex and relationship on self-disclosure. *JSAS Catalog of Selected Documents in Psychology, 7,* 40 (MS. 1470).

Cozby, P. C. (1972). Self-disclosure, reciprocity and liking. *Sociometry, 35,* 151–160.

Cross, S. E., & Madson, L. (1997). Models of the self: Self-construals and gender. *Psychological Bulletin, 122,* 5–37.

Dailey, R. M., & Claus, R. E. (2001). The relationship between interviewer characteristics and physical and sexual abuse disclosures among substance users: A multilevel analysis. *Journal of Drug Issues, 31,* 867–888.

Dainton, M., & Aylor, B. (2002). Routine and strategic maintenance efforts: Behavioral patterns, variations associated with relational length, and the prediction of relational characteristics. *Communication Monographs, 69,* 52–66.

Dainton, M., & Stafford, L. (1993). Routine maintenance behaviors: A comparison of relationship type, partner similarity, and sex differences. *Journal of Social and Personal Relationships, 10*, 255–271.

Dasgupta, S. D. (1998). Gender roles and cultural continuity in the Asian Indian immigrant community in the U.S. *Sex Roles, 38*, 953–974.

Davidson, L. R., & Duberman, L. (1982). Friendship: Communication and interactional patterns in same-sex dyads. *Sex Roles, 8*, 809–822.

Davis, A. J. (1984). Sex-differentiated behaviors in nonsexist picture books. *Sex Roles, 11*, 1–16.

Davis, D., Shaver, P. R., & Vernon, M. L. (2003). Physical, emotional, and behavioral reactions to breaking up: The roles of gender, age, emotional involvement, and attachment style. *Personality and Social Psychology Bulletin, 29*, 871–884.

Davis, M. H., & Oathout, A. (1987). Maintenance of satisfaction in romantic relationships: Empathy and relational competence. *Journal of Personality and Social Psychology, 53*, 397–410.

Deaux, K., & Major, B. (1987). Putting gender into context: An interactive model of gender-related behavior. *Psychological Review, 94*, 369–389.

Deci, E. L., & Ryan, R. M. (1985). The general causality orientations scale: Self-determination in personality. *Journal of Research in Personality, 19*, 109–134.

DeLaria, L. (1995). Ms. DeLaria's dating tips for dykes. In C. Flowers (Ed.), *Out, loud, and laughing* (pp. 57–68). New York: Anchor.

Derlega, V. J., & Chaikin, A. L. (1975). *Sharing intimacy: What we reveal to others and why*. Englewood Cliffs, NJ: Prentice-Hall.

Derlega, V. J., & Chaikin, A. L. (1976). Norms affecting self-disclosure in men and women. *Journal of Consulting and Clinical Psychology, 44*, 376–380.

Derlega, V. J., Winstead, B. A., Wong, P. T. P., & Hunter, S. (1985). Gender effects in an initial encounter: A case where men exceed women in disclosure. *Journal of Social and Personal Relationships, 2*, 25–44.

Deutsch, F. M., Kokot, A. P., & Binder, K. S. (2007). College women's plans for different types of egalitarian marriages. *Journal of Marriage and Family, 69*, 916–929.

Dindia, K., & Allen, M. (1992). Sex differences in self-disclosure: A meta-analysis. *Psychological Bulletin, 112*, 106–124.

Dion, K. K., & Dion, K. L. (2004). Gender, immigrant generation, and ethnocultural identity. *Sex Roles, 50*, 347–355.

Downs, A. C., & Harrison, S. K. (1985). Embarrassing age spots or just plain ugly? Physical attractiveness stereotyping as an instrument of sexism on American television commercials. *Sex Roles, 13*, 9–19.

Eagly, A. H., & Wood, W. (1999). The origins of sex differences in human behavior: Evolved dispositions versus social roles. *American Psychologist, 54*, 408–423.

Eakins, B., & Eakins, R. G. (1978). Verbal turn-taking and exchanges in faculty dialogue. In B. L. Dubois & I. Crouch (Eds.), *Proceedings of the Conference on the Sociology of Languages of American Women* (pp. 53–62). San Antonio, TX: Trinity University Press.

Eastwick, P. W., & Finkel, E. J. (2008). Sex differences in mate preferences revisited: Do people know what they initially desire in a romantic partner? *Journal of Personality and Social Psychology, 94*, 245–264.

Edmondson, C. B., & Conger, J. C. (1995). The impact of mode of presentation on gender differences in social perception. *Sex Roles, 32*, 169–183.

Egland, K. L., Spitzberg, B. H., & Zormeier, M. M. (1996). Flirtation and conversational competence in cross-sex platonic and romantic relationships. *Communication Reports, 9*, 105–117.

Fein, E., & Schneider, S. (2005). *The rules*. New York: Grand Central Publishing.

Feinberg, D. R., Jones, B. C., Law-Smith, M. J., Moore, F. R., DeBruine, L. M., Cornwell, R. E., et al. (2006). Menstrual cycle, trait estrogen level, and masculinity preferences in the human voice. *Hormones and Behavior, 49*, 215–222.

Fink, B., & Penton-Voak, I. S. (2002). Evolutionary psychology of facial attractiveness. *Current Directions in Psychological Science, 11*, 154–158.

Fischer, A. H., & Mosquera, P. M. R. (2001). What concerns men? Women or other men? A critical appraisal of the evolutionary theory of gender differences. *Psychology, Evolution, & Gender, 3*, 5–26.

Fischer, C. S., & Phillips, S. L. (1982). Who is alone? Social characteristics of people with small networks. In L. A. Peplau & D. Perlman (Eds.), *Loneliness: A sourcebook of current theory, research, and theory* (pp. 21–39). New York: Wiley.

Fishman, P. M. (1978). Interaction: The work women do. *Social Problems, 25*, 397–406.

Fletcher, G. J. O., Simpson, J. A., & Thomas, G. (2000). The measurement of perceived relationship quality components: A confirmatory factor analytic approach. *Personality and Social Psychology Bulletin, 26*, 340–354.

Fletcher, G. J. O., Tither, J. M., O'Loughlin, C., Friesen, M., & Overall, N. (2004). Warm and homely or cold and beautiful? Sex differences in trading off traits in mate selection. *Personality and Social Psychology Bulletin, 30*, 659–672.

Flores, E., Tschann, J. M., Marin, B., & Pantoja, P. (2004). Marital conflict and acculturation among Mexican American husbands and wives. *Cultural Diversity and Ethnic Minority Psychology, 10*, 39–52.

Fox, M., Gibbs, M., & Auerbach, D. (1985). Age and gender dimensions of friendship. *Psychology of Women Quarterly, 9*, 489–502.

Fritz, H. L., Nagurney, A. J., & Helgeson, V. S. (2003). Social interactions and cardiovascular reactivity during problem disclosure among friends. *Personality and Social Psychology Bulletin, 29*, 713–725.

Fuiman, M., Yarab, P., & Sensibaugh, C. (1997, July). *Just friends? An examination of the sexual, physical, and romantic aspects of cross-gender friendships*. Paper presented at the annual meeting of the International Network on Personal Relationships, Oxford, OH.

Gagné, F. M., & Lydon, J. E. (2003). Identification and the commitment shift: Accounting for gender differences in relationship illusions. *Personality and Social Psychology Bulletin, 29*, 907–919.

Gagnon, J. H. (1990). The explicit and implicit use of the scripting perspective in sex research. *Annual Review of Sex Research, 1*, 1–43.

Gangestad, S. W., Garver-Apgar, C. E., Simpson, J. A., & Cousins, A. J. (2007). Changes in women's mate preferences across the ovulatory cycle. *Journal of Personality and Social Psychology, 92*, 151–163.

Gangestad, S. W., & Simpson, J. A. (2000). The evolution of human mating: Trade-offs and strategic pluralism. *Behavioral and Brain Sciences, 23*, 573–644.

Gangestad, S. W., & Thornhill, R. (1997). The evolutionary psychology of extrapair sex: The role of fluctuating asymmetry. *Evolution and Human Behavior, 18*, 69–88.

Gangestad, S. W., Thornhill, R., & Carve, C. E. (2002). Changes in women's sexual interests and their partners' mate-retention tactics across the menstrual cycle: Evidence for shifting conflicts of interest. *Proceedings of the Royal Society of London Series B: Biological Sciences, 269*, 975–982.

Ganong, L. H., Coleman, M., Thompson, A., & Goodwin-Watkins, C. (1996). African American and European American college students' expectations for self and for future partners. *Journal of Family Issues, 17*, 758–775.

Garcia, P. A., & Geisler, J. S. (1988). Sex and age/grade differences in adolescents' self-disclosure. *Perceptual and Motor Skills, 67*, 427–432.

Gelfand, M. J., Nishii, L. H., & Raver, J. L. (2006). On the nature and importance of cultural tightness-looseness. *Journal of Applied Psychology, 91*, 1225–1244.

Glick, P., & Fiske, S. T. (1996). The Ambivalent Sexism Inventory: Differentiating hostile and benevolent sexism. *Journal of Personality and Social Psychology, 70*, 491–512.

Gonzales, M. H., & Meyers, S. A. (1993). "Your mother would like me": Self-presentation in the personals ads of heterosexual and homosexual men and women. *Personality and Social Psychology Bulletin, 19*, 131–142.

Goodwin, R. (1999). *Personal relationships across cultures*. Florence, KY: Taylor & Frances/Routledge.

Gray, J. (1992). *Men are from Mars, women are from Venus*. New York: Harper Collins.

Greene, K., & Faulkner, S. L. (2005). Gender, belief in the sexual double standard, and sexual talk in heterosexual dating relationships. *Sex Roles, 53*, 239–251.

Hargie, O. D. W., Tourish, D., & Curtis, L. (2001). Gender, religion, and adolescent patterns of self-disclosure in the divided society of Northern Ireland. *Adolescence, 36*, 665–679.

Harnish, R. J., Abbey, A., & DeBono, K. G. (1990). Toward an understanding of "the sex game": The effects of gender and self-monitoring on perceptions of sexuality and likability in initial interactions. *Journal of Applied Social Psychology, 20*, 1333–1344.

Haselton, M. G., & Gangestad, S. W. (2006). Conditional expression of women's desires and men's mate guarding across the ovulatory cycle. *Hormones and Behavior, 49*, 509–518.

Hazan, C., & Shaver, P. R. (1987). Romantic love conceptualized as an attachment process. *Journal of Personality and Social Psychology, 52*, 511–524.

Helgeson, V. S. (1993). Implications of agency and communion for patient and spouse adjustment to a first coronary event. *Journal of Personality and Social Psychology, 64*, 807–816.

Helgeson, V. S. (1994). Long-distance romantic relationships: Sex differences in adjustment and breakup. *Personality and Social Psychology Bulletin, 20*, 254–265.

Helms, H. M., Proulx, C. M., Klute, M. M., McHale, S. M., & Crouter, A. C. (2006). Spouses' gender-typed attributes and their links with marital quality: A pattern analytic approach. *Journal of Social and Personal Relationships, 23*, 843–864.

Hendrick, C., & Hendrick, S. (1986). A theory and method of love. *Journal of Personality and Social Psychology, 50*, 392–402.

Hendrick, S. S., & Hendrick, C. (1995). Gender differences and similarities in sex and love. *Personal Relationships, 2*, 55–65.

Herold, E. S., & Milhausen, R. R. (1999). Dating preferences of university women: An analysis of the nice guy stereotype. *Journal of Sex & Marital Therapy, 25*, 333–343.

Hickson, F. C. I., Davies, P. M., Hunt, A. J., Weatherburn, P., McManus, T. J., & Coxon, A. P. M. (1992). Maintenance of open gay relationships: Some strategies for protection against HIV. *AIDS Care, 4*, 409–419.

Hill, C. T., Rubin, Z., & Peplau, L. A. (1976). Breakups before marriage: The end of 103 affairs. *Journal of Social Issues, 32*, 147–168.

Hill, C. T., & Stull, D. E. (1987). Gender and self-disclosure: Strategies for exploring the issues. In V. J. Derlega & J. H. Berg (Eds.), *Self-disclosure: Theory, research, and therapy* (pp. 81–100). New York: Plenum.

Holland, D. C. (1992). How cultural systems become desire: A case study of American romance. In R. G. D'Andrade & C. Strauss (Eds.), *Human motives and cultural models* (pp. 61–89). Cambridge, UK: Cambridge University Press.

Holland, J., Ramazanoglu, C., Sharpe, S., & Thomson, R. (1994). Achieving masculine sexuality: Young men's strategies for managing vulnerability. In L. Doyal, J. Naidoo, & T. Wilton (Eds.), *AIDS: Setting a feminist agenda* (pp. 122–148). Philadelphia, PA: Taylor & Francis.

Honeycutt, J. M., Cantrill, J. G., & Greene, R. W. (1989). Examined self-expectations, expectations for future partners, and comparative memory structures for relational escalation: A cognitive test of the sequencing of relational actions and stages. *Human Communication Research, 16*, 62–90.

Hong, S., & Bartley, C. (1986). Attitudes toward romantic love: An Australian perspective. *Australian Journal of Sex, Marriage & Family, 7*, 166–170.

Huston, T. L., & Ashmore, R. D. (1986). Women and men in personal relationships. In R. D. Ashmore & F. K. Del Boca (Eds.), *The social psychology of male-female relations* (pp. 109–132). Hillsdale, NJ: Erlbaum.

Huston, M., & Schwartz, P. (2002). Gendered dynamics in the romantic relationships of lesbians and gay men. In A. E. Hunter & C. Forden (Eds.), *Readings in the psychology of gender: Exploring our differences and commonalities* (pp. 167–178). Needham Heights, MA: Allyn & Bacon.

Hyde, J. S. (2005). The gender similarities hypothesis. *American Psychologist, 60*, 581–592.

Hynie, M., Lalonde, R. N., & Lee, N. S. (2006). Parent-child value transmission among Chinese immigrants to North America: The case of traditional mate preferences. *Cultural Diversity and Ethnic Minority Psychology, 12*, 230–244.

Ickes, W., & Barnes, R. D. (1978). Boys and girls together–and alienated: On enacting stereotyped sex roles in mixed-sex dyads. *Journal of Personality and Social Psychology, 36*, 669–683.

Jack, D. C. (1991). *Silencing the self: Women and depression*. Cambridge, MA: Harvard University Press.

Jacques-Tiura, A. J., Abbey, A., Parkhill, M. R., & Zawacki, T. (2007). Why do some men misperceive women's sexual intentions more frequently than others do? An application of the confluence model. *Personality and Social Psychology Bulletin, 33*, 1467–1480.

Jankowiak, W., & Fischer, E. (1992). Romantic love: A cross-cultural perspective. *Ethnology, 31*, 149–155.

Johnson, C. B., Stockdale, M. S., & Saal, F. E. (1991). Persistence of men's misperceptions of friendly cues across a variety of interpersonal encounters. *Psychology of Women Quarterly, 15*, 463–475.

Johnston, L., Arden, K., Macrae, C. N., & Grace, R. C. (2003). The need for speed: The menstrual cycle and person construal. *Social Cognition, 21*, 89–99.

Kanazawa, S. (2003). Can evolutionary psychology explain reproductive behaviour in the contemporary United States? *Sociological Quarterly, 44*, 291–302.

Kaplan, D. L., & Keys, C. B. (1997). Sex and relationship variables as predictors of sexual attraction in cross-sex platonic friendships between young heterosexual adults. *Journal of Social and Personal Relationships, 14*, 191–206.

Karremans, J. C., & Verwijmeren, T. (2008). Mimicking attractive opposite-sex others: The role of romantic relationship status. *Personality and Social Psychology Bulletin, 34*, 939–950.

Kenrick, D. T., Sadalla, E. K., Groth, G., & Trost, M. R. (1990). Evolution, traits, and the stages of human courtship: Qualifying the parental investment model. *Journal of Personality, 58*, 97–116.

Kiefer, A. K., & Sanchez, D. T. (2007). Scripting sexual passivity: A gender role perspective. *Personal Relationships, 14*, 269–290.

Kiefer, A. K., Sanchez, D. T., Kalinka, C. J., & Ybarra, O. (2006). How women's nonconscious association of sex with submission relates to their subjective sexual arousability and ability to reach orgasm. *Sex Roles, 55*, 93–94.

Kimmel, M. S. (1997). Masculinity as homophobia: Fear, shame,, and silence in the construction of gender identity. In M. M. Gergen & S. N. Davis (Eds.), *Toward a new psychology of gender* (pp. 223–242). Florence, KY: Taylor & Frances/Routledge.

Klinkenberg, D., & Rose, S. (1994). Dating scripts of gay men and lesbians. *Journal of Homosexuality, 26,* 23–35.
Koenig, B. L., Kirkpatrick, L. A., & Ketelaar, T. (2007). Misperception of sexual and romantic interests in opposite-sex friendships: Four hypotheses. *Personal Relationships, 14,* 411–429.
Knapp, M. L. (1984). *Interpersonal communication and human relationships.* Boston, MA: Allyn & Bacon.
Kruger, D. J. (2006). Male facial masculinity influences attributions of personality and reproductive strategy. *Personal Relationships, 13,* 451–463.
Kruger, D. J., Fisher, M., & Jobling, I. (2003). Proper and dark heroes as dads and cads: Alternative mating strategies in British romantic literature. *Human Nature, 14,* 305–317.
Kurdek, L. A., & Schmitt, J. P. (1987). Partner homogamy in married, heterosexual cohabiting, gay, and lesbian couples. *Journal of Sex Research, 23,* 212–232.
Lalonde, R. N., Hynie, M., Pannu, M., & Tatla, S. (2004). The role of culture in interpersonal relationships: Do second generation south Asian Canadians want a traditional partner? *Journal of Cross-Cultural Psychology, 35,* 503–524.
Lalumiere, M. L., Seto, M. C., & Quinsey, V. L. (1995). *Self-perceived mating success and the mating choices of males and females.* Unpublished manuscript.
Lamke, L. K., Sollie, D. L., Durbin, R. G., & Fitzpatrick, J. A. (1994). Masculinity, femininity, and relationship satisfaction: The mediating role of interpersonal competence. *Journal of Social and Personal Relationships, 11,* 535–554.
Laner, M. R., & Ventrone, N. A. (1998). Egalitarian daters/traditionalist dates. *Journal of Family Issues, 19,* 468–477.
Laner, M. R., & Ventrone, N. A. (2000). Dating scripts revisited. *Journal of Family Issues, 21,* 488–500.
Laurenceau, J. P., Barrett, L. F., & Pietromonaco, P. R. (1998). Intimacy as an interpersonal process: The importance of self-disclosure, partner disclosure, and perceived partner responsiveness in interpersonal exchanges. *Journal of Personality and Social Psychology, 74,* 1238–1251.
Levine, R., Suguru, S., Hashimoto, T., & Verma, J. (1995). Love and marriage in eleven cultures. *Journal of Cross-Cultural Psychology, 26,* 554–571.
Levy, B., Ariely, D., Mazar, N., Chi, W., Lukas, S., & Elman, I. (2008). Gender differences in the motivational processing of facial beauty. *Learning and Motivation, 39,* 136–145.
Little, A. C., Jones, B. C., & Burriss, R. P. (2007). Preferences for masculinity in male bodies change across the menstrual cycle. *Hormones and Behavior, 51,* 633–639.
Lydon, J., Fitzsimons, G., & Naidoo, L. (2003). Devaluation versus enhancement of attractive alternatives: A critical test. *Personality and Social Psychology Bulletin, 29,* 349–359.
Maccoby, E. E. (1990). Gender and relationships: A developmental account. *American Psychologist, 45,* 513–520.
MacCorquodale, P. (1989). Gender and sexual behavior. In K. McKinney & S. Sprecher (Eds.), *Human sexuality: The societal and interpersonal context* (pp. 91–112). Westport, CT: Ablex.
MacDonald, G., & Jessica, M. (2006). Family approval as a constraint in dependency regulation: Evidence from Australia and Indonesia. *Personal Relationships, 13,* 183–194.
Mani, L. (1992, Winter). Gender, class, and cultural conflict: Indu Krishnan's knowing her place. *South Asian Magazine for Reflection and Action (SAMAR),* pp. 11–14.
Marshall, T. C. (2008). Cultural differences in intimacy: The influence of gender-role ideology and individualism-collectivism. *Journal of Social and Personal Relationships, 25,* 143–168.
Mayes, S., & Valentine, K. (1979). Sex-role stereotyping in Saturday morning cartoon shows. *Journal of Broadcasting, 23,* 41–50.
McDaniel, A. K. (2005). Young women's dating behavior: Why/why not date a nice guy? *Sex Roles, 53,* 347–359.
McLaughlin, M. L., Cody, M. J., Kane, M. L., & Robey, C. S. (1981). Sex differences in story receipt and story sequencing behaviors in dyadic conversations. *Human Communication Research, 7,* 99–116.
Messman, S. J., Canary, D. J., & Hause, K. S. (2000). Motives to remain platonic, equity, and the use of maintenance strategies in opposite-sex friendships. *Journal of Social and Personal Relationships, 17,* 67–94.
Miller, R. S. (1997). Inattentive and contented: Relationship commitment and attention to alternatives. *Journal of Personality and Social Psychology, 73,* 758–766.
Mongeau, P. A., & Carey, C. M. (1996). Who's wooing whom II? An experimental investigation of date-initiation and expectancy violation. *Western Journal of Communication, 60,* 195–213.
Mongeau, P. A., Hale, J. L., Johnson, K. L., & Hillis, J. D. (1993). Who's wooing whom? An investigation of female initiated dating. In P. J. Kalbfleisch (Ed.), *Interpersonal communication: Evolving interpersonal relationships* (pp. 51–68). Hillsdale, NJ: Erlbaum.
Monsour, M. (2002). *Women and men as friends: Relationships across the life span in the 21st century.* Mahwah, NJ: Erlbaum.

Moore, R. L. (1998). Love and limerence with Chinese characteristics: Student romance in the PRC. In V. C. de Munck (Ed.), *Romantic love and sexual behavior: Perspectives from the social sciences* (pp. 251–283). Westport, CT: Praeger.

Morgan, E. M., & Zurbriggen, E. L. (2007). Wanting sex and wanting to wait: Young adults' accounts of sexual messages from first significant dating partners. *Feminism & Psychology, 17*, 515–541.

Morton, T. L. (1978). Intimacy and reciprocity of exchange: A comparison of spouses and strangers. *Journal of Personality and Social Psychology, 36*, 72–81.

Mulder, M. (1990). Kipsigis women's preferences for wealthy men: Evidence for female choice in mammals. *Behavioral Ecology and Sociobiology, 27*, 255–264.

Murray, S. L., Holmes, J. G. & Griffin., D. W. (1996). The benefits of positive illusions: Idealization and the construction of satisfaction in close relationships. *Journal of Personality and Social Psychology, 70*, 79–98.

Nardi, P. (1992). Seamless souls: An introduction to men's friendships. In P. Nardi (Ed.), *Men's friendships: Research on men and masculinities* (pp. 1–14). Thousand Oaks, CA: Sage.

Neff, K. D., & Suizzo, M. A. (2006). Culture, power, authenticity, and psychological well-being within romantic relationships: A comparison of European Americans and Mexican Americans. *Cognitive Development, 21*, 441–457.

Nolen-Hoeksema, S., & Girgus, J. S. (1994). The emergence of gender differences in depression during adolescence. *Psychological Bulletin, 115*, 424–443.

O'Connor, P. (1992). *Friendships between women: A critical review.* New York: Guilford.

O'Meara, J. D. (1989). Cross-sex friendship: Four basic challenges of an ignored relationship. *Sex Roles, 21*, 525–543.

Oliver, M. B., & Hyde, J. S. (1993). Gender differences in sexuality: A meta-analysis. *Psychological Bulletin, 114*, 29–51.

O'sullivan, L. F., & Byers, S. E. (1995). College students' incorporation of initiator and restrictor roles in sexual dating interactions. *Journal of Sex Research, 29*, 435–446.

Pawlowski, B. (1999). Loss of oestrus and concealed ovulation in human evolution: The case against the sexual selection hypothesis. *Current Anthropology, 40*, 257–275.

Parks, M. R., & Floyd, K. (1996). Meanings for closeness and intimacy in friendship. *Journal of Social and Personal Relationships, 13*, 85–107.

Penton-Voak, I. S., & Chen, J. Y. (2004). High salivary testosterone is linked to masculine male facial appearance in humans. *Evolution and Human Behavior, 25*, 229–241.

Perlman, D., & Fehr, B. (1987). The development of intimate relationships. In D. Perlman & S. Duck (Eds.), *Intimate relationships: Development, dynamics, and deterioration* (pp. 13–42). Thousand Oaks, CA: Sage.

Pleck, J. H. (1976). The male sex role: Definitions, problems, and sources of change. *Journal of Social Issues, 32*, 155–164.

Pleck, J. H., Sonenstein, F. L., & Ku, L. C. (1993). Masculinity ideology: Its impact on adolescent males' heterosexual relationships. *Journal of Social Issues, 49*, 11–29.

Pryor, J. B., & Merluzzi, T. V. (1985). The role of expertise in processing social interaction scripts. *Journal of Experimental Social Psychology, 21*, 362–379.

Puentes, J., Knox, D., & Zusman, M. E. (2008). Participants in "friends with benefits" relationships. *College Student Journal, 42*, 176–180.

Ragsdale, J. D. (1996). Gender, satisfaction level and the use of relational maintenance strategies in marriage. *Communication Monographs, 63*, 354–369.

Rawlins, W. K. (1992). *Communication and social order.* Hawthorne, NY: Aldine de Gruyter.

Regan, P. C. (1996). Rhythms of desire: The association between menstrual cycle phases and female sexual desire. *Canadian Journal of Human Sexuality, 5*, 145–156.

Reis, H. T., Clark, M. S., & Holmes, J. G. (2004). Perceived partner responsiveness as an organizing construct in the study of intimacy and closeness. In D. J. Mashek & A. P. Aron (Eds.), *Handbook of closeness and intimacy* (pp. 201–225). Mahwah, NJ: Erlbaum.

Reis, H. T., Senchak, M., & Solomon, B. (1985). Sex differences in the intimacy of social interaction: Further examination of potential explanations. *Journal of Personality and Social Psychology, 48*, 1204–1217.

Reis, H. T., & Shaver, P. (1988). Intimacy as an interpersonal process. In S. W. Duck (Ed.), *Handbook of personal relationships* (pp. 367–389). Chichester, UK: Wiley.

Rhyne, D. (1981). Bases of marital satisfaction among men and women. *Journal of Marriage and the Family, 43*, 941–955.

Riessman, C. K. (1990). *Divorce talk: Women and men make sense of personal relationships.* New Brunswick, NJ: Rutgers University Press.

Ridgeway, C. L., & Smith-Lovis, L. (1999). Gender and interaction. In J. S. Chafetz (Ed.), *Handbook of the sociology of gender* (pp. 247–270). New York: Kluwer.
Rose, S., & Frieze, I. H. (1989). Young singles' scripts for a first date. *Gender & Society, 3*, 258–268.
Rose, S., & Frieze, I. H. (1993). Young singles' contemporary dating scripts. *Sex Roles, 28*, 499–509.
Rose, S., & Roades, L. (1987). Feminism and women's friendships. *Psychology of Women Quarterly, 11*, 243–254.
Rose, S. M., & Zand, D. (2002). Lesbian dating and courtship from young adulthood to midlife. *Journal of Lesbian Studies, 6*, 85–109.
Rose, S., Zand, D., & Cini, M. (1993). Lesbian courtship scripts. In E. D. Rothblum & K. A. Brehony (Eds.), *Boston marriages: Romantic but asexual relationships among contemporary lesbians* (pp. 70–85). Amherst, MA: University of Massachusetts Press.
Rosenthal, R., Archer, D., DiMatteo, M. R., Kowumaki, J. H., & Rogers, P. O. (1974, September). Body talk and tone of voice: The language without words. *Psychology Today*, pp. 64–68.
Rubin, L. (1985). *Just friends: The role of friendship in our lives.* New York: Harper & Row.
Rubin, L. B. (1990). *Erotic wars: What happened to the sexual revolution?* New York: Farrar, Straus, and Giroux.
Rubin, Z., Hill, C. T., Peplau, L. A., & Dunkel-Schetter, C. (1980). Self-disclosure in dating couples: Sex roles and the ethic of openness. *Journal of Marriage and the Family, 42*, 305–317.
Rubin, Z., Peplau, L. A., & Hill, C. T. (1981). Loving and leaving: Sex differences in romantic attachments. *Sex Roles, 7*, 821–835.
Rudman, L. A., & Fairchild, K. (2007). The F word: Is feminism incompatible with beauty and romance? *Psychology of Women Quarterly, 31*, 125–136.
Rudman, L. A., & Heppen, J. B. (2003). Implicit romantic fantasies and women's interest in personal power: A glass slipper effect? *Personality and Social Psychology Bulletin, 29*, 1357–1370.
Rudman, L. A., & Phelan, J. E. (2007). The interpersonal power of feminism: Is feminism good for romantic relationships? *Sex Roles, 57*, 787–799.
Rusbult, C. E. (1987). Responses to dissatisfaction in close relationships: The exit-voice-loyalty-neglect model. In D. Perlman & S. Duck (Eds.), *Intimate relationships Development, dynamics, and deterioration* (pp. 209–237). Thousand Oaks, CA: Sage.
Rusbult, C. E., Arriaga, X. B., & Agnew, C. R. (2001). Interdependence in close relationships. In G. J. O. Fletcher & M. S. Clark (Eds.), *Blackwell handbook of social psychology: Interpersonal processes* (pp. 359–387). Oxford: Blackwell.
Rusbult, C. E., Drigotas, S. M., & Verette, J. (1994). The investment model: An interdependence analysis of commitment processes and relationship maintenance phenomena. In D. J. Canary & L. Stafford (Eds.), *Communication and relational maintenance* (pp. 115–139). San Diego, CA: Academic Press.
Sapadin, L. A. (1988). Friendship and gender: Perspectives of professional men and women. *Journal of Social and Personal Relationships, 5*, 387–403.
Schaffer, D. R., Pegalis, L., & Cornell, D. P. (1991). Interactive effects of social context and sex–role identity on female self-disclosure during the acquaintance process. *Sex Roles, 24*, 1–19.
Schmitt, D. P. (2005). Fundamentals of human mating strategies. In D. M. Buss (Ed.), *The handbook of evolutionary psychology* (pp. 258–291). Hoboken, NJ: Wiley.
Schmitt, D. P., Alcalay, L., Allensworth, M., Allik, J., Ault, L., Austers, I., et al. (2003). Are men universally more dismissing than women? Gender differences in romantic attachment across 62 cultural regions. *Personal Relationships, 10*, 307–331.
Schmitt, D. P., Shackelford, T. K., Duntley, J. D., Tooke, W., & Buss, D. M. (2001). The desire for sexual variety as a tool for understanding basic human mating strategies. *Personal Relationships, 8*, 425–455.
Schwartz, P. (1994). *Peer marriage: How love between equals really works.* New York: Free Press.
Serewicz, M. C. M., & Gale, E. (2008). First-date scripts: Gender roles, context, and relationship. *Sex Roles, 58*, 149–164.
Shackelford, T. K., & Goetz, A. T. (2007). Adaptation to sperm competition in humans. *Current Directions in Psychological Science, 16*, 47–50.
Sigle-Rushton, W. (2007). *Men's unpaid work and divorce: Reassessing specialisation and trade.* Downloaded fromhttp://www.genet.ac.uk/newsletter/newsletter_feb07.pdf
Simon, W., & Gagnon, J. H. (1986). Sexual scripts: Permanence and change. *Archives of Sexual Behavior, 15*, 97–120.
Snodgrass, S. E. (1985). Women's intuition: The effect of subordinate role upon interpersonal sensitivity. *Journal of Personality and Social Psychology, 49*, 146–155.
Sonnenberg, C. M., Beekman, A. T. F., Deeg, D. J. H., & van Tilburg, W. (2000). Sex differences in late-life depression. *Acta Psychiatrica Scandinivica, 101*, 286–292.

South, S. J. (1991). Sociodemographic differentials in mate selection preferences. *Journal of Marriage and the Family, 53*, 928–940.

Spence, J. T., Helmreich, R. L., & Stapp, J. (1975). Ratings of self and peers on sex-role attributes and their relation to self-esteem and conceptions of masculinity and femininity. *Journal of Personality and Social Psychology, 32*, 29–39.

Sprecher, S. (1989). Premarital sexual standards for different categories of individuals. *Journal of Sex Research, 26*, 232–248.

Sprecher, S. (1994). Two sides to the breakup of dating relationships. *Personal Relationships, 1*, 199–222.

Sprecher, S., Felmlee, D., Metts, S., Fehr, B., & Vanni, D. (1998). Factors associated with distress following the breakup of a close relationship. *Journal of Social and Personal Relationships, 15*, 791–809.

Sprecher, S., & McKinney, K. (1993). *Sexuality*. Thousand Oaks, CA: Sage.

Sprecher, S., & Toro-Morn, M. (2002). A study of men and women from different sides of earth to determine if men are from Mars and women are from Venus in their beliefs about love and romantic relationships. *Sex Roles, 46*, 131–147.

Stafford, L., Dainton, M., & Haas, S. (2000). Measuring routine and strategic relational maintenance: Scale revision, sex versus gender roles, and the prediction of relational characteristics. *Communication Monographs, 67*, 306–323.

Steiner-Pappalardo, N. L., & Gurung, R. A. R. (2002). The femininity effect: Relationship quality, sex, gender, attachment, and significant-other concepts. *Personal Relationships, 9*, 313–325.

Symons, D. (1979). *The evolution of human sexuality*. New York: Oxford University Press.

Talbani, A., & Hasanali, P. (2000). Adolescent females between tradition and modernity: Gender role socialization in south Asian immigrant culture. *Journal of Adolescence, 23*, 615–627.

Tang, T. N., & Dion, K. L. (1999). Gender and acculturation in relation to traditionalism: Perceptions of self and parents among Chinese students. *Sex Roles, 41*, 17–29.

Tashiro, T., & Frazier, P. (2003). "I'll never be in a relationship like that again": Personal growth following romantic relationship breakups. *Personal Relationships, 10*, 113–128.

Tedeschi, R. G., & Calhoun, L. G. (1996). The Post-Traumatic Growth Inventory: Measuring the positive legacy of trauma. *Journal of Traumatic Stress, 9*, 455–471.

Thomas, D. A., & Reznikoff, M. (1984). Sex role orientation, personality structure, and adjustment in women. *Journal of Personality Assessment, 48*, 28–36.

Thompson, E. H., & Pleck, J. H. (1986). The structure of male role norms. *American Behavioral Scientist, 29*, 531–543.

Thornhill, R., & Gangestad, S. W. (2006). Facial sexual dimorphism, developmental stability, and susceptibility to disease in men and women. *Evolution and Human Behavior, 27*, 131–144.

Thornhill, R., Gangestad, S. W., Miller, R., Scheyd, G., McCollough, J. K., & Franklin, M. (2003). Major histocompatibility complex genes, symmetry, and body scent attractiveness in men and women. *Behavioral Ecology, 14*, 668–678.

Tolman, D. L. (1999). Female adolescent sexuality in relational context: Beyond sexual decision making. In N. G. Johnson, M. C. Roberts, & J. Worell (Eds.), *Beyond appearance: A new look at adolescent girls* (pp. 227–246). Washington, DC: American Psychological Association.

Tolman, D. L., Striepe, M. I., & Harmon, T. (2003). Gender matters: Constructing a model of adolescent sexual health. *Journal of Sex Research, 40*, 4–12.

Trepanier, M. L., & Romatowski, J. A. (1985). Attributes and roles assigned to characters in children's writing: Sex differences and sex-role perceptions. *Sex Roles, 13*, 263–272.

Trivers, R. L. (1972). Parental investment and sexual selection. In B. Campbell (Ed.), *Sexual selection and the descent of man, 1871–1971* (pp. 136–179). Chicago, IL: Aldine.

Walker, K. (1994). Men, women, and friendship: What they say, what they do. *Gender & Society, 8*, 246–265.

Walster, E., Aronson, V., Abrahams, D., & Rottman, L. (1966). Importance of physical attractiveness in dating behavior. *Journal of Personality and Social Psychology, 4*, 508–516.

Walzer, S. (2008). Redoing gender through divorce. *Journal of Social and Personal Relationships, 25*, 5–21.

Wellman, B., & Frank, K. A. (2001). Network capital in a multilevel world: Getting support from personal communities. In N. Lin, K. S. Cook, & R. S. Burt (Eds.), *Social capital: Theory and research* (pp. 233–273). Piscataway, NJ: Aldine Transaction.

Williams, K. (2003). Has the future of marriage arrived? A contemporary examination of gender, marriage, and psychological well-being. *Journal of Health and Social Behavior, 44*, 470–87.

Wood, J. W. (1994). *Dynamics of human reproduction: Biology, biometry, demography*. Hawthorne, NY: Aldine de Gruyter.

Wood, J. T., & Inman, C. C. (1993). In a different mode: Masculine styles of communicating closeness. *Journal of Applied Communication Research, 21*, 279–295.

Wong, M. M., & Csikszentmihalyi, M. (1991). Affiliation motivation and daily experience: Some issues on gender differences. *Journal of Personality and Social Psychology, 60*, 154–164.

Youniss, J., & Smollar, J. (1985). *Adolescent relations with mothers, fathers, and friends*. Chicago, IL: University of Chicago Press.

Zimmerman, D. H., & West, C. (1975). Sex roles, interruptions and silences in conversation. In B. Thorne & N. Henley (Eds.), *Language and sex: Difference and dominance* (pp. 105–129). Rowley, MA: Newbury House.

Chapter 13
Gender, Aggression, and Prosocial Behavior

Irene Hanson Frieze and Man Yu Li

In this chapter, we examine research on gender and antisocial as well as prosocial behavior in North America. First we examine the many forms of violent and aggressive behavior that occur in everyday life. These include criminal violence, intimate partner violence, child and elder abuse, sibling violence, peer violence, and violence in the workplace. We also briefly review laboratory studies of aggression with college student samples. Then, we turn to a review of research on gender differences in prosocial behaviors. In this section, we examine empathy, disclosure, helping, and compassionate love. Throughout the chapter, we focus on issues related to gender differences in these behaviors, rather than a complete review of research on all of these topics.

The types of behaviors discussed in this chapter are strongly influenced by cultural factors. Thus, we have not attempted to generalize the findings of US and Canadian studies to other cultures. Culture influences gender-role expectations as well as other norms and role expectations. Bond (2004) argued that cultural socialization affects not only the ways we define different types of behaviors as aggressive but also ideas about what one should do to whom and in what context. Often the goal of cross-cultural comparisons is to understand basic causes of aggression, but interpreting the differences found can be quite complex (Bond, 2004; Wood & Eagly, 2002). We do not attempt to discuss causes of aggression or prosocial behavior in this relatively brief overview.

There is strong evidence that, overall, at least in terms of the types of aggressive behaviors that can be observed in public settings, men and boys tend to do these more than women and girls in many different cultures around the world (e.g., Segall, Ember, & Ember, 1997). There has been much less research on prosocial behavior in other cultures than on aggression, although studies in both areas are limited. Wood and Eagly (2002) suggested that women may engage in more prosocial behavior than men because of the requirements of traditional gender roles, as women typically have more responsibility for the care of children.

Aggression

Defining Aggression

Aggression can be defined in many ways. There is still some disagreement among researchers about how best to define it. Psychologists most often define aggression as *behavior with the intent to harm another* (Geen, 1998). Violent behavior is generally considered aggressive, but does not have to be. Accidental violence would not technically be aggressive if there is no intent to harm the other,

I.H. Frieze (✉)
University of Pittsburgh, Pittsburgh, PA, USA

and aggression does not have to be violent. Forms of nonviolent aggression include verbal hostility, nonverbal hostility, and harming or taking another's property. Saying negative things about someone to someone else is another example of nonviolent aggression. Feelings of resentment, suspicion, or opposition are often associated with aggression (Buss & Durkee, 1957). Many researchers also include withdrawal as a form of aggression, especially when such withdrawal occurs during a conversation or other form of interaction and has a hostile intent (Frieze & McHugh, 1992). Such forms of aggression can be labeled "indirect" aggression.

Another form of aggression has been labeled as "relational aggression" (Crick & Grotpeter, 1995). This is behavior that harms others by damaging interpersonal relationships. At least in children, relational aggression appears to be more commonly done by girls than by boys. Relational aggression can occur through spreading rumors about someone that lead to others disliking them. Excluding others from a group or withdrawing one's friendship is another example of relational aggression. When French and his colleagues (French, Jansen, & Pidada, 2002) asked US children in the fifth and eighth grades to describe a peer they disliked, they were able to code many of the children's responses into categories of physical aggression, verbal aggression, relationship manipulation, social ostracism, and malicious rumors. Verbal aggressiveness was the most common reason listed for not liking someone. Using one of the forms of relational aggression (i.e., ostracizing other children from a group or spreading rumors) was the next most often cited by girls as a reason for disliking someone. Boys were more likely to list someone being physically aggressive as a reason for dislike, although relational aggressiveness was also mentioned. In their discussion of these findings, French et al. pointed out that girls are more likely than boys to engage in relational aggression.

Much of the research on aggression in everyday life concerns physical violence, as this is the most obvious, the most easily measured, and has the greatest consequences for the targets of aggression. Research and popular belief generally show that violent and nonviolent aggression often occur together. Those who are physically violent are usually aggressive in nonviolent ways as well (Marshall, 1994). In this chapter, we consider all of these different forms of aggression with a focus on violence or physical aggression.

Stereotypes of Gender and Aggression

One of our strongest gender stereotypes is that boys and men are more aggressive than girls and women (e.g., Lightdale & Prentice, 1994; Williams & Best, 1982). This association can be seen in a study where college students of both genders were asked about a time they "acted in a masculine way" and a time they "acted in a feminine way." One of the most common themes found for both men and women when they described how they were "masculine" was engaging in some type of aggressive or violent behavior (Signorella & Frieze, 1989).

The association of aggressiveness with masculinity can also be seen in the Bem Sex Role Inventory (BSRI; Bem, 1974), a scale often used to assess self-perceptions of masculinity and femininity. The term "aggressive" is one of the masculine traits included in the BSRI. It is not surprising, given the masculinity items, that Kopper and Epperson (1991) found that both female and male college students who scored high on BSRI masculinity were more likely to be prone to anger and to express that anger toward other people. In another study, both female and male college students who rated themselves as more masculine were more likely to demonstrate aggressive behavior in the laboratory by giving shocks to another student (Hammock & Richardson, 1992).

Given the association of masculinity and aggression in the general public, it is not surprising that researchers have also tended to assume that men and boys are more aggressive than women and girls. Many of the early researchers looked for evidence of gender differences in aggressive children and adolescents. Maccoby and Jacklin (1974), in their classic review of gender differences (primarily in children) in behavior and personality, stated that aggression was one of the four aspects of personality, ability, or behavior in which the genders differed from each other. They argued that boys were more aggressive than girls and believed that boys were more ready to learn and display aggressive behaviors because of biological factors, such as hormones. Another explanation given for greater aggressiveness in boys is their higher likelihood of participating in competition in real-life settings. This desire for competition is seen as leading to increased aggressiveness. Eagly and Steffen (1986), who did a later meta-analysis of gender and aggressive behavior, also argued that men display and receive more aggression than women do, except in situations where gender roles are not salient. However, Eagly and Steffen (1986) disagreed with Maccoby and Jacklin's (1974) conclusion that aggression is one of the largest behavioral gender differences; they argued that equally large gender differences could be seen for helping and nonverbal behavior. Rather than attributing the aggressiveness of men and boys to biological factors, Eagly and Steffen (1986) suggested that difference in beliefs about the consequences of aggression mediated the gender differences in aggressive behaviors. In another review, Bettencourt and Miller (1996) focused on the moderating effect of provocation on aggression. They argued that men and boys respond more aggressively than women and girls do because men are more often provoked. When levels of provocation are controlled, gender differences in aggression are greatly reduced. Bettencourt and Miller argued that provocation attenuates the impact of gender-role norms and thus reduces the gender differences in aggression. Similar to Eagly and Steffen (1986), Bettencourt and Miller (1996) also argued that beliefs about the outcome of any aggressive action predict gender differences in aggression. Such beliefs might include appraisals of possible danger from retaliation or whether or not the level of provocation justifies aggression. Thus, the general argument has been that men and boys do behave in more aggressive ways than women and girls do, on average, but that many social, as well as biological, factors may account for these differences.

Researchers' beliefs about men's greater aggressiveness are also mirrored in self-report studies where people are asked to rate themselves on how often they use various types of aggression. Richardson and Green (2003) summarized 10 different studies with a total of over 1500 respondents and found general support for higher self-reports in men than in women, with some important exceptions. There were differences found in reports of direct and indirect aggression. According to the Richardson Conflict Response Questionnaire (Green, Richardson, & Lago, 1996) which Richardson and Green (2003) used in their study, direct aggression consists of aggressive behaviors such as yelling or screaming at another person, throwing something at someone, pushing, grabbing, shoving, and so on, whereas indirect aggression is defined as harming others in an indirect way such as by making up stories to get others in trouble, spreading rumors about someone, or gossiping. In a series of studies on this type of aggression, Richardson (2005) concluded that direct aggression is used when people feel comfortable acting in the situation. She argued that women generally are not comfortable being aggressive because this violates gender stereotypes. But, when they can do it in private, women are much more likely to use direct aggression. When in a public space women respond to provocation more often with indirect than with direct physical aggression.

In a more recent analysis of gender and aggression, Archer (2004) made the point that researchers need to recognize different kinds of aggression, such as direct physical or verbal hostility and indirect aggression. Indirect aggression might include saying something negative about one person to someone else or withdrawing from an interaction when the other person expects a response (Archer & Coyne, 2005). Archer's (2004) review of previous studies of children indicated that both physical and verbal aggression were more common in boys; gender differences in physical aggression were greater than differences in verbal aggression. However, the data were not clear for indirect aggression. Archer and Cote (2005) believed that it was later in children's development that they began to use indirect aggression and that girls started to use this form of aggression more than boys because of their earlier maturation. They reported no gender differences in indirect aggression in adults.

Controlled Laboratory Studies

An important source of data on gender and aggression comes from studies of college students given tasks in the laboratory. Such studies involve a situation that allows for aggressive responses that do not actually hurt anyone. Thus, the researcher can study actual aggressive *behavior*, rather than relying only on self-reports. A classic technique involves telling the students that they are in a study of the effects of punishment on learning (Geen & O'Neal, 1969). The students are told that they are in the "teacher" condition and are asked to give shocks to other students in the "learning" condition when they did not appear to be learning the material. In actuality, the "learners" are confederates who are asked to pretend not to learn the material and to act as though they are being hurt by the shocks they appear to be receiving. The number and degree of shocks given are used as a measure of aggressiveness. When women are included in such studies, they are often paired with a female "learner," whereas men have a male "learner." Data from this and similar methods indicate that men are more aggressive than women (e.g., Richardson, 2005).

The conclusion about men's greater aggression in these laboratory studies is quite robust, but the studies on which that conclusion is based have a fundamental methodological problem. To control for any possible cross-gender effects, the laboratory studies are generally set up so that men are asked to aggress against other men, whereas women are asked to aggress against other women. This means that the gender of the perpetrator is confounded with the gender of the target. When target gender is one of the variations in the design, it is clear that both women and men are less likely to be aggressive toward a female than toward a male target (Richardson, 2005). Other studies, often conducted outside of the laboratory, have also indicated that men are more often the *targets* of aggression than women are, especially by male aggressors (Frieze, 2005; Graham & Wells, 2001). Both women and men apparently believe that it is not "right" to be aggressive toward women and that others disapprove of such behavior (Baron & Richardson, 1994; Harris & Knight-Bohnhoff, 1996). The highest levels of aggression in the controlled laboratory studies occurred with male study participants, given the opportunity to aggress against another man (Richardson, 2005).

Although the lower levels of stranger aggression against women are often interpreted as a form of "chivalry," another explanation is that women are not believed to provoke violence or otherwise to be as deserving of violence as men are. In support of this idea, a study that included a diverse sample of men and women found that both sexes report more anger toward hypothetical men than women (Brody, Lovas, & Hay, 1995). Laboratory studies further document the effects of perceived insult and anger on aggression. Richardson and her colleagues (Richardson, Leonard, Taylor, & Hammock, 1985) asked men to squeeze a device for measuring hand strength. A female experimenter recorded their scores. In some conditions, the men were told their performance was poor and were further insulted by the female experimenter who said "I thought men were supposed to be strong" or "Maybe you should let me do that." The men were later given an opportunity to aggress against the female experimenter. Those men who were told that they had performed poorly and who were insulted displayed very high levels of aggression against the female experimenter. Thus, when women are seen as threatening, they can certainly become targets of aggression.

Thus, in the body of work on aggression in laboratory and natural settings, one does see some evidence of women's aggressiveness, even toward strangers, but such data depend a great deal on how aggression is defined. Studies of aggression usually focus on physical violence or intentions to injure another person. It is in these types of studies where the gender differences are greatest. Research on other forms of nonviolent aggression, such as manipulation, sometimes shows that women are more likely than men to express aggression in this form (Björkqvist, Lagerspetz, & Kaukiainen, 1992). Women certainly do respond to provocation or to frustration with aggression, just as men do, and women engage in other forms of aggression as well (Bettencourt & Miller, 1996; White & Kowalski, 1994). For example, a recent study of Toronto college students' and university employees' self-reports of aggression while driving a car yielded few gender differences, and both men and women reported engaging in behaviors such as horn honking, swearing at other drivers, and using insulting hand gestures (Hennessy & Wiesenthal, 2001).

Expressions of Aggression in Everyday Life

How is aggression expressed by women and girls and men and boys in their daily lives? We next examine a number of domains in which one can see uncontrolled aggression and violence as it is naturally expressed. Much of the data related to these different types of aggression relies on self-reports. Such data are not ideal and do potentially have biases related to wanting to avoid socially undesirable behavior. However, we believe that it is important to examine these various types of aggression and not to rely only on controlled laboratory studies of college students. In the following section, we review research on personal experience of violence in everyday life, criminal behaviors, intimate partner violence, violence against children and elders, sibling violence, bullying in children, rape, and workplace violence.

Personal Experiences of Violence in Everyday Life

One way of thinking about gender and aggression is to survey people about their own experiences with violence. In a random sample of 1753 adults in Ontario, Canada, people were asked if they had ever been personally involved in a situation with another adult where someone was "pushing, grabbing, hitting, or being physically aggressive in any other way" in the last 12 months (Graham & Wells, 2001). Most people said "no." The 9% who did say "yes" were asked more about the incident. Those who described what happened were more often men and the younger members of the sample. It was estimated that men are 25 times more likely than women to have had such experiences. These data suggest that more men than women live in a violent world, although the large majority of the sample did not recall any violent incident in the last year. Other studies confirm that, even in college samples, men, on average, report having experienced more violence both recently and over their lifetimes than women do (Harris, 1996).

Graham and Wells (2001) further concluded that the types of aggressive experiences reported by women differed from those most often reported by men. For women, the aggression more often involved someone whom they considered an intimate partner and the aggression occurred in the home. The aggression was often associated with jealousy, and the incident was upsetting for these women. For men, the aggression was more often associated with a male stranger, and it occurred in a bar or other public location. Men tended not to be upset by these incidents. Although the researchers did not comment on this, we might assume that some of the men were also involved in intimate partner violence, although this did not seem to be what most men thought about when asked about experiences with aggression. Graham and Wells suggested that men may not take intimate partner violence as seriously as women do, and they may be less likely to remember it. These findings are consistent with other data that indicate that men are generally less likely to show strong negative psychological or emotional reactions to being assaulted, whereas women are more likely to have negative reactions to being assaulted (Acierno, Kilpatrick, & Resnick, 1999).

Gender and Criminal Behavior

Many forms of aggression are illegal, and data on all forms of criminal behavior are collected by the US Department of Justice Bureau of Justice Statistics (BJS). These data come from police and court records as well as from household surveys of national random samples where people are asked about their experiences as a crime victim. According to the Sourcebook of Criminal Justice Statistics (Pastore & Kathleen, 2003), a compilation of both forms of data, in 2002, most of the violent crime arrests were men (83%), and the rate of arrests was higher for men than for women across all kinds of violent crimes, including murder (89%), forcible rape (99%), robbery (90%), and aggravated assault (80%). Thus, men clearly commit much more of this type of aggression than women do.

Men are also more likely than women to be the victims of violent crimes, although the gender difference has decreased in the latter part of the 20th century. By 2006, it was estimated that, for every 1,000 persons aged 12 years and older, the victimization rate for any violent crime was 26.5 for 1000 men and 22.9 for 1000 women (BJS, 2007). Men are more likely than women to be victims of all kinds of violent crimes except sexual assault and rape. The large majority of crimes occur among people who are acquainted. It is interesting to note, though, that women are more likely to be victimized by non-strangers (70%), whereas men are more likely to be victimized by strangers (47%). Furthermore, victimization by an intimate is higher for women (21%) than for men (5%). When considering the data above, readers should note that men are found to be less likely than women to report violent crimes when they experience them. Therefore, victimization rate for men reported above may be underestimated.

Intimate Partner Violence and Aggression

As a result of extensive publicity and research, there is now strong awareness and sympathy in the USA for battered women who are abused by a husband or partner, and there is strong disapproval of men who abuse their wives or girlfriends (Felson, 2002; Frieze, 2008). When people think about intimate partner violence, it is generally very severe, one-sided violence initiated by the man that comes to mind. However, the reality of physical aggression in partnerships is quite different (Frieze, 2008). Unlike the data for gender and aggression in laboratory studies, there is clear evidence that women are *more* likely than men to engage in low-level physical aggression such as hitting, pushing, shoving, or slapping when the target is an intimate partner (Archer, 2000a, 2000b). At the same time, there is a population of severely battered women injured by their intimate partners (e.g., Frieze, 2005). How do we reconcile these two types of data?

One framework for understanding partner violence is to accept the fact that there are many different forms of such violence. Because of the widespread use by researchers of the Conflict Tactics Scale (e.g., Straus, Hamby, Boney-McCoy, & Sugarman, 1996), any time someone indicates use of any form of physical aggression, such as pushing or shoving the partner, the person is classified as "violent." Men, of course, are typically bigger and stronger than women and are more capable of inflicting serious injury. Archer's (2000a) meta-analysis supports the idea that men do use more severe violence with intimate partners. He reported in his summary of many studies of dating and marital violence that 65% of those who had reported any injury were women and 71% of those who had received medical attention were women. Richardson (2005) noted that such data are consistent with laboratory studies of aggressiveness, where men are more likely than women to use the most severe aggressive tactics available to the study participants.

Of course, women can also use serious violence against an intimate partner. Archer's (2000a) data on injury rates indicate that 29% of those who required medical attention for partner violence were men. Because he did not include same-sex couples in his database, these injuries came from female partners. Thus, women can be very violent toward an intimate partner. However, the large majority of partner "violence" consists of acts such as pushing or shoving that do not result in injury and are not seen as serious by those involved. Perhaps because of the severe disapproval of men's violence toward a female partner, these low-level violent actions are more often done by women than by men. Our present methodologies do not easily allow us to differentiate those couples in which more serious aggression occurs from those in which only low-level violence occurs. The severely violent individual is now being classified as an "intimate terrorist," whereas lower level acts of physical aggression are sometimes called "common couple violence" (Johnson & Ferraro, 2000). Once researchers looked at different patterns of partner violence, it became clear that the large majority of couples engage in mutual low-level acts of physical aggression. The severely battered woman, or victim of an intimate terrorist, is relatively uncommon when we consider all of the common acts of low-level violence that actually occur among couples (Frieze, 2008; Williams & Frieze, 2005).

Violence and Aggression Toward Children and Elderly Family Members

Consistent with the data on intimate partners, there is also evidence that women are more likely than men to be violent or aggressive toward children and toward elderly parents or spouses. One reason for this gender difference may be that women spend more time with children and elderly family members who need care and thus have more opportunity for physical and other forms of aggression. Because of this greater exposure, they may also have more experiences of frustration in the course of providing this care.

Data on child abuse are difficult to obtain because children are often unable to report abuse and their adult caretakers are unlikely to report their own violence toward or abuse of these children. The US Department of Health and Human Services (DHHS, 2005) has estimated that over 900,000 children per year are maltreated. The most common form of maltreatment is neglect (61%). Other forms identified included physical abuse (10%) and emotional abuse (5%). Neglect is generally defined as a failure to meet minimal community standards of care. Although neglect can be aggressive, it is typically associated with caretakers' stress and/or lack of parenting skills (Hines & Malley-Morrison, 2005). As women are more often caretakers of children, especially very young children where neglect is most common, it is not surprising that women are blamed for child neglect more often than men are.

Physical child abuse is more clearly identified with aggression. It is typically associated with injuries in children that require medical attention or result in death. Because the signs of physical abuse are more visible, it is more often identified than neglect is, but when caretakers use violence against children that does not result in severe injury, it is unlikely to be noticed by others or reported (Hines & Malley-Morrison, 2005). National rates of reported physical child abuse rose during the 1970s and 1980s, probably because of greater publicity and awareness among the public about this problem. However, rates declined through the years 1990–2004. In an analysis of why this decline occurred, Finkelhor and Jones (2006) argued that a major factor was greater use of prescription drugs, such as Prozac, by caretakers. This suggests that caretakers' stress and depression are major causes of child abuse. But children are also being given medications, and perhaps difficult children have become less difficult as a result of their own use of prescription drugs. As mentioned above, women tend to spend more time with children than men do, thus, as with neglect, mothers are more likely than fathers to commit abuse (Hines & Malley-Morrison, 2005). However, fathers can be abusive of children, too. Men who are highly violent toward their intimate partner also appear to be highly likely to be physically abusive of their children (Frieze, 2005). Predictors of child abuse include parental stress and characteristics of children that make them "difficult." Abusive parents may have learned to be abusive by growing up with parents who abused them. Perhaps because of the very difficult situation in which they find themselves, battered women have high rates of abuse of their own children (Frieze, 2005).

Finally, abuse of the elderly within families is a type of within-family violence that has recently begun to receive researchers' attention. As with children, abuse of the elderly most often involves physical neglect, but it can also include physical violence. Most researchers have argued that female caregivers are more likely than male caregivers to be perpetrators in elder abuse; however, much of this abuse is probably neglect (e.g., Penhale, 2003). Men may be more likely than women to be physically abusive. The National Elder Abuse Incidence Study (NEAIS) data showed that more men (53%) than women (47%) were perpetrators of all kinds of abuse except neglect, and others also have reported that men are more likely than women to be the perpetrators of physical abuse of elders (e.g., Dimah & Dimah, 2003; Penhale, 2003; Weeks, Richards, Nilsson, Kozma, & Bryanton, 2004). However, the data may be affected by biased reporting by social service agencies. One study (Bell, Oyebode, & Oliver, 2004) of 135 social workers, care managers, and home care assistants showed that investigators were more likely to take action and to label the situation as abusive when the caregivers were men than when they were women.

The National Center on Elder Abuse (NCEA, 2004) found that women (66% of cases) were the victims of elder abuse more often than men in an analysis of US data from Adult Protective Services. The National Elder Abuse Incidence Study (NEAIS), which was also done by NCEA (1998), showed more details about the prevalence and pattern of elder abuse. The study was based on using domestic elder abuse data from different agencies, including Adult Protective Services, as well as from individuals in agencies who were trained to have frequent contact with people over 60 years old, such as hospitals and elder care providers, in 20 counties across 15 states. It was found that approximately 450,000 elders were abused or neglected during 1996 in domestic settings. More women than men were found to be victims of all types of elder abuse except abandonment. Data showed that women constituted 76% of emotional abuse cases, 71% of physical abuse cases, 63% of financial exploitation cases, and 60% of neglect cases, whereas men constituted 62% of abandonment cases. More women than men as victims of elder abuse also have been found in other studies (Penhale, 2003; Weeks et al., 2004). Of course, because women are more likely than men to live long enough to be elders, it is unclear how to interpret these data.

Sibling Violence

Sibling violence is quite common; 82% of children in a national study reported having experienced at least one act of sibling violence in the last year (Straus, Gelles, & Steinmetz, 1980). Sibling violence is generally regarded as the most common form of family violence (Hoffman, Kiecolt, & Edwards, 2005). Simonelli, Mullis, Elliott, and Pierce (2002) also found that aggressive behaviors among siblings, including emotional, physical, and sexual aggression, were more common than parental aggression toward children. Although much of this aggression is relatively minor and does not result in injury, it can be extreme. Because of its very high frequency, sibling violence is only labeled as abusive when the target of the violence is much smaller than the perpetrator, when there is frequent violence over long periods of time, when the violent interactions are hidden from others, and when there is serious physical or emotional injury as a result of the aggression (Hines & Malley-Morrison, 2005).

The data on gender differences in sibling violence are complex; gender differences are not consistent, nor are they large. For example, Kettrey and Emery (2006), in a study of college students' recall of violence directed toward the sibling with whom they had had the most disagreements, reported that men were not significantly more likely than women to recall using extreme violence (73 versus 69%), and, for all levels of sibling violence, the students generally reported that the violence was mutual. However, in other samples, more boys than girls are often found to use more extreme forms of violence toward siblings. For example, Noland, Liller, McDermott, Coulter, and Seraphine (2004) recruited a sample of 371 unmarried community college students aged 16–30 years and asked them to recall sibling violence that happened when they were 10–14 years old. Although overall levels of any use of physical violence were about the same for women and men, men were found to be significantly more likely than women to perpetrate sibling violence by hitting with an object, hitting with a fist, smothering with a pillow, holding against the other's will, beating up, choking, and bodily throwing a sibling. Further analysis of sibling dyads showed that aggression in male-to-male dyads often involved hitting with a fist, whereas scratching was more often found in female-to-female dyads. Thus, boys were engaged in the more serious forms of physical aggression more often than girls were.

Conclusions about gender differences in targets of sibling aggression have also been mixed. Goodwin and Roscoe (1990) asked 272 high school students aged 16–19 years to recall sibling violence with their closest-spaced sibling in the past 12 months and found that boys were only slightly more likely than girls (66 versus 64%) to be victims of sibling violence.

However, other data suggest that brother-to-brother sibling violence is the most common. Hoffman et al. (2005) asked 651 college students to recall how often they engaged in sibling violence in their senior year of high school. It was found that boys committed significantly more sibling violence toward their brothers than they did toward their sisters and more than girls did toward their brothers or sisters, although these differences among these sibling pairs were not statistically significant. Brother-to-brother violence ranged from minor to serious violence, such as beating up the brother, threatening him with a weapon, and actually using a weapon against him. Women in this study remembered scratching or hitting their sister more often than men did. The women also recalled using more extreme forms of violence toward brothers than sisters. Both kicking and biting were used by the girls against their brothers.

Aggression in Children: Peer Violence

Children can behave aggressively in the home with family members, as noted above. They can also express aggression toward peers. Such behavior is labeled as peer violence, peer aggression, or bullying. Finkelhor, Turner, and Ormrod (2006) conducted phone interviews of 2030 children aged 10–17 years and adult caregivers of children aged 2–9 years in order to compare peer violence to sibling violence. Although more sibling violence than peer violence was found in younger children, sibling violence declined and peer violence increased as children grew older. Among adolescents (14–17 years of age), rates of peer violence and sibling violence were almost the same.

Forms of peer violence may differ across age groups. Observational studies, which generally involve children in younger age groups, have shown that aggression among peers appears as early as preschool (Crick, Casas, & Mosher, 1997). Preschoolers usually express aggression in less serious forms, such as excluding peers from a play group. Elementary school children may use verbal attacks or physical violence, such as kicking and punching other children (Pepler, Craig, & Roberts, 1998).

When children reach adolescence, peer violence may take a sexual form (Li, Frieze, & Tang, 2008). According to an American Association of University Women (AAUW, 2001) survey of 2,064 eighth to eleventh graders, 79% boys and 83% girls reported having experienced peer sexual harassment in school. Types of harassment were also found to differ across ages. Older students were more likely to have experienced physical forms of sexual harassment, such as being touched, grabbed, or pinched in a sexual way, or to have had someone intentionally brush up against them in a sexual way. Younger students experienced more non-physical sexual harassment, such as being the target of unwanted sexual comments. The differences were greater for boys. Physical forms of sexual harassment experienced by boys increased from 48% of eighth to ninth graders to 56% of tenth to eleventh graders.

Although peer violence can take different forms, researchers do tend to report higher levels of peer violence in boys than in girls. For example, in one observational study of 60 preschoolers, boys received and performed more physical aggression toward their peers than girls did (Ostrov, Woods, Jansen, Casas, & Crick, 2004). In another national study of high school students from the Sourcebook of Criminal Justice Statistics (BJS, 2005a), it was found that 10% of male and 3% of female students reported having carried a weapon to school and 18% of male and 9% of female students had participated in a physical fight in school. Even though these differences are small, they do support the conclusion that there is greater use of physical aggression by older boys than girls. Although this national study only included more serious acts of peer violence by high school students, there are a number of self-report studies about aggression among peers in elementary and secondary school children that did include less serious acts of peer violence. These studies usually show higher rates of peer violence. For example, in Seals and Young's (2003) study of bullying among 454 seventh and eighth graders, boys (32%) were twice as likely as girls (16%) to use this form of aggression.

Gender differences were also found in the targets of peer aggression. A US national study showed that more boys (10%) than girls (6%) reported having been threatened or injured with a weapon on school property (BJS, 2005a). Studies also generally show that more boys than girls are victims of peer sexual harassment (AAUW, 2001; Li et al., 2008; McMaster, Connolly, Pepler, & Craig, 2002). However, in a reversal of this general pattern, Seals and Young (2003) found that more girls (56%) than boys (44%) were victims of peer violence. This atypical finding may be because, in their study, less serious behaviors, such as name calling and exclusion, which are more likely to happen to girls, were included. Seals and Young (2003) also found that most of the peer violence behaviors were directed toward same-sex peers. For boys, 67% of bullying was targeted at other boys; for girls, 88% of bullying was targeted at other girls. Therefore, whether boys or girls are more likely to be the victims of peer violence depends on the level of seriousness of the behaviors as well as the gender of the perpetrators.

A form of peer violence that has recently attracted researchers' interest is cyberbullying, which is defined as "an individual or a group willfully using information and communication involving electronic technologies to facilitate deliberate and repeated harassment or threat to another individual or group by sending or posting cruel text and/or graphics using technological means" (Mason, 2008, p. 323). Electronic technologies include the Internet and text messaging on a cell phone (Mason, 2008; Slonje & Smith, 2008). Adolescents have been found to bully by sending messages to another individual or to forums to which many peers have access (Hinduja & Patchin, 2008). Research on cyberbullying in still in an early stage (Smith et al., 2008), but one of the few studies did show gender differences in cyberbullying. Li (2006) surveyed 264 seventh to ninth graders in Canada and found that boys (22%) were more likely than girls (12%) to be involved in cyberbullying perpetration. There were no gender target effects in this study; girls and boys were equally likely to have been

Rape

Rape is a type of aggression where gender differences are maximized. Rape victims were more than seven times more likely to be women than men in the USA in 2003 according to National Department of Justice data (Pastore & Kathleen, 2003). Arrest rates for perpetrators show that 98.6% of those arrested for committing rape were men; only 1.4% of those arrested were women. Although the statistics change from year to year, this extreme gender difference in rape data has been consistent, although the gender difference in victims has declined somewhat since 2003 in US data.

Although the conclusion that men perpetrate more rapes than women is not questioned, the national Department of Justice data on incidence of rape are widely discounted by researchers because rape data are especially sensitive to the way the questions are phrased. For example, Frieze (1983) reported that, in a sample of married battered women, 43% agreed that "sex is unpleasant because he forces you to have sex," whereas only 34% of that group said that their husbands had raped them. However, 73% of that same group reported having been pressured to have sex. Although the Department of Justice does not use the term "rape" in their data collection, the questions about "forced sexual penetration, involving physical force or psychological coercion" are asked in the context of a survey about experiences as a crime victim. That context may not cue thoughts about rapes that are not defined as "rape" by the victim. This miscategorization is especially likely to occur when the perpetrator is known to the victim (Frieze, 2005).

Laumann, Gagnon, Michael, and Michaels (1994) used both anonymous surveys and interviews in a US national study of sexual behavior. Reports of forced sex were higher for women in the surveys than in the interviews and men were not even asked about rape victimization in the surveys, but some did report it in the interviews. When data from both sources were averaged, 22% of women said that they had ever been forced to have sex by a man, 0.3% by a woman, and 0.5% by both a man and a woman. Among the men, 1% said they had been forced to have sex by a woman, 2% by a man, and 0.4% by both. In addition, 3% of the men and 2% of the women said they had forced someone of the other gender to have sex. Only women were asked about the nature of the relationship in the survey. The large majority of the rapists that the women described were people they knew: 4% were strangers, 19% were acquaintances, 22% were persons known well, 46% were persons with whom they were in love, and 9% were husbands.

These Laumann et al. data, like those of the US Department of Justice, do support the idea that women are much more likely than men to be victimized by rape, but clearly show that there are male victims of rape outside the prison system. (For information about the rape of male prisoners, see Beck, Harrison, and Adams', 2006 report.) The Lauman et al. data also indicate that men are the large majority of rapists, but, again, not the only rapists. Finally, as these data and those of other studies (e.g., Frieze, 2005) indicate, most rapes occur between people who know each other. Stranger rape is actually rare.

The question of how rape is defined arises in other research on unwanted sex. In a widely cited study, Muehlenhard and Cook (1988) asked a large sample of college students about experiences with "unwanted sex." Overall, 98% of the women and 94% of the men said they had been the recipients of this. Unwanted sexual intercourse was reported by 46% of the women and 63% of the men. Participants were also asked to describe the situation and the reasons for the situation. Some of the most common reasons mentioned for unwanted intercourse were that they were seduced (especially common in men, although also common in women), they were drunk, they wanted to gain sexual experience, or they gave in to the other person's request even though they did not really want sex at that time. Patterns were similar for women and men. Only a small percentage of women (6%) and men (7%) reported having been forced. Thus, these situations would not generally be classified as "rape." However, they clearly do show that rape is not the same thing as unwanted sex and that both women and men have these unwanted sexual experiences.

Workplace Violence

Another type of aggression that has recently begun to receive attention from researchers is violence in the workplace. This can come from coworkers, clients, or customers and it can be extremely violent. National US statistics indicate that, in 2005, 466 men and 98 women were victims in 564 workplace homicide cases that included shooting, stabbing, hitting, kicking, and beating (BJS, 2005b).

Other research generally shows that men engage in more workplace violence than women do. Hershcovis and his colleagues (2007) conducted a meta-analysis of 57 studies to analyze the gender effects in workplace violence. They subdivided violence into interpersonal violence (i.e., aggression directed toward an individual person in an organization) and organization violence (i.e., aggression directed at an organization itself). It was found that men engaged in significantly more workplace aggression than women did, both interpersonal aggression and organizational violence. Other studies have shown this same gender difference. Rutter and Hine (2005), in a study of 199 adult employees, subdivided workplace aggression into three subtypes: expressed hostility (i.e., verbal or symbolic aggression, such as verbal assaults or gestures), obstructionism (i.e., acts that hinder coworkers or supervisors from reaching their goals), and overt aggression (i.e., overt violent acts, from property damage to homicide). They reported that men were more likely than women to engage in all three subtypes of workplace aggression. However, in a further analysis of their data, they found that, in all of these subtypes, one reason for the gender difference was that men anticipated a more positive outcome and fewer costs from their violence than women did.

Health-care settings have especially high rates of violence (Bureau of Labor Statistics, 2000). Hatch-Maillette, Scalora, Bader, and Bornstein (2007) found that female staff members were no more likely than male staff in two mental health facilities to be targets of physical assault or threats of physical assault. However, women were significantly more likely than men to be the targets of sexual assaults. Nurses and technicians who worked directly with patients were most at risk for sexual assaults.

Summary of Gender and Aggression Research

As our review indicates, men and boys are generally more likely than women and girls to display aggression. However, it is certainly not the case that women and girls are never aggressive. In some types of situations, they appear to be as aggressive, or perhaps even more aggressive, than men and boys. Also, although researchers have found that men generally do act more aggressively than women do (e.g., Maccoby & Jacklin, 1974; Vierikko, Pulkkinen, Kaprio, Viken, & Rose, 2003), it should be kept in mind that the large majority of these studies, especially of college-aged women, involved aggression against strangers. There is increasing evidence that women are more likely to display aggressive and violent behavior toward people they know than toward strangers (Barber, Foley, & Jones, 1999). This can be seen in terms of intimate partner aggression, as well as aggression against children and the elderly.

Another theme that can be seen in our review of many different types of aggression and violence is that there is a general tendency for people to be more aggressive toward men than toward women. Felson (2002) and others have argued that social norms state that it is more acceptable to be aggressive toward men, thus both men and women may inhibit aggressive behavior more when they are angry at a woman. Researchers need to be more sensitive to this possibility, and the gender of the potential aggressive target needs to be more carefully controlled. Studies that involve women potentially acting aggressively toward other women and men toward other men, all of whom are strangers, probably maximize gender differences.

Prosocial Behavior

Now we turn to the behaviors that facilitate social interactions or benefit others, often classified as prosocial behaviors. A wide range of different types of behaviors have been included under this label by various researchers. In this chapter, we briefly review gender differences in empathy, nurturance, sensitivity to nonverbal communication, helping others, personal disclosure, and compassionate love as some important types of prosocial behavior.

As with aggression and antisocial behavior, there is also a long history of theoretical articles and summaries of empirical research on prosocial behaviors, although the data on gender differences are not as clear in these areas as they are in aggression. In this section, we review some of the classic work and then point out how ideas about the categories of behavior classified as "prosocial" have changed in recent years.

Questions about gender differences in prosocial behavior have not been as visible in the literature on gender differences as have questions about aggression and antisocial behavior, although they have been mentioned. In their classic book, Maccoby and Jacklin (1974) mentioned that gender differences in empathy are negligible and that both men and women are equally empathetic in understanding others' emotional reactions. However, they suggested that better measures of empathy were needed. They also mentioned self-disclosure and reported that gender differences were generally found in studies with younger samples, such that girls disclosed more than boys, but gender differences were not found in adult samples. Other forms of prosocial behavior were not addressed in their early review.

One of the underlying causal factors that may affect prosocial, as well as antisocial, gender differences is that women are believed to care more about other people and about relationships than men do, and women are more likely than men to perceive themselves as prosocial (Gardner & Gabriel, 2004). For example, in an extensive set of studies of vocational interests, Lippa (1998) found that women tend to rate themselves higher in caring for people than things, whereas men tend to rate themselves as higher on the things than on the people dimension. Dyke and Murphy (2006) asked adults with "notable achievements in their work" (p. 359) about how they defined success for themselves. Even within this very select sample, women were more likely than men to mention that their relationships were an important aspect of their personal definition of success. In that study, men more often mentioned money than women did.

The gendered association of women with prosocial behavior, which generally is equated with caring about other people, can be seen in ideas about femininity. Characteristics such as warmth, sensitive to others' needs, and sympathetic are some of the traits on the BSRI femininity subscale (Bem, 1974). Miller, Perlman, and Brehm (2007) pointed out that men are usually encouraged to be instrumental (e.g., assertive, self-reliant, ambitious), whereas women are usually encouraged to be expressive (e.g., warm, tender, compassion, kind, sensitive to others), especially by those who hold traditional gender roles. In general, women are more likely than men to engage in social smiling and eye contact (Hall, 1984). There is also evidence that women engage in more friendly behavior in groups than do men, who tend to be more task-oriented (Eagly & Wood, 1991).

Some researchers have questioned the association between women's roles and caring for others. As Gardner and Gabriel (2004) argued, *both* women and men are motivated to "seek and maintain connection with those around them" (p. 186). The gender difference that is so often reported could be related to the fact that women may be more oriented toward one-on-one relationships, whereas men tend to focus on group belongingness. Baumeister and Sommer (1997) made a similar argument in their analysis of the literature that shows that women are more likely than men are to think of themselves in terms of their relationships with others. They argued that perhaps men are building their close relationships through their wider social networks. This argument implies that some of the reported gender differences in caring for others and for relationships generally might disappear if a more gender-neutral measurement technique weredeveloped.

Empathy, Nurturance, and Sensitivity to Nonverbal Cues

As with other types of aggressive and prosocial behavior, there are many ways to define empathy. Empathy is sometimes associated with caring or concern for another person (sometimes labeled as "sympathy"), although it is also associated with understanding how another person is feeling (Houston, 1990). In more recent studies, these different components of empathy have increasingly been separated. For example, Hall and Mast (2008) defined "interpersonal sensitivity" as "accuracy in processing cues and behaviors in another person" (p. 144). This is sometimes assessed in terms of memory accuracy in describing another person. Other measures of empathy include having tender and concerned feelings for people who are less fortunate than oneself, feeling sorry for people when they are having problems, being protective of others, being emotionally affected by events, and perceiving the self as "soft-hearted" (Smith, 2009, p. 85).

Empathy and sensitivity to other people is typically viewed as more associated with women than with men (Garner & Estep, 2001). Studies based on standard personality inventories do tend to show that women rate themselves higher on empathy than men do (e.g., Lorr, Youniss, & Stefic, 1991; Smith, 2009). One of the explanations for this is that women care more about relationships and people in general than men do. Laboratory studies have shown some support for this idea when reactions of men and women to same-sex peers who are about to experience a high level of shock are examined. Women express more concern about their female peers than men do about their male peers (Garner & Estep, 2001). However, note that these differences could be related to people generally feeling more concern about women than men who are exposed to pain, a finding associated with the aggression literature reviewed earlier.

Another aspect of empathy is being able to judge what others are thinking based on their nonverbal behavior. A good deal of research has indicated that women are generally more accurate judges of nonverbal cues than men are (e.g., Hall, 1978; Hall & Matsumoto, 2004). Hall and Matsumoto (2004) conducted an experiment in which both men and women were asked to judge emotions from facial expressions. Women did better than men in understanding nonverbal cues even when information was minimal. One explanation for this gender difference is, again, that women care more about others than men do, and so they pay greater attention to subtle interpersonal cues. In their review, Miller et al. (2007) suggested that there were no overall gender differences in sensitivity to nonverbal cues. They argued that it was lack of attention and lack of effort that made people insensitive in nonverbal communication, and they concluded that men and women were equally sensitive to nonverbal communication when they were willing to pay attention and put in the needed effort. Another explanation for data that indicate that women are more able to interpret nonverbal communication is that the typical laboratory tasks used to assess nonverbal accuracy relate to emotions or appearance, domains typically associated with femininity and areas in which women may have more interest. However, in a direct test of these two explanations, Hall and Mast (2008) found that, even in a task defined as masculine because it was competitive, women had better recall of information about people they observed than men did. However, the gender difference was greater for the feminine than for the masculine task. Another explanation for gender differences that has been proposed (e.g., Frieze & Ramsey, 1976; Henley, 1973) is that women's sensitivity is related to having lower status than men. However, this idea has never received strong empirical support (Hall & Mast, 2008).

There is some evidence that patterns of empathy may depend on the context and the relationship between the individuals involved. In a study of marital interaction in New Zealand couples, Thomas and his colleagues (Thomas, Fletcher, & Lange, 1997) assessed empathic accuracy, an aspect of empathy that has been labeled by others as "interpersonal sensitivity." Typically, this is measured by having people watch a video of an interaction to determine if they can identify what the other person says he or she was feeling at that time. In a synthesis of studies of general empathic accuracy, Ickes and his colleagues (Ickes, Gesn, & Graham, 2000) argued that, in general, the assumed superiority of women in understanding what others are feeling is rarely found in controlled studies. Many researchers have not found any gender differences, although the results depend on the specific methodology used to assess empathic accuracy. A key variable in understanding when gender differences appear and when they do not seems to be the motivation of the participants. Ickes and his colleagues argued that women, knowing the stereotype that women should be better than men at understanding what others are thinking, try harder to do this when they know that accuracy is being assessed.

Other studies have also shown that the degree of empathy can vary for different types of individuals. In an examination of empathy for rape victims and for rapists, Smith and Frieze (2003) found that college women tended to express relatively more empathy for the (female) rape victims, whereas college men had relatively more empathy for the (male) rapists. However, overall, both sexes were more empathetic toward the female victim than toward the male perpetrator. Women in tats study also rated themselves higher than men did on a standard empathy scale. The researchers noted that empathy for the rapist was not related to the scores on standard empathy measure. In general, researchers have examined empathy for those who are victimized or less fortunate than the participants, but this type of response may be quite different than empathy for people accused of crimes or other antisocial behavior.

Helping Others

During the 1970s and 1980s, a topic of great interest to social psychologists was the investigation of the circumstances in which one person is willing to come to the assistance of another person and the circumstances in which people are apparently not willing to help others. Both environmental and social factors were investigated (see Eagly, 1987). Eagly argued that, because the traditional women's or feminine role encompasses the idea of caring for others, especially those within the family, it is not surprising that women tend to be seen by others as more helpful, kind, and devoted to other people. Studies have consistently shown that women do more caring for children in the home as well as more elder care and care of other family members who need assistance. Even in college samples, women are perceived as more helpful to roommates and friends than men are (Eagly, 1987).

Despite the association of caring and helping with women's role expectations, controlled studies have often shown that men are more likely than women to help others. These studies often involve helping a stranger, sometimes at some risk to the self, in a short-term encounter (Eagly, 1987). Thus, men are probably more likely to do this type of helping, whereas women are more likely to provide assistance to those with whom they are in a relationship. There may also be target effects that further complicate this issue. In a meta-analysis of helping studies, Eagly and Crowley (1986) found that men are especially likely to help women, whereas women are equally likely to help women and men. Men are also more likely to engage in heroic actions. Chivalry is associated with the masculine role, and it is interesting to note that the typical target of chivalrous behaviors is a woman, or someone seen as weak and in need of assistance (Eagly, 1987).

More recent studies of caring for others in daily life indicate that women spend more time than men do in these caring activities. However, men also express caring, but do so by providing for their family financially (Rossi, 2001). Rossi examined many forms of social obligation and found no overall gender differences in feelings of social obligation among adults. But, these feelings change by age. Beginning as young adults, women feel high levels of obligation to their families, and such feelings can be found in women into their 70s. For young men, both work and family obligations are seen as highly important, but, as they get older, the importance of family declines for men while work becomes relatively more important. Both women and men feel a sense of civic obligation that grows beginning in their 50s and becomes increasingly important as they age. The belief that it is important to help others is also related to socioeconomic status. According to Rossi, lower SES groups tend to focus their caring on friends and family, whereas those who are more educated extend their caring to the larger community and to social and political causes. This sociological analysis suggests that, to understand helping as it occurs in the lives of most adults, we need to look beyond college students, who are in a stage of life with relatively few social obligations.

Another form of helping is working in a "helping profession." College women rate the goal of "helping others" as more important for their future careers than college men do (e.g., Olson et al., 2006). Harton and Lyons (2003) looked at why undergraduates chose psychology as a major. Both female and male students reported that concern for others is important to being a good therapist. Harton and Lyons also found that women rated themselves higher in empathy than men did and also reported being more interested than men were in a career in human services or counseling. But, when empathy and interest in human services were controlled, there was no gender difference in wanting to be a psychology major. This suggests that female and male psychology students may be especially high in the desire to help others and possibly in empathy.

More recently, the issue of helping has been associated with volunteering. Penner and Finkelstein (1998) argued that a "prosocial personality" is an important predictor of doing volunteer work. In a large national US study, Marks and Song (2009) found that women overall spent more hours in volunteer work than men did. However, there was no gender difference in providing emotional support to close family members or instrumental support to family and friends. Men were *more* likely to provide instrumental support to less close family and friends. In terms of other measures of helping, women were more likely than men to provide emotional support to family and friends.

Personal Disclosure

Disclosure of personal information about the self is generally classified as prosocial behavior because it contributes to the development of intimacy (Darlega, Metts, Petronio, & Margulis, 1993). In general, people are viewed positively and liked more when they are willing to talk about their personal feelings and share aspects of themselves with another person. There is also evidence that we disclose more to people we already like. However, although the early review done by Maccoby and Jacklin (1974) showed that girls disclose more than boys do, there is no strong evidence that women disclose more than men do overall (Collins & Miller, 1994). In fact, Maccoby and Jacklin (1974) also mentioned that, although gender differences appeared in studies of adolescents, there were no gender differences in adult-level self-disclosures, especially in marriage as husbands and wives were found to disclose equally. There may also be target effects in disclosure. In a meta-analysis of gender and disclosure, it was found that the highest levels of disclosure appear to occur between women in their friendships with women. However, there has been little evidence of any gender difference in disclosure to strangers (Dindia & Allen, 1992).

One of the newer forms of self-disclosure is in blogs or web-logs. Web-logs are often like diaries in which people share personal information with anyone interested in reading it. Because such personal disclosure can have negative effects, many people choose to disguise themselves in these blogs and do not disclose their names or other personal information (Qian & Scott, 2007). Although there are relatively few studies yet on this type of new communication, one study of adolescents showed that girls are less likely than boys to disclose personal information (Huffaker & Calvert, 2005). The researchers suggested that young women's fear of sexual predators might explain their caution.

Blogs can also contain self-promotion and critical statements about others. In a review of informal Internet sources, Pedersen and Macafee (2007) suggested that in the USA women are more likely to offer support and warmth in their blogging, whereas men are more adversarial and self-promoting. In their own research on British bloggers, Pedersen and Macafee found similar patterns of gender differences. Other studies of Internet communication have also yielded gender differences. For example, McKenna, Green, and Gleason (2002) found that those who disclose more on the Internet are more likely to form enduring friendships and that women disclosed more than men did. Bargh, McKenna, and Fitzsimmons (2002) took this finding one step further and looked at Internet communication as compared to face-to-face communication in expressing one's "true self." They defined "true self" as the inner self that one believes is an accurate representation of one's feelings, even if those feelings are not expressed in everyday life. The self that is routinely expressed is considered the "actual self." In a series of studies, the true self was found to be better expressed on the Internet, whereas the actual self was more evident in face-to-face interactions. Perhaps because of the expression of the true self in this format, Internet communication also led to greater idealization of the target of communication, which led to more liking and feelings of closeness. Bargh et al. suggested that such effects could lead to mistaken ideas about the Internet partner and that the relationships may not be sustained in face-to-face communication. Such data suggest that the Internet and other forms of communication, such as text messaging, may be an important area of future research. However, Tyler (2002) cautioned that we can expect to see similar hierarchies maintained in these new forms of communication and that new technologies will not lead to fundamental changes in patterns of communication.

Compassionate Love

Researchers have recently begun talking about another form of prosocial behavior they have labeled as "compassionate love" (Fehr, Sprecher, & Underwood, 2009). This feeling is associated with "the giving of the self for the good of the other" (Fehr & Sprecher, 2009, p. 28), which involves valuing the other person, being open and responsive to that person, and understanding the other person. Behaviors associated with compassionate love include helping, caring, and empathy, which we discussed earlier. Compassionate love is an idea advocated by many religious teachings, but it is one that has only recently been measured or studied by social scientists. Available empirical data indicate that women are more likely than men to experience compassionate love. Women's greater levels of compassionate love can be seen in targets who are close family members as well as strangers.

Perlman and Aragon (2009) critiqued this conceptualization of compassionate love and suggested that love or caring for intimates is quite different than caring for strangers. They noted that correlations between these two different behaviors or motives are at best moderate, and they suggested that additional work is needed to measure this construct more clearly and to determine how it compares to other forms of prosocial behavior. It does appear that different researchers define compassionate love differently and, because of this, measure it differently. One issue is how compassionate love relates to empathy, itself a complex construct that is defined in various ways by different researchers. Understanding compassionate love is an important issue for future studies on gender differences in prosocial behavior.

Future Directions

In our review, we have tried to demonstrate that gender differences can be found in many types of social behaviors. But, we have also shown that context does matter. This can be seen especially in the extensive work on aggression in family settings and in intimate relationships. More research is needed to understand important contextual variables, especially for prosocial behaviors. This work needs to move beyond college samples to people in their everyday lives. Researchers also need to consider issues such as race and ethnicity. Very little has been done to look at social behavior across different groups, but such work is crucial for our greater understanding of humans' antisocial and prosocial behaviors.

As we indicated earlier, it is clear that women and girls and men and boys routinely engage in both aggressive and prosocial behavior. There are individual differences in the tendencies to do each. An examination of why people in general, and men in particular, are more likely to act aggressively is beyond the scope of this chapter, as is a discussion of why certain people are more likely to engage in any of the variety of forms of prosocial behavior outlined above. A general analysis of conditions in which women or men are more or less likely to be aggressive or to act in prosocial ways is also too complex for a detailed discussion. However, in the sections below, we examine a few of the factors that appear to be most relevant for understanding gender differences in these behaviors and describe some of the directions that future work might take.

Interactions Between Aggression and Prosocial Behavior

Although we consider aggression and prosocial behavior as separate categories of behavior in this chapter, there is good evidence that they are related. For example, Kaukiainen et al. (1999), in their study of 526 Finnish early adolescents, found that empathy was negatively correlated with three types of aggression: physical, verbal, and indirect aggression.

Other forms of aggression have also been found to be negatively related to empathy. In a study of 720 students with a mean age 15 years, Jolliffe and Farrington (2006) assessed the role of empathy in bullying and non-bullying male and female students. They divided empathy into cognitive empathy, affective empathy, and total empathy. It was found that, although cognitive empathy was not associated with bullying for boys or girls, affective empathy and total empathy were higher in non-bullying girls than in bullying girls. Although the relationship between empathy and bullying was seen only in girls, Endresen and Olweus (2001) found that, for both boys and girls, higher empathy was associated with lower positive attitude toward bullying and bullying others in their longitudinal study of 2,286 students in Norway. Further investigation showed that, particularly in boys, the gender of the target affected the relationship between empathy and bullying others, such that the relationship was significant in boy-to-boy bullying, but not in boy-to-girl bullying. Therefore, there are no consistent findings for gender differences in the relationship between empathy and bullying, and, as noted earlier, the gender differences might also be complicated by the target of the bullying.

Empathy's relationship to other forms of violence has also been investigated. Partner violence was found to be related to empathic accuracy in Clements, Holtzworth-Munroe, Schweinle, and Ickes's (2007) phone interview study of 71 couples. Lower empathic accuracy was found in violent than in nonviolent men. Violent men also were significantly lower in empathic accuracy than violent women were. Child abuse has also found to be associated with lack of empathy in mothers. In De Paul, Perez-Albeniz, Guibert, Asla, and Ormaechea's (2008) study, mothers who were classified as at high risk for engaging in child physical abuse were found to be lower in two of the three dimensions of empathy used in the study, namely personal distress (i.e., the feeling of discomfort and worry) and perspective taking. However, the study did not include fathers. In another study, Broidy and her colleagues (Broidy, Cauffman, Espelage, Mazerolle, & Piquero, 2003) found that empathy generally was higher in girls than in boys, and it was a protective factor in juvenile offenses for both boys and girls.

All of these studies suggest that the relationship of empathy to aggression is complex and needs more careful study, but that there is a general pattern of negative correlation between them. It appears that particular types of empathy may be related to specific forms of aggression. Researchers need to look at these narrower behaviors in order to understand these relationships better. The relationships found may be different for men and women and for girls and boys. The research reviewed in this chapter makes it clear that gender should always be considered in studies of the interaction between aggression and empathy or other forms of prosocial behavior.

Moving Outside the Laboratory and Considering Social Context

Lack of Social Context in the Laboratory

Eagly (1987) argued that researchers' conclusions about gender differences in behavior are often based on laboratory studies of college students. In such situations, there are few environmental influences that would lead to gender differences. But, in real life, men and women often occupy different roles. It may, indeed, be the demands of men's and women's roles that lead to the widely accepted stereotypes of gender differences and, possibly, to the validity of those stereotypes (Eagly, 1987; Eagly & Wood, 1991). Thus, it is essential that researchers who study aggression or prosocial behavior examine the behavior in settings that resemble people's lives and not just in highly artificial laboratory situations.

The importance of social role can be seen in the many studies that indicate that women and men who work in the same setting tend to be quite similar in values and behavior (Frieze & Olson, 1994). At the same time, women and men do tend to select different types of occupations, perhaps because of a better perceived fit between their own values and the requirements of the occupation (Eagly & Wood, 1991; Frieze & Olson, 1994). In general, the men and women in any given occupation will be more similar than will randomly selected samples, but there is also evidence that, even within these select groups, some gender differences may still be seen. People choose to occupy certain roles, and the choices of these roles are probably of more importance than studying women and men in any particular social niche.

It is also the case that our social environment changes over time. As Twenge (1997) has found, in an extensive meta-analysis of studies of androgyny, the gender differences in androgyny are decreasing over time, primarily because women tend to score higher on the masculine items in more recent studies than they did in the past. Reasons for these changes have not been directly investigated, but a possible explanation is that women are now more involved in the workplace than in earlier years. A tendency for higher career aspirations is especially evident in college women, the sample used in many of the studies examined by Twenge. It will be interesting to see if research questions about gender change over time as people occupy different roles. Psychology of women textbooks published in the 1970s (e.g., Frieze, Parsons, Johnson, Ruble, & Zellman, 1978) included discussions of women's lack of achievement and interest in the workplace. That issue is no longer addressed in recent textbooks.

Effects of Using Psychology Student Samples

Another difficulty in interpreting studies of college students is their particular life stage (Frieze, Sales, & Smith, 1991). At this stage of life, both women and men are preparing for future work roles. There are relatively few gender differences in their social roles. As noted earlier, Eagly's (1987) work suggests that differences in social roles intensify any possible gender differences in personality. Thus, the strong reliance of social and personality researchers on college student samples greatly limits the external validity of their findings. Another complication with psychology student samples, in particular, is that students have selected psychology courses because of their interest in the topic. As noted above, psychology students may be especially high in empathy and other prosocial behaviors, and this might be especially true for the men enrolled in psychology courses. Research that considers sample characteristics in more detail is needed to understand how generalizable psychology student samples really are in understanding aggressive and prosocial behavior.

Gender, Aggression, and Prosocial Behavior in Other Cultures

In this chapter, we have not attempted to generalize the US and Canadian studies to other cultures. Each society has its own stereotypes and unique ways of thinking about the obligations and opportunities associated with various social roles. As we have stated repeatedly, social context must be considered in any research on aggression and prosocial behavior. This will require researchers interested in other cultures first to do basic research to understand these social factors in their own society. Researchers should never assume that findings from one society would necessarily generalize to another.

References

Acierno, R., Kilpatrick, D. G., & Resnick, H. S. (1999). Posttraumatic stress disorder in adults relative to criminal victimization: Prevalence, risk factors, and comorbidity. In P. A. Saigh & J. D. Bremner (Eds.), *Posttraumatic stress disorder: A comprehensive text* (pp. 44–68). Boston, MA: Allyn and Bacon.

American Association of University Women (AAUW). (2001). *Hostile hallways: Bullying, teasing, and sexual harassment in school*. Washington, DC: American Association of University Women Education Foundation.

Archer, J. (2000a). Sex differences in aggression between heterosexual partners: A meta-analytic review. *Psychological Bulletin, 126*, 651–680.

Archer, J. (2000b). Sex differences in physical aggression to partners: A reply to Frieze (2000), O'Leary (2000), and White, Smith, Koss, and Figueredo (2000). *Psychological Bulletin, 126*, 697–702.

Archer, J. (2004). Sex differences in aggression in real world settings: A meta-analytic review. *Review of General Psychology, 8*, 291–322.

Archer, J., & Cote, S. (2005). Sex differences in aggressive behavior: A developmental perspective. In R. E. Tremblay, W. W. Hartup, & J. Archer (Eds.), *Developmental origins of aggression* (pp. 425–443). New York: Guilford.

Archer, J., & Coyne, S. M. (2005). An integrated review of indirect, relational, and social aggression. *Personality and Social Psychology Review, 9*, 212–230.

Barber, M. E., Foley, L. A., & Jones, R. (1999). Evaluations of aggressive women: The effects of gender, socioeconomic status, and level of aggression. *Violence and Victims, 14*, 353–363.

Bargh, J. A., McKenna, K. Y. A., & Fitzsimons, G. M. (2002). Can you see the real me? Activation and expression of the "true self" on the internet. *Journal of Social Issues, 58*, 33–48.

Baron, R. A., & Richardson, D. R. (1994). *Human aggression* (2nd ed.). New York: Plenum.

Baumeister, R. F., & Sommer, K. L. (1997). What do men want? Gender differences and two spheres of belongingness: Comment on Cross and Madson (1997). *Psychological Bulletin, 122*, 38–44.

Beck, A. J., Harrison, P. M., & Adams, D. B. (2007). *Sexual violence reported by correctional authorities, 2006*. Washington, DC: U.S. Department of Justice.

Bell, B., Oyebode, J., & Oliver, C. (2004). The physical abuse of older adults: The impact of the carer's gender, level of abuse indicators, and training on decision making. *Journal of Elder Abuse and Neglect, 16*, 19–44.

Bem, S. L. (1974). The measurement of psychological androgyny. *Journal of Consulting and Clinical Psychology, 42*, 155–162.

Bettencourt, B. A., & Miller, N. (1996). Gender differences in aggression as a function of provocation: A meta-analysis. *Psychological Bulletin, 119*, 422–447.

Björkqvist, K., Lagerspetz, K. M. J., & Kaukiainen, A. (1992). Do girls manipulate and boys fight? Developmental trends in regard to direct and indirect aggression. *Aggressive Behavior, 18*, 117–127.

Bond, M. H. (2004). Culture and aggression—From context to coercion. *Personality and Social Psychology Review, 8*, 62–78.

Brody, L. R., Lovas, G. S., & Hay, D. H. (1995). Gender differences in anger and fear as a function of situational context. *Sex Roles, 32*, 47–78.

Broidy, L., Cauffman, E., Espelage, D. L., Mazerolle, P., & Piquero, A. (2003). Sex differences in empathy and its relation to juvenile offending. *Violence and Victims, 18*, 503–516.

Bureau of Justice Statistics (BJS). (2005a). *High school students reporting victimization experiences and involvement in delinquent activities on school property, by sex, race, ethnicity, and grade level, United States, 2005*. Retrieved July 22, 2008, from http://www.albany.edu/sourcebook/pdf/t3572005.pdf

Bureau of Justice Statistics (BJS). (2005b). *Workplace homicides, by victim characteristics, type of event, and selected occupation and industry, United States, 2003, 2004, and 2005*. Retrieved July 24, 2008, from http://www.albany.edu/sourcebook/pdf/t31352005.pdf

Bureau of Justice Statistics (BJS). (2007). *Criminal victimization 2006*. Washington, DC: U.S. Department of Justice.

Bureau of Labor Statistics. (2000). *Labor force statistics from the current population survey*. Washington, DC: U.S. Government Printing Office.

Buss, A. H., & Durkee, A. (1957). An inventory for assessing different types of hostility. *Journal of Consulting Psychology, 21*, 343–349.

Clements, K., Holtzworth-Munroe, A., Schweinle, W., & Ickes, W. (2007). Empathic accuracy of intimate partners in violent versus nonviolent relationships. *Personal Relationships, 14*, 369–388.

Collins, N. L., & Miller, L. C. (1994). Self-disclosure and liking: A meta-analytic review. *Psychological Bulletin, 116*, 457–475.

Crick, N. R., Casas, J. F., & Mosher, M. (1997). Relational and overt aggression in preschool. *Developmental Psychology, 33*, 579–588.

Crick, N. R., & Grotpeter J. K. (1995). Relational aggression, gender, and social-psychological. *Child Development, 66*, 710–762.

Darlega, V. L., Metts, S., Petronio, S., & Margulis, S. T. (1993). *Self-disclosure*. Newbury Park, CA: Sage.

Department of Health and Human Services (DHHS). (2005). *Child maltreatment 2003*. Washington, DC: U.S. Government Printing Office. Available at http://www.acf.hhs.gov/programs/cb/pubs/cm03/index.htm .

De Paul, J., Perez-Albeniz, A., Guibert, M., Asla, N., & Ormaechea A. (2008). Dispositional empathy in neglectful mothers and mothers at high risk for child physical abuse. *Journal of Interpersonal Violence, 23*, 670–684.

Dimah, K. P., & Dimah, A. (2003). Elder abuse and neglect: Among rural and urban women. *Journal of Elder Abuse and Neglect, 15*, 75–93.

Dindia, K., & Allen, M. (1992). Sex differences in self-disclosure: A meta-analysis. *Psychological Bulletin, 112*, 106–124.

Dyke, L. S., & Murphy, S. A. (2006). How we define success: A qualitative study of what matters most to women and men. *Sex Roles, 55*, 357–371.

Eagly, A. H. (1987). *Sex differences in social behavior: A social-role interpretation*. Hillsdale, NJ: Erlbaum.

Eagly, A. H., & Crowley, M. (1986). Gender and helping behavior: A meta-analytic review of the social psychological literature. *Psychological Bulletin, 100*, 283–308.

Eagly, A. H., & Steffen, V. (1986). Gender and aggressive behavior: A meta-analytic review of the social psychological literature. *Psychological Bulletin, 100*, 309–330.

Eagly, A. H., & Wood, W. (1991). Explaining sex differences in social behavior: A meta-analytic perspective. *Personality and Social Psychology Bulletin, 17*, 306–315.

Endresen, I. M., & Olweus D. (2001). Self-reported empathy in Norwegian adolescents: Sex differences, age trends, and relationship to bullying. In A. C. Bohart & D. Stipek (Eds.), *Constructive and destructive behavior: Implications for family, school, & society* (pp. 147–165). Washington, DC: American Psychological Association.

Fehr, B., & Sprecher, S. (2009). Compassionate love: Conceptual, measurement, and relational issues. In B. Fehr, S. Sprecher, & L. G. Underwood (Eds.), *The science of compassionate love: Theory, research, and applications* (pp. 27–52). Malden, MA: Wiley/Blackwell.

Fehr, B., Sprecher, S., & Underwood, L. G. (Eds.). (2009). *The science of compassionate love: Theory, research, and applications*. Malden, MA: Wiley/Blackwell.

Felson, R. B. (2002). *Violence & gender reexamined*. Washington, DC: American Psychological Association.

Finkelhor, D., & Jones, L. (2006). Why have child maltreatment and child victimization declined? *Journal of Social Issues, 62*, 685–716.

Finkelhor, D., Turner, H., & Ormrod, R. (2006). Kid's stuff: The nature and impact of peer and sibling violence on younger and older children. *Child Abuse & Neglect, 30*, 1401–1421.

French, D. C., Jansen, E. A., & Pidada, S. (2002). United States and Indonesian children's and adolescents' reports of relational aggression by disliked peers. *Child Development, 73*, 1143–1150.

Frieze, I. H. (1983). Investigating the causes and consequences of marital rape. *Signs, 8*, 532–553.

Frieze, I. H. (2005). *Hurting the one you love: Violence in relationships*. Belmont, CA: Wadsworth/Thomson.

Frieze, I. H. (2008). Social policy, feminism, and research on violence in close relationships. *Journal of Social Issues, 64*, 665–684.

Frieze, I. H., & McHugh, M. C. (1992). Power and influence strategies in violent and nonviolent marriages. *Psychology of Women Quarterly, 16*, 449–466.

Frieze, I. H., & Olson, J. E. (1994). Understanding the characteristics and experiences of women in male- and female-dominated fields. In M. R. Stevenson (Ed.), *Gender roles through the life span* (pp. 151–178). Muncie, IN: Ball State University Press.

Frieze, I. H., Parsons, J. E., Johnson, P. B., Ruble, D. N., & Zellman, G. (1978). *Women and sex roles: A social-psychological perspective*. New York: Norton.

Frieze, I. H., & Ramsey, S. J. (1976). Nonverbal maintenance of traditional sex roles. *Journal of Social Issues, 32*(3), 133–141.

Frieze, I. H., Sales, E., & Smith, C. (1991). Considering the social context in gender research: The impact of college students' life stage. *Psychology of Women Quarterly, 15*, 317–392.

Gardner, W. L., & Gabriel, S. (2004). Gender differences in relational and collective interdependence: Implications for self-views, social behavior, and subjective well-being. In A. H. Eagly, A. E. Beall, & R. J. Sternberg (Eds.), *The psychology of gender* (pp. 169–191). New York: Guildford.

Garner, P. W., & Estep, K. M. (2001). Empathy and emotional expressivity. In J. Worell (Ed.), *Encyclopedia of women & gender* (Vol. 1, pp. 391–402). New York: Academic Press.

Geen, R. G. (1998). Processes and personal variables in affective aggression. In R. G. Geen & E. Donnerstein (Eds.), *Human aggression: Theories, research, and implications for social policy* (pp. 1–21). New York: Academic Press.

Geen, R. G., & O'Neal, E. C. (1969). Activation of cue-elicited aggression by general arousal. *Journal of Personality and Social Psychology, 11*, 289–292.

Goodwin, M. P., & Roscoe, B. (1990). Sibling violence and agonistic interactions among middle adolescents. *Adolescence, 25*, 451–467.

Graham, K., & Wells, S. (2001). The two worlds of aggression for men and women. *Sex Roles, 45*, 595–622.

Green, L., Richardson, D., & Lago, T. (1996). How do friendship, indirect, and direct aggression relate? *Aggressive Behaviors, 22*, 81–86.

Hall, J. A. (1978). Gender effects in decoding nonverbal cues. *Psychological Bulletin, 85*, 845–857.

Hall, J. A. (1984). *Nonverbal sex differences: Communication accuracy and expressive style*. Baltimore, MD: Johns Hopkins University Press.

Hall, J. A., & Mast, M. S. (2008). Are women always more interpersonally sensitive than men? Impact of goals and content domain. *Personality and Social Psychology Bulletin, 34*, 144–155.

Hall, J. A., & Matsumoto, D. (2004). Gender differences in judgments of multiple emotions from facial expressions. *Emotion, 4*, 201–206.

Hammock, G. S., & Richardson, D. R. (1992). Predictors of aggressive behavior. *Aggressive Behavior, 18*, 210–229.

Harris, M. B. (1996). Aggressive experiences and aggressiveness: Relationship to ethnicity, gender, and age. *Journal of Applied Social Psychology, 26*, 843–870.

Harris, M. B., & Knight-Bohnhoff, K. (1996). Gender and aggression I: Perceptions of aggression. *Sex Roles, 35*, 1–25.

Harton, H. C., & Lyons, P. C. (2003). Gender, empathy, and the choice of the psychology major. *Teaching of Psychology, 30*, 19–24.

Hatch-Maillette, M. A., Scalora, M. J., Bader, S. M., & Bornstein, B. H. (2007). A gender-based incidence study of workplace violence in psychiatric and forensic settings. *Violence and Victims, 22*, 449–462.

Henley, N. M. (1973). Status and sex: Some touching observations. *Bulletin of Psychometric Society, 2*, 91–93.

Hennessy, D. W., & Wiesenthal, D. L. (2001). Gender, driver aggression, and driver violence: An applied evaluation. *Sex Roles, 44*, 661–676.

Hershcovis, M. S., Turner, N., Barling, J., Arnold, K. A., Dupre, K. E., Inness, M., et al. (2007). Predicting workplace aggression: A meta-analysis. *Journal of Applied Psychology, 92*, 228–238.

Hinduja, S., & Patchin, J. W. (2008). Cyberbullying: An exploratory analysis of factors related to offending and victimization. *Deviant Behaviors, 29*, 129–156.

Hines, D. A., & Malley-Morrison, K. (2005). *Family violence in the United States: Defining, understanding, and combating abuse*. Thousand Oaks, CA: Sage.

Hoffman, K. L., Kiecolt, K. J., & Edwards, J. N. (2005). Physical violence between siblings: A theoretical and empirical analysis. *Journal of Family Issues, 26*, 1103–1130.

Houston, D. A. (1990). Empathy and the self: Cognitive and emotional influences on the evaluation of negative affect in others. *Journal of Personality and Social Psychology, 59*, 859–868.

Huffaker, D. A., & Calvert, S. L. (2005). Gender, identity, and language use in teenage blogs. *Journal of Computer-Mediated Communication, 10*(2), article 1. Retrieved from http://jcmc.indiana.edu/vol10/issue2/huffaker.html

Ickes, W., Gesn, P. R., & Graham, T. (2000). Gender differences in empathetic accuracy: Differential ability or differential accuracy. *Personal Relations, 7*, 95–109.

Johnson, M. P., & Ferraro, K. J. (2000). Research on domestic violence in the 1990s: Making distinctions. *Journal of Marriage and the Family, 62*, 948–963.

Jolliffe, D., & Farrington, D. P. (2006). Examining the relationship between low empathy and bullying. *Aggressive Behavior, 32*, 540–550.

Kaukiainen, A., Bjorkqvist, K., Lagerspetz, K., Osterman, K., Saimivalli, C., Rothberg, S., et al. (1999). The relationships between social intelligence, empathy, and three types of aggression. *Aggressive Behaviors, 25*, 81–89.

Kettrey, H. H., & Emery, B. C. (2006). The discourse of sibling violence. *Journal of Family Violence, 21*, 407–416.

Kopper, B. A., & Epperson, D. L. (1991). Women and anger: Sex and sex-role comparisons in the expression of anger. *Psychology of Women Quarterly, 15*, 7–14.

Laumann, E. O., Gagnon, J. H., Michael, R. T., & Michaels, S. (1994). *The social organization of sexuality: Sexual practices in the United States*. Chicago, IL: University of Chicago Press.

Li, Q. (2006). Cyberbullying in schools: A research of gender differences. *School Psychology International, 27*, 157–170.

Li, M. Y., Frieze, I. H., & Tang, C. S. (2008, June). *Understanding peer sexual abuse: Application of the theory of planned behaviors*. Poster presented at the meeting of the Society for the Psychological Study of Social Issues, Chicago, IL.

Lightdale, J. R., & Prentice, D. A. (1994). Rethinking sex differences in aggression: Aggressive behavior in the absence of social roles. *Personality and Social Psychology Bulletin, 20*, 34–44.

Lorr, M., Youniss, R. P., & Stefic, E. C. (1991). An inventory of social skills. *Journal of Personality Assessment, 57*, 506–520.

Lippa, R. (1998). Gender-related individual differences and the structure of vocational interests: The importance of the people-things dimension. *Journal of Personality and Social Psychology, 74*, 996–1009.

Maccoby, E. E., & Jacklin, C. N. (1974). *The psychology of sex differences*. Stanford, CA: Stanford University Press.

Marks, N. F., & Song, J. (2009). Compassionate motivation and compassionate acts across the adult life course: Evidence from US national studies. In B. Fehr, S. Sprecher, & L. G. Underwood (Eds.), *The science of compassionate love: Theory, research, and applications* (pp. 121–158). Malden, MA: Wiley/Blackwell.

Marshall, L. L. (1994). Physical and psychological abuse. In W. R. Cupach & B. H. Spitzberg (Eds.), *The dark side of interpersonal communication* (pp. 281–311). Hillsdale, NJ: Erlbaum.

Mason, K. L. (2008). Cyberbullying: A preliminary assessment for school personnel. *Psychology in the Schools, 45*, 323–348.

McKenna, K. Y. A., Green A. S., & Gleason, M. E. J. (2002). Relationship formation on the internet: What's the big attraction? *Journal of Social Issues, 58*, 9–31.

McMaster, L. E., Connolly, J., Pepler, D., & Craig, W. M. (2002) Peer to peer sexual harassment in early adolescence: A developmental perspective. *Development and Psychopathology, 14*, 91–105.

Miller, R. S., Perlman, D., & Brehm, S. S. (2007). *Intimate relationships* (4th ed.). Boston, MA: McGraw-Hill.

Muehlenhard, C. L., & Cook, S. W. (1988). Men's self-reports of unwanted sexual activity. *Journal of Sex Research, 24*, 58–72.

National Center on Elder Abuse. (1998). *The National Elder Abuse Incidence Study.* Washington, DC: Author.

National Center on Elder Abuse. (2004). *The 2004 survey of state adult protective services: Abuse of adults 60 years of age or older.* Washington, DC: Author.

Noland, V. J., Liller, K. D., McDermott, R. J., Coulter, M. L., & Seraphine, A. E. (2004). Is adolescent sibling violence a precursor to college dating violence? *American Journal of Health Behavior, 28*, 13–23

Olson, J. E., Frieze, I. H., Wall, S., Zdaniuk, B., Telpuchovskaya, N., Ferligoj, A., et al. (2006). Economic influences on ideals about future jobs in young adults in formerly socialist countries and the United States. *Cross-Cultural Research, 40*, 352–376.

Ostrov, J. M., Woods, K. E., Jansen, E. A., Casas, J. F., & Crick, N. R. (2004). An observational study of delivered and received aggression and social-psychological adjustment in preschool: "This white crayon doesn't work...". *Early Childhood Research Quarterly, 19*, 355–371.

Pastore, A. L., & Kathleen, M. (2003). *Sourcebook of criminal justice statistics 2003.* Washington, DC: U.S. Government Printing Offices.

Pedersen, S., & Macafee, C. (2007). Gender differences in British blogging. *Journal of Computer-Mediated Communication, 12*, 1472–1492.

Penhale, B. (2003). Older women, domestic violence, and elder abuse: A review of commonalities, differences, and shared approaches. *Journal of Elder Abuse and Neglect, 15*, 163–183.

Penner, L. A., & Finkelstein, M. A. (1998). Dispositional and structural determinants of volunteerism. *Journal of Personality and Social Psychology, 74*, 525–537.

Pepler, D., Craig, W. M., & Roberts, W. L. (1998). Observations of aggressive and nonaggressive children on the school playground. *Merrill-Palmer Quarterly, 44*, 55–76.

Perlman, D., & Aragon, R. S. (2009). Compassionate love: Concluding reflections. In B. Fehr, S. Sprecher, & L. G. Underwood (Eds.), *The science of compassionate love: Theory, research, and applications* (pp. 434–452). Malden, MA: Wiley/Blackwell.

Qian, H., & Scott, C. R. (2007). Anonymity and self-disclosure on weblogs. *Journal of Computer Mediated Communication, 12*, 1428–1451.

Richardson, D. S. (2005). The myth of female passivity: Thirty years of revelations about female aggression. *Psychology of Women Quarterly, 29*, 238–247.

Richardson, D. S., & Green, L. R. (2003). Defining direct and indirect aggression: The Richardson Conflict Response Questionnaire. *International Review of Social Psychology, 16*(3), 11–30.

Richardson, D. R., Leonard, K., Taylor, S., & Hammock, G. (1985). Male violence toward females: Victim and aggressor variables. *Journal of Psychology, 119*, 129–135.

Rossi, A. S. (2001). Analysis highlights and overall assessment. In A. S. Rossi (Ed.), *Caring and doing for others: Social responsibility in the domains of family, work, and community* (pp. 505–518). Chicago, IL: University of Chicago Press.

Rutter, A., & Hine, D. W. (2005). Sex differences in workplace aggression: Investigation of moderation and mediation effects. *Aggressive Behaviors, 31*, 254–270.

Seals, D., & Young, J. (2003). Bullying and victimization: Prevention and relationship to gender, grade level, ethnicity, self-esteem, and depression. *Adolescence*, 38, 736–747.

Segall, M. H., Ember, C. R., & Ember, M. (1997). Aggression, crime, and warfare. In J.W. Berry, M. H. Segall, & C. Kagitcibasi (Eds.), *Handbook of cross-cultural psychology: Vol. 3. Social behaviors and applications* (2nd ed., pp. 213–254). Boston, MA: Allyn & Bacon.

Signorella, M. L. & Frieze, I. H. (1989). Gender schemas in college students. *Psychology, 26*(4), 16–13.

Simonelli, C. J., Mullis, T., Elliott, A. N., & Pierce, T. W. (2002). Abuse by siblings and subsequent experiences of violence within the dating relationships. *Journal of Interpersonal Violence, 17*, 103–121.

Slonje, R., & Smith, P. K. (2008). Cyberbullying: Another main type of bullying? *Scandinavian Journal of Psychology, 49*, 147–154.

Smith, T. W. (2009). Loving and caring in the United States: Trends and correlates of empathy, altruism, and related constructs. In B. Fehr, S. Sprecher, & L. G. Underwood (Eds.), *The science of compassionate love: Theory, research, and applications* (pp. 81–119). Malden, MA: Wiley/Blackwell.

Smith, C. A., & Frieze, I. H. (2003). Examining rape empathy from the perspective of the victim and the assailant. *Journal of Applied Social Psychology, 33*, 476–498.

Smith, P. K., Mahdavi, J., Carvalho, M., Fisher, S., Russell, S., & Tippett, N. (2008). Cyberbullying: Its nature and impact in secondary school pupils. *Journal of Child Psychology and Psychiatry, 49*, 376–385.

Straus, M. A., Gelles, R. J., & Steinmetz, S. K. (1980). *Behind closed doors: Violence in the American Family.* Garden City, NY: Doubleday.

Straus, M. A., Hamby, S. L., Boney-McCoy, S., & Sugarman, D. B. (1996). The revised conflict tactics scale (CTS2): Development and preliminary psychometric data. *Journal of Family Issues, 17*, 283–316.

Thomas, G., Fletcher, G. J. O., & Lange, C. (1997). On-line empathetic accuracy in marital interaction. *Journal of Personality and Social Psychology, 72*, 839–850.

Twenge, J. M. (1997). Changes in masculine and feminine traits over time: A meta-analysis. *Sex Roles, 36*, 305–325.

Tyler, T. R. (2002). Is the internet changing social life? It seems the more things change, the more they stay the same. *Journal of Social Issues, 58*, 195–205.

Vierikko, E., Pulkkinen, L., Kaprio, J., Viken, R., & Rose, R. J. (2003). Sex differences in genetic and environmental effects on aggression. *Aggressive Behavior, 29*, 55–68.

Weeks, L. E., Richards, J. L., Nilsson, T., Kozma, A., & Bryanton, O. (2004). A gendered analysis of the abuse of older adults: Evidence from professionals. *Journal of Elder Abuse and Neglect, 16*, 1–15.

White, J. W., & Kowalski, R. M. (1994). Deconstructing the myth of the nonaggressive woman. *Psychology of Women Quarterly, 18*, 487–508.

Williams, J. E., & Best, D. I. (1982). *Measuring sex stereotypes: A thirty-nation study.* Beverly Hills, CA: Sage.

Williams, S. L., & Frieze, I. H. (2005). Patterns of violent relationships, psychological distress, and marital satisfaction in a national sample of men and women. *Sex Roles, 52*, 771–784.

Wood, W., & Eagly, A. H. (2002). A cross-cultural analysis of the behavior of women and men: Implications for the origins of sex differences. *Psychological Bulletin, 128*, 699–727.

Chapter 14
Gender and Group Behavior

Linda L. Carli

In the United States, it appears that the glass ceiling has broken. Women's incomes have risen; among full-time U.S. employees, women now earn 80% of what men earn, compared with only 62% in 1979 (U.S. Bureau of Labor Statistics, 2008a). Women have also made dramatic gains in education and now earn more bachelor's degrees than men do (U.S. National Center for Education Statistics, 2007). Women have greater access to leadership as well. For example, across all organizations in the United States, 26% of CEOs today are women (U.S. Bureau of Labor Statistics, 2008b, Table 11).

Although women have come a long way, they are not yet equal to men. Discrimination in pay (U.S. Government Accountability Office, 2003) and promotion (Maume, 2004) remains. Women continue to be underrepresented in the highest level leadership positions. In business, women hold only 2.4% of CEO (Catalyst, 2008) and 15.6% of top executive positions in the *Fortune* 500 companies (Catalyst, 2007). In U.S. politics, only 16% of Senators and 16.3% of Congressional Representatives are women (Center for the American Woman and Politics, 2008). Women are likewise absent from the highest positions of power in other fields, such as law (Rhode, 2001), higher education (*Chronicle of Higher Education*, 1998), and medicine (Reed & Buddeberg-Fischer, 2001).

The challenges that women face in organizations begin with and derive from obstacles that women face in smaller groups. The goal of this chapter is to examine how a group's gender composition affects its members' behavior and influence and the performance of the group, with a special emphasis on how gender stereotypes undermine women's influence and affect group behavior and performance.

Gender Effects on Group Behavior

Communal and Social Behavior

Research indicates that women exhibit greater amounts of communal behavior than men do, and men exhibit greater amounts of agentic behavior than women do (e.g., Aries, 1976; Berdahl & Anderson, 2005; Carli, 1989; Johnson, Clay-Warner, & Funk, 1996). In interactions with others, men display more dominance, negative behavior, and assertiveness, and women display more warmth, collaboration, and support (Carli, 2001; Carli & Bukatko, 2000; Carli & Olm-Shipman, 2004). For example, men show higher levels of visual dominance, which is the ratio of the amount of time that people

L.L. Carli (✉)
Wellesley College, Wellesley, MA, USA

maintain eye contact while talking to the amount of time that they maintain eye contact while listening to others (Dovidio, Brown, Heltman, Ellyson, & Keating, 1988; Dovidio, Ellyson, Keating, Heltman, & Brown, 1988). And, compared with all-male groups, all-female groups have less hierarchy: There is more equal verbal participation among members (Aries, 1976; Mast, 2001) and more shared leadership (Berdahl & Anderson, 2005) in all-female groups.

Meta-analytic reviews reveal that, compared with women, men talk more ($d = 0.14$), speak more assertively, that is, with speech acts directed at influencing the listener ($d = 0.09$) (Leaper & Ayres, 2007), and interrupt more often to gain the floor ($d = 0.33$) (Anderson & Leaper, 1998). Similarly, reviews indicate that women speak in a more affiliative and communal manner ($d = 0.12$) (Leaper & Ayres, 2007) and smile more at others ($d = 0.41$) (LaFrance, Hecht, & Paluck, 2003). All of the differences are very small except the effect for interrupting, which is small, and the effect for smiling, which is medium in size.

Similar results have been found in meta-analyses that compare the behavior of male and female leaders. Male leaders adopt a more autocratic style of leadership, whereas female leaders exhibit a more democratic style ($d = 0.22$) (Eagly & Johnson, 1990; see also, van Engen & Willemsen, 2004), and men focus more than women do on their subordinates' mistakes and failures ($d = 0.12$) (Eagly, Johannesen-Schmidt, & van Engen, 2003). Female leaders have a more transformational (i.e., coaching and mentoring) style of leadership ($d = 0.10$) and provide rewards to motivate subordinates ($d = 0.13$) (Eagly et al., 2003). These differences are small but consistent. When leading others, relative to women, men are more often directive and penalize poor performance rather than reward good performance. Women more often seek out the opinions of others; reward others; and mentor, support, and reward their subordinates.

Gender effects on group interaction are affected not only by each individual's gender but also by the nature of the group task. Women's agentic behavior increases for tasks that favor women's expertise or that are stereotypically feminine (Dovidio et al., 1988; Eagly & Johnson, 1990; Karakowsky, McBey, & Miller, 2004; McMullen & Pasloski, 1992; Yamada, Tjosvold, & Draguns, 1983). Yet, as evidenced by the greater communality of female than of male leaders, being in a position of authority does not dampen women's communion. In fact, transformational leadership reflects a blend of both agentic and communal behaviors—being a strong role model, problem solving, and effectively completing tasks as well as developing, mentoring, and supporting others (Eagly & Carli, 2007). Thus, having expertise or authority increases women's agentic behavior without necessarily reducing their communal behavior.

In addition to the nature of the group task, gender differences in group behavior also depend on the composition of the group. When gender composition effects are found, they generally reveal that people express more communal behavior toward women than toward men. For example, in a meta-analysis of gender differences in smiling, the gender difference interacts with gender composition such that the gender difference is bigger in same- than mixed-gender interactions (LaFrance et al., 2003). Gender differences in smiling shrink in interactions with women; the most smiling occurs in groups of women and the least in groups of men.

This same pattern occurs for other communal behaviors. With some exceptions (e.g., Myaskovsky, Unikel, & Dew, 2005), in group interactions, higher levels of positive social behaviors are directed at women than at men (Aries, 1976; Carli, 1989; Johnson et al., 1996; Piliavin & Martin, 1978; Wheelan & Verdi, 1992). People speak more warmly to (Hall & Braunwald, 1981) and are more verbally supportive of (Carli, 1989, 1990) women than of men; the greatest warmth shown is in all-female interactions and the least in all-male interactions. Men and women behave more similarly in mixed-gender interactions.

Whereas gender differences in communal behavior generally are more pronounced in same-gender interactions, which reflects greater warmth toward women, with some exceptions (Carli,

1989; Piliavin & Martin, 1978), studies reveal that gender differences in agentic behavior generally are most pronounced in mixed-gender interactions. For example, verbal (Carli, 1990; McMillan, Clifton, McGrath, & Gale, 1977) and visual dominance (Ellyson, Dovidio, & Brown, 1992) are more pronounced in mixed-gender than same-gender interactions. Myaskovsky et al. (2005) found that both women and men showed more task behavior, although not more dominance, in interactions with women. And another study showed that, as the representation of women within groups dropped, so did women's task contributions to the group (Johnson & Schulman, 1989). These results indicate that women are less agentic when interacting with men, and men are more inclined to take charge in interactions with women.

Other factors, such as race or ethnicity and sexual orientation or identity, may moderate gender effects on communal and agentic behavior in groups. Unfortunately, no research to date has examined whether these gender differences are affected by whether group members are gay, lesbian, or transgendered. And little research has explored the effects of race or ethnicity as moderators. Nevertheless, the one study that specifically compared gender differences in communal and agentic group behavior cross-racially did reveal some evidence of a race effect (Filardo, 1996). In that study, which involved Black and White adolescent participants working on a gender-neutral group game, White girls contributed fewer ideas and expressed more positive emotions toward others than did White boys, whereas no gender differences were found for the Black participants.

Social Influence

One aspect of group behavior that is particularly important to group decision making and performance is social influence. For a group to perform well, it must take advantage of the expertise of all of its members, which requires that groups not a priori resist the influence of particular group members. Yet research shows that women have less influence in group interactions than men do.

In a meta-analytic review of 29 studies of gender differences in task-oriented mixed-gender groups, men exerted greater influence and exhibited more leadership behaviors than women did (Lockheed, 1985). Studies reveal that people are more influenced by men than women even in experiments where the behavior of the men and women is manipulated experimentally to be identical (Carli, 2001; DiBerardinis, Ramage, & Levitt, 1984; Schneider & Cook, 1995; Wagner, Ford, & Ford, 1986). For example, in a study of four-person simulated juries, specific case information was given to one or more members of the group, who discussed and reached consensus on the case (Propp, 1995). Results showed that information was more likely to be used by the group in forming their decision when a man had presented it. In the condition in which the information was known to only one person in the group, group members used the information six times more often when it was presented by a man than when it was presented by a woman. Men's greater influence has likewise been revealed in the more frequent emergence of male than female leaders in initially leaderless groups (Eagly & Karau, 1991).

As noted earlier, women show proportionally less task-oriented behavior in groups than men do. In general, emerging as a leader and exerting influence in groups are facilitated by making higher amounts of task contributions (Hawkins, 1995; Ridgeway, 1978; Stein & Heller, 1979; Wood & Karten, 1986). However, it is not the case that women lack influence because they show less task behavior than men do. On the contrary, task contributions by women are more likely to be ignored or to evoke negative reactions (Butler & Geis, 1990; Ridgeway, 1982) and are less likely to influence others than are those by men (Walker, Ilardi, McMahon, & Fennell, 1996).

Gender effects on social influence are moderated by behavior. It might be expected that people who conform to gender roles might have greater influence than those who violate gender-role norms.

In fact, some research has shown that both men and women have greater influence when exhibiting communal or agentic behavior in a gender-stereotypical manner (Burgoon, Dillard, & Doran, 1983; Buttner & McEnally, 1996; Mehta et al., 1989, as cited in Ellyson et al., 1992). Nevertheless, other studies have shown that people grant men greater leeway to behave either in a masculine or in a feminine manner—agentically or communally—whereas women experience greater penalties for behaving agentically (e.g., Bolino & Turnley, 2003; Carli, LaFleur, & Loeber, 1995; Copeland, Driskell, & Salas, 1995; Sterling & Owen, 1982).[1] For example, in a study of dyads, male confederates were equally influential and likeable whether they expressed agreement or disagreement with their partner, but female confederates who disagreed exerted less influence and were considered less likeable than those who agreed (Carli, 2006). In another study, corporate executives indicated whether they would hire a job applicant after having read the applicant's resumé and a transcript of his or her job interview (Buttner & McEnally, 1996). Results revealed that the executives were most persuaded by, and preferred to hire, men who communicated in a manner perceived to be highly competent, by being direct and showing and initiative, rather than men who used a less competent style. The reverse was found for female applicants; the executives reported being least persuaded by, and less likely to hire, a woman who used the style perceived as most competent.

Although people typically are less readily influenced by women than by men, the gender effect on influence is affected by the nature of the group task. Women have greater influence in stereotypical feminine domains than in masculine and gender-neutral domains where men typically exert greater influence. As a result, studies show that, for masculine issues, such as sports and military topics, men are much more persuasive than women, whereas women exert greater influence for feminine issues, such as child care (Gerrard, Breda, & Gibbons, 1990; Falbo, Hazen, & Linimon, 1982; Feldman-Summers, Montano, Kasprzyk, & Wagner, 1980; Javornisky, 1979). Yet men's overall advantage in influence is underscored by their greater influence in gender-neutral contexts (Carli, 1990; Taps & Martin, 1990).

Studies also show that the gender composition of groups affects women's influence. Experimental studies reveal that, unless the task of the group is stereotypically feminine, a condition that undermines men's influence (e.g., Chatman, Boisnier, Berdahl, Spataro, & Anderson, 2005), women have more difficulty influencing other group members when they are in the minority. For example, in one experiment that involved a survival exercise, which participants rated as a masculine task, token

---

[1] Studies on children also reveal that boys who behave communally are not penalized, but girls who behave agentically are, at least by boys (Carli, 2006). Thus, men and boys are allowed more freedom to violate gender norms along communal–agentic dimensions. However, studies show little evidence that men and women are evaluated differently simply for showing cross-gender interests and behaviors (e.g., Lehavot & Lambert, 2007). Not all cross-gender behavior is prohibited. Rather, it is the more negative behaviors associated with each gender that is most unacceptable in the other gender. Specifically, highly dominant agentic behavior (e.g., aggressive, controlling, arrogant) is especially prohibited in women and weak and overly emotional behavior (e.g., weak, melodramatic, gullible) is especially prohibited in men (Prentice & Carranza, 2002). So, people do sometimes penalize men and boys more than women and girls for gender-role violations. For example, boys are penalized more for dressing like girls than vice versa (e.g., Blakemore, 2003; Levy, 1985; Zucker, Wilson-Smith, Kurita, & Stern, 1995), particularly by other boys (Smetana, 1986), and more for acting like sissies than girls who act like tomboys (Martin, 1990). Because behaviors such as dressing and walking like girls and being melodramatic are particularly associated with male homosexuality (Madon, 1997), rejection of men who violate gender norms is likely to reflect homophobia. Studies show negative reactions to homosexuality in men, especially by men (Herek & Capitanio, 1996, 1999; Schope & Eliason, 2004). In the absence of specific information about sexual preference, people may view certain cross-gender behavior in men to be a proxy for homosexuality and respond negatively as a result. This possibility is consistent with evidence that people perceive a stronger link between cross-gender behaviors or traits and sexual orientation in men than in women (McCreary, 1994; Sirin, McCreary, & Mahalik, 2004).

men in groups of women exerted a greater influence than the women did over their groups' decisions, whereas a token woman in a group of men did not increase women's influence (Craig & Sherif, 1986). In another experiment, even though the task was gender neutral, being a token woman reduced women's influence compared with groups that had equal numbers of men and women (Taps & Martin, 1990). Similar findings have been reported in surveys of women in organizational groups, where women reported less influence when they were in the minority than the majority and less influence than men who were in the minority (Izraeli, 1983, 1984).

Organizational studies of variables other than social influence have also documented greater costs for female than for male tokens. Token female employees have more difficulty fitting in than token male employees do (Yoder, 2002). In fact, token men in female-dominated fields actually advance more rapidly than the women do—a phenomenon known as the *glass escalator* (Hultin, 2003; Ott, 1989; Williams, 1992). These findings show that women in the minority, and token women in particular, may find it especially difficult to be influential, whereas the opposite is true for men. Minority status tends to highlight gender stereotypes and elicit greater gender stereotypical behavior (Yoder, 2001). As a result, the lower the percentage of men in a group, the more individual men make task contributions to the group and the less individual women do (Johnson & Schulman, 1989). Minority men's task contributions then enhance their influence in the group (Butler & Geis, 1990; Ridgeway, 1982; Walker et al., 1996). On the other hand, men show more communal behavior toward women than toward other men to the extent that there are proportionally more women present (Johnson et al., 1996; Killen & Naigles, 1995). Thus groups that have a sufficiently high proportion of women may be more open and communal, which tempers men's authority and increases women's influence.

Another factor that potentially contributes to the increased influence of token men and the decreased influence of token women is that men tend to endorse traditional gender roles more than women do (Twenge, 1997). Consequently, men may be especially affected by the gender composition of their group, perhaps relying on gender stereotypes the most when the group contains a token male or female member. Indeed, in one organizational study, male respondents reported greater awareness of gender to the extent that their group contained a very small or a very large percentage of women (Randel, 2002). And the more salient gender was to the men, the more they reported conflict in their group.

Finally, with the exception of the Filardo (1996) study on Black and White adolescents, no research has examined gender differences in influence as a function of group members' heterosexual, gay, lesbian, or transgendered identity or their race. Filardo assessed the extent to which influence attempts failed because such attempts were interrupted by other members of the group. Her results revealed that White girls' influence attempts were interrupted more than White boys' attempts, whereas Black boys and girls were equally likely to be interrupted. Thus, just as with the gender differences in communal and social behavior, gender differences were more pronounced in White than Black participants.

Emergent Leadership

Given men's advantage in social influence, it would not be surprising if men emerged as leaders more often than women in initially leader-less, mixed-gender groups. In fact, a meta-analysis of research that compares men's and women's leader emergence does reveal a general advantage for men. Eagly and Karau (1991) found small- to moderate-sized effects such that men emerged as leaders more than women did on measures of overall leadership ($d = 0.32$) as well as on measures that assessed strictly task-related leadership behaviors ($d = 0.41$). However, they reported a small effect of greater emergent leadership among women for social leadership behaviors ($d = 0.18$). The meta-analysis also revealed that men's overall emergence as leaders diminishes to the extent that the group task involves complex social interactions. When leadership is defined in communal terms or when the group task calls for communal behavior, women experience fewer disadvantages and have a greater opportunity to attain leadership. These results suggest that men's specialization in strictly task-oriented behaviors contributes to their overall emergence as group leaders. This underscores research that shows that leadership is more often associated with agentic behavior, such as task contributions, than with communal behavior (Schein, 2001; Sczesny, 2003).

Another factor that moderates the gender effect on leader emergence is the amount of time that the group interacts. Longer interactions reduce men's advantage in leadership emergence. This may occur because group members obtain more individuating information about each other over time and, as a result, become less affected by gender stereotypes. Alternatively, groups that meet for longer periods of time may require more group cohesion and thus benefit from and reward women's greater contribution of communal behavior in the groups.

As with agentic and communal group behaviors and social influence, the gender effect on leader emergence depends on the gender-typing of the group task. The gender difference is most pronounced for group tasks that are traditionally masculine, and it shrinks for tasks that increasingly favor women's expertise or that are stereotypically feminine. Still, men have the overall leadership advantage because they emerge as leaders more often even for gender-neutral tasks and as often as women do even with clearly feminine tasks.

The gender composition of the group moderates the gender difference in leadership emergence as well. In contrast with research on social influence, where women exerted the least influence when they were tokens or in the minority in their groups, men's advantage in leader emergence is greatest in relatively gender-balanced groups.

Men's Resistance to Women's Influence and Leadership

Studies on gender composition suggest that it may be men in particular who resist women's influence. In fact, research does show this. Men are more influenced by men than by women (Carli, 2001; Ridgeway, 1981). Men also dislike and resist the influence of competent or assertive women more than women do; they prefer and yield in influence more to women who are helpless, indirect, or communal than to women who are very competent or assertive (Carli, 1990; Carli et al., 1995; Ridgeway, 1982; Weimann, 1985). For example, one study revealed that a woman who presented herself in a feminine manner—who preferred traditional gender roles—was perceived to be less competent than a woman who presented herself as less traditionally feminine (Matschiner & Murnen, 1999). In the study, female participants were more influenced by the more competent woman, whereas male participants found the less competent woman to be more influential and likeable.

Further evidence of men's resistance comes from research on hiring preferences. Studies have revealed that men have a stronger preference than do women to hire male job applicants over female applicants, even when the female applicants have credentials that equal or surpass those of their male counterparts (Foschi, Lai, & Sigerson, 1994; Uhlmann & Cohen, 2005). In one study, the men preferred to hire a man when he was slightly superior to a female candidate; the men judged the man more competent and desirable to hire (Foschi et al., 1994). When given evidence that the slightly superior candidate was the woman, men were no more likely to hire her than to hire the man or no one at all. Women evaluated male and female applicants based on their professional records, independent of the applicants' gender.

Men's resistance to women's influence extends to female leaders. Men give female leaders lower evaluations than male leaders for comparable performance, but women's evaluations of leaders are not affected by the leaders' gender (Eagly, Makhijani, & Klonsky, 1992). Men are also more inclined than women to link managerial competence with being a man (Schein, 2001).

Gender Stereotypes and Gender Effects on Group Behavior

People generally have greater influence when they appear knowledgeable and competent. This accounts for the frequent use of professional athletes in advertisements for sneakers and actors portraying physicians in advertisements for medical treatments. In fact, much research has shown a clear link between the extent to which someone is perceived to be competent and that person's ability to influence others (Driskell, Olmstead, & Salas, 1993; Holtgraves & Lasky, 1999; Rhoads & Cialdini, 2002). But competence is not the only determinant of influence. Another important characteristic of influential people is their likeableness; studies confirm that people influence others to a greater degree when they are likable (Carli, 1989; Cialdini, 2001; Wood & Kallgren, 1988). So why do women have less influence in group interactions?

The source of women's disadvantage lies in stereotypes that people hold about men and women. Cross-cultural research reveals considerable consensus about gender stereotypes: Men are considered to possess more agentic qualities, which reflect greater competency and instrumentality, than do women, who are thought to possess more communal qualities than men do. Specifically, men are considered more leader-like, intellectual, analytical, able to think abstractly, and able to solve problems, whereas women are considered kinder, warmer, more expressive, more supportive, and gentler (Williams & Best, 1990).

Where do these stereotypes come from? According to *social role theory*, gender stereotypes reflect the types of roles that women and men typically hold; because of the traditional division of labor in the family, men more often have had the role of financial provider and women more often the role of homemaker (Eagly, 1987; see also Chapter 17). Furthermore, paid occupations are highly gender segregated; men's positions confer higher levels of status and power than women's do. The types of roles more typically held by men more often call for agentic behaviors, whereas types of roles more typically held by women more often call for communal behaviors. Based on their observations of men and women in their typical roles, people infer that men are intrinsically agentic and women intrinsically communal. In fact, these stereotypes do correspond to the types of gender differences found in groups. But they also create different demands on women and men, and the stereotypes interfere with women's authority and influence in groups.

Gender Stereotypes About Agency and the Double Standard

The perception of men's greater agency affects the way people judge men's and women's behavior. When presented with a description of agentic behavior, people recognize the behavior as agentic more quickly when the behavior is exhibited by men than by women (Scott & Brown, 2006). A double standard exists such that women must perform better than men to be considered competent. Experimental research on group interaction shows that, in order for people to perceive a woman as more competent than a man, they must be given very clear and unambiguous evidence of the woman's substantial superiority relative to the man, such as being explicitly told that the woman obtained a much better score on a standardized test (Foschi, Sigerson, & Lebesis, 1995; Pugh & Wahrman, 1983; Shackelford, Wood, & Worchel, 1996; Wagner et al., 1986; Wood & Karten, 1986). With no objective gender differences in actual performance, even in situations where the context has specifically been selected to be gender neutral and to favor neither men's nor women's abilities, men are seen as more competent than women.

Research on the evaluation of women's and men's resumés reveals the same double standard. When profiles include identical resumés, people consider men more qualified than women for masculine or gender-neutral jobs; women's qualifications are considered superior to men's only for traditionally feminine occupations (Davison & Burke, 2000).

When participants are asked to specify what standards would be needed to demonstrate a *high* degree of ability at a task, they set the standard higher for women than for men (Biernat, 2003; Biernat & Kobrynowicz, 1997; Foschi, 1996, 2000). And when asked to indicate what level of performance would be needed to reflect a *minimum* level of skill, people set the minimum lower for women than for men (Biernat & Kobrynowicz, 1997). Thus, people expect low-performing women to perform less well than men, and they demand greater evidence of ability before judging women to be highly competent. Even when people are setting the standard for themselves, women set a higher standard than men do (Foddy & Graham, 1987, as cited in Foschi, 2000, 1996). So, whether people are evaluating themselves or others, they require more evidence of competence from women than from men before concluding that someone's performance or ability is truly excellent.

Higher standards are also applied to female than to male leaders. People believe that women possess less leadership and management skill than men do (Schein, 2001). In a meta-analysis of the evaluation of male and female leaders, Eagly, Makhijani, and Klonsky (1992) reported that female leaders receive somewhat more critical evaluations than male leaders do. The review focused on experimental tests of gender bias and therefore could reveal whether men and women are evaluated differently merely on the basis of their gender. The findings show small effects, such that participants consider male leaders to be more competent ($d = 0.12$) and report feeling more satisfied with men's leadership ($d = 0.16$). In addition, this bias depends on the domain of leadership; when it involved more masculine contexts—business or athletics, say—male leaders received relatively higher ratings. In contexts that involved a feminine domain, such as education, women and men receive comparable ratings for leadership competence. Still, in no domain were women considered superior to men as leaders.

Because people presume that men have more competence than women, particularly for masculine tasks, it is often difficult to recognize highly competent women or women's contributions to group tasks. For example, in an experiment that involved a survival exercise, a stereotypically masculine task, group members had to decide which strategies should be used to survive a wildfire (Thomas-Hunt & Phillips, 2004). Based on participants' individual solutions to the survival exercise, the researchers identified the person within each group who clearly was the most expert; about one-half of the time that person was a woman. There was no objective difference in performance between the female and the male experts. Results revealed that group members rated male experts and nonexperts as having the same level of expertise, which is not surprising considering that participants had no knowledge of the experts' skill at the task, but they rated female experts as having less expertise than female nonexperts. Consequently, female experts exerted less influence over the group decision than nonexpert women did, whereas male experts exerted more influence than nonexpert men did.

Research indicates that a woman's credibility as an expert must be established with compelling evidence before the group is willing to accept her influence. In an experiment that included the NASA "lost-on-the-moon" survival exercise, all-male groups were assigned a female leader, who, in some conditions, was provided ahead of time with a rationale for the correct answers to the exercise, which made her an expert at the task (Yoder, Schleicher, & McDonald, 1998). The expert women were only able to overcome resistance to their influence when group members were explicitly told that the women had received special training that might help the groups accurately complete the survival exercise. In another study, participants read about a work team composed of a man and a woman who had created a successful investment portfolio (Heilman & Haynes, 2005). Again, unless participants were explicitly told that the woman's individual contribution to the project was excellent or were given some other evidence of her exceptional competence at the task, they assumed that she had contributed less than the man had.

In mixed-gender groups, the stereotype that men are more agentic and competent can actually be self-fulfilling and, thus, increase men's task behaviors, influence, and emergence as leaders. Research on *expectation states theory* indicates that gender, like race, education, and other personal attributes, acts as a *status characteristic*, in that it is associated with an individual's relative status in society (Berger, Fisek, Norman, & Zelditch, 1977; Berger & Webster, 2006). When a person possesses relatively high status, people presume that that person will be more competent than someone of lower status. As a result, people seek the opinions of the high-status person and yield to his or her influence more than to someone of low status. This tendency to seek out the opinions of high-status persons and to encourage them to contribute their ideas and to act as task leaders creates a self-fulfilling prophesy: The more individuals make task contributions, the more they enhance their status, increase their influence, and emerge as leaders (Hawkins, 1995; Ridgeway, 1978; Wood & Karten, 1986). Therefore, high-status individuals are not only expected to exhibit higher levels of competence and performance, but these expectations actually increase the probability that they will be more successful in interactions with others and, ultimately, will emerge as leaders. People perceive those of low status, because of their presumed lower competence, to lack legitimacy as authorities, and, as a result, are more likely to ignore them or disregard their ideas. In general, the role of a low-status person is thought to be one of providing support and assistance rather than one of authority and leadership (Meeker & Weitzel-O'Neill, 1985). Consequently, when low-status individuals behave in a status-asserting manner and appear to want authority or leadership, they may be penalized and rejected, which reduces their status further.

Because men typically possess higher status roles and are presumed to be more competent than women, people give men more opportunities than they give women to express their opinions and to direct and lead others. In group settings, this means that men would more often take on the role of task leader by contributing suggestions and opinions, directing the interaction, and eliciting the support of others, which further enhances their status. Women who seem to be very directive and who overtly try to influence the group may be seen as illegitimately attempting to gain status find their contributions at greater risk of being ignored or devalued, which further erodes their status. And, because engaging in task-related behavior is associated with enhancement of a person's status, perceived competence, and chance of emerging as a group leader, men's relative advantage over women could swell.

Gender Stereotypes About Communion and the Double Bind

It is tempting to conclude that, if women could only overcome the perception that they lack competence, they would eliminate any bias against them. But, unfortunately, the stereotype that women have more communal qualities than men do also can be problematic for women. People not only think that women are more communal, but they impose more demands on women than on men to be communal. Women, more than men, are expected to be kind, helpful, warm, and supportive. Because of this expectation, women get little credit for communal behavior but incur penalties for not being communal enough. For instance, researchers who compared reactions to employees who are helpful to their colleagues have reported that people recognize and reward men's helpfulness but not women's (Allen, 2006; Heilman & Chen, 2005).

When women behave in a highly agentic manner, say by taking charge and being directive, they may be seen as lacking communal qualities and thus as violating gender-role norms that require women to be warm, supportive, and helpful (Carli & Eagly, 1999). Likewise, a woman who appears to be very competent may sometimes be perceived as too status asserting or threatening. Strong, assertive, competent women risk being disliked. As a result, displays of warmth and positive social behavior enhance women's influence but have relatively little effect on men's (Carli, 1989, 2006; Ridgeway, 1982; Shackelford et al., 1996). Thus, displays of communal behavior can blunt the threat of women's competence and agency.

In addition to pressures on women to be communal and to conform to the feminine gender role, people expect women to be more communal than men because women lack the status and authority of men, and communal behavior serves to demonstrate a woman's other directedness and lack of interest in status attainment (Lockheed & Hall, 1976; Ridgeway, 2001). These stereotypes derive from the domestic and lower status occupational roles that women more often hold; such roles involve more selflessness and concern for others than men's roles typically do. Women have to be communal, then, because women's traditional roles have typically involved nice, warm behavior and also because of their relatively low status. Low-status individuals are pressured to show communion more than those of high status because people believe low-status individuals lack the legitimacy to take charge and direct others. Therefore, in order to be taken seriously and to have an opportunity to make task-related contributions to a group, lower status individuals must communicate that they have little desire to take charge or lead, lest they be considered uppity.

However, women who appear to be too communal may be seen as lacking agency and competence, which can also undermine their influence. Thus, gender stereotypes create a *double bind* for women. To influence a group, women must overcome doubts about their competence but still not appear too assertive and self-serving. As a result, people are generally more open to a man's influence, regardless of his influence style (Carli, 2001). They give greater scrutiny to a woman's influence style and penalize her for behavior that either fails to establish her competence or is too status asserting and insufficiently warm and nice. Therefore, women often are better liked and have more influence when they inject a degree of communion in their otherwise agentic behavior. People demand a careful balance of competence and warmth from women that they do not require of men.

Considerable research documents penalties against women who behave agentically. For example, studies have shown that people evaluate an exceptional level of managerial competence in women more negatively than they do in men; that is, they see the competent female manager as having a less desirable personality (Heilman, Block, & Martell, 1995; Heilman, Wallen, Fuchs, & Tamkins, 2004). In one study, participants disliked and denigrated a woman described as having exceptional abilities as an engineer or electrician, but did not react negatively to a man with exceptional abilities as a daycare worker or nurse (Yoder & Schleicher, 1996). This negative reaction to women who succeed in masculine domains occurs because such women are thought to lack communion (Heilman & Okimoto, 2007).

Studies have shown that women who interact in a direct competent manner are less well-liked (Burgoon, Jones, & Stewart, 1975; Carli, 1990; Carli et al., 1995; Falbo et al., 1982; Weimann, 1985) and influential (Burgoon et al., 1975; Buttner & McEnally, 1996; Carli, 1990; Tepper, Brown, & Hunt, 1993) than women who interact in a more indirect style. Results show that men are equally persuasive, regardless of their communication style, whereas women exert greater influence only when they communicate in a more indirect manner. Similarly, studies have provided evidence that dominant behavior is less acceptable in women than in men. For example, in one study (Carli, 2006), participants were paired with either a male or a female confederate who interacted with them in either a communal manner, by agreeing with the participants, or in a dominant, manner, by overtly disagreeing with them. Results revealed that women exerted greater influence when communal than when dominant, but men were equally influential in both conditions. Moreover, in that study, people disliked the dominant woman and responded to her dominance with anger, irritation, and hostility, whereas they did not express hostility toward men who were equally dominant. Other research confirms that women who use a self-asserting or dominant style exert less influence than men who use the same style or than women who use a communal style (see Bowles, Babcock, & Lai, 2007; Burgoon, Birk, & Hall, 1991; Burgoon et al., 1983; Mehta, et al., 1989, as cited in Ellyson et al., 1992; Shackelford et al., 1996).

Likewise, women must also avoid self-promotion and instead convey modesty. Women who describe their achievements in a self-promoting manner are perceived as less deserving of recognition or support than less self-promoting women, whereas men are not penalized for self-promotion (Giacalone & Riordan, 1990; Wosinska, Dabul, Whetstone-Dion, & Cialdini, 1996). Consequently, studies have shown that female participants who self-promoted exerted less influence than more modest women did (Carli, 2006; Rudman, 1998), even though people who self-promote are generally considered more competent than their more modest counterparts (Carli, 2006; Miller, Cooke, Tsang, & Morgan, 1992; Rudman, 1998). People consider self-promotion to be less socially sensitive than modesty (Miller et al., 1992), which indicates that self-promoting women are considered less communal than modest women are.

Leadership calls for agency, and people expect leaders to exhibit agentic behavior (Epitropaki & Martin, 2004; Schein, 2001). Nevertheless, female leaders also face the double bind. According to meta-analytic findings, to a small or moderate degree, female leaders are rated less favorably than their male counterparts for leading in an autocratic rather than a democratic manner ($d = 0.30$) (Eagly et al., 1992). On the other hand, the style used by male leaders, democratic or autocratic, has no effect on how they are evaluated or how influential they are.

Gender Effects on Group Performance

Same-Gender Groups

Because men and women exhibit somewhat different patterns of behavior in groups, differences in group performance might be expected depending on the demands of the group task. For example, group tasks that particularly require effective social interaction might favor groups of women, and those that require emphasis on task demands might favor groups of men. In fact, research on gender effects on group performance has revealed mixed findings (Bowers, Pharmer, & Salas, 2000; Wood, 1987), but does provide evidence that women perform well when tasks involve social interaction. Wood's (1987) meta-analysis of laboratory studies show that, overall, studies used tasks that favored men's knowledge and interest, and, unsurprising given this masculine advantage, yielded moderately better overall performance in all-male than all-female groups ($d = 0.39$). Her analysis further revealed that, with task content that favors men's knowledge and interests, male groups outperform female groups only when the task also requires task behavior, but female groups outperform male groups when the task requires social or communal behavior. Thus for a group to perform effectively, its members must not only have expertise at the group task but also exhibit group behavior that fits the demands of the task.

Subsequent studies that used gender-neutral tasks have revealed better performance by all-female groups (Fenwick & Neal, 2001) or no differences between all-female and all-male groups (Henry, Kmet, Desrosiers, & Landa, 2002; Hutson-Comeaux & Kelly, 1996). Myaskovsky and her colleagues (2005) used a stereotypically masculine task (i.e., assembling a radio from its mechanical and electronic parts) and found no performance differences between the male and the female groups. In total, studies of all-male and all-female groups provide little evidence that gender is an important predictor of performance unless the task clearly favors the interest or knowledge of one gender over the other.

Mixed-Gender Groups

What about mixed-gender groups? Does having both male and female members enhance groups' performance? There is reason to assume that, in general, diversity in groups could create advantages for group performance and decision making. Some researchers have claimed that diversity within groups can potentially facilitate group performance compared with more homogenous groups (e.g., Jackson, May, & Whitney, 1995). According to this *information/decision-making* approach, diversity's benefits derive from the fact that diverse groups are likely to have members with more varied perspectives, resources, past experiences, and bases of knowledge than are more homogeneous groups (van Knippenberg & Schippers, 2007). And because such groups consider a wider range of perspectives, reaching consensus is more likely to involve an extended and careful consideration of options, which precludes premature decision making. In particular, groups should benefit most from diversity when they face complex problems or tasks that require innovative or creative solutions (Williams & O'Reilly, 1998).

In contrast, other theorists have made the opposite claim: Group diversity is likely to undermine performance despite the greater breadth of knowledge and information that such groups possess. Instead, diversity can increase the potential for ineffective group processes and can thereby undermine performance; as a result of their differences, group members with varied backgrounds, experiences, and knowledge are more likely to experience conflict and to show in-group/out-group biases, that is to favor group members similar to themselves and denigrate members who are dissimilar (see van Knippenberg & Schippers, 2007). According to *social categorization/social identity* theory, people favor in-groups over out-groups because identifying with desirable groups enhances a person's self-esteem (Bertjan, Ellemers, & Spears, 1999; Tajfel, 1982).

Although the information/decision-making and social categorization/social identity models imply that diversity in knowledge or skill facilitates performance, whereas demographic diversity (i.e., race, gender, nationality) impairs it, there is no clear support for this contention. On the contrary, neither type of diversity has a consistent relation to performance (see Bowers et al., 2000; Webber & Donahue, 2001). Instead, findings on the effects of general diversity are mixed; diversity seems to provide both some benefits and some disadvantages to group performance (Guzzo & Dickson, 1996; van Knippenberg & Schippers, 2007). The same logic applies to gender diversity in groups. Specifically, gains may be expected as a result of the differences in women's and men's style of interaction, but given existing stereotypes about women's communion and men's agency and the resistance to women's influence that stereotypes create, in-group/out-group biases may very well contribute to impaired group performance.

The Wood (1987) meta-analysis of laboratory studies revealed a slight but nonsignificant performance advantage in mixed-gender groups over both all-male and all-female groups. Because the studies in her review generally favored men's expertise and knowledge, Wood noted that all-male groups would be expected to have had greater expertise at their group task than mixed-gender groups and, therefore, should have had the performance advantage. She concluded that lack of evidence for superior performance in all-male groups could have occurred because mixed-gender groups may benefit from a combination of men's agency and women's communion.

Some studies conducted since the Wood (1987) review have shown better performance of mixed-gender groups than same-gender groups (Fenwick & Neal, 2001; Henry et al., 2002; Rogelberg & Rumery, 1996; Schruijer & Mostert, 1997). One such study concerned the effectiveness of groups working on a simulated marketing exercise, a task that is somewhat stereotypically masculine (Fenwick & Neal, 2001). The proportion of women in the groups ranged from 0 to 88%. Comparisons of individual men's and women's marketing ability based on results of a marketing exam revealed no overall objective gender differences. Nevertheless, the gender composition of the group did affect group performance; the higher the proportion of women in the group, the better the group performed. Although the researchers did not measure communal and agentic behavior in the groups, they attributed the enhanced performance of groups with more women to women's more communal style, with its emphasis on shared decision making, which presumably complemented the more agentic and competitive style of the male participants.

In some experiments, researchers have explicitly instructed participants to use a communal or competitive approach to group decision making. Participants in one study worked on a simulated management exercise—a task that was probably somewhat stereotypically masculine (Chatman, Polzer, Barsade, & Neale, 1998). Gender diversity in the study was pooled with diversity based on race and nationality. Members of diverse groups participated more actively and performed better when given communal than when given competitive instructions; the highest degree of creativity, in fact, occurred in the most diverse communal groups. In another experiment, all-female, all-male, and mixed-gender groups worked on a trivia knowledge task, on which men and women performed equally well (Henry et al., 2002). Participants again received instructions to work competitively or communally on the group task. In this case, mixed-gender groups outperformed same-gender groups regardless of the communal or competitive instructions to the groups. Given the absence of gender differences in individuals' performance on the group task in this study, the advantages of the mixed-gender groups cannot be attributed to the greater breadth of knowledge of such groups. Instead, it may be that the particular behavioral styles of participants in mixed-groups facilitated decision making.

Other laboratory studies have shown impaired group performance in mixed-gender groups, primarily because of resistance to women's influence. Even when women possess unique and important information, group members may ignore or devalue it (Propp, 1995; Thomas-Hunt & Phillips, 2004; Yoder et al., 1998). In fact, in the wildfire survival study of reactions to female and male experts, because group members failed to recognize expert women as readily as expert men, groups with female experts performed less well than groups with male experts (Thomas-Hunt & Phillips, 2004). Likewise, in the lost-on-the moon study, unless groups were explicitly told that their female leader had special knowledge about the task, thus legitimating her expertise, groups failed to take advantage of the leader's expertise. Instead, groups with non-legitimated female experts performed no better than groups without experts; non-legitimated female experts were actually less effective at directing group decisions than nonexpert women were (Yoder et al., 1998). These studies demonstrate that female experts may be frustrated in their attempts to share their knowledge, and group performance may suffer as a result.

Given men's greater resistance to women's influence and the disadvantages of token women, women may find it especially difficult to perform well and contribute to their groups when in the minority. In one large-scale study, researchers tested this by examining supervisors' performance ratings of women and men across a wide variety of industries and organizations (Sackett, DuBois, & Noe, 1991). The gender difference in the performance ratings, after controlling for experience and cognitive ability, did show gender composition effects. The gender difference generally favored men when men were in the majority and generally favored women when women were in the majority. Men's better performance was most pronounced when women made up less than 20% of their work groups. Thus groups where women are in the distinct minority undermine women's performance. As a result, such groups may benefit less from women's knowledge and experience than do groups with a more substantial representation of women. So how might resistance to women's influence be overcome?

One method of increasing women's influence is to emphasize to group members that gender diversity can facilitate better group performance. In one study designed to test this, mixed-gender groups worked on a desert survival exercise after having been given one of two instructions: that groups performed better at the exercise either when the groups contained only one gender or when they contained both women and men (Homan, van Knippenberg, Van Kleef, & De Dreu, 2007). In some conditions of the study, prior to working in groups, the female members were given one set of facts needed to solve the exercise, and the male members were given another. Results revealed that, in these conditions, having been first told of the benefits of gender diversity increased open discussion in the groups, and this, in turn, resulted in improved performance.

Other research confirms that men, who are generally more resistant to women's influence, yield more readily to a woman's influence when doing so is likely to benefit them. Under such conditions, men are influenced to a greater degree by competent women than by either women or men who are less competent (Pugh & Wahrman, 1983; Shackelford et al., 1996). So, one way to insure that groups take advantage of gender diversity is to convince group members—and men in particular—that groups make better decisions and experience better outcomes by considering the contributions of all members, including women.

In general, laboratory studies demonstrate that, under certain conditions, mixed-gender groups can outperform same-gender groups, even with stereotypically masculine group tasks. Groups are likely to perform better when members are open to each other's influence, a condition that seems to be more likely when group members show some degree of communal behavior and have open discussions. On the other hand, group performance suffers when women's contributions are ignored or devalued, conditions that seem to be more likely when there is competition and conflict among group members.

Most studies of gender diversity and group conflict have been conducted in naturally occurring work groups and based on surveys of employees or students. In a number of these studies, survey respondents have sometimes reported more conflict or dissatisfaction (Alagna & Reddy, 1985; Alagna, Reddy, & Collins, 1982; Pelled, 1996; Tsui, Egan, & O'Reilly, 1992) and less effective performance in mixed-gender than in same-gender groups (Cummings, Zhou, & Oldham, 1993, as cited in Williams & O'Reilly, 1998; Pelled, 1996; Pelled, Cummings, & Kizilos, 2000). Other studies have shown no effects of a group's gender composition on group conflict or cohesiveness (Pelled, Eisenhardt, & Xin, 1999; Riordan & Shore, 1997; Wheelan, 1996) or on performance (Riordan & Shore, 1997).

Overall, organizational studies on performance in small groups show fewer benefits of gender diversity than laboratory studies do, but it is unclear exactly why this is the case. One difficulty with interpreting the results is that the organizational studies varied in the types of organizations examined, how male dominated the organizations were, the nature of the group task, and other factors, which could have easily affected study findings. Second, in the organizational studies, groups that varied in gender composition probably also varied in other ways that could have affected group outcomes. Third, most of the organizational studies relied on self-reports of performance, which may be less accurate and more prone to biased responses than objective measures.

If performance in work groups is not enhanced by gender diversity, what about gender diversity in leadership positions? Does increasing the proportion of female leaders have benefits? First, there is no evidence that women generally perform less well as leaders. In a meta-analysis of studies that compared male and female leaders' effectiveness, no gender differences were found overall (Eagly,

Karau, & Makhijani, 1995). Women's effectiveness decreased relative to men's to the extent that the organizations were increasingly male dominated, the leader had a higher percentage of male subordinates, and the evaluations of the leaders were subjective rather than objective. These moderator effects are likely to reflect men's resistance to women's influence and are consistent with meta-analytic findings discussed earlier showing male bias in the evaluation of female leaders; for comparable performance, men give female leaders lower evaluations than male leaders (Eagly et al., 1992).

Other studies provide evidence of the particular advantages of women leaders. A meta-analytic review established that transformational leadership, a style of leadership used more often by women than by men, is particularly effective as shown by a large correlation between transformational leadership and leaders' performance ($r = 0.45$) and effectiveness ($r = 0.55$) (Judge & Piccolo, 2004). And organizations perform better with a greater representation of women in positions of authority, on boards of directors and in upper management (Carter, Simkins, & Simpson, 2003; Erhardt, Werbel, & Shrader, 2003; Krishnan & Park, 2005). These findings indicate that the presence of women in leadership positions can be advantageous. Nevertheless, when both the laboratory and the organizational studies are taken into consideration, the general conclusion is that group performance can benefit from gender diversity, but often does not, probably because of increased intra-group conflict and resistance to women's authority and influence.

Future Directions and Conclusion

Gender stereotypes create challenges for women that men do not face. People hold a double standard in evaluating women, and they tend to assume that women are less agentic and competent than men are. At the same time, people demand more communion from women and dislike women who seem too agentic. This creates the double bind, which is more pronounced in mixed- than same-gender group interactions, and especially in groups with few or token women. The double bind contributes to resistance to women's influence and can undermine group performance, as a result.

One limitation of existing research on gender effects on group behavior, influence, and emergent leadership is that, so far, studies have focused on interactions among White participants; little research is available on how race or ethnicity might affect gender differences in groups. Given that gender effects have been linked to men's and women's different social roles and relative status, one might expect African Americans to show smaller gender differences than other ethnic groups. Compared with their male counterparts, African American women have higher labor force participation and, when employed, are more likely to work full time than are European American, Asian American, or Hispanic American women, who have comparable rates of full- and part-time employment (U.S. Bureau of Labor Statistics, 2008, Tables 3, 4, and 8). Indeed, the results of the single study of Black and White participants' communication and influence (Filardo, 1996) are consistent with predictions based on social role and expectation states theories—showing smaller gender effects in African American than white groups. However, further research is needed to confirm these findings and to assess whether gender differences among Asians and Hispanics parallel those among European Americans and whether similar dynamics are found in other parts of the world.

Additional research is also needed to explore whether gender and ethnic background may interact in ethnically diverse groups. In such contexts, predictions based on social role and expectations states theory suggest that women who are ethnic minorities may be doubly disadvantaged in terms of influence and leadership. Indeed, Americans associate being a leader and leadership with being White rather than with being a person of color (i.e., African, Asian, and Hispanic American) (Rosette,

Leonardelli, & Phillips, 2008). Race operates as a status cue (Berger, Rosenholtz, & Zelditch, 1980). Hispanic Americans (Fiske, Cuddy, Glick, & Xu, 2002; Fiske, Xu, Cuddy, Glick, 1999) and African Americans (Berger et al., 1980) are perceived to be relatively low in status, competence, and agency. The situation is somewhat different for Asian American women. People perceive Asians to be competent and agentic, at least to the same degree as European Americans, but less likeable because they are perceived to lack warmth and communal skills (Lin, Kwan, Cheung, & Fiske, 2005). Thus, compared with European American women, Hispanic, Asian, and African American women may have less opportunity to contribute to their group, exert less influence, and emerge less often as leaders.

Resistance to women's authority and influence clearly presents a challenge in mixed-gender groups, and it may be a particular challenge for women of color. More research is needed to explore how best to overcome resistance to women's influence and the increased risk of conflict in diverse groups. Laboratory studies suggest that groups take advantage of diversity and perform best when members are encouraged to behave communally and when they are made aware of the potential benefits of diversity. More carefully conducted field research is needed to test whether these strategies would similarly enhance group performance in organizational settings.

In conclusion, the challenges that women face in small group interactions are a microcosmic reflection of those that women face in organizations and society at large. Women remain underrepresented in positions of authority and continue to experience discrimination in pay and promotion. Yet there is reason to expect improvements in women's status. Increasing numbers of women can be found in positions of authority and leadership. And support for gender equality has risen in many countries around the world (Inglehart & Norris, 2003). If these changes continue, women may find that they are no longer constrained by the double bind. They could then wield greater influence in small task groups, and group performance would benefit as a result.

References

Alagna, S. W., & Reddy, D. M. (1985). Self and peer ratings and evaluations of group process in mixed-sex and male medical training groups. *Journal of Applied Social Psychology, 15,* 31–45.

Alagna, S. W., Reddy, D. M., & Collins, D. L. (1982). Perceptions of functioning in mixed-sex and male medical training groups. *Journal of Medical Education, 57,* 801–803.

Allen, T. D. (2006). Rewarding good citizens: The relationship between citizenship behavior, gender, and organizational rewards. *Journal of Applied Psychology, 36,* 120–143.

Anderson, K. J., & Leaper, C. (1998). Meta-analyses of gender effects on conversational interruption: Who, what, when, where, and how. *Sex Roles, 39,* 225–252.

Aries, E. (1976). Interaction patterns and themes of male, female, and mixed groups. *Small Group Behavior, 7,* 7–18.

Berger, J., Fisek, M. H., Norman, R. Z., & Zelditch, M., Jr. (1977). *Status characteristics and social interactions: An expectation states approach.* New York: Elsevier Science.

Berger, J., Rosenholtz, S. J., & Zelditch, M.,Jrr. (1980). Status organizing processes. *American Sociological Review, 6,* 479–508.

Berger, J., & Webster, M.,Jrr. (2006). Expectations, status, and behavior. In P. J. Burke (Ed.), *Contemporary social psychological theories*(pp. 268–300). Stanford, CA: Stanford University Press.

Berdahl, J. L., & Anderson, C. (2005). Men, women, and leadership centralization in groups over time. *Group Dynamics, 9,* 45–57.

Bertjan, D., Ellemers, N., & Spears, R. (1999). Commitment and intergroup behaviour. In N. Ellemers, R. Spears, & B. Doosje (Eds.), *Social identity: Context, commitment, content* (pp. 84–106). Malden, MA: Blackwell.

Biernat, M. (2003). Toward a broader view of social stereotyping. *American Psychologist, 58,* 1019–1027.

Biernat, M., & Kobrynowicz, D. (1997). Gender and race-based standards of competence: Lower minimum standards but higher ability standards for devalued groups. *Journal of Personality and Social Psychology, 72,* 544–557.

Blakemore, J. E. O. (2003). Children's beliefs about violating gender norms: Boys shouldn't look like girls, and girls shouldn't act like boys. *Sex Roles, 48,* 411–419.

Bolino, M. C., & Turnley, W. H. (2003). Counternormative impression management, likeability, and performance ratings: The use of intimidation in an organizational setting. *Journal of Organizational Behavior, 24*, 237–250.

Bowers, C. A., Pharmer, J. A., & Salas, E. (2000). When member homogeneity is needed in work teams: A meta-analysis. *Small Group Research, 31*, 305–327.

Bowles, H. R., Babcock, L., & Lai, L. (2007). Social incentives for gender differences in the propensity to initiate negotiations: Sometimes it does hurt to ask. *Organizational Behavior and Human Decision Processes, 103*, 84–103.

Burgoon, M., Birk, T. S., & Hall, J. R. (1991). Compliance and satisfaction with physician-patient communication: An expectancy theory interpretation of gender differences. *Human Communication Research, 18*, 177–208.

Burgoon, M., Dillard, J. P., & Doran, N. E. (1983). Friendly or unfriendly persuasion: The effects of violations by males and females. *Human Communication Research, 10*, 283–294.

Burgoon, M., Jones, S. B., & Stewart, D. (1975). Toward a message-centered theory of persuasion: Three empirical investigations of language intensity. *Human Communication Research, 1*, 240–256.

Butler, D., & Geis, F. L. (1990). Nonverbal affect responses to male and female leaders: Implications for leadership evaluations. *Journal of Personality and Social Psychology, 58*, 48–59.

Buttner, E. H., & McEnally, M. (1996). The interactive effect of influence tactic, applicant gender, and type of job on hiring recommendations. *Sex Roles, 34*, 581–591.

Carli, L. L. (1989). Gender differences in interaction style and influence. *Journal of Personality and Social Psychology, 56*, 565–576.

Carli, L. L. (1990). Gender, language, and influence. *Journal of Personality and Social Psychology, 59*, 941–951.

Carli, L. L. (2001). Assertiveness. In J. Worell (Ed.), *Encyclopedia of women and gender: Sex similarities and differences and the impact of society on gender*(pp. 157–168). San Diego, CA: Academic Press.

Carli, L. L. (2001). Gender and social influence. *Journal of Social Issues, 57*, 725–742.

Carli, L. L. (2006, July). *Gender and social influence: Women confront the double bind*. Paper presented at the International Congress of Applied Psychology, Athens, Greece.

Carli, L. L., & Bukatko, D. (2000). Gender, communication, and social influence: A developmental perspective. In T. Eckes & H. M. Trautner (Eds.), *The developmental social psychology of gender* (pp. 295–331). Mahwah, NJ: Erlbaum.

Carli, L. L., & Eagly, A. H. (1999). Gender effects on social influence and emergent leadership. In G. N. Powell (Ed.), *Handbook of gender and work* (pp. 203–222). Thousand Oaks, CA: Sage.

Carli, L. L., LaFleur, S. J., & Loeber, C. C. (1995). Nonverbal behavior, gender, and influence. *Journal of Personality and Social Psychology, 68*, 1030–1041.

Carli, L. L., & Olm-Shipman, C. (2004). *Gender differences in task and social behavior: A meta-analytic review*. Unpublished research, Wellesley College, Wellesley, MA.

Carter, D. A., Simkins, B. J., & Simpson, W. G. (2003). Corporate governance, board diversity, and firm value. *Financial Review,38*, 33–53.

Catalyst. (2007). *2006 Catalyst census of women corporate officers and top earners of the Fortune 500*. http://www.catalyst.org/publication/18/2006-catalyst-census-of-women-corporate-officers-and-top-earners-of-the-fortune-500

Catalyst. (2008). *Women CEOs of the Fortune 1000*. http://www.catalyst.org/publication/271/women-ceos-of-the-fortune-1000

Center for American Women and Politics. (2008). *Facts on women in Congress, 2008*. http://www.cawp.rutgers.edu/fast_facts/levels_of_office/Congress_CurrentFacts.php

Chatman, J. A., Boisnier, A. D., Berdahl, J. L., Spataro, S. E., & Anderson, C. (2005). *The typical, the rare, and the outnumbered: Disentangling the effects of historical typicality and numerical distinctiveness at work*. Working paper, University of California at Berkeley.

Chatman, J. A., Polzer, J. T., Barsade, S. G., & Neale, M. A. (1998). Being different yet feeling similar: The influence of demographic composition and organizational culture on work processes and outcomes. *Administrative Science Quarterly, 43*, 749–780

Chronicle of Higher Education. (1998). Almanac (Vol. 45, No. 1). Washington, DC: Chronicle of Higher Education.

Cialdini, R. B. (2001). *Influence: Science and practice*. Boston: Allyn and Bacon.

Copeland, C. L., Driskell, J. E., & Salas, E. (1995). Gender and reactions to dominance. *Journal of Social Behavior and Personality, 10*, 53–68.

Craig, J. M., &, Sherif, C. W. (1986). The effectiveness of men and women in problem-solving groups as a function of group gender composition. *Sex Roles, 14*, 453–466.

Cummings, A., Zhou, J., & Oldham, G. (1993). *Demographic differences and employee work outcomes: Effects of multiple comparison groups*. Paper presented at the annual meeting of the Academy of Management, Atlanta, GA.

Davison, H. K., & Burke, M. J. (2000). Sex discrimination in simulated employment contexts: A meta-analytic investigation. *Journal of Vocational Behavior, 56*, 225–248.

DiBerardinis, J. P., Ramage, K., & Levitt, S. (1984). Risky shift and gender of the advocate: Information theory versus normative theory. *Group & Organization Studies, 9*, 189–200.

Dovidio, J. F., Brown, C. E., Heltman, K., Ellyson, S. L., & Keating, C. F. (1988). Power displays between men and women in discussions of gender-linked tasks: A multichannel study. *Journal of Personality and Social Psychology, 55*, 580–587.

Dovidio, J. F., Ellyson, S. L., Keating, C. F., Heltman, K., & Brown, C. E. (1988).The relationship of social power to visual displays of dominance between men and women. *Journal of Personality and Social Psychology, 54*, 233–242.

Driskell, J., Olmstead, E. B., & Salas, E. (1993). Task cues, dominance cues, and influence in task groups. *Journal of Applied Psychology, 78*, 51–60.

Eagly, A. H. (1987). *Sex differences in social behavior: A social-role interpretation.* Hillsdale, NJ: Erlbaum.

Eagly, A. H., & Carli, L. L. (2007). *Through the labyrinth: The truth about how women become leaders.* Boston: Harvard Business School Press.

Eagly, A. H., Johannesen-Schmidt, M. C., & van Engen, M. L. (2003). Transformational, transactional, and laissez-faire leadership styles: A meta-analysis comparing women and men. *Psychological Bulletin, 129*, 569–591.

Eagly, A. H., & Johnson, B. T. (1990). Gender and leadership style: A meta-analysis. *Psychological Bulletin, 108*, 233–256.

Eagly, A. H., & Karau, S. J. (1991). Gender and the emergence of leaders: A meta-analysis. *Journal of Personality and Social Psychology, 60*, 685–710.

Eagly, A. H., Karau, S. J., & Makhijani, M. G. (1995). Gender and the effectiveness of leaders: A meta-analysis. *Psychological Bulletin, 117*, 125–145.

Eagly, A. H., Makhijani, M. G., & Klonsky, B. G. (1992). Gender and the evaluation of leaders: A meta-analysis. *Psychological Bulletin, 111*, 3–22.

Ellyson, S. L., Dovidio, J. F., & Brown, C. E. (1992). The look of power: Gender differences in visual dominance behavior. In C. L. Ridgeway (Ed.), *Gender, interaction, and inequality*(pp. 50–80). New York: Springer-Verlag.

Epitropaki, O., & Martin, R. (2004). Implicit leadership theories in applied settings: Factor structure, generalizability, and stability over time. *Journal of Applied Psychology, 89*, 293–310.

Erhardt, M. L., Werbel, J. D., & Shrader, C. B. (2003). Board of director diversity and firm financial performance. *Corporate Governance, 11*, 102–111.

Falbo, T., Hazen, M. D., & Linimon, D. (1982). The costs of selecting power bases or messages associated with the opposite sex. *Sex Roles, 8*, 147–157.

Feldman-Summers, S., Montano, D. E., Kasprzyk, D., & Wagner, B. (1980). Influence attempts when competing views are gender-related: Sex as credibility. *Psychology of Women Quarterly, 5*, 311–320.

Fenwick, G. D., & Neal, D. J. (2001). Effect of group composition on group performance. *Gender, Work, and Organization, 8*, 206–225.

Filardo, A. K. (1996). Gender patterns in African American and white adolescents' social interactions in same-race, mixed-gender groups. *Journal of Personality and Social Psychology, 71*, 71–82.

Fiske, S. T., Cuddy, A. J. C., Glick, P., & Xu, J. (2002). A model of (often mixed) stereotype content: Competence and warmth respectively follow from perceived status and competition. *Journal of Personality and Social Psychology, 82*, 878–902.

Fiske, S. T., Xu, J., Cuddy, A. J. C., & Glick, P. (1999). (Dis)respecting versus (dis)liking: Status and interdependence predict ambivalent stereotypes of competence and warmth. *Journal of Social Issues, 55*, 473–489.

Foddy, M., & Graham, H. (1987). Sex and the double standards in the inference of ability. Presented at the annual meeting of the Canadian Psychological Association, Vancouver, BC.

Foschi, M. (1996). Double standards in the evaluation of men and women. *Social Psychology Quarterly, 59*, 237–254.

Foschi, M. (2000). Double standards for competence: Theory and research. *Annual Review of Sociology, 26*, 21–42.

Foschi, M., Lai, L., & Sigerson. K. (1994). Gender and double standards in the assessment of job applicants. *Social Psychology Quarterly, 57*, 326–339.

Foschi, M., Sigerson, K., & Lebesis, M. (1995). Assessing job applicants: The relative effects of gender, academic record, and decision type. *Small Group Research, 26*, 328–352.

Gerrard, M., Breda, C., & Gibbons, F. X. (1990). Gender effects in couples' decision making and contraceptive use. *Journal of Applied Social Psychology, 20*, 449–464.

Giacalone, R. A., & Riordan, C. A. (1990). Effect of self-presentation on perceptions and recognition in an organization. *Journal of Psychology, 124*, 25–38.

Guzzo, R. A., & Dickson, M. W. (1996). Teams in organizations: Recent research on performance and effectiveness. *Annual Review of Psychology, 47*, 307–338.

Hall, J. A., & Braunwald, K. G. (1981). Gender cues in conversations. *Journal of Personality and Social Psychology, 40*, 270–280.

Hawkins, K. W. (1995). Effects of gender and communication content of leadership emergence in small task-oriented groups. *Small Group Research, 26*, 234–249.

Heilman, M. E., Block, C. J., & Martell, R. F. (1995). Sex stereotypes: Do they influence perceptions of managers? *Journal of Social Behavior and Personality, 10*, 237–252.

Heilman, M. E., & Chen. J. J. (2005). Same behavior, different consequences: Reactions to men's and women's altruistic citizenship behavior. *Journal of Applied Psychology, 90*, 431–441.

Heilman, M. E., & Haynes, M. C. (2005). No credit where credit is due: Attributional rationalization of women's success in male–female teams. *Journal of Applied Psychology, 90*, 905–916.

Heilman, M. E., & Okimoto, T. G. (2007). Why are women penalized for success at male tasks? The implied communality deficit. *Journal of Applied Psychology, 92*, 81–92.

Heilman, M. E., Wallen, A. S., Fuchs, D., & Tamkins, M. M. (2004). Penalties for success: Reactions to women who succeed in male gender-typed tasks. *Journal of Applied Psychology, 89*, 416–427.

Henry, R. A., Kmet, J., Desrosiers, E., & Landa, A. (2002). Examining the impact of interpersonal cohesiveness on group accuracy interventions: The importance of matching versus buffering. *Organizational Behavior and Human Decision Processes, 87*, 25–43.

Herek, G. M., & Capitanio, J. P. (1996). "Some of my best friends": Intergroup contact, concealable stigma, and heterosexuals' attitudes towards gay men and lesbians. *Personality and Social Psychology Bulletin, 22*, 412–424.

Herek, G. M., & Capitanio, J. P. (1999). Sex differences in how heterosexuals think about lesbians and gay men: Evidence from survey context effects. *Journal of Sex Research, 36*, 348–360.

Homan, A. C., van Knippenberg, D., Van Kleef, G. A., & De Dreu, C. K. W. (2007). Bridging faultlines by valuing diversity: Diversity beliefs, information elaboration, and performance in diverse work groups. *Journal of Applied Psychology, 92*, 1189–1199.

Holtgraves, T., & Lasky, B. (1999). Linguistic power and persuasion. *Journal of Language and Social Psychology, 18*, 196–205.

Hultin, M. (2003). Some take the glass escalator, some hit the glass ceiling? Career consequences of occupational sex segregation. *Work and Occupations, 30*, 30–61.

Hutson-Comeaux, S. L., & Kelly, R. J. (1996). Sex differences in interaction style and group task performance: The process-performance relationship. *Journal of Social Behavior & Personality, 11*, 255–275.

Inglehart, R., & Norris, P. (2003). *Rising tide: Gender equality and cultural change around the world*. New York: Cambridge University Press.

Izraeli, D. N. (1983). Sex effects or structural effects? An empirical test of Kanter's theory of proportions. *Social Forces, 62*, 153–165.

Izraeli, D. N. (1984). The attitudinal effects of gender mix in union committees. *Industrial and Labor Relations Review, 37*, 212–221.

Jackson, S. E., May, K. E., & Whitney, K. (1995). Understanding the dynamics of diversity in decision-making teams. In R. A. Guzzo & E. Salas (Eds.), *Team effectiveness and decision making in organizations* (pp. 204–261). San Francisco: Jossey-Bass.

Javornisky, G. (1979). Task content and sex differences in conformity. *Journal of Psychology, 108*, 213–220.

Johnson, C., Clay-Warner, J., & Funk, S. J. (1996). Effects of authority structures and gender on interaction in same sex groups. *Social Psychology Quarterly, 59*, 221–236.

Johnson, R. A., & Schulman, G. I. (1989). Gender-role composition and role entrapment in decision-making groups. *Gender & Society, 3*, 355–372.

Judge, T. A., & Piccolo, R. F. (2004). Transformational and transactional leadership: A meta-analytic test of their relative validity. *Journal of Applied Psychology, 89*, 901–910.

Karakowsky, L., McBey, K., & Miller, D. L. (2004). Gender, perceived competence, and power displays: Examining verbal interruptions in a group context. *Small Group Research, 35*, 407–439.

Killen, M., & Naigles, L. R. (1995). Preschool children pay attention to their addressees: Effects of gender composition on peer disputes. *Discourse Processes, 19*, 329–346.

Krishnan, H. A., & Park, D. (2005). A few good women—on top management teams. *Journal of Business Research, 58*, 1712–1720.

LaFrance, M., Hecht, M. A., & Paluck, E. L. (2003). The contingent smile: A meta-analysis of sex differences in smiling. *Psychological Bulletin, 129*, 305–334.

Lehavot, K., & Lambert, A. J. (2007). Toward a greater understanding of antigay prejudice: On the role of sexual orientation and gender role violation. *Basic and Applied Social Psychology, 29,* 279–292.

Leaper, C., & Ayres, M. M. (2007). A Meta-analytic review of gender variations in adults' language use: Talkativeness, affiliative speech, and assertive speech. *Personality and Social Psychology Review, 11,* 328–363.

Levy, G. D., Taylor, M. G., & Gelman, S. A. (1995).Traditional and evaluative aspects of flexibility in gender roles, social conventions, moral rules, and physical laws. *Child Development, 66,* 515–531.

Lin, M. H., Kwan, V. S. Y., Cheung, A., & Fiske, S. T. (2005). Stereotype content model explains prejudice for an envied outgroup: Scale of anti-Asian American stereotypes. *Personality and Social Psychology Bulletin, 31,* 34–47.

Lockheed, M. E., (1985). Sex and social influence: A meta-analysis guided by theory. In J. Berger & M. Zelditch, Jrr. (Eds.), *Status, rewards, and influence: How expectations organize behavior*(pp. 406–429). San Francisco: Jossey-Bass.

Lockheed, M. E., & Hall, K. P. (1976). Conceptualizing sex as a status characteristic: Application to leadership training strategies. *Journal of Social Issues, 32,* 111–124.

Madon, S. (1997). What do people believe about gay males? A study of stereotype content and strength. *Sex Roles, 37,* 663–385.

Mast, M. S. (2001). Gender differences and similarities in dominance hierarchies in same-gender groups based on speaking time. *Sex Roles, 44,* 537–556.

Maume, D. J.,Jrr. (2004). Is the glass ceiling a unique form of inequality? Evidence from a random-effects model of managerial attainment. *Work and Occupations, 31,* 250–274.

Martin, C. M. (1990). Attitudes and expectations about children with nontraditional and traditional gender roles. *Sex Roles, 22,* 151–165.

Matschiner, M., & Murnen, S. K. (1999). Hyperfemininity and influence. *Psychology of Women Quarterly, 23,* 631–642.

McCreary, D. R. (1994). The male role and avoiding femininity. *Sex Roles, 31,* 517–531.

McMillan, J. R., Clifton, A. K., McGrath, D., & Gale, W. S. (1977). Women's language: Uncertainty or interpersonal sensitivity and emotionality. *Sex Roles, 3,* 545–559.

McMullen, L. M., & Pasloski, D. D. (1992). Effects of communication apprehension, familiarity of partner, and topic on selected "women's language" features. *Journal of Psycholinguistic Research, 21,* 17–30.

Meeker, B. F., & Weitzel-O'Neill, P. A. (1985). Sex roles and interpersonal behavior in task-oriented groups. In J. Berger & M. Zelditch (Eds.), *Status, rewards, and influence* (pp. 379–405). San Francisco: Jossey-Bass.

Mehta, P., Dovidio, J. F., Gibbs, R., Miller, K., Huray, K., Ellyson, S. L., & Brown, C. E. (1989, April). *Sex differences in the expression of power motives through visual dominance behavior.* Paper presented at the annual meeting of the Eastern Psychological Association, Boston.

Miller, L. C., Cooke, L. L., Tsang, J., & Morgan, F. (1992). Should I brag? Nature and impact of positive and boastful disclosures for women and men. *Human Communication Research, 18,* 364–399.

Myaskovsky, L., Unikel, E., & Dew, M. A. (2005). Effects of gender diversity on performance and interpersonal behavior in small work groups. *Sex Roles, 52,* 645–657.

Ott, E. M. (1989). Effects of the male-female ratio at work: Policewomen and male nurses. *Psychology of Women Quarterly, 13,* 41–57.

Pelled, L. H. (1996). Relational demography and perceptions of group conflict and performance: A field investigation. *International Journal of Conflict Management, 7,* 230–246.

Pelled, L. H., Cummings, T. G., & Kizilos, M. A. (2000). The influence of organizational demography on customer-oriented prosocial behavior: An exploratory investigation. *Journal of Business Research 47,* 209–216.

Pelled, L. H., Eisenhardt, K. M., & Xin, K. R. (1999). Exploring the black box: An analysis of work group diversity, conflict, and performance. *Administrative Science Quarterly, 44,* 1–28.

Piliavin, J. A., & Martin, R. R. (1978). The effects of sex composition of groups on style of social interaction. *Sex Roles, 4,* 281–296.

Prentice, D. A., & Carranzo, E. (2002). What women and men should be, shouldn't be, are allowed to be, and don't have to be: The contents of prescriptive gender stereotypes. *Psychology of Women Quarterly, 26,* 269–281.

Pugh, M. D., & Wahrman, R. (1983). Neutralizing sexism in mixed-sex groups: Do women have to be better than men? *American Journal of Sociology, 88,* 746–762.

Propp, K. M. (1995). An experimental examination of biological sex as a status cue in decision-making groups and its influence on information use. *Small Group Research, 26,* 451–474.

Randel, A. E. (2002). Identity salience: A moderator of the relationship between group gender composition and work group conflict. *Journal of Organizational Behavior, 23,* 749–766.

Reed, V., & Buddeberg-Fischer, B. (2001). Career obstacles for women in medicine: An overview. *Medical Education, 35,* 139–147.

Rhoads, K. V., & Cialdini, R. B. (2002). The business of influence: Principles that lead to success in commercial settings. In J. P. Dillard & M. Pfau (Eds.), *The persuasion handbook: Developments in theory and practice* (pp. 513–542). Thousand Oaks, CA: Sage.

Rhode, D. L. (2001). *The unfinished agenda: Women and the legal profession.* Chicago: American Bar Association, Commission on Women in the Profession.

Ridgeway, C. L. (1978). Conformity, group-oriented motivation, and status attainment in small groups. *Social Psychology, 41*, 175–188.

Ridgeway, C. L. (1981). Nonconformity, competence, and influence in groups: A test of two theories. *American Sociological Review, 46*, 333–347.

Ridgeway, C. L. (1982). Status in groups: The importance of motivation. *American Sociological Review, 47*, 76–88.

Ridgeway, C. (2001). Gender, status, and leadership. *Journal of Social Issues, 57*, 637–655.

Riordan, C. M., & Shore, L. M. (1997). Demographic diversity and employee attitudes: An empirical examination of relational demography within work units. *Journal of Applied Psychology, 82*, 342–358.

Rogelberg, S. G., & Rumery, S. M. (1996). Gender diversity, team decision quality, time on task, and interpersonal cohesion. *Small Group Research, 27*, 79–90.

Rosette, A. S., Leonardelli, G. J., & Phillips, K. (2008). The White standard: Racial bias in leader categorization. *Journal of Applied Psychology, 93*, 758–777.

Rudman, L. A. (1998). Self-promotion as a risk factor for women: The costs and benefits of counterstereotypical impression management. *Journal of Personality and Social Psychology, 74*, 629–645.

Sackett, P. R., DuBois, C. L. Z., & Noe, A. W. (1991). Tokenism in performance evaluation: The effects of work group representation on male-female and White-Black differences in performance ratings. *Journal of Applied Psychology, 76*, 263–267.

Scott, K. A., & Brown, D. J. (2006). Female first, leader second? Gender bias in the encoding of leadership behavior. *Organizational Behavior and Human Decision Processes, 101*, 230–242.

Shackelford, S., Wood, W., & Worchel, S. (1996). Behavioral styles and the influence of women in mixed-sex groups. *Social Psychology Quarterly, 59*, 284–293.

Schein, V. E. (2001). A global look at psychological barriers to women's progress in management. *Journal of Social Issues, 57*, 675–688

Schneider, J., & Cook, K. (1995). Status inconsistency and gender: Combining revisited. *Small Group Research, 26*, 372–399.

Schope, R. D., & Eliason, M. J. (2004). Sissies and tomboys: Gender role behaviors and homophobia. *Journal of Gay and Lesbian Social Services, 16*, 73–97.

Schruijer, S. G. L., & Mostert, I. (1997). Creativity and sex composition: An experimental illustration. *European Journal of Work and Organizational Psychology, 6*, 175–182.

Sczesny, S. (2003). A closer look beneath the surface: Various facets of the think-manager—think-male stereotype. *Sex Roles, 49*, 353–363.

Sirin, S. R., McCreary, D. R., & Mahalik, J. R. (2004). Differential reactions to men and women's gender role transgressions: Perceptions of social status, sexual orientation, and value dissimilarity. *Journal of Men's Studies, 12*, 119–132.

Smetana, J. G. (1986). Preschool children's conceptions of sex-role transgressions, *Child Development, 57*, 862–871.

Stein, R. T., & Heller, T. (1979). An empirical analysis between leadership status and participation rates reported in the literature. *Journal of Personality and Social Psychology, 37*, 1993–2002.

Sterling, B. S., & Owen, J. W. (1982). Perceptions of demanding versus reasoning male and female police officers. *Personality and Social Psychology Bulletin, 8*, 336–340.

Stoddard, T., & Turiel, E. (1985). Children's concepts of cross-gender activities. *Child Development, 56*, 1241–1252.

Tajfel, H. (1982). The social psychology of intergroup relations. *Annual Review of Psychology, 33*, 1–39.

Taps, J., & Martin, P. Y. (1990). Gender composition, attributional accounts, and women's influence and likability in task groups. *Small Group Research, 21*, 471–491.

Tepper, B. J., Brown, S. J., & Hunt, M. D. (1993). Strength of subordinates' upward influence tactics and gender congruency effects. *Journal of Applied Social Psychology, 23*, 1903–1919.

Thomas-Hunt, M. C., & Phillips, K. W. (2004). When what you know is not enough: Expertise and gender dynamics in task groups. *Personality and Social Psychology Bulletin, 30*, 1585–1598.

Tsui, A. S., Egan, T. D., & O'Reilly, C. A., III. (1992). Being different: Relational demography and organizational attachment. *Administrative Science Quarterly, 37*, 549–579.

Twenge, J. M. (1997). Attitudes toward women, 1970–1995. *Psychology of Women Quarterly, 21*, 35–51.

Uhlmann, E. L., & Cohen, G. L. (2005). Constructed criteria: Redefining merit to justify discrimination. *Psychological Science, 16*, 474–480.

U.S. Bureau of Labor Statistics. (2008a). *Highlights of women's earnings in 2007.* http://www.bls.gov/cps/cpswom2007.pdf

U.S. Bureau of Labor Statistics. (2008b). *Tables from employment and earnings: Annual averages, household data.* http://www.bls.gov/cps/tables.htm#annual

U.S. Government Accountability Office. (2003). *Women's earnings: Work patterns partially explain difference between men's and women's earnings* (GAO-04-35). http://www.gao.gov/new.items/d0435.pdf

U.S. National Center for Education Statistics. (2007). *Digest of education statistics, 2005.* http://nces.ed.gov/programs/digest/d07/tables/dt07_258.asp.

van Engen, M. L., & Willemsen, T. M. (2004). Sex and leadership styles: A meta-analysis of research published in the 1990s. *Psychological Reports, 94,* 3–18.

van Knippenberg, D., & Schippers, M. C. (2007). Work group diversity. *Annual Review of Psychology, 58,* 515–41

Wagner, D. G., Ford, R. S., & Ford, T. W. (1986). Can gender inequalities be reduced? *American Sociological Review, 51,* 47–61.

Walker, H. A., Ilardi, B. C., McMahon, A. M., & Fennell, M. L. (1996). Gender, interaction, and leadership. *Social Psychology Quarterly, 59,* 255–272.

Webber, S. S., & Donahue L. M. (2001). Impact of highly and less job-related diversity on work group cohesion and performance: A meta-analysis. *Journal of Management, 27,* 141–62.

Weimann, G. (1985). Sex differences in dealing with bureaucracy. *Sex Roles, 12,* 777–790.

Wheelan, S. A. (1996). Effects of gender composition and group status differences on member perceptions of group developmental patterns, effectiveness, and productivity. *Sex Roles, 34,* 665–686.

Wheelan, S. A., & Verdi, A. F. (1992). Differences in male and female patterns of communication in groups: A methodological artifact? *Sex Roles, 27,* 1–15.

Williams, C. L. (1992). The glass escalator: Hidden advantages for men in the "female" professions. *Social Problems, 39,* 41–57.

Williams, J. E., & Best, D. L. (1990). *Measuring sex stereotypes: A multinational study.* Newbury Park, CA: Sage.

Williams K. Y., & O'Reilly C. A. (1998). Demography and diversity in organizations: A review of 40 years of research. *Research in Organizational Behavior, 20,* 77–140

Wood, W. (1987). Meta-analytic review of sex differences in group performance. *Psychological Bulletin, 102,* 53–71.

Wood, W., & Kallgren, C. A. (1988). Communicator attributes and persuasion: Recipients' access to attitude-relevant information in memory. *Personality and Social Psychology Bulletin, 14,* 172–182.

Wood, W., & Karten, S. J. (1986). Sex differences in interaction style as a product of perceived sex differences in competence. *Journal of Personality and Social Psychology, 50,* 341–347.

Wosinska, W., Dabul, A. J., Whetstone-Dion, R., & Cialdini, R. B. (1996). Self-presentational responses to success in the organization: The costs and benefits of modesty. *Basic and Applied Social Psychology, 18,* 229–242.

Yamada, E. M., Tjosvold, D., & Draguns, J. G. (1983). Effects of sex-linked situations and sex composition on cooperation and style of interaction. *Sex Roles, 9,* 541–553.

Yoder, J. D. (2001). Making leadership work more effectively for women. *Journal of Social Issues, 57,* 815–828.

Yoder, J. D. (2002). Context matters: Understanding tokenism processes and their impact on women's work. *Psychology of Women Quarterly, 26,* 1–8.

Yoder, J. D., & Schleicher, T. L. (1996). Undergraduates regard deviation from occupational gender stereotypes as costly for women. *Sex Roles, 34,* 171–188.

Yoder, J. D., Schleicher, T. L., & McDonald, T. W. (1998). Empowering token women leaders: The importance of organizationally legitimated credibility. *Psychology of Women Quarterly, 22,* 209–222.

Zucker, K. J., Wilson-Smith, D. N., Kurita, J. A., & Stern, A. (1995). Children's appraisals of sex-typed behavior in their peers. *Sex Roles, 33,* 703–725.

Chapter 15
Sexual and Gender Prejudice

Ritch C. Savin-Williams, Seth T. Pardo, Zhana Vrangalova, Ryan S. Mitchell, and Kenneth M. Cohen

Sexual prejudice is defined by Herek (2000, p. 19) as "all negative attitudes based on sexual orientation, whether the target is homosexual, bisexual, or heterosexual." Its principal features are an evaluation or judgment directed at social group members because of their sexuality in a manner that ranges from passive negativity to outright hostility (Herek, 2004, 2009). Historically, this prejudice was labeled *homophobia, homonegativism, heterosexism*, and, more recently, *biphobia* and *transphobia*. We prefer the term *sexual prejudice* because it "has the advantage of linking hostility toward homosexuality to the extensive body of social science theory and empirical research on prejudice" (Herek, 2004, p. 17).

Negative attitudes, evaluations, and behaviors are typically targeted at particular sexual orientations and their non-normative (sex or gender atypical) expression in terms of sexual identities, sexual/romantic attractions, and sexual/romantic behavior. Sexual prejudice can be subtle. For example, whereas heterosexual individuals may publicly espouse civil rights for lesbians and gay men as a social group, they may nonetheless experience disgust with same-sex behavior or political activism—expressions of which may "leak out" without their awareness. Thus, it is often challenging for individuals who have, or are erroneously believed to have, same-sex attractions to express their romantic feelings and attractions for members of the same sex.

In this chapter, we broaden our discussion of sexual prejudice to include gender prejudice, which is similarly defined as evaluative negative attitudes and behavior directed at individuals because of their gender orientation, gender identity, or gender expression. We begin with a brief historic overview of the foundation term *homophobia*.

Sexual Prejudice Against Gay and Lesbian Individuals

Homophobia and Its Discontents

Weinberg (1972) coined the term homophobia to describe the fear or the dread of being in proximity to "homosexuals," or people whose sexuality is same-sex oriented. Although popularization of the concept helped to focus attention on negative attitudes and behaviors toward sexual minorities, the word itself was considered by some to be problematic (Herek, 2004). The "phobia" suffix implies a response similar to that of other clinical phobias. We do not deny that a subset of "homophobic" individuals displays such extreme, irrational responses, but this does not characterize the broader

R.C. Savin-Williams (✉)
Cornell University, Ithaca, NY, USA

population who might have reservations about same-sex sexuality that do not rise to the level of a true phobia. To overcome these limitations, researchers either expanded definitions of homophobia explicitly to include non-phobic reactions or abandoned the term altogether.

In the former case, three manifestations of homophobia were commonly recognized: an attitudinal set, a personality dimension, and a cultural phenomenon (Fyfe, 1983). Although a multi-faceted model of homophobia that consisted of cognitive, affective, and behavioral dimensions was proposed (O'Donohue & Caselles, 1993), early assessments tended to emphasize cognitive and affective negativism and disregard the behavioral aspects. Wright, Adams, and Bernat (1999) argued, however, that the homophobia construct should, like other phobias, contain a behavioral component. Thus, some researchers began to include behavioral responses such as violence, discrimination, and harassment (Meyer, 2003), thereby allowing the homophobia construct to transcend that of a true phobia to include all negative reactions to sexual minorities.

Among those who rejected the term homophobia, excessively broad, inclusive meanings were blamed for a loss of precision and for the overemphasis of internal pathology and the underemphasis of social and environmental etiological factors. Hudson and Ricketts (1980) proposed the replacement term *homonegativism*, a concept that combines a spectrum of evaluative and attitudinal reactions with the more traditional antigay affective responses such as anger, fear, disgust, discomfort, and aversion. More recently, *heterosexism* has been used synonymously with homophobia. Herek (2004) rejected this equation as inappropriate because heterosexism more precisely characterizes the cultural norms that *allow* or *encourage* homophobia or homonegativism. That is, heterosexism signifies cultural values that heterosexuality is the only correct, normative, and acceptable expression of sexuality.

Although there is no single, underlying motivation for sexual prejudice, major contributors include belief in rigid gender roles, religious, and moral opposition to same-sex orientations, and in-group domination (Herek, 2004). These issues are discussed below.

Sex and Gender

In their meta-analysis of 112 studies of heterosexuals' attitudes toward gay men and lesbians, Kite and Whitley (1996) found that men report more sexual prejudice than do women, $d = 0.38$, a small to moderate effect size. Such sex differences are not restricted to US and Canadian populations. In a survey of 29 countries, men reported greater overall sexual prejudice, an average of 10 points more on a 100-point scale (Kelley, 2001). Although the strength of these sex differences varied by nation, men reported more negative attitudes in almost every country surveyed.

Kite and Whitley's (1996) meta-analysis also showed that men, unlike women, rate gay men more negatively than they do lesbians, $d = 0.41$, a small to moderate effect. Overall, heterosexual women tend to be more supportive of civil rights, employment protection, and adoption opportunities for gay people and to hold fewer stereotypical beliefs about sexual minorities (Herek, 2002a). One explanation for these sex differences is the importance that men tend to place on masculinity and traditional gender roles when they evaluate others. These gender-role beliefs include stereotypes and strict notions regarding the proper roles of the sexes; those who fail to meet traditional gender-role expectations are evaluated negatively (Deaux & Kite, 1987; Whitley & Ægisdóttir, 2000).

Particularly upsetting to some men may be their perception that gay men and lesbians have intentionally rejected their prescribed gender roles (Theodore & Basow, 2000; Whitley & Ægisdóttir, 2000). That non-masculine men are disliked more than non-feminine women (Madon, 1997; Martin, 1990; McCreary, 1994) suggests that gay men's perceived rejections of the higher status masculine gender role are seen as particularly shameful and unforgivable (Herek, 2002a; Kite & Whitley, 1996; LaMar & Kite, 1998).

Herek (1986) argued that many heterosexual men believe that they must reject gay men in order to fortify their own sense of masculinity. Because masculinity and femininity are portrayed in many cultures as polar opposites, masculinity can be defined by what it is not: femininity or, by association, homosexuality. Following this logic, men who experience their own masculinity as extremely integral to their identity are or would be more sexually prejudiced than men who do not see masculinity as their defining characteristic. Indeed, the most powerful predictor of homophobia in one study of college men was participants' perceived importance of masculinity. That is, men who believed that they did not live up to masculine stereotypes reported more negative self-evaluation and increased prejudice against homosexuals (Theodore & Basow, 2000).

Women are not immune from the effects of gender roles on sexual prejudice. In a sample of undergraduates, those who said that femininity was an integral part of their self-concept were more likely to endorse sexually prejudiced attitudes than were those who did not (Basow & Johnson, 2000). Although this parallels findings from male samples, the effect for women was considerably weaker. In another study, endorsement of conservative gender-role beliefs was related to higher levels of sexual prejudice against lesbians (Wilkinson, 2006). These findings suggest that, although both young women and men evaluate gay men and lesbians based on their adherence to traditional gender roles, women's more relaxed gender role grants them greater flexibility and acceptability than does men's stricter masculinity when gender roles are violated, which could explain why women rate gay men and lesbians more similarly than do heterosexual men (Basow, 1992).

Because gender-role flexibility varies by culture and region, these findings are unlikely to be universal. Indeed, a sample of northeastern Brazilian college students documented slightly higher overall levels of sexual prejudice among women who were also significantly more negative toward lesbians than toward gay men (Proulx, 1997); the men in this sample rated gay men and lesbians equally. Women in this region of Brazil are restricted by traditional gender roles that limit them to being the home-bound partners of men. Deprived of feminist role models common in larger southern Brazilian cities, the female participants viewed lesbianism as the stronger violation of gender roles.

Furthering the gender divide in the evaluation of lesbians and gay men is that, although many heterosexual men disapprove of male homosexuality, they acknowledge that lesbian sexuality affords them erotic appeal (Louderback & Whitley, 1997), and this may thus explain why they dislike lesbians less than gay men. Indeed, after they controlled for the level of erotic value in lesbian sexuality, Louderback and Whitley (1997) found that men's attitudes toward lesbians were no different than their attitudes toward gay men. Heterosexual women report far less erotic value in gay men's sexuality, which may explain why they often report similar attitudes toward gay men and lesbians.

Religion

Religion, especially in association with conservative doctrine, also motivates sexual prejudice. Allport and Ross (1967) distinguished between intrinsic and extrinsic motivation for religious faith and noted that people with an intrinsic faith experience their religion as the primary organizing principle in their lives, whereas people with an extrinsic faith use religion as a means for personal or social achievement. Although intrinsically motivated individuals display lower levels of racial prejudice, they report higher levels of sexual prejudice (Herek, 1987; Rosik, Griffith, & Cruz, 2007; Wilkinson, 2004). Both groups, however, are more sexually prejudiced than non-religiously-oriented people.

People with intrinsic orientations are more likely to internalize the values of their religion, many of which restrict sexuality (Rowatt & Schmitt, 2003). Duck and Hunsberger (1999) surveyed university students regarding the degree to which they believed that racial and sexual prejudice were prohibited by their religious communities. As predicted, racial prejudice was prohibited by most religious groups, and sexual prejudice was either not prohibited or slightly encouraged. Those with intrinsic orientations were less likely than those with extrinsic orientations to engage in prejudice condemned by their church but were more likely to engage in prejudice not condemned by their church (i.e., sexual prejudice).

In-Group Domination

A third major underlying motivation for sexual prejudice is the desire for in-group domination. Social dominance orientation (SDO) is a personality variable defined as "the extent to which one desires that one's in-group dominate and be superior to out-groups" (Pratto, Sidanius, Stallworth, & Malle, 1994, p. 742). To this end, individuals maintain legitimizing myths that disparage out-groups in order to justify their prejudices, such as the superiority of the heterosexual over the homosexual sexual orientation (Altemeyer, 1998; Sidanius & Pratto, 1999; Whitley & Lee, 2000). Because lesbians and gay men are granted lower status than are heterosexuals in North American society, individuals high in SDO hold negative or hostile attitudes toward them (Whitley & Lee, 2000) and believe that heterosexuality is the only "correct" sexual orientation, which legitimizes discrimination and prejudice against lesbians and gay men (Whitley & Ægisdóttir, 2000). Indeed, SDO is a moderate predictor of homophobic attitudes. Men endorse SDO beliefs more than women do, which may partially explain the sex differences in attitudes toward gay men and lesbians (Ekehammar, Akrami, Gylje, & Zakrisson, 2004; Lippa & Arad, 1999; Sibley, Robertson, & Wilson, 2006; Sidanius & Pratto, 1999).

Internalized Homophobia

Internalized homophobia is considered a likely outcome among sexual minorities who face even subtle sexual prejudice and sociocultural heterosexism. In the broadest sense, internalized homophobia involves negative feelings and self-regard due to one's homosexuality (Herek, Cogan, Gillis, & Glunt, 1998). It is also associated with negative evaluations of other sexual minorities and the belief that homosexuality is not a valid sexual orientation or behavioral expression. Homoerotic men tend to experience higher levels of internalized homophobia than do same-sex attracted women, perhaps because they encounter more pervasive, overt forms of sexual prejudice (Herek et al., 1998). Lesbians and gay men with higher internalized homophobia are less likely to disclose their sexuality, suffer greater depression and anxiety, have lower self-esteem, experience greater guilt following sex, and have shorter and less satisfying romantic relationships (Herek et al., 1998; Igartua, Gill, & Montoro, 2003; Ross & Rosser, 1996; Rowen & Malcolm, 2002).

Summary

Lesbians and gay men are frequently viewed as willfully transgressing traditional gender roles, and this sometimes inspires sexual prejudice, especially by heterosexual men against gay men. The desire for in-group domination further contributes to expressed hostility, as does religiosity—particularly among those with an intrinsic and conservative religious orientation. Expressions of hostility lead

Sexual Prejudice Against Bisexual Individuals

Few researchers consider sexual prejudice against bisexuals to be substantially different from prejudice directed against lesbians and gay men. Yet, bisexuals are significantly more likely to be deemed somewhat or very unacceptable (Eliason, 1997), perceived as more likely to be unfaithful to their relationship partners, and believed to be more likely to infect their partners with sexually transmitted diseases (Spalding & Peplau, 1997). Although heterosexuals' attitudes toward homosexuality and bisexuality are highly correlated (Mohr & Rochlen, 1999; Mulick & Wright, 2002), bisexual women and men were rated second lowest among various stigmatized groups; ranked higher only than illegal drug injectors, they were rated lower than all racial, religious, and political minority groups—as well as lower than homosexuals (Herek, 2002b). Furthermore, bisexual women and men reported almost as many sexual orientation-motivated crimes against them as did lesbians and gay men (Herek, Gillis, & Cogan, 1999).

Bisexual writers and activists have long noted that the very existence of bisexuality is often disputed by heterosexuals, lesbians, and gay men, many of whom discriminate against their bisexual friends and lovers (Hutchins & Kaahumanu, 1991; Israel & Mohr, 2004; Ochs, 1996). Prejudice against bisexuals is not limited to the United States; similar patterns have been observed in Germany (Raidt, 2003), the Netherlands (Raidt, 2003), Scotland (Laird, 2004), and Macedonia (Vrangalova, 2005). Unlike sexual prejudice against lesbians and gay men, negative attitudes and hostility toward bisexuals are manifested by both gay and straight individuals, but frequently emanate from different motivations.

Sources of Prejudice: Sex, Gender, and Sexual Orientation

Similar to their attitudes toward gay men and lesbians, heterosexual men report greater bisexual prejudice than do heterosexual women (Herek, 2002b; Hinrichs & Rosenberg, 2002). Also, bisexual men are viewed more negatively than bisexual women and are the least liked and accepted of the four sexual-minority groups (Eliason, 1997; Herek, 2002b). However, when ratings across these four groups are compared, a novel finding emerges: Although heterosexual men consistently rate gay and bisexual *men* less favorably than they do lesbian and bisexual women, heterosexual women rate *bisexual* women and men less favorably than they do lesbians and gay men (Herek, 2002b). Thus, for men it is the sex of the person that matters (nonheterosexual men are judged more harshly), whereas for women it is the sexual orientation that matters (bisexuals of both sexes are judged more harshly). This suggests that men are more concerned about maintaining traditional masculine gender roles, which to them automatically preclude bisexuality or homosexuality, whereas women are more concerned with upholding the monosexual value of binary categories (Herek, 2002b; Steffens & Wagner, 2004).

Among gay men and lesbians, the sex of the rater and of the bisexual person impacts sexual prejudice differently. For more than three decades, lesbians, especially those strongly identified with radical feminism, have been particularly negative toward bisexual women (Blumstein & Schwartz, 1974; Hartman, 2005; Ponse, 1978; Rust, 1995). For example, many lesbians distrust the authenticity of bisexual women's same-sex orientation, and, thus, they prefer to date, befriend, and work with lesbians (Rust, 1995).

Negative attitudes among lesbians and gay men might also reflect insularity following decades of self-contained communities defined by a restricted definition of sexual orientation. Accepting bisexuals as equals or partners requires loosening the borders of communities to the point of rendering them dangerously porous. Perhaps most feared would be a loss of the lesbian and gay communities' status as different or *special* (for a discussion of similar dynamics in Jewish religious communities, referred to as horizontal hostility, see White & Langer, 1999).

Recent research, however, indicates that, despite these concerns, both lesbians and gay men are highly tolerant of bisexuals of both sexes—considerably more tolerant than are heterosexual women and men—though still somewhat skeptical. Although lesbians are more likely than gay men to view bisexuality as a stable identity, they consider men's bisexuality to be more stable than women's bisexuality. Gay men have the opposite view; they believe that women's bisexuality is more enduring because gay men use bisexuality as a safe haven on the way to an eventual gay identity (Mohr & Rochlen, 1999). Regardless, most lesbian and gay groups, publications, and communities now include "bisexual" in their name, and the phrase LGB is ubiquitous.

Further Sources of Prejudice

Stereotyping and misinformation lead many heterosexuals, as well as lesbians and gay men, to view bisexuals as confused about, or as merely experimenting with, their sexuality. Many share the belief that true bisexuality does not exist because no one can possibly be attracted to both sexes. Rather, bisexuals are frequently viewed as essentially same-sex attracted but lying to themselves and others because they are unable to accept their stigmatized attractions, unwilling to face the social challenges that result from embracing a lesbian/gay identity or committed partnership, or reluctant to relinquish the social and interpersonal privileges granted to heterosexuals. Conversely, some believe that bisexuals, particularly bisexual women, are actually heterosexuals who identify as or act bisexual in order to appear "cool" among contemporary peers who view women's bisexuality as enticing (especially to heterosexual men) or in order to experience connectedness and the support of lesbian communities, especially following unsuccessful or abusive heterosexual relations (Hutchins & Kaahumanu, 1991; Ochs, 1996). Adolescents' and young adults' bisexuality is especially suspect and often interpreted as experimentation or questioning (i.e., a transient phase of sexual development that will eventually resolve as individuals either come out as lesbian/gay or return to heterosexuality).

Prejudice also emanates from stereotypes of bisexuals as sexual deviants who are over-sexed, inherently non-monogamous, and irresponsible carriers of HIV and other sexually transmitted infections which they thoughtlessly spread to unsuspecting heterosexual women (via bisexual men) and the lesbian community (via bisexual women). As such, bisexuals are often deemed unsuitable friends or lovers who cheat, abandon, or infect those around them (Israel & Mohr, 2004; Rust, 1995; Spalding & Peplau, 1997). One of the few positive stereotypes, at least among heterosexuals, is the belief that bisexuals are better able to satisfy a partner sexually (Spalding & Peplau, 1997).

In addition to the aforementioned myths and stereotypes, bisexual prejudice is nourished by several other less recognized factors. Some have argued that the unique prejudice against bisexuals might be due to monosexism, a cultural ideology that favors monosexuality (Ochs, 1996; Weiss, 2004). Monosexism holds that individuals should have access to partners of only one sex—either men or women, but not both; this belief is a likely consequence of the human proclivity for establishing binary categories (Ochs, 1996). Monosexism is further fueled by Western views of the sexes as orthogonal, even opposite to each other, which makes it seemingly impossible, if not highly suspect, for anyone to be simultaneously attracted to opposing poles. Rust (2000, p. 206) vividly captured this when she wrote the following: "If one is attracted by a man, how can one simultaneously be attracted by a woman, who is everything a man is not, and nothing that he is?" Bisexuals thus present a quandary because they blur the otherwise distinct boundaries between binary sexual categories. Furthermore, because heterosexuals tend to view bisexuals as more similar to themselves than they do gay men and lesbians (Galupo, Sailer, & St. John, 2004), accepting bisexuality may signify that the "other" sexuality is not so discrepant from their own. In a world in which nonheterosexuality is normatively stigmatized, this is likely to cause affective and cognitive dissonance.

Another source of prejudice is an outgrowth of cultural values that reject anything but heterosexuality and consequently view bisexuality as immoral, if not harmful. Such attitudes result from pervasive ignorance about the nature of bisexual people's lives and identities (Eliason, 2001) and from stereotypes about sexual deviance. Regarding the former, it is commonly assumed that bisexuality necessarily involves equal strength and quality of attraction toward both sexes. Because this occurs rarely (Rust, 2000, 2001; Weinrich & Klein, 2002), observers may erroneously conclude that bisexuality seldom exists. Ochs (1996) argued that such misinformation is enhanced by the invisibility of bisexuality and bisexuals in everyday life. For example, an essential source of information about a person's sexual orientation, their romantic or sexual partner(s), is usually misleading when it comes to bisexuals because unless they are in a polyamorous relationship with at least one partner of each sex (an uncommon scenario; see Rust, 2002), most observers automatically infer that they are either heterosexual or gay, depending on the sex of the current partner. Although visibility might help to remedy this, many bisexuals are apprehensive about speaking openly about their sexuality for fear of rejection by both heterosexual and gay/lesbian communities. Infrequent and negative depictions in the popular media perpetuate stigma and misinformation and thus further undermine accurate representations of bisexuals (Alexander, 2007; Bryant, 2001; Miller, 2002; White, 2002).

Internalized Biphobia

Faced with sexual prejudice from heterosexuals because of their same-sex attractions and from gay men and lesbians because of their other-sex attractions, some bisexuals internalize these negative attitudes, which makes it difficult for them to embrace or even to recognize their own sexuality. Although bisexual writers frequently articulate the negative impact of this dual rejection (Geller, 1990; Hutchins & Kaahumanu, 1991; McLean, 2001), empirical research on internalized bisexual prejudice remains scarce. One study showed that although bisexual men reported higher internalized biphobia than did bisexual women, the scores for both sexes were very low (Dengel, 2006). Studies of internalized homophobia, however, document that, on average, bisexual women and men are more likely to experience self-negating thoughts and feelings than are lesbians and gay men (Ross & Rosser, 1996; Weber, 2008).

Summary

In some respects, sexual prejudice against bisexuals is similar to that experienced by other sexual minorities. In other respects, it is unique and deeply rooted in cultural expectations of monosexuality, the psychological need for simplistic binary categories, identity politics, and ignorance. Gender is a factor, too. On average, women are more hostile toward bisexuals than they are to other monosexual groups, whereas men tend to place bisexuality in the same category as homosexuality. In addition, there is greater hostility toward bisexual men than toward bisexual women, and bisexual men are more likely to internalize negative societal attitudes than are bisexual women.

Gender Prejudice Against Transgender Individuals

The term *gender prejudice* incorporates the negative attitudes, emotional reactions (fear, disgust, anger, discomfort), behavior (harassment, violence), and societal discrimination toward those who are not readily categorized by themselves or others into a binary gender system of man or woman (Bornstein, 1994; Feinberg, 1993, 1996, 2006; Hill, 2003). For reasons similar to those previously discussed, the term gender prejudice supplants the more problematic term *transphobia*, which continues to be used by some writers. *Genderism*, a related concept, characterizes the broad societal attitude that is at the core of gender prejudice and violence (Hill, 2003). The concept reflects a system of beliefs that designate as abnormal or inappropriate transgressions of culturally defined notions of gender and sex and that sanction those who are gender nonconforming. Although most individuals who transgress beyond a "reasonable" level of gender norms are interpersonally and culturally penalized, transgender and self-identified transsexuals suffer the most recrimination.

Here, we explore the contextual origins of gender prejudice as they pertain to transgender (hereafter, "trans") populations in Western cultures and the connections among gender prejudice, sexism, and heterosexism. We review the prevalence and types of gender prejudice that trans people experience and summarize the implications of this for their psychological well-being and social welfare.

Contextual Origins

Western cultural norms typically assume that gender identity, a sense of oneself as a man or a woman, matches biological sex. Typical gender scripts erroneously conceptualize a narrow range of human variation and expression, thereby reducing variability to prescribed gender and sexual boundaries and negating the reality that perceptions of difference are inherently unstable and subjective. Fish (2008) argued that difference is defined by where the baseline is marked, and it is from there that all comparisons are made. Typically, the majority defines the baseline, and minority groups are labeled "fringe" as they are forced to the margins. Thus, although the heterosexual majority perpetuates limitations on the full range of human identity and expression, the true spectrum of sexuality and gender definitions overlap and assume various forms across time (Diamond, 2008; Pardo, 2008).

Particularly exemplary is Western medical institutions' adherence to the deeply rooted notion that there are only two sexes, underscored by the genotypes XX and XY. From birth, individuals are identified by their external genitalia and then socialized according to the prescribed gender association. Yet, genotypes are far more diverse, including X0s and XXYs, and phenotypes vary along a wide feminine/masculine continuum. For example, a healthy female infant born with congenital adrenal hyperplasia may have an enlarged clitoris that is mistaken at birth to be a small or an ambiguous penis. Complete androgen insensitivity among male infants is another intersex condition (also referred to as a "disorder of sexual development") in which an otherwise normative appearing female infant lacks a uterus and has male sex chromosomes.

Despite few empirical reports that document long-term physical harm from untreated intersex conditions (Fausto-Sterling, 2000), standard medical practice has been to correct "nature's mistakes" surgically to facilitate normative sex and gender-role development as well as healthy psychosocial adjustment (Money & Ehrhardt, 1972) with the aid of parents who have been instructed to socialize their children within rigid gender boundaries. Long-term follow-up reports, however, are not necessarily favorable (Colapinto, 2000; Diamond & Sigmundson, 1997). The lesson is not that all sex reassignments are bad, but rather that harm resides in nonconsensual surgical procedures. In fact, several long-term follow-up reports of transsexuals who choose sex reassignment surgery in adulthood highlight improvements in psychological well-being and quality of life after reassignment (Lawrence, 2003; Smith, Van Goozen, Kuiper, & Cohen-Kettenis, 2005).

Western cultures' rigid gender-role assumptions have especially influenced clinical and psychiatric interventions with gender-nonconforming children and adolescents, some of whom report a constellation of cross-dressing behaviors, same-sex erotic attractions, and the desire to be recognized as a member of the other sex. One literature review of children presenting at gender identity clinics concluded that prepubescent boys were 6–19 times more likely to receive therapy referrals than were girls (Zucker, Bradley, & Sanikhani, 1997). Yet, the children's mothers reported that the boys' cross-gender behaviors were mild to moderate, less extreme than those reported among referred girls, which highlights society's greater alarm about gender transgressions by boys. Treatments for gender nonconformity are defended by medical institutions as safe and as facilitating normal sexual and gender-role development (Green, 1987; Money & Lamacz, 1989), despite a dearth of empirical validation for such interventions—or even for the assumption that transsexuality is pathological (Lev, 2004).

Trans individuals may simply be revealing normative variations in gender expression. Whereas some treatment providers continue to encourage trans youths to rehearse gender-"appropriate" behaviors (Bradley & Zucker, 1997), follow-up studies reveal that trans youths experience a lesser reduction of gender-nonconforming behavior than that which was documented in the initial studies. Rather, they reveal that the youths learn better ways to conceal their authentic selves (Swann & Herbert, 1999).

Prevalence of Gender Prejudice

Institutional reports, popular media, and biographical accounts document an abundance of gender prejudice and gender-based violence (Brown & Rounsely, 1996; Feinberg, 1993, 1996, 2006). Stevens-Miller and colleagues (1999) noted that most perpetrators of attacks against trans individuals do not know the sexual orientation of their victims; the common thread is that the victims are gender nonconforming. A recurring survey conducted by the National Coalition of Anti-Violence Programs (NCAVP, 1999) of bias-motivated violence against gender and sexual minorities showed that hate crimes against trans people accounted for one-fifth of all documented murders. A subsequent NCAVP (2007) survey reported increased difficulty in collecting data on trans and gender-nonconforming persons due to a greater range of extant identities and the changing language of gender and sexual identity.

Empirical investigations suggest that, because of their failure to conform to gender expectations, retribution awaits particularly trans youth. Brown and Rounsely (1996) found that trans youths routinely experience taunting, teasing, and bullying at school, and Sausa (2005) reported that nearly all trans youths recalled school-based verbal and physical harassment, which left three-quarters of them feeling unsafe. They felt singled out or traumatized several times a day, such as during gym class, at school events, or when using single-sex restrooms. Lesbian, gay, and bisexual youths confirm that peers verbally harass and physically abuse gender-nonconforming youths more frequently than they do gender-conforming students (D'Augelli, Pilkington, & Hershberger, 2002).

Discrimination against trans people does not end at graduation; rather, it continues to occur across domains, including employment, housing, health care, and peer-to-peer interactions, and sometimes results in premeditated hate crimes. For example, Irwin (2002) reported that among educators, trans individuals were the most likely to experience discrimination or harassment in the workplace, 10–20% more likely than educators who identified as lesbian or gay, respectively. Discriminatory practices included being overlooked for promotion, deprived of opportunities, having their work sabotaged and property destroyed, and verbal threats. Many trans educators felt unsafe being open about their gender identity and were unlikely to take action when harassed. An NCAVP (1999) report suggested that trans persons may be less likely than other people to file formal complaints against coworkers for gender-based discrimination due to fear of negative reprisals or threats of being "outed" at work.

Although few cities in the United States or abroad currently have employment protection and hate crimes legislation for gender-nonconforming or trans people (Lombardi, Wilchins, Priesing, & Malouf, 2001; Minter, 2003), the European Court of Justice (ECJ) and the European Court of Human Rights have begun paving the way for legal protections for trans people (Whittle, Turner, Combs, & Rhodes, 2008). For example, in a civil rights case regarding pensions, the ECJ upheld the Equal Treatment Directive (76/207/EEC), which provides employment protection for trans people. A subsequent case in Europe protected the right of individuals to receive access to goods and services based on gender role rather than on birth sex. France, for instance, specifically protects the right to privacy when it comes to gender reassignment. However, France also maintains one of the most strict transition sequence requirements before a trans individual is permitted to change government-issued identification (Whittle et al., 2008).

Legal protections for European Union trans persons vary widely by member states, and in many states, trans people are uncertain about their rights. It is not surprising that Whittle, Turner, and Al-Alami (2007) recently reported that trans people were repeatedly harassed at work or fired from their jobs as a result of transitioning to live in their preferred gender. Workplace harassment was so pervasive that 42% of respondents not already living full time in their preferred gender reported that the workplace was the reason they had not yet begun their medical transition. Pfafflin and Junge (1998) suggested that gender reassignment can positively impact quality of life; thus, a discriminatory workplace environment can have a substantial effect on well-being.

Consequences of Gender Prejudice

Though much of the extant literature on trans populations focuses on treatment procedures and outcomes (Kahn, 1990; Riseley, 1986; Zucker, 1985, 2005), increased attention is being paid to negative developmental consequences (D'Augelli, Hershberger, & Pilkington, 2001; Denny, 2004; Kahn, 1990). In addition to the challenges of negotiating typical developmental milestones, trans youths' experiences are compounded by their multiple marginalized identities. Like most children, trans youths undergo broad-based pressures to conform to prescribed gender norms, which causes many to recognize early in their development (perhaps as young as age 5) that they are fundamentally different from same-sex peers because of their cross-gender interests, dress style, or play behavior (Ruble, Martin, & Berenbaum, 2007; Ruble, Taylor, et al., 2007; Zucker, 2005). Gender-nonconforming youths are rarely able to articulate to others the reasons why they feel different (Swann & Herbert, 1999).

Left unchecked, the unmediated accumulation of external stresses may lead to an array of unpleasant feelings (e.g., shame, alienation, inadequacy) and psychosocial problems (Meyer, 2003). Trans youths may attempt to cope with victimization and negative emotional backlash by running away from home, dropping out of school, abusing substances, or mutilating themselves (Burgess, 1999; D'Augelli et al., 2001; Klein, 1999; Sausa, 2005). Burgess (1999) noted that negative developmental trajectories may begin during adolescence when trans youths struggle to reconcile the appearance of secondary sexual characteristics with a discordant sex-gender identity. For example, trans youths have reported self-injecting silicone or steroids to create a more feminine or masculine appearance in accordance with their gender identity. Klein (1999) suggested that restricted access to carefully monitored and orchestrated gender transitions can result in increased risk-taking behavior, including self-mutilation, substance abuse, prostitution, and exposure to HIV.

Although the vast majority of discrimination and hate crimes against trans people are unreported—perhaps due to fear of retaliation or limited resources for data collection—signs of progress are evident. Since the 1990s, approximately 100 localities and 13 states have enacted some form of legislation to protect gender identity and/or expression (National Gay and Lesbian Task Force, 2007). Similarly, the European Union through the ECJ and the European Court of Human Rights has decided favorably in several cases that protected the rights of trans and gender-nonconforming people. As a result, non-profit organizations and private agencies now have resources for the collection of national data on trans discrimination and hate crimes. As trans national civil rights legislation expands, small and large businesses are educating their employees about the prevalence of trans-related hate/bias crimes, mandating trainings to increase gender tolerance, and adopting non-discrimination policies aimed at protecting trans people.

Summary

Most individuals, families, and organizations have limited knowledge about the internal experiences and sociocultural challenges that trans youths face. Because of widespread restrictions to gender expression, trans youths struggle to integrate internally driven needs with external sociocultural demands. Whereas supportive opportunities for gender expression can facilitate identity integration and emotional well-being, too often trans youths are labeled mentally ill and censured or punished. At best, these views forestall development and reinforce internalized gender prejudice; at worse, they generate mental illness and contribute to socially sanctioned violence.

Positive Attitudes Toward Sexual Minorities

Although polling data on the attitudes about and beliefs toward lesbians, bisexuals, and gay men are sparse across countries, there are indications that they have become strikingly more positive over the past two decades, especially among younger cohorts. This has been empirically documented primarily in European (especially Scandinavian) countries (Berg-Kelly, 2003; de Graaf, Sandfort, & ten Have, 2006; Steffens & Wagner, 2004; Wichstrøm & Hegna, 2003) and, of course, in the United States. As one index of sexual prejudice, we explore the extent to which positive attitudes toward sexual minorities in the United States characterize today's sexually diverse society.

National US polls have documented falling levels of sexual prejudice against sexual minorities (Campos-Flores, 2008). For example, during the past two decades, a majority of the public has endorsed the acceptability of homosexual relations among consenting adults (Saad, 2007). Only 4 in 10 Americans believe that homosexuality should be discouraged by society (Grossman, 2008a), and, for the first time, most Americans now believe that same-sex marriage is strictly a private decision between two people (Grossman, 2008b). Today, nearly all *Fortune 500* companies include sexual orientation in their non-discrimination policies, and about one-half offer same-sex domestic partner benefits to their employees (Graham, 2005; Gunther, 2006; Weinstein, 2007). A clear majority of the American public believes that homosexuality should be sanctioned as an acceptable alternative lifestyle (Saad, 2007) and that gay men and lesbians should be allowed to serve in the military (Campos-Flores, 2008; Gandossy, 2007).

This pattern of increased acceptance is largely due to two factors: knowing gay people and believing that their sexuality is beyond their control. First, lesbian and gay people have become so ubiquitous that two-thirds of Americans report having a close friend or close acquaintance who is gay; one-third have a family member who is gay (Campos-Flores, 2008). Those who befriend gay people tend to have more positive attitudes toward them (Morrison & Bearden, 2007), though cause and effect are difficult to determine. Second, the public increasingly believes that individuals do not choose their sexual orientation. Whereas 30 years ago, only 1 in 10 US citizens believed that an individual is born gay, today more than 4 in 10 believe that homosexuality is something a person is born with rather than a result of upbringing or the environment (Saad, 2007). Consequently, the majority of the US public believes that sexual orientation cannot be changed (Gandossy, 2007). As Haslam and Levy (2006, p. 478) concluded, this belief matters because "groups that expressed stronger antigay attitudes tended to see homosexuality as potentially alterable, not biologically based, and culturally specific."

Among adolescents and young adults, attitudes toward gay people are especially positive (Savin-Williams, 2005). For example, in recent studies, two-thirds of high school seniors supported the right of same-sex couples to adopt children (Broverman, 2006; Buchanan, 2006; Gandossy, 2007); more than three-fourths of high school seniors favored legalized same-sex marriage or civil unions (Broverman, 2006); and three-fourths of 18–29-year olds maintained that same-sex marriage is a private decision (Grossman, 2008b). Such historically high levels of acceptance can be attributed in part to the proliferation of Gay/Straight Alliances, of which there are now nearly 4,000 in the nation's secondary schools (glsen.org, 2007), and to the frequent portrayal of same-sex desire in the national media. As Doig (2007, p. 49) noted, "During the course of the '90s homosexuality went from being largely invisible to shockingly visible to fairly pedestrian." Despite this progress, however, prejudice against sexual and gender minorities persists.

Future Research Directions

Although discrimination and violence are far from being eradicated, public attitudes toward sexual and gender minorities are ever more accepting and tolerant. With the growing visibility of sexual and gender minorities, the current cohort of youth has become progressively more comfortable with and supportive of nontraditional sexual and gender expressions. Whether these changes among younger generations simply reflect youthful tolerance or a deeper value system that will be preserved with age must be determined. Thus, researchers must continue diligently to assess reasons for the upturn in liberal attitudes and that is necessary to maintain current trends. Little is known developmentally about the establishment and flexibility of these attitudes, such as the age at which opinions about gays and lesbians are fixed. Longitudinal explorations of sexual and gender prejudice may uncover evolving motivations over time and the windows during which interventions might be most effective. Equally important is whether and how these prejudices are reflected in other countries and within subcultures and regions in the United States.

It is also important to establish whether the predictors of sexual prejudice are changing. For example, recent US polls and narratives indicate that a peculiar liberal evangelism has evolved among today's "born again" Christians. When the youthful Azarian Southworth, host of the popular Christian television show *The Remix*, came out as gay, he was neither fired nor subjected to an avalanche of negative response (Southworth, 2008). Indeed, a recent Barna Research Group poll found that four-fifths of young US adults believe that the church has grown too harsh toward gay people. This includes the Catholic Church; a recent study of young Catholics indicated a rejection of church teachings about homosexuality that was tied to their "wisdom of the world" (Maher, Sever, & Pichler, 2008, p. 346); knowing a gay or lesbian person counteracted Catholic antigay dogma. Young US Christians have apparently shifted their attitudes toward gay people to one that emphasizes God's unconditional love and Jesus' ethic of judge not, lest thou be judged (Banerjee, 2008; Murphy, 2008). It is now incumbent on researchers to assess the reasons (e.g., increased contact with sexual minorities? cultural visibility? spiritual revelations?) for this positive shift. Maher et al. (2008) suggested that personal experience with sexual minorities might be the critical factor. Although research has demonstrated that increased exposure to lesbians and gays can diminish negative evaluations, it is unclear whether previously accepting individuals become more negative in light of perceived challenges to traditional religious institutions as sexual minorities struggle for the right to marry. Further research is needed to assess the impact of the evolving legal landscape on sexual and gender prejudice.

Unlike the considerable body of empirical literature on sexual stereotyping and prejudice, qualitative and quantitative investigations of bisexuals are scarce. Needed is understanding both about the views of monosexuals (heterosexuals, gay men, and lesbians) toward bisexuality and about perceived prejudice experienced by bisexuals from monosexuals. In addition, a distinction should be made between those who self-identify as bisexual and those who behave bisexually absent a bisexual identity. The latter are particularly prevalent among certain minority groups, such as Latino/as and African-Americans (Muñoz-Laboy, 2008; Siegel, Schrimshaw, Lekas, & Parsons, 2008), and will likely increase among younger cohorts (Savin-Williams, 2005). It remains unknown whether these groups differently elicit, and subsequently differentially interpret, bisexual prejudice.

Intriguing are the recent advances in biobehavioral assessments of attitudes and the possible contributions they offer for better understanding sexual and gender prejudice. For example, consistent with past research that suggests that heterosexual men experience an unconscious physiological manifestation of their antigay bias (Adams, Wright, & Lohr, 1996), Mahaffey, Bryan, and Hutchison (2005) reported that heterosexual men who rated themselves most biased against gay men had the largest startle eye blink response to pictorial images of gay men who were nude or sexually/romantically engaged. This relationship did not characterize their reactions to pictorial images of lesbians. Heterosexual women had no such physiological manifestations of antigay bias. Perhaps these findings suggest greater potential for change in prejudicial responses among heterosexual women than among heterosexual men or that different interventions are needed to attenuate the sexual prejudices of heterosexual men and women.

Finally, as previously noted, younger cohorts are shifting their attitudes and beliefs about sexual (but perhaps not yet about gender) minorities. When asked, college students endorsed positive stereotypes of gay men as stylish, witty, sensitive, artistic, articulate, attractive, and attuned to the emotional needs of women (Morrison & Bearden, 2007). In another study, youth endorsed positive stereotypes of lesbians as a diverse group consisting of "subtypes," such as *lipstick lesbians* (beauty, sensitivity, maternal instincts), *career-oriented feminists* (proud, successful professional, strong sense of self, open-minded, creative), *soft butches* (athletic, powerful, feminist), and *free spirits* (eccentric, mysterious, nonconformist, persuasive) (Geiger, Harwood, & Hummert, 2006). Acceptance and appreciation of individuals who occupy the poles of gender nonconformity, regardless of their sexuality, remains an unrealized dream—even among younger cohorts. Until then, the time has come for researchers to transcend conventional explorations that focused solely on the negative attitudes toward sexual and gender minorities and to investigate the *positive* attributes that such individuals possess (Savin-Williams, 2005).

References

Adams, H. E., Wright, L. W., Jr., & Lohr, B. A. (1996). Is homophobia associated with homosexual arousal? *Journal of Abnormal Psychology, 105*, 440–445.

Alexander, J. (2007). Bisexuality in the media: A digital roundtable. *Journal of Bisexuality, 7*, 113–124.

Allport, G. W., & Ross, J. M. (1967). Personal religious orientation and prejudice. *Journal of Personality and Social Psychology, 5*, 432–433.

Altemeyer, B. (1998). The other "authoritarian personality." *Advances in Experimental Social Psychology, 30*, 47–92.

Banerjee, N. (2008, June 1). Taking their faith, but not their politics, to the people. *New York Times*. Retrieved June 5, 2008, from www.nytimes.com/2008/06/01/us/01evangelical.html

Basow, S. A. (1992). *Gender: Stereotypes and roles* (3rd ed.). Pacific Grove, CA: Brooks/Cole.

Basow, S. A., & Johnson, K. (2000). Predictors of homophobia in female college students. *Sex Roles, 42*, 391–404.

Berg-Kelly, K. (2003). Adolescent homosexuality: We need to learn more about causes and consequences. *Acta Pædiatrica, 92*, 141–144.

Blumstein, P. W., & Schwartz, P. (1974). Lesbianism and bisexuality. In E. Goode (Ed.), *Sexual deviance and sexual deviants* (pp. 278–295). New York: Morrow.

Bornstein, K. (1994). *Gender outlaw: On men, women, and the rest of us*. New York: Routledge.

Bradley, S. J., & Zucker, K. J. (1997). Gender identity disorder: A review of the past 10 years. *Journal of the American Academy of Child and Adolescent Psychiatry, 36*, 872–880.

Broverman, N. (2006, February 14). By the numbers: Gay rights. *Advocate*, p. 36.

Brown, M. L., & Rounsley, C. A. (1996). *True selves: Understanding transsexualism*. San Francisco, CA: Jossey-Bass.

Bryant, W. M. (2001). Stereotyping bisexual men in film. *Journal of Bisexuality, 1*, 213–219.

Buchanan, W. (2006, March 23). *Poll finds U.S. warming to gay marriage*. Retrieved March 27, 2006, from www.sfgate.com/egi-bin

Burgess, C. (1999). Internal and external stress factors associated with the identity development of transgendered youth. *Journal of Gay and Lesbian Social Services, 10*, 35–47.

Campos-Flores, A. (2008). A gay marriage surge: Public support grows, according to the new *Newsweek* poll. Retrieved December 5, 2008, from www.newsweek.com/id/172399

Colapinto, J. (2000). *As nature made him: The boy who was raised as a girl*. New York: Harper Collins.

D'Augelli, A. R., Hershberger, S. L., & Pilkington, N. W. (2001). Suicidality patterns and sexual orientation-related factors among lesbian, gay, and bisexual youths. *Suicide and Life-Threatening Behavior, 31*, 250–264.

D'Augelli, A. R., Pilkington, N. W., & Hershberger, S. L. (2002). Incidence and mental health impact of sexual orientation victimization of lesbian, gay, and bisexual youths in high school. *School Psychology Quarterly, 17*, 148–167.

Deaux, K., & Kite, M. E. (1987). Thinking about gender. In B. B. Hess & M. M. Ferree (Eds.), *Analyzing gender: A handbook of social science research* (pp. 92–117). Newbury Park, CA: Sage.

de Graaf, R., Sandfort, T. G. M., & ten Have, M. (2006). Suicidality and sexual orientation: Differences between men and women in a general population-based sample from the Netherlands. *Archives of Sexual Behavior, 35*, 253–262.

Dengel, D. W. (2006). *Examining biphobia in heterosexual, homosexual, and bisexual men and women*. Unpublished doctoral dissertation, Temple University.

Denny, D. (2004). Changing models of transsexualism. *Journal of Gay and Lesbian Psychotherapy, 8*, 25–40.

Diamond, L. M. (2008). Female bisexuality from adolescence to adulthood: Results from a 10-year longitudinal study. *Developmental Psychology, 44*, 5–14.

Diamond, M., & Sigmundson, K. (1997). Sex reassignment at birth: Long-term review and clinical implications. *Archives of Pediatrics and Adolescent Medicine, 151*, 298–307.

Doig, W. (2007, July 17). America's real first family. *Advocate*, pp. 46–50.

Duck, R. J., & Hunsberger, B. (1999). Religious orientation and prejudice: The role of religious proscription, right-wing authoritarianism, and social desirability. *International Journal for the Psychology of Religion, 9*, 157–179.

Ekehammar, B., Akrami, N., Gylje, M., & Zakrisson, I. (2004). What matters most to prejudice: Big five personality, social dominance orientation, or right-wing authoritarianism? *European Journal of Psychology, 18*, 463–482.

Eliason, M. J. (1997). The prevalence and nature of biphobia in heterosexual undergraduate students. *Archives of Sexual Behavior, 26*, 317–326.

Eliason, M. (2001). Bi-negativity: The stigma facing bisexual men. *Journal of Bisexuality, 1*, 137–154.

Fausto-Sterling, A. (2000). *Sexing the body: Gender politics and the construction of sexuality*. New York: Basic Books.

Feinberg, L. (1993). *Stone butch blues*. New York: Firebrand Books.

Feinberg, L. (1996). *Transgender warriors: Making history from Joan of Arc to Dennis Rodman*. Boston, MA: Beacon.
Feinberg, L. (2006). *Drag king dreams*. New York: Carroll & Graff.
Fish, S. (2008, June 1). Norms and deviations: Who's to say? *New York Times*. Retrieved June 1, 2008, from fish.blogs.nytimes.com/2008/06/01/norms-and-deviations-whos-to-say/index.html?ref=opinion
Fyfe, B. (1983). "Homophobia" or homosexual bias reconsidered. *Archives of Sexual Behavior, 12*, 549–554.
Galupo, P. M., Sailer, C. A., & St. John, S. C. (2004). Friendships across sexual orientations: Experiences of bisexual women in early adulthood. In R. C. Fox (Ed.), *Current research on bisexuality* (pp. 37–53). New York: Harrington Park Press.
Gandossy, T. (2007, July 7). *Poll majority: Gays' orientation can't change*. Retrieved July 7, 2007, from www.cnn.com/2007/Living/personal
Geiger, W., Harwood, J., & Hummert, M. L. (2006). College students' multiple stereotypes of lesbians: A cognitive perspective. *Journal of Homosexuality, 51*, 165–182.
Geller, T. (Ed.). (1990). *Bisexuality: A reader and sourcebook*. Novato, CA: Times Change.
glsen.org (2007, July 31). Retrieved July 31, 2007, from www.glsen.org
Graham, C. (2005, October 11). Good news at the 500. *Advocate*, p. 60.
Green, R. (1987). *The "sissy boy syndrome" and the development of homosexuality*. New Haven, CT: Yale University Press.
Grossman, C. L. (2008a, June 24). Religion findings show divergence from traditional doctrines. *USA Today*, pp. 1D–2D.
Grossman, C. L. (2008b, June 4). Most say gay marriage private choice. *USA Today*, p. 7D.
Gunther, M. (2006, December 3). *Queer Inc.: How corporate America fell in love with gays and lesbians*. Retrieved December 3, 2006, from www.cnnmoney.com/pt/
Hartman, J. E. (2005). Another kind of 'chilly climate': The effects of lesbian separatism on bisexual women's identity and community. *Journal of Bisexuality, 5*, 61–77.
Haslam, N., & Levy, S. R. (2006). Essentialist beliefs about homosexuality: Structure and implications for prejudice. *Personality and Social Psychology Bulletin, 32*, 471–485.
Herek, G. M. (1986). On heterosexual masculinity: Some psychical consequences of the social construction of gender and sexuality. *American Behavioral Scientist, 29*, 563–577.
Herek, G. M. (1987). Religious orientation and prejudice: A comparison of racial and sexual attitudes. *Personality and Social Psychology Bulletin, 13*, 56–65.
Herek, G. M. (2000). The psychology of sexual prejudice. *Current Directions in Psychological Science, 9*, 19–22.
Herek, G. M. (2002a). Gender gaps in public opinion about lesbians and gay men. *Public Opinion Quarterly, 66*, 40–66.
Herek, G. M. (2002b). Heterosexuals' attitudes toward bisexual men and women in the United States. *Journal of Sex Research, 39*, 264–274.
Herek, G. M. (2004). Beyond "homophobia": Thinking about sexual prejudice and stigma in the twenty-first century. *Sexual Research and Social Policy, 1*, 6–24.
Herek, G. M. (2009). Hate crimes and stigma-related experiences among sexual minority adults in the United States: Prevalence estimates from a national probability sample. *Journal of Interpersonal Violence, 24*, 54–74.
Herek, G. M., Cogan, J. C., Gillis, J. R., & Glunt, E. K. (1998). Correlates of internalized homophobia in a community sample of lesbians and gay men. *Journal of the Gay and Lesbian Medical Association, 2*, 17–25.
Herek, G. M., Gillis, J. R., & Cogan, J. C. (1999). Psychological sequelae of hate-crime victimization among lesbian, gay, and bisexual adults. *Journal of Consulting and Clinical Psychology, 67*, 945–951.
Hill, D. B. (2003). Genderism, transphobia, and gender bashing: A framework for interpreting anti-transgender violence. In B. C. Wallace & R. T. Carter (Eds.), *Understanding and dealing with violence: A multicultural approach* (pp. 113–136). Thousand Oaks, CA: Sage.
Hinrichs, D. W., & Rosenberg, P. J. (2002). Attitudes toward gay, lesbian, and bisexual persons among heterosexual liberal arts college students. *Journal of Homosexuality, 43*, 61–83.
Hudson, W. W., & Ricketts, W. A. (1980). A strategy for the measurement of homophobia. *Journal of Homosexuality, 5*, 357–372.
Hutchins, L., & Kaahumanu, L. (Eds.). (1991). *Bi any other name: Bisexual people speak out*. Boston, MA: Alyson.
Igartua, K. J., Gill, K., & Montoro, R. (2003). Internalized homophobia: A factor in depression, anxiety, and suicide in the gay and lesbian population. *Canadian Journal of Community Mental Health, 22*, 15–30.
Irwin, J. (2002). Discrimination against gay men, lesbians, and transgender people working in education. *Journal of Gay and Lesbian Social Services, 14*, 65–77.
Israel, T., & Mohr, J. J. (2004). Attitudes toward bisexual women and men: Current research, future directions. In R. C. Fox (Ed.), *Current research on bisexuality* (pp. 117–134). New York: Harrington Park Press.

Kahn, T. J. (1990). The adolescent transsexual in a juvenile corrections institution: A case study. *Child and Youth Care Quarterly, 19*, 21–29.

Kelley, J. (2001). Attitudes toward homosexuality in 29 nations. *Australian Social Monitor, 4*, 15–22.

Kite, M. E., & Whitley, B. E. (1996). Sex differences in attitudes toward homosexual persons, behavior, and civil rights: A meta-analysis. *Personality and Social Psychology Bulletin, 22*, 336–353.

Klein, R. (1999). Group work practice with transgendered male-to-female sex workers. *Journal of Gay and Lesbian Social Services, 10*, 95–109.

Laird, N. (2004). *Exploring biphobia: A report on participatory appraisal research workshops in Glasgow and Edinburgh*. Retrieved October 16, 2008, from http://www.stonewall.org.uk/documents/Bisexual_Participatory_Appraisal_Research.pdf

LaMar, L., & Kite, M. (1998). Sex differences in attitudes toward gay men and lesbians: A multidimensional approach. *Journal of Sex Research, 35*, 189–196.

Lawrence, A. A. (2003). Factors associated with satisfaction or regret following male-to-female sex reassignment. *Archives of Sexual Behavior, 32*, 299–315.

Lev, A. I. (2004). *Transgender emergence: Therapeutic guidelines for working with gender-variant people and their families*. Binghamton, NY: Haworth Press.

Lippa, R., & Arad, S. (1999). Gender, personality, and prejudice: The display of authoritarianism and social dominance orientation in interviews with college men and women. *Journal of Research in Personality, 33*, 463–493.

Lombardi, E. L., Wilchins, R. A., Priesing, D., & Malouf, D. (2001). Gender violence: Transgender experiences with violence and discrimination. *Journal of Homosexuality, 42*, 89–101.

Louderback, L. A., & Whitley, B. E., Jr. (1997). Perceived erotic value of homosexuality and sex-role attitudes as mediators of sex differences in heterosexual college students' attitudes toward lesbians and gay men. *Journal of Sex Research, 34*, 175–182.

Madon, S. (1997). What do people believe about gay males? A study of stereotype content and strength. *Sex Roles, 37*, 663–685.

Mahaffey, A. L., Bryan, A., & Hutchison, K. E. (2005). Sex differences in affective responses to homoerotic stimuli: Evidence for an unconscious bias among heterosexual men, but not heterosexual women. *Archives of Sexual Behavior, 34*, 537–545.

Maher, M. J., Sever, L. M., & Pichler, S. (2008). How Catholic college students think about homosexuality: The connection between authority and sexuality. *Journal of Homosexuality, 55*, 325–349.

Martin, C. L. (1990). Attitudes about children with nontraditional and traditional gender roles. *Sex Roles, 22*, 151–165.

McCreary, D. R. (1994). The male role and avoiding femininity. *Sex Roles, 31*, 517–531.

McLean, K. (2001). Living in the double closet: Bisexual youth speak out. *Hecate, 27*, 109–118.

Meyer, I. H. (2003). Prejudice, social stress, and mental health in lesbian, gay, and bisexual populations: Conceptual issues and research evidence. *Psychological Bulletin, 129*, 674–697.

Miller, M. (2002). "Ethically questionable?" Popular media reports on bisexual men and AIDS. *Journal of Bisexuality, 2*, 93–112.

Minter, S. (2003, October). *Representing transsexual clients: Selected legal issues*. Retrieved November 17, 2008, from http://www.transgenderlaw.org/resources/translaw.htm

Mohr, J. J., & Rochlen, A. B. (1999). Measuring attitudes regarding bisexuality in lesbian, gay male, and heterosexual populations. *Journal of Counseling Psychology, 46*, 353–369.

Money, J., & Erhardt, A. (1972). *Man and woman, boy and girl: The differentiation and dimorphism of gender identity from conception to maturity*. Baltimore, MD: Johns Hopkins University Press.

Money, J., & Lamacz, M. (1989). *Vandalized lovemaps: Paraphilic outcome of seven cases in pediatric sexology*. Buffalo, NY: Prometheus Books.

Morrison, T. G., & Bearden, A. G. (2007). The construction and validation of the homopositivity scale: An instrument measuring endorsement of positive stereotypes about gay men. *Journal of Homosexuality, 52*, 63–89.

Mulick, P. S., & Wright, L. W. Jr. (2002). Examining the existence of biphobia in the heterosexual and homosexual populations. *Journal of Bisexuality, 2*, 45–64.

Muñoz-Laboy, M. A. (2008). Familism and sexual regulation among bisexual Latino men. *Archives of Sexual Behavior, 37*, 773–782.

Murphy, T. (2008, June 17). The believers. *Advocate*, pp. 52–58.

National Coalition of Anti-Violence Programs. (1999). *Anti-lesbian, gay, transgender, and bisexual violence in 1999: A report of the National Coalition of Anti-Violence Programs*. Retrieved June 1, 2008, from www.ncavp.org/publications/NationalPubs.aspx

National Coalition of Anti-Violence Programs. (2007). *Anti-lesbian, gay, bisexual and transgender violence in 2007: A report of the National Coalition of Anti-Violence Programs.* Retrieved June 1, 2008, from www.ncavp.org/publications/NationalPubs.aspx

National Gay and Lesbian Task Force. (2007). *Scope of explicitly transgender-inclusive anti-discrimination laws.* Retrieved June 1, 2008, from www.thetaskforce.org/transgender_inclusive_laws

Ochs, R. (1996). Biphobia: It goes more than two ways. In B. A. Firestein (Ed.), *Bisexuality: The psychology and politics of an invisible minority* (pp. 217–239). Thousand Oaks, CA: Sage.

O'Donohue, W., & Caselles, C. E. (1993). Homophobia: Conceptual, definitional, and value issues. *Journal of Psychopathology and Behavioral Assessment, 15*, 177–195.

Pardo, T. (2008). *An exploratory study of identity conceptualization and development in a sample of gender nonconforming biological females.* Unpublished M.A. Thesis, Cornell University.

Pfafflin, F., & Junge, A. (1998). Sex reassignment: Thirty years of international follow-up studies after sex reassignment surgery: A comprehensive review, 1961–1991 [Translated from German into American English by Roberta B. Jacobson and Alf B. Meier]. *International Journal of Transgenderism.* Retrieved November 17, 2008, from http://www.symposion.com/ijt/pfaefflin/1000.htm

Ponse, B. (1978). *Identities in the lesbian world: The social construction of self.* Westport, CT: Greenwood Press.

Pratto, F., Sidanius, J., Stallworth, L. M., & Malle, B. F. (1994). Social dominance orientation: A personality variable predicting social and political attitudes. *Journal of Personality and Social Psychology, 67*, 741–763.

Proulx, R. (1997). Homophobia in northeastern Brazilian university students. *Journal of Homosexuality, 34*, 47–56.

Raidt, T. (2003). *They don't know which side they're on: Biphobia as a result of Western binary thinking and the human need for stability.* Retrieved October 16, 2008, from http://www.tabearaidt.de/Biphobia-TabeaRaidt.pdf

Riseley, D. (1986). Gender identity disorder of childhood: Diagnostic and treatment issues. In W. A. Walters & M. W. Ross (Eds.), *Transsexualism and sex reassignment* (pp. 26–43). New York: Oxford University Press.

Rosik, C. H., Griffith, L. K., & Cruz, Z. (2007). Homophobia and conservative religion: Toward a more nuanced understanding. *American Journal of Orthopsychiatry, 77*, 10–19.

Ross, M. W., & Rosser, B. R. S. (1996). Measurement and correlates of internalized homophobia: A factor analytic study. *Journal of Clinical Psychology, 52*, 15–21.

Rowatt, W. C., & Schmitt, D. (2003). Associations between religious orientation and varieties of sexual experience. *Journal for the Scientific Study of Religion, 42*, 455–465.

Rowen, C. J., & Malcolm, J. P. (2002). Correlates of internalized homophobia and homosexual identity formation in a sample of gay men. *Journal of Homosexuality, 43*, 77–92.

Ruble, D. N., Martin, C., & Berenbaum, S. A. (2007). Gender development. In N. Eisenberg (Ed.), *Handbook of child psychology* (6th ed., Vol. 3, pp. 858–932). New York: Wiley.

Ruble, D. N., Taylor, L., Cyphers, L., Greulich, F. K., Lurye, L. E., & Strout, P. E. (2007). The role of gender constancy in early gender development. *Child Development, 78*, 1121–1136.

Rust, P. C. (1995). *Bisexuality and the challenge to lesbian politics: Sex, loyalty, and revolution.* New York: New York University Press.

Rust, P. C. (2000). Bisexuality: A contemporary paradox for women. *Journal of Social Issues, 56*, 205–221.

Rust, P. C. (2001). Two many and not enough: The meaning of bisexual identities. *Journal of Bisexuality, 1*, 31–68.

Rust, P. C. (2002). Bisexuality: The state of the union. *Annual Review of Sex Research, 13*, 180–240.

Saad, L. (2007, May 29). *Tolerance for gay rights at high-water mark.* Retrieved May 29, 2007, from www.gallup.com/poll/27694/Tolerance-Gay-Rights-HighWater-Mark.aspx

Sausa, L. A. (2005). Translating research into practice: Trans youth recommendations for improving school systems. *Journal of Gay and Lesbian Issues in Education, 3*, 15–28.

Savin-Williams, R. C. (2005). *The new gay teenager.* Cambridge, MA: Harvard University Press.

Sibley, C. G., Robertson, A., & Wilson, M. S. (2006). Exploring the additive and interactive effects of social dominance orientation and right-wing authoritarianism on prejudice and related intergroup attitudes. *Political Psychology, 27*, 755–768.

Sidanius, J., & Pratto, F. (1999). *Social dominance.* New York: Cambridge University Press.

Siegel, K., Schrimshaw, E. W., Lekas, H. M., & Parsons, J. T. (2008). Sexual behaviors of non-gay identified non-disclosing men who have sex with men and women. *Archives of Sexual Behavior, 37*, 720–735.

Smith, Y. S., Van Goozen, S. H., Kuiper, A. J., & Cohen-Kettenis, P. T. (2005). Sex reassignment: Outcomes and predictors of treatment for adolescent and adult transsexuals. *Psychological Medicine, 35*, 89–99.

Southworth, A. (2008, June 17). Unconditional love. *Advocate*, p. 38.

Spalding, L. R., & Peplau, L. A. (1997). The unfaithful lover: Heterosexuals' perceptions of bisexuals and their relationships. *Psychology of Women Quarterly, 21*, 611–625.

Steffens, M. C., & Wagner, C. (2004). Attitudes toward lesbians, gay men, bisexual women, and bisexual men in Germany. *Journal of Sex Research, 41*, 137–149.

Stevens-Miller, M., Plotner, B., Williamson, D., Jackson, M., Monzo, T., & Roder, A. (1999, May). *It's time, Illinois: Report on discrimination and hate crimes against transgendered people in Illinois*. Retrieved June 1, 2008, from www.genderadvocates.org/reports/report2000.pdf

Swann, S., & Herbert, S. E. (1999). Ethical issues in the mental health treatment of gender dysphoric adolescents. *Journal of Gay and Lesbian Social Services, 10*, 19–34.

Theodore, P. S., & Basow, S. A. (2000). Heterosexual masculinity and homophobia: A reaction to the self? *Journal of Homosexuality, 40*, 31–48.

Vrangalova, S. (2005). *Misterijata na seksualnata orientacija: Sovremeni koncepti i makedonski perspektivi [The sexual orientation mystery: Contemporary concepts and Macedonian perspectives]*. Skopje, Macedonia: EGAL.

Weber, G. N. (2008). Using to numb the pain: Substance use and abuse among lesbian, gay, and bisexual individuals. *Journal of Mental Health Counseling, 30*, 31–48.

Weinberg, G. (1972). *Society and the healthy homosexual*. New York: St. Martins.

Weinrich, J. D., & Klein, F. (2002). Bi-gay, bi-straight, and bi-bi: Three bisexual subgroups identified using cluster analysis of the Klein sexual orientation grid. *Journal of Bisexuality, 2*, 109–139.

Weinstein, S. (2007, June 19). Their best foot forward. *Advocate*, pp. 69–70.

Weiss, J. T. (2004). GL vs. BT: The archaeology of biphobia and transphobia within U.S. gay and lesbian community. *Journal of Bisexuality, 3*, 25–55.

White, J. B., & Langer, E. J. (1999). Horizontal hostility: Relations between similar minority groups. *Journal of Social Issues, 55*, 537–559.

White, J. D. (2002). Bisexuals who kill: Hollywood's bisexual crimewave 1985–1995. *Journal of Bisexuality, 2*, 39–54.

Whitley, B. E., & Ægisdóttir, S. (2000). The gender belief system, authoritarianism, social dominance orientation, and heterosexuals' attitudes toward lesbians and gay men. *Sex Roles, 42*, 947–967.

Whitley, B. E., & Lee, S. E. (2000). The relationship of authoritarianism and related constructs to attitudes toward homosexuality. *Journal of Applied Social Psychology, 30*, 144–170.

Whittle, S., Turner, L., & Al-Alami, M. (2007, February). Engendered penalties: Transgender and transsexual people's experiences of inequality and discrimination. *Equalities Review*. Retrieved November 17, 2008, from http://www.pfc.org.uk/files/EngenderedPenalties.pdf

Whittle, S., Turner, L., Combs, R., & Rhodes, S. (2008, April). Transgender EuroStudy: Legal survey and focus on the transgender experience of health care. Retrieved November 17, 2008, from http://www.pfc.org.uk/files/eurostudy.pdf

Wichstrøm, L., & Hegna, K. (2003). Sexual orientation and suicide attempt: A longitudinal study of the general Norwegian adolescent population. *Journal of Abnormal Psychology, 112*, 144–151.

Wilkinson, W. W. (2004). Religiosity, authoritarianism, and homophobia: A multidimensional approach. *International Journal for the Psychology of Religion, 14*, 55–67.

Wilkinson, W. W. (2006). Exploring heterosexual women's anti-lesbian attitudes. *Journal of Homosexuality, 51*, 139–155.

Wright, L. W., Jr., Adams, H. E., & Bernat, J. (1999). Development and validation of the homophobia scale. *Journal of Psychopathology and Behavioral Assessment, 21*, 337–347.

Zucker, K. (1985). Cross-gender identified children. In B. Steiner (Ed.), *Gender dysphoria: Development, research, and management* (pp. 75–174). New York: Plenum.

Zucker, K. (2005). Gender identity disorder in children and adolescents. *Annual Review of Clinical Psychology, 1*, 467–492.

Zucker, K. J., Bradley, S. J., & Sanikhani, M. (1997). Sex differences in referral rates of children with gender identity disorder: Some hypotheses. *Journal of Abnormal Child Psychology, 25*, 217–227.

Part XII
Industrial-Organizational Psychology

Chapter 16
Gender and Occupational Choice

Helen M.G. Watt

Men and women tend to end up in different kinds of occupations. This phenomenon is extraordinarily robust across different settings (see Watt & Eccles, 2008), although there is certainly also cultural variation; good illustrations are women's higher representation in the sciences in India and the former Soviet Socialist Republics than in other countries. Children's literature, role models, vocational high school, and career counseling are some of the ways people get ideas about which careers are appropriate for them. College majors are gender imbalanced, which also sends signals to women who like chemistry and men who like languages that those are not the right places for them. Concerns regarding gendered occupational participation have often focused on women's underrepresentation in STEM (Science, Technology, Engineering, Mathematics) domains based on arguments related to gender equity. Ever since Lucy Sells (1980) identified mathematics as the "critical filter" that limits access to many high-status, high-income careers, others have also argued that many women prematurely restrict their educational and career options by discontinuing their mathematical training in high school or soon after (Bridgeman & Wendler, 1991; Heller & Parsons, 1981; Lips, 1992; Meece, Wigfield, & Eccles, 1990). Women are both less likely to choose careers in STEM fields and more likely to leave those careers if they do enter them (American Association of University Women, 1993, 1998; National Center for Education Statistics [NCES], 1997; National Science Foundation, 1999). In the United States, Australia, and elsewhere, there has been a concentration of research efforts and policy interventions designed to promote girls' and women's participation in mathematics and the sciences over the past 25 years.

The concentration of boys in masculine-typed careers has caused less consternation, probably because female-dominated careers tend to be lower in status and to pay lower salaries. Whether boys pursue their interests and develop their skills in nontraditional domains has been less often a topic of research concern or public interest. However, it is also important to discover the factors that affect boys' and men's educational and occupational choices, and whether they are being pushed into gender-stereotypic careers in the same ways that girls and women are, which could have significant implications for men's career satisfaction and personal well-being. Over the last decade there has been an increasing trend in educational research, policy initiatives, and the media to target boys' educational needs. Such discussions have invariably focused on boys' academic achievement and boys' disaffection with schooling, together with a call for positive male role models among teachers to bring out the best in boys (e.g., House of Representatives Standing Committee on Education and Training, 2002; Lingard, Martino, Mills, & Bahr, 2002; Martin, 2002). In Australia, there has been insistent and vocal concern regarding boys' education and participation in domains gender-typed as

H.M.G. Watt (✉)
Monash University, Melbourne, VIC, Australia

feminine and a call for more efforts to encourage boys' involvement in those domains. An example of this is the ongoing *Inquiry into the Education of Boys* (by the Standing Committee on Employment, Education, and Workplace Relations; Parliament of Australia, House of Representatives, commissioned on 21 March 2000 by the Minister for Education, Training and Youth Affairs; O'Doherty, 1994). I argue from both social justice and human resource perspectives that we should be concerned with the educational opportunities and outcomes of both boys and girls.

Although women have been making gains in entering traditionally male-dominated professions, gender differences persist. Why does a gender imbalance remain, and does it matter? Both genders in male-dominated, masculine-typed occupations report higher levels of job satisfaction than both genders in female-dominated, feminine-typed occupations (Harlan & Jansen, 1987; Jacobs, Chhin, & Bleeker, 2006; Moore, 1985). A possible explanation is that male-dominated occupations generally provide higher levels of income, freedom, and challenge than female-dominated occupations do (Moore, 1985). Yet, the numbers of women in nontraditional occupations continue to be low. As guidance counselors, teachers, and parents help young women to make choices about what fields to pursue, it is important that they encourage girls and women to consider nontraditional fields of interest that are likely to lead to high levels of job satisfaction.

Despite equivalent levels of academic achievement, girls choose fewer advanced STEM courses in senior high school than boys do, and they are less likely to aspire to high-status STEM-related careers than boys are, although they are more likely to be concentrated in lower status STEM professions (e.g., nursing) and other non-STEM caring professions (e.g., teaching). This pattern has been repeatedly identified and is of concern in Australia, the United States, and other countries. Two perspectives inform concerns regarding women's lower participation in STEM fields: (i) an adequate supply of high-quality human capital in the STEM fields is fundamental to any nation's capacity to create and absorb scientific knowledge and to undertake innovative activities, and women represent an underutilized pool that could supplement the critical shortage of people who elect STEM careers and (ii) at an individual level, STEM skills play an important role in expanding or limiting career options (Betz & Hackett, 1983; Lent et al., 2005); mathematics in particular has been identified as the critical filter to many prestigious careers (Sells, 1980), such that women do not share equally in the advantages of the mathematically well prepared.

The first argument is concerned with economic advantage: Participation in advanced science and mathematics education has continually declined in the United States over the last two decades, to the point where there is grave concern about the country's viability to sustain economic growth (see Jacobs, 2005; National Science Board, 2003; National Science Foundation, 2002). Similar concern exists in Australia (Dow, 2003a, 2003b; National Committee for the Mathematical Sciences of the Australian Academy of Science, 2006) and other Western nations. For example, a recent examination showed that only 32% of bachelor's degrees in the United States were in science or engineering (National Science Foundation, 2004) and that there were declines in undergraduate mathematics, engineering, and physical science enrollments through the 1990s of 19, 21, and 13%, respectively (National Science Foundation, 2000). In Australia in 2006, the Department of Education, Science, and Training (DEST) commissioned the Science, Engineering, and Technology (SET) Skills Audit to examine trends in SET demand, supply, and influential factors; the study showed that participation across all education and training sectors was static or declining (DEST, 2006). Global human capital supply issues in STEM are predicted to continue to loom large (Organisation for Economic Cooperation and Development [OECD], 2006) and may impact negatively on countries' economic and social well-being.

The second argument is concerned with social equity and individual well-being. Gender differences in earning potential are important because women are more likely than men to be single, widowed, or single heads of households; therefore, those women are likely to need to support themselves and their dependents financially (see Meece, 2006). Also, both women and men need to develop and deploy their talents and abilities in their work outside the home, as developing and using one's abilities in the workplace substantially impacts general life satisfaction and psychological well-being (Eccles, 1987; Meece, 2006).

The potential talent pool for STEM careers has often been regarded as a "pipeline" that starts in secondary school, flows through university, and empties into the workforce. A pipeline metaphor of supply captures the cumulative nature of STEM education, where early choices to opt out can foreclose or constrain subsequent opportunities. Major transition and decision points provide opportunities for leakage in the STEM pipeline, including the transition between elementary/primary and secondary school, lower and upper secondary school, secondary school and university, undergraduate and graduate education, and throughout employment. These are time points when people may opt out of STEM careers more easily. Figure 16.1 represents this diagrammatically including influential factors at each of the transition points based on an extensive review of the literature. Consideration of gender differences and gendered influences at each critical point in the pipeline is key to interventions designed to promote women's participation.

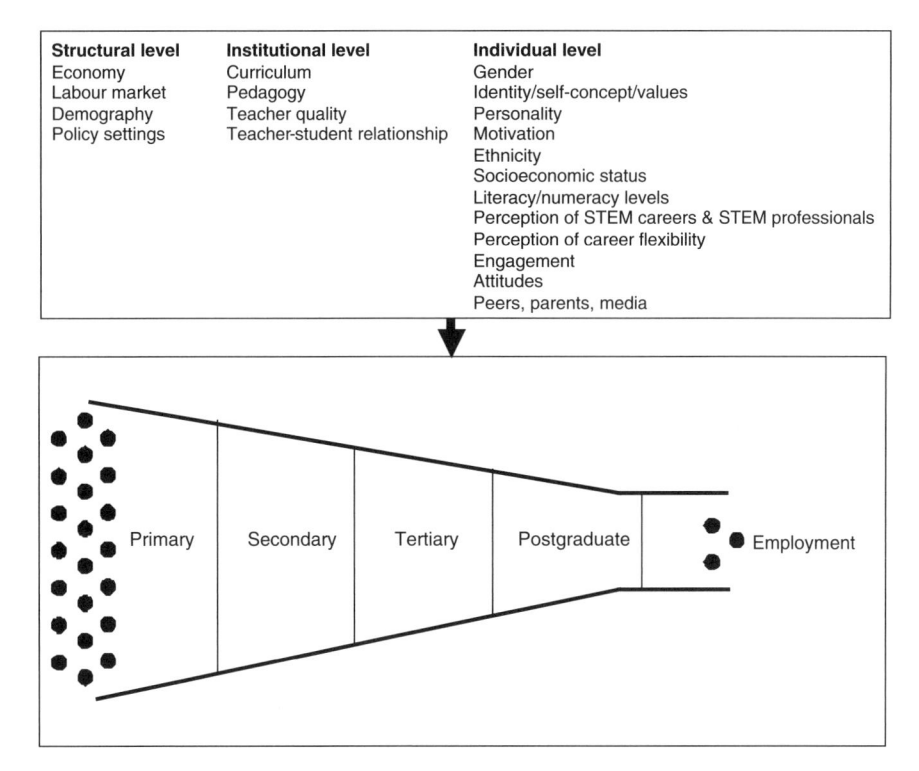

Fig. 16.1 Factors that influence educational and occupational choices at different stages of the STEM pipeline. *Note*: Commonwealth of Australia 2007. This figure is copyright. Apart from any use permitted under the *Copyright Act 1968*, no part may be reproduced by any process without the written permission of the Commonwealth of Australia acting through the Department of Education, Employment and Workplace Relations. The views expressed herein do not necessarily represent the views of the Commonwealth Department of Education, Employment and Workplace Relations

The literature indicates that pathways to STEM careers are defined by a complex and diverse array of factors and that the pipeline is more complex than a sequential funneling effect, whereby structural factors successively filter out girls and women (Watt, Eccles, & Durik, 2006). Such an interpretation does not take into account girls' and women's positive and informed choices as a result of contextual issues such as employability, work-life balance, gender equality, and occupational status (Siann & Callaghan, 2001). Girls and young women may be more likely to consider career options that provide successful role models, rather than those that suggest a "glass ceiling," and to consider their occupational choices in light of family planning. For example, young women's desire for a family-flexible career has been found to predict the decision to opt out of earlier aspirations for a STEM-related career (Frome, Alfeld, Eccles, & Barber, 2008). Because there are fewer women in STEM careers, these careers tend to reflect the values of the men, which, in turn reinforces perceptions that girls and women hold about STEM culture. This is especially the case with the ways in which STEM careers do (or do not) accommodate women's frequent family obligations. Such workplace cultures can affect women's initial aspirations for these careers, impede their progression if they do enter, and deter them from persisting along their career path.

At the far end of the "pipeline," there have also been interventions designed and implemented to meet professional women's needs within STEM careers. It is not clear at the present time how such reforms will change young women's motivation, performance, development, or persistence. Despite a plethora of intervention efforts, particularly targeting the secondary school years, most of these programs have not been formally evaluated. There has also been a lack of longitudinal as opposed to "one-shot" examinations, a lack of large-scale and representative samples rather than small and convenience samples, a lack of representation across diverse samples and sociocultural settings, and a lack of representation and integration across theoretical perspectives. In short, much work is needed in this area. A taxonomy of barriers and supports for girls/women who participate in STEM courses and careers is under development by Fouad, Hackett, and their colleagues (see http://vcc.asu.edu/taxonomy_v1/index.shtml), with the goal of directly translating identified barriers and supports into interventions to promote, sustain, and support girls' and women's participation in STEM pathways. Their developing taxonomy identifies both core obstructive and enabling agents such as parents and family, school, guidance counselors, and other social and individual sources. This taxonomy emphasis reflects the contemporary view that barriers to women's participation in nontraditional careers exist in social structures, rather than in the form of formal barriers as in the past. The cultural context provides norms such as gender-role stereotypes, which impact the formation of individuals' perceptions and motivations, both directly and indirectly, via socializers' beliefs and behaviors (e.g., Fredricks & Eccles, 2002; Frome & Eccles, 1998), such as verbal information, behavioral modeling (Pekrun, 2000), and individuals' own internal schema.

Of course, STEM careers are only one area of work where there are gender differences. Considerably fewer men than women are represented in the arts, humanities, education, and helping professions, such as nursing and social work (e.g., Carrington, 2002; Richardson & Watt, 2006). Although less concern has been expressed in the literature about the underrepresentation of men in these domains, there may well be ramifications for boys' and men's satisfaction and well-being if they do not pursue their interests and abilities in female-dominated careers. It is important that young men feel able to pursue careers outside of STEM fields if this is where their interests and abilities lie. In this chapter I consider influences on occupational choices within STEM and humanities fields, as domains that are respectively male- and female-dominated.

Explanations

Career "choice" presupposes the availability of alternatives as well as the individual freedom to choose from among them. Such an assumption in relation to occupational choice has been regarded as rare, naïve, or even misguided by Özbilgin and his colleagues (Özbilgin, Küskü, & Erdoğmuş,

2005), who reference labor market rigidities of supply and demand, persistent structural and institutionalized forms of discrimination and segregation, and path dependence by prior education and experience in many career fields. Explanations, and therefore interventions, must accommodate both individual and contextual factors at different stages along the "pipeline" (see also Mignot, 2000).

Barriers and Supports

Barriers and supports have been posited to affect career choices indirectly via their impact on individual self-efficacies and interests, however, evidence for both their direct and indirect effects has been identified (e.g., Lent et al., 2005). This indicates that structural and institutional conditions manifest as discrimination and disadvantage both objectively and as internal conditions in conception and imagination (Özbilgin et al., 2005) as individuals filter their experience through a net of expectations and attributions, such that similar phenomena are experienced differently by different people (Sameroff & Feil, 1985). Objective conditions may be more likely to be perceived or experienced as barriers or supports for different subgroups in society. For example, a longitudinal study of men's and women's persistence in science and technology studies at the university level showed that support from parents and teachers contributed weakly to whether women continued their science and technology studies, but strongly to whether men did (Larose et al., 2008). Such results show the critical importance of examining the moderating effects of gender in the links between barriers and supports and individuals' educational and occupational choices. Similarly, others have found ethnicity/race to be important in the development of occupational aspirations (Mau, 1995; Mau & Bikos, 2000; McWhirter, Larson, & Daniels, 1996; Wilson & Wilson, 1992). A recent meta-analysis yielded few differences in occupational aspirations, but significant differences in perceptions of barriers (Fouad & Byars-Winston, 2005), which, in turn, appear differentially to prompt racial/ethnic minority students to foreclose prematurely on career options or to experience greater career indecision (Fouad, 2007).

Gender Stereotypes

Proposed sources of gender stereotypes are many and varied; they include exposure to role models (e.g., Monaco & Gaier, 1992), reinforcement experienced for "gender-appropriate" and "gender-inappropriate" behaviors (e.g., Lamb, Easterbrooks, & Holden, 1980), differential teacher and classroom experiences (e.g., Spender & Sarah, 1992), and the important role played by the media in shaping ideas and attitudes (e.g., Leder, 1992). Key socializers, such as parents and teachers, impact students' outcomes by acting as "interpretors of reality" (Eccles, Arbreton, et al., 1993, p. 154) and through the experiences they provide.

Parents

The importance of parents' beliefs in shaping students' achievement-related attitudes, performance, and career decisions has been established by a large body of literature (see Jacobs, Finken, Griffin, & Wright, 1998), and, over the past 20 years, research based on the Eccles et al. (Parsons, Adler, & Kaczala, 1982) parent socialization model has highlighted the important role parents play (see Jacobs & Eccles, 2000). According to this model, characteristics of the parents, family, and neighborhood, along with characteristics of the child, influence parents' behaviors, general beliefs, and child-specific beliefs, which, in turn, affect parents' behaviors and expectations and, thereby, children's outcomes including their educational and occupational choices. Parents' roles shift from sharing their perspectives and providing exposure, opportunities, and role modeling at early ages to providing encouragement and guidance for activities that are supportive of the child's developing interests in certain occupations (e.g., Eccles, 1994; Jacobs & Eccles, 1992). When parents show enthusiasm they provide a support system to bolster the child's own value for a domain (Gonzalez-DeHass, Willems, & Holbein, 2005). Parents model involvement in valued activities (Jacobs, Davis-Kean, Bleeker, Eccles, & Malanchuk, 2005; Jacobs & Eccles, 2000; Jodl, Michael, Malanchuk, Eccles, & Sameroff, 2001), and, because parents are powerful role models, students come to value what their parents do (Parsons, Adler, & Kaczala, 1982; Eccles, Arbreton, et al., 1993; Whitbeck & Gecas, 1988).

Parents generally have been found to endorse the cultural stereotype of mathematics achievement as more natural for boys (Eccles, Freedman-Doan, Frome, Jacobs, & Yoon, 2000), and verbal or expressive skills as more natural for girls, and to hold gender-differentiated views of their children's academic abilities from a very early age (Eccles, Arbreton et al., 1993). Parents of boys have been reported to stress the importance of productive technical careers for their sons, whereas parents of girls stress the importance of being happy and well adjusted (Willis, 1989). Parents communicate their perceptions to boys through the use of strategies such as withdrawal of privileges for poor work, offering rewards for good performance, discussing the future usefulness of mathematics, and ensuring that homework is done. In addition, parents of boys, particularly fathers, are more likely to tell their sons that they should be ashamed of poor achievement. Such strategies are rarely implemented by parents of daughters (Yee, Jacobs, & Goldsmith, 1986). Parents relay how talented they believe their children to be, and they also can serve as "limit-setters" by communicating their beliefs about their daughters' potentials and abilities (Dickens & Cornell, 1990, p. 9).

Parents' educational expectations for their children during adolescence relate to their adult children's actual educational attainment (Chhin, Jacobs, Bleeker, Vernon, & Tanner, 2005), and parents' earlier gender-typed occupational expectations significantly relate to children's own expectations and actual career choices even 11 years following high school (Jacobs et al., 2006). Although many studies have shown that parents are powerful agents in influencing the goals, choices, and behaviors of their children (Farmer, 1985; Schulenberg, Vondracek, & Crouter, 1984; Trusty, 1998), most have not examined long-term relations between parents' earlier expectations and their children's later career choices because the studies were cross-sectional or spanned only a small number of years. Without additional long-term longitudinal data such as those of Eccles, Jacobs, and colleagues (e.g., Jacobs & Eccles, 1992; Jacobs et al., 2006), it is not possible to study adequately parents' role in constructing and sustaining gendered environments in which adolescents consider future occupations and how adolescents' early speculations translate into actual occupational choices in adulthood.

Peers

Individuation and autonomy development in adolescence is characterized by more time spent with peers and less with parents (Larson & Richards, 1991), and parents' influences may be expanded and challenged by children's peers (Brown, 1990; Kindermann, 1993). Within the domain of mathematics, for example, the class' average value for mathematics has been demonstrated to relate to individual students' values (Frenzel, Pekrun, & Goetz, 2007). Cross-gendered behaviors are more likely than "gender-appropriate" behaviors to cease when criticized by peers. Similarly, "gender-appropriate" behaviors are more likely than "gender-inappropriate" behaviors to be strengthened when praised by peers (Lamb et al., 1980). Because mathematics and English are frequently gender-typed domains, we expect these dynamics to apply. Indeed, boys make a clear gain in status by electing to study advanced mathematics courses, whereas girls who do so gain nothing in the way of status (Cohen & Kosler, 1991).

Teachers

Teachers' own attitudes are related to students' motivations in particular academic domains (Eccles, Arbreton, et al., 1993; Kunter et al., 2008), as are teachers' direct and indirect messages about the value of learning (Brigham, Scruggs, & Mastropieri, 1992; McKinney, Robertson, Gilmore, Ford, & Larkins, 1984; Patrick, Hisley, Kempler, & College, 2000). Classroom practices that have been found to undermine interest and motivation include public competition, frequent drill and practice, and teachers' insincere praise and criticism (e.g., Flink, Boggiano, & Barrett, 1990; Turner et al., 2002). Teachers' preferential treatment of boys in class has been well-established (see Spender, 1982; Spender & Sarah, 1992). Regardless of the gender of the teacher, boys receive more criticism, praise for correct responses, monitoring of work, and general contact with the teacher (Becker, 1981; Brophy & Good, 1974; Hart, 1989; Koehler, 1990; Leder, 1987). Perhaps most disturbing, girls for whom teachers hold high success expectancies have been found to receive the least amount of praise from teachers (Parsons, Kaczala, & Meece, 1982). Spender (1982) found that teachers spent about two-thirds of their classroom interaction time with boys, and boys made about two-thirds of students' comments. She attributed these behaviors to the cultural system in which teachers are embedded, which perceives preferential treatment of boys as the norm and, therefore, fair (Spender, 1981). Over the past 15 years, there have been significant reforms in elementary/primary and secondary school mathematics and science curricula and teaching practices to incorporate more collaborative, problem-focused, and authentic instruction (Meece & Scantlebury, 2006). This happened in response to research that showed that girls take a more active role and respond more favorably in individualized and cooperative learning environments (Kahle & Meece, 1994; Parsons, Kaczala, & Meece, 1982) and that the decontextualized content of the transmissive pedagogies, which have characterized school science and mathematics for generations, do not engage students' interest or commitment (Lyons, 2006).

Media

The male and female role models that children encounter, as well as the role models portrayed in the media, are important broader socialization agents in the development of children's beliefs and values (Signorella, Bigler, & Liben, 1993). Media accounts frequently report difficulties encountered by successful women professionals in balancing job demands with interpersonal needs (Leder, 1992). Such accounts, as well as stereotyped portrayals in films and on television, reinforce the notion that women achieve success at a personal price and that they need to work harder than men do to attain success (Leder, 1992). Clearly, passive nondiscrimination is not an adequate intervention strategy (Eccles & Jacobs, 1986). To counter these gender stereotypes, educators could provide explicit nontraditional role models for children and adolescents.

Ability

Another explanation that has been put forth to explain gender differences in occupational choices relates to different innate abilities for women and men. It is difficult to find a more controversial topic than that of gender differences in mathematical abilities in recent educational research. There is no dispute that, in samples from the general population, women's and men's global mathematical performance is similar (e.g., Hyde, Fennema, Ryan, Frost, & Hopp, 1990; Kimball, 1989; Rosenthal & Rubin, 1982; Tartre & Fennema, 1995). Two comprehensive meta-analyses of approximately 100 research articles each (Friedman, 1989; Hyde, Fennema, & Lamon, 1990) showed that, in samples from the general population, boys' and girls' secondary school mathematical performance is similar. Since then, Hyde and her colleagues have analyzed mathematics achievement data from seven million students in U.S. statewide assessments (Hyde, Lindberg, Linn, Ellis, & Williams, 2008), and they identified uniformly trivial gender differences: 21 indicated better performance by boys, 36 indicated better performance by girls, and 9 showed no difference. The weighted mean effect size was 0.0065, which is consistent with no gender difference. The authors further found that effect sizes for gender differences were similarly small across all ethnic groups. Boys showed slightly more variability in scores, although this could not account for gender differences in participation in STEM fields.

Other researchers have focused on gender differences in spatial skills (Linn & Petersen, 1985) and gender differences among very high achieving students (e.g., the Study of Mathematically Precocious Youth; Lubinski, Benbow, & Sanders, 1993). An influential U.S. study showed that the ratio of men's to women's variability in "space relations" scores on the Differential Aptitude Test generally decreased from 1947 to 1980 (Feingold, 1992), although an interaction effect between year and grade showed that this variance ratio decreased from Grades 8 to 12 in 1947, in 1962 and 1972 it was constant across grades, and in 1980 it increased over grades. Such findings imply that it is necessary to seek explanations beyond biology because these changes are occurring "rather faster than the gene can travel" (Rosenthal & Rubin, 1982, p. 711). Gender differences in mathematical performance have been identified among moderately selective and precocious samples, although Hyde, Fennema, and Lamon (1990) cautioned against the validity of such comparisons because of the different variability within the gender groups being compared (see also Feingold, 1992, 1993). Men and boys are, in fact, overrepresented at both the high *and the low* extremes of mathematical performance (e.g., Lubinski et al., 1993), which some argue means that boys are more often selected for remedial help as well as for gifted programs in mathematics (Willis, 1989).

On the other hand, gender differences in verbal ability are regarded by many as one of the well-established findings in psychology (e.g., Halpern, 1992); most introductory textbooks have presented this as a recognized "fact" (e.g., Atkinson, Atkinson, & Hilgard, 1983; Gleitman, 1981; Hetherington & Parke, 1986; Mussen, Conger, Kagan, & Huston, 1984). A meta-analysis by Hyde and Linn (1988) provided estimates of effect size for gender differences across a range of dimensions of language achievement, including vocabulary, analogies, reading comprehension, speech production, essay writing, anagrams, and general verbal ability. Except for modest effect sizes where girls and women scored higher on measures of general verbal ability, anagrams, and speech production, all other effect sizes were negligible (Hyde & Linn, 1988). A comparison of effect sizes by year of publication (earlier than 1974 versus 1974 and later) was statistically significant, which led the authors to conclude that the gender gap had reduced over time in measured language abilities. The authors concluded that "the magnitude of the gender difference in verbal ability is currently so small that it can effectively be considered to be zero ... the one possible exception is measures of speech production" (Hyde & Linn, 1988, p. 64).

Although recent evidence suggests that biology affects psychological characteristics related to occupational preferences (Berenbaum & Bryk, 2008), recent researchers have emphasized that biology is not destiny, and there are additional effects of social and cultural influences (e.g., Ruble, Martin, & Berenbaum, 2006; Steele, 1997; Wood & Eagly, 2002). It is clear that continued research beyond biology is needed into the antecedents of, and influences on, gendered occupational choices.

Perceived Abilities and Motivations

The expectancy-value model proposed by Eccles and her colleagues (Eccles, 2005; Eccles et al., 1983) sets out the importance of individuals' perceived abilities, motivational values, and background socialization influences in shaping their educational and occupational choices, over and above their demonstrated skills and abilities. This prominent, productive, and highly influential theoretical framework was developed to explain gender differences in mathematics participation and has subsequently been applied to language/literature participation and to different kinds of careers. More recently, the social cognitive career theory of Lent and his colleagues (SCCT; Lent, Brown, & Hackett, 1994, 2000) similarly has emphasized the related constructs of self-efficacy and interest as major influences on career choice.

Part of the explanation for the gender difference in STEM participation lies in the fact that girls have less confidence in their mathematical abilities than boys do, despite similar measured mathematical achievement. Does this mean that girls underestimate their mathematical abilities? In fact, a stronger relationship has been identified between girls' mathematical ability beliefs and achievement than between boys', which suggests that girls may actually be more realistic about their abilities, whereas boys overestimate theirs (Crandall, 1969; Watt, 2005). Boys' higher confidence translates into a spiral of benefits, including enrollment choices that produce advanced mathematical preparation. In contrast, the greater "realism" on the part of girls translates into levels of mathematics participation more commensurate with their abilities, which results in a situation where boys *over-participate,* rather than girls *under-participate,* in advanced mathematics. Given the current critical shortage of people entering mathematics-related careers, it would be silly to suggest that educators discourage boys' participation in order to equalize gender representation. Rather, we should aim to promote greater participation for everyone, but especially girls.

A particularly effective lever for change may be to target girls' lower interest and liking for mathematics, which has strong flow-on effects to their level of mathematics participation in high school and later mathematics-related career choices (Watt, 2006, 2008). Because we know that girls are more likely to be engaged by activities that they see as socially meaningful and important (e.g., Farmer, Rotella, Anderson, & Wardrop, 1998), it is essential that educators make explicit connections between STEM and its social uses and purposes. Adolescents also often have quite inaccurate ideas of which careers involve developed STEM skills (Fouad, 2007), which implies a need to provide more detailed information about STEM skills' relevance for a range of varied careers.

Comparative United States and Australian data have been analyzed to show how gendered choices play out regarding the amount of mathematics students undertake in the U.S. setting, and the difficulty level undertaken in the Australian setting, with prior mathematical achievement controlled (see Watt et al., 2006). No gender difference in the number of senior high school mathematics courses was evident among the U.S. sample, although there were clear gender differences in the Australian sample in which fewer girls both planned to undertake and subsequently actually undertook the higher levels of mathematics. Because Grade 11 in Australia is the first point where students are able to choose their mathematics courses, this means that girls began to opt out of the "pipeline" at their first opportunity. In the U.S. sample, where college-bound youth from this sample's upper-middle class demographic may have thought that they had little choice in how much mathematics to take, most boys and girls similarly undertook the maximum of four courses. The mathematics pipeline, therefore, appears to "leak" later in the U.S. setting, when fewer women elect to study post-secondary mathematics (Bridgeman & Wendler, 1991; Lips, 1992) and when equally prepared women defect from undergraduate mathematics studies at a higher rate (Oakes, 1990). It seems that many women opt out of mathematics when they are given a real choice to do so.

Perceived abilities and intrinsic values are emphasized in the Eccles (Parsons) et al. (1983) expectancy-value model as the most proximal influences on educational and occupational choices (e.g., Eccles, 1984, 1985; Eccles et al., 1983; Eccles, Adler, & Meece, 1984; Meece, Parsons, Kaczala, Goff, & Futterman, 1982; Meece et al., 1990; Watt, 2005; Wigfield, 1994; Wigfield & Eccles, 1992). Intrinsic value is similar to intrinsic motivation as defined by Deci and colleagues (Deci & Ryan, 1985; Deci, Vallerand, Pelletier, & Ryan, 1991) and by Harter (1981); it refers to engaging in a task out of interest or enjoyment.

The influences of perceived abilities and intrinsic values on senior high school mathematics enrollments have been found to exceed the influence of prior mathematical achievement for girls. For boys, perceived abilities and intrinsic values also exert significant, although weaker, influences of similar strength to the impact of their prior mathematical achievement (Watt et al., 2006). In contrast, mathematics-related career aspirations have been found to be directly impacted only by level of senior high school course enrollments (see Watt, 2008), which clearly demonstrates the importance of retaining girls in the mathematics "pipeline" through senior high school as a critical leakage point away from mathematics-related occupations.

English enrollments during senior high school are also substantially predicted by intrinsic values, over and above prior English achievement (Durik, Vida, & Eccles, 2006; Watt 2002, 2008). English-related career plans were predicted equally by ability-related perceptions and utility (or importance) values, whereby boys and girls who believed themselves to be more able in English, and perceived English to be more useful, aspired to careers involving higher English-related skills (Durik et al., 2006; Watt, 2002, 2008). Unlike mathematics, senior high school English enrollments did not mediate the relations between adolescents' English-related motivations and their career plans. It is interesting that these findings suggest that the pipeline argument is less relevant for explaining a continued pattern of lower English participation rates for boys than for girls.

Given the importance of perceived abilities and intrinsic values in determining educational and occupational decisions, it is important to understand their development over time. Identification of points where changes occur can suggest potential causes as well as fruitful points for intervention: Points of gender difference and gender divergence could be particularly helpful in locating gendered barriers and designing interventions. Perceived mathematical abilities have been found to decline fairly linearly through adolescence (Nagy et al., in press; Watt, 2004), as do perceived English abilities (Watt, 2004). Declines in intrinsic values for mathematics and language/literature, however, coincide with changes in curricular structures (Fredricks & Eccles, 2002; Frenzel, Goetz, Pekrun, & Watt, in press; Watt, 2004). These longitudinal studies provide evidence for continued declines after the transition to secondary school that have been well documented in shorter term or cross-sectional research (e.g., Anderman & Midgley, 1997; Midgley, Feldlaufer, & Eccles, 1989a, 1989b; Seidman, Allen, Aber, Mitchell, & Feinman, 1994; Watt, 2000; Wigfield, Eccles, Mac Iver, Reuman, & Midgley, 1991; Yates, 1999). Such declines may be reality based and inevitable due to social comparative processes in which individuals increasingly engage through adolescence (e.g., Nicholls, 1978), but declines also are promoted by the secondary school context through practices such as normative assessment.

Some theorists have suggested that negative changes on transition to junior high school (e.g., Anderman & Midgley, 1997; Midgley et al., 1989a, 1989b; Seidman et al., 1994; Wigfield et al., 1991) are a consequence of concurrent physiological and psychological pubertal changes (e.g., Blyth, Simmons, & Carlton-Ford, 1983; Hill & Lynch, 1983; Rosenberg, 1986; Simmons, Blyth, Van Cleave, & Bush, 1979). This view has been challenged by research that shows how differences in the pre- and post-transition classroom and school environments relate to declining motivations (Eccles & Midgley, 1989, 1990) and, instead, suggests a model of "person-environment fit" whereby the needs of young adolescents are not met by the new junior high school environment. This model is supported by the findings of nonlinear declines in intrinsic values, although perceived abilities appear not to be tied to grade-related changes in the same way.

Gender differences in perceived abilities and intrinsic values in mathematics and language/literature occur in line with gender stereotypes (e.g., Jacobs, Lanza, Osgood, Eccles, & Wigfield, 2002; Watt, 2004). Boys have higher perceived abilities and intrinsic values for mathematics than girls do, whereas girls have higher intrinsic values for language/literature than boys do. There are mixed findings regarding gender differences in perceived English abilities: The U.S. longitudinal study showed that girls had higher ability perceptions than boys did (Jacobs et al., 2002), whereas the Australian longitudinal study indicated no evidence of gender differences in ability-related perceptions, despite higher English achievement levels for girls (Watt, 2004, 2008). No evidence was found in either study for a gender intensification hypothesis (e.g., Eccles, 1987; Hill & Lynch, 1983; Maccoby, 1966); initial gender differences continued to be fairly stable through adolescence (Frenzel et al., in press; Nagy et al., in press; Watt, 2004), which could imply that girls' and boys' perceptions diverge at an earlier age, prior to commencement of secondary school. Because gender differences in perceived abilities and intrinsic values have been identified in early school years (e.g., Eccles, Wigfield, Harold, & Blumenfeld, 1993; Marsh, 1989; Wigfield et al., 1997), it seems that boys and girls begin school already having those gendered perceptions, which have been attributed to socialization experiences in the home and the wider society, such as portrayals of women and men in the media (e.g., Jacobs et al., 2002).

Summary and Directions for Future Research

The occupational landscape is not equal for both genders, nor for minority racial/ethnic groups (Fouad, 2007). In this chapter I have discussed influences on the persistent and enduring problem of women's lower participation in STEM fields, which is important to economic advantage, social equity, and individual well-being, and men's lower representation in female-dominated fields such as language/literature-related careers. The pipeline metaphor was introduced and elaborated to emphasize the need to focus on both individuals' perceptions and motivations and societal barriers and supports. Recommendations that derive from this review to enhance girls' and women's STEM progression and retention include promoting their perceived abilities and intrinsic values, providing them with STEM-related career information and role models, acting to overcome gender-typed messages concerning abilities and opportunities, and attending to gender inequities in barriers and supports at both ends of the pipeline. Recommendations to increase boys' and men's participation in language-related careers are to enhance their interest and liking for language and literary studies and to elaborate its utility value. Of course, this is no simple task.

Advanced mathematical preparation provides a substantial skills and status advantage for further educational and occupational opportunities, yet girls and women appear to opt out of the pipeline once they are given a chance to do so. Results from a German study (Nagy et al., 2008) suggest that forced early specialization may amplify gender differences in students' course selections. Successful participation in post-secondary STEM education has been shown to be associated with less specialization at earlier stages of schooling, which allows fewer points of leakage from the pipeline (Van Langen & Dekkers, 2005). Does this mean that we should more tightly constrain students' mathematics course taking to enhance girls' retention in mathematics through secondary school completion? Should we develop policies to keep girls in the mathematics pipeline for as long as we can? But how long *can* we constrain girls to keep taking mathematics?

Because mathematics-related intrinsic values and perceived abilities are important influences on the extent of girls' and boys' educational and occupational choices, girls' lower intrinsic values and perceived abilities are of particular concern. Such differences are evident even in very young girls and boys. The fact that these gender differences emerge early (as early as Grade 2; Jacobs et al., 2002) implies that they need to be addressed from early childhood, but this does not mean that we should not also address them during secondary school, where there may be much educators can do to increase girls' interest. What we need to be asking is whether factors such as personal relevance, familiarity, novelty, activity level, and comprehensibility, which promote task interest (Hidi & Baird, 1986), are equally addressed for both boys and girls in mathematics classrooms. Eccles and her colleagues have demonstrated that girls are engaged by activities that they perceive to be socially meaningful and important (e.g., Eccles & Vida, 2003), whereas mathematics (and science; DeHart, 1998) is often taught in skills-based, abstract, and decontextualized ways. Making explicit connections between STEM and its social uses and purposes may help to heighten girls' interest. Adolescents also often have quite inaccurate ideas of which careers involve developed scientific and mathematical skills due to negative stereotypes of scientists and mathematicians (e.g., Furlong & Biggart, 1999). Detailed information about the STEM education and skills required for a range of careers would be likely to promote girls' interest when their preferred careers require mathematics or science skills.

A qualitative study of seven women who had "opted out" following completion of an undergraduate mathematics major (Stage & Maple, 1996) showed that interest in mathematics and beliefs about mathematical aptitude *since early childhood* had been the main determinants of the women's decision to complete a mathematics major. Socialization experiences in the home strongly influence children's beliefs and values (Lytton & Romney, 1991), and parents report spending almost no time on mathematics activities with their children (Eccles et al., 2000; Freedman-Doan et al., 2000). This finding is in stark contrast to the emphasis on early reading in the literacy domain; perhaps what is needed is a systematic campaign about the importance of early numeracy experiences. Given the centrality of mathematics interest to choices about mathematics participation and given girls' lower interest in mathematics than boys', it might be worth encouraging parents to focus on engaging in mathematics-related activities such as mathematical puzzles and problem-solving particularly with their young daughters as a possible way to enhance their interest and liking for mathematics. Such recommendations become problematic in cases where parents may not have mathematical skills or interests themselves, although research suggests the need to educate parents about the important roles their opinions and parenting play in their children's later career decisions. Teachers have been able to convince parents that their daughters are talented at mathematics, and then have enlisted the parents' help in encouraging young women to consider advanced mathematics courses and occupations in mathematics-related fields (Eccles, Arbreton, et al., 1993). We need to understand better why it is that girls perceive themselves as having less mathematical talent or ability than boys do, even though they perform similarly. Although girls' perceptions may be more realistic than boys', they nonetheless fail to share as much in the advantages of the mathematically well prepared. Therefore, we need to think very carefully about messages conveyed to girls about their abilities by their teachers, peers, and the media.

It is a fair assumption that the relative absence of women at the end of the STEM pipeline might be an important factor in the choices being made by girls and younger women to move away from those careers. Consequently, there is a need to target both ends of the "pipeline" at once: working to attract individuals to opt in and enforcing explicit policies to change the often unfriendly and unsupportive workplace cultures that might, for example, conflict with women's family responsibilities. STEM careers appear to have remained insufficiently flexible with regard to women's family responsibilities in practice, even if not in policy. There is a need for an explicit policy reform agenda and multi-pronged initiatives aimed at accommodating women's outside-work responsibilities and changing the values of the workplace culture. Until this can be achieved, it may be small wonder that girls and young women elect to specialize in non-STEM occupations as they think ahead about the situation at the end of the "pipeline."

The beginning of the pipeline is an eminently sensible focal point for interventions, before students have implicitly (e.g., affective disengagement, low effort) or explicitly (i.e., enrollment choices) opted out of STEM participation. It may be most sensible to implement preventative measures at this point rather than to focus intervention efforts on attempts to ameliorate substantially reduced participation at later points. Continued investigations into the origins and sources of gender differences in mathematics intrinsic values and self-perceptions promise to shed further light on the reasons for persistent "leaks" from the STEM pipeline for girls. There is also scope for mentorship because women may choose to opt out of STEM courses due to the lack of role models and female networks (Siann & Callaghan, 2001; Van Leuvan, 2004). At the same time, we need to be focused on workplace reforms, which provide family-friendly policies and practices, if we wish to attract girls and women to STEM careers in the long term. Factors that influence individuals' choices at different points in the pipeline are complex and interdependent and require an holistic approach to examining "leaks." This interdependence implies that tackling any one aspect in isolation is unlikely to deliver strong improvements. Although gendered outcomes appear at the level of the individual, a complex set of factors, including the historical legacy of gender differences in STEM domains and interpersonal relations, is involved. Multi-pronged interventions are required to enhance women's participation in STEM, including legal and ideological support at the policy and regulation level, institutional commitment to understand and tackle gendered prejudice and interpersonal measures, such as building networks between female students and providing mentors, and promoting a strong personal awareness that can equip female students with the resolve and vision to counteract the entrenched forms of gendered prejudice that they experience (Küskü, Özbilgin, & Özkale, 2007).

Intrinsic values emerge as a key predictor of choices for language/literature participation in senior high school. Unlike mathematics, English-related ability perceptions do not directly predict English enrollments in senior high school, and gender continues to predict English enrollments significantly even when motivation variables are included in the models (Watt, 2008). Thus, motivations and prior achievement do not fully explain the gender difference by which girls elect to participate more and boys less in language and literary studies; other factors must also be at play. English-related career plans were impacted equally by English ability-related perceptions and utility values. Students who believed themselves to be more able and likely to succeed in English, and students who regarded English as more useful, were those who aspired to highly English-related careers (Watt, 2008).

As with mathematics, and as predicted by expectancy-value theory, ability-related perceptions and values were most important in explaining adolescents' gendered English participation. Different *types* of values were important for different types of choices: As for mathematics, English-related intrinsic values predicted senior high school English course enrollments, whereas utility values influenced English-related career plans. Unlike mathematics, English ability-related perceptions did not impact senior high school course selections but did contribute to career plans. English ability-related perceptions and utility values impacted directly on career plans that would involve language or literary skills; their influence did not operate through senior high school English participation.

In order to encourage boys and young men to aspire to participate in language/literature-related careers, it appears to be most important to target their ability-related beliefs directly, as well as their conceptions regarding the utility of language skills. I believe that it is a dangerous aim to enhance boys' ability beliefs at the expense of girls', and instead recommend targeting boys' lower language/literature *values*, particularly their utility values. It may be less important to worry about boys' lower participation in senior high school English courses, as this does not subsequently determine the language-relatedness of their aspired careers (Watt, 2008). Should we wish to do so, however, it is boys' lower liking for and interest in language/literature that would be most useful to address. Findings imply a focus on boys' lower utility values regarding language/literature through secondary school will be likely to promote boys' and men's participation in language-related careers. That said, I reiterate that other factors are also at play in explaining boys' lower senior high school language/literature course enrollments, such as family influences, lifestyle goals, and social contexts.

Future Directions

I conclude by elaborating three major trends to advance future research in the field. These relate to changes in the world of work, how to contextualize the study of gendered occupational choices, and increased movement toward longitudinal designs, which allow for the study of developmental influences.

The Changing World of Work

The world of work has been impacted by demographic changes within the workforce, emerging technologies, an increasingly globalized economy, and decreased employment security (Fouad, 2007). Rapid changes in the economy and labor force have created a world of work that is now a "moving target" and resulted in the shifting of established notions of careers as resulting from choices made early on toward a view of a series of choices over individuals' working lives (Fouad, 2007, p. 544). Which abilities and values will be the most valuable for individuals to function effectively will be important concerns in this changing environment (Fouad, 2007). Western European beliefs have dominated the career literature until recently, but they may no longer be tenable (Flores & Heppner, 2002). These entail beliefs in individualism and autonomy, affluence, an open opportunity structure, the centrality of work in individuals' lives, and linear and rational processes of career development (see Gysbers, Heppner, & Johnston, 1998). Within the field of gender and occupational choice, there is a strong tradition of theory-based research, which to date has focused on "choice" outcomes, although many individuals either do not have the luxury to choose or do not make their "choices" with awareness, cognition, or volition. Further theoretical developments will need to take into account the degrees of freedom and awareness within which different individuals from different contexts operate. We also need to consider the nature of, and influences on, choices to opt *out* of gender-typed occupational fields, which may involve a different set of processes than simply the reverse of those that explain the choice to opt in.

Contextualization

Consistently strong research evidence for relationships among motivational and achievement-related constructs has accumulated at the level of the individual, whereas contextual effects (e.g., classroom, teachers' influence) have typically been comparatively weaker. Psychologists have worked to conceptualize and measure important individual-level predictors. Similarly sensitive, sound, and robust theories and measurements are needed at the level of context constructs to determine which contextual factors affect psychological beliefs. Integral to this endeavor are decisions concerning the appropriate "grain size." For example, in research concerning gendered educational choices during secondary schooling, is the right grain size the school, the class, friendship networks, the family, or some combination? The important question is which context and level of intensity will provide for better explanation. To complicate matters further, the critical grain size may vary at different developmental points or stages through the pipeline and for different kinds of individuals. Different moderators will need to be examined to determine how processes differ for different groups, as well as continued attention to the psychological mediators via which socio-environmental barriers and supports are construed.

In addition to extra-personal contexts, it will be important to consider intrapersonal contexts and to broaden our theories and measurements to incorporate multiple domains (e.g., career, family) and dimensions (e.g., STEM, humanities, helping professions) of relevance in individuals' lives. Informal barriers may lie in patterns of participation and choice that are functionally related to other patterns of participation and choice (Maines, 1985). This is all the more important in the study of gendered occupational choices because women tend to base their life decisions on a broader set of criteria than men do; women tend to anticipate "contingent futures" in which family plays an important role and where occupational pursuits may be compromised by other commitments (Maines, 1985).

There is a continuing need for psychologists to expand their view of the spectrum of psychological processes, on the one hand, and the array of societal supports and barriers, on the other (Roeser, 2006), and how these interact for different kinds of individuals, at different stages of development, in different contexts. At the macro-contextual level, we need more research that includes diverse samples. Much of the work in this field has been conducted with Western participants, and future researchers could fruitfully sample different racial/ethnic and socioeconomic groups in different countries, for whom there may be quite different patterns of gender influence. Comparative studies from a range of cultures are needed to assess which trajectories may be tied to particular schooling and societal systems. Cross-cultural comparisons provide wonderful *natural experiments* to enable investigations of how different structural features might shape different occupational outcomes for women and men and how trajectories for girls and boys may vary within and across cultures.

Longitudinal Designs

Without longitudinal data, it is not really possible to test the impacts of earlier influences or how processes unfold over time to produce outcomes of interest. We need more long-term longitudinal studies that allow for investigations into the origins of gender differences in occupational choice. At the same time, we also need studies that contain many occasions of measurement to be able to detect the nuances of development and associated influences. These studies will need to be large-scale to permit the kinds of analyses that are now available to researchers as a result of advances in statistical methods, which allow for increasingly sophisticated designs. Rich qualitative data are required within the context of these extensive designs to shed further light on processes and individual particularities, and advances in qualitative software now permit analyses across large numbers of responses.

Greater attention to between-individual variability in trajectories may yield new directions through a closer examination of individuals who demonstrate *positive* development, which may assist in identifying personal factors and social ecologies that promote resilience and well-being. For example, the study of parents who are especially effective in nurturing awareness of nontraditional occupational pathways for their children, schools that promote exemplary mathematics participation among young women or arts and humanities participation among young men, universities that have higher than expected numbers of female STEM or male nursing students, or workplaces that are particularly conducive to work-family balance (Roeser, 2006). To conduct research in this vein implies the need for large-scale, longitudinal, international, interdisciplinary, and collaborative programs of research that involve teams of experts from across different specializations. Although such designs are costly both in terms of time and money, the social and economic costs of *not* bringing our collective resources and expertise to bear on the persistent problem of gendered occupational choices is a greater cost yet.

Acknowledgment I extend my sincere gratitude to Jacquelynne S. Eccles for her continuing generosity and guidance, for her groundbreaking work in this field of inquiry, and for providing an exemplary role model to women in the academy.

References

American Association of University Women (AAUW). (1993). *How schools shortchange girls*. Washington, DC: Author.
American Association of University Women (AAUW). (1998). *Separated by sex: A critical look at single-sex education for girls*. Washington, DC: Author.
Anderman, E. M., & Midgley, C. (1997). Changes in achievement goal orientations, perceived academic competence, and grades across the transition to middle-level schools. *Contemporary Educational Psychology*, 22, 269–298.
Atkinson, R. L., Atkinson, R. C., & Hilgard, E. R. (1983). *Introduction to psychology* (8th ed.). New York: Harcourt Brace Jovanovich.
Becker, J. (1981). Differential treatment of females and males in mathematics classes. *Journal for Research in Mathematics Education*, 12, 40–53.
Berenbaum, S. A., & Bryk, K. L. (2008). Biological contributors to gendered occupational outcome: Prenatal androgen effects on predictors of outcome. In H. M. G. Watt & J. S. Eccles (Eds.), *Gender and occupational outcomes: Longitudinal assessments of individual, social, and cultural influences* (pp. 235–264). Washington, DC: American Psychological Association.
Betz, N. E., & Hackett, G. (1983). The relationship of mathematics self-efficacy expectations to the selection of science-based college majors. *Journal of Vocational Behavior*, 23, 329–345.
Blyth, D. A., Simmons, R. G., & Carlton-Ford, S. (1983). The adjustment of early adolescents to school transitions. *Journal of Early Adolescence*, 3, 105–120.
Bridgeman, B., & Wendler, C. (1991). Gender differences in predictors of college mathematics performance and in college mathematics course grades. *Journal of Educational Psychology*, 83, 275–284.
Brigham, F. J., Scruggs, T. E., & Mastropieri, M. A. (1992). Teacher enthusiasm in learning disabilities classrooms: Effects on learning and behavior. *Learning Disabilities Research & Practice*, 7, 68–73.
Brophy, J. E., & Good, T. (1974). *Teacher-student relationships: Causes and consequences*. New York: Holt, Rinehart, & Winston.
Brown, B. B. (1990). Peer groups and peer culture. In S. S. Feldman & G. R. Elliott (Eds.), *At the threshold: The developing adolescent* (pp. 171–196). Cambridge, MA: Harvard University Press.
Carrington, B. (2002). A quintessentially feminine domain? Student teachers' constructions of primary teaching as a career. *Educational Studies*, 28, 287–303.
Chhin, C. S., Jacobs, J. E., Bleeker, M. M., Vernon, M. K., & Tanner, J. L. (2005). *Great expectations: The relations between parents' early expectations and their children's actual achievements*. Unpublished manuscript.

Cohen, R. M., & Kosler, J. (1991). *Gender equity in high school math: A study of female participation and achievement*. Washington, DC: Office of Educational Research and Improvement, U.S. Department of Education [ERIC Document Reproduction Service No. ED 345 935].

Crandall, V. C. (1969). Sex differences in expectancy of intellectual and academic reinforcement. In C. P. Smith (Ed.), *Achievement-related motives in children* (pp. 11–45). New York: Russell Sage.

Deci, E. L., & Ryan, R. M. (1985). *Intrinsic motivation and self-determination in human behavior*. New York: Plenum.

Deci, E. L., Vallerand, R. J., Pelletier, L. C., & Ryan, R. M. (1991). Motivation and education: The self-determination perspective. *Educational Psychologist*, 26, 325–346.

DeHart, P. H. (1998). Linking science education to the workplace. *Journal of Science Education and Technology*, 7, 329–336.

Department of Education, Science, and Training (DEST). (2006). *Audit of science, engineering & technology skills*. Canberra: Author.

Dickens, M. N., & Cornell, D. G. (1990). *Parental influences on the mathematics self-concept of high-achieving adolescent girls, AEL Minigrant Report No. 20*. Washington, DC: Office of Educational Research and Improvement, U.S. Department of Education [ERIC Document Reproduction Service No. ED 318 207].

Dow, K. L. (2003a). *Australia's teachers: Australia's future - Advancing innovation, science, technology, and mathematics*. [Agenda for action.] Canberra: Commonwealth of Australia.

Dow, K. L. (2003b). *Australia's teachers: Australia's future - Advancing innovation, science, technology, and mathematics*. [Main report.] Canberra: Commonwealth of Australia.

Durik, A. M., Vida, M., & Eccles, J. S. (2006). Task values and ability beliefs as predictors of high school literacy choices: A developmental analysis. *Journal of Educational Psychology*, 98, 382–393.

Eccles, J. (1984). Sex differences in mathematics participation. In M. Steinkamp & M. Maehr (Eds.), *Advances in motivation and achievement* (Vol. 2, pp. 93–137). Greenwich, CT: JAI Press.

Eccles, J. (1985). Model of students' mathematics enrollment decisions. *Educational Studies in Mathematics*, 16, 311–314.

Eccles, J. S. (1987). Gender roles and women's achievement-related decisions. *Psychology of Women Quarterly*, 11, 135–172.

Eccles, J. S. (1994). Understanding women's educational and occupational choices: Applying the Eccles et al. model of achievement-related choices. *Psychology of Women Quarterly*, 18, 585–609.

Eccles, J. S. (2005). Subjective task value and the Eccles et al. model of achievement-related choices. In A. J. Elliot & C. S. Dweck (Eds.), *Handbook of competence and motivation* (pp. 105–121). New York: Guilford.

Eccles, J., Adler, T. F., Futterman, R., Goff, S. B., Kaczala, C. M., Meece, J. L., et al. (1983). Expectancies, values, and academic behaviors. In J. T. Spence (Ed.), *Achievement and achievement motives* (pp. 75–146). San Francisco: Freeman.

Eccles, J., Adler, T., & Meece, J. L. (1984). Sex differences in achievement: A test of alternate theories. *Journal of Personality and Social Psychology*, 46, 26–43.

Eccles, J. S., Arbreton, A., Buchanan, C. M., Jacobs, J., Flanagan, C., Harold, R., et al. (1993). School and family effects on the ontogeny of children's interests, self-perceptions, and activity choices. In J. E. Jacobs (Ed.), *Nebraska Symposium on Motivation, 1992: Developmental perspectives on motivation* (pp. 145–208). Lincoln, NE: University of Nebraska Press.

Eccles, J. S., Freedman-Doan, C., Frome, P., Jacobs, J., & Yoon, K. S. (2000). Gender-role socialization in the family: A longitudinal approach. In T. Eckes, & H. M. Trautner (Eds.), *The developmental social psychology of gender* (pp. 333–360). Mahwah, NJ: Erlbaum.

Eccles, J. S., & Jacobs, J. E. (1986). Social forces shape math attitudes and performance. *Signs*, 11, 367–380.

Eccles, J. S., & Midgley, C. (1989). Stage-environment fit: Developmentally appropriate classrooms for young adolescents. In R. Ames & C. Ames (Eds.), *Research on motivation in education* (Vol. 3, pp. 139–186). New York: Academic Press.

Eccles, J. S., & Midgley, C. (1990). Changes in academic motivation and self-perception during early adolescence. In R. Montemayor, G. R. Adams, & T. P. Gullotta (Eds.), *Advances in adolescent development: From childhood to adolescence* (Vol. 2, pp. 134–155). Newbury Park, CA: Sage.

Eccles, J. S., & Vida, M. (2003, April). *Predicting mathematics-related career aspirations and choices*. Paper presented at the meeting of the Society for Research in Child Development, Tampa, FL.

Eccles, J., Wigfield, A., Harold, R. D., & Blumenfeld, P. (1993). Age and gender differences in children's self- and task perceptions during elementary school. *Child Development*, 64, 830–847.

Farmer, H. S. (1985). Model of career and achievement motivation for women and men. *Journal of Counseling Psychology*, 32, 363–390.

Farmer, H. S., Rotella, S., Anderson, C., & Wardrop, J. (1998). Gender differences in science, math, and technology careers: Prestige level and Holland interest type. *Journal of Vocational Behavior*, 53, 73–96.

Feingold, A. (1992). The greater male variability controversy: Science versus politics. *Review of Educational Research*, 62, 89–90.

Feingold, A. (1993). Joint effects of gender differences in central tendency and gender differences in variability. *Review of Educational Research*, 63, 106–109.

Flink, C., Boggiano, A. K., & Barrett, M. (1990). Controlling teaching strategies: Undermining children's self-determination and performance. *Journal of Personality and Social Psychology*, 59, 916–924.

Flores, Y. L., & Heppner, M. J. (2002). Multicultural career counseling: Ten essentials for training. *Journal of Career Development*, 28, 181–202.

Fouad, N. (2007). Work and vocational psychology: Theory, research, and applications. *Annual Review of Psychology*, 58, 543–564.

Fouad, N. A., & Byars-Winston, A. M. (2005). Cultural context of career choice: Meta-analysis of race/ethnicity differences. *Career Development Quarterly*, 53, 223–233.

Fredricks, J. A., & Eccles, J. S. (2002). Children's competence and value beliefs from childhood through adolescence: Growth trajectories in two male-sex-typed domains. *Developmental Psychology*, 38, 519–533.

Freedman-Doan, C. R., Wigfield, A., Eccles, J. S., Harold, R. D., Arbreton, A. J., & Yoon, K. S. (2000). What am I best at? Grade and gender differences in children's beliefs about ability improvement. *Journal of Applied Developmental Psychology*, 21, 379–402.

Frenzel, A. C., Goetz, T., Pekrun, R., & Watt, H. M. G. (in press). Development of mathematics interest in adolescence: Influences of gender, family, and school context. *Journal of Research on Adolescence*.

Frenzel, A. C., Pekrun, R., & Goetz, T. (2007). Perceived learning environment and students emotional experiences: A multilevel analysis of mathematics classrooms. *Learning and Instruction*, 17, 478–493.

Friedman, L. (1989). Mathematics and the gender gap: A meta-analysis of recent studies on sex differences in mathematical tasks. *Review of Educational Research*, 59, 185–213.

Frome, P. M., Alfeld, C. J., Eccles, J. S., & Barber, B. L. (2008). Is the desire for a family-flexible job keeping young women out of male-dominated occupations? In H. M. G. Watt & J. S. Eccles (Eds.), *Gender and occupational outcomes: Longitudinal assessments of individual, social, and cultural influences* (pp. 195–214). Washington, DC: American Psychological Association.

Frome, P. M., & Eccles, J. S. (1998). Parents' influence on children's achievement-related perceptions. *Journal of Personality and Social Psychology*, 2, 435–452.

Furlong, A., & Biggart, A. (1999). Framing choices: A longitudinal study of occupational aspirations among 13–16 year-olds. *Journal of Education and Work*, 12, 21–36.

Gleitman, H. (1981). *Psychology*. New York: Norton.

Gonzalez-DeHass, A. R., Willems, P. P., & Holbein, M. F. D. (2005). Examining the relationship between parental involvement and student motivation. *Educational Psychology Review*, 17, 66–123.

Gysbers, N., Heppner, M., & Johnston, J. (1998). *Career counseling: Process, issues, and techniques*. Needham Heights, MA: Allyn & Bacon.

Halpern, D. F. (1992). *Sex differences in cognitive abilities* (2nd ed.). Hillsdale, NJ: Erlbaum.

Harlan, C. L., & Jansen, M. A. (1987). The psychological and physical well-being of women in sex-stereotyped occupations. *Journal of Employment Counseling*, 24, 31–39.

Hart, L. (1989). Classroom processes, sex of student, and confidence in learning mathematics. *Journal for Research in Mathematics Education*, 30, 242–260.

Harter, S. (1981). A new self-report scale of intrinsic versus extrinsic orientation in the classroom: Motivational and informational components. *Developmental Psychology*, 17, 300–312.

Heller, K. A., & Parsons, J. E. (1981). Sex differences in teachers' evaluative feedback and students' expectancies for success in mathematics. *Child Development*, 52, 1015–1019.

Hetherington, E. M., & Parke, R. D. (1986). *Child psychology: A contemporary viewpoint* (3rd ed.). New York: McGraw-Hill.

Hidi, S., & Baird, W. (1986). Interestingness: A neglected variable in discourse processing. *Cognitive Science*, 10, 179–194.

Hill, J. P., & Lynch, M. E. (1983). The intensification of gender-related role expectations during early adolescence. In J. Brooks-Gunn & A. C. Petersen (Eds.), *Girls at puberty* (pp. 201–228). New York: Plenum.

House of Representatives Standing Committee on Education and Training. (2002). *Boys: Getting it right*. Canberra: Author.

Hyde, J. S., Fennema, E., & Lamon, S. J. (1990). Gender differences in mathematics performance: A meta-analysis. *Psychological Bulletin*, 107, 139–155.

Hyde, J. S., Fennema, E., Ryan, M., Frost, L. A., & Hopp, C. (1990). Gender comparisons of mathematics attitudes and affect: A meta-analysis. *Psychology of Women Quarterly*, 14, 299–324.

Hyde, J. S., Lindberg, S. M., Linn, M. C., Ellis, A. B., & Williams, C. C. (2008). Diversity: Gender similarities characterize math performance. *Science*, 321, 494–495.

Hyde, J. S., & Linn, M. C. (1988). Gender differences in verbal ability: A meta-analysis. *Psychological Bulletin*, 104, 53–69.

Jacobs, J. E. (2005). Twenty-five years of research on gender and ethnic differences in math and science career choices: What have we learned? *New Directions for Child and Adolescent Development*, 110, 85–94.

Jacobs, J. E., Chhin, C. S., & Bleeker, M. M. (2006). Enduring links: Parents' expectations and their young adult children's gender-typed occupational choices. *Educational Research and Evaluation*, 12, 395–407.

Jacobs, J. E., Davis-Kean, P., Bleeker, M. M., Eccles, J. S., & Malanchuk, O. (2005). 'I can, but I don't want to': The impact of parents, interests, and activities on gender differences in math. In A. M. Gallagher & J. C. Kaufman (Eds.), *Gender differences in mathematics: An integrative psychological approach* (pp. 246–263). New York: Cambridge University Press.

Jacobs, J. E., & Eccles, J. S. (1992). The impact of mothers' gender-role stereotypic beliefs on mothers' and children's ability perceptions. *Journal of Personality and Social Psychology*, 63, 932–944.

Jacobs, J. E., & Eccles, J. S. (2000). Parents, task values, and real-life achievement-related choices. In C. Sansone & J. M. Harackiewicz (Eds.), *Intrinsic and extrinsic motivation: The search for optimal motivation and performance* (pp. 405–439). San Diego, CA: Academic Press.

Jacobs, J. E., Finken, L. L., Griffin, N. L., & Wright, J. D. (1998). The career plans of science-talented rural adolescent girls. *American Educational Research Journal*, 35, 681–704.

Jacobs, J. E., Lanza, S., Osgood, D. W., Eccles, J. S., & Wigfield, A. (2002). Changes in children's self-competence and values: Gender and domain differences across grades one through twelve. *Child Development*, 73, 509–527.

Jodl, K. M., Michael, A., Malanchuk, O., Eccles, J. S., & Sameroff, A. (2001). Parents' roles in shaping early adolescents' occupational aspirations. *Child Development*, 72, 1247–1265.

Kahle, J., & Meece, J. L. (1994). Research on girls in science: Lessons and applications. In D. Gabel (Ed.), *Handbook of research on science teaching* (pp. 1559–1610). Washington, DC: National Science Teachers Association.

Kimball, M. M. (1989). A new perspective on women's math achievement. *Psychological Bulletin*, 105, 198–214.

Kindermann, T. A. (1993). Natural peer groups as contexts for individual development: The case of children's motivation in school. *Developmental Psychology*, 26, 970–977.

Koehler, M. S. (1990). Classrooms, teachers and gender differences in mathematics. In E. Fennema & G. Leder (Eds.), *Mathematics and gender* (pp. 128–148). New York: Teachers' College Press.

Kunter, M., Tsai, Y-M., Klusmann, U., Brunner, M., Krauss, S., & Baumert, J. (2008). Students' and mathematics teachers' perceptions of teacher enthusiasm and instruction. *Learning and Instruction*, 18, 468–482.

Küskü, F., Özbilgin, M., & Özkale, L. (2007). Against the tide: Gendered prejudice and disadvantage in engineering. *Gender, Work, and Organization*, 14, 109–129.

Lamb, M. E., Easterbrooks, M. A., & Holden, G. W. (1980). Reinforcement and punishment among preschoolers. *Child Development*, 51, 1230–1236.

Larose, S., Ratelle, C. F., Guay, F., Senécal, C., Harvey, M., & Drouin, E. (2008). A sociomotivational analysis of gender effects on persistence in science and technology: A 5-year longitudinal study. In H. M. G. Watt & J. S. Eccles (Eds.), *Gender and occupational outcomes: Longitudinal assessments of individual, social, and cultural influences* (pp. 171–192). Washington, DC: American Psychological Association.

Larson, R. W., & Richards, M. H. (1991). Daily companionship in late childhood and early adolescence: Changing developmental contexts. *Child Development*, 62, 284–300.

Leder, G. (1987). Teacher student interaction: A case study. *Educational Studies in Mathematics*, 18, 255–271.

Leder, G. C. (1992). Mathematics and gender: Changing perspectives. In D. A. Grouws (Ed.), *Handbook of research on mathematics teaching and learning* (pp. 597–622). New York: Macmillan.

Lent, R. W., Brown, S. D., & Hackett, G. (1994). Toward a unifying social cognitive theory of career and academic interest, choice, and performance. *Journal of Vocational Behavior*, 45, 79–122.

Lent, R. W., Brown, S. D., & Hackett, G. (2000). Contextual supports and barriers to career choice: A social cognitive analysis. *Journal of Counseling Psychology*, 47, 36–49.

Lent, R. W., Brown, S. D., Sheu, H-B., Schmidt, J., Brenner, B. R., Gloster, C. S., et al. (2005). Social cognitive predictors of academic interests and goals in engineering: Utility for women and students at historically Black universities. *Journal of Counseling Psychology*, 52, 84–92.

Lingard, B., Martino, W., Mills, M., & Bahr, M. (2002). *Addressing the educational needs of boys*. Canberra: Department of Education, Science, and Training.

Linn, M. C., & Petersen, A. C. (1985). Emergence and characterization of sex differences in spatial ability: A meta-analysis. *Child Development*, 56, 1479–1498.

Lips, H. M. (1992). Gender- and science-related attitudes as predictors of college students' academic choices. *Journal of Vocational Behavior*, 40, 62–81.

Lubinski, D., Benbow, C. P., & Sanders, C. E. (1993). Reconceptualizing gender differences in achievement among the gifted. In K. A. Heller, F. J. Monks, & A. H. Pass (Eds.), *International handbook of research and development of giftedness and talent* (pp. 693–707). New York: Pergamon Press.

Lyons, T. (2006). Different countries, same science class: Students' experiences of school science in their own words. *International Journal of Science Education*, 28, 591–613.

Lytton, H., & Romney, D. M. (1991). Parents' differential socialization of boys and girls: A meta-analysis. *Psychological Bulletin*, 109, 267–296.

Maccoby, E. E. (1966). *The development of sex differences*. Stanford, CA: Stanford University Press.

Maines, D. R. (1985). Preliminary notes on a theory of informal barriers for women in mathematics. *Educational Studies in Mathematics*, 16, 303–320.

Marsh, H. W. (1989). Age and sex effects in multiple dimensions of self-concept: Preadolescence to early adulthood. *Journal of Educational Psychology*, 81, 417–430.

Martin, A. J. (2002). *Improving the educational outcomes of boys*. Canberra: Department of Education, Youth, and Family Services.

Mau, W. C. (1995). Educational planning and academic achievement of middle school students: A racial and cultural comparison. *Journal of Counseling and Development*, 73, 518–526.

Mau, W. C., & Bikos, L. H. (2000). Educational and vocational aspirations of minority and female students: A longitudinal study. *Journal of Counseling & Development*, 78, 186–194.

McKinney, C. W., Robertson, C. W., Gilmore, A. C., Ford, M. J., & Larkins, A. G. (1984). Some effects of three levels of teacher enthusiasm on student achievement and evaluation of teacher effectiveness. *Journal of Instructional Psychology*, 11, 119–124.

McWhirter, E. H., Larson, L. M., & Daniels, J. A. (1996). Predictors of educational aspirations among adolescent gifted students of color. *Journal of Career Development*, 23, 97–109.

Meece, J. L. (2006). Introduction: Trends in women's employment in the early 21st century. *Educational Research and Evaluation*, 12, 297–303.

Meece, J. L., Parsons, J. E., Kaczala, C. M., Goff, S. B., & Futterman, R. (1982). Sex differences in math achievement: Toward a model of academic choice. *Psychological Bulletin*, 91, 324–348.

Meece, J. L., & Scantlebury, K. (2006). Gender and schooling: Progress and persistent barriers. In J. Worrell & C. Goodheart (Eds.), *Handbook of girls' and women's psychological health* (pp. 283–291). New York: Oxford University Press.

Meece, J. L., Wigfield, A., & Eccles, J. S. (1990). Predictors of math anxiety and its influence on young adolescents' course enrollment intentions and performance in mathematics. *Journal of Educational Psychology*, 82, 60–70.

Midgley, C., Feldlaufer, H., & Eccles, J. S. (1989a). Change in teacher efficacy and student self- and task-related beliefs in mathematics during the transition to junior high school. *Journal of Educational Psychology*, 81, 247–258.

Midgley, C., Feldlaufer, H., & Eccles, J. S. (1989b). Student/teacher relations and attitudes toward mathematics before and after the transition to junior high school. *Child Development*, 60, 981–992.

Mignot, P. (2000). Metaphor: A paradigm for practice-based research into "career." *British Journal of Guidance & Counselling*, 28, 515–531.

Monaco, N. M., & Gaier, E. L. (1992). Single-sex versus coeducational environment and achievement in adolescent females. *Adolescence*, 27, 579–594.

Moore, H. A. (1985). Job satisfaction and women's spheres of work. *Sex Roles*, 13, 663–678.

Mussen, P. H., Conger, J. J., Kagan, J., & Huston, A. C. (1984). *Child development and personality*. (6th ed.). New York: Harper & Row.

Nagy, G., Garrett, J., Trautwein, U., Cortina, K. S., Baumert, J., & Eccles, J. S. (2008). Gendered high school course selection as a precursor of gendered careers: The mediating role of self-concept and intrinsic value. In H. M. G. Watt & J. S. Eccles (Eds.), *Gender and occupational outcomes: Longitudinal assessments of individual, social, and cultural influences* (pp. 115–143). Washington, DC: American Psychological Association.

Nagy, G., Watt, H. M. G., Eccles, J. S., Trautwein, U., Lüdtke, O., & Baumert, J. (in press). The development of students' mathematics self-concept in relation to gender: Different countries, different trajectories? *Journal of Research on Adolescence*.

National Center for Education Statistics. (1997). *Digest of Education statistics, 1997* [NCES Publication No. 98-015]. Washington, DC: Author.

National Committee for the Mathematical Sciences of the Australian Academy of Science. (2006). *Mathematics and statistics: Critical skills for Australia's future* [The National Strategic Review of Mathematical Sciences Research in Australia.] Canberra: Australian Academy of Science.

National Science Board, Committee on Education and Human Resources, Task force on National Workforce policies for Science and Engineering. (2003). *The science and engineering workforce: Realizing America's potential* [NSB 03-69]. Washington, DC: Author.

National Science Foundation. (1999). *Women, minorities, and persons with disabilities in science and engineering: 1998.* Arlington, VA: Author.

National Science Foundation. (2000). *Women, minorities, and persons with disabilities in science and engineering.* Arlington, VA: Author.

National Science Foundation. (2002). *Higher education in science and engineering: Increasing global capacity.* Arlington, VA: Author.

National Science Foundation. (2004). *Women, minorities, and persons with disabilities in science and engineering.* Arlington, VA: Author.

Nicholls, J. G. (1978). The development of the concepts of effort and ability, perception of own attainment, and the understanding that difficult tasks require more ability. *Child Development*, 53, 310–321.

Oakes, J. (1990). *Lost talent: The underparticipation of women, minorities, and disabled persons in science.* Santa Monica, CA: Rand Corp.

O'Doherty, S. (1994). *Inquiry into boys' education 1994.* Sydney.: Ministry of Education, Training, and Youth Affairs.

Organisation for Economic Co-operation and Development [OECD]. (2006). *Evolution of student interest in science and technology studies* [Policy report]. Paris: Author.

Özbilgin, M., Küskü, F., & Erdoğmuş, N. (2005). Explaining influences on career 'choice': The case of MBA students in comparative perspective. *International Journal of Human Resource Management*, 16, 2000–2028.

Parsons, J. E., Adler, T. F., & Kaczala, C. M. (1982). Socialization of achievement attitudes and beliefs: Parental influences. *Child Development*, 53, 310–321.

Parsons, J. E., Kaczala, C. M., & Meece, J. L. (1982). Socialization of achievement attitudes and beliefs: Classroom influences. *Child Development*, 53, 322–339.

Patrick, B. C., Hisley, J., Kempler, T., & College, G. (2000). "What's everybody so excited about?": The effects of teacher enthusiasm on student intrinsic motivation and vitality. *Journal of Experimental Education*, 68, 1521–1558.

Pekrun, R. (2000). A social-cognitive, control-value theory of achievement emotions. In J. Heckhausen (Ed.), *Motivational psychology of human development* (pp. 143–163). Oxford: Elsevier.

Richardson, P. W., & Watt, H. M. G. (2006). Who chooses teaching and why? Profiling characteristics and motivations across three Australian universities. *Asia-Pacific Journal of Teacher Education*, 34, 27–56.

Roeser, R. W. (2006). On the study of educational and occupational life-paths in psychology: Commentary on the special issue. *Educational Research and Evaluation*, 12, 409–421.

Rosenberg, M. (1986). Self-concept from middle childhood through adolescence. In J. Suls & A. Greenwald (Eds.), *Psychological perspectives on the self* (Vol. 3, pp. 107–136). Hillsdale, NJ: Erlbaum.

Rosenthal, R., & Rubin, D. B. (1982). Further meta-analytic procedures for assessing cognitive gender differences. *Journal of Educational Psychology*, 74, 708–712.

Ruble, D. N., Martin, C. L., & Berenbaum, S. A. (2006). Gender development. In N. Eisenberg (Ed.), *Handbook of child psychology Volume 3: Social, emotional, and personality development.* (6th ed., pp. 858–932). New York: Wiley.

Sameroff, A. J., & Feil, L. A. (1985). Parental concepts of development. In I. E. Sigel (Ed.), *Parental belief systems: The psychological consequences for children* (pp. 83–105). Hillsdale, NJ: Erlbaum.

Schulenberg, J. E., Vondracek, F. W., & Crouter, A. C. (1984). The influence of family on vocational development. *Journal of Marriage and the Family*, 46, 129–143.

Sells, L. W. (1980). Mathematics: The invisible filter. *Engineering Education*, 70, 340–341.

Seidman, E., Allen, L., Aber, J. L., Mitchell, C., & Feinman, J. (1994). The impact of school transitions in early adolescence on the self-system and perceived social context of poor urban youth. *Child Development*, 65, 507–522.

Siann, G., & Callaghan, M. (2001). Choices and barriers: Factors influencing women's choice of higher education in science, engineering, and technology. *Journal of Further and Higher Education*, 25, 85–95.

Signorella, M. L., Bigler, R. S., & Liben, L. S. (1993). Developmental differences in children's gender schemata about others: A meta-analytic review. *Developmental Review*, 13, 147–183.

Simmons, R. G., Blyth, D. A., Van Cleave, E. F., & Bush, D. (1979). Entry into early adolescence: The impact of school structure, puberty, and early dating on self-esteem. *American Sociological Review*, 44, 948–967.

Spender, D. (1981). *The role of teachers: What choices do they have?* Strasbourg: Council of Europe.

Spender, D. (1982). *Invisible women: The schooling scandal.* London: Writers and Readers.

Spender, D., & Sarah, E. (1992). *Learning to lose: Sexism and education* (2nd ed.). London: Women's Press.
Stage, F. K., & Maple, S. A. (1996). Incompatible goals: Narratives of graduate women in the mathematics pipeline. *American Educational Research Journal*, 33, 23–51.
Steele, C. (1997). A threat in the air: How stereotypes shape intellectual identity and performance. *American Psychologist*, 52, 613–629.
Tartre, L. A., & Fennema, E. (1995). Mathematics achievement and gender: A longitudinal study of selected cognitive and affective variables grades 6–12. *Educational Studies in Mathematics*, 28, 199–217.
Trusty, J. (1998). Family influences on educational expectations of late adolescents. *Journal of Educational Research*, 91, 260–270.
Turner, J. C., Midgley, C., Meyer, D. K., Gheen, M., Anderman, E. M., Kang, Y., et al. (2002). The classroom environment and students' reports of avoidance strategies in mathematics: A multimethod study. *Journal of Educational Psychology*, 94, 88–106.
Van Langen, A., & Dekkers, H. (2005). Cross-national differences in participating in tertiary science, technology, engineering, and mathematics education. *Comparative Education*, 41, 329–350.
Van Leuvan, P. (2004). Young women's science/mathematics career goals from seventh grade to high school graduation. *Journal of Educational Research*, 97, 248–267.
Watt, H. M. G. (2000). Measuring attitudinal change in mathematics and English over the first year of junior high school: A multidimensional analysis. *Journal of Experimental Education*, 68, 331–361.
Watt, H. M. G. (2002). *Gendered achievement-related choices and behaviours in mathematics and English: The nature and influence of self-, task- and value-perceptions.* Unpublished doctoral dissertation, University of Sydney.
Watt, H. M. G. (2004). Development of adolescents' self perceptions, values, and task perceptions according to gender and domain in 7th through 11th grade Australian students. *Child Development*, 75, 1556–1574.
Watt, H. M. G. (2005). Explaining gendered math enrollments for NSW Australian secondary school students. *New Directions for Child and Adolescent Development*, 110, 15–29.
Watt, H. M. G. (2006). The role of motivation in gendered educational and occupational trajectories related to maths. *Educational Research and Evaluation*, 12, 305–322.
Watt, H. M. G. (2008). What motivates females and males to pursue sex-stereotyped careers? In H. M. G. Watt & J. S. Eccles (Eds.), *Gender and occupational outcomes: Longitudinal assessments of individual, social, and cultural influences* (pp. 87–113). Washington, DC: American Psychological Association.
Watt, H. M. G., & Eccles, J. S. (Eds.). (2008). *Gender and occupational outcomes: Longitudinal assessments of individual, social, and cultural influences.* Washington, DC: American Psychological Association.
Watt, H. M. G., Eccles, J. S., & Durik, A. M. (2006). The leaky mathematics pipeline for girls: A motivational analysis of high school enrolments in Australia and the USA. *Equal Opportunities International*, 25, 642–659.
Whitbeck, L. B., & Gecas, V. (1988). Value attributions and value transmission between parents and children. *Journal of Marriage and the Family*, 50, 829–840.
Wigfield, A. (1994). Expectancy-value theory of achievement motivation: A developmental perspective. *Educational Psychology Review*, 6, 49–78.
Wigfield, A., & Eccles, J. S. (1992). The development of achievement task values: A theoretical analysis. *Developmental Review*, 12, 265–310.
Wigfield, A., Eccles, J., Mac Iver, D., Reuman, D., & Midgley, C. (1991). Transitions at early adolescence: Changes in children's domain-specific self-perceptions and general self-esteem across the transition to junior high school. *Developmental Psychology*, 27, 552–565.
Wigfield, A., Eccles, J. S., Yoon, K. S., Harold, R. D., Arbreton, A. J. A., Freedman-Doan, C., et al. (1997). Change in children's competence beliefs and subjective task values across the elementary school years: A three-year study. *Journal of Educational Psychology*, 89, 451–469.
Willis, S. (1989). *"Real girls don't do maths": Gender and the construction of privilege.* Waurn Ponds, Australia: Deakin University Press.
Wilson, P. A., & Wilson, J. R. (1992). Environmental influences on adolescent educational aspirations: A logistic transform model. *Youth & Society*, 24, 52–70.
Wood, W., & Eagly, A. H. (2002). A cross-cultural analysis of the behavior of women and men: Implications for the origins of sex differences. *Psychological Bulletin*, 128, 699–727.
Yates, L. (1999). Transitions and the year 7 experience: A report from the 12 to 18 project. *Australian Journal of Education*, 43, 24–41.
Yee, D. K., Jacobs, J., & Goldsmith, R. (1986, April). *Sex equity in the home: Parents' influence on their children's attitudes about mathematics.* Paper presented at the meeting of the American Educational Research Association, San Francisco, CA [ERIC Document Reproduction Service No. ED 280 717].

Chapter 17
Gender and the Division of Labor

Scott Coltrane and Kristy Y. Shih

This chapter focuses on the division of labor between women and men and the distinction commonly drawn between domestic work and paid work. Work performed directly in the service of families – including housework and childcare – is often unacknowledged because of cultural assumptions that a wife or mother should do it in the privacy of the home. Paid work, on the other hand, is much more public and historically associated with men. Holding a job and earning a salary has been considered to be a husband's traditional family obligation, whereas tending to home and children traditionally has been considered a wife's primary obligation (even if she also works outside the home). Why do we make these gendered assumptions, and what impact do these ideals have on individuals and society? In this chapter we investigate these questions by examining how the concept of separate work and family spheres for men and women arose and by exploring how scholars have researched the division of household labor.

Links Between Work and Family

Rosabeth Moss Kanter (1977) was one of the first scholars to point out that it is misleading to treat work and family as separate institutional spheres. She rejected popular beliefs about the separation of workplaces and families, and she called for an examination of the interconnections between the two and the study of how and why people make and sustain attachments to each. Today, most social scientists recognize and appreciate the numerous mutual influences between the workplace and the home (Jacobs & Gerson, 2004; Moen & Coltrane, 2004). Near the end of this chapter we summarize research in this tradition by focusing on some findings about spillover from work to family and from family to work.

Although there are many different linkages between work and family, most researchers have focused on how jobs influence family life. For example, there are many studies of how economic resources and job conditions affect marital functioning, parenting practices, or mental and physical health. In general, longer employment hours, harsher working conditions, and lower wages are associated with more family and health problems, and closely regulated work environments are associated with more restrictive parenting practices. Other work–family studies are focused on the different strategies people use to coordinate market labor and household labor, who does the housework, or how people balance commitments between work and family. Most studies show that job demands have important impacts on families and individuals and that, despite substantial shifts in

S. Coltrane (✉)
University of Oregon, Eugene, OR, USA

women's labor force participation, a belief in separate gender spheres continues to influence the allocation of paid and unpaid work for both men and women (Coltrane & Adams, 2008).

The Cultural Template of Men at Work and Women at Home

Although women are more likely to be employed than ever before, it is still men who tend to be identified most strongly with paid work. Even though dual-earner families (in which both wives and husbands have paid work) now vastly outnumber families in which only the husband is employed, the man's work still tends to count for more than the woman's. In part this is because men still tend to get paid more than women do. According to the US Census Bureau's recent American Community Surveys, men who were employed full time (35+ hours/week) had median earnings of $41,194, whereas women employed full time had median earnings of $31,374 (U.S. Census Bureau, 2005). Although women now make up 47% of the labor force and tend to remain employed when they become mothers, they continue to work slightly fewer hours and to earn significantly less than men. With two earners in most families, there is growing recognition for women's role as breadwinners, but men tend to retain symbolic responsibility for earning money, and they get more credit for doing it than do their female partners (Coltrane, 1996; Gerson, 1993; Hochschild, 2003; Townsend, 2002).

In general, as women's and men's jobs and work histories begin to look more alike, they are likely to share similar family concerns. Recent polls show that over 60% of both American men and women would like to work fewer hours on the job (Jacobs & Gerson, 2004). In addition, 60% of men and 55% of women say that they experience conflict in balancing work, personal, and family life (Bond, Galinsky, & Swanberg, 1998), and the majority of both men and women report that they feel torn between the demands of their job and wanting to spend more time with their family (Gerson, 1993). Because of a belief in separate spheres, it has been easier for some men to believe that they are fulfilling their family commitments by working and being a financial provider. Women, on the other hand, have had to justify why having a job does not make them a bad mother. Pleck (1977) suggested that the boundaries between work roles and family roles are "asymmetrically permeable" for women and men. Men have typically been able to keep family commitments from intruding on their work time and to use job demands to limit family time, though these patterns are converging as men's and women's jobs become more similar (Coltrane, 1996; Gerson, 1993; Jacobs & Gerson, 2004; Williams, 2000).

In contrast to men, women's family obligations have traditionally been allowed to penetrate into their workplace. Women, more often than men, have moved in and out of the labor force, regulated the number of hours they are employed, and sometimes scaled back their career aspirations in response to child care demands and other family needs (Moen, 1985; Presser, 1989; Williams, 2000). Many jobs implicitly favor men by offering benefits and prospects for advancement in a prepackaged form, with expectations for a 40+ hour work week and continuous uninterrupted attachment to the workforce that ignores the demands of maintaining homes and raising young children (Moen & Coltrane, 2004). Results of research over the past few decades have challenged previously taken-for-granted assumptions about the separation of work and family roles for men and women and have focused scholars' attention on the relatively mundane topic of household labor.

History and Importance of Household Labor

Families provide love and support to adults and children, but homes are also workplaces, and households are important parts of the larger economy. Even when families do not directly produce or market goods and services, they keep the economy running by supporting and maintaining adult workers, buying and consuming products, and reproducing the workforce by having babies and socializing children. These domestic activities require labor. In fact, the total amount of time and effort put into feeding, clothing, and caring for family members rivals that spent in all other forms of work in the general economy (Coltrane & Adams, 2008).

Every home is a combination of hotel, restaurant, laundry, and often a childcare and entertainment center. The mundane work that goes into these activities is usually invisible to the people who benefit from it, especially children and husbands, who are the equivalent of nonpaying customers. Cleaning and cooking definitely require work, but even fun activities like parties or holiday gatherings require planning, preparation, service, clean-up, and other behind-the-scenes effort. Although patterns are changing, women continue to perform most of this household labor, even though men do the same sorts of work outside the home for pay as chefs, waiters, or janitors.

Although most people tend to think of domestic activities as "naturally" being women's work, there is enormous variation in who does what both inside and outside the home across historical periods and across cultures. Every society has restrictions on what kinds of work men and women do, but there is no global content to these roles, and studies show that divisions of labor are influenced by specific environmental and social conditions. Activities often associated with women, such as nurturance, domestic chores, and childcare, are sometimes performed by men, and activities often associated with men, such as warfare, hunting, and politics, are sometimes performed by women. Thus, although gender is often used to divide labor, there is no universal set of tasks that can be defined as "women's work" or "men's work" (Coltrane & Adams, 2008).

If the work is not *inherently* gendered, why do many people continue to think that most household labor should be performed by women? A belief in separate work spheres for women and men gained popularity in the USA in the late 1800s. Before the nineteenth century, men, women, and children tended to work side-by-side in family-based agricultural or home production, often doing different chores, but cooperating in the mutual enterprise of running a farm or family business. After the rise of industrialization, most men entered the paid labor force and worked away from home. A romantic ideal of separate spheres emerged to justify the economic arrangement of women staying at home while men left home to earn wages. Women came to be seen as pure, innocent, and loving – traits that made them ideally suited to the "private" sphere of home and family. Popular ideals of womanhood that emerged at this time elevated mothering to a revered status and treated homemaking as a full-time profession (whereas previously women were expected in addition to engage in work on the farm or in the shop). Men who were previously expected to be intimately involved in raising children and running the home were now considered temperamentally unsuited for such duties and were encouraged to find their true calling in the impersonal "public" sphere of work (Coltrane & Adams, 2008).

The type of work it takes to maintain a household has changed over time as well. Before the twentieth century, running the typical household was more physically demanding; most houses lacked running water, electricity, central heating, and flush toilets. Without modern conveniences, people had to do everything by hand, and household tasks were arduous and time consuming, as they still are in some parts of the world. In the nineteenth century, most middle- and upper-class households in the USA also included servants, so live-in maids, cooks, and housekeepers did much of this work. In the twentieth century, indoor plumbing and electricity became widely available, and the invention and distribution of laborsaving appliances changed the nature of housework. By mid-century, the suburbs had multiplied, home ownership had become the norm, and the number of household servants had dropped dramatically. Despite the introduction of modern conveniences, the total amount of time that American women spent on housework was about the same in 1960 as it was in 1920, primarily because standards of comfort rose during this period for most families. When laundry was done by hand, people changed clothes less frequently (unless they had servants to do the washing). With the advent of the washing machine, the average homemaker began to wash clothes more often, as people began to change clothes more frequently. Similarly, standards for personal hygiene, diet, and house cleanliness increased as conveniences such as hot running water, refrigerators, and vacuum cleaners became available, and women became the experts in these matters. Although women's total housework time changed little, there were shifts in the types of tasks performed. Food preparation and meal clean-up consumed somewhat less time, but shopping, child care, and household management took up more time.

This brief historical review ignores many important details about how housework was performed in the past, but it alerts us to the idea that household labor is associated with gender in specific ways and that changes in its allocation reflect larger changes in the economy, the culture, the family, and society. Based on this insight, researchers in the 1970s, 1980s, and early 1990s focused on how household labor remained coded as "women's work" and how, in fact, most of it continued to be performed by women. Nevertheless, this research identified conditions under which divisions of labor might become more equal, and, by the late 1990s, a consensus began to emerge that significant change was occurring, even as older patterns remained (Coltrane, 2000).

Evidence from the USA shows that men's absolute and proportionate contributions to household tasks and childcare over the past three decades have increased dramatically. National cross-time series of time use diary studies show that from the 1960s to the twenty-first century, men's contribution to housework doubled from about 15% to over 30% of the total (Fisher, Egerton, Gershuny, & Robinson, 2006; Robinson & Godbey, 1999). The same studies show that, as rates of employment among American women increased from the 1960s, the time they spent on housework declined substantially (Sullivan, 2006). Although the trends are thus moving in the direction of more sharing, most studies continue to show that, on average, women still perform about twice as much housework as men do. In the rest of the chapter we focus on how social scientists have studied household labor over the past two decades, with special attention to the major theories, research methods, and empirical findings that are evident in the scholarly literature.

Theories of Household Labor

Exchange/Resource theories suggest that household tasks are allocated rationally based on time, resources, and interests of household members. Under this general category we identify two popular general approaches: (a) *Time Availability/Constraints* and (b) *Relative Resources and Economic Dependency*. In part as a reaction to these economically based theories, *Gender* theories posit that the division of housework is influenced by sociocultural gender ideals and dependent on the gendered interaction of household members. *Gender* perspectives include research that utilizes (a) *Socialization and Attitudes toward Gender Roles* and (b) *Gender Construction* approaches. Below we briefly introduce each of these conceptual approaches to household labor research and discuss how they have been employed to explain the allocation of domestic labor.

Exchange/Resource Theories

Time Availability/Constraints

Theories based on time availability/constraints suggest that household labor is allocated according to the availability of household members in relation to the amount of housework that needs to be done (Coverman, 1985; England & Farkas, 1986; Hiller, 1984). From this perspective, those with greater constraints outside the home, especially those who spend more time in paid market work, are expected to spend less time in unpaid housework (Blair & Lichter, 1991; Demo & Acock, 1993). Related indicators of time availability and constraints include employment (e.g., Brines, 1994; Shelton, 1990; Shelton & John, 1996), marital and parental status (e.g., Gupta, 1999; Shelton & John, 1993a; South & Spitze, 1994), and family composition (Gershuny & Robinson, 1988; Shelton, 1992; South & Spitze, 1994). Although these indicators are often presented as gender-neutral in analyses, they are also linked to gender, as women's time is more affected than men's (Bianchi, Milkie, Sayer, & Robinson, 2000; Coltrane, 2000). For example, women perform the majority of "routine" household chores that are time consuming and less flexible or optional (including cooking, meal clean-up, shopping, house cleaning, and laundry, tasks typically labeled "housework"). Men, on the other hand, often perform tasks that are more flexible and can be done at one's own discretion (such as household repairs, lawn care, and car maintenance).

Relative Resources and Economic Dependency

According to theories based on the relative resources hypothesis, the division of household labor is primarily determined by the amount of structural resources (i.e., education and income) each partner brings to the relationship (Blumberg & Coleman, 1989). Those who possess a greater amount of resources are assumed to have more power in deciding how household labor is allocated, and those with fewer resources and less power are expected to do more of it (Blood & Wolfe, 1960). The division of housework, thus, is an outcome of negotiation between individuals who use available resources to bargain for their best interests (Brines, 1993).

Another variant of relative resources is derived from neoclassical economic theory. Based on the specialization of each partner in either market or nonmarket labor, this perspective suggests that couples divide household labor to maximize overall household efficiency or utility (Becker, 1981). For example, men's comparative advantage in wage earning results in their concentration in the labor market, whereas women's comparative advantage in domestic labor results in their concentration on nonmarket work (Bianchi et al., 2000). Similarly, economic dependency approaches argue that, because wives are assumed to be economically dependent on their husbands, they are likely to trade doing housework for economic security (Brines, 1993, 1994).

Critiques of Exchange and Resource Perspectives

Time availability, economic, and resource exchange perspectives provide only a partial picture of how couples and families decide on the allocation of housework. These theories assume a gender-neutral approach that emphasizes rational choice and exchange principles. With some exceptions (see, for example, Brines, 1994; Greenstein, 2000; Pyke, 1994), exchange and resource theories fail to consider and analyze why some people (or one gender) would have more resources than others (but see Blumberg & Coleman, 1989, for a gender-sensitive resource theory). If divisions of household labor are based solely on time availability, relative resources, or economic exchanges, we would assume that housework would be shared more equally once women gained the opportunity for market employment (because they would have less time and more resources to bargain for doing less housework). Such predictions, however, are not supported fully by previous research (Berk, 1985; Coltrane, 2000; Thompson & Walker, 1989). Studies have shown that employed women continue to spend longer hours in housework than their male counterparts do, even though the hours they spend on housework have decreased in recent decades (Bianchi et al., 2000; Bianchi, Robinson, & Milkie, 2006; Robinson & Godbey, 1999; Sullivan, 2006; Sullivan & Gershuny, 2001). As a consequence, some scholars have argued that the division of housework is not simply a rational response to market conditions based on resources and time availability but should be understood by considering how it is influenced by cultural conceptions of gender, by the extent to which individuals believe in gender differences, and by differences in power between men and women.

Gender Theories

In addition to the gender-neutral exchange and resource approaches noted above, research in the past two decades has focused on how gender relations shape couples' negotiation and sharing of household labor. Researchers who utilize a gender perspective have aimed to explain why there is no simple trade-off between the hours spent in paid and unpaid labor between women and men (Ferree, 1990; Greenstein, 1996) and the symbolic as well as interactional nature of housework (Berk, 1985; Coltrane, 1989; West & Zimmerman, 1987).

Socialization and Attitudes Toward Gender Roles

Role theorists often conceive of gender as a property that is inherent in the individual, rather than as something that is socially and culturally produced and interactively maintained. In this view, what children learn from socialization agents (e.g., family, peers, schools, the media) "produces masculine and feminine attitudes, motivations, and personalities that will fit children into their adult roles" (Lorber, 1994, pp. 1–2). Socialization and gender role theories posit that the process of socialization is a major determinant of the gendered division of household labor. Such approaches assume that differential socialization of women and men contributes to their different roles in the family and shapes how household labor is divided. According to functionalist socialization and gender role theories (e.g., Parsons & Bales, 1955), women are described as occupying the "expressive role" and thus assume responsibility for taking care of family members and performing household chores. Men are, complementarily, socialized to occupy the "instrumental role," to become providers for their families, and to interface with public institutions.

Although some changes may be possible, gender role theories typically assume that gendered personality characteristics, such as women's abilities or preferences for performing housework and parenting, are relatively static. Researchers who utilize this perspective generally have focused on the socialization of individuals (especially children) into "proper" gender roles and behaviors, but early attempts to link gender identity or gendered personality type (e.g., "masculine" or "feminine") with household divisions of labor were largely unsuccessful. Nevertheless, gender role theories assume that those who are socialized to gender-segregated work will conform to those beliefs and practices, and most research confirms this hypothesis (Coltrane, 2000). For example, men and women with more "traditional" gender attitudes tend to share less housework, whereas those with "nontraditional" or egalitarian gender attitudes tend to share more housework (Adams, Coltrane, & Parke, 2007; Arrighi & Maume, 2000; Greenstein, 1996).

Gender Construction

The gender construction approach emphasizes the symbolic aspects of gender and situates gender in social interaction rather than viewing it as a personality trait (West & Fenstermaker, 1993; West & Zimmerman, 1987). This newer approach to theorizing gender rejects the assumption that people are rigidly socialized into gender roles or have fixed gendered personalities that last a lifetime. Following this perspective, many researchers have focused on the interactional aspects of gender to explain why men and women perform different household tasks and why power imbalances within families persist (see, for examples, Berk, 1985; Ferree, 1991; Hochschild, 2003; Pestello & Voydanoff, 1991). The gender construction perspective focuses on routine interaction and the accomplishment of gender and suggests that doing housework is also "doing gender" (Berk, 1985; West & Fenstermaker, 1993). Performing certain household tasks not only provides opportunities to establish oneself as a competent member of a gender category but also serves to affirm and reproduce gendered selves and behaviors (Coltrane, 1989; DeVault, 1991). For women, cooking the evening meals or taking care of children (but not repairing the cars) is "doing gender" (i.e., it confirms and reinforces an identity as a woman rather than a man). Through the symbolic enactment of gender relations, couples not only do come to view certain household tasks as "feminine" or "masculine" duties (Bianchi et al., 2000) but also participate in activities that conform to their gender category and resist those that do not. By avoiding "feminine" tasks such as cooking, cleaning, and laundry men lay claim to a masculine self and invoke masculine privilege. Thus, women's and men's performance of different tasks helps to define their interpersonal relations and constructs the gender order.

Although many researchers have set up studies to test which theory better explains observed patterns, the research often provides mixed empirical results. As we discuss below, researchers have found support for the time availability/constraints, relative resources, and gender perspectives, but, almost as often, they have failed to find strong and consistent predictors, especially when many possible predictors are considered simultaneously (Bianchi et al., 2000; Coltrane, 2000; Davis, Greenstein, & Marks, 2007; Goldberg & Perry-Jenkins, 2007). Such findings suggest that the above theories are not mutually exclusive and that combinations of factors probably best explain how and why household labor is allocated. Before reviewing empirical findings about household labor allocation, we discuss the typical methods used in its study.

Methods of Studying Household Labor

How is household labor defined and measured? According to most studies, household labor refers to unpaid work done to maintain family members and/or a home (Shelton & John 1996). Although this concept can include child minding, household management, and various kinds of emotional labor, most housework studies have tended to exclude these less visible or overlapping types of "work" from study (Coltrane, 2000; Ferree, 1990; Thompson & Walker, 1989). Large-sample national surveys conducted in the USA show that the five most time-consuming major household tasks (excluding direct childcare) include (a) meal preparation or cooking, (b) housecleaning, (c) shopping for groceries and household goods, (d) washing dishes or cleaning up after meals, and (e) laundry, including washing, ironing, and mending clothes (Blair & Lichter, 1991; Robinson & Godbey, 1999). These routine household tasks, typically called "housework," not only are the most time consuming but also are less optional and less able to be postponed than other household tasks such as gardening or household repairs (Coltrane, 2000; DeMaris & Longmore, 1996). Although some people find pleasure in doing some of these tasks (e.g., cooking), most women and men report that they do not enjoy doing the routine housework (DeVault, 1991; Robinson & Milkie, 1998). Residual household tasks such as house repairs, yard care, driving other people, or paying bills are also measured in many household labor studies. These more time flexible and discretionary tasks are often labeled as "other household labor" and are typically included in measures of "total household labor." Earlier studies in the home economics and time use traditions tended to measure absolute hours of total household labor for all men and all women, but more recent studies have tended to focus on couple dynamics, favoring the use of proportional measures and data collected for men and women in the same household, including consideration of the gender-typing of specific tasks.

Information about household labor is most often collected using time diaries or survey questions. In time diary studies, randomly selected individuals are asked to complete logs to account for time spent on various activities, usually for a 24-hour period, with results collected via phone, mail, or in person (Robinson & Godbey, 1999). Time diaries generally are considered to generate the most accurate (and lower) estimates of time spent on specific activities by individuals. With a primary focus on time use, these results often include less information about individual attitudes or other aspects of family life but are well suited for making cross-national or cross-time comparisons.

National, regional, and local survey research studies (whether by phone, mail, or in person) generally cover a broader range of topics, and, when they focus on family issues, they are increasingly likely to include direct questions about time spent on household labor. Respondents typically are asked how much time they "usually" spend per week on specific household activities or how much time they spent "yesterday" on selected activities. Comparisons with time diary studies show that results are highly correlated but that direct question surveys produce estimates of time spent that are significantly higher, especially for frequently performed activities. For less frequently performed activities, survey questions may produce lower estimates, especially if the period of recall is long. Both women and men tend to overestimate their own contributions in direct question surveys and to double-count time spent in simultaneous activities (Coltrane, 2000). When survey respondents are asked for proportional estimates of household labor performance (e.g., "Who does the house cleaning? – always me, mostly me, shared equally, mostly my partner, always my partner") the share of the total is approximately equal to estimates derived from data collected from time diaries (Sullivan, 1997). Proportional measures are sometimes difficult to interpret because they cannot be used for all households (e.g., single-person households are excluded), do not measure how much time is spent on housework (e.g., a paid housekeeper might do most of the work), and do not reflect the source of change (e.g., is a shift toward sharing due to wives doing less or husbands doing more?). Some surveys ask for global proportional estimates or how much time respondents spend in a typical week on "housework" or "household labor," whereas others ask for these assessments about a list of specific tasks, subsequently aggregated into composite measures. Although most published data come from surveys or time diary studies, scholars who assess the allocation of household labor also use other research techniques such as in-depth interviews, direct observations, and historical comparative methods (Coltrane, 2000).

Predictors of Household Labor: Empirical Findings

As we refine our techniques for studying household labor and learn more about the conditions that lead to the performance of various household tasks, we should be able to estimate how and why men and women allocate responsibility for this labor. To help specify these conditions and allocation processes, we summarize household labor research findings from the past two decades based on several general types of predictors. Women's and men's employment status and hours, earnings, education, attitudes toward gender roles, age and life course stages, marital and parental status, and union types have all been identified as important predictors in past research.

Women's and Men's Employment

Research on the effects of women's and men's employment on the household division of labor generally supports the time availability hypothesis. That is, those who spend more time in paid market work tend to spend less time in unpaid housework. Most studies show women's employment status to be negatively associated with time spent in housework (Brines, 1994; Shelton & John, 1996). Data from national time-dairy studies also suggest that employed women perform one-third less housework than their non-employed counterparts do (Robinson & Godbey, 1999), which supports the time availability hypothesis as well as the relative resource hypothesis. Not only do employed women cut back their time on housework, but they also tend to shift some household chores to the weekends. Although employed mothers reduce their housework time considerably, they do not reduce their contribution to childcare (Bianchi et al., 2006). Similarly, the longer the hours a woman is employed in the labor force, the less time she spends performing housework (Bianchi et al., 2000). Research has also shown women's employment status (Cunningham, 2007) and employment hours (Blair & Lichter, 1991; Coltrane & Ishii-Kuntz, 1992; Davis & Greenstein, 2004; Demo & Acock, 1993) to be associated with increases in their spouses' participation and sharing of household chores. In general, dual-income couples share more housework than do couples in male-breadwinner households (DeMeis & Perkins, 1996; Sullivan, 1997).

In contrast, men's employment produces inconsistent and mixed effects on their participation in household labor. Studies show that men's employment status (i.e., full time vs. part time) has no significant effect on the amount of time they invest in household labor (Sanchez, 1993; Shelton & John, 1996). Some studies show no association between men's employment hours and their participation in housework (Almeida, Maggs, & Galambos, 1993; Sullivan, 1997). However, other researchers have found that men's employment hours have a negative association with housework time; men who are employed fewer hours share more household chores than those employed longer hours do (Coltrane & Ishii-Kuntz, 1992; Greenstein, 1996; South & Spitze, 1994). Others have found men's employment hours to be associated with the types of housework they perform (Blair & Lichter, 1991). For example, men who are employed longer hours tend to perform less routine housework and more discretionary tasks, such as maintenance and repairs.

Earnings

Examination of the effects of earnings on housework yield fairly consistent results. Generally, women with higher earnings enjoy more equal division of household labor. Some researchers distinguish between women's relative and absolute earnings (Coltrane, 2000), and their studies suggest that smaller income gaps between husbands and wives create a more equal division of labor (Blair & Lichter, 1991; Kamo & Cohen, 1998). Women's higher relative earnings decrease their time in household labor (Cunningham, 2007). This, however, does not mean that women's higher income increases men's participation in housework (Brines, 1994; Gupta, 2006). Other studies show women's housework to be dependent on their absolute earnings rather than on their spouse's earnings or on women's income relative to that of their spouse (Gupta, 2006, 2007). By examining women's absolute earnings, Gupta was able to extend and challenge both the economic dependency and the gender construction theoretical frameworks. He suggested that housework is better predicted by women's own earnings (economic autonomy) than by their economic dependency.

Furthermore, women's earnings may only be predictive of housework allocation insofar as they do not exceed their husbands' earning (Bittman, England, Sayer, Folbre, & Matheson, 2003). In contradiction of simple resource theories, couples who deviate from normative earning patterns (e.g., men make less than women) are often found to have more traditional divisions of household labor (Bittman et al., 2003; Brines, 1994; Greenstein, 2000; Pyke, 1994; Tichenor, 2005). Especially among married men in lower income households, the more a husband is dependent on his wife's income, the less routine housework he is likely to perform, a finding that is interpreted to support gender construction or display theories (Brines, 1994).

Education

Similar to employment, women's educational attainment has been found to be negatively associated with their time spent in performing housework (Brines, 1994; Sanchez & Thomson, 1997; South & Spitze, 1994). Not only do women with higher levels of education tend to do less housework, but these women are also more likely than those with less education to purchase domestic help (Cohen, 1998). Women's relative education has also been found to affect their partners' levels of housework sharing. Women with equal or more education than their husbands tend to have husbands who share more housework (Davis & Greenstein, 2004). In contrast, men's educational attainment has been found to associate positively with time spent in housework (Batalova & Cohen, 2002; Bergen, 1991; Presser, 1994; Shelton & John, 1996; South & Spitze, 1994). In general, men with more education tend to contribute more to housework than those with less education do, though there is some question as to whether these correlational findings reflect unmeasured egalitarian gender ideals more than educational attainment per se.

Age and the Life Course

Studies suggest that, in general, younger women perform less housework and tend to share more of it with their spouses than do women who are older (Coltrane, 2000). In a recent cross-national study, younger men also were found to share a greater amount of housework than do those who are older (Batalova & Cohen, 2002). In addition, for some older women, the meanings and perceptions of housework change as they age (Altschuler, 2004). Researchers have examined the division of housework in later life, including transitions to retirement (Solomon, Acock, & Walker, 2004; Szinovacz, 2000) and widowhood (Utz, Reidy, Carr, Nesse, & Wortman, 2004). Some studies suggest that retirement does have an influence on the division of labor, especially when the husband retires and the wife continues to work (Szinovacz, 2000). Further, the effects of change in retirement are also related to gender roles and marital dependence. For example, Solomon and colleagues (2004) found that egalitarian women increased their investment in routine chores after retirement, whereas egalitarian men did not. Others found no significant changes in retirement on the gendered division of labor (Robinson & Spitze, 1992; Ward, 1993). In addition, late-life widowhood significantly alters men's and women's time in household labor, such that widowers perform significantly more housework than married men do, whereas widows performed significantly less housework than married women do (Utz et al., 2004).

Attitudes Toward Gender Roles

Studies show that women's and men's attitudes toward gender roles are consistent predictors of housework sharing (Artis & Pavalko, 2003; Blaisure & Allen, 1995; Brayfield, 1992; Greenstein, 1996; Lye & Biblarz, 1993; Potuchek, 1992; Shelton & John, 1993a; Thompson & Walker, 1989). Married men who have more egalitarian attitudes in early adulthood are also likely to participate more in routine housework later in life (Cunningham, 2005). Cross-national studies also suggest a significant relationship between more egalitarian attitudes toward gender roles and less traditional divisions of labor (Batalova & Cohen, 2002; Crompton & Harris, 1999). In addition, couples are more likely to share housework when wives feel more strongly about the sharing of both paid and non-paid work and about equality between women and men (Coltrane, 2000). The congruence of attitudes between spouses is also important. Those who share similar attitudes are more likely to translate them into actual practice, and when both spouses hold more traditional attitudes, they share less housework than when both spouses share more egalitarian attitudes (Greenstein, 1996; MacDermid, Huston, & McHale, 1990).

Marital Status and Union Type

Marital status and union type have also been found to be associated with the amount of housework men and women perform. Married women consistently perform more housework than do women who are single or cohabiting, whereas married men perform less housework than do their single or cohabiting counterparts (Davis et al., 2007; Nock, 1998; Perkins & DeMeis, 1996; Shelton & John, 1993a). This finding suggests that being married entails more housework for women and less for men. Results of longitudinal studies further suggest that men who form couple households reduce their housework time (Gupta, 1999). Cross-national comparisons shed some light on the possible effects of premarital cohabitation on attitudes toward gender roles and household division of labor. For example, Batalova and Cohen (2002) used survey data from 22 countries and found that former cohabiters bring more egalitarian expectations and experiences to their subsequent marriages, which, in turn, are conducive to a more egalitarian division of labor.

Lesbian and Gay Couples and Families

Until recently, there was little research on the division of household labor among lesbian and gay couples. Generally, studies that focus on the comparison between lesbian/gay and heterosexual couples have shown that role division in lesbian/gay couples is more egalitarian than that of their heterosexual counterparts (Chan, Brooks, Raboy, & Patterson, 1998; McPherson, 1994; Patterson, 2000; Peplau & Spalding, 2000; Solomon, Rothblum, & Balsam, 2005). Lesbian mothers not only share housework more equally than other mothers but also express greater preference for equality in the division of family labor. Some researchers who focus on the details of daily life have argued that the general belief that same-sex couples share housework does not match the actual practice of how specific tasks are accomplished (Carrington, 1999). For example, even though lesbian and gay couples in Carrington's study presented their relationship and the division of domestic labor as fair and equal, his ethnographic data suggested that these couples utilized hegemonic concepts of gender in their discussions of division of housework. Similar to patterns found in heterosexual couples (see Hochschild, 2003), Carrington found discrepancies between gay and lesbian couples' ideal of egalitarianism and the reality of housework division based on power and status differentials in their everyday life.

Among lesbian couples, both biological and non-biological mothers tend to share housework and family decision making relatively evenly (Chan et al., 1998; Patterson, Sutfin, & Fulcher, 2004; Sullivan, 1996), except in the area of childcare, where biological mothers tend to spend more time than their partners do (Goldberg & Perry-Jenkins, 2007; Johnson & O'Connor, 2002). More time spent on childcare, however, does not necessarily make the biological mother the more primary parent (Goldberg & Perry-Jenkins, 2007).

A few studies have been done to compare gay and lesbian couples on levels of housework sharing, and these offer varied findings and explanations. For example, Kurdek (1993) found that lesbian couples were more likely to share equally in domestic tasks than were gay couples. In a more recent study, gay and lesbian partners without children were found to be similar in the relative frequency of housework performed in their households; gay couples were more likely to have one partner who specialized in particular tasks (Kurdek, 2007). In contrast to typical gender stereotypes, Blumstein and Schwartz (1983) and Carrington (1999) reported that lesbian couples do *less* housework than do gay couples. Blumstein and Schwartz explained their finding by speculating that lesbians do less housework because they regard housework as a symbol associated with women's lower status in society. Carrington, on the other hand, attributed his finding to the fact that gay couples have more income and larger living spaces than do lesbian couples.

Race and Ethnicity

Housework researchers have also begun to examine how racial/ethnic differences are associated with the division of household labor. Most previous studies have focused on comparisons between African American and European American couples and families (Bergen, 1991; Broman, 1988; Hossain & Roopnarine, 1993; John & Shelton, 1997; Kamo & Cohen, 1998; Orbuch & Eyster, 1997; Sanchez & Thomson, 1997); only a handful of studies have examined the division of household labor in other racial/ethnic families. Generally, studies that include African American couples suggest that Black men are more likely to share housework than White men are (Broman, 1993; Orbuch & Custer, 1995); however, Black women are still responsible for almost twice the housework that Black men perform. Common predictors of housework have been found to have different effects for Black couples and White couples, partly because of Blacks' more egalitarian gender attitudes and the smaller employment and earning gap between spouses (Orbuch & Eyster, 1997).

Several researchers have examined the division of household labor among Latino/a families, and they reported contradictory results. Some studies show that Latino/a families share housework slightly more than their European American counterparts do (Mirande, 1997; Shelton & John, 1993b), whereas others suggest there is less sharing of housework among Latino/a families (Golding, 1990; Pinto & Coltrane, 2009). Most studies, however, suggest that Latino/a couples share housework in response to factors similar to those that affect their European American counterparts, including relative earnings, employment patterns, and gender ideals (Coltrane & Valdez, 1993; Herrera & del Campo, 1995; Pinto & Coltrane, 2009).

Recently, housework scholars have argued for the importance of examining the division of labor from an intersectional perspective that focuses on race–class–gender connections simultaneously (e.g., Dillaway & Broman, 2001). They argued that, even though race and class differences may affect women's satisfaction with the division of household labor, such connections have been overlooked in previous research. Although there is still little research on social class differences in the division of labor among racial/ethnic and immigrant families, some evidence suggests that middle- and upper-middle class immigrant women enjoy more egalitarian relations than lower-class women do (Chen, 1992; Coltrane & Valdez, 1993; Espiritu, 1999; Pyke, 2004; Toro-Morn, 1995). For example, Chen (1992) found that Taiwanese immigrant men in the professional class tend to be more egalitarian and to participate more in household labor than do their counterparts in the working and small business owner classes. Despite theories that suggest that it is primarily culture that determines gender roles in ethnic minority families, some recent studies show that economic resources and practical constraints shape housework allocation in poor immigrant Latino/a families, as they often do in wealthier European American families (Pinto & Coltrane, 2009).

Outcomes of Household Labor

Marital Happiness, Marital Satisfaction, and Marital Quality

Marital happiness, satisfaction, and quality have been found to be positively related to the amount of housework spouses share (Erickson, 1993; Orbuch &Eyster, 1997; Pina & Bengtson, 1993; Suitor, 1991). That is, generally, the more work that is shared between spouses, the higher the reported levels of marital satisfaction and happiness. Further, satisfaction with the division of household labor has been found to be a greater predictor of marital satisfaction across the life course than many other predictors, such as age, education, and women's employment status (Suitor, 1991). In addition, men are found to be more satisfied when they perform more and their partners perform less child care, and women are found to be more satisfied when their spouses undertake more childcare responsibilities (Stevens, Kiger, & Mannon, 2005).

Studies also suggest the importance of congruent attitudes and actions between spouses. For example, spouses who have similar attitudes are generally found to be happier in, and more satisfied with, their marriages (McHale & Crouter, 1992; Perry-Jenkins & Crouter, 1990). Couples who have incongruent expectations are less happy, less satisfied with the marriage, and more likely to end their relationships (Cooke, 2006; Hohmann-Marriott, 2006).

Marital satisfaction has also been found to be positively associated with men's and women's performance of emotion work, including expressions of affection and appreciation (Erickson, 1993; Stevens et al., 2005). Both male and female respondents report higher levels of marital satisfaction when their partners increase their emotion work and expressiveness (Stevens et al., 2005). This suggests that the emotion work performance a spouse does may serve as an indicator of his/her investment in the relationship.

In addition, marital satisfaction is significantly related to how women and men perceive fairness in their housework contributions and in the couple's division of labor. When more egalitarian individuals (i.e., those with nontraditional gender attitudes) perceive unequal division of housework, they tend to be less satisfied with their relationships (Kluwer, Heesink, & Van de Vliert, 1997; Lye & Biblarz, 1993). Women report greater satisfaction when they see themselves as doing less housework than their female friends and when they perceive their husbands as doing more housework than other men do (Himsel & Goldberg, 2003). The same study found that men tend to report that they are more satisfied when their wives do more housework than their mothers did. Both men and women who believe that they perform more than their fair share of housework report lower levels of marital satisfaction than do those who perceive fairness in the couple's division of labor (Frisco & Williams, 2003). This is especially true for men. Further, Frisco and Williams (2003) found that women who perceive unfairness in the division of housework are more than twice as likely as their counterparts who perceive fairness to divorce (see also Cooke, 2006; Hohmann-Marriott, 2006).

An Emerging Focus on Fairness Evaluations

Fairness evaluation research has attracted much attention from housework researchers since the 1990s (Coltrane, 2000). As noted above, researchers have found that those who think that domestic work is divided fairly tend to be happier with their relationships. But recent research in this area also aims to uncover reasons why a majority of women do not view their housework contributions as unfair, even though they are typically responsible for about two-thirds of the total household labor. Most research shows that couples' evaluations of fairness generally do not utilize 50% as the mark of equality (Lennon & Rosenfeld, 1994). And, as suggested above, there are often discrepancies in what men and women consider as their fair share. On average, women consider the division to be fair when they contribute approximately 66% of total housework, whereas men consider it fair when they contribute about 36% of household tasks (Lennon & Rosenfeld, 1994). Consistent with national trends based on time diary analysis, women see themselves as doing slightly less housework than their own mothers did, whereas men perceive their participation to be greater than that of their own fathers (Himsel & Goldberg, 2003). When compared with their parents' generation, men report that their wives do slightly more housework than their own mothers did, and women report that their husbands do more than their own fathers did.

Several factors contribute to one's perceptions of fairness, such as social comparison (Grote, Clark, & Moore, 2004; Grote, Naylor, & Clark, 2002; Himsel & Goldberg, 2003), enjoyment and competence (Grote et al., 2002), and types of housework (Bartley, Blanton, & Gilliard, 2005). Individuals often make social comparisons with their own parents, spouses, friends, and peers. Whereas men tend to draw on more traditional gender-based divisions of labor by comparing their contribution to those of their same-sex peers, women are more likely to compare their own contributions to those of their spouses, which suggest that women base their evaluations of fairness on principles of marital equality (Gager & Hohmann-Marriott, 2006). Other studies, however, suggest that women's perception of equality is based on comparisons with the relationships of other women (Blaisure & Allen, 1995; Hochschild, 2003; Pina & Bengston, 1993; Ward, 1993).

The types of housework regularly performed also influence couples' perception of fairness. Bartley and colleagues (2005) found that time spent in "low-control" tasks (including those typically identified as "women's work" that are routine, repetitive, and not easily subject to rescheduling) increases both men's and women's sense of inequity and unfairness. However, time involved in "high-control" (traditionally "men's work") tasks does not impact perceptions of equity.

As noted above, perceived fairness is also related to marital satisfaction and relationship quality (Blair, 1993; Dance & Gilbert, 1993; Frisco & Williams, 2003; Gjerdingen & Center, 2005; Meier, McNaughton-Cassill, & Lynch, 2006; Wilkie, Ferree, & Ratcliff, 1998). Perceived fairness is positively associated with good quality marital interaction and closeness, which, in turn, contributes to greater marital satisfaction. Further, perceived fairness is negatively associated with marital conflict, rates of divorce, and depression (Frisco & Williams, 2003; Pina & Bengtson, 1993). In addition, perceived fairness may affect individuals' personal and social relations. For example, individuals who perceive their housework contribution as fair are more likely to report having greater social support than those who perceive their load as inequitable (Van Willigen & Drentea, 2001).

Psychological Adjustment

Studies have also pointed to the direct and indirect effects of the division of housework on individuals' psychological adjustment, especially depression. Doing large amounts of repetitive housework has been linked to more depressive symptoms for women, and sometimes for men (Barnett & Shen, 1997; Glass & Fujimoto, 1994). Women display fewer depressive symptoms when housework appears to be fairly distributed, whereas they display higher rates of depression when housework distribution appears to be unfair (Glass & Fujimoto, 1994; Lennon & Rosenfeld, 1994). Other studies show that perceived inequality predicts more psychological distress than the actual amount of housework performed (Bird, 1999).

Work–Family and Family–Work Spillover

Changes in family and work lives in the past few decades have contributed to an increase in scholarship on work–family balance and spillover. Research suggests that work/family spillover is reciprocal: work affects family life (work-to-family spillover) and family influences work (family-to-work spillover). In the empirical literature, work-to-family spillover has received more attention than family-to-work spillover until recently (Dilworth, 2004; Eagle, Miles, & Icenogle, 1997; Higgins & Duxbury, 1992). Spillover effects can be both positive and negative (the latter is sometimes referred to as work–family conflict). Positive spillover promotes better functioning across work and family domains, whereas negative spillover is associated with adverse outcomes such as stress, depression, poor physical health, and heavy alcohol use (Grzywacz & Marks, 2000).

Gender-based spillover effects have also been suggested, such that men are more affected by work-to-family spillover, and women are more affected by family-to-work spillover (Pleck, 1977). Drawing on the gender role approach noted above, this model suggests that gender roles require men to prioritize paid employment over family life and women to prioritize family obligations over paid employment. For example, studies have shown that employed mothers experience more negative family-to-work spillover than employed fathers do (Crouter, 1984; Dilworth, 2004; Keene & Reynolds, 2005), and this is especially true for women with young children.

Several factors discussed earlier affect family/work spillover. Stevens and colleagues (Stevens, Minnotte, & Kiger, 2004) found men's ages and women's employment status to be significant predictors of work–family spillover. Men between the ages of 31 and 40 years reported the highest level of such work-to-family spillover. Women employed full time reported higher work-to-family spillover than those employed part time.

With regard to family-to-work spillover, men's levels of education and time spent away from work to care for a sick child are significant predictors of greater negative spillover (Dilworth, 2004). Employment status (full time vs. part time) and number of work hours per week predicted negative spillover for both men and women (Dilworth, 2004; Stevens et al., 2004). Although some research shows the number of children to be predictive, other work suggests that the age of children has a greater effect on mothers' family-to-work spillover. For example, negative spillover effects are greater for mothers with younger, especially preschool-aged, children (Dilworth, 2004; Stevens et al., 2004). In addition, marital and family life satisfactions have been found to affect family-to-work spillover differentially. For example, one study shows marital satisfaction to have no significant effect on negative spillover, but low levels of family life satisfaction to be one of the strongest predictors of negative family-to-work spillover for both women and men (Dilworth, 2004). However, others found relationship satisfaction to be associated with positive family-to-work spillover for men and satisfaction with housework arrangements to be associated with positive spillover for women (Stevens, Minnotte, Mannon, & Kiger, 2007). In addition, men's satisfaction with their performance of status enhancement in support of their partner's career (e.g., making sure one's partner has enough time for work commitments and building goodwill with a partner's colleagues) was associated with decreased negative family-to-work spillover.

Concluding Comments and Future Directions

Many people – especially women – derive satisfaction from doing housework because these activities symbolize love and care for family members (DeVault, 1991). At the same time, because housework continues to be relegated to wives and daughters, it is typically analyzed as part of a larger system of gender inequality (Coltrane & Adams, 2008). Although some tasks are enjoyable, most people do not like routine housework, and, when financially able, most hire others to do some of the work. Because many hired domestic workers are poor women of color, this system perpetuates class and race inequalities and socializes privileged children to expect to be waited on by disadvantaged women (Glenn, Chang, & Forcey, 1994). In studying the division of labor, researchers have an opportunity to document how these interlocking systems of gender, class, and race inequalities play out in people's everyday lives.

As evident from the above review of literature, the field of household labor research is now a relatively mature area of study that has attracted substantial scholarly attention, and many recent advances in the field have been informed by relying on theories of gender and inequality. Several theories have been advanced to explain how and why housework gets divided and how it affects men, women, children, and society at large. Empirical research has contributed to our understanding of who does what inside households, but this research has not been able to adjudicate fully among competing theories, and much work remains to be done. We still know relatively little about the division of household labor in racial/ethnic families, gay/lesbian families, immigrant families, and in countries outside of the USA, Europe, and other developed nations.

New sources of multinational time use diary data are now available for making comparisons across countries and across time, which will allow researchers to answer more complicated questions about how people use time and how different social and political conditions are associated with different divisions of labor. The Multinational Time Use Survey (MTUS) is a collection of harmonized time use diary surveys based on nationally representative samples from over 20 countries from the early 1960s to 2000 and beyond.[1] The MTUS diary surveys of many European countries around the year 2000 are part of the Harmonized European Time Use Study (HETUS) – a project coordinated by EUROSTAT with the aim of creating comparable and standardized time use statistics across European countries.[2] In addition, the American Heritage Time Use Study (AHTUS) puts together major national samples of time diary-based studies in the USA since the 1960s with the purpose of creating historically comparable time use statistics.[3] These data sets can be used to track change over time in specific countries and to compare the pace or scale of change across countries, and, when combined with data on economic conditions, social indicators, and government policies, they may provide the basis for predicting or influencing such change (Sullivan, Coltrane, McAnnally, & Altintas, 2009).

There are other related areas of research (e.g., paid domestic labor practices and experiences, work and family policy formation and implementation, cultural conceptions of housework) that could not be included in this review because of space limitations but are nonetheless important. We expect that analyses of such topics will increase as the sorts of data described above become available and as the organization of paid and unpaid work continues to change. We hope that this review reveals some of the important questions that have been raised and, more important, shows that more research questions can be asked about how gender and household labor are related. We trust that the next generation of household labor researchers will address such questions and help us to understand better the relation between gender and the organization of everyday life.

---

[1] The MTUS is available from the Centre for Time Use Research, University of Oxford. For more information access http://www.timeuse.org/.

[2] More information on HETUS is available at https://www.testh2.scb.se/tus/tus/.

[3] The AHTUS is available from the Centre for Time Use Research, University of Oxford. For more information access http://www.timeuse.org/.

References

Adams, M., Coltrane, S., & Parke, R. D. (2007). Cross-ethnic applicability of the gender-based attitudes toward marriage and child rearing scales. *Sex Roles, 56*, 325–339.

Almeida, D., Maggs, J., & Galambos, N. (1993). Wives' employment hours and spousal participation in family work. *Journal of Family Psychology, 7*, 233–244.

Altschuler, J. (2004). Meaning of housework and other unpaid responsibilities among older women. *Journal of Women & Aging, 16*, 143–159.

Arrighi, B., & Maume, D. (2000). Workplace subordination and men's avoidance of housework. *Journal of Family Issues, 21*, 464–487.

Artis, J. E., & Pavalko, E. K. (2003). Explaining the decline in women's household labor: Individual change and cohort differences. *Journal of Marriage and Family, 65*, 746–761.

Barnett, R., & Shen, Y.-C. (1997). Gender, high- and low-schedule-control housework tasks, and psychological distress: A study of dual-earner couples. *Journal of Family Issues, 18*, 403–428.

Bartley, S., Blanton, P., & Gillard, J. (2005). Husbands and wives in dual-earner marriages: Decision-making, gender role attitudes, division of household labor, and equity. *Marriage and Family Review, 37*, 69–94.

Batalova, J., & Cohen, P. (2002). Premarital cohabitation and housework: Couples in cross-national perspective. *Journal of Marriage and Family, 64*, 743–755.

Becker, G. (1981). *A treatise on the family.* Cambridge, MA: Harvard University Press.

Bergen, E. (1991). The economic context of labor allocation: Implications for gender stratification. *Journal of Family Issues, 12*, 140–157.

Berk, S. F. (1985). *The gender factory: The apportionment of work in American households.* New York: Plenum.

Bianchi, S. M., Milkie, M. A., Sayer, L. C., & Robinson, J. P. (2000). Is anyone doing the housework? Trends in the gender division of household labor. *Social Forces, 79*, 191–228.

Bianchi, S. M., Robinson, J. P., & Milkie, M. A. (2006). *Changing rhythms of American family life.* New York: Russell Sage.

Bird, C. E. (1999). Gender, household labor, and psychological distress: The impact of the amount and division of housework. *Journal of Health and Social Behavior, 40*, 32–45.

Bittman, M., England, P., Sayer, L., Folbre, N., & Matheson, G. (2003). When does gender trump money? Bargaining and time in household work. *American Journal of Sociology, 109*, 186–214.

Blair, S. L. (1993). Employment, family, and perceptions of marital quality among husbands and wives. *Journal of Family Issues, 14*, 178–203.

Blair, S. L., & Lichter, D. (1991). Measuring the division of household labor: Gender segregation of housework among American couples. *Journal of Family Issues, 12*, 91–113.

Blaisure, K., & Allen, K. (1995). Feminists and the ideology and practice of marital equality. *Journal of Marriage and the Family, 57*, 5–19.

Blood, R., & Wolfe, D. (1960). *Husbands and wives.* New York: Free Press.

Blumberg, R., & Coleman, M. (1989). A theoretical look at the balance of power in the American couple. *Journal of Family Issues, 10*, 225–250.

Blumstein, P., & Schwartz, P. (1983). *American couples: Money, work, sex.* New York: Morrow.

Bond, J. T., Galinsky, E., & Swanberg, J. E. (1998). *The 1997 national study of the changing workforce.* New York: Families and Work Institute.

Brayfield, A. (1992). Employment resources and housework in Canada. *Journal of Marriage and the Family, 54*, 19–30.

Brines, J. (1993). The exchange value of housework. *Rationality and Society, 5*, 302–340.

Brines, J. (1994). Economic dependency, gender, and the division of labor at home. *American Journal of Sociology, 100*, 652–688.

Broman, C. (1988). Household work and family life satisfaction of Blacks. *Journal of Marriage and the Family, 50*, 743–748.

Broman, C. (1993). Race differences in marital well-being. *Journal of Marriage and the Family, 55*, 724–732.

Carrington, C. (1999). *No place like home: Relationships and family life among lesbians and gay men.* Chicago: University of Chicago Press.

Chan, R. W., Brooks, R. C., Raboy, B., & Patterson, C. J. (1998). Division of labor among lesbian and heterosexual parents: Associations with children's adjustment. *Journal of Family Psychology, 12*, 402–419.

Chen, H. S. (1992). *Chinatown no more: Taiwan immigrants in contemporary New York.* Ithaca, NY: Cornell University Press.

Cohen, P. (1998). Replacing housework in the service economy: Gender, class, and race-ethnicity in service spending. *Gender & Society, 12*, 219–231.

Coltrane, S. (1989). Household labor and the routine production of gender. *Social Problems, 36*, 473–490.

Coltrane, S. (1996). *Family man: Fatherhood, housework, and gender equity*. New York: Oxford University Press.

Coltrane, S. (2000). Research on household labor: Modeling and measuring the social embeddedness of routine family work. *Journal of Marriage and the Family, 62*, 1208–1233.

Coltrane, S., & Adams, M. (2008). *Gender and families*. Lanham, MD: Rowman & Littlefield.

Coltrane, S., & Ishii-Kuntz, M. (1992). Men's housework: A life-course perspective. *Journal of Marriage and the Family, 54*, 43–57.

Coltrane, S., & Valdez, E. (1993). Reluctant compliance: Work/family role allocation in dual-earner Chicano families. In J. Hood (Ed.), *Men, work, and family* (pp. 151–175). Thousand Oaks, CA: Sage.

Cooke, L. P. (2006). "Doing" gender in context: Household bargaining and risk of divorce in Germany and the United States. *American Journal of Sociology, 112*, 442–72.

Coverman, S. (1985). Explaining husbands' participation in domestic labor. *Sociological Quarterly, 26*, 81–97.

Crompton, R., & Harris, F. (1999). Attitudes, women's employment and the changing domestic division of labour. In R. Crompton (Ed.), *Restructuring gender relations and employment* (pp. 279–315). Oxford: Oxford University Press.

Crouter, A. C. (1984). Spillover from family to work: The neglected side of the work-family interface. *Human Relations, 37*, 425–442.

Cunningham, M. (2005). Gender in cohabitation and marriage: The influence of gender ideology on housework allocation over the life course. *Journal of Family Issues, 26*, 1037–1061.

Cunningham, M. (2007). Influences of women's employment on the gendered division of household labor over the life course: Evidence from a 31-year panel study. *Journal of Family Issues, 28*, 422–444.

Dance, L., & Gilbert, L. (1993). Spouses' family work participation and its relation to wives' occupational level. *Sex Roles, 28*, 127–145.

Davis, S. N., & Greenstein, T. N. (2004). Cross-national variations in the division of household labor. *Journal of Marriage and Family, 66*, 1260–1271.

Davis, S. N., Greenstein, T. N., & Marks, J. P. G. (2007). Effects of union type on division of household labor: Do cohabiting men really perform more housework? *Journal of Family Issues, 28*, 1246–1272.

DeMaris, A., & Longmore, M. A. (1996). Ideology, power, and equity: Testing competing explanations for the perception of fairness in household labor. *Social Forces, 74*, 1043–1071.

DeMeis, D., & Perkins, H. (1996). "Supermoms" of the nineties: Homemaker and employed mothers' performance and perceptions of the motherhood role. *Journal of Family Issues, 17*, 776–792.

Demo, D., & Acock, A. (1993). Family diversity and the division of domestic labor: How much have things really changed? *Family Relations, 42*, 323–331.

DeVault, M. (1991). *Feeding the family: The social organization of caring as gendered work*. Chicago: University of Chicago Press.

Dillaway, H., & Broman, C. (2001). Race, class, and gender differences in marital satisfaction and divisions of household labor among dual-earner couples: A case for intersectional analysis. *Journal of Family Issues, 22*, 309–327.

Dilworth, J. E. (2004). Predictors of negative spillover from family to work. *Journal of Family Issues, 25*, 241–261.

Eagle, B., Miles, E., & Icenogle, M. (1997). Interrole conflicts and the permeability of work and family domains: Are there gender differences? *Journal of Vocational Behavior, 50*, 168–184.

England, P., & Farkas, G. (1986). *Households, employment, and gender: A social, economic, and demographic view*. New York: Aldine.

Erickson, R. (1993). Reconceptualizing family work: The effect of emotion work on perceptions of marital quality. *Journal of Marriage and the Family, 55*, 888–900.

Espiritu, Y. L. (1999). Gender and labor in Asian immigrant families. *American Behavioral Scientist, 42*, 628–647.

Ferree, M. M. (1990). Beyond separate spheres: Feminism and family research. *Journal of Marriage and the Family, 52*, 866–884.

Ferree, M. M. (1991). The gender division of labor in two-earner marriages: Dimensions of variability and change. *Journal of Family Issues, 12*, 158–180.

Fisher, K., Egerton, M., Gershuny, J. I., & Robinson, J. P. (2006). *Gender convergence in the American Heritage Time Use Study (AHTUS)*. Social Indicators Research. DOI 10.1007/s11205-006-9017-y.

Frisco, M. L., & Williams, K. (2003). Perceived housework equity, marital happiness, and divorce in dual-earner households. *Journal of Family Issues, 24*, 51–73.

Gager, C. T., & Hohmann-Marriott, B. (2006). Distributive justice in the household: A comparison of alternative theoretical models. *Marriage and Family Review, 40*, 5–42.

Gershuny, J., & Robinson, J. (1988). Historical changes in the household division of labor. *Demography, 25*, 537–552.

Gerson, K. (1993). *No man's land: Men's changing commitment to family and work.* New York: Basic Books.

Gjerdingen, D. K., & Center, B. A. (2005). First-time parents' postpartum changes in employment, childcare, and housework responsibilities. *Social Science Research, 34*, 103–116.

Glass, J., & Fujimoto, T. (1994). Housework, paid work, and depression among husbands and wives. *Journal of Health and Social Behavior, 35*, 179–191.

Glenn, E. N., Chang, G., & Forcey, L. R. (Eds.). (1994). *Mothering: Ideology, experience, and agency.* New York: Routledge.

Goldberg, A., & Perry-Jenkins, M. (2007). The division of labor and perceptions of parental roles: Lesbian couples across the transition to parenthood. *Journal of Social and Personal Relationships, 24*, 297–318.

Golding, J. (1990). Division of household labor, strain, and depressive symptoms among Mexican Americans and Non-Hispanic Whites. *Psychology of Women Quarterly, 14*, 103–117.

Greenstein, T. N. (1996). Husbands' participation in domestic labor: Interactive effects of wives' and husbands' gender ideologies. *Journal of Marriage and the Family, 58*, 585–595.

Greenstein, T. N. (2000). Economic dependence, gender, and the division of labor in the home: A replication and extension. *Journal of Marriage and Family, 62*, 322–335.

Grote, N. K., Clark, M. S., & Moore, A. (2004). Perceptions of injustice in family work: The role of psychological distress. *Journal of Family Psychology, 18*, 480–492.

Grote, N. K., Naylor, K. E., & Clark, M. S. (2002). Perceiving the division of family work to be fair: Do social comparisons, enjoyment, and competence matter? *Journal of Family Psychology, 16*, 510–522.

Grzywacz, J. G., & Marks, N. F. (2000). Family-work, work-family spillover, and problem drinking during midlife. *Journal of Marriage and the Family, 62*, 336–348.

Gupta, S. (1999). The effects of marital status transitions on men's housework performance. *Journal of Marriage and the Family, 61*, 700–711.

Gupta, S. (2006). Her money, her time: Women's earnings and their housework hours. *Social Science Research, 35*, 975–999.

Gupta, S. (2007). Autonomy, dependency, or display? The relationship between married women's earnings and housework. *Journal of Marriage and Family, 69*, 399–417.

Herrera, R., & del Campo, R. (1995). Beyond the superwoman syndrome: Work satisfaction and family functioning among working-class, Mexican American women. *Hispanic Journal of Behavioral Sciences, 17*, 49–60.

Higgins, C. A., & Duxbury, L. E. (1992). Work-family conflict: A comparison of dual-career and traditional-career men. *Journal of Organizational Behavior, 13*, 389–411.

Hiller, D. (1984). Power dependence and division of family work. *Sex Roles, 10*, 1003–1019.

Himsel, A. J., & Goldberg, W. A. (2003). Social comparisons and satisfaction with the division of housework: Implications for men's and women's role strain. *Journal of Family Issues, 24*, 843–866.

Hochschild, A. R. [with Machung, A.]. (2003). *The second shift* (2nd ed.). New York: Avon.

Hohmann-Marriott, B. E. (2006). Shared beliefs and union stability of married and cohabiting couples. *Journal of Marriage and Family, 68*, 1015–1028.

Hossain, Z., & Roopnarine, J. (1993). Division of household labor and child care in dual-earner African-American families with infants. *Sex Roles, 29*, 571–583.

Jacobs, J., & Gerson, K. (2004). *The time divide: Work, family and gender inequality.* Cambridge, MA: Harvard University Press.

John, D., & Shelton, B. (1997). The production of gender among Black and White women and men. *Sex Roles, 36*, 171–193.

Johnson, S., & O'Connor, E. (2002). *The gay baby boom: The psychology of gay parenthood.* New York: New York University Press.

Kamo, Y., & Cohen, E. L. (1998). Division of household work between partners: A comparison of Black and White couples. *Journal of Comparative Family Studies, 29*, 131–146.

Kanter, R. M. (1977). *Work and family in the United States: A critical review and agenda for research and policy.* New York: Russell Sage Foundation.

Keene, J. R., & Reynolds, J. R. (2005). The job costs of family demands: Gender differences in negative family-to-work spillover. *Journal of Family Issues, 26*, 275–299.

Kluwer, E., Heesink, J., & Van de Vliert, E. (1997). The marital dynamics of conflict over the division of labor. *Journal of Marriage and the Family, 59*, 635–653.

Kurdek, L. (1993). The allocation of household labor in gay, lesbian, and heterosexual married couples. *Journal of Social Issues, 49*, 127–139.

Kurdek, L. A. (2007). The allocation of household labor by partners in gay and lesbian couples. *Journal of Family Issues, 28*, 132–148.

Lennon, M., & Rosenfeld, S. (1994). Relative fairness and the division of housework: The importance of options. *American Journal of Sociology, 100*, 506–531.

Lorber, J. (1994). *Paradoxes of gender.* New Haven, CT: Yale University Press.

Lye, D., & Biblarz, T. (1993). The effects of attitudes toward family life and gender roles on marital satisfaction. *Journal of Family Issues, 14*, 157–188.

MacDermid, S., Huston, T., & McHale, S. (1990). Changes in marriage associated with the transition to parenthood: Individual differences as a function of sex-role attitudes and changes in the division of household labor. *Journal of Marriage and the Family, 52*, 475–486.

McHale, S., & Crouter, A. (1992). You can't always get what you want – incongruence between sex-role attitudes and family work roles and its implications for marriage. *Journal of Marriage and the Family, 54*, 537–547.

McPherson, D. (1994). *Gay parenting couples: Parenting arrangements, arrangement satisfaction, and relationship satisfaction.* Unpublished doctoral dissertation, Pacific University Graduate School of Psychology.

Meier, J., McNaughton-Cassill, M., & Lynch, M. (2006). The management of household and childcare tasks and relationship satisfaction in dual-earner families. *Marriage and Family Review, 40*, 61–88.

Mirande, A. (1997). *Hombres et machos: Masculinity and Latino culture.* Boulder, CO: Westview.

Moen, P. (1985). Continuities and discontinuities in women's labor force activity. In J. G. H. Elder (Ed.), *Life course dynamics: Trajectories and transitions, 1968–1980* (pp. 113–155). Ithaca, NY: Cornell University Press.

Moen, P., & Coltrane, S. (2004). Families, theories, and social policy. In V. Bengtson, D. Klein, A. Acock, K. Allen, & P. Dilworth-Anderson (Eds.), *Sourcebook of family theory and research* (pp. 534–556). Thousand Oaks, CA: Sage.

Nock, S. (1998). *Marriage in men's lives.* New York: Oxford University Press.

Orbuch, T., & Custer, L. (1995). The social context of married women's work and its impact on Black husbands and White husbands. *Journal of Marriage and the Family, 57*, 333–345.

Orbuch, T., & Eyster, S. (1997). Division of household labor among Black couples and White couples. *Social Forces, 76*, 301–332.

Parsons, T., & Bales, R. (1955). *Family: Socialization and interaction process.* New York: Free Press.

Patterson, C. (2000). Family relationships of lesbians and gay men. *Journal of Marriage and the Family, 62*, 1052–1969.

Patterson, C., Sutfin, E., & Fulcher, M. (2004). Division of labor among lesbian and heterosexual parenting couples: Correlates of specialized versus shared patterns. *Journal of Adult Development, 11*, 179–189.

Peplau, L., & Spalding, L. (2000). The close relationship of lesbians, gay men, and bisexuals. In C. Hendrick & S. Hendrick (Eds.), *Close relationships: A sourcebook* (pp. 111–124). Thousand Oaks, CA: Sage.

Perkins, H., & DeMeis, D. (1996). Gender and family effects on the second-shift domestic activity of college-educated young adult. *Gender & Society, 10*, 78–93.

Perry-Jenkins, M., & Crouter, A. (1990). Men's provider-role attitudes: Implications for household work and marital satisfaction. *Journal of Family Issues, 11*, 136–156.

Pestello, F., & Voydanoff, P. (1991). In search of mesostructure in the family: An interactionist approach to division of labor. *Symbolic Interaction, 14*, 105–128.

Pina, D., & Bengtson, V. (1993). The division of household labor and wives' happiness – Ideology, employment, and perceptions of support. *Journal of Marriage and the Family, 55*, 901–912.

Pinto, K., & Coltrane, S. (2009). Divisions of labor in Mexican origin and Anglo families: Structure and culture. *Sex Roles, 60*, 482–495.

Pleck, J. H. (1977). The work-family role system. *Social Problems, 24*, 417–427.

Potuchek, J. (1992). Employed wives' orientations to breadwinning: A gender theory analysis. *Journal of Marriage and the Family, 54*, 548–558.

Presser, H. B. (1989). Can we make time for children? *Demography, 26*, 523–554.

Presser, H. B. (1994). Employment schedules among dual-earner spouses and the division of household labor by gender. *American Sociological Review, 59*, 348–364.

Pyke, K. (1994). Women's employment as a gift or burden? Marital power across marriage, divorce, and remarriage. *Gender & Society, 8*, 73–91

Pyke, K. (2004). Immigrant families in the U.S. In J. L. Scott, J. Treas, & M. P. Richards (Eds.), *The Blackwell companion to the sociology of the family* (pp. 253–269). New York: Blackwell.

Robinson, J., & Godbey, G. (1999). *Time for life* (2nd ed.). State College, PA: Pennsylvania State University Press.

Robinson, J. P., & Milkie, M. A. (1998). Back to the basics: Trends in and role determinants of women's attitudes toward housework. *Journal of Marriage and the Family, 60*, 205–218.

Robinson, J., & Spitze, G. (1992). Whistle while you work? The effect of household task performance on women's and men's well-being. *Social Science Quarterly, 73*, 844–861.

Sanchez, L. (1993). Women's power and the gendered division of domestic labor in the third world. *Gender & Society, 7*, 434–459.

Sanchez, L., & Thomson, E. (1997). Becoming mothers and fathers: Parenthood, gender, and the division of labor. *Gender & Society, 11*, 747–772.

Shelton, B. (1990). The distribution of household tasks: Does wife's employment status make a difference? *Journal of Family Issues, 11*, 115–135.

Shelton, B. (1992). *Women, men, and time: Gender differences in paid work, housework, and leisure.* Westport, CT: Greenwood.

Shelton, B., & John, D. (1993a). Does marital status make a difference? Housework among married and cohabiting men and women. *Journal of Family Issues, 14*, 401–420.

Shelton, B., & John, D. (1993b). Ethnicity, race, and difference: A comparison of White, Black, and Hispanic men's household labor time. In J. Hood (Ed.), *Men, work, and family* (pp. 131–150). Thousand Oaks, CA: Sage.

Shelton, B., & John, D. (1996). The division of household labor. *Annual Review of Sociology, 22*, 299–322.

Solomon, C. R., Acock, A. C., & Walker, A. J. (2004). Gender ideology and investment in housework: Postretirement change. *Journal of Family Issues, 25*, 1050–1071.

Solomon, S. E., Rothblum, E. D., & Balsam, K. F. (2005). Money, housework, sex, and conflict: Same-sex couples in civil unions, those not in civil unions, and heterosexual married siblings. *Sex Roles, 52*, 561–575.

South, S., & Spitze, G. (1994). Housework in marital and nonmarital households. *American Sociological Review, 59*, 327–347.

Stevens, D., Kiger, G., & Mannon, S. (2005). Domestic labor and marital satisfaction: How much or how satisfied? *Marriage and Family Review, 37*, 49–67.

Stevens, D. P., Minnotte, K. L., & Kiger, G. (2004). Differences in work-to-family and family-to-work spillover among professional and nonprofessional workers. *Sociological Spectrum, 24*, 535–551.

Stevens, D. P., Minnotte, K. L., Mannon, S. E., & Kiger, G. (2007). Examining the "neglected side of the work-family interface": Antecedents of positive and negative family-to-work spillover. *Journal of Family Issues, 28*, 242–262.

Suitor, J. (1991). Marital quality and satisfaction with the division of household labor across the family life cycle. *Journal of Marriage and the Family, 53*, 221–230.

Sullivan, M. (1996). Rozzie and Harriet? Gender and family patterns of lesbian coparents. *Gender & Society, 10*, 747–767.

Sullivan, O. (1997). The division of housework among "remarried" couples. *Journal of Family Issues, 18*, 205–223.

Sullivan, O. (2006). *Changing gender relations, changing families: Tracing the pace of change over time.* Lanham, MD: Rowman & Littlefield.

Sullivan, O., Coltrane, S., McAnnally, L., & Altintas, E. (2009). Father-friendly policies and time use data in a cross-national context: Potential and prospects for future research. *Annals of the American Academy of Political and Social Science, 624*, 234–257.

Sullivan, O., & Gershuny, J. (2001). Cross-national changes in time-use: Some sociological (hi)stories re-examined. *British Journal of Sociology, 52*, 331–347.

Szinovacz, M. (2000). Changes in housework after retirement: A panel study. *Journal of Marriage and Family, 62*, 78–92.

Thompson, L., & Walker, A. (1989). Gender in families: Women and men in marriage, work, and parenthood. *Journal of Marriage and the Family, 51*, 845–871.

Tichenor, V. (2005). Maintaining men's dominance: Negotiating identity and power when she earns more. *Sex Roles, 53*, 191–205.

Toro-Morn, M. (1995). Gender, class, family, and migration: Puerto Rican women in Chicago. *Gender & Society, 9*, 712–726

Townsend, N. W. (2002). *The package deal: Marriage, work, and fatherhood in men's lives.* Philadelphia: Temple University Press.

U.S. Census Bureau. (2005). *Income, earnings, and poverty from the 2004 American Community Survey* (American Community Survey Reports, ACS-01). Washington DC: U.S. Census Bureau.

Utz, R. L., Reidy, E. B., Carr, D., Nesse, R., & Wortman, C. (2004). The daily consequences of widowhood: The role of gender and intergenerational transfers of subsequent housework performance. *Journal of Family Issues, 25*, 683–712.

Van Willigen, M., & Drentea, P. (2001). Benefits of equitable relationships: The impact of sense of fairness, household division of labor, and decision making power on perceived social support. *Sex Roles, 44,* 571–597.
Ward, R. (1993). Marital happiness and household equity in later life. *Journal of Marriage and the Family, 55,* 427–438.
West, C., & Fenstermaker, S. (1993). Power and the accomplishment of gender. In P. England (Ed.), *Theory on gender: Feminism on theory* (pp. 151–174). New York: Aldine deGruyter.
West, C., & Zimmerman, D. (1987). Doing gender. *Gender & Society, 1,* 121–151.
Wilkie, J., Ferree, M., & Ratcliff, K. (1998). Gender and fairness: Marital satisfaction in two-earner couples. *Journal of Marriage and the Family, 60,* 577–594.
Williams, J. (2000). *Unbending gender: Why family and work conflict and what to do about it.* Oxford: Oxford University Press.

Chapter 18
The Gendered Nature of Workplace Mistreatment

Vicki J. Magley, Jessica A. Gallus, and Jennifer A. Bunk

There is a fairly vast literature on workplace violence and aggression; two entire books recently were published on the topic (Griffin & O'Leary-Kelly, 2004; Kelloway, Barling, & Hurrell, 2006). A gap exists, however, in the analysis of the gendered nature of such experiences. Although empirical and theoretical accounts have appeared here and there, an overview of this scattered work is due. Hence, our goal for the present chapter is to provide a summary of the research and thinking on ways in which workplace violence and aggression are gendered phenomena.

Why is a gendered lens on this issue of value? Although workplace aggression and violence are important to organizations due to its negative impact on employee well-being (and, ostensibly, on overall productivity), it does not affect men and women equally. A recent meta-analysis of 57 studies showed that men were more likely than women to be aggressive at work (Hershcovis et al., 2007). Further, in a study of attorneys practicing in US federal courts, nearly 75% of female attorneys, but only 50% of male attorneys, reported having experienced some intermix of incivility and sexual harassment in the previous 5 years (Cortina et al., 2002). Why are there such stable and significant differences? Readers of this volume might not even consider such a question necessary, and we certainly do not want to "preach to the choir" and provide what might seem like an endless list of statistics and theories. But, for those who perhaps are first-time consumers of this literature, we offer the following summary.

Conceptual Space of Workplace Mistreatment

Before we go any further, we want to be sure that we are clear in what we mean by "workplace mistreatment." There are several conceptually overlapping forms of workplace mistreatment, and it is important to understand the similarities and differences among them before we discuss issues of gender more specifically. Types of workplace mistreatment abound in the literature, including incivility (e.g., Andersson & Pearson, 1999), deviance (e.g., Bennett & Robinson, 2000), aggression (e.g., Neuman & Baron, 1997), bullying (e.g., Rayner & Hoel, 1997), and sexual harassment (e.g., Fitzgerald, Gelfand, & Drasgow, 1995).

Andersson and Pearson (1999) developed a framework specifically for the purposes of differentiating and defining workplace incivility, but it is also useful for making sense of some of the several classes of mistreatment. In an overlapping Ven diagram, they fit several kinds of mistreatment into the larger conceptual areas of antisocial and deviant behaviors. Robinson and Bennett

V.J. Magley (✉)
University of Connecticut, Storrs-Mansfield, CT, USA

(1995) defined organizational deviance as behaviors that "violate significant organizational norms" (p. 556). Thus, the common thread among several forms of mistreatment is that they are antisocial and, thus, have the capability of harming an organization and/or its members, and they violate workplace norms.

Andersson and Pearson (1999) further differentiated among aggression, violence, and incivility. According to their framework, violence is a specific form of aggression because it is a high-intensity, physically aggressive behavior with intent to harm the target, in contrast to incivility, which is a *low*-intensity deviant behavior with *ambiguous* intent. Thus, some acts of incivility may be deliberately aggressive; for example, a worker might deliberately make a rude comment to a coworker. Other incivility acts, however, are not meant to harm the target. For example, a worker might not notice a colleague's greeting and that colleague may take it as a personal slight.

There are other forms of workplace mistreatment mentioned in the literature that are not included in Andersson and Pearson's (1999) diagram but fit into this framework as well. For example, one particular form of workplace mistreatment that has received increased attention is workplace bullying. It is one of the only forms of workplace mistreatment, besides sexual harassment, to receive attention in legal circles (e.g., Tuna, 2008). The study of workplace bullying began in Scandinavia (e.g., Einarsen & Skogstad, 1996; Leymann, 1990) and soon spread to other European countries (e.g., Lee, 2000; Quine, 2001; Rayner & Hoel, 1997). It has been defined as a kind of aggressive behavior that occurs at least once per week for at least 6 months and involves either a structural or an interpersonal power imbalance between the target and the instigator(s) (e.g., Einarsen, 1999; Einarsen, Hoel, Zapf, & Cooper, 2003). Rayner and Hoel (1997) defined five categories of bullying that include threat to professional status, threat to personal standing, isolation, overwork, and destabilization. Given that bullying occurs with the intent to harm the target, it can be considered a pervasive form of aggression that overlaps somewhat with incivility.

Sexual harassment is another form of workplace mistreatment that has been discussed in gendered ways. The psychological definition of sexual harassment (i.e., unwanted sex-related behavior at work that is appraised by the recipient as offensive or threatening; Fitzgerald, Swan, & Magley, 1997) has traditionally included three types of harassment: gender harassment, unwanted sexual attention, and sexual coercion (Fitzgerald et al., 1995; Fitzgerald, Shullman, Bailey, & Richards, 1988). Gender harassment consists of any behaviors that convey misogynist or homophobic attitudes. Unwanted sexual attention, as the name implies, is any kind of sexual attention that is unwanted and unreciprocated. These first two kinds of sexual harassment are what would fall under the legal definition of a *hostile working environment*. The last type of harassment, sexual coercion, mirrors the legal term *quid pro quo*, which involves attempts to make job rewards contingent on sexual cooperation.

Sexual harassment is, thus, another form of antisocial, deviant workplace behavior that can be relatively high in intensity, and the intent to harm the target is present. What differentiates it from other forms of high-intensity, calculated forms of mistreatment (e.g., aggression) is that it is sexualized in nature – either by subtly demeaning members of a certain sex (or sexual orientation) or by more blatantly using sexual attention in an inappropriate and/or intimidating manner.

In sum, the number of possible constructs in the larger workplace aggression and violence literature exceeds what we can possibly manage within a single chapter. Hence, given the legal importance of sexual harassment and workplace bullying, as well as our own specializations in sexual harassment and incivility, we focus our chapter on these three constructs. As we are able, and as appropriate, we also include relevant research on the umbrella area of workplace aggression.

Chapter Overview

We begin our summary of the literature with a discussion of theories about the etiology of each of these forms of mistreatment, and we focus particularly on theories that emphasize, or are relevant to, gender. Note that complete descriptions of the origins of each of these theories appear elsewhere in the literature; for example, see Cortina and Berdahl (2008) on sexual harassment or either of the books (Griffin & O'Leary-Kelly, 2004; Kelloway et al., 2006) mentioned earlier for general aggression summaries. Next, we review the research findings on gender differences in incidence of workplace mistreatment, as this information certainly forms the basis for why the larger topic is relevant to gender studies. We then move on to the more psychological studies of the process by which these negative experiences impact targets. We consider how men and women appraise their experiences differently, as well as how they are differently affected. Although we raise questions for future research throughout the chapter, we conclude with a few more broad-brushed thoughts on the directions for this area of research.

Gendered Frameworks of the Antecedents of Workplace Mistreatment

Until psychologists and employers have an understanding of the causes of workplace mistreatment, they cannot even begin to intervene in any systematic or potentially successful manner. Hence, we begin with gendered frameworks for understanding the antecedents of workplace mistreatment. Given the complexity of the different types of mistreatment, we consider them one by one, beginning with sexual harassment.

Sexual Harassment

Although researchers have suggested a number of factors that lead to sexual harassment, one of the most frequently cited contributing factors is power – whether this is in the form of the status of the perpetrator or the desire to dominate the target (Cleveland & Kerst, 1993; Timmerman & Bajema, 2000; Wayne, 2000).[1] Recent research suggests that sexual harassment occurs as a means of protecting one's gender-related social status. Specifically, Berdahl (2007a, p. 641) argued that sexual harassment "derogates, demeans, or humiliates an individual based on that individual's sex" and that harassers engage in such behavior to protect their own sex-based social status. What exactly does this mean? Social status is derived in a number of ways, and one such way is through gender. Being part of one gender group or another can be an empowering or a disempowering experience simply because of the rewards or punishments that accompany being female or male. More men than women tend to reap the benefits associated with gender, as is obvious in any consideration of societal and organizational disparities (e.g., laws that punish women but not men for the same acts, unequal pay between the sexes, a greater number of men in leadership positions in organizations). To maintain this position of power associated with "maleness," some men will sexually harass women as a means of preventing women from infiltrating the dominant social position in society and, more specifically, at work. Women who

---

[1] Although there is a small body of research that documents harassment from less to more empowered individuals, known as contrapower harassment (e.g., DeSouza & Fansler, 2003; McKinney, 1990), we focus here on the more common occurrence of harassment that originates from someone with greater power.

challenge men by displaying traditionally masculine characteristics or by successfully navigating male-dominated cultures may be particularly susceptible to this hostile form of harassment (Berdahl, 2007a).

It is important to note that sexual desire is missing from discussions of sex-based harassment, and this omission is certainly purposeful. Harassment based on maintaining the existing gender hierarchy is thought to have little to do with sexual attraction and everything to do with dominance and power. Although the layperson's understanding of sexual harassment may include notions of love spurned or romantic requests unrequited, Berdahl (2007a, 2007b) noted that some forms of sexual expression at work may be benign and in some instances may be conducive to building positive relationships. It is certainly not uncommon to hear stories of spouses who first met on the job. Of course, the notion that certain sexual behaviors can be viewed by targets as flattering or welcome further complicates our understanding of why sexual harassment occurs and what constitutes sexual harassment from the perspective of the target (e.g., Magley, Hulin, Fitzgerald, & DeNardo, 1999). Greater understanding of this appraisal process is long overdue and is particularly relevant to a gender analysis of the ample literature that documents gender differences in perceptions of harassment severity (c.f., meta-analysis by Rotundo, Nguyen, & Sackett, 2001).

Incivility

Theoretical frameworks are noticeably absent from the incivility literature. However, an exception that is relevant here, as it incorporates gender, is Cortina's (2008) recent theory of selective incivility. In it, she suggested that, under certain circumstances, these subtly rude behaviors can be forms of rogue sexism (and/or racism). Based on the social psychological literature on modern discrimination, the main idea of this theory is that, because modern society does not accept and even punishes overt sexism, instigators who hold sexist beliefs may engage in *selective incivility* by mistreating the targets of their beliefs (e.g., a man with sexist attitudes toward women targets only women). Incivility is not overtly sexist in and of itself because these behaviors are simply rude and discourteous and not gendered in nature, but, because of the instigator's underlying beliefs and motives, selective incivility can be labeled covert sexism.

In her multi-level theory, Cortina (2008) discussed person-, organization-, and societal-level predictors of selective incivility. She also discussed the potential interaction between person and organization by suggesting that, for example, covert discrimination (under the guise of incivility) can occur when workers do not necessarily hold sexist beliefs but are members of an organization that seems to promote such beliefs. In an effort to preserve their own identity ("I'm not sexist") but to fit in with their workplace, such individuals may engage in selective incivility.

Cortina's (2008) selective incivility theory makes several important contributions in the understanding of how gender, race, and incivility intersect. First of all, simply exploring this intersection is a contribution by itself, as it is an oft-neglected area for incivility researchers. It also provides a framework for understanding why women, and particularly women of color, may be especially vulnerable to modern day discrimination. By taking a perpetrator's perspective, which is something that is not often done is this area of research, Cortina (2008) provided a mechanism for understanding *why* individuals might engage in incivility. The theory also suggests the idea that, even though it may be harder to pinpoint, discrimination does continue to exist in modern organizations, and selective incivility should be taken just as seriously as its less subtle counterparts (e.g., sexual harassment). Of course, from a practical standpoint, pinpointing selective incivility in organizations may be difficult because, to put it simply – how can we see something that, given its ambiguity, is hidden? However, the challenge of removing the mask of unseen injustice is a worthwhile endeavor.

Indeed, there are several challenges for researchers who want to study the relationship between gender and incivility. Future theoretical work should build upon selective incivility theory by answering such questions as the following: Are there other gendered motives, besides discrimination, for engaging in incivility? What about organizational power issues? Are there inherent gender differences that make the experience of incivility different for women and men? Clearly, the next-generation of incivility researchers have the potential to do quite interesting work with a gendered lens.

Buss' Framework of Aggression

Most research on workplace bullying and aggression concerns the antecedents that contribute to such behavior and the resulting outcomes. For example, Neuman and Baron (1998) proposed a three-part model that includes an extensive list of social (e.g., unfair treatment, norm violations), situational (e.g., electronic performance monitoring, downsizing), and individual (e.g., Type A personality, low self-monitoring) antecedents to aggression. In addition, Glomb (2002) examined antecedents (e.g., job-related stress, organizational injustice) and individual-level outcomes (e.g., job-related stress, need to "get away" from work environment). Although these models of aggression are certainly helpful, they tell us little about the role of gender in contributing to aggressive behavior.

More to the point, no formalized theoretical discussions of the gendered nature of other forms of workplace mistreatment (e.g., aggression, deviance, bullying) exist, despite empirical studies of whether men and women differ in their experiences of such behaviors, either as perpetrators or targets. Although we summarize this material later in the chapter, here we want to consider briefly how one typology of aggression – Buss' (1961) aggression framework – might be useful in understanding the role of gender in workplace mistreatment. Specifically, Buss proposed that aggression can be viewed in three dichotomies: active–passive, physical–verbal, and direct–indirect. Active aggression perpetrators inflict harm to the target through various actions such as criticizing, insulting, or threatening, whereas passive perpetrators are more likely to withhold information that is important to the target. Physical forms of aggression include assaulting the target, whereas verbal forms of aggression include yelling, swearing, and insults. Finally, direct forms of aggression are intended to harm the target directly, whereas indirect forms of aggression are intended to cause injury to something the target values (e.g., yelling at the target versus yelling at the target's child).

What does Buss' framework have to do with gender? Given the traditional social expectation for women to comply with social demands instead of expressing stereotypically masculine traits such as anger and aggression (Kopper & Epperson, 1996), it would not be surprising to find that women are more likely to engage in verbal, passive, and indirect forms of aggression, whereas men are more likely to engage in physical, direct, and active aggression. According to social role theory, physical, cultural, ecological, and socioeconomic contexts pressure women and men to behave in accordance with their designated roles in society (Eagly & Mitchell, 2004). Within patriarchal societies, men typically assume roles with greater status and power. Given this power, men may have an easier time engaging in aggressive behaviors without negative consequence to themselves (i.e., getting away with the aggressive behaviors) and may even be expected to engage in such behaviors. Further, societal expectations of men and women may explain why women who behave aggressively experience fear and anxiety regarding their actions (Douglas & Martinko, 2001).

More research is needed to illuminate how gender influences experiences and perpetration of workplace aggression. Not only would this aid in our understanding of perpetrators and targets, but it would also help to determine whether women and men engage in different types of aggression and, if so, what the outcomes of that aggression are.

Contextual Influences on Mistreatment

Although social roles and norms have been implicated in the above analysis of gender and workplace aggression, the workplace context in and of itself can certainly affect the incidence and experience of mistreatment. Specifically, one's workgroup may be a particularly influential part of the experience and/or the perpetration of mistreatment. Glomb (2002) found that angry feelings or experiences in workgroup settings escalated to more damaging aggression. As one member of a workgroup experiences mistreatment of some form, others are simultaneously exposed to the same behavior, even if it is not directed at them. These subtle experiences are known as *ambient stimuli*, or stimuli that are potentially available to all group members. The pervasive impact of a workgroup on individuals' attitudes and behaviors may be due to ambient stimuli such that workgroup members' actions act as cues to others about what will and will not be tolerated within the group (Hackman, 1992), which ultimately has the potential to perpetuate and/or escalate the mistreatment.

Similarly, George (1990) found that workgroups are often characterized by a particular affective tone or consistent affective reaction. For example, groups that are composed of individuals who tend to be enthusiastic and excited could be characterized as groups with a positive affective tone. In regard to mistreatment, if hostility, anger, harassment, and/or incivility are consistently present in individual members of a workgroup, the workgroup can be said to have a negative affective tone, which could inhibit positive and foster negative behaviors (George, 1990; Robinson & O'Leary-Kelly, 1998).

In addition to the influence of the workgroup, the larger organizational climate may impact targets' experiences of, and potential perpetration of, mistreatment. Considerable work has been done on the impact of organizations' climate on the incidence of sexual harassment. Specifically, sexual harassment is less prevalent within positive social climates and when women and men work in gender-equitable climates (Timmerman & Bajema, 2000). Furthermore, organizations that create climates that do not tolerate and clearly discourage harassment through rules, policies, and procedures have lower incidence of sexual harassment than other organizations do (Fitzgerald, Drasgow, Hulin, Gelfand, & Magley, 1997; Fitzgerald, Drasgow, & Magley, 1999; Williams, Fitzgerald, & Drasgow, 1999). Perceptions of an intolerant climate not only predict respondents' reports of their own sexual harassment experiences but also that of their workgroup members (Glomb et al., 1997), which provides reassurance that the results reviewed above are not simply response bias artifacts.

Although none of the above contextual factors explicitly incorporates gender, there are several studies that suggest that the context is experienced differently by men and women. Fitzgerald and colleagues (1999) found that organizational tolerance of sexual harassment is a somewhat stronger predictor of sexual harassment for women (path coefficient $= 0.39$) than for men (path coefficient $= 0.24$). Similarly, Bergman and Henning (2008) found that gender moderated the same perceived tolerance–sexual harassment relationship such that the relationship was considerably stronger for women (0.63) than for men (0.18). Further, recent research has shown that women who worked in a climate intolerant of sexual harassment but who, nonetheless, found themselves sexually harassed suffered from intensified negative work-related outcomes (e.g., lower job satisfaction and affective commitment, greater job withdrawal; Kath, Swody, Magley, Bunk, & Gallus, 2009).

Gendered Profiles of Targets and Perpetrators

There is more gender research in the area of incidence and perpetration of workplace mistreatment. It is to this literature that we now turn.

Incivility

Research on general, rude experiences in the workplace has shown that approximately 70% of respondents report experiences of incivility (Cortina, Magley, Williams, & Langhout, 2001). Women are more likely to be the recipients of incivility (Cortina et al., 2001), and men are more likely to be the perpetrators (e.g., Einarsen & Skogstad, 1996). In their groundbreaking study on incivility, Pearson, Andersson, and Porath (2000) found that men were twice as likely as women to be instigators. In addition, men were seven times more likely to perpetrate incivility when the target was of lower status, whereas women were just as likely to behave uncivilly to their superiors as they were to their subordinates (Pearson et al., 2000). This pattern demonstrates that women's perpetration of incivility may be based more on individual than contextual variables as such experiences do not seem to be linked to organizational power or status.

What can we make of the incongruence between the genders in terms of who behaves uncivilly? Does the greater perpetration of incivility by men suggest that they are by nature more rude? One possible explanation for this difference is that women are more likely to rate potentially uncivil experiences as offensive or rude (Berdahl & Moore, 2006; Lim, Cortina, & Magley, 2008). It is also possible that the higher incidence of perpetration by men reflects society's greater tolerance for men to treat others in a manner that is normally considered unacceptable. It is interesting that other preliminary research in this area suggests that men who work in an organizational climate that tolerates incivility are more likely than women to perpetrate it. Women's rudeness is more apt to be related to their own uncivil experiences, whereas men are more influenced by organizational norms for such behaviors (Gallus, Matthews, Bunk, Barnes-Farrell, & Magley, 2006).

Bullying

Research indicates that 4–5% of employees are targets of bullying and that the bullying lasts, on average, about 3 years (Rayner & Hoel, 1997). Unlike incivility, which may come from subordinates, peers, or managers, most targets of bullying report that the mistreatment comes from someone with greater organizational status – usually their direct manager or a senior manager in the company (Adams, 1997; Rayner, 1997). The gender of the perpetrators reflects the management structure of most organizations; the rate of female perpetrators is lower than that of male perpetrators, which may be due to the fact that women occupy fewer management positions than men do.

Results of research on targets of bullying and gender are mixed. A study of bullying in a university setting indicated that women reported having been targets more often than men did (Bjorkqvist, Osterman, & Hjelt-Back, 1994), yet it is unclear whether these results would translate to more traditional work settings. Other researchers have found that women and men experience similar incidence rates of bullying (Rayner & Hoel, 1997; Vartia & Hytti, 2002). Although this may be the case in most work settings, Hoel, Cooper, and Faragher (2001) found that gender impacts bullying dynamics at higher organizational levels. For instance, female senior managers were more than twice as likely as their male counterparts to experience bullying. The intensity of such experiences was also more severe for women, as 4.5% reported having been bullied on a regular basis, but none of the men did (Hoel et al., 2001).

One finding that is consistent across the bullying research is that men are more likely to be targeted by other men than by women (Lewis & Orford, 2005; Rayner & Hoel, 1997). Whether this is due to actual bullying rates or because of men's reluctance to label bullying from women as such remains to be seen. In addition, the prevalence of same-sex bullying of men (62.2%) is much higher than that of same-sex bullying of women (37.3%; Hoel et al., 2001).

Sexual Harassment

Given that, on average, men tend to have more power than do women in Western societies, it is no surprise that the majority of harassment occurs from men to women. This has been the most extensively studied type of what is referred to as "opposite-sex" sexual harassment (OSSH; Stockdale, Visio, & Batra, 1999). Estimates of men's sexual harassment of women in the workplace usually range from 40 to 80% (Firestone & Harris, 2003). This broad range may be explained by the greater incidence of sexual harassment in certain types of organizations, particularly those with definitive hierarchies and power differentials (e.g., the military; Ilies, Hauserman, Schwochau, & Stibal, 2003).

Significantly less is known about the other type of OSSH, that is, women's harassment of men, although researchers have offered a few explanations for such behavior. The first explanation mirrors Berdahl's (2007a) sex-based harassment theory and suggests that men who threaten women's sex-based status are more likely to be sexually harassed by women. This is certainly an unusual kind of sex-based harassment in that women generally have less social power than men do. It is possible that such harassment is more prevalent in female-dominated arenas, such as child care or nursing, in an attempt to keep men from progressing in areas where women are traditionally viewed as more competent. It is also possible that women's harassment of men is a form of approach-based harassment (Stockdale, Gandolfo-Berry, Schneider, & Cao, 2004) or harassment that consists of sexual advances or unwanted sexual attention. This is unlikely, though, as men seldom view the sexual advances of women as bothersome or harassing (Berdahl, 2007a; Berdahl, Magley, & Waldo, 1996). Despite these possibilities, the harassment of men by women warrants further empirical examination so that we can understand what motivates such behavior.

If sex-based harassment is intended to help one gender group maintain their status over another, how, then, do we explain same-sex sexual harassment (SSSH; Stockdale et al., 1999)? Although women are the traditional targets of sexual harassment, SSSH is more prevalent among men. In fact, a study of federal employees showed that nearly 21% of men's harassment was done by other men, whereas only 1–3% of women's harassment was done by other women (US Merit Systems Protection Board, 1981, 1995). Magley and colleagues (Magley, Waldo, Drasgow, & Fitzgerald, 1999) found similar results in a military sample: 52% of men's harassment was perpetrated by other men, but less than 2% of women's harassment was perpetrated by other women. At first glance, one might assume that the higher rate of SSSH for men is indicative of homosexuality. Although there is some debate as to the motivation behind such harassment, the great majority of research suggests that the sexual harassment of men by other men is a form of rejection-based harassment in which the perpetrator attempts to punish or humiliate the target (Magley, Waldo, et al., 1999; Stockdale et al., 2004; Waldo, Berdahl, & Fitzgerald, 1998). This is typically done as a means of "gender policing" or forcing the target to conform to stereotypical or exaggerated gender roles. In the case of man-to-man harassment, gender policing may be done to assure that men are maintaining hypermasculine standards, which have to do with antifemininity, dominance, and subordination of women (Stockdale et al., 1999; Stockdale et al., 2004). Enforcement of the heterosexual masculine gender role is a means some men use to maintain the superiority of men in general; men who are not considered "manly" or who exhibit characteristics associated with femininity (e.g., nurturing, passive, sensitive) are punished (Magley, Waldo, et al., 1999). The emphasis on the ultra-masculine in man-to-man harassment has led some researchers to refer to such behavior as "not man enough" harassment (Berdahl, 2007a).

The majority of sexual harassment research has been focused on the most prevalent type of harassment, that is, OSSH with the man as the perpetrator and the woman as the target. Although this is certainly understandable considering incidence rates, future researchers should continue to explore SSSH of both men and women. Special attention should be paid to women's SSSH, given that we know so little about this type of harassment. Given the low incidence rates of SSSH for women, being a target of such harassment may be a very isolating and detrimental experience. In addition, akin to the development of the SSSH construct for men, more work needs to be done in terms of defining what constitutes SSSH for women. Perhaps the existing constructs of sexual harassment experiences do not fully capture the type of harassment that occurs from woman to woman, which could give the false impression that the incidence rates of this type of harassment are very low.

Workplace Aggression/Violence

What do we know about the perpetrators of workplace violence and aggression? For one, men are more likely than women to engage in aggression, whether physical or psychological (e.g., Baron, Neuman, & Geddes, 1999; Rutter & Hine, 2005; for a meta-analysis, see Hershcovis et al., 2007). Men are also more likely than women to view aggression as acceptable behavior (Douglas & Martinko, 2001). In fact, men are more likely than women are to seek revenge, perhaps because gender norms make such behavior more socially acceptable for men (Douglas & Martinko, 2001). Although social role theory predicts these gender differences in perpetration of aggression, the same theoretical explanation is not supported for gender differences in the expression of anger. Specifically, some studies have shown that women are more likely than men to express anger and hostility, whereas other studies have found no differences (Kopper & Epperson, 1996).

What are the characteristics of the perpetrators of workplace violence and aggression? Researchers have found that trait anger, attitude toward revenge, and previous exposure to aggressive cultures contribute to workplace aggression (e.g., Aquino, Tripp, & Bies, 2001). Perpetrators are described as hot tempered and have been found to have a difficult time controlling their anger (Glomb, 2002). The perception that someone is threatening their self-esteem or position in the organization can also precipitate perpetration (Glomb, 2002). Past antisocial behavior and alcohol or drug abuse also contribute to violence and aggression at work (Elliott & Jarrett, 1994; Jockin, Arvey, & McGue, 2001; LeBlanc & Barling, 2004).

Although incidents of workplace violence and aggression appear, on the surface, to be gender blind in terms of victimization, there are still a number of factors that contribute to being targeted (Budd, Arvey, & Lawless, 1996). Individuals who work at night or in the early morning, work alone, or have jobs where they must protect valuable assets are more likely to be killed on the job, whereas supervisors and those who handle cash are more likely to be threatened but not physically attacked (Budd et al., 1996). As noted by LeBlanc and Barling (2004), the most extreme workplace aggression, or what the majority of people would consider workplace violence (e.g., homicide, physical assault), is perpetrated by outsiders. The US National Institute for Occupational Safety and Health (NIOSH) reported that homicide was the second leading cause of job-related deaths in the United States in 1993, and this was also the case in a study by the U.S. Bureau of Labor Statistics in 1995 (Schat & Kelloway, 2000).

Reactions to Workplace Mistreatment

It would not be a bold statement to claim that different people react differently to similar workplace mistreatment encounters. This idea is central to Lazarus and Folkman's (1984) cognitive appraisal theory, which suggests that, as we attempt to make meaning of the events that occur in our lives, cognitive appraisal is a key part of this meaning-making system. An appraisal is essentially an evaluation of an encounter. For example, when people experience workplace mistreatment, they may ask themselves: "Did this bother me? How much? Will this happen again? Was it my fault? Can I cope with this?" The answers to these questions will determine the individual's reactions, both proximal and distal, to this event. Cognitive appraisal theory thus serves as a very useful framework for exploring potential gender differences in reactivity to mistreatment.

Appraisal Processes

One form of appraisal identified by Lazarus and Folkman (1984) is primary appraisal. This is an evaluation of how much a particular encounter actually matters to one's well-being. Some encounters may be appraised as benign because the individual does not think the experience caused any harm. Other encounters may be appraised as stressful because they are harmful or threatening. In addition, for an encounter to be appraised as stressful, the individual needs to *notice* its potentially harmful aspects.

Research findings relevant to gender and the primary appraisal of mistreatment experiences suggest that women are more sensitive to their interpersonal environments than men are. For example, in what is now considered classic work in nonverbal communication, Hall (1987) demonstrated that women are better than men at noticing and reading nonverbal interpersonal cues. Thus, women may be more likely than men to notice subtle nonverbal cues that may indicate mistreatment, especially when the mistreatment is of low intensity and ambiguous, such as with incivility. Men may be less likely to *notice* subtle mistreatment when it is happening to them (and others), and, therefore, they may be less likely to appraise these kinds of situations as stressful. There is some empirical evidence to support this claim, as it has been found that women are more likely than men to assess mistreatment experiences as offensive and/or inappropriate (e.g., Hendrick, Hendrick, Slapion-Foote, & Foote, 1985; Konrad & Gutek, 1986; Montgomery, Kane, & Vance, 2004). We should be clear here – the message is not that women are "too sensitive" and/or "can't take the heat," but that, because they are more sensitive to their interpersonal environments, they may more readily notice and understand the subtleties that often constitute mistreatment.

Another explanation that is relevant to cognitive appraisal for why there may be gender differences in reactivity to mistreatment has to do with organizational power – and the fact that women often have relatively little of it. Tiedens, Ellsworth, and Mesquita (2000) have used social stereotypes to explain the effects that social hierarchies have on appraisals. Because of what they call "sentimental stereotypes," high-status workers are perceived more positively than low-status workers, and, consequently, low-status workers are more likely to be blamed for negative events. As mentioned above, part of cognitive appraisal involves asking questions about fault and coping potential. In a situation where a male supervisor mistreats a female subordinate, she may think that it was her fault ("I brought this on. I deserved it.") and/or she may believe, because of her lack of power, that she has few resources to cope with the mistreatment. Thus, we cannot ignore the powerful role that organizational status can play in shaping women's and men's appraisals of, and reactions to, workplace mistreatment.

Note that the operative word in the previous sentence is "can." In contrast to the substantial literature on research participants' perceptions of hypothetical mistreatment experiences (see Rotundo et al., 2001, for a meta-analysis of this research), there simply is very little research on targets' appraisals of their own experiences and how those appraisals might influence their responses and outcomes. Cortina and Magley (2009) recently examined overall appraisals of incivility, and they found that this form of mistreatment does trigger mildly negative appraisals, most notably annoyance and frustration. On the other hand, sexual harassment appraisals have been found to be more offensive and upsetting; Schneider, Swan, and Fitzgerald (1997) reported that over one-half of the women in their samples who had experienced sexual harassment labeled their experiences as such. Men, on the other hand, rated their sexual harassment experiences, on average, as "not at all" to "slightly upsetting" (Waldo et al., 1998). Unfortunately, there is no research to date that explicitly compares how men and women appraise workplace mistreatment; future research might benefit from such a comparison.

Coping Processes

Once workplace mistreatment is, indeed, noticed, targets determine whether and how to respond to the treatment. As Ben-Zur and Yagil (2005, p. 84) aptly stated, "a variety of coping strategies are used in dealing with aggressive behaviours in the workplace." Their brief review of coping with workplace mistreatment – including bullying, verbal aggression, and sexual harassment – demonstrates that employees use a full range of coping strategies to manage their experiences, including avoiding the perpetrator, requesting assistance either from organizational representatives or friends and family, and even quitting the job. Cortina and Magley (2009) found a similar range of coping responses to experiences of workplace incivility.

We strongly believe that it is important to emphasize that there is no "right" way to cope with experiences of mistreatment. Some individuals may feel more comfortable using active coping strategies, such as standing up to the perpetrator or seeking social support, whereas other targets may employ passive strategies, such as minimizing or denying the importance of their experiences. Despite the number of coping methods available to targets of mistreatment, organizations tend to favor (or at least purport to favor) assertive responses to mistreatment. Unfortunately, many of these organizations encourage such responses yet fail to take individual characteristics (e.g., comfort with being assertive) or organizational factors (e.g., perpetrator power, climate for mistreatment) into account (Bergman, Langhout, Palmieri, Cortina, & Fitzgerald, 2002). As Magley (2002, p. 944) noted, the "appropriate" response to mistreatment is often thought to be assertion, and targets who do not cope assertively are judged accordingly:

> One consequence of framing women's responses purely as a continuum of assertiveness is that responses other than assertiveness can be interpreted as weakness on the part of the recipient or evidence that she did not handle it properly.

Research from the general coping literature suggests that, although women utilize virtually all coping strategies more frequently than men do, when researchers control for each individual's coping frequency overall, women and men cope in gender-stereotyped ways: Women emote and men act (Tamres, Janicki, & Helgeson, 2002). Hence, the expectation that women should assert themselves by standing up to their perpetrator or by reporting the behavior to their managers leaves such women in a double-bind. Given stereotypical gender roles, reporting may not be the best course of action for women, as acting outside of gender expectations is often viewed negatively (Eagly & Mitchell,

2004). This may explain in part why, in response to bullying, men are more likely than women to use assertive strategies (Olafsson & Johannsdotir, 2004).

In regard to sexual harassment, Gruber and Smith (1995) noted that the majority of women respond with non-assertive techniques such as minimization or avoidance. The current laws regarding sexual harassment reflect the burden that is unduly placed on targets in terms of expectations for how they should cope with their experiences. In 1998, the US Supreme Court established the "affirmative defense" to sexual harassment by declaring that organizations would not be liable for sexual harassment claims if the target did not make reasonable attempts to use established organizational complaint procedures (Bergman et al., 2002). However, recent studies have demonstrated that negative outcomes of sexual harassment are often exacerbated when targets report and that reporting may *not* in fact be a "reasonable" course of action for most targets (Bergman et al., 2002; Gruber & Smith, 1995); this was found to be particularly true for male targets in a secondary analysis of the US Merit Systems data conducted by Stockdale (1998). Assertiveness is generally used when the harassment is severe, when the perpetrator is someone other than the target's supervisor, and when the gender composition of the group is skewed such that the target works in a group of mostly men. Unfortunately, little is known about differences in sexual harassment reporting between men and women, given the few studies on the sexual harassment experiences of men.

Companies should first assess organizational culture and climate to ascertain whether assertive responses and/or reporting would be tolerated in the organization. It is likely that in organizations where assertive responses are deemed unacceptable (whether formally or informally), targets who assert and/or report could suffer a variety of negative consequences (e.g., decreased job satisfaction and organizational commitment; increased work and job withdrawal). Also, organizations ought to consider individual characteristics of the target before touting the benefits of particular coping strategies. For example, companies that promote the use of assertive responses to mistreatment may actually be inducing stress in individuals who are not naturally assertive. The act of standing up to or reporting the perpetrator may be more stressful than the mistreatment itself for such individuals. Unfortunately, though, Cortina and Magley (2003) found that targets of high-frequency workplace mistreatment who did not speak out about their experiences suffered the greatest psychological and physical harm.

More research is needed on how targets cope with workplace mistreatment – particularly in light of how coping is thought to buffer the stress associated with such experiences. One serious limitation in the present research is that it lacks a common framework from which clear generalizations can be based. Perhaps the most widely used assessment within the general stress and coping literature is the COPE (Carver, Scheier, & Weintraub, 1989), which is both theoretically and empirically solid. The health psychology literature provides some insights into two coping-related constructs that might be of value for organizational researchers to examine: meaning making and optimism. Individuals who have found meaning (i.e., an enhanced appreciation for life and recognition of its fragility; Bower, Kemeny, Taylor, & Fahey, 2003) in the midst of tragedy fare better than those who became overwhelmed by the traumatic event. Those who have heightened optimism also fare better than those with a more pessimistic outlook (Stanton, Revensen, & Tennen, 2007). For example, breast cancer patients who found meaning in their diagnosis were more likely to experience positive emotions (Bower et al., 2005), and those who were more optimistic were found to have better adjustment 1 year after the diagnosis (Stanton et al., 2007). Consideration of how the targets of workplace mistreatment might benefit from finding meaning in their experiences – perhaps in developing compassion for others suffering from similar mistreatment or propelling targets to change the dynamics of their workgroup or the larger organization – could be an interesting avenue for future research. In addition, as it is thought that heightened levels of optimism increase an individual's propensity to seek social support as well as to practice approach-oriented coping strategies, an examination of whether greater optimism facilitates how targets discuss their experiences with supportive others and with organizational representatives (e.g., Human Resource professionals) could also prove interesting. Certainly, adding gender to the mix in both of these areas could only be helpful.

Escalating Aggression

A final reaction to workplace mistreatment that we need to consider is the possibility of further, potentially even worse, aggression. In particular, it is worth highlighting that mistreatment experiences do not occur in a vacuum It takes (at least) two people to form a mistreatment episode, and it is possible that milder forms of mistreatment (e.g., incivility) can spiral into more severe forms (e.g., physical violence). Such a social interactionist approach (e.g., Felson & Tedeschi, 1993), which highlights the motives and actions of both the actor and the target, was taken by Andersson and Pearson (1999) in their work on the incivility spiral. They discussed how mild incivility can spiral out of control due to the desire to retaliate and save face. Thus, the initial actor can become the target, and this can lead to severe forms of mistreatment, such as physical violence. Although the idea that such spirals occur in workplaces certainly makes theoretical sense, it is not very well established empirically, in part because workplace violence incident rates are quite low. Privacy issues might also prevent our complete understanding of the spiral process as assessments of the motives and experiences of both parties are difficult to procure.

Although Andersson and Pearson (1999) did not explicitly address gender issues, they did discuss topics that have the potential to be gendered. For example, one of the fuels that fires the incivility spiral is the need for revenge, and revenge is a traditionally masculine motivation. This begs the questions of whether men may be more likely than women to engage in spiraling. Indeed, Pearson and Porath (2005) found that, when targeted with incivility, men are more likely than women to engage in retribution. Women, on the other hand, are more likely to avoid the instigator. Pearson and Porath concluded that the worst case scenario might be two men who take turns being actor and target, as the intensity of the mistreatment heightens each time they switch roles.

Does this mean, then, that, in order to curtail incivility spirals in work environments, men need to learn how to tone down their instinct to seek revenge? This is admittedly a bit of a stretch, but playing Devil's Advocate can raise some interesting points. First, we have to remember that we are dealing with survey results. Just because men *report* engaging in retribution more often than women do does not mean that it actually happens. Further, we also have to remember that, even if men do engage in retribution more often than women do, turning the incivility spiral (and other potential mistreatment problems in organizations) into a "men's issue" belies the larger organizational context in which mistreatment occurs. For example, as mentioned previously, climate can play a large role in guiding people's actions. If two men engage in mistreatment in a workplace climate where these kinds of behaviors are not tolerated, their actions may be less likely to spiral out of control than would be the case in a climate where these behaviors are accepted. The message for organizations, then, is to reflect carefully on how much civility, respect, and fair treatment *truly* are valued and rewarded in their workplace.

The Impact of Workplace Mistreatment: Is It the Same for Women and Men?

Perhaps one of the most important reasons that workplace mistreatment is a concern is its broad negative effects. Not only are there negative consequences for the victims of workplace mistreatment, but there is increased awareness that witnesses are also negatively affected and that there is damage to larger organizational processes and general employee behavior. The meta-analytic evidence of the impact of generalized harassment (Bowling & Beehr, 2006) and sexual harassment (Willness, Steel, & Lee, 2007) is irrefutable; both damage targets' work satisfaction and commitment, as well as their physical and emotional well-being. Given that Glomb and Cortina (2006) have recently reviewed these general, negative consequences in great detail, in this final section we focus particularly on gender differences within this literature. Although in previous sections of this chapter we have addressed specific forms of workplace mistreatment separately, there is simply not enough research to make that demarcation an effective one here. Instead, we carefully review studies with respect to the type of consequence.

Psychological and Physical Consequences

Whether workplace mistreatment has a differential impact on psychological and physiological outcomes is, to date, virtually a toss-up. Richman, Rospenda, and colleagues (Richman, Shinsako, Rospenda, Flaherty, & Freels, 2002; Rospenda, Fujishiro, Shannon, & Richman, 2008) documented similar longitudinal effects of sexual harassment on men's and women's depression and anxiety. In a cross-sectional study of military personnel, Magley et al. (1999) also found that men and women experienced nearly identical impairments to their psychological well-being and health satisfaction as a result of having experienced sexual harassment. Finally, incivility was similarly negatively linked to both the mental and the physical health of both women and men (Lim et al., 2008).

On the other hand, Richman et al. (2002) found that generalized workplace hostility predicted women's psychological distress, but not men's. However, this is the only research that documents more serious consequences for women with respect to psychological and physical domains. Although sexual harassment was associated with more negative current mental health for both men and women, the associations with depression and general mental health (but not PTSD) were stronger for men than for women at higher levels of sexual harassment (Street, Gradus, Stafford, & Kelly, 2007). Kaukiainen and colleagues (2001) reported stronger correlations between experienced workplace aggression and physical symptoms, psychological symptoms (including depression and anxiety), and psychosocial problems (e.g., family, work, interpersonal problems) among male employees than among female employees. Finally, Rospenda et al. (2008) found that both sexual harassment and generalized workplace hostility predicted increases in problem drinking 1 year later for men but not for women.

Work-Related Consequences

In the first research to consider gender differences in job-related consequences of sexual harassment, Gutek (1985; Konrad & Gutek, 1986) found that women were much more likely than men to report adverse job-related outcomes (e.g., transferring or quitting a job) of sexual harassment. This effect was supported by a meta-analysis that specifically considered the impact of nonsexual aggression on job satisfaction (Lapierre, Spector, & Leck, 2005). However, the preponderance of the research does point more to similar, rather than dissimilar, effects of workplace mistreatment on work-related consequences for women and men. Although Stockdale (1998) hypothesized that female military personnel would suffer more seriously from experiences of sexual harassment than would male personnel, she did not find support for this with respect to turnover intentions and perceptions of work. This lack of gender difference replicated across a host of work-related outcomes (e.g., satisfaction with one's supervisor, coworkers, and the work itself; organizational commitment; self-reported workgroup productivity). Cortina and colleagues (Cortina et al., 2002; Lim et al., 2008) have examined the possibility that incivility experiences might affect men and women differently but have found that not to be the case for work and supervisor satisfaction, general job satisfaction, job stress, and turnover intentions.

Conclusion and Directions for Future Research

Throughout the chapter, we have offered suggestions for additional research. There are a few remaining areas that we would like to highlight here, as we conclude. First is a concern for vulnerable workers. The power disparities felt by young workers, token workers, and gay men and lesbians remind us that it is important to recognize that vulnerability is not only manifested in people's gender. Second, we are fascinated by the sheer lack of examination of contextual factors that might differentially influence the occurrence of workplace mistreatment for women and men. Bergman and Henning (2008) recently published research that documents that the influence of an organization's tolerance for sexual harassment on employees' actual harassment experiences was much stronger for women ($r = 0.63$) than for men ($r = 0.18$). In that organizational cultures can be changed, we find this line of research to be of great practical value and would like to see more like it. Finally, there is truly a general paucity of research on how men and women cope with their workplace mistreatment. Again, from an intervention perspective, this type of research could be helpful in improving employees' working lives.

If there is one main conclusion to be drawn from our review of the literature, it is that much more can be – and needs to be – done to understand how, when, and why workplace mistreatment differs for women and men and how to prevent it. Although we are quite familiar with this literature, we were surprised at how few researchers have examined gender differences in the occurrence of, processing of, and impact of workplace mistreatment. We hope that our review will spark interest in future researchers, who will make important discoveries about the mistreatment process and the role that gender plays in it.

References

Adams, A. (1997). Bullying at work. *Journal of Community and Applied Social Psychology, 7*, 177–180.
Andersson, L. M., & Pearson, C. M. (1999). Tit for tat? The spiraling effect of incivility in the workplace. *Academy of Management Review, 24*, 452–471.
Aquino, K., Tripp, T. M., & Bies, R. J. (2001). How employees respond to personal offense: The effects of blame attribution, victim status, and offender status on revenge and reconciliation in the workplace. *Journal of Applied Psychology, 86*, 52–59.
Baron R. A., Neuman J. H., & Geddes D. (1999). Social and personal determinants of workplace aggression: Evidence for the impact of perceived injustice and the Type A Behavior Pattern. *Aggressive Behavior, 25*, 281–296.
Bennett, R. J., & Robinson, S. L. (2000). Development of a measure of workplace deviance. *Journal of Applied Psychology, 85*, 349–360.
Ben-Zur, H., & Yagil, D. (2005). The relationship between empowerment, aggressive behaviours of customers, coping, and burnout. *European Journal of Work and Organizational Psychology, 14*, 81–99.
Berdahl, J. L. (2007a). Harassment based on sex: Protecting social status in the context of gender hierarchy. *Academy of Management Review, 32*, 641–658.
Berdahl, J. L. (2007b). The sexual harassment of uppity women. *Journal of Applied Psychology, 92*, 425–437.
Berdahl, J. L., Magley, V. J., & Waldo, C. R. (1996). The sexual harassment of men? Exploring the concept with theory and data. *Psychology of Women Quarterly, 20*, 527–547.

Berdahl, J. L., & Moore, C. (2006). Workplace harassment: Double jeopardy for minority women. *Journal of Applied Psychology, 91*, 424–436.

Bergman, M. E., & Henning, J. B. (2008). Sex and ethnicity as moderators in the sexual harassment phenomenon: A revision and test of Fitzgerald et al. (1994). *Journal of Occupational Health Psychology, 13*, 152–167.

Bergman, M. E., Langhout, R. D., Palmieri, P. A., Cortina, L. M., & Fitzgerald, L. F. (2002). The (un)reasonableness of reporting: Antecedents and consequences of reporting sexual harassment. *Journal of Applied Psychology, 87*, 230–242.

Bjorkqvist, K., Osterman, K., & Hjelt-Back, M. (1994). Aggression among university employees. *Aggressive Behaviour, 20*, 27–33.

Bower, J. E., Kemeny, M. E., Taylor, S. E., & Fahey, J. L. (2003). Finding positive meaning and its association with natural killer cell cytotoxicity among participants in a bereavement-related disclosure intervention. *Annals of Behavioral Medicine, 25*, 146–155.

Bower, J. E., Meyerowitz, B. E., Desmond, K. A., Bernaards, C. A., Rowland, J. H., & Ganz, P. A. (2005). Perceptions of positive meaning and vulnerability following breast cancer: Predictors and outcomes among long-term breast cancer survivors. *Annals of Behavioral Medicine, 29*, 236–245.

Bowling, N. A., & Beehr, T. A. (2006). Workplace harassment from the victim's perspective: A theoretical model and meta-analysis. *Journal of Applied Psychology, 91*, 998–1012.

Budd, J. D., Arvey, R. D., & Lawless, P. (1996). Correlates and consequences of workplace violence. *Journal of Occupational Health Psychology, 1*, 197–210.

Buss, A. H. (1961). *The psychology of aggression.* New York: Wiley.

Carver, C. S., Scheier, M. F., & Weintraub, J. K. (1989). Assessing coping strategies: A theoretically based approach. *Journal of Personality and Social Psychology, 56*, 267–283.

Cleveland, J. N., & Kerst, M. E. (1993). Sexual harassment and perceptions of power: An under-articulated relationship. *Journal of Vocational Behavior, 42*, 49–67.

Cortina, L. M. (2008). Unseen injustice: Incivility as modern discrimination in organizations. *Academy of Management Review, 33*, 55–75.

Cortina, L. M., & Berdahl, J. L. (2008). Sexual harassment in organizations: A decade of research in review. In J. Barling & C. L. Cooper (Eds.), *The Sage handbook of organizational behavior, Vol. 1: Micro approaches* (pp. 469–497). Thousand Oaks, CA: Sage.

Cortina, L. M., Lonsway, K. A., Magley, V. J., Freeman, L. V., Hunter, M., Collinsworth, L. L., et al. (2002). What's gender got to do with it? Incivility in the federal courts. *Law and Social Inquiry, 27*, 235–270.

Cortina, L. M., & Magley, V. J. (2003). Raising voice, risking retaliation: Events following interpersonal mistreatment in the workplace. *Journal of Occupational Health Psychology, 8*, 247–265.

Cortina, L. M., & Magley, V. J. (2009). Patterns and profiles of response to incivility in the workplace. *Journal of Occupational Health Psychology, 14*, 272–288.

Cortina, L. M., Magley, V. J., Williams, J. H., & Langhout, R. D. (2001). Incivility in the workplace: Incidence and impact. *Journal of Occupational Health Psychology, 6*, 64–80.

DeSouza, E., & Fansler, A. G. (2003). Contrapower sexual harassment: A survey of students and faculty members. *Sex Roles, 48*, 519–542.

Douglas, S. C., & Martinko, M. J. (2001). Exploring the role of individual differences in the prediction of workplace aggression. *Journal of Applied Psychology, 86*, 547–559.

Eagly, A. H., & Mitchell, A. A. (2004). Social role theory of sex differences and similarities: Implications for the sociopolitical attitudes of women and men. In M. A. Paludi (Ed.), *Praeger guide to the psychology of gender* (pp. 183–206). Westport, CT: Praeger.

Einarsen, S. (1999). The nature and causes of bullying at work. *International Journal of Manpower, 20*, 16–27.

Einarsen, S., Hoel, H., Zapf, D., & Cooper, C. L. (2003). The concept of bullying at work: The European tradition. In S. Einarsen, H. Hoel, D. Zapf, & C. L. Cooper (Eds.), *Bullying and emotional abuse in the workplace: International perspectives in research and practice* (pp. 3–30). London: Taylor & Francis.

Einarsen, S., & Skogstad, A. (1996). Bullying at work: Epidemiological findings in public and private organizations. *European Journal of Work and Organizational Psychology, 5*, 185–201.

Elliott, R. H., & Jarrett, D. T. (1994). Violence in the workplace: The role of Human Resource Management. *Public Personnel Management, 23*, 287–299.

Felson, R. B., & Tedeschi, J. T. (Eds.). (1993). *Aggression and violence: Social interactionist perspectives.* Washington, DC: American Psychological Association.

Firestone, J. M., & Harris, R. J. (2003). Perceptions of effectiveness of responses to sexual harassment in the US Military, 1988 and 1995. *Gender, Work, and Organizations, 10*, 43–64.

Fitzgerald, L. F., Drasgow, F., Hulin, C. L., Gelfand, M. J., & Magley, V. J. (1997). Antecedents and consequences of sexual harassment in organizations: A test of an integrated model. *Journal of Applied Psychology, 82*, 578–589.

Fitzgerald, L. F., Drasgow, F., & Magley, V. J. (1999). Sexual harassment in the armed services: A test of an integrated model. *Military Psychology, 11*, 329–343.

Fitzgerald, L. F., Gelfand, M. J., & Drasgow, F. (1995). Measuring sexual harassment: Theoretical and psychometric advances. *Basic and Applied Social Psychology, 17*, 425–445.

Fitzgerald, L. F., Shullman, S. L., Bailey, N., & Richards, M. (1988). The incidence and dimensions of sexual harassment in academia and the workplace. *Journal of Vocational Behavior, 32*, 152–175.

Fitzgerald, L. F., Swan, S., & Magley, V. J. (1997). But was it really sexual harassment? Legal, behavioral, and psychological definitions of the workplace victimization of women. In W. O'Donohue (Ed.), *Sexual harassment: Theory, research, and treatment* (pp. 5–28). Needham Heights, MA: Allyn & Bacon.

Gallus, J. A., Matthews, R. A., Bunk, J. A., Barnes-Farrell, J. L., & Magley, V. J. (2006, March). The role of climate and gender in understanding the experience and perpetration of workplace incivility. In R. A. Matthews (Chair), *Occupational health psychology: A graduate student consortium*. Symposium presented at the NIOSH-APA "Work, Stress, and Health 2006" Conference, Miami, FL.

George, J. M. (1990). Personality, affect, and behavior in groups. *Journal of Applied Psychology, 75*, 107–116.

Glomb, T. M. (2002). Workplace anger and aggression: Informing conceptual models with data from specific encounters. *Journal of Occupational Health Psychology, 7*, 20–36.

Glomb, T. M., & Cortina, L. M. (2006). The experience of victims: Using theories of traumatic and chronic stress to understand individual outcomes of workplace abuse. In E. K. Kelloway, J. Barling, & J. J. Hurrell, Jr. (Eds.), *Handbook of workplace violence* (pp. 517–534). Thousand Oaks, CA: Sage.

Glomb, T. M., Richman, W. L., Hulin, C. L., Drasgow, F., Schneider, K. T., & Fitzgerald, L. F. (1997). Ambient sexual harassment: An integrated model of antecedents and consequences. *Organizational Behavior and Human Decision Processes, 71*, 309–328.

Griffin, R. W., & O'Leary-Kelly, A. M. (2004). *The dark side of organizational behavior*. San Francisco: Jossey-Bass.

Gruber, J. E., & Smith, M. D. (1995). Women's responses to sexual harassment: A multivariate analysis. *Basic and Applied Social Psychology, 17*, 543–562.

Gutek, B. A. (1985). *Sex and the workplace: Impact of sexual behavior and harassment on women, men, and organizations*. San Francisco: Jossey-Bass.

Hackman, J. R. (1992). Group influences on individuals in organizations. In M. D. Dunnette & L. M. Hough (Eds.), *Handbook of industrial organizational psychology* (Vol. 3, pp. 199–267). Palo Alto, CA: Consulting Psychologists Press.

Hall, J. A. (1987). On explaining gender differences: The case of nonverbal communication. In P. Shaver & C. Hendrick (Eds.), *Sex and gender: Review of personality and social psychology* (Vol. 7, pp. 177–201). Newbury Park, CA: Sage.

Hendrick, S., Hendrick, C., Slapion-Foote, M. J., & Foote, F. H. (1985). Gender differences in sexual attitudes. *Journal of Personality and Social Psychology, 48*, 1630–1642.

Hershcovis, M. S., Turner, N., Barling, J., Arnold, K. A., Dupré, K. E., Inness, M., et al. (2007). Predicting workplace aggression: A meta-analysis. *Journal of Applied Psychology, 92*, 228–238.

Hoel, H., Cooper, C. L., & Faragher, B. (2001). The experience of bullying in Great Britain: The impact of organizational status. *European Journal of Work and Organizational Psychology, 10*, 443–465.

Ilies, R., Hauserman, N., Schwochau, S., & Stibal, J. (2003). Reported incidence rates of work-related sexual harassment in the United States: Using meta-analysis to explain reported rate disparities. *Personnel Psychology, 56*, 607–631.

Jockin, V., Arvey, R. D., & McGue, M. (2001). Perceived victimization moderates self-reports of workplace aggression and conflict. *Journal of Applied Psychology, 86*, 1262–1269.

Kath, L. M., Swody, C. A., Magley, V. J., Bunk, J. A., & Gallus, J. (2009). Workgroup climate for sexual harassment as a moderator of the relationship between individuals' experiences of sexual harassment and job-related outcomes. *Journal of Occupational and Organizational Psychology, 82*, 159–182.

Kaukiainen, A., Salmivalli, C., Björkqvist, K., Österman, K., Lahtinen, A., Kostamo, A., et al. (2001). Overt and covert aggression in work settings in relation to the subjective well-being of employees. *Aggressive Behavior, 27*, 360–371.

Kelloway, E. K., Barling, J., & Hurrell, J. J., Jr. (2006). *Handbook of workplace violence*. Thousand Oaks, CA: Sage.

Konrad, A. M., & Gutek, B. A. (1986). Impact of work experiences on attitudes toward sexual harassment. *Administrative Science Quarterly, 31*, 422–438.

Kopper, B. A., & Epperson, D. L. (1996). The experience and expression of anger: Relationships with gender, gender role socialization, depression, and mental health functioning. *Journal of Counseling Psychology, 43*, 158–165.

Lapierre, L. M., Spector, P. E., & Leck, J. D. (2005). Sexual versus nonsexual workplace aggression and victims' overall job satisfaction: A meta-analysis. *Journal of Occupational Health Psychology, 10*, 155–169.

Lazarus, R. S., & Folkman, S. (1984). *Stress, appraisal, and coping.* New York: Springer.

LeBlanc, M. M., & Barling, J. (2004). Workplace aggression. *Current Directions in Psychological Science, 13*, 9–12.

Lee, D. (2000). An analysis of workplace bullying in the U.K. *Personnel Review, 29*, 593–612.

Lewis, S. I., & Orford, J. (2005). Women's experiences of workplace bullying: Changes in social relationships. *Journal of Community and Applied Social Psychology, 15*, 29–47.

Leymann, H. (1990). Mobbing and psychological terror at workplaces. *Violence & Victims, 5*, 119–126.

Lim, S., Cortina, L. M., & Magley, V. J. (2008). Personal and workgroup incivility: Impact on work and health outcomes. *Journal of Applied Psychology, 93*, 95–107.

Magley, V. J. (2002). Coping with sexual harassment: Reconceptualizing women's resistance. *Journal of Personality and Social Psychology, 83*, 930–946.

Magley, V. J., Hulin, C. L., Fitzgerald, L. F., & DeNardo, M. (1999). Outcomes of self-labeling sexual harassment. *Journal of Applied Psychology, 84*, 390–402.

Magley, V. J., Waldo, C. R., Drasgow, F., & Fitzgerald, L. F. (1999). The impact of sexual harassment on military personnel: Is it the same for men and women? *Military Psychology, 11*, 283–302.

McKinney, K. (1990). Sexual harassment of university faculty by colleagues and students. *Sex Roles, 23*, 421–438.

Montgomery, K., Kane, K., & Vance, C. M. (2004). Accounting for differences in norms of respect: A study of assessments of incivility through the lenses of race and gender. *Group & Organization Management, 29*, 248–268.

Neuman, J. H., & Baron, R. A. (1997). Aggression in the workplace. In R. Giacalone & J. Greenberg (Eds.), *Antisocial behavior in organizations* (pp. 37–67). Thousand Oaks, CA: Sage.

Neuman, J. H., & Baron, R. A. (1998). Workplace violence and workplace aggression: Evidence concerning specific forms, potential causes, and preferred targets. *Journal of Management, 24*, 391–419.

Olafsson, R. F., & Johannsdotir, H. L. (2004). Coping with bullying in the workplace: The effect of gender, age, and type of bullying. *British Journal of Guidance and Counseling, 32*, 319–333.

Quine, L. (2001). Workplace bullying in nurses. *Journal of Health Psychology, 6*, 73–84.

Pearson, C. M., Andersson, L. M., & Porath, C. L. (2000). Assessing and attacking workplace incivility. *Organizational Dynamics, 29*, 123–137.

Pearson, C. M., & Porath, C. L. (2005). On the nature, consequences, and remedies of workplace incivility: No time for "nice?" Think again. *Academy of Management Executive, 19*, 7–18.

Rayner, C. (1997). The incidence of workplace bullying. *Journal of Community and Applied Social Psychology, 7*, 199–208.

Rayner, C., & Hoel, H. (1997). A summary review of the literature related to workplace bullying. *Journal of Community and Applied Social Psychology, 7*, 181–191.

Richman, J. A., Shinsako, S. A., Rospenda, K. M., Flaherty, J. A., & Freels, S. (2002). Workplace harassment/abuse and alcohol-related outcomes: The mediating role of psychological distress. *Journal of Studies on Alcohol, 63*, 412–419.

Robinson, S. L., & Bennett, R. J. (1995). A typology of deviant workplace behaviors: A multidimensional scaling study. *Academy of Management Journal, 38*, 555–572.

Robinson, S. L., & O'Leary-Kelley, A. M. (1998). Monkey see, monkey do: The influence of work groups on the antisocial behavior of employees. *Academy of Management Journal, 41*, 658–672.

Rospenda, K. M., Fujishiro, K., Shannon, C. A., & Richman, J. A. (2008). Workplace harassment, stress, and drinking behavior over time: Gender differences in a national sample. *Addictive Behaviors, 33*, 964–967.

Rotundo, M., Nguyen, D., & Sackett, P. R. (2001). A meta-analytic review of gender differences in perceptions of sexual harassment. *Journal of Applied Psychology, 86*, 914–922.

Rutter, A., & Hine, D. W. (2005). Sex differences in workplace aggression: An investigation of moderation and mediation effects. *Aggressive Behavior, 31*, 254–270.

Schat, A. C. H., & Kelloway, E. K. (2000). Effects of perceived control on the outcomes of workplace aggression and violence. *Journal of Occupational Health Psychology, 5*, 386–402.

Schneider, K. T., Swan, S., & Fitzgerald, L. F. (1997). Job-related and psychological effects of sexual harassment in the workplace: Empirical evidence from two organizations. *Journal of Applied Psychology, 82*, 401–415.

Stanton, A. L., Revenson, T. A., & Tennen, H. (2007). Health psychology: Psychological adjustment to chronic disease. *Annual Review of Psychology, 58*, 565–592.

Stockdale, M. S. (1998). The direct and moderating influences of sexual-harassment pervasiveness, coping strategies, and gender on work-related outcomes. *Psychology of Women Quarterly, 22*, 521–535.

Stockdale, M. S., Gandolfo-Berry, C., Schneider, B. W., & Cao, F. (2004). Perceptions of the sexual harassment of men. *Psychology of Men & Masculinity, 5*, 158–167.

Stockdale, M. S., Visio, M., & Batra, L. (1999). The sexual harassment of men: Evidence for a broader theory of sexual harassment and sex discrimination. *Psychology, Public Policy, and Law, 5*, 630–664.

Street, A. E., Gradus, J. L., Stafford, J., & Kelly, K. (2007). Gender differences in experiences of sexual harassment: Data from a male-dominated environment. *Journal of Consulting and Clinical Psychology, 75*, 464–474.

Tamres, L. K., Janicki, D., & Helgeson, V. S. (2002). Sex differences in coping behavior: A meta-analytic review and an examination of relative coping. *Personality and Social Psychology Review, 6*, 2–30.

Tiedens, L. Z., Ellsworth, P. C., & Mesquita, B. (2000). Sentimental stereotypes: Emotional expectations for high- and low-status groups members. *Personality and Social Psychology Bulletin, 26*, 560–575.

Timmerman, G., & Bajema, C. (2000). The impact of organizational culture on perceptions and experiences of sexual harassment. *Journal of Vocational Behavior, 57*, 188–205.

Tuna, C. (2008, August 4). Lawyers and employers take the fight to "workplace bullies." *Wall Street Journal*, p. B6.

U.S. Merit Systems Protection Board. (1981). *Sexual harassment in the federal workplace: Is it a problem?* Washington, DC: U.S. Government Printing Office.

U.S. Merit Systems Protection Board. (1995). *Sexual harassment in the federal workplace: Trends, progress, and continuing challenges.* Washington, DC: U.S. Government Printing Office.

Vartia, M., & Hytti, J. (2002). Gender differences in workplace bullying among prison officers. *European Journal of Work and Organizational Psychology, 11*, 113–126.

Waldo, C. R., Berdahl, J. L., & Fitzgerald, L. F. (1998). Are men sexually harassed? If so, by whom? *Law and Human Behavior, 22*, 59–79.

Wayne, J. H. (2000). Disentangling the power bases of sexual harassment: Comparing gender, age, and position power. *Journal of Vocational Behavior, 57*, 301–325.

Williams, J. H., Fitzgerald, L. F., & Drasgow, F. (1999). The effects of organizational practices on sexual harassment and individual outcomes in the military. *Military Psychology, 11*, 303–328.

Willness, C. R., Steel, P., & Lee, K. (2007). A meta-analysis of the antecedents and consequences of workplace sexual harassment. *Personnel Psychology, 60*, 127–162.

Chapter 19
Gender and Leadership: Negotiating the Labyrinth

Ronit Kark and Alice H. Eagly

There is no topic with more profound implications for gender equality than leadership. Gender equality cannot be attained until women and men share leadership equally. With unfettered access of women to leadership, the policies of organizations and governments would balance the concerns of women and men more equitably. Yet, women and men are not equally represented as leaders in any contemporary nation. Therefore, it is essential that people committed to furthering gender equality understand what enhances the access of women and men to leadership and their ability to perform well in leader roles. To foster this understanding, we focus this chapter on explaining why women have less access to leadership than men do, especially to roles that confer high levels of power and authority. We also explore women's considerable progress in attaining such roles in many nations. An understanding of both women's advancement and their continuing lack of equality with men illuminates the changes needed to produce gender equality.

The first issue we address is whether the typically greater family responsibilities of mothers than fathers are the main deterrent to women's rise as leaders. The second issue is whether people are prejudiced against women as leaders and, therefore, discriminate against them as candidates for leadership roles and resist their authority once they occupy these roles. Such prejudicial pressures can affect women's leadership behavior. The third issue is whether challenges to women as leaders reside at least in part in the structure and culture of organizations. As we argue in this chapter, the conjunction of these several considerations produces paths to leadership that are decidedly more challenging for women than for men—challenges that can be metaphorically described by a *labyrinth* that women traverse to attain power and authority and exercise it effectively (Eagly & Carli, 2007).

Given that all individuals possess identities in addition to their gender, the multifaceted challenges to leadership that individuals face can differ depending on attributes such as sexual orientation, race, and ethnicity. Throughout the chapter, we remain cognizant of the different contours that these intersectionalities impose on men's and women's leadership (Shields, 2008).

Representation of Women in Leader Roles

Although women in Western nations have achieved more access to leadership than at any other period in history, equal representation remains a distant goal. Nevertheless, the increase of women in managerial roles is substantial (United Nations Development Programme, 2008; see Fig. 19.1). In many nations between one-quarter and one-half of the occupants of such roles are women. Overall in

R. Kark (✉)
Bar-Ilan University, Ramat Gan, Israel

J.C. Chrisler, D.R. McCreary (eds.), *Handbook of Gender Research in Psychology*,
DOI 10.1007/978-1-4419-1467-5_19, © Springer Science+Business Media, LLC 2010

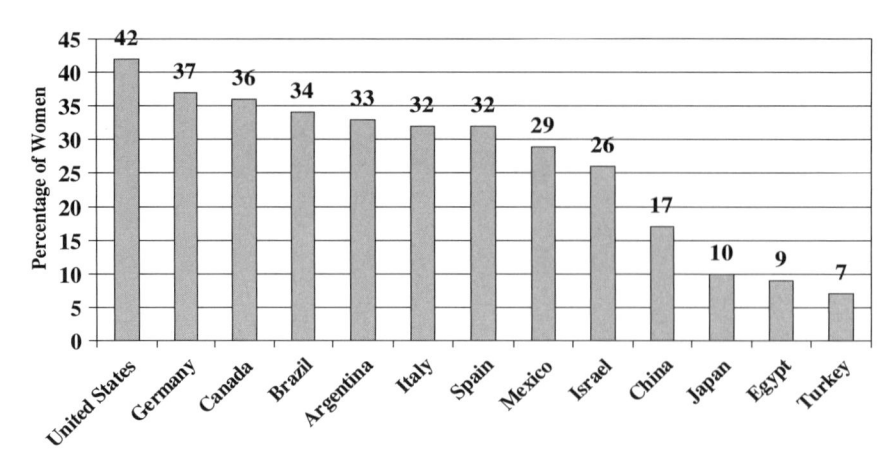

Fig. 19.1 Percentage of women among managers, legislators, and senior officials in selected nations. Data from the United Nations Development Programme (2008)

the United States, 11% of employed men and 9% of employed women have management positions (U.S. Bureau of Labor Statistics, 2008); however, the women are concentrated at lower and middle levels of management. Across all economic sectors, substantially more men than women occupy positions that confer major decision-making authority and the ability to influence others' pay or promotions (Smith, 2002).

A low representation of women is most evident among executives in the most valuable corporations in the business sector. For example, in the United States *Fortune* 500, women account for only 2% of chief executive officers, 16% of corporate officers, and 15% of members of boards of directors (Catalyst, 2008). In the largest publicly quoted companies in the European Union, women account for only 4% of the presidents and 11% of the members of the highest decision-making bodies (European Commission, 2007). The underrepresentation of women from some minority groups in leadership roles, relative to their numbers in the population, is generally even greater than that of White women. In U.S. management, White and Asian women are better represented than Black and Hispanic/Latina women are (U.S. Bureau of Labor Statistics, 2008).

Women usually have more access to power outside of large corporations, especially in the non-profit sector. Women constitute 26% of chief executives in the United States when all organizations are considered; among ethnic minorities of both sexes, 4% of chief executives are Black, 4% Asian, and 5% Hispanic (U.S. Bureau of Labor Statistics, 2008). Women are 23% of college and university presidents and 53% of the chief executives of foundations and charitable giving programs, and they hold 27% of the top federal civil service jobs (Eagly & Carli, 2007).

Women's representation as political leaders is also on the rise in many nations, as shown by statistics on women in national parliaments. Nevertheless, this representation is generally well below 50% (see Fig. 19.2), and the world average is only 18% (Inter-Parliamentary Union, 2008). Among the members of the U.S. 110th Congress, 17% were women; among members of both sexes, 8% were Black, 1% Asian, and 5% Hispanic (Infoplease, 2008). Some of the global variation in parliamentary representation reflects many nations' and political parties' introduction of quotas to ensure a certain percentage of female candidates or office holders. Quotas are ordinarily effective in increasing the proportion of parliamentary seats held by women (Dahlerup, 2006).

Women are active as community leaders and entrepreneurs in many nations, but exact statistics are unknown. In the United States, small-group studies conducted in universities and with juries

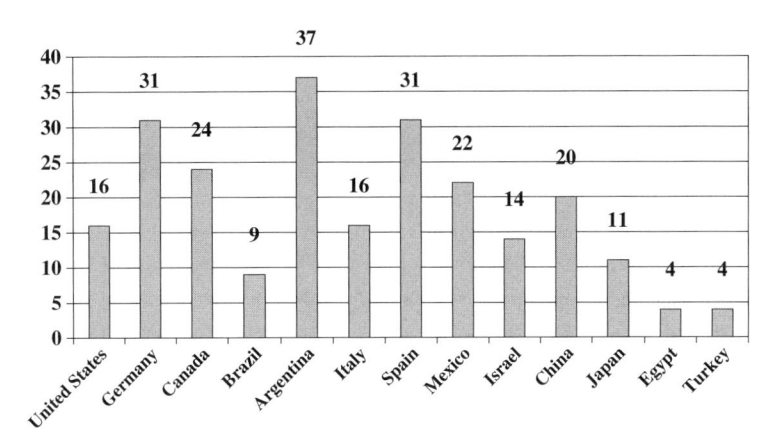

Fig. 19.2 Percentage of seat of parliament (lower house) held by women in selected nations. Data from the United Nations Development Programme (2008)

assembled to hear court cases, settings in which leadership emerges spontaneously, men emerged as leaders more often than women did, but there is some evidence that women are increasing in these leadership roles as well (see Eagly & Carli, 2007).

Work–Family Issues

The most obvious answer to the question of why more men than women occupy leader roles is that a division of labor dictates that women have greater domestic responsibilities, which limit their employment outside of the home. For most women, the path to workplace advancement involves negotiating trade-offs between family and employment.

The idea that family commitments compromise women's careers is consistent with economists' traditional human capital theories, which argue that wages and promotion reflect people's investment in qualities that increase their value in labor markets, such as education, training, and workforce experience. Women's human capital investments have risen steeply in recent years, with large gains in education. In most Western nations, women now earn more university degrees than men do (United Nations Development Programme, 2008). In the United States, for example, women now earn 58% of bachelor's degrees and the majority of advanced degrees (U.S. National Center for Educational Statistics, 2007). However, there is one important area in which women lag behind men—the amount and consistency of their participation in the labor force. Although women's participation has increased greatly in most nations, their participation rates and weekly employment hours have remained lower than those of men (United Nations Development Programme, 2008).

Women's lesser participation in the labor force stems in large part from their domestic responsibilities. Even though time diary studies have demonstrated that men accomplish more household chores and childcare than they once did (e.g., Bianchi, Robinson, & Milkie, 2006), women still do the majority of such work in virtually all nations (United Nations Development Programme, 2008). These responsibilities, especially childcare, cause some women to drop out of the labor force entirely, at least while their children are young, and others to lower their hours of paid work. These family-related accommodations slow women's workplace advancement.

Single parents ordinarily do not have the same options as married parents because they have to fulfill both provider and homemaker roles. Even though the employment hours are more similar for single mothers and fathers than for married ones, single fathers typically have longer work hours than single mothers (Sayer, Cohen, & Casper, 2004). Single fathers are able to have these longer hours because most of them live together with their own parents or other adults who can share domestic responsibilities with them. Single mothers typically do not have such living arrangements.

When mothers remain employed full-time, they generally face demands that can make their lives rushed and time-stressed—demands that are typically greater than those faced by fathers. Even highly paid women usually face family–employment trade-offs, which often result in postponing having children or foregoing childbearing altogether. Such pressures are especially intense for women in professional and managerial careers, which often require very long hours, although the high income of some of these women can mitigate these pressures (Eagly & Carli, 2007). Men in high-level careers typically do not encounter the same family–employment dilemmas because they generally have wives who either are not employed or have shorter work hours than their own.

Nations, cultures, races, and religions differ in their norms regarding family size and motherhood, and, as a result, fertility rates (Remennick, 2008). For example, in Israel, the expectation that women will have children is strong, and the fertility rate is very high compared with other industrialized nations (e.g., 2.9 vs. 1.9 in the United States and 1.3 in Germany; United Nations Development Programme, 2008). In Israel, few women without children occupy leadership positions (Herzog, 1999; Kark, 2007). A list of the 50 most influential women in the Israeli economy, which was published by the prominent newspaper *Ha'aretz* in 2003, included only two women who were not mothers. In comparison, approximately 40% of the women in the top percentile of wage earners in the United States do not have children (Hewlett, 2002). Given the high cultural value of bearing children and Israeli women's aspirations for advancement, social norms and practical arrangements support the combination of managerial careers and mothering (Frenkel, 2008). However, although these arrangements, in Israel and other countries with family-friendly policies, may allow mothers to hold leadership positions, they may also bring disadvantage. A recent 20-nation study showed that family-friendly policies (e.g., long maternity leaves) paradoxically widen the gender wage gap and contribute to a lesser representation of women in high-status and high-earning managerial positions (Mandel & Semyonov, 2005).

Women's domestic responsibilities do not fully account for their underrepresentation as leaders. This conclusion emerges from economists' and sociologists' large-scale surveys of wages and promotions. Such studies typically determine whether adjusting for human capital variables (e.g., education, job experience), family characteristics (e.g., marriage and children), and structural factors (e.g., occupational segregation) can account for women's lesser advancement and lower wages. The nearly unanimous conclusion is that such variables account for only a portion of these gender gaps (e.g., Blau & Kahn, 2006; Maume, 1999).

Discrimination and Prejudice

As women's domestic responsibilities are only one factor that influences their representation as leaders, other factors must also be important. The usual suspect is discrimination—that is, the possibility that women receive fewer opportunities for leadership than do men with equivalent qualifications. The gender gap in wages and promotions that social scientists cannot explain with human capital variables can represent discrimination, although psychological variables such as personal preferences, which are not considered in such studies, could also be important.

To obtain clearer evidence of discrimination, some social scientists have conducted experiments that equate job applicants in all respects other than the attribute (race or sex) that is suspected to trigger discrimination. Many of these experiments include resumes presented to students and other participant groups, but other experiments are more naturalistic audit studies in which job applications or actual applicants are presented to employers. Although most of these audit studies have addressed racial and ethnic discrimination, some have examined sex discrimination (see review by Riach & Rich, 2002). In addition to discrimination against people of color, the findings show a high incidence of sex discrimination against women in more senior jobs that yield higher status and wages and against both sexes when they applied for jobs dominated by the other sex. Also, Davison and Burke (2000) meta-analyzed the results of 49 experiments in simulated employment contexts and found that in male-dominated jobs (e.g., auto salesperson, life insurance agent), men were slightly preferred over identically qualified women (mean $d = 0.34$). However, in female-dominated jobs (e.g., secretary, director of a day care center), women were slightly preferred over identically qualified men (mean $d = -0.26$). Another important finding that emerged from experiments as well as correlational studies is that mothers are especially likely to be targets of workplace discrimination (Correll, Benard, & Paik, 2007; Heilman & Okimoto, 2008).

Discrimination is consequential for women's access to leadership roles because most roles that confer substantial power, authority, and high wages are male-dominated. As we explain in subsequent sections, discrimination against women is particularly potent in roles associated with men.

Gender and Leader Stereotypes

Given that sex discrimination is illegal in many industrialized nations, its continuing presence may seem puzzling. In many contexts, blatant expressions of discrimination have disappeared. Yet, discrimination continues to proceed, often in covert, subtle, and even unintentional forms (e.g., Dovidio & Gaertner, 2004). People can discriminate unknowingly by means of "mindless" processes that operate beyond their conscious awareness. Those who engage in discrimination may believe that they are merely choosing the best person for the job or otherwise acting in an unbiased manner when in fact they are biased against women and minorities (e.g., Lane, Banaji, Nosek, & Greenwald, 2007).

How does this happen? Our beliefs about social groups often bias our judgments of individual group members (e.g., Darley & Gross, 1983; von Hippel, Sekaquaptewa, & Vargas, 1995). The potential for prejudice against women as leaders is present when people hold a stereotype about women that is incongruent with the qualities that they believe are required for success in leader roles. Even when an *individual* woman actually has the qualities thought necessary for leadership, people may believe that she does not "have what it takes" for success as a leader. This outcome then elicits a less favorable attitude toward persons who are stereotypically mismatched than to those who are matched with the requirements of a leader role (Eagly & Karau, 2002; Heilman, 2001). Such an attitude constitutes prejudice when the stereotypically matched and mismatched individuals are objectively equivalent on the attributes that contribute to effective leadership. A common result is discriminatory behaviors toward mismatched individuals.

Are women vulnerable to prejudice because of the beliefs that people ordinarily hold about women? Extensive research has examined gender stereotypes, which consist of the attributes that people believe characterize men or women (e.g., Newport, 2001; for a review, see Kite, Deaux, & Haines, 2008). Unlike investigations of actual sex or gender differences in traits (e.g., Costa, Terracciano, & McCrae, 2001), gender stereotypes refer to consensual beliefs regarding such traits. Such stereotypes are pervasive and widely shared by both men and women.

Prominent in the content of gender stereotypes are two themes: the *communal* qualities of women and the *agentic* qualities of men (e.g., Deaux & Lewis, 1984). Generally, the communal stereotype refers to an interpersonally sensitive orientation by which individuals are concerned with the welfare of others and with interpersonal relationships. Women are stereotypically viewed as kind, helpful, and empathic as well as motivated by needs for nurturance and affiliation. In contrast, the agentic stereotype refers to a self-interested, task-focused orientation by which individuals are concerned with mastery, dominance, and control. Men are stereotypically viewed as ambitious, competent, competitive, and individualistic as well as motivated by needs for autonomy, aggression, dominance, achievement, and endurance. In addition, gender stereotypes encompass other themes having to do with, for example, cognitive abilities and physical characteristics (Cejka & Eagly, 1999; Deaux & Lewis, 1984). Moreover, any difference observed between a man and a woman is likely to be incorporated, at least temporarily, into beliefs about how men and women differ in general (Prentice & Miller, 2006). Nonetheless, communion and agency predominate in gender stereotypes.

These cultural stereotypes, which are part of a society's shared knowledge, encompass two types of beliefs: expectations about what members of these groups are actually like and what they should be like (Heilman, 2001). Expectations about the actual characteristics of group members are known as *descriptive beliefs*; an example is the belief that men behave in an active, assertive manner. Expectations about what group members should be like are known as *prescriptive beliefs*; an example is the belief that men should behave in an active, assertive manner. Although descriptive and prescriptive beliefs generally encompass the same qualities, they diverge in some respects. For example, less positive descriptive beliefs that men are overbearing and insensitive and women are whiny and complaining (e.g., Diekman & Eagly, 2000; Kark & Waismel-Manor, 2005) are descriptive but not prescriptive.

Do gender stereotypes disadvantage women? The answer depends on the qualities that people expect in leaders. Although these expectations depend to some extent on the setting in which leadership takes place, research has established that people generally believe that leaders are especially well endowed with agentic qualities, such as ambition, confidence, self-sufficiency, and dominance, and less well endowed with communal qualities (e.g., Powell, Butterfield, & Parent, 2002). For example, the role of a business executive is thought to require attributes such as action-oriented, decisive, and competitive (e.g., Martell, Parker, Emrich, & Crawford, 1998). Descriptions of most leader roles are strongly infused with cultural masculinity (Atwater, Brett, Waldman, DiMare, & Hayden, 2004).

Given such stereotypes about leaders, there is considerable incompatibility between beliefs about what it means to be a good leader and what it means to be a woman (e.g., Agars, 2004; Eagly & Karau, 2002; Powell et al., 2002). The resulting perception of leaders as more similar to men than to women received support in research by Schein (1973, 2001), who labeled this phenomenon the "think manager—think male" effect. In Schein's studies respondents rated women, men, or successful middle managers on traits that are stereotypical of women or men. The results showed that managers were perceived considerably more similar to men than to women. This perceived fit between what is managerial and what is masculine has proven to be relatively durable since the early 1970s. Yet, recent research has yielded some weakening of the "think manager—think male" effect among some, but not all, samples (Duehr & Bono, 2006; Sczesny, Bosak, Neff, & Schyns, 2004).

Despite the general tendency for men to be regarded more positively than women in leader roles, specific role requirements can moderate or reverse this tendency. For example, an analysis of archival performance evaluations showed that women received lower performance evaluations than did men in line managerial positions, which hold greater organizational and decision-making power. In contrast, women received higher performance evaluations than did men in staff managerial positions, where the role includes support for line managers (Lyness & Heilman, 2006). Further support for the "lack of fit" basis of evaluating leaders is evidence that women's chances of emerging as a leader are increased by tasks that are socially complex (Eagly & Karau, 1991) or stereotypical of women (Ritter & Yoder, 2004).

Not only are women perceived as less suitable than men to higher level positions in general but also they are regarded as more suited than men to manage organizations that are failing and, thus, in organizational crisis. As demonstrated by Haslam and Ryan (2008), people tend to "think female" when appointing managers of failing companies. Evidently women's stereotypical qualities of being understanding, intuitive, and creative are viewed as particularly appropriate for crisis management in companies that are in precarious circumstances. Of course, the risk of personal and organizational failure is high for managers who accept such positions.

Are these ideas about women, men, and leadership important? It might seem reasonable that gender stereotypes are inconsequential in employment settings. However, gender remains important in workplaces, and it is, in fact, the first thing we notice about people. Gender cues often automatically evoke gender stereotypes. Although stereotypes associated with people's other attributes compete with gender stereotypes, such individuating information does not necessarily cancel the effects of gender stereotypes in workplaces (Heilman & Eagly, 2008). Instead, merely classifying a person as male or female automatically evokes associations of masculine and feminine qualities with them (e.g., Banaji & Hardin, 1996; Ito & Urland, 2003). These mental associations, or stereotypes, can be influential even when people are unaware of their presence (e.g., Sczesny & Kühnen, 2004). Stereotyping can make individual men and women appear to be more similar to their respective societal stereotypes than they actually are. Because people act on their construals of others, not on others' actual qualities, implicit and explicit beliefs about gender and leadership affect how people evaluate individuals' potential for leadership and react to their attempts to exert leadership (Heilman, 2001; Rudman & Glick, 2001).

Cultural stereotypes of gender become more complex when we take into consideration the multiple intersecting identities that individuals may have (e.g., gender, race, class, sexual orientation). For example, racial and ethnic stereotypes also contain attributes disadvantageous for leadership, such that African Americans are often stereotyped as antagonistic and lacking competence, Hispanics as uneducated and unambitious, and Asian Americans as quiet and unassertive (e.g., Madon et al., 2001; Niemann, Jennings, Rozelle, Baxter, & Sullivan, 1994). Therefore, when subjected to stereotyping based on gender and race, women of color may have a double disadvantage as managers and as applicants for managerial roles.

Disadvantage can also intensify at the intersection between gender and sexual orientation. Stereotypes of homosexuality appear to conform to what has been called an "implicit inversion theory," whereby homosexuals are regarded as similar to cross-sex heterosexuals—that is, gay men as more feminine than straight men and lesbians as more masculine than straight women (Kite & Deaux, 1987). Although this perception of masculinity might be expected to advantage lesbians for leadership, complexity enters because many people perceive homosexuality as an immoral lifestyle choice that violates religious doctrines (Ragins, Cornwell, & Miller, 2003). Consider that a Gallup poll revealed that 6 of 10 Americans believe that homosexual behavior is morally wrong (Newport, 1998). Such data suggest that lesbians and gay men who disclose their sexual orientation at work are in danger of experiencing discrimination. A study of over 500 U.S. lesbian and gay employees showed that their disclosure of sexual orientation at work was related to their perceptions of workplace discrimination and lack of advancement (Ragins & Cornwell, 2001). To the extent that these subjective reports are valid, lesbian and gay employees can face restricted upward mobility, a phenomenon sometimes labeled as the "lavender ceiling" (Friskopp & Silverstein, 1996). Such attitudes can undermine not only their access to leadership but also their acceptance as worthy, ethical leaders and role models (Fassinger, Shullman, & Stevenson, in press).

The Effects of Incompatible Leader and the Gender Roles

Given the prevalence of gender and leader stereotypes and their tendency to operate below conscious awareness, the effects of these stereotypes are pervasive. As we have indicated, descriptive gender stereotypes can result in even fully qualified women being viewed as not having what is needed for most leader roles. Perceived as deficient in essential leader qualities, women have reduced access to leadership, particularly where leadership has an especially agentic definition.

The descriptive aspects of stereotypes can also act as self-fulfilling prophecies. Realization that others hold certain expectations about one's behavior can trigger confirmation of these expectations. In fact, gender stereotypes have yielded some of the clearest demonstrations that people behaviorally confirm their interaction partners' beliefs (see review by Geis, 1993). Therefore, if a colleague at work believes that a woman is not assertive enough to be an effective manager, these expectancies can influence her behavior in a stereotype-conforming direction. The confirmation of gender-based expectations maintains, propagates, and justifies people's stereotypes about the leadership ability of women and men.

Another way that the descriptive aspect of stereotypes can affect leader behavior is that they can trigger women's anxiety and undermine their willingness to put themselves forward as potential leaders. Such an effect appeared in research on stereotype threat in which presenting participants with gender stereotypical portrayals of women prior to a group task caused the women (but not the men) to indicate less interest in being the group leader and more interest taking a follower role (Davies, Spencer, & Steele, 2005). In addition, many demonstrations of stereotype threat pertain to racial stereotyping, whereby African Americans' concerns about confirming stereotypes of lack of competence cause their performance to falter on academic tasks (see Steele, Spencer, & Aronson, 2002). Therefore, Black women may be challenged by both gender and race stereotypes, thus compounding the challenges that they face.

Prescriptive gender stereotypes also can lead to less favorable evaluations of women than of objectively equivalent men who occupy leader roles. The prescriptive aspect of gender stereotypes places competing demands on women leaders, who face a dilemma—in fact, a double bind (Eagly & Carli, 2007). The prescriptions for the female gender role stipulate that women should be especially communal, and the prescriptions for most leadership roles stipulate that leaders should be especially agentic. The resulting dilemma is that highly communal female leaders may be criticized for not being agentic enough and not properly taking charge and highly agentic female leaders may be criticized for lacking communion and not being nice enough. In this way, female leaders are often in a lose–lose situation. If their behavior confirms the gender stereotype, they are not thought to be acting as a proper leader, but if their behavior is consistent with the leader stereotype, they are not thought to be acting as a proper woman. Violating either of these stereotypes can lower evaluations of them and their performance (e.g., Cuddy, Fiske, & Glick, 2004; Eagly & Karau, 2002; Heilman, Wallen, Fuchs, & Tamkins, 2004; Rudman & Glick, 2001). Female leaders can alleviate this dilemma to some extent by exhibiting both agentic and communal behavior (Johnson, Murphy, Zewdie, & Reichard, 2008; see also Eagly & Carli, 2007)

In support of this reasoning, a meta-analysis of the results of experiments that varied the sex of leaders but held other attributes constant showed that the prejudicial devaluation of women's leader behaviors is somewhat pronounced when leader behaviors are stereotypically masculine, especially when they are autocratic or directive (mean $d = 0.30$ for autocratic leadership; Eagly, Makhijani, & Klonsky, 1992). Thus, a male manager who acts in a forceful or assertive manner is perceived as behaving appropriately and displaying leadership, whereas a female leader who behaves in exactly the same way is vulnerable to being regarded as unacceptably pushy. Male managers, in contrast, suffer no penalty when they manifest the more collaborative and democratic leadership styles that are more typical of women (Eagly et al., 1992).

Gender biases that disadvantage women as leaders may emerge quite early during the encoding stage of information processing (Scott & Brown, 2006; see also Foti, Knee, & Baekert, 2008). Specifically, participants in experiments had difficulty encoding leadership behaviors into the underlying prototypical leadership traits of assertiveness when the agentic behavior was enacted by a woman. This phenomenon would make it difficult for women to be perceived as possessing the qualifications for leader roles.

Given the double bind whereby women can be criticized for being both like and unlike leaders, women can find leadership challenging. Influence—the ability to affect the beliefs or behaviors of others—is required for effective leadership. Because of the double bind, people may resist a woman's influence, particularly in masculine settings. Sometimes they resist her because they think she lacks communion, so they don't like her. Sometimes they resist her because they think she lacks agency and competence, so they don't respect her. Yet people have greater influence when they appear both agentically competent and warm. So for women to gain influence, the double bind requires a difficult balancing act (Eagly & Carli, 2007).

Although the balancing act that women managers endure on the basis of their gender can be challenging enough, women of color can face additional pressures—the "invisibility vise" described by Bell and Nkomo (2001, p. 149). Black women managers reported that their White colleagues feel more comfortable with Blacks who suppress their racial identity in the workplace, yet these women often prefer to maintain a strong, "visible," racial identity. A clash of this type can place African Americans, and perhaps other minorities, under pressures specific to their race and ethnicity. As one manager noted, in reference to the expectation that she assimilate and avoid expressing her racial identity: "When they get comfortable with you, you become invisible" (Bell & Nkomo, 2001, p. 150; see also hooks, 1989). It is not surprising, therefore, that, among female managers, Black women, more than White women, reported resistance and challenge to their authority from bosses, subordinates, and colleagues (Bell & Nkomo, 2001). In addition, Hispanic female (and male) managers in the United States reported experiencing ambiguity about their colleagues' acceptance of their ethnicity. However, they were more likely to question whether there were negative implications of ethnicity than were the Black managers, who usually believed that their race did matter (Cianni & Romberger, 1991).

Special pressures are also evident for male leaders from groups with lower social status. For example, because Black men are associated with threat, disarming mechanisms (e.g., babyfaceness) may facilitate the success of Black male executives by mitigating such perceptions. Although prior research showed that babyfaceness negatively correlated with the success of White men in high leadership positions (e.g., Rule & Ambady, 2008; Zebrowitz & Montepare, 2005), Black male CEOs were significantly more babyfaced than White male CEOs (Livingston & Pearce, 2009). In addition, babyfaced Black CEOs tended to lead more prestigious corporations and to have higher salaries than mature-faced Black CEOs; these relations did not emerge for White CEOs.

To understand the leadership challenges that women and minority men face, it is necessary to study the structure and culture of the organizations within which leadership takes place. Impediments to leadership can reside in the traditions and practices of organizations just as much as in the minds of the individuals who inhabit these organizations.

Organizational Barriers to Women's Leadership

Although it may seem that organizations provide equal advancement opportunities for women and men, their social structure and culture often create more challenges to women than to men. These challenges are inherent in organizations' formal roles, rules, and procedures as well as their tacit rules and norms of conduct. In both structure and culture, organizations present women with many impediments to advancement (e.g., Acker, 1990; Calás & Smircich, 1992; Fletcher, 1999; Martin, 1990). Although few of these features were expressly designed to exclude women and, in fact, can appear to be gender neutral, they often pose more difficulties to women than to men.

It is not surprising that many aspects of organizations implicitly favor men's leadership because, traditionally, many men and very few women held leader roles in most organizations. Therefore, organizations developed traditions that fit men's lifestyles and preferences. These masculine traditions have become exacerbated because, in recent decades, organizations have come to represent an implicit model of an ideal employee who can be called on to work long hours and to make many personal sacrifices for the organization. This ideal employee has few encumbrances that could limit devotion to the job and certainly few family responsibilities (Acker, 1990; Martin, 1996; Kark & Waismel-Manor, 2005; Williams, 2000). In the next sections, we explore the implications of this ideal employee model and analyze those aspects of organizations that most disadvantage women.

Demands for Long Hours and Relocation

One common feature of managerial positions, especially those with higher levels of authority, is a demand for continuous availability. In general, managerial, professional, and technical workers have longer than average work weeks (Jacobs & Gerson, 2004). Willingness to work very long hours can be an important qualification for rising to higher positions, especially if organizations focus more on amount of work than on the productivity or the quality of employees' contributions. Working nights and weekends demonstrates commitment to the organization, even when such efforts are not really necessary (Brett & Stroh, 2003; Rapoport, Bailyn, Fletcher, & Pruitt, 2002). In global markets, availability at all hours and frequent travel can be required of managers to meet the needs of international business partners. In addition to long hours, managers may encounter demands to relocate for new assignments or higher positions in other cities or countries.

Long hours reduce the number of highly paid workers that organizations must employ. Thus, this pattern can be attractive to organizations especially during periods of downsizing. However, requiring more work from fewer employees often creates stress (Armstrong-Stassen, 2005) and can reduce organizational performance (McElroy, Morrow, & Rude, 2001). Moreover, long hours can reflect managers' lack of planning and discipline concerning what work really needs to be done and how to organize to accomplish tasks efficiently (Bailyn, 2002).

In many organizations, long hours of work are not an official job requirement but are regarded as an aspect of appropriate behavior (Bolino, 1999; Kark & Waismel-Manor, 2005). Long hours are an aspect of *organizational citizenship behavior*, which consists of discretionary behavior that is not explicitly recognized by the formal reward system and that in the aggregate promotes the functioning of the organization (Organ, 1988). Such behavior encompasses conscientiousness, which involves going well beyond minimally required levels of work attendance and punctuality, which can be exaggerated to include coming to work early, staying late, and refraining from taking breaks (Morrison, 1994).

In general, men are more able than women to increase their work hours and limit their time away from the job because of their lesser domestic responsibility (Acker, 1990; Hochschild, 1989; Martin, 1990). This situation contributes to the reputation of men as good organizational citizens (Kark & Waismel-Manor, 2005). Women experience greater stress from extremely long work hours because they are less likely than men to be able to shift domestic responsibilities to a partner (Davidson & Fielden, 1999).

In anticipation of stresses from very time-consuming job demands, women in high-status careers tend to forego or delay childbearing (e.g., Hewlett, 2002), and some quit their jobs when they have a child. For example, one U.S. study showed that 37% of women with very strong educational credentials voluntarily dropped out of employment at some point, but only 24% of similarly qualified men did (Hewlett & Luce, 2005). Among women with one or more children, this percentage rose to 43%. The main reason that these women relinquished employment was for "family time," but for men it was usually to change careers. The situation is similar in many other industrialized nations. In the Netherlands, for example, 11% of women who had their first child stopped working altogether and 49% reduced their hours of paid work. In contrast, the great majority of men continued to work for as many hours as they did before their first child was born (Portegijs, Hermans, & Lalta, 2006).

Masculine Organizational Culture

Organizations often manifest a culture that makes it hard for women to fit in and to advance to leadership positions. For example, in one U.S. survey, women in managerial and professional jobs most frequently cited "a male-dominated work culture" as a barrier to their advancement (Manuel, Shefte, & Swiss, 1999).

Masculine values and "doing masculinity" at work are manifested in many ways that go beyond being totally devoted to one's job with few family entanglements. For example, everyday activities on the job often feature sports and military terminology such as "slam dunk" and "getting flack" (Eagly & Carli, 2007). An especially dedicated employee may be labeled a "good solider" (Organ, 1988; Kark & Waismel-Manor, 2005). A tendency in many nations for senior political and business roles to be held by former military officers results in the military culture being carried into other organizational spheres. Military and sports discourse, because it is more familiar and comfortable for men, tends to favor their presence in the upper echelons of power.

Masculine values may also be communicated in the recreational activities pursued by workplace colleagues. For example, in the United States, meetings of Wal-Mart managers and executives included quail hunting expeditions and visits to strip clubs. One manager received feedback that she would not advance any further at Wal-Mart because she did not hunt or fish (Featherstone, 2004). Other leisure activities may be organized around masculine team sports, such as basketball (Eagly & Carli, 2007). In a study of oral histories of managers' daily experiences, women described their exclusion from social events that they perceived to lead to career advantage, such as golf games and bowling leagues (Cianni & Romberger, 1991). Masculine traditions are also evident even in the design of features of the organizational environment, for example, a speaker's podium appropriate for men's, but not women's, average height.

Although many work organizations maintain a masculine culture, there are certain types of organizations that are ordinarily highly masculine, such as the police and the military. In such organizations women and minority men may have a harder time fitting in (Silvestri, 2003; see also Chapter 28). For example, in the police, women's presence has been met with covert and overt hostility, and the employment of lesbians and gay men as police officers has been found to be especially threatening in this occupation that values traditional masculinity and middle-class morality (Miller, Forest, & Jurik, 2003; Shilts, 1980).

Women generally are less likely to approve of masculine organizational culture than men are, even though many women end up conforming to it (van Vianen & Fischer, 2002). Although accommodation is no doubt one of the main ways for women to advance in masculine organizations, this approach can make some women feel that they are not authentically expressing their own identities and preferences (Eagly, 2005). Alternatively, those women and men who do not fit with masculine organizational culture sometimes invent nuanced ways of advancing while transforming the culture so that it becomes more inclusive of diverse values and preferences (see Meyerson, 2001).

Barriers to Building Social Capital

Social capital consists of relationships between people and the mutual obligation and support that develop from these relationships. Social capital in one's workplace and profession is crucial to career advancement (Brass, 2001). Managers' social capital, especially their relationships with people in other organizations, fosters their progress upward through organizational hierarchies (e.g., Seibert, Kraimer, & Liden, 2001). Such relationships can yield valuable information, access to help and resources, sharing of creative ideas, and career sponsorship.

Organizational research has often shown that women have less social capital than men do (Eagly & Carli, 2007). One of the difficulties that women face is that social networks in organizations tend to be segregated by sex. Both sexes often form social networks dominated by their own sex, and women can experience exclusion from informal "old boys' networks" (Ibarra, 1992). Segregated networks are not optimal for women's advancement because networks populated by men are generally more powerful. Yet, women can experience gains from relationships with other women, especially in terms of social support, role modeling, and information about overcoming discrimination (Forret & Dougherty, 2004; Timberlake, 2005). Role modeling of other women can have a meaningful effect on women's motivation and ability to lead (Adler, 2008). More generally, female managers and male managers from minority groups need to form more diverse networks and more contacts outside their work teams in order to advance, whereas White male managers can draw on homogenous networks (Ibarra, 1995).

The concentration of power in networks dominated by White men tends to limit women's social capital (see review by Timberlake, 2005) as well as that of men who are members of racial minority groups. Both female and male managers of color can have even less access to White male-dominated social networks than White women do (Catalyst, 2006; Ibarra, 1995). A U.S. survey indicated that only 59% of the Black female managers reported having White men in their networks, whereas 91% of the White female managers did (Bell & Nkomo, 2001). Furthermore, African American women often reported that they felt themselves to be outsiders in their own organizations. Minority women's gender and race set them apart from the White male executives. These women's networking strategies generally involve connecting with other women, especially other minority women, and attempting to make some inroads into men's networks (Catalyst, 2006).

Mentoring relationships, which provide one way of gaining social capital, tend to enhance individuals' career progress (Allen, Eby, Poteet, Lentz, & Lima, 2004). Mentors who hold powerful positions are in a position to offer considerable career facilitation. Yet, mentoring relationships also tend to form along same-sex lines. Race can also affect mentoring, and one study showed that Black women were less likely than White women and Black men to receive mentoring from the highest status managers, who generally are White men (Thomas, 1990).

Women's deficit in social capital may seem paradoxical, given that they acknowledge the importance of networking (e.g., Manuel et al., 1999) and, on average, have better relational skills than men do, as shown, for example, on tests of emotional intelligence (e.g., Brackett, Rivers, Shiffman, Lerner, & Salovey, 2006). However, women's relational skills are often directed to work that has little bearing on advancement (Fletcher, 1999). For example, managerial women are more likely than managerial men to focus on mentoring followers and attending to their individual needs (Eagly, Johannesen-Schmidt, & van Engen, 2003). Employees who were promoted at a fast pace focused instead on high visibility tasks and not on the less visible relational tasks that are nonetheless crucial for the success of the organization's projects, such as assisting others who have heavy workloads (Kark & Waismel-Manor, 2005). Moreover, many of these relational tasks, such as coordination and the collection of information, are vulnerable to being devalued as easy (De Pater, van Vianen, Fischer, & van Ginkel, 2009). Ironically, by providing much of the social glue that helps organizations to function smoothly, women may fail to advance.

Women's deficits in social capital follow in part from the increased work hours that are inherent in extensive networking. Useful relationships can be forged, for example, from after-dinner drinks with colleagues or weekend golf outings with potential clients and customers. Even during ordinary work hours, informal networking can be difficult for women if influential networks are composed almost entirely of men. In these contexts, women usually have less legitimacy and influence and, therefore, benefit less than men from participation.

Challenges of Obtaining Desirable Assignments

One of the benefits of social capital is that it facilitates opportunities to gain appropriately demanding assignments, known as developmental job experiences. Becoming recognized for solving problems acknowledged as challenging speeds advancement to upper level management, but social capital is a prerequisite for winning the chance to take on such projects (e.g., McCauley, Ruderman, Ohlott, & Morrow, 1994). Given women's generally lesser social capital, it is not surprising that they often lack such opportunities (e.g., Lyness & Thompson, 2000).

Women's difficulties in obtaining developmental job experiences are compounded by their occupancy of managerial roles that serve staff functions, such as human resources and public relations, rather than line functions, which are usually seen as more critical to the success of organizations. Given stereotypical norms about whether women or men are optimal for various types of management, men are more often channeled into line management, with its better opportunities to ascend into senior leadership.

Despite women's difficulties in obtaining demanding assignments, other evidence shows that some women are placed, more often than comparable men, in highly risky positions, a phenomenon labeled the *glass cliff* (Ryan & Haslam, 2007). When companies are facing financial downturns and declining performance, executives have a fairly high risk of failure. Companies may be more willing to have female executives take these risks, and women may be more willing to accept such positions, given their lesser prospects for obtaining more desirable positions or their lack of access to networks that might steer them away from such jobs. Both this glass cliff and fewer developmental job experiences deny women access to the "good" assignments that maximize opportunities for showing oneself as a high-potential manager.

Leadership Effectiveness

Our consideration of discrimination and organizational barriers raises the question of how women compare to men when they reach leadership positions in organizations. Are they effective leaders? Answers have emerged in three traditions of research: (a) studies that relate organizations' effectiveness to the percentages of women among their executives; (b) studies that assess the effectiveness of individual male and female leaders; and (c) studies that compare the effectiveness of the leadership styles of men and women. We now review evidence based on these three different approaches.

Organizational Effectiveness of Gender-Integrated Executive Teams

Groups that bring together individuals from multiple identity groups may outperform more homogeneous groups because they ordinarily include members with different ways of representing and solving problems (Hong & Page, 2004; Page, 2007). Such groups may be more successful than groups composed of individuals selected exclusively for their high ability because the best solutions to complex problems generally result from teams whose members apply different tools and abilities. The challenge is to leverage this potential by lessening the conflict, communication barriers, and lack of mutual respect that can develop in identity-diverse groups (e.g., Polzer, Milton, & Swann, 2002; see review by van Knippenberg & Schippers, 2007).

Business organizations produce financial data that can serve as one measure of the association between effectiveness and diversity. Catalyst (2004), which is a research and advisory organization dedicated to advancing women's careers, analyzed data from the *Fortune* 500, the 500 largest corporations in the United States as defined by their revenues. The researchers used appropriate measures of financial performance for the period 1996–2000 and found that the companies with the highest representation of female executives (top 25%) fared substantially better than the companies with the lowest representation (bottom 25%). A similar study of European-based companies compared those with greatest gender diversity in top management with average performance in their economic sector and showed better financial performance in companies with gender diversity (Desvaux, Devillard-Hoellinger, & Baumgarten, 2008). In a more advanced U.S. study that took into account numerous control variables, researchers examined the relation between women's percentage in the top management teams of the *Fortune* 1000 companies and their financial performance from 1998 to 2000 (Krishnan & Park, 2005). The findings showed that companies with larger percentages of women in their top management groups had better financial performance (see also Carter, Simkins, & Simpson, 2003; Erhardt, Werbel, & Shrader, 2003).

Earlier U.S. studies produced more ambiguous outcomes (e.g., Shrader, Blackburn, & Iles, 1997). For example a British study yielded no relation between board gender diversity and financial performance in the FTSE 100, the largest corporations in the United Kingdom. (Vinnicombe & Singh, 2003). Judge (2003) inspected these data and observed that, of the 10 companies with the highest percentage of women on their boards, six had underperformed relative to the mean performance of FTSE 100 companies. In contrast, the five companies with the lowest percentage of women on their boards (i.e., no women at all) had all performed better than the FTSE 100 average. This result led Judge to conclude that "corporate Britain may well be better off without women on the board" (p. 21).

Ryan and Haslam (2005, 2007) took issue with Judge's views. They examined the contexts in which women were appointed to leadership positions by comparing companies' performance before and after the appointment of male or female board members, and their analysis revealed that the appointment of a female director was *not* associated with a subsequent drop in company performance. Instead, in a time of a general financial downturn, companies that appointed a woman actually experienced a marked *increase* in share price followed by a period of share price stability, although, in relative terms, the companies were still performing poorly. The studies further showed that companies that appointed a woman to their board had experienced poor performance in the months *preceding* the appointment. Consistent with the glass cliff phenomenon, women may have privileged access to such highly risky positions and, thus, reap the blame for organizational failure (Haslam & Ryan, 2008; Ryan & Haslam, 2005).

These studies reveal some of the complexities of assessing the effectiveness of women in executive positions. Data from a wider span of years and data from more nations might allow stronger causal inferences. Nonetheless, recent studies show that women's participation as business leaders can coincide with economic gains for corporations.

Effectiveness of Individual Male and Female Leaders

The second approach to assessing the effectiveness of female and male leaders entails a comparison of their performance. A meta-analysis was conducted to explore the results of 96 such studies (Eagly, Karau, & Makhijani, 1995). The studies included assessments of managers in organizational settings and, in a few instances, leaders of small laboratory groups. The male and female leaders who were compared held the same or generally comparable roles. Researchers typically determined leaders' effectiveness by having people (i.e., subordinates, peers, superiors, or leaders themselves) subjectively rate how well the leaders performed. These evaluations are not necessarily unbiased and may well be affected by prejudice against women leaders, especially in male-dominated settings. However, because leaders cannot be effective unless others accept their leadership, these evaluations, however biased, serve as a relevant measure of how well an individual leads.

The findings of this meta-analysis suggest that the effectiveness of male and female leaders depends on the context in which they lead (Eagly et al., 1995). Specifically, men's effectiveness as leaders surpassed women's in roles that were male-dominated or masculine in other ways (e.g., military) and in positions associated with a higher proportion of male subordinates (or when effectiveness was assessed by ratings performed by a higher proportion of men; see also Bowen, Swim, & Jacobs, 2000). However, women were found to be somewhat more effective than men in roles where women were more numerous (e.g., educational, governmental, and social service organizations).

The meta-analysis included additional data derived from a panel of judges assembled to give ratings of the leader roles. Those data showed that women exceeded men in effectiveness in leader roles perceived as attractive to women and as requiring stereotypical feminine characteristics (e.g., cooperativeness, the ability to get along well with others). Men exceeded women in effectiveness in roles perceived as attractive to men and as requiring stereotypical masculine characteristics (e.g., directiveness, the control of others). Overall, effectiveness tracked gender stereotyping quite closely.

This meta-analysis also showed that female managers fared particularly well in effectiveness, relative to male managers, in middle-level leadership positions. This finding is understandable, given middle management's usual demands for complex interpersonal skills (e.g., Paolillo, 1981), most of which are encompassed in the stereotypically feminine communal repertoire of behaviors.

These results suggest that leader roles that are highly male-dominated or culturally masculine in their demands present particular challenges to women because of their incompatibility with people's expectations about women. This incompatibility not only restricts women's access to such leadership roles but also can compromise the effectiveness of the women who occupy these roles. When leader roles are extremely masculine, people may suspect that women are not qualified for them, and they often resist women's authority (Carli, 1999; Eagly & Karau, 2002; Heilman, 2001). Sexual harassment and other potential forms of resistance to women's leadership remain potent factors in such environments (Stockdale & Bhattacharya, 2009).

Taken together, these findings imply that women leaders in masculine settings are likely to encounter difficulties in gaining authority and feeling accepted and comfortable (e.g., Lyness & Thompson, 2000; Silvestri, 2003; Wajcman, 1998). Further, women in highly masculine domains often have to contend with criticisms that they lack the toughness and competitiveness needed to succeed. In such settings, it is difficult for women to build relationships and gain acceptance in influential networks (Timberlake, 2005). Given these hurdles, advancing in a highly male-dominated hierarchy requires a highly competent, strong, and persistent woman. She has to avoid the threats to her confidence that other people's doubts and criticisms can elicit.

Women's vulnerability in male-dominated settings is especially evident for women of color and for lesbians and gay men. For example, Black female managers who were interviewed in a survey believed that they were held to a higher standard than their White female colleagues, even when the credentials of the Black women were extraordinary. Sixty-five percent of the Black women who participated in a national survey indicated that they had to outperform their White colleagues for the same rewards and credibility (Bell & Nkomo, 2001). Gay men and lesbians also are likely to experience more discrimination in male-dominated than in female-dominated contexts, given that men have more negative attitudes toward homosexuality than women do (see meta-analysis by Kite & Whitley, 1996). Research has confirmed that heterosexism, especially directed toward lesbians, is pronounced in work environments with male supervisors and primarily male work teams, especially when these teams are homogeneously White (Ragins et al., 2003).

Leadership Style and Leaders' Effectiveness

The third approach to examining the effectiveness of female and male leaders concerns the effectiveness of their leadership styles. Due to the growing numbers of women in managerial positions, many people have wondered whether there is a leadership style that distinguishes female leaders from male leaders.

Many academic writers have claimed that there are no differences in leadership style between women and men in the same leadership position (e.g., Bass, 1990; Vecchio, 2002). In support of gender similarity, managerial roles surely suppress behavioral differences when men and women occupy the same role. Men and women are generally selected for roles by similar criteria, and they are under the same pressures to fulfill the tasks of the roles.

Contrary claims that women's leadership style differs from men's initially came from writers of popular books on leadership (e.g., Helgesen, 1990; Rosener, 1995). The evidence they offered was based on their impressions of the women they have surveyed or interviewed. In support of their claims, gender roles do not disappear in employment settings—they continue to have some influence and, thereby, to some extent foster gender stereotypical behavior. Given the double bind cross-pressures from leadership roles and the feminine gender role, it is not surprising that female leaders report that finding an appropriate and effective leadership style is one of their greatest challenges. In fact, a study of *Fortune* 1000 female executives showed that 96% rated as *critical* or *fairly important* that they develop a style with which male managers are comfortable (Catalyst, 2000).

The issues of leadership style are best resolved by meta-analyses, which take all of the relevant studies into account and integrate the results quantitatively. Two meta-analyses have compared the leadership styles of men and women who occupy the same or similar leadership roles. The first of these included the classic literature on leadership style, which emphasized the distinction between task-oriented and relationship-oriented styles and between autocratic and democratic styles (Eagly & Johnson, 1990; see also van Engen & Willemsen, 2004). The findings did not confirm the gender-stereotypic expectation that women lead in an interpersonally oriented style and men in a task-oriented style. Yet, female leaders tended to adopt a somewhat more democratic or participative style and a somewhat less autocratic or directive style than male leaders did (mean $d = 0.22$). However, this relatively small difference became especially small in more male-dominated leadership roles. Without a critical mass of other women to affirm the legitimacy of a more collaborative, participative style, female leaders evidently tend to opt for whatever style is typical of their male colleagues.

Given the double bind that we emphasized earlier, women no doubt are more readily accepted as leaders when they share power by being collaborative. Yet, a collaborative style is not necessarily better than a directive one. These styles' effectiveness is contingent on various features of group and organizational environments (see meta-analyses by Foels, Driskell, Mullen, & Salas, 2000; Gastil, 1994). Under some circumstances, democratic and participative styles are effective, and, under other circumstances, autocratic and directive styles are effective.

The second meta-analysis included the more recently developed research literature on transformational and transactional leadership styles (see Avolio, 1999; Bass, 1998). Transformational leadership has been widely accepted as a model of contemporary good managerial practice and is, in fact, correlated with leaders' effectiveness (see the meta-analysis by Judge & Piccolo, 2004). Such leadership involves establishing oneself as a role model by gaining followers' trust and confidence. Transformational leaders state future goals, develop plans to achieve them, and innovate, even when their organization is generally successful. They mentor and empower followers by encouraging them to develop their full potential. As this description of transformational leadership suggests, it is neither masculine nor feminine when considered in its entirety but, instead, culturally androgynous. Yet, because of some of its elements, especially the mentoring and empowering of subordinates, it appears to be slightly more aligned with the feminine than the masculine gender role (Duehr & Bono, 2006; Kark, 2004).

Transformational leadership differs from transactional leadership, which is rooted in give-and-take relationships that appeal to subordinates' self-interest. One aspect of transactional leadership that is quite effective is rewarding satisfactory performance by followers; attending to followers' mistakes and failures is much less effective. Yet another potential leadership style, labeled *laissez-faire*, involves a general failure to take responsibility for managing. This approach is quite ineffective (Judge & Piccolo, 2004).

A meta-analysis of 45 studies included all available research that had assessed leadership style according to the distinctions between transformational, transactional, and laissez-faire leadership (Eagly et al., 2003). That analysis established small gender differences, such that women were generally more transformational in leadership style (mean $d = -0.10$) and also more transactional in terms of providing rewards for satisfactory performance (mean $d = -0.13$). Women's transformational leadership was especially evident in their focus on developing and mentoring followers and attending to their individual needs (mean $d = -0.19$). In contrast, men were more likely than women to emphasize followers' mistakes and failures (mean $d = 0.12$). In addition, men were more likely than women to wait until problems become severe before intervening (mean $d = 0.12$) and more likely to shirk responsibility for managing (mean $d = 0.16$). Although these more negative and ineffective styles were more common among men, they were relatively uncommon among leaders of both sexes.

Given that men have greater access to leadership than women do, it is startling to find even these small meta-analytic differences showing that women obtained higher ratings than men did on the components of leadership style that relate positively to effectiveness and that men obtained higher ratings than women did on the transactional and laissez-faire styles, which do not enhance effectiveness. The implications of these style findings for effectiveness were corroborated by the somewhat better performance of female managers than male managers on the effectiveness measures used in the studies included in the meta-analysis.

The causes of these differences in women's and men's leadership may lie in several factors: (a) the ability of the transformational repertoire (and rewarding behaviors) to resolve some of the typical incongruity between the leadership roles and the feminine gender role because these styles are not distinctively masculine; (b) gender roles' influence on women's leadership by means of the spillover and internalization of gender-specific norms, which would facilitate the somewhat feminine aspects of transformational leadership; and (c) prejudicial evaluations whereby a double standard for entering into managerial roles produces more highly skilled female than male leaders (Eagly et al., 2003; Kark, 2004).

At the intersection of gender and leadership, although empirical findings are limited, different cultural backgrounds can shape leadership styles along with gender. For example, there are claims that African American women have an especially self-confident, assertive style (Sanchez-Hucles & Davis, in press; Parker, 2005; Parker & Ogilvie, 1996) and that Asian leaders manifest a collectivistic orientation that emphasizes group harmony (Cheung & Halpern, in press; Kawahara, Esnil, & Hsu, 2007) and benevolently paternalistic behaviors (Ayman & Korabik, in press). In addition, female leaders of color, due to their dual marginality in countries where they are a minority, may be particularly concerned about integrity and justice, especially related to the inclusion and fair treatment of diverse individuals. Gay and lesbian managers' behavior may also be shaped by their experience of discrimination and marginality, which perhaps fosters greater sensitivity to employees' emotions and needs for respect, as well as greater ability to build environments that embrace change, nonconformity, and risk taking (Hexter, 2007; Snyder, 2006).

Although empirical evidence about the effectiveness of such aspects of leadership style is absent, these somewhat different leadership styles could produce advantages for several reasons. One reason is that leaders from different backgrounds may be advantaged by their ability to modify and switch between minority and majority perspectives, depending on their immediate cultural context (Molinsky, 2007). Women and men from racial, ethnic, and sexual minority groups generally have multicultural experience because they have learned to negotiate both minority and majority cultures. Multicultural competence may also foster flexibility and openness to change (Musteen, Barker, & Baeten, 2006), as well as creative cognitive processes and problem-solving strategies (Leung, Maddux, Galinsky, & Chiu, 2008).

Finally, having one's abilities challenged on the basis of membership in a group traditionally excluded from leadership sometimes can inspire people to outstanding performance. In fact, research has shown that women who are confident about their leadership ability are not deterred by statements that women have less leadership ability than men do; instead, they react by exhibiting even more competence than they would in the absence of an explicit challenge (Hoyt & Blascovich, 2007, 2009). In addition, it is plausible that diverse leaders perform especially well to the extent that they had to meet a higher standard to attain leadership roles in the first place (see review by Biernat, 2005).

The bottom line on leadership style and gender is that women and men in the same leadership position do differ, but not by very much. Many women do lead with behaviors that are tinged with culturally feminine qualities. Differences between women and men may be more pronounced when women are in a position of lower access to power in comparison to their male colleagues (Keshet, Kark, Pomerantz-Zorin, Koslowsky, & Schwarzwald, 2006). But the good news for women is that these less masculine ways of leading have gained cultural currency as the traditionally masculine command-and-control style has become less admired than in the past (Eagly & Carli, 2007; Kark, 2004). This shift reflects the greater complexity of modern organizations. A modern manager gains less from ordering others about and more from assembling a team of smart, motivated subordinates who together figure out how to solve problems.

Mapping Future Research Directions

There is a saying that "we all travel the same journey; however, some people have better maps." In this chapter we have charted the different trails, routes, and road maps of men and women in their journeys to attain leadership positions and function effectively as leaders. We have addressed the importance of the typically greater family responsibilities of women in slowing their rise in organizational hierarchies, explored the effects of prejudice and discrimination against women as leaders and potential leaders, and examined the effects of the structure and culture of organizations. These considerations together produce paths to leadership that are decidedly more labyrinthine for women than for men. In light of these challenges, we discussed research findings regarding the effectiveness of women's and men's leadership. We further considered the different leadership journeys taken by women and men from diverse identity groups based on race, sexual orientation, ethnicity, and nationality.

Our review of the literature on gender and leadership points to several valuable directions for future research. First, although research has shown that the organizational and cultural context of leadership is important, studies have so far focused on only a few aspects of context. For example, studies of the glass cliff (e.g., Ryan & Haslam, 2007) showed a tendency to appoint women to leadership positions when organizations are in crisis. Also, Ely and Meyerson (2008) showed that establishing an organizational culture that is less masculine and that does not favor macho behaviors, even in masculine environments (e.g., oil rigs), can improve organizational effectiveness and safety and also foster a more inclusive environment for women. Because the power imbalance between men and women takes different forms depending on organizational, political, cultural, and historical circumstances (e.g., Mohanty, 1991), it is essential to focus on a wide range of contextual characteristics to further our understanding of gender and leadership.

Second, studies of the influence of women's and men's identities on aspiration for leadership and leader behavior are still quite limited. Although the most popular measures of gender are based on self-reports of agentic and communal dimensions of personality, gender role and identity can take different forms (see review by Wood & Eagly, 2009). Also, gender identity intersects with identities based on other group memberships such as race, ethnicity, nationality, and religion (Bowleg, 2008). These varied, intersecting identities are marked by the power disparities and status differences that accompany membership in various societal groups. Understanding identity processes is crucial to the successful management of diversity in contemporary organizations (Rink & Ellemers, 2009). Therefore, future researchers should attempt to attain a more comprehensive understanding of the simultaneous effects of different aspects of identity on leadership.

Third, most studies of gender and leadership are cross-sectional and, thereby, neglect the importance of change over time. Given the extraordinary change in women's roles in the last half of the twentieth century, it is important to understand how these social changes have affected and continue to affect women's opportunities for leadership. Also relatively unexplored are the changes that occur in the careers of men and women as they initially attain leadership roles and maintain themselves in them. Do the initial barriers and resistances that women often encounter erode over time as they earn legitimacy through good performance? Do women then have more freedom these days to display authentic behaviors that express their identities as women, and does such freedom, if it exists, also allow racial, ethnic, and sexual minority leaders to express their identities? Longitudinal studies could be conducted to explore the ways in which time and associated experiences shape expectations toward leaders from groups traditionally excluded from leadership. In addition, developmental studies could focus on different life stages to reveal how aspirations for leadership are fostered in earlier life experiences in families, schools, and communities.

Fourth, although scholarly discourse on leadership is typically presented as gender neutral, gender is implicit in the theories and concepts. Leadership theories and concepts not only reflect existing organizational structures but also support and reproduce the existing order by shaping understanding of effective leadership. Researchers who draw on critical perspectives on leadership (e.g., Fletcher, 2004; Kark, 2004) have opportunities to rethink leadership theories to take account of gender and power dynamics. We challenge theorists and researchers of leadership to consider new perspectives and to navigate roads not yet taken (see Eagly & Chin, in press). Such shifts in understanding could potentially affect the practice of leadership and, thereby, ease the now-difficult leadership journeys undertaken by women and people from other groups whose access to leadership opportunities are limited.

References

Acker, J. (1990). Hierarchies, jobs, bodies: A theory of gendered organizations. *Gender & Society, 4*, 139–158.
Adler, N. J. (2008). I am my mother's daughter: Early developmental influences on leadership. *European Journal of International Management, 2*, 6–21.
Agars, M. D. (2004). Reconsidering the impact of gender stereotypes on the advancement of women in organizations. *Psychology of Women Quarterly, 28*, 103–111.
Allen, T. D., Eby, L. T., Poteet, M. L., Lentz, E., & Lima, L. (2004). Career benefits associated with mentoring for proteges: A meta-analysis. *Journal of Applied Psychology, 89*, 127–136.
Armstrong-Stassen, M. (2005). Coping with downsizing: A comparison of executive-level and middle managers. *International Journal of Stress Management, 12*, 117–141.
Atwater, L. E., Brett, J. F., Waldman, D., DiMare, L., & Hayden, M. V. (2004). Men's and women's perceptions of the gender typing of management subroles. *Sex Roles, 50*, 191–199.
Avolio, B. J. (1999). *Full leadership development: Building the vital forces in organizations.* Thousand Oaks, CA: Sage.
Ayman, R., & Korabik, K. (in press). Leadership: Why gender and culture matter. *American Psychologist.*
Bailyn, L. (2002). Time in organizations: Constraints on, and possibilities for, gender equity in the workplace. In R. J. Burke & D. L. Nelson (Eds.), *Advancing women's careers: Research and practice* (pp. 262–272). Malden, MA: Blackwell.
Banaji, M. R., & Hardin, C. D. (1996). Automatic stereotyping. *Psychological Science, 7*, 136–141.
Bass, B. M. (1990). *Bass & Stogdill's handbook of leadership: Theory, research, and managerial applications.* New York: Free Press.
Bass, B. M. (1998). *Transformational leadership: Industrial, military, and educational impact.* Mahwah, NJ: Erlbaum.
Bell, E. J. E., & Nkomo, S. M. (2001). *Our separate ways: Black and White woman and the struggle for professional identity.* Boston, MA: Harvard Business School Press.
Bianchi, S. M., Robinson, J. P., & Milkie, M. A. (2006). *Changing rhythms of American family life.* New York: Russell Sage.
Biernat, M. (2005). *Standards and expectancies: Contrast and assimilation in judgments of self and others.* New York: Psychology Press.
Blau, F. D., & Kahn, L. M. (2006). The gender pay gap: Going, going …but not gone. In F. D. Blau, M. C. Brinton, & D. B. Grusky (Eds.), *The declining significance of gender?* (pp. 37–66). New York: Russell Sage Foundation.
Bolino, M. C. (1999). Citizenship and impression management: Good soldiers or good actors? *Academy of Management Review, 24*, 82–98.
Bowleg, L. (2008). When Black + lesbian + woman # Black lesbian woman: The methodological challenges of qualitative and quantitative intersectionality research. *Sex Roles, 59*, 312–325
Bowen, C., Swim, J. K., & Jacobs. R. R. (2000). Evaluating gender biases on actual job performance of real people: A meta-analysis. *Journal of Applied Social Psychology, 30*, 2194–2215.
Brackett, M. A., Rivers, S. E., Shiffman, S., Lerner, N., & Salovey, P. (2006). Relating emotional abilities to social functioning: A comparison of self-report and performance measures of emotional intelligence. *Journal of Personality and Social Psychology, 91*, 780–795.

Brass, D. J. (2001). Social capital and organizational leadership. In S. J. Zaccaro & R. J. Klimoski (Eds.), *The nature of organizational leadership: Understanding the performance imperatives confronting today's leaders* (pp. 132–152). San Francisco, CA: Jossey-Bass.

Brett, J. M., & Stroh, L. K. (2003). Working 61 hours a week: Why do managers do it? *Journal of Applied Psychology, 88*, 67–78.

Calás, M. B., & Smircich, L. (1992). Re-writing gender into organization theorizing: Directions from feminist perspectives. In M. Reed & M. Hughes (Eds.), *Rethinking organization: New directions in organization theory and analysis* (pp. 227–253). London: Sage.

Carli, L. L. (1999). Gender, interpersonal power, and social influence. *Journal of Social Issues, 55*, 81–99.

Carter, D. A., Simkins, B. J., & Simpson, W. G. (2003). Corporate governance, board diversity, and firm value. *Financial Review, 38*, 33–53.

Catalyst. (2000). *Across three cultures Catalyst finds top barriers to women's professional advancement.* Retrieved September 20, 2008, from https://www.catalyst.org/press-release/29/across-three-cultures-catalyst-finds-top-barriers-to-womens-professional-advancement

Catalyst. (2004). *Women and men in U.S. corporate leadership: Same workplace, different realities?* Retrieved March 12, 2007, from http://www.catalyst.org/file/74/women%20and%20men%20in%20u.s.%20corporate%20leadership%20same%20workplace,%20different%20realities.pdf

Catalyst. (2006). *Connections that count: The informal networks of women of color in the United States.* Retrieved September 20, 2008, from http://www.catalyst.org/file/25/women%20of%20color%20-%20connections%20that%20count.pdf

Catalyst. (2008). *Catalyst 2008 census of the Fortune 500 reveals women gained little ground advancing to business leadership positions.* Retrieved December 14, 2008, from http://www.catalyst.org/press-release/141/catalyst-2008-census-of-the-fortune-500-reveals-women-gained-little-ground-advancing-to-business-leadership-positions

Cejka, M. A., & Eagly, A. H. (1999). Gender-stereotypic images of occupations correspond to the sex segregation of employment. *Personality and Social Psychology Bulletin, 25*, 413–423.

Cheung, F. M., & Halpern, D. F. (in press). Women at the top: Powerful leaders define success as work + family. *American Psychologist.*

Cianni, M., & Romberger, B. (1991). Belonging in the corporation: Oral histories of male and female White, Black, and Hispanic managers. *Academy of Management Proceedings*, 358–362.

Correll, S. J., Benard, S., & Paik, I. (2007). Getting a job: Is there a motherhood penalty? *American Journal of Sociology, 112*, 1297–1338.

Costa, P., Terracciano, A., Jr., & McCrae, R. R. (2001). Gender differences in personality traits across cultures: Robust and surprising findings. *Journal of Personality and Social Psychology, 81*, 322–331.

Cuddy, A. J. C., Fiske, S. T., & Glick, P. (2004). When professionals become mothers, warmth doesn't cut the ice. *Journal of Social Issues, 60*, 701–718.

Dahlerup, D. (2006). *Women, quotas, and politics.* New York: Routledge.

Darley, J. M., & Gross, P. H. (1983). A hypothesis-confirming bias in labeling effects. *Journal of Personality and Social Psychology, 44*, 20–33.

Davidson, M. J., & Fielden, S. (1999). Stress and the working women. In G. N. Powell (Ed.), *Handbook of gender and work* (pp. 413–426). Thousand Oaks, CA: Sage.

Davies, P. G., Spencer, S. J., & Steele, C. M. (2005). Clearing the air: Identity safety moderates the effects of stereotype threat on women's leadership aspirations. *Journal of Personality and Social Psychology, 88*, 276–287.

Davison, H. K., & Burke, M. J. (2000). Sex discrimination in simulated employment contexts: A meta-analytic investigation. *Journal of Vocational Behavior, 56*, 225–248.

Deaux, K., & Lewis, L. L. (1984). Structure of gender stereotypes: Interrelationships among components and gender label. *Journal of Personality and Social Psychology, 46*, 991–1004.

De Pater, I. E., van Vianen, A. E. M., Fischer, A. H., & van Ginkel, W. P. (2009). Challenging experiences: Gender differences in task choice. *Journal of Managerial Psychology, 24*, 4–28.

Desvaux, G., Devillard-Hoellinger, S., & Baumgarten, P. (2008). *Women matter: Gender diversity, a corporate performance driver.* Paris: McKinsey.

Diekman, A. B., & Eagly, A. H. (2000). Stereotypes as dynamic constructs: Women and men of the past, present, and future. *Personality and Social Psychology Bulletin, 26*, 1171–1188.

Dovidio, J. F., & Gaertner, S. L. (2004). Aversive racism. In M. P. Zanna (Ed.), *Advances in experimental social psychology* (Vol. 36, pp. 1–52). San Diego, CA: Academic Press.

Duehr, E. E., & Bono, J. E. (2006). Men, women, and managers: Are stereotypes finally changing? *Personnel Psychology, 59*, 815–846.

Eagly, A. H. (2005). Achieving relational authenticity in leadership: Does gender matter? *Leadership Quarterly, 16*, 459–474.
Eagly, A. H., & Carli, L. L. (2007). *Through the labyrinth: The truth about how women become leaders.* Boston, MA: Harvard Business School Press.
Eagly, A. H., & Chin, J. L. (in press). *Diversity and leadership in a changing world. American Psychologist.*
Eagly, A. H., Johannesen-Schmidt, M. C., & van Engen, M. L. (2003). Transformational, transactional, and laissez-faire leadership styles: A meta-analysis comparing women and men. *Psychological Bulletin, 129*, 569–591.
Eagly, A. H., & Johnson, B. (1990). Gender and leadership style: A meta-analysis. *Psychological Bulletin, 108*, 233–256.
Eagly, A. H., & Karau, S. J. (1991). Gender and the emergence of leaders: A meta-analysis. *Journal of Personality and Social Psychology, 60*, 685–710.
Eagly, A. H., & Karau, S. J. (2002). Role congruity theory of prejudice toward female leaders. *Psychological Review, 109*, 573–598.
Eagly, A. H., Karau, S. J., & Makhijani, M. G. (1995). Gender and the effectiveness of leaders: A meta-analysis. *Psychological Bulletin, 117*, 125–145.
Eagly, A. H., Makhijani, M. G., & Klonsky, B. G. (1992). Gender and the evaluation of leaders: A meta-analysis. *Psychological Bulletin, 111*, 3–22.
Ely, R., & Meyerson, D. (2008). Unmasking manly men. *Harvard Business Review, 86*, 20.
Erhardt, N. L., Werbel, J. D., & Shrader, C. B. (2003). Board of director diversity and firm financial performance. *Corporate Governance, 11*, 102–111.
European Commission. (2007, December 17). *Decision-making in the top 50 publicly quoted companies.* Retrieved July 7, 2008, from http://ec.europa.eu/employment_social/women_men_stats/out/measures_out438_en.htm
Fassinger, R., Shullman, S., & Stevenson, M. (in press). Toward an affirmative lesbian, gay, bisexual, transgender leadership paradigm. *American Psychologist.*
Featherstone, L. (2004). *Selling women short: The landmark battle for workers' rights at Wal-Mart.* New York: Basic Books.
Fletcher, J. K. (1999). *Disappearing acts: Gender, power, and relational practice at work.* Cambridge, MA: MIT Press.
Fletcher, J. K. (2004). The paradox of postheroic leadership: An essay on gender, power, and transformational change. *Leadership Quarterly, 15*, 647–661.
Foels, R., Driskell, J. E., Mullen, B., & Salas, E. (2000). The effects of democratic leadership on group member satisfaction: An integration. *Small Group Research, 31*, 676–701.
Forret, M. L., & Dougherty, T. W. (2004). Networking behaviors and career outcomes: Differences for men and women? *Journal of Organizational Behavior, 25*, 419–437.
Foti, R. J., Knee, R. E., Jr., & Backert, R. S. G. (2008). Multi-level implications of framing leadership perceptions as a dynamic process. *Leadership Quarterly, 19*, 178–194.
Frenkel, M. (2008). Reprogramming femininity? The construction of gender identities in the Israeli hi-tech industry between global and local gender orders. *Gender, Work, and Organizations, 15*, 352–374.
Friskopp, A., & Silverstein, S. (1996). *Straight jobs, gay lives: Gay and lesbian professionals, the Harvard Business School, and the American workplace.* New York: Touchstone.
Gastil, J. (1994). A meta-analytic review of the productivity and satisfaction of democratic and autocratic leadership. *Small Group Research, 25*, 384–410.
Geis, F. L. (1993). Self-fulfilling prophecies: A social psychological view of gender. In A. E. Beall & R. J. Sternberg (Eds.), *The psychology of gender* (pp. 9–54). New York: Guilford.
Haslam, S. A., & Ryan, M. K. (2008). The road to the glass cliff: Differences in the perceived suitability of men and women for leadership positions in succeeding and failing organizations. *Leadership Quarterly, 19*, 530–546.
Heilman, M. E. (2001). Description and prescription: How gender stereotypes prevent women's ascent up the organizational ladder. *Journal of Social Issues, 57*, 657–674.
Heilman, M. E., & Eagly, A. H. (2008). Gender stereotypes are alive, well, and busy producing workplace discrimination. *Industrial and Organizational Psychology, 1*, 393–398.
Heilman, M. E., & Okimoto, T. G. (2008). Motherhood: A potential source of bias in employment decisions. *Journal of Applied Psychology, 93*, 189–198.
Heilman, M. E., Wallen, A. S., Fuchs, D., & Tamkins, M. M. (2004). Penalties for success: Reactions to women who succeed at male gender-typed tasks. *Journal of Applied Psychology, 89*, 416–427.
Helgesen, S. (1990). *The female advantage: Woman's ways of leadership.* New York: Doubleday.
Herzog, H. (1999). *Gendering politics: Women in Israel.* Ann Arbor, MI: University of Michigan Press.
Hexter, R. J. (2007, May–June). On being out as a college president. *Gay & Lesbian Review Worldwide*, pp. 4–5.

Hewlett, S. A. (2002). *Creating a life: Professional women and the quest for children.* New York: Talk Miramax Books.
Hewlett, S. A., & Luce, C. B. (2005). Off-ramps and on-ramps: Keeping talented women on the road to success. *Harvard Business Review, 83*, 43–54.
Hochschild, A. (1989). *The second shift.* New York: Viking.
Hong, L., & Page, S. E. (2004). Groups of diverse problem solvers can outperform groups of high-ability problem solvers. *Proceedings of the National Academy of Sciences, 101*, 16385–16389.
hooks, b. (1989). *Talking back: Thinking feminist, thinking black.* Boston, MA: South End Press.
Hoyt, C. L., & Blascovich, J. (2007). Leadership efficacy and women leaders' responses to stereotype activation. *Group Processes and Intergroup Relations, 10*, 595–616.
Hoyt, C. L., & Blascovich, J. (2009). The role of self-efficacy and stereotype activation on cardiovascular, behavioral, and self-report responses in the leadership domain. *Leadership Quarterly, 20*, 233–249.
Ibarra, H. (1992). Homophily and differential returns: Sex differences in network structure and access in an advertising firm, *Administrative Science Quarterly, 37*, 422–447.
Ibarra, H. (1995). Race, opportunity, and diversity of social circles in managerial networks. *Academy of Management Journal, 38*, 673–703.
Infoplease. (2008). *Minorities and women in the 110th Congress.* Retrieved March 17, 2008, from http://www.infoplease.com/us/government/women-minorities-110th-congress.html
Inter-Parliamentary Union. (2008). *Women in national parliaments* (situation as of July 31, 2008). Retrieved on September 1, 2008, from http://www.ipu.org/wmn-e/world.htm
Ito, T. A., & Urland, G. R. (2003). Race and gender on the brain: Electrocortical measures of attention to the race and gender of multiply categorizable individuals. *Journal of Personality and Social Psychology, 85*, 616–626.
Jacobs, J. A., & Gerson, K. (2004). *The time divide: Work, family, and gender inequality.* Cambridge, MA: Harvard University Press.
Johnson, S. K., Murphy, S. E., Zewdie, S., & Reichard, R. J. (2008). The strong, sensitive type: Effects of gender stereotypes and leadership prototypes on the evaluation of male and female leaders. *Organizational Behavior and Human Decision Processes, 106*, 39–60.
Judge, E. (2003, November 11). Women on board: Help or hindrance? *Times*, p. 21.
Judge, T. A., & Piccolo. R. F. (2004). Transformational and transactional leadership: A meta-analytic test of their relative validity. *Journal of Applied Psychology, 89*, 901–910.
Kark, R. (2004). The transformational leader: Who is (s)he? A feminist perspective. *Journal of Organization Change Management, 17*, 160–176.
Kark, R. (2007). Women in the land of milk, honey, and high technology: The Israeli case. In R. Burke & M. Mattis (Eds.), *Women and minorities in science, technology, engineering, and mathematics: Opening the pipeline* (pp. 101–127). Cheltenham, UK: Elgar.
Kark, R., & Waismel-Manor, R. (2005). Organizational citizenship behavior: What's gender got to do with it? *Organization, 12*, 889–917.
Kawahara, D. M., Esnil, E. M., & Hsu, J. (2007). Asian American women leaders: The intersection of race, gender, and leadership. In J. L. Chin, B. Lott, J. K. Rice, & J. Sanchez-Hucles (Eds.), *Women and leadership: Transforming visions and diverse voices* (pp. 297–313). Malden, MA: Blackwell.
Keshet, S., Kark, R., Pomerantz-Zorin, L., Koslowsky, M., & Schwarzwald, J. (2006). Gender, status, and the use of power strategies. *European Journal of Social Psychology, 36*, 105–117.
Kite, M. E., & Deaux, K. (1987). Gender belief systems: Homosexuality and the implicit inversion theory. *Psychology of Women Quarterly, 11*, 83–96.
Kite, M. E., Deaux, K., & Haines, E. L. (2008). Gender stereotypes. In F. L. Denmark & M. A. Paludi (Eds.), *Psychology of women: A handbook of issues and theories* (2nd ed., pp. 205–236). Westport, CT: Praeger.
Kite, M. E., & Whitley, B. E., Jr. (1996). Sex differences in attitudes toward homosexual persons, behaviors, and civil rights: A meta-analysis. *Personality and Social Psychology Bulletin, 22*, 336–353.
Krishnan, H. A., & Park, D. (2005). A few good women—On top management teams. *Journal of Business Research, 58*, 1712–1720.
Lane, K. A., Banaji, M. R., Nosek, B. A., & Greenwald, A. G. (2007). Understanding and using the Implicit Association Test IV: What we know (so far) about the method. In B. Wittenbrink & N. Schwarz (Eds.), *Implicit measures of attitudes* (pp. 59–102). New York: Guilford.
Leung, A. K., Maddux, W. W., Galinsky, A. D., & Chiu, C. (2008). Multicultural experience enhances creativity: The when and how. *American Psychologist, 63*, 169–181.
Livingston, R. W., & Pearce, N. A. (2009). The teddy bear effect: Facial cues of warmth benefit Black CEOs. *Psychological Science, 20*, 1229–1236.

Lyness, K. S., & Heilman, M. E. (2006). When fit is fundamental: Performance evaluations and promotions of upper-level female and male managers. *Journal of Applied Psychology, 91*, 777–785.

Lyness, K. S., & Thompson, D. E. (2000). Climbing the corporate ladder: Do female and male executives follow the same route? *Journal of Applied Psychology, 85*, 86–101.

Madon, S., Guyll, M., Aboufadel, K., Montiel, E., Smith, A., Palumbo, P., et al. (2001). Ethnic and national stereotypes: The Princeton trilogy revisited and revised. *Personality and Social Psychology Bulletin, 27*, 996–1010.

Mandel, H., & Semyonov, M. (2005). Family policies, wage structures, and gender gaps: Sources of earnings inequality in 20 countries. *American Sociological Review, 70*, 949–968.

Manuel, T., Shefte, S., & Swiss, D. J. (1999). *Suiting themselves: Women's leadership styles in today's workplace.* Cambridge, MA: Radcliffe Public Policy Institute and the Boston Club.

Martell, R. F., Parker, C., Emrich, C. G., & Crawford, M. S. (1998). Sex stereotyping in the executive suite: "Much ado about something." *Journal of Social Behavior and Personality, 13*, 127–138.

Martin, J. (1990). Deconstructing organizational taboos: The suppression of gender conflict in organizations. *Organization Science, 1*, 339–359.

Martin, P. Y. (1996). Gendering and evaluating dynamics: Men, masculinities, and managements. In D. L. Collinson & J. Hearn (Eds.), *Men as managers, managers as men* (pp. 186–209). London: Sage.

Maume, D. J., Jr. (1999). Occupational segregation and the career mobility of White men and women. *Social Forces, 77*, 1433–1459.

McCauley, C. D., Ruderman, M. N., Ohlott, P. J., & Morrow, J. E. (1994). Assessing the developmental components of managerial jobs. *Journal of Applied Psychology, 79*, 544–560.

McElroy, J. C., Morrow, P. C., & Rude, S. N. (2001). Turnover and organizational performance: A comparative analysis of the effects of voluntary, involuntary, and reduction-in-force turnover. *Journal of Applied Psychology, 86*, 1294–1299.

Meyerson, D. E. (2001). *Tempered radicals: How people use difference to inspire change at work.* Boston, MA: Harvard Business School Press.

Miller, S. L., Forest, K. B., & Jurik, N. C. (2003). Diversity in blue: Lesbian and gay police officers in a masculine occupation. *Men and Masculinities, 5*, 355–385.

Mohanty, C. T. (1991). Under Western eyes: Feminist scholarship and colonial discourses. In C. T. Mohanty, A. Russo, & L. Torres (Eds.), *Third world women and the politics of feminism* (pp. 51–80). Bloomington, IN: Indiana University Press.

Molinsky, A. (2007). Cross-cultural code switching: The psychological challenges of adapting behavior in foreign cultural interactions. *Academy of Management Review, 32*, 622–640.

Morrison, E. W. (1994). Role definitions and organizational citizenship behavior: The importance of the employee's perspective. *Academy of Management Journal, 37*, 1543–1567.

Musteen, M., Barker, V. L., III, & Baeten, V. L. (2006). CEO attributes associated with attitude toward change: The direct and moderating effects of CEO tenure. *Journal of Business Research, 59*, 604–612.

Newport, F. (1998, July). Americans more likely to believe sexual orientation due to environment, not genetics. *Gallup Poll Monthly*. Retrieved September 5, 2008, from Gallup Brain, http: www.brain.gallup.com

Newport, F. (2001, February 21). *Americans see women as emotional and affectionate, men as more aggressive*: Gender specific stereotypes persist in recent Gallup poll. Retrieved September 13, 2009, from Gallup Brain, http://brain.gallup.com

Niemann, Y. F., Jennings, L., Rozelle, R. M., Baxter, J. C., & Sullivan, E. (1994). Use of free responses and cluster analysis to determine stereotypes of eight groups. *Personality and Social Psychology Bulletin, 20*, 379–390.

Organ, D. W. (1988). *Organizational citizenship behavior: The good soldier syndrome.* Lexington, MA: Lexington Books.

Page, S. E. (2007). *The difference: How the power of diversity creates better groups, firms, schools, and societies.* Princeton, NJ: Princeton University Press.

Paolillo, J. G. P. (1981). Managers' self assessments of managerial roles: The influence of hierarchical level. *Journal of Management, 7*, 43–52.

Parker, P. S. (2005). *Race, gender, and leadership: Re-envisioning organizational leadership from the perspectives of African American women executives.* Mahwah, NJ: Erlbaum.

Parker, P. S., & Ogilvie, D. T. (1996). Gender, culture, and leadership: Toward a culturally distinct model of African-American women executives' leadership strategies. *Leadership Quarterly, 7*, 189–214.

Polzer, J. T., Milton, L. P., & Swann, W. B., Jr. (2002). Capitalizing on diversity: Interpersonal congruence in small work groups. *Administrative Science Quarterly, 47*, 296–324.

Portegijs, W., Hermans, B., & Lalta, V. (2006). *Emancipatiemonitor 2006.* The Hague: Sociaal Cultureel Planbureau.

Powell, G. N., Butterfield, D. A., & Parent, J. D. (2002). Gender and managerial stereotypes: Have the times changed? *Journal of Management, 28*, 177–193.

Prentice, D. A., & Miller, D. T. (2006). Essentializing differences between women and men. *Psychological Science, 17*, 129–135.

Ragins, B. R., & Cornwell, J. M. (2001). Pink triangles: Antecedents and consequences of perceived workplace discrimination against gay and lesbian employees. *Journal of Applied Psychology, 86*, 1244–1261.

Ragins, B. R., Cornwell, J. M., & Miller, J. S. (2003). Heterosexism in the workplace: Do race and gender matter? *Group & Organization Management, 28*, 45–74.

Rapoport, R., Bailyn, L., Fletcher, J. K., & Pruitt, B. H. (2002). *Beyond work-family balance: Advancing gender equity and workplace performance.* San Francisco, CA: Jossey-Bass.

Remennick, L. (2008). Contested motherhood in the ethnic state: Voices from an Israeli postpartum ward. *Ethnicities, 8*, 199–226.

Riach, P. A., & Rich, J. (2002). Field experiments of discrimination in the market place. *Economic Journal, 112*, F480–F518.

Rink, F., & Ellemers, N. (2009). Managing diversity in work groups: How identity processes affect diverse work groups. In M. Barreto, M. K. Ryan, & M. T. Schmitt (Eds.), *The glass ceiling in the 21st century: Understanding barriers to gender inequality* (pp. 281–303). Washington, DC: American Psychological Association.

Ritter, B. A., & Yoder, J. D. (2004). Gender differences in leader emergence persist even for dominant women: An updated confirmation of role congruity theory. *Psychology of Women Quarterly, 28*, 187–193.

Rosener, J. B. (1995). *America's competitive secret: Women managers.* New York: Oxford University Press.

Rudman, L. A., & Glick, P. (2001). Prescriptive gender stereotypes and backlash toward agentic women. *Journal of Social Issues, 57*, 743–762.

Rule, N. O., & Ambady, N. (2008). The face of success: Inferences from chief executive officers' appearance predict company profits. *Psychological Science, 19*, 109–111.

Ryan, M. K., & Haslam, S. A. (2005). The glass cliff: Evidence that women are over-represented in precarious leadership positions. *British Journal of Management, 16*, 81–90.

Ryan, M. K., & Haslam, S. A. (2007). The glass cliff: Exploring the dynamics surrounding the appointment of women to precarious leadership positions. *Academy of Management Review, 32*, 549–572.

Sanchez-Hucles, J., & Davis, D. D. (in press). *Diverse voices in leadership: The role of gender, race, and identity. American Psychologist.*

Sayer, L. C., Cohen, P. N., & Casper, L. M. (2004). *The American people: Women, men, and work.* New York: Russell Sage Foundation.

Schein, V. E. (1973). The relationship between sex role stereotypes and requisite management characteristics. *Journal of Applied Psychology, 57*, 95–100.

Schein, V. E. (2001). A global look at psychological barriers to women's progress in management. *Journal of Social Issues, 57*, 675–688.

Scott, K. A., & Brown, D. J. (2006). Female first, leader second? Gender bias in the encoding of leadership behavior. *Organizational Behavior and Human Decision Processes, 101*, 230–242.

Sczesny, S., Bosak, J., Neff, D., & Schyns, B. (2004). Gender stereotypes and the attribution of leadership traits: A cross-cultural comparison. *Sex Roles, 51*, 631–645.

Sczesny, S., & Kühnen, U. (2004). Meta-cognition about biological sex and gender-stereotypic physical appearance: Consequences for the assessment of leadership competence. *Personality and Social Psychology Bulletin, 30*, 13–21.

Seibert, S. E., Kraimer, M. L., & Liden, R. C. (2001). A social capital theory of career success. *Academy of Management Journal, 44*, 219–237.

Shields, S. A. (2008). Gender: An intersectionality perspective. *Sex Roles, 59*, 301–311.

Shilts, R. (1980, January). Gay police. *Police Magazine,* pp. 32–33.

Shrader, C. B., Blackburn, V. B., & Iles, P. (1997). Women in management and firm financial performance: An exploratory study. *Journal of Managerial Issues, 9*, 355–372.

Silvestri, M. (2003). *Women in charge: Policing, gender, and leadership.* Portland, OR: Willan.

Smith, R. A. (2002). Race, gender, and authority in the workplace: Theory and research. *Annual Review of Sociology, 28*, 509–542.

Snyder, K. (2006). *The G quotient: Why gay executives are excelling as leaders . . . and what every manager needs to know.* San Francisco, CA: Jossey-Bass.

Steele, C. M., Spencer, S. J., & Aronson, J. (2002). Contending with group image: The psychology of stereotype and social identity threat. In M. P. Zanna (Ed.), *Advances in experimental social psychology* (pp. 379–440). San Diego, CA: Academic Press.

Stockdale, M. S., & Bhattacharya, G. (2009). Sexual harassment and the glass ceiling. In M. Barreto, M. K. Ryan, & M. T. Schmitt (Eds.), *The glass ceiling in the 21st century: Understanding barriers to gender inequality* (pp. 171–199). Washington, DC: American Psychological Association.

Timberlake, S. (2005). Social capital and gender in the workplace. *Journal of Management Development, 24*, 34–44.

Thomas, D. A. (1990). The impact of race on managers' experiences of developmental relationships (mentoring and sponsorship): An intra-organizational study. *Journal of Organizational Behavior, 11*, 479–492.

U.S. Bureau of Labor Statistics. (2008). *Household data, annual averages: Employed persons by detailed occupation, sex, race, and Hispanic or Latino ethnicity*. Retrieved March 17, 2008, from http://www.bls.gov/cps/cpsaat11.pdf

U.S. National Center for Educational Statistics. (2007). *Digest of education statistics, 2007*. Retrieved September 20, 2008, from http://nces.ed.gov/programs/digest/d07/ch_1.asp

United Nations Development Programme. (2008). *Human development report 2007–2008*. New York: Oxford University Press.

van Engen, M. L., & Willemsen, T. M. (2004). Sex and leadership styles: A meta-analysis of research published in the 1990s. *Psychological Reports, 94*, 3–18.

van Knippenberg, D., & Schippers, M. C. (2007). Work group diversity. *Annual Review of Psychology, 58*, 515–541.

van Vianen, A. E. M., & Fischer, A. H. (2002). Illuminating the glass ceiling: The role of organizational culture preferences. *Journal of Occupational and Organizational Psychology, 75*, 315–337.

Vecchio, R. P. (2002). Leadership and gender advantage. *Leadership Quarterly, 13*, 643–671.

Vinnicombe, S., & Singh, V. (2003). Women-only management training: An essential part of women's leadership development. *Journal of Change Management, 3*, 294–306.

von Hippel, W., Sekaquaptewa, D., & Vargas, P. (1995). On the role of encoding processes in stereotype maintenance. In M. Zanna (Ed.), *Advances in experimental social psychology* (Vol. 27, pp. 177–254). San Diego, CA: Academic Press.

Wajcman, J. (1998). *Managing like a man: Women and men in corporate management*. University Park, PA: Pennsylvania State University Press.

Williams, J. (2000). *Unbending gender: Why family and work conflict and what to do about it*. New York: Oxford University Press.

Wood, W., & Eagly, A. H. (2009). Gender identity. In M. Leary & R. Hoyle (Eds.), *Handbook of individual differences in social behavior.* (pp. 109–125). New York: Guilford.

Zebrowitz, L. A., & Montepare, J. M. (2005). Appearance does matter. *Science, 308*, 1565–1566.

Part XIII
Health Psychology

Chapter 20
Gender, Health, and Health Behaviors

Christina Lee

One of the most well-established gender differences in health is that men die earlier than women. Men's life expectancy, worldwide, averages 4 years less than women's (Population Reference Bureau, 2008). This chapter explores some of the individual and social reasons behind this difference in life expectancy, as well as differences in behaviors related to wellness and quality of life among women and men.

It is often assumed that differences in health and longevity between men and women are biological in origin, but in fact the vast majority of gender differences can be explained by differences in health-related behavior, which, in turn, are strongly influenced by social and cultural expectations about appropriate behaviors and attitudes among women and men. Thus, most of the difference in life expectancy and in health is explicable by social and cultural aspects of gender. Men's and women's relationships with their bodies, their health behaviors, and their health concerns are strongly dictated by cultural expectations about masculinity and femininity.

Life Expectancy

The fact that gender differences in life expectancy are strongly influenced by social, cultural, and behavioral factors is illustrated by differences in the size of the gender gap between regions and over time. In Eastern Europe, for example, men's life expectancy is currently 11 years less than women's, and the difference is greatest in Russia, where the difference in life expectancy is 13 years (59 for men and 72 for women). By contrast, men's life expectancy is 5 years less than women's in northern Europe, 3 years less in east Asia (including China and Japan) and in North America, and only 1 year less in sub-Saharan Africa (Population Reference Bureau, 2008).

Overall life expectancies, and the magnitude of gender differences, are associated with changes in social and economic circumstances. This can be seen dramatically when there are major political disruptions. For example, life expectancy in Russia was 64 years among men and 74 among women in 1989, before the fall of the Soviet Union. By 1993, it was 59 years among men and 73 among women (Conradi, 1994). In the absence of epidemics of infectious disease or all-out war, this drop of 5 years in average life expectancy among men in only 4 calendar years, during which life expectancy among women fell by only 1 year, is unprecedented. It is discussed in greater depth later in this chapter, but the fact that the drop was so much larger among men suggests that men and women were differentially affected by the political upheavals in ways that affected men profoundly.

C. Lee (✉)
University of Queensland, Brisbane, QLD, Australia

J.C. Chrisler, D.R. McCreary (eds.), *Handbook of Gender Research in Psychology*,
DOI 10.1007/978-1-4419-1467-5_20, © Springer Science+Business Media, LLC 2010

There are also contemporaneous differences between subpopulations within countries, a fact that makes it clear that cultural, social, environmental, and behavioral factors must play a major role in men's and women's life expectancies. In Australia, for example, the average age at death is 83 among women and 78 among men, but among the indigenous subpopulation (approximately 2% of the total population) life expectancy is only 65 years among women and 59 years among men (Australian Bureau of Statistics, 2006a). In Russia, research on mortality rates in that country in the 1990s showed that Jewish men lived on average 11 years longer than other men and Jewish women lived 2 years longer than other women (Shkolnikov, Andreev, Anson, & Meslé, 2004). Differences like these cannot have simple biological explanations but must be related to different health behaviors and different patterns of life among men and women and among people of different ethnicities.

Health Behaviors

To understand the reasons underlying differences in life expectancy, it is important to understand the relationships between individual behavior and life expectancy. The major causes of death in developed countries have changed substantially over the past few generations. For the first one-half of the twentieth century, the major causes of death in the United States were infectious diseases such as influenza, pneumonia, tuberculosis, and gastroenteritis. Advances in medical treatment, particularly the discovery of antibiotics, mean that the risk of premature death from infection is now much lower, and the most prevalent causes of death are cancers and cardiovascular diseases. Although genetic predispositions explain some of the risk of dying from these conditions, individual behaviors explain a great deal of the risk. In particular, cigarette smoking, misuse of alcohol and other drugs, a sedentary lifestyle, and poor diet have been estimated to explain well over one-half of all premature deaths (Australian Institute of Health & Welfare, 2006). These individual choices are embedded in a social and cultural context, which differs for men and women.

A widely used contemporary model for understanding health and life expectancy involves a hierarchy of determinants that influence each other sequentially, starting with the broadest sociocultural factors and ending at the individual's biological state. According to this model, the most "upstream" factors are broad settings such as the country's cultural, political, and economic system. These constrain and partially determine access to resources such as education, employment, and health services and determine the levels of availability of resources and how access is distributed between women and men and also across other social categories, such as wealth, ethnicity, religion, or political affiliation. Access to these resources, in turn, influences knowledge, attitudes, and opportunities to choose whether or not to adopt or avoid individual health behaviors. The health behaviors are immediate causes of biological risks such as obesity, high blood pressure, and immune function, which are the proximal causes of illness and death (Turrell, Oldenburg, McGuffog, & Dent, 1999). Thus, individual choice is important, but it must be seen in the context of broader factors that constrain choice: Women in countries in which they are not permitted to attend school, drive cars, or to leave the house unaccompanied, for example, have fewer opportunities to make healthy or unhealthy choices than do women in societies that afford human rights to all people regardless of gender.

The importance of behavioral risk factors in determining mortality is illustrated by a prospective population-based study of British men. The overall rate of heart attacks, both fatal and non-fatal, declined by 62% in the 25 years between 1978 and 2002, and this trend has been investigated in several countries. Hardoon et al. (2008), in Britain, showed that almost one-half of this decline could be explained by reductions in cigarette smoking and by changes in diet and physical activity, which had affected weight, serum cholesterol, and blood pressure. In a recent meta-analysis, which combined large population-based studies from several countries, Nocon et al. (2008) showed that physical activity reduced the risk of cardiovascular-related mortality by 35% and of all-cause mortality by 33%. Thus, individual decisions about health behaviors have a major influence on the health, well-being, and life expectancy of the population overall.

Gender differences in behavioral risk factors are remarkably consistent across countries. Australia is typical of developed countries: Men have higher rates of smoking and alcohol abuse than do women, whereas women are more likely than men are to be sedentary but more likely to eat a healthy diet high in fruit and vegetables (Australian Institute for Health & Welfare, 2006). The international epidemiological literature shows that this is a consistent pattern across all developed countries. In general, and with the exception of physical activity, men choose to engage in more health-damaging behaviors and women choose to engage in more health-protective behaviors (e.g., Stronegger, Freidl, & Rasky, 1997; Uitenbroek, Kerekovska, & Festchieva, 1996). Men in all cultures are more likely than women to eat a diet high in animal fats and low in fruit and vegetables (Prättälä et al., 2007), to smoke and to drink alcohol at unsafe levels (Holtzman, Powell-Griner, Bolen, & Rhodes, 2000), and to be overweight or obese (Holtzman et al., 2000). The only health-promoting behavior that is consistently engaged in by men more than by women is physical activity (Australian Bureau of Statistics, 2006b; Shaw & Henderson, 2000).

Vandevijvere et al. (2008), in a national survey of Belgians, found that women were more likely to eat fruit and men more likely to eat meat and starchy foods. Diets tended to be better in older groups, but there was a large gap between actual and recommended diets for both genders. Blanck, Gillespie, Kimmons, Seymour, and Serdula (2008) found that women in the United States also ate more fruit and vegetables than did men. Diets had not improved between 1994 and 2005, despite intensive public education campaigns. Such data are explained by the fact that there is more to individual decisions about health risk behaviors than knowledge, and the factors that might affect individual choices may differ by gender. This, in turn, suggests that campaigns to improve health behaviors at a population level must be carefully nuanced and targeted to specific groups if they are to be effective.

There is evidence that the reasons behind gender differences in health behaviors lie in cultural prescriptions for men and for women. Choices about health behaviors are strongly embedded in hegemonic and traditional views of the ideal man as tough and physical, as hard working, and as unconcerned about his own safety and well-being, and in cultural constructions that regard these characteristics as superior and advantageous despite their obvious capacity to harm (Petersen, 1998). By contrast, traditional cultural models of femininity position women as concerned about their own and their families' health, as risk-avoidant, and as well-informed about matters to do with health, diet, and well-being (Lee, 1998; Sherr & St Lawrence, 2000).

Although – and with the exception of physical activity – women have lower levels of "traditional" risk factors than do men, there are other behaviors that relate strongly to health and are perhaps more problematic for women than for men. The most important of these is that set of individual behaviors and choices that cluster around physical appearance, a topic with very strongly gendered cultural meanings. Women may be less likely than men to eat to excess, but they are more likely to engage in unhealthy restrictive practices related to diet and body shape. Anorexia nervosa, the most extreme example of restrictive eating, has the highest death rate of any psychiatric disorder. The annual death rate among sufferers is 10 times as high as the general population (Birmingham, Su, Hlynsky, Goldner, & Gao, 2005), and it does appear that the "classic" eating disorders of anorexia and bulimia nervosa are considerably more common among women than among men. For example, the lifetime prevalence rate of anorexia nervosa in the United States is just under 1% among women and only 0.3% among men and for bulimia nervosa the rates are around 1.5% for women and 0.5% for men (Kessler, Chiu, Dernier, & Walters, 2005).

However, the gender difference is less clear-cut than it might appear if one looks only at extreme clinical disorders. If we broaden the definition of disordered eating to include subclinical syndromes, gender differences become small to nonexistent (Striegel-Moore & Bulik, 2007). The most serious restrictive disorders are most common among women, although it has been argued that even this difference is not as strong as is believed. Anorexia nervosa in men tends to be underdiagnosed or misdiagnosed as loss of appetite as a result of depression (Lee & Owens, 2002).

Both anorexia nervosa and bulimia nervosa certainly are recorded among men (Buckley, Freyne, & Walsh, 1991; Carlat & Camargo, 1991), but the patterns of their eating disorders serve to illustrate the gendered forces that influence these conditions. Men who develop eating disorders are likely to be involved in occupations such as modeling or dancing, or sporting activities, such as diving or horse racing, which demand low body fat, and bulimia in particular seems to be more common in homosexual than heterosexual men (Carlat & Camargo, 1991). No such patterns are seen among women because in modern societies *all* women, regardless of their occupational or sporting interests, are evaluated according to body weight and shape.

The abuse of steroids is another strongly gendered behavior that has potential health risks, and it is so widespread as to be a significant public health problem (Sjöqvist, Garle, & Rane, 2008). It can been seen in some senses as a sort of "male version" of anorexia nervosa – both involve the use of unhealthy and potentially fatal practices in an effort to achieve a gender-specific "ideal" body shape. Although steroid abuse is less likely than anorexia nervosa to have fatal consequences, long-term use does have severe physical and mental side effects, including liver damage, infertility, sexual dysfunction, extreme violence, mood swings, and anger (Sjöqvist et al., 2008). In a study of adolescents in Norway, Pallesen, Jøsendal, Johnsen, Larsen, and Molde (2006) found that 3.6% of male students reported having used anabolic-androgenic steroids. In the areas of competitive sport in which steroid use is most obviously beneficial, steroid use is common and regarded as normal. Blouin and Goldfield (1995), for example, found that 78% of a sample of male competitive bodybuilders reported having used anabolic steroids, as did 20% of male recreational bodybuilders. Thus, concerns about physical appearance lead to choices to engage in risky behaviors among both men and women, but the nature of those behaviors varies strongly according to gender.

Health Service Use and Health-Related Symptoms

Compounding the problem that men's lifestyles tend to be generally less healthy than women's is evidence that men generally make less use of health care and screening services than do women (e.g., Schappert, 1999). This difference is found even when researchers account for the fact that women are likely to use health services for reasons other than illness, such as advice concerning pregnancy and contraception (e.g., Stoverinck, Lagro-Janssen, & Weel, 1996). There is also some evidence to suggest that men are slower to acknowledge symptoms of illness (e.g., van Wijk, Huisman, & Kolk, 1999), but – as for disordered eating – findings in this area are less clear-cut than might be expected. A survey of the general population in Scotland (Macintyre, Ford, & Hunt, 1999) found that men were just as willing as women to report symptoms and to seek health care, and no more likely to discount symptoms that might be considered "trivial" or emotional in nature. Another survey by the same group (Wyke, Hunt, & Ford, 1998) showed that men were less likely than women to report experience of various symptoms, but those who did report symptoms were equally likely to have seen a doctor about them. And a study of men and women with colds (Macintyre, 1993) found that men were actually more likely than women to overrate the severity of their symptoms, by comparison with an objective clinical observer. Thus, differences between men and women are more complex and nuanced than they might at first appear.

It is popularly believed that women experience – or at least report – more minor illnesses and more physical symptoms of malaise (e.g., headaches, backaches) than do men and that this is somehow linked to biological differences between men and women. However, this assumption is not supported when the evidence is examined carefully. Macintyre, Hunt, and Sweeting (1996) showed that the pattern of gender differences in morbidity is complex. Whether gender differences exist at all, and their direction and magnitude, differs according to the particular symptom or illness studied, the life stage of the people compared, and other socioeconomic conditions that vary by gender and that appear to have a direct effect on well-being. For example, Macintyre et al. used large national data sets to show that men and women were equally likely to complain of back trouble, colds and flu, and nasal congestion. Women were more likely than men to report worry, nerves, tiredness, faintness, and headaches, but men were more likely to report hearing problems and heart palpitations. For some symptoms the pattern varied with age: for example, stiff or painful joints were more common among men than women in younger age groups, but more common among women than men in older age groups.

The inadequacy of biological explanations is also demonstrated by several pieces of research, which show that variability in health-care use and symptom recognition is largely explained by the effects of socioeconomic and work-related variables, but not by gender. Women are more likely than men to work in low-grade, unpleasant, repetitive, and boring jobs. Several different teams of researchers have demonstrated that gender differences in malaise, physical symptoms, and medical help-seeking between men and women can actually be explained by their different working conditions and levels of seniority: In other words, it is not being a woman that leads to high levels of symptoms, but having a low-level and unpleasant working life (Emslie, Hunt, & Macintyre, 1999a, 1999b; Feeney, North, Head, Canner, & Marmot, 1998). This suggests that the crucial question is not why men report fewer symptoms and make less use of health services, but why women have poorer working conditions than men do, and the answers to these questions go back to the "upstream" factors described earlier: Women's restricted access to educational and financial resources in comparison to men's.

It has also been argued that simply assessing reports of symptoms and number of visits to health professionals is less relevant to the actual health outcomes of men and women than is understanding whether men and women differ in their reasons for seeking health services and in their experiences of the health-care system (Kandrack, Grant, & Segall, 1991). Some qualitative research (e.g., Seymour-Smith, Wetherell, & Phoenix, 2002) has demonstrated that men's interactions with medical practitioners are less satisfactory than women's. Doctors' approach to consultations is affected by assumptions that men will not discuss symptoms or emotions and that wives and girlfriends often take responsibility for deciding when men need to seek medical advice, making appointments for them, and even attending consultations to explain the problem. It is argued that the health-care system is a "feminine" space in which men do not feel comfortable, and this has been used to explain why men may be more reluctant than women to seek help and less willing than women are to articulate their problems when they do see a physician (Seymour-Smith, 2008). Thus, the relationships between gender on the one hand and health service use and symptoms on the other hand demonstrate that gender is more complex and more variable than a simple categorization of people as men or women.

Gendered Patterns of Risk

In taking a more complex look at the differences between men and women that are relevant to their health, it is worth noting that individual risk behaviors such as sedentariness, smoking, alcohol abuse, and use of illicit drugs are not independent of each other. Rather, they tend to occur together and also to co-occur with behaviors that put individuals at risk of accidental injury. And, although clustering of risk behaviors has been observed across many populations, it is also the case that the nature of the clusters tends to differ by gender. For example, Wu, Rose, and Bancroft (2006) found different patterns of risk behaviors among adolescents in the United States. They identified a subgroup of boys who were likely to be involved in fights, to drink alcohol, and to participate in physical activity and a subgroup of girls who used a cluster of unhealthy behaviors that all appeared to target weight loss, including unsustainable diets, bulimic behaviors, and smoking. It is notable that these two different clusters are related to culturally valued aspects of masculinity and femininity; the choice of risky (and healthy) behaviors is one way in which women and men enact culturally defined gender roles. Among young Americans, gendered clusters of risk behaviors have also been shown to differ across ethnic backgrounds, which reflects differences between cultural subgroups (Weden & Zabin, 2005).

One popular belief, often used to excuse unhealthy habits, is that positive health behaviors can counteract negative ones, so that, for example, young men who abuse alcohol may do so without harm as long as they also exercise regularly. However, the evidence tends to dispute this. For example, it is not the case that physical activity can counteract the ill effects of behavioral risk factors. It does not totally counteract the negative effects of obesity (Orsini et al., 2008) nor does it have any mitigating effect on the effects of smoking, although smokers who are physically active do appear to be more interested in smoking cessation (Deruiter, Faulkner, Cairney, & Veldhuizen, 2008). And, although many people believe that smoking can help to control weight, a review of the evidence (Chiolero, Faeh, Paccaud, & Cornuz, 2008) showed that, in fact, prolonged smoking gradually affects the body's insulin resistance, which in turn has the effect of increased body weight as well as the risk of diabetes in the longer term. Therefore, the idea that clusters of gender-typed behaviors may in some way cancel each other out is not supported by the evidence.

Behaviors that are normalized in young men may be part of a "deviant" cluster among girls. For example, a survey of U.S. 12th-grade students (Elliott, Shope, Raghunathan, & Waller, 2006) showed that young women who engaged in high-risk driving (i.e., speeding, street racing, drink-driving) were more likely than other girls to use alcohol and marijuana, but high-risk driving young men did not differ from other young men in their patterns of drug and alcohol use. High-risk driving is one strategy by which young men can demonstrate their toughness and masculinity, but these behaviors are less consistent with a feminine stereotype; thus, high-risk behaviors are associated with other deviant behaviors among young women but not among young men.

Similar findings from other countries suggest that unhealthy behavioral choices are part of the expression of mainstream masculinity in many countries but tend to be somewhat more deviant among women. For example, surveys of Brazilian university students in 1996 and 2001 (Wagner, de Andrade Stempliuk, Zilberman, Barroso, & de Andrade, 2007) showed that use of tobacco, alcohol, and illicit drugs was higher among male than among female students and that the use of these substances had increased between the time of the two surveys. Similarly, among Swedish university students (Andersson, Johnsson, Berglund, & Öjehagen, 2007), men were more likely than women to report problem drinking.

Why Do Individual Health Behaviors Differ by Gender?

The evidence that men and women choose somewhat different patterns of health-related behavior is clear. But this raises the question of what might influence and constrain these individual choices. In this section I examine both individual and social factors that might explain these differences. At the individual level, men and women appear to have different attitudes toward and perceptions of health-related behaviors, and these are likely to affect differences in behavioral choices. For example, Toll et al. (2008) showed that women and men perceive the risks and benefits of smoking differently. Women smokers, for example, seemed to be more influenced by the belief that smoking aids weight control. Potter, Pederson, Chan, Aubut, and Koval (2004) found that weight concerns were more important in young women's than in young men's decisions to take up smoking. Qualitative research with adolescents in Scotland also identified strong gender differences in the nature of attitudes toward smoking. Girls were concerned about the smell of smoking and its effect on their appearance, and boys were concerned about negative effects on fitness and sporting ability (Amos & Bostock, 2007). These differences are congruent with gendered cultural prescriptions: Women should be concerned about their physical appearance and the impression they make on others, whereas men should be concerned about fitness and strength. This demonstrates that gender affects the attitudes underlying decisions about smoking: Women and men are socialized to think about smoking in different ways and to relate choices about smoking to broader concerns about themselves as gendered beings.

In general, societies position knowledge and concern about health as a feminine issue. Men are generally less likely than women to express an interest in making health-related lifestyle changes (Gabhainn et al., 1999), and they tend to know less about health and healthy lifestyles than do women. A survey of rural Australian men (O'Kane, Craig, Black, & Sutherland, 2008) indicated that those with poor health habits generally agreed that they would need a major health care before they would consider changing their behavior. These findings appear to arise from cultural institutions that position men as ignorant about their health and women as responsible not only for their own health but also for that of their children and of the men in their lives. Lyons and Willott (1999), for example, have analyzed the way in which the popular media direct information about men's health and health behaviors toward their wives and mothers. This establishes and reinforces the views that men should not concern themselves with health issues and, indeed, that they are incapable of caring for their own health.

In married couples, women are likely to try to control health-related aspects of their husbands' behavior such as diet and alcohol use, but men are much less likely to try to control those same aspects of their wives' behavior (Umberson, 1992). Men who lose a partner, whether through divorce (Umberson, 1992) or widowhood (Clayton, 1990), show negative changes in health behaviors to a much greater extent than do women, and this is particularly the case for diet, alcohol intake, and use of other drugs (Byrne, Raphael, & Arnold, 1999). These self-harming attitudes and behaviors among men are consistent with a concept of masculinity that places value on a disregard for the long-term health consequences of one's actions and that views taking care of one's body as evidence that one is "soft" or overly concerned with appearance (Petersen, 1998). The widespread and continuing stigmatization of gay men means that any suggestion of a "typically feminine" concern for appearance is strongly rejected by young men who generally, and regardless of their actual sexual orientation or interest, wish to avoid any suggestion that they might be homosexual (Hargreaves & Tiggemann, 2006).

Physical activity is an important component of any discussion of health-related behaviors because of its strong relationships with health and well-being, but it differs in several important ways from other widely investigated topics such as alcohol use, smoking, drug use, and diet. As already indicated, it is one of the very few positive health behaviors that are adopted more often by men than by women. The explanation for this can again be found in the social and cultural context. Adopting physical activity is different from adopting other healthy patterns of behavior in at least one important regard. It takes a significant investment of time and resources: 30 minutes of continuous exercise on most days of the week is the minimum recommended for cardiovascular fitness and heart health, but 60–90 minutes of exercise per day is needed for weight loss and maintenance of healthy weight (Johannsen, Redman, & Ravussin, 2007). By contrast, avoiding cigarette smoking or drug use takes no additional time or economic resources, although it may require substantial changes to social interactions and lifestyle and adopting a healthy diet takes little or no more time or money than eating unhealthy food.

Individuals' ability to commit this level of time is affected by a number of gender-relevant factors, and this goes some way to explaining the observed gender differences. In particular, women work longer hours than men do, even though they are paid for fewer of them. Unpaid domestic labor continues to be inequitably distributed between women and men: The 2005 British Time Use study showed that women's total work time was about 2 hours a week greater than men's but that men were paid for about two-thirds of their work, whereas women were paid for just over one-third of theirs (Lader, Short, & Gershuny, 2006). Similar findings from Australia (Australian Bureau of Statistics, 2008) also demonstrate that women of all ages have significantly less leisure time than do men.

Women's leisure is further constrained by the "ethic of care" (e.g., Shaw & Henderson, 2000), the cultural prescription that women should always put the needs of others before their own interests. Women internalize this ethic, thus their leisure time is more likely than men's to be constrained and interrupted by the needs of family members or by the social expectations that women are available for volunteer work, running errands, driving children around, and otherwise tending to the needs of others, in a way that is not paralleled for men. Notions that femininity is incompatible with fitness, strength, or physical capacity (Choi, 2000) further undermine women's ability to find space in their lives for regular healthy exercise.

Gender differences in health behaviors may also be affected by the assumptions and stereotypes held by health service providers and the general public. For example, U.S. physicians are significantly less likely to prescribe smoking cessation medications for women than they are for men (Steinberg, Akincigil, Delnevo, Crystal, & Carson, 2006). Although heart disease and cancer occur in roughly equal proportions among men and women, cultural norms regard heart disease as primarily a "male" disease and cancer primarily "female." Clarke, van Amerom, and Binns (2007), for example, analyzed mass print media articles about heart disease and found that the majority of articles were explicitly or implicitly directed at men and that the discourse suggested that heart disease was almost an inevitable consequence of leading a successful masculine life (characterized as involving aggression, hard physical work, and a failure to rest or care adequately for oneself). By contrast, a Canadian survey (McCreary, Gray, & Grace, 2006) showed that both men and women incorrectly believe that cancer is primarily a disease of women, which may be one factor underlying lower rates of screening and higher cancer risk behaviors among men.

Other Social and Demographic Categories

Gender differences in risk behaviors and attitudes are reasonably consistent across countries and can be explained to some degree by commonalities in beliefs, attitudes, and concerns related to gender and its expression through behavioral choices. However, the differences are more complex than they might appear and – as already suggested – vary not only at the level of individual men and women but also according to social, cultural, and demographic factors. For example, gender differences in alcohol and drug use were found to be stronger in urban than in rural locations in the United States (Diala, Muntaner, & Walrath, 2004). Rodham, Hawton, Evans, and Weatherall (2005), in a survey of British high school students' use of drinking, smoking, and drugs, found the expected gender differences, but found equally strong differences between ethnic groups in choice of substance and level of use. Motivations for health-related behavior also differ by ethnic identity: Fulkerson and French (2003) studied U.S. adolescents' motivations for smoking and found that the extent of smoking for weight control varied by ethnic background: Black girls were the only group of girls who generally did not report weight control as a motivation for smoking, whereas among boys, the only group without this pattern were White boys. Such findings suggest the need for a more complex approach to understanding unhealthy choices and to the promotion of healthy choices in the multiethnic and pluralistic societies of the developed world.

The emphasis on complexity and variability so far in this chapter stresses the underlying argument that gender differences in risk behaviors do not arise from essential and immutable differences between female and male human beings. Rather, they arise from social and cultural definitions of masculinity and femininity and are aspects of the ways in which men and women express themselves as gendered individuals in different societies. The interaction of individual behavioral choices and sociocultural aspects of gender is exemplified in Spain, where smoking trends among men and women have been analyzed in relation to historical changes, particularly the second wave of feminism. Schiaffino et al. (2003) found that Spanish men's smoking rates increased, and age at initiation dropped, from the 1950s to the 1980s, after which smoking rates began to fall, particularly among men of high socioeconomic status. This pattern broadly parallels changes that were occurring in other countries at the same time. Women's smoking rates, by contrast, were extremely low until the 1960s, but then showed a rapid increase to converge with men's rates. This pattern has been explained in terms of social and cultural change in Spain at that time. The Spanish culture moved quite rapidly from a traditional one, in which it was generally accepted that women's behavior was and should be more restricted than was men's, including a perception that women who smoked were deviant or lacked respectability, to a more modern and egalitarian society characterized by changes in women's roles and opportunities. In this context smoking became, for many women, a symbol of their equality with men.

Socioeconomic Context

Gender is arguably the most important social category in human societies: the first thing we notice about someone, the most important cue for determining how we should behave toward someone. But other social differences also affect health behaviors. Gender differences interact with the well-established phenomenon of the "socioeconomic gradient." This term refers to the well-established observation that there is a correlation between socioeconomic disadvantage and poor health. Gradients are consistently found for health and well-being, health behaviors, and life expectancy. In Australia, Siahpush (2004) has argued that smoking is so strongly linked to socioeconomic status that smoking rate can be used as an excellent measure of the social disadvantage of any particular social group. Socioeconomic gradients are also found for physical activity: Azevedo et al. (2007), for example, in a population-based survey of Brazilian adults, found that men were more active than women at all ages, particularly in early adulthood, but that higher socioeconomic status was also predictive of high levels of physical activity.

Socioeconomic gradients tend to be stronger for men than for women. For example, Ginter and Hulanska (2007) showed a much greater socioeconomic gradient in life expectancy among men than among women in Slovakia. However, gradients in health risk behaviors vary widely according to country as well as gender. Generally, in developed countries the socioeconomically disadvantaged tend to have the highest rates of unhealthy behaviors such as smoking and alcohol abuse, but the reverse effect is seen in some, but not all, developing countries. Bloomfield, Grittner, Kramer, and Gmel (2006) explored socioeconomic gradients in alcohol consumption in 15 different countries and found great variety in the distribution of problem drinking. Level of education (a widely used marker of socioeconomic status) was positively associated with problem drinking in some countries and negatively in others; men and women showed similar patterns in some countries and not in others. A further analysis (Kuntsche et al., 2006) showed that socioeconomic patterns of heavy drinking varied, particularly among women, depending on the level of social welfare and gender equity in a country. These complex, and at times contradictory, findings illustrate the fact that gender differences are not straightforward. Rather, gender is one of several social categories, including ethnicity and socioeconomic status, that are differentially associated with various health-related attitudes and behaviors.

Gender Convergence

There is some evidence for a recent historical trend toward a closer convergence between men and women in health-related behaviors in several countries, and this appears to be related to convergence in social attitudes and expectations of men's and women's behavior. For example, a large national survey on alcohol and alcohol-related conditions in the United States shows that the gender difference in both low-risk drinking and alcohol abuse is smaller in younger generations, as women's drinking increases to match that of men (Keyes, Grant, & Hasin, 2008). It is argued that this arises from a reduction in social pressures on women to conform to an outmoded gender stereotype that placed great importance on a woman's public reputation for modesty and for self-control. Similar patterns have been found in other Western countries and with other methodologies. Sweeting and West (2003), for example, studied the leisure activities of adolescents in western Scotland and found that gender differences in use of legal and illegal drugs had disappeared between 1987 and 1999. They hypothesized that cultural changes that reduced the social value of girls' reputations as "respectable" had also removed one barrier to risk-taking among those girls. Gender convergence in alcohol consumption was also demonstrated in New Zealand (McPherson, Casswell, & Pledger, 2004), and again the researchers argued that it was a consequence of convergence in social roles, attitudes, and expectations among young women and young men.

Convergence also has been observed across some other social categories, but not always consistently. For example, a Centers for Disease Control and Prevention (CDC, 2007) study of changes in rates of physical activity in the United States. between 2001 and 2005 showed that physical activity rates rose more quickly among women than they did among men, and more quickly among Blacks than among other ethnic groups, which has led to an attenuation of previously strong gender and ethnic differences. On the other hand, surveys of Australian adolescents (Okely, Booth, Hardy, Dobbins, & Denney-Wilson, 2008) showed that rates of physical activity had risen equally among both boys and girls between 1985 and 2004, which means that the gender differences were maintained.

Gender and Socioeconomic Status in Developing and Emerging Countries

The discussion so far has focused mainly on developed countries, but rates of risky individual behaviors – particularly smoking, alcohol abuse, and unhealthy diets – are increasing rapidly in developing countries and, in some places, are completely negating the health gains that have been made through the control of infectious diseases and reduction of child mortality (World Health Organization [WHO], 2008). Smoking rates have been dropping steadily in developed countries, where restrictions are increasingly placed on the promotion of smoking and restrictions on contexts in which smoking is acceptable or legal, and as a consequence tobacco companies are increasingly promoting smoking in the much larger populations of India, China, and other countries of the developing world (WHO, 2008). Gender differences in smoking, and indeed in other substance use, in those countries are considerably greater than in developed countries.

For example, a national survey of drug use in India conducted in 1995–1996 (Neufeld, Peters, Rani, Bonu, & Broomer, 2005) demonstrated patterns that were very different in some ways from those in Western countries. Overall, individual risk behaviors were less common than in Western countries; the national prevalence of cigarette smoking was estimated to be 16%, chewing tobacco use 14%, and alcohol use 4%. However, gender differences were much greater: Men were 25 times more likely than women to smoke, four times more likely to chew tobacco, and 10 times more likely to drink alcohol. Gender roles are more traditional and more clearly delineated in India than in Western countries; women's position is socially inferior to men's, and this is reflected in very different sets of health-related behaviors. A further issue in countries with relatively limited health service availability is that women may be denied access to services. For example, Borooah (2004) showed that Indian girls were significantly less likely than boys to be adequately fed and to be fully immunized. However, this effect was strongest when the mother was illiterate, and Borooah (2004) argued that gender was by no means as strong a disadvantage as poverty. Similarly, Neufeld et al. (2005) found that members of the lowest ranking castes, and people in rural areas, had greater levels of risk behavior and lower levels of appropriate health care than did other Indians.

Gender differences in risk behaviors in the former Soviet Union provide another example of the interactions between cultural and economic factors and individual behaviors and attitudes, which again emphasizes the fact that gender differences in health behavior must be understood in the specific context in which they occur. Russia was mentioned at the beginning of this chapter as the country with the greatest gender difference in life expectancy in the world, and this appears to be explained mainly by an equally great discrepancy in health risk behaviors, notably alcohol abuse and tobacco use.

Life expectancy among Russian men (but not women) fell sharply in the 1980s and 1990s, after the collapse of the Soviet Union, and Leon et al. (2007) have shown that the change mirrored very high and rapidly increasing rates of alcohol consumption; almost one-half of the deaths among Russian men of working age are explicable by alcohol abuse. In a comparison of eastern and western European countries, Rehm et al. (2007) found that the overall death rate from alcohol-related causes among working-age individuals was 10 times as high in Russia as it was in Sweden; it was also five times as high for Russian men as for Russian women. The evidence that alcohol is the main underlying cause of men's excess mortality in Russia is incontrovertible; Men, Brennan, Boffetta, and Zaridze (2003) have argued that the individual choice to abuse alcohol must be understood in the context of underlying economic and societal factors. The collapse of the state means that there are very few positive strategies by which men can express their masculinity: poverty, high unemployment, corruption, and the weakening of the rule of law all undermine more positive strategies among men.

It is notable that women in general appear to be less affected by poverty or social upheaval than do men, and in Russia they did not adopt heavy alcohol use to anything like the same extent. But over the same period, the Russian birth rate dropped dramatically. The total fertility rate (estimated lifetime births per woman) in Russia dropped from 1.9 in 1992 to 1.3 in 2001 (Population Reference Bureau, 2003). A total fertility rate of 2.1 per woman is required to maintain a country's population, and this continued low rate, in combination with the high death rate among men, high rates of emigration, and low rates of immigration, means that the total population of Russia is predicted to decrease by 23% by 2050. This suggests that men and women have reacted in gendered ways to the breakdown of social order and security: men by alcohol abuse and women by choosing not to bring children into an unstable society. It is notable that the same time period that has seen these gendered trends in health behaviors in Russia has also seen massive increases in the steepness of the socioeconomic gradient: Murphy, Bobak, Nicholson, Rose, and Marmot (2006) demonstrated that the differences in life expectancy according to educational level became much greater between 1989 and 2001, and again this effect was much stronger for men than for women.

High-Risk Activities

So far I have dealt mainly with "traditional" health risk behaviors such as smoking and alcohol abuse. These behaviors are strongly related to the serious chronic illnesses that are the major causes of death among both women and men and higher rates of these behaviors among men explain much of the difference in life expectancy. However, in most Western countries, the causes of death with the greatest gender differences are not coronary heart disease and cancer, but accidents, violence, and suicide. These affect people across the life span, but the age range 20–34 has the highest risk. Mortality in younger age groups has a disproportionate effect on average life expectancies, and it is this age group that has the strongest gender difference in death rates. This supports the view that it is not diseases of old age but behavioral factors, especially high-risk activities, that explain a major proportion of the gender difference in life expectancy (Smith, 1993).

Risk-taking, violence, and suicide are not generally included in the same category as those behaviors that are associated with early onset of chronic disease, but their effects on well-being and on life expectancy are profound and their relationships with gender are very strong. Worldwide, injuries account for approximately 1 in 8 deaths among men and boys and 1 in 14 deaths among women and girls (MacKenzie, 2000). Injuries represent one of the leading causes of death and disability throughout the world, and, because they affect young people disproportionately, they make a major contribution to life years lost and to lives with acquired disability (Krug, Sharma, & Lozano, 2000). We tend to think about accidental injuries as isolated incidents that result from individual carelessness or bad luck, rather than from socially defined aspects of masculine behavior, but the gender differences suggest that there is again a strong gender component.

Gender differences in risk of accidental injury or death are demonstrated even in early childhood in many countries. Surveys from Argentina (Murgio, Mila, Manolio, Maurel, & Ubeda, 1999), Australia (Lam, Ross, & Cass, 1999), Austria (e.g., Eberl et al., 2008; Schalamon et al., 2007), the United Arab Emirates (Bener, Hyder, & Schenk, 2007), and the United States (Danseco, Miller, & Spicer, 2000; Stone, Lanphear, Pomerantz, & Khoury, 2000) have consistently shown that boys are approximately twice as likely as girls to be severely injured or killed in playground accidents and falls. Gender differences in injury rates are even higher among adults: Men are two to three times as likely as women are to die from injuries (Australian Bureau of Statistics, 2006a; Li & Baker, 1996).

Patterns of accidental death are reflected in patterns of severe and debilitating injury. Evidence from several countries shows that men are between two and five times as likely as women to be admitted to hospital as a result of injuries of all kinds. For example, Gardiner, Judson, Smith, Jackson, and Norton (2000) found that 75% of intensive care admissions in Auckland were men and boys. Watson and Ozanne-Smith (2000) showed that 62% of all medically recorded injuries in Victoria, Australia, including three-quarters of all fatal injuries, were sustained by men and boys. In Israel, Haik et al. (2007) found that men and boys were twice as likely as women and girls to be hospitalized for burns. Men are also three to four times as likely as women to experience spinal cord injuries, and their injuries tend to be more severe, which means that that they are likely to experience greater levels of disability over a longer period of time (Nobunaga, Go, & Karunas, 1999; van Asbeck, Post, & Pangalila, 2000).

Kolakowsky-Hayner et al. (1999) also found that the majority of spinal cord and traumatic brain injury patients were young men, and further that most were heavy drinkers. As suggested earlier, health behaviors tend to cluster in gender-specific ways, and it seems that it is a combination of traditionally masculine-typed health behaviors and traditionally male-dominated recreational and sporting activities that places individuals at high risk of these major injuries. This finding is consistent with that of Ryb, Dischinger, Kufera, and Soderstrom (2007), who surveyed drivers who had been admitted to hospital following car accidents. Among this group, those who smoked – most of whom were male – were also more likely to have had previous accidents; more likely to have been hospitalized for other, non-traffic-related injuries; less likely to wear seatbelts; more likely to drink and drive; and more likely to use alcohol and illicit drugs.

In other words, accidents appear to be more likely to occur among people who are enacting a traditional masculine script that includes reckless behaviors and substance abuse. Interventions to improve safety or to reduce risk, on the roads and in other contexts, might benefit from an understanding that accidents do not occur at random but are more likely to occur among people who take other risks.

The excess representation of men in rates of accidental injury and death is consistent across countries and across occupational, traffic-related, and recreational circumstances. Work-related serious injuries and deaths are significantly more common among men than among women. Caradoc-Davies and Hawker (1997) used New Zealand data to estimate the rate of work-related injury for men to be twice that for women. This is particularly observable in physically demanding and hazardous occupations, which are characterized by a high preponderance of male workers. For example, a Welsh study showed that men suffered 11 times as many work-related burns as women did; it was young men in physical occupations who were at highest risk (Munnoch, Darcy, Whallett, & Dixon, 2000). In the United States, men are several times as likely as women to be injured on farms (Mongin et al., 2007) or in factory work (Wong, Lincoln, Tielsch, & Baker, 1998). But these gender differences are almost entirely explained by differences in men's and women's involvement in high-risk occupations. In fact, several studies have shown that, when differential rates of involvement between men and women are taken into account, women are actually slightly more likely than men to be injured or killed in manufacturing, agriculture, or other high-risk occupations (e.g., Hansen & Jensen, 1998; Mongin et al., 2007).

Similar patterns are found in other domains. Men and boys have much higher rates of sporting accidental injury and death (e.g., Williams, Wright, Currie, & Beattie, 1998). But once again, this effect is entirely explained by higher levels of sporting involvement among men and boys. In fact, women and girls who do play competitive sport are consistently shown to be more prone to musculoskeletal injury than are men and boys (e.g., Ingram, 2008; Powell & Barber-Foss, 2000).

Similarly, men are more likely than women to experience traffic-related accidents, and they are three times as likely as women to be killed in motor vehicle accidents (Li, Baker, Langlois, & Kelen, 1998). Men also have several times the rate of women of injury or death in bicycle accidents (e.g., Li & Baker, 1996; Welander, Ekman, Svanstrom, Schelp, & Karlsson, 1999). But, again, these observed differences are almost entirely explained by gender differences in exposure, including time and distance traveled (Li & Baker, 1996; Li et al., 1998; Lourens, Vissers, & Jessurun, 1999).

What this suggests is that it is not the risk behaviors of individual men that require understanding, but the social forces that lead to the gender differences in choice of occupation and recreational activity. Taking risks – whether by engaging in health risk behavior or by doing dangerous things – is an aspect of culturally defined masculinity. There is evidence (e.g., Harris, Jenkins, & Glaser, 2006) that women expect greater negative outcomes and less pleasure across a wide range of risky activities. These include those that increase the risk of chronic disease, those that increase the risk of injury, and those that are associated with social and economic risks, such as gambling. Even among children, boys perceive less risk than do girls in the same situation (Morrongiello & Rennie, 1998). Differences are observable early in life and are transmitted at least in part by parental attitudes and behaviors. Boys are socialized from an early age to expose themselves to risk. Research (Morrongiello & Dawber, 2000; Morrongiello & Hogg, 2004) shows that mothers react differently to small boys' and girls' risk-taking. They tend to caution their daughters to avoid risk, but either encourage sons or assume that boys' risk behaviors are "natural" and not amenable to change.

The gendered patterns in accidental injury and death are mirrored by gendered patterns in physical violence. The masculine nature of crime, and particularly violent crime, is readily demonstrated. An analysis based on Australian police reports (Mukherjee, Carach, & Higgins, 1997), for example, indicates that men vastly outnumber women as perpetrators of every category of crime; the gender difference is largest for crimes of violence, where the difference is approximately tenfold.

Again, the gender differences are not straightforward. Men are far more likely than women to be the victims of violent crime in general, but women are disproportionately likely to be the victims of family violence. To take murder as the most dramatic example, only 25% of all murders are classified as "intimate homicides," that is, involving current or former partners, but in almost 80% of those crimes the perpetrator is male and the victim female (Carach & James, 1998). By contrast, around 75% of the victims of nonintimate homicides are men (Pratt & Deosaransingh, 1997), as are 75% of the perpetrators (Carach & James, 1998). These are Australian data, and population-based murder rates differ considerably between countries – six times as high in the United States as in the United Kingdom, for example (National Campaign Against Violence and Crime, 1998) – but the gender ratios remain relatively constant.

Psychological research on other violent crimes, such as assault, has focused almost exclusively on violence within relationships and has ignored assault outside the family. Assault by an acquaintance or stranger in a public place is the most common form of assault reported to the police (Victoria Police, 1997) and is overwhelming perpetrated by young men against other young men. By contrast, incidents of family violence reported to the police are almost entirely perpetrated by men against women (Victoria Police, 1997). It must, however, be remembered that not all crimes are reported to the police and that family violence in particular is vastly underreported; less than one-third of these crimes are ever reported to any authority (Löbmann, Greve, Wetzels, & Bosold, 2003). Further, there is evidence to show that family violence has much more severe emotional and physical consequences for the victim than assault by a stranger does. There are several reasons for this. One is that family violence is more likely to be repeated and habitual, rather than a single incident; another, perhaps more important, factor is that violence within a relationship or family represents a major betrayal of trust that can seriously affect a person's ability to form or maintain relationships in other contexts (Löbmann et al., 2003). Family violence has been shown to lead to a plethora of serious physical and emotional problems for the victims, including bodily pain, gynecological problems, depression, low self-esteem, panic disorder, difficulties in forming later relationships, and increased risk of later sexual abuse (e.g., Loxton, Schofield, Hussain, & Mishra, 2006; Watson, Taft, & Lee, 2007).

Attention has been placed on the reluctance of law enforcement systems to treat domestic violence against women as serious criminal assault, and feminists have been influential in changing cultural attitudes toward taking family crime considerably more seriously, although there is a long way to go before women in all countries are genuinely protected from assault in the home (e.g., Coker, Smith, McKeown, & King, 2000). At the same time, however, violent assault between young men, particularly alcohol-fuelled brawls and violence in sporting contexts, is viewed by some sections of the population, including the police, as a private or trivial matter, or as normal social behavior in certain circumstances and locations (Lee & Owens, 2002). Thus, young men may internalize a view that violent crime and victimization are normal aspects of masculine life.

Parallel to the gender disparities in accidental injury and violent crime is the gender disparity in suicide. Suicide is more common among men/boys than among women/girls at all age groups in all Western countries. Lee, Collins, and Burgess (1999) showed that, among U.S. children and adolescents, suicide is four times as common among boys and men as among women and girls. Among adults in Western societies, men also commit suicide at around four times the rate of women (Taylor, Morrell, Slaytor, & Ford, 1998; Yip, 1998). It is interesting that this gender difference is not apparent in Asian countries. Yip (1998) demonstrated that men's and women's suicide rates are roughly equal in Hong Kong, and the rate in mainland China is actually somewhat lower for men than for women (Yip, Callanan, & Yuen, 2000), which, again, suggests that explanations are to be found in social and cultural factors rather than in anything innately self-destructive about men.

The evidence supports the view that it is marginalized men who are at highest risk of suicide. Lee et al. (1999) showed that suicide rates are highest among migrant, indigenous, gay, and other minority men. Consistent with the earlier discussion of socioeconomic gradients, marginalization, poverty, and social isolation appear to affect men more strongly and negatively than they do women. For example, Taylor et al. (1998) demonstrated that low socioeconomic status is a more important predictor of suicide for men than for women, which suggests that women may be better able to draw on other resources (e.g., social support) when their economic resources are limited. Similarly, loss of a partner affects men more negatively than women. In the United States, divorced men have twice the suicide rate of married men, whereas there is no difference among women (Kposowa, 2000). In Hong Kong, where there is no overall gender difference in suicide rates, elderly single or widowed men are at increased risk (Yip, Chi, & Yu, 1998). Men in all countries appear to be less able than women to cope with change and loss, and the reasons behind this difference are, again, likely to be found in cultural and social expectations rather than in biological differences.

Future Directions

I have argued that gender differences in health-related behaviors, and in associated attitudes, must be understood from the perspective of sociocultural forces, which encourage men and women to engage in gender-stereotypic behavior in order to differentiate themselves as much as possible from the other sex. Thus, the causes of gender differences in health behavior arise from a social process, whereby men are socialized to disregard knowledge about healthy lifestyles and to choose harmful behaviors, as one way of acting out the masculine script, whereas women are socialized to be cautious with their own health and protective of the health of others. Cultural assumptions about masculinity and femininity include the stereotypes that men should be strong, brave, stoical, and insensitive to pain and that women should take responsibility for the health and health behaviors of the men in their lives.

Research and theorizing about the ways in which gender affects health behaviors and risk-taking is not well developed, and in the next few decades there are several areas, currently under-researched, in which the field could usefully expand. In this final section I briefly discuss two such areas.

Lesbian, Gay, Bisexual, and Transgender (LGBT) Health Issues

The majority of this chapter has been written from a perspective that implicitly assumes that all people are clearly and unambiguously male or female and that most people are straightforwardly heterosexual. This is, of course, far from the case, and there is an extensive literature that examines the well-being of people who fall under the broad category of "queer." This includes people who are sexually attracted to people of the same sex, either exclusively or in addition to attraction to the other sex, as well as people whose biological sex and their psychological or "felt" gender are in conflict.

The majority of this work has focused on lesbians and gay men, a sizable minority who experience considerable social stigma. Despite good evidence that homosexuality is a normal variant of human sexuality, almost all societies continue to discriminate against homosexual people. Although the extent is highly variable, lesbians and gay men consistently experience rejection, legal discrimination, ridicule, and, at times, violence (O'Hanlan, Dibble, Hagan, & Davids, 2004). There is convincing evidence that lesbians and gay men experience poorer mental health than do heterosexual people and that this is best explained by the stresses associated with prejudice and stigma (e.g., Meyer, 2003). Evidence from a number of different countries also shows that lesbians and gay men are more likely than others to engage in unhealthy behaviors. For example, a survey of Boston lesbians (Roberts, Patsdaughter, Grindel, & Tarmina, 2004) showed that lesbians have high rates of smoking and alcohol abuse and lower than average use of cancer screening. Similarly, a survey of gay men in Geneva (Wang, Häusermann, Vounatsou, Aggleton, & Weiss, 2007) showed that those men were more likely than average to report high levels of physical symptoms, to smoke, and to have high cholesterol and high blood pressure, although they were less likely than other men to be overweight. Further, lesbians and gay men have difficulty accessing appropriate health services or are subjected to criticism and the attitude that, whatever their presenting health issue, their "real problem" lies in their sexuality (O'Hanlan et al., 2004).

To date, health psychology has documented the health consequences that stigma and rejection have for LGBT individuals but has done little to develop strategies to combat these issues. Perhaps the only exception to this is the extensive work that has been done in many countries to prevent HIV infection and to assist people living with HIV. Although HIV occurs primarily among heterosexual people in Africa, it is most prevalent among gay men in Western countries, and living with the actuality or the threat of HIV infection is a daily stressor that affects the health of many gay men (Cochran & Mays, 2007). Important future directions in health psychology include interventions to promote a broader understanding of LGBT individuals as well as development of strategies that target the well-being of these individuals directly.

It is important to understand that lesbians, gay men, and people with other sexualities live in a predominantly heterosexist world, in which assumptions about men's and women's lives start with the first question anyone asks ("Is it a boy or a girl?"). Thus one cannot simply assume that – for example – gay men's lives and health concerns parallel those of heterosexual women or that transgender individuals can unproblematically adopt their "felt" gender. Further, there is as much variability among LGBT people as among anyone else, and the variables of social class, ethnicity and religion interact strongly with sexual orientation.

Indigenous, Migrant, and Bicultural Individuals

Throughout the world, the health of indigenous peoples tends to be noticeably poorer than that of members of the colonizing cultures. Stephens, Nettleton, Porter, Willis, and Clark (2005) have pointed out that indigenous people's health is worse than that of others in every country, and they pointed to social marginalization, lack of access to services, and, perhaps more important, lack of access to decision-making and policy development, which has meant that indigenous health services have been under-funded and under-resourced in almost every nation. For example, in the United States, funding of healthcare for indigenous people is not mandated as it is for mainstream Medicare recipients, and the discretionary nature of the budget means that expenditure has consistently been insufficient (Westmoreland & Watson, 2006).

In Australia, successive governments have targeted indigenous health and health behaviors, yet reviews show that health indices, including health risk behaviors, health service use, and life expectancy, as well as levels of violence, family breakdown, unemployment, and low education, are not improving (Hunter, 2003). It appears that efforts to intervene with indigenous issues tend to use strategies that have been rejected or discredited in other areas. For example, Australian efforts to improve indigenous health behaviors such as substance abuse have often involved coercive strategies or legal force, rather than the harm-minimizing, persuasive techniques that have been shown to work in other contexts (e.g., Brady, 2007; Maher, 2004). Good health obviously is predicted by much the same variables among indigenous populations as among nonindigenous populations. Richmond, Ross, and Egeland (2007), for example, showed that the self-rated health of indigenous Canadians, particularly women, was strongly predicted by social support.

Clearly indigenous health is an important issue, but one that has barely been addressed. It is perhaps unsurprising, then, that there has been little attention paid to the gendered nature of indigenous health, and this is an area in which health psychology has a very long way to go.

The health of indigenous people shares issues with health concerns for migrant and bicultural people. The assumption that individuals can be categorized according to their ethnicity has been current in mainstream psychology for decades, but most people in Western societies identify with more than one ethnic or cultural group. Migration complicates matters for many people. For example, 21% of the Australian population was born in other countries, but 61% identify as having at least one ethnicity other than, or in addition to, Australian (Department of Immigration and Multicultural Affairs, 2001). The social impact of racism, which means that members of ethnic minorities have reduced educational, vocational, and developmental opportunities, and thus poorer health, is well documented (e.g., Funkhouser & Moser, 1990), but the ways in which ethnicity interacts with gender is a topic for future research. In particular, the ways in which young people brought up in the migrant culture of their parents or grandparents interact with mainstream cultures is of concern, and this is an area in which gender is clearly important.

This chapter demonstrates that a significant proportion of the difference in longevity between men and women is explicable in terms of culturally mediated attitudes and individual behaviors. Mainstream psychology is silent on this issue or simply makes the assumption that women and men are intrinsically different from each other. Attempts to understand the forces that promote unhealthy choices need to be informed by an understanding of gender and how it is expressed in a range of cultures and subcultures.

References

Amos, A., & Bostock, Y. (2007). Young people, smoking and gender: A qualitative exploration. *Health Education Research*, 22, 770–781.

Andersson, C., Johnsson, K. O., Berglund, M., & Öjehagen, A. (2007). Alcohol involvement in Swedish university freshmen related to gender, age, serious relationship, and family history of alcohol problems. *Alcohol and Alcoholism*, 42, 448–455.

Australian Bureau of Statistics. (2006a). *Deaths, Australia, 2004.* [Cat no 3302.0]. http://www.ausstats.abs.gov.au/ausstats/subscriber.nsf/0/FE3EED4BB4BCE497CA2570CF007458EB/$File/33020_2004.pdf. Accessed 11th October 2008.

Australian Bureau of Statistics (2006b). *Physical activity in Australia: AsSnapshot,* 2004–05. [Cat no 4835.0.55.001]. http://www.abs.gov.au/ausstats/abs@.nsf/mf/4835.0.55.001. Accessed 11th October 2008.

Australian Bureau of Statistics. (2008). *How Australians use their time, 2006.* [Cat no 4153.0]. http://www.abs.gov.au/ausstats/abs@.nsf/mf/4153.0. Accessed 11th October 2008.

Australian Institute for Health and Welfare (2006). *Australia's health, 2006.* Canberra: Author.

Azevedo, M. R., Araújo, C. L., Reichert, F. F., Siqueira, F. V., da Silva, M. C., & Hallal, P. C. (2007). Gender differences in leisure-time physical activity. *International Journal of Public Health, 52,* 8–15.

Bener, A., Hyder, A. A., & Schenk, E. (2007). Trends in childhood injury mortality in a developing country: United Arab Emirates. *Accident & Emergency Nursing, 15,* 228–233.

Birmingham, C. L., Su, J., Hlynsky, J. A., Goldner, E. M., & Gao, M. (2005). The mortality rate from anorexia nervosa. *International Journal of Eating Disorders, 38,* 143–146.

Blanck, H. M., Gillespie, C., Kimmons, J. E., Seymour, J. D., & Serdula, M. K. (2008). Trends in fruit and vegetable consumption among U.S. men and women, 1994–2005. *Prevention of Chronic Diseases, 5,* A35.

Bloomfield, K., Grittner, U., Kramer, S., & Gmel, G. (2006). Social inequalities in alcohol consumption and alcohol-related problems in the study countries of the EU concerted action Gender, Culture and Alcohol Problems: A Multi-national Study. *Alcohol and Alcoholism, 41*(Suppl 1), 26–36.

Blouin, A. G., & Goldfield, G. S. (1995). Body image and steroid use in male body builders. *International Journal of Eating Disorders, 18,* 159–165.

Borooah, V. K. (2004). Gender bias among children in India in their diet and immunization against disease. *Social Science & Medicine, 58,* 1719–1731.

Brady, M. (2007). Equality and difference: Persisting historical themes in health and alcohol policies affecting indigenous Australians. *Journal of Epidemiology & Community Health, 61,* 759–763.

Buckley, P., Freyne, A., & Walsh, N. (1991). Anorexia nervosa in males. *Irish Journal of Psychological Medicine, 8,* 15–18.

Byrne, G. J. A., Raphael, B., & Arnold, E. (1999). Alcohol consumption and psychological distress in recently widowed older men. *Australian and New Zealand Journal of Psychiatry, 33,* 740–747.

Carach, C., & James, M. (1998). *Homicide between intimate partners in Australia.* [Report No. 90.] Canberra: Australian Institute of Criminology.

Caradoc-Davies, T., & Hawker, A. (1997). The true rates of injury among workers in New Zealand: Comparing 1986 and 1991. *Disability and Rehabilitation, 19,* 285–292.

Carlat, D. J., & Camargo, C. A. (1991). Review of bulimia nervosa in males. *American Journal of Psychiatry, 148,* 831–843.

Centers for Disease Control and Prevention. (2007). Prevalence of regular physical activity among adults – United States, 2001 and 2005. *Morbidity & Mortality Weekly Report, 56,* 1209–1212.

Chiolero, A., Faeh, D., Paccaud, F., & Cornuz J. (2008). Consequences of smoking for body weight, body fat distribution, and insulin resistance. *American Journal of Clinical Nutrition, 87,* 801–809.

Choi, P. (2000). *Femininity and the physically active woman.* London: Routledge.

Clarke, J., van Amerom, G., & Binns, J. (2007). Gender and heart disease in the mass print media: 1991, 1996, 2001. *Women & Health, 45,* 17–35.

Clayton, P. J. (1990). Bereavement and depression. *Journal of Clinical Psychiatry, 51*(Suppl), 34–38.

Cochran, S. D., & Mays, V. M. (2007). Physical health complaints among lesbians, gay men, and bisexual and homosexually-experienced heterosexual individuals: Results from the California Quality of Life Survey. *American Journal of Public Health, 97,* 2048–2055.

Coker, A. L., Smith, P. H., McKeown, R. E., & King, M. J. (2000). Frequency and correlates of intimate partner violence by type: Physical, sexual, and psychological battering. *American Journal of Public Health, 90,* 553–559.

Conradi, P. (1994). Life expectancy in Russia falls. *British Medical Journal, 308,* 553.

Danseco, E. R., Miller, T. R., & Spicer, R. S. (2000). Incidence and costs of 1987–1994 childhood injuries: Demographic breakdowns. *Pediatrics, 105,* E27.

Department of Immigration and Multicultural Affairs. (2001). *Immigration – Federation to century's end.* Retrieved from http://www.immi.gov.au/media/publications/statistics/federation/federation.pdf

Deruiter, W. K., Faulkner, G., Cairney, J., & Veldhuizen, S. (2008). Characteristics of physically active smokers and implications for harm reduction. *American Journal of Public Health, 98,* 925–931.

Diala, C. C., Muntaner, C., & Walrath, C. (2004). Gender, occupational, and socioeconomic correlates of alcohol and drug abuse among U.S. rural, metropolitan, and urban residents. *American Journal of Drug and Alcohol Abuse, 30,* 409–428.

Eberl, R., Schalamon, J., Singer, G., Ainoedhofer, H., Petnehazy, T., & Hoellwarth, M. E. (2008). Analysis of 347 kindergarten-related injuries. *European Journal of Pediatrics*, published online. 7th May 2008, doi: 10.1007/s00431-008-0723-0

Elliott, M. R., Shope, J. T., Raghunathan, T. E., & Waller, P. F. (2006). Gender differences among young drivers in the association between high-risk driving and substance use/environmental influences. *Journal of Studies on Alcohol, 67*, 252–260.

Emslie, C., Hunt, K., & Macintyre, S. (1999a). Gender differences in minor morbidity among full time employees of a British university. *Journal of Epidemiology and Community Health, 53*, 465–475.

Emslie, C., Hunt, K., & Macintyre, S. (1999b). Problematizing gender, work, and health: The relationship between gender, occupational grade, working conditions and minor morbidity in full-time bank employees. *Social Science and Medicine, 48*, 33–48.

Feeney, A., North, F., Head, J., Canner, R., & Marmot, M. (1998). Socioeconomic and sex differentials in reason for sickness absence from the Whitehall II Study. *Occupational and Environmental Medicine, 55*, 91–98.

Fulkerson, J. A., & French, S. A. (2003). Cigarette smoking for weight loss or control among adolescents: Gender and racial/ethnic differences. *Journal of Adolescent Health, 32*, 306–313.

Funkhouser, S. W., & Moser, D. K. (1990). Is health care racist? *Advances in Nursing Science, 12*, 47–55.

Gabhainn, S. N., Kelleher, C. C., Naughton, A. M., Carter, F., Flanagan, M., & McGrath, M. J. (1999). Socio-demographic variations in perspectives on cardiovascular disease and associated risk factors, *Health Education Research, 14*, 619–628.

Gardiner, J. P., Judson, J. A., Smith, G. S., Jackson, R., & Norton, R. N. (2000). A decade of intensive care unit trauma admissions in Auckland. *New Zealand Medical Journal, 113*, 327–330.

Ginter, E., & Hulanská, K. (2007). Social determinants of health in Slovakia. *Bratislava Medical Journal, 108*, 477–479.

Haik, J., Liran, A., Tessone, A., Givon, A., Orenstein, A., & Peleg, K. (2007). Burns in Israel: Demographic, etiologic, and clinical trends, 1997–2003. *Israeli Medical Association Journal, 9*, 659–662.

Hansen, H. L., & Jensen, J. (1998). Female seafarers adopt the high risk lifestyle of male seafarers. *Occupational and Environmental Medicine, 55*, 49–51.

Hardoon, S. L., Whincup, P. H., Lennon, L. T., Wannamethee, S. G., Capewell, S., & Morris, R. W. (2008). How much of the recent decline in the incidence of myocardial infarction in British men can be explained by changes in cardiovascular risk factors? Evidence from a prospective population-based study. *Circulation, 117*, 598–604.

Hargreaves, D. A., & Tiggemann, M. (2006). "Body image is for girls": A qualitative study of boys' body image. *Journal of Health Psychology, 11*, 567–576.

Harris, C. R., Jenkins, M., & Glaser, D. (2006). Gender differences in risk assessment: Why do women take fewer risks than men? *Judgment and Decision Making, 1*, 48–63.

Holtzman, D., Powell-Griner, E., Bolen, J. C., & Rhodes, L. (2000). State- and sex-specific prevalence of selected characteristics: Behavioral Risk Factor Surveillance System 1996 and 1997. *Morbidity and Mortality Weekly Report, 49*(6), 1–39.

Hunter, E. (2003). Staying tuned to developments in Indigenous health: Reflections on a decade of change. *Australasian Psychiatry, 11*, 418–422.

Ingram, J. G. (2008). Epidemiology of knee injuries among boys and girls in US high school athletics. *American Journal of Sports Medicine, 36*, 1116–1122.

Johannsen, D. L., Redman, L. M., & Ravussin, E. (2007). The role of physical activity in maintaining a reduced weight. *Current Atherosclerosis Reports, 9*, 463–471.

Kandrack, M., Grant, K. R., & Segall, A. (1991). Gender differences in health-related behaviour: Some unanswered questions. *Social Science and Medicine, 32*, 579–590.

Kessler, R. C., Chiu, W. T., Dernier, O., & Walters, E. E. (2005). Prevalence, severity, and comorbidity of 12-month *DSM-IV* disorders in the National Comorbidity Survey replication. *Archives of General Psychiatry, 62*, 617–627.

Keyes, K. M., Grant, B. F., & Hasin, D. S. (2008). Evidence for a closing gender gap in alcohol use, abuse, and dependence in the United States population. *Drug and Alcohol Dependence, 93*, 21–29.

Kolakowsky-Hayner, S. A., Gourley, E. V., Kreutzer, J. S., Marwitz, J. H., Cifu, D. X., & McKinley, W. O. (1999). Pre-injury substance abuse among persons with brain injury and persons with spinal cord injury. *Brain Injury, 13*, 571–581.

Kposowa, A. J. (2000). Marital status and suicide in the National Longitudinal Mortality Study. *Journal of Epidemiology and Community Health, 54*, 254–261.

Krug, E. G., Sharma, G. K., & Lozano, R. (2000). The global burden of injuries. *American Journal of Public Health, 90*, 523–526.

Kuntsche, S., Gmel, G., Knibbe, R. A., Kuendig, H., Bloomfield, K., Kramer, S., et al. (2006). Gender and cultural differences in the association between family roles, social stratification, and alcohol use: A European cross-cultural analysis. *Alcohol and Alcoholism, 41*(Suppl), 37–46.

Lader, D., Short, S., & Gershuny, J. (2006). *The time use survey, 2005.* London: Office for National Statistics.

Lam, L. T., Ross, F. I., & Cass, D. T. (1999). Children at play: The death and injury pattern in New South Wales, Australia, July 1990–June 1994. *Journal of Paediatrics and Child Health, 35*, 572–577.

Lee, C. (1998). *Women's health: Psychological and social perspectives.* London: Sage.

Lee, C. J., Collins, K. A., & Burgess, S. E. (1999). Suicide under the age of eighteen: A 10-year retrospective study. *American Journal of Forensic Medicine and Pathology, 20*, 27–30.

Lee, C., & Owens, R. G. (2002). *The psychology of men's health.* London, UK: Open University Press.

Leon, D. A., Saburova, L., Tomkins, S., Andreev, E., Kiryanov, N., McKee, M., et al. (2007). Hazardous alcohol drinking and premature mortality in Russia: A population based case-control study. *Lancet, 369*, 2001–2009.

Li, G., & Baker, S. P. (1996). Exploring the male-female discrepancy in death rates from bicycling injury: The decomposition method. *Accident Analysis and Prevention, 28*, 537–540.

Li, G., Baker, S. P., Langlois, J. A., & Kelen, G. D. (1998). Are female drivers safer? An application of the decomposition method. *Epidemiology, 9*, 379–384.

Löbmann, R., Greve, W., Wetzels, P., & Bosold, C. (2003). Violence against women: Conditions, consequences, and coping. *Psychology, Crime, & Law, 9*, 309–331.

Lourens, P. F., Vissers, J. A., & Jessurun, M. (1999). Annual mileage, driving violations, and accident involvement in relation to drivers' sex, age, and level of education. *Accident Analysis and Prevention, 31*, 593–597.

Loxton, D., Schofield, M., Hussain, R., & Mishra, G. (2006). History of domestic violence and physical health in mid-life. *Violence Against Women, 12*, 715–731.

Lyons, A. C., & Willott, S. (1999). From suet pudding to superhero: Representations of men's health for women. *Health, 3*, 283–302.

Macintyre, S. (1993). Gender differences in the perceptions of common cold symptoms. *Social Science & Medicine, 36*, 15–20.

Macintyre, S., Ford, G., & Hunt, K. (1999). Do women "over-report" morbidity? Men's and women's responses to structured prompting on a standard question on long standing illness. *Social Science & Medicine, 48*, 89–98.

Macintyre, S., Hunt, K., & Sweeting, H. (1996). Gender differences in health: Are things really as simple as they seem? *Social Science & Medicine, 42*, 617–624.

MacKenzie, E. J. (2000). Epidemiology of injuries: Current trends and future challenges. *Epidemiological Review, 22*, 112–119.

Maher, L. (2004). Drugs, public health, and policing in indigenous communities. *Drug and Alcohol Review, 23*, 249–251.

McCreary, D. R., Gray, R. E., & Grace, S. L. (2006). Gender differences in cancer mortality risk perceptions and screening behaviors among adults 40–60 years of age. *International Journal of Men's Health, 5*, 53–63.

McPherson, M., Casswell, S., & Pledger, M. (2004). Gender convergence in alcohol consumption and related problems: Issues and outcomes from comparisons of New Zealand survey data. *Addiction, 99*, 738–748.

Men, T., Brennan, P., Boffetta, P., & Zaridze, D. (2003). Russian mortality trends for 1991–2001: Analysis by cause and region. *British Medical Journal, 327*, 964.

Meyer, I. H. (2003). Prejudice, social stress, and mental health in lesbian, gay, and bisexual populations: Conceptual issues and research evidence. *Psychological Bulletin, 129*, 674–697.

Mongin, S. J., Jensen, K. E., Gerberich, S. G., Alexander, B. H., Ryan, A.D., Renier, C. M., et al. (2007). Agricultural injuries among operation household members: RRIS-II 1999. *Journal of Agricultural Safety & Health, 13*, 295–310.

Morrongiello, B. A., & Dawber, T. (2000). Mothers' responses to sons and daughters engaging in injury-risk behaviors on a playground: Implications for sex differences in injury rates. *Journal of Experimental Child Psychology, 76*, 89–103.

Morrongiello, B. A., & Hogg, K. (2004). Mothers' reactions to children misbehaving in ways that can lead to injury: Implications for gender differences in children's risk taking and injuries. *Sex Roles, 50*, 103–118.

Morrongiello, B. A., & Rennie, H. (1998). Why do boys engage in more risk taking than girls? The role of attributions, beliefs, and risk appraisals. *Journal of Pediatric Psychology, 23*, 33–43.

Mukherjee, S., Carach, C., & Higgins, K. (1997). *A statistical profile of crime in Australia.* [Research and Public Policy Series, No. 7.] Canberra: Australian Institute of Criminology.

Munnoch, D. A., Darcy, C. M., Whallett, E. J., & Dixon, W. A. (2000). Work-related burns in South Wales 1995–96. *Burns, 26*, 565–570.

Murgio, A., Fernandez Mila, J. F., Manolio, A., Maurel, D., & Ubeda, C. (1999). Minor head injury at paediatric age in Argentina. *Journal of Neurosurgical Sciences, 43*, 15–23.

Murphy, M., Bobak, M., Nicholson, A., Rose, R., & Marmot, M. (2006). The widening gap in mortality by educational level in the Russian Federation, 1980–2001. *American Journal of Public Health, 96*, 1293–1299.

National Campaign Against Violence and Crime. (1998). *Fear of crime, Commonwealth of Australia*. Canberra: Australian Government Publishing Service.

Neufeld, K. J., Peters, D. H., Rani, M., Bonu, S., & Broomer, R. K. (2005). Regular use of alcohol and tobacco in India and its association with age, gender, and poverty. *Drug and Alcohol Dependence, 77*, 283–291.

Nobunaga, A. I., Go, B. K., & Karunas, R. B. (1999). Recent demographic and injury trends in people served by the Model Spinal Cord Injury Care Systems. *Archives of Physical Medicine and Rehabilitation, 80*, 1372–1382.

Nocon, M., Hiemann, T., Müller-Riemenschneider, F., Thalau, F., Roll, S., & Willich, S. N. (2008). Association of physical activity with all-cause and cardiovascular mortality: A systematic review and meta-analysis. *European Journal of Cardiovascular Prevention & Rehabilitation, 15*, 239–246.

O'Hanlan, K. A., Dibble, S. L., Hagan, H. J. J., & Davids, R. (2004). Advocacy for women's health should include lesbian health. *Journal of Women's Health, 13*, 227–234.

O'Kane, G. M., Craig, P., Black, D., & Sutherland, D. (2008). Riverina Men's Study: A preliminary exploration of the diet, alcohol use, and physical activity behaviours and attitudes of rural men in two Australian New South Wales electorates. *Rural & Remote Health, 8*, 851.

Okely, A. D., Booth, M. L., Hardy, L., Dobbins, T., & Denney-Wilson, E. (2008). Changes in physical activity participation from 1985 to 2004 in a statewide survey of Australian adolescents. *Archives of Pediatric & Adolescent Medicine, 162*, 176–180.

Orsini, N., Bellocco, R., Bottai, M., Pagano, M., Michaelsson, K., & Wolk, A. (2008). Combined effects of obesity and physical activity in predicting mortality among men. *Journal of Internal Medicine, 264*, 442–451.

Pallesen, P., Jøsendal, O., Johnsen, B., Larsen, S., & Molde, H. (2006). Anabolic steroid use in high school students. *Substance Abuse & Misuse, 41*, 1705–1717.

Petersen, A. (1998) *Unmasking the masculine: "Men" and "identity" in a sceptical age*. London: Sage.

Population Reference Bureau. (2003). *Reproductive health trends in Eastern Europe and Eurasia*. http://www.prb.org/pdf/ReproductiveHealthTrendsEE.pdf. Accessed 8th July 2008.

Population Reference Bureau. (2008). *2007 World population data sheet*. http://prb.org/pdf07/07WPDS_Eng.pdf. Accessed 7th July 2008.

Potter, B. K., Pederson, L. L., Chan, S. S. H., Aubut, J. L., & Koval, J. J. (2004). Does a relationship exist between body weight, concerns about weight, and smoking among adolescents? An integration of the literature with an emphasis on gender. *Nicotine & Tobacco Research, 6*, 397–425.

Powell, J. W., & Barber-Foss, K. D. (2000). Sex-related injury patterns among selected high school sports. *American Journal of Sports Medicine, 28*, 385–391.

Pratt, C., & Deosaransingh, K. (1997). Gender differences in homicide in Contra Costa County, California: 1982–1993. *American Journal of Preventive Medicine, 13*(6 Suppl), 19–24.

Prättälä, R., Paalanen, L., Grinberga, D., Helasoja, V., Kasmel, A., & Petkeviciene, J. (2007). Gender differences in the consumption of meat, fruit, and vegetables are similar in Finland and the Baltic countries. *European Journal of Public Health, 17*, 520–525.

Rehm, J., Sulkowska, U., Mańczuk, M., Boffetta, P., Powles, J., Popova, S., et al. (2007). Alcohol accounts for a high proportion of premature mortality in central and eastern Europe. *International Journal of Epidemiology, 36*, 458–467.

Richmond, C., Ross, N., & Egeland, G. M., (2007). Societal resources and thriving health: A new approach for understanding health of indigenous Canadians. *American Journal of Public Health, 97*, 1827–1833.

Roberts, S., Patsdaughter, C. A., Grindel, C. G., & Tarmina, M. S. (2004). Health-related behaviors and cancer screening of lesbians: Results of the Boston Lesbian Health Project II. *Women & Health, 39*(4), 41–55.

Rodham, K., Hawton, K., Evans, E., & Weatherall, R. (2005). Ethnic and gender differences in drinking, smoking, and drug taking among adolescents in England: A self-report school-based survey of 15 and 16 year olds. *Journal of Adolescence, 28*, 63–73.

Ryb, G. E., Dischinger, P., Kufera, J., & Soderstrom, C. (2007). Smoking is a marker of risky behaviors independent of substance abuse in injured drivers. *Traffic Injury Prevention, 8*, 248–252.

Schalamon, J., Eberl, R., Ainoedhofer, H., Singer, G., Spitzer, P., Mayr, J., et al. (2007). School accidents in Austria. *Pediatric Surgery International, 23*, 861–865.

Schappert, S. M. (1999). Ambulatory care visits to physician offices, hospital outpatient departments, and emergency departments: United States 1997. *Vital and Health Statistics, 143*, 1–39.

Schiaffino, A., Fernandez, E., Borrell, C., Salto, E., Garcia, M., & Borras, J. M. (2003). Gender and educational differences in smoking initiation rates in Spain from 1948 to 1992. *European Journal of Public Health, 13*, 56–60.

Seymour-Smith, S. (2008). "Blokes don't like that sort of thing": Men's negotiation of a troubled self-help group identity. *Journal of Health Psychology, 13*, 785–797.

Seymour-Smith, S., Wetherell, M., & Phoenix, A. (2002). "My wife ordered me to come!": A discursive analysis of doctors' and nurses' accounts of men's use of general practitioners. *Journal of Health Psychology, 7*, 253–267.

Shaw, S. M., & Henderson, K. A. (2000). Physical activity, leisure, and women's health. In L. Sherr & J. St Lawrence (Eds.), *Women, health, and the mind* (pp. 339–354). London: Wiley.

Sherr, L., & St Lawrence, J. (Eds.). (2000). *Women, health, and the mind*. London: Wiley.

Shkolnikov, V. M., Andreev, E. M., Anson, J., & Meslé, F. (2004). The peculiar pattern of mortality of Jews in Moscow, 1993–95. *Population Studies, 58*, 311–329.

Siahpush, M. (2004). Smoking and social inequality. *Australian & New Zealand Journal of Public Health, 28*, 297.

Sjöqvist, F., Garle, M., & Rane, A. (2008). Use of doping agents, particularly anabolic steroids, in sports and society. *Lancet, 371*, 1872–1882.

Smith, D. W. E. (1993). *Human longevity*. Oxford: Oxford University Press.

Steinberg, M. B., Akincigil, A., Delnevo, C. D., Crystal, S., & Carson, J. L. (2006). Gender and age disparities for smoking-cessation treatment. *American Journal of Preventive Medicine, 30*, 405–412

Stephens, C., Nettleton, C., Porter, J., Willis, R., & Clark, S. (2005). Indigenous peoples' health: Why are they behind everyone, everywhere? *Lancet, 365*, 10–13.

Stone, K. E., Lanphear, B. P., Pomerantz, W. J., & Khoury, J. (2000). Childhood injuries and deaths due to falls from windows. *Journal of Urban Health, 77*, 26–33.

Stoverinck, M. J., Lagro-Janssen, A. L., & Weel, C.V. (1996). Sex differences in health problems, diagnostic testing, and referral in primary care. *Journal of Family Practice, 43*, 567–576.

Striegel-Moore, R. H., & Bulik, C. M. (2007). Risk factors for eating disorders. *American Psychologist, 62*, 181–198.

Stronegger, W. J., Freidl, W., & Rasky, E. (1997). Health behaviour and risk behaviour: Socioeconomic differences in an Austrian rural county. *Social Science and Medicine, 44*, 423–426.

Sweeting, H., & West, P. (2003). Young people's leisure and risk-taking behaviours: Changes in gender patterning in the west of Scotland during the 1990s. *Journal of Youth Studies, 6*, 391–412.

Taylor, R., Morrell, S., Slaytor, E., & Ford, P. (1998). Suicide in urban New South Wales, Australia 1985–1994: Socio-economic and migrant interactions. *Social Science and Medicine, 47*, 1677–1686.

Toll, B. A., Salovey, P., O'Malley, S. S., Mazure, C. M., Latimer, A., & McKee, S. A. (2008). Message framing for smoking cessation: The interaction of risk perceptions and gender. *Nicotine & Tobacco Research, 10*, 195–200.

Turrell, G., Oldenburg, B., McGuffog, I., & Dent, R. (1999). *Socioeconomic determinants of health: Toward a national research program and a policy and intervention agenda*. Canberra: Ausinfo.

Uitenbroek, D. G., Kerekovska, A., & Festchieva, N. (1996). Health lifestyle behaviour and socio-demographic characteristics: A study of Varna, Glasgow, and Edinburgh. *Social Science and Medicine, 43*, 367–377.

Umberson, D. (1992). Gender, marital status, and the social control of health behaviour. *Social Science and Medicine, 34*, 907–917.

van Asbeck, F. W., Post, M. W., & Pangalila, R. F. (2000). An epidemiological description of spinal cord injuries in The Netherlands in 1994. *Spinal Cord, 38*, 420–424.

Vandevijvere, S., De Vriese, S., Huybrechts, I., Moreau, M., Temme, E., De Henauw. S., et al. (2008). The gap between food-based dietary guidelines and usual food consumption in Belgium, 2004. *Public Health Nutrition*, published online 22nd April 2008, doi: 10.1017/S1368980008002164

van Wijk, C. M. G., Huisman, H., & Kolk, A. M. (1999). Gender differences in physical symptoms and illness behavior: A health diary study. *Social Science and Medicine, 49*, 1061–1074.

Victoria Police. (1997). *Crime statistics 1995/96*. Melbourne, Australia: Victoria Police Family Violence Project Office.

Wagner, G. A., de Andrade Stempliuk, V., Zilberman, M. L., Barroso, L. P., & de Andrade, A. G. (2007). Alcohol and drug use among university students: Gender differences. *Revista Brasileira de Psiquiatria, 29*, 123–129.

Wang, J., Häusermann, M., Vounatsou, P., Aggleton, P., & Weiss, M. G. (2007). Health status, behavior, and care utilization in the Geneva Gay Men's Health Survey. *Preventive Medicine, 44*, 70–75.

Watson, W. L., & Ozanne-Smith, J. (2000). Injury surveillance in Victoria, Australia: Developing comprehensive injury incidence estimates, *Accident Analysis and Prevention, 32*, 277–286.

Watson, L. F., Taft, A. J., & Lee, C. (2007). Age at menarche, first intercourse, and first birth: Associations with experiences of violence among a national population sample of young Australian women. *Women's Health Issues, 17*, 281–289.

Weden, M. M., & Zabin, L. S. (2005). Gender and ethnic differences in the co-occurrence of adolescent risk behaviors. *Ethnicity & Health, 10*, 213–234.

Welander, G., Ekman, R., Svanstrom, L., Schelp, L., & Karlsson, A. (1999). Bicycle injuries in western Sweden: A comparison between counties. *Accident Analysis and Prevention, 31*, 13–19.

Westmoreland, T., & Watson, K. R. (2006). Fulfilling the hollow promises made to indigenous people: Redeeming hollow promises – The case for mandatory spending on health care for American Indians and Alaska Natives. *American Journal of Public Health, 96*, 600–605.

Williams, J. M., Wright, P., Currie, C. E., & Beattie, T. F. (1998). Sports-related injuries in Scottish adolescents aged 11–15. *British Journal of Sports Medicine, 32*, 291–296.

Wong, T. Y., Lincoln, A., Tielsch, J. M., & Baker, S. P. (1998). The epidemiology of ocular injury in a major US automobile corporation. *Eye, 12*, 870–874.

World Health Organisation. (2008). *WHO report on the global tobaccoe Epidemic, 2008: The MPOWER package*. Geneva: Author.

Wu, T. Y., Rose, S. E., & Bancroft, J. M. (2006). Gender differences in health risk behaviors and physical activity among middle school students. *Journal of School Nursing, 22*, 25–31.

Wyke, S., Hunt, K., & Ford, G. (1998) Gender differences in consulting a general practitioner for common symptoms of minor illness. *Social Science and Medicine, 46*, 901–906.

Yip, P. S. (1998). Suicides in Hong Kong and Australia. *Crisis, 19*, 24–34.

Yip, P. S., Callanan, C., & Yuen, H. P. (2000). Urban/rural and gender differentials in suicide rates: East and West. *Journal of Affective Disorders, 57*, 99–106.

Yip, P. S., Chi, I., & Yu, K .K. (1998). An epidemiological profile of elderly suicides in Hong Kong. *International Journal of Geriatric Psychiatry, 13*, 631–637.

Chapter 21
Gender, Stress, and Coping

Amy Zwicker and Anita DeLongis

Gender Differences in Stress and Coping

Despite an extensive literature on stress and coping, it is difficult to pinpoint ways of coping that, as a rule, are adaptive or maladaptive. Coping is a dynamic process, one that is shaped by characteristics of the person and situation (DeLongis & Holtzman, 2005; Folkman, Lazarus, Dunkel-Schetter, DeLongis, & Gruen, 1986). What is stressful to one individual in one situation may not be stressful to another person or to the same person in a different situation. This dynamic nature of stress and coping poses many challenges and requires that researchers pay adequate attention to the personal and situational context in which stress and coping occur. Across all cultures, to various degrees, there are differences in the stressful situations to which men and women are exposed. It follows, then, that gender may be an important factor to consider in understanding the dynamics of the stress process. The purpose of this chapter is to review theory and research on stress and coping in the context of gender. Our approach here is to consider gender not as a variable to be controlled in research but rather as an important contextual variable to be considered in understanding stress and coping.

Models of Stress and Coping

In order to build an understanding of the differences in women's and men's stress and coping patterns, it is important first to have an understanding of stress and coping more generally. The transactional model of stress and coping (Lazarus & DeLongis, 1983; Lazarus & Folkman, 1984) suggests that stress is experienced when an individual confronts an event that is relevant to his or her well-being and taxes or exceeds his or her coping resources. This model argues that the individual and the environment must be considered in relation to one another. In other words, a negative event may or may not be deemed stressful by a given individual depending on the individual's cognitive appraisal of the event and his or her ability to cope with the event.

It is posited that individuals engage in two types of stress appraisals: primary and secondary. When making a primary appraisal, the individual evaluates what is at stake in the situation. That is, the situation is determined to be either irrelevant, positive, or stressful. Situations are appraised as stressful when they entail harm or loss, the threat of potential harm or loss, or challenge. Whether the individual experiences stress as a result of the stressor also depends on her or his secondary

A. Zwicker (✉)
University of British Columbia, Vancouver, BC, Canada

appraisal of the event. Secondary appraisal occurs when a person considers what coping resources and options are available and can be brought to bear on the situation. As such, an individual may not experience much stress, even when facing a harmful or threatening event, if that individual believes that her or his coping resources are sufficient to manage the stressor. Alternatively, an event that is not particularly threatening or harmful may be perceived as stressful to an individual if coping resources are insufficient to manage the event.

The appraisal process can be illustrated by imagining two different drivers, each with a flat tire. The first driver has never changed a flat tire and is running late for an important meeting, whereas the second driver is out for a leisurely afternoon drive and happens to be an auto mechanic. The same stressor—a flat tire—should be more stressful for our first driver given that it will be appraised as a threat to his or her ability to meet work demands. In addition, this driver may feel that his or her ability to cope with the situation (e.g., change the tire) is poor. Appraising the situation as threatening and feeling ill-equipped to cope with, it would be likely to lead the driver to experience much more stress than would our second driver, for whom the consequences of the flat tire would be less threatening and, by drawing upon his or her automotive background, he or she would likely cope more easily with the challenge.

Coping refers to cognitive and behavioral efforts to manage stress. Coping was initially conceptualized in the transactional model as either problem focused, which includes efforts directed toward changing some aspects of the stressful situation, or emotion focused, which includes efforts to manage one's emotions during the stressful episode. In a contextual model that builds on the transactional model, attention is paid to the interpersonal context in which the stress process occurs (DeLongis & Holtzman, 2005). Here, a third facet of coping is posited. Relationship-focused coping includes efforts directed toward managing and maintaining close relationships during times of stress (Coyne & Smith, 1991; DeLongis & O'Brien, 1990).

A contextual model of stress and coping is depicted in Fig. 21.1. In this model, it is argued that the interplay of personal and situational characteristics is evident at every stage of the stress process. For example, characteristics such as gender, personality, age, income, education, and past experiences affect the likelihood of exposure to stressful situations. Along with these person characteristics, situational factors such as the novelty, predictability, event uncertainty, imminence, and duration of the situation (Lazarus & Folkman, 1984; O'Brien & DeLongis, 1997) also play a role in the appraisal of the situation as stressful. Person and situation variables influence the selection of coping

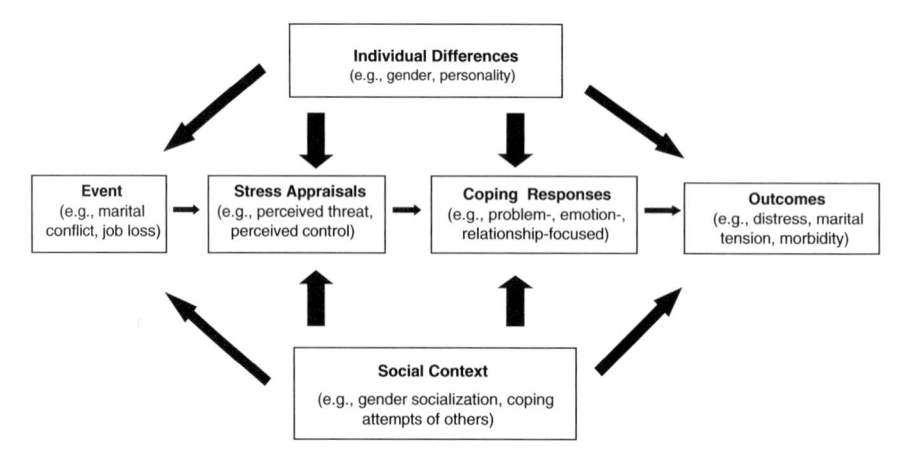

Fig. 21.1 Contextual model of stress and coping process

methods and the success of coping methods in dealing with the stressor; in other words, personal and situational differences make up the context in which people cope with stressful events.

Among situational factors, interpersonal features of stressors, such as who else is involved in the situation (O'Brien & DeLongis, 1997) and how these others are responding (Marin, Holtzman, DeLongis, & Robinson, 2007), are among the most influential in the stress process. Indeed, interpersonal stressors, as compared to other types of stressors (e.g., work stress), tend to have the most impact in everyday life (Bolger, DeLongis, Kessler, & Schilling, 1989). From this interpersonal and contextual focus has emerged a literature on "dyadic coping" (Revenson, Kayser, & Bodenman, 2005) that examines the stress and coping of both members of a couple in tandem to predict the outcomes of stress.

In this chapter, we first discuss gender differences in sources of stress. Work stress, stress arising in interpersonal relationships, and stress arising in the context of chronic illness are examined in detail, largely because they are three contexts in which important gender differences reliably emerge. In addition, they are common stressors for the majority of adults. Close relationships are a central arena in which people experience and cope with stress (DeLongis & Holtzman, 2005). Even when sources of stress originate outside the context of a close relationship, much of the individual's coping with that stress may be undertaken with the support of and in collaboration with a close other. "How was your day?" is the prototypical first question asked as family members arrive home, and coping efforts may be planned or adjusted in light of the response of others. Without an examination of how people cope with stress within the context of close relationships, we are unlikely ever to understand fully why and how some people thrive in the face of stress while others flail. For many adults, the marital relationship is a primary relationship. Given this, we draw upon the marital literature as a key context in which to examine gender differences in stress and coping. This literature has obvious limitations for understanding gender differences, as it draws almost entirely upon studies of heterosexual couples. There is, unfortunately, a dearth of studies of couples outside of a traditional marital context, and we are therefore limited in the conclusions we can draw based upon this literature.

Following our discussion of sources of stress, we discuss gender differences in coping, namely, in the use of social support as a coping resource. The considerable amount of research that shows reliable gender differences in all aspects of social support suggests that it may be the coping resource that differs most by gender. We conclude the chapter by presenting research on culture, diversity, and discrimination to highlight special issues and limitations in the extant literature on gender, stress, and coping and also to provide direction for future research.

Gender Differences in Stress and Coping: Considered in Context

There is a popular notion that men tend to engage in more problem-focused coping, whereas women use more emotion-focused coping to deal with stress. This arises in part from common gender stereotypes such as the independent, task-oriented man and the dependent, emotionally expressive woman (e.g., Bem, 1974). There is some support in the literature for this notion. For example, a study of community-residing men and women revealed that, across the course of a year, men reported significantly higher levels of problem-focused coping than did women. Women, on the other hand, reported significantly higher levels of emotion-focused coping than did men (Folkman & Lazarus, 1980). At first glance, these results seem to suggest that men and women cope in ways that fit with common gender stereotypes. However, important gender differences also emerged in the types of stressors that were reported in the study. That is, men reported significantly more work-related stressors, and women reported significantly more family-related and health-related stressors. For both men and women, work stressors were associated with greater use of problem-focused coping, whereas family and health stressors were linked more strongly to emotion-focused coping. When exposure to these different types of stressors was controlled, the gender difference in emotion-focused coping vanished, and the gender difference in problem-focused coping was reduced.

This finding illustrates the need to consider stress and coping in context. That is, the participants coped in ways that matched the stressor; differences in coping arose from differences in the types of stressors experienced by women and men as opposed to from gender differences in coping, per se. As a result, it is important to consider where in the stress and coping processes gender differences arise and how the differences carry through other phases of the stress and coping process. In the following sections we consider gender differences in stress and coping, looking specifically at the stressors that tend to be reported most often by women and by men, namely gender differences in interpersonal, health, and work stress.

Coping with Interpersonal Stress

Relationships can be a great resource in that the support of others can help women and men to cope with stressors. However, attention needs to be paid to the distinction between relationships as a source of support and as a source of stress (Coyne & DeLongis, 1986). We first discuss relationships as a source of stress, in and of themselves, and then as a context in which to cope with other stressors. The supportive role of relationships is discussed later in the social support section of this chapter.

Research suggests that women are at increased risk of experiencing interpersonal stress. For example, women report that interpersonal conflict is the most common and distressing form of stress they face (Taylor et al., 2000). This may arise, in part, because women tend to be more integrated within social networks, an issue we discuss again when we highlight the benefit of social integration, namely, increased social support. However, greater social integration can also lead to increased exposure to interpersonal stressors. For example, Kessler and McLeod (1984) found that women's increased interpersonal integration and empathic concern for others in their social network exposes them to more "network events." That is, women are distressed not only by the life events that affect them personally but also by the life events that affect others who are important to them. In addition, women tend to appraise interpersonal stressors as more stressful. The tendency for women to appraise interpersonal situations as more stressful has been found when men and women have been asked to rate the severity of interpersonal situations (Krajewski & Goffin, 2005) and when physiological responses to interpersonal stress have been recorded (Kiecolt-Glaser & Newton, 2001). Taken together, this research suggests that interpersonal relationships create more stress for women than for men.

Interpersonal relationships have important implications in the lives of both men and women. A close, intimate relationship with a partner, whether or not acknowledged via marriage, is reported to be the most central relationship for most adults. The presence of such a relationship is reliably related to lower morbidity and mortality rates in partnered than in single people (House, Umberson, & Landis, 1988). However, such relationships are, of course, not always supportive. Conflictual relationships are not only a source of stress but they also may isolate individuals by limiting their ability to obtain support from outside of the relationship (Coyne & DeLongis, 1986). These findings suggest that stress in close relationships may decrease well-being not only directly but also indirectly by contributing to social isolation.

Research suggests that conflict in close relationships also bears directly on physical and mental health. For example, a recent review of the literature regarding the effects of marriage on health indicated that poorer marital functioning was related to poorer self-reported health for both women and men (Kiecolt-Glaser & Newton, 2001). However, the same review revealed that marital conflict may exact a greater physiological toll on women than on men. For example, Kiecolt-Glaser and Newton pointed to considerable evidence that marital conflict is related to poorer cardiovascular functioning (e.g., increased blood pressure), immune functioning (e.g., decreased lymphocyte proliferative responses), and endocrine functioning (e.g., increased cortisol and norepinephrine release) in women than in men. This increased physiological reactivity in women is striking given the general tendency for men to display more physiological reactivity to acute stressors in laboratory settings, including tasks such as public speaking or performing mental arithmetic in front of an audience. In other words, these findings do not represent a general increase in stress reactivity in women, but rather a specific pattern of increased reactivity to interpersonal stressors (Kiecolt-Glaser & Newton, 2001). These findings suggest that women appear to endure more stress than men do in a troubled marriage. In fact, research we present later in this chapter on gender differences in social support shows that marriage confers greater benefit to men than to women.

It was noted earlier that coping behavior is highly situation specific. For example, work-related stress often elicits problem-focused coping, whereas health-related stress often elicits emotion-focused coping (Folkman & Lazarus, 1980). Interpersonal stressors are associated with relationship-focused coping. O'Brien and DeLongis (1996) found that the use of one form of relationship-focused coping, namely empathic responding, tended to be elicited by stress in close relationships, for example, stress involving a close family member or friend.

In a study of the role of empathic responding in coping with marital stress (O'Brien, DeLongis, Pomaki, Puterman, & Zwicker, 2009) we found that, although the use of empathic responding did not vary by gender, the effects of empathic responding did. For men, increases in empathic responding were associated with immediate increases in marital tension. For women, the opposite effect was found; marital tension was diffused. For both husbands and wives, the longer term effect of empathic responding was a diffusion of marital tension. The emotional attunement and communication involved in empathic responding may defuse tension more rapidly for women than for men due to women's preferences for staying engaged and in communication during times of marital conflict (Carstensen, Gottman, & Levenson, 1995; Gottman, 1998). This illustrates a conflict that can arise from coping—what may be beneficial coping for the individual may be costly to the relationship or what may be beneficial to the relationship may be costly to the individual (Coyne & Smith, 1991).

Our discussion of interpersonal stress thus far has focused on studies conducted in Western countries. It is imperative that we do not assume that these findings generalize across cultures. In the following example, and in our discussion of work-related stress in different cultures, it is clear that the cultural milieu in which women and men live influences stress and coping. Gender roles are an important variable that differs across cultures and consequently helps to explain differences in interpersonal distress across cultures. Rheman and Holtzworth-Munroe (2006) examined interpersonal distress in North American and Pakistani couples and found important differences in communication patterns in these more egalitarian and more patriarchal societies, respectively. They examined the demand–withdraw pattern in which one partner is emotionally demanding or critical of the other and the other partner withdraws or defends her- or himself in order to retreat from the demands (Christensen & Heavey, 1990). This communication pattern is considered a hallmark of marital distress in Western samples. In their study, Rheman and Holtzworth-Munroe found that the demand–withdraw communication pattern was also related to relationship distress in Pakistani couples.

However, the relationship of gender to the demand and withdrawal roles varies across cultures. In Western samples it has been found that women fill the demanding role, whereas men withdraw. It is tempting to conclude that these behaviors are inherent to women and men, respectively; however, cross-cultural work shows that these roles are not tied to gender so much as they are to power differentials. In their study, Rheman and Holtzworth-Munroe (2006) replicated the common finding that women make more demands and husbands withdraw in their sample of North American couples, but the pattern was reversed in their sample of couples from Pakistan. They drew from the Marital Structure Hypothesis (Eldridge & Christensen, 2002) to explain the reversed demand–withdraw roles filled by men and women across these two cultures. This theory suggests that there is more room to negotiate or contest gender roles in more egalitarian marriages; the same is not true of more traditional marriages. As such, women in more egalitarian marriages tend to make demands as a way to bring about change (e.g., request more help with household labor and childcare), whereas men tend to withdraw as a way to maintain the status quo. In contrast, men in more traditional marriages such as those in Pakistan may exercise their power by making demands. Women in these more traditional marriages may withdraw given that it would be inappropriate to contest or negotiate the demands from their positions of lesser power. Although the demand–withdraw pattern is related to interpersonal distress in both Western and non-Western societies, it is very clear that the cultural context and gender roles within this context must be considered carefully in order to understand the function of this behavior.

Coping with Chronic Illness

As is clear in our discussion of the classic demand–withdraw pattern described above, the coping engaged in by one member of a dyad, although perhaps meeting his or her own needs, is not necessarily of benefit to the other member of a dyad or larger social unit. On the other hand, in the context of coping with chronic illness, coping behavior is frequently of benefit primarily to others and not necessarily directly beneficial to the person engaged in the coping. The finding that one may prioritize the well-being of a partner or the relationship at one's personal expense is not uncommon here. For example, Coyne and Smith (1991) studied husbands who had suffered a myocardial infarction (MI) and their wives, and they found that after 6 months the MI wives were at least as distressed as the patients were. Wives' distress was predicted by their use of relationship-focused coping, in particular, protective buffering. Protective buffering is a form of relationship-focused coping that entails hiding concerns, denying worries, and yielding to the partner to avoid disagreements. From this it was concluded that the wives' use of relationship-focused coping represented the cost of caring; it may represent a trade-off between their personal distress and the recovery of the patient. A follow-up to this study revealed that patient self-efficacy was also related to the spouse's use of relationship-focused coping (Coyne & Smith, 1994). Increases in patient self-efficacy were related to wives' use of more protective buffering and patients' use of less protective buffering and more active engagement. Active engagement consists of involving the partner in discussions, inquiring about how the partner feels, and other constructive communal problem-solving strategies (Coyne & Smith, 1991). So it seems that the extent to which wives shelter their concerns from the patients, and the patients invoke their wives' active support without concealing their worries or concerns, the patients may benefit and the wives may suffer.

It is tempting to conclude that these findings represent gender differences in coping with illness, although it is not clear if that is actually the case. Because all of the patients in this study were men and all of the spouses were women, it could also be that coping differences arise due to patient and partner roles as opposed to gender roles per se. Many studies of the ways in which couples cope with illness have focused on specific illnesses such as breast cancer, prostate cancer, and rheumatoid arthritis. Given that these illnesses occur exclusively or predominantly in one gender as opposed to the other, differences in outcomes that are attributed to being the patient as opposed to the partner are often confounded with differences in outcomes that might also be explained by one gender as opposed to the other. In a recent meta-analysis, Hagedoorn, Sanderman, Bolks, Tuinstra, and Coyne (2008) examined the relationship between gender and patient–partner roles for couples in which one person had received a cancer diagnosis. It was found that gender, as opposed to patient or partner status, was a better predictor of distress. That is, women reported a greater level of distress regardless of whether they were patient or partner. Similarly, a study of patients coping with rheumatic disease showed that male patients had the lowest levels of distress, female patients had the highest levels of distress, and their male and female partners had moderate levels of distress and fell between the two patient groups (Revenson, Abraído-Lanza, Majerovitz, & Jordan, 2005). Again, women faced greater distress regardless of their patient–partner status. These important findings help to explain the often contradictory results in the literature on the relative adjustment of patients and partners to illness; gender is a critical component in this relationship that, if ignored, can greatly confuse the picture.

Why is it, then, that women fair more poorly, regardless of whether they are themselves ill or are partner to someone with an illness? First, it is important to note that the interdependent coping and support processes that characterize couples imply that illness impacts both the patient and the partner emotionally and practically (Hagedoorn et al., 2008). Women may fair more poorly when they are the partner of an ill man because of their relational self-construal; the well-being of women is affected by the well-being of those around them, more so than is the case for men (Berg & Upchurch, 2007; Hagedoorn et al., 2008; Kessler & McLeod, 1984). Further to this, as we have discussed, wives' greater tendency to use protective buffering to cope with their husbands' illness (Badr, 2004; Coyne & Smith, 1991, 1994) reveals a possible conflict between this situation-specific coping and women's typical coping patterns. That is, whereas women seem to respond to their husbands' illnesses by putting on a brave face and sheltering their husbands from their worries, the broader literature on women's coping patterns suggests that women prefer to get their thoughts and feelings out in the open by talking with close others (Cohen & Wills, 1985). This conflict may contribute to the increased distress that women face as partners to ill husbands. Not only do women tend to engage in protective buffering when their partners are ill, they also engage in protective buffering, avoidance coping, and are less likely to solicit support when they themselves are the patients (Badr, 2004). The protective stance that women take when they are both patients and partners of the patients is likely to contribute to the higher distress rates reported by women, regardless of their illness role, and this helps to explain why male patients and partners do not face as much distress.

Another factor that may contribute to the interesting finding that ill husbands fair better than their healthy wives is the quality of social support that husbands receive from their wives. Not only are wives reported to be better providers of social support (Cutrona, 1996; Neff & Karney, 2005) but they preferentially provide, and are deemed better providers of, emotional support specifically (Verhofstadt, Buysse, & Ickes, 2007). Emotional support may be the most influential type of support for patient well-being. For example, Hagedoorn et al. (2008) suggested that the term "caregiver" is often incorrectly ascribed to the partner of patients with chronic illness because it is assumed that the partner takes on additional responsibilities to aid in the patient's recovery. With illnesses such as cancer, however, partners often do not assume major responsibilities in terms of assisting medical management or activities of daily living. Instead, partners more often assume the role of providing emotional support. In line with this, a study of the relationship between the functional impairment of cancer patients and their preference for different types of support showed that declining functional ability did not predict an increased desire for instrumental support (Manne, Alfieri, Taylor, & Dougherty, 1999). Declining functional ability did, however, predict increased desire for emotional support in female, but not in male, patients. Thus, even though these female patients were experiencing difficulty with instrumental tasks, they preferred emotional support that would help them to deal with the stress that accompanied their functional decline rather than instrumental support that would compensate for their functional decline. Men tend more often to provide instrumental support (Verhofstadt et al., 2007), and, consequently, female patients may face a gap between their needs for emotional support and the support received from their male partner. Men, on the other hand, will benefit, whether they are the patient or partner, from women's tendency to provide emotional support that aids in adjustment to illness.

It is important to keep in mind that these results are relative; that is, both women and men are distressed when coping with illness and other interpersonal stressors. The fact that research consistently shows that women are more distressed when facing interpersonal stressors and when coping with other stressors such as illness in the context of a relationship follows from their strong attunement to others in their social networks or their communality (Helgeson, 1994; Kessler & McLeod, 1984). Perhaps because men are socialized to be more agentic in their strivings, stressors in the workplace present a common source of stress to men (Helgeson, 1994).

Coping with Work-Related Stress

Whereas women more often report that interpersonal stressors are distressing, men consistently cite workplace stressors as more distressing. This is not surprising given that work figures prominently in the masculine identity (Helgeson, 1994). However, with dramatic increases in the number of women who join men in the labor force, particularly across the past few decades, workplace stress is shared by men and women alike. Work overload and job insecurity are commonly reported by both women and men as major stressors in the workplace (Tennant, 2001). However, men and women also experience workplace stress that is unique or, at least, more common to their gender.

It has been argued that societal change has not kept up with the changing role of women in the workplace, which in many occupations remains a masculine environment (Fielden & Cooper, 2002; Shaffer, Joplin, Bell, Lau, & Oguz, 2000). This implies that women face unique stressors and, indeed, there is a large literature on the work stressors with which women must cope, over and above the work stress that they share with men (for comprehensive reviews, see Fielden & Cooper, 2002; Greenglass, 2002). The unique stressors that women face in the workforce include gender harassment (Piotrkowski, 1998), decreased control (Krajewski & Goffin, 2005), fewer career prospects (Nelson & Quick, 1985), and conflict of work with childrearing and domestic duties, for which most women still hold the majority of responsibility (Long & Cox, 2000). Women face sex-based discrimination in the workforce; the stress of discrimination based on sex, sexual orientation, and race is discussed in greater detail later in this chapter. The changing face of the workplace also poses stress for men; men have historically defined themselves as providers, and the influx of women into the workplace, along with corporate downsizing and restructuring, means that men are increasingly faced with the need to re-evaluate their roles in the workplace and at home (Burke, 2002). It is clear that men and women do face different sources of stress within the workplace; the extent to which these differences in stress exposure influence the well-being of men and women, however, must be considered in light of stress appraisals and coping resources within the workplace.

Men and women differ in their primary appraisals of sources of stress in the workplace. It is not surprising that women tend to appraise situations characterized by victimization, the need to behave assertively, and their own non-nurturant behavior as more distressing, whereas men tend to appraise their own performance failures, subordination to women, and intellectual inferiority as more distressing (Bekker, Nijssen, & Hens, 2001). Gender also yields differences in secondary stress appraisals; one of the key variables that have been found to be related to gender differences in the selection of coping options is control. Numerous studies have shown that women are often at the bottom of the organizational hierarchy; they are less likely to occupy high-status positions in the workforce, positions that include more executive tasks, participation, and autonomy, and they face fewer opportunities for advancement (Bekker et al., 2001; Greenglass, 2002; Piotrkowski, 1998). The result is that women perceive less control and fewer opportunities to affect change in the workplace.

These gender differences in secondary stress appraisal have important implications for the selection of coping skills that are brought to task. Research has demonstrated the integral role of perceived control in coping by experimentally manipulating hypothetical sources of work-related stress. For example, Krajewski and Goffin (2005) developed vignettes in which workplace stress was represented by work overload. In one condition, participants were asked how they would cope in response to an independent work overload (e.g., extra work assigned to them directly by their employer), whereas in a second condition participants were asked how they would respond to an interpersonal work overload (e.g., one in which the employer required that all of the employees meet in order to negotiate who would take on the additional workload). No gender differences in coping arose in the independent work overload condition; however, women reported more emotion-focused coping in the interpersonal work overload condition. It is important to note that women also perceived less control relative to men in the interpersonal work overload condition, which helps to explain why, when faced with the same task of negotiating which employee would assume the extra work, women more often used emotion-focused coping, whereas men more often used problem-focused coping.

The broader literature on stress and coping has shown that people tend to use more problem-focused coping when a situation is seen as changeable, whereas emotion-focused coping is often reserved for situations in which the person perceives little opportunity to change the situation (Folkman et al., 1986). As a result of their relatively greater positions of control, studies have shown that men use more problem-focused coping in the workplace (Folkman & Lazarus, 1980). When researchers have eliminated power differentials by examining men and women who share similar positions, coping differences tend to disappear. For example, McDonald and Korabik (1991) found that men and women who occupy management positions with equivalent decision-making latitude, access to resources, and control tend to cope similarly by taking direct action to solve problems on the job. The increased use of problem-focused coping by men in the workplace is particularly effective given that research shows that they benefit more from this type of coping. Gonzalez-Morales, Peiro, Rodriguez, and Greenglass (2006) found that men experienced less psychological and psychosomatic distress when problem-focused coping was used. For women, the benefit of problem-focused coping was not as great; they experienced decreased psychological distress, but no differences were found in terms of psychosomatic complaints. One can see that if the researchers had considered only one of these outcomes, either psychological distress or psychosomatic complaints, a different pattern of results would have been revealed. This highlights one of the methodological challenges in this field: the importance of specifying effects of stress on particular outcomes and not assuming that a method of coping that is effective for improving one outcome is necessarily effective for all.

There are also differences between women and men in the seeking of social support in the workplace. Across a wide range of stressors, women seek out more social support than men do (Taylor et al., 2000). Gender differences in social support are discussed in detail in the following section; however, social support differences, as they pertain to coping with work stress, will be highlighted here. Women are more likely than men to solicit support in the form of seeking advice, information, practical assistance, and emotional support when coping with work stress (Greenglass, 2002). Not only do women seek more support, but they benefit more from that support. Gonzalez-Morales and her colleagues (2006) found that female employees' increased use of social support was related to fewer psychosomatic complaints. Contrary to this, social support appeared to be harmful for male employees; their increased social support was related to more psychological and psychosomatic complaints. Gonzalez-Morales et al. argued that men are not as able to benefit from social support because men are socialized in ways that discourage emotional expression and encourage goal-directed, independent coping efforts. As a result, the distress that men face when they use social support to cope with work stress may arise from using a coping method that is not "allowed" by their gender role.

This discussion of stress and coping in the workplace indicates that there are consistent gender differences in (1) exposure to sources of stress in the workplace, (2) primary and secondary appraisals of work stress, (3) coping, (4) social support, and (5) outcomes. The notion that men and women are categorically different in the ways they cope with work stress is not well supported. Instead, it is clear that most of these gender differences arise from gender distinctions in the broader social context in which men and women live. Given this, variations in gender roles that arise in different cultural contexts should result in differences in gender-related work stress across cultures. The following examples suggest that this is indeed the case.

The research discussed above was all conducted in Western countries where there is substantial legislation that strives to curb sex discrimination in the workplace. It has been found that gender is more often used to evaluate employees in countries such as the People's Republic of China (including Hong Kong) where legislation is not enforced as strongly as in other countries (Shaffer et al., 2000). Shaffer et al. suggested that more negative attitudes exist toward women in Hong Kong and other parts of the People's Republic of China relative to the United States and that these negative attitudes are related to greater distress in working women. Although there is not a great deal of research that compares cultural differences in work stress, this example serves to remind us that the cultural context shapes the stress and coping process in men and women. It is also important to keep in mind that all of the differences between the ways men and women cope with work stressors exist among a great many similarities. For example, despite the pattern discussed above in which certain contextual factors (e.g., control appraisals) facilitate more problem-focused coping in men, both women and men use more problem-focused coping than emotion-focused coping in the workplace (Folkman & Lazarus, 1980; Gonzalez-Morales et al., 2006).

Gender Differences in Social Support

As noted above, women, more often than men, tend to seek out social support to cope with a wide range of stressors, of which work-related stress is only one example. Social support is a key resource in the stress and coping process; evidence shows that it lessens the negative impact of stress and is related to better health (for reviews, see DeLongis, Holtzman, Puterman, & Lam, in press; Taylor, 2007). The effects of social isolation are not trivial; epidemiological studies indicate that social isolation is a risk factor for morbidity and mortality that is comparable in effect size to other well-known risk factors such as smoking and obesity (House et al., 1988). Just as the evidence for the benefits of social support is strong, so too is the evidence for gender differences in social support.

As we discuss in this chapter, the extent to which women, more often than men, seek out social support in times of stress has been noted as one of the most robust gender differences in human behavior (Taylor et al., 2000). Not only do women seek out more social support, they hold a more favorable perception of the effectiveness of social support as a coping resource, they provide support to others more frequently, and the support they provide is judged by support recipients to be better than that provided by men (Barbee et al., 1993; Cohen & Wills, 1985; Greenglass, 2002; Neff & Karney, 2005; Taylor et al., 2000; Thoits, 1991). It is not surprising, then, that both men and women tend to turn to women more often for support; married men more often turn to their wives and married women more often turn to other women (Taylor et al., 2000). Taylor (2002) has even implicated social support in the longer life span that women enjoy relative to men. This brief overview of gender differences in social support suggests that social support may be more integral to the lives of women; this does not suggest, however, that men do not benefit from social support.

Structural and Functional Aspects of Support

Before we examine these substantial gender differences in social support more closely, it should be noted that social support has been conceived of and measured in many different ways, which adds some confusion to this field. We briefly review and emphasize these conceptual and methodological distinctions as we discuss the ways in which social support contributes to the stress and coping process and the ways in which this contribution differs for men and women.

More often than not, social support brings benefits to those on the receiving end. Cohen and Wills (1985) reviewed the literature on social support and concluded that there is evidence to suggest that (1) social support improves well-being irrespective of whether one is facing stress and (2) social support improves well-being by protecting against the negative effects of stress. These are known as the direct effect and buffering models, respectively. Cohen and Wills noted that empirical support is most often found for the direct effect of social support when structural aspects of support are measured. Structural aspects include the number of supportive people in the network and the degree of integration within that network. Empirical support for the buffering model is more often found when functional aspects of support are measured. The functional categories most often described in the literature include (1) informational support, such as providing knowledge and advice, (2) tangible support, such as providing material resources and services, and, (3) emotional support, such as providing acceptance and understanding (Schaefer, Coyne, & Lazarus, 1981).

Given that supportive behaviors can serve quite different functions, social support is better able to buffer the ill-effects of stress when the type of support matches the needs elicited by the stress; this is known as the matching hypothesis (Cohen & Wills, 1985). In keeping with a contextual model of stress and coping, the needs elicited by a particular stressor will differ based on contextual variables such as gender; indeed, evidence suggests that what is an effective buffer for men in a certain situation might not be an effective buffer for women in the same situation. For example, perhaps because women are socialized to be more comfortable having intimate discussions about thoughts and emotions, emotional support has been found to be a better stress buffer for women, whereas instrumental support is a better buffer for men (Bellman, Forster, Still, & Cooper, 2003; Barbee et al., 1993; Cohen & Wills, 1985; Greenglass, 2002). With this in mind, our understanding of the role of social support in the well-being of men and women can be improved if specific functions of social support are examined rather than limiting our discussion to the broader concept of overall social support.

Gender socialization has been raised as one explanation for gender differences in social support, but other explanations such as biobehavioral mechanisms have been implicated as well. Taylor and her colleagues (2000) reviewed animal and human literature on sex differences in response to stress. They concluded that evidence supports conceptualization of the stress response in women as a "tend-and-befriend" response as opposed to the traditional "fight-or-flight" response that is more descriptive of the stress response in men. These authors argued that women have evolved to be more nurturing in order to protect themselves and their offspring during times of stress (e.g., tending) and to create and maintain social networks that serve as resources in times of stress (e.g., befriending). In effect, women are more integrated in their social networks, and this integration is of benefit in times of stress. Taylor et al. pointed out that research on neuroendocrine underpinnings of the fight-or-flight response has been conducted predominantly with male animal subjects and is, in part, mediated by testosterone. Research with female subjects instead suggests that there is considerable evidence that the female neuroendocrine response to stress is mediated by oxytocin, other sex-linked hormones, and endogenous opioids. This neuroendocrine response has been linked to maternal and affiliative behaviors in both animals and humans, and, along with cultural and socialization factors that maintain these behaviors, it is at the root of the tend-and-befriend theory. It is not within the scope of this chapter to describe at length the social, evolutionary, and biological theories that give rise to gender differences in the creation and maintenance of social networks. We intend here only to bring awareness of the broad origins of gender differences in social support behaviors and focus our attention instead on the behavior itself and its relationship to stress and coping for women and men.

Perceived vs. Received Social Support

The social support literature makes a distinction between perceived support and received support. This distinction is of great consequence because perceived support and received support often have opposite relationships with outcomes. Many studies have shown that people benefit from the perception that support will be available when needed, whereas received support has sometimes been found to have either no effect or harmful effects on well-being (e.g., Bolger & Amarel, 2007; Helgeson, 1993; Lindorff, 2000). There is very little research to explain the mechanisms through which received support has this surprisingly harmful effect on well-being, although a number of theories have been proposed. For example, it has been proposed that receiving support may lead an individual to feel overly dependent and indebted to the provider or to face threats to self-esteem (Bolger & Amarel, 2007).

Does gender change the relationships between perceived support, received support, and well-being? There is preliminary evidence to suggest that it might. For example, Lindorff (2000) found that both men and women reported decreases in health strain when they perceived support; yet when participants reported receiving support, men, but not women, reported increases in health strain. This interesting gender difference in the outcome of receiving support fits well with theories that suggest that receiving social support might be related to self-esteem threat and feelings of dependence. Given that men are socialized to cope with stress in independent and instrumental ways, the receipt of emotional support may conflict with the masculine gender role and thus increase the negative consequences for men (Greenglass, 2002; Lindorff, 2000). However, the Lindorff study was cross-sectional in nature, so the direction of the relationship between received emotional support and health strain cannot be confirmed. In keeping with the broader theory that receipt of social support seems to come with some cost, it could be that emotional support led to increased health strain for men, as proposed above. Alternatively, it could be that men who were facing more health strain evoked more emotional support from others. Further research is needed to confirm the direction of the relationship between received social support and negative consequences for men.

One way that researchers are teasing apart the relationship between perceived support, received support, and well-being is by examining support processes in dyadic relationships. Bolger, Zuckerman, and Kessler (2000) used this methodology, and they found that there are many support interactions that one partner describes providing to the other that the other partner makes no report of receiving. They coined the term invisible support to describe received support that goes unnoticed by the recipient, and they found that invisible support predicted adjustment to stress. This finding is in keeping with the above discussion given that the recipients of invisible support are receiving the benefits of being supported without the costs of realizing that they have received support.

A second study (Bolger & Amarel, 2007) of invisible support in an experimental setting helps to explain why invisible support brings benefits, although more overt forms of support may not. It was found that cognitive appraisal plays a crucial mediating role between social support and outcomes for individuals under stress; stress levels either remained unchanged or were exacerbated when individuals made the appraisal that the support provider viewed them as inefficacious. It is not surprising that overt support behaviors were more likely to lead individuals to make the appraisal that the support provider viewed them as inefficacious and, consequently, that those receiving overt support faired more poorly in adjusting to a stressor. Invisible support, which was less likely to lead to appraisals of inefficacy, was related to decreases in stress response. This experiment was conducted in an all female sample, however, so the results do not speak to possible gender differences. Examination of possible gender differences in invisible support might prove to be a fruitful direction for research. As is evident throughout our discussion of social support, independence and instrumentality are tied closely to the masculine gender role and may contribute to harsher self-evaluations when men receive overt social support. Following from this, we posit that the differential benefits of invisible and overt support may be gendered, with greater differences apparent for men. Finally, it should be noted that not all research on invisible support has shown it to be effective. In a study of mostly female patients with rheumatoid arthritis, it was found that support reported as provided by the spouse was unrelated to the patient's disease course unless it was identified as received by the patient (Lehman, DeLongis, Pratt, Collins, & Esdaille, 2008).

Social Support Networks

As mentioned earlier, the benefits of social support are enjoyed not only by women; it may be, though, that men form different types of support networks and draw upon their networks in different ways than women do. For men, more so than for women, the support derived from marriage seems to be critical. Kiecolt-Glaser and Newton (2001) reviewed the literature on marriage and its relationship to health and found that, although marriage confers mental and physical health protection to both men and women, the protective benefits of a supportive marriage are substantially greater for men than for women. Unmarried women face a 50% increase in mortality relative to married women, whereas unmarried men face a 250% increased mortality rate relative to married men. What can explain the relative increase in benefit that men derive from marriage that women do not? One explanation is that men do not have as many supportive outlets outside of marriage. For example, whereas women tend to form larger support networks that include multiple people in whom they can confide, men tend to confide primarily in their spouse (Cutrona, 1996; Taylor et al., 2000).

Another explanation for the protective benefits that marriage provides to men arises from the *support gap* theory (Cutrona, 1996). This theory suggests that husbands receive more frequent and more helpful support from their wives than they provide to their wives. Although this theory is supported by a great deal of evidence, there is also considerable debate about the relative differences in husbands' and wives' ability to support one another. This debate is fueled by inconsistencies in the social support literature that arise from the variability in conceptual and methodological approaches to social support research. That is, studies that measure self-reported levels of social support tend to find results that differ from those of observational studies in which supportive interactions are observed in a laboratory setting (Neff & Karney, 2005; Verhofstadt et al., 2007).

To illustrate, in self-report studies, both women and men often report that women provide superior support to their husbands, whereas observational studies often fail to find evidence of gender differences in support provision (Neff & Karney, 2005; Verhofstadt et al., 2007). In these laboratory studies husbands and wives are asked to discuss a personal problem or insecurity, with the idea that this situation allows ample opportunity to solicit and provide support to one another. Under these circumstances, gender differences in spousal support have not emerged. One can conclude from this that women and men have a similar capacity to support their spouses (Neff & Karney, 2005; Verhofstadt et al., 2007). How, then, do we explain the common perception that women are better support providers? The answer may be in the timing of support provision.

Neff and Karney (2005) conducted a study that provides strong evidence for the notion that support provision by women is better matched to changing stress levels in their spouses. They compared support provision in husbands and wives in observational laboratory settings and in self-reported daily diaries. Overall, they found that men and women were rated by trained observers as providing equal amounts of support to one another during the discussion interactions and that, on average, men and women reported receiving equal levels of support from their spouses across a 7-day period. So it would seem that men and women are equally capable of supporting one another. However, a closer look at the match between the severity of stress experienced by one partner and the provision of support by the other revealed a different picture. When they took changing stress levels into account, Neff and Karney (2005) found that, when husbands discussed more severe problems in the laboratory setting, wives provided more positive support and were rated as better support providers. This finding was not replicated when wives reported more severe problems and husbands, in turn, were providing support. This trend emerged from the diary data as well. In between-subject comparisons it was found that those husbands who reported the greatest stress levels also perceived greater levels of support from their wives, whereas wives in the sample who reported the greatest levels of stress did not perceive greater levels of support from their husbands. In fact, the most distressed wives reported increases in negative behaviors from their husbands, such as criticism, blame, or inconsiderate advice. When they used more stringent within-subject comparisons, the researchers found that, across the 7-day study period, stress levels were related to support provision for both husbands and wives, such that days in which one spouse reported more stress, that spouse perceived an increase in support from the other spouse. However, stress levels in wives were also related to negative behaviors in their husbands such that on days in which wives reported higher stress levels, they perceived more negative behaviors from their husbands.

The Neff and Karney study provides strong support for the notion that, although women and men are both quite capable of supporting their partners, women are more attuned to changing stress levels in their partners, and they increase support provision accordingly when their husbands face increased stress. When wives experience greater distress, their husbands also provide support; however, this support provision may be undermined by accompanying increases in negative behaviors (Neff & Karney, 2005). An alternative conclusion is that, when women face increased stress, they are more likely to make negative appraisals of their husbands' support behaviors and fail to give them credit where credit is due. Neff and Karney concluded that this was unlikely given that the within-subject analysis showed that it was not only that stressed wives reported negative responses from their husbands, but wives under stress also reported increased support. This is an indication that wives do not hold a global bias to perceive their husbands' behavior negatively during times of stress and are, in fact, willing to give credit for supportive behaviors when that credit is due. In addition, the laboratory condition showed that husbands did not succeed in providing increased support to wives facing increased stress; the fact that support behaviors in this condition were rated by trained observers precludes the possibility that the gender difference, at least in the observational condition, arose from a negatively biased perception on the part of the wives.

Although it seems likely that the findings reported by Neff and Karney reflect real gender differences in support provision as opposed to gender differences in self-reporting tendencies, self-report biases are a limitation in this area of research that need to be carefully considered. Many studies of social support have participants report the extent to which they provide or receive support. The use of self-report to study supportive behavior comes with limitations such as the possibility that the recall of support behaviors may be biased by gender roles. For example, one study (Porter et al., 2000) showed that, when men and women were asked to complete a trait measure that assessed the extent to which they tend to use different coping methods to respond to marital and work stress, women reported using social support more often than did men to cope with stress. However, when these participants completed daily diaries to report coping skills used to deal with situation-specific daily stressors, there were no gender differences in the use of social support. Based on this discrepancy it was concluded that recall may be biased by gender role heuristics and may not reflect actual behavioral differences. The Porter et al. study suggests that measuring stress and coping behaviors with daily diaries would more accurately capture the behaviors that are occurring. This method is particularly useful when one considers alternative methods such as observational studies, which may only capture capabilities of men and women to provide support to one another in situations designed to elicit support; these capabilities do not necessarily play out in the day-to-day context of coping with stress (e.g., Neff & Karney, 2005).

Stress, Coping, and Gender in Diverse Populations

Our discussion of gender thus far has been based primarily on research conducted in Western cultures. It cannot be assumed that these patterns generalize to other cultures. We have highlighted research that suggests that cultural factors, namely cultural differences in gender socialization and workplace rules and laws, are important predictors of gender differences in stress and coping in the work domain (Shaffer et al., 2000). Similarly, the study by Rheman and Holtzworth-Munroe (2006) is an excellent example of cultural differences in gender roles that relate to marital distress. Given the broader social context in which all stress and coping processes occur, cultural factors must be incorporated into our understanding of gender, stress, and coping outside of the three domains we discuss in this chapter. Similarly, the literature discussed in the preceding section is limited in that it largely ignores minority populations within Western culture such as lesbian, gay, and bisexual (LGB) populations. Although the literature on stress, coping, and gender in ethnic minorities and in LGB populations within Western cultures is limited, the increased stress facing members of ethnic and sexual minorities calls for further exploration of stress and coping of men and women in minority groups.

The concept of minority stress is based on the assumption that minority stress is unique: It is additive to general stressors faced by all people, it is chronic, and it arises from socially based processes, institutions, and structures (Meyer, 2003). In other words, members of minority groups (e.g., groups based on categories of socioeconomic status, disability, race/ethnicity, gender, or sexuality) must cope not only with personal events but also with the chronic social stress that arises from belonging to a less powerful or stigmatized group. This extra burden leads to poorer outcomes for minority group members. For example, research supports the claim that gay men and lesbians represent one of the most stressed groups in society (Iwasaki & Ristock, 2007). In his comprehensive theory of minority stress, Meyer (2003) drew clear links between the experience of this increased stress in the LGB population and the higher mental illness rates that are found in LGB, relative to heterosexual, populations. To consider lesbians, bisexuals, and gay men as *one group*, however, is probably an oversimplification.

Perhaps because research on particular minority groups is relatively scarce, the authors who have explored the stress and coping process seem to have looked broadly at the common sources of stress that are unique to the minority population as a whole. As a result, it is more difficult to make conclusions about stress and coping in female minority group members than in male minority group members. However, a small body of research points to the need to consider the role of gender within the context of other roles. For example, one study showed that gay men and lesbians identify different sources of minority stress; gay men more often reported stressors related to violence and harassment, whereas lesbians reported more family-based stressors (Lewis, Derlega, Berndt, Morris, & Rose, 2001). There is further reason to study gay men and lesbians separately in that lesbians are more likely to face sex discrimination in addition to homophobia (Szymanski & Chung, 2003). The term "intersectionality" has been used to conceptualize the way that individuals' multiple roles interact to shape their experience, and it may provide a framework for understanding the ways in which gender interacts with minority stress to predict well-being (Iwasaki & Ristock, 2007).

The interaction of gender with minority status in racial groups has been studied as well. For example, allostatic load scores are higher in Black than in White adults and, more specifically, in Black women relative to Black men and White women (Geronimus, Hicken, Keene, & Bound, 2006). These differences widen with age. Allostatic load, or the repeated wear and tear on bodily systems that arises from repeated stress exposure, appears to be greater in Black women because they face both sex and race discrimination. Although one might assume that poverty explains the vulnerability of Black women, to the contrary, the difference in allostatic load scores in Black and White women was particularly pronounced among those who were not poor. Instead it seems to be the case that both gender and race influence differences in exposure to stress experiences that draw heavily upon coping resources and leave their mark on biological systems (Geronimus et al., 2006).

Although these studies of minority groups suggest that women face increased vulnerability due to "double jeopardy" (Geronimus et al., 2006), opposing views exist in the literature as well. For example, it has been suggested that the multiple roles with which minority women can identify create some ambiguity in their attributions about stress. For example, in a sample of racially diverse young adults, it was found that men reported more perceived discrimination than did women, and this discrimination among men predicted anxiety and depression (Cassidy, O'Connor, Howe, & Warden, 2004). The relationship of discrimination with anxiety and depression was mediated by personal and ethnic self-esteem in men, whereas in women discrimination was directly related to anxiety, but not to depression, and self-esteem did not mediate the relationship. The authors concluded that discrimination may be more stressful for men because they identify more with their ethnicity, whereas the tendency for women to identify more with interpersonal relationships may be a better predictor of women's well-being. It is clear that further research must be done to sort out the complex relationships between gender and other roles within the stress and coping process.

What Can We Conclude About Stress and Coping in Women and Men?

In this chapter we have shown that, for reasons ranging from female and male physiology to gender socialization, women and men experience and respond to stress in different ways. Despite numerous gender differences in the stress and coping literature, however, it is difficult to isolate specific gender-based stressors or ways of coping. This difficulty is simply a reflection of the critical role of the personal and situational contexts in which individuals experience and cope with stress. With that said, there are general trends, such as the propensity for men to engage more often in problem-focused coping, whereas women more often respond to stress by soliciting support. Because of the strong ties between these stress and coping patterns and gender socialization, it is possible that generational changes in gender socialization, such as increasing shifts toward gender-neutral socialization, may bring about more similarities in the experience of and response to stress for women and men (Berg & Upchurch, 2007; Gonzalez-Morales et al., 2006). It is also possible that these trends vary by class, race, sexual orientation, and other unidentified characteristics and contexts.

The story emerging in this chapter, and in the literature, is that women report more stressors, experience these stressors as more intense, and, consequently, enlist more coping efforts in their response to stress (Krajewski & Goffin, 2005). However, the outcomes of stress are not all negative, despite this predominant focus in the literature and in this chapter. Stress can also lead to post-traumatic growth, also referred to as perceived benefits, positive adjustment/adaptation, benefit finding, or thriving. Research suggests that women, more often than men, realize these beneficial outcomes of stress (Kesimci, Goral, & Gencoz, 2005). In addition, the increased stress that women face may be tempered by their ability to engage in and benefit more from social support. In particular, whereas husbands benefit primarily from the support of a wife, women benefit from more opportunities to cope dyadically in additional relationships outside of marriage (e.g., with female friends)—it has been argued that this is increasingly important in our society in which men and women tend to marry later, and there are increasing numbers of men and women who do not (or cannot) marry at all (Berg & Upchurch, 2007). Considerations such as these give a more complete picture of stress adaptation in men and women.

It is also possible that reports of increased stress among women represent a tendency by women to overreport stress or men to underreport stress, in studies where stress and coping are measured by self-report. It is difficult to eliminate this concern altogether, even though, for example, studies of the reporting habits of men and women have found women's reporting behavior to be closely tied to actual symptoms such as medical symptoms that steer morbidity rates (Verbrugge, 1989). It is tempting to push for greater use of observational studies in order to quantify stress and coping more objectively and assuage this concern. However, carefully designed studies, such as that by Neff and Karney (2005), demonstrate that stress and coping behaviors observed in laboratory settings do not always map onto stress and coping behaviors that occur in the context of day-to-day life. Instead, daily process designs may help to increase the reliability and validity of self-reported stress and coping behavior by capturing stress and coping behaviors close to their real-time occurrence, thus reducing recall error (DeLongis & Holtzman, 2005; Tennen, Affleck, Coyne, Larsen, & DeLongis, 2006) and reducing the tendency to report in line with gender stereotypes (Porter et al., 2000).

Finally, it is important to reiterate that the gender differences in stress and coping that have been highlighted in this chapter exist among a great many similarities in women's and men's stress and coping. For example, as was noted in the discussion of work stress, there are many gender differences in the experience of stress and coping in the workplace. However, there are also great commonalities, such as that men and women both tend to use more problem-focused coping than emotion-focused coping to deal with work-related stress (Folkman & Lazarus, 1980; Gonzalez-Morales et al., 2006). Through the use of a contextual framework in this examination of stress and coping, it was possible to pinpoint precise factors that contribute to the relative gender differences that do arise, and, at the same time, to highlight the fundamental stress and coping process that is shared among men and women.

Future Directions for Research on Gender, Stress, and Coping

Following from perhaps the most noteworthy limitation in this field of research, an important area of future inquiry is gender differences in stress and coping among different minority groups. There is an obvious methodological advantage to studies of stress and coping within married couples because many social contextual factors (e.g., family income and lifestyle factors) are controlled, which allows greater power to examine gender differences. However, this heteronormative approach is also flawed; it neglects the experience of those not living within the context of a marital relationship, and it may not generalize to LGB couples. Future researchers should examine stress and coping in a more inclusive way, studying LGB populations, as well as those from diverse cultural backgrounds. In the currently available literature on heterosexual, primarily White couples, differences in stress and coping are often attributed to differences between men and women more generally. Yet, these gender differences may arise not only from gender per se but also from different roles assumed within a relationship. Studies of same-sex couples will allow us to make clearer conclusions about stress and coping differences within couples that arise from gender differences or from the assumption of roles within a relationship that may or may not be tied to gender. Whereas gender may be confounded with roles (e.g., provider, nurturer) within heterosexual couples, this confound does necessarily not exist within same-sex couples.

Another line of research that would benefit from closer examination is that of gender differences in the receipt of social support. Social support is generally assumed to be an asset in coping with stress. In this chapter we discuss research that shows that women more often elicit and benefit from social support. It has been suggested that men do not benefit as much from social support because the receipt of such support is contradictory to the ways in which men are socialized to be independent and, thus, may threaten a man's self-esteem (e.g., Greenglass, 2002; Lindorff, 2000). As such, invisible support, as coined by Bolger and colleagues (Bolger & Amarel, 2007; Bolger et al., 2000) may be more supportive for men than for women. Future researchers who strive to discern ways in which social support can be delivered in inadvertent "invisible" ways may produce results that lead to improved outcomes for all support receivers, especially for male support receivers. Along these lines, future research would benefit from more attention to the particulars of support. That is, most studies to date have assessed global perceptions of support receipt or availability, and the behavioral basis for these perceptions is often unclear or entirely ignored. Are there particular supportive actions that are beneficial to the health and well-being of the support recipient? Are there other supportive actions that, although offered in a spirit of support, are actually detrimental to the health and well-being of the recipient? And do such effects vary by characteristics (such as neuroticism) of the support provider or recipient? Such questions, and an examination of related gender differences, are likely not only to provide important insight into basic stress and coping processes but also to form the groundwork for the development of evidence-based stress management interventions.

Acknowledgments The preparation of this manuscript was supported by graduate fellowships to the first author from the Natural Sciences and Engineering Research Council of Canada, the Michael Smith Foundation for Health Research, and the British Columbia Medical Services Foundation, and an operating grant to the second author from the Social Science and Humanities Research Council of Canada.

References

Badr, H. (2004). Coping in marital dyads: A contextual perspective on the role of gender and health. *Personal Relationships, 11*, 197–211.

Barbee, A. P., Cunningham, M. R., Winstead, B. A., Derlega, V. J., Gulley, M. R., Vankeelov, P. A., et al. (1993). Effects of gender role expectations on the social support process. *Journal of Social Issues, 49*, 175–190.

Bekker, M. H. J., Nijssen, A., & Hens, G. (2001). Stress prevention training: Sex differences in types of stressors, coping, and training effects. *Stress and Health, 17*, 207–218.

Bellman, S., Forster, N., Still, L., & Cooper, C. L. (2003). Gender differences in the use of social support as a moderator of occupational stress. *Stress and Health, 19*, 45–58.

Bem, S. L. (1974). The measurement of psychological androgyny. *Journal of Consulting and Clinical Psychology, 42*, 155–162.

Berg, C. A., & Upchurch, R. (2007). A developmental-contextual model of couples coping with illness across the adult life span. *Psychological Bulletin, 133*, 920–954.

Bolger, N., & Amarel, D. (2007). Effects of social support visibility on adjustment to stress: Experimental evidence. *Journal of Personality and Social Psychology, 92*, 458–475.

Bolger, N., DeLongis, A., Kessler, R. C., & Schilling, E. A. (1989). The emotional effects of daily stress. *Journal of Personality and Social Psychology, 57*, 808–818.

Bolger, N., Zuckerman, A., & Kessler, R. C. (2000). Invisible support and adjustment to stress. *Journal of Personality and Social Psychology, 71*, 953–961.

Burke, R. J. (2002). Men, masculinity, and health. In D. L. Nelson & R. J. Burke (Eds.), *Gender, work stress, and health* (pp. 35–54). Washington, DC: American Psychological Association.

Carstensen, L. L., Gottman, J. M., & Levenson, R. W. (1995). Emotional behavior in long-term marriage. *Psychology and Aging, 10*, 140–149.
Cassidy, C., O'Connor, R. C., Howe, C., & Warden, D. (2004). Perceived discrimination and psychological distress: The role of personal and ethnic self-esteem. *Journal of Counseling Psychology, 51*, 329–339.
Christensen, A., & Heavey, C. L. (1990). Gender and social structure in demand-withdraw pattern of marital conflict. *Journal of Personality and Social Psychology, 59*, 73–81.
Cohen, S., & Wills, T. A. (1985). Stress, social support, and the buffering hypothesis. *Psychological Bulletin, 98*, 310–357.
Coyne, J. C., & DeLongis, A. (1986). Going beyond social support: The role of social relationships in adaptation. *Journal of Consulting and Clinical Psychology, 54*, 454–460.
Coyne, J. C., & Smith, D. A. F. (1991). Couples coping with a myocardial infarction: A contextual perspective on wives' distress. *Journal of Personality and Social Psychology, 61*, 404–412.
Coyne, J. C., & Smith, D. A. F. (1994). Couples coping with myocardial infarction: Contextual perspective on patient self-efficacy. *Journal of Family Psychology, 8*, 1–13.
Cutrona, C. E. (1996). *Social support in couples*. Thousand Oaks, CA: Sage.
DeLongis, A., & Holtzman, S. (2005). Coping in context: The role of stress, social support, and personality in coping. *Journal of Personality, 73*, 1633–1656.
DeLongis, A., Holtzman, S., Puterman, E., & Lam, M. (in press). Dyadic coping: Support from the spouse in times of stress. In J. Davila & K. Sullivan (Eds.), *Social support processes in intimate relationships*. New York: Oxford University Press.
DeLongis, A., & O'Brien, T. (1990). An interpersonal framework for stress and coping: An application to the families of Alzheimer's patients. In M. A. P. Stephens, J. H. Crowther, S. E. Hobfoll, & D. L. Tennenbaum (Eds.), *Stress and coping in later-life families* (pp. 221–239). New York: Hemisphere.
Eldridge, K. A., & Christensen, A. (2002). Demand-withdraw communication during couple conflict: A review and analysis. In P. Noller & J. A. Feeney (Eds.), *Understanding marriage: Developments in the study of couple interaction* (pp. 289–322). New York: Cambridge University Press.
Fielden, S. L., & Cooper, C. L. (2002). Managerial stress: Are women more at risk? In D. L. Nelson & R. J. Burke (Eds.), *Gender, work stress, and health* (pp. 19–34). Washington, DC: American Psychological Association.
Folkman, S., & Lazarus, R. S. (1980). An analysis of coping in a middle aged community sample. *Journal of Health and Social Behavior, 21*, 219–239.
Folkman, S., Lazarus, R. S., Dunkel-Schetter, C., DeLongis, A., & Gruen, R. J. (1986). Dynamics of a stressful encounter: Cognitive appraisal, coping, and encounter outcomes. *Journal of Personality and Social Psychology, 50*, 992–1003.
Geronimus, A. T., Hicken, M., Keene, D., & Bound, J. (2006). "Weathering" and age patterns of allostatic load scores among Blacks and Whites in the United States. *American Journal of Public Health, 96*, 826–833.
Gonzalez-Morales, G., Peiro, J. M., Rodriguez, I., & Greenglass, E. R. (2006). Coping and distress in organizations: The role of gender in work stress. *International Journal of Stress Management, 13*, 228–248.
Gottman, J. M. (1998). Psychology and the study of marital processes. *Annual Review of Psychology, 49*, 169–97.
Greenglass, E. (2002). Work stress, coping, and social support: Implications for women's occupational well-being. In D. L. Nelson & R. J. Burke (Eds.), *Gender, work stress, and health* (pp. 85–96). Washington, DC: American Psychological Association.
Hagedoorn, M., Sanderman, R., Bolks, H. N., Tuinstra, J., & Coyne, J. C. (2008). Distress in couples coping with cancer: A meta-analysis and critical review of role and gender effects. *Psychological Bulletin, 134*, 1–30.
Helgeson, V. S. (1993). Two important distinctions in social support: Kind of support and perceived versus received. *Journal of Applied Social Psychology, 23*, 825–845.
Helgeson, V. S. (1994). Relation of agency and communion to well-being: Evidence and potential explanations. *Psychological Bulletin, 116*, 412–428.
House, J. S., Umberson, D., & Landis, K. R. (1988). Structures and processes of social support. *Annual Review of Sociology, 14*, 293–318.
Iwasaki, Y., & Ristock, J. L. (2007). The nature of stress experienced by lesbians and gay men. *Anxiety, Stress, & Coping, 20*, 299–319.
Kesimci, A., Goral, F. S., & Gencoz, T. (2005). Determinants of stress-related growth: Gender, stressfulness of the event, and coping strategies. *Current Psychology, 24*, 68–75.
Kessler, R. C., & McLeod, J. D. (1984). Sex differences in vulnerability to undesirable life events. *American Sociological Review, 49*, 620–631.
Kiecolt-Glaser, J. K., & Newton, T. (2001). Marriage and health: His and hers. *Psychological Bulletin, 127*, 472–503.

Krajewski, H. T., & Goffin, R. D. (2005). Predicting occupational coping responses: The interactive effect of gender and work stressor context. *Journal of Occupational Health Psychology, 10,* 44–53.

Lazarus, R. S., & DeLongis, A. (1983). Psychological stress and coping in aging. *American Psychologist, 38,* 245–254.

Lazarus, R. S., & Folkman, S. (1984). *Stress, appraisal, and coping.* New York: Springer.

Lehman, A., DeLongis, A., Pratt, D., Collins, D., & Esdaille, J. (2008). Is invisible social support effective – or is support in the eye of the beholder? Manuscript submitted for publication.

Lewis, R. J., Derlega, V. J., Berndt, A., Morris, L. M., & Rose, S. (2001). An empirical analysis of stressors for gay men and lesbians. *Journal of Homosexuality, 42,* 63–88.

Lindorff, M. (2000). Is it better to perceive than receive? Social support, stress, and strain for managers. *Psychology & Health Medicine, 5,* 271–286.

Long, B. C., & Cox, R. S. (2000). Women's ways of coping with employment stress: A feminist contextual analysis. In P. Dewe, M. Leiter, & T. Cox (Eds.), *Coping, health, and organizations* (pp. 109–123). London: Taylor & Francis.

Manne, S., Alfieri, T., Taylor, K., & Dougherty, J. (1999). Preferences for spousal support among individuals with cancer. *Journal of Applied Social Psychology, 29,* 722–749.

Marin, T., Holtzman, S., DeLongis, A., & Robinson, L. (2007). Coping and the response of others. *Journal of Social and Personal Relationships, 24,* 951–969.

McDonald, L. M., & Korabik, K. (1991). Sources of stress and ways of coping among male and female managers. *Journal of Social Behavior and Personality, 6,* 185–198.

Meyer, I. H. (2003). Prejudice, social stress, and mental health in lesbian, gay, and bisexual populations: Conceptual issues and research evidence. *Psychological Bulletin, 129,* 674–697.

Neff, L. A., & Karney, B. R. (2005). Gender differences in social support: A question of skill or responsiveness. *Journal of Personality and Social Psychology, 88,* 79–90.

Nelson, D. L., & Quick, J. C. (1985). Professional women: Are distress and disease inevitable? *Academy of Management Review, 10,* 206–218.

O'Brien, T. B., & DeLongis, A. (1996). The interactional context of problem-, emotion-, and relationship-focused coping: The role of the Big Five personality factors. *Journal of Personality, 64,* 775–813.

O'Brien, T., & DeLongis, A. (1997). Coping with chronic stress: An interpersonal perspective. In B. H. Gottlieb (Ed.), *Coping with chronic stress* (pp. 161–190). New York: Plenum.

O'Brien, T., DeLongis, A., Pomaki, G., Puterman, E., & Zwicker, A. (2009). Couples coping with stress: The role of empathic responding. *European Psychologist, 14,* 18–28.

Piotrkowski, C. S. (1998). Gender harassment, job satisfaction, and distress among employed White and minority women. *Journal of Occupational Health Psychology, 3,* 33–43.

Porter, L. S., Marco, C. A., Schwartz, J. E., Neale, J. M., Shiffman, S., & Stone, A. A. (2000). Gender differences in coping: A comparison of trait and momentary assessments. *Journal of Social and Clinical Psychology, 19,* 480–498.

Revenson, T. A., Abraído-Lanza, A. F., Majerovitz, S. D., & Jordan, C. (2005). Couples coping with chronic illness: What's gender got to do with it? In T. A. Revenson, K. Kayser, & G. Bodenmann (Eds.), *Couples coping with stress: Emerging perspectives on dyadic coping* (pp. 137–156). Washington, DC: American Psychological Association.

Revenson, T. A., Kayser, K., & Bodenmann, G. (2005). *Couples coping with stress: Emerging perspectives on dyadic coping.* Washington, DC: American Psychological Association.

Rheman, U. S., & Holtzworth-Munroe, A. (2006). A cross-cultural analysis of the demand-withdraw marital interaction: Observing couples from a developing country. *Journal of Consulting and Clinical Psychology, 74,* 755–766.

Schaefer, C., Coyne, J. C., & Lazarus, R. S. (1981). The health-related functions of social support. *Journal of Behavioral Medicine, 4,* 381–406.

Shaffer, M. A., Joplin, J. R. W., Bell, M. P., Lau, T., & Oguz, C. (2000). Disruptions to women's social identity: A comparative study of workplace stress experiences by women in three geographic regions. *Journal of Occupational Health Psychology, 5,* 441–456.

Szymanski, D. M., & Chung, Y. B. (2003). Internalized homophobia in lesbians. *Journal of Lesbian Studies, 7,* 115–125.

Taylor, S. E. (2002). *The tending instinct: How nurturing is essential to who we are and how we live.* New York: Holt.

Taylor, S. E. (2007). Social support. In H. S. Friedman & R. C. Silver (Eds.), *Foundations of health psychology* (pp. 145–171). New York: Oxford University Press.

Taylor, S. E., Klein, L. C., Lewis, B. P., Gruenewald, T. L., Gurung, R. A. R., & Updegraff, J. A. (2000). Behavioral responses to stress in females: Tend-and-befriend, not fight-or-flight. *Psychological Review, 107,* 411–429.

Tennant, C. (2001). Work-related stress and depressive disorders. *Journal of Psychosomatic Research, 51,* 697–704.

Tennen, H., Affleck, G., Coyne, J. C., Larsen, R. J., & DeLongis, A. (2006). Paper and plastic in daily diary research. *Psychological Methods, 11*, 112–118.

Thoits, P. A. (1991). Gender differences in coping with emotional distress. In J. Eckenrode (Ed.), *The social context of coping* (pp. 107–138). New York: Plenum.

Verbrugge, L. M. (1989). The twain meet: Empirical explanations of sex differences in health and mortality. *Journal of Health and Social Behavior, 30*, 282–304.

Verhofstadt, L. L., Buysse, A., & Ickes, W. (2007). Social support in couples: An examination of gender differences using self-report and observational methods. *Sex Roles, 57,* 267–282.

Chapter 22
Gender and Health-Care Utilization

Cheryl Brown Travis, Andrea L. Meltzer, and Dawn M. Howerton

There are three compelling reasons to understand the utilization of health care. First, understanding the full range of factors that shape the utilization of health care is important for determining the health-care needs of individuals, for developing health resources and the training of care providers, as well as for planning programs aimed at the prevention, promotion, or protection of health. Second, access to care, the availability of care, and the quality and efficacy of care are essential components of social justice. Disparities in care associated with gender, ethnicity, age, education, or income are alarming and erode the fundamental trust in fairness on which democracy is based. Third, both the structure and the utilization of health care have a massive impact on the economic stability of nations. For example, data from the Organization for Economic Co-operation and Development (OECD) indicate that the United States spends about 15.3% of its gross domestic product on health care, whereas European countries with esteemed health-care systems spend far less: Spain 8.1%, United Kingdom 8.1%, Sweden 9.1%, Germany 10.6%, Switzerland 11.6% (National Center for Health Statistics, 2007).

One might assume that any difference between women and men in the utilization of care would be largely due to pregnancy and birth. Surely these are important factors, but even when these are set aside, there remain noteworthy gender differences in many areas: usual sources of care, ambulatory care and physician visits, preventive care such as screenings and immunizations, emergency care, hospitalization and medical procedures, use of medications and pharmaceuticals, and general preventive care. As discussed later, these differences derive, in part, from gender role orientation, health beliefs, patterns of employment and of lifestyle, health insurance, and variations in quality of care. Many of these dimensions of health and health care are influenced by sexism and racism. In the following sections we outline patterns of access and health-care use and then offer discussion of related gender and equity considerations for four specific areas of health care: long-term care and Alzheimer's disease, cancer, diabetes, and sexual and reproductive health.

Health-Care Access and Utilization

Access to a usual source of care is a fundamental cornerstone of health care not only for good health care but also for controlling health-care costs. Having a consistent source of care enhances preventive measures (e.g., prenatal care, blood pressure testing, immunizations), timely interventions, better

C.B. Travis (✉)
University of Tennessee, Knoxville, TN, USA

monitoring of treatment, continuous care, lower rates of hospitalization, shorter hospital stays, and overall lower health-care costs. Access to a consistent source of care also contributes to a reduction in the use of more costly emergency department services (McWilliams, Meara, Zaslavsky, & Ayanian, 2007). A consistent source of care at any age reduces the overall costs of care because a reliable source of care enables timely interventions that are less invasive and more effective. For example, compared to individuals with continuous health coverage, individuals in the United States who were previously uninsured and later became eligible for Medicare coverage had 13% higher physician visits and 51% higher medical expenditures (Adams, Lucas, Barnes, & National Center for Health Statistics, 2008). Consistent sources of care vary in terms of whether there is a particular provider or group of providers who are the consistent contact point for a patient, whether the individual patient can speak by phone with this provider, and whether there is emergency coverage after hours or on weekends. Many factors influence access to a consistent source of care, including perceived health status, access to transportation, and the availability of providers, as well as employment and health insurance.

Gender is certainly a central variable in health status, access to and utilization of care, and quality of care. Nonetheless, comparisons based on gender are incomplete without consideration of the social and economic conditions that may underlie gender patterns. For example, individual assessment of health status is one factor that shapes physician visits and general use of health services. In general, men and women have very similar assessments of their health. However, there are large differences in self-rated health status associated with income (National Center for Health Statistics, 2007). Individuals who are near poverty level are much less likely to report good health and instead report fair or poor health and patterns associated with educational level parallel those for income level. Thus, any observed gender differences in health status and in the use of care may be secondary to broad socioeconomic factors.

Although there is a common belief that health care is readily available throughout the United States, this is far from the truth. In general, access to private health insurance has declined from past decades. For example, in 1984, 76.8% of the population under age 65 had private health insurance, but, in 2006, that figure dropped to 69.2% (U.S. Census Bureau, 2007a).[1] The most recent data indicate that about 47 million Americans (15.8%) under the age of 65 are without any health insurance and do not have access even through Medicaid (Crimmel, 2007a, 2007b). For those under age 65, health insurance is based most commonly on employment; however, one must be employed by a business that offers health insurance or be a family member of such an employee in order to be covered; in many instances women have coverage not as a policy holder but rather as a dependent. Even when families are covered by employer-based insurance programs, the size of the annual deductible that must be paid by the employee is substantial. The average deductible for family coverage increased by 28.6% in only 4 years from $958 in 2002 to $1,232 in 2005 and deductibles for single individuals with employer-based insurance rose 46% (Cherry, Woodwell, Rechtsteiner, & National Center for Health Statistics, 2007). In small firms with less than 50 employees, these deductible amounts were higher. This system puts children at risk because they are dependent on parents' ability to obtain employment that offers meaningful health-care coverage. Other countries do not link health care to the means of economic production.

Most insurance plans in the United States are group plans obtained through an employer, and, because men are more likely than women to belong to unions and to work for employers that offer such plans, men have somewhat better coverage. But gender is not always the principal or most

---

[1] URL for spreadsheet data for table 136, p. 415, Health United States 2007 – ftp://ftp.cdc.gov/pub/Health_Statistics/NCHS/Publications/Health_US/hus07tables/Table136.xls

salient basis for inequity; much larger differences are associated with race and ethnicity. Among the approximately 47 million people without health insurance in the United States, there are large differences by race and ethnicity: 10.4% are European Americans, 19.5% are African Americans, 17.7% are Asian Americans or Pacific Islanders, and 31.1% are Hispanic (U.S. Census Bureau, 2007b).

Ambulatory Care

Ambulatory care may involve physician office visits, outpatient visits, or emergency department visits associated with hospitals. Typically, individuals in the United States have approximately 3.3 office visits annually, for a national population total of 963 million visits (Cherry et al., 2007). On average, direct consultation with a physician averages 19 minutes; roughly 19% of physician visits last less than 10 minutes, but some 73% of visits range up to 30 minutes (Cherry et al., 2007). Although the *rate* of physician visits usually is highest for infants under 1 year, the greatest *number* of visits occurs for patients aged 45–64, which represents the upward age shift for the population as a whole. Gender plays a key role in these visits because, throughout their lives, women are encouraged to have preventive care and screening visits (e.g., tests for cervical cancer pap tests, birth control consultation, and mammograms). In addition, women typically bring their infants and children for care, and, at the same time, they may have informal consultations about their own health. Women above the age of 15 make approximately 87,000 preventive care visits annually (about 50% of all preventive care visits), whereas men of the same age make approximately 37,000 visits (or about 20% of visits; Cherry et al., 2007). (The remaining percent of preventive care visits are associated with children under the age of 15.) Women also monitor the health of other adult family members, encourage spouses and partners to seek care, and may seek services for older siblings, parents, or in-laws. To this extent, women often are the family brokers of health care.

Chronic conditions account for a high number of physician visits. The most common chronic conditions associated with ambulatory care are hypertension, arthritis, hyperlipidemia, and diabetes. Even when women and men have the same condition, women tend to make higher use of physician services (Rosemann, Laux, & Szecsenyi, 2007). Osteoarthritis provides one example where women tend to have more physician visits than do men (Kaur, Stechuchak, Coffman, Allen, & Bastian, 2007). This is also true among armed service veterans, and chronic pain from any source is an area where women are more likely than men to have physician visits (Verbrugge, 1995; Verbrugge & Juarez, 2001). Some of these visits are linked to chronic pain associated with bone and joint conditions, such as osteoarthritis, that are more common among women than among men (Schiller, Kramarow, & Dey, 2007).

Although not a chronic condition, falls and the injuries associated with them are a frequent reason for seeking rehabilitation and assistance in living as well as initial physician treatment (National Center for Health Statistics, 2007). Total injuries that require immediate medical attention reveal an excess among boys and men. There are about 22 million emergency department visits annually by men/boys and about 19 million by women/girls of all ages in the United States (Cherry et al., 2007).

Medications

In general, the rate of medical prescriptions (at least one in the past month) is consistently higher for women than for men across different racial/ethnic groups (Olfson, Marcus, Druss, Elinson et al., 2002; Olfson, Marcus, Druss, & Pincus, 2002; Pincus et al., 1998). Among individuals 18 years or older, some of the most frequently prescribed medications associated with health-care visits in the United States are metabolic agents (18%) such as drugs for cholesterol lowering (statins) and blood glucose regulators for diabetics, cardiovascular agents (17%), central nervous system agents (analgesics 13%, psychotropic medications 9%), and medications for gastrointestinal conditions (8%) (National Center for Health Statistics, 2007).

Overall gender differences for antidepressants associated with physician or outpatient visits are particularly notable. Antidepressant use is even higher when the general prevalence is estimated by household interviews conducted by the U.S. Centers for Disease Control and Prevention (CDC), such as the National Health and Nutrition Examination Survey (NHANES). Prescription of antidepressant medications increased substantially with the development of selected serotonin reuptake inhibitors (SSRIs) marketed under brand names such as Prozac, Paxil, Zoloft, and Lexapro (Stone, Viera, & Parman, 2003). The fact that these drugs are also useful in treating anxiety, migraines, and pain associated with diabetic neuropathy contributes to the high number of prescriptions (Miranda & Cooper, 2004). As we discuss more fully later, women may more readily convey emotional distress to their physicians and thus receive more prescriptions. However, gender differences may also be due to under diagnosis of men, especially minority men, who have depression but mask it with bravado or stoicism (DeFrances, Hall, & National Center for Health Statistics, 2007). It is also quite likely that physicians are reluctant to prescribe antidepressants to men who may be more likely than women to be self-medicating their depression (or anxiety) with alcohol or other illicit drugs. (See also Chapter 7.)

Hospital Admissions and Procedures

Across the United States, there are annually about 34 million admissions to short-stay hospitals (Kozak, DeFrances, Hall, & National Center for Health Statistics, 2006), approximately 21 million of these are women and 14 million are men (Travis, 2005). Men receive about 17 million procedures and women receive about 27 million procedures. If hospitalizations are adjusted for birthing, the number of admissions for women and men are effectively equal. This is true for virtually all age groups beyond childbearing years, with some slight excess in hospitalizations among men. Even when obstetrical procedures are controlled, the types of procedures patients receive while hospitalized vary notably by gender. For example, cardiovascular procedures are dramatically higher for men (23%) than for women (15%) (Kozak et al., 2006).

Despite similarities in general hospitalization admissions and in many procedures, birth and related obstetrical procedures account for a substantial amount of health-care utilization. In any given year, roughly four million women are hospitalized to give birth, and they receive almost seven million procedures. Medical procedures typically associated with hospital births include episiotomy, rupture of membranes, induced labor, and repair of lacerations associated with the birthing. The National Hospital Discharge Survey records that over one million of the roughly four million births involved Cesarean surgery (Graves, Gillum, & National Center for Health Statistics, 1997). The upward trend in Cesareans has been steady, from 220 per 1,000 births in 1994 (Kozak et al., 2006) to 300 per 1,000 births in 2004 (Klebanov & Jemmott, 1992). This trend reflects a growing medicalization of birth, a matter of concern to feminists and many health providers. It has been accompanied by the perspective that birth is an unnatural and dangerous event that should be managed by professionals and technical interventions. Furthermore, cascading effects from early interventions may contribute to later complications and the need for surgery. Finally, there has been a long-standing practice to perform surgery for all births subsequent to Cesarean procedures.

Gender Stereotypes and Physician–Patient Communication

Traditional and stereotyped views of gender (rugged men, fragile women) contribute to health-care utilization for a range of problems. For both men and women, traditional gender roles increase health-care use in some instances and make it less likely in others. Sometimes these effects seem to be mediated by beliefs about biology, at other times by beliefs about the efficacy of health care itself, and on other occasions by dynamics of the physician–patient interaction.

Gender Stereotypes

Victorian views of (middle- and upper-class White) women included frailty as a key component of femininity. Women were assumed to be prone to hysteria, insomnia, and nervousness. This surely supported hierarchical and patronizing patterns of physician–patient interactions. At the same time, medical developments in anesthesia and in surgical instrumentation, such as forceps used in birth, facilitated increasingly invasive procedures, especially in obstetrics and gynecology. Such surgery was in part supported by the lingering concept that any woman could periodically be afflicted with a wandering uterus that might cause any variety of complaints.

Although the idea of a wandering uterus has become passé, women's sexual and reproductive biology continues to provide an interpretive backdrop for many psychological and physical symptoms. In the context of a patriarchal belief system, women themselves may locate the cause of some symptoms in the menstrual cycle as opposed, for example, to heart disease. One study provides an interesting illustration. Women deceived into believing they were premenstrual often reported more negative physical symptoms than did women who were told they were mid-cycle (Ruble, 1977). Women may be especially ready to find a link between their own hostile moods and their reproductive biology because it is socially unacceptable for women to feel or to express anger, and attributions to hormonal biology relieve the woman from some responsibility (Chrisler, Rose, Dutch, Sklarsky, & Grant, 2006). In fact, much of the understanding of premenstrual syndrome seems to be based on popular belief rather than scholarly research (Raofi & Schappert, 2006).

The conceptual linking of women's cyclic biology to a plethora of signs and symptoms may also contribute to the higher prescriptions of psychotropic medications for women. Although women receive a greater *number of* prescriptions for psychotropes, it is due, in part, to the greater frequency of wellness visits by women than by men (Travis, 1988). If we control for the greater frequency of visits among women and instead look at the *rate* of such prescriptions as a function of patient age, a different picture emerges. Rates of these prescriptions *per 1,000 physician visits* are close to equal for women and men until after age of 45, an age that coincides with social themes of general decline in women's physical vigor, cognitive ability, appearance, and sexuality as antecedents to menopause. After age 45, the rate of psychotrope prescriptions levels out for men but continues to rise steeply for women until after age 65 (Travis, 1988; Travis & Meltzer, 2008). This is exactly the time frame of premenopausal and menopausal changes when women are likely to report sleep disorders and nervousness that can be treated by sedatives and tranquilizers. It is also a time period when an increasingly sedentary lifestyle may contribute to restless sleep or the inability to relax. Treatment of these assorted menopausal conditions with psychotropes often falls in the realm of off-label prescriptions for which the psychotrope is not approved and may not be effective (Barsky, Peekna, & Borus, 2001).

Reporting Style

Gender differences in reporting style may contribute to differential use of medications. Women tend to report more numerous and more frequent bodily symptoms than men do (Berger, Levant, McMillan, Kelleher, & Sellers, 2005; Levant et al., 2003; 2006). The pattern occurs in community samples as well as among medical patients and seems to persist across a range of study designs. A variety of explanations have been offered for the readiness of women to disclose symptoms and for men to remain silent on vulnerabilities and maintain a pose of bravado. One consideration is that more complete reporting of symptoms combined with the cultural view of women as weaker may have a synergistic effect. Women are thorough about reporting and are not likely to be socially sanctioned for doing so. Culturally at least, women have less to lose by disclosing symptoms, whereas men who do so may think they are admitting to a fundamental flaw in their masculinity.

Cultural constructions of masculinity generally call for restraint in any behavior associated with femininity, and disclosures of illness or personal problems certainly fall into this category. Even when men report pain or other symptoms to their wives, they may present a pose of bravado and bonhomie to physicians (authority figures who are most often male). Men's reluctance to disclose weakness or vulnerability underlies in part a general avoidance of mentioning emotions that convey distress. The pattern of minimizing unacceptable emotions is sufficiently common among men to support the notion of a normative alexithymia (Courtenay, 2000). This general difficulty in recognizing and describing feelings (or any symptoms of vulnerability or weakness) may partially explain men's incomplete reporting styles.

Other considerations suggest that gender differences in reporting may not emerge directly from gender role or personal style. Because women as a group make more wellness physician visits, they may simply be more adept and efficient in reporting symptoms. Women may have a better understanding of the importance of providing a full disclosure in the process of diagnosis and treatment. Concomitant health conditions and life history may also shape reporting; for example, the greater prevalence of depression among women may contribute to more negativity about general health and a tendency to report more symptoms. A life history that includes traumatic events may also contribute to more symptom reporting by both women and men and might include a history of childhood abuse or trauma during military deployment.

Health Beliefs and Physician–Patient Communication

Men and women may vary in general health vigilance and beliefs about the general efficacy of health-care interventions, which is complicated by the fact that options available to demonstrate masculinity are often unhealthy (Courtenay, McCreary, & Merighi, 2002). Men tend to hold riskier beliefs and to engage in riskier behavior than women do (Karoly, Ruehlman, & Lanyon, 2005). For example, beliefs and intentions about controlling health outcomes may shape adherence to lifestyle changes, such as diet, smoking cessation, and compliance with medication regimens. Various scales have been developed to measure health locus of control and other multidimensional factors (Street, Krupat, Bell, Kravitz, & Haidet, 2003). However, personal internal traits are not sufficient to account for the range and variety of gender patterns in utilization of health care.

Important elements of health decision making and use of health-care resources emerge in a dynamic interaction between physician and patient. Indeed, a major motivation for the women's health movement was dissatisfaction with the failure of health providers to supply information or choices to patients. Initial patient communication about symptoms and follow-up discussions are critical to case conceptualization, to diagnosis, and to treatment plans. Mutuality and responsiveness in physician–patient interactions and in partnership building tend to be reciprocal (Beck, Daughtridge, & Sloane, 2002). Further, physician interaction styles that involve empathy, reassurance, and patient-centered questioning have been associated with improved clinical outcomes (Levinson et al., 1999). Resolving conflicts and differences of opinion can be problematic, but advice for health-care providers includes open discussion and active involvement by the patient (West, 1993).

The emergent and interactive features of the physician–patient relationship reflect partly the cultural modes of "doing gender" as described by Candace West (Roter & Hall, 1998). The somewhat more ready use of collaborative styles by female than by male providers is surely one factor in the gendered aspects of physician–patient encounters (Bylund & Makoul, 2002; Roter & Hall, 1998), but, in any case, physicians of either gender are more likely to express empathy and to engage in relationship building with women patients (Badger et al., 1999). For example, male physicians have been found to be more likely to explore depressive symptomology with female patients, which perhaps contributes to some of the higher recognition of these conditions among women themselves (Boston Women's Health Book Collective, 1971; Dreifus, 1977; Ehrenreich & English, 1973; Munch, 2006; Ruzek, 1978; Zimmerman, 1987). These complex and often subtle patterns highlight the possibility that stereotypes and bias can creep systematically into health care.

Some key themes emerge with respect to health care in each of these areas. Although individual beliefs and lifestyles influence health status and utilization of care, the consistent universal factor is the cost of care, insurance, and the likelihood that there will be a consistent source of care. Simply having insurance is not a guarantee of ready access to care, and insurance plans vary greatly in what they cover and deductible costs that must be born by the policy holder. For example, a full course of chemotherapy depends in part on patient reactions to the toxic side effects of various elements in the chemotherapy regimen. Some chemotherapy agents (e.g., carboplatin, marketed by Bristol Myers Squibb as Paraplatin) have lower incidence of remote neuropathy or other toxic side effects, yet insurance companies can and do deny claims for this agent in favor of less expensive ones that have more side effects. Similarly, the ability of a patient to tolerate a full course of chemotherapy may depend in part on the ability to control nausea. One of the more effective antiemetics, Zofran, marketed by GlaxoSmithKline, is also more expensive, and insurance companies may deny claims in favor of other less costly, less effective, medications; the generic version, ondansetron, costs $17.50 for one pill.[2]

Alzheimer's Disease and Long-Term Care

Alzheimer's disease is now the fifth leading cause of death for those over the age of 65 (Alzheimer's Disease International, 2006) and was estimated, in 2002, to be the fourth leading cause of death among developed nations (Centers for Disease Control and Prevention, 2008). Approximately 5.2 million Americans are afflicted with Alzheimer's disease, and death rates are higher among women than among men (23.8 and 17.7, respectively, per 100,000 persons). Risk factors for Alzheimer's disease include increased age, high blood pressure, history of head trauma, poor heart health, and being female (perhaps because women tend to live longer than men) (Plassman et al., 2007). Blacks are more likely than Whites to develop the disease, and one protective factor seems to be years of

---

[2]Personal communication from a patient.

education (Paganini-Hill & Henderson, 1994). Although the disease remains incurable, it does not remain untreatable.

In the past, estrogen was prescribed to female Alzheimer's patients due to the belief that its depletion through menopause was linked to the development of Alzheimer's (Paganini-Hill & Henderson, 1994). It was thought that estrogen would be helpful in controlling the symptoms of menopause and also in delaying the onset of dementia (Alzheimer's Disease Education & Referral Center, 2003). Unfortunately, this was not the case. Recent research suggests that estrogen, especially when combined with progestin, can actually increase a woman's risk for dementia, as well as her risk for a heart attack, breast cancer, stroke, blood clots, hip fractures, and colon cancer (National Institutes of Health, 2007).

Currently, three promising treatments work to slow the progression of Alzheimer's and to help patients to live comfortably with the disease. The treatments include prescriptions, lifestyle changes, and antioxidant supplements. The FDA has approved a number of cholinesterase inhibitors[3] to treat mild to moderate symptoms and Memantine[4] to treat moderate to severe symptoms (Centers for Disease Control and Prevention, 2008). Research suggests that lifestyle changes (e.g., physical exercise, mental exercise, social interaction) may prevent mental decline (Centers for Disease Control and Prevention, 2008). In addition to prescription medications and lifestyle changes, Vitamin E, omega-3 fatty acids, and various antioxidant supplements have also produced promising results in combating the advancement of the disease (Greenberg-Dotan, Reuveni, Simon-Tuval, Oksenberg, & Tarasiuk, 2007).

Long-Term Care

In 2006, there were 16,000 nursing home facilities that were certified by Medicare and Medicaid (Centers for Disease Control and Prevention, 2004), and nearly 1.5 million Americans resided in a nursing home (National Center for Health Statistics, 2007). The nursing home resident age-adjusted rate for women 65 years and over tends to be nearly twice that for men (40.4 compared with 24.1 per 1,000 population, age-adjusted) Part of the gender difference may be due to the fact that, prior to nursing home admission, more men (61.7%) than women (45%) are invited to live with family members (Centers for Disease Control and Prevention, 2004; National Center for Health Statistics, 2007). Rates are also higher for Black than White people (49.9 and 34, respectively) (Centers for Disease Control and Prevention, 2004), which may reflect poverty and limited resources.

Of those admitted to nursing homes, 9.9% are specifically afflicted with Alzheimer's disease and senile dementia ("Alzheimer's Association – Lotsa Helping Hands," 2008; Frytak et al., 2008). These patients had 944 days of care (Frytak et al., 2008), and we explore Alzheimer's disease in detail because Alzheimer's patients in assisted living and nursing home facilities often require more care than the average patient (Greenberg-Dotan et al., 2007). Alzheimer's patients are more likely to suffer broken bones, accidental injuries, and falls than are other nursing home patients (Burton et al., 2001). Despite the fact that they are already in a health-care facility, nursing home residents with Alzheimer's disease are less likely to visit a physician or to be hospitalized than are those without

---

[3]Cholinesterase inhibitors work to prevent the breakdown of acetylcholine in the brain. Acetylcholine is a chemical that helps to bridge connections between synapses important to learning and memory; these inhibitors work to slow the progression of Alzheimer's disease (Centers for Disease Control and Prevention, 2008).

[4]Memantine works to regulate glutamate (also important to learning and memory) and delays the progression of Alzheimer's disease in some patients.

Alzheimer's (Burton et al., 2001). Overall, those with dementia had fewer medical appointments after suffering from a fever or from an infection than did others with the same symptoms (Centers for Disease Control and Prevention, 2004). Nevertheless, among Alzheimer's patients, men are slightly more likely (8.3%) than women (6.3%) to be hospitalized for specialized care (Centers for Disease Control and Prevention, 2004). Not only are men in nursing homes more likely to be hospitalized but they (9.7%) are also somewhat more likely than women (7.7%) to visit the emergency room (Centers for Disease Control and Prevention, 2004). It is not clear whether this reflects relatively poor health status among men or under utilization of care for women.

There are also racial differences in specific nursing home care practices. For example, the use of physical restraints on Alzheimer's patients is common in nursing homes, but it is more common among Black patients. When physical restraint is used within the nursing home, Blacks are more likely than Whites to be restrained, with bed rails (20.3% versus 12.7%), side rails (26.5% versus 24.3%), and chair restraint (4.1% versus 3.2%) (Centers for Disease Control and Prevention, 2004). Bed rail and chair restraint use are similar among male and female patients; however, side rail restraints are used slightly more often with women (26.5%) than men (24.3%) (Richardson, Sullivan, Hill, & Yu, 2007). A variety of hypotheses might explain these patterns. Use of restraints may reflect greater deterioration and frailty among women or Black patients, perhaps because their diagnosis, and therefore treatment, was delayed or perhaps because admission to a nursing facility was delayed because of financial hardships. Less palatable is the possibility that women and racial minority patients may receive less attention and simply may be seen as more bothersome.

When compared to other patients in the last 30 days of life, Alzheimer's patients are less likely to receive aggressive medical care (Centers for Disease Control and Prevention, 2004) such as dialysis, to be admitted into the intensive care unit, to be put on a ventilator, and/or to receive pulmonary artery monitoring. Also, men are more likely than women to be provided nourishment via a feeding tube when the opportunity arises (7.4 and 5.3%, respectively) (Gessert, Haller, Kane, & Degenholtz, 2006). Some of these disparities may be due to the location of the nursing home. Those living in a rural area are less likely than those living in an urban area to receive medical services toward the end of life (American Cancer Society, 2008). However, it is not likely that there are relatively more women and racial minorities in rural facilities.

Cancer

Cancer is a disease process that affects cell biology and internal molecular processes of over 100 different organ systems. Cancer cells typically (though not always) have a distorted shape, divide and multiply at a faster than normal rate, fail to differentiate into normally functioning cells, fail to repair themselves, and/or fail to regress or die.[5] One-half of all men and one-third of all women will develop some form of cancer in their lifetimes (Pleis & Lethbridge-Cejku, 2007). In 2006, there were 6.5 million (6.6%) men and 9.3 million (7.8%) women who had ever been diagnosed with cancer (Peleg-Oren, Sherer, & Soskolne, 2003).

Significant sex and race disparities emerge in the utilization of health-care resources for different types of cancer. Women are more likely than men to receive screenings for most cancers (with the exception of lung cancer) and to have higher survival rates for most types of cancer, whereas men are more likely than women to receive aggressive treatments as well as combination treatments. When coping with the psychosocial stressors of cancer, women tend to be more emotionally expressive,

---

[5] A kind of pre-programmed cell death called apoptosis.

whereas men are reliant upon their partners. These patterns are consistent with gender roles; women are expressive and rely on a wide range of social support, whereas men suppress their emotions and express their problems within a small social group (Espey et al., 2007).

In 2008, roughly 565,650 Americans are expected to die from cancer, which accounts for one of every four deaths. Though this number is extremely high, cancer death rates have recently been on a slow decline. Overall, cancer death rates decreased by 2.1% per year between 2002 and 2004 (Kung, Hoyert, Xu, & Murphy, 2008), almost *twice* the decrease from 1975 to 2001 at 1.1% per year. However, cancer remains the second leading cause of death in the United States for both women and men (Kung et al., 2008), though women experienced greater improvements in mortality from 2004 to 2005. Surveillance, Epidemiology, and End Results (SEER) databases indicate that men have a more than 40% greater likelihood of dying than women do (at age-adjusted rates) (American Cancer Society, 2008).

The most common forms of cancer in the United States are skin cancer, colorectal cancer (i.e., colon, rectal, or bowel cancer), breast cancer, prostate cancer, and lung cancer. Although there are many types of cancer, in this section we focus on breast, prostate, lung, and colon cancers.

Breast Cancer

The most commonly diagnosed form of cancer for women is breast cancer, with an age-adjusted incidence rate of 126.1 per 100,000 women per year, based on the 2000 census population data (Reis et al., 2008). Black women have a lower incidence of breast cancer than White women do, yet they continue to have a higher death rate (1.4 Black women to every White woman) (Maloney et al., 2006; O'Malley et al., 2001). This racial disparity is shaped by a number of causes, including socioeconomic status, access to care, personal and family history of breast problems, and education level (Otto et al., 2003; Tabar et al., 2003).

Yearly mammograms starting at age 40 can reduce the risk of mortality by almost 40%. Women with female physicians or who have an obstetrician/gynecologist as their general practitioner are more likely than other women to have yearly mammograms (O'Malley et al., 2001). However, there is racial disparity among those who actually receive yearly mammograms. Physicians recommend mammograms most often to White women, though it is suggested that this difference may be a result of the lower socioeconomic status and limited access to care among racial minority women (Maloney et al., 2006).

A study conducted at the Breast Evaluation Clinic at Eastern Virginia Medical School evaluated the use of mammograms, sentinel lymph node (SLN) biopsies,[6] and treatment among breast cancer patients. After the researchers controlled for equal socioeconomic status and access to care, White women received both mammograms (81%) and SLN biopsies (75%) more frequently than did Black women (56 and 42%, respectively). Among this sample, when mammograms were utilized, 100% of the Black women tested had abnormal cells, whereas only 76% of the White women did (Fisher et al., 1995), which suggests that mammograms are being used for disease confirmation among Black women but as a preventative measure among White women. No racial differences were found in subsequent treatment.

---

[6] A procedure associated with breast cancer surgery in which the lymph node closest to the breast tumor (sentinel lymph node) is removed and examined under a microscope in order to determine whether or not cancer cells are present. This biopsy provides an estimate of the likelihood that the cancer has metastasized by entering the lymph system.

Once diagnosed with breast cancer, there are a number of different treatment options available including lumpectomy, mastectomy, lymph node dissection, chemotherapy, radiation therapy, and hormonal therapy. Less invasive lumpectomy followed by radiation therapy, in the early stages of breast cancer, has been found to be as safe and effective as mastectomy (Zuckerman, 2008). However, a large majority of breast cancer patients, particularly older women and/or those with lower incomes, are still receiving mastectomies (Zuckerman, 2008). One reason for this may be that it is actually less expensive to perform a mastectomy than to provide a lumpectomy followed by radiotherapy. Individuals covered under private insurance and in urban settings are more likely to receive the combination treatment rather than mastectomy (Scalliet & Kirkove, 2007). One rationale for decisions about surgical procedures is patient age; older patients are not often advised to receive combination treatment because it is believed their cancer is at a more advanced stage and therefore more aggressive. However, this is not the case; patients over the age of 65 or 70 benefit from postoperative radiotherapy just as much as younger patients do, and, therefore, they should have all options available to them (American Cancer Society, 2008).

Men are also affected by breast cancer but at a significantly lower rate. In 2008, an estimated 0.01 per 100,000 men were expected to be diagnosed and 0.002 per 1,000,000 men were estimated to die as a result of the disease (Csillag, 2005). Very little research exists with regard to possible sex differences in treatment effectiveness, though some gender differences have been documented in treatment utilization. Being male increases the probability of receiving radiotherapy following a mastectomy (American Cancer Society, 2008). One possible explanation for this may be that men's tumor to breast size ratio is typically higher than women's.

Prostate Cancer

Among men, the most commonly diagnosed form of cancer is prostate cancer, with an age-adjusted incidence rate of 38.4 per 100,000 men, based on the 2000 census population data (Bennett et al., 1998; Potosky et al., 1999; Robbins, Whittemore, & Van Den Eeden, 1998). Yearly screening tests such as the prostate-specific antigen (PSA) blood test and the digital rectal examination (DRE) are helpful in detecting prostate cancer in its early stages. Known barriers to prostate cancer screening include advanced age, low socioeconomic status, and racial minority status (U.S. Cancer Statistics Working Group, 2007). Black men have a higher incidence rate of prostate cancer than White men do (217.5 and 134.5 per 100,000, respectively) as well as a higher mortality rate (56.1 and 23.4 per 100,000, respectively) (Klabunde, Potosky, Harlan, & Kramer, 1998). In addition, Black men receive less screening for prostate cancer, are more likely to be diagnosed at an advanced stage, and receive aggressive treatments (i.e., radical prostatectomy[7]) less often than White men do (Allen, Kennedy, Wilson-Glover, & Gilligan, 2007; Gillian, Wang, Levin, Kantoff, & Avorn, 2004). These racial disparities may be explained in part by lack of insurance and financial resources, mistrust of the health-care system by Black men, lack of responsiveness by the health-care systems to Black men, and differences in how Black and White men understand and manage threats to male sexuality (Allen et al., 2007). In Western societies, sexual prowess is a defining feature of the masculine gender role, and techniques used in prostate cancer screening, such as the DRE, threaten masculinity for many heterosexual men. Prostate cancer survivors are often concerned about loss of masculinity or sexual function following treatment (National Cancer Institute, 2008).

---

[7] A major surgery that is performed under general anesthesia to remove the entire prostate gland and some of the tissue around it.

There are four standard treatments for prostate cancer: watchful waiting, surgery (i.e., pelvic lymphadenectomy, radical prostatectomy), radiation therapy, and hormone therapy. Other treatments such as cryosurgery, chemotherapy, biological therapy, and high-intensity focused ultrasound are currently being tested in clinical trials (Underwood et al., 2004). Black and Hispanic men are less likely than non-Hispanic White men to receive prostatectomy, radiotherapy, brachytherapy, and combinations thereof (Sadetsky et al., 2005). Robotic surgery, which results in less blood loss and shorter hospital stays, is an increasingly available option. However, robotic machines cost over $1 million, and the cost of an individual surgery is roughly $1,000 more than conventional surgery. Following a radical prostatectomy, socioeconomic status (SES) plays a significant role in access to care and utilization of health services (e.g., use of general practitioners, mental health professionals, oncologists); SES is mediated by ethnicity and education (Robbins, Yin, & Parikh-Patel, 2007).

Once diagnosed with prostate cancer, Black men have a lower survival rate than other ethnic groups. Diagnosed Black men often are younger, at a more advanced stage of the disease, receive less treatment with surgery or radiation therapy and have lower socioeconomic status. After each of these potentially modifiable disparities is controlled, racial differences in prostate cancer survival diminish (Jones, Underwood, & Rivers, 2007). Remaining differences may be due to comorbidities among Blacks as well as to an increased risk of prostate cancer recurrence (Burns & Mahalik, 2008).

Men who receive radical prostate cancer treatments with a large number of side effects (i.e., sexual dysfunction, osteoporosis, fatigue) suffer from a decreased well-being if they do not feel comfortable expressing themselves emotionally to others (Burns & Mahalik, 2008). In Western societies, masculine gender role stereotypes make it difficult for men to be emotionally expressive. Following radical treatments, men who have clinicians who work to reduce embarrassment and shame as well as encourage them to participate in support groups have increased well-being than those who do not receive encouragement (Heller, 2006).

One in six men will be afflicted with prostate cancer in his lifetime, whereas one in eight women will be diagnosed with breast cancer in her lifetime. Though both are equally serious health issues in the United States, the publicity, effort, and funding for breast cancer research are far greater than that allocated to prostate cancer (National Cancer Institute, 2006). In 2007, an estimated $551.1 million was spent on breast cancer research, whereas $305.6 million was spent on prostate cancer research (U.S. Department of Defense, 2008). In the 2008 fiscal year, the Congressionally Directed Medical Research Program, one of the top supporters of health research, appropriated $138 million to breast cancer research and only $80 million to prostate cancer research (Stewart, Bertoni, Staten, Levine, & Gross, 2007). There is a disparity not only in funding but also in clinical trials; finding men willing to participate in prostate cancer clinical trials, as well as physicians willing to support new research, is challenging (Heller, 2006). This difference in funding and clinical trial enrollment may be a result of women's greater willingness to be vocal and to campaign for the need to find a breast cancer cure. In addition, the discomfort men experience, both physically and emotionally, during prostate cancer screening exams may help to explain the gender differences in cancer health-care utilization (American Cancer Society, 2008). For example, two common side effects of radical prostatectomy and radiotherapy include incontinence and impotence. In a society where men's sexual performance is highly valued, these threats may hinder men from participating in clinical trials and demanding treatment as often as women with breast cancer do.

Lung Cancer

After breast cancer in women and prostate cancer in men, lung cancer is the second most common form of diagnosed cancer among both men and women in the United States with an incidence rate of 144.2 per 100,000 (89 per 100,000 men and 55.2 per 100,000 women) based on the 2000 age-adjusted census population (American Cancer Society, 2008; Mortality Trends for Selected Smoking-Related Cancers and Breast Cancer in the United States, 1950–1990, 1993), and it is the leading cause of cancer-related deaths (Shugarman, Bird, Schuster, & Lynn, 2008). The prevalence of lung cancer among men is slowly declining (from 102 cases per 100,000 in 1984 to 73.6 in 2004), whereas women's rates have come to a plateau after a period of increase.

Once diagnosed with lung cancer, gender differences in patterns of health-care utilization emerge. Women are slightly more likely than men to utilize inpatient services (85.8 and 85.1%, respectively), skilled nursing facility services (28.2 and 23.1%, respectively), home health services (49.8 and 41.5%, respectively), and hospice services (53.0 and 48.6%, respectively) (Shugarman et al., 2008). There are no significant gender differences among the utilization of outpatient services[8] and physician services. Further, though lung tumors are predominantly located in the upper lobes for both women and men, there are differences in surgical procedures. Men most often receive surgical removal of an entire lung (pneumonectomy), whereas women are more apt to receive a partial lung removal (segmentectomy) (de Perrot et al., 2000; Olak & Colson, 2004).

Colorectal Cancer

Colorectal cancer is the third most common form of cancer in both men and women with an estimated 148,810 (77,250 men and 71,560 women) new cases in 2008 (American Cancer Society, 2008). Proper colorectal screening (yearly fecal occult blood testing [FOBT] and a sigmoidoscopy, colonoscopy, or double-contrast barium enema) every 5–10 years reduces mortality rates. In fact, the prevalence of colorectal cancer is on a slow decline thanks to increased screening and early detection.

Men are more likely than women to receive screening for colon cancer. Among those being screened there are gender differences by type of screening (Donovan & Syngal, 1998). Although colonoscopy is a superior method of screening (McMahon et al., 1999), women are more likely to receive a combination of FOBTs, barium enemas, and sigmoidoscopies, whereas men are more likely to receive colonoscopies (Rosen & Schneider, 2004). Consequently, women most often receive screenings that are less complete (i.e., exams that involve only the lower portion of the colon). This gender difference may be explained in part by the common belief that colorectal cancer is a man's disease, and the focus on breast cancer rather than colon cancer screening for women may have resulted in a delayed utilization of colorectal screening by women (Podolsky, 2000). It also may be explained partially by the high cost of a colonoscopy and the fact that women may have health insurance plans that require higher deductibles.

Differential screening also is evidenced in the interaction of gender and weight. Individuals who are considered obese (a body mass index [BMI] between 30 and 34.9) and morbidly obese (a BMI 35 or higher) have a greater risk of colorectal cancer and a higher associated mortality rate (Rosen & Schneider, 2004). Despite the link between obesity and colorectal cancer, women who are classified as "morbidly obese" are significantly less likely than women with "normal" BMI to be screened for colorectal cancer (37.1 and 42.7%, respectively); these differences are not observed among men (Rosen & Schneider, 2004). These obesity-related patterns may be a result of a combination of patient and physician factors. In Western societies, there is a clear bias and stigmatization against obese individuals, particularly women.

---

[8]Outpatient services tend to encompass medical procedures, surgeries, tests, etc., that are performed in a medical setting and do not require an overnight stay. Although home health services by definition occur without a hospital stay, they are considered social-support services, much like hospice.

Diabetes

Approximately 24 million Americans are afflicted with diabetes, and another 57 million are presumed to be prediabetic with an increased risk of developing diabetes in the future (Roe, McNamara, & Motheral, 2002). Currently, 11.2% of men and 10.2% of women suffer from diabetes; one-half of them are over 60 years of age (National Diabetes Statistics, 2005). In 2005 diabetes accounted for 24.6 deaths per 100,000 persons, age-adjusted rate, within the United States (National Center for Health Statistics, 2007), and those with diabetes are two to four times more likely than those without diabetes to suffer a stroke or to die from heart disease (National Diabetes Fact Sheet, 2007). Complications related to diabetes made it the seventh leading cause of death in the United States during the year of 2006.

Health Effects

Gender differences in the cascading health effects related to diabetes contribute to differential utilization of physician visits, hospitalization, and surgery. For example, 2005 data indicate that the age-adjusted prevalence of visual impairment was 19.3% among women and 16.2% among men (Centers for Disease Control and Prevention, 2005). Data on visual impairment generally reflect physician visits as opposed to hospitalization. However, hospital discharge data indicate that men have higher rates than women of several other conditions, such as peripheral artery disease, ulceration, and neuropathy. For example, the age-adjusted hospital discharge rate for peripheral artery disease was nearly 40% greater among men than among women, the discharge rate for ulcerations/inflammations/infections was nearly 60% greater among men than among women, and the neuropathy[9] rate was around 23% greater among men than among women (McKeever, Weston, Hubbard, & Fogarty, 2005). This may be because diabetes among men is more resistant to standard treatments, which leads to an increase in related health effects. It is also possible that men are less watchful in the management of their diabetes and therefore suffer more complications. The posture of invincibility and self-sufficiency required by the traditional masculine gender role surely contributes to a cavalier attitude toward preventive health and may lead to delays in diagnosis and treatment.

In addition to biomedical health effects associated with diabetes, over 25% of diabetic patients report clinical depression (Centers for Disease Control and Prevention, 2007), and depression is especially common among older women with diabetes (Centers for Disease Control and Prevention, 2007; Finkelstein et al., 2003). Depressive symptoms tend to worsen as diabetes progresses, which makes regular care plans difficult to follow and increases complications of the disease (Musen et al., 2006). Those with both diabetes and depression are more likely to seek medical attention and to spend more time in the hospital than are diabetics without depression (Middleton, Hing, & Xu, 2007). Women are slightly more likely than men (11.7 and 8.1%, respectively) voluntarily to seek outpatient care when coping with depression (Finkelstein et al., 2003); this might be due to machismo among men and reluctance to admit vulnerability (see Chapter 7). Treatment for major depression may help to decrease medical costs especially if treatment helps to decrease overall medical attention (Johnson, Pohar, & Majumdar, 2006).

---

[9]The CDC (2005) defines neuropathy as a nerve disease with complications including weakness in the muscles, pain, and numbness.

Diabetes and Utilization of Care

Although individuals of every age and from every walk of life could become afflicted with diabetes, utilization of health care is not always equally distributed. Limited access to care and limited financial means surely contribute to differences in utilization. Among diabetic patients under age 65 (and therefore not covered by Medicare), women, especially Black women and Latinas, are less likely than men to have medical insurance (McCall, Sauaia, Hamman, Reusch, & Barton, 2004). Without health insurance and access to regular care, the cost is simply prohibitive for individuals who otherwise must pay out-of-pocket costs. The average 10-year cost to manage diabetes for an individual has been estimated at just over $33,500 for Type I diabetes and around at $38,000 for Type II diabetes (Harris, 2001). Among those with type II diabetes, Latinos/as (66%) are less likely than African Americans (89%) and European Americans (91%) to be covered by medical insurance (Harris, 1999).

Racial disparities persist even among those with private insurance (Adams et al., 2005). African Americans and Latinos/as are less likely than European Americans to monitor their blood glucose and to have their cholesterol checked, and they are more likely to suffer from high blood pressure (Harris, Eastman, Cowie, Flegal, & Eberhardt, 1999). In addition, Non-Hispanic Black women and Mexican American men are more likely than those in all other groups to display lower levels of glycemic control (Harris, 1999, 2001). Given that patient education would be more likely when there is regular access to health care and health insurance, one should not be surprised that African Americans and Latinos/as are among those who have poorly controlled diabetes and hypertension (Klarenbach & Jacobs, 2003).

Despite U.S. patterns, racial and ethnic disparities are less dramatic in other countries. For example, diabetic patients in Canada are more likely than patients in the United States to have contact with a physician, to have an eye specialist, and to have had an overnight hospital stay in the past year (Brown et al., 2005). Lower quality of care and poorer outcomes in the United States than in Canada remain even in well-managed care settings. In the United States, poorer and less educated diabetic patients receive fewer dilated eye exams (Klarenbach & Jacobs, 2003). Men are 12% less likely than women to make optometry visits and 19% less likely to stay overnight in the hospital. In addition, compared to Canadian health practice, diabetic patients in the United States are one-half as likely to visit any type of health professional, including psychologists (Norris, Engelgau, & Narayan, 2001).

Interventions and Programs

Not withstanding disparities in health care for diabetics and numerous complications associated with diabetes, there are some hopeful trends. Research suggests that educational interventions that include patient interaction improve patients' glycemic control, weight, and fat intake (California Medi-Cal Type 2 Diabetes Study Group, 2004). Three intervention strategies and educational programs offer good examples: Project DIRECT (Diabetes Intervention Reaching and Educating Communities Together), the National Diabetes Education Program (NDEP), and the SEARCH for Diabetes in Youth Study. Funded by the Centers for Disease Control and Prevention, Project DIRECT is the largest community-based diabetes program in the United States, and it works to reduce the burdens of diabetic care within the African American community (*National Diabetes Education Program*, 2008). Primary efforts of the DIRECT program are focused on health promotion, community outreach, and increasing regular patient monitoring of blood glucose levels. Public and private partners work together to promote early diagnosis of diabetes through the National Diabetes Education Program (NDEP). The goal of NDEP is to delay, if not to prevent, the onset of diabetes and also to improve treatment outcomes for minority groups at risk of the disease (Centers for Disease Control and Prevention, 2007). The SEARCH for Diabetes in Youth Study works to find trends within the diabetic youth populations afflicted with Type I and Type II diabetes, which also focuses on minority populations (Crooks & Baur, 2005). Together, these intervention strategies and programs could help to combat, compound, and reduce disparities in diabetes health-care utilization.

Sexual and Reproductive Health

Historically, there has been a sexual double standard in which sex before marriage was acceptable for men but not for women. Although belief in a sexual double standard is not as widely held today (Hinchliff, Gott, & Galena, 2004), it continues to have an impact. Consistent with society's view of moral femininity, women do not want to be perceived as overly sexually active; yet, images of women as simultaneously innocent and sexual seem to be effective in marketing products to women. Although women often present themselves in a sexually objectified manner, it is not as acceptable for women as it is for men to have multiple sexual partners (see Volume I, Chapter 15).

Being sexually active and having a number of sexual partners puts individuals at an increased risk for unwanted pregnancy and sexually transmitted diseases, and, therefore, they should see physicians on a routine basis for screenings. When individuals go to family practitioners, clinics, or specialists, men are more likely than women to discuss sexual health issues (Hinchliff et al., 2004). When women see a general practitioner, sexual health is often not discussed unless it is in the context of reproductive health, particularly if the physician is male (Dixon-Woods et al., 2001). In fact, most physicians believe that women do not want to discuss sexual health with male medical professionals. Further, stigma and embarrassment accompany discussions of sexual health by women in many societies (Lurie et al., 1993). The sex of the physician affects the kind of preventive care or screening that women receive. Women who see a female physician are much more likely to have annual Pap tests and mammograms (Nurnberg et al., 2008; Nurnberg, Hensley, Lauriello, Parker, & Keith, 1999).

Traditional gender roles place much of the burden of sexual and reproductive health on women's shoulders. Consequently, sexual and reproductive health services are one medical domain in which men are often underserved (Finer, Darroch, & Frost, 2003). For example, even when family planning clinics offer services for men (e.g., sexually transmitted disease testing) only 14% of clients are likely to be male (Kalmuss & Tatum, 2007). In addition, there is a dearth of guidelines regarding what formal screening or sexual and reproductive health services men should receive. Any standards that have been developed differ from document to document and often focus only on adolescent boys, ignoring the needs of adult men (Frost, 2006).

Women's most common forms of ambulatory care for sexual and reproductive health are clinical gynecological services, including Pap smears and pelvic exams. However, the majority of these patients are White women (72%) with a minimum of a high school education (90%) and adequate incomes (Kalmuss & Tatum, 2007). Testicular examinations are the most common sexual and reproductive health services for men; 35% of men receive these exams each year. However, among these men, more than one-half report that testicular examinations are the *only* form of sexual and reproductive health service they receive (Centers for Disease Control and Prevention, 2006). Further, it is important to notice differences in the aims of reproductive health services for women and men. Among women, the focus is on sexual and reproductive health as well as cancer screening (e.g., Pap smears, pelvic exams), whereas for men the focus is mostly cancer screening (e.g., testicular, prostate exams).

In contrast to long-term care associated with Alzheimer's disease, sexual and reproductive health typically requires immediate or short-term interventions that encompass a broad array of needs, conditions, and care, including reproductive tract cancer screening, sexually transmitted diseases, screening for human immunodeficiency virus (HIV) and acquired immunodeficiency syndrome (AIDS), contraception and abortion, sterilization, assisted fertility, pregnancy, and childbirth. Given limitations of space and time, we focus here on sexually transmitted diseases.

Sexually transmitted diseases (STDs) are a major component of sexual and reproductive health with an estimated 19 million new STD cases in the United States each year, and nearly one-half of these cases are young people between the ages of 19 and 24 (Brackbill, Sternberg, & Fishbein, 1999). Based on the 1992 U.S. National Health and Social Life Survey (NHSLS), most individuals with STDs reported seeking treatment at a private practice (49%); others went to "other clinics" (8%), the emergency room (7%), an STD clinic (5%), or a family planning clinic (5%); 26% did not report where they sought treatment (Nathanson, 1977). The source of treatment varies by gender: Women are significantly more likely to seek STD treatment at private practices, whereas men are more likely to go to an emergency room, an STD clinic, or a family planning clinic. As previously mentioned, this difference may be because women are more likely to see health-care providers of all kinds on a regular basis (Kalmuss & Tatum, 2007).

HIV/AIDS

In 2006, there were an estimated 56,300 new HIV infections (Centers for Disease Control and Prevention, 2008). Clear sex disparities exist with regard to the prevalence of HIV. Seventy-three percent of new infections are among men, of whom 53% are gay or bisexual. Preventive measures for many STDs (e.g., increased education or safer sex practices) are aimed at both men and women; however, research and treatment of HIV and AIDS are predominantly aimed at men. Further, homosexual men are targeted for HIV/AIDS education and treatment more than heterosexual men and women (Box, Olsen, Oddone, & Keitz, 2003).

Among women with HIV, increased responsibilities in family care and child-rearing could be possible barriers to access to care and to utilization of health services. However, once diagnosed, HIV-positive men and women receive similar care and have similar utilization of health services (e.g., primary care visits, emergency room visits, annual admission, rates, lengths of stay for hospitalizations) (National Center for Health Statistics, 1999).

Among HIV/AIDS patients, there are disparities in hospitalizations and procedures. Since 1997, data show a decrease in hospitalization among both male and female HIV/AIDS patients (DeFrances, Cullen, Kozak, & National Center for Health Statistics, 2007; Fleishman & Hellinger, 2003; Popovic, Kozak, & National Center for Health Statistics, 2000; Popovic & National Center for Health Statistics, 2001). This decline has been attributed to increased antiretroviral therapies as well as improved HIV/AIDS prevention efforts, which in turn have decreased the death rate and consequently reduced the need for hospital care. Individuals admitted to hospitals for HIV-related illness have predominantly been men (at a ratio of 2–3 for every woman), but this gap has narrowed over time; the hospital admissions among men with HIV/AIDS have declined at a steeper rate than admissions among comparable women (Palella et al., 1998).

Although public opinion generally holds that a diagnosis of HIV/AIDs is fatal, there have been dramatic advances in treatments that extend healthy years of life (World Health Organization, 2004).

Highly Active Antiretroviral Therapy (HAART),[10] an aggressive HIV treatment aimed at suppressing the disease's progress, has had moderate levels of success (Chu & Selwyn, 2008; Gebo et al., 2005; Shapiro et al., 1999). Despite evidence for good efficacy, United States data reveal gender and racial disparities among individuals receiving HAART. Men are more likely than women to receive HAART (odds ratio of 1.23), and Blacks are less likely than Whites to receive HAART (odds ratio of 0.86) (Ofotokun, Chuck, & Hitti, 2007). One explanation for this may be women make up a minority of those in clinical trials ("National Institutes of Health Revitalization Act of 1993: Clinical Research Equity Regarding Women and Minorities," 1993). Even when women in the United States are included in trials, there are no National Institutes of Health (NIH) guidelines that require separate analysis of efficacy or safety for women. In fact the regular inclusion of women in clinical trials required an act of Congress (Travis & Meltzer, 2008) to stipulate that government-funded clinical trials sponsored by NIH[11] include them. Even so, researchers are permitted to exclude women if they provide a rationale for doing so. One such rationale for the exclusion of women is almost always available, specifically, that women may become pregnant during a drug trial, with possible teratogenic effects on the fetus.

Future Directions

Future research regarding gender and health-care utilization must continue to incorporate the intersectionality of gender and other dimensions of identity. Feminist theory acknowledges that gender is not always the primary locus of identity or of oppression (Canadian Research Institute for the Advancement of Women [CIRAW], 2006; Landrine, 1995). This perspective extends beyond ethnicity to include ability, age, chronic health conditions, immigrant status, economic class, and sexualities. Although single variable analysis can bring to light previously indistinct patterns and problem areas; solutions will inevitably require holistic approaches.

Incorporating social and psychological dimensions as well as biomedical elements in analysis of trends, explanations, and best practices is another fruitful area of research and policy. In fact, what is judged as normal or ideal for personal identity is often intimately related to health status, utilization of services, and the effectiveness of coping with illness. These multilayered aspects can be seen in the use of primary prevention as well as tertiary care. Because these "soft" dimensions have not historically been integrated with biomedical analysis, qualitative methods are probably essential to identifying fruitful lines of research. There is, after all, substantial variation among men as well as among women that cannot be reflected in standard national or international databases. Clues to holistic social and psychological dynamics are much more likely to emerge in personal narrative.

Access to and use of care is never just about gender, it requires a look at funding and economic factors that make care more or less available. Although health status is typically linked to individual age and health behaviors, one reasonably could argue that the biggest determinant of health is socioeconomic status. Future research directions in practice patterns must incorporate structural context with the social–psychological factors. For example, utilization of care is heavily shaped by structural factors such as the availability of services, especially access to a regular care provider,

---

[10] The regimen consists of three or more different drugs from different classes, such as two nucleoside reverse transcriptase inhibitors (NRTIs) and a protease inhibitor (PI), two NRTIs and a non-nucleoside reverse transcriptase inhibitors (NNRTIs), or other combinations.

[11] Clinical trials funded solely by corporations or private foundations do not fall under the requirement to include women.

and this is heavily determined by the structure of health-care funding. Part of the structural context is also based on the relative weight accorded prevention, protection, and cost efficiency within a particular health-care system. In this light, we have noted persistent barriers and deficiencies in the availability of comprehensive health care. Although the data discussed here are primarily derived from U.S. patterns and sources, the interplay of socioeconomic factors with access to and quality of care is relevant in all countries. The relative emphasis given to prevention, wellness, safety, quality of care, and overall costs in health care reflects values that vary cross-culturally. These, in turn, are moderated by population pressures, natural resources, domestic productivity, governmental systems, and, too often, by international competition and conflict.

References

Adams, A. S., Zhang, F., Mah, C., Grant, R. W., Kleinman, K., Meigs, J. B., et al. (2005). Race differences in long-term diabetes management in an HMO. *Diabetes Care, 28*, 2844–2849.

Adams, P. F., Lucas, J. W., Barnes, P. M., & National Center for Health Statistics. (2008). Summary health statistics for the U.S. Population: National health interview survey 2006. *Vital and Health Statistics, series 10*(236), 1–113.

Allen, J. D., Kennedy, M., Wilson-Glover, A., & Gilligan, T. D. (2007). African-American men's perceptions about prostate cancer: Implications for designing educational interventions. *Social Science & Medicine, 64*, 2189–2200.

Alzheimer's Association – Lotsa Helping Hands. (2008). Retrieved June 10, 2008, from http://www.alz.org/we_can_help_lotsa_helping_hands.asp

Alzheimer's Disease Education & Referral Center. (2003). *Detailed questions and answers about the women's health initiative and the women's health initiative memory study*. Retrieved September 1, 2008, from http://www.alzheimers.org/nianews/detailedQ&A56.htm

Alzheimer's Disease International. (2006). *Dementia in the Asia Pacific region: The epidemic is here*. Retrieved from http://www.alz.co.uk/research/files/apreport.pdf

American Cancer Society. (2008). *Cancer facts & figures, 2008*. Retrieved July 20, 2008, from http://www.cancer.org/downloads/STT/2008CAFFfinalsecured.pdf

Badger, L. W., Berbaum, M., Carney, P. A., Dietrich, A. J., Owen, M., & Stem, J. T. (1999). Physician-patient gender and the recognition and treatment of depression in primary care. *Journal of Social Service Research, 25*(3), 21–39.

Barsky, A. J., Peekna, H. M., & Borus, J. F. (2001). Somatic symptom reporting in women and men. *Journal of General Internal Medicine, 16*, 266–275.

Beck, R. S., Daughtridge, R., & Sloane, P. D. (2002). Physician-patient communication in the primary care office: A systematic review. *Journal of the American Board of Family Medicine, 15*, 25–38.

Bennett, C. L., Ferreira, M. R., Davis, T. C., Kaplan, J., Weinberger, M., Kuzel, T., et al. (1998). Relation between literacy, race, and stage of presentation among low-income patients with prostate cancer. *Journal of Clinical Oncology, 16*, 3101–3104.

Berger, J. M., Levant, R., McMillan, K. K., Kelleher, W., & Sellers, A. (2005). Impact of gender role conflict, traditional masculinity ideology, alexithymia, and age on men's attitudes toward psychological help seeking. *Psychology of Men & Masculinity, 6*, 73–78.

Boston Women's Health Book Collective. (Ed.). (1971). *Our bodies ourselves*. New York: Simon & Schuster.

Box, T. L., Olsen, M., Oddone, E. Z., & Keitz, S. A. (2003). Healthcare access and utilization by patients infected with human immunodeficiency virus: Does gender matter? *Journal of Women's Health, 12*, 391–397.

Brackbill, R. M., Sternberg, M. R., & Fishbein, M. (1999). Where do people go for treatment of sexually transmitted diseases? *Family Planning Perspectives, 31*, 10–15.

Brown, A. F., Gregg, E. W., Stevens, M. R., Karter, A. J., Weinberger, M., Safford, M. M., et al. (2005). Race, ethnicity, socioeconomic position, and quality of care for adults with diabetes enrolled in managed care. *Diabetes Care, 28*, 2864–2870.

Burns, S. M., & Mahalik, J. R. (2008). Treatment type and emotional control as predictors of men's self-assessed physical well-being following treatment for prostate cancer. *Psychology of Men & Masculinity, 9*, 55–66.

Burton, L. C., German, P. S., Gruber-Baldini, A. L., Hebel, J. R., Zimmerman, S., & Magaziner, J. (2001). Medical care for nursing home residents: Differences by dementia status. *Journal of the American Geriatrics Society, 49*, 142–147.

Bylund, C. L., & Makoul, G. (2002). Empathic communication and gender in the physician-patient encounter. *Patient Education and Counseling, 48,* 207–216.

California Medi-Cal Type 2 Diabetes Study Group. (2004). Closing the gap: Effect of diabetes case management on glycemic control among low-income ethnic minority populations. *Diabetes Care, 27,* 95–103.

Canadian Research Institute for the Advancement of Women (CIRAW). (2006). *Intersectional feminist frameworks: An emerging vision.* Retrieved November 16, 2008, from http://www.criaw-icref.ca/CRIAW%20Focus/The%20IFFs-%20An%20Emerging%20Vision_e.pdf

Centers for Disease Control and Prevention. (2004). *National nursing home survey.* Retrieved November 9, 2008, from http://www.cdc.gov/nchs/about/major/nnhsd/ResidentTables.htm

Centers for Disease Control and Prevention. (2005). *Diabetes complications.* Retrieved August 8, 2008, from http://www.cdc.gov/diabetes/statistics/complications_national.htm

Centers for Disease Control and Prevention. (2006). *STD surveillance, 2006.* Retrieved August 2, 2008, from http://www.cdc.gov/std/stats/trends2006.htm

Centers for Disease Control and Prevention. (2007). *Search for diabetes in youth.* Retrieved November 9, 2008, from http://www.cdc.gov/diabetes/projects/diab_children.htm

Centers for Disease Control and Prevention. (2008). *Estimates of new HIV infections in the United States.* Retrieved August 3, 2008, from http://www.cdc.gov/hiv/topics/surveillance/resources/factsheets/incidence.htm

Cherry, D. K., Woodwell, D. A., Rechtsteiner, E. A., & National Center for Health Statistics. (2007). National ambulatory medical care survey: 2005 summary. *Advance Data from Vital and Health Statistics, 29*(387), 1–40.

Chrisler, J. C., Rose, J. G., Dutch, S. E., Sklarsky, K. G., & Grant, M. C. (2006). The pms illusion: Social cognition maintains social construction. *Sex Roles, 54,* 371–376.

Chu, C., & Selwyn, P. A. (2008). Current health disparities in HIV/AIDS. *AIDS Reader, 18,* 144–146, 152–158.

Courtenay, W. H. (2000). Engendering health: A social constructionist examination of men's health beliefs and behaviors. *Psychology of Men & Masculinity, 1,* 4–15.

Courtenay, W. H., McCreary, D. R., & Merighi, J. R. (2002). Gender and ethnic differences in health beliefs and behaviors. *Journal of Health Psychology, 7,* 219–231.

Crimmel, B. L. (2007a). *Co-pays and coinsurance percentages for employer-sponsored health insurance in the private sector, by firm size classification, 2002–2005. [Statistical brief #189. November 2007. Medical Expenditure Panel Survey. Agency for Healthcare Research and Quality].* Retrieved July 21, 2008, from http://www.meps.ahrq.gov/mepsweb/data_files/publications/st189/stat189.pdf

Crimmel, B. L. (2007b). *Deductibles for employer-sponsored health insurance in the private sector, by firm size classification, 2002–2005.[Medical Expenditure Panel Survey. Agency for Healthcare Research and Quality].* Retrieved November 10, 2008, from http://www.meps.ahrq.gov/mepsweb/data_files/publications/st190/stat190.pdf

Crooks, R., & Baur, K. (2005). *Our sexuality* (9th ed.). Belmont, CA: Wadsworth.

Csillag, C. (2005). Radiotherapy after mastectomy more common in men. *Lancet Oncology, 6,* 547–547.

de Perrot, M., Licker, M., Bouchardy, C., Usel, M., Robert, J., & Spiliopoulos, A. (2000). Sex differences in presentation, management, and prognosis of patients with non-small cell lung carcinoma. *Journal of Thoracic and Cardiovascular Surgery, 119,* 21–26.

DeFrances, C. J., Cullen, K. A., Kozak, L. J., & National Center for Health Statistics. (2007). National hospital discharge survey: 2005 annual summary with detailed diagnosis and procedure data. *Vital and Health Statistics, series 13*(165), 1–218.

DeFrances, C. J., Hall, M. J., & National Center for Health Statistics. (2007). National hospital discharge survey 2005. *Advance Data from Vital and Health Statistics, 13*(385), 1–20.

Dixon-Woods, M., Stokes, T., Young, B., Phelps, K., Windridge, K., & Shukla, R. (2001). Choosing and using services for sexual health: A qualitative study of women's views. *Sexually Transmitted Infections, 77,* 335–339.

Donovan, J. M., & Syngal, S. (1998). Colorectal cancer in women: An underappreciated but preventable risk. *Journal of Women's Health, 7,* 45–48.

Dreifus, C. (Ed.). (1977). *Seizing our bodies.* New York: Vintage Books.

Ehrenreich, B., & English, D. (1973). *Complaints and disorders: The sexual politics of sickness.* New York: Feminist Press.

Espey, D. K., Wu, X. C., Swan, J., Wiggins, C., Jim, M. A., Ward, E., et al. (2007). Annual report to the nation on the status of cancer, 1975–2004, featuring cancer in American Indians and Alaska Natives. *Cancer, 110,* 2119–2152.

Finer, L. B., Darroch, J. E., & Frost, J. J. (2003). Services for men at publicly funded family planning agencies, 1998–1999. *Perspectives on Sexual and Reproductive Health, 35,* 202–207.

Finkelstein, E. A., Bray, J. W., Chen, H., Larson, M. J., Miller, K., Tompkins, C., et al. (2003). Prevalence and costs of major depression among elderly claimants with diabetes. *Diabetes Care, 26,* 415–420.

Fisher, B., Anderson, S., Redmond, C. K., Wolmark, N., Wickerham, D. L., & Cronin, W. M. (1995). Reanalysis and results after 12 years of follow-up in a randomized clinical trial comparing total mastectomy with lumpectomy with or without irradiation in the treatment of breast cancer. *New England Journal of Medicine, 333*, 1456–1461.

Fleishman, J. A., & Hellinger, F. H. (2003). Recent trends in HIV-related inpatient admissions 1996–2000: A 7-state study. *Journal of Acquired Immune Deficiency Syndrome, 34*, 102–110.

Frost, J. J. (2006, September). *Source of contraceptive and reproductive health services: 2002 national survey of family growth*. Paper presented at the Title X Family Planning Program Grantee Meeting: Policy, Research, and Service. Sponsored by the Office of Population Affairs (OPA), Office of Family Planning, (OPA/OFP).

Frytak, J. R., Henk, H. J., Zhao, Y., Bowman, L., Flynn, J. A., & Nelson, M. (2008). Health service utilization among alzheimer's disease patients: Evidence from managed care. *Alzheimer's & Dementia, 4*, 361–367.

Gebo, K., Fleishman, J., Conviser, R., Reilly, E., Korthuis, P., Moore, R., et al. (2005). Racial and gender disparities in receipt of highly active antiretroviral therapy persist in a multistate sample of HIV patients in 2001. *Journal of Acquired Immune Deficiency Syndrome, 38*, 96–103.

Gessert, C. E., Haller, I. V., Kane, R. L., & Degenholtz, H. (2006). Rural-urban differences in medical care for nursing home residents with severe dementia at the end of life. *Journal of the American Geriatrics Society, 54*, 1199–1205.

Gillian, G. T., Wang, P. S., Levin, R., Kantoff, P. W., & Avorn, J. (2004). Racial differences in screening for prostate cancer in the elderly. *Archives of Internal Medicine, 164*, 1858–1864.

Graves, E. J., Gillum, B. S., & National Center for Health Statistics. (1997). National hospital discharge survey: 1994 annual summary. *Vital and Health Statistics, 13*(128), 1–59.

Greenberg-Dotan, S., Reuveni, H., Simon-Tuval, T., Oksenberg, A., & Tarasiuk, A. (2007). Gender differences in morbidity and health care utilization among adult obstructive sleep apnea patients. *Sleep, 30*, 1173–1180.

Harris, M. I. (1999). Racial and ethnic differences in health insurance coverage for adults with diabetes. *Diabetes Care, 22*, 1679–1682.

Harris, M. I. (2001). Racial and ethnic differences in health care access and health outcomes for adults with type 2 diabetes. *Diabetes Care, 24*, 454–459.

Harris, M. I., Eastman, R. C., Cowie, C. C., Flegal, K. M., & Eberhardt, M. S. (1999). Racial and ethnic differences in glycemic control of adults with type 2 diabetes. *Diabetes Care, 22*, 403–408.

Heller, A. (2006). *The great dichotomy: Breast cancer versus prostate cancer*. Retrieved November 11, 2008, from http://www.associatedcontent.com/article/80165/the_great_dichotomy_breast_cancer_versus.html

Hinchliff, S., Gott, M., & Galena, E. (2004). GPs' perceptions of the gender-related barriers to discussing sexual health in consultations: A qualitative study. *European Journal of General Practice, 10*(2), 56–60.

Johnson, J. A., Pohar, S. L., & Majumdar, S. R. (2006). Health care utilization and costs in the decade after identification of type 1 and type 2 diabetes. *Diabetes Care, 29*, 2403–2408.

Jones, R. A., Underwood, S. M., & Rivers, B. M. (2007). Reducing prostate cancer morbidity and mortality in African American men: Issues and challenges. *Clinical Journal of Oncology Nursing, 11*, 865–872.

Kalmuss, D., & Tatum, C. (2007). Patterns of men's use of sexual and reproductive health services. *Perspectives on Sexual and Reproductive Health, 39*(2), 74–78.

Karoly, P., Ruehlman, L. S., & Lanyon, R. I. (2005). The assessment of adult health care orientations: Development and preliminary validation of the Multidimensional Health Profile-Health Functioning Index (MHP-H) in a national sample. *Journal of Clinical Psychology in Medical Settings, 12*(1), 79–91.

Kaur, S., Stechuchak, K. M., Coffman, C. J., Allen, K. D., & Bastian, L. A. (2007). Gender differences in health care utilization among veterans with chronic pain. *Journal of General Internal Medicine, 22*, 228–233.

Klabunde, C. N., Potosky, A. L., Harlan, L. C., & Kramer, B. S. (1998). Trends and Black/White differences in treatment for nonmetastatic prostate cancer. *Medical Care, 36*, 1337–1348.

Klarenbach, S. W., & Jacobs, P. (2003). International comparison of health resource utilization in subjects with diabetes. *Diabetes Care, 26*, 1116–1122.

Klebanov, P. K., & Jemmott, J. B. (1992). Effects of expectations and bodily sensations on self-reports of premenstrual symptoms. *Psychology of Women Quarterly, 16*, 289–310.

Kozak, L. J., DeFrances, C. J., Hall, M. J., & National Center for Health Statistics. (2006). National hospital discharge survey: 2004 annual summary with detailed diagnosis and procedure data. *Vital and Health Statistics, 13*(162), 1–218.

Kung, H. C., Hoyert, D. L., Xu, J., & Murphy, S. L. (2008). Deaths: Final data for 2005. *National Vital Statistics Report, 56*(10), 1–121, from http://www.cdc.gov/nchs/data/nvsr/nvsr156/nvsr156_110.pdf

Landrine, H. (Ed.). (1995). *Bringing cultural diversity to feminist psychology: Theory, research, and practice*. Washington, DC: American Psychological Association.

Levant, R. F., Good, G. E., Cook, S. W., O'Neil, J. M., Smalley, K., Owen, K., et al. (2006). The Normative Male Alexithymia Scale: Measurement of a gender-linked syndrome. *Psychology of Men & Masculinity, 7,* 212–224.

Levant, R. F., Richmond, K., Majors, R. G., Inclan, J. E., Rossello, J. M., Heesacker, M., et al. (2003). A multicultural investigation of masculinity ideology and alexithymia. *Psychology of Men & Masculinity, 4,* 91–99.

Levinson, W., Gorawara-Bhat, R., Dueck, R., Egener, B., Kao, A., Kerr, C., et al. (1999). Resolving disagreements in the patient-physician relationship: Tools for improving communication in managed care. *Journal of the American Medical Association, 282,* 1477–1483.

Lurie, N., Slater, J., McGovern, P., Ekstrum, J., Quam, L., & Margolis, K. (1993). Preventive care for women – does the sex of the physician matter? *New England Journal of Medicine, 329,* 478–482.

Maloney, N., Koch, M., Erb, D., Schneider, H., Goffman, T., Elkins, D., et al. (2006). Impact of race on breast cancer in lower socioeconomic status women. *Breast Journal, 12*(1), 58–62.

McCall, D. T., Sauaia, A., Hamman, R. F., Reusch, J. E., & Barton, P. (2004). Are low-income elderly patients at risk for poor diabetes care? *Diabetes Care, 27,* 1060–1065.

McKeever, T. M., Weston, P. J., Hubbard, R., & Fogarty, A. (2005). Lung function and glucose metabolism: An analysis of data from the third National Health and Nutrition Examination Survey. *American Journal of Epidemiology, 161,* 546–556.

McMahon, L. F., Jr., Wolfe, R. A., Huang, S., Tedeschi, P., Manning, W., Jr., & Edlund, M. J. (1999). Racial and gender variation in use of diagnostic colonic procedures in the Michigan Medicare population. *Medical Care, 37,* 712–717.

McWilliams, J. M., Meara, E., Zaslavsky, A. M., & Ayanian, J. Z. (2007). Health of previously uninsured adults after acquiring Medicare coverage. *Journal of the American Medical Association, 298,* 2886–2894.

Middleton, K. R., Hing, E., & Xu, J. (2007). National Hospital Ambulatory Medical Care Survey: 2005 outpatient department summary. *Advance Data from Vital and Health Statistics, 13*(389), 1–35. Retrieved from http://www.cdc.gov/nchs/data/ad/ad389.pdf

Miranda, J., & Cooper, L. A. (2004). Disparities in care for depression among primary care patients. *Journal of General Internal Medicine, 19,* 120–126.

Mortality Trends for Selected Smoking-Related Cancers and Breast Cancer – United States, 1950–1990. (1993). *Morbidity and Mortality Weekly Report, 42,* 863–866.

Munch, S. (2006). The women's health movement: Making policy, 1970–1995. *Social Work in Health Care, 43*(1), 17–32.

Musen, G., Lyoo, I. K., Sparks, C. R., Weinger, K., Hwang, J., Ryan, C. M., et al. (2006). Effects of type 1 diabetes on gray matter density as measured by voxel-based morphometry. *Diabetes, 55,* 326–333.

Nathanson, C. (1977). Sex, illness, and medical care: A review of data, theory, and methods. *Social Science and Medicine, 11,* 13–25.

National Cancer Institute. (2006). Cancer research funding. *National Cancer Institute: Fact Sheet.* Retrieved September 1, 2008, from www.cancer.gov/cancertopics/factsheet/NCI/research-funding

National Cancer Institute. (2008). *Prostate cancer treatment.* Retrieved September 1, 2008, from www.cancer.gov/cancertopics/pdq/treatment/prostate/Patient/page4

National Center for Health Statistics. (1999). *New data show AIDS patients less likely to be hospitalized.* Retrieved August 2, 2008, from http://www.cdc.gov/nchs/pressroom/99news/97nhds.htm

National Center for Health Statistics. (2007). *Health United States, 2007 with chartbook on trends in the health of Americans.* Retrieved August 2, 2008, from http://www.cdc.gov/nchs/data/hus/hus07.pdf

National Diabetes Education Program. (2008). Retrieved May 10, 2008, from http://www.cdc.gov/diabetes/ndep/workgroups.htm

National Diabetes Fact Sheet. (2007). *General information and national estimates on diabetes in the United States.* Retrieved November 8, 2008, from http://www.cdc.gov/diabetes/pubs/pdf/ndfs_2007.pdf

National Diabetes Statistics. (2005). Retrieved May 10, 2008, from http://diabetes.niddk.nih.gov/dm/pubs/statistics/index.htm#7

National Institutes of Health. (2007). *Alzheimer's disease medications fact sheet.* Retrieved November 9, 2008, from http://www.nia.nih.gov/NR/rdonlyres/5178456B-4E16-4A71-A704-46637C6FE61B/8734/Alzheimers_Disease_Medications_Factsheet1107.pdf

National Institutes of Health Revitalization Act of 1993: Clinical Research Equity Regarding Women and Minorities. (1993). Retrieved September 3, 2008, from http://orwh.od.nih.gov/inclusion/revitalization.pdf

Norris, S. L., Engelgau, M. M., & Narayan, K. M. V. (2001). Effectiveness of self-management training in type 2 diabetes. *Diabetes Care, 24,* 561–587.

Nurnberg, H. G., Hensley, P. L., Heiman, J. R., Croft, H. A., Debattista, C., & Paine, S. (2008). Sildenafil treatment of women with antidepressant-associated sexual dysfunction: A randomized controlled trial. *Journal of the American Medical Association, 300*, 395–404.

Nurnberg, H. G., Hensley, P. L., Lauriello, J., Parker, L. M., & Keith, S. J. (1999). Sildenafil for women patients with antidepressant-induced sexual dysfunction. *Psychiatric Services, 50*, 1076–1078.

O'Malley, M. S., Earp, J. A., Hawley, S. T., Schell, M. J., Mathews, H. F., & Mitchell, J. (2001). The association of race/ethnicity, socioeconomic status, and physician recommendation for mammography: Who gets the message about breast cancer screening? *American Journal of Public Health, 91*, 49–54.

Ofotokun, I., Chuck, S. K., & Hitti, J. E. (2007). Antiretroviral pharmacokinetic profile: A review of sex differences. *Gender Medicine, 4*(2), 106–119.

Olak, J., & Colson, Y. (2004). Gender differences in lung cancer: Have we really come a long way, baby? *Journal of Thoracic and Cardiovascular Surgery, 128*, 346–351.

Olfson, M., Marcus, S. C., Druss, B., Elinson, L., Tanielian, T., & Pincus, H. A. (2002). National trends in the outpatient treatment of depression. *Journal of the American Medical Association, 287*, 203–209.

Olfson, M., Marcus, S. C., Druss, B., & Pincus, H. A. (2002). National trends in the use of outpatient psychotherapy. *American Journal of Psychiatry, 159*, 1914–1920.

Otto, S. J., Fracheboud, J., Looman, C. W., Broeders, M. J., Boer, R., Hendriks, J. H., et al. (2003). Initiation of population-based mammography screening in Dutch municipalities and effect on breast-cancer mortality: A systematic review. *Lancet, 361*, 1411–1417.

Paganini-Hill, A., & Henderson, V. W. (1994). Estrogen deficiency and risk of Alzheimer's disease in women. *Journal of Epidemiology, 140*, 256–261.

Palella, F. J., Delaney, K. M., Moorman, A. C., Loveless, M. O., Fuhrer, J., Satten, G. A., et al. (1998). Declining morbidity and mortality among patients with advanced human immunodeficiency virus infection. *New England Journal of Medicine, 338*, 853–860.

Peleg-Oren, N., Sherer, M., & Soskolne, V. (2003). Effect of gender on the social and psychological adjustment of cancer patients. *Social Work in Health Care, 37*(3), 17–34.

Pincus, H. A., Tanielian, T. L., Marcus, S. C., Olfson, M., Zarin, D. A., Thompson, J., et al. (1998). Prescribing trends in psychotropic medications: Primary care, psychiatry, and other medical specialties. *Journal of the American Medical Association, 279*, 526–531.

Plassman, B. L., Langa, K. M., Fisher, G. G., Heeringa, S. G., Weir, D. R., Ofstedal, M. B., et al. (2007). Prevalence of dementia in the United States: The aging, demographics, and memory study. *Neuroepidemiology, 29*, 125–132.

Pleis, J. R., & Lethbridge-Cejku, M. (2007). Summary health statistics for U.S. Adults: National health interview survey, 2006. *Vital and Health Statistics, 10*(235), 1–153.

Podolsky, D. K. (2000). Going the distance – the case for true colorectal-cancer screening. *New England Journal of Medicine, 343*, 207–208.

Popovic, J. R., Kozak, L. J., & National Center for Health Statistics. (2000). National hospital discharge survey. 1998 annual summary with detailed diagnosis and procedure data. *Vital and Health Statistics, 13*(148), 1–203.

Popovic, J. R., & National Center for Health Statistics. (2001). National hospital discharge survey. 1999 annual summary with detailed diagnosis and procedure data. *Vital and Health Statistics, series 13*(151), 1–214.

Potosky, A. L., Merrill, R. M., Riley, G. F., Taplin, S. H., Barlow, W., Fireman, B. H., et al. (1999). Prostate cancer treatment and ten-year survival among group/staff HMO and fee-for-service Medicare patients – health maintenance organization. *Health Services Research, 34*, 525–546.

Raofi, S., & Schappert, S. M. (2006). Medication therapy in ambulatory medical care: United States, 2003–04. *Vital and Health Statistics, 13*(163), 1–48.

Reis, L. A. G., Melbert, D., Krapcho, M., Stinchcomb, D. G., Howlader, N., Horner, M. J., et al. (2008). *Breast cancer SEER stat fact sheets.* [SEER cancer statistics review, 1975–2005, based on November 2007 SEER data submission, posted 2008. Division of cancer control and population sciences, National Cancer Institute]. Retrieved November 9, 2008, from http://seer.cancer.gov/statfacts/html/breast.html

Richardson, S. S., Sullivan, G., Hill, A., & Yu, W. (2007). Use of aggressive medical treatments at the end of life: Differences between patients with and without dementia. *Health Research and Educational Trust, 42*, 183–200.

Robbins, A. S., Whittemore, A. S., & Van Den Eeden, S. K. (1998). Race, prostate cancer survival, and membership in a large health maintenance organization. *Journal of the National Cancer Institute, 90*, 986–990.

Robbins, A. S., Yin, D., & Parikh-Patel, A. (2007). Differences in prognostic factors and survival among White men and Black men with prostate cancer, California, 1995–2004. *American Journal of Epidemiology, 166*, 71–78.

Roe, C. M., McNamara, A. M., & Motheral, B. R. (2002). Gender- and age-related prescription drug use patterns. *Annals of Pharmacotherapy, 36*, 30–39.

Rosemann, T., Laux, G., & Szecsenyi, J. (2007). Osteoarthritis: Quality of life, comorbidities, medication, and health service utilization assessed in a large sample of primary care patients. *Journal of Orthopaedic Surgery and Research, 2,* 1–9.

Rosen, A. B., & Schneider, E. C. (2004). Colorectal cancer screening disparities related to obesity and gender. *Journal of General Internal Medicine, 19,* 332–338.

Roter, D. L., & Hall, J. A. (1998). Why physician gender matters in shaping the physician-patient relationship. *Journal of Women's Health, 7,* 1093–1097.

Ruble, D. N. (1977). Premenstrual symptoms: A reinterpretation. *Science, 197,* 291–292.

Ruzek, S. (1978). *The women's health movement: Feminist alternatives to medical control.* New York: Praeger.

Sadetsky, N., Lubeck, D., Latini, D. M., Pasta, D. J., Kayakami, J., DuChane, J., et al. (2005). Demographics, insurance coverage, and utilization of medical services in newly diagnosed prostate cancer – data from CaPSURE. *Managed Care Interface, 18,* 25–30.

Scalliet, P. G. M., & Kirkove, C. (2007). Breast cancer in elderly women: Can radiotherapy be omitted? *European Journal of Cancer, 43,* 2264–2269.

Schiller, J. S., Kramarow, E. A., & Dey, A. N. (2007). Fall injury episodes among noninstitutionalized older adults: United States, 2001–2003. *Advance Data from Vital and Health Statistics, 21*(392), 1–16.

Shapiro, M. F., Morton, S. C., McCaffrey, D. F., Senterfitt, J. W., Fleishman, J. A., Perlman, J. F., et al. (1999). Variations in the care of HIV-infected adults in the United States: Results from the HIV cost and services utilization study. *Journal of the American Medical Association, 281,* 2305–2315.

Shugarman, L. R., Bird, C. E., Schuster, C. R., & Lynn, J. (2008). Age and gender differences in medicare expenditures and service utilization at the end of life for lung cancer decedents. *Womens Health Issues, 18,* 199–209.

Stewart, J. H., Bertoni, A. G., Staten, J. L., Levine, E. A., & Gross, C. P. (2007). Participation in surgical oncology clinical trials: Gender-, race/ethnicity-, age-based disparities. *Annals of Surgical Oncology, 14,* 3328–3334.

Stone, K. J., Viera, A. J., & Parman, C. L. (2003). Off-label applications for SSRIs. *American Family Physician, 68,* 498–504.

Street, R. L., Jr., Krupat, E., Bell, R. A., Kravitz, R. L., & Haidet, P. (2003). Beliefs about control in the physician-patient relationship: Effect on communication in medical encounters. *Journal of General Internal Medicine, 18,* 609–616.

Tabar, L., Yen, M. F., Vitak, B., Chen, H. H., Smith, R. A., & Duffy, S. W. (2003). Mammography service screening and mortality in breast cancer patients: 20-year follow-up before and after introduction of screening. *Lancet, 361,* 1405–1410.

Travis, C. B. (1988). *Women and health psychology: Mental health issues.* Hillsdale, NJ: Erlbaum.

Travis, C. B. (2005). Heart disease and gender inequity. *Psychology of Women Quarterly, 29,* 15–23.

Travis, C. B., & Meltzer, A. L. (2008). Women's health: Biological and social systems. In F. L. Denmark & M. A. Paludi (Eds.), *Psychology of women: A handbook of issues and theories* (2nd ed., pp. 353–399). Westport, CT: Praeger.

U.S. Cancer Statistics Working Group. (2007). *United States cancer statistics: 1999–2004, incidence and mortality web-based report.* Retrieved August 27, 2008, from www.cdc.gov/uscs

U.S. Census Bureau. (2007a). *Annual social and economic supplements: Historical health insurance tables.* Retrieved July 12, 2008, from http://www.census.gov/hhes/www/hlthins/historic/hihistt1.htm

U.S. Census Bureau. (2007b). *Health insurance coverage: 2007 highlights.* Retrieved September 15, 2008, from http://www.census.gov/hhes/www/hlthins/hlthin07/hlth07asc.html

U.S. Department of Defense. (2008). *Current research programs.* Retrieved September 1, 2008, from http://cdmrp.army.mil/

Underwood, W., De Monner, S., Ubel, P., Fagerline, A., Sanda, M. G., & Wei, J. T. (2004). Racial/ethnic disparities in the treatment of localized/regional prostate cancer. *Journal of Urology, 171,* 1504–1507.

Verbrugge, L. M. (1995). Women, men, and osteoarthritis. *Arthritis Care and Research, 8,* 212–220.

Verbrugge, L. M., & Juarez, L. (2001). Profile of arthritis disability. *Public Health Reports, 116* (Suppl. 1), 157–179.

West, C. (1993). Reconceptualizing gender in physician-patient relationships. *Social Science & Medicine, 36,* 57–66.

World Health Organization. (2004). *Scaling up antiretroviral therapy in resource-limited settings: Treatment guidelines for a public health approach.* Retrieved September 3, 2008, from http://www.who.int/hiv/pub/prev_care/en/arvrevision2003en.pdf

Zimmerman, M. K. (1987). The women's health movement: A critique of medical enterprise and the position of women. In B. B. Hess & M. M. Ferree (Eds.), *Analyzing gender: A handbook of social science research* (pp. 442–472). Thousand Oaks, CA: Sage.

Zuckerman, D. (2008). *Mastectomy v. lumpectomy: Who decides?* Retrieved August 11, 2008, from http://www.center4research.org/bc071502.html

Chapter 23
Gender Issues in the Diagnosis and Treatment of Chronic Illness

Vivian S. Hwang and Sharon Danoff-Burg

Chronic illness will more than likely touch each one of us through the course of our lifetimes, whether directly or indirectly. In the United States, 7 of every 10, or more than 1.7 million, people die each year due to a chronic illness (Centers for Disease Control and Prevention [CDC], 2008a), and 1 of every 10, or 25 million, people experience major disabilities and limitations in activity due to the course and symptoms of chronic diseases (CDC, 2008a). According to the Global Burden of Disease study conducted by the World Health Organization (WHO, 2008a) in 2004, non-communicable diseases accounted for 6 of every 10 deaths worldwide. The debilitating effects of chronic illnesses and their treatments lead to a decreased quality of life for men and women who suffer from chronic conditions, as well as for their families, spouses, and friends.

As the prevalence rates of chronic diseases have shifted in the last century, heart disease and stroke have gained the top and third positions in leading causes of death for Americans (Anderson & Smith, 2005). Cardiovascular diseases are also the leading cause of death worldwide, approximately 32% of all deaths in women and 27% in men (WHO, 2008a). Of the estimated 59 million deaths worldwide in 2004, almost 13 million were caused by either coronary heart disease or some form of cerebrovascular disease (WHO, 2008a).

In the United States, cancer is the second leading cause of death (Anderson & Smith, 2005). Contrary to popular perceptions, lung cancer accounts for the most cancer-related deaths in both men and women, and an estimated 161,840 lung cancer deaths (29% of all cancer deaths) were expected to occur in 2008 (American Cancer Society, 2008). Rates of death among men with lung cancer have decreased since 1990; however, rates among women have continued to increase through the decades, though the prediction is that rates will reach a plateau. Lung cancer consistently has accounted for more cancer-related deaths in women than has breast cancer since 1987. Prostate and breast cancers account for the most estimated new cases of cancer for men and women, respectively, whereas lung cancer accounts for the second most new cases, and colorectal cancers rank third for both women and men.

Some of these patterns change when researchers include rates in the developing areas of the world, although lung cancer still accounts for the most deaths worldwide; stomach and liver cancers follow (Mackay, Jemal, Lee, & Parkin, 2006). The estimated number of cancer-related deaths in 2002 across the world was 7 million, and by 2020 it is projected that more than 16 million new cancer cases will emerge and lead to 10 million expected deaths (Mackay et al., 2006). Lung, breast, colorectal, stomach, and prostate cancers are the most common worldwide in terms of new cases and deaths, though there are gender differences. Breast and cervical tumors are most common in women,

---

V.S. Hwang (✉)
University at Albany, State University of New York, Albany, NY, USA

except in some areas of east Asia, where stomach cancers are prevalent. For men, lung and prostate cancers dominate, although liver cancer is prevalent in some parts of Africa and Asia. Lung cancer still remains, across genders, the most common cancer, both in terms of new cases and deaths, and 80% of lung cancer cases in men and women are caused by tobacco smoking (Mackay et al., 2006).

Age-adjusted morbidity and mortality rates for cardiovascular disease (CVD), cancer, and diabetes are higher for men than for women (Kung, Hoyert, Xu, & Murphy, 2008). Men are more likely to die from these diseases, and sooner, than women, whereas women are more likely to live with these chronic conditions for many years in later life. In addition, other chronic illnesses, such as autoimmune disorders, which include over 80 separate conditions, affect women more than men in terms of overall prevalence. A single prevalence rate for all of these conditions is unavailable, as epidemiology studies tend to focus on reports of separate diseases (National Institutes of Health [NIH], 2003). Jacobson, Gange, Rose, and Graham (1997) reviewed studies of 24 autoimmune disorders in the United States and estimated 237,200 new cases in 1996 – approximately 172,700 in women (1.3 for every 1,000 women) and 64,500 in men (0.5 for every 1,000 men). Multiple sclerosis (MS) is an example of an autoimmune disease that is more common in women than in men. In the United States, MS is two to three times more common in women than in men (National Multiple Sclerosis Society, 2008). Globally, this female to male ratio is estimated to be two women for every man diagnosed with MS (WHO, 2008b). Systemic lupus erythematosus (SLE) and rheumatoid arthritis (RA) are other autoimmune diseases that occur at disproportionate rates among women (Petri, 2000; Theis, Helmick, & Hootman, 2007).

One chronic illness that retains prevalence among American men relative to women is HIV/AIDS. In 2006, men were estimated to account for approximately three-quarters of HIV cases in the United States (CDC, 2008b). The epidemic is particularly severe among ethnic minority men and among men of all ethnic groups who have sex with men. It is important to note, however, that the number of cases is estimated to be growing fastest among women, particularly ethnic minority women, relative to other groups. For example, in 2006 the HIV prevalence rate for African American women was nearly 18 times the rate for European American women. According to the World Health Organization (WHO, 2008c), approximately one-half of the people worldwide with HIV are women, and this has been true since the late 1990s. Due to a host of biopsychosocial factors, women and men are differentially affected by the illness. For instance, in sub-Saharan Africa, the area of the world most heavily affected by HIV, women aged 15–59 years have a much higher AIDS mortality rate than do men in the same age range (WHO, 2008a).

Researchers (e.g., Grieg, Peacock, Jewkes, & Msimang, 2008) have emphasized that gender is an essential key to understanding and addressing the global HIV/AIDS epidemic. In their recent article, Grieg et al. (2008) discussed how factors such as violence against women, the practice of transactional sex in the context of poverty, and concepts of masculinity that equate manhood with dominance contribute to the spread and impact of the virus. This perspective has led international HIV/AIDS researchers (see WHO, 2008c) to become concerned about women's limited access to quality education and their economic dependence on men, which has led to interest in microfinance and skills training initiatives. With regard to health services, programs aimed at prevention of mother-to-child transmission are needed, as is comprehensive post-rape health care. A gendered perspective also prioritizes efforts to increase use of HIV services among men, who may be reluctant to seek testing or treatment. With regard to interventions targeting men, Grieg and colleagues also referred to the effectiveness of Promundo, a nongovernmental organization, in challenging normative gender attitudes among Brazilian men in order to increase condom use.

As illustrated in the previous paragraph about HIV/AIDS, any discussion of women's and men's experiences of chronic illness requires more than mere consideration of prevalence and mortality rates. As medical treatments for chronic illnesses advance, more and more people now have to adjust to living with illness. The term *chronic*, therefore, takes on a new, extended meaning; rather than a description of the biological course of the disease, its definition now encompasses the psychological experience of coping with and living with the disease as well (Stanton & Revenson, 2007). Living with a chronic illness is a unique experience for each individual within the context of society and culture. Researchers have investigated and identified gender-specific differences in prevalence, health-care costs, and treatment patterns among men and women with chronic illnesses (Stock, Stollenwerk, Redaelli, Civello, & Lauterbach, 2008), but the psychosocial effects of these differences should also be considered in order to gain a better understanding of the unique experiences that these women and men face.

Disease Knowledge, Screening, and Diagnosis

Disease Knowledge

The general knowledge and perceptions about chronic illnesses held by women and men can affect preventive screening practices and timely diagnosis of an illness. Illnesses such as prostate cancer in men and breast cancer in women are given a wide range of media and medical attention, which affects the risk perceptions held by the public. For instance, McCreary, Gray, and Grace (2006) found that men and women overestimated mortality risks for these two illnesses, as indicated by their beliefs that prostate cancer is the leading cause of death in men and that breast cancer is the leading cause of death in women.

When a population is unaware of the risk factors associated with highly prevalent diseases, health behaviors such as seeking screening, symptom reporting, and timely treatment may be affected. For example, although women tend to have more cardiovascular risk factors than men do, including elevated cholesterol, central obesity (or abdominal obesity, as measured and compared against national standards), and low high-density lipoprotein cholesterol (Ong, Tso, Lam, & Cheung, 2008), most women do not recognize CVD as the leading cause of death among women, and the majority of women report not being well informed about heart disease and stroke or not having effective communication with their health-care providers regarding their cardiovascular health (Hart, 2005; Mosca et al., 2000; Mosca, Ferris, Fabunmi, & Robertson, 2004). This misunderstanding is especially true for younger women; more women aged 25–44 years than women aged 65 or older incorrectly identified breast cancer as the leading cause of death (Mosca et al., 2000). Women are also more likely than men to have uncontrolled hypertension, even if they have been treated (Ostchega, Hughes, Wright, McDowell, & Louis, 2008). Beyond biological factors, researchers posit that this may be explained by many health-care professionals downplaying the cardiovascular risk status of women and being less likely to suggest preventive measures for female patients (Ostchega et al., 2008). The lack of recognition among women and their health-care providers regarding cardiovascular disease risk prompted the assembly of an expert panel by the American Heart Association, which recently published updated, evidence-based guidelines and clinical recommendations for preventing CVD in women, which were grouped into interventions geared toward lifestyle, risk factors, and preventive drugs (Mosca et al., 2007).

Gender differences in CVD knowledge and risk perception are not consistent across the literature, however (Jensen & Moser, 2008). Knowledge and risk perception among women and men may vary across other factors such as ethnicity/race, age, educational level, and perceptions of good health (Pace, Dawkins, Wang, Person, & Shikany, 2008; Tullmann & Dracup, 2005; Victor et al., 2008). For example, Homko et al. (2008) found that participants who were female or from rural areas were more knowledgeable about CVD than were participants who were male or from urban areas. One generally held belief, reported throughout the literature, is that, despite inconsistencies and disparities between groups, overall awareness of CVD risk and knowledge remains low. Educational interventions aimed at increasing awareness of disease risks may motivate lifestyle changes such as diet, exercise, and stress management that will ultimately benefit the health of those at risk for CVD (Daubenmier et al., 2007).

We have used the example of CVD to illustrate lack of disease knowledge and risk perception as related to gender, but it is important to note that this issue is not limited to cardiovascular problems. Cancer risk perception and worry also have been examined with respect to gender difference. Research (McQueen, Vernon, Meissner, & Rakowski, 2008) indicates that men reported higher risk perception, whereas women reported more frequent cancer worry. Thus, similar concerns for other chronic illnesses should be considered, investigated, and brought to public attention as well.

Screening Practices

As noted above, knowledge and perceptions of illness risk may influence health behaviors such as preventive screening for particular diseases. For example, colorectal cancer screening rates remain low in the United States, despite the fact that it is the second leading cause of cancer-related death in American men and women (American Cancer Society, 2008). Lack of awareness and lack of physician recommendation are among the most commonly reported barriers to undergoing colorectal cancer screening (Seeff et al., 2004). Improving colorectal cancer screening rates requires an understanding of factors associated with barriers and facilitators of cancer screening, including gender differences, awareness and risk perceptions, and health-care coverage. Although colorectal cancer screening has increased over the years, men still report higher prevalence of testing for colorectal cancer than women do (Meissner, Breen, Klabunde, & Vernon, 2006). This is a phenomenon that differs from other types of screenings (e.g., mental health, other types of cancer), wherein men report lower rates of screening practices than do women. The distinction may be that colorectal cancer is more traditionally viewed as a man's disease, and therefore, women may be less likely to perceive risk or seek information about screening practices (Podolsky, 2000).

A recent study showed that those who had health insurance were more than twice as likely as those without to be screened for colorectal cancer, though this relation differed by gender (de Bosset, Atashili, Miller, & Pignone, 2008). After they controlled for age and annual household income, the researchers found that men with health insurance were more likely to report colorectal cancer screening than were men without insurance, but this effect did not hold for women. In contrast, Hsia and colleagues (Hsia, Kemper, Kiefe, et al., 2000) found that health insurance status was among the list of positive determinants of screening among women, including mammograms, Pap smears, and colorectal cancer screening. This association was strongest for women under 65 years of age, a finding that may be explained by the fact that older women (i.e., over 65 years of age) in the United States are eligible for Medicare. For the younger women in this sample, a lack of health insurance was associated with a lack of cancer screening. Although the older women in the sample had Medicare, the type of insurance coverage they reported was associated with screening practices. Those who reported that they had Medicare and a prepaid plan were more likely to have had a mammogram than those reporting that they had Medicare and a fee-for-service plan (Hsia, Kemper, Kiefe, et al., 2000). Furthermore, in a sample of older women, health insurance status was found to be a significant determinant of regular health-care provider utilization, even when researchers controlled for perceived health, chronic conditions, and past serious medical illnesses (Hsia, Kemper, Sofaer, et al., 2000).

Body weight may also influence screening practices, and evidence has shown that this association differs by gender (Heo, Allison, & Fontaine, 2004; Rosen & Schneider, 2004). Whereas men who were categorized as either overweight or obese were more likely to have obtained screening for colorectal cancer than were men of normal weight, women who were categorized as obese were less likely than were normal weight women to have obtained screening. Heo et al. (2004) speculated that the gender disparity might have been due to physicians' more vigorous encouragement of cancer screening in their overweight and obese male patients, as well as to differences between women and men in such factors as body image and self-esteem. This could be an important point in understanding barriers to cancer screening, as weight has been shown to be related to higher rates of chronic illnesses.

Early Disease Diagnosis

It is clear that early diagnosis and treatment of illnesses such as hypertension and cancer are important for better health outcomes; however, early detection of some chronic illnesses that disproportionately affect women, such as SLE and RA, is not always possible (Leeb, Weber, & Smolen, 1998). RA often has been considered a relatively benign, "wait and see" disease, but this stance is problematic in light of evidence that aggressive treatment early on in the disease course may lead to better health outcomes, such as functional improvement and less joint damage (Combe, 2007; Egsmose et al., 1995; Fleischmann, Stern, & Iqbal, 2005; Goekoop-Ruiterman et al., 2008). One study (Nell et al., 2004) of the effects of very early therapy with disease-modifying antirheumatic drugs identified a possible optimal window of time in the first year (especially within the first 3 months of therapy) in which treatment for RA is highly successful. As patients with RA experience a substantial increase in work disability (at least 50% are work-disabled within 10 years of disease onset; Weinblatt, 1996), functional status with regard to employment is a major concern. Therefore, studies that show that early diagnosis and treatment of rheumatic disease lead to better functioning and less work disability have important implications for the quality of life of RA patients and their families (Puolakka et al., 2005).

Reaction to Diagnosis

Gender differences in coping with illness generally have been recognized in the literature and are discussed later in this chapter; however, gender differences during the more specific time period directly after illness diagnosis have not been as widely investigated by psychological researchers. Longitudinal research on women and men with lung cancer suggests that gender differences in functioning, particularly emotional functioning, may exist in the time period close to diagnosis and before treatment (Lövgren, Tishelman, Sprangers, Koyi, & Hamberg, 2008). Lövgren et al. (2008) found that women reported more problems and more intensity of problems related to emotional functioning directly after diagnosis than men did, though the emotional and physical functioning of both men and women improved significantly over time.

A qualitative study (McCaughan & McKenna, 2007) of men newly diagnosed with cancer identified men's discomfort in the hospital setting, which affected the extent to which they asked for information regarding their diagnosis. Most of the diagnosis and treatment information received by these men was obtained from the male patients' female relatives. Addis and Mahalik (2003) argued for increasing men's adaptive help-seeking strategies, given that much of the research literature suggests that men are less likely than women to seek professional help. These authors discussed the strengths and weaknesses of research focused on gender-role socialization – in contrast to typical "sex differences" research – in the context of men's help seeking. They posited that men's internalization of masculine norms, such as emotional stoicism and self-reliance, is related to their help-seeking resistance (Addis & Mahalik, 2003).

Rather than ignoring the variable of gender or treating it as statistical covariate, researchers should consider the potential influence of gender on patients' responses to diagnosis. In addition, researchers should attempt to recruit patients closer to the time of diagnosis in order to determine ways in which women and men may differ and how gender-role socialization may affect decision-making related to treatment and coping.

Adjustment to Chronic Illness

Adjustment to chronic illness includes the reaction to an initial diagnosis, as well as the adaptation and level of functioning that follow a diagnosis. The diagnosis of a chronic illness challenges and confronts people with new situations that may require them to adapt and change their habitual coping strategies (de Ridder, Geenen, Kuijer, & van Middendorp, 2008). Several characteristics of adjustment to chronic illness have emerged in the literature (Stanton & Revenson, 2007; Stanton, Revenson, & Tennen, 2007). The nature of adjustment is multifaceted and requires adaptation across all domains of life. Adjustment is a dynamic process that changes and develops over time after diagnosis. Adjustment is also heterogeneous across individuals of different genders, cultures, and diseases. Both positive and negative indicators are relevant to adjustment to chronic illness, though it has not been until recently that the literature has reflected the importance of considering positive indicators.

Stanton, Collins, and Sworowski (2001) outlined at least five ways in which positive adjustment to chronic illness has been conceptualized, whether explicitly or implicitly, in research studies. The first of these is mastery of adaptive, illness-related tasks, such as managing symptoms and pain, navigating the health-care system, communicating with health-care providers, and gathering ample information about the disease and treatment. Taylor (1983) highlighted that an individual's sense of mastery over her or his life as well as a search for meaning in the context of a threatening event are key for successful adjustment. For example, women with RA have described the experience of managing their disorder in terms of developing a sense of mastery in coping with their symptoms, especially in implementing strategies that allow them to carry out gendered roles and tasks (Shaul, 2005). Mastery over these tasks can vary greatly depending upon many individual factors, as well as the patient's experience in the medical system. For example, providers have been shown to be more likely to choose optimal pain treatment for men than for women following surgery, which suggests that gender influences physicians' decision-making (Green & Wheeler, 2003). Such differences in treatment can impact patients' interactions with providers, and qualitative data from women with chronic pain highlight the stigmas and pressure felt by female patients to present themselves and their illness as credible (Werner & Malterud, 2003).

Second, the absence of psychological disorders as a form of positive adjustment in patients with chronic illness has also interested researchers; depression, adjustment disorders, and anxiety disorders have been particularly well-studied with medical samples. Research on depression in chronically ill populations has identified risk factors, including female sex, younger age, particular chronic illnesses, marital/relationship status, disease severity, lack of social support, and family history of depression (Bamer, Cetin, Johnson, Gibbons, & Ehde, 2008; Egede, 2007; Patten, Metz, & Reimer, 2000; Schane, Woodruff, Dinno, Covinsky, & Walter, 2008).

The third conceptualization is the focus on emotion in the experience of chronic illness. Patients' reports of negative affect have received particular attention in the literature on adjustment (Stanton et al., 2001). However, a focus only on depressive symptoms or diminished functioning reveals an incomplete picture of an individual's disease experience and quality of life. If we are to understand the experience of people living with chronic illness, the study of positive adjustment is very important as well (Stanton & Revenson, 2007). Studies have shown that people living with illness report not only positive affect but also personal growth that has resulted from the disease experience; finding benefits in an otherwise negative situation may predict better disease outcomes (e.g., Carver & Antoni, 2004; Danoff-Burg & Revenson, 2005). Understanding patients' perceptions of growth in response to illness may facilitate the specification of protective factors and targeted intervention goals. With regard to the question of whether gender moderates the relation between benefit finding or perceptions of growth and adjustment outcomes, a meta-analytic review was inconclusive in part due to the fact that many of the studies were conducted with samples that were either all male or all female (Helgeson, Reynolds, & Tomich, 2006).

Fourth, researchers have examined how people with chronic illness perceive their quality of life in the face of challenges to various domains, including the physical, social, functional, sexual, and emotional. Women and adolescent girls have been shown to report worse quality of life than men and adolescent boys with a chronic illness (e.g., Arrington-Sanders et al., 2006; Di Marco et al., 2006; van Jaarsveld et al., 2002). For example, McEntee and Badenhop (2000) found that women with cardiopulmonary problems reported significantly lower quality of life than their male counterparts before entering a rehabilitation program, although they made greater gains and improvement than men did after the 12-week program.

Some research has suggested that gender differences in quality of life among chronic illness patients may be a result of women's higher rates of particular health problems (e.g., autoimmune disorders) and also the fact that women, on average, live longer than men and therefore experience more health problems over time (Kaplan, Anderson, & Wingard, 1991). Rather than focusing on base rates, other researchers have emphasized that it is more culturally acceptable for women to voice distress and concerns, whereas men are often expected to deny signs of vulnerability and assume stoicism in the face of the chronic illness experience (Kaplan et al., 1991).

The last of these five conceptualizations of adjustment involves the maintenance of adequate functional status. The degree of functional limitations is an aspect of adjustment that should be considered, as it varies with individual experience. Depending on a person's functioning and goals prior to diagnosis, the level of interference and duration of difficulties can have either minimal or major impact upon adjustment. For example, women in committed romantic partnerships with men are often responsible for the vast majority of household responsibilities whether they have been diagnosed with a chronic illness or not. For a woman with rheumatic disease, bearing the brunt of disproportionate household and family responsibilities can take a physical and emotional toll. These women carry the double burden of managing illness symptoms and household responsibilities (Danoff-Burg & Revenson, 2000), which exemplifies differences in the types or amounts of stressors that women and men coping with chronic illness often face.

Gender Differences in Adjustment to Chronic Illness

Gender Differences in Psychological Adjustment

Findings have been inconsistent regarding gender differences in the association of chronic illness and psychosocial distress. However, much of the research mirrors the differences seen in medically healthy samples, wherein women report more depressive symptoms (e.g., Hagedoorn, Buunk, Kuijer, Wobbes, & Sanderman, 2000; see also Chapter 7).

In a study (Di Marco et al., 2006) of 202 patients with chronic obstructive pulmonary disease (COPD) and 114 age- and sex-matched healthy participants, prevalence of depression and anxiety symptoms in the patient sample was significantly higher (18.8 and 28.2%, respectively) than in the control group (3.5 and 6.1%, respectively). Women with COPD reported higher levels of anxiety and depression and worse symptom-related quality of life than men with COPD. Moreover, the researchers observed a stronger association between depression and dyspnea in women than in men with COPD, which provides some support for a link between psychological adjustment and health status in chronically ill women.

In a study (van Jaarsveld et al., 2002) of men and women with CVD, quality of life was observed to be significantly lower 1 year after diagnosis than it was at premorbid levels. However, quality of life in women was significantly lower than quality of life in men at all assessment periods. One possible explanation for this difference may be that, consistent with other studies, women reported more severe CVD symptoms than did men. In addition, gender differences in quality of life 1 year after diagnosis in this sample were accounted for by women's lower premorbid quality of life, advanced age, and higher number of comorbid conditions.

Although women reported symptoms and greater overall distress more frequently than did men in a sample of 149 cancer patients (Keller & Heinrich, 1999), general satisfaction with life did not differ between genders. Women's distress was related to their physical condition, whereas men's distress was related to their psychological condition. The role of social support also differed between men and women in this study. Men's distress tended to diminish with spousal support, though women's distress was unrelated to spousal support. The researchers suggested that higher distress in women may lead to finding more effective ways of coping and, therefore, result in adjustment comparable to men's with regard to levels of life satisfaction.

A study (Hampton & Frombach, 2000) of cancer patients' experience of traumatic stress during treatment indicated that women experienced the medical environment as more stressful than did men, and the perceived intensity of medical treatment was the principal predictor of higher PTSD scores for the female cancer patients. Although that study demonstrated worse adjustment for women during medical treatment, other studies have indicated that men show poorer adjustment outcomes than women do. For example, a study (Kiviruusu, Huurre, & Aro, 2007) of young adults showed that men with chronic illness (e.g., migraine, asthma, diabetes) were more depressed than a comparison sample of healthy men, but no similar difference was found between depression scores for women with chronic illness and a comparison sample of healthy women. Of the four subgroups examined, men with chronic illness were the most depressed, and healthy men were the least depressed. A study of people with cancer (Peleg-Oren, Sherer, & Soskolne, 2003) showed that men reported more difficulties than women did in social adjustment and psychological distress, especially in dealing with fear, paranoia, anxiety, depression, and hostility, though not all results were statistically significant.

Rather than simply asking which gender shows better adjustment to illness, researchers would be wise to investigate how women and men might respond differently along different dimensions of quality of life. For example, among patients with rectal cancer, women reported worse global health and physical functioning, as well as higher scores on treatment strain and fatigue after surgery, whereas men reported difficulties with sexual enjoyment, which created high levels of strain (Schmidt et al., 2005). Different reactions to illness may be linked with issues of feminine and masculine identity held by patients. Whereas women often articulate their identities along interpersonal lines (e.g., mother, friend), men often conceptualize their identities in terms of strength and independence. Therefore, it is not surprising that chronic illnesses, which involve symptoms that can threaten these valued aspects of identity, may be experienced differently across genders.

For example, Solimeo (2008) showed that, among older adults with Parkinson's disease, women's concerns tended to be related to maintaining social roles and relationships, whereas men were concerned about others' perception of their physical attributes. In addition, the ways in which men and women may view threats to their masculinity or femininity may vary by age, ethnicity, and access to health care. For example, Liburd, Namageyo-Funa, and Jack (2007) discussed how meanings of manhood and masculinity affect African American men coping with Type II diabetes, including their interactions with health-care systems. Werner and Malterud (2003) indicated that some women who struggle with health-care professionals' gendered perceptions of their patients might use the strategy of "overdoing" their symptoms and expressing extreme femininity in order to gain credibility with their doctors.

Although psychosocial distress and psychological disorders, such as depression and PTSD, are associated with disability, pain, and disease severity, the aforementioned studies demonstrate that physical aspects of chronic illness do not fully explain observable gender differences in adjustment. The influences of gender-role socialization, gender-linked personality traits, and interpersonal context should be considered, as individual patients do not adjust to their illness in a vacuum, but rather as active agents in their environments.

Agency and Communion

In recent years, an interesting body of research has emerged regarding the effect of gender-linked personality traits on physical health. In particular, the gender-related traits of agency and communion have received attention, as agency represents one aspect of masculinity and communion represents one aspect of femininity (Bakan, 1966; Spence, 1984). Helgeson (1994) theorized that women and men are socialized to adopt different behavior patterns and social roles, and these differences may enhance or undermine emotional and physical well-being. Specifically, men are more likely to develop characteristics related to agency, defined as a focus on the self and autonomy, whereas women are more likely to develop characteristics related to communion, defined as a focus on other people and relationships. For example, agency includes self-assertion, self-protection, and self-direction, whereas communion involves group participation, cooperation, and the formation of attachments. Of course, men and women may possess both agentic and communal characteristics; nonetheless, women, on average, score higher on measures of communion, and men, on average, score higher on measures of agency (Helgeson, 1994).

Both agency and communion are required for optimal well-being; however, problems may occur when one exists in the absence of the other: agency unmitigated by communion (i.e., unmitigated agency) or communion unmitigated by agency (i.e., unmitigated communion). Unmitigated communion involves focusing on other people's needs to the detriment of one's own well-being, which clearly could have a negative impact on an individual's own psychological and physical health. Similarly, unmitigated agency, which involves a focus on the self to the exclusion of others, can contribute to an individual's poor health. Possible pathways include lack of social support; difficulty expressing emotions; and a level of hostility, arrogance, or psychological reactance that impedes willingness to follow advice from medical professionals or loved ones (Helgeson, 2003; Helgeson & Fritz, 1999).

Indeed, with regard to physical health, negative outcomes have been found among those who score high on unmitigated communion, presumably because these individuals are overinvolved with others and fail to attend to their own needs (Helgeson & Fritz, 1998). For example, unmitigated communion has been linked to poor health behavior among cardiac patients as measured by an index of smoking, exercise, diet, stress, and relaxation (Helgeson & Fritz, 1999). In addition, unmitigated communion has been associated with low adherence to physicians' instructions among cardiac patients (Fritz, 2000; Helgeson, 1993), functional disability among adults with RA (Trudeau, Danoff-Burg, Revenson, & Paget, 2003), and poor metabolic control among adolescents with diabetes (Helgeson & Fritz, 1996; Helgeson, Escobar, Siminerio, & Becker, 2007). Patients with chronic illness who have high levels of unmitigated communion may feel deprived of the opportunity to care for others (e.g., Danoff-Burg, Revenson, Trudeau, & Paget, 2004). During the onset of recovery, they are likely to neglect their own health as they attempt to restore their caregiving role (Helgeson & Fritz, 2000). In contrast to unmitigated communion, the less extreme and more socially desirable construct of communion appears to be unrelated to most health outcomes, although it has been positively related to adaptive interpersonal outcomes, including adjustment to chronic illness (e.g., Fritz & Helgeson, 1998; Mosher & Danoff-Burg, 2007).

The gender-related trait of agency is typically related to measures of positive physical and mental well-being. In contrast, unmitigated agency is often linked to negative outcomes. These relations have been found among patients with prostate cancer (Helgeson & Lepore, 1997), heart disease (Helgeson, 1990, 1993), and RA (Trudeau et al., 2003). In a study of college students (Danoff-Burg, Mosher, & Grant, 2006), unmitigated agency was associated with a variety of maladaptive behaviors related to health and well-being, including binge eating, reckless driving (e.g., driving 20 or more miles per hour over the speed limit), use of illicit drugs, and negative consequences of substance use (e.g., fighting and damaging property). In contrast, as hypothesized, agency was associated with positive health behaviors, including physical activity, healthy eating patterns, and good dental hygiene. Unmitigated communion was not significantly correlated with any of the behaviors measured, but communion was related to binge eating. That unexpected finding was not replicated in a follow-up study (Mosher & Danoff-Burg, 2008), whereas the aforementioned link between unmitigated agency and binge eating was replicated even after depressive symptoms were controlled.

In the above studies of agency, communion, and their unmitigated counterparts, participant gender was controlled in the analyses, and, therefore, did not account for the relation between personality and behavior. Rather, the authors argued that their findings contribute to the literature on aspects of gender roles that may be costly to individuals of either gender and, at times, to those with whom they interact (Snell, Belk, & Hawkins, 1987). In a broader sense, findings such as these highlight the importance of attending to social roles and personality factors in health rather than focusing exclusively on gender differences.

Dyadic Coping and the Interpersonal Context

Research that focuses only on individual aspects of coping with chronic illness runs the risk of missing important aspects of the individual's interpersonal context. A person's experience with chronic illness does not occur in isolation, but rather in a web of interpersonal interactions that include the individual's health-care providers and social support network. This social support network encompasses both macrolevel sources of support, such as an illness community or local communities (e.g., church, school, work environment), and more intimate, microlevel sources of support, such as significant others, friends, family, and pets.

According to Lazarus and Folkman's (1984) cognitive appraisal model of stress and coping, an individual assesses and evaluates her or his dynamic relationship with the environment and appraises the significance of that transaction and the amount of threat it may pose. Coping with stress can be directed toward altering the problem or toward regulating the emotional response. Lazarus and

Folkman's model includes seeking social support as one possible type of coping strategy, but the overall model does not emphasize interpersonal facets of coping. People experience chronic illness and other stressors within the context of their interpersonal relationships. Although individuals are likely to be coping within the context of a broad support network (Chrisler & Parrett, 1995), committed romantic relationships have been shown to be among the most important (Revenson, Kayser, & Bodenmann, 2005). These relationships provide a primary source of social support, as well as a deeper level of intimacy and support for individuals (Revenson, 1994). Examination of both individual and interpersonal facets of coping within a couple allows researchers to understand how both partners negotiate coping and share the illness experience (Coyne & Smith, 1991). Relationship-focused coping has been conceptualized as including both *active engagement*, which involves involvement in decision-making and problem-solving activities, and *protective buffering*, which is the extent to which partners may deny their worries about the illness or defer to their partners in order to avoid disagreements (Coyne & Smith, 1991).

Much of the research thus far on couples coping with chronic illness has focused on breast cancer, which limits our ability to interpret gender differences. However, recent studies have included women with RA and their partners (e.g., Majerovitz & Revenson, 1994), men with prostate cancer and their partners (e.g., Banthia et al., 2003), and mixed-gender samples of couples coping with different cancers (e.g., Hagedoorn et al., 2000; Northouse, Mood, Templin, Mellon, & George, 2000) or congestive heart failure (CHF; Rohrbaugh et al., 2002). These studies allow us to consider the effects of role (e.g., patient or caregiver) as well as the effects of gender. For example, a study (Hagedoorn et al., 2000) of couples in which one person had cancer revealed that female patients and female partners of patients perceived more distress and lower quality of life than did women in couples not dealing with illness. In contrast, men's level of distress depended on their role: Male patients' scores were similar to female patients' and female partners' scores on measures of psychological distress and quality of life, whereas male partners of patients and men in healthy couples reported lower levels of distress and higher levels of quality of life. A longitudinal study (Northouse et al., 2000) of colon cancer patients and their spouses during the first year following surgical treatment examined each partner's appraisal of illness, resources, concurrent stress, and adjustment. Results suggested that spouses reported significantly more distress and less social support than patients did. Furthermore, gender differences emerged. Women reported more distress, more role problems, and less marital satisfaction than men did, regardless of whether they were patients or caregivers.

Results of a study (Banthia et al., 2003) of men with prostate cancer and their spouses support the idea that the association between coping and distress is dependent on the quality of dyadic functioning. Even when patients reported maladaptive coping strategies, those who were in stronger relationships were less distressed than those in more dysfunctional dyads. Men with prostate cancer and their partners may respond differently to the illness experience, which was evidenced in this study by low correlations between spouses and patients on most variables. Results also indicated that marital factors did not moderate the relation between coping and distress in spouses as they did in patients. In a study (Rohrbaugh et al., 2002) of couples in which one partner had CHF, wives of male patients reported substantially more psychological distress than did husbands of female patients. Variations in perceptions of marital quality may be important in interpreting this finding, given that wives of male patients reported lower marital quality and tended to describe themselves as less stable emotionally.

A study (Badr, 2004) that compared couples in which both spouses were healthy to couples in which one spouse had a chronic illness showed that coping may vary both by gender and by health status. When husbands were ill, they focused on obtaining network support and actively engaging their wives. Healthy husbands, however, engaged in protective buffering when their wives were the ones dealing with illness. Marital adjustment was associated with congruent patterns in gagement but complementary patterns (i.e., one partner scored high and the other scored protective buffering. This suggests that interventions might encourage spouses to communi-ively with each other about the illness experience and that patients and spouses both might benefit from learning how to recognize protective buffering in their partners and how to respond with appropriate support.

A recent meta-analysis of studies of couples coping with cancer points to women as more distressed than men, regardless of whether they are patients or partners of a patient (Hagedoorn, Sanderman, Bolks, Tuinstra, & Coyne, 2008). Based on a total of 6,179 participants, the authors reported $d = 0.30$. The effects of patient–partner roles on distress dropped out when gender was taken into account, which fail to support the idea that patients are more distressed than their caregivers or vice versa. The researchers discussed the limitations of work in this area, such as the small number of studies that compare couples with illness to control couples and the basing of conclusions about gender and patient–partner roles on data for illnesses that primarily affect only women or only men. Consequently, the researchers suggested that future studies in this area should no longer focus solely on patient–partner status or gender alone, and more attention should be paid to mediating factors, such as interpersonal processes, in the impact of cancer on patients and their partners. Future researchers should also use a theoretical framework that highlights the primacy of gender and includes influences of stress and coping processes that are not limited to the illness experience, but are also indicative of how couples cope with other stressful experiences in their lives.

Directions for Future Research

Sexual Minority Status

One pertinent area for further study of gender in relation to chronic illness adjustment is that of sexual minority status. As awareness increases about how sexual minority status can impact risk factors for chronic illness, symptom report, treatment seeking, and communication with health-care providers, researchers can shed light upon how these influences then impact patients' psychological well-being and physical health. Although research in this area is not extensive, accumulating evidence supports the need for further study of sexual minority status and its subsequent influence on gender, illness, and health care.

One subfield of research in this area is concerned with the prevalence of diagnosis and risk factors for some chronic illnesses. For example, for lesbians there are factors that might increase risk of developing breast cancer and result in a later breast cancer diagnosis. These factors include health and screening behaviors, as well as risk factors that lesbian and bisexual women are more likely than heterosexual women to experience. These risk factors include a higher rate of engaging in health-compromising behaviors, such as smoking and heavy alcohol use, consuming fewer fruits and vegetables daily, being overweight, and having less access to regular sources of health care (Diamant, Wold, Spritzer, & Gelberg, 2000; Valanis et al., 2000). In addition, lesbians are more likely than heterosexual women to report depression and antidepressant use (Case et al., 2004). Although it seems that preventive screening practice among lesbians has increased in recent years, studies have shown that up to 10% of lesbians still do not obtain Pap smears to detect cervical cancer (Roberts, 2006). However, despite the possible differences in behaviors and risk factors between lesbian and heterosexual women, actual prevalence rates of breast cancer in women of sexual minority status remain varied (Cochran et al., 2001).

Another area that requires further investigation is communication between health-care providers and sexual minority patients. This is a research area in which dissemination of data to clinicians can have a direct impact on patients' physical and psychological health outcomes. Research has shown that multiple dimensions of the patient–provider relationship (e.g., general communication, HIV-specific communication, overall satisfaction, and participatory decision making) are associated with better medication adherence in patients with HIV infection and are, therefore, important avenues for intervention (Schneider, Kaplan, Greenfield, Li, & Wilson, 2004). Interviews with sexual minority women with breast cancer identified a need for doctors' respect for the patient's sexual orientation, as well as for their female partners (Boehmer & Case, 2006). More recently, the topic of communicating effectively with transgender patients (e.g., sensitivity regarding patients' preferences for which name and gender they prefer) has begun t o be discussed in medical journals (Northen, 2008; Samuel & Ziritsky, 2008).

A related dimension of the patient–provider interaction is that of disclosure. Given that people of sexual minority status may be at high risk for particular health problems, it is important that these patients disclose relevant information to their health-care providers. Among a sample of men who reported sexual contact with men, more than one-third (39%) reported not having disclosed that sexual contact to their medical providers (Bernstein et al., 2008). Furthermore, disclosure was less likely among African American, Hispanic, and Asian men and among men who reported sexual contact with women within 1 year of the study. Men who had ever been tested for HIV were twice as likely to have disclosed. Risk-based assessment such as HIV screening is contingent upon health-care providers' knowledge of a patient's potentially heightened risk, and, therefore, these findings highlight the need for more open communication between patients and providers. Too often, however, inaccurate assumptions held by health-care providers about their patients' sexual behavior create a barrier to effective communication and patient interaction (Bonvicini & Perlin, 2003; Christensen, 2005). Heterosexist assumptions may be conveyed not only verbally but also through the language used in medical forms (e.g., request for "marital status"). Health-care providers who express homophobic attitudes or who operate under heterosexist assumptions about patients and their families face the risk of creating an uncomfortable environment, missing critical health information, and compromising the quality of care.

Adverse health consequences may occur when patients are not provided with opportunities for disclosure. One study (Cole, Kemeny, Taylor, & Visscher, 1996) showed that, among gay and bisexual men, the incidence of cancer and particular infectious diseases was related to the degree to which participants concealed their sexual identity, and this effect was not attributable to demographic characteristics, health behavior patterns, or measures of affect and social desirability. These findings led the investigators to examine whether disease progression was more rapid among gay men who concealed their sexual orientation. Indicators of HIV progression included time period to a critically low CD4 T-lymphocyte level, time period to AIDS diagnosis, and time period to AIDS mortality. On each of these measures, HIV infection progressed more rapidly in a dose-response fashion according to the degree to which participants concealed their homosexual identity (Cole, Kemeny, Taylor, Visscher, & Fahey, 1996). Similarly, another group of researchers found that concealment of homosexuality was associated with lower CD4 cell count, greater social constraints, less social support, and greater levels of depressive symptoms (Ullrich, Lutgendorf, & Stapleton, 2003). These data have important implications for the role of open, understanding communication between patients and health-care providers.

Cultural and Religious Implications

Another area in which more research is needed is the interactional nature of gender and race/ethnicity in influencing health. One study (Read & Gorman, 2006) of whether and how racial/ethnic differences play a role in gender differences showed health disparities across both dimensions. For example, in a sample comprised of European American, African American, Mexican, Puerto Rican, and Cuban adults, European American and Mexican women and men reported better health outcomes than the other groups. In contrast, African Americans, in particular women, reported the most life-threatening conditions. Within each racial/ethnic group, women fared worse than men in terms of functional impairments, and women in each group (except for Mexican women) reported worse functioning than European American men. Although studies such as this begin to tease apart the impact of gender and race/ethnicity on health, future researchers should focus on culture-specific factors (e.g., acculturation, perceptions, and attitudes) and their interplay with gender-specific factors in adjustment to illness. Much as research on gender differences without a contextual analysis of gender-role socialization and other psychosocial variables is only a first step in understanding the influence of gender in adjustment, the reporting of racial/ethnic differences without further consideration of cultural variables, such as culture-based norms and acculturation, fails to paint a full picture of adjustment.

An important direction for multicultural consideration in health care is to examine differences among ethnic groups in the ways that people adjust to illness, as well as their attitudes toward and perceptions of the illness experience. In addition, within-group differences and their possible influences must be examined, as evidence in cultural research – as in gender research – supports the presence of considerable within-group variability (Sue & Dhindsa, 2006). Further research on how cultural norms influence gender roles within cultures would allow us to appreciate the transactional relationship between these factors, as they may reveal different adjustment processes that different ethnic groups experience within the context of a chronic illness.

Religion is an important component of culture, and its function as an important coping resource and source of social support should be addressed. For example, when asked about coping strategies and social support, Latinas with arthritis reported engaging in various activities to be the most common coping strategy, followed religion and prayer (Abraído-Lanza, Guier, & Revenson, 1996). The women in this sample relied more on their family members (especially daughters) than on their friends for social support. These results may reflect culture-based coping strategies, as well as cultural norms, such as familism. Another study (Abraído-Lanza, Vásquez, & Echeverría, 2004) highlighted the relation between religious activities and active coping strategies in a sample of 200 Latinos and Latinas with arthritis and indicated that religious coping is not a passive form of coping but rather is associated with action-oriented responses to pain and chronic illness. In contrast, another study (Biggar et al., 1999) showed that, when faced with HIV, African American women relied on prayer but reported that prayer was less important in coping with their illness than non-HIV-infected women reported it would be if they had a chronic illness.

It should be noted that, although we have highlighted cultural issues primarily in this section of the chapter, culture-related factors and their influences on gender pervade all aspects of the chronic illness experience. Research on specific cultural variables that contribute to differences in coping strategies, social support, psychological well-being, and quality of life in the face of chronic illness among women and men of different ethnicities is a rich area waiting to be explored in more depth.

Conclusion

As researchers come to realize more fully a biopsychosocial conceptualization of health and illness, factors, both individual and contextual, that can influence a patient's adjustment to the diagnosis and treatment of chronic illness must be considered. Adjustment to chronic illness affects not only the patient but also the patient's family and social network. Therefore, the transactional relation between the person and his or her environment cannot be ignored. Gender is one such factor that has a great influence on behavioral processes (e.g., health habits), environmental processes (e.g., interpersonal relations), and physical as well as psychological outcomes (e.g., depression). Researchers thus far have done much to illustrate that women and men do not necessarily experience chronic illness in the same way; however, there is still much to be examined to delineate specific ways in which they might differ.

To date, much of the research on psychological aspects of chronic illness has been gender specific, that is, focused solely on either men or women in the context of a gender-specific disease. Some researchers who do include both women and men as research participants treat gender as a variable to be statistically controlled, or they report gender differences without further analysis or interpretation. However, other researchers have recognized that merely reporting gender differences is not a sufficient explanation, and they have progressed to examining related psychosocial variables such as gender roles. Methodological questions, such as the best ways to operationalize and assess these variables and compare them across gender, remain to be answered. Most studies of gender in chronic illness have been cross-sectional. Few have utilized longitudinal designs with premorbid measures of quality of life and physical and psychological symptom severity that would facilitate interpretation of gender differences in terms of patients' functioning before diagnosis and across the illness course. Moreover, issues of culture, sexual orientation, socioeconomic status, and access to health care are just some of the topics that need to be studied with regard to the processes through which they interact with gender. The progress in research thus far allows us to begin formulating a biopsychosocial conceptualization of how all of these facets of adjustment to chronic illness affect women and men, and this conceptualization should drive future research on chronic illness.

References

Abraído-Lanza, A. F., Guier, C., & Revenson, T. A. (1996). Coping and social support resources among latinas with arthritis. *Arthritis Care and Research, 9,* 501–508.

Abraído-Lanza, A. F., Vásquez, E., & Echeverría, S. E. (2004). En las manos de Dios [in God's hands]: Religious and other forms of coping among Latinos with arthritis. *Journal of Consulting and Clinical Psychology, 72,* 91–102.

Addis, M. E., & Mahalik, J. R. (2003). Men, masculinity, and the contexts of help seeking. *American Psychologist, 58,* 5–14.

American Cancer Society. (2008). *Cancer facts and figures 2008.* Atlanta, GA: American Cancer Society.

Anderson, R. N., & Smith, B. L. (2005). Deaths: Leading causes for 2002. *National Vital Statistics Reports, 53,* 1–92.

Arrington-Sanders, R., Yi, M. S., Tsevat, J., Wilmott, R. W., Mrus, J. M., & Britto, M. T. (2006). Gender differences in health-related quality of life of adolescents with cystic fibrosis. *Health and Quality of Life Outcomes, 4,* doi:10.1186/1477-7525-4-5.

Badr, H. (2004). Coping in marital dyads: A contextual perspective on the role of gender and health. *Personal Relationships, 11,* 197–211.

Bakan, D. (1966). *The duality of human existence.* Chicago, IL: Rand McNally.

Bamer, A. M., Cetin, K., Johnson, K. L., Gibbons, L. E., & Ehde, D. M. (2008). Validation study of prevalence and correlates of depressive symptomatology in multiple sclerosis. *General Hospital Psychiatry, 30,* 311–317.

Banthia, R., Malcarne, V. L., Varni, J. W., Ko, C. M., Sadler, G. R., & Greenbergs, H. L. (2003). The effects of dyadic strength and coping styles on psychological distress in couples faced with prostate cancer. *Journal of Behavioral Medicine, 26,* 31–52.

Bernstein, K. T., Liu, K., Begier, E. M., Koblin, B., Karpati, A., Murrill, C. (2008). Same-sex attraction disclosure to health care providers among New York City men who have sex with men. *Archives of Internal Medicine, 168,* 1458–1464.

Biggar, H., Forehand, R., Devine, D., Brody, G., Armistead, L., Morse, E., et al. (1999). Women who are HIV infected: The role of religious activity in psychosocial adjustment. *AIDS Care, 11,* 195–199.

Boehmer, U., & Case, P. (2006). Sexual minority women's interactions with breast cancer providers. *Women & Health, 44*(2), 41–58.
Bonvicini, K. A., & Perlin, M. J. (2003). The same but different: Clinician-patient communication with gay and lesbian patients. *Patient Education and Counseling, 51*, 115–122.
Carver, C. S., & Antoni, M. H. (2004). Finding benefit in breast cancer during the year after diagnosis predicts better adjustment 5 to 8 years after diagnosis. *Health Psychology, 23*, 595–598.
Case, P., Austin, S. B., Hunter, D. J., Manson, J. E., Malspeis, S., Willett, W. C., et al. (2004). Sexual orientation, health risk factors, and physical functioning in the nurses' health study II. *Journal of Women's Health, 13*, 1033–1047.
Centers for Disease Control and Prevention (CDC). (2008a). *Chronic disease overview*. Retrieved May 15, 2008, from http://www.cdc.gov/nccdphp/overview.htm
Centers for Disease Control and Prevention (CDC). (2008b). *HIV/AIDS surveillance report, 2006*. Atlanta, GA: U.S. Department of Health and Human Services.
Chrisler, J. C., & Parrett, K. L. (1995). Women and autoimmune disorders. In A. L. Stanton & S. J. Gallant (Eds.), *The psychology of women's health: Progress and challenges in research and application* (pp. 171–195). Washington, DC: American Psychological Association.
Christensen, M. (2005). Homophobia in nursing: A concept analysis. *Nursing Forum, 40*, 60–71.
Cochran, S. D., Mays, V. M., Bowen, D., Gage, S., Bybee, D., Roberts, S. J., et al. (2001). Cancer-related risk indicators and preventive screening behaviors among lesbians and bisexual women. *American Journal of Public Health, 91*, 591–597.
Cole, S. W., Kemeny, M. E., Taylor, S. E., & Visscher, B. R. (1996). Elevated physical health risk among gay men who conceal their homosexual identity. *Health Psychology, 15*, 243–251.
Cole, S. W., Kemeny, M. E., Taylor, S. E., Visscher, B. R., & Fahey, J. L. (1996). Accelerated course of human immunodeficiency virus infection in gay men who conceal their homosexual identity. *Psychosomatic Medicine, 58*, 219–231.
Combe, B. (2007). Early rheumatoid arthritis: Strategies for prevention and management. *Clinical Rheumatology, 21*, 27–42.
Coyne, J. C., & Smith, D. A. (1991). Couples coping with a myocardial infarction: A contextual perspective on wives' distress. *Journal of Personality and Social Psychology, 61*, 404–412.
Danoff-Burg, S., & Revenson, T. A. (2000). Rheumatic illness and relationships: Coping as a joint venture. In K. B. Schmaling & T. G. Sher (Eds.), *The psychology of couples and illness: Theory, research, and practice* (pp. 105–133). Washington, DC: American Psychological Association.
Danoff-Burg, S., & Revenson, T. A. (2005). Benefit-finding among patients with rheumatoid arthritis: Positive effects on interpersonal relationships. *Journal of Behavioral Medicine, 28*, 91–103.
Danoff-Burg, S., Mosher, C. E., & Grant, C. A. (2006). Relations of agentic and communal personality traits to health behavior and substance use among college students. *Personality & Individual Differences, 40*, 353–363.
Danoff-Burg, S., Revenson, T. A., Trudeau, K. J., & Paget, S. A. (2004). Unmitigated communion, social constraints, and psychological distress among women with rheumatoid arthritis. *Journal of Personality, 72*, 29–46.
Daubenmier, J. J., Weidner, G., Sumner, M. D., Mendell, N., Merritt-Worden, T., Studley, J., et al. (2007). The contribution of changes in diet, exercise, and stress management to changes in coronary risk in women and men in the multisite cardiac lifestyle intervention program. *Annals of Behavioral Medicine, 33*, 57–68.
de Bosset, V., Atashili, J., Miller, W., & Pignone, M. (2008). Health insurance–related disparities in colorectal cancer screening in Virginia. *Cancer Epidemiology Biomarkers and Prevention, 17*, 834–837.
de Ridder, D., Geenen, R., Kuijer, R., & van Middendorp, H. (2008). Psychological adjustment to chronic disease. *Lancet, 372*, 246–255.
Diamant, A. L., Wold, C., Spritzer, K., & Gelberg, L. (2000). Health behaviors, health status, and access to and use of health care: A population-based study of lesbian, bisexual, and heterosexual women. *Archives of Family Medicine, 9*, 1043–1051.
Di Marco, F., Verga, M., Reggente, M., Casanova, F. M., Santus, P., Blasi, F., et al. (2006). Anxiety and depression in COPD patients: The roles of gender and disease severity. *Respiratory Medicine, 100*, 1767–1774.
Egede, L. E. (2007). Major depression in individuals with chronic medical disorders: Prevalence, Correlates, and association with health resource utilization, lost productivity, and functional disability. *General Hospital Psychiatry, 29*, 409–416.
Egsmose, C., Lund, B., Pettersson, H., Berg, E., Brodin, U., & Trang, L. (1995). Patients with rheumatoid arthritis benefit from early 2nd line therapy: 5 year follow-up of a prospective double blind placebo controlled study. *Journal of Rheumatology, 22*, 2208–2213.

Fleischmann, R. M., Stern, R. L., & Iqbal, I. (2005). Treatment of early rheumatoid arthritis. *Modern Rheumatology, 15*, 153–162.

Fritz, H. L. (2000). Gender-linked personality traits predict mental health and functional status following a first coronary event. *Health Psychology, 19*, 420–428.

Fritz, H. L., & Helgeson, V. S. (1998). Distinctions of unmitigated communion from communion: Self-neglect and overinvolvement with others. *Journal of Personality and Social Psychology, 75*, 121–140.

Goekoop-Ruiterman, Y. P., de Vries-Bouwstra, J. K., Allaart, C. F., van Zeben, D., Kerstens, P. J., Hazes, J. M., et al. (2008). Clinical and radiographic outcomes of four different treatment strategies in patients with early rheumatoid arthritis (the BeSt study): A randomized, controlled trial. *Arthritis & Rheumatism, 58*, S126–S135.

Green, C. R., & Wheeler, R. C. (2003). Physician variability in the management of acute post-operative pain and cancer pain: A quantitative assessment of the Michigan experiences. *Pain Medicine, 4*, 8–20.

Grieg, A., Peacock, D., Jewkes, R., & Msimang, S. (2008). Gender and AIDS: Time to act. *AIDS, 22*, S35–S43.

Hagedoorn, M., Buunk, B. P., Kuijer, R. G., Wobbes, T., & Sanderman, R. (2000). Couples dealing with cancer: Role and gender differences regarding psychological distress and quality of life. *Psycho-Oncology, 9*, 232–242.

Hagedoorn, M., Sanderman, R., Bolks, H. N., Tuinstra, J., & Coyne, J. C. (2008). Distress in couples coping with cancer: A meta-analysis and critical review of role and gender effects. *Psychological Bulletin, 134*, 1–30.

Hampton, M. R., & Frombach, I. (2000). Women's experience of traumatic stress in cancer treatment. *Health Care for Women International, 21*, 67–76.

Hart, P. L. (2005). Women's perceptions of coronary heart disease: An integrative review. *Journal of Cardiovascular Nursing, 20*, 170–176.

Helgeson, V. S. (1990). The role of masculinity as a prognostic predictor of heart attack severity. *Sex Roles, 22*, 755–774.

Helgeson, V. S. (1993). Implications of agency and communion for patient and spouse adjustment to a first coronary event. *Journal of Personality and Social Psychology, 64*, 807–816.

Helgeson, V. S. (1994). Relation of agency and communion to well-being: Evidence and potential explanations. *Psychological Bulletin, 116*, 412–428.

Helgeson, V. S. (2003). Gender-related traits and health. In J. Suls, & K. A. Wallston (Eds.), *Social psychological foundations of health and illness* (pp. 367–394). Malden, MA: Blackwell.

Helgeson, V. S., Escobar, O., Siminerio, L., & Becker, D. (2007). Unmitigated communion and health among adolescents with and without diabetes: The mediating role of eating disturbances. *Personality and Social Psychology Bulletin, 33*, 519–536.

Helgeson, V. S., & Fritz, H. L. (1996). Implications of unmitigated communion and communion for adolescent adjustment to type I diabetes. *Women's Health, 2*, 163–188.

Helgeson, V. S., & Fritz, H. L. (1998). A theory of unmitigated communion. *Personality and Social Psychology Review, 2*, 173–183.

Helgeson, V. S., & Fritz, H. L. (1999). Unmitigated agency and unmitigated communion: Distinctions from agency and communion. *Journal of Research in Personality, 33*, 131–158.

Helgeson, V. S., & Fritz, H. L. (2000). The implications of unmitigated agency and unmitigated communion for domains of problem behavior. *Journal of Personality, 68*, 1031–1057.

Helgeson, V. S., & Lepore, S. J. (1997). Men's adjustment to prostate cancer: The role of agency and unmitigated agency. *Sex Roles, 37*, 251–267.

Helgeson, V. S., Reynolds, K. A., & Tomich, P. L. (2006). A meta-analytic review of benefit finding and growth. *Journal of Consulting and Clinical Psychology, 74*, 797–816.

Heo, M., Allison, D. B., & Fontaine, K. R. (2004). Overweight, obesity, and colorectal cancer screening: Disparity between men and women. *BMC Public Health, 4*, doi:10.1186/1471-2458-4-53.

Homko, C. J., Santamore, W. P., Zamora, L., Shirk, G., Gaughan, J., Cross, R., et al. (2008). Cardiovascular disease knowledge and risk perception among underserved individuals at increased risk of cardiovascular disease. *Journal of Cardiovascular Nursing, 23*, 332–337.

Hsia, J., Kemper, E., Kiefe, C., Zapka, J., Sofaer, S., Pettinger, M., et al. (2000). The importance of health insurance as a determinant of cancer screening: Evidence from the women's health initiative. *Preventive Medicine, 31*, 261–270.

Hsia, J., Kemper, E., Sofaer, S., Bowen, D., Kiefe, C. I., & Zapka, J. (2000). Is insurance a more important determinant of healthcare access than perceived health? Evidence from the women's health initiative. *Journal of Women's Health & Gender-Based Medicine, 9*, 881–889.

Jacobson, D. L., Gange, S. J., Rose, N. R., & Graham, N. M. H. (1997). Epidemiology and estimated population burden of selected autoimmune disease in the United States. *Clinical Immunology and Immunopathology, 84*, 223–243.

Jensen, L. A., & Moser, D. K. (2008). Gender differences in knowledge, attitudes, and beliefs about heart disease. *Nursing Clinics of North America, 43*, 77–104.

Kaplan, R. M., Anderson, J. P., & Wingard, D. L. (1991). Gender differences in health-related quality of life. *Health Psychology, 10*, 86–93.

Keller, M., & Henrich, G. (1999). Illness-related distress: Does it mean the same for men and women? Gender aspects in cancer patients' distress and adjustment. *Acta Oncologica, 38*, 747–755.

Kiviruusu, O., Huurre, T., & Aro, H. (2007). Psychosocial resources and depression among chronically ill young adults: Are males more vulnerable? *Social Science & Medicine, 65*, 173–186.

Kung, H. C., Hoyert, D. L., Xu, J., & Murphy, S. L. (2008). Deaths: Final data for 2005. *National Vital Statistics Reports, 56*, 1–124.

Lazarus, R. S., & Folkman, S. (1984). *Stress appraisal and coping*. New York: Springer.

Leeb, B. F., Weber, K., & Smolen, J. S. (1998). Rheumatoid arthritis: Diagnosis and screening. *Disease Management and Health Outcomes, 4*, 315–324.

Liburd, L. C., Namageyo-Funa, A., & Jack, L., Jr. (2007). Understanding "masculinity" and the challenges of managing type-2 diabetes among African American men. *Journal of the National Medical Association, 99*, 550–558.

Lövgren, M., Tishelman, C., Sprangers, M., Koyi, H., & Hamberg, K. (2008). Symptoms and problems with functioning among women and men with inoperable lung cancer: A longitudinal study. *Lung Cancer, 60*, 113–124.

Mackay, J., Jemal, A., Lee, N. C., & Parkin, D. M. (2006). *The cancer atlas*. Atlanta: American Cancer Society.

Majerovitz, S. D., & Revenson, T. A. (1994). Sexuality and rheumatic disease: The significance of gender. *Arthritis Care and Research, 7*, 29–34.

McCaughan, E., & McKenna, H. (2007). Information-seeking behavior of men newly diagnosed with cancer: A qualitative study. *Journal of Cancer Nursing, 16*, 2105–2113.

McCreary, D. R., Gray, R. E., & Grace, S .L. (2006). Gender differences in cancer mortality risk perceptions and screening behaviors among adults 40–60 years of age. *International Journal of Men's Health, 5*, 53–63.

McEntee, D. J., & Badenhop, D. T. (2000). Quality of life comparisons: Gender and population difference in cardiopulmonary rehabilitation. *Heart & Lung, 29*, 340–347.

McQueen, A., Vernon, S. W., Meissner, H. I., & Rakowski, W. (2008). Risk perceptions and worry about cancer: Does gender make a difference? *Journal of Health Communication, 13*, 56–79.

Meissner, H. I., Breen, N., Klabunde, C. N., & Vernon, S. W. (2006). Patterns of colorectal cancer screening uptake among men and women in the United States. *Cancer Epidemiology, Biomarkers & Prevention, 15*, 389–394.

Mosca, L., Banka, C. L., Benjamin, E. J., Berra, K., Bushnell, C., Dolor, R. J., et al. (2007). Evidence-based guidelines for cardiovascular disease prevention in women: 2007 update. *Circulation, 115*, 1481–1501.

Mosca, L., Ferris, A., Fabunmi, R., & Robertson, R. M. (2004). Tracking women's awareness of heart disease: An American Heart Association national study. *Circulation, 109*, 573–579.

Mosca, L., Jones, W. K., King, K. B., Ouyang, P., Redberg, R. F., & Hill, M. N. (2000). Awareness, perception, and knowledge of heart disease risk and prevention among women in the United States. *Archives of Family Medicine, 9*, 506–515.

Mosher, C., & Danoff-Burg, S. (2007). College students' life priorities: The influence of gender and gender-linked personality traits. *Gender Issues, 24*, 21–33.

Mosher, C. E., & Danoff-Burg, S. (2008). Agentic and communal personality traits: Relations to disordered eating behavior, body shape concern, and depressive symptoms. *Eating Behaviors, 9*, 497–500.

National Institutes of Health. (2003). *Autoimmune diseases research plan*. Retrieved January 15, 2009, from http://www.niaid.nih.gov/dait/pdf/ADCC_report.pdf

National Multiple Sclerosis Society. (2008). *Epidemiology of MS: National MS Society*. Retrieved May 4, 2008, from http://www.nationalmssociety.org/about-multiple-sclerosis/who-gets-ms/epidemiology-of-ms/index.aspx

Nell, V. P., Machold, K. P., Eberl, G., Stamm, T. A., Uffmann, M., & Smolen, J. S. (2004). Benefit of very early referral and very early therapy with disease-modifying anti-rheumatic drugs in patients with early rheumatoid arthritis. *Rheumatology, 43*, 906–914.

Northen, S. (2008). Pride and prejudice. *Nursing Standard, 22*, 18–22.

Northouse, L. L., Mood, D., Templin, T., Mellon, S., & George, T. (2000). Couples' patterns of adjustment to colon cancer. *Social Science & Medicine, 50*, 271–284.

Ong, K. L., Tso, A. W. K., Lam, K. S. L., & Cheung, B. M. Y. (2008). Gender difference in blood pressure control and cardiovascular risk factors in Americans with diagnosed hypertension. *Hypertension, 51*, 1142–1148.

Ostchega, Y., Hughes, J. P., Wright, J. D., McDowell, M. A., & Louis, T. (2008). Are demographic characteristics, health care access and utilization, and comorbid conditions associated with hypertension among U.S. adults? *American Journal of Hypertension, 21*, 159–165.

Pace, R., Dawkins, N., Wang, B., Person, S., & Shikany, J. M. (2008). Rural African Americans' dietary knowledge, perceptions, and behavior in relation to cardiovascular disease. *Ethnicity & Disease, 18*, 6–12.

Patten, S. B., Metz, L. M., & Reimer, M. A. (2000). Biopsychosocial correlates of lifetime major depression in a multiple sclerosis population. *Multiple Sclerosis, 6*, 115–120.

Peleg-Oren, N., Sherer, M., & Soskolne, V. (2003). Effect of gender on the social and psychological adjustment of cancer patients. *Social Work in Health Care, 37*, 17–33.

Petri, M. (2000). Systemic lupus erythematosus: Women's health issues. *Bulletin on the Rheumatic Diseases, 49*, 1–3.

Podolsky, D. K. (2000). Going the distance: The case for true colorectal-cancer screening. *New England Journal of Medicine, 343*, 207–208.

Puolakka, K., Kautiainen, H., Möttönen, T., Hannonen, P., Korpela, M., Hakala, M., et al. (2005). Early suppression of disease activity is essential for maintenance of work capacity in patients with recent onset rheumatoid arthritis: Five-year experience from the Finnish Rheumatoid Arthritis Combination-Therapy trial (FIN-RACo). *Arthritis & Rheumatism, 52*, 36–41.

Read, J. G., & Gorman, B. K. (2006). Gender inequalities in U.S. adult health: The interplay of race and ethnicity. *Social Science & Medicine, 62*, 1045–1065.

Revenson, T. A. (1994). Social support and marital coping with chronic illness. *Annals of Behavioral Medicine, 16*, 122–130.

Revenson, T. A., Kayser, K., & Bodenmann, G. (2005). *Couples coping with stress: Emerging perspectives on dyadic coping*. Washington, DC: American Psychological Association.

Roberts, S. J. (2006). Health care recommendations for lesbian women. *Journal of Obstetric, Gynecologic, and Neonatal Nursing, 35*, 583–591.

Rohrbaugh, M. J., Cranford, J. A., Shoham, V., Nicklas, J. M., Sonnega, J. S., & Coyne, J. C. (2002). Couples coping with congestive heart failure: Role and gender differences in psychological distress. *Journal of Family Psychology, 16*, 3–13.

Rosen, A. B., & Schneider, E. C. (2004). Colorectal cancer screening disparities related to obesity and gender. *Journal of General Internal Medicine, 19*, 332–338.

Samuel, L., & Zaritsky, E. (2008). Communicating effectively with transgender patients. *American Family Physician, 78*, 648–650.

Schane, R. E., Woodruff, P. G., Dinno, A., Covinsky, K. E., & Walter, L. C. (2008). Prevalence and risk factors for depressive symptoms in persons with chronic obstructive pulmonary disease. *Journal of General Internal Medicine, 23*, 1757–1762.

Schmidt, C. E., Bestmann, B., Kuchler, T., Longo, W. E., Rohde, V., & Kremer, B. (2005). Gender differences in quality of life of patients with rectal cancer. A five-year prospective study. *World Journal of Surgery, 29*, 1630–1641.

Schneider, J., Kaplan, S. H., Greenfield, S., Li, W., & Wilson, I. B. (2004). Better physician-patient relationships are associated with higher reported adherence to antiretroviral therapy in patients with HIV infection. *Journal of General Internal Medicine, 19*, 1096–1103.

Seeff, L. C., Nadel, M. R., Klabunde, C. N., Thompson, T., Shapiro, J. A., Vernon, S. W., et al. (2004). Patterns and predictors of colorectal cancer test use in the adult U.S. population. *Cancer, 100*, 2093–2103.

Shaul, M. P. (2005). From early twinges to master: The process of adjustment to living with rheumatoid arthritis. *Arthritis & Rheumatism, 8*, 290–297.

Snell, W. E., Belk, S. S., & Hawkins, R. C. (1987). Alcohol and drug use in stressful times: The influence of the masculine role and sex-related personality attributes. *Sex Roles, 16*, 359–373.

Solimeo, S. (2008). Sex and gender in older adults' experience of Parkinson's disease. *Journal of Gerontology, 63B*, S42S48.

Spence, J. T. (1984). Masculinity, femininity, and gender-related traits: A conceptual analysis and critique of current research. In B. A. Maher & W. B. Maher (Eds.), *Progress in experimental personality research* (pp. 1–97). San Diego, CA: Academic Press.

Stanton, A. L., Collins, C. A., & Sworowski, L. A. (2001). Adjustment to chronic illness: Theory and research. In A. Baum, T. A. Revenson, & J. E. Singer (Eds.), *Handbook of health psychology* (pp. 387–403). Mahwah, NJ: Erlbaum.

Stanton, A. L., & Revenson, T. A. (2007). Adjustment to chronic disease: Progress and promise in research. In H. S. Friedman & R. C. Silver (Eds.), *Foundations of health psychology* (pp. 203–233). New York: Oxford University Press.

Stanton, A. L., Revenson, T. A., & Tennen, H. (2007). Health psychology: Psychological adjustment to chronic disease. *Annual Review of Psychology, 58*, 565–592.

Stock, S. A. K., Stollenwerk, B., Redaelli, M., Civello, D., & Lauterbach, K. W. (2008). Sex differences in treatment patterns of six chronic diseases: An analysis from the German statutory health insurance. *Journal of Women's Health, 17*, 343–354.

Sue, S., & Dhindsa, M. K. (2006). Ethnic and racial health disparities research: Issues and problems. *Health Education & Behavior, 33*, 459–469.

Taylor, S. (1983). Adjustment to threatening events: A theory of cognitive adaptation. *American Psychologist, 38*, 1161–1173.

Theis, K. A., Helmick, C. G., & Hootman, J. M. (2007). Arthritis burden and impact are greater among U.S. women than men: Intervention opportunities. *Journal of Women's Health, 16*, 441–453.

Tullmann, D. F., & Dracup, K. (2005). Knowledge of heart attack symptoms in older men and women at risk for acute myocardial infarction. *Journal of Cardiopulmonary Rehabilitation, 25*, 33–39.

Trudeau, K. J., Danoff-Burg, S., Revenson, T. A., & Paget, S. A. (2003). Agency and communion in people with rheumatoid arthritis. *Sex Roles, 49*, 303–311.

Ullrich, P. M., Lutgendorf, S. K., & Stapleton, J. T. (2003). Concealment of homosexual identity, social support and CD4 cell count among HIV-seropositive gay men. *Journal of Psychosomatic Research, 54*, 205–212.

Valanis, B. G., Bowen, D. J., Bassford, T., Whitlock, E., Charney, P., & Carter, R. A. (2000). Sexual orientation and health: Comparisons in the women's health initiative sample. *Archives of Family Medicine, 9*, 843–853.

van Jaarsveld, C. H., Sanderman, R., Ranchor, A. V., Ormel, J., van Veldhuisen, D. J., & Kempen, G. I. (2002). Gender-specific changes in quality of life following cardiovascular disease: A prospective study. *Journal of Clinical Epidemiology, 55*, 1105–1112.

Victor, R. G., Leonard, D., Hess, P. Bhat, D. G., Jones, J., Vaeth, P. A., et al. (2008). Factors associated with hypertension awareness, treatment, and control in Dallas County, Texas. *Archives of Internal Medicine, 168*, 1285–1293.

Weinblatt, M. E. (1996). Rheumatoid arthritis: Treat now, not later! *Annals of Internal Medicine, 124*, 773.

Werner, A., & Malterud, K. (2003). It is hard work behaving as a credible patient: Encounters between women with chronic pain and their doctors. *Social Science & Medicine, 57*, 1409–1419.

World Health Organization. (2008a). *The global burden of disease: 2004 update*. Geneva: WHO Press.

World Health Organization. (2008b). *Atlas: Multiple sclerosis resources in the world, 2008*. Geneva: WHO Press.

World Health Organization. (2008c). *Report on the global HIV/AIDS epidemic, 2008*. Geneva: WHO Press.

Part XIV
Special Topics in Applied Psychology

Chapter 24
Gender in Sport and Exercise Psychology

Diane L. Gill and Cindra S. Kamphoff

In this chapter, gender psychology meets sport and exercise psychology. For many readers, this is a first meeting, and an introduction is in order. Sport and exercise psychology is located in a much different context than most of the other psychology areas covered in this handbook. Although academic and clinical psychologists have engaged in sport and exercise psychology research or consulted with athletes and exercisers, for the most part, sport and exercise psychology faculty, courses, graduate programs, and research activities are found in departments of kinesiology or exercise and sport science. Our colleagues and research collaborators are predominantly exercise physiologists, biomechanists, and motor behavior researchers, with an occasional sociocultural sport studies scholar in the mix. Other than a few graduate students in focused sport and exercise psychology concentrations, most of our students aim for professional careers in sports medicine, health and fitness, or physical education. Although sport and exercise psychology draws its scholarly base from psychology, it also draws from kinesiology. Thus, sport and exercise psychology reflects kinesiology's emphasis on the physical and biological processes, and its roots in kinesiology/physical education provide a unique social–historical context, as discussed in the next section of this chapter. Moreover, that orientation and context is particularly relevant to gender psychology.

Gender is a pervasive influence throughout society, and this certainly is evident in sport and exercise settings. Indeed, the sport world seems to exaggerate and highlight gender. Sport and physical activities remain largely sex-segregated and male-dominated, and both research and professional practice emphasize elite, competitive sport. Sport and exercise psychology research reflects the gendered cultural boundaries of elite sport and also reflects kinesiology's emphasis on the physical and biological processes. Given the context, it is not surprising that sport and exercise psychology lags behind other areas within psychology in addressing gender issues and incorporating feminist and multicultural perspectives.

In psychology, as in most academic areas, it is typically women who raise and address gender issues as they become visible and active in areas that have been dominated by men. In psychology today, women outnumber men in many areas and gender issues are recognized and addressed by both, and for both, women and men. That is not the case for sport and exercise psychology. For example, the 2007 American Psychological Association (APA, 2008) membership data indicate that 45.3% are men and 54.3% are women. In APA Division 47 (Exercise and Sport Psychology) men are the clear majority at 69.1%; women make up 30.8% of the membership. It might also be noted that the Division 47 membership at 83.3% White is less racially and ethnically diverse than the larger APA membership, which is 66.3% White. As noted earlier, most sport and exercise psychology

---

D.L. Gill (✉)
University of North Carolina, Greensboro, NC, USA

scholars are not in psychology departments. Kinesiology and Exercise and Sport Science departments typically emphasize the biosciences and tend to be dominated by men. Within this context, masculine values are so prominent that they are rarely questioned, and it is not surprising that gender issues are typically raised by women, and often involve neglected women's issues and experiences. Thus, much of the research reviewed in this chapter is on women with no comparable work on men. The short and somewhat glib explanation is that all the other sport and exercise psychology work is on men and masculine issues. The more nuanced explanation is that few men (and actually few women) address gender issues in sport and exercise; the masculine, elite, competitive sport model is rarely questioned, and gender is not usually recognized as anything to do with men.

Framework for Gender in Sport and Exercise Psychology

In contrast to dominant paradigms within kinesiology/exercise science, but in line with current gender psychology, we recognize the intertwined nature of gender and multiple cultural diversity issues. Gender issues have been addressed in psychology for some time, with the initial focus on the psychology of women and a gradual incorporation of other gender issues, including the psychology of men and masculinity. Recently, the APA (2007) developed and approved Guidelines for Psychological Practice with Girls and Women; the guidelines recognize the diversity among women and note that disparities still persist despite tremendous gains for women in many areas. There are similar APA guidelines related to lesbian, gay, and bisexual clients (APA, 2000), older adults (APA, 2004), and multicultural education, research, practice, and organizational change (APA, 2003), all of which explicitly highlight the intersections of gender and culture. Similarly, our guiding framework for this chapter draws from both gender scholarship and the growing multicultural psychology scholarship.

Our framework is also informed by cultural *sport* studies scholarship, which highlights the unique social–historical context of sport in relation to gender. For example, sport studies scholar M. Ann Hall has been a clear voice for feminist and cultural studies perspectives within sport and kinesiology for some time. Hall (1996) has argued that gender influences everyone and that simple, dichotomous categories cannot explain real-world behavior. We all have multiple, intersecting identities, and the mix of identities and power relations vary with time and context. Hall has also called for moves away from theory and into the real world through professional work and social action. Feminist and cultural analysis perspectives are common in the current sport studies literature, and in this chapter we draw on that scholarship. Gender psychology, multicultural psychology, and cultural sport studies all emphasize the three themes that form the framework for this chapter: (a) multiple, intersecting cultural identities, (b) power relations within the cultural context, and (c) moving beyond scholarship to social action and advocacy.

Social–Historical Context of Sport and Physical Activity

Sport and other physical activities have a unique (and gendered) context. Sport not only highlights gender but also highlights the biological/physical and the competitive/hierarchical – both are masculine values. *Citius, Altius, Fortius* – the Olympic motto – translates as "swifter, higher, stronger," which underscores that sport is competitive and hierarchical as well as physical. However, highly structured, male-dominated, competitive sport is a relatively modern phenomenon. Both women and men engaged in physical activities throughout history, and specific activities, behaviors, and cultural meanings varied across time and location. For readers who want more detail, sport history scholars, particularly Roberta Park (1987) and Betty Spears (1978) have provided detailed and insightful accounts of women's sport and physical activity and elsewhere Gill (1995) described the early roots and development of women's place in the history of sport psychology.

Early Women's Sport and Physical Education

Roberta Park's commentary and historical analysis on physical activity and sport include some enlightening insights on women and gender. In a 1987 essay published in the book *From "Fair Sex" to Feminism*, she described how organized sport became a major vehicle for defining and acting out gender roles following the US Civil War. Based on British and American writing, she argued that gender roles were more exaggerated and more clearly linked with sport in the USA than in the UK Early women's rights leaders referenced physical activity. Elizabeth Cady Stanton was a particularly strong advocate of women's physical activity, and in an 1855 paper (cited in Park, 1987, p. 1577) she rejected "man's claim to physical superiority" and stated that "We cannot say what the woman might be physically, if the girl were allowed all the freedom of the boy, in romping, swimming, climbing and playing ball." As Park noted, men's sport became very public, but women's sport, with a few exceptions, was largely cloistered until the 1970s. Thus, modern sport has been defined and dominated by the masculine model.

As Park (1987), Gill (1995), and others have noted, women's physical education provided a woman-oriented environment for sport and physical activity long before the women's movement of the 1970s. Physical activities were part of the curriculum in the first women's colleges. Vassar opened in 1865, and it required callisthenic exercises; Wellesley also required callisthenics and sports when it opened in 1874. Wellesley also became the most influential program for training women physical educators when it merged with the Boston Normal School of Gymnastics. Graduates established women's physical education programs in public schools and colleges, organized and run by women to promote women's development and achievement, at a time when few women held academic positions in psychology or other fields. The philosophy and approach of these early women physical educators set a context that was quite different from the men's sport model, which has prevailed to become our current sport model. Specifically, they advocated putting athletes first, preventing exploitation, downplaying competition, emphasizing enjoyment and sportsmanship, and promoting activity for all rather than just an elite few, as expressed in the classic statement "A game for every girl and every girl in a game" (National Amateur Athletic Federation [NAAF], 1930, p. 41).

From the 1970s to Today's Gendered Sport

In the USA the 1972 passage of Title IX of the Educational Amendments Act, which prohibits sex discrimination in all programs that receive federal financial assistance, was a highlight of the Women's Liberation Movement. Title IX also marked the beginning of the move away from that early model of women's sport toward today's competitive sport programs for both men and women. Title IX covered the full range of educational programs, but athletics proved particularly contentious. Although change has been slowed by challenges that continue even today, Title IX dramatically changed sport in US society. Indeed, women's and girls' athletic participation has exploded in the last generation. Still, the numbers do not equal the numbers for boys and men; women and girls make up about 40% of the high school and college athletes. More important, the sport social context, although still gendered, has changed. The average man may be taller, faster, and stronger than the average woman, but biological sex is only part of the gender mix. All the meanings, social roles, expectations, and power relations related to gender must be considered within the sport context. As many sport studies scholars (e.g., Hall, 1996; Park, 1987) have argued, the public attention to the increasing numbers of girls and women in competitive sports masks the decline in intramural and recreational sports opportunities for the larger numbers of girls and boys, and men and women, who are not as physically elite and competitive. With the merger of the former women's physical education programs into general physical education programs that quickly became heavily male-dominated, the ideals of the early leaders lost out. We no longer have "a game for every girl" (or boy).

Even within competitive sport, including today's highly visible female athletes, gender influence is clear. It is important to go beyond participation numbers to consider power and privilege: "Who makes the rules?" In the larger society and in sport, White men hold the power positions. Sue (2004) illustrated the power differential by noting that although White men make up just 33% of the US population, they hold 80% of tenured faculty positions, 92% of *Forbes* 400 CEO-level positions, 80% of the seats in the House of Representatives, 84% of the Senate seats, and, of special interest here, *99% of the athletic team owners*. Note that it is the elite sport (athletics) context that exhibits the most exaggerated gender power relations. The power differential is not confined to professional sports, and it reflects the unique social–historical context of sport and physical activity.

Before the 1972 passage of Title IX, more than 90% of women's athletic teams in the United States were coached by women and had a woman athletic director. Vivian Acosta and Linda Carpenter (Carpenter & Acosta, 2008) have clearly documented the continuous decline in the number of women coaches since then. In their most recent 2008 update (available at: http://www.acostacarpenter.org) they reported that participation in women's athletics is at the highest level ever, but the representation of women as coaches remains low at 42.8%. The proportion of female athletic directors (21.3%), head athletic trainers (27.3%), and sports information directors (11.3%) has risen but remains far below men's numbers. Acosta and Carpenter also indicated that only 2–3% of men's teams are coached by a female head coach. Gender bias and White male privilege may not totally explain the declining numbers of female coaches, but Kamphoff's (2006) dissertation research clearly shows that female coaches within collegiate athletics experience marginalization, devaluation, and homophobia. The female former coaches that she interviewed reported fewer resources, lower salaries, more responsibilities, and less administrative support than their male counterparts did.

The lack of female coaches is a worldwide issue that has been documented in several countries. In Canada, one in five senior coaches is women (Laberge, 1992). Data from New Zealand indicate that only 26% of women's Olympic teams and only 1% of men's Olympic teams are coached by a woman (Kamphoff, Armentrout, & Leberman, 2008). In the UK, less than one-quarter of active coaches are women, and there are no female head coaches of men's national teams (Norman, 2008). Similarly, data from the Women's National Basketball Association (WNBA) in the USA indicate that only 5 of 19 (36%) of head coaches of WNBA teams are women, and no women are head coaches of men's professional teams (Lapchick, Lerner, & Zahn, 2008).

To examine the experiences of women coaching men (the 2–3% of US collegiate coaches that Acosta and Carpenter reported), Kamphoff, Armentrout, Driska, and Daniels (2009) interviewed 15 of the 39 women who coach men at the Division I level. In actuality, most of the 39 women coached a combined men and women's cross country/track and field program; in fact, only 2 of the 39 women coached a men's only team. Of the 15 women interviewed, all were extremely decorated athletes who typically had experience competing at the Olympic or other international level. Yet regardless of their athletic accomplishments, these women described a culture of discrimination and the difficulty of gaining respect from administrators, parents, and male athletes. Several were asked to apply for their position and were unaware of the opportunity to coach men before they were hired. Many had never considered the possibility that women could coach men at this level.

Leanne Norman (2008) argued that the coaching system in the UK has contributed to the inferior status of female coaches. Her data support the conclusion that coaching can be an isolating profession for women and that the cultural value of men as superior leaders, coaches, and athletes has impacted women's opportunities. She argued that the UK coaching system is failing women coaches. In a commentary on Norman's paper, Kamphoff (2008) similarly argued that the US coaching system is failing female coaches. She explained that the lack of coaching opportunities in the USA for women coaches is "indicative of the gendered culture and organization of sport" with a clear privileging of men and the prevailing view that a "good coach" is a man. Kamphoff argued that a radical change must take place in the patriarchal culture of sport to improve the experiences of female coaches worldwide.

Richard Lapchick's annual *Racial and Gender Report Cards* clearly show racial and gender inequities in sport, with little progress. White men dominate coaching, even of women's teams. The 2005 *Racial and Gender Report Card* (Lapchick, 2006) indicated that Whites holds approximately 90% of the head coaching positions in all US athletic divisions. The number of Black men coaching division I basketball reached an all time high of 25.2%. The number of Black women who coach increased to 9.3%, but that is still far below the proportion of Black women who play basketball (43.7%). Numbers of coaches of other racial/ethnic identities are too small to be counted, and athletic administrators remain solidly White men. Clearly, sport is gendered and elite; White men hold the power and women of color are noticeably absent in leadership roles.

Gender and Physical Activity/Exercise Participation

Sex segregation is not as obvious in physical activity settings other than competitive athletics, but gender influence is clear. Women and men may exercise in the same fitness center, but the aerobics and yoga classes are predominantly women's spaces, whereas the men dominate the free weights area. Census data and public health reports indicate that physical activity is limited by gender, race, class, and by physical attributes. Physical activity decreases across the adult lifespan, although men are more active than women and racial/ethnic minorities are less active across all age groups (Pratt, Macera, & Blanton, 1999; U.S. Department of Health and Human Services [USDHHS], 2000). For example, Kimm et al. (2002) used a large national database to track girls' physical activity levels across adolescence. Physical activity declined dramatically, so that, at age 18–19, 56% of Black girls and 31% of White girls reported no regular physical activity. In one of the few studies to examine social class, Crespo, Ainsworth, Keteyian, Heath, and Smit (1999) found greater inactivity in less privileged social classes and women and girls more inactive in all social class groups. Crespo (2005) called for professionals to consider unique needs and cultural constraints when giving advice on exercise. Rimmer (2005) noted that people with physical disabilities are one of the most inactive segments of the population and argued that organizational policies, discrimination, and social attitudes are the real barriers to physical exercise.

These disparities in physical activity are of particular concern as public health and social justice issues. Disparities in physical activity mirror many of the health disparities that receive attention from funding agencies and health researchers (USDHHS, 2003). Based on considerable evidence that inactivity is a risk factor for most major diseases and that physical activity is a key behavior in health promotion, the Healthy People 2010 report (USDHHS, 2000) cited physical activity as a leading indicator of public health.

Sport and exercise psychologists could advance psychology in the public interest by applying our expertise to promote *physical activity for all*, so that the benefits for health and well-being are not limited to the elite. To do that, sport and exercise psychology must expand the research base on gender and culture, translate that research into culturally competent professional practice, and advocate for social justice within sport and physical activity.

Gender Scholarship in Sport and Exercise Psychology

Despite the gendered context of sport, the diversity of participants, and the need for cultural competence, sport and exercise psychology research seldom addresses gender or multicultural issues, and professional practice focuses on elite sport. Gender scholarship in sport and exercise psychology has followed gender scholarship within psychology in shifting from sex differences, to gender roles, to social processes. However, sport and exercise psychology has followed behind at quite a distance and has not caught up with more recent moves to multicultural perspectives.

Fisher, Butryn, and Roper (2003) called for the application of cultural studies perspectives to expand sport psychology research and practice. Cultural studies deals with the interrelated issues of social difference, distribution of power, and social justice. However, sport and exercise psychology has not heeded that call. Gender research focuses on gender differences in athletic participation with little attention to the social context and lacks critical, feminist analyses; research on other aspects of cultural diversity is rarely found in our primary journals.

Duda and Allison (1990) first identified the lack of research on race/ethnicity; they reported that less than 4% of the published papers in sport and exercise psychology journals considered race/ethnicity, and most of those were simply sample descriptions. Ram, Starek, and Johnson (2004) updated that report by reviewing articles in sport and exercise psychology research journals published between 1987 and 2000 for both race/ethnicity and sexual orientation content. They found that only 20% of the articles made reference to race/ethnicity and 1.2% to sexual orientation. More important, those few articles provided few insights, and Ram et al. concluded that there has been no systematic attempt to include the experiences of marginalized groups in sport and exercise research.

Kamphoff, Araki, and Gill (2004) surveyed the Association for Applied Sport Psychology (AASP) conference programs from the first conference in 1986 to the 2003 conference and found a slight increase in the percentage of abstracts that addressed diversity issues, from 11.5% in 1986 to 19.2% in 1994, but no further change from 1995 to 2003. Most of those few abstracts contained simple comparisons of gender differences with little insightful analysis. It might be noted that, even though those AASP conferences were held in the USA, a significant number of first authors were from other countries (70/29.2% in 1995, 81/23.1% in 2003). Arnett (2008) recently argued that psychology and the APA journals are too narrowly focused on the USA. His review of major psychology journals from 2003 to 2007 indicated that 73% of first authors were from the USA and another 14% from the English-speaking countries of Canada, the UK, Australia, and New Zealand. We (Kamphoff et al., 2004) found that international authors of AASP abstracts came from 16 different countries. Although we have not surveyed all sport and exercise psychology journal articles, the review of AASP abstracts and a quick review of the editorial boards of our three main journals suggest that sport and exercise psychology may be more global, albeit dominated by English-speaking counties, than the larger field of psychology. The editors of the three main journals (*Journal of Sport & Exercise Psychology*, *Journal of Applied Sport Psychology*, and *The Sport Psychologist*) come from three countries (USA, UK, and Australia); editorial boards of both *JSEP* and *JASP* are about one-third non-USA, and *TSP* has a majority (54.8%) from outside the USA. In terms of gender distribution, one editor is a woman, and about one-third of each of the editorial board members are women.

Given the limitations of the sport and exercise psychology literature, we have drawn relevant research from both sport studies and gender psychology sources. In this section we review the research on gender in sport and exercise psychology and highlight scholarship that is in line with our guiding framework (see Gill, 2007, for a more detailed review).

Gender Differences and Gender Roles

Sex differences are still discussed in popular reports and some exercise and sport science research, which probably reflects the biological emphasis of kinesiology programs. For example, in conducting a brief online literature search for current research on "gender, men, and sport," we found that the majority of the citations were reports on sex differences – usually with physiological, biomechanical, or performance outcome measures. Yet, gender psychology has clearly moved beyond the search for sex differences. For example, Hyde (2005) recently reviewed 46 meta-analyses of the extensive gender differences literature and concluded that results support the *gender similarities hypothesis*. That is, men and women are more alike than different, and overstated claims of gender differences cause harm and limit opportunities. Gender similarities also hold in sport and physical activities. Despite the dominance of biological sex differences approaches in kinesiology, some current sport and exercise psychology scholars (e.g., Gill, 2007; Krane, 2001) recognize that gender is complicated by a host of social psychological factors.

Much of the sport and exercise psychology research on gender emphasizes personality, following the lead of Bem (1978) and Spence and Helmreich (1978), who developed models and measures of stereotypically masculine and feminine personality traits and behavior in the 1970s. Although the masculine and feminine categories and measures have fallen out of favor, much sport and exercise psychology gender research is still based on that early work. For example, Spence and Helmreich (1978) reported that most female collegiate athletes were either androgynous or masculine-typed, in contrast to non-athlete female college students who were most often classified as feminine. That prompted a host of studies in the sport psychology literature that generally yielded similar findings (e.g., Harris & Jennings, 1977). One recent study (Koca & Asci, 2005) in that line expanded our Western cultural perspective by surveying a large Turkish sample. As with Western samples, Turkish female athletes scored higher than female non-athletes on masculine-typed traits, and the authors suggested that both female and male athletes must be competitive, assertive, independent, and willing to take risks – all traditionally masculine-typed characteristics.

Overall, this line of research suggests that female athletes possess more masculine personality characteristics than do female non-athletes, but this conclusion is not particularly enlightening. The higher masculinity scores of female athletes probably reflect an overlap with competitiveness, which can be measured directly without invoking gender roles. For example, a series of studies with the Sport Orientation Questionnaire (SOQ; Gill & Deeter, 1988), which measures sport achievement orientation along three dimensions of competitiveness, win orientation, and goal orientation, showed that, although men scored higher than women on competitiveness and win orientation, gender differences were minimal and not particularly interesting. Differences between athletes and non-athletes were much stronger and more consistent (Gill, 1993). In a study of international and university athletes and non-athletes from Taiwan (Kang, Gill, Acevedo, & Deeter, 1990), there were strong differences between athletes and non-athletes, but minimal gender differences on any SOQ scores. With one unique sample of ultramarathoners, there were low win orientations, but very high goal orientations and no gender differences on any scores (Gill, 1993). Overall, gender differences in competitiveness are limited and seem to reflect opportunity and experience in competitive sport; gender influence is most evident when there is an emphasis on social comparison and winning within the sport context.

Other researchers have reported similar findings. McNally and Orlick (1975) introduced a cooperative broomball game to children in both urban Canada and the northern territories, and they found that girls were more receptive than boys, but northern children were more receptive than urban children. Duda (1986) reported similar results with Navajo and European American children in the southwestern USA; European American boys were the most win-oriented and placed the most emphasis on athletic ability. Weinberg and colleagues (2000) found men to score higher on competitive, extrinsic, and social recognition motives for sport and physical activity and women to score higher on fitness, fun, and teamwork motives across three countries (USA, Australia, and New Zealand); these differences fit gender stereotypes.

Gender Roles and Gender Conflict

It has been suggested that the sport environment, with its emphasis on masculine behaviors and values, leads to gender role conflict in female participants. Despite the popular appeal of the gender role conflict argument, and several studies on the topic (e.g., Desertrain & Weiss, 1988; Sage & Loudermilk, 1979), there is little evidence that female athletes experience conflict. Clearly, sport is gendered, and gender stereotypes are prevalent and influential as confirmed in considerable research (e.g., Krane, Choi, Baird, Aimar, & Kauer, 2004). However, it does not necessarily result in role conflict.

Gilenstam, Karp, and Henriksson-Larsen (2008) investigated gender roles and conflict with female ice hockey players in Sweden, and Fallon and Jome (2007) interviewed US female rugby players. In both studies, the women clearly perceived the stereotypes and stigma associated with these "masculine" sports activities. However, they did not personally experience a high level of conflict. The Swedish hockey players recognized the gender stereotypes and inequities in men's and women's sport but generally were content with the situation and apparently held traditional Western views of masculinity and femininity. The rugby players perceived conflicting expectations associated with stereotypes, but did not seem to experience conflict as they had several strategies for resolving or avoiding it. Although we might expect similar conflicting expectations for men in more feminine-type sports (e.g., figure skating), we know of no research within sport and exercise psychology that addresses these issues with men.

Gender Stereotypes

Today, most researchers look beyond the male–female and masculine–feminine dichotomies to developmental and social cognitive models with an emphasis on stereotypes and perceptions. Although actual personality and ability differences are small and inconsistent, gender stereotypes are pervasive (e.g., Deaux, 1984; Deaux & Kite, 1993; see Chapter 2 and Volume I, Chapter 15). People tend to exaggerate minimal differences into larger perceived differences, and these perceptions influence gender behaviors and relations.

Gender stereotypes certainly exist within sport. In her classic analysis, Eleanor Metheny (1965) concluded that it is *not socially appropriate* for women to engage in contests in which the resistance of the *opponent* is overcome by bodily contact (e.g., football or any contact sports), the resistance of a *heavy object* is overcome by direct application of bodily force (e.g., shot put), or the body is projected into or through space over long distances or for extended periods of time (e.g., high jump). As Metheny noted, many of the sports considered more appropriate for women (e.g., badminton, archery, golf) de-emphasize strength and body contact in favor or skill and grace; however, such sports are not inappropriate for men and do not conflict directly with gender stereotypes for men. Metheny also noted that, even in those sports, "there is no serious competition in which women are matched against men. Rather in those sports in which men and women participate together, they play as partners, with women generally accepting the supporting rather than the dominant role" (p. 55).

Metheny offered her analyses over 50 years ago, before the more visible participation of girls and women in more varied sports today. Still, gender stereotypes in the USA did not fade away with the implementation of Title IX. Kane and Snyder (1989) confirmed the gender stereotypes associated with sports and identified physicality (i.e., an emphasis on physical muscularity, strength, and power) as the key masculine features. Riemer and Visio (2003) recently re-examined Metheny's stereotypes. They found some shifts but still confirmed clear gender stereotyping of several sports; (American) football and wrestling were rated as boys' sports, and aerobics and gymnastics were rated as girls' sports. Riemer and Visio noted that more sports were considered appropriate for both boys and girls, particularly basketball and soccer. As they suggested, the increasing visibility of girls and women in these sports changed the social context and stereotypes. Even in 1965, before Title IX and the increased visibility of female athletes, Metheny (1965) took a broader social perspective and recognized that stereotypes depend on the context; she stated that "…socially sanctioned images of femininity and masculinity are always relative. They differ from culture to culture, and from group to group within a given social organization" (p. 48).

Indeed, the immediate and larger cultural context has changed, particularly for women and girls in sport and exercise. However, gender stereotypes persist, and some work suggests that those stereotypes may be even more restrictive for boys and men than for women and girls. Although we think of sport as a stereotypically masculine activity and assume that girls and women are the only ones restricted, several studies (Koivula, 1995; Riemer & Visuo, 2003) suggest that boys are more restricted than girls in terms of physical activity choices and behaviors. For example, Schmalz and Kerstetter (2006) recently investigated gender stereotypes with a sample of 8- to 10-year-old boys and girls who were both surveyed and interviewed. The research confirmed that young children recognize the gender stereotypes and stigma associated with certain activities and also confirmed that girls have more latitude than boys do in crossing gender boundaries. The interview data paralleled findings with older samples and hinted at perceived links between gender and sexuality, as the children referred to "girly" activities and noted that boys' activities were more aggressive.

Gender Bias in the Media

Research (e.g., Messner, Duncan, & Jensen, 1993) indicates that media coverage reflects gender bias. Female athletes receive much less coverage than male athletes do, and the type of coverage differs by gender, with the emphasis on athletic ability and masculinity for men, but on feminine characteristics and physical attractiveness for women. In an analysis of *Monday Night Football*, Trujillo (1995) examined the way the male body is reproduced in media coverage where traditional images of masculinity are represented. His data support three main patriarchal images of the male body and football: (1) the body as tool: football as work, (2) the body as weapon: football as war, and (3) the body as object of gaze: (watching) football as pleasure. Trujillo argued that the hegemonic masculinity represented in *Monday Night Football* has serious consequences for both men and women because the coverage marginalizes women, gay men, and some ethnic minority men. In a study of National Collegiate Athletic Association (NCAA) basketball tournaments and US Open tennis coverage, Messner et al. (1993) noted less stereotyping than reported by previous researchers but still found considerable gender marking (e.g., "women's final four" but just the "final four" for men) and gendered hierarchy of naming (i.e., women referred to as girls, young ladies, or women; but men never referred to as boys).

Gender marking may be appropriate when symmetrical, as it was for most of the tennis coverage (Messner et al., 1993), but dissimilar marking labels women as "other." Gendered language was also apparent in comments about men's strength and emotional reasons for failure cited more often for women. Messner et al. (1993), who noted that "dominants" in society typically are referred to by last names and subordinates by first names, found first names used over 50% of the time to refer to women but only 10% of the time for men. Also, the few male athletes referred to in the media by their first names were Black basketball players.

Recent studies reveal some improvement, but gender bias persists. Capranica and colleagues (2008) examined Italian coverage of the 2004 Olympics. The coverage was not balanced, in that female athletes received less media attention. However, they found that audience "appreciation" of men's and women's events was balanced, after they took into account the differences in coverage. Kian, Vincent, and Mondello (2008) examined the 2006 NCAA basketball tournament coverage in four major outlets (two newspapers and two online sources) and reported that, although there was some shift in media representation, the coverage still reflected the typical "gender order" with exclusion and trivialization of women's games. Their analysis of 508 articles revealed six themes that suggest gender bias:

He was always on my mind. Even when writing about women's events, sportswriters mentioned the men's tournament, players, or coaches.

She must have played with the boys to get that good. Articles on standout female players suggested that they had improved by playing with boys or men.

First football, then men's basketball, and then everything else. Although articles were about the basketball tournament, football was often mentioned.

Parents are noteworthy, especially athletic fathers. Parents were often mentioned, and the athletic or coaching experiences of fathers were especially common (mothers' athletic experiences were seldom mentioned).

Race only matters for men. The stereotype that African Americans are naturally superior athletes whereas European American athletes work hard to overcome lack of natural talent was noted in a few cases, but only in reference to male athletes.

Straight is great, but gay is nowhere. There were no references to gay men or lesbians in these articles, but references to heterosexual spouses or partners were common in articles on men's basketball.

The themes found by Kian et al. are similar to those in other research on media coverage; there has been some improvement, but still gender stereotypes remain common. The persistent gender stereotypes in sport media reports may partially reflect the persistent gender imbalance among those who do the reporting and their supervisors. More specifically, the sports media are heavily dominated by White men. Richard Lapchick recently released the 2008 *Racial and Gender Report Card of the Associated Press Sports Editors*, which is available online at The Institute for Diversity and Ethics in Sport (www.tidesport.org). The 2008 report, which was requested by the Associated Press Sports Editors (APSE), gave APSE websites and newspapers a grade of *C* for racial hiring practices and an *F* for gender hiring practices. In the executive summary, Lapchick noted little change from 2006; the biggest change was in the percent of African American columnists, which increased from 7.4 to 10.7%. In 2008, women made up 11.5% of the total staff, which actually was a decrease from 2006 when women made up 12.6% of total staff. Of the sports editors, who are in the most powerful position, 94% were men and 94% were White, but White men heavily dominated all positions; 87% of reporters were White and 91% were men. Given that the sports reporters do not come close to representing the diversity of the athletes, let alone the wider population or readers/viewers, gender bias in the media is not surprising. As Lapchick noted in the press release, the APSE is at least taking steps in the right direction by studying the issues.

Gender and Self-perceptions in Sport

Gender stereotypes and media bias are of concern because we act on them in ways that exaggerate minimal gender differences and restrict opportunities for everyone. Social development and social cognitive models (e.g., Bandura, 1986; Eccles, 1985) that frame much of the sport and exercise psychology research and serve as a basis for many programs suggest that the social environment, with its gender restrictions, is a key influence on self-perceptions and motivation. Restrictive gender stereotypes and self-perceptions are a particular concern for children as they are developing perceptions of physical activity and behaviors that will carry into their adult lives. Girls and boys have similar physical capabilities and could well be engaged in the same activities, but sport organizations, the media, parents, teachers, and most adults support "gender-appropriate" activities for children.

Gender, Expectations, and Participation

The continuing research of developmental psychologist Jacqueline Eccles and her colleagues is particularly relevant to sport and exercise psychology. Eccles' (1985; Eccles, Barber, Jozefowicz, Malenchuk, & Vida, 1999) developmental model incorporates the social context along with both expectations and values as determinants of achievement behaviors. Expectations and values are influenced by gender role socialization, the stereotyped expectations of others, and sociocultural norms, as well as individual characteristics and experiences. Eccles and Harold (1991) confirmed that the model holds for sport achievement, that gender influences children's sport achievement perceptions and behaviors at a very young age, and that these gender differences seem to be the product of gender role socialization. Eccles has often addressed sport competence; she has consistently found larger gender differences in sport competence than in other domains and that gender differences in perceptions are much larger than gender differences in actual sport-related skills.

Fredericks and Eccles' (2004) review of the literature on parental influence and youth sport involvement revealed that parents held gender-stereotyped beliefs about athletics and provided more opportunities and encouragement to sons than to daughters. Fredericks and Eccles (2005) examined these hypotheses with children from a large longitudinal study. They found that mothers and fathers did hold gender-stereotyped beliefs and practices and that parents' perceptions of the child's ability were related to the child's beliefs and participation. Their results confirmed that boys had higher perceived competence, valued athletics more, and had higher sport participation, despite the absence of gender differences in motor proficiency, which suggests the strong influence of socialization factors.

Because of the gender issues in physical self-perceptions, physical activity has a tremendous potential to enhance girls' and women's sense of competence and control. Some research supports the testimonials of women who report that physical activity programs lead to enhanced self-esteem and a sense of physical competence. Several studies (Brown & Harrison, 1986; Choi, 2000; Holloway, Beuter, & Duda, 1988; Krane et al., 2004) confirm that exercise programs, particularly weight and strength training, enhance self-perceptions of female participants. Research also suggests that exercise is associated with stronger self-efficacy and physical self-perceptions (Caruso & Gill, 1992; McAuley, Bane, & Mihalko, 1995). Tiggemann and Williamson (2000), in one of the few studies to include both women and men and a wide age range (16–60 years), found a negative relationship between exercise and self-perceptions for the younger women, but a positive relationship for mature women and for both young and mature men. The results suggest either developmental changes or different social processes are operating for the young women.

Conception and Ebbeck (2005) explored the benefits of physical activity for domestic abuse survivors – women who clearly can benefit from programs that foster empowerment and competence. The participants reported that physical activity gave them a sense of accomplishment, enhanced mental and physical states, and a greater sense of being "normal." Although the study was limited in scope, it offers promising directions for using physical activity to enhance well-being of these and other women who have been disempowered or experienced trauma.

Women who are not physically skilled, or who have physical disabilities, may particularly benefit from physical activity, but often confront barriers to participation. Henderson and Bedini (1995) found that women with disabilities reported that physical activities had leisure, therapeutic, and health value, but still some saw little value for physical activity in their lives. Blinde and McCallister (1999) interviewed adult women aged 19–54 years with physical disabilities and found that they participated in more fitness than sport activities, participated to maintain functional capabilities, and valued intrinsic gains (perceived competence, enhanced body image, and control).

Physical Activity, Gender, and Body Image

Body perceptions are particularly relevant to sport and exercise psychology. Research on body image (see Chapter 8) indicates that most women recognize and strive for an aesthetic ideal that is much less than ideal in terms of physical and mental health. Boys and men also have body image concerns, but the literature indicates that body image concerns are gender-related and that girls' and women's body images are much more negative. Girls are particularly concerned with physical beauty and maintaining the culturally ideal thin shape, whereas boys are more concerned with size, strength, and power. Some have suggested that sport and exercise settings exaggerate body image issues and encourage unhealthy behaviors for both women and men, but the research is mixed.

Body Image and Sport Participation

Some researchers have found positive relationships between participation in sport and body perceptions (Hausenblas & Mack, 1999), but others have found negative relationships (Davis, 1992). Krane, Waldron, Michalenok, and Stiles-Shipley (2001) found that athletes reported positive affect and a positive body image when they considered themselves in the athletic context, but a more negative body image as well as maladaptive behaviors (e.g., disordered eating) in other social contexts. Cox and Thompson (2000) similarly reported that elite female soccer players were confident in their athletic bodies but experienced more general dissatisfaction and anxiety related to other aspects of their bodies. Greenleaf (2002) explored body image issues with competitive female athletes and found that they recognized the conflict between their athletic bodies and social ideals, but the incongruence did not seem problematic.

Body Image, Sport, and Eating Disorders

Justine Reel and colleagues examined body image, eating disorders, and pressures in cheerleading and dance, activities assumed to highlight body issues. Reel and Gill (1996) found strong relationships between body dissatisfaction and eating disorders in cheerleaders; high school cheerleaders reported fewer pressures than their college counterparts but exhibited greater body dissatisfaction and disordered eating. In a study of college female dancers, Reel, SooHoo, Jamieson, and Gill (2005) found that, although social physique anxiety and eating disorder scores were moderate, the dancers overwhelmingly reported pressures to lose weight with unique pressures related to mirrors, performance advantages, and getting major roles.

Greenleaf (2005) has connected her research on body image in sport and exercise psychology with self-objectification theory (Fredrickson & Roberts, 1997) and reported that higher self-objectification was related to body shame, appearance anxiety, and disordered eating among physically active women. Similarly, Muscat and Long (2008) used objectification theory in exploring relationships among critical comments about the body and disordered eating in female collegiate athletes and recreational sports participants. They found no differences between the athletes and other sport participants on disordered eating, although athletes did report having received more critical comments. In line with objectification theory, those who recalled more critical comments had more negative emotional responses to the comments and more disordered eating.

Body Image and Physical Activity

Some researchers have examined body image with the wider range of physical activity settings. Hausenblas and Fallon (2002) found that exercise behavior was the strongest predictor of body satisfaction for men, but it was not a predictor for women. Berman, DeSouza, and Kerr (2005) extended that work with recreational exercisers and found that, although women cited numerous benefits of physical activity, weight and appearance were the key motivators for exercise. Berman et al. further explored the direction of the relationship and reported that weight/appearance concerns prompted physical activity; there was no evidence for reverse effects. Daubenmier (2005) investigated self-perceptions of female participants in yoga, aerobics, and non-yoga/non-aerobic activities and found that yoga participants had more positive self-perceptions with higher body satisfaction and less disordered eating.

Body Image and Muscularity

Most sport and exercise psychology research on body image and gender has focused on women, but recently the work has extended to men and muscularity. The popular book *The Adonis Complex* (Pope, Phillips, & Olivardia, 2000) suggested that boys and men may be obsessed with body appearance and engage in unhealthy behaviors, including excessive exercise, steroid abuse, and disordered eating in order to mold their bodies. That body image disorder is often referred to as *muscle dysmorphia*. Pope and colleagues (Pope, Choi, Olivardia, & Phillips, 1997) have described signs of muscle dysmorphia and reported that male weightlifters with muscle dysmorphia have more mood disturbances and eating disorders than those without muscle dysmorphia. A large study conducted in conjunction with the National Collegiate Athletic Association (NCAA) showed that 1.1% of female athletes met diagnostic criteria for bulimia nervosa and 9.2% presented subclinical bulimia and anorexia, whereas no male athletes met diagnostic criteria and only 0.01% presented with subclinical bulimia (Johnson, Powers, & Dick, 1999). Despite the low numbers, body image issues for boys and men are of concern in sport and exercise psychology. The issues may well be more prominent in other exercise and physical activity settings and may well be both under-reported and under-recognized. As researchers (Anderson, 1992; Beals, 2003) have noted, our tendency to think of body image and eating disorders as women's issues may keep both participants and professionals from recognizing men's problems.

Some research (e.g., Markula, 1995) suggests that women, as well as men, are concerned with muscularity and a strong but thin body. Kyrejto, Mosewich, Kowalski, Mack, and Crocker (2008) investigated drive for muscularity (DFM) and noted that most researchers focus on men and assume that men have a greater drive for muscularity. However, Kyrejto et al. noted that DFM has typically been defined and measured with a focus on "bulking up" or muscle size. When they assessed DFM with a focus on muscle "tone" they found that women were just as concerned about muscularity as were men. Moreover, men and women used similar strategies to develop their muscles; physical activity was by far the most common strategy for both men and women.

Overall, research on body perceptions and physical activity suggests that body image concerns are powerful, gender-related, and vary with the sport and cultural context. Sport and exercise psychologists who understand the role of gender and culture in body perceptions can help to promote healthy sport and exercise behaviors.

Physical Activity and Adolescent Development

Several researchers and community service professionals (e.g., Danish, Fazio, Nellen, & Owens, 2002; Hellison et al., 2000) have promoted sport and activity programs for positive youth development. Their research supports benefits for both girls and boys, and other recent work has explored intersections of gender, race, and class. The U.S. President's Council on Physical Fitness and Sport (1997) report *Physical Activity and Sport in the Lives of Girls* noted the physical benefits of sport and physical activity (e.g., motor skill development, fitness, reproductive function, body density, immune function), gave special attention to the psychosocial benefits (e.g., self-concept, emotional well-being, social competence), and concluded with a call for activity programs for girls.

Richman and Shaffer (2000) found a positive relationship between pre-college sport participation and self-esteem in college women. They reported that sport participation led to more positive body image, physical competencies, and less adherence to gender stereotypes, and those intervening variables led to greater self-esteem. Pedersen and Seidman (2004) investigated team sport participation and self-esteem with a large sample of adolescent girls from diverse racial/ethnic backgrounds, and they found that team sport participants scored higher than non-participants on self-esteem and athletic self-evaluation.

Miller, Sabo, Farrell, Barnes, and Melnick (1999) used data from the Centers for Disease Control and Prevention's (CDC) national 1995 *Youth Risk Behavior Survey* of high school students to explore gender and sexuality in the sport context and to address the practical question "Does sport reduce the risk of teen pregnancy?" The survey sample purposely included similar numbers of Black/African American, Hispanic/Latino/a, and White/European American youth. Results indicated that girls who participated in sport were indeed at less risk for teen pregnancy. Those girls reported lower rates of sexual experience, fewer partners, later age of first intercourse, higher rates of contraception use, and lower rates of past pregnancies. Boys in sport also reported higher contraceptive use, but on other measures they reported more sexual experience. Miller and colleagues suggested that athletic participation for girls leads to less adherence to conventional cultural scripts and more social/personal resources in sexual bargaining. Sport for boys provides similar resources but strengthens boys' commitment to traditional masculine scripts. In addition to the main results on sport and sexual behaviors, Miller et al. (1999) reported that boys had higher sport participation rates than did girls and that Whites had the highest participation of the three race/ethnic groups; Hispanic youth reported the lowest participation rates.

In one particularly relevant report, Erkut, Fields, Sing, and Marx (1996) explored the experiences (including sport experiences) that influenced urban girls from five ethnic backgrounds (Native

American, African American, European American, Asian/Pacific Islander, and Latina). When the girls were asked "What activities make you feel good about yourself?" athletics was the most common response. When asked about why the activity made them feel good, the most common response was mastery or competence (e.g., "I'm good at it") followed by enjoyment. Erkut et al.'s large, diverse sample and the many variations in findings highlight the importance of cultural contexts in the lives of these girls and raise many questions for sport and exercise psychology.

The Tucker Center (2007) recently released a 10-year update on their influential 1997 report on girls and physical activity. The 2007 report provides updated research summaries on the psychological, sociocultural, and physiological dimensions of girls' physical activity along with recommendations for best practices in programs, policies, and in future research (available at: www.tuckercenter.org). The recommendations in the psychosocial category highlight supportive practices that promote intrinsic motivation, mastery orientation, positive self-perceptions, social development, coping skills and mental health, and general engagement and empowerment. Sociocultural best practices emphasize positive gender confirmation and challenging limiting and unhealthy stereotypes. Physiological practices emphasize regular moderate-to-vigorous physical activity in fostering lifestyle activity.

Gender and Sexuality in Sport and Physical Activity

Sexuality and sexual orientation are clearly linked with gender. That link is particularly strong in sport and physical activity, but, with a few notable exceptions, particularly the work of Vikki Krane (Krane, 2001; Krane & Barber, 2003), sport and exercise psychology research has contributed little to our understanding of that link. The scholarship on sexual orientation and sport is typically found in sport studies and focuses on women, homophobia, and competitive athletics. Greg Herek (2000) prefers the term *sexual prejudice*, which denotes an attitude involving hostility or dislike, to homophobia, which is typically understood as an irrational fear and implies psychopathology. Sexual prejudice is the more appropriate term for our chapter, but related sport studies scholarship often refers to homophobia.

Homophobia and Professional Sport

Gender and sexuality in sport have different meanings and implications for women and men. As Michael Messner (1996, p. 225) has argued, the "dualities of *lesbian versus heterosexual* and *gay versus heterosexual*" have been differently constructed for women and men in sport. It is quite clear in our society, even without a critical cultural analysis, that sport for men is closely linked with masculinity and heterosexuality, but sport for women disrupts gender constructions. As Messner (1996) noted, the equation is clear for men: athleticism = masculinity = heterosexuality. However, for women, the equation is more paradoxical: athleticism? femininity? heterosexuality?

Many people assume that sport attracts lesbians (though, of course, not gay men), but there is no inherent relationship between sexual orientation and sport. No doubt, homophobia has kept more heterosexual women than lesbians out of sports, and homophobia restricts the behavior of all women in sport. Moreover, Messner (1992) suggested that homophobia probably restricts men in sport even more than it restricts women. Men who deviate from the heterosexual norm within the homophobic athletic culture often face ridicule, harassment, or physical violence. Hence, few male athletes tell others if they are gay. For readers who want more detail, Eric Anderson's (2005) book *In the Game:*

Gay Athletes and the Cult of Masculinity provides detailed and insightful accounts of interviews with over 60 gay male athletes at the high school, college, and professional levels.

Messner (1992) described sport as a powerful force that socializes boys and men into a restricted masculine identity and argued that homophobia leads all boys and men (gay or straight) to conform to a narrow definition of masculinity. "Real men" compete and avoid anything feminine that might lead them to be branded a "sissy." One successful elite athlete interviewed by Messner noted that he was interested in dance as a child but instead threw himself into athletics as a football and track jock. He reflected that he probably could have been a dancer but wanted the macho image of the athlete. Messner (1992) linked homophobia with misogyny; sport bonds men together as superior to women. For example, consider the widespread use of sexist and homophobic terms to derogate boys and men in sport (e.g., "fag," "you throw like a girl"). We expect to see men dominate women, and we are uncomfortable with bigger, stronger women who take on the active, dominant roles expected of athletes.

Griffin (1998) has written extensively on homophobia in sport and physical education, with a focus on connections among sexism, heterosexism, and sport. Broad (2001) took an activist approach and argued that women's sport participation may be interpreted as queer resistance and a "gendered unapologetic," that is, rather than downplaying masculine qualities, women in sport claim those qualities. Despite the visibility of a few prominent lesbian athletes, most remain closeted, and those involved with women's athletics often go out of the way to avoid any appearance of lesbianism. The former female coaches that Kamphoff (2006) interviewed provided examples of rampant homophobia in US collegiate coaching; the coaches clearly felt pressure to act as heterosexuals, regardless of their sexual orientation, to fit into the collegiate system.

Sexual Prejudice in Non-professional Sport and Physical Activity

Few scholars have examined sexual prejudice outside of competitive athletics in wider physical activity settings. Although scholarly research in sport and physical activity settings is limited, reports from the National Gay and Lesbian Task Force Policy Institute (Rankin, 2003) and Human Rights Watch (2001), as well as observations and anecdotal evidence, suggest that organized sport is a particularly hostile environment for sexual minority youth and that fitness clubs, sports medicine facilities, and recreational physical activity programs do not welcome gay men and lesbians.

In one of the few empirical studies, Morrow and Gill (2003) reported that both physical education teachers and students witnessed high levels of homophobic and heterosexist behaviors in public schools, but teachers failed to confront those behaviors. Over 60% of the teachers and students reported having seen homophobia, and over 50% of the gay/lesbian youth reported having experienced homophobia. The good news is that over 75% of the teachers said that they want safe, inclusive physical education, but the bad news is that over 50% of those teachers themselves reported that they had *never* confronted homophobia.

In subsequent research with undergraduates in exercise and sport science, Gill, Morrow, Collins, Lucey, and Schultz (2006) examined attitudes toward racial/ethnic minorities, older adults, and persons with disabilities, as well as sexual minorities. Overall, attitudes of our pre-professional students reflect sexual prejudice. Evaluation scores were markedly more negative for both gay men and lesbians than for other minority groups; male students were especially negative toward gay men.

Krane (2001; Krane & Barber, 2003) and her colleagues have drawn connections among gender, sexism, and heterosexism and have applied social identity theory as a framework for their research and advocacy work (e.g., Krane & Barber, 2003). Barber and Krane (2005) offered suggestions for considering gender and sexuality in sport psychology practice. For example, they called for sport psychology consultants to educate themselves, to create an atmosphere in which homophobic

Sexual Harassment in Sport and Exercise

Sexual harassment has clear gender connotations and relevance to sport and exercise psychology. Given the prevalence of sexual harassment and sexual assault in society in general and specifically in educational settings, female athletes are much more likely to present problems related to these issues than to eating disorders or other clinical issues. Considerable psychological research (e.g., Koss, 1990; see Chapter 18) and public attention demonstrate the prevalence of sexual harassment. Sport studies scholars have addressed this, but the sport and exercise psychology literature is nearly silent on the topic.

Lenskyj (1992) discussed sexual harassment in sport, drew ties to power relations and the ideology of male athletes, and noted unique concerns for female athletes. Sport (as a nonfeminine activity) may elicit derisive comments; team uniforms are revealing; male coaches are often fit and conventionally attractive; female athletes spend a lot of time training and thus less time in general social activity than other girls and women do; coaches are authoritarian; and in some sports (e.g., figure skating), merit is equated with conventional heterosexual attractiveness.

It is interesting that sexual harassment and abuse have received more attention at the international level than in the USA, which dominates much of the sport and exercise psychology literature. At the 2001 International Society of Sport Psychology Congress, Kari Fasting of Norway and Celia Brackenridge of the UK (2001) organized a symposium on sexual harassment and abuse; the presenters came from around the world. Their talks converged on common feminist themes and clearly showed the prevalence of sexual harassment and abuse throughout the sport world. Their collective works indicate that the sport climate fosters sexual harassment and abuse; that young, elite female athletes are particularly vulnerable; that neither athletes nor coaches have education or training about the issues; and that both research and professional development are needed in sport and exercise psychology to address issues of sexual harassment and abuse (Brackenridge, 1997; Brackenridge & Kirby, 1997; Bringer, Brackenridge, & Johnston, 2001; Kirby & Wintrup, 2001; Leahy, Pretty, & Tenenbaum, 2001; Volkwein, 2001; Volkwein, Schnell, Sherwood, & Livezey, 1997).

As part of a larger Norwegian Women's Project, Fasting, Brackenridge, and Walseth (2007) interviewed 25 elite female athletes about their experiences with sexual harassment. They found that the athletes had experienced negative emotions (e.g., anger, disgust, fear) and had exhibited more internal, individual responses than externally focused collective responses. Fasting et al. argued that sport organizations must change to challenge and eradicate sexual harassment, and their findings suggest that sport psychology consultants have a role in providing athletes with the skills to avert or confront sexual harassment. As the work of Fasting, Brackenridge, and their colleagues reminds us, sexual harassment and assault probably occur much more often than we recognize in sport and physical activity. Both women and men must be aware of issues, and sport and exercise psychology professionals can promote educational efforts and social action.

Advancing Gender Research and Social Action in Sport and Exercise Psychology

Our review of the literature on gender in sport and exercise psychology suggests several areas in which gender influences parallel those in other contexts and also highlights the unique gender context of sport and exercise. For example, like research in other areas of psychology, the sport and exercise psychology research on gender has moved beyond dichotomies of biological sex and masculine-feminine gender roles to emphasize social perceptions and processes. Still, gender stereotypes are more persistent in sport and exercise than in most settings. Most sport activities are clearly linked with masculine values and behaviors, and gender role and heterosexist stereotypes clearly limit behaviors for both men and women. The emphasis on the physical body in sport and exercise clearly brings body image issues into play, and research connects body perceptions, which clearly are gendered, with sport and exercise behaviors, including disordered eating. The research is limited in all ways and allows few strong conclusions. The gender research has focused on women, which brings neglected issues and experiences to our attention, but sport and exercise psychology scholars have far to go to understand gender and its influence on both women and men in physical activity settings.

Scholarship in sport and exercise psychology could advance the field by following the themes that form our chapter's framework to advance sport and exercise psychology research on gender and move toward more culturally competent professional practice. Some researchers cited here have addressed the first theme by considering the intersections of gender and culture, and a few have gone deeper to address the second theme by investigating power relations. Even fewer scholars have addressed the third theme by calling for cultural competence and social action in sport and exercise psychology practice.

Sport and exercise psychologists can look to a few psychologists who have incorporated these themes in their professional roles and provided models and directions. William Parham (2005) has offered useful guidelines for consulting with culturally diverse athletes based on his professional practice and drawing on multicultural psychology. His guidelines reflect our framework and suggest that sport and exercise psychology is culturally limited, with its emphasis on independence, competitiveness, and individual striving. In a commentary, Gridley (2005) affirmed much of Parham's advice, but added more emphasis on the persistent homophobia in sport, and with her more community-oriented approach and Australian base, she moves outside Western-based psychology.

Ruth Hall has eloquently addressed the intersections of gender, race, and sexuality in drawing on her clinical experiences to discuss the role of exercise in therapy with African American women (Hall, 1998) and more explicitly trying to "shake the foundation" of sport psychology in discussing the marginalization of women of color in sport (Hall, 2001). Researchers who take up the challenges of Parham, Grider, and Hall by incorporating multicultural perspectives, examining power relations, and engaging in active research that serves participants can help sport and exercise psychology to advance our understanding of gender and provide more inclusive empowering sport and exercise programs. Specifically, research on gender must consider the social context and cultural intersections, look beyond numbers for the social dynamics and power relations, and move to action for social justice by researching and advocating for sport and physical activity that promotes health and well-being for all women and men.

References

American Psychological Association. (2000). Guidelines for psychotherapy with gay, lesbian, and bisexual clients. *American Psychologist, 55,* 1440–1451.

American Psychological Association. (2003). Guidelines on multicultural education, training, research, practice, and organizational change for psychologists. *American Psychologist, 58,* 377–402.

American Psychological Association. (2004). Guidelines for psychological practice with older adults. *American Psychologist, 59,* 236–260.

American Psychological Association. (2007). Guidelines for psychological practice with girls and women. *American Psychologist, 62,* 949–979.

American Psychological Association. (2008). APA membership statistics. Accessed on November 23, 2008, from http://memforms.apa.org/apa/cli/mbdirsearch/mestat.cfm

Anderson, A. F. (1992). Eating disorders in male athletes: A special case? In K. D. Brownell, J. Rodin, & J. H. Wilmore (Eds.), *Body weight and performance in athletes: Disorders of modern society* (pp. 172–188). Philadelphia: Lea & Febiger.

Anderson, E. (2005). *In the game: Gay athletes and the cult of masculinity.* Albany, NY: State University of New York Press.

Arnett, J. J. (2008). The neglected 95%: Why American psychology needs to become less American. *American Psychologist, 63,* 602–614.

Bandura, A. (1986). *Social foundations of thought and action: A social-cognitive theory.* Englewood Cliffs, NJ: Prentice-Hall.

Barber, H., & Krane, V. (2005). The elephant in the locker room: Opening the dialogue about sexual orientation on women's sport teams. In M. B. Anderson (Ed.), *Sport psychology in practice* (pp. 265–285). Champaign, IL: Human Kinetics.

Beals, K. A. (2003). Mirror, mirror on the wall, who is the most muscular one of all? Disordered eating and body image disturbances in male athletes. *ACSM's Health & Fitness Journal, 7*(2), 6–11.

Bem, S. L. (1978). Beyond androgyny: Some presumptuous prescriptions for a liberated sexual identity. In J. Sherman & F. Denmark (Eds.), *Psychology of women: Future directions for research* (pp. 1–23). New York: Psychological Dimensions.

Berman, E., DeSouza, M. J., & Kerr, G. (2005). A qualitative examination of weight concerns, eating, and exercise behaviors in recreational exercisers. *Women in Sport and Physical Activity Journal, 14,* 24–38.

Blinde, E. M., & McCallister, S. G. (1999). Women, disability, and sport and physical fitness activity: The intersection of gender and disability dynamics. *Research Quarterly for Exercise and Sport, 70,* 303–312.

Brackenridge, C. (1997). Playing safe: Assessing the risk of sexual abuse to elite child athletes. *International Review for the Sociology of Sport, 32,* 407–418.

Brackenridge, C., & Kirby, S. (1997). "He owned me basically...": Women's experience of sexual abuse in sport. *International Review for the Sociology of Sport, 32,* 115–130.

Bringer, J. D., Brackenridge, C. H., & Johnston, L. H. (2001). A qualitative study of swimming coaches' attitudes toward sexual relationships in sport. In A. Papaioannou, M. Goudas, & Y. Theodorkis (Eds.), *International Society of Sport Psychology 10th World Congress of Sport Psychology: Vol. 4 Programme & Proceedings* (pp. 187–189). Thessaloniki, Greece: Christodoulidi Publications.

Broad, K. L. (2001). The gendered unapologetic: Queer resistance in women's sport. *Sociology of Sport Journal, 18,* 181–204.

Brown, R. D., & Harrison, J. M. (1986). The effects of a strength training program on the strength and self-concept of two female age groups. *Research Quarterly for Exercise and Sport, 57,* 315–320.

Capranica, L., Tessitore, A., D'Artibale, E., Cortis, C., Casella, R., Camilleri, E., et al. (2008). Italian women's television coverage and audience during the 2004 Athens Olympic Games. *Research Quarterly for Exercise and Sport, 79,* 101–115.

Carpenter, L. J., & Acosta, R.V. (2008). *Women in intercollegiate sport: A longitudinal, national study thirty-one year update 1977–2008.* Retrieved March 20, 2008, from http://www.acostacarpenter.org

Caruso, C., & Gill, D. L. (1992). Strengthening self-perceptions through exercise. *Journal of Sports Medicine and Fitness, 32,* 416–427.

Choi, P. Y. L. (2000). *Femininity and the physically active woman.* Philadelphia: Taylor & Francis.

Conception, R. Y., & Ebbeck, V. (2005). Examining the physical activity experience of survivors of domestic violence in relation to self-views. *Journal of Sport and Exercise Psychology, 27,* 197–211.

Cox, B., & Thompson, S. (2000). Multiple bodies: Sportswomen, soccer, and sexuality. *International Review for the Sociology of Sport, 35,* 5–20.

Crespo, C. J. (2005). Physical activity in minority populations: Overcoming a public health challenge. *The President's Council on Physical Fitness and Sports Research Digest, 6*(2).

Crespo, C. J., Ainsworth, B. E., Keteyian, S. J., Heath, G. W., & Smit, E. (1999). Prevalence of physical inactivity and its relations to social class in U.S. adults: Results from the Third National Health and Nutrition Examination Survey, 1988–1994. *Medicine & Science in Sports & Exercise, 31,* 1821–1827.

Danish, S. J., Fazio, R. J., Nellen, V. C., & Owens, S. S. (2002). Teaching life skills through sport: Community-based programs to enhance adolescent development. In J. L. VanRaalte & B. W. Brewer (Eds.), *Exploring sport and exercise psychology* (2nd ed., pp. 269–288). Washington, DC: American Psychological Association.

Daubenmier, J. J. (2005). The relationship of yoga, body awareness, and body responsiveness to self-objectification and disordered eating. *Psychology of Women Quarterly, 29,* 207–219.

Davis, C. (1992). Body image, dieting behaviors, and personality factors: A study of high –performance female athletes. *International Journal of Sport Psychology, 23*, 179–192.

Deaux, K. (1984). From individual differences to social categories: Analysis of a decade's research on gender. *American Psychologist, 39*, 105–116.

Deaux, K., & Kite, M. (1993). Gender stereotypes. In F. L. Denmark & M. A. Paludi (Eds.), *Psychology of women: A handbook of issues and theories* (pp. 107–139). Westport, CT: Greenwood.

Desertrain, G. S., & Weiss, M. R. (1988). Being female and athletic: A case for conflict? *Sex Roles, 18*, 567–582.

Duda, J. L. (1986). A cross-cultural analysis of achievement motivation in sport and in the classroom. In L. VanderVelden & J. Humphrey (Eds.), *Psychology and sociology of sport: Current selected research* (Vol. 1, pp. 115–134). New York: AMS Press.

Duda, J. L., & Allison, M. T. (1990). Cross-cultural analysis in exercise and sport psychology: A void in the field. *Journal of Sport & Exercise Psychology, 12*, 114–131.

Eccles, J. S. (1985). Sex differences in achievement patterns. In T. Sonderegger (Ed.), *Nebraska Symposium of Motivation, 1984: Psychology and gender* (pp. 97–132). Lincoln, NE: University of Nebraska Press.

Eccles, J. S., Barber, B., Jozefowicz, D., Malenchuk, O., & Vida, M. (1999). Self-evaluation of competence, task values, and self-esteem. In N. G. Johnson, M. C. Roberts, & J. Worell (Eds.), *Beyond appearance: A new look at adolescent girls* (pp. 53–84). Washington, DC: American Psychological Association.

Eccles, J. S., & Harold, R. D. (1991). Gender differences in sport involvement: Applying the Eccles expectancy-value model. *Journal of Applied Sport Psychology, 3*, 7–35.

Erkut, S., Fields, J. P., Sing, R., & Marx, F. (1996). Diversity in girls' experiences: Feeling good about who you are. In B. J. R. Leadbeater & N. Way (Eds.), *Urban girls: Resisting stereotypes, creating identities* (pp. 53–64). New York: New York University Press.

Fasting, K., & Brackenridge, C. (2001, June). *Sexual harassment and abuse in sport – Challenges for sport psychology in the new millennium*. Symposium presented at the World Congress of Sport Psychology, Skiathos, Greece.

Fasting, K., Brackenridge, C., & Walseth, K. (2007). Women athletes' personal responses to sexual harassment in sport. *Journal of Applied Sport Psychology, 19*, 419–433.

Fallon, M. A., & Jome, L. M. (2007). An exploration of gender-role expectations and conflict among women rugby players. *Psychology of Women Quarterly, 31*, 311–321.

Fisher, L. A., Butryn, T. M., & Roper, E. A. (2003). Diversifying (and politicizing) sport psychology through cultural studies: A promising perspective. *Sport Psychologist, 17*, 391–405.

Fredericks, J. A., & Eccles, J. S. (2004). Parental influences on youth involvement in sports. In M. R. Weiss (Ed.), *Developmental sport and exercise psychology: A lifespan perspective* (pp. 145–164). Morgantown, WV: Fitness Information Technology.

Fredericks, J. A., & Eccles, J. S. (2005). Family socialization, gender, and sport motivation and involvement. *Journal of Sport & Exercise Psychology, 27*, 3–31.

Fredrickson, B. L., & Roberts, T.-A. (1997). Objectification theory. *Psychology of Women Quarterly, 21*, 173–206.

Gilenstam, K., Karp, S., & Henriksson-Larsen, K. (2008). Gender in ice hockey: Women in a male territory. *Scandinavian Journal of Medicine & Science in Sports, 18*, 235–249.

Gill, D. L. (1993). Competitiveness and competitive orientation in sport. In R. N. Singer, M. Murphey, & L. K. Tennant (Eds.), *Handbook on research in sport psychology* (pp. 314–327). New York: Macmillan.

Gill, D. L. (1995). Women's place in the history of sport psychology. *Sport Psychologist, 9*, 418–433.

Gill, D. L. (2007). Gender and cultural diversity. In G. Tenenbaum & R.C. Eklund (Eds.), *Handbook of sport psychology* (3rd ed., pp. 823–844). Champaign, IL: Human Kinetics.

Gill, D. L., & Deeter, T. E. (1988). Development of the Sport Orientation Questionnaire. *Research Quarterly for Exercise and Sport, 59*, 191–202.

Gill, D. L., Morrow, R. G., Collins, K. E., Lucey, A. B., & Schultz, A. M. (2006). Attitudes and sexual prejudice in sport and physical activity. *Journal of Sport Management, 20*, 554–564.

Greenleaf, C. (2002). Athletic body image: Exploratory interviews with former competitive female athletes. *Women in Sport and Physical Activity Journal, 11*, 63–74.

Greenleaf, C. (2005). Self-objectification among physically active women. *Sex Roles, 52*, 51–62.

Gridley, H. (2005). Commentary on chapter 11. In M. B. Anderson (Ed.), *Sport psychology in practice* (pp. 217–221). Champaign, IL: Human Kinetics.

Griffin, P. S. (1998). *Strong women, deep closets: Lesbians and homophobia in sport*. Champaign, IL: Human Kinetics.

Hall, M. A. (1996). *Feminism and sporting bodies*. Champaign, IL: Human Kinetics.

Hall, R. L. (1998). Softly strong: African American women's use of exercise in therapy. In K. F. Hays (Ed.), *Integrating exercise, sports, movement and mind: Therapeutic unity* (pp. 81–100). New York: Haworth Press.

Hall, R. L. (2001). Shaking the foundation: Women of color in sport. *Sport Psychologist, 15*, 386–400.

Harris, D. V., & Jennings, S. E. (1977). Self-perceptions of female distance runners. *Annals of the New York Academy of Sciences, 301*, 808–815.

Hausenblas, H., & Mack, D. E. (1999). Social physique anxiety and eating disorders among female athletic and nonathletic populations. *Journal of Sport Behavior, 22*, 502–512.

Hausenblas, H., & Fallon, E. (2002). Relationship among body image, exercise behavior, and exercise dependence symptoms. *International Journal of Eating Disorders, 32*, 179–185.

Hellison, D., Cutworth, N., Kallusky, J., Martinek, T., Parker, M., & Stiehl, J. (2000). *Youth development and physical activity*. Champaign, IL: Human Kinetics.

Henderson, K. A., & Bedini, L. A. (1995). "I have a soul that dances like Tina Turner, but my body can't": Physical activity and women with disability impairments. *Research Quarterly for Exercise and Sport, 66*, 151–161.

Herek, G. M. (2000). Psychology of sexual prejudice. *Current Directions in Psychological Science, 9*, 19–22.

Holloway, J. B., Beuter, A., & Duda, J. L. (1988). Self-efficacy and training for strength in adolescent girls. *Journal of Applied Social Psychology, 18*, 699–719.

Human Rights Watch. (2001). Hatred in the hallways: Violence and discrimination against lesbian, gay, bisexual, and transgender students in U.S. schools. *American Journal of Health Education, 32*, 302–306. Full report Retrieved June 6, 2005, from http://www.hrw.org/reports/2001/uslgbt/toc.htm

Hyde, J. S. (2005). The gender similarities hypothesis. *American Psychologist, 60*, 581–592.

Johnson, C., Powers, J. S., & Dick, R. (1999). Athletes and eating disorders: The National Collegiate Athletic Association study. *International Journal of Eating Disorders, 26*, 179–188.

Kamphoff, C. (2006). *Bargaining with patriarchy: Former women coaches' experiences and their decision to leave collegiate coaching*. Unpublished Doctoral Dissertation, University of North Carolina at Greensboro.

Kamphoff, C. (2008). The U.K. coaching system is failing women coaches: A commentary. *International Journal of Sport Science and Coaching, 3*, 469–473.

Kamphoff, C., Araki, K., & Gill, D. (2004, Fall). *Diversity issues in AAASP*. AAASP Newsletter, pp. 26–27.

Kamphoff, C., Armentrout, S. M., Driska, A., & Daniels, C. (2009, April). *Women's experiences as Division I head coaches of men's teams*. Paper presented at the American Alliance of Health, Physical Education, Recreation, and Dance International Conference, Tampa, FL.

Kamphoff, C., Armentrout, S. M., & Leberman S. (2008, May). *Women as elite coaches: Strategies for sport and social change*. Paper presented at Remember is to Resist: 40 Years of Sport and Social Change International Conference, Toronto, Canada.

Kane, M. J., & Snyder, E. (1989). Sport typing: The social "containment" of women. *Arena Review, 13*, 77–96.

Kang, L., Gill, D. L., Acevedo, E. D., & Deeter, T. E. (1990). Competitive orientations among athletes and nonathletes in Taiwan. *International Journal of Sport Psychology, 21*, 146–152.

Kian, E. M., Vincent, J., & Mondello, M. (2008). Masculine hegemonic hoops: An analysis of media coverage of March madness. *Sociology of Sport Journal, 25*, 223–242.

Kimm, S. Y. S., Glynn, N. W., Kriska, A. M., Barton, B. A., Krosenberg, S. S., Daniels, S. R., et al. (2002). Decline in physical activity in Black girls and White girls during adolescence. *New England Journal of Medicine, 347*, 709–715.

Kirby, S. L., & Wintrup, G. (2001). Running the gauntlet: An examination of initiation/hazing and sexual abuse in sport. In A. Papaioannou, M. Goudas, & Y. Theodorkis (Eds.), *International Society of Sport Psychology 10th World Congress of Sport Psychology*: Vol. 4 Programme & Proceedings (p. 186). Thessaloniki, Greece: Christodoulidi Publications.

Koca, C., & Asci, F. H. (2005). Gender role orientation in Turkish female athletes and non-athletes. *Women in Sport and Physical Activity Journal, 14*, 86–94.

Koivula, N. (1995). Ratings of gender appropriateness of sports participation: Effects of gender-based schema processing. *Sex Roles, 33*, 543–557.

Koss, M. P. (1990). The women's mental health research agenda. *American Psychologist, 45*, 374–380.

Krane, V. (2001). We can be athletic and feminine, but do we want to? Challenging hegemonic femininity in women's sport. *Quest, 53*, 115–133.

Krane, V., & Barber, H. (2003). Lesbian experiences in sport: A social identity perspective. *Quest, 55*, 328–346.

Krane, V., Choi, P. Y. L., Baird, S. M., Aimar, C. M., & Kauer, K. J. (2004). Living the paradox: Female athletes negotiate femininity and muscularity. *Sex Roles, 50*, 315–329.

Krane, V., Waldron, J., Michalenok, J., & Stiles-Shipley, J. (2001). Body image concerns in female exercisers and athletes. *Women in Sport and Physical Activity Journal, 10*, 17–54.

Kyrejto, J. W., Mosewich, A. D., Kowalski, K. C., Mack, D. E., & Crocker, P. R. E. (2008). Men's and women's drive for muscularity: Gender differences and cognitive behavioral correlates. *International Journal of Sport and Exercise Psychology, 6*, 69–84.

Laberge, S. (1992). Employment situation of higher performance coaches in Canada. *Sport Canada, 3*(1), 1–49.

Lapchick, R. (2006). *The 2005 Racial and Gender Report Card.* Retrieved March, 2008, from http://www.bus.ucf.edu/sport

Lapchick, R. (2008). *The 2008 Racial and Gender Report Card of the Associated Press Sports Editors.* Retrieved June 28, 2008, from http://www.tidesport.org

Lapchick, R., Lerner, C., & Zahn, J. (2008). *The 2008 Women's National Basketball Association Racial and Gender Report Card.* The Institute for Diversity and Ethics in Sport. Retrieved October 15, 2008, from http://www.bus.ucf.edu/sport/public/downloads/2008_WNBA_RGRC_PR.pdf

Leahy, T., Pretty, G., & Tenenbaum, G. (2001). "Once I got into the elite squad, it was a lot easier for him to get me": Sexual abuse in organised sport – A comparison of elite and club athletes' experiences. In A. Papaioannou, M. Goudas, & Y. Theodorkis (Eds.), *International Society of Sport Psychology 10th World Congress of Sport Psychology: Programme & Proceedings* (Vol. 4, pp. 190–192). Thessaloniki, Greece: Christodoulidi Publications.

Lenskyj, H. (1992). Unsafe at home base: Women's experiences of sexual harassment in university sport and physical education. *Women in Sport & Physical Activity Journal, 1,* 19–33.

Markula, P. (1995). Firm but shapely, fit but sexy, strong but thin: Postmodern aerobicizing female bodies. *Sociology of Sport Journal, 15,* 109–137.

McAuley, E., Bane, S., & Mihalko, S. (1995). Exercise in middle-aged adults: Self-efficacy and self-presentational outcomes. *Preventive Medicine, 24,* 319–328.

McNally, J., & Orlick, T. (1975). Cooperative sport structures: A preliminary analysis. *Mouvement, 7,* 267–271.

Messner, M. A. (1992). *Power at play: Sports and the problem of masculinity.* Boston: Beacon Press.

Messner, M. A. (1996). Studying up on sex. *Sociology of Sport Journal, 13,* 21–237.

Messner, M. A., Duncan, M. C., & Jensen, K. (1993). Separating the men from the girls: The gendered language of televised sports. In D. S. Eitzen (Ed.), *Sport in contemporary society: An anthology* (4th ed., pp. 219–233). New York: St. Martin's Press.

Metheny, E. (1965). Symbolic forms of movement: The feminine image in sports. In E. Metheny (Ed.), *Connotations of movement in sport and dance* (pp. 43–56). Dubuque, IA: Brown.

Miller, K. E., Sabo, D. F., Farrell, M. P., Barnes, G. M., & Melnick, M. J. (1999). Sports, sexual behavior, contraceptive use, and pregnancy among female and male high school students: Testing cultural resource theory. *Sociology of Sport Journal, 16,* 366–387.

Morrow, R. G., & Gill, D. L. (2003). Perceptions of homophobia and heterosexism in physical education. *Research Quarterly for Exercise and Sport, 74,* 205–214.

Muscat, A. C. & Long, B. C. (2008). Comments about body shape and weight: Disordered eating of female athletes and sport participants. *Journal of Applied Sport Psychology, 20,* 1–24.

National Amateur Athletic Federation, Women's Division. (1930). *Women and athletics.* New York: Barnes.

Norman, L. (2008). The U.K. coaching system is failing women coaches. *International Journal of Sport Science and Coaching, 3,* 447–467.

Parham, W. D. (2005). Raising the bar: Developing an understanding of athletes from racially, culturally, and ethnically diverse backgrounds. In M. B. Anderson (Ed.), *Sport psychology in practice* (pp. 201–215). Champaign, IL: Human Kinetics.

Park, R. J. (1987). Sport, gender and society in a transatlantic Victorian perspective. In J. A. Mangan & R. J. Park (Eds.), *From "fair sex" to feminism: Sport and socialization of women in the industrial and postindustrial eras* (pp. 58–93). London: Cass.

Pedersen, S., & Seidman, E. (2004). Team sport achievement and self-esteem development among urban adolescent girls. *Psychology of Women Quarterly, 28,* 412–422.

Pope, H. G., Gruber, A. J., Choi, P., Olivardia, R. & Phillips, K. A. (1997). Muscle dysmorphia: An unrecognized form of body dysmorphic disorder. *Psychosomatics, 38,* 548–557.

Pope, H. G., Phillips, K. A., & Olivardia, R. (2000). *The Adonis complex: The secret crisis of male body obsession.* New York: Free Press.

Pratt, M., Macera, C. A., & Blanton, C. (1999). Levels of physical activity and inactivity in children and adults in the United States: Current evidence and research issues. *Medicine and Science in Sport and Exercise, 31,* 526–533.

President's Council on Physical Fitness and Sports. (1997). *Physical activity and sport in the lives of girls: Physical and mental health dimensions from an interdisciplinary approach.* Washington, DC: Department of Health and Human Services.

Ram, N., Starek, J., & Johnson, J. (2004). Race, ethnicity, and sexual orientation: Still a void in sport and exercise psychology. *Journal of Sport & Exercise Psychology, 26,* 250–268.

Rankin, S. R. (2003). *Campus climate for gay, lesbian, bisexual, and transgender people: A national perspective.* New York: National Gay and Lesbian Task Force Policy Institute. Retrieved June 6, 2005, from: http://www.thetaskforce.org/reslibrary

Reel, J. J., & Gill, D. L. (1996). Psychosocial factors related to eating disorders among high school and college female cheerleaders. *Sport Psychologist, 10*, 195–206.

Reel, J. J., SooHoo, S., Jamieson, K. M., & Gill, D. L. (2005). Femininity to the extreme: Body image concerns among college female dancers. *Women in Sport and Physical Activity Journal, 14*, 39–51.

Richman, E. L., & Shaffer, D. R. (2000). "If you let me play sports": How might sport participation influence the self-esteem of adolescent females. *Psychology of Women Quarterly, 24*, 189–199.

Riemer, B. A., & Visio, M. E. (2003). Gender-typing of sports: An investigation of Metheny's classification. *Research Quarterly for Exercise and Sport, 74*, 193–204.

Rimmer, J. H. (2005). The conspicuous absence of people with disabilities in public fitness and recreation facilities: Lack of interest or lack of access? *American Journal of Health Promotion, 19*, 327–329.

Sage, G. H., & Loudermilk, S. (1979). The female athlete and role conflict. *Research Quarterly, 50*, 88–96.

Schmalz, D. L., & Kerstetter, D. L. (2006). Girlie girls and manly men: Children's stigma consciousness of gender in sports and physical activities. *Journal of Leisure Research, 38*, 536–557.

Spears, B. (1978). Prologue: The myth. In C. A. Ogelsby (Ed.), *Women and sport: From myth to reality* (pp. 1–15). Philadelphia, PA: Lea & Febiger.

Spence, J. T., & Helmreich, R. L. (1978). *Masculinity and femininity*. Austin, TX: University of Texas Press.

Sue, D. W. (2004). Whiteness and ethnocentric monoculturalism: Making the "invisible" visible. *American Psychologist, 59*, 761–769.

Tiggemann, M., & Williamson, S. (2000). The effect of exercise on body satisfaction and self-esteem as a function of gender and age. *Sex Roles, 43*, 119–127.

Trujillo, N. (1995). Machines, missiles, and men: Images of the male body on ABC's *Monday Night Football*. *Sociology of Sport Journal, 12*, 403–423.

Tucker Center for Research on Girls and Women in Sport. (2007). *The 2007 Tucker Center Research Report on developing physically active girls: An evidence-based multidisciplinary approach*. Retrieved January, 19, 2008, from Tucker Center for Research on Girls & Women in Sport, University of Minnesota Web site: http://www.tuckercenter.org/projects/tcrr/default.html

U.S. Department of Health and Human Services (USDHHS). (2000). *Healthy people 2010*. Washington, DC: Author.

U.S. Department of Health and Human Services (USDHHS). (2003). *National healthcare disparities report*. Washington, DC: Author.

Volkwein, K. A. E. (2001). Sexual harassment of women in athletics vs. academia. In A. Papaioannou, M. Goudas & Y. Theodorkis (Eds.), *International Society of Sport Psychology 10th World Congress of Sport Psychology*: Vol. 4. *Programme & Proceedings* (p. 183). Thessaloniki, Greece: Christodoulidi Publications.

Volkwein, K. A. E., Schnell, F. I., Sherwood, D., & Livezey, A. (1997). Sexual harassment in sports: Perceptions and experiences of female student athletes. *International Review for the Sociology of Sport, 32*, 283–296.

Weinberg, R., Tennenbaum, G., McKenzie, A., Jackson, S. J., Anshel, M., Grove, R., et al. (2000). Motivation for sport and physical activity: Relationships to culture, self-reported activity levels, and gender. *International Journal of Sport Psychology, 31*, 321–346.

Chapter 25
Ethical and Methodological Considerations for Gender Researchers in Forensic Psychology

Kenneth V. Heard

Forensic psychology is a broad and rapidly growing field that encompasses the intersection of psychology and the law. Although psychologists have been involved with research on forensically relevant subjects and have consulted on forensic issues for over 100 years, the field has been in a period of expansion and professionalization since the 1970s. As is often the case during the growth of a profession, there remains some disagreement about the boundaries, definitions, and terminologies that form the common understanding of what forensic psychology is, what minimum or common training standards are necessary or sufficient for forensic psychology as a discipline, and what criteria must be met for an individual to be labeled a "forensic psychologist." Despite this, there appears to be increasing consensus that there is a significant distinction to be drawn between psychologists who provide direct professional services in forensic contexts and psychologists whose interaction with the legal system is less frequent, direct, or applied. The American Psychological Association (APA, 2009, Para. 1), in recognizing Forensic Psychology as an area of specialization, specified that

> Forensic psychology is the professional practice by psychologists who foreseeably and regularly provide professional psychological expertise to the judicial system. Such professional practice is generally within the areas of clinical psychology, counseling psychology, neuropsychology, and school psychology, or other applied areas within psychology involving the delivery of human services, by psychologists who have additional expertise in law and the application of applied psychology to legal proceedings.

Likewise, the American Psychology-Law Society (APA Division 41) published the Specialty Guidelines for Forensic Psychologists

> to provide more specific guidance to forensic psychologists in monitoring their professional conduct when acting in assistance to courts, parties to legal proceedings, correctional and forensic mental health facilities, and legislative agencies (Committee on Ethical Guidelines for Forensic Psychologists, 1991, p. 655).

Although under revision, the current draft of the Specialty Guidelines retains the assumption that forensic psychologists are specifically those engaged in applied practice to the legal system. This may be reasonable in some respects, given that the majority of Division 41 members identify themselves as clinicians. Furthermore, all US states license "psychologists" as applied practitioners, and some, but not all, require an additional certification to perform some court-related services. Not all writers agree with this narrow definition, but I adopted it for the purposes of this chapter. This is not to diminish the importance of forensic researchers but to remain consistent with the terminology that is most commonly recognized within the legal system. Psychologists from all disciplines engage in forensically relevant research, and this chapter focuses on the work of researchers rather than on applied practice.

K.V. Heard (✉)
University of Rhode Island, Kingston, RI, USA

Defining Gender

The definition of "gender" is far more complex. In general, the prevailing concept of gender in most forensic contexts is that of biological sex. For example, the assignment of a transgendered person to a men's or women's correctional facility will generally be decided by biological sex as determined by the current state of the person's genitalia (c.f., Peek, 2004). The exception is in those specific cases where defining gender is *in and of itself* the issue under consideration. In these instances, psychological, sexual, and social identities may become influential or even deciding factors when a person's gender is "determined" by the courts for legal purposes. For the purposes of this chapter, I use gender in a broader sense that encompasses social and cultural aspects of identity, roles, and behavior, but the reader should be aware that much of the published literature in legal and forensic scholarship may use the term in its narrower sense.

Methodological and Epistemological Pluralism in Gender Research

More than in many other areas of psychology, gender researchers have developed and advocated for a variety of methodological perspectives, such as qualitative, critical, and constructivist (c.f., Rabinowitz & Martin, 2001). Context, culture, politics, and various other considerations play an important role in how research is conceptualized, implemented, interpreted, and received, both at the level of the individual research study and at the level of the epistemological assumptions that underlie programs of research. In the interest of grounding this chapter, I disclose that my own perspective is one of scientific realism in the sense that I believe that there is some objective reality "out there" that exists independently of our culture and understanding. I do not believe that we can obtain objective knowledge in the sense of a "God's eye" perspective, but that we can gain a more probabilistic understanding of that reality and that different competing methods and theories may be differentially effective and accurate in characterizing it. A variety of competing methods and models can help to mitigate the influence of various biases and cognitive limitations in the ongoing effort to develop an understanding of reality with incrementally greater verisimilitude, but the application of the scientific method has had unparalleled success compared to alternative models. Beyond this, the actors in forensic contexts are not necessarily interested in academic arguments about epistemology. Forensic researchers should recognize that legislative bodies, the courts, and other legal systems have immediate pragmatic concerns and will often have limited or no use for such theoretical discussions (c.f., Faust & Heard, 2003a, 2003b). Judges, administrators, and legislators may have an intellectual interest in these issues, but, at a fundamental level, decision-making in legal, administrative, and legislative settings often requires the evaluation of the relative merit of competing assertions (e.g., guilty or not guilty; competent or incompetent). These demands can be incompatible with the ways that some social scientists conceptualize knowledge (c.f., Meehl, 1971/1991). Failure to acknowledge this may hinder the ability of forensic researchers to have a meaningful impact outside of academia. Important research findings may be easily attacked, dismissed, misunderstood, or ignored when communicated in language that decision makers do not find relevant.

The Goals of This Chapter and a Final Disclaimer

As noted above, forensic psychology covers a very wide range of subjects. An adequate treatment of any individual topic (e.g., the role of gender in child custody arrangements, gender differences in the effectiveness of prison rehabilitation programs, the effect of gender on the career paths of attorneys and law enforcement personnel) could warrant an individual chapter or a book, and so a thorough review of the existing literature is well beyond the scope of this chapter. Consequently, I focus on methodological concerns specific to forensic research and attempt to identify main areas of consideration with gender-relevant illustrations.

The material in this chapter is written with the US legal system in mind, and so much of it will not necessarily apply to other nations. There is also considerable variation between the various federal, state, and local jurisdictions within the USA, so readers should consider the content of this chapter in the most appropriate context. The legal landscape can also change dramatically and abruptly as a result of legislation or judicial precedent, which could require a reconsideration of the content, organization, and conclusions of this chapter. Last, this chapter is intended to highlight areas for researchers to consider; it is not to provide legal advice. When confronted with questions or dilemmas, researchers should seek appropriate and qualified consultation.

General Considerations in Research in Forensic Contexts

Standards for Forensic Research Relative to Research in Other Contexts

Decisions in forensic contexts can have substantial consequences for the individuals and populations affected by them. They may be binding, life-altering, or irreversible in ways that exceed the decisions made in many other venues. Forensic research has the potential to inform these decisions for good or ill. As a consequence, forensic researchers have an obligation to adhere to the best possible methodological standards and to the practice and policy standards of the field to minimize the risk that bad science causes harm to the public. Researchers should anticipate that there is a potential for the misuse and abuse of their research by individuals with a political agenda or who might otherwise have a stake in legal outcomes. Sentences in written communications that may easily be taken out of context, or conclusions that are not calibrated to the strength of the data, can have unforeseen and unintended consequences when they enter the public sphere in the media, litigation, or policy debates. Even assuming that all parties involved have the best of intentions, forensic researchers should be mindful of the fact that many consumers of their work will not have significant (or any) formal training in the conduct and interpretation of science, and so it is particularly important for researchers to be as clear and thoughtful in their reports and communications as possible. Once poor research, or a misinterpretation (or misrepresentation) of good research, has made its way into the public sector, it may take years of effort for the damage to be undone (if it can be).

A second reason for exercising care in the interpretation and reporting of results is that failure to do so may undermine the efforts of psychologists to work toward social change. Forensic researchers are often drawn to the area due to an interest in advocacy and social justice. Statements that are not adequately supported, that are stronger than the underlying data, or that can be taken as evidence of bias may be seized upon to discredit the researcher or those who rely upon the researcher's efforts in forming their opinions. It is critical to recognize that forensic psychologists cannot allow advocacy to overtake objectivity or the strength of data. Johnson, Krafka, and Cecil (2000) and Krafka, Dunn, Johnson, Cecil, and Miletich (2002) reported that judges identified expert witnesses who abandon objectivity and overstep the reliability of their data as among the more frequent problems that they encounter when dealing with expert witnesses.

Forensically relevant research may be subject to far greater scrutiny than research in other areas. During litigation, for example, particular studies may be dissected and challenged on a point-by-point basis. Individual studies, researchers, and even bodies of research may become tainted in the eyes of policy makers and the public as a result of such examination. Even exemplary research may be compromised by inflammatory rhetoric or incautious statements. This is not to advocate for or to defend the ad hominem attack but to highlight the potential damage to efforts to create positive change that can result when researchers do not fully appreciate the risks involved. Because issues related to social justice evoke strong, and not necessarily reasoned, opinions, there will always be individuals who are predisposed to be hostile to research findings that do not comport with their beliefs. Research communications in forensically relevant areas should be written in anticipation of potential attacks so as to defuse them in advance.

In line with this discussion, researchers who anticipate that the subject of their research may be utilized within legal proceedings would be advised to familiarize themselves with the standards for the admissibility of expert witness testimony in court, in particular those established by the Federal Rules of Evidence (Committee on the Judiciary, House of Representatives, 2006) and *Daubert v. Merrell Dow Pharmaceuticals* (1993). Before an expert witness can testify, she or he must be proffered to the court and certified as an expert. The process of certification may include, among other considerations, an evaluation of the reliability, or scientific merit, of the proposed testimony. If the judge decides that the expert's proposed testimony does not meet some minimum standard of scientific merit for presentation at trial, he or she can refuse to certify the expert and admit the testimony into evidence. In addition, an attorney may file a formal motion to exclude the testimony of a proposed expert witness by challenging the scientific foundation of her or his testimony. Limited data suggest that social science experts may face greater rates of exclusion based on such challenges than do their colleagues in the natural or physical sciences (Bursoff, 1999; Nordberg, 2006).

Space precludes extensive discussion of what is a complex and fluid landscape, but there has been extensive discussion of evidentiary issues in the peer-reviewed psychological literature. Forensically relevant research cannot influence legal proceedings if, based on an evaluation of scientific rigor or trustworthiness, it does not pass the threshold for admissibility in court.

Forensic Versus Therapeutic Roles

Both the APA Code of Ethics (American Psychological Association, 2002) and the Division 41 Specialty Guidelines (Committee on Ethical Guidelines for Forensic Psychologists, 1991) caution against dual-role relationships. Forensic research and practice entail a different relationship with participants than does typical therapeutic practice, and the roles may be fundamentally incompatible (Greenberg & Shuman, 1997). This presents a challenge in many areas of forensic research that concern victimized, disadvantaged, incarcerated, or hospitalized populations. In some cases, a treatment context may be the best way to recruit research participants; in others, treating clinicians may be the only ones with reasonable access to the population of interest. As some individuals have a strong individual or cultural memory of mistreatment by researchers in the past, a prior treatment relationship may be an effective way of gaining sufficient good will and trust to secure their participation. In general, dual-role relationships are to be avoided unless there is a clear and appropriate justification that substantially outweighs any possible risks. Researchers must give careful consideration to potential role conflicts in these circumstances and take appropriate precautions to safeguard the rights and well-being of participants and the methodological integrity of research.

Ethical Issues in Forensic Research

It should go without saying that the standard ethical considerations apply to research in the forensic arena. However, there are specific challenges or considerations that are of greater salience or complexity in research with forensic populations. Psychologists engaged in forensic research often study behavior that is covert, embarrassing, dangerous, stigmatizing, or illegal, and they often work with vulnerable, marginalized, or disadvantaged populations. This presents specific risks and liabilities to research participants, to the researchers themselves, and to the institutions that employ them. This section is not intended to be comprehensive but to highlight a number of specific considerations of importance.

Confidentiality and Anonymity

Participants in forensic research may be placed at risk for significant and life-altering consequences if their identity can be tied to their data, or, in some cases, if their participation in and of itself becomes known. Consider the following illustration: A psychologist is conducting research on the relationship between substance abuse and recidivism in sex offenders on probation. Participants come to the researcher's office to provide self-report data on a monthly basis, which may include data on substance use amounts, frequency, and patterns as well as data on sexual fantasies, cognitions, and behaviors. It is possible that law enforcement personnel might seek access to those records in the course of the investigation of a particular offense, either because a known participant is a suspect or because the offense took place in the neighborhood of the clinic. Law enforcement personnel might also conceivably seek to obtain records in an effort to uncover offenses that have not been reported, or probation officials might take an interest in whether a participant is meeting the terms of his or her release. It is unusual, but researchers have been arrested (Armstrong, 1993; Inciardi, 1993), interrogated by police (Bourgois, 1989), or threatened with legal sanctions for refusing to cooperate with a legal investigation or court proceedings (Brajuha & Hallowell, 1986; Scarce, 2005; Yablonsky, 1968).

In a treatment setting, the confidentiality of records in the face of these inquiries is normally secure due to the privileged status of communications in the treatment relationship. Some breaches of confidentiality may be legal or mandated (e.g., the suspicion of child abuse, cooperation with a child abuse investigation, or a specific threat of harm to self or others), but, outside of these narrow circumstances, the patient's right to confidentiality is well established as an ethical and legal standard. However, this privilege does not automatically extend to research protocols, even if the researcher holds a clinical degree.

It has been argued within academic circles that academic research should receive privileged status as research on topics of social importance may require the investigation of covert or illegal behavior (Leo, 1995). To date, court rulings on the protection of research data have been mixed. In some cases, judges have extended privileged status to research records, but, in others, they have ruled that the interest of the public outweighs the researcher's ethical obligation to protect the anonymity or confidentiality of participants. In practice, court-ordered disclosure of research records is very rare, but there have been some exceptions. However, in principle, a psychologist in a research relationship with a participant does not automatically enjoy the same confidentiality protections as a psychologist does in a therapist–client relationship.

Two of the most significant cases involving the subpoena of researchers' records concern graduate students conducting field research. In the first of these, a student (Brajuha) was conducting observational research in a restaurant. Brajuha's research journals were subpoenaed after a suspicious fire. (His presence in the days preceding the fire was coincidental; he was not there to research criminal activities nor was he suspected in the case.) Although he complied with the requirement to provide testimony before the grand jury, he resisted turning over his written records and cited his ethical obligation to protect the confidentiality of his participants. In his ruling, Judge Weinstein stated that, although a scholar has no absolute right to refuse to testify or to the confidentiality of research records, the interest of the public in the investigation and prosecution of crime must be balanced against the societal interest in protecting the integrity of scientific research (*In Re Grand Jury Subpoena Dated January 4, 1984, 583 F. Supp. 991,* 1984). As Brajuha had already testified as to what he had witnessed, the judge ruled that the prosecution had not demonstrated a compelling justification for release of Brajuha's journals. The prosecution appealed this ruling. The appellate court acknowledged that scholars might enjoy a limited privilege akin to that of journalists but ruled that Brajuha had not provided sufficient evidence to support his assertion that such privilege should apply at all and that, if it did, it did not necessarily apply to the entirety of his notes. As the existing record did not provide sufficient facts to determine the merits of the claim, the lower court's decision to deny the subpoena was reversed and remanded for further testimony. Judge Winter's written decision in this case states that the mere claim of scholarly privilege is not sufficient in and of itself.

> Surely the application of a scholar's privilege, if it exists, requires a threshold showing consisting of a detailed description of the nature and seriousness of the scholarly study in question, of the methodology employed, of the need for assurances of confidentiality to various sources to conduct the study, and of the fact that the disclosure requested by the subpoena will seriously impinge upon that confidentiality. (*In Re Grand Jury Subpoena Dated January 4, 1984*, 750 F.2d 223, 1984).

Judge Winter went on to note that the direct knowledge of illegal acts is not subject to any such privilege. Brajuha and the prosecutors subsequently reached an agreement in which he turned over his notes in redacted form (Brajuha & Halliwell, 1986). Consequently, a final ruling on the legal status of these records at the appellate level was not made.

In the second case, Scarce was interrogated by the FBI and subpoenaed to testify at a federal grand jury during the prosecution of members of the Animal Liberation Front in 1993. Scarce refused to testify based on the assurances of confidentiality he made during his research on radical environmental movements that allegedly engaged in acts of terrorism. He was jailed for 5 months for contempt of court before the judge released him, but no clear precedent was established (Scarce, 2005).

Violations of anonymity or confidentiality in forensic research may produce more than a risk of embarrassment or legal consequences; participants, and even potential participants, may be placed at risk for physical harm under some circumstances. For example, Newman (2006) reported a case in which a researcher collected data on secret police activities in a totalitarian state. He took extensive measures to protect the identity of his informants for fear that they would be harmed or killed if their identities became known. More commonly, individuals involved in, or who are witness to, criminal activity could be placed in danger from their peers, adversaries, or individuals with power over them if it became known that they were even approached for research purposes, irrespective of whether they were willing to participate. For example, such communications could arouse suspicion that a gang member or prisoner is a police informant. Vulnerable populations such as coerced sex workers, battered spouses, and abused children may be subjected to violent retaliation for speaking to an unknown third party. This danger may exist even if the individual has said nothing to the researcher beyond "I can not talk to you."

The most immediate protection against forced disclosure is to ensure that data is de-identified to secure the anonymity of participants. This may be problematic, particularly with small-sample research or research that employs idiographic methods. For example, there are currently 179 judgeships approved by the US Congress within the federal court of appeals. As the judges' identities and biographies are public record, the collection of even limited demographic data as part of survey would quickly allow for the identification of some respondents from this population. In such a case, no guarantee of anonymity can be offered. The researcher who collects in-depth qualitative data also should be aware of the implications of collecting potentially identifiable data from participants. The goal of an idiographic study is to produce a rich and detailed account of an individual, system, or event, but the inclusion of such specific detail in published reports can jeopardize the anonymity of the participant(s). Even if the researcher alters or disguises elements of a case study in an effort to preserve participants' anonymity, it may not be possible to anticipate which specific elements will result in identification. Seemingly insignificant details may be sufficient for identification in the context of other information known to third parties or may be quite salient and informative to someone with close knowledge of the participant(s). This is a growing concern, given the increasing ability of the public to access and cross-reference scholarly materials through the Internet. Third parties, or the participants themselves, can be in a position to link an individual to her or his specific responses, to identify where a participant fits within a research design, and to examine the conclusions drawn by a researcher about the participants within the study.

Forensic researchers may be in a position to obtain stronger guarantees against forced disclosure of confidential research records. The US National Institutes of Health (NIH) can issue a certificate of confidentiality to researchers who are engaged in research with human subjects that involves sensitive information such as sexual preference, substance use, or illegal activities. The certificate provides a shield for the researcher against any forced disclosure of identifying information in the face of subpoena. The NIH issues these certificates on a discretionary basis based on individual review of the proposed research. NIH (2002) reported that legal challenges to the protection provided by these certificates are rare and that such challenges generally have not been successful. The US Supreme Court has declined to hear one such challenge, but the court could certainly change this stance in the future. Research conducted by government employees or federally funded research that involves embarrassing, stigmatizing, or illegal behavior could be granted additional privacy protections through other mechanisms. For example, research funded through the US Department of Justice enjoys statutory protection against the forced disclosure of personally identifiable information provided that the researcher has complied with appropriate review and documentation processes.

There is a potential conflict between these protections and the public's right to gain access to data and records collected with public funds under the federal Freedom of Information Act (FOIA). This applies to all records produced by federal agencies and employees or that are the result of professional activities paid for with federal money. Records or correspondence generated by private citizens (e.g., grant applications) become government records once they are submitted. The purpose of the FOIA is to promote transparency in government by preventing the government from needlessly withholding information from the public. Federal agencies may withhold records requested through the FOIA under a number of exceptions and exemptions, including information that is prohibited from disclosure by another federal law and information that involves matters of personal privacy. The standard for balancing the need to preserve the privacy of individuals against the public's right to transparency and access to information was established by the US Supreme Court in *Department of State v. Washington Post* (1982). In this decision, the court held that an agency seeking to withhold records in response to a FOIA request must establish that a proposed or potential invasion of privacy is "clearly unwarranted." This standard errs strongly on the side of disclosing information, and so it is reasonable to anticipate that researchers would be ordered to release their records and data in response to such a request. The release could be in a redacted form that allows for the protection of the identities of specific participants, but there is no guarantee that this would be the case. Therefore, researchers working within or through the federal government, or who are supported with federal funding, should recognize that an FOIA request could require the violation of any assurances of confidentiality and anonymity offered, a fact that should be made explicit as part of informed consent. The fact that promises were inappropriately made, even in good faith, is not an effective legal defense against forced disclosure.

Furthermore, subsequent to the passage of the FOIA, all US states adopted similar legislation, although the specific standards, exceptions, and exemptions vary greatly. A psychologist who conducts research as an employee of a state university that receives federal funding could therefore be subject to requests via either mechanism. Researchers should undertake an examination of the limits of confidentiality and anonymity applicable to their research based on their funding source and agency affiliations.

The anonymity and confidentiality of research records presents additional problems in institutional settings, such as forensic inpatient mental health units or correctional facilities. Institutional records in these settings may be accessible to employees who do not have a professional need for access. For example, correctional staff may be in a position to examine inmate medical records whether or not this is within the bounds of the law or prison regulations. Inmates may have access to records in the course of other activities, such as custodial work as part of prison employment or rehabilitation. The use of electronic records systems mitigates this concern as file access is monitored, but research data may not be housed within these systems, even were it appropriate to do so. A researcher's records may not be classified as institutional records, but the issue of access may still remain. Due to safety and security considerations, non-research staff often have access to a researcher's office space. Records "secured" in a locked office, therefore, are not necessarily secure in all circumstances.

A final threat to participants' welfare due to breach of anonymity may arise from accidental public disclosure of the nature of the research itself. Consider, again, the example of a psychologist conducting research on the relationship between substance abuse and recidivism in sex offenders on probation. Individuals in neighboring offices or buildings, through casual observation or ordinary curiosity, could take an interest in the activities that take place in the psychologist's office. Mail accidentally delivered to the wrong address, or the recognition of a single participant as a sex offender (e.g., from pictures distributed as part of offender registration and community notification programs) could alert the public to the population under study. As a consequence, *all* individuals seen coming and going from the researcher's office could come under suspicion, with the possibility of negative consequences.

Harm

A wide range of additional risks and ethical dilemmas can emerge that are particular to forensic research. Researchers have observed illegal actions during field research on offenders (Perrone, 2006), law enforcement personnel (Marquart, 1986), and corrections officers (Van Maanen, 1982). This can create an ethical dilemma in which the researcher may have an obligation to report such acts, even if it means compromising one's role or effectiveness as a researcher. It may also place the researcher in the position of being complicit in, or a material witness to, specific crimes, which could increase the researcher's vulnerability to the subpoena of research records.

A related concern during observational research is the effect of participants' reactance to observation with the possible risk of increasing the likelihood of crime by inducing specific criminal acts.

Decker and Van Winkle (1996) reported that, during their research on criminal street gangs, participants offered to provide demonstrations of criminal acts. In this case, the researchers reported that they declined these offers and that they made no effort to encourage illicit behavior, but it is not clear whether the criminal acts they did observe would have occurred in the absence of their involvement. There was an explicit braggadocio on the part of participants in this case, which makes it obvious that reactance was a potential problem, but this will not always be so unambiguous. It may not be possible to assess accurately the degree to which the researcher's efforts may alter the likelihood of crime in either a positive or a negative direction.

Of even greater concern is the possibility of participation in illegal activities as part of participant observation (Adler, 1990; Ferrell, 1997; Polsky, 1969). For example, informants may expect the researcher to serve as a look-out, to consume illegal drugs, or engage in other activities that are themselves illegal or are in service of illegal acts. It could occur for practical reasons (e.g., an offender unexpectedly needs someone to hold a flashlight and asks the researcher for assistance) or as part of the vetting process some individuals may use to determine whether they would be willing to participate in the study. This dilemma is unusual, but such behavior is almost certainly unethical, even in the name of establishing sufficient trust to allow research to proceed. Some might argue that the commission of misdemeanors with the goal of accurately assessing the nature and extent of harmful and covert activities (e.g., forced sexual trafficking of women and children) serves a greater good and higher ethical standard. Such activities should be investigated, but researchers should consider the role that they occupy in comparison to journalists or members of law enforcement. Despite the potential for social value to result from research on such issues, it is not clear that the forensic researcher is the appropriate party to engage in investigations that require the commission of illegal actions. In such cases, if appropriate boundaries cannot be set, then an alternative method should probably be employed and additional efforts aimed at encouraging the appropriate agents to become more actively involved.

Research on illegal activities may also carry with it a risk of physical danger to the researcher. For example, efforts to interview criminals can involve the risk of direct physical violence, and it is common for witnesses of crimes to be threatened or worse in order to encourage or guarantee their silence. Observational research in the natural setting is the most obvious circumstance that exposes the researcher to this risk, but it may also occur during efforts to identify and recruit participants for interviews, surveys, or other data collection. As discussed below, research on covert activity or highly marginalized populations may require recruitment methods such as direct face-to-face outreach or the use of snowball sampling. In either case, the risk of violence is increased relative to other sampling methods. Approaching individuals engaged in illegal activity may present an immediate threat to the researcher from potential participants. Word of mouth that a researcher is seeking participants on illegal activity may also attract the attention of individuals with a vested interest in discouraging that behavior: those who fear that the researcher is a member of law enforcement or cooperating with law enforcement or those who otherwise do not want attention of any kind drawn to their community or behavior.

The level of connection between researchers and informants that is created through participant observation may create atypical forms of risk or exploitation. For example, Perrone (2006) described a case in which a reliable and established informant intervened to protect her against a sexually aggressive third party, which resulted in a physical altercation. In addition, sexual involvement between researchers and informants during participant observation may be more common than social science researchers have been willing to admit, and this raises serious concerns for the protection of vulnerable participants from exploitation and about the introduction of bias in data collection (Goode, 2002).

It should be noted that the majority of the specific examples cited above come from ethnography and participant observation, methodologies that may create more complicated ethical dilemmas than other forms of research do (Leo, 1996). In addition, many of these cases are not recent; some predate the establishment of current standards for the protection of human subjects in social research. Scarce (2005) is perhaps the most salient recent case of legal complications that resulted from forensically relevant research, and he, by his own admission, failed to apply for Institutional Review Board (IRB) approval for his study. It is entirely possible that his imprisonment could have been avoided entirely had he followed the ethical and legal requirements for research with human subjects.

Informed Consent

Many populations of forensic interest present complications in terms of obtaining legitimate informed consent. In the USA the rates of intellectual compromise, psychiatric and neuropsychological disorder, limited education, functional illiteracy, and English as a second language are higher than the norm within the general population. Heightened vulnerability to deception, participants' perception of coercion, greater risk of psychological distress or harm due to limited coping resources, and challenges in assuring the adequacy of debriefing are all issues that confront the forensic researcher who works with vulnerable populations. This can require a more careful assessment of the degree to which a participant fully understands the potential risks and benefits associated with a given study. The requirement to avoid coercion is complicated by the characteristics and circumstances of many potential participants in forensic research. Individuals who are under correctional supervision, or who are involved in court proceedings (e.g., persons involved in family court who are negotiating child custody or seeking adoption), may perceive that negative consequences could result from a refusal to participate. Such a belief could be fostered or reinforced, rightly or wrongly, by other actors within the legal system. An attorney, for example, might encourage participation in a proposed study as part of her or his ethical obligation to pursue the best interests of the client. It is reasonable for an attorney to presume that an individual's willingness to participate in research would be looked upon favorably by a judge. Participation could be portrayed as evidence of pro-social attitudes and, in the case of clinical trials (e.g., research on substance abuse intervention, anger management, or parenting skills), as evidence of a commitment to treatment. Prisoners are, by statute, protected from potential negative consequences based on their agreement or refusal to participate in research. Ordinary citizens seeking child custody, adoption rights, or to avoid entering correctional supervision do not enjoy the same protection. The degree to which judges take these things into consideration is not known.

The possibility of benefit (real or imagined) due to research participation, does not, in and of itself, constitute coercion in most cases. The marginal utility of a given incentive for participation (whether direct or indirect) will vary depending on the population and individual in question. It is reasonable to assume that the power of monetary reward varies based on an individual's socioeconomic status or that the attractiveness of a parental skills program may be stronger for a parent in danger of losing custody of his or her children due to state intervention. The opportunity to receive treatment during clinical trials may be an extraordinary incentive for an active heroin addict. Given the vulnerability of many forensic populations, and the significant life consequences they can experience as a result of decisions made in legal contexts, the possibility of coercion requires careful consideration. Ethical absolutists, or those with an overdetermined view of the effect of differential of power relations on individual choice, may suggest that research that includes the possibility of a reward with high marginal utility constitutes coercion for all practical purposes. However, refusal to do research on vulnerable populations due to the belief that they are fundamentally incompetent to make free and informed decisions about their participation compounds their marginalized status. Taken to the extreme, it is a "paternalistic" attitude that reinforces stigma and perpetuates their societal disadvantages. Just as one cannot "burn the village in order to save it," one cannot ethically "protect" individuals and populations by sustaining their vulnerability.

A final challenge in the ethics of consent occurs in the context of naturalistic observation when individuals are not informed that they are under observation. It is assumed that individuals enjoy certain fundamental privacy rights and that observational research may be an infringement on those rights. For many purposes, there is a presumption that when an individual engages in public behavior, she or he has, in essence, consented to some level of observation. The evaluation of the ethics of a proposed unobtrusive observational study requires consideration of the degree to which individuals have an expectation of privacy and the degree to which they would experience distress were they to know that they were under systematic, rather than casual, observation. In effect, a judgment is made about whether a reasonable person would consent to this observation if the researcher's presence and role were revealed. As research in forensic psychology often involves examining behavior that is covert, the evaluation of privacy expectations and potential for distress becomes more complex. Individuals are likely to have different levels of desire for privacy for the same behavior, such as entering a door, when the door leads to a shoe store as opposed to a location known as a place for the sale and use of illegal drugs. In the latter case, although no criminal activity is directly witnessed, the level of intrusion is arguably greater. Humphreys' (1970) classic study "Tearoom Trade," which involved the covert naturalistic observation of men engaging in anonymous sex in public restrooms, is perhaps the best known invasion of privacy by a researcher.

Disclosure of Potential Conflict of Interest

In the past 20 years there has been increasing consensus that researchers have an obligation to disclose conflicts of interest that could be perceived as compromising the integrity of their results (e.g., the sponsorship of medical research by pharmaceutical or medical device manufacturers). Many professional journals now require the disclosure of any real or perceived conflict of interest as a condition of publication, but there is no generally recognized standard. Psychologists are often retained by attorneys to provide consultation in the course of litigation. Consider that an attorney files a class action lawsuit on behalf of a group of plaintiffs who allege psychological injuries due to sexual harassment in a hostile work environment. In this case, the attorney might request that a psychologist conduct a research study with the goal of establishing the presence, nature, severity, and consequences of symptoms, the results of which could be used in support of the suit. It can be ethical for a psychologist to conduct such a study provided that the attorney does not have inappropriate influence in the design and implementation of the research and that the psychologist is compensated for time, effort, and expertise without regard to the results obtained. The fact that an attorney is the funding source for the research is not a priori evidence that the research is biased or that anything unethical has occurred, but the potential for conflict of interest remains. The interests of an attorney funding research are no less vested than are those of the manufacturer of a new medical device funding research on its safety and effectiveness.

If potential or perceived conflict of interest is disclosed, then the research can be given due scrutiny with that information in mind. However, disclosure that research has been funded for the purpose of litigation has not been a requirement in the professional literature. It is difficult to gauge the frequency with which such studies have entered the literature or the degree to which any of those that have may have been compromised. The potential consequences can perhaps be illustrated with reference to the alleged association between vaccination and the onset of autism in children. Methodologically sound studies continue to indicate that there is no causal relationship (Brown, Berkovic, & Scheffer, 2007; Halsey & Hyman, 2001; Madsen et al., 2002; Madsen & Vestergaard, 2004), but the financial and human cost of these continued assertions is enormous. Rates of harmful childhood diseases have increased due to declining immunization rates, and previously well-controlled diseases have had resurgent outbreaks or reemerged as endemic. Hundreds of millions of dollars have been spent in legal fees and in research monies that could have been spent productively elsewhere. The emotional toll on parents who erroneously believe that they have caused their children irreparable harm is perhaps the most terrible result. As of this writing, the principle author of the 1988 report that triggered this controversy is under investigation by the UK's General Medical Counsel for potential ethical violations, and evidence that suggests data manipulation and misrepresentation has emerged. In addition

> Further questions arise about the motivations of [the study's author]...*The Sunday Times* reported that he worked for lawyers, and that many of the families were either litigants or were part of networks through which they would sue. Far from routine referrals, as they appeared, many of them had made contact with one another (Deer, 2009).

It remains to be seen whether these reports are true, but, if they are substantiated, the possibility that undue influence arose from the context in which the study occurred is obviously of concern. As noted above, research that is conducted in support of litigation is not necessarily ethically or methodologically compromised. However, disclosure of this context (if the allegation is true) could have resulted in more critical reviews prior to publication of the study and perhaps a more measured response by the public. The need for full disclosure when research is funded, in full or in part, by attorneys for the purposes of litigation seems clear, and it should become a standard editorial policy for journals in the field.

Interstate Research

Forensic psychologists may, under some circumstances, conduct professional activities outside of the state that has issued their professional licensure. There is increasing awareness that interjurisdictional licensure presents a variety of legal, pragmatic, and ethical challenges for clinicians conducting clinical assessments for litigation purposes. States vary widely in the restrictions that exist on clinical practice by psychologists whose licenses are issued by another state and in the procedures that a psychologist must follow in order to obtain legal authorization to engage in professional activities (Tucillo, DeFilippis, Denney, & Dsurney, 2002). Performing clinical activities in violation of relevant licensing laws is unethical and can result in significant consequences for a psychologist.

Psychologists who conduct research across state lines may unknowingly place themselves at risk, even if they do not hold a professional license or do not intend to conduct professional activities that are therapeutic in nature. For example, it is estimated that there are approximately 1500 women imprisoned in the USA for sex crimes (Center for Sex Offender Management, 2007). Due to the small size and wide geographic dispersion of this participant pool, a psychologist conducting research that involves interviews or assessments with this population could be forced to travel to a number of different states in order to attain a representative sample size that is large enough to allow for adequate statistical power. In other circumstances, an attorney could commission a research study as part of a class action lawsuit (e.g., gender-based employment discrimination or the effects of gender stereotypes in educational outcomes) and retain a psychologist with expertise in that particular area to conduct the research.

In either case, the state licensing board could determine that licensure, or some form of prior approval by the board, is required in order for the researcher to engage in actions that fall within, or overlap with, the bounds of regulated clinical practice according to local statutes. The conceptual distinction between clinical and research activities could be, in at least some cases, based on role and intent: Interviews, surveys, and various measures may be employed in the service of either process. It could be argued that the therapeutic relationship and goal of providing treatment renders the administration of an MMPI-2 a clinical, rather than a research, activity, but this is not necessarily the case, and the boundaries may be ambiguous. The local licensing body, and not the researcher, has legal authority to make that determination. Consequently, researchers should give due consideration to the local laws that govern the professional activities in which they intend to engage prior to undertaking them in another jurisdiction, and they should seek consultation as necessary.

Methodological Issues in Forensic Research

Sampling

Obtaining access to participants can present a tremendous challenge to forensic researchers in some cases. The development of a well-specified and representative sampling frame can be extremely difficult when the study concerns covert, stigmatized, or illegal activities. Investigations of the homeless, drug users, or prostitutes are examples of these populations, as there are no adequate "registries" to allow for the identification of members of the population for sampling purposes. In other cases, an adequate sampling frame may exist, but there are statutory or institutional limitations on access to records. One can create sampling frames through known points of institutional contact (e.g., shelters, treatment programs, emergency rooms, probation offices), but these frames may not capture the population of interest adequately. Even if such frames are sufficiently representative, many forensically relevant populations are typified by transient and unstable lifestyles, or efforts to conceal identities, which render contact information unreliable for research purposes. The response rate for mailed surveys or phone interviews is reduced as a result of population characteristics in these cases, and the attrition rate of longitudinal research is elevated. Snowball sampling, which utilizes the social networks of initial participants to identify and recruit subsequent participants, suffers from selection bias but may be a viable solution to the problem of sampling transient or unstable populations within a community setting.

Even when a reasonable sampling frame can be identified or developed, forensic research often relies on non-probability samples which can, in some case, be so non-representative that meaningful generalizations, and sometimes meaningful conclusions, cannot be drawn. For example, an important line of research concerns the effect of different child custody arrangements on the welfare of children following their parents' divorce. In general, despite an official policy that requires such decisions to be made in the best interest of the child, mothers gain physical and legal custody at far higher rates than fathers do. This suggests that the courts continue to make custody decisions in accordance with the "tender years" doctrine that presumes that a mother's nurturance during a child's youth is more beneficial to the child's development than that of the father (Kelly, 2007; Kushner, 2006). Limited research has shown that children raised in single-father families are at risk for poorer social, psychological, and health outcomes than those raised in single-mother families (Breivik & Olweus, 2006; Demuth & Brown, 2004; Jablonska & Lindberg, 2007).

The underlying problem with the results of most, if not all, research in this area is the non-equivalence of single mothers and single fathers as parents for reasons that have nothing to do with gender. As the continued influence of the "tender years" doctrine results in an ongoing bias toward adjudicating custody decisions in favor of the mother, the characteristics of the parents in cases where the father is granted sole custody may be skewed. In such cases, it is possible that the father is an extraordinary parent, who is an outlier relative to his peers. A finding of no difference between single-mother and single-father families, or an advantage for single-father families, would therefore provide no meaningful information about the relative merit of awarding sole custody to typical or average fathers. It is also possible that fathers are more likely to be awarded sole custody in those cases where the mother is markedly dysfunctional due to significant psychopathology, addiction, or is unavailable due to other factors (e.g., incarceration). In these cases, a finding of increased risk for negative outcomes for children in single-father families may well be due to the damage done in the family environment prior to the divorce. Research based on samples of different family structures as determined by the courts bears this fundamental flaw, and it is not clear how successful efforts to control for these factors has been.

A meaningful way to compare single-father and single-mother families would be to examine the psychological health and ultimate outcomes for children who have lost a parent not through divorce, but through unfortunate illness or accident. This method is an application of Group Membership by Chance (Faust & Ackley, 1998): Relatively healthy families with more typical parents are "selected" into single-mother and single-father configurations by random factors. The design remains quasi-experimental, and it is necessary to control for variables that might predispose individuals to terminal illness or accidental death, but such a design could be more informative in examining the relative effects of parent's gender on child outcomes.

Additional problems in sampling may be present within more controlled settings such as prisons and forensic psychiatric facilities. For example, prisoners may be transferred, moved to a more or less restrictive environment, have schedule changes and disruptions due to court appearances with little warning, or be released abruptly into the community. A relatively short delay between establishing the sampling frame and initiating data collection can result in poor response rates, participant attrition, or a lack of treatment fidelity due to missed appointments.

Efforts to engage in research within agencies or institutions may present other complications in terms of participant access. In addition to the usual processes associated with IRB review and grant applications, there will normally be additional layers of review process within the institution itself. At a minimum, this will extend the time frame for the completion of research, but it can also present a barrier to obtaining access to participants. Closed institutions, such as police departments and correctional facilities, may or may not have a documented policy for reviewing requests for subject access, which leaves the decision to higher level administrators in the institutional hierarchy. Even if policies do exist, decisions to allow research within an institution may have more to do with institutional needs than with issues related to the protection of human subjects or the merits of the research design. Administrators may determine that allowing a researcher access to staff members presents an additional and unnecessary demand on overburdened personnel or may not want personnel to devote time to activities deemed of less, or far less, importance relative to their daily job responsibilities. Administrators may also be concerned that allowing access to institutional personnel could have negative ramifications in the form of adverse publicity, exposure to legal liability, compromised funding, placing professional advancement at risk, or inviting interference in the operations of the facility from legislative or other administrative bodies. This concern is justified, even if the institution itself is run with the utmost professionalism and competence. A single public report that is critical of some specific event or aspect of the institution's operations or policies can produce a substantial backlash against the institution, its administrators, and its staff, whether that criticism is justified or not. Given that law enforcement and correctional personnel may view researchers as potential reformers, as activists, or as having a political agenda that is incompatible with that of the institution, the request for access to participants may be viewed with suspicion. The perceived risks of allowing such access can easily outweigh any perceived benefits.

Even if the administration of an institution approves access to personnel as participants, the researcher may face an additional hurdle. A large portion of employees within public institutions such as prisons, law enforcement agencies, and forensic psychiatric facilities are members of labor unions, and union leadership may share concerns similar to those of the administration. In addition, if participation in research is not already part of a collective bargaining agreement, union leadership may perceive allowing the membership to participate in research as a "give back" in the current contract, or as having a potential impact upon upcoming labor negotiations (e.g., allowing participation could be viewed as undermining a future argument that a facility is understaffed or that job duties are excessive). In either case, labor leaders may discourage or forbid participation as perceived risks may outweigh potential benefits to allowing access to participants.

As a final example, all actors within the legal realm are potential participants of interest for research in forensic psychology. The distribution of gender across the legal profession is asymmetric: a disproportionate number of attorneys and judges are male, men hold a substantial dominance in leadership positions within the field, and they earn greater compensation than their female colleagues do. There has been an increase in women's participation in all areas, and gender parity in American Bar Association-approved law schools was achieved in 2002 (American Bar Association Commission on Women in the Profession, 2006). There is a strong societal interest in examining all aspects of issues related to career selection and advancement, and the impact of gender disparities in legal venues may affect the creation, administration, implementation, and outcome of legal processes for all involved. The American Bar Association, the National Center for State Courts, the Federal Judicial Center's Research Division, and various state agencies all provide ample statistical data and a variety of research reports, but it can be difficult for the independent social science researcher to gain access to judges and attorneys as study participants.

Measurement

Whenever possible, psychologists should follow the standards set forth in the Standards for Educational and Psychological Testing (American Educational Research Association [AERA], American Psychological Association [APA], and National Council on Measurement in Education [NCME], 1999) when conducting research that involves tests, measures, or assessment procedures, and they should acknowledge the limitations that failure to do so places on their analysis and conclusions. Research can, by necessity, involve the use of experimental measures, the use of established measures for unvalidated purposes, or the use of measures with populations for which they were not originally designed. If research required perfection in advance, research in important areas could not be conducted, but it is essential for researchers to match the strength of their conclusions to the reliability and validity of their methods of assessment, interpretation, and data integration. Adherence to the standards is particularly important in forensically relevant research, given the impact forensic psychology can have on individual lives and on society in general through litigation, public policy, and law. Psychologists who depend upon the results of research may be hindered in their effectiveness to the extent that they must depend upon the work of researchers who have employed inadequate testing, measurement, assessment, and data integration methods.

When conducting research on forensic populations, careful consideration must be given to the effects of the forensic status of participants on the validity of assessment and measurement.

Potential pitfalls include failure to assess response bias adequately and the more general problem of a pervasive lack of adequately validated tests and measures for minority populations who are overrepresented in many forensic contexts.

Response Bias

Biased responding, in the form of conscious and systematic efforts to present oneself as more or less capable, socially desirable, or symptomatic is a problem within forensic research that can create a substantial or even critical threat to the validity of findings. The past 20 years has seen a substantial increase in attention to response bias and an acknowledgement that psychologists cannot reliably identify manipulated test performance without including formal measures of response bias and comparing the consistency of test results with other data sources (c.f., Reynolds, 1997; Rogers, 2008).

In research on attitudes, beliefs, and behaviors that are potentially stigmatizing or that run counter to social norms, there is a risk that participants will skew their responses in the direction of what they perceive to be socially acceptable. Unpopular attitudes or beliefs (e.g., racism, acceptance of sexual violence) and illicit or stigmatized behavior (e.g., driving while intoxicated, acts perceived by some as sexually deviant) are often minimized or denied by participants. Stand-alone scales to measure social desirability exist (e.g., the Marlowe-Crowne Social Desirability Scale; Crowne & Marlowe, 1960), but the utility of such measures is limited. Even if participants can be identified as having a response bias in the direction of the socially desirable, there is no empirically validated method for determining the effect of this bias on most measures relevant to forensic research. In the absence of such correction factors, it can only be argued that the results are invalid to some degree; how invalid they are cannot be established.

An alternate method for reducing the effects of social desirability is to decrease the intimacy of data collection. Research indicates that disclosure of personal information on sensitive or embarrassing topics increases as interpersonal immediacy decreases. The use of paper surveys in place of personal interviews, or Internet data collection instead of paper surveys, may reduce the impact of social desirability (Supple, Aquilino, & Wright, 1999). The use of on-line surveys is increasingly popular in social science literature (c.f., Birnbaum, 2004; Buchanan, 2000; Reips, 2002). If handled appropriately, Internet-based studies can entail no more risk to participants (Kraut et al., 2004) than traditional methods do. Special attention to the assurance of confidentiality and anonymity of responses regarding illicit or stigmatizing behavior is required. Reduced computer literacy in marginalized or disadvantaged populations may require additional safeguards during the informed consent process to ensure that participants truly understand the limits and hazards associated with the control and security of Internet data. Anonymous and confidential responses are neither if they can be traced back to a particular ISP address.

An additional safeguard that can be used to reduce response bias and protect the anonymity of participants during the conduct of research on illegal or stigmatizing activities is the utilization of statistical models that estimate the prevalence of a characteristic or behavior that individuals may not wish to disclose (e.g., covert or illegal sexual behavior, sexual orientation, a history of sexual assault). The Unmatched Count Technique allows participants to provide accurate information about sensitive subjects without directly admitting to any specific behavior (c.f., Dalton, Wimbush, & Daily, 1994; Wimbush & Dalton, 1997). Participants are provided with groups of statements, each of which includes one item of interest and a series of foils, and asked to indicate how many of the statements within each group are true without identifying which statement(s) they have endorsed. For example,

How many of the following statements are true for you?

Q1: Have you ever been the victim of a hate crime based on sexual orientation?
Q2: Have you ever been employed as a retail salesperson?
Q3: Have you ever ridden a motorcycle?

A comparison group performs the same task but receives only the foils. Differences in the number of items endorsed between the two groups allow for a statistical estimate of the base rate for the sensitive items. Provided the number, and content, of the foils avoids placing the participants in a position in which they must endorse *all* items within a group, it is not possible to determine whether the item of interest is one of the items a participant has endorsed.

In contrast, the Randomized Response Techniques (RRT; Christofides, 2003; Warner, 1965) also presents participants with a group of statements including the item of interest and one or more foils, but participants select one of the questions in the group *at random* to answer correctly. Participants utilize a coin toss or the roll of a die to determine to which question they will respond.

Roll the die and answer *one* of the following questions. If you roll a 1 or 2, answer Q1; if you roll a 3 or 4, answer Q2; if you roll a 5 or 6, answer Q3.

Q1: Have you ever been the victim of a hate crime based on sexual orientation?
Q2: Have you ever been employed as a retail salesperson?
Q3: Have you ever ridden a motorcycle?

The participant does not indicate to which question she or he has responded but provides an answer for the group of items. As the participant has control of the randomizer (e.g., coin, die), and no record of the random result is kept, it is not possible for the researcher to know which question the participant has answered. The base rate for behaviors, or the proportion of participants who answered items in particular direction, can be estimated statistically.

Another form of RRT presents participants with the sensitive items only, and they are instructed to answer them either truthfully or falsely depending on the result of a coin toss or die roll. Thus, if a participant's response to the question "Have you ever been the victim of a hate crime based on sexual orientation?" is "true," it is unknown whether the participant is answering this question honestly or not. When these methods are employed correctly, participants' responses to the sensitive items are, in effect, anonymous. RRT generally produces more valid estimates of population parameters for sensitive data than more conventional methods (e.g., interviews, direct survey questions) do (Lensvelt-Mulders, Hox, Van der Heijden, & Maas, 2005).

The feigning, exaggeration, or malingering of symptoms and deficits is a pervasive problem within many areas of forensic assessment, although the base rate is not as well characterized as one would wish (c.f., Mittenberg, Patton, Canyock, & Condit, 2002). Likewise, faking good, in the sense of minimizing or denying symptoms, or attempting to demonstrate competence, psychological health, and abilities beyond what one possesses, can also be a problem in forensic contexts (e.g., child custody disputes). For obvious reasons, much of the existing research has been aimed at detecting response bias in the context of applied clinical assessment. The degree to which response bias affects measurement in a pure research context, in which external gain based on the results is not necessarily a factor, is unknown. At a minimum, forensic researchers should give consideration to the possibility of dishonest responding by participants during data collection, and research in this area is warranted. The evaluation of research reports and archival data based on data from correctional populations or populations from medico-legal contexts should include attention to the assessment of response bias by the original authors.

Despite a proliferation of stand-alone measures for the detection of response bias, significant limitations on our ability to detect response bias remain. A portion of the difficulty is due to the psychometric limitations of the available methods. Here again, if malingering is identified by one or more stand-alone measures, it does little but cast doubt upon all other measurements employed. In the absence of validated methods to "correct" for response bias, we can only know that our results, in whole or in part, may be invalid to some degree. Consequently, measures that have validity checks incorporated within them may be preferable to stand-alone measures for many research purposes.

The interaction of gender with malingering is an area that has not received sufficient attention. There are two areas of malingering detection research for which gender may be of particular importance. One method of conducting research in malingering detection is the examination of "known groups." As malingerers do not often confess their manipulations to researchers, research of this type is often conducted with participants whose feigning has been independently verified or whose status as malingerers is highly suspected. As men are disproportionately represented within the correctional population, the recruitment of an adequate number of known or suspected female malingerers for research purposes within any given institution is challenging at best. (This is a lesser barrier in studying malingering in civil contexts.) A second area of malingering detection with potential gender effects is the development of measures based on discrepancies between the known course, presentation, and pattern of symptoms associated with specific disorders and stereotypical conceptions held by the public. To the extent that gender has an influence on sources of information about disorder, women and men may engage in different strategies when feigning disorder. Knowledge (accurate or not) of the effects of head injury derived from stereotypically "masculine" entertainment (e.g., contact sports) may vary from knowledge derived from stereotypically "feminine" entertainment (e.g., soap operas). Obviously, the boundaries between women's and men's entertainment preferences are not rigid, and there are common, non-gendered, sources of information as well. However, the utility of examining gender differences in symptom presentation may be viable, and it is worthy of investigation.

Fairness and Bias in Measurement

Fairness and bias in measurement are two separable but related issues that take on additional importance in forensic research. Bias is a purely statistical property of measures related to such issues as differential item functioning and relative predictive accuracy. In contrast, fairness is value judgment about measures and their interaction with society (for a full discussion, see the Standards for Educational and Psychological Testing; AERA, APA, & NCME, 1999). The inappropriate utilization of tests that are statistically biased against distinguishable groups, or the differential availability of unbiased tests, are examples of how the two concepts interact. Issues of fairness and test bias both emerge as strong concerns in forensic psychology given the overrepresentation of men and of minority populations in many forensic contexts. Base rate differences in the frequencies of criminal behavior, arrest, and incarceration of men and women create a circumstance in which classes of female offenders are under-researched within the criminal justice system (c.f., Dickens et al., 2007; Freeman & Sandler, 2008; Girshick, 2002; Roe-Sepowitz & Krysik, 2008). Consequently, the majority of measures developed to predict recidivism, categorize offenders within taxonomies, and diagnose disorders of forensic significance (e.g., psychopathy) have been developed on and validated for use with male offenders (Lillenfeld, 1998; Nicholls, Ogloff, Brink, & Spidel, 2005). Research on these topics with female offenders lags behind, in some cases substantially. In one sense, this may be appropriate, as a strong case can be made that focusing attention on the offenders who are the most common and dangerous is a rational strategy. This makes sense in terms of protecting the interests of the public at large from criminal offenders. However, this circumstance places women in a disadvantaged position in their interactions with the legal system when social science research has, or could have, a bearing on their outcomes.

Problems with bias and fairness are even more prominent for forensic researchers who conduct research with culturally diverse populations. Full and appropriate statistical analysis of test bias has not been undertaken for a majority of the tests and assessments that are available. The use of a demographically representative sample for establishing test norms, although often appropriate, does not allow for the identification of underlying statistical bias within the test itself (e.g., differential item functioning).

The validity of tests is not universal and must be established for each distinct population and for specific purposes. Reliability coefficients may vary, and test items may perform differently within different populations. The measurement characteristics, and the predictive or diagnostic equivalence of tests, are uncertain until the necessary research has been conducted. Test results are, in many cases, less reliable and valid to some unknown degree when used with populations different from the standardization sample, and it is not necessarily possible to know which cases will be so affected. In an effort to improve the validity of measures, researchers may be tempted to make ad hoc modifications to standardized administration, scoring, and interpretive procedures when employing them within populations different from that of the standardization sample; such accommodations do not necessarily improve the reliability or validity of tests and might even compromise them further. As the number and extent of violations of standardization increases, the reliability and validity of measures probably deteriorates to some unknown degree. Research on the review of items by cultural experts for potential bias indicates that such experts cannot accurately identify which test items are statistically biased (Anastasi & Urbina, 1997). Even if they could, there is no sound reason to believe that they would be able to make substitutions or modifications to items that would produce item equivalence in the absence of formal research. Consequently, one can have no confidence that modifying standard procedures in an effort to minimize the impact of culture on tests produces results that are more valid and reliable than results produced through adherence to standardization. In either case, test results are compromised, and the conclusions drawn from research in these circumstances are rendered questionable.

The same general concerns about the reliability and validity of results also apply to the translation of tests and test items. Very few measures available in the USA have been developed for use with participants who are not native speakers of English. Many instruments in use are, again, ad hoc modifications created by individuals who possess some degree of bilingualism (Artiola i Fortuny & Mullaney, 1997). This is not a sufficient method for test translation, which requires a formal process of translation-back-translation by more than one individual with excellent proficiency in both languages involved (c.f., International Test Commission, 2000a, 2000b). The degree of compromise may be worse when tests with inadequate translation are employed, but even the results of research with the best possible translation practices must be interpreted with caution as the reliability, validity, and equivalence of the results of translated tests is unknown until evaluated with formal study.

Finally, even to the extent that individual measures may possess adequate psychometric properties in general, there are often significant problems with the norms for many tests. In many cases, norms are piecemeal; different researchers and practitioners have published normative data based on small local samples with varied characteristics (Mitrushina, Boone, Razani, & D'Elia, 2005; Strauss, Sherman, & Spreen, 2006). These norms can vary substantially in quality and in the degree to which they provide adequate representation based on gender and other demographic variables. Beyond this general problem, a more subtle one permeates test norms that has a differential impact on marginalized or disenfranchised populations. In the construction of test norms researchers or test developers may employ a series of exclusion criteria to select the sample. For example, in an effort to establish the functioning of neurologically healthy and intact individuals on a neuropsychological test, the developers may exclude from the normative sample individuals with a history of concussion, neurological or psychiatric disease, seizures, syncope, substance use, those who are currently on various medications, and/or those who have other health conditions that could affect test scores. The result can be that the final normative sample is based on individuals who are atypical relative to the general population. The prevalence of each of the exclusion criteria in the general population is such that many, if not most, individuals have the potential to be excluded from the study based on one or more criteria, which obviously renders the sample non-representative. The "normal" population becomes, in fact, "super-normal." Normative samples of this type very often have above-average health, education, and IQ scores. As a consequence, the average performance in the general population may appear to be below average in comparison, and the average performance within disenfranchised groups may appear to be poor or pathological. Data on IQ or education are not always collected or reported, and so this bias in the normative sample is not always readily apparent.

In sum, the availability of psychometrically sound measures with adequate norms and known reliability and validity for use in diverse, disadvantaged, and disenfranchised populations is the exception rather than the rule for many purposes (see Chapter 4). Social scientists engaged in forensic research should recognize the substantial impact that poor instrumentation has on the strength and quality of the conclusions that can be legitimately drawn from research. Failure to do so compromises the integrity of the research literature; increases the likelihood of bad outcomes at the individual, community, and legislative levels; and contributes to the continued marginalization of large segments of society. Although most psychologists are aware of the need to take diversity into account in their research and practice activities, this general awareness has not yet produced the testing and assessment methods necessary to respond adequately to this need. Many areas of research would benefit from addressing this fundamental concern instead of pressing ahead in an attempt to conduct research with inadequate methods.

Reliance on Simulation Research

For ethical and pragmatic reasons, it is sometimes necessary to utilize analogue or simulation research in forensic psychology. Research on the functioning and decision-making of juries is one example. Social scientists have a keen interest in jury research, given the concern that various factors (including the gender and sexual orientation of any and all participants in the legal process) could have an inappropriate influence on outcomes with the potential for substantial individual and societal harm. As a foundation of the legal system, jury processes cannot be compromised by any outside intrusion. Jury deliberations are secret, and recordings or transcriptions are illegal, which prevents the subsequent evaluation of archival data. Likewise, research on malingering frequently involves analogue studies in which participants are instructed to complete tests *as if* they were seeking to feign disorder and escape detection. As noted above, malingerers rarely identify themselves for research purposes.

The impact of simulation methods on the external validity of research probably varies, and perhaps considerably, depending on the topic under investigation. No matter what efforts have been made to increase the ecological validity of a research study, there are aspects of real life situations that cannot be simulated adequately. It is one thing to make a recommendation for the death penalty after spending an afternoon pretending to serve on a jury for research purposes; it is quite another to make such a recommendation after days or perhaps weeks of trial process with the fate of a specific individual in question. This is not to say that simulation research should not be undertaken, or that it cannot be informative, but the gap between the laboratory and real life must be acknowledged explicitly. If the disconnect is substantial enough, there is no basis for utilizing the research results for advocacy, court testimony, or policy formation.

Reliance on Self-report

Overreliance on self-report is a significant problem in forensic research. For example, Haney (2003) conducted a study of the rates of self-reported psychiatric symptoms among prisoners in so-called supermax correctional facilities. These facilities are designed to hold prisoners who present an ongoing risk to others as evidenced by violent assaults on staff and other inmates, sexual exploitation, and running criminal organizations. Inmates typically are placed on 23-hour solitary lockdown, with limited or no access to social contact or to educational, recreational, and rehabilitative programming. Among the criticisms raised about this form of incarceration is the potential for adverse psychological effects caused by this extreme level of isolation (Mears & Watson, 2006). Haney's methodology consisted of conducting face-to-face interviews in which inmates were asked whether they had experienced any of a list of psychiatric symptoms. A large percentage of inmates reported that they were experiencing a wide variety of symptoms. The number and severity of methodological flaws in the study as reported is impressive. The research utilized an ad hoc interview schedule with unknown reliability or validity, contained no assessment for malingering, collected no baseline or historical data to determine rates or severity of symptoms reported prior to entering the isolation unit, used no objective measures (such as psychiatric and hospital records), and used comparison groups from different time periods that were assessed with different methods. There is no indication in the report that either the interviewer or the participants were blind to the purpose of the study. The validity of self-reports of symptoms from this population is questionable at best. In addition to the high rates of character disorder that were likely to be present in the sample, there are obvious motivations, such as complaining to improve their circumstances or creating problems for correctional staff and administrators, that could bias symptom reporting. It is also notable that the bulk of the symptoms reported by inmates related to anxiety and sleep disorder. This is partially an artifact of the methodology in that they were not asked about other symptom groups. However, the possibility that drug-seeking behavior influenced symptom reports is not acknowledged in the report.

It would be one thing had Haney acknowledged the limitations of the study and calibrated the conclusions appropriately. Instead, the conclusions offered are made in the strongest possible language, and the author drew a causal connection between extreme isolation and symptoms. As designed, the study can only provide evidence that this population complains and, perhaps, that the complaints are consistent with those identified in other studies. This is an extreme example, but the reliance on self-report in research with forensic populations represents an obvious and substantial threat to the validity of research.

Archival Data

Researchers in forensic psychology have access to an extraordinary quantity and diversity of archival data developed by state and governmental agencies in the USA and abroad, as well as those that are made available through private foundations and international agencies and networks (c.f., Mosher, Miethe, & Phillips, 2002; Riedel, 2000). The Inter-University Consortium for Political and Social Research and the National Archive of Criminal Justice Data alone provide access to an extensive array of data sets relevant to forensic psychology. Space precludes substantial discussion of the challenges associated with the analysis of secondary data, but there are three points that are particularly relevant to the goals of this chapter that should be discussed.

First, the individuals who record and report data are often stakeholders with a vested interest in the statistics reported. Crime statistics can be inflated or minimized dramatically in response to the needs of the reporting agency. Reports of high crime rates may serve the purpose of justifying larger budget requests, and reports of lower crime rates may provide a demonstration that changes in leadership, law, policy, enforcement, or intervention methods have had a beneficial effect. The manipulation of crime statistics for financial and political gain is well documented (Mosher et al., 2002).

Second, the integrity of archival data sets collected over time can be compromised by changes in data collection methods. Changes in reporting protocols, technology, policy, and funding over the course of years or decades can produce the appearance of trends that are wholly artifactual in nature. There is often a fundamental lack of equivalence between different data sets that cover the same phenomena or within data sets over time. Even small changes in the numerator and denominator of prevalence rates due to methodological changes can produce very large swings, which can lead to the misimpression of dramatic trends or changes in the frequency or extent of social phenomena.

Last, a problem with all research based on archival data is the absence of control over what data are collected and how. For example, the Federal Bureau of Investigation's (FBI) Uniform Crime Reporting program (UCR) defines forcible rape as "the carnal knowledge of a female forcibly and against her will" (FBI, 2004, p. 18). Men, by definition, cannot be victims of forcible rape within this reporting system (although they can be victims of assault or "other sex offenses"). In contrast, the FBI's National Incident Based Reporting System does not define rape by the sex of the victim, but by the match between the victim and the perpetrator(s) of the offense. A sexual assault can be identified as rape if one or more of the active perpetrators is not of the same sex as the victim (FBI, 1992). By this standard, men can be raped by women, but not by men, and women cannot be raped by women. Similarly, many states have restrictions that exclude gay, lesbian, or transgendered individuals from domestic violence statutes (Girshick, 2002), which renders crimes against them invisible within official statistics.

Conclusion and Directions for Future Research

Gender is not a prominent topic in forensic psychology, which could lead some to conclude that not much gender-related research has been done in this area. However, as I reviewed the literature in preparation for writing this chapter, I discovered the opposite to be true. The problem is that so much literature exists that a summation and critical review of gender-relevant research in forensic psychology requires, *at minimum*, a volume of its own. There is substantial variation in the quality and quantity of research available to researchers on the diverse interactions of gender with forensic psychology, and the available literature is scattered across a wide range of academic disciplines. Given the importance of the subject matter, the production of such a volume would be an important step in the development of the field. A clearer understanding and integration of the extant literature, with careful consideration given to the methodological concerns outlined above, would provide researchers with a conceptual map of the field and highlight specific topics that demand attention.

In general, I offer three suggestions for future research on forensic and legal issues related to gender. First, as research on forensic topics has the potential to be utilized in the courtroom, future research should, when possible and appropriate, be conducted with recognition of standards of admissibility for expert witness testimony. Research cannot inform court decisions if it does not meet minimum standards for admission. In my opinion, there are many areas of gender-relevant testimony that, although popular or accepted among some groups of psychologists, would be unlikely to withstand a determined effort to exclude them based on issues of scientific merit. The admission of testimony in the past is, at best, an indirect measure of the strength of its scientific foundation. In fact, the admissibility of testimony that is "shaky" or of questionable scientific merit may not even be challenged as part of trial strategy; it may be advantageous to allow a weak expert to testify and then expose the flaws of the case during cross-examination. Attorneys are becoming increasingly capable in cross-examining psychologists in an effort to shed light on any deficiencies in their testimony. This is not a criticism of attorneys or of the adversarial process; the expert bears the responsibility to ensure that her or his testimony is based upon sufficient facts. Researchers should be aware of the level of scrutiny to which their research may be submitted, lest valuable findings be excluded or dismissed during the legal process. Bodies of existing research should be reevaluated in this light and remediated where possible. A useful step in this direction for many areas of existing inquiry would be to address the methodological considerations outlined in this chapter.

Second, future research should be directed at improving the standards of measurement researchers employ and developing measures that are not biased against individuals based on gender in its broadest sense. The psychometric quality of measures used in many areas of psychology is often inadequate, and this is true in forensic psychology as well. The strength and validity of conclusions will always be limited by the quality of the measures employed. Adherence, to the extent possible, to the Standards for Educational and Psychological Testing (AERA, APA, & NCME, 1999) is essential for researchers on forensic topics. Even if we assume that measures do have adequate reliability and validity when normed and researched in the general population, it is not clear, a priori, which measures might demonstrate statistical bias when researchers compare heterosexual and gay, lesbian, or transgendered populations. Simple inclusion of diverse populations within normative samples does not address test bias; research must be conducted to establish its presence or absence.

Finally, given the disproportionate representation of minority groups within many forensic contexts, it is unfortunate that inadequate attention to diversity issues remains a concern within the field. Forensic psychology may, in some ways, have a better record than other areas of the field, but considerable improvement remains warranted.

References

Adler, P. (1990). Ethnographic research in hidden populations: Penetrating the drug world. In E. Lambert (Ed.), *The collection and interpretation of data from hidden populations* (pp. 96–112). [DHHS Publication Number NDA 90-1678]. Bethesda, MD: National Institute on Drug Abuse.

American Bar Association Commission on Women in the Profession. (2006). *Charting our progress: The status of women in the profession today.* Chicago, IL: American Bar Association.

American Educational Research Association (AERA), American Psychological Association (APA), & National Council on Measurement in Education (NCME). (1999). *Standards for educational and psychological testing.* Washington, DC: American Educational Research Association.

American Psychological Association. (2002). Ethical principles of psychologists and code of conduct. *American Psychologist, 57*, 1060–1073.

American Psychological Association. (2009). *Archival description: Specialty of forensic psychology.* Retrieved January 8, 2009, from http://www.apa.org/crsppp/archivforensic.html

Anastasi, A., & Urbina, S. (1997). *Psychological testing* (7th ed.). Upper Saddle River, NJ: Prentice-Hall.

Armstrong, G. (1993). Like that Desmond Morris. In D. Hobbs & T. May (Eds.), *Interpreting the field: Accounts of ethnography* (pp. 2–43). Oxford: Clarendon.

Artiola i Fortuny, L., & Mullaney, H. A. (1997). Neuropsychology with Spanish speakers: Language use and proficiency issues for test development. *Journal of Clinical and Experimental Neuropsychology, 19*, 615–622.

Birnbaum, M. H. (2004). Human research and data collection via the internet. *Annual Review of Psychology, 55*, 803–832.

Bourgois, P. (1989). In search of Horatio Alger: Culture and ideology in the crack economy. *Contemporary Drug Problems, 16*, 619–649.

Brajuha, M., & Hallowell, L. (1986). Legal intrusion and the politics of fieldwork: The impact of the Brajuha case. *Urban Life, 14*, 454–478.

Breivik, K., & Olweus, D. (2006). Adolescents' adjustment in four post-divorce family structures: Single mother, stepfather, joint physical custody, and single father families. *Journal of Divorce and Remarriage, 44*, 99–25.

Brown, N. J., Berkovic, S. F., & Scheffer, I. E. (2007). Vaccination, seizures and "vaccine damage." *Current Opinion in Neurology, 20*, 181–187.

Buchanan, T. (2000). Potential of the internet for personality research. In H. M. Birnbaum (Ed.), *Psychological experiments on the internet* (pp. 121–265). San Diego, CA: Academic Press.

Bursoff, D. N. (1999). *Table of cases.* Unpublished manuscript.

Center for Sex Offender Management. (2007). *Female sex offenders.* Silver Spring, MD: Author.

Christofides, T. C. (2003). A generalized randomized response technique. *Metrika, 57*, 195–200.

Committee on Ethical Guidelines for Forensic Psychologists. (1991). Specialty guidelines for forensic psychologists. *Law and Human Behavior, 15*, 655–665.

Committee on the Judiciary, House of Representatives. (2006). *Federal rules of evidence.* Washington, DC: U.S. Government Printing Office.

Crowne, D. P., & Marlowe, D. (1960). A new scale of social desirability independent of psychopathology. *Journal of Consulting Psychology, 24*, 349–354.

Dalton, D. R., Wimbush, J. C., & Daily, C. M. (1994). Using the unmatched count technique (UCT) to estimate base rates for sensitive behavior. *Personnel Psychology, 47*, 817–828.

Daubert v. Merrell Dow Pharmaceuticals, Inc., 509 U. S. 579 (1993).

Decker, S. H., & Van Winkle, B. (1996). *Life in the gang: Family, friends, and violence.* New York: Cambridge University Press.

Deer, B. (2009, February 8) Hidden records show MMR truth. *Sunday Times.* Retrieved March 15, 2009, from http://www.timesonline.co.uk/tol/life_and_style/health/article5683643.ece

Demuth, S., & Brown, S. L. (2004). Family structure, family processes, and adolescent delinquency: The significance of parental absence versus parental gender. *Journal of Research in Crime and Delinquency, 41*, 58–81.

Department of State v. Washington Post, 456 U.S. 595 (1982).

Dickens, G., Sugarman, P., Ahmad, F., Edgar, S., Hofberg, K., & Tewari, S. (2007). Gender differences amongst adult arsonists at psychiatric assessment. *Medical Sciences and the Law, 47*, 233–238.

Faust, D., & Ackley, M. A. (1998). Did you think it was going to be easy? Some methodological suggestions for the investigation and development of malingering-detection techniques. In C. R. Reynolds (Ed.), *Detection of malingering during head injury litigation* (pp. 1–54). New York: Plenum.

Faust, D., & Heard, K. V. (2003a). Biased experts: Strategies for identifying and demonstrating unfair practices. In I. Z. Schultz & D. O. Brady (Eds.), *Psychological injuries at trial* (pp. 1706–1739). Chicago, IL: American Bar Association.

Faust, D., & Heard, K. V. (2003b). Objectifying subjective injury claims. In I. Z. Schultz & D. O. Brady (Eds.), *Psychological injuries at trial* (pp. 1686–1705). Chicago, IL: American Bar Association.

Federal Bureau of Investigation (FBI). (1992). *Uniform crime reporting handbook* (NIBRS ed.). Clarksville, WV: Author.

Federal Bureau of Investigation (FBI). (2004). *Uniform crime reporting handbook.* Clarksburg, WV: Author.

Ferrell, J. (1997). Criminological verstehen: Inside the immediacy of crime. *Justice Quarterly, 14*, 3–23.

Freeman, N. J., & Sandler, J. C. (2008). Female and male sex offenders: A comparison of recidivism patterns and risk factors. *Journal of Interpersonal Violence, 23*, 1394–1413.

Girshick, L. (2002). *Woman-to-woman sexual violence: Does she call it rape?* Boston: Northeastern University Press.

Goode, E. (2002). Sexual involvement and social research in a fat civil rights organization. *Qualitative Sociology, 25*, 501–534.

Greenberg, S. A., & Schuman, D. W. (1997). Irreconcilable conflict between therapeutic and forensic roles. *Professional Psychology, 28*, 50–57.

Halsey, N.A., & Hyman, S. L. (2001). Measles-mumps-rubella vaccine and autistic spectrum disorders: Report from the New Challenges in Childhood Immunization Conference convened in Oak Brook, Illinois, June 12–13, 2000. *Pediatrics, 107*, E84

Haney, C. (2003). Mental health issues in long-term solitary and "supermax" confinement. *Crime and Delinquency, 49*, 124–156.

Humphreys, L. (1970). *Tearoom trade.* Chicago: Aldine.

In Re Grand Jury Subpoena Dated January 4, 1984, 583 F. Suppl. 991 (1984).

In Re Grand Jury Subpoena Dated January 4 1984, 750 F. 2d 223 (1984).

Inciardi, J. A. (1993). Some considerations on the methods, dangers, and ethics of crack house research. In J. A. Inciardi, D. Lockwood, & A. Potieger (Eds.), *Women and crack cocaine* (pp. 147–157). New York: Macmillan.

International Test Commission (ITC). (2000a). *ITC guidelines for test use.* Retrieved November 17, 2008, from http://www.intestcom.org/guidelines/index.php

International Test Commission (ITC). (2000b). *ITC guidelines on adapting tests.* Retrieved November 17, 2008, from http://www.intestcom.org/guidelines/index.php

Jablonska, B., & Lindberg, L. (2007). Risk behaviors, victimization, and mental distress among adolescents in different family structures. *Social Psychiatry and Psychiatric Epidemiology, 42,* 656–664.

Johnson, M. T, Krafka, C., & Cecil, J. S. (2000). *Expert testimony in federal civil trials: A preliminary analysis.* Washington, DC: Federal Judicial Center.

Kelly, J. B. (2007). Children's living arrangements following separation and divorce: Insights from empirical and clinical research. *Family Process, 46,* 35–52.

Krafka, C., Dunn, M. A., Johnson, M. T., Cecil, J. S., & Miletich, D. (2002). Judge and attorney experiences, practices, and concerns regarding expert testimony in federal civil trials. *Psychology, Public Policy, & Law, 8,* 309–332.

Kraut, R., Olson, J., Banaji, M., Bruckman, A., Cohen, J., & Couper, M. (2004). Psychological research online: Report of the Board of Scientific Affairs' Advisory Group on the Conduct of Research on the Internet. *American Psychologist, 59,* 105–117.

Kushner, M. A. (2006). In whose best interest: The ruling or the children? *Journal of Divorce and Remarriage, 44* (3/4), 17–30.

Lensvelt-Mulders, G. J. L. M., Hox, J. J., Van der Heijden, P. G. M., & Maas, C. J. M. (2005). Meta-analysis of randomized response research: Thirty-five years of validation. *Sociological Methods & Research, 33,* 319–348.

Leo, R. A. (1995). Trial and tribulations: Courts, ethnography, and the need for evidentiary privilege for academic researchers. *American Sociologist, 26,* 113–134.

Leo, R. A. (1996). The ethics of deceptive research roles reconsidered: A response to Kai Erickson. *American Sociologist, 27,* 122–128.

Lillenfeld, S. O. (1998). Methodological advances and developments in the assessment of psychopathy. *Behavior Research and Therapy, 36,* 99–125.

Madsen, K. M., Hviid, A., Vestergaard, M., Schendel, D., Wolfram, J., Thorsen, P., et al. (2002). A population-based study of measles, mumps, and rubella vaccination and autism. *New England Journal of Medicine, 374,* 1477–1482.

Madsen, K. M., & Vestergaard, M. (2004). MMR vaccination and autism: What is the evidence for a causal association? *Drug Safety, 27,* 831–840.

Marquart, J. (1986). Doing research in prison: The strengths and weaknesses of full participation as a guard. *Justice Quarterly, 3,* 15–32.

Mears, D., & Watson, J. (2006). Toward a fair and balanced assessment of supermax prisons. *Justice Quarterly, 23,* 232–270.

Meehl, P. E. (1971/1991). Law and the fireside inductions: Some reflections of a clinical psychologist. In C. A. Anderson & K. Gunderson (Eds.), *Paul E. Meehl: Selected philosophical and methodological papers* (pp. 440–480). Minneapolis, MN: University of Minnesota Press.

Mitrushina, M., Boone, K. B., Razani, J., & D'Elia, L. F. (2005). *Handbook of normative data for neuropsychological assessment* (2nd ed.). New York: Oxford University Press.

Mittenberg, W., Patton C., Canyock, E., & Condit, D. (2002). Base rates of malingering and symptom exaggeration. *Journal of Clinical and Experimental Neuropsychology, 24,* 1094–1102.

Mosher, C. J., Miethe, T. D., & Phillips, D. M. (2002). *The mismeasure of crime.* Thousand Oaks, CA: Sage.

National Institutes of Health, Office of Extramural Research. (2002). *Frequently asked questions on certificates of confidentiality.* Retrieved March, 15, 2009, from http://grants.nih.gov/grants/policy/coc/faqs.html

Newman, W. L. (2006). *Social research methods: Qualitative and quantitative approaches* (6th ed.). Boston, MA: Allyn & Bacon.

Nicholls, T. L., Ogloff, J. R., Brink, J., & Spidel, A. (2005). Psychopathy in women: A review of its clinical usefulness for assessing risk for aggression and criminality. *Behavioral Sciences and the Law, 23,* 779–802.

Nordberg, P. B. (2006). *Psychologists & psychiatrists.* Retrieved February 21, 2006, from, http://www.daubertontheweb.com/psychologists.html

Peek, C. (2004). Breaking out of the prison hierarchy: Transgender prisoners, rape, and the eighth amendment. *Santa Clara Law Review, 44,* 1211–1212.

Perrone, D. (2006). New York club kids: A contextual understanding of club drug use. In B. Sanders (Ed.), *Drugs, clubs, and young people* (pp. 26–49). Aldershot, UK: Ashgate.

Polsky, N. (1969). *Hustlers, beats, and others.* Garden City, NY: Anchor.

Rabinowitz, V. C., & Martin, D. (2001). Choices and consequences: Methodological issues in the study of gender. In R. Unger (Ed.), *Handbook of the psychology of women and gender* (29–52). New York: Wiley.

Reips, U. (2002). Standards for internet-based experimenting. *Experimental Psychology, 49*, 243–256.

Reynolds, C. R. (Ed.). (1997). *Detection of malingering during head injury litigation.* New York: Springer.

Riedel, M. (2000). *Research strategies for secondary data: A perspective for criminology and criminal justice.* Thousand Oaks, CA: Sage.

Roe-Sepowitz, D., & Krysik, J. (2008). Examining the sexual offenses of female juveniles: The relevance of childhood maltreatment. *American Journal of Orthopsychiatry, 78*, 405–412.

Rogers, R. (Ed.). (2008). *Clinical assessment of malingering and deception* (3rd ed.). New York: Guilford.

Scarce, R. (2005). *Contempt of court: A scholar's battle for free speech.* Lanham, MD: Alta Mira Press.

Strauss, E., Sherman, E. M. S., & Spreen, O. (2006). *A compendium of neuropsychological tests: Administration, norms, and commentary* (3rd ed.). New York: Oxford University Press.

Supple, A. J., Aquilino, W. S., & Wright, D. L. (1999). Collecting sensitive self-report data with laptop computers: Impact on the response tendencies of adolescents in a home interview. *Journal of Research on Adolescents, 9*, 467–488.

Tucillo, J. A., DeFilippis, J. A., Denney, R. L., & Dsurney, J. (2002). Licensure requirements for interjurisdictional forensic evaluations. *Professional Psychology, 33*, 377–383.

Van Maanen, J. (1982). Fieldwork on the beat. In J. Van Maanen, J. Dabbs, & R. R. Faulkner (Eds.), *Varieties of qualitative research* (pp. 103–151). Beverly Hills, CA: Sage.

Warner, S. (1965). Randomized response: A survey technique for eliminating evasive answer bias. *Journal of the American Statistical Association, 60*, 63–69.

Wimbush, J. C., & Dalton, D. R. (1997). Baserate for employee theft: Convergence of multiple methods. *Journal of Applied Psychology, 82*, 756–763.

Yablonsky, L. (1968). On crime, violence, LSD, and legal immunity for social sciences. *Criminologica, 3*, 148–149.

Chapter 26
The Treatment of Gender in Community Psychology Research

Sharon M. Wasco and Meg A. Bond

Since the founding of the field, community psychology has held attention to diversity as a central tenet, and the inclusion of gender issues has long been considered particularly compatible with core frameworks (Angelique & Cully, 2000, 2003; Mulvey, 1988; Swift, Bond, & Serrano-Garcia, 2000). Although community psychology covers topics that overlap with interests of other subfields of psychology, the field is distinctive in its adoption of systemic paradigms for the study of these widely ranging topics. We begin this chapter by discussing the fit between attending to gender in our research and the guiding values and principles of community psychology. We then turn to an assessment of how the field has actually incorporated gender issues into research published in the leading journals of community psychology in the USA. We present several exemplars to highlight the predominant themes related to the treatment of gender within community psychology and emphasize the field's contribution to understanding gender as a process variable and as a contextual variable.

The Field of Community Psychology

The field of community psychology is perhaps best described by a few core principles. One such principle is the importance of being explicit about guiding values in research and action (Rappaport, 1977; Rudkin, 2004). Community psychologists, individually and collectively, emphasize individual and family wellness, sense of community, respect for human diversity, citizen participation, collaboration, strengths-based approaches, and the importance of empirical grounding (Dalton, Elias, & Wandersman, 2007). There is also an emphasis on prevention and the integration of theory, research, and action to promote social justice and social change. These guiding principles can be traced back to the emergence of community psychology in the USA in the 1960s[1] and have been reinforced and refined over the last 40 years (Bennett et al., 1966; Wilson, Hayes, Greene, Kelly, & Iscoe, 2003).

Community psychology incorporates a systemic analysis of social issues, and the majority of work is guided by a social ecological perspective that understands human behavior as a function of

---

S.M. Wasco (✉)
University of Massachusetts Lowell, Lowell, MA, USA

The order of authorship does not reflect authors' relative contributions, which are inseparable.

[1] We focus here primarily on the academic discipline of community psychology, organized within the Society for Research and Action: Division 27 of the American Psychological Association, which is the primary professional association of community psychologists and the cornerstone of community psychology in the USA. There is a rich history of community psychology movements internationally (see Reich, Riemer, Prilleltensky, & Montero, 2007a). The impetus and local historical context for the evolution of community psychology varies considerably by location.

the person and her or his environment (Kelly, 1968, 1986; Trickett, 1986; Trickett, Kelly, & Vincent, 1985). The broader field of psychology has long focused on individual differences in mental processes and behavior; the social ecological perspective embraced by community psychologists widens the focus to the influences of *extra*-individual factors – such as social support, neighborhood climate, group dynamics, organizational climate, and cultural practices, and beliefs – in diverse people's lives. Community psychology is guided by the assertions that "community research and action require explicit attention to and respect for diversity among peoples and settings" and "human competencies and problems are best understood by viewing people within their social, cultural, economic, geographic, and historical contexts" (Mission statement for the Society for Community Research and Action: Division 27 of the American Psychological Association, http://www.scra27.org/about.html).

There are also shared values about the process of community psychology research and action, including that community psychology not be practiced alone within the confines of an office or a university. Rather, community psychologists value work conducted in the community through collaboration with others in order to integrate the acquisition of knowledge with the utilization of the knowledge to promote change. Community psychologists' embrace of diversity extends beyond appreciation of human diversity, as they are trained to recognize and utilize, where appropriate, multiple epistemologies and methodologies. These types of values and priorities, the hallmarks of community psychology, are applied across a wide range of research topics and community problems (e.g., gender-based violence, discrimination, poverty, homelessness, HIV/AIDS, substance abuse).

The field's emphasis on empowerment, social justice, and the role of structural inequality and social conditions on well-being has led many authors to make the case that the values, frameworks, and methods of community psychology have a unique compatibility with feminist analyses (see for example, Bond, Hill, Mulvey, & Terenzio, 2000a, 2000b; Campbell & Wasco, 2000; Cosgrove & McHugh, 2000; Mulvey, 1988; Oliver & Hammerton, 1992). There are shared values for research that incorporate self-reflection, attention to the relationship between researchers and participants, and acknowledgment of the intersectionality of such influences as gender, ethnicity/race, and class. Indeed, there has been explicit attention to women's issues and to feminist methods and analysis over the years (Bond & Mulvey, 2000). Scholars in the field have not, however, published a systematic review of research on men and masculinity in major community psychology outlets.

Most past work in this spirit has focused on appraisals of the state of research related to women within the field. Scholars have yet to publish a systematic review of research on men and masculinity in a major community psychology outlet. For example, Swift and colleagues (2000) systematically reviewed the community psychology journals to identify the topics of particular relevance to women's lives. They found work on varied family and relationship patterns (e.g., issues in the lives of lesbians and the impact of divorce), workforce participation (e.g., work–family issues, sexual harassment, barriers to full participation), carework (e.g., for young children, for people with special needs, for the elderly), health and reproduction (e.g., eating disorders, AIDS, adolescent pregnancy), violence against women in its many forms, and the problems of poverty and homelessness. Swift et al. (2000) also pointed to work focused on understanding issues of particular relevance to women of color and to the intersections of gender with other dimensions of diversity.

Angelique and Cully (2000, 2003) have published two reviews of community psychology's attention to women's issues. In their earlier study, they conducted a content analysis of all articles in the *American Journal of Community Psychology* (*AJCP*) and the *Journal of Community Psychology* (*JCP*) from 1973 to 1997. Although they found less attention to women's issues than they had hoped, they emphasized that there was progress over time both in the number of articles considered "women relevant" and in the incorporation of feminist perspectives and analyses. They also noted that women's mental health and motherhood were the most addressed content areas. Their later analysis of the same journals documented a continuing trend from 1998 to 2000 toward more feminist research and highlighted some noteworthy exemplars.

In the current chapter, we sought to complement past work that has tracked the coverage of topics of particular relevance to women's lives by broadening our examination to understand the treatment of gender in community psychology research across all topics and participant populations. Given that entire chapters, and even sections, in this volume are devoted to many of the substantive topics that are of concern to community psychologists (e.g., education, life span development, discrimination and harassment, homophobia, sexism, health and well-being, stress and coping, health care utilization, workplace equity issues), we believe that the most important contribution that a chapter on gender in community psychology can make to this handbook may be conceptual and/or philosophical in nature. Thus, the primary focus of this chapter is not to summarize research areas that may be considered men's or women's issues; rather we explore the ways in which gender is treated in the conceptualization and conduct of community psychology research across a wide range of community phenomena. Specifically, we analyzed the ways that "gender" and "sex" have been approached in research published by two primary community psychology journals. For the purposes of this review, we defined research as the systematic collection of data, which were then subjected to some degree of analysis. We included action research, descriptive research, and case studies in addition to experimental work; we examined qualitative and content analyses that yielded frameworks in addition to quantitative projects that tested for statistical significance. This approach afforded an opportunity to assess the extent to which the field's stated emphasis on attending to intersecting and multileveled dimensions of diversity offers particular insights for expanding gender research in psychology. Our findings highlighted the importance of thinking about gender as an ecological, or contextual, variable.

Conceptualization of Gender

There are several interpretations and uses of the word "gender." As per one of the guiding principles in our field – the appreciation of diversity – we understand gender as one of the key ways in which people are different from each other. We believe that many of these differences are social constructions, that is, that they are learned behaviors or human choices shaped by social, cultural, and historical forces. As one of many dimensions of social identity, gender has its own influences on the human experience, but it also interacts with other dimensions of social identity (e.g., ethnicity, sexual orientation, disability). Gender differences are typically described in binary ways, that is, as differentiations between femininity and masculinity. However, the dichotomization of the phenomena is misleading because masculinity and femininity may be experienced in a wide range of manners; variations are often influenced by such factors as ethnic background, class, age, cohort, and sexual orientation (Unger & Crawford, 1992; Unger & Sanchez-Hucles, 1993).

As mentioned above, gender interacts with all dimensions of human diversity, but there are two that are particularly notable because of their close relationship to gender: biological sex and sexual orientation. Though sex, based on chromosomal make-up and reproductive anatomy, is an important determinant of gender, sex and gender are different concepts. A key difference is that sex is biologically determined and thus similar across cultures, whereas gender is neither. As mentioned above, gender is the set of socially constructed meanings attached to sex that are inextricably linked to the cultural and historical context of a specific place. Our primary focus in this chapter is on gender.

Sexual orientation is another dimension of human diversity that is related to, but clearly separate from, gender. Though many gay, lesbian, and bisexual individuals and communities have challenged traditional notions of gender, and gender expectations are at times conflated with sexual orientation (e.g., a man's choice of a pink shirt may be derided as "gay"), sexual orientation refers to a person's sexual attraction to others. We have not tried to review all community psychology research related to sexual orientation; however, such work was included when there was an explicit attempt to look at the ways in which gendered dynamics, expectations, stereotypes, bias, and discrimination (including homophobia) influence people's lives.

We focus this chapter on three related questions: How is gender treated in the community psychology literature? How has the treatment of gender evolved over the 40 years since the field was founded? What insights, if any, can community psychology research provide about how gender affects the important contexts of community life?

Method

To examine gender research within the field of community psychology, we conducted a content analysis of work published in the two largest academic journals devoted to community psychology, the *American Journal of Community Psychology* (*AJCP*) and the *Journal of Community Psychology* (*JCP*), between 1973 (when both journals were founded) and 2007.[2] Limiting the search to these two major publication outlets is an approach that has been used by many other community psychologists to summarize the work of the field (e.g., Angelique & Culley, 2000, 2003; Bernal & Enchautegui-de-Jesus, 1994; Loo, Fong, & Iwamasa, 1988; Lounsbury, Leader, Meares, & Cook, 1980; Speer et al., 1992). One of the advantages of using these two journals is that they are the longest standing journals of community psychology, both in the USA and abroad, which allowed for a historical analysis over time. The combined total number of articles from these two journals cataloged in the *PsycINFO* database at the time of our literature search (i.e., from 1973 to 2007) was 2,973.

We began by searching the *PsycINFO* database for articles in both journals that contained *gender* in the title or abstract, and we found 133 articles. This number seemed low, and we suspected that we were missing many articles of interest, so we then expanded our search to include additional terms. The terms *sex difference(s)* yielded 48 additional articles, and *feminist* and *feminism* yielded an additional 20 articles, for a total of 201 articles that included at least one of those terms. We then examined these articles for additional criteria for inclusion in our content analysis. First, the article had to be a research report, which we defined as subjecting empirical data to some level of analysis. We excluded ($n = 25$) articles that did not meet our criteria (e.g., introductions to special issues, strictly theoretical pieces, literature reviews, and commentaries not based on systematic content analyses). We also excluded ($n = 2$) articles that were not clearly focused on gender or sex (i.e., the terms were embedded in the phrases "men who had same-gender sex" and "inspired by a literary-feminist reading of biblical texts"). There were a few papers in the initial sample ($n = 7$) that treated gender as though it were a distraction from the main constructs of interest or an influence to be minimized, or controlled, methodologically. We excluded these particular articles from our content analysis as well, which left 167 publications in our sample.

---

[2]Neither of these journals is published by the American Psychological Association, so, unlike APA journals, the abstracts have remained consistent in length over the years.

Once the literature was identified, three raters (the two authors of this chapter and a graduate student in community social psychology) worked independently to code all 167 abstracts using a three-category coding schema. Although we began with a general sense of these categories, the specific criteria for coding were developed inductively through a process of coding and discussion among raters. The final categories represent three major ways that community psychology has treated gender in research and practice over the years: as a *grouping variable*, as a *process variable*, and as a *contextual variable*. Descriptions of these categories are provided below with the results. All three raters marked each abstract with one or more of the three codes, and we met collectively to share our codes and resolve discrepancies. Where there was disagreement, the coders discussed the issues until consensus was reached.

The coding scheme we created to classify the scholarship on gender provided a framework for organizing the work of community psychologists in this chapter; however, these codes are probably not exhaustive and are definitely not mutually exclusive. We discovered that it was not possible to formulate mutually exclusive categories because many times there were multiple treatments of gender within a single research report. Thus, abstracts were given a primary code as well as secondary code(s) when appropriate.

Once all abstracts were coded, we noted emerging themes within each category and chose exemplars to present here. Many full research reports were obtained, reviewed, and summarized. For abstracts where gender seemed to be a minor consideration, full research reports were not reviewed. We gave special attention to the articles that best exemplify what we have classified as the three major treatments of gender in community psychology research. Finally, we included the year of publication as a variable in order to look at fluctuation in number of publications and treatment of gender over the years since *AJCP* and *JCP* began publishing. We used 5-year blocks of time to create seven discrete time periods: 1973–1977, 1978–1982, 1983–1987, 1988–1992, 1993–1997, 1998–2002, and 2003–2007. We then conducted frequency analyses to document how gender has been treated in this body of work over time.

Our approach to the literature search limits this chapter in a few ways. First, by restricting our search to *AJCP* and *JCP*, we knowingly excluded outlets where community psychologists might publish gender-related research (e.g., *Journal of Human Sexuality, Journal of Prevention and Intervention in the Community, Journal of Social Issues, Psychology of Men & Masculinity, Psychology of Women Quarterly, Sex Roles*) because it is impossible to assess accurately which authors in these journals consider themselves community psychologists. Although *AJCP* and *JCP* include research by authors from all over the world, limiting our search to two journals also left out international journals that include the work of community psychologists such as the *Journal of Community and Applied Social Psychology* (UK), *Community, Work, & Family* (the Netherlands), *the Australian Community Psychologist*, and *Psychology in Society* (South Africa). We return to the issue of international contributions in the last section of the chapter. It is possible that our choice of search terms might have led us to overlook research on men that incorporated a gender analysis. Finally, our sampling of the literature did not necessarily include research on some substantive topics that are inherently gendered (e.g., parenting and other forms of caregiving, rape, and other forms of interpersonal violence). For example, the abstract of a comparative study of stress among mothers and fathers of deaf children (Hagborg, 1989) did not contain a search term and thus was not included in our review despite the fact that the author examined gender differences. Although our approach runs the risk of overlooking some substantive contributions of community psychology to scientific knowledge on gender, the approach did allow us to observe systematically the ways that community-based researchers treat gender as a psychological construct.

Observations

Our initial survey of the literature was guided by the primary question: How is gender treated in community psychology research? Our review confirmed what others have found as they explored related questions (e.g., Angelique & Culley, 2000; Swift et al., 2000), which is that there is very little literature in these community journals that identifies gender as the primary focus of the research. Instead, we found that gender-related issues have been incorporated into the study of a wide range of substantive research topics. The literature we reviewed covered a variety of core concepts in community psychology (e.g., prevention science, stress and coping, social support and help seeking, sense of community, empowerment), focused on a plethora of social issues and problem areas (e.g., mentoring, homelessness, drug and alcohol dependence, adolescent pregnancy), and addressed a variety of special populations (e.g., minority urban youth, Mexican migrant laborers, disadvantaged African American women, Navajo adolescents).

The coding scheme that we developed through iterative abstract review and discussion provides additional answers to how community psychologists treat the construct of gender. In about 80% of these substantively diverse articles ($n = 134$; 80.2%), the community researchers treated gender as a *grouping* variable. A few research reports ($n = 13$; 7.8%) presented ways that gender impacts the research and action process, which we have called gender as a *process* variable. The authors of 20 articles (12%) treated gender as what we have termed a *contextual* variable, which means that the researchers considered gender-related values and/or dynamics as embedded qualities of the context/s being studied. These treatments of gender are discussed in greater detail below.

Gender as a Grouping Variable

The majority of articles in our sample (80.2%) treated gender as a *grouping* variable, that is, as an individual difference that could be used to divide participants into meaningful subgroups for comparison. Gender was treated as a static property or characteristic of each participant, which then allowed for group comparisons between women and men or boys and girls in regard to some topic of interest. Despite the wide variety of research topics included here, several themes regarding the treatment of gender did emerge through iterative review. The themes describe sometimes subtle variations in conceptualizations of gender as a grouping variable and are as follows: (a) gender as a descriptive variable, (b) gender as a demographic variable, (c) gender as a risk or protective factor, (d) gender as a moderating variable, (e) gender as an individual-level variable within a contextual or ecological model, and (f) gender as an intersecting variable. The themes are not mutually exclusive, and the commonality across all themes is the use of gender to compare two groups of people.

Gender as a Descriptive Variable

In most articles where authors treated gender as a grouping variable, gender differences were often presented in a descriptive way – as observations about the participants or communities included in the research. Rather than being grounded in some theory about gender, differences between women and men were explored in these studies because it was interesting or practically relevant to do so. In some studies, being male was associated with a problematic variable of interest. For example, Romero, Carvajal, Volle, and Orduña (2007) found that, relative to women, men reported more stress due to discrimination or prejudice, immigration, and acculturation, which the authors called *bicultural stress*. Other studies documented an association between being female and some negative outcomes; for example, in the transition to parenthood in a Chinese cultural context, women reported higher stress, more psychological symptoms, and lower marital satisfaction than men did (Luo, 2006). Less frequently, more positive outcomes were associated with being a man or a woman. For example, Schwarzer, Hahn, and Schröder (1994) reported that, compared to women, men from the former East Germany were more socially active following the reunification of East and West Germany. Zlotnick, Robertson, and Lahiff (1999) found that, among homeless persons, being a woman was associated with more residential stability. Whether the association between gender and the variable(s) of interest was framed as positive or negative may often be a matter of tradition and/or convenience (i.e., the available standardized measures are often worded and scaled in ways that measure the presence of a negative phenomenon).

Because community psychology advocates a strengths-based approach (e.g., Rappaport, 1977), it is worth noting that far more of the published research on gender differences is conducted in a way that, intentionally or not, uncovers deficits – or associations between gender group membership and some negative phenomenon. In a study of gender differences among Native American adolescents, Mitchell and Beals (1997) directly addressed some of the philosophical, conceptual, and empirical issues within the strengths vs. deficit debate. They measured negative and positive behaviors separately, that is, *not* as two opposing ends of the same continuum. They found that, in their words, "these were neither 'good' kids nor 'bad' kids; as a group, they represented a complex mixture of both problem and positive behaviors" (p. 277). The authors used a statistical technique (multi-sample confirmatory factor analysis) that allowed them to test their elaborate measurement model on subgroups within their sample, including boys and girls. They found seven significant differences by gender. This work was successful in documenting, analyzing, and describing aspects of human experience – including gender – in ways that move beyond simple linear correlations.

Mitchell and Beals used multi-sample confirmatory factor analysis to evaluate relationships between variables for boys and for girls concurrently, whereas other community researchers interested in gender differences have used separate models for women and men (Whitbeck, Hoyt, & Yoder, 1999) or a series of model comparisons to look at differences between men and women. For example, by comparing two models (one for each gender), Conger, Conger, Matthews, and Elder (1999) found that, although both girls and boys are at risk for problems when families experience economic pressure, there were gender differences in the nature of the relationships between economic hardship and problem manifestation. Family economic stress had a more negative impact on boys' than on girls' sense of mastery, but girls experienced more emotional distress than boys did when there were such declines in mastery. Similarly, Pretty and McCarthy (1991) used subgroups analysis with regression equations and found that different aspects of the psychosocial work climate predicted psychological sense of community for women and for men. They found that support from others was important for the sense of community of all workers but that the sources of support varied by gender and by job position. Among managers, peer cohesion was the strongest predictor of sense of community for men, whereas women seemed to benefit from supervisors' support. In contrast, male nonmanagers' sense of community was related to supervisors' support and female non-mangers' sense of community to support from peers. Work pressure had an impact on sense of community for both women and men, but for men the impact was positive, and for women it was negative.

Regardless of how the variables were operationalized or analyzed, it is notable that the majority of the studies suggested no consistent gender differences in the main phenomena of interest. For example, there were no differences between men and women in sleep disturbances or community violence exposure (Cooley-Quille & Lorion, 1999), the communication patterns (Klaw, Huebsch, & Humphreys, 2000) or content of postings (Salem, Bogat, & Reid, 1997) of on-line mutual help groups, changes in school and peer microsystems during normative transition to high school (Seidman, Aber, Allen, & French, 1996), predictors of physical and sexual victimization among homeless persons (Roll, Toro, & Ortola, 1999), or subjective well-being of Korean Americans after the Sa-i-gu riots in Los Angeles (Sasao & Chun, 1994). The authors of the studies we highlight employed methodological strategies to compare the same set of hypothesized relationships by looking both within and across gender groups. These analytic approaches allowed community researchers to acknowledge similarity in human experiences (i.e., economic pressure on family leads to problems for both boys and girls; both men and women experience psychological sense of community at work) even as they pointed out the gendered nature of these experiences.

Gender as a Demographic Variable

Some community psychologists have treated gender as a demographic variable. The distinction we saw between treating gender as a demographic and descriptive variable was primarily that some researchers used the word "demographic" to describe gender, whereas others did not. Because demography is the study of structure and change in human populations, researchers who wittingly chose to label gender as a demographic variable may have signaled an assumption of societal-level explanations for differences between women and men. Researchers who used the term demographic and interpreted the gender differences, as opposed to just noting them, tended to place emphasis on societal factors. For example, Jackson and Heatherington's (2006) survey of young Jamaicans showed demographic differences (age, gender, social class, and rural vs. urban location) in negative attitudes toward people with mental illness. When they interpreted their results, including gender differences, the authors highlighted Jamaican and American cultural influences.

There were times, however, when the use of the language of demography, as opposed to the psychological term "individual difference variable," was more semantic than interpretative. In other words, in some studies the inclusion of gender as a demographic variable did not result in social, cultural, or regional interpretations nor was there any theoretical basis for expecting or explaining differences between men and women. For example, Hanson, Smith, Kilpatrick, and Freedy (2000) used careful sampling strategies associated with sociological surveys to conduct a large-scale telephone survey of South Central and other Los Angeles county residents regarding exposure to traumatic events and fear of crime, yet they reported gender differences descriptively. Nonetheless, we suggest that (even purely semantic) treatment of gender as a demographic variable makes gender's social construction salient.

Gender as a Risk or Protective Factor

A focus on prevention and health promotion as a way to improve individual, group, and community well-being is central to the field of community psychology. Thus, another way of treating gender that reflects community psychology's approach to solving social problems is to frame gender as a risk or protective factor. In other words, some authors described gender membership as having an impact positively or negatively on some specific problem. For example, in their analysis of risk and protective factors related to suicide, O'Donnell, O'Donnell, Wardlaw, and Stueve (2004) reported that risk factors for both suicidal ideation and suicide attempts included "being female" (p. 37). On the other hand, Rauh, Parker, Garfinkel, Perry, and Andrews (2003) found that being a boy was a risk factor for poor reading scores, and Mason, Chapman, and Scott (1999) reported that being a boy increased an individual's risk of having a severe emotional disturbance or an emotional handicap. Unger, Kipke, Simon, Montgomery, and Johnson (1997) studied homeless youth and reported that girls were at increased risk for depression, whereas boys were at increased risk for alcohol abuse. Though the authors of these studies invoked a prevention framework, this treatment of gender as a risk or protective factor is problematic because the politics of identity, substantial gender variation across cultures/contexts, and basic ethical considerations make it difficult to prevent one's biological status as male or female or to promote masculinity over femininity, or vice versa.

We argue that suggesting that gender is a risk factor is essentially the same as comparing groups of women and men and noting the ways in which they differ in amount of distress in some particular aspect of their lives. When placed in a risk factor framework, gender functions as an easily measured proxy for other resources and social conditions that vary by gender (e.g., social norms that encourage girls to please others and normalize boys' use of aggression). Thus, the treatment of gender as a risk factor may uncover gender differences in the problems community psychologists are invested in solving (e.g., suicide, depression, substance abuse), but, in doing so, this treatment only raises further questions about what factors and processes put one gender at risk or protect the other gender. We believe that prevention or promotion efforts ultimately will need to intervene to address those conditions, factors, or processes for which gender serves as a proxy variable. For example, rather than targeting one gender over another, programs should be designed to reduce potentially harmful aspects of masculinity (e.g., risk-taking and impulsivity) or femininity (e.g., passivity, rumination), as well as to promote healthy behaviors and social competencies in ways that are meaningful to both girls and boys.

Gender as an Influence on Other Variables in a Theoretical Relationship

Another approach to research used by community psychologists who seek to identify preconditions for particular individual outcomes is to consider how gender affects both predictor variables (often conceptualized as a risk/protective factors) and the outcome variable/s (whether defined as distress or well-being). Within these studies, gender is again treated as a grouping variable but conceptualized as moderating the relationship between two other sets of variables. For example, Rosario, Salzinger, Feldman, and Ng-Mak (2003) looked at the relationship between youths' exposure to violence and delinquent behavior and found that the relationship was moderated by gender in some fairly complex ways. Support from peers buffered the effects of witnessing violence on subsequent delinquent behavior for boys, whereas, for girls, support from guardians was a more effective buffer. Some studies have identified factors that serve a protective function for girls, whereas the very same variable is a risk factor for boys. For example, a study of the relationship between family conflict and conduct problems showed that, in general, greater parental attachment attenuated the relationship between family conflict and behavior problems among adolescent girls, but actually exacerbated the relationship for adolescent boys (Formoso, Gonzales, & Aiken, 2000).

In some similarly structured studies, gender differences were found in the predictor and/or the outcome variables, but not necessarily in the relationship between the two. For example, in a study of the association between religious involvement and the risk behaviors of youth, researchers found gender differences in religious involvement but did not find that the relationship between religiosity and risk behavior was actually different for boys and girls (Scott, Munson, McMillen, & Ollie, 2006). Similarly, some of the studies we reviewed examined how intervention effectiveness might vary by gender of participants (e.g., Edwards, 1979; Hüsler, Werlen, & Blakeney, 2005; Ialongo et al., 1999). Many researchers have assessed the differential impact of specific prevention programs on the mental health or problem behaviors of female and male participants, and some showed that the intervention was more successful for boys/men, whereas others were more successful for girls/women. These studies are conceptually akin to those that examine the role of gender in the relationship between risk factors and outcomes. Other intervention studies that examined how the dynamics of the particular intervention strategy (i.e., the process as opposed to the outcome) might be influenced by gender are explored in more depth when we look at gender as a process variable.

Gender as an Individual-Level Difference Variable Within an Ecological Framework

Community researchers also considered gender as an individual difference variable within ecological analyses of social outcomes. For example, Duncan, Duncan, Okut, Strycker, and Hix-Small (2003) utilized a multilevel design to examine contributors to neighborhood collective efficacy by considering indicators at the neighborhood level (i.e., mobility, racial/ethnic make-up, crime reports), at the family level (i.e., marital status, family income), and at the individual level (i.e., gender, age). This particular study showed no gender differences; however, a multileveled study of neighborhoods showed that perceptions of safety varied by gender as well as by contextual characteristics such as neighborhood income (Mulvey, 2002). In a study of Lowell, Massachusetts over 14 years, Mulvey found that women felt less safe than men did, both downtown and in their own neighborhoods, and that residents of lower income neighborhoods felt less safe than did their counterparts from higher income neighborhoods. However, ratings of general quality of life varied with economic conditions but not by gender, which prompted Mulvey to suggest that a lack of safety may be experienced by women as "natural, or just the way things are" (p. 675).

Other similarly structured studies have included gender differences in multileveled analyses of academic climate for lesbian, gay, and bisexual (LGB) students on a college campus (Waldo, 1998) and academic achievement of African American adolescents (Seyfried, 1998). Waldo found not only that LGB students experienced the academic climate at a large state university as more negative than did heterosexual students but also that women and racial/ethnic minorities (regardless of sexual orientation) were "more aware of this negativity and contributed to it less" (p. 745) than did men or European American students. Seyfried looked at the interaction between student characteristics (including gender), family environment, and teacher perceptions of social skills in determining academic success as measured by grade point average. The inclusion of gender as an individual difference variable within a broader set of comparisons is consistent with the guiding values and ecological framework of community psychology. Studies such as these further our knowledge of how gender might interact with contextual factors, such as neighborhood income or campus climate, to affect individuals' sense of well-being.

Gender as an Intersecting Variable

In many of the articles, community psychologists explored gender conjointly with race, ethnicity, and one or more other demographic variables (e.g., age). This treatment of gender illustrates the ways that gender, as one aspect of social identity, interacts with other aspects of social identity in diverse groups of people. For example, Snowden (2001) used data from a large household survey to test a hypothesis that, when compared to European Americans, African Americans would exhibit higher levels of social embeddedness, a construct that taps into community well-being and social support. The findings, however, suggested a different pattern for men than for women. African American men were more socially embedded than European American men were, but African American women were, with few exceptions, less socially embedded than European American women were. Thus, the author noted that work designed to compare ethnic differences on this topic must be qualified by gender.

Gonzalez, Alegria, and Prihoda (2005) examined attitudes toward seeking mental health treatment based on data from a large epidemiological sample. They replicated a common finding that men reported more negative attitudes toward help seeking than women did. However, their sample was predominantly European American, and when race/ethnicity was considered, they found that the gender difference was not significant for Latinos/as or African Americans in willingness to seek help, comfort talking with a professional, or embarrassment about help seeking. Both Snowden and

Gonzalez and colleagues documented how gender and ethnicity interact to create a complex set of relationships in the variables of interest. Understanding the intersecting nature of gender – how, for example, it is intricately wrapped up with ethnicity – helps to illustrate the indirect ways that gender permeates psychological phenomena.

Gender as a Process Variable

The second subset of articles we reviewed ($n = 13$) conceptualized gender as an influential factor in the process of community research and/or action. Here, community psychologists examined the gendered aspects of interactions among researchers, collaborators, or participants in the community action or research project. Community psychologists have conducted research on whether gender match, when both members of a dyad share the same gender, influences research and practice processes such as research participants' responses to phone surveys (Sasao, 1994), the impact of mental health services on clients (Fujino, Okazaki, & Young, 1994; Stack, Lannon, & Miley, 1983), and the effectiveness of mentoring for protégés (Grossman & Rhodes, 2002). These studies also examined ethnic/racial match, which underscores community psychologists' conceptualization of gender as one aspect of a multidimensional social identity. Common premises were that more positive change can occur in longer-lasting relationships and that matching by gender or other social identity variables might increase the duration or quality of relationships that are the cornerstone of community research and action (e.g., mentor–protégé, facilitator–participant, therapist–client, interviewer–informant).

A pattern of gender and ethnic match was documented in descriptive work of naturally occurring relationships in various communities. For example, in their interviews with Latino/a adolescents, Sanchez and Reyes (1999) found that most participants described the mentors in their lives as individuals who shared their gender and ethnicity and who often were family members. Similarly, Darling, Hamilton, Toyokawa, and Matsuda (2002) found that college students in both the USA and Japan described mentoring functions as occurring most frequently in relationships with adults (rather than peers), with relatives (rather than unrelated persons), and with others of the same gender. In addition to documenting gender match as it naturally exists in understudied communities (Sanchez & Reyes, 1999) and cross-culturally (Darling et al., 2002), community psychologists have also assessed the impact of gender match in relationships designed for community studies and interventions.

Overall, community psychologists' evaluations of gender match in research and action have resulted in mixed findings. Assessments of interventions have not consistently supported the premise that gender matching leads to longer or more effective relationships. Grossman and Rhodes (2002) reported that women's gender matching was related to somewhat higher rates of termination in formal mentoring relationships (e.g., Big Brother-Big Sister programs). The opposite was true in Fujino et al.'s (1994) survey of Asian American women receiving mental health services. These researchers found that having a female therapist (gender match condition) was associated with reduced premature termination and increased time in treatment overall but not statistically associated with client functioning at discharge (Fujino et al., 1994).

Community researchers have also looked beyond the dyad to examine gender match in interventions with groups of individuals. Here, researchers considered the gender composition of the group (i.e., whether groups were comprised of members of the same gender only or were mixed by gender) as well as the match between group facilitator and group participants. An understanding of the impact of gender in groups is important not only because community psychologists can control the gender composition and facilitator match in the design of interventions but also because descriptive research has shown significant differences in gender composition in naturally occurring community settings. For example, in a comparative case study, Mowbray, Cohen, Harris, and Trosch (1992) found that services for homeless individuals with mental illnesses faced unique challenges because of differences in gender composition of clients across the three sites they studied.

Jemmott, Jemmott, Fong, and McCaffree (1999) conducted a study of moderators of effectiveness of HIV risk-reduction interventions that systematically tested effects of gender in the implementation of community-based interventions. The researchers wanted to know which characteristics of interventions, under which circumstances, had the greatest impact on success. They had numerous specific hypotheses to test two basic predictions: (1) that matching characteristics (such as gender and race) of facilitators and participants would lead to more effectiveness and (2) that single-gender groups would be more conducive to discussions about sensitive topics and lead to more effective HIV risk-reduction interventions. This research is notable for its experimental design (including a sophisticated blocking design and random assignment of participants to conditions) and statistical analysis of complex interaction effects. The authors examined differences between students who received the intervention of interest and those in a control group over time (pre-intervention, post-intervention, after 3 months, and after 6 months) and demonstrated positive and sustained effects of the intervention (e.g., stronger condom use intentions). However, they found no empirical support for gender match or gender composition as a moderator of intervention effectiveness. The effects of the intervention did not vary by facilitator's race or gender, participant's gender, or the gender composition of the intervention group (Jemmott et al., 1999).

Gender match in traditional research activities has also received some attention from community psychologists. In a relatively early article, Argentino, Kidd, and Bogart (1977) examined three ways that gender might influence the process of doing experimental research with college-aged participants. They hypothesized that experimenter's gender, participant's gender, and type of housing (same sex vs. mixed sex) would all significantly affect self-reported attitudes toward women. They found no main effect for experimenter's gender, but effects for the gender composition of participant's housing, participant's gender, and the interaction between the experimenter's and the participant's gender were all significant. There were no differences between male and female participants when the experimenter was a man, but when the experimenter was a woman, women reported significantly more liberal attitudes than did men. Argentino and colleagues (1977) used their results to suggest that researchers "use experimenters of both sexes to avoid biasing the data" (p. 188). This is in slight contrast to suggestions of the author of a more recent study of the role of gender in conducting telephone survey research with Asian Americans. Sasao (1994) matched interviewer ethnicity to several different Asian American groups (i.e., Chinese, Japanese, Korean, Vietnamese) and found no statistically significant effects of the interviewer's gender on any of the participants' responses. However, he did report anecdotes that suggest that male respondents may have been reluctant to disclose personal information to a female stranger, and he called for more systematic study of gender and age-match in interview studies.

Taken together, these articles indicate community psychologists' interest in the various ways that gender influences the process of activities of the field, including research, intervention, and action. The pattern of findings regarding gender match and gender composition in the research conducted by community psychologists has not been consistent; however, the number of studies included in the present review is relatively small. What is important to our thesis is the way gender can affect the design of research or action projects and can shape the nature of relationships among those involved (e.g., power dynamics, sense of safety, openness) (see also Campbell, Sefl, Wasco, & Ahrens, 2004). The notions of creating settings and understanding contexts are central to the field of community psychology, and in the next section we describe work that has treated gender as one of the forces that shapes our social environments, which we also call social contexts or social ecologies.

Gender as a Contextual Variable

Thinking ecologically involves moving beyond treating gender as a demographic grouping variable, or even a process variable, to conceptualizing gendered influences as dynamic forces that become part of the settings that define and affect peoples' lives. This conceptual paradigm challenges community psychologists to conduct gender research aimed at increased understanding of contexts (i.e., characteristics of relationships, neighborhoods, organizations, societies, and/or cultures) that are shaped by gender-related forces. We identified 20 community psychology journal articles in which the authors explored the impact of gender narratives, gender roles, gender expectations, and/or gendered relations on participants' day-to-day lives. These articles fall into three themes: (a) individual gender-related attitudes as context, (b) relationships as context, and (c) cultural narratives about gender as context. In many of these articles, gender was conceptualized as just one dimension of diversity that intersected with ethnicity, SES, sexual orientation, and disability.

Individual Gender-Related Attitudes as Context

One subset of these articles focused on how the adoption of beliefs or attitudes about gender, gender roles, and gender identity affected people in their daily lives. These articles remained at an individual level of analysis (i.e., assessed the impact of an individual's attitudes on individual outcomes), but nonetheless generated knowledge about how social forces related to gender can impact individuals' well-being through the adoption of sociocultural gender-based ideologies.

For example, Kulik and Rayyan (2003) examined the impact of gender role attitudes among Jewish and Arab couples living in Israel. Even though they found that the Jewish and Arab participants differed in self-reported values about the gender-related division of labor within families (Arabs in their study held more traditional attitudes toward gender roles), gender role attitudes were found to predict psychological well-being in both groups. Participants who held more egalitarian attitudes experienced lower burnout and greater life satisfaction. Jackson (1997) examined how mothers' attitudes toward leaving children in the care of others affected the women's well-being. Although comfort with child care is not a direct measure of the gender-based attitudes of the low-income African American women in the study, it can be argued that discomfort with the idea of non-maternal care is at least partially rooted in gender-based values about who should be caring for one's children. The women who worked more hours and who expressed a preference for employment were the ones who said that they had greater life satisfaction. That is, those who had not adopted stereotypical beliefs about women's roles were happier. The common thread between these two studies is that the adoption of more traditional attitudes about gender roles was associated with more negative individual outcomes.

There may be exceptions to the negative impact of traditional gender roles. One study in our sample of the literature suggested cross-cultural variation in the effect of traditional attitudes toward gender roles. A study by Kulis, Marsiglia, and Hurdle (2003) established a link between gender-related beliefs and substance abuse outcomes in a largely Mexican American sample of middle school children. The authors explored the relationship between acculturation, gender, and self-ratings of "gender-typed traits and behaviors" (which yielded four groups that they labeled aggressive masculinity, assertive masculinity, affective femininity, and submissive femininity) and alcohol and drug use. Findings indicated that the femininity/masculinity variable had more explanatory power than gender itself (as a grouping variable). Furthermore, the authors also found that the impact of gender-typed traits and values was mediated by ethnicity and acculturation. The authors interpreted these results to suggest that the adoption of some aspects of culturally ascribed gender roles may have a protective impact as the relationship between machismo and substance use was lower for Latino than for non-Latino boys. The relationship between traditional cultural values and substance abuse issues for girls was not addressed.

Relationships as Context

Some community researchers have explored how gender-based dynamics within relationships (e.g., dyadic, group, neighborhood) relate to outcomes of substantive interest. For example, in a very early study (Eiswirth-Neems & Handal, 1978) of heterosexual couples the researchers assessed how men's and women's feelings about maternal occupational status affected their relationships and their family culture. They found that the attitudes of husbands and wives, when considered individually, failed to show an effect on family culture; however, when a husband's attitude was negative and the woman liked her job, family climate was less cohesive. Here, it was the relationship context (i.e., the conflict in values about gendered work expectations) – not the individual-level beliefs – that had a significant impact.

Gender-related relationship characteristics have also been considered as they relate to HIV/AIDS prevention. St. Lawrence, Wilson, Eldridge, Brasfield, and O'Bannon (2001) explored how the risks for women in new heterosexual relationships are different than for those in established relationships. Condom use was higher in new relationships where risk of infection is associated with the prior history of this new partner than in established relationships where the risk is associated with a partner's extra-relationship behavior. Wingood and DiClemente (1998) also examined relationship correlates of condom use. Their study showed that condom use among a group of African American women was associated with partner cooperation and shared beliefs about condoms. They also found that condom use was associated with women's adoption of behaviors that are arguably heavily gendered (e.g., sexual assertiveness) and beliefs about how hard it is to find an eligible man. They found that noncondom use was related to women's concern that asking a partner to use condoms might "compromise the stability in the sexual relationship" (p. 47). Thus, they argued that women's nonuse of condoms must be understood in the context of gendered beliefs about heterosexual relationships and the sexual division of power.

The question about the impact of relationship dynamics has been particularly basic to work on intimate partner violence, which has often concerned the ways in which abuse is shaped by relational power asymmetries. Community psychologists have contributed to the broader literature on this theme and have urged nuanced and dynamic understandings of how gender affects the relational context of abusive relationships. For example, the author (Ristock, 2003) of a study of relationship violence in the lives of 80 lesbians emphasized the need for conceptual frameworks that allow for fluctuating power dynamics and that consider power in a relational manner vs. as a static quality or as an unchanging quality associated with one partner.

Community psychologists have also looked at how gender-related factors might influence neighborhood relationships and thereby shape responses to social problems. Saegert (1989) studied the ways that the availability of community supports combined with gender, race, and age to shape the responses to housing concerns among a group of low-income Black women. Frye (2007), on the other hand, found that neighborhood qualities do not always trump individual attitudes. She examined how neighborhood social cohesion might combine with attitudes toward intimate partner violence to predict the likelihood of taking some sort of action to stop the violence, and she found that personal attitudes were the only statistically significant predictor.

The over-riding theme of these studies is the importance of looking closely at the relational context of people's lives in a dynamic and nuanced way in order to understand which conditions foster the emergence of personal and social problems. Taken together, these studies provide insights into the dynamic connections between gender influences, relational context, and individual well-being (i.e., the ways in which gendered values and beliefs help to shape relationships and how the resulting qualities of relationships can influence the emergence of social problems and/or access to resources) for both women and men. In other words, gender-related dynamics can influence the quality of important relationships, and this influence is somewhat independent of the gender status of the individuals in the relationship.

Cultural Narratives About Gender as Context

A third theme in research that treated gender as a contextual variable was the examination of how people are affected by cultural beliefs about gender that become embedded in the settings where people live and work. In other words, some researchers looked at the impact of shared gender narratives (conceptualized as embedded qualities of community and organizational contexts) on individuals' well-being. These studies are different from those that assessed individuals' gender-related beliefs and those that assessed gender-related qualities of close relationships in that the researchers assessed the impact of values shared and embraced by a larger group, whether it is a cultural, community, or organizational group.

In an early *JCP* special issue on "Women in the Community," Comas-Diaz (1988) discussed the ways in which community paradigms for work with Latinas need to incorporate attention to the sociocultural and gender-related aspects of these women's contexts. She explored the particular case of male dominance within the Puerto Rican culture. In line with this call for sociocultural sensitivity, other researchers have examined the ways in which traditional gender relations within cultural groups can be a barrier to HIV/AIDS prevention work. For example, De Jesus (2007) studied the issue within a Cape Verdean community; Ortiz-Torres, Serrano-Garcia, and Torres-Burgos (2000) described specific Latin values, such as machismo and marianismo, that affect HIV/AIDS prevention work in Puerto Rico. These studies are important contributions to the reconceptualizion of HIV/AIDS as a community problem embedded in a set of cultural values about gender and gender roles. A particularly nuanced look at how cultural beliefs about gender shape expressions of social problems in communities was provided by Hamby (2000). She looked at how men's authority and restrictiveness as expressed by some Native American tribes are related to violence against women in these communities, and she found that the incidence of violence among Native communities depends on the tribe's traditions related to gender, class, and power.

We also identified a study that explored the impact of sociocultural gender narratives on people with learning disabilities (McDonald, Keys, & Balcazar, 2007). These researchers documented ways that men experienced cultural beliefs about men's competence as intensifying social judgments about learning disabilities as "illegitimate" (p. 152), whereas female participants thought that cultural narratives about the dependence of people with disabilities "further exacerbated already pejorative narratives about women" (p. 154). Although the sample was quite small, the researchers suggested ways in which gender narratives seemed to vary across ethnic groups to affect the study participants' lives.

In addition to looking at cultural gender narratives, community-based researchers have explored the reciprocal relationship between gender-related qualities of more immediate social settings and the psychological and behavioral experiences of people in those settings. For example, Kulik (1998) documented how community characteristics affect the adoption of gender stereotypes among young people. She found that, compared to adolescents who lived in more urban areas of Israel, those who grew up on kibbutzim had more liberal attitudes toward gender roles. This research did not directly explore which specific aspects of these different communities (i.e., living arrangements, division of labor, values, and beliefs) reinforced and shaped the cultural narratives about gender that became dominant across the settings. However, it does add to an ecological understanding of the relationship between individuals and their environments as reciprocal and involving a process of mutual adaptation. Individuals' beliefs about gender are not only shaped by environmental characteristics; once formed, such attitudes or stereotypical beliefs become part of the gendered culture of the social environment, which in turn can influence members of the setting.

One type of social environment that has received particular attention in the community psychology literature is organizational settings (e.g., schools and workplaces). Community psychologists have explored the ways that the gendered nature of these settings can affect people in both negative (e.g., violent acts) and positive (e.g., organizational commitment) ways. For example, one study (Khoury-Kassabri, Benbenishty, Astor, & Zeira, 2004) guided by an ecological perspective included gender-related variables at multiple levels in the prediction of school violence. The researchers considered gender as an individual difference variable but also as a school-level variable (i.e., gender ratio of the school) along with other school-level variables (i.e., class size, school climate), family variables (i.e., income), and neighborhood characteristics (i.e., neighborhood income). Not only was gender itself related to violence (boys experienced more violence than girls did), but school-level gender ratio was also related (the higher the percentage of boys in the school, the greater the overall violence). This treatment of gendered phenomena as part of an organizational context was also adopted by Morris, Shinn, and DuMont (1999). They examined how elements of an organization's culture (operationalized as the mean perceptions of management fairness, support, and sensitivity to human diversity) affected organizational commitment among police officers. They found that higher perceptions of fairness and support (but not sensitivity to diversity) were related to higher levels of organizational commitment.

The primary commonality among the articles that we discuss in this section is the way in which these community researchers have treated gender as a social force that exerts an influence on important contexts of people's lives. As mentioned earlier, many of these researchers have asked individual participants to provide their own perceptions of their context, and thus, many of the studies are still essentially at the individual level of analysis (i.e., they incorporate individuals' perceptions of contexts vs. direct assessment of contextual variables.) Nonetheless, the research described here was designed to uncover the ways in which gendered influences are dynamic and constantly shaping the settings within which people live, work, and play. From a social ecological or systemic perspective, gender is not merely a descriptor of individuals or a demographic variable. It is not restricted to a variable at the individual level of analysis. All of these studies are based on an assumption that people are embedded in layers of context that are affected by gender dynamics and that these ecological levels of analysis have independent and interactive influences on human experience and behavior.

A Look at Gender Treatment Over Time

A secondary goal for this chapter was to provide a historical analysis. How has community psychology's treatment of gender changed over time? In line with prior observations that the community psychology literature on women has increased over the years (Angelique & Culley, 2000, 2003; Bond & Mulvey, 2000; Swift et al., 2000), we hypothesized that (1) the amount of gender research may have increased over time and that (2) conceptualizations of gender may have become more nuanced in recent years and thus led to more work that deviates from the popular treatment of gender as a grouping variable. As described above, we grouped the abstracts in 5-year blocks, starting in 1973, when both the *AJCP* and the *JCP* were first published, and then conducted frequency analysis to examine these trends over time.

Our analysis of the top two journals in the field between 1973 and 2007 revealed 2973 total articles, 167 of which met the criteria for inclusion in this content analysis. Thus, less than 6% of the scholarship published in the leading community psychology journals has included a gender analysis, even broadly construed. There was, however, evidence that the amount of community psychology research on gender has increased with time. In the first 5 years of the journals' existence (1973–1977), only 10 gender-related studies were published. In the most recent 5 years (2003–2007), there were nearly five times as many articles ($n = 49$). About one-half of the gender-related articles we found in our literature searches ($n = 101$) were published between 1998 and 2007, which suggests an increase in such work over time. The highlights of the most recent decade (1998–2007), which included two special issues on feminism and community psychology in the *American Journal of Community Psychology* (Bond et al., 2000a, 2000b) and two syntheses of the feminist literature that have already been mentioned in this chapter (Angelique & Culley, 2000, 2003), suggest that specific interests in gender still tend to focus on traditionally defined "women's issues," and there has yet to be a special issue on men and masculinity. However, we feel cautiously optimistic in predicting a continued interest in gender research among a broader set of community psychologists and other community-based researchers in the future.

Our examination of the treatment of gender by time period indicated trends that suggest some evolution in the conceptualization of gender over time. A greater proportion of work published in recent time blocks treated gender as a contextual or ecological variable. The proportion of work that treated gender as a contextual variable increased from 0% in the first time period (1973–1977) to 19.4% in the most recent current time period (2003–2007). Similarly, the number of published articles that treated gender as a process variable has fluctuated over the past 25 years, with a peak of 15% of all gender-related publications between 1998 and 2002. Treatment of gender as a difference variable has held steady as the most popular treatment of gender across time periods, though there has been a slight downward trend over the years, from 90% of the articles published between 1973 and 1977 to 80.6% in recent years (between 2003 and 2007). Table 26.1 displays the frequency distributions for primary codes by 5-year time blocks. Though we did not examine the factors that contributed to changes in gender research, the trends in how researchers treat gender are likely to be related to many factors including an increase in the number of graduate training programs in community psychology, more diversity among community researchers, more sophisticated statistical and analytic techniques that allow for more complex modeling, and more nuanced thinking about gender in general.

Reflections and Future Directions

Our exploration of gender research in community psychology suggests that there is limited published research that focuses directly on gender, which is consistent with past reviews of the community literature (Angelique, Campbell, & Culley, 2001; Angelique & Culley, 2000, 2003; Harper & Schneider, 2003; Swift et al., 2000). We also found that, when community psychologists explicitly consider the influence of gender on their substantive issue of choice, they are most likely to treat gender as a grouping variable. However, we also found evidence that community psychology offers a tradition of scholarship that contributes insights for gender research in psychology. These contributions are reflected in the studies that treated gender as process and/or contextual variables.

In the final section of this chapter, we reflect upon three interconnected themes that emerged from our review. These themes reflect distinctive contributions that community psychology can make to the psychological research literature on gender and, simultaneously, frame challenges for ongoing

Table 26.1 Treatment of gender in community psychology research reports from 1973 until 2007 (n = 167)

Treatment of gender	1973–1977 n	1973–1977 %	1978–1982 n	1978–1982 %	1983–1987 n	1983–1987 %	1988–1992 n	1988–1992 %	1993–1997 n	1993–1997 %	1998–2002 n	1998–2002 %	2003–2007 n	2003–2007 %	Total n	Total %
Grouping variable	9	90	23	92	12	92	17	74	16	80	28	70	29	81	134	80
Process variable	1	10	0	0	1	8	3	13	2	10	6	15	0	0	13	8
Contextual variable	0	0	2	8	0	0	3	13	2	10	6	15	7	19	20	12

Note: Percentage values are rounded to the nearest whole number.

research in the field. These themes are redefining dualisms, conceptualizing gender systemically, and adopting critical consciousness as a criterion for quality research. We discuss the ways in which these three themes present both conceptual and methodological challenges for conducting community-based gender research.

Redefining Dualisms

Consistent with the work of gender scholars from many disciplines (see Barnett & Rivers, 2004; Deaux & Major, 1987; Hyde, 2005; Unger, 1996), the work discussed in this chapter has yielded few enduring socially significant gender differences. As communities of people, our attitudes, behaviors, and psychological experiences can be notably similar across gender groups. The limited utility of reifying differences between men and women becomes more striking as our conceptualizations of two naturally occurring, biologically determined, and immutable sex categories (i.e., male, female) are challenged by the growing awareness and inclusion of intersexed and transgendered persons, sometimes called the "third gender," in our communities. However, having said that, contextually grounded and ecologically relevant research and practice still require that community psychologists do not minimize the significant ways that how one "does gender" shapes individuals' perceptions, treatment, and access to resources (Fine, 1992).

Despite community psychology's value of social justice and our use of oppression theories to recognize systemic forces and structures that privilege agent identities (e.g., heterosexuals, men) over target identities (e.g., gay men/lesbians, women), our review did not find as much empirical work as we had anticipated related to gendered oppression. Therefore, we suggest that one of the challenges community psychology faces is how to highlight differential experiences and treatment of women and men so that they can be adequately addressed with community intervention, prevention, and advocacy efforts – without framing the gender per se of the primary actor(s) as the causal factor.

There is a tension here. Throughout the chapter we have made an argument, consistent with feminist and community theory, that researchers should not focus much attention on dichotomizing gender and looking for difference. Instead we advocate for contextual understandings of gender dynamics that are socially constructed through family and peer influences; role opportunities within school, church, neighborhood, workplace, and other settings; as well as broad-based cultural and social norms. However, we now raise a concern that by *not* treating gender as dichotomous variable at times (i.e., without directly comparing those who identify as women and those who identify as men) we may render certain power differentials invisible and be unable to document the social injustices done to women and, at times, men. In a sense, we emerged from our review less critical than we might have been about the frequent use of gender as a grouping variable; rather we advocate more multileveled analyses of gender differences and more focus on the ways in which the gender differences are interpreted.

The problems of sexual and domestic violence, which represent extreme acts of power and control, can help to illustrate this point. On one hand, both men and women commit acts of sexual and domestic violence, and both men and women are victims of these acts (see Tjaden & Thoennes, 2000). Especially when the experiences of children are taken into account, girls and boys endure physical and sexual abuse at the hands of abusers of both genders (Finkelhor & Dzuiba-Leatherman, 1992; Stevenson & Gajarsky, 1991; U.S. Department of Health and Human Services, 2007). Furthermore, most men (probably over 80%) do not rape or batter women (Abbey & McAuslan, 2004; Kessler, Molnar, Feurer, & Applebaum, 2001), and some women physically and sexually abuse their partners in same-sex (McClennen, 2005; Ristock, 2003) and cross-sex relationships (Kernsmith, 2005; Richardson, 2005). On the other hand, the majority of known cases of domestic and sexual violence are acts committed most often by men against women (Koss et al., 1994; Renzetti, Edleson, & Bergen, 2001). Although one's gender cannot be used to predict whether one will be a victim/perpetrator of these kinds of interpersonal violence, few would deny that women and girls do suffer disproportionately from sexual and domestic violence.

For some who study these problems, gender is understood to be a locus of oppression, and sexual and domestic violence are often conceptualized along a continuum of power and control wielded by men (the agent identity) against women (the target identity). The term *violence against women*, preferred by some because it acknowledges that women, in particular, are most hurt by these forms of violence, tends to essentialize gender so that being a woman is fundamental to being a victim of the kinds of acts included in the umbrella term (e.g., rape, stalking, abuse by a partner). Other behaviorally specific terms such as *family violence, intimate partner violence*, and *sexual assault* are not only gender-neutral but they rightly ground the act of violence in the context of families, intimate relationships, and sexual encounters. However, these terms may ignore the hierarchical nature of families, intimate relationships, and sexual encounters and/or minimize the extent to which men harm women. Recently, the term *gender-based* (or *gendered*) *violence* has emerged to describe these acts. These semantics indicates a conceptual shift that acknowledges gender dynamics related to power and control in sexual and relationship violence without relying on the man/woman dichotomy.

At the heart of striking this balance between revealing gender-based injustices and avoiding static views of gender may be an understanding of power and oppression that moves beyond stereotypes of women and men. Adopting such an approach will require removing hidden assumptions (e.g., that men are more aggressive than women) from surveys and questionnaires; vigilance in recruiting participants from diverse groups, including transgendered persons who may be difficult to identify; and collaborating with community members to interpret, disseminate, and use research results to improve individual and community wellness. We challenge community psychologists to resist a pull to essentialize gender differences and continue to document the differences between women and men that are manifestations of sexism and other forms of gender discrimination including homophobia, misunderstanding of transgendered persons, and biases against men.

Conceptualizing Gender Systemically

In order to understand how gender differences might reflect oppressive and/or discriminatory practices (as opposed to fundamental group differences), community psychology research needs to incorporate a systemic understanding of gender. Thus, the second challenge in advancing gender research in community psychology is to expand the ways in which we conceptualize and analyze gender at extra-individual levels (e.g., familial, organizational, cultural). Some of the research that we reviewed here treated gender as a contextual variable and examined the impact of collective narratives, expectations, and beliefs that are shaped by societal values concerning gender and gender roles. Some of the researchers were able to go beyond gender as an individual characteristic and consider the ways it can influence the social contexts of people's lives. Although these examples demonstrate some approaches that community-based researchers have taken to meet this challenge, the extent of this type of inquiry remains limited.

Research related to diversity in community and organizational settings may provide a useful example here. The vast majority of the community psychology research on diversity documents discriminatory treatment (e.g., related to inequitable treatment, harassment, access to services). As we argue above, it is useful to document differences in the treatment because the approach can reveal sites of inequality. However, our understanding of the processes that lead to differential treatment will remain limited unless we expand research to identify the qualities of communities and organizations that contribute to these inequities.

There is a long tradition within community psychology that emphasizes the assessment of settings (Kelly, 1966; Kelly, Ryan, Altman, & Stelzner, 2000; Linney, 2000; Moos, 1973, 1994, 2002, 2003; Seidman, 1988, 1990; Shinn, 1996; Shinn & Toohey, 2003). Behavior setting theory (Barker, 1968; Schoggen, 1989), in particular, has received considerable attention and, although critiqued and revised (Perkins, Burns, Perry, & Neilsen, 1988), has guided some research in community psychology (see Brown, Shepherd, Wituk, & Meissen, 2007; Zimmerman et al., 1991). There is also a growing literature on the intersections between the fields of organization studies and community psychology that emphasizes the importance of organizational characteristics for individual participants. There is, in fact, a special issue of *JCP* devoted to this topic (Boyd & Angelique, 2007).

However, very little of the past work has been developed to assess gender-related concerns. None of the community psychology pioneers tackled the challenge of understanding the gendered nature of settings. The special issue of *JCP* included only one article that dealt directly with diversity (Griffith, Childs, Eng, & Jeffries, 2007) and none that focused explicitly on gender. Some have, however, attempted to define the contextual factors that support meaningful inclusion of women within community and organizational settings. For example, in her summary of multiple studies, Bond (1999) proposed a culture of connection and the recognition of multiple realities as key qualities of organizational settings that support diversity. She also suggested that organizational practices that incorporate values for autonomy and pressures for sameness serve as countervailing values (see also Bond, 2007). Nonetheless, we are still left with the challenge of how to explore these proposed qualities in a more systematic way.

One of the major barriers to research that incorporates gender at a systemic level is the lack of easily accessible measures that operationalize gender at systemic levels. Recording individuals' gender (whether a person is a man or a woman) is an easy proxy, and available research methodologies tend to be more conducive to gender differences research (Cosgrove & McHugh, 2000; Shinn & Perkins, 2000; Unger, 1996). The contextual factors influenced by gender that lead to differences in women's vs. men's experiences are harder to capture – especially as psychologists, where the majority of our work is based on individual queries. A review of validated measures related to diversity in organizational settings (Bond et al., 2007) identified only 5 of 46 measures that assessed issues at an organizational level, and these measures still involved asking individuals for their perceptions of the organization.

Community psychologists have struggled with the measurement challenge for decades, have tailored scales, collaborated across disciplines, and borrowed from the scholarship of our colleagues in biology, sociology, political science, and economics (Shinn & Rapkin, 2000). Assessments of representation (e.g., gender ratios at different levels of the organization), shared values (e.g., organizational culture, informal team dynamics, sense of community), and organizational practices (e.g., assessments of formal policies) are approaches that have some potential. Cross-cultural community-based research on gender, like a few of the studies reviewed here (i.e., Darling et al., 2002; Gonzalez et al., 2005; Khoury-Kassabri et al., 2004; Kulik & Rayyan, 2003), also has great potential to enrich research from a contextual perspective because comparative studies provide more easily measured variability in cultural determinants of gender differences, such as values, gender role expectations, or family structures.

Critical Consciousness as Essential to Quality Research

An anchor for analyses of the impact of gender-based ideologies is a classic *AJCP* article by Albee (1982) entitled "The politics of nature and nurture." Albee, an early leader in community psychology, argued that scientists' explanations of group differences are influenced by their values and politics.

Albee looked at researchers' explanations for both gender and race differences, and he made a powerful case for how individual belief systems vis-à-vis gender affected all aspects of the research process.

From early on, the field of community psychology has advocated for a critical consciousness of multiple and intersecting social identities of all people involved in a community project, including the researchers themselves, and for reflection upon how gender similarities and differences influence relationships within the project. Articles that described authors' personal experiences in gendered relationships contribute to gender scholarship in a way that is consistent with feminist research in general and feminist community psychology specifically (Campbell & Wasco, 2000). In a field that is often defined less by what we research and more by how research is done (i.e., in a collaborative fashion with the community, incorporating values for diversity and social justice), these articles show how work in community psychology – the research and action – is itself gendered. Interactions between trainers and workshop participants, mentors and protégées, social change agents and constituents, or researchers and participants are all relationships that are influenced by social and cultural facets of gender.

Articles from a special issue on diversity challenges (Harrell & Bond, 2006) tell stories of how aspects of the authors' social identities, including gender, became salient in the work they were doing (e.g., Langhout, 2006; Vasquez, 2006). These narratives were excluded from our formal analysis of the community literature because they did not meet our criteria. However, they offer observations relevant to the discussion of gendered processes in community research and action as they described issues in forming collaborative relationships, engaging with diverse groups, choosing methods, and collecting data.

In one of these articles, Vasquez (2006), a Latino, described how he and his African American male co-facilitator responded to challenges from a participant in one of their workplace diversity workshops. Vasquez explored how intersections of race, class, and gender might have shaped this European American man's reaction, including the ways in which his working class status could have made it difficult for him to embrace the workshop material on privilege. Vasquez acknowledged the complexity of social identities and wrote about the intersecting layers of gender expectations and ethnicity as he raised questions about whether the facilitation challenges would have been different if he and his co-facilitator were women or from different ethnic backgrounds. Although Vasquez did not draw any definitive conclusions, his questions are informative.

In another article about the challenges and rewards of doing work in diverse communities, Langhout (2006), a European American woman, situated herself within multiple social identities (race, class, gender, and age) to discuss her experience working with a predominantly African American community. Langhout shared how, through exchanges with an African American graduate student, she came to see that, in her relationships with African American community gardeners, she "had highlighted my gender (female) and class (working class background) identities in a way that enabled me to ignore my race (White) identity and privilege" (p. 270). This article encourages community researchers to ask existential and philosophical questions such as "How do I see myself and how does this relate to how my collaborators see me?" (p. 273).

These examples emphasize an issue that emerged from the content analysis of research on gender matching that other social identity variables, such as ethnicity, matter as well (e.g., Jemmott et al., 1999; Sanchez & Reyes, 1999; Sasao, 1994). Both Vasquez and Langhout highlighted the way that gender interacts with other dimensions of diversity. They recognized gender as an important part of people's multidimensional and socially constructed identities and, in these cases, as the common link between the community psychologist and the participants in the community work. This commonality is a potential resource for bridging other kinds of differences, such as race, age, and class, yet simultaneously it has the potential to blind the psychologist to the other important differences. An ongoing process of self-reflection as described by the contributors of the special issue on diversity challenges (Bond & Harrell, 2006; Harrell & Bond, 2006) may help community psychologists to maintain awareness of gender similarities, differences, and other forms of privilege in order to avoid such blindness in future work.

Freire (1970, 1973) advocated critical questioning of the historical and social situation, what he sometimes called "reading the world," as an essential step in changing oppressive elements of society. If community psychology is to forward a social justice agenda in increasingly diverse communities, accurately perceiving gendered power dynamics in our research and action would be important. The kinds of experiences and insights shared by Langhout and Vasquez are probably common to many community psychologists and are discussed at psychological conferences, workshops, and other gatherings. This type of discourse, however, is not frequently found in peer-reviewed journals because limited journal space is usually reserved for the results of empirical research. Recently, Prilleltensky (2003, 2008) advocated that community psychologists not only reflect on the connections between political and psychological factors that affect wellness and justice in our research interpretations but that the merit of community research and action be evaluated on the extent to which it takes those psychopolitical factors into account. A special issue of *JCP* on this relatively new concept of psychopolitical validity (Speer, Newbrough & Lorion, 2008) contributed multiple perspectives on how to assess power in the practice of community psychology, and, although none of the articles explicitly discussed gendered power dynamics, this recent trend in the field is consonant with our current call for a critical consciousness of gender in community-based research.

In coming years, international community psychology may be able to offer particular insight into critical consciousness and gender research. Community psychologists have a presence, though always on the fringe of the larger subdisciplines of psychology, in at least 38 countries around the world (Reich, Riemer, Prilleltensky, & Montero, 2007b), and the organization of the first International Conference on Community Psychology in 2006 suggests that disciplinary engagement across national boundaries is increasing and global perspectives are gaining recognition in the field. Although contributions of community psychologists from many countries may not be readily available through outlets such as peer-reviewed journals, we believe that research being done outside the USA, often with strong traditions in liberation theory, will ultimately help community psychologists grapple with the challenges in gender research outlined here.

As mentioned earlier, culturally comparative work easily exposes the contextual aspects of gendered human experiences. In addition, Reich, Riemer, Prilleltensky, and Montero (2007c) have identified poverty, power, and inequality as topic areas in community psychology that transcend international boundaries. They suggested that as community psychologists fighting oppression based on gender and sexual orientation (e.g., in Australia, Canada, and the USA) share epistemologies, theories, and methodologies with community psychologists who are working against the residual impact of colonization (e.g., in South Africa, Cameroon, and New Zealand), the relationship between individual well-being and sociocultural conditions will probably be triangulated, thereby reinforcing the need for transformative change of these conditions.

Conclusion

Conceptual frameworks and values embraced by community psychologists around the globe pose particular challenges and opportunities for research on gender. Although the absolute number of community-based psychological studies on gender is underwhelming, the thematic insights that emerged from our review highlight some of the points of synergy between contemporary approaches to gender research and the principles of community psychology. Although the fit between feminism and community psychology has been noted in several outlets, we would like to complement that earlier work by asserting that these approaches are relevant to understanding and empowering individuals across the gender spectrum. We are hopeful that reducing dichotomous conceptualizations, assessing contextual and systemic factors, and being critically conscious of power in the study of gender can increase the kind of knowledge about men's and women's experiences that is necessary to build and sustain healthy communities.

Acknowledgments We are grateful to Rebecca Edwards for her insightful research assistance and to Michelle Fine, James G. Kelly, and the editors of this volume for their helpful feedback on an earlier version of this chapter.

References

Abbey, A., & McAuslan, P. (2004). A longitudinal examination of male college students' perpetration of sexual assault. *Journal of Consulting and Clinical Psychology, 72*, 747–756.

Albee, G. (1982). The politics of nature and nurture. *American Journal of Community Psychology, 10*, 4–36.

Angelique, H., Campbell, R., & Culley, M. (2001). The anemic state of women's health in community psychology. *Community Psychologist, 34*, 22–24.

Angelique, H., & Culley, M. (2000). Searching for feminism: An analysis of community psychology literature relevant to women's concerns. *American Journal of Community Psychology, 28*, 793–813.

Angelique, H., & Culley, M. (2003). Feminism found: An examination of gender consciousness in community psychology. *Journal of Community Psychology, 31*, 189–209.

Argentino, C., Kidd, A., & Bogart, K. (1977). The effects of experimenter's sex and subject's sex on the attitudes toward women of fraternity, sorority, and mixed-dormitory residents. *Journal of Community Psychology, 5*, 186–188.

Barker, R. G. (1968). *Ecological psychology: Concepts and methods for studying the environment of human behavior.* Stanford, CA: Stanford University Press.

Barnett, R., & Rivers, C. (2004). *Same difference: How gender myths are hurting our relationships, our children, and our jobs.* New York: Basic Books.

Bennett, C., Anderson, L., Cooper, S., Hassol, L., Klein, D., & Rosenblum, G. (1966). *Community Psychology: A Report of the Boston Conference on the Education of Psychologists for Community Mental Health.* Boston, MA: Boston University.

Bernal, G., & Enchautegui-de-Jesus, N. (1994). Latinos and Latinas in community psychology: A review of the literature. *American Journal of Community Psychology, 22*, 531–558.

Bond, M. A. (1999). Gender, race, and class in organizational contexts. *American Journal of Community Psychology, 27*, 327–355.

Bond, M. A. (2007). *Workplace chemistry: Promoting diversity through occupational change.* Hanover, NH: University Press of New England.

Bond, M. A., & Harrell, S. (2006). Diversity challenges in community research and action: The story of a special issue of AJCP. *American Journal of Community Psychology, 37*, 157–165.

Bond, M. A., Hill, J., Mulvey, A., & Terenzio, M. (Eds.). (2000a). Special issue part I: Feminism and community psychology I [Special issue]. *American Journal of Community Psychology, 28*(5), 585–755.

Bond, M. A., Hill, J., Mulvey, A., & Terenzio, M. (Eds.). (2000b). Special issue part II: Feminism and community psychology II [Special issue]. *American Journal of Community Psychology, 28*(6), 759–911.

Bond, M. A., Kalaja, A., Markkanen, P., Cazeca, D., Daniel, S., Tsurikova, L., et al. (2007). *Expanding our Understanding of the Psychosocial Work Environment: A Compendium of Measures of Discrimination, Harassment and Work-Family Issues* (Publication No. 2007-127). Cincinnati, OH: National Institute for Occupational Safety and Health (NIOSH).

Bond, M. A., & Mulvey, A. (2000). A history of women and feminist perspectives in community psychology. *American Journal of Community Psychology, 28*, 599–630.

Boyd, N., & Angelique, H. (Eds.). (2007). Exploring the intersection of organization studies and community psychology [Special issue]. *Journal of Community Psychology, 35*(3), 277–416.

Brown, L., Shepherd, M., Wituk, S., & Meissen, G. (2007). How settings change people: Applying behavior setting theory to consumer-run organizations. *Journal of Community Psychology, 35*, 399–416.

Campbell, R., Sefl, T., Wasco, S. M., & Ahrens, C. E. (2004). Doing community research without a community: Creating safe space for rape survivors. *American Journal of Community Psychology, 33*, 253–260.

Campbell, R., & Wasco, S. M. (2000). Feminist approaches to social science: Epistemological and methodological tenets. *American Journal of Community Psychology, 28*, 773–792.

Comas-Diaz, L. (1988). Mainland Puerto Rican women: A sociocultural approach. *Journal of Community Psychology, 16*, 21–31.

Conger, R., Conger, K. J., Matthews, L., & Elder, G. (1999). Pathways of economic influence on adolescent adjustment. *American Journal of Community Psychology, 27*, 519–541.

Cooley-Quille, M., & Lorion, R. (1999). Adolescents' exposure to community violence: Sleep and psychophysiological functioning. *Journal of Community Psychology, 27*, 367–375.

Cosgrove, L. & McHugh, M. (2000). Speaking for ourselves: Feminist methods and community psychology. *American Journal of Community Psychology, 28*, 815–838.

Dalton, J. H., Elias, M. J., & Wandersman, A. (2007). *Community psychology: Linking individuals and communities* (2nd ed.). Belmont, CA: Thomson.

Darling, N., Hamilton, S., Toyokawa, T., & Matsuda, S. (2002). Naturally occurring mentoring in Japan and the United States: Social roles and correlates. *American Journal of Community Psychology, 30*, 245–270.

Deaux, K., & Major, B. (1987). Putting gender into context: An interactive model of gender-related behavior. *Psychological Review, 94*, 369–389.

De Jesus, M. (2007). HIV/AIDS and immigrant Cape Verdean women: Contextualized perspectives of Cape Verdean community advocates. *American Journal of Community Psychology, 39*, 121–131.

Duncan, T., Duncan, S., Okut, H., Strycker, L., & Hix-Small, H. (2003). A multilevel contextual model of neighborhood collective efficacy. *American Journal of Community Psychology, 32*, 245–252.

Edwards, D. (1979). Effects of midterm integration on state and trait anxiety in Black and White elementary school children. *American Journal of Community Psychology, 7*, 57–70.

Eiswirth-Neems, N., & Handal, P. (1978). Spouses' attitudes toward maternal occupational status and effects on family climate. *Journal of Community Psychology, 6*, 168–172.

Fine, M. (1992). *Disruptive voices: The transgressive possibilities of feminist research*. Ann Arbor, MI: University of Michigan Press.

Finkelhor, D., & Dziuba-Leatherman, J. (1992). Victimization of children. *American Psychologist, 49*, 173–183.

Formoso, D., Gonzales, N., & Aiken, L. (2000). Family conflict and children's internalizing and externalizing behavior: Protective factors. *American Journal of Community Psychology, 28*, 175–199.

Freire, P. (1970). *Pedagogy of the oppressed*. New York: Continuum.

Freire, P. (1973). *Education for critical consciousness*. New York: Continuum.

Frye, V. (2007). Informal social control of intimate partner violence against women: Exploring personal attitudes and perceived neighborhood social cohesion. *Journal of Community Psychology, 35*, 1001–1018.

Fujino, D., Okazaki, S., & Young, K. (1994). Asian-American women in the mental health system: An examination of ethnic and gender match between therapist and client. *Journal of Community Psychology, 22*, 164–176.

Gonzalez, J., Alegria, M., & Prihoda, T. (2005). How do attitudes toward mental health treatment vary by age, gender, and ethnicity/race in young adults? *Journal of Community Psychology, 33*, 611–629.

Griffith, D., Childs, E., Eng, E., & Jeffries, V. (2007). Racism in organizations: The case of a county public health department. *Journal of Community Psychology, 35*, 287–302.

Grossman, J., & Rhodes, J. (2002). The test of time: Predictors and effects of duration in youth mentoring relationships. *American Journal of Community Psychology, 30*, 199–219.

Hagborg, W. J. (1989). A comparative study of parental stress among mothers and fathers of deaf school-age children. *Journal of Community Psychology, 17*, 220–224.

Hamby, S. (2000). The importance of community in a feminist analysis of domestic violence among American Indians. *American Journal of Community Psychology, 28*, 649–669.

Hanson, R., Smith, D., Kilpatrick, D., & Freedy, J. (2000). Crime-related fears and demographic diversity in Los Angeles county after the 1992 civil disturbances. *Journal of Community Psychology, 28*, 607–623.

Harper, G. W., & Schneider, M. (2003). Oppression and discrimination among lesbian, gay, bisexual, and transgendered people and communities: A challenge for community psychology. *American Journal of Community Psychology, 31*, 243–252.

Harrell, S., & Bond, M. A. (2006). Listening to diversity stories: Principles for practice in community research and action. *American Journal of Community Psychology, 36*, 364–376.

Hüsler, G., Werlen, E., & Blakeney, R. (2005). Effects of a national indicated preventive intervention program. *Journal of Community Psychology, 33*, 705–725.

Hyde, J. S. (2005). The gender similarities hypothesis. *American Psychologist, 60*, 581–592.

Ialongo, N., Werthamer, L., Kellam, S., Brown, C., Wang, S., & Lin, Y. (1999). Proximal impact of two first-grade preventive interventions on the early risk behaviors for later substance abuse, depression, and antisocial behavior. *American Journal of Community Psychology, 27*, 599–641.

Jackson, A. (1997). Effects of concerns about child care among single, employed Black mothers with preschool children. *American Journal of Community Psychology, 25*, 657–673.

Jackson, D., & Heatherington, L. (2006). Young Jamaicans' attitudes toward mental illness: Experimental and demographic factors associated with social distance and stigmatizing opinions. *Journal of Community Psychology, 34*, 563–576.

Jemmott, J., Jemmott, L., Fong, G., & McCaffree, K. (1999). Reducing HIV risk-associated sexual behavior among African American adolescents: Testing the generality of intervention effects. *American Journal of Community Psychology, 27*, 161–187.

Kelly, J. G. (1966). Ecological constraints on mental health services. *American Psychologist, 21*, 535–539.

Kelly, J. G. (1968). Toward an ecological conception of preventive interventions. In J. Carter (Ed.), *Research contributions from psychology to community mental health* (pp. 75–99). New York: Behavioral Publications.

Kelly, J. G. (1986). Content and process: An ecological view of the interdependence of practice and research. *American Journal of Community Psychology, 14*, 581–605.

Kelly, J. G., Ryan, A. M., Altman, B. E., & Stelzner, S. P. (2000). Understanding and changing social systems: An ecological view. In J. Rappaport & E. Seidman (Eds.), *Handbook of community psychology* (pp. 133–159). New York: Kluwer/Plenum.

Kessler, R. C., Molnar, B. E., Feurer, I. D., & Appelbaum, M. (2001). Patterns and mental health predictors of domestic violence in the United States: Results from the National Comorbidity Survey. *International Journal of Law and Psychiatry, 24*, 487–508.

Kernsmith, P. (2005). Exerting power or striking back: A gendered comparison of motivations for domestic violence perpetration. *Violence and Victims, 20*, 173–185.

Khoury-Kassabri, M., Benbenishty, R., Astor, R., & Zeira, A. (2004). The contributions of community, family, and school variables to student victimization. *American Journal of Community Psychology, 34*, 187–204.

Klaw, E., Huebsch, P. D., & Humphreys, K. (2000). Community patterns in an on-line mutual help group for problem drinkers. *Journal of Community Psychology, 28*, 535–546.

Koss, M. P., Goodman, L. A., Browne, A., Fitzgerald, L. F., Keita, G. P., & Russo, N. F. (1994). *No safe haven: Male violence against women at home, at work, and in the community*. Washington DC: American Psychological Association.

Kulik, L. (1998). Effect of gender and social environment of gender role perceptions and identity: Comparative study of kibbutz and urban adolescents in Israel. *Journal of Community Psychology, 26*, 533–548.

Kulik, L., & Rayyan, F. (2003). Spousal relations and well-being: A comparative analysis of Jewish and Arab dual-earner families in Israel. *Journal of Community Psychology, 31*, 57–73.

Kulis, S., Marsiglia, F., & Hurdle, D. (2003). Gender identity, ethnicity, acculturation, and drug use: Exploring differences among adolescents in the Southwest. *Journal of Community Psychology, 31*, 167–188.

Langhout, R. (2006). Where am I? Locating myself and its implications for collaborative research. *American Journal of Community Psychology, 37*, 267–274.

Linney, J. A. (2000). Assessing ecological constructs and community context. In J. Rappaport & E. Seidman (Eds.), *Handbook of community psychology* (pp. 647–668). New York: Kluwer/Plenum.

Loo, C., Fong, K. T., & Iwamasa, G. (1988). Ethnicity and cultural diversity: An analysis of work published in community psychology journals, 1965–1985. *Journal of Community Psychology, 16*, 332–348.

Lounsbury, J., Leader, D., Meares, E., & Cook, M. (1980). An analytic review of research in community psychology. *American Journal of Community Psychology, 8*, 415–441.

Luo, L. (2006). The transition to parenthood: Stress, resources, and gender differences in a Chinese society. *Journal of Community Psychology, 34*, 471–488.

Mason, C., Chapman, D., & Scott, K. (1999). The identification of early risk factors for severe emotional disturbances and emotional handicaps: An epidemiological approach. *American Journal of Community Psychology, 27*, 357–381.

McClennen, J. C. (2005). Domestic violence between same gender partners. *Journal of Interpersonal Violence, 20*, 149–154.

McDonald, K., Keys, C., & Balcazar, F. (2007). Disability, race/ethnicity, and gender: Themes of cultural oppression, acts of individual resistance. *American Journal of Community Psychology, 39*, 145–161.

Mitchell, C., & Beals, J. (1997). The structure of problem and positive behavior among American Indian adolescents: Gender and community differences. *American Journal of Community Psychology, 25*, 257–288.

Moos, R. (1973). Conceptualizations of human environments. *American Psychologist*, *28*, 652–665.
Moos, R. (1994). *The Social Climate Scales: A user's guide* (2nd ed.). Palo Alto, CA: Consulting Psychologists Press.
Moos, R. (2002). The mystery of human context and coping: An unraveling of clues. *American Journal of Community Psychology*, *30*, 67–88.
Moos, R. (2003). Social contexts: Transcending their power and their fragility. *American Journal of Community Psychology*, *31*, 1–14.
Morris, A., Shinn, M., & DuMont, K. (1999). Contextual factors affecting the organizational commitment of diverse police officers: A levels of analysis perspective. *American Journal of Community Psychology*, *27*, 75–105.
Mowbray, C., Cohen, E., Harris, S., & Trosch, S. (1992). Serving the homeless mentally ill: Mental health linkage. *Journal of Community Psychology*, *20*, 215–227.
Mulvey, A. (1988). Community psychology and feminism: Tensions and commonalities. *Journal of Community Psychology*, *16*, 70–83.
Mulvey, A. (2002). Gender, economic context, perceptions of safety, and quality of life: A case study of Lowell, Massachusetts (U.S.A.) 1982–96. *American Journal of Community Psychology*, *30*, 655–679.
O'Donnell, L., O'Donnell, C., Wardlaw, D., & Stueve, A. (2004). Risk and resiliency factors influencing suicidality among urban African American and Latino youth. *American Journal of Community Psychology*, *33*, 37–49.
Oliver, P., & Hammerton, H. (1992). Women, peace, and community psychology: A common agenda for social change. In D. Thomas & A. Veno (Eds.), *Psychology and social change* (pp. 55–73). Palmerston North, New Zealand: Dunmore Press.
Ortiz-Torres, B., Serrano-Garcia, I., & Torres-Burgos, N. (2000). Subverting culture: Promoting HIV/AIDS prevention among Puerto Rican and Dominican women. *American Journal of Community Psychology*, *28*, 859–882.
Perkins, D., Burns, T., Perry, J., & Nielsen, K. (1988). Behavior setting theory and community psychology: An analysis and critique. *Journal of Community Psychology*, *16*, 355–372.
Pretty, G., & McCarthy, M. (1991). Exploring psychological sense of community among women and men of the corporation. *Journal of Community Psychology*, *19*, 351–361.
Prilleltensky, I. (2003). Understanding, resisting, and overcoming oppression: Toward psychopolitical validity. *American Journal of Community Psychology*, *31*, 195–201.
Prilleltensky, I. (2008). The role of power in wellness, oppression, and liberation: The promise of psychopolitical validity. *Journal of Community Psychology*, *36*, 116–136.
Rappaport, J. (1977). *Community psychology: Values, research, and action*. New York: Holt, Rinehart, & Winston.
Rauh, V., Parker, F., Garfinkel, R., Perry, J., & Andrews, H. (2003). Biological, social, and community influences on third-grade reading levels of minority head start children: A multilevel approach. *Journal of Community Psychology*, *31*, 255–278.
Reich, S. M., Riemer, M., Prilleltensky, I., & Montero, M. (Eds.). (2007a). *International community psychology: History and theories*. New York: Springer.
Reich, S. M., Riemer, M., Prilleltensky, I., & Montero, M. (2007b). Introduction: The diversity of CP internationally. In S. M. Reich, M. Riemer, I. Prilleltensky & M. Montero (Eds.), *International community psychology: History and theories* (pp. 1–12). New York: Springer.
Reich, S. M., Riemer, M., Prilleltensky, I., & Montero, M. (2007c). Conclusion: History and theories of community psychology around the globe. In S. M. Reich, M. Riemer, I. Prilleltensky, & M. Montero, (Eds.), *International community psychology: History and theories* (pp. 415–436). New York: Springer.
Renzetti, C. M., Edleson, J. L., & Bergen, R. K. (2001). *Sourcebook on violence against women*. Thousand Oaks, CA: Sage.
Richardson, D. S. (2005). The myth of female passivity: Thirty years of revelations about female aggression. *Psychology of Women Quarterly*, *29*, 238–247.
Ristock, J. (2003). Exploring dynamics of abusive lesbian relationships: Preliminary analysis of a multisite, qualitative study. *American Journal of Community Psychology*, *31*, 329–341.
Roll, C., Toro, P., & Ortola, G. (1999). Characteristics and experiences of homeless adults: A comparison of single men, single women, and women with children. *Journal of Community Psychology*, *27*, 189–198.
Romero, A., Carvajal, S., Volle, F., & Orduña, M. (2007). Adolescent bicultural stress and its impact on mental well-being among Latinos, Asian Americans, and European Americans. *Journal of Community Psychology*, *35*, 519–534.
Rosario, M., Salzinger, S., Feldman, R., & Ng-Mak, D. (2003). Community violence exposure and delinquent behaviors among youth: The moderating role of coping. *Journal of Community Psychology*, *31*, 489–512.
Rudkin, J. K. (2004). *Community psychology: Guiding principles and orienting concepts*. Upper Saddle River, NJ: Prentice Hall.

Saegert, S. (1989). Unlikely leaders, extreme circumstances: Older Black women building community households. *American Journal of Community Psychology, 17*, 295–316.

Salem, D., Bogat, G., & Reid, C. (1997). Mutual help goes on-line. *Journal of Community Psychology, 25*, 189–207.

Sanchez, B., & Reyes, O. (1999). Descriptive profile of the mentorship relationships of Latino adolescents. *Journal of Community Psychology, 27*, 299–302.

Sasao, T. (1994). Using surname-based telephone survey methodology in Asian-American communities: Practical issues and caveats. *Journal of Community Psychology, 22*, 283–295.

Sasao, T., & Chun, C. (1994). After the Sa-i-gu (April 29) Los Angeles Riots: Correlates of subjective well-being in the Korean-American community. *Journal of Community Psychology, 22*, 136–152.

Schwarzer, R., Hahn, A., & Schröder, H. (1994). Social integration and social support in a life crisis: Effects of macrosocial change in East Germany. *American Journal of Community Psychology, 22*, 685–706.

Schoggen, P. (1989). *Behavior settings: A revision and extension of Roger G. Barkers's ecological psychology*. Stanford, CA: Stanford University Press.

Scott, L., Munson, M., McMillen, J., & Ollie, M. (2006). Religious involvement and its association to risk behaviors among older youth in foster care. *American Journal of Community Psychology, 38*, 223–236.

Seidman, E. (1988). Back to the future, community psychology: Unfolding a theory of social interventions. *American Journal of Community Psychology, 16*, 3–24.

Seidman, E. (1990). Pursuing the meaning and utility of social regularities for community psychology. In P. Tolan, C. Keys, F. Chertok, & L. Jason (Eds.), *Researching community psychology* (pp. 91–100). Washington, DC: American Psychological Association.

Seidman, E., Aber, J., Allen, L., & French, S. (1996). The impact of the transition to high school on the self-esteem and perceived social context of poor urban youth. *American Journal of Community Psychology, 24*, 489–515.

Seyfried, S. (1998). Academic achievement of African American preadolescents: The influence of teacher perceptions. *American Journal of Community Psychology, 26*, 381–402.

Shinn, M. (Ed.) (1996). Ecological assessment [Special issue]. *American Journal of Community Psychology, 24*(1).

Shinn, M., & Perkins, D. N. T. (2000). Contributions from organizational psychology. In J. Rappaport & E. Seidman (Eds.), *Handbook of community psychology* (pp. 615–641). New York: Kluwer/Plenum.

Shinn, M., & Rapkin, B. (2000). Cross-level research without cross-ups in community psychology. In J. Rappaport & E. Seidman (Eds.), *Handbook of community psychology* (pp. 669–695). New York: Kluwer/Plenum.

Shinn, M., & Toohey, S. (2003). Community contexts of human welfare. *Annual Review of Psychology, 54*, 427–459.

Snowden, L. (2001). Social embeddedness and psychological well-being among African-Americans and Whites. *American Journal of Community Psychology, 29*, 519–536.

Speer, P., Dey, A., Grigg, P., Gibson, C., Lubin, B., & Hughey, J. (1992). In search of community: An analysis of community psychology research, 1984–1988. *American Journal of Community Psychology, 20*, 195–209.

Speer, P. W., Newbrough, J. R., & Lorion, R. P. (2008). The assessment of power through psychopolitical validity [Special issue]. *Journal of Community Psychology, 36*(2), 113–268.

Stack, L., Lannon, P., & Miley, A. (1983). Accuracy of clinicians' expectancies for psychiatric rehospitalization. *American Journal of Community Psychology, 11*, 99–113.

Stevenson, M. R., & Gajarsky, W. M. (1991). Unwanted childhood sexual experiences relate to later revictimization and male perpetration. *Journal of Psychology & Human Sexuality, 4*, 57–70.

St. Lawrence, J., Wilson, T., Eldridge, G., Brasfield, T., & O'Bannon, R. (2001). Community-based interventions to reduce low income, African American women's risk of sexually transmitted diseases: A randomized controlled trial of three theoretical models. *American Journal of Community Psychology, 29*, 937–964.

Swift, C., Bond, M. A., & Serrano-Garcia, I. (2000). Women's empowerment: A review of community psychology's first twenty-five years. In J. Rappaport & E. Seidman (Eds.), *Handbook of community psychology* (pp. 857–896). New York: Kluwer/Plenum.

Tjaden, P., & Thoennes, N. (2000). *Full report of the prevalence, incidence, and consequences of violence against women: Findings from the national violence against women survey*. Washington, DC: National Institute of Justice.

Trickett, E. (1986). Consultation as a preventative intervention: Comments on ecologically based case studies. *Prevention in Human Services, 4*, 187–204.

Trickett, E., Kelly, J. G., & Vincent, T. (1985). The spirit of ecological inquiry in community research. In E. C. Susskind & D. C. Klein (Eds.), *Community research: Methods, paradigms, and applications* (pp. 283–333). New York: Praeger.

Unger, R. (1996). Using the master's tools: Epistemology and empiricism. In S. Wilkinson (Ed.), *Feminist social psychologies: International perspectives* (pp. 165–181). Buckingham, UK: Open University Press.

Unger, R., & Crawford, M. (1992). *Women and gender: A feminist psychology*. New York: McGraw-Hill.

Unger, J., Kipke, M., Simon, T., Montgomery, S., & Johnson, C. (1997). Homeless youths and young adults in Los Angeles: Prevalence of mental health problems and the relationship between mental health and substance abuse disorders. *American Journal of Community Psychology, 25,* 371–394.

Unger, R., & Sanchez-Hucles, J. (1993). Integrating culture: Implications for the psychology of women. *Psychology of Women Quarterly, 17,* 365–372.

U.S. Department of Health and Human Services, Administration on Children, Youth, and Families. (2007). *Child maltreatment 2005.* Washington, DC: U.S. Government Printing Office.

Vasquez, H. (2006). Facing resistance in waking up to privilege. *American Journal of Community Psychology, 37,* 183–189.

Waldo, C. (1998). Out on campus: Sexual orientation and academic climate in a university context. *American Journal of Community Psychology, 26,* 745–774.

Whitbeck, L., Hoyt, D., & Yoder, K. (1999). A risk-amplification model of victimization and depressive symptoms among runaway and homeless adolescents. *American Journal of Community Psychology, 27,* 273–296.

Wilson, B. D. M., Hayes, E., Greene, G., Kelly, J. G., & Iscoe, I. (2003). Community psychology. In D. K. Freedheim (Ed.), *Handbook of psychology* I: *History of psychology* (pp. 431–449). New York: John Wiley.

Wingood, G., & DiClemente, R. (1998). Partner influences and gender-related factors associated with noncondom use among young adult African American women. *American Journal of Community Psychology, 26,* 29–51.

Zimmerman, M., Reischl, T., Seidman, E., Rappaport, J., Toro, P., & Salem, D. (1991). Expansion strategies of a mutual help organization. *American Journal of Community Psychology, 19,* 251–278.

Zlotnick, C., Robertson, M., & Lahiff, M. (1999). Getting off the streets: Economic resources and residential exits from homelessness. *Journal of Community Psychology, 27,* 209–224.

Chapter 27
Gender and Media: Content, Uses, and Impact

Dara N. Greenwood and Julia R. Lippman

Although research offers compelling evidence to suggest that men and women are far more similar than they are different across a wide variety of domains, our *perceptions* of gender difference can lead us to believe that men and women do inhabit distinct gendered universes and can trigger self-fulfilling prophecies that confirm these expectations. These perceptions can even guide how academics choose to interpret the research literature. Hyde's (2005) review of 46 meta-analyses supports a "gender similarities hypothesis," namely, the magnitude of gender differences across these studies as measured by effect size is small or negligible in over three quarters of the cases assessed. Put differently, a "small" effect size (i.e., $d < 0.35$; Hyde, 2005) means that 85% of the distributions for women and men overlap. This is not to say that a 15% difference in distributions is an insignificant percentage, but it certainly illustrates that emphasizing difference to the exclusion of similarity paints an inaccurate picture. Further, where moderate or large gender differences did emerge, they were often the product of social context. For example, women are more likely than men to smile when they know they are being observed (LaFrance, Hecht, & Paluck, 2003, as cited in Hyde, 2005). The latter finding suggests that a given social situation may be of paramount importance in the apparent differences between men and women.

The social environment can influence the manifestation of present attitudes and behaviors, but it is also a powerful shaping force throughout the lifespan. In their discussion of a social cognitive approach to gender development, Bussey and Bandura (2004) suggested that the mass media, in addition to ongoing input from parents and peers, offer a "pervasive cultural modeling of gender roles" (p. 108). It is not just children who assimilate cultural models, however; research on the phenomenon of "possible selves" (Markus & Nurius, 1986) suggests that over the course of our lives, we continue to draw hoped for as well as feared selves from "the categories made salient by the individual's particular sociocultural and historical context and from the *models, images, and symbols provided by the media* and by the individual's immediate social experiences" (p. 954, emphasis added).

So how does the media environment contribute to our gendered perceptions and experiences? With a few exceptions, the basic cognitive and emotional processes by which media exert an impact tend to be similar for both men and women. The most robust gender differences exist at the level of media representation and content and the selective exposure patterns that are, in part, a response to gender-typed content. In order to understand how media affect women and men, it is crucial first to understand systematic gender differences in media content, as well as any gender differences that emerge with respect to the quality and quantity of media use.

D.N. Greenwood (✉)
University of Michigan, Ann Arbor, MI, USA

Media Content: Quantity and Quality of Gender Representation

At the most basic level, the mere presence – or lack thereof – of men and women in various media tells us something about the existing gender power dynamic. Because women make up more than one-half of the actual population, their under- or non-representation in the symbolic social landscape of the mass media may reflect and contribute to a cultural climate in which women are less valued than men. Indeed, as Gerbner and Gross (1976) famously articulated, "Representation in the fictional world signifies social existence; absence means symbolic annihilation" (p. 182). Although research suggests that, in terms of sheer numbers, progress has been made toward equitable representation (Signorielli & Bacue, 1999), we still have quite a distance to go. However, the gender disparity in representation grows or shrinks depending upon which particular forms of media are investigated.

Research on US media content indicates that men and women are represented at a ratio of approximately 3:2 in scheduled television programming (Elasmar, Hasegawa, & Brain, 1999; Glascock, 2001; Greenberg & Worrell, 2007; Harwood & Anderson, 2002; Lauzen, Dozier, & Cleveland, 2006; Signorielli & Bacue, 1999; Signorielli & Kahlenberg, 2001) and commercials (Stern & Mastro, 2004). Similar figures have been obtained in content analyses of scheduled television programming in Britain (Coyne & Archer, 2004) and of television commercials in Korea (Kim & Lowry, 2005) and New Zealand (Furnham & Farragher, 2000). However, two separate content analyses of British television commercials (Furnham & Farragher, 2000; Nassif & Gunter, 2008) and one of Saudi Arabian television commercials (Nassif & Gunter, 2008) showed that men and women enjoyed roughly equal representation. The latter finding, in particular, indicates that numbers represent only part of the story. A consideration of the qualitative dimensions of representation is also needed; indeed, the same study showed that women on Saudi Arabian television were cast in dependent or stereotypically feminine roles – and thus reflected the real-life experiences of Saudi Arabian women – far more often than men were. Although the studies cited do not even begin to account for most countries, they do represent studies conducted on media in countries that are geographically and politically disparate. More important, they indicate both that the trend of women's under-representation is more than an American peculiarity and that the trend is by no means universal.

However, these general figures obscure some significant differences within particular forms of entertainment media. For example, in the 1990s women were typically featured in greater numbers in comedies than in dramas (Elasmar et al., 1999; Signorielli & Bacue, 1999). Further, women appearing in comedies had proportionally greater speaking time than women appearing in dramas (Glascock, 2001). Why might this be? In her work on racial representation in entertainment media, Coleman (2000) argued that dramas with Black casts have failed in part because they require (White) audiences to take Blacks seriously – something that, at least in the USA, they might not yet have been prepared to do. By way of imperfect analogy, the data on women's representation presented here are highly suggestive of the same phenomenon. Viewing audiences may be reluctant to take women seriously in dramatic roles. Recent programming has indicated that we are, however, moving in a progressive direction – there are currently female leads in highly rated recurring crime dramas (*Medium, The Closer*) not to mention the hugely successful so-called dramedies (*Sex and the City, Desperate Housewives*). Given increasing visibility, however, it becomes increasingly important to consider and compare the quality of gendered representations, which we address below.

The general figures presented above also obscure some significant findings regarding subpopulations. Although the aforementioned studies do not purport to account for heterosexual characters specifically, in practice, given the infrequency with which queer characters appear in the media, that is what they have, for the most part, done. A content analysis of 125 major characters in sitcoms showed that only 3 (2%) were clearly anything other than heterosexual (Fouts & Inch, 2005). Although reliable statistics regarding the prevalence of various sexual orientations are hard to come by, most estimates place the prevalence rate of homosexuality at considerably higher than 3%. For example, one study showed that 11.1% of respondents self-identified as homosexual or bisexual (Bagley & Tremblay, 1998). Thus, gay individuals are grossly under-represented in the mass media.

All three of the nonheterosexual sitcom characters identified by Fouts and Inch (2005) were gay men (there were no lesbian or bisexual characters). This means that, as with studies of presumably heterosexual populations, among homosexuals, men are represented more frequently than women are. This disparity may reflect the relative power gay men and lesbians are afforded. And, although cable television shows such as the *The L Word* have increased the number of lesbian characters on television of late, scholars have noted that lesbian representations frequently function to reinforce the status quo: Same-sex sexual behavior between women is often depicted as a temporary experimental departure from their underlying heterosexual "nature" and is often designed to be titillating to male viewers (Diamond, 2005).

With regard to the intersection of gender and age representation in entertainment media, those over 65 – both men and women – are among the most under-represented relative to their actual numbers in the population as measured by US Census data (Harwood & Anderson, 2002; Signorielli, 2004). However, the "social age" (a measure that determines a character's "age" based on what phase of the life cycle he or she appears to be in) of women in this age group is much more likely to be categorized as "elderly" (83% of women vs. 66% of men). By contrast, one in three men with an apparent chronological age of over 65 was rated as "middle aged," whereas just over one in seven women were categorized (Signorielli & Bacue, 1999). This trend continues in the 50–64 age range: One in four women in this age group was categorized as elderly, whereas only 1 in 10 men in this age group was categorized (Signorielli, 2004). In other words, women are cast in roles that make them seem older than they are more frequently and at earlier ages than men are.

Is children's media any different than media targeted to adults? Research on violence in the media suggests that children are more susceptible than adults to media influence because they are still in the process of developing social cognitive structures – a learning process influenced by stimuli observed in both interpersonal and mediated contexts (Huesmann, Moise-Titus, Podolski, & Eron, 2003; see also Dubow, Huesmann, & Greenwood, 2006, for a review of media socialization moderators, processes, and effects). This suggests that the representations to which children are exposed are of special concern. M. Larson (2001) found that girls and boys were represented with near equal frequency in commercials that aired during children's programming. However, the figures from a study on Federal Communications Commission-mandated educational television are strikingly similar to those from studies of television targeted to adults (Barner, 1999). And figures from a study of favorite television programs of first and second graders show that 35.4% of minor characters and only 29.6% of major characters were female (Aubrey & Harrison, 2004). As Aubrey and Harrison noted, children might well interpret this imbalance as reflective of the relative importance of men and women in society.

If the gender skew in children's television seems like cause for alarm, the gender imbalance in video game characters is even more problematic. In one study of video games, 72% of the characters were male, whereas only 14% were female (the remainder were of an undeterminable gender) (Beasley & Standley, 2002); in another study, only 15% of games were found to have at least one female hero or action character and fully 30% of the games that had human characters had no female characters at all (Dietz, 1998). The cultural view of video games also indicates that they are "still a man's game" (Ivory, 2006): In recent studies there were more than three times more men than women featured in advertisements for video games (Scharrer, 2004) and more than five times more men than women pictured in video game magazines (Miller & Summers, 2007). Online reviews of video games showed similar patterns: Men and boys were significantly more likely to be mentioned at all (75 vs. 42% of reviews) or to be shown in images associated with the reviews (78 vs. 32% of reviews; Ivory, 2006).

Statistics on the gender breakdown in various media paint an incomplete picture, however. Just as important – if not more so – are the ways the genders are represented when they are present. When a group is already under-represented, the characters and personae that are visible carry an increased burden of fair representation; however, diverse and equitable representations tend to go hand in hand with the quantity of roles available to a particular group (Mastro & Stern, 2003). Although some of the literature on media coverage of sports suggests that progress toward equitable coverage has been made in recent years (Cunningham, Sagas, Sartore, Amsdern, & Schellhase, 2004; King, 2007), research on magazines headlines (Davalos, Davalos, & Layton, 2007) and prime-time television (Signorielli & Bacue, 1999) indicates that media messages about gender roles continue to draw on stereotypical notions of gender.

In the USA, men are more likely than women to be shown in a paid position of labor (Glascock & Preston-Schreck, 2004; Signorielli, 2004; Signorielli & Bacue, 1999; Stern & Mastro, 2004). This is especially true of senior adults: In a content analysis of television commercials, 40.3% of senior men were shown as workers, whereas only 2.4% of senior women were (Stern & Mastro, 2004). However, the findings are more mixed for studies conducted in countries other than the USA. Although studies conducted in Germany (Döring & Pöschl, 2006), Indonesia (Furnham, Mak, & Tanidjojo, 2000), and Korea (Kim & Lowry, 2005) indicate that men are shown as paid laborers more frequently than women are, a pair of content analyses conducted in Britain and New Zealand showed a non-significant gender difference on this measure (Furnham & Farragher, 2000). Women, on the other hand, are more likely either not to work or to be in a role that does not allow their employment status to be determined (Signorielli & Kahlenberg, 2001; Stern & Mastro, 2004). Significant gender differences also emerge for job status: Men are more likely to be depicted as bosses (Glascock, 2001) and professionals (Glascock & Preston-Schreck, 2004; Stern & Mastro, 2004; but see Signorielli & Kahlenberg, 2001, for non-significant differences), although women's representation in the latter category showed a significant increase between the 1970s and the 1990s (Signorielli & Bacue, 1999). In light of these findings, perhaps it should not come as a surprise that a content analysis of women's magazine headlines conducted in the USA showed that only 3–4% of headlines dealt with "career or finance" (Davalos et al., 2007).

Whereas men are more likely to be shown engaged in paid labor, women are far more likely to be shown engaged in domestic labor (Glascock & Preston-Schreck, 2004; Stern, 2005; Stern & Mastro, 2004). And it is not just women who are doing household chores: The same pattern was found for girls in television commercials, who were far more likely than boys to be shown doing household labor. This gender difference only increased with age, which underscores the role that socialization processes play in the division of labor: By young adulthood, women were twice as likely as men to be shown performing domestic chores; by middle adulthood, women were *five* times more likely than men to be shown performing domestic chores (Stern & Mastro, 2004). Not only are women far more likely to be shown doing such chores, but when men do attempt to do housework, they are often portrayed as incapable of completing the task at hand without a woman's assistance (Kaufman, 1999) or else the chore they performed leads to a negative consequence (Scharrer, Kim, Lin, & Liu, 2006). This not only underscores women's obligation to take charge of domestic details but may reinforce problematic assumptions that women are more naturally suited to domestic work. Further, these kinds of gendered messages about the division of household labor may dissuade men from participating, for fear of failing at the task.

Just as women's roles in the (media-represented) home largely conform to gender-stereotypical norms, so, too, do their roles in their families. Women are more likely than men to be portrayed as married (Glascock, 2001; Glascock & Preston-Schreck, 2004), and married women are less likely to be portrayed as working outside the home than are single or formerly married women (Signorielli & Kahlenberg, 2001). What's more, when married women do work outside the home, they are less likely than their unmarried counterparts to be in white-collar positions (Elasmar et al., 1999). Men, on the other hand, are significantly more likely than women to be of unknown marital and parental status (Glascock, 2001), which is important because it suggests that, unlike women, men can be defined in ways other than through their associations with their spouses or children. It is not surprising that women are generally portrayed as responsible for more childcare than are men (Glascock, 2001; Glascock & Preston-Schreck, 2004), although men may participate in some areas such as teaching, reading to, eating with, and playing with children – but only with boys (Kaufman, 1999). However, although the qualified progress media representations of men have made certainly deserves recognition, lavishing praise on men for performing some childcare duties misses the point: It is still the case that real-world mothers who fail to attend to every detail of childcare are regarded as failures (and often come to see themselves as failures), and this phenomenon may be fueled by media messages that define parenting as solely a woman's responsibility (Douglas & Michaels, 2004).

Whereas home and family have traditionally been considered women's domains, sports and athleticism have traditionally been associated with men. However, there are some indications that there has been significant progress toward more egalitarian coverage – progress explicitly noted in both American (Cunningham et al., 2004) and British (King, 2007) studies that compared earlier sports coverage to more recent coverage. Furthermore, non-significant gender differences have been found for several indicators of quality of coverage, such as the amount of space devoted to each story and the likelihood that photographs associated with stories will be in color (Crossman, Vincent, & Speed, 2007; Huffman, Tuggle, & Rosengard, 2004). Despite this progress, though, men continue to receive more overall coverage (Billings, Halone, & Denham, 2002; Crossman et al., 2007; Huffman et al., 2004), and this coverage often expresses a gender bias that highlights male athletes' athleticism but emphasizes female athletes' appearance, personality, and background (Billings et al., 2002). Some of this bias may reflect internalized gender stereotypes being externalized by female journalists. Although sports journalists are still overwhelmingly male (Billings et al., 2002; Huffman et al., 2004; King, 2007), female sports broadcasters are more likely than their male colleagues to comment on the personality or appearance of female athletes (Billings et al., 2002). African American men are especially likely to be portrayed as athletes (Coltrane & Messineo, 2000) and to be described as having "natural athletic ability," whereas their European American male counterparts are more likely to be described as having basketball "court smarts" (Eastman & Billings, 2001; Stone, Perry, & Darley, 1997).

Perhaps the most well-researched topic on gender differences has been in the area of physical appearance. Female characters in US media are consistently rated as more attractive (Aubrey & Harrison, 2004; Harwood & Anderson, 2002), thinner (Glascock & Preston-Schreck, 2004; Klein & Shiffman, 2005), more sexualized (Plous & Neptune, 1997; Tanner-Smith, Williams, & Nichols, 2006), less muscular (Baker & Raney, 2007; Miller & Summers, 2007), and younger (Greenberg & Worrell, 2007; Signorielli, 2004) than their male counterparts. These asymmetries in gender representation are particularly noteworthy because they suggest that men are more powerful – physically and psychologically – than women are, a representational bias that has been documented for decades (e.g., Goffman, 1979). The consequences and reach of this symbolically rendered power dynamic cannot be under-stated: In addition to increasing women's tendency to self-objectify (Fredrickson & Roberts, 1997), and in addition to reflecting and contributing to a cultural climate of sexual aggression and harassment (Donnerstein & Berkowitz, 1981; Rudman & Borgida; 1995), the tendency for women to be portrayed with a lower face-to-body ratio than men (known as face-ism) may be associated with lower perceptions of women's intelligence and ambition (Archer, Iritani, Kimes, &

Barrios, 1983). Further, new research shows that female politicians who represent themselves (in online photographs) with higher face-to-body ratios have more pro-feminist voting records (Konrath & Schwarz, 2007). This suggests that something as subtle as small distinctions in face-to-body ratios may reflect important social and political belief systems.

Women of color tend to incur a double penalty when it comes to media representation. For example, Latinas, who are dramatically under-represented in comparison to their actual population numbers, are more likely than other ethnic groups to be shown in sexualized poses or as children in television commercials (Coltrane & Messineo, 2000; Mastro & Stern, 2003). Black women, on the other hand, are less likely than White women to be shown in sexualized poses but are more likely than White women to be shown in submissive poses (Millard & Grant, 2006). Past research has also indicated that Black women are more likely than White women to be shown wearing animal prints within the pages of fashion magazines (Plous & Neptune, 1997), a trend that may insinuate that Black women are more primitive and sexually motivated than White women are.

The association between femininity and physical beauty manifests itself in entertainment media in a number of different ways: Women's magazine headlines disproportionately make reference to the importance of physical attractiveness (Davalos et al., 2007), female cartoon characters are far more likely to be physically attractive (which, in turn, has significant positive associations with happiness, intelligence, and romantic activities and significant negative correlations with physical problems, anger, and antisocial behavior) than male characters (Klein & Shiffman, 2006), and parenting magazines send the message that appearance is important for girls more often than any other gender-stereotypical message (Spees & Zimmerman, 2002). These messages, in combination with research evidence that suggests that women whose looks are aligned with cultural ideals of beauty are awarded real socioeconomic benefits, such as increased likelihood of being hired (Marlowe, Schneider, & Carnot, 1996) and higher salaries once hired (Frieze, Olson, & Russell, 1991), can lead women and girls to internalize the message that nothing is more important than the way they look (Fredrickson & Roberts, 1997). In line with this, research shows that perceived physical attractiveness was the sole predictor of young girls' wishful identification with a female television character, but for boys, wishful identification was predicted by perceived intelligence of a favorite male character (Hoffner, 1996). Although recent Disney movies depict more adventurous, less stereotypical female heroes (e.g., Mulan, Pocahontas), one need only note the latest "Princess" craze and its shopping mall embodiment (i.e., theme stores in which young girls can spend the day putting on makeup, having their hair done, and trying on ball gowns) or catch the eye of one of the hyper-glamorous and sexualized "Bratz Dolls" to realize that young girls are still being taught powerful lessons about the central role that physical appearance plays in everyday life.

The dominant feature of current media-perpetuated conceptualizations of female beauty is thinness, as exemplified by the 94% of women's magazine covers that display thin models or celebrities (Malkin, Wornian, & Chrisler, 1999). This message is echoed in other media formats: 12% of female characters (of all weights) on prime-time situation comedies are shown restricting their dietary intake (Fouts & Burggraf, 1999), perhaps to elicit the positive feedback from male characters that is positively correlated with thinness (Fouts & Burggraf, 1999) or to avoid the negative feedback – 80% of which is reinforced by audience laughter – with which thinness is negatively correlated (Fouts & Burggraf, 2000). When male characters elicit negative comments from female characters, it is uncorrelated with their actual body size or audience laughter; it is only male characters' self-deprecating jokes about their own weight that is meaningfully related to their body size and audience response (Fouts & Vaughn, 2002). This suggests that, when men deviate from an ideal body size, it is a less serious social offense and a greater opportunity for good natured self-parody than is the case for women.

It is important to note, however, that, although the media representations of idealized female beauty and size are ubiquitous and powerful, the emphasis on a muscular and sexualized male body has also been increasing in recent decades (Rohlinger, 2002). In some respects, equating masculinity with muscularity is no different than equating femininity with thinness. Both place an emphasis on the body, both only recognize a single body type as desirable, and both lead people to unhealthy extremes in their efforts to obtain the "perfect" body. In both cases, these unhealthy extremes may be driven by distortions: Just as women tend to underestimate the weight men perceive as ideal (Fallon & Rozin, 1985), men may overestimate the degree to which high levels of muscularity are valued by women (Frederick, Fessler, & Hasleton, 2005). Of course, one way in which the two ideals do differ is that muscles are part and parcel of a physically powerful body, which stands in contrast to the purely visual statement that a thin female physique makes. However, these images serve to reinforce the conflation of masculinity with physical dominance, and men are hardly immune to the effects of such images. The impact of exposure to idealized images on both women and men is discussed later in the chapter.

If the cultural ideal of femininity values and rewards physical beauty above all else, the cultural ideal of masculinity prizes physical aggressiveness. And just as defining femininity narrowly leads to stereotypical and, ultimately, damaging representations, so, too, does defining masculinity in narrow terms. Scharrer (2001) argued that "hypermasculinity" – that is, "macho" portrayals of masculinity – is positively correlated with physical aggression. Put another way, the media teach us that part of being a "real man" is being physically aggressive. In a similar vein, Dill and Thill (2007) noted that nearly one-third of images of male video game characters are portrayed as both hypermasculine and aggressive.

Male characters in media content that ranges from British television (Coyne & Archer, 2004) to newspaper comics (Glascock & Preston-Schreck, 2004) to film (Stern, 2005) are typically found to be higher in physical aggression than female characters. This finding has held for studies that used composite or unspecified measures of aggression to examine children's educational television (Barner, 1999), Portuguese advertisements aimed at children (Neto & Furnham, 2005), and video game magazines (Dill & Thill, 2007). However, researchers who have separated verbal aggression from physical aggression have usually found that female characters are higher in the former, an effect demonstrated in British television (Coyne & Archer, 2004), American television (Glascock, 2001), advertisements aired during American children's television programming (Larson, 2001), and newspaper comics (Glascock & Preston-Schreck, 2004). Coyne and Archer (2004) argued for the importance of studying indirect (or relational) aggression, which, like verbal aggression, is exhibited more frequently by women and girls than by men and boys. These differences highlight the importance of treating physical, verbal, and indirect aggression as separate constructs. However, there is a conflation of media form and aggressive style. Glascock (2001) found that women in prime-time television comedies were more likely to be both more physically and verbally aggressive than men were, whereas the reverse was true in television dramas. This, once again, alerts us to the idea that the mass media are not yet comfortable taking women's aggression seriously.

All of this is not meant to imply that women in the media do not sometimes exhibit physical aggression. But images of women in video games are far more likely than those of men to embody both aggression and sexuality (Dill & Thill, 2007), which is of particular concern given that one indicator of hypermasculinity (and one that positively predicts aggression) is a "callused attitude toward women or sex" (Scharrer, 2001, p. 620). This means that not only is a callused attitude toward women and sex positively correlated with aggression in male characters but images of female characters appear to encourage this association.

News media are similarly problematic. News coverage of women involved in crimes suggests that as long as women "stay in their (culturally prescribed) place," they will be portrayed positively. Women who stray from this place, however, are demonized. For example, when women commit crimes, they typically receive more lenient treatment from the news media than do men. However, there is an important exception to this rule: When women commit crimes that transgress traditional gender roles (e.g., violent crime, causing harm to a child), they receive *harsher* coverage than men (Grabe, Trager, Lear, & Rauch, 2006). Similarly, coverage of rape victims invariably employs either a "virgin" or "vamp" narrative. The former frames the victim as "innocent," and the latter implies that the victim in some way "asked for it" (Benedict, 1992). Benedict noted that a woman's transgression of – or failure to adhere to – traditional gender roles is one of the criteria that increase the likelihood of her being framed as a "vamp." Women are not the only ones who suffer at the hands of news directors: There is a well-documented bias in the news against African American men, who are over-represented as criminals. European American men, on the other hand, are under-represented as criminals (Dixon & Maddox, 2005; Gilliam, Iyengar, Simon, & Wright, 1997).

This portrait of gender representation across various forms of media content appears rather bleak given the social, political, and economic advances that women have made in the last few decades. And, although it is a fairly crude breakdown of the current landscape and does not provide the kind of nuanced and often more optimistic analyses that more in-depth cultural studies analyses offer (see Lotz, 2006), it is still important to keep these basic trends in mind as we move on to the consideration of selective media use. A recent interview with a few Emmy-nominated actresses highlights the qualified progress that television shows have made with regard to female roles. Although Calista Flockhart noted that, "you see women getting more interesting roles, playing more protagonists, more vivid characters," and Kyra Sedgwick agreed that, "We're no longer just the girlfriend or the wife," Brooke Shields commented that, "There are so many reasons they give for tossing you out as an actress: too tall, too short, too blonde, not blonde enough, too pretty, not pretty enough, too fat, too thin, too old. There's always something you aren't going to be" (Reuters, 2008). It seems that, at the moment, while some things change, other things stay the same.

Gender and Media Use: Video Games, Internet, Sexual Material, and Film Genres

In addition to understanding how women and men are represented in various forms of media content, it is important to understand whether male and female media consumers differ in their selective exposure to specific media content. This gives us valuable information regarding *who* is exposed to *which* messages about gender and provides an informed starting point for understanding how women and men may be impacted by their media habits. Further, understanding men's and women's perceptions of media content gives us additional information about how gendered messages and images are being received by media consumers. There are a few key forms of media that have garnered a fair amount of academic attention regarding gender differences in selective use and exposure: video games, new media use (internet, cell phones), pornography, and specific movie genres.

Video Games

Research on gender differences and video games centers on both quantity and quality of game play. In general, men and boys are more likely to play video games than girls and women are (Lucas & Sherry, 2004; Ogletree & Drake, 2007), and they are more likely to play violent video games in particular (Anderson & Dill, 2000). This is not surprising given the data cited above that male video game characters outnumber female characters at a 3:1 ratio or greater. However, these differences are less pronounced in younger populations (Bickham et al., 2006, Calvert, Rideout, Woolard, Barr, & Strouse, 2005), and there are some notable exceptions. For example, Bickham et al. (2006) found that, although boys spend more time playing electronic games than girls do overall, when games were examined by genre, no significant differences were found for "sensorimotor" games (e.g., racing, shooting), a form of game that made up 35% of all game play. It was educational games, which constituted 13% of game play, that showed a gender skew; European American girls played those games more often than other groups did.

Lucas and Sherry (2004) sampled a college population and found that 88% of men and 55% of women reported that they play video games at least once per week. Men also played more hours per week than women did. Even when the researchers limited their sample to men and women with some interest/experience in game playing, men reported significantly greater intensity of gratifications (e.g., challenge, arousal, diversion, social interaction) across the board than women did, although both men and women rated the "challenge" motivation (e.g., "I find it very rewarding to get to the next level") highest. It is interesting that "arousal" (e.g., "I find that playing video games raises my level of adrenalin") was the second most common gratification cited by women, whereas "social interaction" (i.e., using video games as an excuse to spend time with friends) was the second highest rated gratification for men. This violates traditional assumptions, and indeed some research findings (e.g., Hartmann & Klimmt, 2006), that women prefer activities that have a social interaction component and that men prefer media that "pumps them up" (as in the research on gender differences in music use; Larson, 1995). However, this difference may also speak to the tendency for men to socialize via competitive play and to the possibility that women who play video games may be less socially oriented than women who are not interested in video games. Of course, the latter two possibilities are hard to disentangle from the reality that many video games are designed for and marketed toward boys and men. This brings up questions regarding gender difference in selective use of particular kinds of video games.

Lucas and Sherry (2004) found that women rated "traditional" games (e.g., trivia, puzzles) as more enjoyable than men did, whereas men rated "physical enactment" games (e.g., fighter games, sports) and "imagination" games (e.g., role playing, action adventure) as more enjoyable than women did. The researchers pointed out that women show a bias in favor of games that do not require mental rotation, which the researchers attributed to evolved sex differences in "natural cognitive abilities," and they concluded that video game designers should try to engage women by capitalizing on the "gatherer" abilities they do have (e.g., "landmark memory"). The researchers did note, however, that by increasing game play overall girls and women would also be "reaping the benefit of increasing their mental rotation skills, navigational ability and their confidence in managing a complex and competitive virtual world" (p. 519). The latter suggestion implies, quite rightly, that even so-called natural abilities are clearly sensitive to socialization and learning processes. (See Volume I, Chapter 13, and also Volume I, Chapter 16, for discussion of these issues.)

Additional support for the improvement of spatial skills from computer game play has been reported: Feng, Spence, and Pratt (2007) showed that a 10-hour training session with action video games reduced or eliminated any pre-existing gender differences between male and female non-game players from pre-test to post-test. Further, although there may be some evolutionary explanations for why men and boys routinely score higher on mental rotation tasks, the targeted marketing of toys and games that teach spatial rotation may also serve to inhibit young girls' interests and hence lower their chances to hone their spatial skills. Finally, other problematic features may be confounded with games that require mental rotation skill. Research on German women's perceptions of single-person action games shows that these types of games may be less appealing to women, in part, because they contain stereotypic and sexualized representations of women as well as violence (Hartmann & Klimmt, 2006). The creation of engaging video games with female and male characters who do not conform to either aggressive or sexualized stereotypes would be an excellent starting point for addressing some of these obstacles.

New Media

Initial research on gender differences in internet and computer use was informed by an apparent "digital divide" between men and women. Indeed, earlier research showed that boys scored appreciably higher than girls did on computer use and perceived computer efficacy (Whitley, 1997). However, recent findings from a Pew Internet and American Life project report suggest that, as of the year 2000, men and women have been utilizing the internet in relatively equal numbers (Fallows, 2005). Beyond this, some qualitative differences emerged: Women invest more time in e-mail communication and use of e-mail to maintain intimate relationships more than men do. This is consistent with other research that has shown that women are more likely to use the internet for communicating (e.g., e-mail), whereas men use it more to browse content on the internet (Jackson, Ervin, Gardner, & Schmitt, 2001). However, some researchers found no qualitative difference in the nature of men's and women's internet use (Shaw & Gant, 2002; Thayer & Ray, 2006), and still other research showed that men were more likely to use gaming sites, to have their own web pages, and to download more online materials than women do, but women were not more likely to use e-mail than men were (Joiner et al., 2005). Thus, the extent to which men and women are truly utilizing the internet in different ways remains open for debate and future inquiry.

The Pew Internet and American Life Project (Fallows, 2005) also suggests that age interacts with gender when it comes to frequency of internet use, as younger women outpace younger men in online behaviors, and older men outpace older women in frequency of internet use. This is in line with Selwyn, Gorard, Furlong, and Madden's (2003) study of users in England and Wales in which approximately three quarters of the individuals aged 61 and older who were surveyed reported no use of computers in the last year; however, more women than men fell into the non-user category, whereas the reverse pattern occurred in the user category. Among very young children, however, gender differences in computer knowledge and use are not pronounced. Calvert et al. (2005) surveyed parents about their children's computer use and found that boys and girls start using computers in a diverse number of ways at the same age. For example, by 5 years, over one-half of children surveyed could turn on a computer on their own, use a mouse, and use a computer without aid from a parent. The only gender difference of note was that boys had greater ability to load a CD-rom than girls did. No gender differences emerged for game play on a randomly selected day, which the authors interpreted as an optimistic sign that, at least for young children, computer games may be more gender neutral in their target appeal. They also noted that socialized roles for game play may be less pronounced at earlier ages.

The most recent statistics on high school students also suggest that boys and girls are using the internet at similar rates (1–2 hours/day), but boys report significantly more gaming online than girls do (Willoughby, 2008). The extent to which there are qualitative differences in web use as a function of gender is unclear. This is consistent with another study (Gross, 2004) that showed that male adolescents were more likely than their female peers to be "heavy gamers," a difference that accounted for boys' greater time spent online. However, the latter study also showed that the most common online activities for both girls and boys were socializing (instant messenger and e-mail) and visiting websites to download music.

Research on gender differences in cell phone use also shows a bit of a mixed picture. For example, results of another survey by the Pew Internet and American Life Project (Rainie & Keeter, 2006) showed that individuals who reported using only cell phones (vs. using both land lines and cell phones) were most often younger (<30 years) men. The same study also showed that men were more likely than women to endorse the statement that they "couldn't live without their mobile phone" (p. 8). Other research has shown that men and women may utilize cell phones for different purposes, in line with stereotypical gender-role behavior; for example, a study of Taiwanese college students showed that women were more likely to use their cell phones to keep up with friends and family, whereas men were more likely to use their cell phones for information seeking, at least according to self-report (Wei & Lo, 2006). Chesley (2006) found few basic differences between women and men, with the exception that husbands' use of cell phones at one time predicted the probability that their wives would use a cell phone at a later time, whereas the reverse trend (wives influencing husbands' use of cell phones) was not obtained. The researcher noted that this might indicate men's perceived role as the "technology expert" of the household (p. 606).

Finally, a large scale survey on both internet and mobile phone use showed that, although women were more likely than men to be "non-users" of the internet, no significant gender differences arose for mobile phone use (Rice & Katz, 2003). And, no gender differences were found in the Pew research study (Rainie & Keeter, 2006) with regard to various uses of and attitudes about cell phones, such as frequency of sending and receiving text messages, making calls to pass the time, feeling pressured to answer the phone even when it is perceived as interfering with another activity, and using cell phones to vote in an "American Idol-type television contest" (p. 9). In general, it seems that any glaring gender differences in terms of frequency or type of new media use are on the decline.

Newer research on young adults and internet use has focused more specifically on the burgeoning phenomenon of social networking sites (SNS). These are multi-purpose websites that enable users to post and share various forms of personal information (e.g., favorite books and movies, photographs, "status updates" that provide moment to moment information about what the user is doing, thinking, or feeling) with other users to whom they have granted access. In most cases they also allow users to communicate with one another via comments or e-mails. Recent research shows that women are more avid users of SNS than men are overall, although when the sites are considered separately, the difference is more pronounced for *MySpace* than for *Friendster* or *Facebook* (Hargittai, 2008).

When it comes to perceptions of male and female users and their motivations, research shows that some striking double standards may be in effect. For example, in one study (Walther, Van der Heide, Kim, Westerman, & Tong, 2008) researchers exposed participants to fictionalized websites ostensibly owned by a man or a woman (a picture of pre-tested "neutral" attractiveness was used to designate the profile owner) and manipulated the tone of the messages left on their profiles. The positive comments indicated that the profile owner was the "life of the party last night" and had a fun trip to Las Vegas planned with friends. The negative comments insinuated that the profile owner had gotten too drunk and left a party with a "nasty slob" and that another friend was not impressed by how "trashed" he/she was. Participants' ratings of the profile owners' perceived attractiveness showed an unanticipated interaction between gender and comment. Specifically, positive comments were associated with increased perceptions of a female profile owner's attractiveness, but negative comments were associated with decreased perceptions of her attractiveness. However, the opposite trend emerged for the male profile owner; that is, negative comments were associated with increased perceptions of his attractiveness and positive comments were associated with decreased attractiveness perceptions. The researchers noted that this interaction effect may be attributed to a "sexual double standard" (p. 45), in which promiscuous drunken encounters raise men's social status but lower women's. They cautioned that, in addition to simply reflecting social biases that occur in everyday life, social networking sites like Facebook may become part of a larger observational learning environment in which "bad boys" are rewarded and "bad girls" are denigrated.

A qualitative investigation of motivations for using social networking sites, conducted by the Office for Communications Regulation and Research in the UK (Office of Communication, 2008), is an instructive example of the kinds of gender biases that can influence perceptions of internet use. Fifty-two participants who ranged in age from 11 to 35 and older completed self-report measures of SNS use and also participated in smaller in-depth interviews regarding their perceptions of SNS and various motivations for using them. Based on respondents' feedback, a number of subgroups were identified on the basis of their motivations for using SNS. No gender differences emerged for categories of "non-users" (those who lacked technological expertise or who were concerned about personal safety) and "intellectual rejecters" (those who thought social networking sites were a waste of time). Men and boys were more likely to be labeled as "functional" users who went online for instrumental purposes (such as downloading music). What is most striking, however, is the gender distinction between "alpha socializers" and "attention seekers." Men and boys were more likely to be coded as "alpha socializers" (those who go online for "flirting, meeting new people"), whereas women and girls were more likely to be coded as "attention seekers" (those who go online for "posting photos to get comments from others"). The comments offered about these groups indicate that users' stereotyped perceptions may have affected their judgments. For example, "Attention seekers" incurred disparaging comments from others: "She seems really vain; 20 pictures of herself but no pictures of her friends" (boy); or "I think some [girls] feel self-conscious…so they'll put explicit pictures up and hope people say they look good and then they'll feel better about themselves" (girl). However, it is "alpha socializers" who explicitly proclaimed attention-seeking motivations (e.g., "I like being the centre of attention and this is a wicked and fun way of doing it") as well as superficial requirements for friend-adding (e.g., "I'd add anyone who is fit"). So how is it that women and girls who post photos are considered superficial and self-conscious, whereas men and boys who are explicitly engaged in both attention-seeking and superficial use behaviors are considered "alpha socializers"? More work is needed to probe the gender stereotypes that may be reflected and perpetuated by social networking sites and, indeed, by the research organizations that report on them.

Sexually Explicit Content

Gender differences in exposure to sexually explicit materials may reflect the skewed targeting of sexual content toward men. Indeed, "Explicit sexual materials have traditionally been designed by men and for men…they have a distinctly macho and hypermasculinized orientation" (Harris & Scott, 2002, p. 311). However, long-standing taboos regarding women's involvement with erotica of any kind may also depress both use and/or reports of use, which makes it a challenge to get an accurate assessment of the quantity or quality of sexual material viewed by women.

The gender-typed nature of sexual content in the media may influence both selective exposure as well as attitudes toward the content, which may then feed back into more general attitudes about sex. For example, Peter and Valkenberg (2006) found that both gender and perceived realism of sexually explicit internet content explain the link between exposure and attitudes. Specifically, men, who report greater exposure to sexually explicit online content than women do, also tend to believe that "sex on the internet is similar to sex in real life" (p. 648; one of four perceived realism items, adapted from Busselle, 2001), which mediates the link between exposure and recreational attitudes toward sex (e.g., "Sex is a game between males and females"; p. 648). These associations held up after the researchers controlled for other relevant variables, such as age of pubertal onset, religiosity, level of sexual experience, and exposure to sexual media content outside of the internet. The authors acknowledged that the correlational nature of the research does not rule out the possibility that recreational attitudes toward sex influence internet use or that the two variables may be influencing each other reciprocally, but the researchers highlighted the important role that perceived realism plays in the link between exposure and attitudes. This is consistent with the results of other research; perceived realism has also been found to moderate the link between media violence viewing in childhood and later aggression in adult men (Huesmann et al., 2003). Media that are perceived to be reflective of life as it is may function as a validating echo chamber for superficial sexual attitudes cultivated through other channels (such as peers) and may obscure the contributions that media make to the development of these attitudes.

Gender differences in selective exposure to sexual television content may also be linked to stereotyped attitudes toward sex. Ward (2002) found that, for both women and men, hours spent watching music videos as well as being motivated to view in order to learn about social life (e.g., "to help me understand the world"; p. 5) predicted increased endorsement of sexual stereotypes (e.g., men are sex-driven, women are sex objects, dating is a game). However, for women, but not for men, viewing soap operas also predicted perceptions of peer sexual activity, presumably due to women's higher selective exposure to this genre. Further, manipulated exposure to sexual content from prime-time television programming increased women's but not men's endorsement of gender-role stereotypes. Ward explained this difference in light of men's initially higher endorsement of stereotypes, in combination with women's increased consumption of and receptivity to prime-time programs such as the female-centered "dramedy" *Ally McBeal* and the long-running and hit situation comedy *Friends*. Other researchers (Hawk, Vanwesenbeeck, de Graaf, & Bakker, 2006) found that men reported more sexual content gleaned from television, internet, and radio, whereas women reported more sexual content exposure from magazines. In line with this apparent selection effect, women rated books and magazines as more informative about sex than men did, whereas men ranked television and internet as more valuable sources of sexual information than women did.

The above research underscores the importance of carefully analyzing the content of sexual media targeted to men and women, as well as those media's impact. If women and men are attending to, and therefore receiving, different (stereotyped) messages about sex and gender, this may have dramatic and possibly problematic implications for the expectations men and women bring into heterosexual relationships. Indeed, research shows that increased exposure to sexually oriented television is associated with different sexual expectations in male and female viewers – namely, women who watch more sexually oriented television programs anticipate engaging in sexual behavior earlier in a relationship than do women who watch fewer sexually oriented programs, whereas men who watch more sexually oriented television programs anticipate a broader range of sexual activities than do their male peers who watch fewer sexually oriented programs (Aubrey, Harrison, Kramer, & Yellin, 2003).

We know substantially less about how individuals respond to gay sexual content in the media. In general, and as noted earlier in this chapter, gay characters have been dramatically under-represented in mainstream media programs (Fisher, Hill, Grube, & Gruber, 2007). A recent content meta-analysis of the last three decades of US prime-time TV programming indicated that depictions of homosexual content (e.g., two men kissing) have increased to 0.38 occurrences per hour in 2002, after being virtually invisible in 1975 and peaking once in the mid-1980s and again in 2000 (Hetsroni, 2007). Further, Fisher et al. (2007) observed that the majority of gay content occurred in comedic or contrived contexts (e.g., Reality TV shows), which may increase the likelihood of stereotyped or negative portrayals. The researchers concluded that "nonheterosexual individuals will continue to receive few media messages about healthy and responsible sexual relationships" (p. 185). There is some indication, however, that exposure to positive gay media exemplars (e.g., Ellen DeGeneres,

Will Truman) may foster more positive perceptions of gay individuals (Bonds-Raacke et al., 2007; Schiappa, Gregg, & Hewes, 2006). Schiappa et al. (2006) proposed that increased "parasocial contact" with positive gay portrayals may both reinforce and enhance real-world perceptions of gay individuals.

Film Genres

Video games and sexually explicit media are not the only entertainment media genres that are highly gendered in terms of consumption and marketing. Research has shown that women tend to seek out and enjoy romantic films and so-called tearjerkers more than men do (Oliver, 1993; Oliver, Weaver, & Sargent, 2000). Many of these movies are referred to derogatorily as "chick flicks," which ostensibly renders them unpalatable for men's viewing. Gender typing of movie genres begins early; young children can identify whether a movie is likely to be more appealing to boys or girls, a phenomenon that is also associated with more gender-stereotyped media preferences. Oliver and Green (2001) showed boys and girls' previews of both *Teenage Mutant Ninja Turtles* (*TMNT*) and *Beauty and the Beast* (*BAB*) and asked them to describe whether the film would be more appealing to boys, girls, or both. *TMNT* was perceived as appealing more to boys than to girls, and the most commonly cited reason for this was the violent content. This suggests that, at an early age, children are using violent content as a proxy for boys' enjoyment. Although the modal response for *BAB* was that it would appeal to "both boys and girls" (perhaps due in part to the scary beast, which may have neutralized some of the more stereotypically feminine themes in the movie), the next most common response was that it would be most appealing to girls. The top reason cited for this appeal was the gender of the protagonist. This suggests that children understand the pleasure of identification with a lead character in a film, but it also suggests that boys may opt not to see a film simply because it has a female protagonist and thus is not perceived as relevant to them.

It is interesting that, in Oliver and Green's (2001) study, boys who stereotyped *BAB* as appealing mostly to girls enjoyed the movie significantly less than did girls who stereotyped the movie as appealing mostly to girls, and girls who stereotyped *TMNT* as a boys' movie enjoyed the movie significantly less than boys who held the same perceptions. The researchers noted that it is hard to tell whether a child's own liking for the preview in question influenced their perceptions of whether it was a "girls'" or "boys'" movie, or whether the stereotype influenced their enjoyment ratings, but they cautioned film makers to avoid overtly gender-typed programming in order to elicit more gender-neutral responses. Stereotyped perceptions, which might lead boys and girls to avoid movie content that they might otherwise enjoy, should also be debunked whenever possible. Indeed, research on adults' perceptions shows that both men and women assume that "most men" would not enjoy a romantic movie on a date, despite retrospective autobiographical reports to the contrary; men in fact reported a relatively high mean enjoyment level (rated 5 of 7) of such films (Harris et al., 2004).

Another commonly cited explanation for gender differences in movie preferences is that women embrace and experience emotion more strongly and willingly than men do. Research has shown that women score higher on a "Need for Affect" scale (Maio & Esses, 2001), which in turn predicts involvement with sad media news themes such as Princess Diana's death. Similarly, Oliver (1993) found that women score higher than men on her "Sad Film scale" (e.g., "I enjoy feeling strong emotions in response to sad movies"; "It feels good to cry when watching a sad movie"). However, this phenomenon is at least partly socialized or learned. Indeed, Oliver also found that, even after she controlled for gender, individuals who scored higher on a measure of stereotypically feminine-typed personality traits (as measured by the Bem Sex Role Inventory) also reported greater enjoyment of sad films.

Specific media may even be used strategically (if not necessarily consciously) as a vehicle for the socialization of gendered emotion. A small body of literature has focused on the gendered socialization that accompanies the viewing of horror films (see Mundorf & Mundorf, 2003, for a review). For example, Zillmann, Weaver, Mundorf, and Aust (1986) found that men who watched a horror film in the company of a distressed woman (confederate) were more likely to enjoy the experience than were men who viewed the film in the company of a woman who did not display a fright reaction. Conversely, women who watched a horror film in the company of an unfazed or bold man (confederate) enjoyed the film more than did women who viewed it in the company of a frightened man. Sparks (1991) replicated this finding and added a physiological dimension – for men, delight was more highly correlated with arousal (as measured by galvanic skin response) than it was for women. The researcher suggested that this might reflect evolutionary gender differences in responses to threat – men ostensibly needed to master their fear to be successful in hunting and combat, whereas women ostensibly needed to avoid threat to protect their children and themselves. However, as noted above, it is certainly possible that men and women are socialized to interpret their own and each others' reactions through stereotypical lenses. In support of this idea, Mundorf, Weaver, and Zillmann (1989) found that men overestimated women's fear response to a horror film clip relative to the women's actual response, and women who scored higher on a measure of traditional femininity significantly underestimated men's fright responses relative to men's actual response.

In sum, when it comes to video games, internet sites, sexual content, and film genres, men and women may selectively tune in to different media environments whose content may reinforce and exacerbate gender stereotypes, as well as justify ongoing selective avoidance of media that target the other gender. A final important question to ask is whether gender differences have been documented in the realm of media effects.

Key Areas of Impact: Aggression, Self/Sexual Objectification, and Stereotypes

In addition to understanding systematic differences in gender representation and use of mass media, it is crucial to understand how media representations stand to influence those who are exposed to them. Research on media effects has been predominantly focused on the negative impact that media may have on individuals' perceptions of themselves and others. Specifically, the consequences of exposure to media violence, sexist/sexual media representations, and gender stereotypes have been central foci of empirical scrutiny.

Aggression

All things being equal, the processes (e.g., temporary activation of aggressive schemas, long-term observational learning) that link exposure to violent media and aggressive thoughts and behavior tend to affect men and women in similar ways. However, the intermediary variables that moderate such a link – selective exposure to aggressive media content, identification with physically aggressive characters, and existing tendencies toward aggression – tend to be more common in men than in women and hence make men's aggression in response to violent media a more widespread phenomenon than is women's aggression. As described in the previous section, men are more likely than women to play violent video games (Anderson & Dill, 2000; Bickham et al., 2006; Lucas & Sherry, 2004) and to prefer violent films (Bushman, 1995). In addition, because the vast majority of physically violent film and video game characters tend to be male, there are many more opportunities for boys and men than for girls and women to identify with glorified violent characters. An instructive example comes from Eyal and Rubin's (2003) study in which men reported greater identification with violent media characters than women did; however, men were also significantly more likely to choose a same-sex media character than were women (who were about equally likely to choose a male as a female aggressive character).

Identification may also interact with qualitative distinctions between aggressive male and female characters as well as existing aggressive schemas and social norms that locate men's aggression within an idealized "hypermasculine" template. A psychologically compelling case study by Coleman (2002) shows how a particular representation of African American men's violence both resonated with and glamorized the life experiences of a young black boy (Caryon) and ultimately resulted in a heinous copycat murder spree following repeated exposure to the film *Menace II Society*. Coleman noted that his experiences with entertainment media provided Caryon with "A Black manhood, framed by and (re)produced through media spectacle (e.g., celebrities and Hollywood films) that affirmed an identity position marked by power – sexual conquest, aggression/violence, and wealth" (p. 269). Longitudinal work by Huesmann et al. (2003) also showed that identification with same-sex aggressive characters may have a more powerful exacerbating effect on adult aggression for men than for women. Although same-sex character identification predicted adult aggression for both men and women 15 years later, the interaction between identification and exposure increased aggression for men only. This difference may reflect qualitative differences in male and female aggressive characters in the 1970s and 1980s, as well as social norms that inhibit women's but encourage men's aggressive behaviors.

When media characters *do* offer women appealing opportunities for identification and idealization, some expected associations tend to emerge. For example, Greenwood (2007) found greater aggressive tendencies among women who reported greater idealization of (i.e., wishful identification with) female action heroes. It is interesting that women who felt more similar to favorite female action heroes did not report greater aggressive tendencies. This may be due to the multi-dimensional appeal that characters such as Sydney Bristow (of *Alias*) or Buffy the Vampire Slayer offer young women. Indeed, participants were just as, if not more, likely to describe a female action hero as smart, confident, witty, and attractive as they were to describe her as one who "kicks ass." More research is needed to track both the development of aggressive female characterizations as well as the dispositional motivations that attract viewers to them.

Self/Sexual Objectification

The processes that link exposure to idealized media images and body image concerns tend to affect men and women in similar ways. In addition to the vast literature that documents the deleterious effects of exposure to idealized media images on women's mood and body image (Botta, 1999; Groesz, Levine, & Murnen, 2002; Stice, Schupak-Neuberg, Shaw, & Stein, 1994), there are now numerous studies that show that exposure to idealized media images is associated with decreases in men's body satisfaction and/or increases in their drive to attain an idealized physique (Agliata & Tantleff-Dunn, 2004; Barlett, Vowels, & Saucier, 2008; Giles & Close, 2008; Hatoum & Belle, 2004). In both cases, media images are theorized to activate an unrealistically high standard of physical appearance that primes unfavorable actual-ideal comparisons among viewers, and, for both women and men, the effects of media exposure tend to be more pronounced for those with pre-existing body image concerns (Hamilton & Waller, 1993; Harrison, Taylor, & Marske, 2006; Heinberg & Thompson, 1995). Further, some researchers have found that exposure to idealized female bodies is associated with increased anxiety and body image concerns among men (Johnson, McCreary, & Mills, 2007; Lavine, Sweeney, & Wagner, 1999), which suggests that unrealistically high standards of female beauty have negative repercussions for men as well as for women.

What is different for men and women, however, are the quantity and quality of body image messages in the media that target men and women, in conjunction with existing social norms and schemas that dictate how important it is to obtain an idealized physical appearance. Fredrickson and Roberts (1997) described the phenomenon of self-objectification, which they argued is unique to women because they are much more likely to be sexually objectified both in everyday life and in the myriad media images that feature women as sex objects for visual consumption. The theory proposes that women are socialized to view themselves from an outsider's perspective, which leads to ongoing monitoring of their physical appearance, a task that depletes both cognitive and psychological resources. In support of this idea, the now famous "swimsuit study" (Fredrickson, Roberts, Noll, Quinn, & Twenge, 1998) shows that women who were made to wear swimsuits while taking a math test did significantly worse on the test than did women made to wear sweaters while they worked, whereas men showed no difference in math performance as a function of their outfit. Further, women in the swimsuit condition scored higher on emotions such as revulsion and disgust than men did, whereas men in swimsuit condition scored higher on emotions such as sheepishness and shyness than women did. This illustrates important gender differences in the nature and intensity of self-conscious emotions elicited by wearing revealing clothing, such as bathing suits.

Research conducted since this original study, however, has shown that self-objectification is not solely a women's experience. When men were made to wear Speedos (form-fitting bathing suits) instead of the swim shorts they wore in the original study, only a main effect of condition and gender were obtained – that is, although men still outperformed women, participants in the sweater condition outperformed those in the swimsuit condition regardless of gender or ethnicity (Hebl, King, & Lin, 2004). The researchers found that, although White "women are generally more susceptible to negative experiences related to body image, men and members of other ethnic groups more typically resilient to these experiences can be negatively affected by situations that induce a state of self-objectification" (Hebl et al., p. 1328). A more recent study shows that for European American boys, exposure to muscular ideals in video game magazines predicts an increase in the drive for muscularity at a later time, after initial drive for muscularity was controlled (Harrison & Bond, 2007). The results of this study invite the speculation that aggressive and muscular models in the mass media might not only activate aggressive tendencies in young men but concerns about body size and strength as well.

So, once more, the processes and effects of self-objectification may be similar for women and men, but the extent to which each gender encounters social environments that trigger self-objectification and the kind of images that inspire such tendencies are different. Research has also shown differences in objectification tendencies and triggers within gender, on the basis of sexual orientation. Martins, Tiggemann, and Kirkbride (2007) proposed that, because of multiple converging factors – the general increase in sexualized images of men in the media, the increasing if subtle targeting of the gay male population by advertisers, and the emphasis on physical appearance in gay social life – gay men may be more susceptible to chronic self-objectification than straight men are. Indeed, they found that gay men reported greater self-objectification tendencies (e.g., emphasizing how one's body looks over what one's body can do), body shame, and body dissatisfaction than straight men did, and experimental manipulation of self-objectification showed that gay men's body shame increased in the swimsuit (vs. sweater) condition, whereas straight men's body shame was unaffected by what they were wearing. This research highlights both the universality and the complex nuances associated with gender differences, media, and body image concerns.

Research on African American women and body image is complex: Some research shows that African American viewers, despite the fact that they watched more television overall than other groups do, appear to be less influenced by mainstream standards of thinness (Schooler, Ward, Merriwether, & Caruthers, 2004), perhaps because of the greater diversity of body types afforded the few powerful women of color in the mass media (e.g., Queen Latifah, Oprah Winfrey), in-group norms that espouse inner beauty and self-acceptance, and different sites of body anxiety (e.g., hair, clothes; see Rubin, Fitts, & Becker, 2000) than are typically discussed and measured. However, other research shows that African American women who idealize media models may be more vulnerable than their European American counterparts to body image concerns (Botta, 2000). It is too early to tell what effect Tyra Banks' hit series *America's Next Top Model* will have on African American women's self and body image. Visibility is certainly preferable to invisibility, but at what cost? It is refreshing to see African American women being incorporated into mainstream standards of beauty, but given that mainstream beauty norms remain unrealistically tall and thin, and given that the show itself is an explicit endorsement of an industry that deifies women who adhere to these standards, it may be premature to celebrate.

The ubiquity of sexually objectified media images of women not only impacts women's views of their own bodies but also has negative effects on men's perceptions of women. A fair amount of research attention has been paid to the potentially problematic effects of men's exposure to sexualized images of women (for overviews of this literature, see Brown, 2003, and Harris & Scott, 2002). Of particular concern are media depictions of women who initially refuse or fight aggressive sexual advances and then ultimately seem to be aroused and excited by the encounter. These types of scenes may perpetuate the idea that when women say no, they really mean yes (one among many rape myths; Kahlor & Morrison, 2007). The scenes have at least two very serious implications: (1) Sexual violence becomes associated with sexual arousal, even men without sexually aggressive tendencies may find these types of scenes arousing (Malamuth & Check, 1983), and (2) such exposure may desensitize men to the consequences of real-life rape scenarios and motivate more "blame the victim" attributions in the context of a criminal trial (Linz, Donnerstein, & Penrod, 1984). However, even sexual media content that is less egregious in its portrayal of women can have attitudinal and behavioral consequences.

A complex and thought-provoking study by Rudman and Borgida (1995) indicates that men exposed to sexually objectifying advertisements of women (e.g., car and beer ads) not only showed specific activation of sexual stereotypes in a lexical decision task (faster responses to words such as "babe" and "bimbo") but behaved in a more sexualized manner toward a female confederate who was ostensibly interviewing for an actual or hypothetical job. Existing individual differences in the likelihood to engage in sexual harassment (as measured by the Likelihood to Sexually Harass Scale, Pryor, 1987) also predicted increased sexualized behavior but did not overpower the main effect for media exposure. Further, the men primed with sexist advertisements perceived the female job applicants as less qualified but more hirable, a finding that Rudman and Borgida (1995) noted "suggest[s] (at best) that inappropriate criteria were used a basis for hiring the confederate and (at worst) that some subjects' motivations for hiring were suspect" (p. 510). The study demonstrates that even brief exposure to sexist or sexualized media content can activate inappropriate scripts for social behavior.

Stereotyping: Media Threats and Solutions

Gender stereotypes that pervade the mass media may have direct consequences for women's intellectual performance and career aspirations. Davies, Spencer, Quinn, and Gerhardstein (2002) theorized that sexist media depictions might activate stereotype threat (Steele, 1997) conditions, under which women may fear being negatively evaluated on the basis of a prevalent stereotype (e.g., women are not good with numbers) and may consequently dis-identify with or underperform in domains (e.g., math) in which they are not expected to do well. To test this idea, Davies et al. (2002) exposed men and women to television commercials that portrayed women in either a gender-stereotypical (e.g., showing heightened excitement over brownie mixes or acne medication), a gender counter-stereotypical (e.g., an attractive woman who displayed expertise in automotive engineering), or a non-human control condition and then measured the extent to which these images facilitated access to gender-role stereotypes (via a lexical decision task) and the extent to which the activation of gender-role stereotypes mediated the link between exposure and math test performance. Results showed that gender-stereotypical commercials activated gender-role stereotypes for both men and women. Further, it was only women for whom the activated stereotype was self-relevant and, thus, only women for whom the stereotype mediated the link between exposure and math performance.

Two subsequent studies conducted by Davies et al. (2002) showed that exposure to sexist (vs. neutral) advertisements reduced the number of math items women attempted and reduced the likelihood of women reporting that they would attempt quantitatively based (and lucrative) careers such as engineering or computer science. The researchers concluded that the media may perpetuate this myth, which may in turn perpetuate the troubling consequences associated with gender stereotypes. Researchers have also examined the career implications of other media-perpetuated myths about gender that abound in traditional fairy tales. Rudman and Heppen (2003) found that women who implicitly linked their romantic partner to traditional, fairy tale notions of paternalistic chivalry were also less likely to report wanting high status and high-paying careers. For men, no consistent associations between implicit romantic associations and career ambitions emerged. The authors coined the term "glass slipper effect" to explain that idealized notions of femininity are incongruent with power and ambition and may contribute to and reflect obstacles to economic and social equality.

Stereotypical representations of gender in the mass media also interact with racial stereotypes to affect individuals' perceptions and behavior. For example, the earlier described media bias in which African American male athletes are considered successful due to innate physical prowess rather than to intellectual performance, whereas European American male athletes are credited for utilizing more cognitive skills, also has consequences for sports performance. Stone, Lynch, Sjomeling, and Darley (1999) found that, when a sports task was framed as indicative of "sports intelligence," African American men performed worse than when the task was framed as indicate of "natural ability"; the reverse effect occurred for European American men. The researchers explained these findings in terms of a stereotype threat effect. Namely, evaluation apprehension may be most pronounced and disruptive when a stereotype that favors an out-group is primed. Other research has shown that certain genres of music can activate double stereotypes of race and gender and influence perceptions of African American targets (Gan, Zillmann, & Mitrook, 1997; Johnson, Trawalter, & Dovidio, 2000). For example, Johnson et al. (2000) found that priming individuals with violent rap music (vs. non-violent rap music) increased the likelihood of judging a subsequent African American male target (vs. European American male target) in accordance with negative racial stereotypes. Similarly, Gan et al. (1997) found that exposing European American participants to sexually themed music videos of African American women (vs. romantic-themed videos or control) negatively influenced European Americans' perceptions of a subsequent African American female target.

All is not entirely bleak when it comes to racial stereotypes and the media, however. Dasgupta and Greenwald (2001) found that when exposed not only to positive Black male exemplars (e.g., Denzel Washington) but also to negative White exemplars (e.g., Jeffrey Dahmer), individuals showed a reduced implicit racial bias, and the effect of the priming manipulation was still in evidence a day later. The researchers concluded that, "if media representations were to become more balanced, reminding people of both admired members of outgroups and less-than-stellar members of ingroups with emphasis on their group membership, the combined effect may be able to shift implicit prejudices and stereotypes" (p. 808).

Conclusion and Future Directions

Though our review is by no means exhaustive, we have summarized some of the more well-studied areas with regard to gender and media content, use, and impact. It seems that the allegedly different planets from which women and men are sometimes assumed to hail may be an artifact of the gender-stereotyped landscape of the mass media, the selective attention it elicits from men and women, and the resultant effects it has on our perceptions of ourselves and each other. Not given its proper due in this chapter is the positive impact that media can have on consumers' gender perceptions. This is partly reflective of the bias in the research (people have an ostensibly adaptive and natural tendency to be more attuned to negative than positive stimuli; e.g., Pratto & John, 1991) and partly reflective of the sexist world in which we continue to live. Focusing on the potentially destructive impact of entertainment media is, in many ways, a useful awakening; it is not uncommon to hear female undergraduates at the beginning of a course on gender and media say that they believe women and men are now on equal footing and that the obstacles that stood in their grandmothers' and mothers' way are no longer relevant to their lives. However, as Mares and Woodard (2001) pointed out in their meta-analytic review of prosocial media effects on children's social behavior, the mechanisms that drive negative media effects should also be relevant to positive media effects. In fact, plenty of research energy and money are being spent on investigating the positive effects that media have, particularly on public health. One recent innovation in development is the idea of using video games to teach urban young adults about safe sex behaviors by relying on the psychological mechanisms that make video games both appealing and influential (Farrar, Snyder, Barta, & Lin, 2007). Other research has underscored the powerful role that the internet (a medium for which few consistent gender differences in use emerge) plays in giving voice to previously marginalized social groups, such as south Asian women (Mitra, 2004) or gay individuals (McKenna & Bargh, 1998).

By the end of the term if our students still find themselves feeling a bit discouraged in response to the gender biases that continue to pervade the mass media, it is useful to remind them that stereotypic attitudes and behaviors exist at the individual level as well as the group level, and so can be changed at the individual level. We can arm ourselves with information and education, and we can start early. We can choose not to default to the color-coded path of least resistance in toy stores. We can encourage "and" rather than "or" approaches to creative play, even if we cannot immediately supplant traditional gendered icons: Barbie can, after all, drive a dump truck, and the Incredible Hulk can bake cupcakes. We can try to inhibit our impulse to praise new parents by telling them their baby boy looks strong and their baby girl looks beautiful. We can become role models of gender equality within our own relationships, families, and careers. These types of shifts can happen at the industry level as well. As Glascock (2001) found, more women behind the scenes of prime-time television translated into more women in front of the camera.

Researchers can continue to take systematic stock of the evolution of media content, use, and effects – filling gaps, reconciling inconsistencies, and developing and testing new ways to promote positive and counter-stereotypic images and messages. Counter-stereotypic gender content should be thoroughly examined to determine men's and women's emotional responses and implicit as well as explicit shifts in self and other perceptions following exposure. Attitudinal moderators should also be studied; how do individuals who endorse more sexist attitudes respond to traditional vs. non-traditional media content? To keep in mind the larger ecological niche in which individuals develop and maintain their gender-role attitudes, interactions among media use, peer, and family influences should also be assessed systematically. Further, researchers should attend not only to shifting representations of various social groups but to the media habits of and effects on audiences that are diverse with respect to age, ethnicity, sexual orientation, and nation of origin.

Finally, research on gender and media must be informed by ongoing dialogue between scholars in communication studies and in psychology, between quantitative and qualitative assessments, and among content, uses, and effects studies. Just as our assumptions about gender difference (vs. similarity) can limit the kinds of research questions we ask and conclusions we draw, the assumptions we make about disciplinary and methodological differences can obscure constructive opportunities for intellectual and empirical collaboration.

References

Agliata, D., & Tantleff-Dunn, S. (2004). The impact of media exposure on males' body image. *Journal of Social and Clinical Psychology, 23*, 7–22.

Anderson, D. A., & Dill, K. E. (2000). Violent games and aggressive thoughts, feelings, and behaviors in the laboratory and in life. *Journal of Personality and Social Psychology, 78*, 772–790.

Archer, D., Iritani, B., Kimes, D. D., & Barrios, M. (1983). Face-ism: Five studies of sex differences in facial prominence. *Journal of Personality and Social Psychology, 45*, 725–735.

Aubrey, J. S., & Harrison, K. (2004). The gender-role content of children's favorite television programs and its links to their gender-related perception. *Media Psychology, 6*, 111–146.

Aubrey, J. S., Harrison, K., Kramer, L., & Yellin, J. (2003). Variety versus timing: Gender differences in college students' sexual expectations as predicted by exposure to sexually oriented television. *Communication Research, 30*, 432–460.

Bagley, C., & Tremblay, P. (1998). On the prevalence of homosexuality and bisexuality, in a random community survey of 750 men aged 18 to 27. *Journal of Homosexuality, 36*(2), 1–18.

Baker, K., & Raney, A. A. (2007). Equally super? Gender-role stereotyping of superheroes in children's animated programs. *Mass Communication & Society, 10*, 25–41.

Barner, M. R. (1999). Sex-role stereotyping in FCC-mandated children's educational television. *Journal of Broadcasting & Electronic Media, 43*, 551–564.

Barlett, C. P., Vowels, C. L., & Saucier, D. A. (2008). Meta-analyses of the effects of media images on men's body-image concerns. *Journal of Social and Clinical Psychology, 27*, 279–310.

Beasley, B., & Standley, T. C. (2002). Shirts vs. skins: Clothing as an indicator of gender role stereotyping in video games. *Mass Communication & Society, 5*, 279–293.

Benedict, H. (1992). *Virgin or vamp: How the press covers sex crimes*. New York: Oxford University Press.

Bickham, D. S., Vandewater, E. A., Huston, A. C., Lee, J. H., Caplovitz, A. G., & Wright, J. C. (2006). Predictors of children's electronic media use: An examination of three ethnic groups. *Media Psychology, 5*, 107–137.

Billings, A. C., Halone, K. K., & Denham, B. E. (2002). "Man, that was a pretty shot": An analysis of gendered broadcast commentary surrounding the 2000 men's and women's NCAA Final Four basketball championships. *Mass Communication & Society, 5*, 295–315.

Bonds-Raacke, J. M., Cady, E. T., Schlegel, R., Harris, R. J., & Firebaugh, L. (2007). Remembering gay/lesbian media characters: Can Ellen and Will improve parents' attitudes toward homosexuals? *Journal of Homosexuality, 53*, 19–34.

Botta, R. (1999). Television images and adolescent girls' body image disturbance. *Journal of Communication, 49*, 22–41.

Botta, R. (2000). The mirror of television: A comparison of Black and White adolescents' body image. *Journal of Communication*, 144–159.

Brown, D. (2003). Pornography and erotica. In J. Bryant, D. Roskos-Ewoldson, & J. Cantor (Eds.), *Communication and emotion: Essays in honor of Dolf Zillmann* (pp. 221–253). Mahwah, NJ: Erlbaum.

Bushman, B. J. (1995). Moderating role of trait aggressiveness in the effects of violent media on aggression. *Journal of Personality and Social Psychology, 69*, 950–960.

Busselle, R. W. (2001). Television exposure, perceived realism, and exemplar accessibility in the social judgment process. *Media Psychology, 3*, 43–67.

Bussey, K., & Bandura, A. (2004). Social cognitive theory of gender development and functioning. In A. H. Eagly, A. E. Beall, & R. J. Sternberg (Eds.), *The psychology of gender* (2nd ed., pp. 92–119). New York: Guilford.

Calvert, S. L., Rideout, V. J., Woolard, J. L., Barr, R. F., & Strouse, G. A. (2005). Age, ethnicity, and socioeconomic patterns in early computer use: A national survey. *American Behavioral Scientist, 48*, 590–607.

Chesley, N. (2006). Families in a high-tech age: Technology usage patterns, work and family correlates, and gender. *Journal of Family Issues, 27*, 587–608.

Coleman, R. R. M. (2000). *African American viewers and the Black situation comedy: Situating racial humor.* New York: Garland.

Coleman, R. R. M. (2002). The Menace II Society copycat murder case and thug life: A reception study with a convicted criminal. In R. R. M. Coleman (Ed.), *Say it loud: African American audiences, media, and identity* (pp. 249–284). New York: Routledge.

Coltrane, S., & Messineo, M. (2000). The perpetuation of subtle prejudice: Race and gender imagery in 1990s television advertising. *Sex Roles, 42*, 363–389.

Coyne, S. M., & Archer, J. (2004). Indirect aggression in the media: A content analysis of British television programs. *Aggressive Behavior, 30*, 254–271.

Crossman, J., Vincent, J., & Speed, H. (2007). "The times they are a-changin": Gender comparisons in three national newspapers of the 2004 Wimbledon championships. *International Review for the Sociology of Sport, 42*, 27–41.

Cunningham, G. B., Sagas, M., Sartore, M. L., Amsden, M. L., & Schellhase, A. (2004). Gender representation in the *NCAA News*: Is the glass half full or half empty? *Sex Roles, 50*, 861–870.

Dasgupta, N., & Greenwald, A. G. (2001). On the malleability of automatic attitudes: Combatting automatic prejudice with images of admired and disliked individuals. *Journal of Personality and Social Psychology, 81*, 800–814.

Davalos, D. B., Davalos, R. A., & Layton, H. S. (2007). Content analysis of magazine headlines: Changes over three decades? *Feminism & Psychology, 17*, 250–258.

Davies, P. G., Spencer, S. J., Quinn, D. M., & Gerhardstein, R. (2002). Consuming images: How television commercials the elicit stereotype threat can restrain women academically and professionally. *Personality and Social Psychology Bulletin, 28*, 1615–1628.

Diamond, L. M. (2005). "I'm straight, but I kissed a girl": The trouble with American media representations of female-female sexuality. *Feminism & Psychology, 15*, 104–110.

Dietz, T. L. (1998). An examination of violence and gender role portrayals in video games: Implications for gender socialization and aggressive behavior. *Sex Roles, 38*, 425–442.

Dill, K. E., & Thill, K. P. (2007). Video game characters and the socialization of gender roles: Young people's perceptions mirror sexist media depictions. *Sex Roles, 57*, 851–864.

Dixon, T. L., & Maddox, K. B. (2005). Skin tone, crime news, and social reality judgments: Priming the stereotype of the dark and dangerous Black criminal. *Journal of Applied Social Psychology, 35*, 1555–1570.

Donnerstein, E., & Berkowitz, L. (1981). Victim reactions in aggressive erotic films as a factor of violence against women. *Journal of Personality and Social Psychology, 41*, 710–724.

Döring, N., & Pöschl, S. (2006). Images of men and women in mobile phone advertisements: A content analysis of advertisements for mobile communication systems in selected popular magazines. *Sex Roles, 55*, 173–185.

Douglas, S. J., & Michaels, M. W. (2004). *The mommy myth: The idealization of motherhood and how it has undermined all women.* New York: Free Press.

Dubow, E., Huesmann, R., & Greenwood, D. (2006). Media and youth socialization: Underlying processes and moderators of effects. In J. Grusec & P. Hastings (Eds.), *Handbook of socialization* (pp. 404–430). New York: Guilford.

Eastman, S. T., & Billings, A. C. (2001). Biased voices of sports: Racial and gender stereoptyping in college basketball announcing. *Howard Journal of Communications, 12*, 183–201.

Elasmar, M., Hasegawa, K., & Brain, M. (1999). The portrayal of women in U.S. prime- time television. *Journal of Broadcasting & Electronic Media, 44*, 20–34.

Eyal, K., & Rubin, A. M. (2003). Viewer aggression and homophily, identification, and parasocial relationships with television characters. *Journal of Broadcasting & Electronic Media, 47*, 77–98.

Fallon, A. E., & Rozin, P. (1985). Sex differences in perceptions of desirable body shape. *Journal of Abnormal Psychology, 94*, 102–105.

Fallows, D. (2005). How women and men use the internet. *Pew Internet & American Life Project, December 28, 2005.* http://www.pewinternet.org/pdfs/PIP_Women_and_Men_online.pdf Accessed on October 20, 2008.

Farrar, K., Snyder, L., Barta, W., & Lin, C. A. (2007, May). *Creating positive sexual media effects using a video game.* Paper presented at the annual meeting of the International Communication Association, San Francisco, CA.

Feng, J., Spence, I., & Pratt, J. (2007). Playing an action video game reduces gender differences in spatial cognition. *Psychological Science, 18*, 850–855.

Fisher, D. A., Hill, D. L., Grube, J. W., & Gruber, E. L. (2007). Gay, lesbian, and bisexual content on television: A quantitative analysis across two seasons. *Journal of Homosexuality, 52*, 167–188.

Fouts, G., & Burggraf, K. (1999). Television situation comedies: Female body images and verbal reinforcements. *Sex Roles, 40*, 473–481.

Fouts, G., & Burggraf, K. (2000). Television situation comedies: Female weight, male negative comments, and audience reaction. *Sex Roles, 42*, 925–932.

Fouts, G., & Inch, R. (2005). Homosexuality in TV situation comedies: Characters and verbal comments. *Journal of Homosexuality, 49*(1), 35–45.

Fouts, G., & Vaughan, K. (2002). Television situation comedies: Male weight, negative references, and audience reactions. *Sex Roles, 46*, 439–442.

Frederick, D. A., Fessler, D. M. T., & Haselton, M. G. (2005). Do representations of male muscularity differ in men's and women's magazines? *Body Image, 2*, 81–86.

Fredrickson, B. L., & Roberts, T. A. (1997). Objectification theory: Toward understanding women's lived experiences and mental health risks. *Psychology of Women Quarterly, 21*, 173–206.

Fredrickson, B. L., Roberts, T. A., Noll, S. M., Quinn, D. M., & Twenge, J. M. (1998). That swimsuit becomes you: Sex differences in self-objectification, restrained eating, and math performance. *Journal of Personality and Social Psychology, 75*, 269–284.

Frieze, I. H., Olson, J. E., & Russell, J. (1991). Attractiveness and income for men and women in management. *Journal of Applied Social Psychology, 21*, 1037–1059.

Furnham, A., & Farragher, E. (2000). A cross-cultural content analysis of sex-role stereotyping in television advertisements: A comparison between Great Britain and New Zealand. *Journal of Broadcasting & Electronic Media, 44*, 415–436.

Furnham, A., Mak, T., & Tanidjojo, L. (2000). An Asian perspective on the portrayal of men and women in television advertisements: Studies from Hong Kong and Indonesian television. *Journal of Applied Social Psychology, 30*, 2341–2364.

Gan, S., Zillmann, D., & Mitrook, M. (1997). Stereotyping effect of Black women's sexual rap on White audiences. *Basic and Applied Social Psychology, 19*, 381–399.

Gerbner, G., & Gross, L. (1976). Living with television: The violence profile. *Journal of Communication, 26*, 172–199.

Giles, D. C., & Close, J. (2008). Exposure to 'lad magazines' and drive for muscularity in dating and non-dating young men. *Personality and Individual Differences, 44*, 1610–1616.

Gilliam, F. D., Iyengar, S., Simon, A., & Wright, O. (1997). Crime in Black and White: The violent, scary world of local TV news. In S. Iyengar & R. Reeves (Eds.), *Do the media govern? Politicians, voters, and reporters in America* (pp. 287–295). Thousand Oaks, CA: Sage.

Glascock, J. (2001). Gender roles on prime-time network television: Demographics and behaviors. *Journal of Broadcasting & Electronic Media, 45*, 656–669.

Glascock, J., & Preston-Schreck, C. (2004). Gender and racial stereotypes in daily newspaper comics: A time-honored tradition? *Sex Roles, 51*, 423–431.

Goffman, E. (1979). *Gender advertisements*. London: Macmillan.

Grabe, M. E., Trager, K. D., Lear, M., & Rauch, J. (2006). Gender in crime news: A case study test of the chivalry hypothesis. *Mass Communication & Society, 9*, 137–163.

Greenberg, B. S., & Worrell, T. R. (2007). New faces on television: A 12-season replication. *Howard Journal of Communication, 18*, 277–290.

Greenwood, D. (2007). Are female action heroes risky role models? Character identification, idealization, and viewer aggression. *Sex Roles, 57*, 725–732.

Groesz, L. M., Levine, M. P., & Murnen, S. K. (2002). The effect of experimental presentation of thin media images on body satisfaction: A meta-analytic review. *International Journal of Eating Disorders, 31*, 1–16.

Gross, E. (2004). Adolescent internet use: What we expect, what teens report. *Applied Developmental Psychology, 25*, 633–649.

Hamilton, K., & Waller, G. (1993). Media influences on body size estimation in anorexia and bulimia: An experimental study. *British Journal of Psychiatry, 162*, 837–840.

Hargittai, E. (2008). Whose space? Differences among users and nonusers of social network sites. *Journal of Computer-Mediated Communication, 13*, 276–297.

Harris, R. J., Hoekstra, S. J., Scott, C. L., Sanborn, F. W., Dodds, L. A., & Brandenburg, J. D. (2004). Autobiographical memories for seeing romantic movies on a date: Romance is not just for women. *Media Psychology, 6*, 257–284.

Harris, R. J., & Scott, C. L. (2002). Effects of sex in the media. In J. Bryant & D. Zillman (Eds.), *Media effects: Advances in theory and research* (pp. 307–331). Mahwah, NJ: Erlbaum.

Harrison, K., & Bond, B. J. (2007). Gaming magazines and the drive for muscularity in preadolescent boys: A longitudinal examination. *Body Image, 4*, 269–277.

Harrison, K., Taylor, L. D., & Marske, A. L. (2006). Women's and men's eating behavior following exposure to ideal-body images and texts. *Communication Research, 33*, 507–529.

Hartmann, T., & Klimmt, C. (2006). Gender and computer games: Exploring females' dislikes. *Journal of Computer-Mediated Communication, 11*, 910–931.

Harwood, J., & Anderson, K. (2002). The presence and portrayal of social groups on prime-time television. *Communication Reports, 15*, 81–97.

Hatoum, I. J., & Belle, D. (2004). Mags and abs: Media consumption and bodily concerns in men. *Sex Roles, 51*, 397–407.

Hawk, S. T., Vanwesenbeeck, I., de Graaf, H., & Bakker, F. (2006). Adolescents' contact with sexuality in mainstream media: A selection-based perspective. *Journal of Sex Research, 43*, 352–363.

Hebl, M. R., King, E. B., & Lin, J. (2004). That swimsuit becomes all of us: Ethnicity, gender, and vulnerability to self-objectification. *Personality and Social Psychology Bulletin, 30*, 1322–1331.

Heinberg, L. J., & Thompson, J. K. (1995). Body image and televised images of thinness and attractiveness: A controlled laboratory investigation. *Journal of Social and Clinical Psychology, 14*, 325–338.

Hetsroni, A. (2007). Three decades of sexual content on prime-time network programming: A longitudinal meta-analytic review. *Journal of Communication, 57*, 318–348.

Hoffner, C. (1996). Children's wishful identification and parasocial interaction with favorite television characters. *Journal of Broadcasting and Electronic Media, 40*, 389–402.

Huesmann, L. R., Moise-Titus, J., Podolski, C., & Eron, L. (2003). Longitudinal relations between children's exposure to TV violence and their aggressive and violent behavior in young adulthood: 1977–1992. *Developmental Psychology, 39*, 201–221.

Huffman, S., Tuggle, C. A., & Rosengard, D. S. (2004). How campus media cover sports: The gender-equity issue, one generation later. *Mass Communication & Society, 7*, 475–489.

Hyde, J. S. (2005). The gender similarities hypothesis. *American Psychologist, 60*, 581–592.

Ivory, J. (2006). Still a man's game: Gender representation in online reviews of video games. *Mass Communication & Society, 9*, 103–114.

Jackson, L. A., Ervin, K. S., Gardner, P. D., & Schmitt, N. (2001). Gender and the internet: Women communicating, men searching. *Sex Roles, 44*, 363–379.

Johnson, P. J., McCreary, D. R., & Mills, J. S. (2007). Effects of exposure to objectified male and female media images on men's psychological well being. *Psychology of Men & Masculinity, 8*, 95–102.

Johnson, J. D., Trawalter, S., & Dovidio, J. F. (2000). Converging interracial consequences of exposure to violent rap music on stereotypical attributions of Blacks. *Journal of Experimental Social Psychology, 36*, 233–251.

Joiner, R., Gavin, J., Duffield, J., Brosnan, M., Crook, C., Durndell, A., et al. (2005). Gender, internet identification, and internet anxiety: Correlates of internet use. *CyberPsychology and Behavior, 8*, 371–378.

Kahlor, L., & Morrison, D. (2007). Television viewing and rape myth acceptance among college women. *Sex Roles, 56*, 729–739.

Kaufman, G. (1999). The portrayal of men's family roles in television commercials. *Sex Roles, 41*, 439–458.

Kim, K., & Lowry, D. T. (2005). Television commercials as a lagging social indicator: Gender role stereotypes in Korean television advertising. *Sex Roles, 53*, 901–910.

King, C. (2007). Media portrayals of male and female athletes. *International Review for the Sociology of Sport, 42*, 187–199.

Klein, H., & Shiffman, K. S. (2005). Thin is "in" and stout is "out": What animated cartoons tell viewers about body weight. *Eating and Weight Disorders, 10*, 107–116.

Klein, H., & Shiffman, K. S. (2006). Messages about physical attractiveness in animated cartoons. *Body Image, 3*, 353–363.

Konrath, S., & Schwarz, N. (2007). Do male politicians have big heads? Face-ism in Online self-representations of politicians. *Media Psychology, 10*, 436–448.

Larson, R. (1995). Secrets in the bedroom: Adolescents' private use of media. *Journal of Youth and Adolescence, 24*, 535–550.

Larson, M. (2001). Interactions, activities, and gender in children's television commercials: A content analysis. *Journal of Broadcasting & Electronic Media, 45*, 41–56.

Lauzen, M. M., Dozier, D. M., & Cleveland, E. (2006). Genre matters: An examination of women working behind the scenes and on-screen portrayals in reality and scripted prime-time programming. *Sex Roles, 55*, 445–455.

Lavine, H., Sweeney D., & Wagner, S. H. (1999). Depicting women as sex objects in television advertising: Effects on body dissatisfaction. *Personality and Social Psychology Bulletin, 25*, 1049–1058.

Linz, D. G., Donnerstein, E., & Penrod, S. (1984). The effects of multiple exposure to filmed violence against women. *Journal of Communication, 34*, 130–147.

Lotz, A. (2006). *Redesigning women: Television after the network era*. Chicago: University of Illinois Press.

Lucas, K., & Sherry, J. L. (2004). Sex differences in video game play: A communication-based explanation. *Communication Research, 31*, 499–523.

Maio, G. R., & Esses, V. M. (2001). The need for affect: Individual differences in the motivation to approach or avoid emotions. *Journal of Personality, 69*, 583–615.

Malamuth, N. M., & Check, J. V. (1983). Sexual arousal to rape depictions: Individual differences. *Journal of Abnormal Psychology, 92*, 55–67.

Malkin, A. R., Wornian, K., & Chrisler, J. C. (1999). Women and weight: Gendered messages on magazine covers. *Sex Roles, 40*, 647–655.

Mares, M., & Woodard, E. H. (2001). Prosocial effects on children's social interactions. In D. G. Singer & J. L. Singer (Eds.), *The handbook of children and the media* (pp. 415–445). Thousand Oaks, CA: Sage.

Markus, H., & Nurius, P. (1986). Possible selves. *American Psychologist, 41*, 954–969.

Marlowe, C. M., Schneider, S. L., & Carnot, E. (1996). Gender and attractiveness biases in hiring decisions: Are experienced managers less biased? *Journal of Applied Psychology, 81*, 11–21.

Martins, Y., Tiggemann, M., & Kirkbride, A. (2007). Those speedos become them: The role of self-objectification in gay and heterosexual men's body image. *Personality and Social Psychology Bulletin, 33*, 634–647.

Mastro, D. E., & Stern, S. R. (2003). Representations of race in television commercials: A content analysis of prime-time advertising. *Journal of Broadcasting & Electronic Media, 47*, 638–647.

McKenna, K. Y. A., & Bargh, J. A. (1998). Coming out in the age of the internet: 'Demarginalization' through virtual group participation. *Journal of Personality and Social Psychology, 75*, 681–694.

Millard, J. E., & Grant, P. R. (2006). The stereotypes of Black and White women in fashion magazine photographs: The pose of the model and the impression she creates. *Sex Roles, 54*, 659–673.

Miller, M. K., & Summers, A. (2007). Gender differences in video game characters' roles, appearances, and attire as portrayed in video game magazines. *Sex Roles, 57*, 733–742.

Mitra, A. (2004). Voices of the marginalized on the Internet: Examples from a website for women of south Asia. *Journal of Communication, 54*, 492–510.

Mundorf, N., & Mundorf, J. (2003). Gender socialization of horror. In J. Bryant, D. Roskos-Ewoldson, & J. Cantor (Eds.), *Communication and emotion: Essays in honor of Dolf Zillmann* (pp. 155–178). Mahwah, NJ: Erlbaum.

Mundorf, N., Weaver, J., & Zillmann, D. (1989). Effects of gender roles and self-perceptions on affective reactions to horror films. *Sex Roles, 20*, 655–673.

Nassif, A., & Gunter, B. (2008). Gender representation in television advertisements in Britain and Saudi Arabia. *Sex Roles, 58*, 752–760.

Neto, F., & Furnham, A. (2005). Gender-role portrayals in children's television advertisements. *International Journal of Adolescence and Youth, 12*, 69–90.

Office of Communications. (2008, April 2). *Annex 3: Social networking qualitative research report*. London: Author. www.ofcom.org.uk/advice/media_literacy/medlitpub/medlitpubrss/socialnetworking/annex3.pdf. Retrieved June 30, 2008.

Ogletree, S. M., & Drake, R. (2007). College students' video game participation and perceptions: Gender differences and implications. *Sex Roles, 56*, 537–542.

Oliver, M. B. (1993). Exploring the paradox of the enjoyment of sad films. *Human Communication Research, 19*, 315–342

Oliver, M. B., & Green, S. (2001). Development of gender differences in children's responses to animated entertainment. *Sex Roles, 45*, 67–88.

Oliver, M. B., Weaver, J. B., III, & Sargent, S. L. (2000). An examination of factors related to sex differences in enjoyment of sad films. *Journal of Broadcasting & Electronic Media, 44*, 282–300.

Peter, J., & Valkenberg, P. M. (2006). Adolescents' exposure to sexually explicit on-line material and recreational attitudes toward sex. *Journal of Communication, 56*, 639–660.

Plous, S., & Neptune, D. (1997). Racial and gender biases in magazine advertising. *Psychology of Women Quarterly, 21*, 627–644.

Pratto, F., & John, O. P. (1991). Automatic vigilance: The attention grabbing power of negative social information. *Journal of Personality and Social Psychology, 61*, 380–391.

Pryor, J. B. (1987). Sexual harassment proclivities in men. *Sex Roles, 17*, 269–290.

Rainie, L., & Scott, K. (2006). Technology and media use: How Americans use their cell phones. *Pew Internet & American Life Project, April, 2006*. http://www.pewinternet.org/pdfs/PIP_Cell_phone_study.pdf. Accessed on October 21, 2008.

Reuters. (2008). Actresses trade quips ahead of Emmy nominations. Retrieved July 13, 2008, from http://www.nytimes.com

Rice, R. E., & Katz, J. E. (2003). Comparing internet and mobile phone usage: Digital divides of usage, adoption, and dropouts. *Telecommunications Policy, 27*, 597–623.

Rohlinger, D. A. (2002). Eroticizing men: Cultural influences on advertising and male objectification. *Sex Roles, 46*, 61–74.

Rubin, L. R., Fitts, M. L., & Becker, A. E. (2000). Whatever feels good in my soul: Body ethics and aesthetics among African American and Latino women. *Culture, Medicine, and Psychiatry, 27*, 49–75.

Rudman, L. A., & Borgida, E. (1995). The afterglow of construct accessibility: The behavioral consequences of priming men to view women as sexual objects. *Journal of Experimental Social Psychology, 31*, 493–517.

Rudman, L. A., & Heppen, J. B. (2003). Implicit romantic fantasies and women's interest in personal power: A glass slipper effect? *Personality and Social Psychology Bulletin, 29*, 1357–1370.

Scharrer, E. (2001). Tough guys: The portrayal of hypermasculinity and aggression in televised police dramas. *Journal of Broadcasting & Electronic Media, 45*, 615–634.

Scharrer, E. (2004). Virtual violence: Gender and aggression in video game advertisements. *Mass Communication & Society, 7*, 393–412.

Scharrer, E., Kim, D. D., Lin, K., & Liu, Z. (2006). Working hard or hardly working? Gender, humor, and the performance of domestic chores in television commercials. *Mass Communication & Society, 9*, 215–238.

Schiappa, E., Gregg, P. B., & Hewes, D. E. (2006). Can one TV show make a difference? *Will & Grace* and the parasocial contact hypothesis. *Journal of Homosexuality, 51*, 15–37.

Schooler, D. L., Ward, M., Merriwether, A., & Caruthers, A. (2004). Who's that girl? Television's role in the body image development of young White and Black women. *Psychology of Women Quarterly, 28*, 38–47.

Selwyn, N., Gorard, S., Furlong, J., & Madden, L. (2003). Older adults' use of information and communications technology in everyday life. *Ageing & Society, 23*, 561–582.

Shaw, L. H., & Gant, L. M. (2002). Users divided? Exploring the gender gap in internet use. *CyberPsychology and Behavior, 5*, 517–527.

Signorielli, N. (2004). Aging on television: Messages relating to gender, race, and occupation in prime time. *Journal of Broadcasting & Electronic Media, 48*, 279–301.

Signorielli, N., & Bacue, A. (1999). Recognition and respect: A content analysis of prime-time television characters across three decades. *Sex Roles, 40*, 527–544.

Signorielli, N., & Kahlenberg, S. (2001). Television's world of work in the nineties. *Journal of Broadcasting & Electronic Media, 45*, 4–22.

Sparks, G. G. (1991). The relationship between distress and delight in males' and females' reactions to frightening films. *Human Communication Research, 17*, 625–637.

Spees, J. M. G., & Zimmerman, T. S. (2002). Gender messages in parenting magazines: A content analysis. *Journal of Feminist Family Therapy, 14*(3–4), 73–100.

Steele, C. M. (1997). A threat in the air: How stereotypes shape intellectual identity and performance. *American Psychologist, 52*, 613–629.

Stern, S. R. (2005). Self-absorbed, dangerous, and disengaged: What popular films tell us about teenagers. *Mass Communication & Society, 8*, 23–38.

Stern, S. R., & Mastro, D. E. (2004). Gender portrayals across the life span: A content analytic look at broadcast commercials. *Mass Communication & Society, 7*, 215–236.

Stice, E., Schupak-Neuberg, E., Shaw, H. E., & Stein, R. I. (1994). Relation of media exposure to eating disorder symptomatology: An examination of mediating mechanisms. *Journal of Abnormal Psychology, 103*, 836–840.

Stone, J., Lynch, C. I., Sjomeling, M., & Darley, J. M. (1999). Stereotype threat effects on Black and White athletic performance. *Journal of Personality and Social Psychology, 77*, 1213–1227.

Stone, J., Perry, Z. W., & Darley, J. M. (1997). "White men can't jump": Evidence for the perceptual confirmation of racial stereotypes following a basketball game. *Basic and Applied Social Psychology, 19*, 291–306.

Tanner-Smith, E. E., Williams, D. T., & Nichols, D. (2006). Selling sex to radio program directors: A content analysis of *Radio & Records* magazine. *Sex Roles, 54*, 675–686.

Thayer, S. E., & Ray, S. (2006). On-line communication preferences across age, Gender, and duration of internet use. *CyberPsychology and Behavior, 9*, 432–440.

Walther, J. B., Van der Heide, B., Kim, S., Westerman, D., & Tong, S. T. (2008). The role of friends' appearance and behavior on evaluations of individuals on *Facebook*: Are we known by the company we keep? *Human Communication Research, 34*, 28–49.

Ward, L. M. (2002). Does television exposure affect emerging adults' attitudes and assumptions about sexual relationships? Correlational and experimental confirmation. *Journal of Youth and Adolescence, 31*, 1–15.

Wei, R., & Lo, V. (2006). Staying connected while on the move: Cell phone use and social connectedness. *New Media & Society, 8*, 53–72.

Whitley, B. E. (1997). Gender differences in computer-related attitudes and behavior: A meta-analysis. *Computers in Human Behavior, 13,* 1–22.

Willoughby, T. (2008). A short-term longitudinal study of Internet and computer game use by adolescent boys and girls: Prevalence, frequency of use, and psychosocial predictors. *Developmental Psychology, 44,* 195–204.

Zillmann, D., Weaver, J. B., Mundorf, N., & Aust, C. F. (1986). Effects of an opposite sex companion's affect to horror on distress, delight, and attraction. *Journal of Personality and Social Psychology, 51,* 586–594.

Chapter 28
Gender and Military Psychology

Angela R. Febbraro and Ritu M. Gill

The focus of this chapter is on major themes in research and theory in the field of gender and military psychology. The chapter includes a summary and discussion of psychological research and theory regarding selected topics in the field of gender and the military, as well as suggestions for future research. At the outset, it is important to explicate the meta-theoretical approach that is adopted in this chapter in regard to the concept of gender. Thus, "gender" is considered in broad terms, primarily from a social constructionist and/or societal theoretical perspective (Hare-Mustin & Maracek, 1988). From this perspective, the psychology of women and men is viewed as predominantly socially constructed, although the importance of embodiment, or the relationship between psychological experience and physical/biological experience, is acknowledged (Bayer & Malone, 1998). Further, the implications of sexual orientation within a heterosexist, patriarchal society, which includes the military as a significant societal institution, is also considered. The chapter also refers to the experiences of military men and women as they may differ with respect to race, ethnicity, and class. Although the focus of this chapter is on the experiences of both men and women in the military context, it should be stated at the outset that research in this area has focused predominantly on women and that the topic of men and the military, from a gendered perspective, is an area that is ripe for needed research.

The content of this chapter bears some connection to the set of chapters in the "Industrial-Organizational Psychology" section, as the military constitutes one example of a workplace or "occupational choice" in which gender-related issues regarding career progression, division of labor, and sexual harassment, among other career concerns, may figure prominently. As such, the major topic areas discussed in this chapter include the following five areas: (a) gender and military career segregation; (b) gender and military career progression; (c) gender and harassment in the military; (d) work–family issues in the military; and (e) gay men and lesbians in the military. The final portion of the chapter provides an integrative summary and conclusion and presents suggestions for future research.

Gender and Military Careers: Segregation and Progression

Within most cultures, the military is a patriarchal institution; that is, the military is dominated by men numerically and is defined by traditional masculine values and practices, such as an emphasis on

A.R. Febbraro (✉)
Defence R&D Canada, Toronto, ON, Canada

emotional toughness, physical strength, and war-fighting (Nelson & Robinson, 2002). Indeed, within Western cultures, key military values (e.g., aggression, courage, strength) are important aspects of traditional, socialized masculinity, and "soldier" is an early career goal for many boys, most of whom, beginning at an early age, are given war-related toys and games, such as toy soldiers, toy guns, G.I. Joe dolls, and video games that contain violent and war-related images, whereas this is much less often the case for girls (Crawford & Unger, 2000). However, although joining the military is not a traditional career choice for girls and women and although women constitute a numerical minority in most countries' militaries, women generally join the military (in the all-volunteer context) for reasons similar to those of men: for the challenge and adventure, for educational and career opportunities, and to serve their country (Tanner, 1999). However, women are generally more likely than men to leave the military (especially the most male-dominated parts of the military, such as the combat arms), and to leave for family-related reasons, whereas men are more likely to leave the military for career-related reasons, such as better opportunities for promotion in the civilian world (see Bourgon, 2007). Thus, there are important gender-related differences in the experiences of women and men in the military context. Two such areas of experience, namely career segregation and career progression, are discussed below.

Gender and Occupational Segregation

The focus here is on the representation of women and men within different military occupational categories (i.e., gender-based occupational or career segregation), as well as different environmental elements (e.g., army, navy, air force). For instance, as will be discussed in more detail, Canadian research suggests that women are more likely than men to serve in supportive military roles (e.g., health-related and administrative military occupations) than in operational roles (e.g., the combat arms), and they are relatively more likely than men to serve in the air force than in the army (Winslow, Browne, & Febbraro, 2007). In some nations, women, like men, are permitted to serve in all military occupational roles, including the combat arms, but in the USA and the UK, women are excluded from direct combat roles, despite the fact that many US military women have lost their lives in conflict-ridden areas while serving in non-combat roles. As will be discussed, the reasons given by government officials for the exclusion of women from combat roles encompass a number of assumptions and stereotypes about psychological gender differences, such as the assumption that women are not emotionally tough or aggressive enough to fight effectively and the assumption that mixed-gender units would undermine the "male bonding" that is needed in combat units (Febbraro & McCann, 2003). The latter is also a major reason why gay men and lesbians are still not allowed to serve openly in the US military. This issue is discussed in a later section of this chapter.

To date, many North Atlantic Treaty Organization (NATO) countries and other allied nations have made significant progress toward increasing gender integration in their militaries by removing limitations on the roles of women. For example, Canada, the Czech Republic, Denmark, Hungary, Spain, the Netherlands, Norway, Sweden, Austria, Germany, and Ireland all allow women to serve in combat arms occupations (Davis & McKee, 2004). However, combat exclusions remain in place in Australia, France, Turkey, and, as mentioned, the UK and the USA (Davis & McKee, 2004; Harries-Jenkins, 2004).

For some nations, the removal of the combat exclusion for women was a result of political and legal pressures imposed on the military. In Canada, for instance, the employment of women in the combat arms was a direct result of a human rights court ruling imposed on the Canadian Forces (CF) in 1989. The one exclusion to the court order, submarine service, was removed in March 2001. Since the 1989 court ruling, the CF has made considerable strides in gender integration. Canadian women have participated in a wide range of domestic and international military operations, from humanitarian relief to peacekeeping to war-fighting. In May 2006, Captain Nichola Goddard became the first woman in Canadian history to be killed while serving on the front lines in a direct (and official) combat role and the first female member of the Canadian military to be killed in combat since World War II. It is interesting that the Canadian public's response to the death of Captain Goddard in a battle with the Taliban raised few questions in reference to appropriate gender roles. Instead, there was an overwhelming focus on the fact that Canada had lost a competent, dedicated soldier, regardless of gender (Davis, 2007). However, as will be discussed, although women are beginning to be appointed to senior operational leadership positions in the CF, women have not progressed in large numbers to the most senior ranks, particularly in the combat arms, where they account for only 3.9% of officers and 1.4% of non-commissioned members (NCMs; Holden & Tanner, 2001). Further, the concentration of women in the CF continues to be in the more traditional support areas such as medical and dental occupations (Bourgon, 2007; Committee on Women in NATO Forces, 2003). Indeed, taken together, women constituted nearly 70% of officers in the medical and dental (44%) and other support (25%) occupational categories in the CF (regular force) in 2006 (Bourgon, 2007).

Similarly, in Belgium, the most "female-friendly" unit is the Medical Service, with 21.4% women, whereas the army, the most traditional service, has the smallest proportion of female personnel (6.7%). Further, Belgian military women are under-represented (and men are over-represented) in the combat arms: In 2005, there were only 6 women in infantry (0.4%), 13 female personnel in armor (1.5%), and 6 female pilots (1.5%) in the air force. The highest percentages of women were found in administration, communications, and information systems in the army (13.2 and 11%, respectively; Manigart, 2007). Following a similar pattern, in the Netherlands, only 13% of all female soldiers in the army were in combat units, whereas the percentages of women in combat functions in the navy and the air force were much higher (33 and 21%, respectively). Moreover, women are poorly represented in technical units; the reverse is true for support units, in which women are very well represented (approximately 70%; Richardson, Bosh, & Moelker, 2007). US military women are the most heavily concentrated in the air force (20%) and the least concentrated in the Marine Corps (6%); further, as mentioned earlier, they are excluded from serving in direct combat roles (Moskos, 2007).

In Brazil, women are still not allowed to join the navy fleet, the most important career in the navy; the greatest advances in terms of gender integration have occurred in the Brazilian Air Force; and the army was the last service to allow women's participation, which in 2006 stood at 2% (Castro, 2007). As is the case in many countries (see Soeters & van der Meulen, 2007), the Brazilian Army is the service in which the participation of women is the most unequal in terms of career opportunity. According to Castro (2007), the main reason for this is the prejudiced belief that women cannot endure traditional army activities for physical and psychological reasons. Similarly, in the South African (S.A.) military, most women still serve in traditional women's roles, although since 1996 there have been female crews in the infantry, artillery, and armored corps of the army, as well as in the air force as pilots and in the navy on ships (Heinecken, 2007). Further, although women in the South African National Defence Force (SANDF) are permitted to serve in all ranks and positions, including combat roles, the real issue for S.A. military women is whether they will do so in a gender-friendly environment, given the fact that cultural attitudes that assume women to be inferior and subordinate have remained unchanged. For example, S.A. women on deployment have been the target of abuse, sexual violence, and other forms of gender-based violence (Heinecken, 2007).

As has been the case for the militaries of other countries, women in the Israeli Defence Forces (IDF) have been most often posted to clerical, support, or "caretaking" (teaching or social welfare) roles, consistent with traditional gender-role expectations, stereotypes, and norms. The integration of women is still limited, and the most significant struggle is over inclusion into the last bastions of male exclusivity, combat roles. As a result of external legal and political pressures, and the internal pressure of some commanders, the IDF has been forced to integrate women into such roles as pilots and naval commanders and into the artillery and light infantry (Lomskey-Feder & Ben-Ari, 2007). However, although Israeli women may volunteer for combat assignments, in practice the IDF does not take all eligible women, but rather selects the number that it needs to meet personnel quotas each year, and, once a combat unit deploys, women soldiers are generally evacuated (Norris, 2007). Thus, it can be seen that, consistent with traditional roles and views of masculinity and femininity, women tend to be found in supportive roles in the militaries of Western nations, whereas men predominate in operational roles, such as the combat arms.

Gender, Combat, and the "Warrior Ethic"

Davis and McKee (2004) argued that the real obstacle to women's full participation in the military today has little to do with their physical and psychological abilities but rather concerns social and cultural issues that characterize a "warrior" framework. They suggested that military policy and doctrine in Canada, for example, are increasingly dominated by the terms "warrior ethos," "warrior culture," and "warrior spirit" and that the combat-focused warrior framework, as opposed to the role of the soldier as peacekeeper, has gained emphasis and legitimacy as a schema for describing the entire military. They viewed this "warrior creep" as unwarranted by current and future military requirements (e.g., changes in technology that obviate the need for "brute strength") and as inimical to the integration of women, as well as increasing proportions of men, as the values and lifestyles of democratic societies evolve. Thus, despite women's service in the combat arms in Canada, women have not served in the so-called assaulter roles in Canada's elite anti-terrorist unit, Joint Task Force (JTF) 2. Although women are not formally excluded from such roles, the physical standards have been set so high that very few women can be expected to meet them or, if they do, to survive the subsequent training process that functions to "weed out" candidates. The question here is whether or not the standards applied reflect actual *bona fide* job requirements (Davis & McKee, 2004).

As noted earlier, a number of countries continue to exclude women from combat roles. Moreover, the reasons given for this exclusion encompass a number of assumptions and stereotypes about psychological gender differences, and about masculinity and femininity, including the assumption that men, but not women, are emotionally tough or aggressive enough to fight effectively, and the assumption that mixed-gender units will undermine the "male bonding" that is needed in order for combat units to fight effectively (Febbraro & McCann, 2003). In regard to aggression, psychological research suggests that the genders are much more alike than different in this area and that, where gender differences are found, they tend to be small and context- or culture-specific, rather than universal (see Chapter 13). Thus, although men may be more aggressive than women on average (e.g., within a North American cultural context), women can be just as aggressive as men, depending on the circumstances (Eagly, Karau, & Makhijani, 1995; Eagly & Steffen, 1986).

Furthermore, given the changing nature of warfare, and current gender socialization, it may be that women are more likely than men to possess the psychological attributes, such as conflict resolution skills, negotiation skills, and communication skills, needed for combat in certain contexts. Indeed, the U.N. resolution 1325 is intended to reinforce the role of women in conflict resolution. The Dutch military, for example, comply with this resolution and integrate gender perspectives into peacekeeping operations. The objective is to deploy female soldiers in peace support operations because of the constructive roles that they are assumed to be able to play (Richardson et al., 2007). However, although such policies may help to further gender integration, they are nevertheless premised on socially constructed but de-contextualized generalizations about the abilities and characteristics of men and women, in the same way that policies that exclude women from combat roles are based on overgeneralizations about gender differences.

For instance, there are numerous examples of women's aggressiveness in military contexts. Although warfare may be more prevalent among men, history has shown that women have fought effectively in wars in direct physical combat, both disguised as men and openly as women, and in both single-gender and mixed-gender units (Goldstein, 2001). In addition to the extensive use of women in revolutionary, guerrilla, and partisan warfare (e.g., among the Eritrean rebels and the Sandinistas), women fought in the Serbian and Russian armies in World War I (e.g., in the "Battalion of Death"), during the Russian Civil War, and for the army of North Vietnam (and, to a lesser extent, South Vietnam) in the Vietnam War (Goldstein, 2001). In World War II, hundreds of thousands of Soviet women served in combat as snipers, machine gunners, artillery women, and tank women – probably the largest case of women's participation in direct combat in modern history (Goldstein, 2001). Throughout such wars, women's combat experience has also included dragging wounded comrades away from the battlefield. Furthermore, evidence of women's ability to serve effectively in combat roles continues to the present context, for example, in Afghanistan.[1]

Another argument against the inclusion of women in combat roles concerns the negative impact on unit cohesion and "male bonding" that it is assumed would result from the inclusion of women. Counter to this argument, there is a substantial body of psychological research that demonstrates that effective mixed-gender bonding regularly occurs within police and fire departments and that successful mixed-gender bonding has occurred, for example, among Eritrean rebels (in which 35% of the frontline troops were reportedly women) and in numerous other military contexts (Thomas & Thomas, 1993). During Operation Desert Storm, for instance, the combat support units, ships, and aircrews that included women performed their mission well, even under direct fire. There is also evidence to suggest that mixed-gender units may perform even more effectively than single-gender units in some cases, as they did in North Vietnam and El Salvador, for example. Some American commanders of experienced mixed-gender units have noticed a similar pattern of positive dynamics: The women often worked harder to gain approval, and the men worked harder not to be undone. This was apparent, for instance, in the Persian Gulf. These experiences are also supported by studies conducted by the U.S. Army Research Institute that showed that women in combat support units did not adversely affect unit performance; by Canadian military research that showed that the assignment of women to non-traditional roles in land, air, and sea environments did not have negative impacts on operational effectiveness (Hoiberg, 1991); and by Danish research that showed that women performed just as well as men in land and sea combat roles (Goldstein, 2001). In general, research indicates that cohesion and bonding are not adversely affected in mixed-gender groups and that the genders can work together effectively, especially when women are not a novelty in a unit and when women and men are deployed in the field (Goldstein, 2001). According to Paul E. Roush (1991), a retired US Marine Corps colonel, bonding requires three elements: organization for a common goal, the presence of or potential for danger, and a willingness to sacrifice. None of these is gender-specific (Thomas & Thomas, 1993). Rather, cohesion is affected by group solidarity, leadership, and the adequacy of support and command channels, and bonding is primarily related to situation, circumstance, and environment – in other words, to a commonality of experience that is shared by everyone in the group (Goldstein, 2001; Hoiberg, 1991). Although none of these is related to gender, and although many countries have now had at last some experience with mixed-gender units with little evidence of

---

[1] Also note that at the time of this writing, 97 US military women have lost their lives in the Iraq War, although not officially serving in combat roles (Mooney, 2008).

negative impacts on effectiveness, cohesion, or readiness, the assumption that cohesion or bonding would be undermined by the presence of women in combat units persists, for example, in the US and UK militaries, despite the lack of evidence.

Gender Differences in Occupational Stratification

Statistics from several countries demonstrate the persistence of gender-based occupational stratification in the military, such that the under-representation of women, and the over-representation of men, tends to be greatest at the most senior ranks. In other words, there is still a glass ceiling for military women in different parts of the world. For example, according to figures released by the Director of Military Gender Integration and Employment Equity (DMGIEE) in 2003, women accounted for 14.1% of CF officers and 11.9% of NCMs; overall, 12.4% of CF members were women. More recent statistics in 2007 indicate that women constitute about 9.6% of senior officers in the CF regular force and 7.7% of senior officers in the CF reserve force (Davis, 2007). Women also constitute about 9.6% of senior NCMs in the CF regular force and about 12.8% of senior NCMs in the CF reserve force (Davis, 2007). However, there are inter-service differences. In 2003, the Committee on Women in NATO forces reported that women comprised 16.6% of the Canadian Air Force (14.8% of officers and 17.3% of NCMs); 11.5% of the Navy (15.9% of officers and 10.2% of NCMs); and 9.6% of the Army (11.8% of officers and 9.2% of NCMs). Presently, there are only 4 female generals in the CF (all at the Brigadier-General/Commodore rank) and 13 full colonels serving, and most of these senior women are in National Defence Headquarters, as opposed to in operational settings (Davis, 2007). Further, the rate of progress of women into the senior ranks (Major and above for officers, Sergeant and above for NCMs) is not generally comparable to that of their male counterparts (Holden & Tanner, 2001). Perhaps of greatest concern, the attrition rate for women in the combat arms has been high (in some cases six times higher than the rate for men; Tanner, 1999; see also Bourgon, 2007).

This pattern of gender-related occupational stratification in the CF is evident in the militaries of other countries, as well (Moskos, 2007). The percentage of women in the US military has increased dramatically in recent decades: In 1970 women (mainly nurses) made up only 2% of the military (1% of the enlisted force and 4% of the officer force), but by 2004 women comprised 15% of both the enlisted force and the officer force (Moskos, 2007). Further, in 2004 the proportion of US military women was highest in the air force (20%), followed by the army (15%), the navy (14%), and the Marine Corps (6%). Moreover, US military women have been disproportionately represented in the lower enlisted and lower officer levels in all four services (Moskos, 2007).

Although the specifics vary among nations, similar patterns of gender-related occupational stratification (i.e., under-representation of women at the most senior ranks; over-representation of women at the lowest ranks; but overall increases in the representation of women in the military over time) exist in nations as diverse as Brazil, South Africa, Eritrea, India, Israel, the UK, France, Germany, Belgium, and the Netherlands (see Soeters & van der Meulen, 2007). Female warriors in the Eritrean People's Liberation Front (EPLF) provide an interesting counter-example to the military experiences of many countries, particularly those in which liberation movements have waged guerrilla warfare. By 1979, women constituted 13% of the fighters and 30% of the EPLF as a whole. As of 1993, women made up 34% of the EPLF. The EPLF had a higher percentage of women than any other liberation army in the world. Further, the women fighters were among the few women in the world who have played an exemplary role in attaining independence. For these women warriors, participation in the revolution offered an alternative approach to traditional gender roles (and in some cases, an escape from an arranged marriage). However, no women fighters ever achieved the highest officer ranks. Further, toward the end of the revolution, a more traditional gendered division of labor in allotting military tasks became increasingly prevalent in the EPLF. Thus, the EPLF was not free from gender bias, despite revolutionary ideology concerning gender equality (Tessema, 2007).

As indicated earlier, gender differences in career progression have also been evident in the promotion rates of men and women in the military. For instance, evidence suggests that average promotion rates in the CF (e.g., between 1989 and 1997) have tended to be higher for men than for women in the senior officer ranks, although the differences have not always been statistically significant (Tanner, 1999). Average promotion rates for senior NCM ranks also tended to be higher for men than for women during this time period, and many of the differences reached statistical significance. A more extensive analysis of promotions to the senior ranks of officers and NCMs was conducted in 1995 (Bender, Tanner, & Tseng, 1995a, 1995b). These studies included additional factors, such as eligibility rates, women's share of enrolments, women's share of promotions, time in rank, and time in previous rank, but the findings were similar, in that there were discrepancies in the promotion patterns in the senior ranks for men and women (Tanner, 1999).

Career Progression of Ethnic or Visible Minorities in the Military

In any consideration of career progression and occupational stratification, it is important to examine the intersection of race and gender. For instance, in the case of the US military, the proportion of African American women has increased markedly from 1980 to 2004, especially in the army (Moskos, 2007). African Americans account for 23% of all female army officers and 42% of all army enlisted women, which makes them the largest group of female soldiers. Also noteworthy is the intersection of race and gender in attrition. For men of any race and for Black women, about one-third do not complete their enlistment; for White women, however, the attrition rate is over 1.5 times higher than for men or Black women (e.g., in the army, less than 50% of White women complete their initial enlistment). As the reasons for these differences are unclear, this is an area that warrants future research.

Gender, Career Progression, and Leadership

Psychological research suggests that one explanation for the slow progress of women into leadership positions in general, and, therefore, the glass ceiling that still exist in the military and many other organizational contexts, involves the critical role that gender stereotyping plays in leadership appraisals and concepts (e.g., Boldy, Wood, & Kashy, 2001; Eagly et al., 1995; Rice, Yoder, Adams, Priest, & Prince, 1984). Despite numerous studies that show women's leadership effectiveness, and only small gender differences in leadership style (e.g., Eagly, Johannesen-Schmidt, & van Engen, 2003; Eagly & Johnson, 1990; Eagly et al., 1995; Vecchio, 2002), there is still the widespread belief, first demonstrated over 30 years ago (O'Leary, 1974; Schein, 1973, 1975), that women are not suited for leadership positions. Thus, the stereotype of "effective leader" remains masculine in content (Boyce & Herd, 2003). Indeed, numerous studies suggest that there is a strong cultural association between traditional notions of masculinity and concepts of leadership, including military leadership (e.g., Boyce & Herd, 2003). In the CF, for example, stereotypes about leaders include physical characteristics (e.g., tall, broad-shouldered, loud voice), behaviors (e.g., touching or other nonverbal behavior during interpersonal interactions, conversational styles), and other attributes (e.g., interests, participation in specific social rituals) that may exclude women but actually have little to do with effective leadership (Hill, 2001). Indeed, although the psychological literature has demonstrated women's leadership effectiveness in many settings, one noteworthy exception has been the military context. Eagly and colleagues' (1995) meta-analytic review of 76 studies of leadership effectiveness in the military setting, for instance, concluded that women performed less effectively than men in this context. However, this gender difference was found even when the genders engaged in equivalent leadership behaviors, which suggests that the gender difference reflects a stereotype, or bias, rather than a true performance difference. A similar finding was obtained more recently by Boldry et al. (2001) in their study of women and men in the Texas A&M University Corps of Cadets: Men more than women were judged to possess the motivation and leadership qualities necessary for effective military performance (e.g., competitiveness, physical fitness, independence, self-confidence), whereas women were judged to possess more feminine attributes that are believed to impair effective leadership performance (e.g., being helpful, kind, gentle, emotionally expressive) – despite the fact that men and women did not differ on objective measures of military leadership performance (see also Adams, 1984; Rice et al., 1984).

Eagly and colleagues (1995) have offered *role congruity theory* as an explanation for the gender stereotyping of leadership positions and its effects. According to this theory, perceptions of the appropriate roles for the two genders may conflict with expectations regarding leadership roles, especially when an occupation is held predominantly by one gender. For example, female leaders may be evaluated negatively when they violate gender-role expectations by adopting masculine leadership behaviors and by failing to exhibit feminine leadership behaviors in a male-dominated context (Eagly & Johnson, 1990). Role congruity theory also suggests, however, that the "male managerial model" (i.e., the assumption that leaders must be male or masculine) may pose barriers for women who aspire to leadership positions. This is because women who engage in feminine behaviors, in accordance with their gender role, may be seen as unable to behave in a way that is congruent with "appropriate" leadership behaviors. As noted above, however, even when women engage in the same (masculine) leadership behaviors as men do, women may be evaluated negatively.

As a whole, results of psychological research reflect the dilemma that female leaders face. On the one hand, women may not be perceived as leaders simply by virtue of their gender – unless, perhaps, they act in masculine ways. On the other hand, when women do act in masculine ways (e.g., autocratically), their performance ratings may suffer, especially if they are being rated by men in a male-dominated environment. This "catch-22" seems especially pertinent to the military context, where attributes of masculinity have traditionally been encouraged. Indeed, the psychological attributes required of a successful soldier or military leader (e.g., decisiveness, confidence, assertiveness) are also stereotypic of men, whereas the stereotypic qualities attributed to women (e.g., kindness, emotional expressiveness) are explicitly rejected (Boldry, et al., 2001; Diekman & Eagly, 2000; see also Rice, Instone, & Adams, 1984).[2]

---

[2]Since the early work of Bakan (1966) on communal versus agentic traits, and the early studies by Broverman and colleagues on traits attributed to men and women (e.g., Broverman, Broverman, Clarkson, Rosenkrantz, & Vogel, 1970; Broverman, Vogel, Broverman, Clarkson, & Rosenkrantz, 1972), a strong consensus has formed within the psychological and scientific community regarding what constitutes stereotypic masculine and feminine traits (see also Bem, 1974; Boyce & Herd, 2003). When applied to leadership, these communal and agentic traits suggest that feminine stereotypic forms of leadership are interpersonally oriented and collaborative, whereas masculine stereotypic forms of leadership are task-oriented and dominating (Eagly, Makhijani, & Klonsky, 1992). These gender stereotypic aspects of leadership style also mirror Bales' early (1950) distinction between *socioemotional* and *task* leaders; the distinction between the *interpersonally oriented* and *task-oriented* aspects of leadership (or between *consideration* and *initiation of structure*) emphasized in classic studies on leadership (e.g., Stogdill, 1963); and between *democratic* versus *autocratic* (or *participative* versus *directive*) styles of leadership (e.g., Vroom & Yetton, 1973).

In a similar vein, Yoder's (1999) study of the experiences of the first female cadets to attend the U.S. Military Academy at West Point, a training ground for military leaders, found that, instead of learning to be leaders, the women became passive observers who were often criticized for their "non-command voices" and peripheral importance (Yoder, 1999). Moreover, almost one-half the women in Yoder's study reported feeling overprotected as cadets, a circumstance incompatible with the leadership role but one that conforms readily to the feminine role. Yoder found that, in a setting that defined cadets in masculine terms, the women struggled to create a new role, that of "woman cadet," and to disassociate themselves from femininity. For example, women shunned their skirted uniform and instead tried to blend in by wearing trousers (Yoder, 1999).

On the other hand, Febbraro's (2003) study of women in the CF combat arms, which included both leaders and followers (NCMs) as participants, provided some evidence that a cultural change, or cultural integration, is beginning to occur in the combat arms. For example, when speaking in general terms about leadership effectiveness, the majority of participants saw value in both masculine and feminine leadership characteristics; that is, they spoke of effective leadership in androgynous terms, as drawing on or integrating both traditionally masculine and feminine characteristics. Furthermore, most of the female leaders did not believe that they must adopt a masculine style in order to be perceived as effective by others. Perhaps one of the strongest indications of a cultural change is the finding that each one of the women described feminine attributes (e.g., interpersonal skills) as important aspects of their own leadership style. Similarly, Boyce and Herd (2003) found that female cadet leaders perceived successful officers as having characteristics commonly ascribed to both women and men (see also Eagly et al., 2003; Yoder, 1983). However, Febbraro's (2003) study also provided evidence that cultural assimilation is still prevalent in the CF combat arms: That alongside a cultural change in the CF combat arms as a result of the presence of women or femininity, women are also assimilating to an existing culture in the combat arms. One piece of evidence concerns the negative implications that participants perceived in relation to female leaders who adopt feminine styles of leadership (or feminine characteristics exhibited by female leaders), such as lack of respect from peers/followers. For instance, participants warned against a female leader adopting feminine roles or a feminine physical appearance; they warned against a female leader being "sexually provocative" or being seen as a "sex object;" and they warned against a female leader being perceived as too caring or compassionate. Such warnings are reminiscent of the concerns of the female cadets studied by Yoder (1999) (see also Marshall, 1993). In contrast, and somewhat counter to what would be expected from role congruity theory (Eagly et al., 1995), relatively few of the participants anticipated any negative implications arising from a female leader exhibiting a masculine leadership style and/or masculine characteristics. The participants who did anticipate such negative implications warned against a female leader being too "loud or aggressive." Such findings suggest that perceptions of gender and leadership remain highly complex and gender-based in the military context and that dilemmas continue to figure prominently in the psychological experience of female leaders.

Gender and Harassment in the Military

Over the past several decades the reduction or elimination of various forms of discrimination against social groups and individuals has become both a social concern and a legal issue, especially in democratic societies (Holden & Davis, 2004). One of the more abhorrent forms of discrimination is harassment. Harassment is a particularly salient issue within military organizations, for, as we have seen, women and minority groups continue to be significantly under-represented in many areas, and their small numbers and relative newcomer status make them vulnerable to discrimination and harassment (Holden & Davis, 2004; Korabik, 2005). The psychological literature indicates that women in organizations whose workforce is primarily male-dominated, and in which job duties are stereotypically masculine, encounter greater problems with sexual harassment than do women whose workforce is female-dominated and stereotypically feminine. Indeed, the prevalence of sexual harassment has been found to be considerably higher for women who work in military organizations than for women who work in female-dominated occupations (Gill & Febbraro, 2008).

Workplaces that are male-dominated are more likely to emphasize sexual aggression and sexual posturing and to belittle femininity (see Crawford & Unger, 2000). For instance, male-dominated environments such as the military tend to be more physically hostile and intimidating than other work environments, and men are more likely to physically mark their work environment with sexually objectifying material, sexual comments, and sexual jokes (Gruber, 1998). In accordance with this, Corbett (2007) noted that many female soldiers have reported being sexually assaulted, harassed, and raped by fellow soldiers and officers. Sexual harassment can also be seen as an abuse of power, a reflection of the low status of women, and a means of social control. Because men generally have greater authority, status, and material power in the workplace, they are able to force their sexual attentions on women. Male-dominated organizations, such as the military, legitimize harassment by claiming that it is minor problem and by treating women who complain as though they are "crazy" (Crawford & Unger, 2000).

The focus of this section is on the gender-based harassment that has been experienced by military personnel in various nations. In particular, the experiences of military women with sexual harassment are discussed, along with the psychological implications of such experiences. Included also is a discussion of the harassment experiences of racial or ethnic minorities. Although there has been much discussion about the harassment experiences of US military women (e.g., Tailhook, the Iraq War) and at US military academies, recent cross-national research suggests the possibility that such incidents may be on the decline (Winslow et al., 2007). In addition, this section addresses the harassment experiences of military (heterosexual) men; that is, we will examine what, if any, research has been conducted in this area, and whether this may be a fruitful area for future research.

Harassment Experiences of Military Personnel

Throughout the 1980s and the 1990s, a number of policies, programs, and training initiatives to reduce or eliminate gender harassment were introduced into Western militaries. Surveys were designed to determine the experiences and perceptions of military members concerning harassment in order to provide a measure of the effectiveness of those policies and programs. Thus, over time, in certain Western militaries, indicators as to whether the reported rates of harassment have remained stable, decreased, or increased have begun to be established. Notwithstanding national differences in how harassment was defined and in survey methodology,[3] we offer an analysis of the results of surveys conducted in four nations: Australia, Canada, New Zealand, and the USA (see Holden & Davis,

---

[3] Although the countries used many identical and similar questionnaire items and agreed considerably on what types of behavior constitute harassment, they also varied in their definitions of harassment. Some of the surveys provided a definition of harassment, others provided a list of harassment behaviors, and some provided both a definition and a list of harassment behaviors. Some asked respondents directly if they have been harassed, which may provide a different or lower rate of sexual harassment than if respondents are asked if they have experienced any of a series of categories of unwanted sexual behaviors. Researchers in Australia, Canada, and the USA used definitions of the various forms of harassment but also a list of behaviors (Holden & Davis, 2004). The surveys also varied in terms of whether they were administered within certain service environments (navy, army, and air force), across defense forces as a whole (regular and reserve force personnel), across defense departments (military and civilian personnel), and in terms of the time frame over which harassment was reported, the location of the harassment, the activity during which the harassment occurred, and the status of the alleged offender (Holden & Davis, 2004).

2004, for more details). Holden and Davis (2004) drew a number of general conclusions discussed below on the basis of their examination of these studies, despite differences in methodologies and definitions across surveys.

In 1995 the *Australian Defence Force: Career and Family Study*, which was a replication of a 1987 study administered only to female military members, was conducted in order to assess the incidence of harassment in the Australian military. A comparison of the 1995 results to the 1987 results showed that that the incidence of all types of harassment of servicewomen had declined over the 8-year time period. The types of harassment included gender harassment/hostile workplace (the most frequently reported category of harassment, which fell from 40 to 34%), unwanted sexual attention (which fell from 24 to 15%), and sexual coercion (which fell from 2 to 1%). In the 1995 survey, which had been administered to 5,000 regular force men and women (with an overall response rate of 62%), 26% of men reported having experienced gender harassment/hostile workplace; 5% reported unwanted sexual attention; and 0.4% reported sexual coercion. In addition, analysis of a 1995 *Sexual Experiences Questionnaire* (SEQ), which measures five types of sexual harassment (gender harassment, seductive behavior, sexual bribery, sexual coercion, and sexual assault) showed that women were several times more likely than men to experience most harassment behaviors, but that up to 60% of men described offensive gender-related behaviors in their work environment. Further, the *Survey of Your Experiences of Unacceptable Behaviour in the Military* was administered to a sample of 5,000 Australian Defence Force (ADF) personnel (2,500 women and 2,500 men) in October 2000, with the SEQ to measure harassment behaviors (the overall response rate was 47.2%). Overall, 77.3% of female and 63.6% of male respondents indicated that they had experienced at least one of the behaviors listed on the SEQ. The survey also measured experience of unacceptable workplace behavior on the basis of 14 items that ranged from teasing to harassment based on skin color, religion, age, etc. Overall, 81.9% of female and 73.3% of male respondents reported having observed at least one of these behaviors in the previous 12 months.

In 1992, the CF administered a personal harassment survey to approximately 5,700 regular force members. This survey asked respondents whether or not they had experienced personal harassment, sexual harassment, or abuse of authority; respondents were also given a list of behaviors that could be considered harassing. Personal harassment was defined as unsolicited behavior by an individual that is directed at or is offensive to another individual based on personal characteristics, such as race, religion, gender, physical characteristics, or mannerisms, and that a reasonable person ought to have known would be unwelcome; it excludes sexual harassment. Sexual harassment was defined as a type of harassment that has a sexual purpose or is of a sexual nature, including, but not limited to, touching, leering, and the display of pornographic material. Abuse of authority was defined as the misuse of authority to undermine, sabotage, or otherwise interfere with the career of another individual, including, but not limited to, intimidation, threats, blackmail, coercion, or unfairness in the distribution of work assignments, in the provision of training or promotional opportunities, or in the provision of job references. Of the almost 73% who responded, 26.2% of women and 2% of men believed that they had been subjected to sexual harassment; 32.6% of women and 19.4% of men believed that they had been subjected to personal harassment; and 31.5% of women and 28.9% of men believed that they had been subjected to abuse of authority while performing CF duties during the past 12 months.

A follow-up harassment survey was conducted in 1998, which replicated many of the questions asked in 1992 and included a fourth type of harassment – hazing. Hazing was defined as any activity that is part of an initiation ceremony or rite of passage that offends, demeans, belittles, or humiliates those who participate; it might include, but is not limited to, bullying. The 1998 survey was administered to a sample of 2,290 regular and reserve force members and 2,340 CF personnel undergoing qualification and pre-qualification training. For the regular force, 39% of women and 24% of men in the CF reported having experienced one or more of the four types of harassment examined. For the reserve personnel, about 30% of women and 20% of men reported having experienced any of the four types of harassment in the last 12 months. For the training sample, 28% of women and 16% of men reported having experienced some form of harassment in the past 12 months. A comparison of the results for the regular force from 1992 to 1998 shows a decline in the incidence of abuse of authority, personal harassment, and sexual harassment. The most notable decline for women was in the rate of sexual harassment, from 26% in 1992 to 14% in 1998 (personal harassment reported by women declined from 32.6% in 1992 to 30% in 1998; abuse of authority reported by women declined from 31.5% in 1992 to 29% in 1998). The incidence of harassment generally decreased for men as well (for personal harassment, from 19.4% in 1992 to 14% in 1998, and for abuse of authority, from 28.9% in 1992 to 19% in 1998). However, the incidence of sexual harassment reported by men increased from 2% in 1992 to 3% in 1998, although such a small difference was probably due to random error.

In 1995 a harassment survey was created by the New Zealand Defence Force (NZDF) based on the CF Personal Harassment Questionnaire and the US Department of Defense (DoD) Harassment Survey. The survey was sent out to 10% of the military and civilian populations; approximately 1,160 people were sent the survey, and the response rate was 80%. Results indicate that women experienced relatively greater levels of general harassment based on gender, harassment of a sexual nature, and harassment based on physical characteristics. Also, proportionately more women than men reported having experienced sexually harassing behaviors; approximately 30% of women had experienced sexual teasing, and between 13 and 20% (depending on the service) reported having experienced unwelcome or offensive touching, leaning over, or pinching.

As indicated earlier, there has been much discussion about the harassment experiences of US military women (e.g., Tailhook, the Iraq War) and at US military academies. For example, in 1991 a major scandal (referred to as the US Navy's Tailhook scandal) occurred at the convention of navy fighter pilots in Las Vegas, Nevada. Male pilots sexually assaulted female Navy personnel and brought national shame to the navy (see Moskos, 2007). In 1996, incidents of male sergeants sexually harassing female recruits in training camps shook the army. Shortly thereafter, charges of sexual abuse were brought against an army sergeant major (who was subsequently found not guilty). In 2005, a national commission was established to examine reports of widespread sexual harassment in the military academies. Yet, ironically, these scandals also provided an impetus for the opening up of roles for women; for instance, the 1991 Tailhook scandal at the navy pilots' convention facilitated the opening up of combat aircraft and warships to women (Moskos, 2007).

The US 1995 Department of Defense Sexual Harassment Survey consisted of three forms: Form A, which produced the first baseline data on sexual harassment in the active duty services, was sent to over 30,000 personnel in 1995 and was completed by 46%. Results indicate a decline in self-reported sexual harassment from 1988 to 1995. In 1988, 64% of active duty military women and 17% of active duty military men reported having experienced unwanted, uninvited sexual attention while at work in the year prior to the survey, as compared to the 55% of women and 14% of men who reported this in 1995. Form B of the survey was sent to over 50,000 personnel, and 58% responded. Results indicate that 78% of women and 38% of men reported having experienced one or more of the harassment behaviors listed in the survey during the previous 12 months. However, when respondents were asked whether they had considered any of the behaviors that they experienced to be sexual harassment, about one-third of the women and nearly three-quarters of the men said that none of their experiences constituted harassment (Holden & Davis, 2004). This may be because such behaviors have been normalized within North American culture (Crawford & Unger, 2000).

The 1996 US Armed Forces Equal Opportunity Survey (AFEOS) was administered to over 76,000 personnel in all ranks in the army, navy, Marine Corps, air force, and coast guard; the usable return rate was 53% (Holden & Davis, 2004). Overall, 81% of junior enlisted, 76% of senior enlisted, and 67% of officers indicated that, in the previous year, they or their family had experienced one of the 42 potential incidents related to racial or ethnic harassment or discrimination. Although members of all racial and ethnic groups perceived insensitivity, harassment, and discrimination, members of minority racial and ethnic groups (Black, Hispanic, Asian/Pacific Islander, and Native Americans/Alaskan Natives) indicated that they had encountered more of these types of problems than White respondents did. Women and men were equally likely to report having experienced at least 1 of 10 behaviors identified as an "offensive encounter" (66 and 64%, respectively), behaviors that most closely paralleled the unwanted or uninvited behaviors described in the 1995 DoD Sexual Harassment Survey. Although there were variations in the proportions of men and women who reported an offensive encounter among different racial or ethnic groups, overall, junior enlisted members were most likely to report offensive encounters (74%), followed by senior enlisted members (67%), and officers (49%).

The US Naval Equal Opportunity and Sexual Harassment Survey (NEOSH) was administered in the navy every other year between 1989 and 1999. Stratified random samples of active duty enlisted and officer personnel were identified for all surveys to allow for comparison of the data over 10 years. Response rates were 60% in 1989, 48% in 1991, 41% in 1993, 40% in 1995, 45% in 1997, and 30% in 1999/2000. In the 1989 survey, 42% of enlisted women and 26% of female officers reported that they had been sexually harassed during the 1-year survey period while on duty on a base or ship or while off duty. In comparison, 4% of enlisted men and 1% of male officers reported having being sexually harassed during the same period. A comparison of the results of the 1989 and 1991 surveys showed a statistically significant increase in the percentage of female officers and enlisted men who reported having been harassed. The 1991 survey showed that 44% of enlisted women, 33% of female officers, 8% of the enlisted men, and 2% of the male officers reported that they had been sexually harassed during the 1-year period.

By 1997, however, survey findings of self-reported sexual harassment were significantly lower than the 1989 and 1991 findings for enlisted women and female officers: 23% of enlisted women and 13% of female officers reported having experienced sexual harassment behavior, an absolute decrease of 21% for enlisted women and 20% for female officers over the 6-year period between 1991 and 1997. The self-reported incident rate for male officers declined and remained steady at 1% for the 1995 and 1997 surveys, and the incident rates for male enlisted members decreased to 3% in 1995 and remained at 3% in 1997. Responses to the 1999/2000 NEOSH survey reflect a lower percentage of respondents who reported experiences of harassment in the past 12 months compared to previous baseline rates, and there was a significant decline among the female officers who reported sexual harassment by senior supervisors.

The 1995, 1997, and 1999/2000 NEOSH surveys also asked respondents about experiences of racial or ethnic and gender discrimination during the previous 12 months. Results showed that Black enlisted respondents were the most likely to report experiences of racial or ethnic discrimination (41% in 1995, 34% in 1997), and White officers were the least likely to report racial or ethnic discrimination (5% in 1995 and 1997). Enlisted women were the most likely to report experience of gender discrimination (43% in 1995 and 36% in 1997), and male officers were the least likely to report experience of gender discrimination (4% in 1995, 5% in 1997). Overall, experiences of discrimination declined among all personnel from 1995 to 1997, with the exception of male officers, whose self-reports reflected a slight increase in gender discrimination. However, initial results of the 1999/2000 NEOSH surveys indicate that racial minorities had not experienced a decline in certain racial discrimination behaviors, and approximately one-third of enlisted women and female officers continued to report gender discrimination (Holden & Davis, 2004).

Conclusions from the Harassment Surveys

The results of the harassment surveys show both converging and diverging themes. First, there seems to be general agreement across nations and militaries as to what constitutes harassment, and the incidence of some forms of harassment has been sufficiently high as to represent a significant problem for all of the militaries studied (Holden & Davis, 2004). Further, the most recent results from each of the four nations indicate that the forms of sexual harassment most and least commonly experienced are similar in each nation. Of those who reported having experienced harassment, up to 86% reported having experienced it in the form of jokes, comments, teasing, and questions. On the other hand, actual or attempted rape, sexual assault, and violence were the least likely to be reported. Although the incident rates in this area were quite low (from less than 1 to 3.7%), all nations reported some of these serious harassment behaviors.

Further, reported harassment rates varied considerably, depending on the type of harassment being measured, the demographic characteristics of the respondent (such as gender and military rank), when the survey was administered, and the nation. At one end of the spectrum, 0.4% of male respondents in the ADF in 1994 reported experience of sexual coercion, whereas 64% of female respondents in the USA in 1988 reported experiences of unwanted, uninvited, sexual attention. The available data consistently show that proportionately more women than men are subjected to various forms of harassment.

Survey results also indicate an overall decrease in the reported incident rates of harassment, for both women and men, throughout the 1990 s. Overall absolute decreases in reported incident rates of harassment could be due to a number of factors, including greater emphasis on harassment prevention programs, the creation and implementation of anti-harassment policies, and the visible commitment of senior leadership to eradicate harassment from the military environment. On the other hand, lower rates of reported harassment may also result from fear of the consequences of reporting or lack of confidence that military leadership will effectively and fairly address harassment in the military work environment (Holden & Davis, 2004). For instance, the literature suggests that a decrease in harassment reports may be attributed to fear of losing one's job, being derogated by colleagues, being labeled as a troublemaker, or believing that the formal complaint process will be counterproductive. Indeed, research indicates that women who use the sexual harassment label are often blamed for the incident and their reports are perceived as untrustworthy (Marin & Guadagno, 1999). Thus, it is estimated that 69–90% of sexual assaults in the military go unreported and that reports of sexual abuse are often rebuffed by military officials (Hunter, 2008; Lyons, 2008). Furthermore, more recent statistics suggest that 23–41% of US female troops/veterans reported having experienced physical sexual assault (Hunter, 2008; Lyons, 2008), which challenges the notion that sexual harassment (at least in the US military) is necessarily on the decline.

Furthermore, women who report sexual harassment may be denigrated for violating gender norms and role expectations, where characteristics such as passivity and nurturance are stereotypically associated with the feminine gender role and independence or assertiveness are stereotypically associated with the masculine gender role (Bem, 1974). It may be more consistent with gender-role expectations for women to accept and respond passively to sexually aggressive behavior from men. Women who violate gender-role expectancies by demonstrating stereotypic masculine characteristics tend to be targets for sexual harassment; for instance, Berdahl (2007) found that, among women who worked in male-dominated jobs, those who had relatively masculine personality characteristics, experienced greater sexual harassment than women who had more feminine characteristics. The more women deviated from traditional gender roles and characteristics, the more they were targeted for sexual harassment. In addition, women who report sexual harassment may violate gender-role expectancies for what constitutes a "good" employee (Marin & Guadagno, 1999). For instance, success in jobs may involve conforming to social rules and norms in order to avoid conflicts. Women who report and label sexual harassment risk being labeled a troublemaker or viewed as an employee who is not a "team player."

In terms of implications for job-related operations, research indicates that sexual harassment may lead to lower satisfaction with colleagues and supervisors, lower commitment to the military, lower work productivity, and lower general job performance (Gill & Febbraro, 2008). For instance, Magley, Waldo, Drasgow, and Fitzgerald (1999) found that women in the US military who had experienced unwanted gender-related behaviors were less satisfied with their work, co-workers, and supervisors; less committed to the military; and less productive. The researchers also found that women's psychological well-being suffered as they reported greater anxiety and depression, which contributed to lower work productivity. In the literature, sexual harassment has consistently been found to have adverse effects on job satisfaction and organizational commitment (Dansky & Kilpatrick, 1997; Fitzgerald, Drasgow, & Magley, 1999; Munson, Miner, & Hulin, 2001; Schneider, Swan, & Fitzgerald, 1997).

A recent study of perceptions and experiences of sexual harassment among 26 women in the CF regular force combat arms indicates that six of the women, who were NCMs, did not feel safe reporting harassment and believed that when harassment is reported it will be dismissed (Gill & Febbraro, 2008). They also revealed that, when a woman reports harassment, she is blamed for the incident. Harassment was also noted as expected by women in male-dominated fields. These results suggest that, although military organizations have made strides in dealing with sexual harassment, there is a need to create an environment for women in the military that facilitates the harassment reporting process so that complainants do not experience negative consequences that interfere with their work productivity and feelings of safety (Gill & Febbraro, 2008).

Indeed, other research suggests that serious psychological consequences may result from experiences of harassment. Targets of sexual harassment report fear, anger, self-questioning, and self-blame (Koss, 1990). Women frequently describe the experience of harassment as degrading, disgusting, and humiliating (Crawford & Unger, 2000). Women who are sexually harassed report more negative psychological symptoms than do other women, including anxiety, depression, decreased satisfaction with life, and greater symptoms of post-traumatic stress disorder (PTSD; see also Koss, 1990). They may also suffer lowered self-esteem, impaired social relationships, and overall lowered satisfaction with their lives. Further, Hunter (2008) and Lyons (2008) noted that military sexual assaults led to PTSD in more cases (60%) than other types of trauma (42%) and that women who experienced military sexual assault were three times more likely to have PTSD than women who were sexually assaulted in other contexts (e.g., childhood, civilian) and nine times more likely than women who had no sexual assault history. Further, sexual harassment need not be severe to have negative consequences; college women who were sexually harassed, even at "low levels," reported more negative feelings about themselves, their peers, their professors, and the campus, felt less competent academically, and were more likely to leave school than women who were not harassed. The economic costs of sexual harassment can also be quite high and may include, for example, higher levels of absenteeism and a greater desire to leave the company. Women who have been sexually harassed have been found to be less satisfied with their work, their co-workers, and their supervisors (Crawford & Unger, 2000).

It is clear, therefore, that sexual harassment may result in various forms of disrupted psychological well-being for women. In addition to the fact that women are generally more likely than men to experience harassment, there are other important gender differences (or gender-related trends) that also need to be taken into account in considering harassment, particularly in the military context. One difference between male and female *perpetrators* of harassment is their status. Men who harass are likely to be in supervisory positions and thus have power over the women whom they harass, but women who initiate harassment typically do not occupy such positions, giving them relatively little power to demand or coerce sexual favors from the men with whom they work. In other words, men who are harassed by women are generally not at risk of losing their careers because of the sexual behavior of women at work. Women's careers, on the other hand, are more often endangered by sexual harassment. Indeed, over 30% of employed women have experienced some negative job consequences as a result of sexual harassment, compared to around 10% of men (Gutek, 1985). These problems included quitting their jobs, asking for transfers, or losing their jobs for refusing to have sex with employers or supervisors (Brannon, 1999).

To date, however, there has been comparatively little research on the impact of sexual harassment on men's psychological health, particularly in the military context, or on the harassment of gay men and lesbians in the military. These are clearly areas in need of further research. For example, a survey of employed men and women revealed that a certain form of gender harassment was reported by men but not by women: This type of harassment came from other men and involved comments about the target man not living up to standards of manliness by showing too much concern or sympathy for women. That is, a man who failed to share a joke that is derogatory toward women might be censured by other men who enjoyed the joke (Brannon, 1999). Furthermore, it has been estimated that 9% of male military members may be victims of sexual assault (Hunter, 2008; Lyons, 2008), which suggests that the harassment of military men may be *more* prevalent than indicated in earlier surveys. Perhaps the military's attention to it and the enhanced training has helped men to recognize and label their experiences as harassment.

Work–Family Issues in the Military

Research on work–family issues in the military suggests that balancing work and family with a military career continues to be a challenge, particularly for military women. Research on women in the CF, for example, has indicated that women are more likely than men to leave the CF due to difficulties in balancing work and family responsibilities (see Bourgon, 2007; Pickering, 2006). Similarly, research conducted in the USA indicates that military women often face similar difficulties because of their role as mothers (Ganderton, 2002; Holden & Tanner, 2001; Thomas, 1997; Vinokur, Pierce, & Buck, 1999). Indeed, many military and feminist theorists have argued that the military constitutes a "total institution" that views its demands as superceding any competing family or personal needs. Similarly, Segal (1986) has described both work and family as "greedy institutions" that compete for the commitment, loyalty, time, and energy of their members and that place military women, in particular, in a tenuous position of sacrifice and compromise between the two roles (see also Albano, 1994; Bourg & Segal, 1999; Bowen, Orthner, & Zimmerman, 1993; McFadyen, Kerpelman, & Adler-Baeder, 2005; Vinokur et al., 1999). Thus, according to results from the Canadian Forces Attrition Information Questionnaire (CFAIQ), which collected CF attrition data from 1992 to 1999, key factors associated with decisions to leave the CF were issues related to workplace fairness, family, civilian opportunities, career issues, and posting issues. Although family issues such as separation and stability were of concern to 18–20% of navy, army, and air force respondents, these concerns, as well as staying home to raise a family, dominated the decisions by women, in particular, to leave the military. More recent data suggest that, in about two-thirds of cases, family reasons figure prominently in the decisions of women to leave the Canadian military (Bourgon, 2007).

Below we explore some of the issues involved in balancing work and family in the military context, primarily from a North American perspective. However, the section also includes a cross-national comparison of work–family policies in the militaries of different nations, which indicates that there is a great deal of diversity in the policies of different nations with respect to work and family issues. Some nations offer many more family-supportive policies and programs to their military personnel than others do. Comprehensive family programs, which recognize the increasing diversity of military service members and the evolving nature of military families, are necessary to maintain combat readiness and to continue to recruit and retain highly skilled personnel, both women and men (Febbraro, in press).

Balancing Work and Family in the Military Context

To date, a great deal of psychological research suggests that various types of family-supportive programs and policies in the workplace (including the military) have a positive impact on productivity, job satisfaction, and organizational commitment. Research also indicates that a supportive supervisor or leader is significantly related to higher job satisfaction, fewer problems with childcare, less work-to-family interference, and less stress (Bourg & Segal, 1999; Britt & Dawson, 2005). Further, support from partners, friends, and relatives is associated with lower levels of depressive symptoms and less perceived stress among military women (Kelley et al., 2002), and it is also associated with women's decisions to join the military (Tanner, 1999). Similarly, a spouse's attitudes toward military service have been related to the recruitment, retention, morale, and commitment of married military members (Bourg & Segal, 1999).

In the Canadian military, there are concerns that not enough is being to improve overall family support (Ganderton, 2002). Duxbury and Higgins (2001) conducted a large-scale survey on work–life balance in the Canadian Department of National Defence (DND) and found that 44% of CF members, but only 14% of civilian employees, reported that work interferes with family. When asked whether DND's environment supports work–life balance, only 25% of the CF respondents agreed with this statement, but only 40% of DND civilian employees did. Unlike for civilian personnel, the CF has no formal policy for telework or compressed work weeks for military personnel. As Ganderton (2002) explained, this approach reflects a military culture that places a high value on "face time" at the workplace and that remains skeptical of both the capability for and the optics of individual off-site productivity (i.e., co-workers often believe that teleworkers are not really working or are working less than those who work on-site). Thus, a recent study of perceptions of quality-of-life initiatives among 2,847 CF members identified family as a factor that the CF needs to address in order to improve quality of life for CF members and their families (Jeffries, 2001). For example, CF members thought that more choice in postings, and longer postings, could benefit the family and increase family stability. Thus, although a number of quality of life or "family-friendly" policies have been instituted in the CF (see Holden & Tanner, 2001),[4] such policies often are not implemented

---

[4] For example, the CF provides a Military Family Support Program (MFSP) at all locations where a significant number of Canadian military families are stationed. This program promotes health and social well-being; provides needed information and referral; assists in the prevention of individual, family, and community breakdown; buffers lifestyle stresses; enhances coping skills; and aids individuals or families in distress. Similarly, Military Family Resource Centres (MFRCs) have been established that employ child care coordinators who are responsible for coordinating child care services and emergency child care requirements; for screening caregivers and other facilities; for liaising with the community; and for providing enhanced child care options and information to families (Holden & Tanner, 2001). There is also a Family Care Assistance (FCA) program that provides financial assistance to single-parent families and to service couples who are required by the CF to be absent from home at the same time (Holden & Tanner, 2001).

consistently, and individuals are frequently dependent on the willingness of their superiors to grant them (Holden & Tanner, 2001).

Febbraro's (2003) study of women in the CF combat arms showed some of the difficulties that military women face in balancing work and family. Several participants in the study spoke of the difficulties of balancing family life with the demands of military life. In fact, some attributed military women's higher attrition to the difficulties associated with balancing work and family. This echoes previous research that shows the role of work–family conflict in the attrition of military women (see Ganderton, 2002). Some participants expressed concerns about the impact of taking a full year of maternity leave, or of pregnancy itself, on one's career, and several participants spoke about the difficult sacrifices that a military career can demand from a family. Regarding perceptions of the level of support from the CF for family concerns, some of the women in Febbraro's study, particularly NCMs, perceived a lack of support for family from the CF, despite the CF's official family-supportive stance.

These findings raise concerns in light of previous research that suggests the importance of various types of family-supportive programs and policies in terms of their positive effects on productivity, job satisfaction, time spent on the job, absenteeism, turnover, use of sick leave, organizational commitment, and organizational effectiveness (Bourg & Segal, 1999; Ganderton, 2002). Furthermore, previous research has shown that perceptions of the degree to which the military is supportive of families affects adaptation to and satisfaction with military life in general and with specific demands of the military lifestyle, such as deployment separation (Bourg & Segal, 1999). Work–life imbalance associated with role overload and work-to-family interference, on the other hand, brings with it increased stress levels, physical health problems, and decreased work and global life satisfaction levels, all of which erode personal productivity, commitment, and, ultimately, retention, and overall force readiness (Ganderton, 2002). Indeed, McCreary, Thompson, and Pastò (2003) found, in a sample of CF personnel, that family concerns were associated with all measured dimensions of psychological well-being, including depression, hyper-alertness, anxiety, and somatic complaints. Work–life balance initiatives can help to reverse these trends and thus increase overall retention and recruitment, as well as gender integration (Ganderton, 2002). All in all, Bourg and Segal (1999) suggested that responsiveness to families on the part of the military will lessen the degree of conflict between the two "greedy" institutions of the military and the family.

Work–Family Policies in the Militaries of Various Countries

In recent years, the civilian world has sought to address the challenge of balancing work and family by introducing a broad range of work–life balance initiatives, including telework (working from home or a remote office), flextime (changing the start and end times of the work day), job sharing (sharing a full-time position with another employee), compressed work week (working full-time hours in fewer than 5 days), and part-time work (reducing the number of hours worked each day or week) (Ganderton, 2002). Other offerings in the civilian context include paid leave days for personal/family reasons, on-site or subsidized child care, eldercare services, employee assistance programs, and leaves of absence for maternity, professional development, or personal sabbaticals (Ganderton, 2002). Although not all programs would fit within the operational context of all organizations or be suitable for all occupations – and, indeed, there are limits on what is practically feasible in the military – it is nevertheless important that organizations such as the military develop workplace programs that respond to pervasive employee/member needs or provide a menu of optional benefits that can respond to individual needs for work–life balance (Ganderton, 2002). Further, a flexible portfolio of initiatives could respond to a diverse range of needs of single, married, and common-law personnel, with or without children, both women and men (Ganderton, 2002).

According to the recent report by the Committee on Women in the NATO Forces (CWINF, 2003), a challenge for many military families is finding suitable care for their children during times of deployment. Some countries address this issue by offering relatives free travel to help care for children or offering to send children to relatives without any costs to the family. Some countries offer workplace kindergarten care for members' children and allow members to work from home to help alleviate stress, and a number of countries offer their members the option of working flexible hours and have instituted flexible career options. Still other nations offer a "regionalized commitment" to their military members that allows them to remain in a specific posting for a period of time. This gives members and their families greater stability and has had the effect of greater retention. In addition, allowing service couples to serve together (e.g., to be posted together and/or posted close to family), increasing the number and access to child care facilities, and offering a children's education allowance are some of the other actions taken by many NATO countries to retain members. Further, the majority of NATO nations have instituted some type of program or policy concerning maternity/parental leave, flexible work arrangements (e.g., flextime, career breaks for child care or professional development, part-time work, a reduction of the work day for childcare, breastfeeding leave), child care, gender awareness policies and programs, and equality of treatment (CWINF, 2003). Other family supportive policies and practices include allowing military personnel time off for family emergencies and non-emergency family activities (e.g., children's school events), encouraging and supporting family-oriented work unit activities, providing a means for deployed soldiers to communicate with their families, providing relocation assistance, and informing soldiers and spouses about spouse employment programs (Bourg & Segal, 1999). These programs and policies demonstrate that, although practical and operational constraints must be considered, modern militaries can provide a wide range of work–family balance initiatives for their members.[5] As Kelley and colleagues (2002) have argued, it is important to develop a military culture that recognizes and respects family responsibilities as well as the evolving and diverse nature of military families.

Gay Men and Lesbians in the Military

Since the 1980 s the position of gay men and lesbians in the military has been the subject of debate and research. In terms of civil/human rights and identity politics, there have been clear parallels with the position of women in the military. On the other hand, gay men and lesbians have still had to fight their own struggle in order to gain legal access to military forces. Although, they have generally been successful in doing so, their daily lives as enlisted and officers have not been free from prejudice and discrimination. This section of the chapter focuses on issues of specific concern to gay men and lesbians in the military. In particular, we examine the policies of different nations toward the service of gay men and lesbians in the military and, more important, the psychological assumptions that underlie these policies. For instance, the US government does not currently allow gay men and lesbians to serve openly in the military, and follows a "don't ask, don't tell" policy, in part because of assumptions made about differences between the psychological nature of gay men and lesbians compared to heterosexual men and women and about the impact of these assumed differences on unit cohesion and operational effectiveness. Even in countries where "don't ask, don't tell" is not the official policy, it may be perceived by the parties involved as the preferred coping strategy (Soeters & van der Meulen, 2007).

---

[5]For more details on the policies and programs of NATO nations, see Committee on Women in NATO Nations (2003).

Cross-National Comparisons of Policies Concerning Lesbians and Gay Men in the Military

Through most of the history of the Canadian military, homosexuals were classified as deviants and were considered a threat to good order and discipline. In 1967, sexual relations between same-gender consenting adults ceased to be a criminal offense. However, until the mid-1970 s the process for disposal of homosexual cases remained virtually unchanged (Pinch, 1984). The 1985 review of the equal rights provision of the Charter of Human Rights and Freedoms, which found the CF as potentially in violation, was responsible for 6 years of study and debate over the issue of lesbians and gay men in the military. Surveys of the CF about the impact of allowing homosexuals to serve were conducted in 1986 and 1991; the results showed that military personnel, especially men, were against the lifting of the ban. Male personnel were negative about all aspects of service with homosexuals. Most said that they would refuse to share living accommodations with known homosexuals, and many, particularly those in combat units, said that they would refuse to work with individuals who were openly homosexual (Gade, Segal, & Johnson, 1996). Despite CF resistance to the presence of lesbians and gay men, the Canadian Federal Court concluded that there was no compelling evidence for the ban and determined that the CF was in violation of the Charter of Rights and Freedoms by restricting the military service of homosexuals. The CF complied with the court's decision and lifted the ban on homosexuals in 1992. The integration of lesbians and gay men into the CF has been a relative success, in part because the approach was deliberately low-key (Gade et al., 1996).

So far, the policy changes and their practical implementation seem to have progressed smoothly. None of the dire predictions about performance, recruitment, retention, and violent reactions have proven correct. Part of the reason for the successful implementation was the immediate and full support of the policy change by the leaders in the Department of National Defence and the CF (Gade et al., 1996). In addition, in contrast to the issue of gender integration, special attention was directed away from homosexuals, rather than toward them as a special case. Still, findings from the 2004 Army Culture and Climate Survey and the 2003 CROP Army Organizational Culture Survey (Capstick, Farley, Wild, & Parkes, 2005) suggest that, although diversity is generally accepted in the army, a large segment of army men, in particular, indicate that lesbians and gay men are not acceptable as workmates, which suggests that attitudinal barriers may still be prevalent.

The situation for gay men and lesbians in the military is often even more difficult. In the Brazilian military, although homosexual behavior is no longer legally punishable, gay men and lesbians are seen as victims of a behavioral deviation that threatens the technical and moral functioning of the military institution. Gay men, for instance, are seen as unable to control their impulses or to respect moral precedents conducive to a profession (see Castro, 2007). In South Africa, homosexuality is legally permitted, but negative attitudes still prevail (Heinecken, 2007). A recent survey showed that substantial prejudice and stereotypes regarding gay men and lesbians continue to exist. These range from concerns about the impact that homosexuals may have on the spread of HIV/AIDS, possible abuse of authority (seniors harassing juniors), the impact that "openly gay" personnel may have on morale, and the impact on combat effectiveness, the sharing of facilities, and issues of morality. Most of those surveyed thought that homosexuals are still "in the closet" because they are afraid of being rejected, oppressed, victimized, criticized, or publicly judged. To address these negative attitudes, it has been recommended that more needs to be done to remove stereotypes and misperceptions about homosexuality in the SANDF through awareness campaigns (Heinecken, 2007).

In the USA, the "don't ask, don't tell" policy regarding gay men and lesbians is based on the belief that a lifting of the ban on gay men and lesbians in the military would undermine unit cohesion and operational readiness, result in an increase in violence, and lead to a lessening of the privacy rights of straight soldiers. Further, each one of these beliefs reflects assumptions about fundamental differences between the psychological nature of gays men and lesbians compared to heterosexual men and women. In contrast, however, empirical research conducted in the militaries of 24 countries that have lifted their bans on gay men and lesbians has shown that the lifting of bans has not resulted in any of those consequences (Belkin & Bateman, 2003). Further, psychological research does not support the notion of fundamental psychological differences between homosexuals and heterosexuals (Crawford & Unger, 2000).

In most European countries, homosexuality is not subject to punishment. However, the personnel management of the German Bundeswher long assumed that a gay soldier would be restricted in aptitude and capacity for duty and that a gay officer would negatively influence the troops' operational readiness and discipline. In the past this meant that most homosexuals, though liable to conscription, were not called to arms if their sexual orientation became known and that volunteers were refused if they confessed their homosexuality during their preliminary medical examination. If a soldier's homosexuality was revealed while in a position of authority, it usually meant the loss of a command status. This situation changed in 2000 when it was declared by the German government that homosexuality no longer justified restrictions with regard to a soldier's employment and status. This does not mean, however, that the issue of homosexuality in the German military has been solved completely, as there is still a great deal of uncertainty with regard to the "correct behavior" toward homosexuals, and great efforts will be needed to reduce homophobic attitudes among soldiers (Biehl, Klein, & Kümmel, 2007).

In contrast to many other nations, in Belgium, the official policy regarding lesbians and gay men in the military is one of respecting people's diverse sexual orientations. There are examples of lesbians and gay men of all ranks who have publicly come out and affirmed their sexual orientations. There is also at least one case of a transsexual non-commissioned officer (NCO) who, while on active duty, underwent surgery (reimbursed by social security) in order to become a woman and then remained in her position. The head of her service informed her colleagues of her operation in order to smooth her integration. At the time of this writing this individual is still working in the same service with the same colleagues, apparently without any major problems (Manigart, 2007).

Integrative Summary, Conclusions, and Future Research Directions

In this chapter, we have identified a number of themes pertaining to selected topics in the field of gender and military psychology. Along with these themes, a number of suggestions for future research are suggested in the areas of gender and military career segregation; gender and military career progression; gender and harassment in the military; work–family issues in the military; and gay men and lesbians in the military.

First, military women still appear to be concentrated in the traditional military occupational categories, such as health-related support roles, and, in some nations, notably the USA and UK, women are still excluded from frontline combat. Second, although evidence suggests that the representation of women in the militaries of many Western countries is increasing, there is also evidence of a persistent gender-based glass ceiling: Women are less likely than men to reach the most senior military ranks, and women's promotion rates still tend to be lower than men's. Future researchers will need to investigate the factors involved in these gender differences in promotion rates, and studies will be needed to track changes in patterns of gender-related career progression and occupational segregation. In addition, future researchers should examine the pattern of over-representation and under-representation of African Americans (both men and women) in the US military, depending on service and rank, and should address the question of why, for instance, attrition is so high among White women in the US military.

The third area explored in this chapter pertains to gender harassment in the military. Evidence suggests that such harassment (especially sexual harassment) may be decreasing. Yet, harassment, in its many forms, is still an issue for the militaries of many nations. In particular, research is lacking on the effects of gender harassment on military men, and relatively little systematic research has been conducted on the harassment of gays and lesbians. These are areas that clearly warrant future research. In addition, research on contra-power harassment in the military context, in which subordinates harass superiors is needed, as this type of harassment affects both male and female supervisors (Clapp, Chrisler, & Devlin, 2008).

The fourth area examined in this chapter involved the difficulties associated with balancing military work and family. Although many nations have made progress in terms of developing "family-friendly" policies for military personnel, challenges remain. Many countries are still lacking in the development of a comprehensive, yet flexible, set of work–family policies. Moreover, there are indications that simply having formal work–family policies are not enough – that there are gaps between formal and informal organizational policies, or between *policies* and *practice* (Bourg & Segal, 1999). In particular, future researchers should focus on the development, implementation, and evaluation of innovative work–family policies, as well as their actual use, as these will be critical to the policies' success. This will involve a better understanding of military culture and of how that culture facilitates or hinders work–family balance. In addition, future researchers should explore work–family issues for military men, as research is lacking in this area.

The final topic addressed in this chapter concerns gay men and lesbians in the military. It is clear that policies that exclude gay men and lesbians from military service (or prejudices against lesbians and gay men) are based on fundamental assumptions about gender and gender-appropriate behavior. It has been argued that such assumptions ultimately rest upon problematic, empirically unsupported notions about the dichotomous nature of masculinity and femininity, about the nature and sexual behavior of gay men and lesbians, and about the effects on operational cohesion of allowing gay men and lesbians to serve openly in the military. Future researchers should focus on efforts to reduce or eliminate prejudice against lesbians and gay men within patriarchal, heterosexist cultures and institutions, including military institutions. For instance, the highlighting of cross-national research that demonstrates the *lack* of negative effects associated with the presence of lesbians and gay men the military (e.g., Belkin & Bateman, 2003) can play a role in reducing such prejudice.

It is clear from the psychological research reviewed in this chapter that gender differences, when they are found in a military context, are not inherent, timeless, or universal, but rather are a function of social, cultural, societal, national, and historical arrangements and practices. Similarly, military organizations themselves are changing and evolving, not static or monolithic, entities. Thus, it is anticipated that a future chapter on gender and military psychology will reflect changes in such arrangements, practices, and contexts and will draw new psychological insights and conclusions about gender in the military context.

References

Adams, J. (1984). Women at West Point: A three-year perspective. *Sex Roles, 11*, 525–541.
Albano, S. (1994). Military recognition of family concerns: Revolutionary war to 1993. *Armed Forces & Society, 20*, 283–302.
Bakan, D. (1966). *The duality of human existence*. Chicago: Rand McNally.
Bales, R. F. (1950). *Interaction process analysis: A method for the study of small groups*. Reading, MA: Addison-Wesley.
Bayer, B., & Malone, K. R. (1998). Feminism, psychology, and matters of the body. In H. J. Stam (Ed.), *The body and psychology* (pp. 94–199). London: Sage.

Belkin, A., & Bateman, G. (Eds.). (2003). *Don't ask, don't tell: Exploring the debates on the gay ban in the U.S. Military.* Boulder, CO: Lynne Rienner.

Bem, S. L. (1974). The measurement of psychological androgyny. *Journal of Consulting and Clinical Psychology, 42,* 155–162.

Bender, P., Tanner, L., & Tseng, S. (1995a). *A preliminary analysis of career progression of female officers in the Canadian Forces* (PRT Research Note 3/95). Ottawa: Department of National Defence.

Bender, P., Tanner, L., & Tseng, S. (1995b). *A preliminary analysis of career progression of female NCMs in the Canadian Forces* (PRT Research Note 4/95). Ottawa: Department of National Defence.

Berdahl, J. (2007). The sexual harassment of uppity women. *Journal of Applied Psychology, 92*(2), 425–437.

Biehl, H., Klein, P., & Kümmel, G. (2007). Diversity in the German armed forces. In J. Soeters & J. van der Meulen (Eds.), *Cultural diversity in the armed forces: An international comparison* (pp.171–184). London: Routledge.

Boldy, J., Wood, W., & Kashy, D. A. (2001). Gender stereotypes and the evaluation of men and women in military training. *Journal of Social Issues, 57,* 689–705.

Boldry, J., Wood, W., & Kashy, D. A. (2001). Gender stereotypes and the evaluation of men and women in military training. *Journal of Social Issues, 57*(4), 689–705.

Bourg, C., & Segal, M. (1999). The impact of family supportive policies and practices on organizational commitment to the Army. *Armed Forces & Society, 25,* 633–652.

Bourgon, L. (2007). *The CF as employer of choice: The key for successful gender integration.* Kingston: Canadian Forces College.

Bowen, G. L., Orthner, D. K., & Zimmerman, L. I. (1993). Family adaptation of single parents in the United States Army: An empirical analysis of work stressors and adaptive resources. *Family Relations, 42,* 293–304.

Boyce, L. A. & Herd, A. M. (2003). The relationship between gender role stereotypes and requisite military leadership characteristics. *Sex Roles, 49,* 365–378.

Brannon, L. (1999). *Gender: Psychological perspectives.* Boston, MA: Allyn & Bacon.

Britt, T. W., & Dawson, C. R. (2005). Predicting work-family conflict from workload, job attitudes, group attributes, and health: A longitudinal study. *Military Psychology, 17,* 203–227.

Broverman, I. K., Broverman, D. M., Clarkson, F. E., Rosenkrantz, P., & Vogel, S. R. (1970). Sex-role stereotypes and clinical judgments of mental health. *Journal of Consulting and Clinical Psychology, 34,* 1–7.

Broverman, I. K., Vogel, S. R., Broverman, D. M., Clarkson, F. E., & Rosenkrantz, P. S. (1972). Sex-role stereotypes: A current appraisal. *Journal of Social Issues, 28,* 59–78.

Capstick, M., Farley, K., Wild, W., & Parkes, M. A. (2005). *Canada's soldiers: Military ethos and Canadian values in the 21st century army. The major findings of the Army Culture and Climate Survey and the Army Socio-Cultural Survey.* Ottawa: Director General Land Capability Development.

Castro, C. (2007). Diversity in the Brazilian armed forces. In J. Soeters & J. van der Meulen (Eds.), *Cultural diversity in the armed forces: An international comparison* (pp. 64–76). London: Routledge.

Clapp, S. K., Chrisler, J. C., & Devlin, A. S. (2008, May). *Contrapower sexual harassment of military officers.* Poster presented at the meeting of the Association for Psychological Science, Chicago, IL.

Committee on Women in NATO Forces (CWINF). (2003, June). *Proceedings from the meeting of the committee on women in NATO forces.* Ottawa, Canada.

Corbett, S. (2007). The women's war. *New York Times Magazine,* March 18, pp. 40–55.

Crawford, M., & Unger, R. (2000). *Women and gender: A feminist psychology.* Boston, MA: McGraw-Hill.

Dansky, B. S. & Kilpatrick, D. G. (1997). Effects of sexual harassment. In W. O'Donahue (Ed.), *Sexual harassment: Theory, research, & treatment* (pp. 152–174). Boston, MA: Allyn & Bacon.

Davis, K. D. (Ed.). (2007). *Women and leadership in the Canadian Forces: Perspectives and experience.* Kingston: Canadian Defence Academy Press.

Davis, K. D., & McKee, B. (2004). Women in the military: Facing the warrior framework. In F. C. Pinch, A. T. MacIntryre, & P. Browne (Eds.), *Challenge and change in the military: Gender and diversity issues* (pp. 52–75). Canadian Forces Leadership Institute, Canadian Defence Academy, Winnipeg, Canada: Winnipeg, Wing Publishing Office, 17 Wing.

Diekman, A. B., & Eagly, A. H. (2000). Stereotypes as dynamic constructs: Women and men of the past, present, and future. *Personality and Social Psychology Bulletin, 26,* 1171–1188.

Duxbury, L., & Higgins, C. (2001). *Summary of key findings from Supportive Work Environment Survey (2001): Department of National Defence.* Ottawa, Canada: Director of Strategic Human Resources.

Eagly, A. H., Johannesen-Schmidt, M. C., & van Engen, M. L. (2003). Transformational, transactional, and laissez-faire leadership styles: A meta-analysis comparing women and men. *Psychological Bulletin, 129,* 569–591.

Eagly, A. H., & Johnson, B. T. (1990). Gender and leadership style: A meta-analysis. *Psychological Bulletin, 108,* 233–256.

Eagly, A. H., Karau, S. J., & Makhijani, M. G. (1995). Gender and the effectiveness of leaders: A meta-analysis. *Psychological Bulletin, 117,* 125–145.

Eagly, A. H., Makhijani, M. G., & Klonsky, B. G. (1992). Gender and the evaluation of leaders: A meta-analysis. *Psychological Bulletin, 111,* 3–22.

Eagly, A. H., & Steffen, V. J. (1986). Gender and aggressive behavior: A meta-analytic review of the social psychological literature. *Psychological Bulletin, 100,* 309–330.

Febbraro, A. R. (2003). *Women, leadership and gender integration in the Canadian combat arms: A qualitative study* (DRDC Toronto TR 2003-170). Toronto: Defence Research and Development Canada, Toronto.

Febbraro, A. R. (in press). Discourses of family among women in the Canadian Forces combat arms. In P. Browne (Ed.), *Women, family and their leadership experience in the Canadian Forces: Negotiating the right balance.* Kingston: Canadian Forces Leadership Institute.

Febbraro, A. R., & McCann, C. (2003, May). Demystifying the "feminine mythtique": Or, women and combat can mix. *Gazette on the Net.* (On-line publication of the U.S. Marine Corps.).

Fitzgerald, L. F., Drasgow, F., & Magley, V. J. (1999). Sexual harassment in the armed forces: A test of an integrated model. *Military Psychology, 11*(3), 329–343.

Gade, P., Segal, D. & Johnson, E. (1996). The experience of foreign militaries. In G. Herek, J. Jobe, & R. Carney (Eds.), *Out in force: Sexual orientation and the military* (pp. 106–139). Chicago: University of Chicago Press.

Ganderton, S. L. (2002). *Work-life balance: Implementing flexible initiatives to improve retention and complete integration of women in the Canadian Forces.* Toronto: Canadian Forces College.

Gill, R. M., & Febbraro, A. R. (2008, October). *Sexual harassment among women in the Canadian Forces combat arms.* Paper presented at the NATO RTO HFM-158 Symposium on Impacts of Gender Differences on Conducting Operational Activities, Antalya, Turkey.

Goldstein, J. S. (2001). *War and gender: How gender shapes the war system and vice versa.* New York: Cambridge University Press.

Gruber, J. E. (1998). The impact of male work environments and organizational policies on women's experiences of sexual harassment. *Gender & Society, 12,* 301–320.

Gutek, B. A. (1985). *Sex and the workplace.* San Francisco: Jossey-Bass.

Hare-Mustin, R., & Marecek, J. (1988). The meaning of difference: Gender theory, postmodernism, and psychology. *American Psychologist, 43,* 455–464.

Harries-Jenkins, G. (2004). Institution to occupation to diversity: Gender in the military today. In F. C. Pinch, A. T. MacIntryre, & P. Browne (Eds.), *Challenge and change in the military: Gender and diversity issues* (pp. 26–51). Canadian Forces Leadership Institute, Canadian Defence Academy, Winnipeg, Canada: Winnipeg, Wing Publishing Office, 17 Wing.

Heinecken, L. (2007). Diversity in the South African armed forces. In J. Soeters & J. van der Meulen (Eds.), *Cultural diversity in the armed forces: An international comparison* (pp. 77–94). London: Routledge.

Hill, S. A. (2001). *Identification of women's leadership in the Canadian Forces* (CFLI Research Note RN02-01). Kingston: Canadian Forces Leadership Institute.

Hoiberg, A. (1991). Military psychology and women's role in the military. In G. Reuven & D. A. Mangelsdorff (Eds.), *Handbook of military psychology* (pp. 725–739). Chichester, UK: Wiley.

Holden, N. J., & Davis, K. D. (2004). Harassment in the military: Cross-national comparisons. In F. C. Pinch, A. T. MacIntryre, & P. Browne (Eds.), *Challenge and change in the military: Gender and diversity issues* (pp. 97–121). Canadian Forces Leadership Institute, Canadian Defence Academy, Winnipeg, Canada: Winnipeg, Wing Publishing Office, 17 Wing.

Holden, N. J., & Tanner, L. M. (2001*). An examination of current gender integration policies in TTCP countries.* Director Strategic Human Resource Coordination Personnel Operational Research Team & Director Military Gender Integration and Employment Equity (ORD Report R2001/01). Ottawa, Canada: Department of National Defence.

Hunter, M. (2008). Sexual abuse: Another source of military trauma, *The National Psychologist, 17,* 11.

Jeffries, J. E. (2001). *Quality of life in the Canadian Forces: Qualitative analysis of the Quality of Life Questionnaire for CF Members.* Ottawa: Director Human Resources Research and Evaluation.

Kelley, M. L., Hock, E., Jarvis, M. S., Smith, K. M., Gaffney, M. A., & Bonney, J. F. (2002). Psychological adjustment of Navy mothers experiencing deployment. *Military Psychology, 14,* 199–216.

Korabik, K. (2005). *Leadership and diversity in the Canadian Forces: A conceptual model and research agenda* (DRDC Toronto CR 2005-243). Toronto: Defence R&D Canada, Toronto.

Koss, M. P. (1990). The women's mental health research agenda: Violence against women. *American Psychologist, 45,* 374–380.

Lomskey-Feder, E., & Ben-Ari, E. (2007). Diversity in the Israel defence forces. In J. Soeters & J. van der Meulen (Eds.), *Cultural diversity in the armed forces: An international comparison* (pp. 125–139). London: Routledge.

Lyons, J. (2008). Intimate relationships and the military. In S. M. Freeman, B. Moore & A. Freeman (Eds.), *In harm's way: A psychological treatment for pre- and post deployment*. New York: Routledge.

Magley, V. J., Waldo, C., Drasgow, F., & Fitzgerald, L. (1999). The impact of sexual harassment on military personnel: Is it the same for men & women? *Military Psychology, 11*, 283–302.

Manigart, P. (2007). Diversity in the Belgian armed forces. In J. Soeters & J. van der Meulen (Eds.), *Cultural diversity in the armed forces: An international comparison* (pp. 185–199). London: Routledge.

Marin, A. J. & Guadagno, R. E. (1999). Perceptions of sexual harassment victims as a function of labeling & reporting. *Sex Roles, 41*, 912–940.

Marshall, J. (1993). Organizational cultures and women managers: Exploring the dynamics of resilience. *Applied Psychology, 42*, 313–322.

McCreary, D. R., Thompson, M. M., & Pastò, L. (2003). The impact of family concerns on the pre-deployment well-being of Canadian Forces personnel. *Canadian Journal of Police and Security Services, 1*, 33–40.

McFadyen, J., Kerpelman, J., & Adler-Baeder, F. (2005). Examining the impact of workplace support: Work-family fit and satisfaction in the US military. *Family Relations, 54*, 131–144.

Mooney, K. (2008, July 2). Female U.S. casualties more common in Iraq War. *The Nation*. Retrieved from http://www.cnsnews.com/ViewNation.asp?Page=/Nation/archive/200807/NAT20080702a.html

Moskos, C. (2007). Diversity in the armed forces of the United States. In J. Soeters & J. van der Meulen (Eds.), *Cultural diversity in the armed forces: An international comparison* (pp. 15–30). New York: Routledge.

Munson, L. J., Miner, A. G., & Hulin, C. (2001). Labeling sexual harassment in the military: An extension & replication. *Journal of Applied Psychology, 86*, 293–303.

Nelson, A., & Robinson, B. W. (2002). *Gender in Canada* (2nd ed.). Toronto: Prentice-Hall.

Norris, M. (2007, October 1). Roles for women in US Army expand. *National Public Radio*. Retrieved from http://www.npr.org/templates/story/story.php?storyId=14869648

O'Leary, V. (1974). Some attitudinal barriers to occupational aspirations in women. *Psychological Bulletin, 81*, 809–826.

Pickering, D. I. (2006). *The relationship between work-life conflict/work-life balance and operational effectiveness in the Canadian Forces* (DRDC Toronto TR 2006-243). Toronto: Defence Research and Development Canada, Toronto.

Pinch, P. (1984). *Perspectives on organizational change in the Canadian Forces* (Research Report 1657, NTIS No. ADA277746). Alexandria, VA: Army Research Institute for the Behavioral and Social Sciences.

Rice, R. W., Instone, D., & Adams, J. (1984). Leader sex, leader success, and leadership process: Two field studies. *Journal of Applied Psychology, 69*, 12–31.

Rice, R. W., Yoder, J. D., Adams, J., Priest, R. F., & Prince, H. T. (1984). Leadership ratings for male and female military cadets. *Sex Roles, 10*, 885–901.

Richardson, R., Bosch, J., & Moelker, R. (2007). Diversity in the Dutch armed forces. In J. Soeters & J. van der Meulen (Eds.), *Cultural diversity in the armed forces: An international comparison* (pp. 200–214). London: Routledge.

Roush, P. E. (1991, April). *Rethinking who fights our wars – and why*. Paper presented at the Harvard Law School Symposium on Women in the Military, Cambridge, MA.

Schein, V. E. (1973). The relationship between sex-role stereotypes and requisite management characteristics. *Journal of Applied Psychology, 57*, 95–100.

Schein, V. E. (1975). The relationship between sex-role stereotypes and requisite management characteristics among female managers. *Journal of Applied Psychology, 60*, 340–344.

Schneider, K. S., Swan, & Fitzgerald, L. (1997). Job-related & psychological effects of sexual harassment in the workplace: Empirical evidence from two organizations. *Journal of Applied Psychology, 82*, 401–415.

Segal, M. (1986). The military and the family as greedy institutions. *Armed Forces & Society, 13*(1), 9–38.

Soeters, J., & van der Meulen, J. (Eds.). (2007). *Cultural diversity in the armed forces: An international comparison*. London: Routledge

Stogdill, R. M. (1963). *Manual for the Leader Behavior Description Questionnaire – Form XII*. Columbus, OH: Bureau of Business Research, Ohio State University.

Tanner, L. (1999). *Gender integration in the Canadian Forces: A quantitative and qualitative analysis*. Director General Military Human Resources Policy & Planning, Directorate of Military Gender Integration & Employment Equity, & Director General Operational Research Directorate of Operational Research (Corporate, Air & Maritime) (ORD Report R9901). Ottawa: Department of National Defence.

Tessema, M. T. (2007). Diversity in the Eritrean armed forces. In J. Soeters & J. van der Meulen (Eds.), *Cultural diversity in the armed forces: An international comparison* (pp. 95–110). London: Routledge.

Thomas, V. (1997, May). *A re-examination of gender differences in voluntary attrition from hard sea occupations*. CASA Consulting for the Personnel Research Team, Ottawa: National Defence Headquarters.

Thomas, P. J., & Thomas, M. D. (1993). Mothers in uniform. In F. W. Kaslow (Ed.) *The military family in peace and war* (pp. 25–47). New York: Springer.

Vecchio, R. P. (2002). Leadership and gender advantage. *Leadership Quarterly, 13*, 643–671.

Vinokur, A. D., Pierce, P. F., & Buck, C. L. (1999). Work-family conflicts of women in the Air Force: Their influence on mental health and functioning. *Journal of Organizational Behaviour, 20*, 865–878.

Vroom, V. H., & Yetton, P. W. (1973). *Leadership and decision-making*. Pittsburgh, PA: University of Pittsburgh Press.

Winslow, D., Browne, P., & Febbraro, A. (2007). Diversity in the Canadian Forces. In J. Soeters & J. van der Meulen (Eds.), *Cultural diversity in the armed forces: An international comparison* (pp. 31–47). New York: Routledge.

Yoder, J. D. (1983). Another look at women in the United States Army: A comment on Woelfel's article. *Sex Roles, 9*, 285–288.

Yoder, J. D. (1999). *Women and gender: Transforming psychology*. Upper Saddle River, NJ: Prentice-Hall.

Author Index

A

Aamodt, M. G., Vol-I: 438
Aaron, D. J., Vol-I: 187
Abbey, A., Vol-II: 283–284, 631
Abdel-Shaheed, J., Vol-I: 240
Abdul-Quader, A. S., Vol-I: 187
Abell, S. C., Vol-I: 544
Aber, J. L., Vol-II: 388, 619
Abraham, S. F., Vol-I: 458
Abrahams, D., Vol-II: 287
Abrahams, S., Vol-I: 225, 328
Abraído-Lanza, A. F., Vol-II: 501, 554
Abramson, L. Y., Vol-I: 545; Vol-II: 96, 136, 142, 146
Abu Odeh, L., Vol-I: 119
Acacio, J. C., Vol-I: 329
Acevedo, E. D., Vol-II: 569
Acierno, R., Vol-II: 316
Acker, J., Vol-II: 452
Ackerman, P. L., Vol-I: 301
Ackerman, S. J., Vol-II: 235
Ackley, M. A., Vol-II: 600
Acock, A. C., Vol-II: 405, 409–410
Acosta, R. V., Vol-II: 566
Acton, W., Vol-I: 471
Adams, A. S., Vol-II: 531
Adams, C., Vol-I: 323
Adams, H. E., Vol-II: 360, 371
Adams, J., Vol-II: 677–678
Adams, M., Vol-II: 402–403, 406, 416
Adams, P. F., Vol-II: 518
Adams, R. B. Vol-I: 431
Adams, S., Vol-II: 141
Aday, L. A., Vol-I: 180
Addis, M. E., Vol-I: 51, 53–55, 136, 145; Vol-II: 135, 137, 223–226, 228, 230, 234–236, 241, 267, 545–546
Ader, D. N., Vol-I: 197, 199
Adler, N. J., Vol-II: 454
Adler, P., Vol-II: 595
Adler, T. F., Vol-II: 383–384, 388
Adler-Baeder, F., Vol-II: 686
Ægisdóttir, S., Vol-II: 360, 362
Affleck, G., Vol-II: 511
Afifi, W. A., Vol-II: 283

Agars, M. D., Vol-II: 448
Agarwal, P., Vol-II: 292
Aggleton, P., Vol-II: 486
Agliata, D., Vol-II: 167, 658
Agnew, C. R., Vol-II: 294
Agostini, L., Vol-I: 496
Agras, W. S., Vol-I: 86
Agronick, G., Vol-I: 19
Agronick, G. S., Vol-I: 566
Ahlers, R. H., Vol-I: 328
Ahluwalia, J., Vol-I: 309
Ahmed, F., Vol-I: 194
Ahrens, C. E., Vol-II: 624
Aiken, L., Vol-II: 621
Aikin, K. J., Vol-I: 144
Aimar, C. M., Vol-II: 570
Ainsworth, B. E., Vol-II: 567
Aitken, L., Vol-I: 180
Akers, J., Vol-I: 107
Akimoto, S. A., Vol-I: 198
Akincigil, A., Vol-II: 478
Akrami, N., Vol-II: 362
Alagna, S. W., Vol-II: 350
Al-Alami, M., Vol-II: 368
Álava, M. J., Vol-I: 322
Albano, S., Vol-II: 686
Albee, G., Vol-II: 633–634
Albert, M. S., Vol-I: 227
Albrecht, R., Vol-I: 535
Albritton, K., Vol-I: 183
Aldarondo, E., Vol-II: 271–272
Alegria, M., Vol-II: 622
Aleman, A., Vol-I: 223
Alexander, A. M., Vol-II: 165
Alexander, G. M., Vol-I: 236–237, 322, 325
Alexander, J. F., Vol-II: 255, 269
Alexander, J. M., Vol-I: 457
Alexander, M. G., Vol-I: 481–482, 487
Alfeld, C. J., Vol-II: 382
Alfieri, A., Vol-I: 530
Alfieri, T., Vol-II: 501
Algoe, S. B., Vol-I: 413
Ali, A., Vol-II: 9, 91–105

Alibakhshi, G., Vol-I: 390
Alindogan, J., Vol-II: 173
Alison, J. A., Vol-I: 54
Alkon, A., Vol-I: 442
Allen, A., Vol-II: 67
Allen, E., Vol-I: 307
Allen, G. L., Vol-I: 330
Allen, J. D., Vol-II: 527
Allen, K. D., Vol-II: 519
Allen, L., Vol-II: 388
Allen, L. S., Vol-I: 217, 225
Allen, M., Vol-I: 440, 475, 479; Vol-II: 21
Allen, M. J., Vol-I: 319
Allen, O., Vol-I: 547
Allen, T. D., Vol-II: 454
Allgood-Merten, B., Vol-I: 544; Vol-II: 24, 30
Allik, J., Vol-I: 441
Allison, D. B., Vol-II: 159, 545
Allison, M. T., Vol-II: 568
Allison, S., Vol-II: 48
Allon, N., Vol-II: 167
Alloy, L. B., Vol-II: 142, 144, 146
Allport, G. W., Vol-II: 80, 361
Allwood, C. M., Vol-I: 163
Almeida, D., Vol-II: 409
Almeida, D. M., Vol-I: 87, 530
Almeida, O. P., Vol-I: 224
Almeida, R. V., Vol-II: 255, 261–262, 269–270
Almeida-Filho, N., Vol-II: 195
Aloisi, A. M., Vol-I: 241–242
Altabe, M. N., Vol-I: 153
Altemeyer, B., Vol-I: 194; Vol-II: 362
Altermatt, E. R., Vol-I: 283
Altintas, E., Vol-II: 416
Altman, B. E., Vol-II: 633
Altmann, D., Vol-I: 220
Altschuler, J., Vol-II: 410
Alvarez, J. M., Vol-I: 516
Amarel, D., Vol-II: 506, 512
Amaro, H., Vol-I: 548, 549
Ambady, N., Vol-I: 284, 353, 412–413, 433, 438; Vol-II: 451
Ambwani, S., Vol-II: 204
Amos, A., Vol-II: 477
Amparo, E. G., Vol-I: 224
Amponsah, B., Vol-I: 326
Amunts, K., Vol-I: 239
An, C., Vol-II: 228
Anastasi, A., Vol-II: 80, 605
Andayani, S., Vol-I: 432
Anderberg, U. M., Vol-I: 241
Anderman, E. M., Vol-II: 388–389
Andersen, A., Vol-I: 54
Andersen, A. E., Vol-II: 170, 172
Andersen, J. H., Vol-I: 242
Anderson, A. S., Vol-I: 456
Anderson, C., Vol-I: 429

Anderson, C. A., Vol-I: 198
Anderson, C. M., Vol-II: 226
Anderson, D., Vol-I: 505, 510
Anderson, D. A., Vol-II: 651, 657
Anderson, D. E., Vol-I: 412
Anderson, D. R., Vol-I: 505, 511
Anderson, E., Vol-II: 541
Anderson, H., Vol-I: 111
Anderson, J. P., Vol-II: 547
Anderson, K. J., Vol-I: 414; Vol-II: 338
Anderson, N., Vol-II: 71
Anderson, R. N., Vol-II: 228
Anderson, S., Vol-I: 68
Andersson, C., Vol-II: 476
Andersson, L. M., Vol-II: 423–424, 429, 435
Andrade, A. G., Vol-II: 476
Andrade, L., Vol-II: 134
Andreev, E. M., Vol-II: 472
Andrews, G., Vol-II: 228
Andrews, H., Vol-II: 620
Andrews, J. A., Vol-I: 548
Andrzejewski, S. A., Vol-I: 438
Aneja, A., Vol-I: 501
Aneshensel, C. S., Vol-I: 544
Angelique, H., Vol-II: 613–614, 616, 618, 628–629, 633
Angold, A., Vol-I: 548; Vol-II: 133, 137
Anhalt, K., Vol-I: 68
Annett, M., Vol-I: 325
Ansell, E. B., Vol-II: 26
Ansfield, M. E., Vol-I: 412
Anson, J., Vol-II: 472
Anstiss, V., Vol-I: 460
Antes, J. R., Vol-I: 330
Anthony, J. C., Vol-I: 547
Anton, S. D., Vol-I: 456
Antoni, M. H., Vol-I: 547
Antonovsky, A., Vol-II: 35
Antonucci, T. C., Vol-I: 559, 570
Antshel, K. M., Vol-II: 236
Anuar, K., Vol-I: 328
Aoki, Y., Vol-I: 436
Appenzeller, S. N., Vol-II: 116
Apperloo, M. J., Vol-I: 483
Applebaum, S., Vol-I: 248
Apt, C., Vol-I: 485
Aquilino, W. S., Vol-II: 602
Aquino, K., Vol-II: 431
Arad, S., Vol-II: 362
Aragon, R. S., Vol-II: 328
Aragon, S. R., Vol-I: 290
Arai, Y., Vol-I: 236
Araki, K., Vol-II: 568
Arbisib, P. A., Vol-II: 76
Arbreton, A., Vol-II: 383–385
Archer, D., Vol-I: 412–413, 441; Vol-II: 295
Archer, J., Vol-I: 14, 147, 168, 193, 546; Vol-II: 15, 313, 316

Archibald, A. B., Vol-I: 202
Arciniega, G. M., Vol-II: 226
Arczynski, A., Vol-II: 235
Arden, K., Vol-II: 287
Arden, R., Vol-I: 302
Argentino, C., Vol-II: 624
Arias, E., Vol-II: 228
Aries, E., Vol-I: 385, 394; Vol-II: 337–338
Aries, E. J., Vol-I: 380–381, 385, 388, 393–394
Arieti, S., Vol-I: 352
Arisaka, O., Vol-I: 236
Arkowitz, H., Vol-II: 235
Arluke, A., Vol-I: 396–397
Armentrout, S. M., Vol-II: 566
Armstrong, G., Vol-II: 591
Armstrong, J. D., Vol-I: 368
Armstrong, J. G., Vol-II: 209
Armstrong-Stassen, M., Vol-II: 452
Arnau, R. C., Vol-I: 242
Arnett, C., Vol-I: 456
Arnett, J. J., Vol-II: 568
Arnold, A. P., Vol-I: 217
Arnold, E., Vol-II: 477
Arnold, K. D., Vol-I: 350–351
Aro, H., Vol-II: 548
Aron, A., Vol-II: 66
Aron, R. H., Vol-I: 330
Aronson, J., Vol-I: 84–85, 327, 353, 430; Vol-II: 450
Aronson, V., Vol-II: 287
Arras, R. E., Vol-I: 53
Arredondo, P., Vol-II: 231, 260
Arriaga, X. B., Vol-II: 294
Arrighi, B., Vol-I: 406
Arrindell, W. A., Vol-I: 145
Arrington-Sanders, R., Vol-II: 547
Arthur, A. E., Vol-I: 516
Artiola i Fortuny, L., Vol-II: 605
Artis, J. E., Vol-II: 410
Arvey, R. D., Vol-I: 431
Asch, S. E., Vol-I: 319
Asci, F. H., Vol-II: 569
Ashbaker, M., Vol-I: 435
Asher, S. J., Vol-II: 297
Ashmore, M., Vol-II: 169
Ashmore, R. D., Vol-I: 496–497; Vol-II: 166, 289, 293
Ashworth, P., Vol-I: 103
Asla, N., Vol-II: 329
Asmussen, L., Vol-I: 540
Asrani, S., Vol-I: 236
Astor, R., Vol-II: 628
Astur, R. S., Vol-I: 221, 321, 328–329
Atashili, J., Vol-II: 544
Atkins, B., Vol-I: 381, 387
Atkinson, D. R., Vol-II: 200, 233
Atkinson, J. W., Vol-II: 41–42, 55, 200, 233, 386
Atkinson, R. C., Vol-II: 386
Atkinson, R. L., Vol-II: 386

Atlis, M. M., Vol-II: 78–79
Atlisa, M. M., Vol-II: 76
Attie, I., Vol-I: 544
Atwater, L. E., Vol-II: 448
Aube, J., Vol-I: 545; Vol-II: 23, 43
Aubrey, J. S., Vol-I: 97, 475; Vol-II: 645, 647, 655
Aubry, S., Vol-I: 514
Aubry, T., Vol-II: 204
Aubut, J. L., Vol-II: 477
Auerbach, C. F., Vol-II: 258, 272
Auerbach, D., Vol-II: 282
Ault-Riche, M., Vol-II: 255
Aupont, M., Vol-I: 139; Vol-II: 113
Aust, C. F., Vol-II: 657
Austin, D., Vol-I: 111
Avalos, L., Vol-II: 173
Avants, B., Vol-I: 307
Avero, P., Vol-I: 442
Avery, P. G., Vol-II: 115
Aviram, O., Vol-I: 242
Avis, J. M., Vol-II: 255–256
Avolio, B. J., Vol-I: 418; Vol-II: 459
Avorn, J., Vol-II: 527
Axel, R., Vol-I: 247
Ayala, G., Vol-II: 145
Ayanian, J. Z., Vol-II: 518
Aylor, B., Vol-II: 293, 296
Ayman, R., Vol-II: 460
Ayotte, V., Vol-II: 31
Ayral-Clause, O., Vol-I: 345
Ayres, M. M., Vol-I: 414; Vol-II: 338
Azevedo, M. R., Vol-II: 479

B

Ba'tki, A., Vol-I: 309
Baartmans, B. J., Vol-I: 332
Babcock, L., Vol-I: 383–385; Vol-II: 347
Babey, S. H., Vol-II: 30
Bachman, J. G., Vol-II: 224
Bachmann, G., Vol-I: 480–481
Backes, R. C., Vol-I: 269
Bäckman, L., Vol-I: 240, 248
Bäckström, T., Vol-I: 459
Bacue, A., Vol-II: 644–646
Badenhop, D. T., Vol-II: 547
Bader, S. M., Vol-II: 322
Badger, L. W., Vol-II: 523
Badgett, M. V., Vol-I: 66
Badgett, M. V. L., Vol-II: 139
Badia, X., Vol-I: 171
Badr, H., Vol-II: 501, 551
Baenninger, M., Vol-I: 308, 326–327
Baer, J., Vol-I: 349–351, 354
Baeten, V. L., Vol-II: 460
Bagley, C., Vol-II: 645
Bahr, M., Vol-II: 379
Bahrke, M. S., Vol-II: 162

Bailey, J. M., Vol-I: 225–226, 510–512
Bailey, N., Vol-II: 424
Bailyn, L., Vol-II: 452
Baird, M. K., Vol-II: 205
Baird, S. M., Vol-II: 570
Baird, W., Vol-II: 390
Bajema, C., Vol-II: 425, 428
Bakan, D., Vol-I: 135, 415, 421; Vol-II: 56, 549, 678
Bakeman, R., Vol-I: 541
Baker, D. P., Vol-I: 307
Baker, K., Vol-II: 647
Baker, N. L., Vol-I: 9, 105
Baker, S., Vol-I: 219
Baker, S. P., Vol-II: 482–483
Baker, S. W., Vol-II: 116
Baker-Sperry, L., Vol-II: 166
Bakker, F., Vol-II: 655
Balaban, T., Vol-I: 510
Balcazar, F., Vol-II: 627
Bales, R. F., Vol-I: 134; Vol-II: 23, 406, 678
Ballard, C. G., Vol-II: 97
Balleine, B. W., Vol-II: 115
Ballou, M., Vol-II: 64, 73, 83, 198, 202
Balogun, A. O., Vol-II: 155
Balogun, J. A., Vol-II: 155
Balsam, K. F., Vol-II: 138–139, 411
Baltes, M. M., Vol-I: 569–570
Baltes, P. B., Vol-I: 566–567
Bamer, A. M., Vol-II: 546
Banaji, M., Vol-I: 281
Banaji, M. R., Vol-I: 35, 196, 198, 497, 517; Vol-II: 447, 449
Bancroft, J., Vol-I: 459, 485
Bancroft, J. M., Vol-II: 476
Bandura, A., Vol-I: 84, 474, 508; Vol-II: 64, 70, 573, 643
Bandura, M. M., Vol-I: 239, 266
Bane, S., Vol-II: 573
Banerjee, N., Vol-II: 371
Bangerter, A., Vol-I: 201
Bankey, R., Vol-II: 100
Banks, A., Vol-I: 483
Banthia, R., Vol-II: 551
Baranowski, M., Vol-I: 195
Barban, L., Vol-II: 195
Barbaranelli, C., Vol-I: 172
Barbaree, H. E., Vol-I: 367
Barbee, A. P., Vol-II: 504–505
Barber, B. L., Vol-II: 382, 573
Barber, H., Vol-II: 577–578
Barber, M. E., Vol-II: 322
Barber-Foss, K. D., Vol-II: 483
Barbur, J. L., Vol-I: 237
Barbuto, J. E., Vol-II: 93–94
Bardwick, J. M., Vol-I: 27
Barenbaum, N. B., Vol-II: 53
Bargad, A., Vol-I: 139, 149
Bargh, J. A., Vol-I: 196; Vol-II: 327, 662

Barkan, A. L., Vol-I: 459, 464
Barker, E. T., Vol-II: 134, 164
Barker, M., Vol-I: 198
Barker, R. G., Vol-II: 633
Barker, V. L., Vol-II: 460
Barkley, C. L., Vol-I: 329
Barlett, C. P., Vol-I: 567; Vol-II: 658
Barling, J., Vol-II: 423, 431
Barlow, D. H., Vol-I: 479
Barn, R., Vol-II: 195
Barner, M. R., Vol-II: 645, 649
Barnes, G. M., Vol-II: 576
Barnes, M. L., Vol-I: 417
Barnes, N. W., Vol-II: 144
Barnes, P. M., Vol-II: 518
Barnes, R. D., Vol-II: 295
Barnes-Farrell, J. L., Vol-II: 429
Barnett, A. M., Vol-I: 221, 323
Barnett, R. C., Vol-I: 560, 562, 570, 572; Vol-II: 65, 414, 631
Barnfield, A. M. C., Vol-I: 321
Baron, A. S., Vol-I: 497, 517
Baron, J., Vol-I: 182, 567
Baron, R. A., Vol-II: 314, 423, 427, 431
Baron, R. M., Vol-I: 3, 86; Vol-II: 3
Baron-Cohen, S., Vol-I: 220, 300, 309
Barr, L., Vol-II: 30
Barr, R. F., Vol-II: 651
Barrett, A. E., Vol-I: 530–531, 572
Barrett, F. L., Vol-I: 436, 439
Barrett, K., Vol-I: 186
Barrett, L., Vol-I: 259
Barrett, L. F., Vol-II: 294
Barrett, S. E., Vol-II: 263–264
Barrios, M., Vol-II: 648
Barron, F., Vol-I: 350
Barroso, L. P., Vol-II: 476
Barry, K., Vol-I: 107
Barsade, S. G., Vol-II: 349
Barsky, A. J., Vol-II: 521
Barsky, J., Vol-II: 43
Barsky, R. D., Vol-I: 328
Bart, M., Vol-I: 290
Barta, W., Vol-II: 662
Bartels, M., Vol-I: 239
Bartko, W. T., Vol-I: 537
Bartky, S., Vol-II: 156, 170–171
Bartle-Haring, S., Vol-II: 204
Bartlett, C., Vol-II: 166
Bartlett, N. H., Vol-II: 125
Bartley, C., Vol-II: 289
Bartley, S., Vol-II: 414
Barton, J. J. S., Vol-I: 221
Barton, P., Vol-II: 531
Bartoshuk, L. M., Vol-I: 246
Bartsch, D., Vol-I: 462
Baruch, G. K., Vol-I: 560, 562, 572

Basow, S., Vol-I: 388
Basow, S. A., Vol-I: 7, 277–291; Vol-II: 7, 296, 360–361
Bass, B. M., Vol-I: 418; Vol-II: 458–459
Bastian, L. A., Vol-II: 519
Batalova, J., Vol-II: 410–411
Bateman, G., Vol-II: 691–692
Bates, C. J., Vol-I: 456–457
Bates, J. E., Vol-I: 140, 151
Batra, L., Vol-II: 430
Battle, A., Vol-I: 569
Baucom, D. H., Vol-II: 265–266, 268
Bauer, C. F., Vol-I: 317
Baum, B. J., Vol-I: 246
Baumeister, R. F., Vol-I: 64, 193, 485, 499; Vol-II: 24, 31, 289, 324
Baumgarten, P., Vol-II: 456
Baur, K., Vol-II: 532
Baxter, J. C., Vol-II: 449
Bayard, D., Vol-I: 392
Bayer, B., Vol-II: 671
Bazelier, F. G., Vol-I: 457, 459
Beall, A. E., Vol-I: 167; Vol-II: 168
Beals, J., Vol-II: 619
Beals, K. A., Vol-II: 575
Beals, K. P., Vol-I: 66, 480
Bearden, A. G., Vol-II: 370–371
Bearman, S. K., Vol-I: 544; Vol-II: 155–156
Beasley, B., Vol-II: 645
Beaton, D., Vol-I: 171
Beattie, T. F., Vol-II: 483
Beatty, J., Vol-I: 362
Beatty, W. W., Vol-I: 247, 330
Beaty, L. A., Vol-I: 541
Beauchaine, T. P., Vol-II: 138
Beautrais, A. L., Vol-II: 135
Beaver, A. S., Vol-II: 103
Bechtold, K. T., Vol-I: 510
Beck, A. T., Vol-II: 80
Beck, R. S., Vol-II: 523
Beck, S., Vol-I: 330
Becker, A. E., Vol-II: 167
Becker, B. J., Vol-I: 318
Becker, D., Vol-II: 193
Becker, G., Vol-II: 405
Becker, J., Vol-I: 226; Vol-II: 385
Becker, J. B., Vol-I: 534
Becker, J. R., Vol-I: 307
Becker, M. W., Vol-I: 330
Beckjord, E., Vol-II: 82
Bedini, L. A., Vol-II: 574
Beehr, T. A., Vol-II: 436
Beekman, A. T. F., Vol-II: 297
Beer-Borst, S., Vol-I: 456, 462
Beere, C. A., Vol-I: 133–134
Behar, R., Vol-I: 109–111, 117
Behrendt, G., Vol-II: 290
Behrendt, R., Vol-I: 517

Beier, M. E., Vol-I: 301
Beilock, S. L., Vol-I: 433
Bein, A., Vol-II: 204
Bein, E., Vol-II: 145
Bein, F. L., Vol-I: 330
Beitel, P. A., Vol-I: 326; Vol-II: 229
Bekker, M. H. J., Vol-II: 502–503
Belahsen, R., Vol-II: 160
Belenky, M., Vol-I: 105
Belenky, M. F., Vol-I: 32, 198
Belhekar, V. M., Vol-II: 26
Belitsky, C. A., Vol-II: 96
Belk, S. S., Vol-I: 52; Vol-II: 550
Belkin, A., Vol-II: 691–692
Bell, A. P., Vol-I: 475
Bell, B., Vol-II: 318
Bell, E., Vol-I: 398
Bell, E. J. E., Vol-II: 451, 454, 458
Bell, M. P., Vol-II: 502
Bell, R., Vol-I: 456
Bell, R. A., Vol-II: 522
Bell, R. R., Vol-II: 283
Belle, D., Vol-II: 101, 658
Bellman, S., Vol-II: 505
Bem, D., Vol-I: 363
Bem, D. J., Vol-II: 67
Bem, S., Vol-I: 192, 366, 382
Bem, S. L., Vol-I: 14, 28, 47, 50, 52, 84, 134–135, 150, 192, 197, 203, 352, 354, 363–364, 421, 499, 508, 512, 532; Vol-II: 14, 21–22, 287, 294–295, 312, 323, 497, 569, 678, 684
Benard, S., Vol-II: 447
Benardete, E., Vol-I: 236
Ben-Ari, A., Vol-I: 67
Ben-Ari, E., Vol-II: 674
Benbenishty, R., Vol-II: 628
Benbow, C. P., Vol-I: 304, 310, 317; Vol-II: 386
Bender, P., Vol-II: 677
Benedetti, F., Vol-I: 240
Benedict, H., Vol-II: 650
Bener, A., Vol-II: 482
Benet-Martínez, V., Vol-I: 160, 166, 170–171
Benetti-McQuoid, J., Vol-II: 435
Bengtson, V., Vol-II: 413–414
Bengtsson, S., Vol-I: 249
Benjamin, L. T., Vol-I: 25
Bennett, C. L., Vol-II: 527, 613
Bennett, G. K., Vol-I: 320
Bennett, K. C., Vol-I: 117
Bennett, M., Vol-I: 496, 500
Bennett, R. J., Vol-II: 423
Ben-Porath, Y. S., Vol-I: 70, 80–81
Benson, B., Vol-I: 456
Bentler, P., Vol-I: 146; Vol-I: 115
Bentler, P. M., Vol-I: 140, 151; Vol-II: 24
Benwell, B., Vol-I: 398

Ben-Zeev, T., Vol-II: 21
Ben-Zeev, T. A., Vol-I: 284
Ben-Zur, H., Vol-II: 433
Bepko, C. S., Vol-II: 94–95, 102, 104, 255, 257
Berberich, D. A., Vol-II: 74
Berdahl, J. L., Vol-II: 337–338, 340, 425–426, 429–431, 684
Beren, S. E., Vol-II: 156
Berenbaum, S., Vol-I: 501
Berenbaum, S. A., Vol-I: 140, 219–220, 222, 279, 510, 527; Vol-II: 368, 387
Berent, S., Vol-I: 227
Berg, C. A., Vol-II: 501, 510–511
Berg, G. E., Vol-I: 246
Berg, K., Vol-II: 144
Berg, P., Vol-II: 153
Bergemann, N., Vol-I: 223
Bergen, E., Vol-II: 410, 412
Bergen, R. K., Vol-II: 632
Berger, J. M., Vol-I: 138; Vol-II: 14, 345, 352, 522
Berger, P. A., Vol-I: 49
Berger, P. L., Vol-I: 51
Bergeron, K. B., Vol-I: 458
Bergeron, M., Vol-II: 208–209
Bergers, G. P. A., Vol-I: 457
Berg-Kelly, K., Vol-II: 369
Berglund, H., Vol-I: 249
Berglund, M., Vol-II: 476
Bergman, B., Vol-I: 111, 113
Bergman, M. E., Vol-II: 428, 433–434, 437
Bergvall, V., Vol-I: 401
Berk, S. F., Vol-II: 405–407
Berkman, L. F., Vol-II: 139, 145
Berkovic, S. F., Vol-II: 598
Berkowitz, L., Vol-II: 647
Berman, E., Vol-II: 575
Berman, L. S., Vol-II: 572
Bermúdez, J., Vol-I: 172
Bernal, G., Vol-II: 233, 273, 616
Bernal, J. D., Vol-I: 200
Bernard, J., Vol-II: 225
Bernat, J., Vol-II: 360
Berndt, A., Vol-II: 509
Berndt, T. J., Vol-I: 530, 538
Bernieri, F. J., Vol-I: 413, 438
Bernstein, J., Vol-I: 328–329
Bernstein, K. T., Vol-II: 553
Bernstein, S., Vol-I: 508
Berquist, B. E., Vol-II: 113
Berry, J. W., Vol-I: 161–164, 326
Berscheid, E., Vol-II: 69, 281
Berson, Y., Vol-I: 418
Berthiaume, F., Vol-I: 240, 320
Berthoz, A., Vol-I: 329
Bertjan, D., Vol-II: 348
Bertoni, A. G., Vol-II: 528
Bertrand, R., Vol-I: 227

Bertsch, T., Vol-I: 113
Berzonsky, M. D., Vol-I: 536
Bessenoff, G. R., Vol-II: 167
Best, D. I., Vol-II: 312, 343; Vol-I: 133, 150, 169–170, 173
Best, L. A., Vol-I: 202
Bettencourt, B. A., Vol-I: 440; Vol-II: 313, 315
Bettinger, M., Vol-I: 64; Vol-II: 257
Bettner, L. G., Vol-I: 238
Betz, N. E., Vol-I: 43, 51; Vol-II: 24, 155, 380
Beuter, A., Vol-II: 573
Beutler, L. E., Vol-II: 221
Bevington, D., Vol-I: 191
Bharadwaj, R., Vol-I: 347
Bhatia, S., Vol-I: 106, 109
Bhattacharya, G., Vol-II: 457
Bhavnani, K., Vol-I: 106
Bianchi, S. M., Vol-II: 405, 407, 409, 445
Biblarz, T., Vol-II: 410, 413
Bickham, D. S., Vol-II: 651, 657
Bieber, I., Vol-I: 61
Biehl, H., Vol-II: 691
Biehl, M., Vol-I: 441
Biernat, M., Vol-II: 344, 460
Bies, R. J., Vol-II: 431
Bieschke, K. J., Vol-II: 64
Biggar, H., Vol-II: 554
Biggart, A., Vol-II: 390
Biggs, E., Vol-I: 198
Bigler, R. S., Vol-I: 282, 500, 503, 512, 516–517; Vol-II: 385
Biglia, B., Vol-I: 118
Bijl, R. V., Vol-II: 135, 224
Bikos, L. H., Vol-II: 383
Bilash, I., Vol-I: 246
Billings, A. C., Vol-II: 647
Billson, J. M., Vol-II: 227
Billy, J. O. G., Vol-II: 65
Bimbi, D. S., Vol-I: 64
Bimler, D., Vol-I: 237
Binder, K. S., Vol-II: 299
Bing, J., Vol-I: 401
Binns, J., Vol-II: 478
Binson, D., Vol-I: 186
Binsted, G., Vol-I: 221, 323
Birch, L. L., Vol-I: 544
Bird, C. E., Vol-II: 414, 529
Birk, T. S., Vol-II: 347
Birkby, J., Vol-I: 241
Birkett,, M., Vol-I: 290
Birmingham, C. L., Vol-II: 473
Birnbaum, M. H., Vol-II: 602
Birrell, P., Vol-II: 214
Birren, J. E., Vol-I: 348
Bischof, W. F., Vol-I: 329
Bishop, F., Vol-I: 110
Bitan, T., Vol-I: 245

Bittman, M., Vol-II: 409
Bjorklund, D. F., Vol-I: 263, 265, 473
Bjorkqvist, K., Vol-II: 315, 429
Black, D., Vol-I: 187; Vol-II: 477
Black, K. N., Vol-I: 195
Blackburn, V. B., Vol-II: 456
Blaine, B., Vol-I: 497
Blair, J., Vol-I: 186
Blair, S. L., Vol-II: 405, 407, 409, 414
Blaisure, K., Vol-II: 410, 414
Blake, J., Vol-I: 141
Blake, S. M., Vol-I: 548
Blakemore, J. E. O., Vol-I: 144, 501; Vol-II: 340
Blakeney, R., Vol-II: 621
Blanch, R. J., Vol-I: 330
Blanchard, R., Vol-I: 483–484; Vol-II: 117
Blanchard-Fields, F., Vol-I: 567
Blanchette, I., Vol-I: 200, 202
Blanck, H. M., Vol-II: 473
Blankenship, V., Vol-II: 50, 53
Blanton, C., Vol-II: 567
Blanton, P., Vol-II: 414
Blascovich, J., Vol-II: 460
Blatt, S. J., Vol-II: 139
Blau, F. D., Vol-II: 446
Blauwkamp, J. M., Vol-II: 170
Blazer, D. G., Vol-II: 134
Blazina, C., Vol-I: 145; Vol-II: 225–226, 229
Bleeker, M. M., Vol-II: 380, 384
Blevins, N., Vol-II: 161
Blinde, E. M., Vol-II: 574
Bliss, G. K., Vol-II: 295
Blix, A. G., Vol-II: 160
Blix, G. G., Vol-II: 160
Block, C. J., Vol-II: 346
Block, J., Vol-II: 95
Blood, R., Vol-II: 405
Bloom, B. L., Vol-II: 297
Bloomfield, K., Vol-II: 480
Blouin, A. G., Vol-II: 474
Blow, F. C., Vol-II: 188, 193–194
Bluck, S., Vol-I: 567
Blum, J. E., Vol-I: 238
Blum, R. W., Vol-II: 156
Blum, S. A., Vol-II: 200
Blumberg, F. C., Vol-II: 228
Blumberg, H., Vol-I: 396
Blumberg, R., Vol-II: 405
Blumenfeld, P., Vol-II: 389
Blumstein, P., Vol-I: 64, 66, 390
Blumstein, P. W., Vol-II: 292, 363, 412
Blundell, J. E., Vol-I: 458–459, 464
Blyth, D. A., Vol-II: 389
Bobak, M., Vol-II: 482
Boca, S., Vol-I: 440
Bochner, A., Vol-I: 114

Bockting, W. O., Vol-II: 111–112
Bodenmann, G., Vol-II: 551
Bodine, A., Vol-I: 195
Bodo, C., Vol-I: 218
Boehmer, A. L., Vol-I: 218
Boehmer, U., Vol-I: 7, 179–188; Vol-II: 7, 113–114, 553
Boesch, E. E., Vol-I: 163
Boffetta, P., Vol-II: 481
Bogaert, A. F., Vol-I: 367
Bogart, K., Vol-II: 624
Bogat, G., Vol-II: 619
Boggiano, A. K., Vol-II: 385
Boggs, C. D., Vol-II: 73, 193
Bograd, M., Vol-II: 255–256, 262
Bohan, J., Vol-I: 103, 401
Bohan, J. S., Vol-I: 32, 60, 72, 103, 108; Vol-II: 64, 66, 73
Bohon, L. M., Vol-I: 327
Boisnier, A. D., Vol-II: 340
Boldizar, J. P., Vol-I: 135
Boldy, J., Vol-II: 677
Bolen, J. C., Vol-II: 473
Boles, D., Vol-I: 325
Bolger, N., Vol-II: 497, 506, 512
Bolin, A., Vol-II: 115
Bolino, M. C., Vol-II: 340, 452
Bolks, H. N., Vol-II: 501, 552
Bombardier, C., Vol-I: 171
Bond, B. J., Vol-II: 659
Bond, J. T., Vol-II: 402
Bond, M. A., Vol-II: 613–636
Bond, M. H., Vol-II: 311
Bond, S., Vol-II: 160
Bonds-Raacke, J. M., Vol-I: 549; Vol-II: 166, 656
Boneva, B., Vol-II: 282
Boney-McCoy, S., Vol-II: 316
Bonica, C., Vol-I: 540
Bonifazi, M., Vol-I: 242
Bono, J. E., Vol-II: 448, 459
Bonu, S., Vol-II: 481
Bonvicini, K. A., Vol-II: 553
Boone, K. B., Vol-II: 605
Booraem, C., Vol-I: 382
Boorstin, D. J., Vol-I: 344
Booth, J. R., Vol-I: 245
Booth, M. L., Vol-II: 480
Borden, K. A., Vol-I: 323
Borders, L. D., Vol-I: 135, 151
Borghetti, D., Vol-I: 239
Borgida, E., Vol-II: 647, 660
Boring, E. G., Vol-I: 20, 24, 25
Borkenau, P., Vol-II: 412–413
Borker, R., Vol-I: 385–386, 389
Born, M., Vol-II: 71
Bornstein, B. H., Vol-II: 322
Bornstein, K., Vol-I: 369; Vol-II: 123, 366
Borooah, V. K., Vol-II: 481

Boroughs, M., Vol-II: 156, 163
Borowiecki, J., Vol-I: 53
Borowiecki, J. J., Vol-II: 166, 172
Borus, J. F., Vol-II: 521
Bosak, J., Vol-I: 421; Vol-II: 448
Bosco, A., Vol-I: 330
Bosold, C., Vol-II: 484
Bosson, J., Vol-I: 397
Bostock, Y., Vol-II: 477
Both-Orthman, B., Vol-I: 458
Botta, R., Vol-II: 167, 172, 658, 660
Botvin, G. J., Vol-I: 546
Bouchard, T. J., Vol-II: 19
Boucher, M., Vol-II: 235
Bound, J., Vol-II: 510
Bourg, C., Vol-I: 90; Vol-II: 686–689, 692
Bourgois, P., Vol-II: 591
Bourgon, L., Vol-II: 672–673, 676, 686
Bowen, C., Vol-II: 457
Bowen, D. J., Vol-I: 7, 179–188, 246, 464; Bowen, D. J., Vol-II: 114
Bowen, G. L., Vol-II: 686
Bowen, K. R., Vol-I: 301
Bower, J. E., Vol-II: 434
Bowers, A. M. V., Vol-II: 64
Bowers, C. A., Vol-II: 347–348
Bowers, K. S., Vol-I: 354
Bowker, G. C., Vol-II: 112
Bowlby, J., Vol-II: 281
Bowlby, J. W., Vol-I: 329
Bowleg, L., Vol-II: 461
Bowles, H. R., Vol-II: 347
Bowling, N. A., Vol-II: 436
Bowman, M., Vol-I: 329
Box, T. L., Vol-II: 533
Boxer, A. W., Vol-I: 535
Boyatzis, R., Vol-II: 49–50
Boyce, L. A., Vol-II: 677–679
Boyce, W. T., Vol-I: 442
Boyd, N., Vol-II: 633
Boyd-Franklin, N., Vol-II: 259
Boyle, D. E., Vol-I: 539
Boyle, P. A., Vol-II: 141
Boysen, G. A., Vol-I: 194; Vol-II: 231
Bozionelos, G., Vol-II: 23
Bozionelos, N., Vol-II: 23
Brabeck, M. M., Vol-I: 35, 317, 325
Brackbill, R. M., Vol-II: 533
Brackenridge, C. H., Vol-II: 579
Brackett, M. A., Vol-I: 439; Vol-II: 454
Bradbard, M., Vol-I: 515
Bradbard, M. R., Vol-I: 511, 515
Bradbury, H., Vol-I: 118, 122
Bradford, J., Vol-I: 66, 186; Vol-II: 114
Bradley, S. J., Vol-II: 112–114, 116–118, 122
Bradley, D. B., Vol-I: 164
Bradley, D. W., Vol-I: 147

Bradley, K., Vol-I: 278
Bradley, R. H., Vol-II: 225
Bradley, S. J., Vol-I: 141–142, 495, 510–511
Brady, K. L., Vol-I: 285
Brady, M., Vol-II: 487
Brain, M., Vol-II: 644
Braithwaite, V. A., Vol-I: 265, 325
Brajuha, M., Vol-II: 591–592
Brake, B., Vol-I: 263, 312
Brammer, M. J., Vol-I: 247, 464
Brand, G., Vol-I: 248
Brand, P., Vol-II: 50
Brandes, J. L., Vol-I: 241
Brandimonte, M. A., Vol-I: 330
Brannon, L., Vol-II: 686
Brannon, R., Vol-I: 44, 52, 136, 145, 150, 286
Brasfield, T., Vol-II: 626
Brass, D. J., Vol-II: 454
Brathwaite, A., Vol-II: 226
Braun, L., Vol-I: 64
Braun, V., Vol-I: 201, 392
Braunwald, K. G., Vol-II: 338
Brausch, A. M., Vol-II: 153
Braverman, L., Vol-II: 255
Brawer, M. K., Vol-I: 568
Bray, P., Vol-I: 243
Brayfield, A., Vol-II: 410
Brebner, J., Vol-I: 435
Breda, C., Vol-II: 340
Breedlove, S. M., Vol-I: 217, 270, 323
Breen, N., Vol-II: 544
Breggin, P., Vol-II: 97
Brehany, K., Vol-I: 456
Brehm, S. S., Vol-II: 323
Breivik, K., Vol-II: 599
Brener, N. D., Vol-II: 65
Brennan, D., Vol-I: 330
Brennan, P., Vol-II: 481
Brescoll, V., Vol-I: 194–195
Brescoll, V. L., Vol-I: 431
Bretherton, D., Vol-II: 202, 205
Bretschneider, J. G., Vol-I: 481
Brett, J. F., Vol-II: 448, 452
Brett, J. M., Vol-II: 448, 452
Brewer, H., Vol-II: 158
Brewer, M. B., Vol-I: 516
Brewis, A. A., Vol-II: 160
Bricheno, P., Vol-I: 288
Brickman, D., Vol-I: 507
Bridgeman, B., Vol-I: 304; Vol-II: 379, 388
Bridgest, S. T., Vol-I: 284
Briere, J., Vol-II: 70, 80, 208–209, 214
Briggs, P. T., Vol-I: 219
Brigham, F. J., Vol-II: 385
Brignone, B., Vol-I: 239
Brines, J., Vol-II: 405, 409–410
Bringer, J. D., Vol-II: 579

Brink, J., Vol-II: 604
Brinkmann, S., Vol-I: 106
Brinsmead-Stockham, K., Vol-II: 287
Brislin, R. W., Vol-I: 161–163, 169–173
Briton, N. J., Vol-I: 430–432
Britt, T. W., Vol-II: 687
Broad, K. L., Vol-II: 578
Broaddus, M., Vol-I: 505
Broadnax, S., Vol-I: 497
Brod, H., Vol-I: 51
Brodsky, A., Vol-II: 191
Brodsky, A. M., Vol-I: 29–30
Brody, C., Vol-I: 390
Brody, L. E., Vol-I: 304
Brody, L. R., Vol-I: 8, 429–448; Vol-II: 314
Brody, N., Vol-II: 68
Broidy, L., Vol-II: 329
Brolese, A., Vol-I: 329
Broman, C., Vol-II: 412
Bronfenbrenner, U., Vol-I: 528; Vol-II: 287
Bronk, E., Vol-I: 223
Brooker, R. J., Vol-I: 445
Brooks, G., Vol-I: 43, 46
Brooks, G. R., Vol-I: 45; Vol-II: 222, 224–225, 229, 232, 253–273
Brooks, R. C., Vol-II: 411
Brooks, W. M., Vol-I: 227, 264
Brooks-Gunn, J., Vol-I: 527–550
Broomer, R. K., Vol-II: 481
Brophy, J. E., Vol-II: 385
Broverman, D. M., Vol-I: 28; Vol-II: 64, 188, 678
Broverman, I. K., Vol-I: 28; Vol-II: 64, 73, 104, 188, 192–193, 678
Broverman, N., Vol-II: 370
Brown, A. F., Vol-II: 531
Brown, B. B., Vol-I: 537, 540, 549; Vol-II: 384
Brown, C., Vol-I: 352
Brown, C. E., Vol-I: 389, 414; Vol-II: 168, 338–339, 343
Brown, C. S., Vol-I: 282; Vol-I: 497–499, 516
Brown, D. J., Vol-II: 51, 343, 451, 660
Brown, D. K., Vol-I: 243
Brown, D. M., Vol-I: 457
Brown, G. K., Vol-II: 70
Brown, J. D., Vol-I: 542; Vol-II: 30
Brown, L., Vol-I: 68, 138
Brown, L. M., Vol-I: 105
Brown, L. S., Vol-I: 30, 35; Vol-II: 64, 83, 92, 94–95, 191–192, 196, 209, 234
Brown, M., Vol-I: 60, 71
Brown, M. L., Vol-II: 367
Brown, N. J., Vol-II: 598
Brown, R., Vol-I: 516
Brown, R. D., Vol-II: 573
Brown, S. D., Vol-II: 387
Brown, S. J., Vol-II: 346
Brown, S. L., Vol-I: 323; Vol-II: 599
Brown, S. P., Vol-II: 205
Brown, T. H., Vol-I: 573
Brown-Collins, A., Vol-I: 192
Browne, P., Vol-II: 672
Brownell, K. D., Vol-II: 167
Brownlee, K., Vol-II: 75
Brownmiller, S., Vol-II: 157
Brubaker, B. S., Vol-I: 264
Bruch, M. A., Vol-II: 24, 233
Brucken, L., Vol-I: 516
Bruggeling, E. C., Vol-I: 239
Brummett, B. H., Vol-II: 29
Bruns, C. M., Vol-II: 187–215
Brunstein, J. C., Vol-II: 43–44, 48, 53, 57
Brunswik, E., Vol-I: 416
Bryan, A., Vol-II: 371
Bryan, A. I., Vol-I: 20, 24
Bryan, J., Vol-I: 528, 532
Bryant, A., Vol-II: 170
Bryant, K. J., Vol-I: 329
Bryant, K., Vol-II: 112, 123, 125
Bryant, W. M., Vol-II: 365
Bryanton, O., Vol-II: 318
Bryden, M. P., Vol-I: 218, 221, 263, 300, 318, 325
Brydon-Miller, M., Vol-I: 113
Bryk, K. L., Vol-II: 387
Bub, K., Vol-I: 87
Buch, E. D., Vol-I: 106
Buchanan, C. M., Vol-I: 534
Buchanan, T., Vol-II: 602
Buchanan, W., Vol-II: 370
Buck, C. L., Vol-II: 686
Buck, L., Vol-I: 247
Buck, M., Vol-I: 195
Buckley, P., Vol-II: 474
Buckley, T., Vol-II: 169
Buckner, C., Vol-II: 150
Buckner, J. P., Vol-I: 437, 446
Buckwalter, J. G., Vol-I: 244
Budd, J. D., Vol-II: 431
Buddeberg-Fischer, B., Vol-II: 337
Buechel, C., Vol-I: 195, 197, 199, 202, 204, 372–373
Bugental, D. E., Vol-I: 438
Buhrke, R. A., Vol-II: 284
Bui, U., Vol-II: 233
Bukatko, D., Vol-II: 337
Bukowski, W. M., Vol-II: 122
Bulik, C. M., Vol-I: 460; Vol-II: 473
Bulka, D., Vol-I: 567
Buller, D. J., Vol-I: 260–262, 272
Bullis, J., Vol-I: 433
Bullock, H. E., Vol-II: 101
Bunk, J. A., Vol-II: 11, 423–437
Buntaine, R. L., Vol-I: 435
Bunting, A. B., Vol-I: 52
Burchard, E. G., Vol-I: 179
Burchinal, M., Vol-I: 87

Burg, A., Vol-I: 236
Burgess, C., Vol-II: 368
Burgess, L. H., Vol-I: 226
Burgess, M. C. R., Vol-I: 97
Burgess, S. E., Vol-II: 485
Burgess, S. R., Vol-I: 97
Burggraf, K., Vol-II: 167, 648
Burghauser, R., Vol-I: 246
Burgoon, M., Vol-I: 392; Vol-II: 340, 346–347
Burke, B. L., Vol-II: 235
Burke, M. E., Vol-I: 183
Burke, M. J., Vol-II: 344, 447
Burke, P., Vol-II: 118
Burke, R. J., Vol-I: 437; Vol-II: 502
Burkhardt, K. J., Vol-I: 163
Burkitt, J., Vol-I: 223, 330
Burleson, B. R., Vol-II: 23, 253
Burleson, M. H., Vol-II: 287
Burman, D. D., Vol-I: 245
Burman, E., Vol-I: 117, 198, 203; Vol-II: 66
Burn, S. M., Vol-II: 281
Burnam, M. A., Vol-II: 137
Burns, J. W., Vol-I: 443
Burns, N. R., Vol-I: 223
Burns, S. M., Vol-II: 528
Burns, T., Vol-II: 633
Burrell, N., Vol-I: 475
Burridge, A., Vol-II: 226
Burriss, L., Vol-I: 442
Burriss, R. P., Vol-II: 286
Bursik, K., Vol-I: 435
Bursoff, D. N., Vol-II: 590
Burton, L. A., Vol-I: 442
Burton, L. C., Vol-II: 524–525
Burwell, R. A., Vol-II: 167
Busby, L., Vol-II: 171
Busby, R. A., Vol-I: 323
Busch, H., Vol-II: 43
Bush, D., Vol-II: 389
Bushman, B. J., Vol-II: 657
Bushnell, M. C., Vol-I: 240, 243
Buss, A. H., Vol-II: 154, 312, 427
Buss, D. M., Vol-I: 49, 84, 167–168, 194, 201–202, 259, 261, 473, 481; Vol-II: 253, 281, 284–286, 300
Buss, K. A., Vol-I: 445
Busselle, R. W., Vol-II: 654
Bussey, K., Vol-I: 84, 474, 508; Vol-II: 643
Buswell, B. N., Vol-I: 299, 431; Vol-II: 30
Butcher, J. N., Vol-I: 14, 135; Vol-II: 15, 70, 76–79
Butler, D., Vol-II: 339, 341
Butler, J., Vol-I: 120, 194, 201, 260, 368
Butler, R., Vol-I: 345, 566
Butler, S., Vol-I: 330
Butryn, T. M., Vol-II: 568
Butterfield, D. A., Vol-II: 448
Butterworth, M., Vol-I: 368
Buttner, E. H., Vol-II: 340, 346

Buunk, A. P., Vol-II: 288
Buunk, B. P., Vol-II: 548
Buysse, A., Vol-II: 501
Byars-Winston, A. M., Vol-II: 383
Byers, E. S., Vol-II: 299
Byers, S. E., Vol-II: 299
Bylund, C. L., Vol-II: 523
Byne, W., Vol-I: 217, 225
Byrne, B. M., Vol-I: 172
Byrne, G. J. A., Vol-II: 477
Byron, K., Vol-I: 438

C

Cabaj, R. P., Vol-I: 64
Cabanac, M., Vol-I: 458
Cabe, N., Vol-II: 230
Cabrera, N. J., Vol-II: 229
Cacioppo, J. T., Vol-I: 239
Cadinu, M., Vol-I: 433
Cady, E. T., Vol-I: 549; Vol-II: 565
Cafri, G., Vol-I: 54; Vol-II: 99, 153, 156–157, 160–163, 172
Cain, D. P., Vol-I: 221
Cain, V. A., Vol-II: 228
Cairney, J., Vol-II: 476
Cairns, B., Vol-I: 397
Cairns, R., Vol-I: 397
Calás, M. B., Vol-II: 452
Caldera, Y., Vol-I: 502
Caldwell, L. D., Vol-II: 227, 236
Caldwell, M. A., Vol-II: 282
Caldwell, N. D., Vol-II: 144
Caldwell-Colbert, A. T., Vol-II: 460
Cale, E. M., Vol-II: 96
Calhoun, L. G., Vol-II: 297
Calkins, M. W., Vol-I: 21–27
Callaghan, M., Vol-II: 382, 391
Callanan, C., Vol-II: 485
Callanan, M. A., Vol-I: 307, 445
Calloway, D. H., Vol-I: 458
Calogero, R. M., Vol-I: 10, 86, 91; Vol-II: 10, 153–174
Calvert, S. L., Vol-I: 515; Vol-II: 327, 651–652
Calvo, M. G., Vol-I: 442
Camara, W. J., Vol-II: 72
Camarata, S., Vol-I: 301
Camargo, C. A., Vol-II: 474
Cameron, B. A., Vol-I: 457
Cameron, C. E., Vol-I: 21
Cameron, D., Vol-I: 118, 195, 381, 387, 397–398
Cameron, J. A., Vol-I: 516
Cameron, L., Vol-I: 517
Cameron, R. P., Vol-I: 544
Camfield, T. M., Vol-I: 21
Camic, P. M., Vol-I: 103, 121–122
Cammarota, J., Vol-II: 272
Campbell, A., Vol-I: 396–397, 496
Campbell, B., Vol-I: 534

Campbell, D. T., Vol-I: 81, 161, 164–165, 171–173
Campbell, I. C., Vol-I: 247, 464
Campbell, J. D., Vol-II: 24
Campbell, K. L., Vol-II: 54
Campbell, R. T., Vol-I: 187
Campbell, R., Vol-II: 614, 624, 629, 634
Campbell, T. L., Vol-I: 172
Campos, D., Vol-II: 43
Campos-Flores, A., Vol-II: 369–370
Canada, K., Vol-I: 285
Canary, D. J., Vol-II: 283, 293, 296
Canetto, S. S., Vol-I: 569
Canner, R., Vol-II: 475
Cannon, L. W., Vol-I: 108
Cánovas, R., Vol-I: 328
Cantor, J., Vol-I: 68, 542; Vol-II: 166
Cantrill, J. G., Vol-II: 291
Canyock, E., Vol-II: 603
Cao, F., Vol-II: 430
Capdevila, R., Vol-I: 365
Capitanio, J. P., Vol-II: 340
Capitanio, J., Vol-I: 68
Caplan, J., Vol-I: 403
Caplan, J. B., Vol-I: 84; Vol-II: 91
Caplan, P., Vol-I: 403
Caplan, P. J., Vol-I: 9, 29, 84, 318; Vol-II: 9, 64, 73, 91–105, 192, 196
Capodilupo, C., Vol-II: 227
Capotosto, L., Vol-I: 285
Cappelleri, J. C., Vol-II: 76
Capranica, L., Vol-II: 572
Caprara, G. V., Vol-I: 172
Capshew, J. H., Vol-I: 24
Capstick, M., Vol-II: 690
Carach, C., Vol-I: 484
Caradoc-Davies, T., Vol-II: 483
Card, N. A., Vol-I: 546
Carey, C. M., Vol-II: 290
Carey, M., Vol-I: 485, 487
Carlat, D. J., Vol-II: 474
Carli, L., Vol-I: 380, 383, 387
Carli, L. L., Vol-I: 411, 419; Vol-II: 10, 337–352
Carlson, E. R., Vol-I: 31
Carlson, L., Vol-II: 50
Carlson, R., Vol-I: 31
Carlson, T. S., Vol-II: 271
Carlsson, I., Vol-I: 353
Carlton-Ford, S., Vol-II: 389
Carney, D. R., Vol-I: 417
Carnot, E., Vol-II: 648
Carp, F. M., Vol-I: 573
Carpenter, C., Vol-II: 171
Carpenter, D., Vol-II: 479
Carpenter, K., Vol-II: 159
Carpenter, L. J., Vol-II: 566
Carr, D. S., Vol-II: 296, 410
Carranza, E., Vol-I: 198

Carrere, S., Vol-II: 265
Carrico, A., Vol-II: 21
Carrier, B., Vol-I: 243
Carrington, B., Vol-II: 382
Carrington, C., Vol-II: 411–412
Carroll, J., Vol-II: 9, 174
Carroll, J. B., Vol-I: 263
Carroll, R., Vol-I: 487
Carroll, S. A., Vol-I: 439
Carson, D. K., Vol-I: 457
Carson, J. L., Vol-II: 478
Carson, K. A., Vol-I: 219
Carstensen, L. L., Vol-I: 437, 566–567; Vol-II: 499
Carter, B., Vol-II: 255
Carter, C. S., Vol-I: 249
Carter, D. A., Vol-II: 351, 456
Carter, D. B., Vol-I: 515
Carter, G., Vol-I: 330; Vol-II: 228
Carter, J. D., Vol-I: 411, 413, 415, 446
Carter, P., Vol-I: 319
Caruso, C., Vol-II: 573
Caruso, D. R., Vol-I: 418, 439
Caruthers, A., Vol-II: 171, 660
Carvajal, S., Vol-II: 618
Carve, C. E., Vol-II: 286
Carver, C. S., Vol-II: 434, 547
Carver, P. R., Vol-I: 142, 498–499, 512
Carver, R. A., Vol-II: 43, 53
Casanova, E. M., Vol-II: 160
Casas, J. F., Vol-II: 319–320
Casas, J. M., Vol-II: 236
Case, P., Vol-II: 552–553
Case, S-E., Vol-I: 119
Caselles, C. E., Vol-II: 360
Casey, K. L., Vol-I: 242, 243
Casey, M. B., Vol-I: 317, 325, 332
Cash, T. F., Vol-I: 150, 567; Vol-II: 153–154, 156, 158–160, 163, 173
Casper, L. M., Vol-II: 446
Caspi, A., Vol-I: 535, 543, 548
Cass, D. T., Vol-II: 482
Cass, V. C., Vol-I: 541
Cassidy, A., Vol-I: 195, 202
Cassidy, C., Vol-I: 510
Cassidy, J. W., Vol-I: 243
Casswell, S., Vol-II: 480
Castelli, L., Vol-I: 517
Castle, D. J., Vol-II: 161
Castro, C., Vol-II: 673, 690
Catanese, K. R., Vol-II: 289
Catrell, A. K., Vol-II: 69
Catsambis, S., Vol-I: 310
Cattarin, J. A., Vol-II: 162
Cattell, H. E. P., Vol-II: 69, 80
Cattell, R. B., Vol-II: 80
Cauffman, E., Vol-I: 536; Vol-II: 329
Caviness, V. S., Vol-I: 217

Caws, P., Vol-II: 94
Caygill, L., Vol-I: 496
Ceccarelli, I., Vol-I: 241
Ceci, S. J., Vol-I: 283, 300
Cecil, J. S., Vol-II: 589
Ceder, I., Vol-I: 332
Cejka, M. A., Vol-II: 448
Cella, K., Vol-II: 260
Cella, S., Vol-I: 544
Cellerino, A., Vol-I: 239
Center, B. A., Vol-II: 414
Cermele, J., Vol-II: 103
Cerone, L. J., Vol-I: 239, 325
Cervantes, C. A., Vol-I: 445
Cetin, K., Vol-II: 546
Chabanne, V., Vol-I: 330
Chagnon, N., Vol-I: 269
Chaiken, S., Vol-I: 457, 460, 567
Chaikin, A. L., Vol-II: 294
Chakraborty, P., Vol-II: 98
Chalifoux, B., Vol-II: 101
Chamberlain, K., Vol-II: 228
Chambless, D. C., Vol-II: 221
Chambless, D. L., Vol-II: 197, 202–203
Chan, C., Vol-I: 64, 65; Vol-II: 288, 293
Chan, C. W., Vol-I: 236
Chan, N., Vol-I: 247, 462
Chan, R., Vol-I: 67
Chan, R. W., Vol-II: 411
Chan, S. S. H., Vol-II: 477
Chang, E. L., Vol-I: 328
Chang, G., Vol-II: 416
Chang, K. T., Vol-I: 330
Chang, L., Vol-I: 241
Chang, S., Vol-II: 288, 293
Chang, T., Vol-II: 226, 228, 232, 234
Chang, Y. F., Vol-I: 187
Chang-Schneider, C., Vol-II: 31
Channer, K. S., Vol-I: 242
Chantala, K., Vol-I: 530
Chaplin, T. M., Vol-I: 435, 437, 445
Chapman, D., Vol-II: 620
Chapman, M., Vol-I: 45
Chapman, T. K., Vol-I: 114
Charles, M., Vol-I: 278
Charles, R., Vol-I: 350
Charles, S. T., Vol-I: 567
Charleston, S. I., Vol-I: 328
Charlton, K., Vol-I: 413
Charlton, R., Vol-I: 568
Charmaz, K., Vol-I: 111
Charyton, C., Vol-I: 351
Chase, C., Vol-I: 194
Chase, S. E., Vol-I: 108, 111
Chase, T. N., Vol-I: 226
Chasiotis, A., Vol-II: 43
Chatman, C. M., Vol-I: 497

Chatman, J. A., Vol-II: 340, 349
Chattha, H. K., Vol-II: 75
Chavous, T. M., Vol-I: 285, 496
Chawla, P., Vol-I: 438
Cheater, F., Vol-II: 228
Check, J. V., Vol-II: 660
Chen, C., Vol-I: 307
Chen, H. S., Vol-II: 412
Chen, J. T., Vol-I: 179
Chen, J. Y., Vol-II: 286
Chen, Y., Vol-I: 438
Chen. J. J., Vol-I: 345
Cheney, M. M., Vol-I: 247, 462
Cheng, J. H. S., Vol-I: 288
Chentsova-Dutton, Y. E., Vol-I: 435, 437–438, 442
Cherney, I., Vol-I: 263
Cherney, I. D., Vol-I: 320, 322, 515
Chernovetz, M. E., Vol-II: 24
Cherrier, M. M., Vol-I: 223
Cherry, D. K., Vol-II: 518–519
Chesler, P., Vol-I: 27, 347; Vol-II: 73, 188, 192
Chesley, N., Vol-II: 653
Chesney, G. L., Vol-I: 238
Chester, A., Vol-II: 202, 205
Chester, N. L., Vol-II: 42, 45–46, 49, 53
Cheung, A., Vol-II: 352
Cheung, B. M. Y., Vol-II: 543
Cheung, F. M., Vol-I: 166, 170; Vol-II: 460
Cheung, P., Vol-I: 369
Chevrier, E., Vol-I: 319, 322
Chew, J., Vol-II: 205
Chhin, C. S., Vol-II: 380, 384
Chi, I., Vol-II: 485
Chi, Q., Vol-I: 248
Chia, S., Vol-I: 475
Chiappa, K. H., Vol-I: 243
Chiarello, C., Vol-I: 324
Child, P., Vol-I: 497
Childs, E., Vol-II: 633
Childs, G., Vol-I: 289
Chin, J., Vol-I: 30
Chin, J. L., Vol-II: 224, 462
Chiolero, A., Vol-II: 476
Chipman, K., Vol-I: 222
Chiu, C., Vol-I: 160; Vol-II: 70, 460
Chiu, W. T., Vol-II: 473
Chivers, M. L., Vol-I: 225
Chodorow, N., Vol-I: 32, 473; Vol-II: 117
Chodorow, N. J., Vol-I: 50
Choi, E., Vol-I: 420
Choi, J., Vol-I: 222, 263, 265, 318–319, 321, 328–329
Choi, N., Vol-I: 135
Choi, P., Vol-II: 158, 478, 575
Choi, P. Y. L., Vol-II: 570, 573
Choo, P., Vol-II: 297
Choprac, A., Vol-I: 246
Chovil, N., Vol-I: 438

Chrisler, J. C., Vol-I: 1–15, 110, 348, 352, 361–374, 433, 444, 566; Vol-II: 1–15, 97–98, 104, 159, 161, 167–168, 174, 205, 521, 551, 648, 692
Christensen, A., Vol-II: 499
Christensen, M., Vol-II: 553
Christensen, P. N., Vol-I: 446; Vol-II: 168
Christenson, A., Vol-II: 265–267
Christians, C. G., Vol-I: 106
Christofides, T. C., Vol-II: 603
Christova, P. S., Vol-I: 239
Chrousos, G. P., Vol-I: 534
Chryssochoou, X., Vol-I: 199
Chu, C., Vol-II: 534
Chu, J. Y., Vol-I: 137, 150
Chubb, N. H., Vol-II: 30
Chuck, S. K., Vol-II: 534
Chun, C., Vol-II: 620
Chung, W. C. J., Vol-II: 116
Chung, Y. B., Vol-I: 509
Church, A. T., Vol-I: 166, 170
Church, J., Vol-I: 327
Chusmir, L., Vol-II: 44, 46
Chusmir, L. H., Vol-I: 354
Cialdini, R. B., Vol-II: 343, 347
Cianni, M., Vol-II: 451, 453
Ciarlo, J. A., Vol-II: 224
Ciarrochi, J., Vol-I: 439; Vol-II: 236, 242
Cimadevilla, J. M., Vol-I: 328
Cini, M. A., Vol-II: 292
Citera, M., Vol-I: 96
Civello, D., Vol-II: 543
Claes, M. E., Vol-II: 281
Clapp, S. K., Vol-II: 692
Clark, E. V., Vol-I: 361
Clark, H. H., Vol-I: 197; Vol-II: 361
Clark, J., Vol-I: 241
Clark, M., Vol-I: 187
Clark, M. D., Vol-II: 104, 192–193
Clark, M. P., Vol-I: 25
Clark, M. S., Vol-II: 282, 295, 414
Clark, R. A., Vol-II: 282
Clark, S., Vol-II: 486
Clarke, J., Vol-II: 478
Clarke, L. H., Vol-II: 174
Clarke, P. G., Vol-I: 222
Clarke, S., Vol-I: 390
Clarkson, F. E., Vol-I: 28; Vol-II: 104, 188, 678
Clarkson, R. F., Vol-II: 72
Claus, R. E., Vol-II: 295
Clayton, P. J., Vol-I: 477
Clay-Warner, J., Vol-II: 337
Clegg, D. J., Vol-I: 247
Clements, K., Vol-II: 329
Clements-Nolle, K., Vol-II: 120–122
Clendenen, V. I., Vol-I: 462
Cleveland, E., Vol-II: 644
Cleveland, J. N., Vol-II: 425

Clifton, A. K., Vol-II: 339
Clifton, A., Vol-I: 380
Clinchey, B. M., Vol-I: 32
Clinchy, B., Vol-I: 105
Clinchy, B. M., Vol-I: 198
Clipp, E. C., Vol-I: 574
Clore, G. L., Vol-I: 434, 436, 439
Close, J., Vol-I: 567; Vol-II: 658
Clossick, M. L., Vol-II: 255
Cloud, J., Vol-I: 290
Cloutier, J., Vol-II: 285
Coates, J., Vol-I: 117, 385, 390, 394
Coats, E. J., Vol-I: 416, 421, 438, 444
Cochran, S. D., Vol-I: 63, 65, 69, 480; Vol-II: 103, 133, 137–138, 144, 224, 229, 232, 234–236, 486, 552
Cochran, S. V., Vol-I: 6, 43–55; Vol-II: 6, 135, 230, 232–235
Cochrane, G. H., Vol-II: 172
Code, L., Vol-I: 32
Cody, M. J., Vol-II: 295
Coffee, A., Vol-I: 241
Coffman, C. J., Vol-II: 519
Cogan, J., Vol-I: 67, 69
Cogan, J. C., Vol-II: 161, 362–363
Cohane, G., Vol-I: 53
Cohane, G. H., Vol-II: 225
Cohen, D., Vol-II: 91, 96
Cohen, D. S., Vol-I: 330
Cohen, E., Vol-I: 249; Vol-II: 624
Cohen, E. L., Vol-II: 409–410, 412
Cohen, G. L., Vol-II: 342
Cohen, I. T., Vol-I: 458–459, 464
Cohen, J., Vol-I: 298, 309, 477
Cohen, L., Vol-I: 393
Cohen, L. L., Vol-I: 147, 151; Vol-II: 170
Cohen, P. N., Vol-II: 446
Cohen, R. M., Vol-II: 385
Cohen, R. S., Vol-I: 142–143
Cohen, S., Vol-II: 501, 504–505
Cohen-Kettenis, P. T., Vol-I: 222, 224–225, 270, 324; Vol-II: 115–116, 367
Cohn, L., Vol-I: 54; Vol-II: 170
Coie, J., Vol-I: 397
Coker, A. L., Vol-II: 485
Coker, D. R., Vol-I: 514
Cokley, K. O., Vol-I: 285
Colapinto, J., Vol-I: 260; Vol-II: 366
Colburne, K. A., Vol-I: 501
Cole, C. M., Vol-I: 224
Cole, E. R., Vol-I: 193
Cole, J. R., Vol-I: 345, 354
Cole, K. L., Vol-II: 209
Cole, P. M., Vol-I: 435
Cole, S. W., Vol-II: 141, 553
Cole-Harding, S. F., Vol-I: 483
Cole-Kelly, K., Vol-II: 255
Coleman, E., Vol-I: 72, 368; Vol-II: 112

Coleman, M., Vol-II: 289, 405
Coleman, R. R. M., Vol-II: 644, 658
Coleman, S. M., Vol-II: 113
Collaer, M. L., Vol-I: 225, 320, 322
College, G., Vol-II: 385
Colley, A., Vol-I: 394
Collins, A., Vol-I: 244
Collins, C. A., Vol-II: 546
Collins, D. L., Vol-II: 507
Collins, D. W., Vol-I: 221, 319
Collins, K. A., Vol-II: 485
Collins, K. E., Vol-II: 578
Collins, N. L., Vol-II: 326
Collins, P. A., Vol-I: 511
Collins, P. H., Vol-I: 32, 105, 108–109
Collins, W. A., Vol-I: 540
Collinsworth, L. L., Vol-I: 282
Collman, P., Vol-I: 506
Colom, R., Vol-I: 322
Colön, D., Vol-I: 325
Colson, Y., Vol-II: 529
Colten, M. E., Vol-I: 186
Coltrane, S., Vol-II: 11, 401–416, 647–648
Coluccia, E., Vol-I: 265, 330
Colvin, C. R., Vol-I: 413, 417
Colwill, N., Vol-II: 295
Comas-Díaz, L., Vol-I: 30, 35; Vol-II: 192–193, 261–262, 627
Combe, B., Vol-II: 545
Combs, R., Vol-II: 368
Compas, B., Vol-I: 544
Compas, B. E., Vol-I: 545; Vol-II: 82
Conception, R. Y., Vol-II: 574
Condit, D., Vol-II: 603
Condon, B., Vol-I: 330
Conforti, K., Vol-II: 235
Conger, J., Vol-I: 59, 70
Conger, J. C., Vol-II: 283
Conger, J. J., Vol-II: 386
Conger, K. J., Vol-II: 619
Conger, R. D., Vol-I: 543, 544; Vol-II: 139, 619
Conkright, L., Vol-I: 515
Conn, S. R., Vol-II: 80
Connell, R. W., Vol-I: 51; Vol-II: 169, 225–227
Connellan, J., Vol-I: 309
Connelly, S., Vol-I: 143
Conner, M., Vol-I: 456
Connidis, I. A., Vol-I: 572
Connolly, C. M., Vol-II: 258
Connolly, J., Vol-I: 540; Vol-II: 320
Conrad, P., Vol-I: 194
Conradi, P., Vol-II: 471
Conroy, D., Vol-II: 48
Constable, R. T., Vol-I: 328
Constantian, C. A., Vol-II: 50
Constantine, M. G., Vol-I: 34
Constantinople, A., Vol-I: 150, 192, 204, 366; Vol-II: 22

Contreras, M. J., Vol-I: 322
Conway, L., Vol-II: 113–115
Conway, M., Vol-II: 144
Conway-Turner, K., Vol-I: 572
Cook, C. M., Vol-I: 221, 323
Cook, E. P., Vol-II: 94
Cook, J., Vol-I: 285
Cook, J. A., Vol-I: 105, 109
Cook, K., Vol-II: 339
Cook, M., Vol-II: 616
Cook, S., Vol-I: 139
Cook, S. W., Vol-II: 321
Cook, T. D., Vol-I: 81, 161, 164
Cooke, D. J., Vol-II: 74
Cooke, E. P., Vol-I: 14; Vol-II: 15
Cooke, L. L., Vol-II: 347
Cooke, L. P., Vol-II: 413
Cooley-Quille, M., Vol-II: 619
Coolidge, F. L., Vol-II: 67
Coombes, L., Vol-I: 117
Cooper, C. L., Vol-II: 424, 429, 502, 505
Cooper, H., Vol-I: 413
Cooper, J., Vol-I: 510, 515
Cooper, K., Vol-II: 120
Cooper, L. A., Vol-II: 520
Cooper, M. L., Vol-II: 23
Cooper, R. M., Vol-I: 246
Cooper, R. S., Vol-I: 179
Cooper, S. P., Vol-II: 195
Copeland, C. L., Vol-II: 340
Coquillon, E., Vol-I: 118
Corballis, M. C., Vol-I: 239
Corbett, S., Vol-II: 680
Corbin, J., Vol-I: 111
Corby, B. C., Vol-I: 498, 512–513
Cordova, J., Vol-I: 437, 439
Corenlius, L., Vol-I: 180
Corker, M., Vol-I: 32
Cormier, H., Vol-II: 170
Cormier, J. F., Vol-II: 164–165
Corneal, D. A., Vol-I: 544
Cornell, D. G., Vol-II: 384
Cornell, D. P., Vol-II: 295
Cornuz, J., Vol-II: 476
Cornwell, J. M., Vol-II: 449
Correll, S. J., Vol-II: 447
Corrigall, E. A., Vol-I: 95
Corrigan, S. A., Vol-I: 458
Cortina, L. M., Vol-II: 423, 425–426, 429, 433–437
Cosgrove, L., Vol-I: 103, 108, 362, 364, 381–382, 400–401, 403–404; Vol-II: 64, 73, 92, 94–95, 98–100, 192, 196, 633
Costa, P., Vol-I: 442
Costa, P. T. Jr., Vol-I: 560; Vol-II: 25–28, 81, 447
Costa, P. T. J., Vol-I: 170
Costanzo, M., Vol-I: 412–413
Costello, E. J., Vol-I: 548; Vol-II: 133, 137, 144

Costenbader, V. K., Vol-I: 435
Costrich, N., Vol-I: 383
Cote, S., Vol-II: 313
Cotrufo, P., Vol-I: 544
Coulter, M. L., Vol-II: 319
Counts, M., Vol-I: 330
Couper-Leo, J., Vol-I: 323
Coupland, J., Vol-I: 394
Courchesne, E., Vol-I: 217
Cournoyer, R. J., Vol-II: 137
Courtenay, W. H., Vol-I: 48, 53, 535, 568; Vol-II: 170, 224, 228, 522
Courtois, C., Vol-II: 195, 208
Cousins, A. J., Vol-II: 286
Covatto, A. M., Vol-I: 539
Coverman, S., Vol-II: 405
Covinsky, K. E., Vol-II: 546
Cowan, G., Vol-I: 387, 510
Cowan, R. L., Vol-I: 237
Cowie, C. C., Vol-II: 531
Cox, B., Vol-II: 574
Cox, B. D., Vol-I: 319
Cox, D., Vol-I: 263
Cox, R. S., Vol-II: 502
Coyle, A., Vol-I: 192
Coyne, J. C., Vol-II: 139, 496, 498–501, 505, 511, 551–552
Coyne, J., Vol-I: 146
Coyne, S. M., Vol-II: 313, 644, 649
Cozby, P. C., Vol-II: 295
Cozza, T. M., Vol-I: 137
Craeynest, M., Vol-I: 497
Craft, R. M., Vol-I: 241–242
Craig, D., Vol-I: 388
Craig, J. M., Vol-II: 341
Craig, P., Vol-II: 477
Craig, W., Vol-I: 540
Craig, W. M., Vol-II: 319–320
Craik, F. I. M., Vol-I: 568
Cramer, P., Vol-I: 432
Cramond, B., Vol-I: 7, 343–355
Crandall, C. S., Vol-II: 167
Crandall, V. C., Vol-II: 387
Crane, D. R., Vol-II: 272
Crane, M., Vol-I: 508
Crawford, J., Vol-I: 115
Crawford, J. K., Vol-I: 535; Vol-II: 165
Crawford, M., Vol-I: 20, 33, 103, 198, 327, 361–365, 381–383, 388, 484
Crawford, M. S., Vol-II: 34, 64–65, 67, 71, 73, 168, 448, 615, 672, 680, 682, 685, 691
Cremato, F., Vol-I: 544
Crerand, C. E., Vol-II: 162
Crespo, C. J., Vol-II: 567
Creswell, J. W., Vol-I: 112, 123
Crick, N. R., Vol-I: 546; Vol-II: 312, 319–320
Crimmel, B. L., Vol-II: 518

Cristofaro, T. N., Vol-I: 500, 505
Crittenden, N., Vol-I: 439
Crocker, J., Vol-I: 194, 496–497
Crocker, P. R. E., Vol-II: 576
Crockett, L. J., Vol-I: 543
Crombez, G., Vol-I: 497
Crompton, R., Vol-II: 410
Cronbach, L. J., Vol-I: 349
Crooks, R., Vol-II: 532
Croom, G., Vol-I: 65
Cross, S. E., Vol-I: 429; Vol-II: 294–295, 297
Crossley, M. L., Vol-I: 114, 116, 118
Crossman, J., Vol-II: 647
Crouch, I., Vol-I: 381
Crouter, A. C., Vol-I: 143, 144, 501, 511, 536–537, 544, 570–571; Vol-II: 296, 384, 413, 415
Crowe, P. A., Vol-I: 539
Crowley, C., Vol-I: 541
Crowley, K., Vol-I: 307
Crowley, M., Vol-II: 326
Crowne, D. P., Vol-II: 602
Crusco, A. H., Vol-I: 458
Cruz, Z., Vol-II: 361
Crystal, S., Vol-II: 478
Csank, P. A. R., Vol-II: 144
Csikszentmihalyi, M., Vol-II: 232, 282
Csillag, C., Vol-II: 527
Cuddy, A. J. C., Vol-II: 352, 450
Cui, L., Vol-I: 249
Cullen, K. A., Vol-II: 533
Cullen, P. C., Vol-II: 97
Culley, M., Vol-I: 616, 618, 628–629
Cummings, A. L., Vol-I: 548
Cummings, T. G., Vol-II: 350
Cunningham, A., Vol-I: 548
Cunningham, G. B., Vol-II: 647
Cunningham, J. G., Vol-I: 431
Cunningham, M. R., Vol-II: 409–410
Cunningham, S. J., Vol-II: 21
Currie, C. E., Vol-II: 483
Curtis, J., Vol-I: 569
Curtis, L., Vol-II: 282
Cusack, J., Vol-II: 242
Cusak, J., Vol-II: 236
Custer, H., Vol-I: 438
Custer, L., Vol-II: 412
Cutler, S. E., Vol-II: 137
Cutmore, T. R. H., Vol-I: 328
Cutrona, C. E., Vol-II: 501, 507
Czaja, S. J., Vol-II: 137

D

D'Agostino, H., Vol-II: 156
D'Alessandro, L. M., Vol-I: 244
d'Anna, S., Vol-I: 236
D'Arcy, C., Vol-II: 228

D'Augelli, A. R., Vol-I: 68, 545; Vol-II: 120, 136, 138, 367–368
D'Elia, L. F., Vol-II: 605
Dabbs, J. M. Vol-I: 328, 330; Vol-I: 226
Dabul, A. J., Vol-II: 347
Dadds, M., Vol-I: 436
Dahl, S., Vol-II: 207
Dahlerup, D., Vol-II: 444
Dahlheimer, D., Vol-I: 67
Dahlstrom, L. E., Vol-II: 76
Dahlstrom, W. G., Vol-II: 70
Dahms, T. L., Vol-II: 201
Dailey, R. M., Vol-II: 295
Daily, C. M., Vol-II: 602
Dainton, M., Vol-II: 293, 296
Daiuto, A. D., Vol-II: 266
Dalton, D. R., Vol-II: 602
Dalton, J. H., Vol-II: 613
Dalvit, S. P., Vol-I: 458
Dalvit-McPhillips, S., Vol-I: 459, 464
Daly, J., Vol-I: 117
Damasio, H., Vol-I: 217
Dana, M., Vol-II: 168
Dance, L., Vol-II: 414
Daniel, S., Vol-II: 271
Daniels, C., Vol-II: 566
Daniels, J. A., Vol-II: 383
Danish, S. J., Vol-II: 576
Dankoski, M. E., Vol-II: 255
Danner, C. C., Vol-II: 206, 208
Danoff-Burg, S., Vol-II: 12, 541–555
Danseco, E. R., Vol-II: 482
Dansky, B. S., Vol-II: 685
Danziger, K., Vol-I: 204
Darcy, C. M., Vol-II: 483
Dargel, A., Vol-II: 51
Dark, L., Vol-I: 68
Darlega, V. L., Vol-II: 326
Darley, J. M., Vol-II: 447, 647, 661
Darling, N., Vol-II: 623, 633
Dar-Nimrod, I., Vol-I: 194, 374
Darroch, J. E., Vol-II: 532
Darrow, C. N., Vol-I: 44
Dasgupta, N., Vol-II: 661
Dasgupta, S. D., Vol-II: 292–293
Dash, A. S., Vol-I: 238
Dash, X., Vol-I: 238
Dasti, J., Vol-II: 124
Daubenmier, J. J., Vol-II: 544, 575
Daughtridge, R., Vol-II: 523
Davalos, D. B., Vol-II: 646, 648
Davalos, R. A., Vol-II: 646
David, D., Vol-I: 44, 136, 145, 150
David, L., Vol-I: 47, 48, 145
Davids, R., Vol-II: 486
Davidson, J., Vol-I: 49
Davidson, K., Vol-I: 431

Davidson, L., Vol-II: 272
Davidson, L. R., Vol-II: 294
Davidson, M. J., Vol-II: 452
Davidson, R. J., Vol-I: 242; Vol-II: 54
Davies, A. P., Vol-I: 193
Davies, D. C., Vol-I: 216–217
Davies, I. J., Vol-I: 218
Davies, K., Vol-I: 505
Davies, P. G., Vol-II: 450, 661
Davis, A. J., Vol-II: 141, 290
Davis, A. M., Vol-I: 119
Davis, B., Vol-I: 83
Davis, B. J., Vol-II: 228
Davis, C., Vol-II: 158, 574
Davis, D. D., Vol-II: 460
Davis, E., Vol-I: 368
Davis, G. A., Vol-I: 350
Davis, J. H., Vol-I: 108–109, 113–115
Davis, K. D., Vol-II: 672, 674, 676, 679–684
Davis, K. E., Vol-II: 233
Davis, M. H., Vol-I: 438; Vol-II: 295
Davis, P. J., Vol-I: 445
Davis, R. H., Vol-I: 49
Davis, R., Vol-II: 70, 81, 97
Davis, S., Vol-I: 483
Davis, S. N., Vol-I: 108–109, 113–115, 505; Vol-II: 407, 409–411
Davis, W. N., Vol-II: 171
Davis-Kean, P., Vol-II: 384
Davison, G., Vol-I: 62
Davison, H. K., Vol-II: 344, 447
Davitz, J. R., Vol-II: 438
Davy, B., Vol-I: 456–457, 464
Dawber, T., Vol-II: 484
Dawes, R. M., Vol-II: 94, 193
Dawkins, N., Vol-II: 543
Dawson, C. R., Vol-II: 687
Day, A. L., Vol-I: 439
Day, R., Vol-II: 50
De Amicis, L., Vol-I: 517
de Andrade Stempliuk, V., Vol-II: 476
de Andrade, A. G., Vol-II: 476
De Backer, C., Vol-I: 398
de Bosset, V., Vol-II: 544
De Bourdeaudhuij, I., Vol-I: 497
de Castro, J. M., Vol-I: 456–457, 462
De Dreu, C. K. W., Vol-II: 350
de Graaf, H., Vol-II: 655
de Graaf, R., Vol-II: 135, 224, 369
De Haan, E. H. F., Vol-I: 321
De Jesus, M., Vol-II: 627
de la Motte, D., Vol-I: 348
De Lisi, R., Vol-I: 319, 328
De Pater, I. E., Vol-II: 455
De Paul, J., Vol-II: 329
de Perrot, M., Vol-II: 529
De Reus, L. A., Vol-I: 563

de Ridder, D., Vol-II: 546
de St. Aubin, E., Vol-I: 563–564
De Vries, G. J., Vol-II: 116
de Wied, M., Vol-I: 242
Deacon, S. A., Vol-II: 255
Dean, C., Vol-II: 97
Dean, J. T., Vol-II: 195
Dean, L., Vol-I: 69
Deane, F. P., Vol-II: 236, 242
Deary, I. J., Vol-I: 301–302
Deaux, K., Vol-I: 28, 84, 88, 197, 364–365, 429, 496; Vol-II: 67, 69, 71, 75–76, 296, 360, 447–449, 570, 631
deBeauvoir, S., Vol-I: 197
DeBono, K. G., Vol-II: 283
DeBord, K. A., Vol-II: 226
DeBro, S. C., Vol-II: 68
Deci, E. L., Vol-II: 297, 388
Decker, S. H., Vol-II: 595
Deeb, S. S., Vol-I: 237
Deeg, D. J. H., Vol-II: 297
Deer, B., Vol-II: 598
Deeter, T. E., Vol-II: 569
DeFilippis, J. A., Vol-II: 598
Deforche, B., Vol-I: 497
DeFrances, C. J., Vol-II: 520, 533
Degelman, D., Vol-I: 194
Degenholtz, H., Vol-II: 525
DeGraffinreid, C. R., Vol-I: 184
DeHart, P. H., Vol-II: 390
Deinhart, A., Vol-II: 255–256
Deiss, V., Vol-I: 463
Dekkers, H., Vol-II: 390
DeKoekkoek, P. D., Vol-I: 573
del Campo, R., Vol-II: 412
Del Zotto, M., Vol-I: 239
DeLamater, J. D., Vol-I: 431
Delaney, J., Vol-II: 169
DeLaria, L., Vol-II: 292
Delbridge, R., Vol-I: 395, 397
Delnevo, C. D., Vol-II: 478
DeLoache, J. S., Vol-I: 509
DeLongis, A., Vol-II: 495–512
Delon-Martin, C., Vol-I: 249
Delva, J., Vol-I: 570
DeMaris, A., Vol-II: 137, 407
DeMeis, D., Vol-II: 409, 411
DeMers, S., Vol-I: 354
Demo, D., Vol-II: 405, 409
Demolar, G. L., Vol-I: 247
DeMoss, K., Vol-I: 354
Dempsey, D., Vol-I: 64
Demuth, C., Vol-I: 110
Demuth, S., Vol-II: 599
DeNardo, M., Vol-II: 426
DeNavas-Walt, C., Vol-II: 123
Dengel, D. W., Vol-II: 365

Denham, B. E., Vol-II: 647
Denislic, M., Vol-I: 240
Denmark, F. L., Vol-I: 20, 27
Denmark, F., Vol-I: 371
Denney, R. L., Vol-II: 598
Denney-Wilson, E., Vol-II: 480
Dennis, W. D., Vol-II: 225
Denny, D., Vol-II: 119, 368
Dent, R., Vol-II: 472
Denzin, N. K., Vol-I: 106, 108, 119, 122
Deo, S., Vol-II: 26
Deogracias, J. J., Vol-I: 141
Deosaransingh, K., Vol-II: 484
DePaulo, B. M., Vol-I: 412, 413
Depner, C., Vol-II: 43
Dépret, E., Vol-I: 418
Derbyshire, S. W., Vol-I: 242
Derbyshire, S. W. G., Vol-I: 242
Derlega, V. J., Vol-II: 294–295, 509
Dernier, O., Vol-II: 473
Derogatis, L. R., Vol-II: 209
Deruiter, W. K., Vol-II: 476
Desaulniers, J., Vol-II: 21
Desertrain, G. S., Vol-II: 570
Desmarais, S., Vol-I: 569
DeSouza, E., Vol-II: 425
DeSouza, M. J., Vol-II: 575
Despres, J. P., Vol-I: 457
Desrosiers, E., Vol-II: 347
Desvaux, G., Vol-II: 456
Deutsch, F. M., Vol-II: 299
Devaud, L. L., Vol-I: 365
DeVault, M., Vol-II: 407, 415
Devillard-Hoellinger, S., Vol-II: 456
Devine, P. G., Vol-I: 418, 431
Devineni, T., Vol-I: 323
Devlin, A. S., Vol-I: 328–329; Vol-II: 692
DeVoe, M., Vol-I: 567
DeVore, I., Vol-I: 267
Devos, T., Vol-I: 196, 198
Dew, M. A., Vol-II: 338
Dey, A. N., Vol-II: 519
deZwaan, M., Vol-I: 86
Dhillon, P. K., Vol-I: 347
Dhindsa, M. K., Vol-II: 554
Di Ceglie, D., Vol-II: 115, 125
Di Dio, L., Vol-II: 23
Di Marco, F., Vol-II: 547–548
Diala, C. C., Vol-II: 478
Diamant, A. L., Vol-II: 552
Diamond, L., Vol-I: 368, 480
Diamond, L. M., Vol-I: 64, 66, 72, 262, 540–541, 549; Vol-II: 140, 366, 645
Diamond, M., Vol-I: 194, 367; Vol-II: 366
Diaz, R. M., Vol-I: 187; Vol-II: 145–146
Diaz, S. F., Vol-II: 162
Dibble, S. L., Vol-II: 486

DiBerardinis, J. P., Vol-II: 339
Dick, R., Vol-II: 575
Dickens, G., Vol-II: 604
Dickens, M. N., Vol-II: 384
Dickson, M. W., Vol-II: 348
DiClemente, R., Vol-II: 626
DiDomenico, L., Vol-II: 172
Diekman, A. B., Vol-I: 84, 90, 421, 570, 572; Vol-II: 448, 678
Diener, E., Vol-I: 434, 436
Diener, M. L., Vol-I: 431
Dietz, T. L., Vol-II: 645
DiFranceisco, W., Vol-I: 487
Dijksterhuis, A., Vol-I: 418
Dill, K. E., Vol-II: 649, 651, 657
Dillard, J. P., Vol-II: 340
Dillard, J., Vol-I: 392
Dillaway, H., Vol-II: 174, 412
Dillaway, H. E., Vol-I: 568
Dilworth, J. E., Vol-II: 415
Dimah, A., Vol-II: 318
Dimah, K. P., Vol-II: 318
DiMare, L., Vol-II: 448
DiMatteo, M. R., Vol-I: 413, 441; Vol-II: 295
Dimberg, U., Vol-I: 434, 438
Dinda, K., Vol-II: 21
Dindia, K., Vol-I: 440; Vol-II: 282–283, 294, 300, 327
Dingstad, G. I., Vol-I: 463
Dinno, A., Vol-II: 546
Dion, K. K., Vol-II: 157, 292, 301, 347
DiPlacido, J., Vol-I: 63, 68
Diquinzio, P., Vol-II: 117
Dischinger, P., Vol-II: 483
Ditrano, C., Vol-II: 272
Dittmar, H., Vol-I: 566–567; Vol-II: 154
Ditty, K. M., Vol-I: 243
Diver, M. J., Vol-I: 242
Diversi, M., Vol-I: 110–111, 119
Dixon, T. L., Vol-II: 650
Dixon, W. A., Vol-I: 24, 483
Dixon-Woods, M., Vol-II: 532
Dixson, A. D., Vol-I: 114
Dobbins, T., Vol-II: 480
Dobie, T. G., Vol-I: 245
Dobson, K. S., Vol-II: 141
Dobson, S. H., Vol-I: 330
Docherty, K. J., Vol-I: 226
Dochin, E., Vol-I: 238
Docter, R., Vol-I: 486
Dodd, G. H., Vol-I: 248
Dodder, R. A., Vol-I: 135
Dodge, K. A., Vol-II: 70
Doherty, R. W., Vol-I: 434
Dohrenwend, B. P., Vol-II: 137–138
Doig, W., Vol-II: 370
Dokecki, P., Vol-II: 272
Dolan-Del Vecchio, K., Vol-II: 262, 269–271

Dolezal, C. L., Vol-I: 140
Don, M., Vol-I: 243
Donaghy, E., Vol-I: 183
Donahue, L. M., Vol-II: 348
Donahue, M., Vol-I: 445
Donaldson, J. S., Vol-I: 194
Donaldson, M., Vol-I: 51
Donnerstein, E., Vol-II: 647, 660
Donovan, J. M., Vol-II: 529
Donzella, B., Vol-I: 242
Doorn, C. D., Vol-I: 224
Doran, N., Vol-I: 392
Doran, N. E., Vol-II: 340
Döring, N., Vol-II: 646
Dorn, L. D., Vol-I: 534
Dorner, G., Vol-I: 217
Doroszewicz, K., Vol-I: 167
Dorsch, K. D., Vol-I: 535, 567
Dosanih, N., Vol-I: 117
Doss, B. D., Vol-II: 225
Dottl, D. A., Vol-I: 242
Dottolo, A. L., Vol-I: 20, 36
Doty, R. L., Vol-I: 248
Double, K. L., Vol-I: 244
Doucet, A., Vol-II: 229
Doucet, J., Vol-II: 101
Dougherty, J., Vol-II: 501
Dougherty, T. W., Vol-II: 454
Douglas, S. C., Vol-II: 427, 431
Douglas, S. J., Vol-II: 647
Douvan, E., Vol-II: 43
Dovidio, J. F., Vol-I: 389, 414, 416–417; Vol-II: 147, 338–339, 447, 661
Dow, K. L., Vol-II: 380
Downey, G., Vol-I: 540; Vol-II: 140–141
Downey, J., Vol-I: 226
Downey, R., Vol-I: 463
Downing, N. E., Vol-I: 146, 148–149
Downs, A. C., Vol-I: 52, 143; Vol-II: 287
Doyle, A., Vol-I: 501, 531
Doyle, J. A., Vol-I: 47, 52; Vol-II: 104
Dozier, D. M., Vol-II: 644
Dozois, D. J., Vol-II: 141
Dracup, K., Vol-II: 543
Dragowski, E. A., Vol-II: 195
Draguns, J. G., Vol-II: 338
Draijer, N., Vol-II: 100
Drake, R., Vol-II: 650
Drakich, J., Vol-I: 388–389, 393–394
Drapeau, V., Vol-I: 457
Drasgow, F., Vol-II: 423, 428, 430, 685
Drasin, H., Vol-I: 549
Dreger, A. D., Vol-I: 194
Dreifus, C., Vol-II: 523
Drentea, P., Vol-II: 414
Drescher, J., Vol-I: 61
Drewnowski, A., Vol-I: 457; Vol-II: 156

Drigotas, S. M., Vol-II: 294
Driscoll, A. K., Vol-II: 138
Driscoll, I., Vol-I: 227, 264
Driska, A., Vol-II: 566
Driskell, J. E., Vol-II: 340, 343, 459
Droit-Volet, S., Vol-I: 463
Drummond, K. D., Vol-I: 142
Drummond, M. J. N., Vol-II: 124, 169–170
Druss, B., Vol-II: 519
Dsurney, J., Vol-II: 598
Du, R., Vol-I: 238
Duan, C., Vol-I: 1; Vol-II: 1
Dubas, J. J. S. D., Vol-I: 414
Dubas, J. S., Vol-I: 327
Dubb, A., Vol-I: 307
Dubbs, S. L., Vol-II: 288
Dubé, E. M., Vol-I: 540
Duberman, L., Vol-II: 294
Dubois, B., Vol-I: 380–381
DuBois, C. L. Z., Vol-II: 349
Dubow, E., Vol-II: 645
Duck, R. J., Vol-II: 362
Duckers, S., Vol-I: 456
Duda, J. L., Vol-II: 568, 570, 573
Dudek, S. Z., Vol-I: 350
Duehr, E. E., Vol-II: 448, 459
Duff, S. J., Vol-II: 323
Duffy, J., Vol-I: 283
Duffy, S. M., Vol-I: 64
Duffy, V. B., Vol-I: 246–247
Duggan, S. J., Vol-II: 158
Duggan, S. L., Vol-II: 535
Dugger, M., Vol-I: 328
Duka, T., Vol-I: 224
Duke, M. P., Vol-I: 414
Dumont, A., Vol-I: 27
DuMont, K., Vol-II: 137, 628
Dunbar, K., Vol-I: 200, 202
Dunbar, R., Vol-I: 396
Dunbar, R. I. M., Vol-I: 259
Duncan, G. H., Vol-I: 240, 243
Duncan, L., Vol-I: 327
Duncan, L. E., Vol-I: 9, 566; Vol-II: 9, 41–58
Duncan, M. C., Vol-II: 571
Duncan, S., Vol-I: 388
Duncan, T., Vol-II: 622
Duncombe, D., Vol-II: 173
Dunham, Y., Vol-I: 497
Dunkel-Schetter, C., Vol-II: 294, 495
Dunlop, L., Vol-II: 169
Dunn, C., Vol-II: 235
Dunn, E., Vol-I: 497
Dunn, M. A., Vol-II: 589
Duntley, J. D., Vol-II: 285
Dupuy, P., Vol-II: 94
Durbin, R. G., Vol-I: 296
Durik, A. M., Vol-I: 431, 485; Vol-II: 48, 381, 388

Durkee, A., Vol-II: 312
Durrant, J. D., Vol-I: 243
Dutch, S. E., Vol-II: 521
Duxbury, L. E., Vol-II: 415, 687
Dweck, C. S., Vol-I: 284, 307; Vol-II: 67, 70
Dworkin, S. F., Vol-I: 241
Dworkin, S. H., Vol-II: 161
Dye, L., Vol-I: 458–459, 464
Dyke, L. S., Vol-II: 323
Dykes, J., Vol-I: 515
Dyrenfurth, I., Vol-I: 226

E
Eagle, B., Vol-II: 415
Eagly, A., Vol-I: 106, 402
Eagly, A. H., Vol-I: 11, 35, 84, 89–90, 167–168, 195, 198, 201, 203, 262, 313, 411, 415, 419–422, 430, 438, 475, 481, 569, 570, 572; Vol-II: 11, 13, 20–21, 33, 68, 153, 168, 170, 282, 288, 311, 313, 324–326, 329, 338–339, 341, 343, 346–347, 350–351, 387, 427, 433–462
Eakins, B., Vol-I: 390; Vol-II: 295
Eakins, G., Vol-I: 390
Eakins, R. G., Vol-II: 295
Eals, M., Vol-I: 221, 263, 265, 321, 325
Easterbrooks, M. A., Vol-II: 383
Eastin, M., Vol-II: 167
Eastman, R. C., Vol-II: 531
Eastman, S. T., Vol-II: 647
Easton, A., Vol-I: 187
Eastwick, P. W., Vol-I: 168; Vol-II: 287–288
Eaton, W., Vol-II: 134
Ebbeck, V., Vol-II: 574
Eberhardt, M. S., Vol-II: 531
Eberl, R., Vol-II: 482
Ebersole, P., Vol-I: 352
Ebner, N. C., Vol-I: 566
Eby, L. T., Vol-II: 454
Eccles, J., Vol-I: 281, 284, 297, 310
Eccles, J. S., Vol-I: 143, 306, 374, 497, 510, 528, 531–532, 534, 569; Vol-II: 379, 381–385, 387–390, 394
Echeverri, F., Vol-I: 247
Echeverría, S. E., Vol-II: 554
Eck, B. A., Vol-II: 154, 170
Eckel, L. A., Vol-I: 218; Vol-II: 74
Eckenrode, J., Vol-II: 76
Eckert, P., Vol-I: 385, 390
Eckes, T., Vol-I: 517
Ecuyer-Dab, I., Vol-I: 263, 267, 269–270, 325–326, 330
Eddins, R., Vol-II: 226
Edelen, M. O., Vol-I: 547
Edelsky, C., Vol-I: 388–390
Eder, D., Vol-I: 395–396, 540
Edgar, M. A., Vol-I: 225
Ediger, E., Vol-II: 99
Edison, M. I., Vol-I: 285

Edleson, J. L., Vol-II: 632
Edmondson, C. B., Vol-II: 283
Edwards, D., Vol-II: 621
Edwards, J. N., Vol-II: 318
Edwards, K., Vol-I: 435
Edwards, P. C., Vol-I: 267
Edwards, R., Vol-I: 106
Edwards, S., Vol-I: 53
Edwards, T., Vol-I: 368
Egan, J., Vol-II: 225
Egan, S. K., Vol-I: 142, 150, 192, 497–499, 512, 529, 531
Egan, T. D., Vol-II: 350
Egede, L. E., Vol-II: 546
Egeland, G. M., Vol-II: 487
Egerton, M., Vol-II: 404
Eggermont, J. J., Vol-I: 243
Eggins, S., Vol-I: 396
Egland, K. L., Vol-II: 283
Egsmose, C., Vol-II: 545
Ehde, D. M., Vol-II: 546
Ehrbar, R. D., Vol-II: 111
Ehrenfeld, J., Vol-II: 204
Ehrenreich, B., Vol-II: 523
Ehrensaft, M. K., Vol-I: 546–547
Ehrhardt, A. A., Vol-I: 140, 260; Vol-II: 116
Ehrlich, S. B., Vol-I: 318
Eibach, R., Vol-I: 198
Eichenfield, E., Vol-II: 222
Eichenfield, G. A., Vol-I: 45
Eichorn, D., Vol-I: 535
Eichstedt, J. A., Vol-I: 500–501
Einarsen, S., Vol-II: 424, 429
Einon, D., Vol-II: 169
Einstein, A., Vol-II: 187
Eisenberg, M. E., Vol-II: 140
Eisenberg, N., Vol-I: 242, 435; Vol-II: 174
Eisenbud, L., Vol-I: 511
Eisenhardt, K. M., Vol-II: 350
Eisler, R., Vol-I: 53–54, 145
Eisler, R. M., Vol-I: 51–52, 146, 285; Vol-II: 123
Eisner, E., Vol-I: 120
Eiswirth-Neems, N., Vol-II: 626
Ekehammar, B., Vol-II: 362
Ekins, R., Vol-II: 112
Ekman, P., Vol-I: 412
Ekman, R., Vol-II: 483
Ektor-Andersen, J., Vol-I: 241
Elasmar, M., Vol-II: 644, 647
Elder, G., Vol-II: 46, 619
Elder, G. H. Vol-I: 532–543, 559, 574; Vol-II: 139
Eldridge, G., Vol-II: 626
Eldridge, K. A., Vol-II: 500
Eldridge, N. S., Vol-II: 263–264
Elhai, J. D., Vol-II: 76
Elias, L., Vol-I: 221, 264, 321, 328–329

Elias, L. J., Vol-I: 222
Elias, M. J., Vol-II: 613
Eliason, M. J., Vol-II: 340, 363, 365
Eliason, M., Vol-I: 68
Elinson, L., Vol-II: 519
Ellemers, N., Vol-II: 348, 461
Ellermeier, W., Vol-I: 241
Ellickson, P. L., Vol-I: 547
Elliot, A. J., Vol-II: 44
Elliot, L. B., Vol-I: 566
Elliott, A. N., Vol-I: 482; Vol-II: 318
Elliott, D., Vol-I: 322
Elliott, G., Vol-I: 533
Elliott, M. R., Vol-II: 476
Elliott, R. H., Vol-II: 431
Ellis, A., Vol-I: 299
Ellis, A. B., Vol-I: 262, 531; Vol-II: 386
Ellis, C., Vol-I: 107, 114–115
Ellis, J., Vol-I: 186–187
Ellis, J. B., Vol-I: 151
Ellis, J. M., Vol-I: 186
Ellis, L., Vol-I: 483
Ellsworth, P. C., Vol-I: 435; Vol-II: 432
Ellyson, S. L., Vol-I: 389, 414, 416; Vol-II: 338–340, 347
Elms, A. C., Vol-I: 29
Else-Quest, N. M., Vol-I: 445
Elston, D., Vol-I: 462, 464
Ely, R., Vol-II: 461
Elze, D. E., Vol-I: 545; Vol-II: 114, 125
Embaye, N., Vol-I: 71
Ember, C. R., Vol-I: 160, 162, 167, 269; Vol-II: 311
Ember, M., Vol-I: 160, 164, 167, 269; Vol-II: 311
Embretson, S. E., Vol-II: 76, 81–82
Emery, B. C., Vol-II: 319
Emmerich, W., Vol-I: 503
Emory, L. E., Vol-I: 224
Emrich, C. G., Vol-II: 448
Emslie, C., Vol-I: 51; Vol-II: 475
Emswiller, T., Vol-I: 28
Enchautegui-de-Jesus, N., Vol-II: 616
Enck, P., Vol-I: 245
Endicott, J., Vol-II: 98
Endo, S., Vol-I: 246
Endresen, I. M., Vol-II: 328
Endsley, R., Vol-I: 511
Endsley, R. C., Vol-I: 511, 515
Eng, E., Vol-II: 633
Engelgau, M. M., Vol-II: 531
Engeln-Maddox, R., Vol-II: 166
England, P., Vol-II: 405, 409
Englar-Carlson, M., Vol-I: 10, 45; Vol-II: 10, 221–243
Engleson, S. A., Vol-I: 52
Englis, B. G., Vol-II: 166
English, D., Vol-II: 523

English, K. M., Vol-I: 242
English, L., Vol-I: 363
Enke, J., Vol-I: 395–396
Enns, C. Z., Vol-II: 191, 197, 201–202, 205
Enriquez, V. G., Vol-I: 34
Epitropaki, O., Vol-II: 347
Epley, M. L., Vol-I: 329
Epp, J. R., Vol-I: 226
Epperson, D. L., Vol-II: 196, 312, 427, 431
Epstein, C., Vol-I: 381–382, 401
Epstein, M., Vol-I: 6, 133–152
Epstein, N. B., Vol-II: 6, 265, 268
Epstein, R., Vol-I: 382
Epstein, S., Vol-I: 193
Epting, F., Vol-II: 231
Epting, L. K., Vol-I: 224
Erb, M., Vol-I: 239
Erdoğmuş, N., Vol-II: 382
Erhardt, M. L., Vol-II: 351
Erhardt, N. L., Vol-II: 456
Erickson, M. J., Vol-II: 531
Erickson, R., Vol-II: 413
Erickson, S. J., Vol-II: 141
Erikson, E., Vol-I: 528, 560
Erikson, E. H., Vol-I: 560–562, 565–566; Vol-II: 56, 58
Erikson, J. M., Vol-I: 560
Erikson, K. B., Vol-II: 193, 196
Erkanli, A., Vol-II: 133, 137
Erkut, S., Vol-I: 332; Vol-II: 576–577
Erly, A. M., Vol-II: 265
Ernst, D., Vol-I: 197
Ernst, M., Vol-I: 219
Eron, L., Vol-II: 645
Erskine, J. A. K., Vol-I: 460, 462, 464
Ersland, L., Vol-I: 324
Ervin, K. S., Vol-II: 652
Escobar, O., Vol-II: 550
Esdaille, J., Vol-II: 507
Esnil, E. M., Vol-II: 460
Espelage, D. L., Vol-I: 290; Vol-II: 329
Espey, D. K., Vol-II: 526
Espila, A. M., Vol-I: 224
Espin, O. M., Vol-I: 34, 35
Espínola, M., Vol-I: 328
Espinoza, P., Vol-I: 198
Espiritu, Y. L., Vol-II: 412
Esses, V., Vol-I: 195
Esses, V. M., Vol-II: 656
Esseveld, J., Vol-I: 107
Essex, M. J., Vol-I: 97
Essick, G. K., Vol-I: 246
Estep, K. M., Vol-II: 324
Etcoff, N., Vol-II: 156, 164
Ethier, K. A., Vol-I: 429
Evaldsson, A., Vol-I: 397
Evans, C., Vol-I: 540
Evans, E., Vol-II: 478

Evans, E. M., Vol-I: 531
Evans, J. D., Vol-I: 568
Evans, L., Vol-I: 505
Evans, M., Vol-II: 225
Evans, P. C., Vol-II: 166
Evans, W. J., Vol-I: 249
Evardone, M., Vol-I: 322
Eve, R. A., Vol-I: 330
Everson, H. T., Vol-II: 72
Ewashen, C., Vol-II: 205
Exner, J. E. Jr., Vol-II: 70
Eyal, K., Vol-II: 658
Eyre, H. L., Vol-I: 435
Eyssell, K. M., Vol-I: 436
Eyster, S., Vol-II: 412–413

F
Fabes, R. A., Vol-I: 219, 500
Fabrigar, L. R., Vol-I: 151
Fabunmi, R., Vol-II: 543
Facio, E., Vol-I: 572
Factor, R. J., Vol-I: 369
Faeh, D., Vol-II: 476
Fagot, B. I., Vol-I: 504–505, 510–511
Fahey, J. L., Vol-II: 434, 553
Fairbank, J. A., Vol-II: 137
Fairchild, K., Vol-II: 298
Faith, M. S., Vol-II: 159, 164
Fajen, B. R., Vol-I: 266
Falbo, T., Vol-I: 383; Vol-II: 340, 346
Falkner, A., Vol-I: 66
Fallon, A. E., Vol-II: 649
Fallon, E., Vol-II: 575
Fallon, M. A., Vol-II: 570
Fallows, D., Vol-II: 652
Falomar-Pichastor, J. M., Vol-I: 194
Fansler, A. G., Vol-II: 425
Faraday, M. M., Vol-I: 457
Farage, M. A., Vol-I: 223
Faragher, B., Vol-II: 429
Fargo, J. D., Vol-I: 288
Farkas, G., Vol-II: 405
Farley, K., Vol-II: 690
Farmer, H. S., Vol-I: 384, 387
Farragher, E., Vol-II: 644, 646
Farrar, K., Vol-II: 662
Farrell, M. P., Vol-II: 576
Farrington, D. P., Vol-II: 328
Fassinger, R. E., Vol-II: 205
Fasteau, M. F., Vol-I: 44
Fasting, K., Vol-II: 579
Fauldi, S., Vol-II: 117
Faulkner, G., Vol-II: 476
Faulkner, S. L., Vol-II: 283, 289, 299–300
Faust, D., Vol-II: 588, 600
Fausto-Sterling, A., Vol-I: 83, 194; Vol-II: 366
Fay, C., Vol-II: 162

Fazio, R. J., Vol-II: 576
Featherstone, L., Vol-II: 453
Febbraro, A. R., Vol-II: 12, 671–692
Fechner, P. Y., Vol-I: 533
Fedigan, L. M., Vol-I: 200
Fedoroff, I. C., Vol-I: 456
Feeney, A., Vol-II: 475
Fehr, B., Vol-II: 282, 297, 327
Feigal, J., Vol-I: 67
Feil, L. A., Vol-II: 383
Fein, E., Vol-II: 290
Feinberg, D. R., Vol-II: 286
Feinberg, L., Vol-II: 366–367
Feine, J. S., Vol-I: 240
Feingold, A., Vol-I: 150, 300–303, 305, 318, 567; Vol-II: 139, 155, 386
Feingold, J., Vol-II: 27, 30
Feinman, J., Vol-II: 388
Feinstein, J., Vol-I: 383
Feiring, C., Vol-I: 527, 529, 540
Feist, G. J., Vol-I: 354
Feld, S., Vol-II: 43, 55
Feldbaum, M., Vol-I: 194
Feldlaufer, H., Vol-II: 388
Feldman, C. M., Vol-II: 210
Feldman, J. F., Vol-I: 140
Feldman, R., Vol-II: 621
Feldman, R. S., Vol-I: 421, 438
Feldman, S., Vol-I: 533
Feldman-Summers, S., Vol-II: 340
Feldt, T., Vol-II: 27, 35
Félix-Ortiz, M., Vol-I: 165
Feller, R. P., Vol-I: 246
Felmlee, D., Vol-II: 297
Felson, R. B., Vol-II: 316, 323, 435
Feng, B., Vol-II: 253
Feng, J., Vol-I: 307, 328; Vol-II: 70, 651
Fennell, M. L., Vol-II: 339
Fennema, E., Vol-I: 303, 317, 531; Vol-II: 386
Fenstermaker, S., Vol-II: 406–407
Fenwick, G. D., Vol-II: 347, 349
Ferguson, A. D., Vol-I: 65
Ferguson, L., Vol-I: 397
Ferguson, M., Vol-I: 393
Ferguson, M. J., Vol-II: 170
Ferguson, T. J., Vol-I: 435
Fergusson, D. M., Vol-II: 135–136
Fernandez, E., Vol-II: 120
Fernandez, L. C., Vol-I: 20
Ferraro, K. J., Vol-II: 317
Ferree, M. M., Vol-II: 372, 406–407, 414
Ferrell, J., Vol-I: 595
Ferrera, D., Vol-I: 134
Ferrera, D. L., Vol-I: 47
Ferris, A., Vol-II: 543
Fertman, C. I., Vol-II: 30
Fessler, D. M. T., Vol-II: 649

Festchieva, N., Vol-II: 473
Feurer, I. D., Vol-II: 631
Fichman, L., Vol-I: 545
Fidell, L., Vol-I: 88
Field, E. F., Vol-I: 220
Fielden, S. L., Vol-II: 452, 502
Fielding, N., Vol-I: 123
Fields, A. W., Vol-I: 329
Fields, J. P., Vol-II: 576
Filardo, A. K., Vol-II: 339, 341, 351
Filipek, P. A., Vol-I: 217
Fillingim, R. B., Vol-I: 241
Finch, S., Vol-I: 456
Fine, E., Vol-I: 114
Fine, M., Vol-I: 35, 103, 106, 108, 110, 114, 118; Vol-II: 272, 631
Fine, M. G., Vol-I: 392
Finegan, J. K., Vol-I: 220
Finemore, J., Vol-II: 156
Finer, L. B., Vol-II: 532
Finger, T. E., Vol-I: 246, 248
Fingerhut, A., Vol-I: 480
Fink, B., Vol-II: 286
Fink, P. J., Vol-II: 111
Finkel, E. J., Vol-II: 287–288
Finkelhor, D., Vol-II: 317, 319, 631
Finkelstein, E. A., Vol-II: 530
Finkelstein, J. S., Vol-I: 35
Finken, L. L., Vol-II: 383
Finlay, F., Vol-I: 398
Finlay, L., Vol-I: 109
Finlayson, T. L., Vol-I: 570
Finley, S., Vol-I: 119
Finn, S. E., Vol-II: 197
Firebaugh, L., Vol-I: 549
Firestein, B., Vol-I: 66, 72; Vol-II: 193
Firestone, J. M., Vol-II: 430
Firestone, L., Vol-I: 242
Fisch, H., Vol-I: 568
Fischer, A. H., Vol-I: 430, 434–435, 441–442; Vol-II: 282, 453, 455
Fischer, A. R., Vol-I: 136, 149; Vol-II: 200, 226, 238
Fischer, C. S., Vol-II: 297
Fischer, E., Vol-II: 292
Fischer, H., Vol-I: 240
Fischer, R., Vol-I: 172, 246
Fisek, M. H., Vol-II: 345
Fish, J., Vol-I: 186
Fish, S., Vol-II: 366
Fish, V., Vol-II: 95
Fishbein, M., Vol-II: 533
Fisher, B., Vol-II: 526
Fisher, D. A., Vol-II: 655
Fisher, H., Vol-I: 480
Fisher, K., Vol-II: 404
Fisher, L. A., Vol-II: 568
Fisher, M., Vol-II: 232, 285

Fisher, M. L., Vol-I: 398
Fisher, T. D., Vol-I: 481–482, 487
Fishman, P. M., Vol-II: 295
Fiske, A. P., Vol-I: 1; Vol-II: 1
Fiske, D. W., Vol-I: 173, 388
Fiske, S., Vol-I: 485
Fiske, S. T., Vol-I: 1, 144, 147–148, 168, 198, 418; Vol-II: 1, 70, 137, 290, 352, 450
Fitting, S., Vol-I: 322
Fitts, M. L., Vol-II: 660
Fitzgerald, L., Vol-I: 43, 51
Fitzgerald, L. F., Vol-II: 228, 230, 423–424, 426, 428, 430, 433, 685
Fitzgerald, R. W., Vol-I: 266
Fitzpatrick, J. A., Vol-II: 296
Fivush, R., Vol-I: 70, 437, 445–446; Vol-II: 141
Flaherty, J. A., Vol-II: 436
Flanagan, M. B., Vol-I: 245
Flannagan, D., Vol-I: 515
Flannery-Schroeder, E., Vol-II: 159
Fleeson, W., Vol-II: 29, 34
Flegal, K. M., Vol-II: 531
Fleischmann, R. M., Vol-II: 545
Fleishman, J. A., Vol-II: 533
Fleming, A. S., Vol-I: 548
Fleming, E. C., Vol-II: 173
Fleming, J., Vol-II: 47–48
Fletcher, G. J. O., Vol-II: 21, 284, 293, 325
Fletcher, J. K., Vol-II: 452, 454, 462
Flett, G., Vol-I: 457
Flett, G. L., Vol-I: 567; Vol-II: 99
Flick, U., Vol-I: 113
Flinchbaugh, L. J., Vol-I: 548
Flink, C., Vol-II: 385
Flitter, J. M. K., Vol-II: 76
Floor, E., Vol-II: 54
Flores, E., Vol-II: 301
Flores, Y. L., Vol-II: 392
Flowers, J., Vol-I: 382
Floyd, F. J., Vol-I: 541
Floyd, K., Vol-II: 282
Flynn, M., Vol-II: 139
Fodor, E. M., Vol-II: 43, 53–54
Fodor, I. G., Vol-I: 382
Foehr, U. G., Vol-I: 542
Foels, R., Vol-II: 459
Fogarty, A., Vol-II: 530
Fogel, G. I., Vol-I: 50
Folbre, N., Vol-II: 409
Foley, L. A., Vol-II: 196, 322
Folkman, S., Vol-II: 432, 495–497, 499, 503–504, 511
Fonda, S. J., Vol-I: 227
Fong, G., Vol-II: 624
Fong, K. T., Vol-II: 616
Fonow, M. M., Vol-I: 105, 109
Fontaine, K. R., Vol-II: 545
Foote, F. H., Vol-II: 432

Forbes, G. B., Vol-I: 159–173
Forcey, L. R., Vol-II: 416
Ford, G., Vol-II: 474
Ford, J. G., Vol-I: 183–184
Ford, M. J., Vol-II: 385
Ford, P., Vol-II: 485
Ford, R. S., Vol-II: 339
Ford, T. W., Vol-II: 339
Fordham, S., Vol-I: 290
Forest, K. B., Vol-II: 453
Formoso, D., Vol-II: 621
Forouzan, E., Vol-II: 74
Forret, M. L., Vol-II: 454
Forster, N., Vol-II: 505
Foschi, M., Vol-II: 342–344
Foster, R. A., Vol-I: 195
Foti, R. J., Vol-II: 451
Fouad, N. A., Vol-II: 382–383, 387–389, 392
Foucault, M., Vol-I: 32, 108, 202, 368, 402–403; Vol-II: 112
Fouts, G., Vol-II: 167, 644–645, 648
Fox, C. J., Vol-I: 221
Fox, D., Vol-I: 31, 35
Fox, K. V., Vol-I: 107, 119
Fox, M., Vol-II: 282, 284
Fox, R., Vol-I: 63, 65
Fox-Keller, E., Vol-I: 30
Fox-Rushby, J., Vol-I: 171
Fraley, R. C., Vol-I: 484
Frances, A., Vol-II: 95, 116
Frank, A. W., Vol-I: 115
Frank, K. A., Vol-II: 281
Franklin, A. J., Vol-II: 227
Fransson, P., Vol-I: 240
Franz, B. T., Vol-II: 138
Franz, C., Vol-II: 46, 56
Franz, C. E., Vol-I: 560, 562–563, 571
Franzoi, S. L., Vol-II: 154
Frazier, P., Vol-II: 297
Frederick, D. A., Vol-II: 157, 164, 649
Fredericks, J. A., Vol-II: 573
Fredricks, J. A., Vol-I: 531; Vol-II: 382, 388
Fredrickson, B., Vol-I: 567
Fredrickson, B. L., Vol-I: 91; Vol-II: 117, 153–157, 170–171, 575, 647–648, 659
Freed, A., Vol-I: 401
Freedman, E. G., Vol-I: 202
Freedman, R., Vol-II: 167
Freedman-Doan, C. R., Vol-II: 390
Freedy, J., Vol-II: 620
Freels, S., Vol-II: 436
Freeman, D., Vol-I: 159, 259
Freeman, N. J., Vol-II: 604
Freidl, W., Vol-II: 473
Freire, P., Vol-II: 635
Freitas, A. L., Vol-II: 140–141
French, D. C., Vol-II: 312

French, J. R. P. Vol-I: 416
French, S. A., Vol-II: 156, 479
French, S., Vol-II: 619
Frenkel, M., Vol-II: 446
Frenzel, A. C., Vol-I: 444; Vol-II: 385, 388–389
Freud, S., Vol-I: 61, 199–200, 471–472, 560
Freund, A. M., Vol-I: 566
Freund, H. J., Vol-I: 244
Frey, K. S., Vol-I: 496, 503, 510–511
Freyd, J., Vol-II: 214
Freyne, A., Vol-II: 474
Frick, K. M., Vol-I: 321
Frick, P. J., Vol-I: 547
Fridell, S. R., Vol-I: 510–511; Vol-II: 117
Friedan, B., Vol-I: 361
Frieden, G., Vol-II: 272
Friederici, A. D., Vol-I: 244–245
Friedman, B. N., Vol-II: 164
Friedman, C. K., Vol-I: 280
Friedman, H., Vol-II: 75
Friedman, K., Vol-I: 542; Vol-II: 171
Friedman, L., Vol-II: 386
Friedman, R. C., Vol-I: 50
Friesen, M., Vol-II: 284
Frieze, I., Vol-I: 10, 88, 381
Frieze, I. H., Vol-I: 193, 371, 391; Vol-II: 10, 290–292, 311–330, 648
Frijda, N. H., Vol-I: 225, 324
Frijters, J. E. R., Vol-I: 457
Frisco, M. L., Vol-II: 413–414
Frisen, A., Vol-II: 156, 165
Friskopp, A., Vol-II: 449
Fritschy, J. M., Vol-I: 365
Fritz, H. L., Vol-II: 295, 549–550
Fritz, S. M., Vol-I: 93
Frohlich, D., Vol-II: 282
Frombach, I., Vol-II: 548
Frome, P., Vol-II: 384
Frome, P. M., Vol-I: 306; Vol-II: 382
Frost, J. A., Vol-I: 245
Frost, J. J., Vol-II: 532
Frost, L. A., Vol-II: 386
Frye, C. A., Vol-I: 247
Frye, V., Vol-II: 626
Frytak, J. R., Vol-II: 524
Fuchs, D., Vol-II: 346, 450
Fuiman, M., Vol-II: 283
Fujimoto, T., Vol-II: 414
Fujino, D., Vol-II: 623
Fujioka, T., Vol-I: 497
Fujishiro, K., Vol-II: 436
Fukuyama, M. A., Vol-I: 65
Fulcher, M., Vol-II: 411
Fulkerson, J. A., Vol-II: 161, 479
Fuller-Iglesias, H., Vol-I: 559
Fullerton, S. M., Vol-I: 186
Fung, H. H., Vol-I: 567

Funk, S. J., Vol-II: 337
Funkhouser, S. W., Vol-II: 487
Fuqua, D. R., Vol-I: 135; Vol-II: 284
Furlong, A., Vol-II: 390
Furlong, J., Vol-II: 652
Furman, W., Vol-I: 540
Furneaux, E. C., Vol-I: 246
Furnham, A., Vol-II: 160, 644, 646, 649
Furumoto, L., Vol-I: 20–21
Futterman, R., Vol-II: 388
Fyfe, B., Vol-II: 360

G

Gaab, N., Vol-I: 244
Gabbard, G. O., Vol-II: 20
Gabhainn, S. N., Vol-II: 477
Gable, R., Vol-I: 47
Gable, R. K., Vol-I: 145, 280
Gabriel, K. I., Vol-I: 329
Gabriel, S., Vol-I: 499; Vol-II: 323–324
Gabriel, S. L., Vol-I: 285
Gabrieli, J. D. E., Vol-II: 66
Gaddis, A., Vol-I: 535
Gade, P., Vol-II: 690
Gaertner, S. L., Vol-II: 147, 447
Gager, C. T., Vol-II: 414
Gagné, F. M., Vol-II: 294
Gagne, P., Vol-II: 111, 114, 123
Gagnon, J. H., Vol-I: 478; Vol-II: 289, 321
Gaier, E. L., Vol-II: 383
Gainor, K. A., Vol-I: 59–60, 70–71
Gajarsky, W. M., Vol-II: 631
Galaburda, A. M., Vol-I: 239
Galambos, N., Vol-II: 409
Galambos, N. L., Vol-I: 87, 147, 530–532, 536–538, 548; Vol-II: 134, 164
Galdas, P. M., Vol-II: 228
Gale, E., Vol-II: 290–291
Gale, W., Vol-I: 380
Gale, W. S., Vol-II: 339
Galea, L. A., Vol-I: 221, 329
Galen, B. R., Vol-I: 527, 546
Galena, E., Vol-II: 532
Galibois, N., Vol-I: 391, 399–400
Galinsky, A. D., Vol-II: 460
Galinsky, E., Vol-II: 402
Gallagher, A. M., Vol-I: 304, 308
Gallagher, R., Vol-I: 180
Gallant, S., Vol-II: 98
Gallop, R., Vol-II: 95
Gallus, J. A., Vol-II: 11, 423–437
Galton, F., Vol-I: 204, 344, 348
Galupo, P. M., Vol-II: 365
Gammell, D. J., Vol-II: 96
Gamson, J., Vol-I: 108
Gan, S., Vol-II: 661
Gandara, B., Vol-I: 241

Ganderton, S. L., Vol-II: 686–689
Gandevia, S. C., Vol-I: 242–243
Gandolfo-Berry, C., Vol-II: 430
Gandossy, T., Vol-II: 369–370
Gange, S. J., Vol-II: 542
Gangestad, S. W., Vol-I: 168; Vol-II: 285–286
Ganis, G., Vol-I: 328
Ganley, A. L., Vol-II: 201
Gannon, L., Vol-I: 195, 197, 199, 372–373
Ganong, L. H., Vol-II: 289, 291, 299
Gant, L. M., Vol-II: 652
Gao, M., Vol-II: 473
Garber, J., Vol-I: 66
Garcia, C., Vol-I: 398
Garcia, P. A., Vol-II: 295
Gard, D. E., Vol-II: 35
Gard, M. G., Vol-II: 35
Gardiner, J. P., Vol-II: 482
Gardiner, M., Vol-II: 168
Gardner, C., Vol-I: 393
Gardner, H., Vol-I: 345
Gardner, K. E., Vol-I: 537
Gardner, P. D., Vol-II: 652
Gardner, R. M., Vol-II: 164, 173
Gardner, W. L., Vol-I: 499; Vol-II: 323–324
Garfinkel, P. E., Vol-I: 165
Garfinkel, R., Vol-II: 620
Gariepy, J., Vol-I: 397
Garle, M., Vol-II: 474
Garner, D. M., Vol-I: 165; Vol-II: 159
Garner, P. W., Vol-II: 324
Garnets, L., Vol-I: 50; Vol-II: 139
Garnets, L. D., Vol-I: 64–66, 72
Garofalo, R., Vol-I: 69; Vol-II: 138
Garrel, D., Vol-I: 458
Garrick, D., Vol-II: 205
Gartlehner, G., Vol-II: 97
Gartner, R. B., Vol-II: 230
Gartrell, N., Vol-I: 483
Gartrell, N. K., Vol-I: 226
Garver-Apgar, C. E., Vol-II: 286
Gary, T. L., Vol-I: 10
Gastil, J., Vol-II: 459
Gates, G., Vol-I: 187
Gates, G. J., Vol-I: 187
Gaulin, S. J., Vol-I: 325
Gaulin, S. J. C., Vol-I: 266, 268–269, 323
Gault, U., Vol-I: 115
Gauthier, R., Vol-II: 511
Gautier, T., Vol-I: 218, 529
Gauvin, L., Vol-II: 165
Gavey, N., Vol-I: 103, 117
Gaze, C. E., Vol-I: 308, 319, 328
Gazzaniga, M. S., Vol-I: 222
Ge, X., Vol-I: 543–544; Vol-II: 139
Geary, D. C., Vol-I: 263, 265–266, 317, 326
Gebo, K., Vol-II: 534

Gecas, V., Vol-II: 384
Geddes, D., Vol-II: 431
Gee, J., Vol-I: 307
Geen, R. G., Vol-II: 311, 314
Geenen, R., Vol-II: 546
Geertz, C., Vol-I: 104
Geiger, J. F., Vol-I: 323
Geiger, W., Vol-II: 371
Geis, F. L., Vol-II: 339, 341, 450
Geisler, J. S., Vol-II: 295
Gelberg, L., Vol-II: 552
Gelfand, M., Vol-I: 384
Gelfand, M. J., Vol-II: 301, 423, 428
Geller, T., Vol-II: 365
Gelles, R. J., Vol-II: 318
Gelman, S. A., Vol-I: 502, 505–506, 515–516
Gelso, C. J., Vol-II: 231
Gencoz, T., Vol-II: 511
Genero, N. P., Vol-II: 213
Gentile, D., Vol-II: 229
Gentile, D. A., Vol-I: 364–365
Gentry, M., Vol-I: 280
George, J. M., Vol-II: 428
George, T., Vol-II: 551
Georgopoulos, A. P., Vol-I: 239
Gerbner, G., Vol-II: 167, 644
Gergen, K. J., Vol-I: 103, 116, 119–120, 122, 151
Gergen, M., Vol-I: 103, 107–110, 113, 116–117, 120, 122, 167
Gergen, M. M., Vol-I: 33, 103–123, 562
Gerhardstein, R., Vol-II: 660
Geronimus, A. T., Vol-II: 510
Gerrard, M., Vol-II: 76, 340
Gerschick, T. J., Vol-I: 112
Gershkovich, I., Vol-II: 43
Gershuny, J. I., Vol-II: 404–405, 478
Gerson, K., Vol-II: 401–402, 452
Gerson, M., Vol-I: 572
Gerstmann, E. A., Vol-I: 148–149
Geschwind, N., Vol-I: 239
Gesn, P. R., Vol-I: 438; Vol-II: 21, 325
Gessert, C. E., Vol-II: 525
Gettman, H., Vol-I: 384
Gevins, A., Vol-I: 238
Ghiz, L., Vol-II: 174
Giacalone, R. A., Vol-II: 347
Giacomini, M., Vol-I: 198
Gianetto, R. M., Vol-I: 438
Giannopoulos, C., Vol-II: 144
Giaschi, D., Vol-I: 221
Gibb, B. E., Vol-II: 146
Gibbon, A. E., Vol-II: 103
Gibbons, F. X., Vol-II: 340
Gibbons, J. L., Vol-II: 225
Gibbons, L. E., Vol-II: 546
Gibbons, M. B. C., Vol-II: 234
Gibbs, J., Vol-II: 195

Gibbs, M., Vol-II: 282
Gibson, E. L., Vol-I: 456
Gibson, P. R., Vol-II: 94
Gidycz, C. A., Vol-II: 137
Gifford, R., Vol-I: 412
Gilbert, A. N., Vol-I: 248
Gilbert, L. A., Vol-I: 29; Vol-II: 201–202, 211–212, 223, 237, 414
Gilbert, P., Vol-II: 35
Gilboa, E., Vol-II: 141
Gilenstam, K., Vol-II: 570
Giles, D. C., Vol-I: 567; Vol-II: 658
Gill, D. L., Vol-II: 12, 563–580
Gill, K., Vol-II: 362
Gill, R. M., Vol-II: 671–692
Gillespie, B. L., Vol-I: 146; Vol-II: 123
Gillespie, C., Vol-II: 473
Gillespie, J. M., Vol-I: 240
Gillespie, W. T., Vol-I: 328–329
Gilliam, F. D., Vol-II: 650
Gillian, G. T., Vol-II: 527
Gilligan, C., Vol-I: 31–32, 105, 113, 198, 528, 531; Vol-II: 117, 188, 253, 266
Gilligan, T. D., Vol-II: 527
Gillihan, S. J., Vol-II: 253
Gillis, J., Vol-I: 67, 69
Gillis, J. R., Vol-II: 362–363
Gillon, E., Vol-II: 236
Gillum, B. S., Vol-II: 520
Gilman, S. E., Vol-I: 63, 68; Vol-II: 135, 167, 224
Gilmartin, P. P., Vol-I: 330
Gilmore, A. C., Vol-II: 385
Gilmore, D. D., Vol-I: 133, 150
Gilstrap, C. M., Vol-II: 23
Giltay, E. J., Vol-I: 224
Ginsburg, H. J., Vol-I: 392–393
Ginter, E., Vol-II: 479
Giordani, B., Vol-I: 227
Giordano, J., Vol-II: 255
Girdler, S. S., Vol-I: 436
Girelli, L., Vol-I: 323
Girgus, J. S., Vol-I: 543; Vol-II: 297
Girshick, L., Vol-II: 604, 608
Gitelson, I. B., Vol-I: 147
Givens, J. E., Vol-II: 538
Gjerde, P. F., Vol-I: 203
Gjerdingen, D. K., Vol-II: 414
Gladstone, T., Vol-II: 142
Gladue, B. A., Vol-I: 226
Glanville, E. V., Vol-I: 246
Glascock, J., Vol-II: 644, 646–647, 649, 662
Glaser, B. G., Vol-I: 111
Glaser, D., Vol-II: 484
Glass, B., Vol-I: 1; Vol-II: 1
Glass, J., Vol-II: 414
Gleason, J. H., Vol-II: 165
Gleason, M. E. J., Vol-II: 327

Glebova, T., Vol-II: 204
Gleitman, H., Vol-II: 386
Glenn, E. N., Vol-II: 416
Glick, P., Vol-I: 144, 147–148, 151, 168, 198; Vol-II: 137, 290, 352, 449–450
Glidden, C. E., Vol-II: 197, 212
Glomb, T. M., Vol-II: 427–428, 431, 436
Gluck, J., Vol-I: 322, 567
Gluckman, M., Vol-I: 396
Glucksberg, S., Vol-I: 200
Glunt, E., Vol-I: 69
Glunt, E. K., Vol-II: 362
Gmel, G., Vol-II: 480
Gnisci, A., Vol-I: 321
Go, B. K., Vol-II: 483
Godbey, G., Vol-II: 404–405, 407–409
Goekoop-Ruiterman, Y. P., Vol-II: 545
Goetz, A. T., Vol-II: 286
Goetz, T., Vol-I: 444; Vol-II: 385, 388
Goff, S. B., Vol-II: 388
Goffin, R. D., Vol-II: 498, 502–503, 510
Goffman, E., Vol-II: 647
Gohm, C. L., Vol-I: 439
Gokee-Larose, J., Vol-II: 166
Golbeck, S. L., Vol-I: 319–320
Gold, D., Vol-I: 349, 531
Gold, S. N., Vol-II: 76
Goldberg, A., Vol-I: 540; Goldberg, A., Vol-II: 407, 411
Goldberg, H., Vol-I: 44
Goldberg, L. R., Vol-II: 28
Goldberg, W. A., Vol-II: 413–414
Goldberger, N., Vol-I: 105
Goldberger, N. R., Vol-I: 32, 198
Golden, A. M., Vol-I: 194
Golden, C., Vol-I: 364, 368–369
Goldenberg, J. L., Vol-II: 169
Goldfield, A., Vol-II: 167
Goldfield, G. S., Vol-II: 474
Goldfried, A. P., Vol-II: 140
Goldfried, M. R., Vol-I: 63; Vol-II: 141
Golding, J., Vol-II: 412
Golding, J. M., Vol-II: 98
Goldin-Meadow, S., Vol-I: 318
Goldner, E. M., Vol-II: 473
Goldner, V., Vol-II: 255
Goldsmith, H. H., Vol-I: 445
Goldsmith, R., Vol-II: 384
Goldstein, D., Vol-I: 319
Goldstein, G., Vol-I: 322
Goldstein, J. S., Vol-II: 675
Golombok, S., Vol-I: 70
Gomez, G., Vol-I: 277
Gong, E. J., Vol-I: 458, 464
Gonsiorek, J., Vol-I: 62, 64, 69
Gonzales, M. H., Vol-II: 285
Gonzales, N., Vol-II: 621
Gonzalez, J., Vol-II: 633

Gonzalez, Z., Vol-I: 459
Gonzalez-DeHass, A. R., Vol-II: 384
Gonzalez-Morales, G., Vol-II: 503–504, 510
Good, G., Vol-I: 45
Good, G. E., Vol-I: 45, 49, 51, 53, 136, 150; Vol-II: 123, 135, 137, 222–226, 228–229, 237–238, 241
Good, L., Vol-II: 170
Good, R. H., Vol-I: 83
Good, T., Vol-II: 385
Goode, E., Vol-II: 595
Gooden, A. M., Vol-I: 281, 505
Gooden, M. A., Vol-I: 281, 505
Goodenow, C., Vol-I: 290
Goodman, E., Vol-I: 69; Vol-II: 138
Goodrich, T. G., Vol-II: 263
Goodrich, T. J., Vol-II: 253–255, 260, 263
Goodwin, M. H., Vol-I: 385, 396–397
Goodwin, M. P., Vol-II: 319
Goodwin, R. D., Vol-I: 445; Vol-II: 133
Goodwin, S. A., Vol-I: 418
Goodwin, T. M., Vol-I: 246
Goodwin-Watkins, C., Vol-II: 289
Gooren, L. G. J., Vol-II: 113
Gooren, L. J. G., Vol-I: 224–225, 324; Vol-II: 115–116
Gootjes, L., Vol-I: 239
Goral, F. S., Vol-II: 511
Gorard, S., Vol-II: 652
Gordon, A. H., Vol-I: 242, 432, 442
Gordon, D. A., Vol-I: 110–111
Gordon, E., Vol-I: 392
Gordon, J. H., Vol-I: 483
Gordon, J. R., Vol-I: 570
Goris, Y., Vol-I: 325
Gorman, B. K., Vol-II: 553
Gorski, R., Vol-I: 218
Gorski, R. A., Vol-I: 217, 225, 483; Vol-II: 115
Gosling, A. L., Vol-II: 255
Gotay, C. C., Vol-I: 184
Gotlib, I. H., Vol-I: 445; Vol-II: 141
Gotoh, K., Vol-I: 247
Gott, M., Vol-II: 532
Gottlieb, A., Vol-II: 169
Gottman, J. M., Vol-I: 437, 440; Vol-II: 265, 268, 499
Gouchie, C., Vol-I: 222
Gough, H. G., Vol-I: 134
Gould, M. S., Vol-I: 68
Gow, J., Vol-II: 171
Grabe, M. E., Vol-II: 650
Grabe, S., Vol-I: 87, 95, 150; Vol-II: 142, 154
Graber, J. A., Vol-I: 8, 527–550
Grabowski, T. J., Vol-I: 217
Grace, A. D., Vol-I: 304, 306
Grace, R. C., Vol-II: 287
Grace, S. L., Vol-II: 478, 543
Gradus, J. L., Vol-II: 436
Grady, W. R., Vol-II: 65
Graham, C., Vol-I: 479; Vol-II: 369

Graham, J. R., Vol-II: 70
Graham, K., Vol-II: 314–315
Graham, N. M. H., Vol-II: 542
Graham, T., Vol-I: 438; Vol-II: 21, 325
Grant, B., Vol-II: 135, 230
Grant, B. F., Vol-II: 133, 480
Grant, C. A., Vol-II: 550
Grant, K. R., Vol-II: 475
Grant, K., Vol-I: 35
Grant, L., Vol-I: 284
Grant, M. C., Vol-II: 521
Grant, P. R., Vol-II: 648
Grant, R. W., Vol-II: 521
Grauerholz, E., Vol-II: 171
Grauerholz, L., Vol-II: 166
Graves, A. R., Vol-II: 253
Graves, E. J., Vol-II: 520
Gray, C., Vol-I: 289
Gray, D., Vol-I: 64
Gray, J., Vol-I: 379, 386, 394;
Gray, J., Vol-II: 290
Gray, J. J., Vol-I: 90, 535; Vol-II: 160, 167, 172
Gray, J. L., Vol-II: 159
Gray, R., Vol-I: 108
Gray, R. E., Vol-II: 478, 543
Grayson, C., Vol-II: 137
Graziano, W. G., Vol-I: 434
Graziottin, A., Vol-I: 483
Green, A. S., Vol-II: 327
Green, C. R., Vol-II: 546
Green, E., Vol-I: 412
Green, L., Vol-I: 285
Green, L. R., Vol-II: 313
Green, R., Vol-I: 224, 324; Vol-II: 115–117, 367
Green, R. J., Vol-I: 64; Vol-II: 255, 257–258, 263
Green, S., Vol-I: 264, 321; Green, S., Vol-II: 656
Green, S. M., Vol-I: 221
Greenberg, B. S., Vol-II: 167, 644, 647
Greenberg, S., Vol-II: 524
Greenberg, S. A., Vol-II: 590
Greenberg, T., Vol-I: 68
Greenberg-Dotan, S., Vol-II: 524
Greene, A. L., Vol-II: 545
Greene, B., Vol-I: 35, 64–65, 68, 72; Vol-II: 103, 192–193, 255, 259–260, 262–263
Greene, G., Vol-II: 613
Greene, K., Vol-II: 289, 299–300
Greene, R. L., Vol-II: 78–79
Greene, R. W., Vol-II: 291
Greenfield, M., Vol-I: 396
Greenfield, P., Vol-II: 66
Greenfield, P. M., Vol-I: 162–163, 169–171, 173; Vol-II: 66, 78
Greenfield, S., Vol-II: 553
Greenglass, E., Vol-II: 502–506, 512
Greenglass, E. R., Vol-II: 503
Greenleaf, C., Vol-II: 574–575

Greenman, Y., Vol-I: 464
Greeno, G. G., Vol-I: 459
Green-Powell, P., Vol-I: 112, 116
Greenstein, T. N., Vol-II: 405–407, 409–411
Greenwald, A., Vol-I: 200, 281
Greenwald, A. G., Vol-II: 447, 661
Greenwald, S., Vol-II: 447, 661
Greenway, F. L., Vol-I: 456
Greenwood, D., Vol-II: 12, 645, 658
Greenwood, D. N., Vol-II: 643–663
Greenwood, G., Vol-I: 187
Greenwood, R. M., Vol-I: 105
Greer, K. M., Vol-I: 195
Gregersen, E. A., Vol-I: 392
Gregg, P. B., Vol-II: 656
Gregory, W. L., Vol-II: 287
Grellert, E. A., Vol-I: 140
Greulich, F. K., Vol-I: 496
Greve, W., Vol-II: 484
Gridley, H., Vol-II: 580
Grieg, A., Vol-II: 542
Grieve, F. G., Vol-II: 99
Griffin, C., Vol-I: 110; Vol-II: 112
Griffin, D. W., Vol-II: 294
Griffin, N. L., Vol-II: 383
Griffin, P. S., Vol-II: 578
Griffin, R. W., Vol-II: 423, 425
Griffith, D., Vol-II: 633
Griffith, L. K., Vol-II: 361
Grilo, C. M., Vol-II: 156
Grimes, C., Vol-I: 397
Grimshaw, G. M., Vol-I: 220
Grindel, C. G., Vol-II: 486
Grittner, U., Vol-II: 480
Groesz, L., Vol-I: 86, 97
Groesz, L. M., Vol-I: 97; Vol-II: 156, 159, 658
Grogan, S., Vol-I: 456–457, 462–463; Vol-II: 153–155, 160, 166–168, 171
Grön, G., Vol-I: 330
Gross, C. P., Vol-I: 184; Gross, C. P., Vol-II: 528
Gross, E., Vol-II: 652
Gross, J., Vol-I: 437, 440
Gross, J. J., Vol-I: 432, 434
Gross, L., Vol-II: 167, 644
Gross, P. H., Vol-II: 447
Grossman, A. H., Vol-II: 120
Grossman, C. L., Vol-II: 369–370
Grossman, J., Vol-II: 623
Grossman, M., Vol-I: 434
Grossman, S., Vol-II: 81
Grossmann, T., Vol-I: 244
Grote, N. K., Vol-II: 414
Grotevant, H. D., Vol-I: 562
Groth, G., Vol-II: 285
Grotpeter, J. K., Vol-II: 312
Grov, C., Vol-I: 64
Grover, G. N., Vol-I: 458

Grover, V. P., Vol-II: 155, 158
Grube, J. W., Vol-II: 655
Gruber, A. J., Vol-I: 53; Vol-II: 158–159, 166
Gruber, E. L., Vol-II: 655
Gruber, J. E., Vol-II: 434, 680
Gruen, R. J., Vol-II: 495
Gruenfeld, D. H., Vol-I: 429
Grumbach, M. M., Vol-I: 534
Grunberg, N. E., Vol-I: 457, 459–460
Grzywacz, J. G., Vol-II: 415
Guadagno, R. E., Vol-II: 684
Guanipa, C., Vol-II: 255
Gubin, A., Vol-I: 418
Gubrium, J. F., Vol-I: 103, 122
Guest, S., Vol-I: 246
Guibert, M., Vol-II: 329
Guier, C., Vol-II: 554
Guille, C., Vol-II: 161
Guillemin, F., Vol-I: 171
Guiso, L., Vol-I: 262, 300, 303–305, 307–308, 313
Gulko, J., Vol-I: 501
Gullette, M., Vol-I: 567
Gulyas, B., Vol-I: 249
Gundersen, H. J., Vol-I: 217
Gunnar, M. R., Vol-I: 445
Gunn-Gruchy, C. D., Vol-II: 69
Gunter, B., Vol-II: 644
Gunther, M., Vol-II: 369
Güntürkün, O., Vol-I: 222, 245, 270
Gunz, A., Vol-II: 45
Gupta, S., Vol-II: 405, 409, 411
Gur, R., Vol-I: 307
Gur, R. C., Vol-I: 217, 245, 279, 307, 325
Gur, R. E., Vol-I: 279
Gurian, M., Vol-I: 278–281, 287–288
Gurin, G., Vol-II: 55
Guroff, J. J., Vol-II: 195
Gurung, R. A. R., Vol-II: 296
Gutek, B. A., Vol-II: 432, 436, 686
Guthrie, J. F., Vol-I: 456
Guthrie, R. V., Vol-I: 25
Gutierrez, M., Vol-II: 200
Gutmann, D., Vol-I: 444, 565
Guttormson, H. E., Vol-II: 271
Gutwin, C., Vol-I: 221
Guzman, R., Vol-II: 122
Guzzo, R. A., Vol-II: 348
Gygax, L., Vol-I: 512
Gylje, M., Vol-II: 362
Gysbers, N., Vol-II: 392

H
Haake, S., Vol-II: 228
Haas, A., Vol-I: 392
Haas, K. B., Vol-I: 167
Haas, S., Vol-II: 296
Hacker, S., Vol-I: 363

Hackett, G., Vol-II: 197, 201–203, 205, 380, 382
Hackler, A. H., Vol-II: 228
Hackman, J. R., Vol-II: 428
Haddad, M. E., Vol-I: 496
Haddock, G., Vol-I: 195
Hadjiyannakis, K., Vol-II: 136
Hadley, D., Vol-I: 330
Hafetz, J., Vol-I: 442
Hagan, H. J. J., Vol-II: 486
Hagan, R., Vol-I: 504
Hagborg, W. J., Vol-II: 617
Hagedoorn, M., Vol-II: 501, 548, 551–552
Hagen, J. W., Vol-I: 21
Hahn, A., Vol-II: 619
Hahn, E. D., Vol-I: 147, 151
Hahn, J., Vol-II: 78, 79
Haidet, P., Vol-II: 522
Haidt, J., Vol-II: 169
Haier, R. J., Vol-I: 279
Haig, D., Vol-I: 365
Haik, J., Vol-II: 482–483
Haiken, E., Vol-II: 163, 166
Haines, E. L., Vol-II: 447
Hajszan, T., Vol-I: 217
Halari, R., Vol-I: 222, 324
Halberstadt, A. G., Vol-I: 136, 421, 438
Halbert, C. H., Vol-I: 7, 179–188
Halbreich, U., Vol-I: 222–223
Haldane, D., Vol-I: 319
Haldeman, D., Vol-II: 117
Haldeman, D. C., Vol-I: 62; Vol-II: 227
Hale, J. L., Vol-II: 290
Halford, W. K., Vol-II: 268
Halim, M. L., Vol-I: 8, 495–518
Hall, J. A., Vol-I: 8, 136, 411–421, 429–448; Vol-II: 8, 324–325, 338, 432, 523
Hall, J. R., Vol-II: 347
Hall, K. P., Vol-II: 346
Hall, M. A., Vol-II: 564, 566
Hall, M. J., Vol-II: 520
Hall, R. L., Vol-II: 225, 259–260, 262–263, 580
Hall, W. S., Vol-I: 144
Hallahan, M., Vol-I: 412
Hallberg, L. R-M., Vol-I: 111, 113
Haller, I. V., Vol-II: 525
Hallfors, D. D., Vol-I: 536
Hall-Hoffarth, D., Vol-I: 329
Halliday, G. M., Vol-I: 244
Halliwell, E., Vol-I: 566–567; Vol-II: 154
Hallowell, L., Vol-II: 591–592
Halone, K. K., Vol-II: 647
Halpern, C. T., Vol-I: 534, 536
Halpern, D. F., Vol-I: 236, 238, 301, 303, 309, 318, 323–324; Vol-II: 68, 70, 386, 460
Halpert, S. C., Vol-I: 68
Halsey, N. A., Vol-II: 598
Halstead, K., Vol-II: 258

Halverson, C. F., Vol-I: 508, 515; Vol-I: 511
Ham, M., Vol-I: 544
Hamann, S., Vol-I: 483
Hamberg, K., Vol-II: 545
Hambleton, R. K., Vol-I: 170–171; Vol-II: 67, 76, 81–82
Hamburg, P., Vol-II: 167
Hamby, B. A., Vol-II: 225
Hamby, S., Vol-II: 627
Hamby, S. L., Vol-II: 316
Hamill, R., Vol-II: 158
Hamilton, D. A., Vol-I: 227, 264
Hamilton, E. A., Vol-I: 570
Hamilton, J., Vol-II: 98
Hamilton, K., Vol-II: 658
Hamilton, M. C., Vol-I: 195, 361, 363, 373, 505
Hamilton, S., Vol-II: 94, 193, 623
Hamilton, W. D., Vol-I: 260
Hamm, J. P., Vol-I: 324
Hamman, R. F., Vol-II: 531
Hammar, M. L., Vol-I: 246
Hammen, C. L., Vol-II: 82
Hammer, T., Vol-I: 105
Hammerstein, S. K., Vol-I: 475
Hammerton, H., Vol-II: 614
Hammock, G., Vol-II: 314
Hammock, G. S., Vol-II: 312
Hammond, B., Vol-II: 122
Hammond, W. P., Vol-I: 150; Vol-II: 226
Hampson, E., Vol-I: 84, 220–224, 227, 239, 270, 323–324
Hampson, E. A., Vol-I: 222
Hampson, J. G., Vol-I: 194
Hampson, J. L., Vol-I: 194
Hampson, S. E., Vol-I: 548
Hampton, M. R., Vol-II: 548
Hancock, K. A., Vol-I: 6, 59–72
Handa, R. J., Vol-I: 226
Handal, P., Vol-II: 626
Handelsman, J., Vol-I: 313
Haney, C., Vol-II: 607
Hanish, L. D., Vol-I: 219
Hankin, B. L., Vol-II: 96, 134, 142
Hanna, E., Vol-II: 230
Hansbrough, E., Vol-I: 542
Hansen, A. M., Vol-I: 242
Hansen, H. L., Vol-II: 438
Hanson, G. R., Vol-I: 548
Hanson, R., Vol-II: 620
Hansson, R. O., Vol-I: 573; Vol-II: 24
Harackiewicz, J., Vol-II: 48
Harasty, J., Vol-I: 244
Haraway, D., Vol-I: 105
Haraway, D. J., Vol-I: 194, 202
Harcourt, J., Vol-II: 114, 125
Hardin, C. D., Vol-II: 77, 449
Harding, S., Vol-I: 30–32, 36, 103, 105, 395–396, 398–399

Hardoon, S. L., Vol-II: 472
Hardy, L., Vol-II: 480
Hardy, R., Vol-II: 165
Hare, R. D., Vol-II: 74
Harel, F., Vol-I: 319
Hare-Mustin, R., Vol-I: 381–382, 387, 403
Hare-Mustin, R. T., Vol-I: 20, 29–31, 33, 193, 197; Vol-II: 64, 66, 83, 117–118, 253, 255, 671
Hargie, O. D. W., Vol-II: 282, 295
Hargittai, E., Vol-II: 253
Hargreaves, D., Vol-II: 170
Hargreaves, D. A., Vol-II: 477
Hargreaves, D. J., Vol-I: 349
Harlan, C. L., Vol-II: 380
Harlan, L. C., Vol-II: 527
Harlow, J. A., Vol-I: 237
Harmon, T., Vol-II: 284
Harnish, R. J., Vol-II: 283
Harold, R., Vol-I: 281
Harold, R. D., Vol-II: 389, 573
Harper, B., Vol-II: 171
Harper, G. W., Vol-II: 629
Harré, R., Vol-I: 541
Harrell, S., Vol-II: 634–635
Harrell, W. A., Vol-I: 329
Harries-Jenkins, G., Vol-II: 672
Harrington, D. M., Vol-I: 352, 354
Harris, A., Vol-I: 285
Harris, A. C., Vol-I: 499
Harris, B., Vol-I: 133
Harris, C., Vol-I: 150–151
Harris, C. R., Vol-II: 484
Harris, D. V., Vol-II: 531, 569
Harris, F., Vol-II: 410
Harris, J. R., Vol-I: 282
Harris, L., Vol-I: 283
Harris, L. J., Vol-I: 330, 348
Harris, M. B., Vol-I: 314–315
Harris, M. I., Vol-II: 531
Harris, R., Vol-II: 166
Harris, R. J., Vol-I: 549; Vol-II: 430, 654–656, 660
Harris, S., Vol-II: 624
Harris, V. A., Vol-I: 194
Harrison, D., Vol-I: 437
Harrison, J. M., Vol-II: 573
Harrison, K., Vol-I: 150; Vol-II: 159, 161, 163, 166–167, 645, 647, 655, 658–659
Harrison, L., Vol-I: 64, 363
Harrison, P. M., Vol-II: 321
Harrison, S. J., Vol-I: 374
Harrison, S. K., Vol-II: 287
Hart, G., Vol-II: 228
Hart, L., Vol-II: 385
Hart, P. L., Vol-II: 543
Hart, R., Vol-I: 330
Harter, S., Vol-I: 497, 528–529, 532; Vol-II: 30, 388
Hartman, J. E., Vol-II: 363

Hartmann, H. I., Vol-I: 571
Hartmann, T., Vol-II: 651–652
Harton, H. C., Vol-II: 326
Hartsen, K. M., Vol-II: 43
Hartsock, N., Vol-I: 105
Harway, M., Vol-I: 54; Vol-II: 255
Harwood, J., Vol-II: 371, 644–645, 647
Harzing, A., Vol-I: 172
Hasanali, P., Vol-II: 288
Hasegawa, K., Vol-II: 644
Haselton, M. G., Vol-I: 168; Vol-II: 286
Hasher, L., Vol-I: 432
Hashim, A., Vol-I: 365
Hashimoto, T., Vol-II: 289
Hasin, D., Vol-II: 159
Hasin, D. S., Vol-II: 133–134, 146, 480
Haskell, S. M., Vol-II: 192
Haslam, N., Vol-I: 1, 194, 197; Vol-II: 1, 27, 370
Haslam, S. A., Vol-I: 193; Vol-II: 449, 455–456, 461
Hassett, J. M., Vol-I: 220
Hassler, M., Vol-I: 348, 354
Hatano, G., Vol-I: 162–163
Hatch-Maillette, M. A., Vol-II: 322
Hatfield, E., Vol-I: 239, 481; Vol-II: 297
Hathaway, S. R., Vol-II: 78–79
Hatoum, I. J., Vol-II: 658
Hatzenbuehler, M. L., Vol-II: 9, 133–147
Haug, F., Vol-I: 115
Haught, C., Vol-I: 200
Haugrud, S., Vol-I: 462
Hause, K. S., Vol-II: 283, 296, 300
Hausenblas, H., Vol-II: 574–575
Hauser, S., Vol-I: 564
Hauserman, N., Vol-II: 430
Häusermann, M., Vol-II: 486
Hausman, B. L., Vol-II: 115, 117, 121
Hausmann, M., Vol-I: 222, 245, 270
Havens, M. D., Vol-I: 323
Hawgood, G., Vol-I: 328
Hawk, S. T., Vol-II: 655
Hawker, A., Vol-II: 483
Hawkins, K. W., Vol-II: 339, 345
Hawkins, R. C., Vol-I: 52; Vol-II: 550
Hawton, K., Vol-II: 478–479
Hay, D. H., Vol-II: 314
Hayati, M., Vol-I: 328
Hayden, H. A., Vol-II: 156
Hayden, M. V., Vol-II: 448
Hayes, C. W., Vol-I: 438
Hayes, D., Vol-I: 463
Hayes, E., Vol-II: 613
Hayes, J. A., Vol-II: 231
Hayes, K., Vol-I: 290
Haynes, M. C., Vol-II: 345
Hays, D. G., Vol-II: 205
Hays, J., Vol-I: 185
Hayslip, B. Jr., Vol-II: 174

Hayward, C., Vol-I: 86, 543–544
Hazan, C., Vol-I: 262; Vol-II: 281
Hazen, M. D., Vol-I: 383; Vol-II: 340
Head, J., Vol-II: 475
Healy, D., Vol-II: 107
Healy, J. M., Vol-I: 566
Healy, S. D., Vol-I: 325
Heaphy, B., Vol-I: 565
Heard, K. V., Vol-II: 12, 587–609
Heath, G. W., Vol-II: 567
Heatherington, L., Vol-I: 620
Heatherton, T. F., Vol-II: 167, 285
Heaton, R. K., Vol-I: 568
Heavey, C. L., Vol-II: 265–266, 499
Hebert, K., Vol-I: 226
Hébert, M., Vol-II: 208–209
Hebl, M. R., Vol-I: 446; Vol-II: 157, 167–168, 172, 659
Hecht, M. A., Vol-I: 89, 411, 437–438; Vol-II: 21, 338, 643
Heckathorn, D. D., Vol-I: 187
Heckhausen, J., Vol-I: 573
Hedden, T., Vol-II: 66
Hederstierna, C., Vol-I: 244
Hedges, L. V., Vol-I: 299, 302, 304–305, 318
Heerey, E. A., Vol-I: 420
Heesacker, M., Vol-I: 437; Vol-II: 232
Heesink, J., Vol-II: 413
Hegarty, M., Vol-I: 328–329
Hegarty, P., Vol-I: 7, 191–204, 372–373
Hegna, K., Vol-II: 369
Heider, F., Vol-I: 200
Heil, M., Vol-I: 239, 319, 322
Heilman, M. E., Vol-II: 345–346, 447–450, 457
Heimberg, R. G., Vol-II: 136, 140, 142
Heinberg, L. J., Vol-II: 153, 159, 658
Heine, S. J., Vol-I: 161, 194, 374
Heinecken, L., Vol-II: 673, 690
Heining, M., Vol-I: 247, 464
Heins, J. A., Vol-I: 330
Heinze, H., Vol-I: 442
Heinze, H. J., Vol-I: 324
Heisenberg, W., Vol-II: 187
Heitkemper, M. M., Vol-I: 241
Helaire, L., Vol-I: 285
Helbing, N., Vol-I: 503
Helgesen, S., Vol-II: 458
Helgeson, V. S., Vol-I: 421; Vol-II: 23, 25, 295, 297, 433, 502, 506, 547, 549–550
Heller, A., Vol-II: 528
Heller, D., Vol-II: 33–34
Heller, K. A., Vol-II: 379
Heller, T., Vol-II: 339
Hellinger, F. H., Vol-II: 533
Hellison, D., Vol-II: 576
Hellstrom, B., Vol-I: 241
Helm, B., Vol-I: 47
Helmick, C. G., Vol-II: 542

Helmreich, R., Vol-I: 146, 515
Helmreich, R. L., Vol-I: 14, 47, 52, 134–136, 144, 146–147, 150–152, 192; Vol-II: 14, 22–23, 295, 569
Helmreich, R. M., Vol-I: 366
Helms, B. J., Vol-I: 145
Helms, H. M., Vol-II: 296
Helms, J. E., Vol-II: 65–66, 68, 72
Helson, R., Vol-I: 26, 350–351, 566–568, 570–571
Helt, M., Vol-I: 327
Heltman, K., Vol-I: 389, 414; Vol-II: 338
Helwig-Larson, M., Vol-II: 21
Henderson, K. A., Vol-I: 90; Vol-II: 167, 473, 478, 574
Henderson, L. A., Vol-I: 242–243
Henderson, V. W., Vol-II: 524
Henderson-King, D., Vol-I: 573; Vol-II: 163
Henderson-King, E., Vol-I: 573; Vol-II: 163
Hendrick, C., Vol-II: 289, 299–300, 432
Hendrick, S. S., Vol-II: 289, 299–300, 432
Hengst, J. A., Vol-I: 114
Henley, M., Vol-I: 387–388, 399
Henley, N., Vol-I: 27–28, 381–382, 399, 402
Henley, N. M., Vol-I: 412, 418, 421; Vol-II: 168, 325
Henley, P., Vol-I: 278–279, 281, 287–288
Henne, J., Vol-II: 145
Hennessy, D. W., Vol-II: 315
Henning, J. B., Vol-II: 428, 437
Henning, J., Vol-I: 354
Henning, K., Vol-I: 478
Henning, S. L., Vol-I: 94
Henninger, D., Vol-I: 442
Henrie, R. L., Vol-I: 330
Henriksson-Larsen, K., Vol-II: 570
Henriques, J., Vol-I: 118
Henry, K. D., Vol-I: 25
Henry, R. A., Vol-II: 347, 349
Hens, G., Vol-II: 502
Hensley, P. L., Vol-II: 532
Henwood, K., Vol-I: 111
Heo, M., Vol-II: 545
Hepburn, A., Vol-I: 33, 121
Heppen, J. B., Vol-II: 290, 661
Heppner, M., Vol-II: 392
Heppner, M. J., Vol-II: 392
Heppner, P. P., Vol-II: 24, 226
Herbert, S. E., Vol-II: 367–368
Herbozo, S., Vol-II: 166–168
Herd, A. M., Vol-II: 677–679
Herdman, M., Vol-I: 171
Herdt, G., Vol-I: 133, 150
Herek, G., Vol-II: 139
Herek, G. M., Vol-I: 60, 67–69; Vol-II: 139, 193, 340, 359–363, 577
Herlitz, A., Vol-I: 323
Herman, C. P., Vol-I: 8, 455–466; Vol-II: 8, 167
Herman, J., Vol-II: 95
Herman, J. F., Vol-I: 264–265, 329–330
Herman, J. L., Vol-II: 190, 195–196, 208, 214

Herman, R., Vol-I: 483
Herman-Giddens, M. E., Vol-I: 533
Hermann, D., Vol-I: 236
Hermann, K. S., Vol-II: 24
Hermann, M. G., Vol-II: 42
Hermans, B., Vol-II: 453
Hernandez, P., Vol-II: 262, 269–270
Herold, E. S., Vol-I: 393; Vol-II: 286
Héroux, G., Vol-I: 326
Herrera, R., Vol-II: 412
Herrmann, D. J., Vol-I: 327
Hershberger, S., Vol-I: 68
Hershberger, S. L., Vol-I: 545; Vol-II: 138, 367–368
Hershcovis, M. S., Vol-II: 322, 423, 431
Hertz, R., Vol-I: 111
Herzberger, S. D., Vol-II: 160
Herzog, D. B., Vol-II: 167
Herzog, H., Vol-II: 446
Hess, N., Vol-I: 397
Hess, U., Vol-I: 431, 434–435
Hesse-Biber, S. N., Vol-I: 3, 103, 112–113, 122; Vol-II: 3, 168
Hetherington, E. M., Vol-II: 386
Hetherington, M. M., Vol-I: 456, 462
Hetsroni, A., Vol-II: 655
Hewes, D. E., Vol-II: 656
Hewitt, C., Vol-I: 547
Hewitt, P. L., Vol-II: 99
Hewlett, S. A., Vol-II: 446, 453
Hewstone, M., Vol-I: 497
Hexter, R. J., Vol-II: 460
Heyman, G. D., Vol-I: 501, 506, 517
Heyman, R. E., Vol-II: 268
Heyns, R. W., Vol-II: 42, 49
Hicken, M., Vol-II: 510
Hicks, B. M., Vol-II: 74
Hicks, G. R., Vol-I: 549
Hicks, K. L., Vol-II: 158
Hickson, F. C. I., Vol-II: 292
Hidi, S., Vol-II: 390
Higginbotham, E., Vol-I: 108
Higgins, C. A., Vol-II: 415, 687
Higgins, E. T., Vol-I: 196, 530
Higgins, K., Vol-II: 484
Highnote, S. M., Vol-I: 237
Hilgard, E. R., Vol-II: 386
Hill, A., Vol-II: 525
Hill, C. A., Vol-I: 144
Hill, C. E., Vol-II: 203
Hill, C. T., Vol-II: 294–295, 297
Hill, D. A., Vol-I: 114
Hill, D. B., Vol-II: 366
Hill, D. L., Vol-II: 655
Hill, E. M., Vol-I: 320, 322
Hill, J., Vol-I: 196; Vol-II: 614
Hill, J. P., Vol-I: 530, 536; Vol-II: 389
Hill, M., Vol-II: 202

Hill, M. S., Vol-II: 156, 200
Hill, R. A., Vol-I: 243
Hill, S. A., Vol-II: 678
Hiller, D., Vol-II: 405
Hiller, J., Vol-I: 480, 483
Hillier, L., Vol-I: 64
Hillis, J. D., Vol-II: 290
Hilsenroth, M. J., Vol-II: 235
Hilt, L. M., Vol-II: 9, 133–147
Hilton, J. L., Vol-I: 197
Himsel, A. J., Vol-II: 413–414
Hinchliff, S., Vol-II: 532
Hinduja, S., Vol-II: 320
Hine, D. W., Vol-II: 322, 431
Hine, T. J., Vol-I: 328
Hines, D. A., Vol-I: 94; Vol-II: 317–319
Hines, M., Vol-I: 84, 224, 270, 279, 307, 317, 324
Hing, E., Vol-II: 530
Hinrichs, D. W., Vol-II: 363
Hinsz, V. B., Vol-II: 446
Hirakata, M., Vol-I: 330
Hirsch, E. S., Vol-I: 456
Hirsch, L. S., Vol-I: 137
Hirschfeld, M., Vol-II: 111
Hisley, J., Vol-II: 385
Hitchcock, A., Vol-I: 191, 196
Hitti, J. E., Vol-II: 534
Hix-Small, H., Vol-II: 622
Hjelt-Back, M., Vol-II: 429
Hlynsky, J. A., Vol-II: 473
Ho, C., Vol-II: 199
Ho, D., Vol-II: 139
Hoard, M. K., Vol-I: 317
Hoban, M. C., Vol-I: 458
Hobbs, W., Vol-I: 329
Hochschild, A. R., Vol-II: 402, 407, 411, 414, 452
Hodges, C., Vol-I: 517
Hodges, E. V. E., Vol-I: 498
Hodges, S. D., Vol-I: 438; Vol-II: 21
Hodgetts, D., Vol-II: 228
Hoek, A., Vol-I: 483
Hoek, H. W., Vol-I: 247
Hoel, H., Vol-II: 423–424, 429–430
Hoenig, J., Vol-II: 115
Hofer, J., Vol-II: 43
Hofferth, S., Vol-II: 225
Hoffman, B. J., Vol-II: 50
Hoffman, C., Vol-I: 194, 198
Hoffman, D., Vol-II: 98
Hoffman, G. E., Vol-I: 266
Hoffman, K. L., Vol-II: 318–319
Hoffman, M. A., Vol-I: 225
Hoffman, M. L., Vol-II: 23
Hoffman, R. M., Vol-I: 135, 151
Hoffner, C., Vol-II: 648
Hofman, M., Vol-II: 116
Hofman, M. A., Vol-I: 224

Hogan, J. D., Vol-I: 20, 159
Hogan, K., Vol-II: 242
Hogg, K., Vol-II: 484
Hogue, M., Vol-I: 91
Hohmann-Marriott, B. E., Vol-II: 413–414
Hoiberg, A., Vol-II: 675
Hoke, L., Vol-II: 95
Holahan, C. K., Vol-I: 136; Vol-II: 23
Holbein, M. F. D., Vol-II: 384
Holbrook, T., Vol-I: 54
Holbrook, T. M., Vol-II: 170
Holden, G. W., Vol-II: 383
Holden, N. J., Vol-II: 673, 676, 679–684, 686–688
Holder, A., Vol-II: 227
Holderness, C. C., Vol-I: 535
Holding, C. S., Vol-I: 329
Holding, D. H., Vol-I: 329
Holdsworth, M., Vol-I: 327
Holdsworth, M. J., Vol-I: 327
Holland, D. C., Vol-II: 291
Holland, J., Vol-II: 282
Holliday, H., Vol-I: 397
Hollingworth, L. S., Vol-I: 23, 27, 81
Hollon, S. D., Vol-II: 82
Holloway, J. B., Vol-II: 573
Hollway, W., Vol-I: 117–118
Holm, S. L., Vol-II: 144
Holmbeck, G. N., Vol-I: 536
Holmes, J. G., Vol-II: 282, 294
Holmes, J., Vol-I: 381, 389, 394–395
Holmes, L. D., Vol-I: 259
Holmes, M., Vol-I: 194
Holmes, R., Vol-I: 389, 394
Holmes, S., Vol-I: 53; Vol-II: 123
Holmes, W. C., Vol-II: 230
Holmqvist, K., Vol-II: 156
Holning, L., Vol-I: 187
Holstein, J. A., Vol-I: 103, 122
Holstrom, A. J., Vol-II: 167
Holt, C. L., Vol-I: 151
Holt, K. E., Vol-II: 156, 165
Holtgraves, T., Vol-II: 343
Holtzman, D., Vol-II: 473
Holtzman, S., Vol-II: 495–497, 504, 511
Holtzworth-Munroe, A., Vol-II: 329, 499–500, 509
Holve, K., Vol-I: 354
Homan, A. C., Vol-II: 350
Homko, C. J., Vol-II: 543
Hondagneu-Sotelo, P., Vol-I: 112
Honeycutt, J. M., Vol-II: 291
Hong, K. E., Vol-II: 120
Hong, L., Vol-II: 456
Hong, M., Vol-I: 442
Hong, S., Vol-II: 289
Hong, Y., Vol-I: 160; Vol-II: 70
Hong, Z., Vol-I: 531
Honnold, J., Vol-I: 186

Hook, E. B., Vol-I: 246
Hook, J. N., Vol-I: 227
Hooker, E., Vol-I: 59, 62, 204
Hooks, b., Vol-I: 104
Hooks, B., Vol-II: 451
Hootman, J. M., Vol-II: 542
Hoover, H. D., Vol-I: 244
Hopcroft, R. L., Vol-I: 164
Hopkins, J. R., Vol-II: 225
Hopkins, N., Vol-I: 496
Hopp, C., Vol-II: 386
Hops, H., Vol-I: 544
Hopwood, C., Vol-II: 204
Horan, P. F., Vol-I: 220
Horgan, T. G., Vol-I: 411, 413–414, 438, 446
Horn, S. S., Vol-I: 538
Horne, A., Vol-II: 224
Horne, S. G., Vol-I: 69
Horner, M. S., Vol-I: 28; Vol-II: 47–48
Horwood, L. J., Vol-II: 135
Hossain, Z., Vol-II: 412
Hou, J., Vol-I: 319
Hough, J. C., Vol-I: 516
Houk, C. P., Vol-I: 194
House, A. T., Vol-I: 139; Vol-II: 113
House, J. S., Vol-II: 498, 504
Houser-Marko, L., Vol-II: 45
Houston, B. K., Vol-I: 322
Houston, D. A., Vol-II: 324
Houtz, J. C., Vol-I: 349
Howard, C., Vol-II: 228
Howard, K. I., Vol-II: 224
Howard, R. W., Vol-I: 25
Howe, C., Vol-II: 510
Howe, K. G., Vol-I: 286
Howerton, M. W., Vol-I: 11
Hox, J. J., Vol-II: 603
Hoyer, W. D., Vol-II: 229
Hoyert, D. L., Vol-II: 526, 542
Hoyt, C. L., Vol-II: 460
Hoyt, D., Vol-II: 619
Hrdy, S. B., Vol-I: 474
Hruda, L., Vol-I: 502
Hsia, J., Vol-II: 544
Hsiung, R. C., Vol-II: 229
Hsu, J., Vol-II: 460
Hu, L., Vol-I: 146
Huang, Y., Vol-I: 98
Hubbard, G., Vol-I: 183
Hubbard, R., Vol-II: 530
Hubner, J. J., Vol-II: 31
Hudson, J., Vol-II: 158
Hudson, W. W., Vol-II: 360
Huebner, D. M., Vol-I: 186; Vol-II: 170
Huebsch, P. D., Vol-II: 619
Huesmann, L. R., Vol-II: 655, 658

Huesmann, R., Vol-II: 645
Huettel, S. A., Vol-I: 329
Huffaker, D. A., Vol-II: 327
Huff-Corzine, L., Vol-I: 463
Huffman, S., Vol-II: 647
Hugdahl, K., Vol-I: 324
Hughes, I. A., Vol-I: 194
Hughes, J. P., Vol-II: 543
Hughes, M., Vol-II: 134
Hughes, T. L., Vol-I: 187; Vol-II: 161
Huguet, P., Vol-I: 284, 289
Hui, S. P., Vol-I: 236
Huisman, H., Vol-II: 474
Hulanská, K., Vol-II: 479
Hulin, C. L., Vol-II: 426, 428, 685
Hultcrantz, M., Vol-I: 244
Hultin, M., Vol-II: 341
Hummel, D. D., Vol-I: 320
Hummert, M. L., Vol-II: 371
Humphreys, K., Vol-II: 619
Humphreys, L., Vol-II: 597
Hund-Georgiadis, M., Vol-I: 245
Hunsberger, B., Vol-II: 362
Hunsley, J., Vol-II: 204
Hunt, E., Vol-I: 329
Hunt, E. B., Vol-I: 322
Hunt, K., Vol-II: 228, 474–475
Hunt, M. D., Vol-II: 346
Hunt, M. G., Vol-II: 24
Hunter, A. E., Vol-I: 36
Hunter, B., Vol-I: 363
Hunter, B. A., Vol-I: 144
Hunter, E., Vol-II: 487
Hunter, J., Vol-I: 63–64, 545
Hunter, M., Vol-II: 684–686
Hunter, S., Vol-II: 295
Hurd, L. C., Vol-I: 567
Hurd, S., Vol-I: 185
Hurdle, D., Vol-II: 625
Hurlbert, D., Vol-I: 485
Hurrell, J. J. Jr., Vol-II: 423
Hurst, N., Vol-I: 194, 198
Hurt, M. M., Vol-I: 139
Hurtaldo, A., Vol-I: 105
Husaini, B. A., Vol-II: 228
Huselid, R. F., Vol-II: 23
Hüsler, G., Vol-II: 621
Huss, E., Vol-I: 119
Hussain, R., Vol-II: 484
Huston, A., Vol-I: 502
Huston, A. C., Vol-I: 501, 505, 510, 514–515; Vol-II: 386
Huston, M., Vol-II: 292
Huston, T., Vol-II: 411
Huston, T. L., Vol-I: 562, 571; Vol-II: 289, 293
Hutchins, L., Vol-II: 363–365
Hutchison, K. E., Vol-II: 371
Hutson-Comeaux, S. L., Vol-I: 432–433; Vol-II: 347
Huttenlocher, J., Vol-I: 318, 326
Huurre, T., Vol-II: 548
Huynh, S. C., Vol-I: 236
Hwang, C. P., Vol-II: 165
Hwang, K., Vol-I: 162
Hwang, V. S., Vol-II: 541–555
Hyams, M., Vol-I: 113
Hyde, J. S., Vol-I: 7–8, 35, 87, 89, 91, 139, 149–150, 193–195, 262, 280, 282, 297–313, 317–318, 362, 412, 431, 445, 471–488, 531, 545, 549, 569–570; Vol-II: 7–8, 30, 97, 136, 142, 146, 154, 156, 171, 253, 281, 299–300, 386, 569, 631, 643
Hyde, R. J., Vol-I: 246
Hyder, A. A., Vol-II: 482
Hyers, L., Vol-I: 393
Hyers, L. L., Vol-II: 170
Hyman, S. L., Vol-II: 598
Hynan, D. J., Vol-II: 81
Hynes, K., Vol-I: 439
Hynie, M., Vol-II: 288
Hytti, J., Vol-II: 429

I

Iachini, T., Vol-I: 321
Iacoviello, B. M., Vol-II: 234
Ialongo, N., Vol-II: 621
Iaria, G., Vol-I: 221
Ibarra, H., Vol-II: 454
Icenogle, M., Vol-II: 415
Ickes, W., Vol-I: 413–414, 438; Vol-II: 21, 295, 325, 501
Igartua, K. J., Vol-II: 362
Iijima, M., Vol-I: 236
Ikeda, M., Vol-I: 246
Ilardi, B., Vol-II: 29
Ilardi, B. C., Vol-II: 339
Iles, P., Vol-II: 456
Ilies, R., Vol-II: 430
Imel, Z. E., Vol-II: 221
Imperato-McGinley, J., Vol-I: 218, 263, 321, 529
Impett, E. A., Vol-I: 138; Vol-II: 117
Inch, R., Vol-II: 644–645
Inciardi, J. A., Vol-II: 591
Inclan, J. E., Vol-II: 261–262
Inglehart, R., Vol-II: 352
Ingram, D., Vol-I: 220
Ingram, J. G., Vol-II: 483
Inhelder, B., Vol-I: 319
Inman, C. C., Vol-II: 283, 294
Instone, D., Vol-II: 678
Inzlicht, M., Vol-I: 284; Vol-II: 21
Iqbal, I., Vol-II: 545
Irfan, N., Vol-I: 456
Iribarne, L., Vol-I: 328
Iritani, B., Vol-II: 647
Irwin, J., Vol-II: 367
Irwin, W., Vol-I: 242
Irwing, P., Vol-I: 301

Iscoe, I., Vol-II: 613
Isensee, R., Vol-I: 64
Isgor, C., Vol-I: 323
Ishii-Kuntz, M., Vol-II: 409
Ishikawa, T., Vol-I: 328
Ismail, A. I., Vol-I: 570
Israel, J. B., Vol-I: 238
Israel, T., Vol-II: 363–364
Israeli, D., Vol-I: 121
Issakidis, C., Vol-II: 228
Istar, A., Vol-II: 258
Ito, T. A., Vol-II: 449
Itoh, M., Vol-I: 245
Ivanenko, Y. P., Vol-I: 329
Ivory, J., Vol-II: 645–646
Ivry, R. B., Vol-I: 222
Iwamasa, G., Vol-II: 616
Iwamoto, D. K., Vol-I: 53
Iwasaki, Y., Vol-II: 509–510
Iyengar, S., Vol-II: 650
Izendoorn, R., Vol-I: 321
Izraeli, D. N., Vol-II: 341

J

Jablonska, B., Vol-II: 599
Jack, D. C., Vol-I: 105; Vol-II: 94, 96, 102, 295
Jack, L. Jr., Vol-II: 549
Jacklin, C., Vol-I: 193
Jacklin, C. N., Vol-I: 28, 88, 194, 240, 298, 317, 322, 514, 536; Vol-II: 313, 322–323, 326
Jackson, A., Vol-II: 625
Jackson, B., Vol-II: 74
Jackson, C., Vol-I: 289
Jackson, D., Vol-II: 620
Jackson, J. M., Vol-I: 284
Jackson, L. A., Vol-II: 652
Jackson, M. A., Vol-II: 228
Jackson, R., Vol-II: 482
Jackson, S., Vol-I: 117
Jackson, S. E., Vol-II: 348
Jackson, S. J., Vol-II: 482
Jacob, S., Vol-I: 248
Jacobi, C., Vol-I: 86
Jacobi, L., Vol-II: 159
Jacobs, D. H., Vol-II: 91, 96
Jacobs, E. C., Vol-I: 327
Jacobs, G. H., Vol-I: 237
Jacobs, J. A., Vol-II: 452
Jacobs, J. E., Vol-I: 306, 374; Vol-II: 380, 384–385, 389–390
Jacobs, J., Vol-I: 281; Vol-II: 384, 401–402
Jacobs, L. F., Vol-I: 266, 329
Jacobs, P., Vol-II: 531
Jacobs. R. R., Vol-II: 457
Jacobson, D. L., Vol-II: 542
Jacobson, K. M., Vol-I: 187
Jacobson, L., Vol-I: 306

Jacobson, N. S., Vol-II: 265–267
Jacques-Tiura, A. J., Vol-II: 284
Jaffee, S. R., Vol-I: 474
Jager, G., Vol-I: 321
Jager, R., Vol-I: 267
Jägle, H., Vol-I: 237
Jago, B., Vol-I: 115
Jahoda, G., Vol-I: 222
Jain, E., Vol-I: 442
James, D., Vol-I: 388–390, 393–394
James, J. B., Vol-II: 65
James, M., Vol-II: 484
James, R. D., Vol-I: 186
James, T. W., Vol-I: 321
James, W. H., Vol-I: 226
Jameson, K. A., Vol-I: 237
Jamieson, K. M., Vol-II: 575
Jamison, W., Vol-I: 320, 327
Jäncke, L., Vol-I: 324
Janicki, D., Vol-II: 433
Jankowiak, W., Vol-II: 292
Janowsky, J., Vol-I: 222
Janowsky, J. S., Vol-I: 223
Jansen, E. A., Vol-II: 312, 320
Jansen, M. A., Vol-II: 380
Jansen-Osmann, P., Vol-I: 239, 319, 322, 329
Janssen, E., Vol-I: 479, 485
Jansz, J., Vol-II: 236
Janzon, L., Vol-I: 241
Jarrett, D. T., Vol-II: 431
Jarrin, D., Vol-I: 456
Jarvik, L. F., Vol-I: 238
Jasper, K., Vol-II: 168
Jastrow, J., Vol-I: 22
Javornisky, G., Vol-II: 340
Jay, T., Vol-I: 391–392
Jayaratne, T. E., Vol-I: 194
Jayaratne, T., Vol-I: 110
Jeffries, J. E., Vol-II: 687
Jeffries, V., Vol-II: 633
Jemal, A., Vol-II: 541
Jemmott, J. B., Vol-II: 51, 54, 520; Vol-II: 624, 634
Jemmott, L., Vol-II: 624, 634
Jenkins, M., Vol-II: 407, 411, 413
Jenkins, S., Vol-II: 47, 56
Jenkins, S. R., Vol-II: 161
Jennings, L., Vol-II: 449
Jennings, S. E., Vol-II: 569
Jensen, J., Vol-II: 483
Jensen, K. E., Vol-II: 571
Jensen, L. A., Vol-II: 543
Jessell, T. H., Vol-I: 236
Jessica, M., Vol-II: 11, 288
Jessurun, M., Vol-II: 483
Jewkes, R., Vol-II: 542
Jibotian, K. S., Vol-I: 195

Jobling, I., Vol-II: 285
Jockin, V., Vol-II: 431
Jodl, K. M., Vol-II: 384
Joffe, T. H., Vol-I: 217
Johannesen-Schmidt, M. C., Vol-I: 84, 422; Vol-II: 338, 454, 677
Johannsdotir, H. L., Vol-II: 434
Johannsen, D. L., Vol-II: 478
John, D., Vol-II: 405, 407, 409–412
John, O. P., Vol-I: 434; Vol-II: 35, 45, 81
Johnsen, B., Vol-II: 458, 474
Johnsen, B. H., Vol-I: 239
Johnson, A., Vol-I: 24–25
Johnson, B. T., Vol-I: 150; Vol-II: 338, 677–678
Johnson, B. W., Vol-I: 324–325
Johnson, C., Vol-II: 337–338, 341, 620
Johnson, C. B., Vol-II: 284
Johnson, C. C., Vol-I: 288
Johnson, E., Vol-II: 690
Johnson, E. M., Vol-I: 571
Johnson, E. S., Vol-I: 220
Johnson, F., Vol-I: 385, 394
Johnson, F. L., Vol-I: 392
Johnson, H. M., Vol-I: 433
Johnson, J., Vol-I: 244, 380; Vol-II: 568
Johnson, J. A., Vol-II: 530
Johnson, J. D., Vol-II: 661
Johnson, J. T., Vol-I: 430, 436
Johnson, K., Vol-I: 119; Vol-II: 361
Johnson, K. L., Vol-II: 290, 546
Johnson, L. L., Vol-I: 510
Johnson, M. P., Vol-II: 317
Johnson, M. T., 589
Johnson, N. G., Vol-II: 117
Johnson, P. B., Vol-II: 330
Johnson, P. J., Vol-I: 98, 567; Vol-II: 659
Johnson, R. A., Vol-II: 339, 341
Johnson, S., Vol-I: 393, 397–398; Vol-II: 411
Johnson, S. B., Vol-I: 197, 199
Johnson, S. K., Vol-II: 450
Johnson, S. M., Vol-I: 67
Johnson, S. P., Vol-I: 318
Johnson, T., Vol-II: 257
Johnson, V., Vol-I: 474–475, 486; Vol-II: 190
Johnson, W., Vol-II: 162
Johnson, W. G., Vol-I: 464
Johnsson, K. O., Vol-II: 476
Johnston, E., Vol-I: 24–25
Johnston, J., Vol-II: 392
Johnston, L., Vol-I: 460
Johnston, L. D., Vol-II: 224
Johnston, L. H., Vol-II: 579
Johnston-Robledo, I., Vol-I: 8, 35, 361–374; Vol-II: 8, 97
Joiner, R., Vol-II: 652
Joiner, T., Vol-II: 139
Joiner, T. E., Vol-II: 194

Jolliffe, D., Vol-II: 328
Jolly, A., Vol-II: 228
Jome, L. M., Vol-II: 200, 570
Jonas, K., Vol-I: 418
Jonasson, Z., Vol-I: 264, 323
Jones, A. K., Vol-I: 242
Jones, B. C., Vol-II: 286
Jones, B. E., Vol-II: 104
Jones, C., Vol-I: 544
Jones, C. M., Vol-I: 265, 269–270, 325
Jones, C. R., Vol-I: 196
Jones, D., Vol-I: 394
Jones, D. C., Vol-I: 535; Vol-II: 165–166
Jones, D. P., Vol-I: 307
Jones, D. W., Vol-I: 245
Jones, E. E., Vol-I: 194
Jones, J., Vol-II: 160
Jones, J. C., Vol-I: 479
Jones, K. S., Vol-I: 240
Jones, L., Vol-II: 317
Jones, L. C., Vol-I: 516
Jones, R. A., Vol-II: 528
Jones, S. B., Vol-II: 346
Jones, S. H., Vol-I: 111
Jones, T. H., Vol-I: 242
Jones, W. H., Vol-II: 24
Jönsson, F. U., Vol-I: 248
Joplin, J. R. W., Vol-II: 502
Jordan, C., Vol-II: 501
Jordan, C. L., Vol-I: 270, 323
Jordan, J., Vol-I: 105; Vol-II: 237
Jordan, K., Vol-I: 324
Jordan, T. J., Vol-I: 225
Jøsendal, O., Vol-II: 474
Josephs, R. A., Vol-I: 222; Vol-II: 20
Josselson, R., Vol-I: 116, 563, 570
Jost, A., Vol-I: 217
Jost, J. T., Vol-II: 35
Jouvent, R., Vol-I: 329
Jovanovic, J., Vol-I: 283, 326
Joyner, K., Vol-II: 136, 138, 142
Jozefowicz, D., Vol-II: 573
Juarez, L., Vol-II: 519
Judd, C. M., Vol-I: 500
Judd, P., Vol-II: 101
Judge, E., Vol-II: 456
Judge, T. A., Vol-II: 351, 459
Judson, J. A., Vol-II: 482
Juillard, E., Vol-I: 463
Julien, D., Vol-II: 266
Jung, D. I., Vol-I: 418
Jung, J., Vol-I: 173; Vol-II: 167
Junge, A., Vol-II: 368
Juni, S., Vol-I: 52, 136
Juntunen, D. L., 200, 211
Jurik, N. C., Vol-II: 453
Jussab, F., Vol-I: 328

K

Kaahumanu, L., Vol-II: 363–365
Kaas, A. L., Vol-I: 240
Kaczala, C. M., Vol-II: 383–385
Kaergaard, A., Vol-I: 242
Kaestle, C. E., Vol-I: 536
Kagan, D. M., Vol-II: 118
Kagan, J., Vol-I: 512; Vol-II: 386
Kagawa, M., Vol-II: 155
Kahle, J., Vol-II: 385
Kahle, J. B., Vol-I: 288
Kahlenberg, S., Vol-II: 644, 646–647
Kahlor, L., Vol-II: 660
Kahn, A. S., Vol-I: 31; Vol-II: 55
Kahn, L. M., Vol-II: 446
Kahn, R., Vol-I: 566–567
Kahn, T. J., Vol-II: 368
Kahneman, D., Vol-I: 196, 199
Kail, R., Vol-I: 319
Kail, R. V., Vol-I: 264, 322, 329
Kaiser, C. R., Vol-II: 138, 143
Kalcik, S., Vol-I: 390
Kalinka, C. J., Vol-II: 299
Kalish, C. W., Vol-I: 500, 506
Kallai, J., Vol-I: 328, 330
Kallgren, C. A., Vol-II: 343
Kallivayalil, D., Vol-II: 199
Kalmuss, D., Vol-II: 532–533
Kaluzny, G., Vol-I: 96
Kamali, B., Vol-I: 118
Kaminiski, P. L., Vol-II: 174
Kaminski, P. L., Vol-II: 31–32
Kamo, Y., Vol-II: 409, 412
Kamphoff, C. S., Vol-II: 12, 563–580
Kanazawa, S., Vol-I: 199; Vol-II: 285
Kandel, E. R., Vol-I: 236
Kando, T., Vol-I: 368
Kandrack, M., Vol-II: 475
Kandzari, D. E., Vol-I: 180
Kane, K., Vol-II: 432
Kane, M. J., Vol-II: 571
Kane, M. L., Vol-II: 295
Kane, R. L., Vol-II: 525
Kanfer, R., Vol-I: 301
Kang, L., Vol-II: 569
Kanner, A., Vol-I: 146
Kansaku, K., Vol-I: 245
Kanter, R. M., Vol-II: 401
Kantoff, P. W., Vol-II: 527
Kantor, R., Vol-I: 387
Kaplan, A., Vol-I: 105
Kaplan, A. R., Vol-I: 246
Kaplan, B. J., Vol-II: 73
Kaplan, D. L., Vol-II: 283
Kaplan, E., Vol-I: 236
Kaplan, R. M., Vol-I: 547
Kaplan, S., Vol-II: 229
Kaplan, S. H., Vol-II: 553
Kappers, A. M., Vol-I: 240
Kaprio, J., Vol-II: 322
Karakowsky, L., Vol-II: 338
Karau, S. J., Vol-I: 411, 419–421; Vol-II: 339, 341, 351, 447–450, 457, 674
Kareken, D. A., Vol-I: 249
Kark, R., Vol-II: 13, 443–462
Karlsson, A., Vol-II: 483
Karney, B. R., Vol-II: 501, 504, 507–509, 511
Karol, D., Vol-II: 69
Karoly, P., Vol-II: 522
Karp, S., Vol-II: 570
Karremans, J. C., Vol-II: 294
Karten, S. J., Vol-I: 389, 393; Vol-II: 339, 343, 345
Karunas, R. B., Vol-II: 483
Kaschak, E., Vol-I: 10; Vol-II: 10, 187–215
Kashy, D. A., Vol-II: 677
Kaslow, N., Vol-II: 142
Kasper, S., Vol-I: 444
Kasprzyk, D., Vol-II: 340
Kass, S. J., Vol-I: 328
Kasser, T., Vol-I: 194
Kassinove, H., Vol-I: 393
Kath, L. M., Vol-II: 428
Kathleen, M., Vol-II: 316, 321
Katkin, E. S., Vol-I: 443
Katz, A. N., Vol-I: 354
Katz, D. L., Vol-II: 99
Katz, J. E., Vol-II: 653
Katz, M., Vol-II: 121–122
Katz, M. L., Vol-I: 184
Katz, P. A., Vol-I: 47, 501, 503, 516–517
Katz, S., Vol-I: 567–568
Kauer, K. J., Vol-II: 570
Kaufman, G., Vol-II: 646–647
Kaufman, J., Vol-I: 329
Kaufman, J. C., Vol-I: 304, 308
Kaufman, J. S., Vol-I: 179
Kaufman, S. B., Vol-I: 323
Kaukiainen, A., Vol-II: 315, 328, 436
Kaur, S., Vol-II: 519
Kautzman, D., Vol-I: 462
Kaw, E., Vol-I: 114
Kawachi, I., Vol-II: 139, 145
Kawahara, D. M., Vol-II: 460
Kawakami, K., Vol-II: 147
Kay, G., Vol-I: 133
Kayano, M., Vol-I: 165
Kayser, K., Vol-II: 497, 551
Keane, T., Vol-I: 383
Keating, C. F., Vol-I: 389, 414; Vol-II: 338
Keating, D. P., Vol-I: 528; Vol-II: 32
Keating, J. P., Vol-I: 195
Keel, P. K., Vol-II: 155, 161
Keelan, J. P., Vol-II: 157
Keenan, C., Vol-I: 69

Keenan, J. P., Vol-I: 244
Keene, D., Vol-II: 510
Keene, J. R., Vol-II: 415
Keery, H., Vol-I: 88; Vol-II: 153, 164
Kegan, R., Vol-I: 560, 563
Kehily, M., Vol-I: 282
Keil, J. E., Vol-II: 160
Keita, G. P., Vol-II: 97
Keith, J. R., Vol-I: 226, 269
Keith, S. J., Vol-II: 532
Keitz, S. A., Vol-II: 533
Kelen, G. D., Vol-II: 483
Kelleher, W., Vol-I: 138; Vol-II: 522
Keller, A., Vol-I: 248
Keller, A. J., Vol-I: 221, 323
Keller, C. J., Vol-I: 352, 354
Keller, E. F., Vol-I: 200, 202; Vol-II: 189
Keller, H., Vol-I: 110, 346
Keller, L. B., Vol-I: 569
Keller, M., Vol-II: 134, 548
Keller, M. B., Vol-II: 195
Kellermann, S., Vol-I: 245
Kelley, H. H., Vol-I: 200
Kelley, J., Vol-II: 360
Kelley, M. L., Vol-I: 687, 689
Kelley, W. M., Vol-II: 285
Kelloway, E. K., Vol-II: 423, 425, 431
Kelly, A., Vol-I: 388; Vol-II: 268
Kelly, D. M., Vol-I: 329–330
Kelly, E., Vol-II: 166
Kelly, F. D., Vol-I: 536
Kelly, J., Vol-I: 383
Kelly, J. A., Vol-I: 389
Kelly, J. B., Vol-II: 599
Kelly, J. G., Vol-II: 613–614, 633
Kelly, J. R., Vol-I: 432–433
Kelly, K., Vol-II: 255, 436
Kelly, L., Vol-II: 173
Kelly, R. J., Vol-II: 347
Keltner, D., Vol-I: 429, 431, 435
Kemeny, M. E., Vol-II: 141, 434, 553
Kemp, D. T., Vol-I: 243
Kempel, P., Vol-I: 324
Kemper, E., Vol-II: 544
Kempler, T., Vol-II: 385
Kenagy, G. P., Vol-II: 114, 121
Kenna, J. C., Vol-II: 115
Kennealy, P. J., Vol-II: 74
Kennedy, C. R., Vol-I: 243
Kennedy, D. N., Vol-I: 217
Kennedy, G., Vol-II: 230
Kennedy, M., Vol-II: 527
Kennedy, R. E., Vol-I: 545
Kenny, D. A., Vol-I: 3, 86; Vol-II: 3
Kenrick, D. T., Vol-II: 285
Keogh, E., Vol-I: 241
Kerekovska, A., Vol-II: 473

Kerkstra, A., Vol-I: 411, 419–420
Kern, J., Vol-I: 383
Kern, M. K., Vol-I: 241
Kerns, K. A., Vol-I: 220
Kernsmith, P., Vol-II: 631
Kerpelman, J., Vol-II: 686
Kerr, G., Vol-II: 575
Kerr, J. E., Vol-I: 226
Kershner, J. R., Vol-I: 354
Kersker, J. L., Vol-I: 329
Kerst, M. E., Vol-II: 425
Kerstetter, D. L., Vol-II: 571
Keshet, S., Vol-II: 460
Kesimci, A., Vol-II: 511
Kessels, R. P. C., Vol-I: 223, 321
Kessenich, J. J., Vol-II: 154
Kessler, R., Vol-I: 63
Kessler, R. C., Vol-II: 96, 133–135, 137, 140, 224, 473, 497–498, 501–502, 506, 631
Kessler, S., Vol-I: 105, 112, 120, 194, 364
Kessler, S. J., Vol-I: 192, 194, 260
Ketay, S., Vol-II: 66
Ketelaar, T., Vol-II: 283
Keteyian, S. J., Vol-II: 567
Kettrey, H. H., Vol-II: 319
Keyes, K. M., Vol-II: 146, 480
Keyes, S., Vol-I: 515
Keys, C., Vol-II: 627
Keys, C. B., Vol-II: 283
Keysar, B., Vol-I: 200
Khouri, H., Vol-II: 140
Khoury, J., Vol-II: 482
Khoury-Kassabri, M., Vol-II: 628, 633
Kian, E. M., Vol-II: 572
Kidd, A., Vol-II: 624
Kidd, L., Vol-I: 183
Kidd, S., Vol-I: 163
Kidder, L., Vol-I: 383
Kiecolt, K. J., Vol-II: 318
Kiecolt-Glaser, J. K., Vol-I: 443; Vol-II: 498–499, 507
Kiefe, C. I., Vol-II: 544
Kiefer, A. K., Vol-II: 291, 299
Kiesinger, C. E., Vol-I: 107, 109
Kiesner, J., Vol-I: 433
Kiessling, F., Vol-II: 43
Kiger, G., Vol-II: 413, 415
Kilborn, B., Vol-I: 159
Kilgus, M. D., Vol-II: 118
Killen, J. D., Vol-II: 544
Killian, L. T., Vol-II: 101
Killian, T. M., Vol-II: 101
Kilmartin, C., Vol-I: 54
Kilmartin, C. T., Vol-II: 225
Kilpatrick, D., Vol-II: 620
Kilpatrick, D. G., Vol-II: 137, 195, 316, 685
Kim, D. D., Vol-II: 646
Kim, J., Vol-I: 511

Kim, K., Vol-II: 644, 646
Kim, S., Vol-II: 653
Kim, U., Vol-I: 162–163, 166
Kimball, M. M., Vol-I: 304, 505; Vol-II: 386
Kimberley, B. P., Vol-I: 243
Kimble, T. D., Vol-I: 236
Kimerling, R., Vol-II: 74
Kimes, D. D., Vol-II: 648
Kimm, S. Y. S., Vol-II: 567
Kimmel, A. J., Vol-II: 123
Kimmel, A., Vol-I: 398
Kimmel, D., Vol-I: 65–66
Kimmel, E., Vol-I: 33, 103
Kimmel, E. B., Vol-I: 20
Kimmel, M., Vol-I: 133; Vol-II: 225–226
Kimmel, M. S., Vol-II: 282, 291
Kimmel, S. B., Vol-II: 170
Kimmons, J. E., Vol-II: 473
Kimura, D., Vol-I: 49, 216, 220–223, 239, 263, 265–266, 279, 319, 321, 324, 329
Kincheloe, J. L., Vol-I: 290
Kinchla, M., Vol-I: 456
Kindermann, T. A., Vol-II: 384
King, A., Vol-II: 171
King, C., Vol-II: 646, 647
King, D., Vol-II: 112
King, E. B., Vol-II: 157
King, J., Vol-I: 277
King, L. A., Vol-II: 45
King, M. J., Vol-II: 98, 485
King, S. E., Vol-II: 230
King, S. S., Vol-I: 283
Kinnish, K. K., Vol-I: 72
Kinnunen, U., Vol-II: 27
Kinsey, A., Vol-I: 204, 486
Kinsey, A. C., Vol-I: 66
Kinsey, B. L., Vol-I: 317
Kipke, M., Vol-II: 620
Kipp, K., Vol-I: 473
Kippax, S., Vol-I: 115
Kirasic, K. C., Vol-I: 330
Kirby, S. L., Vol-II: 579
Kirk, S. A., Vol-II: 105
Kirkbride, A., Vol-I: 98; Vol-II: 156, 659
Kirkland, J., Vol-I: 237
Kirkley, B., Vol-I: 383
Kirkove, C., Vol-II: 527
Kirkpatrick, K. L., Vol-II: 35
Kirkpatrick, L. A., Vol-II: 283
Kirk-Smith, M., Vol-I: 248
Kiselica, M. S., Vol-II: 224, 232–233, 235–237
Kissling, E. A., Vol-I: 393
Kitano, K., Vol-II: 120
Kitayama, S., Vol-I: 441; Vol-II: 26, 56
Kitazawa, S., Vol-I: 245
Kite, M. E., Vol-I: 195, 480; Vol-II: 360–361, 447, 449, 458

Kite, M., Vol-II: 570
Kitzinger, C., Vol-I: 35, 110, 117–118, 192, 194, 199, 201, 382; Vol-II: 192
Kiviruusu, O., Vol-II: 548
Kivnick, H. Q., Vol-I: 560
Kizilos, M. A., Vol-II: 350
Klabunde, C. N., Vol-II: 527, 544
Klaczynski, P. A., Vol-I: 501
Klarenbach, S. W., Vol-II: 531
Klaw, E., Vol-II: 619
Klebanov, P. K., Vol-II: 520
Kleck, R. E., Vol-I: 431
Klein, A., Vol-II: 161, 163
Klein, D. J., Vol-II: 547
Klein, E. B., Vol-I: 44
Klein, F., Vol-I: 66, 72; Vol-II: 365
Klein, H., Vol-II: 167, 647–648
Klein, K. J., Vol-II: 21
Klein, K. J. K., Vol-I: 438
Klein, L. C., Vol-I: 457, 459–460
Klein, P., Vol-II: 291
Klein, R., Vol-II: 368–369
Klein, S., Vol-I: 240, 243
Klesges, R. C., Vol-I: 462
Klieme, E., Vol-I: 318
Klimmt, C., Vol-II: 651–652
Kline, R. B., Vol-I: 151
Kling, K. C., Vol-I: 299, 431, 569; Vol-II: 30
Klinger, R. L., Vol-I: 64
Klinkenberg, D., Vol-II: 292
Klöckner, C., Vol-I: 420
Klohnen, E. C., Vol-II: 45
Klonoff, E. A., Vol-I: 148, 192; Vol-II: 195
Klonsky, B. G., Vol-II: 343–344, 450
Klosterhalfen, S., Vol-I: 245
Kluckhohn, C., Vol-I: 160
Klump, K. L., Vol-II: 161
Klute, M. M., Vol-II: 296
Kluwer, E., Vol-II: 413
Kmet, J., Vol-II: 347
Knapp, D., Vol-I: 329
Knapp, M. L., Vol-I: 412
Knee, R. E. Jr., Vol-II: 451
Knickmeyer, R. C., Vol-I: 220
Kniffin, K., Vol-I: 396
Knight, C., Vol-II: 169
Knight-Bohnhoff, K., Vol-II: 314
Knott, J. A., Vol-I: 308, 319
Knox, D., Vol-II: 283
Knox, R., Vol-II: 242
Koberg, C. S., Vol-I: 354
Kobrynowicz, D., Vol-II: 344
Koca, C., Vol-II: 569
Koch, J., Vol-I: 281–283, 287, 289
Koch, P., Vol-I: 485
Kochanek, K. D., Vol-II: 228
Koehler, M. S., Vol-II: 385

Koelsch, S., Vol-I: 244
Koenig, A. M., Vol-I: 430, 438, 569
Koenig, B. L., Vol-II: 283–284
Koenig-Nobert, S., Vol-I: 461
Koeske, R., Vol-I: 88, 381
Koeske, R. D., Vol-I: 193, 371
Koestner, R., Vol-I: 545; Vol-II: 23, 43–46, 49, 56
Koff, E., Vol-I: 535, 544
Kohlberg, L., Vol-I: 260, 528; Vol-II: 188
Kohlberg, L. A., Vol-I: 496
Kohlman, M., Vol-I: 96
Koivula, N., Vol-II: 571
Kokot, A. P., Vol-II: 299
Kolakowsky-Hayner, S. A., Vol-II: 483
Kolaric, G. C., Vol-I: 531
Kolb, D., Vol-I: 395, 397
Kolk, A. M., Vol-I: 145; Vol-II: 474
Koller, V., Vol-I: 404
Kollock, P., Vol-I: 390
Kolo, L. L., Vol-I: 323
Komar, J., Vol-II: 33
Komesaroff, P., Vol-I: 117
Konik, J., Vol-I: 362, 565
Konrad, A. M., Vol-I: 95, 150–151; Vol-II: 432, 436
Konrath, S., Vol-II: 648
Kopper, B. A., Vol-II: 312, 427, 431
Koppeschaar, H. P. F., Vol-I: 223, 321
Korabik, K., Vol-II: 460, 503, 679
Korchmaros, J., Vol-I: 195–196
Korchmaros, J. N., Vol-I: 195, 199
Kornman, C. L., Vol-II: 205
Korol, D. L., Vol-I: 323
Koropeckyj-Cox, T., Vol-I: 573
Korszun, A., Vol-I: 241
Kosler, J., Vol-II: 385
Koslowsky, M., Vol-II: 460
Koss, M. P., Vol-II: 137, 330, 579, 632, 685
Kosslyn, S. M., Vol-I: 328
Kosutic, I., Vol-II: 254, 269
Kotre, J., Vol-I: 563
Kouznetsova, N., Vol-I: 432
Kovacs, M., Vol-II: 134
Koval, J. J., Vol-II: 477
Kowalski, K. C., Vol-II: 576
Kowalski, R. M., Vol-II: 315
Kowumaki, J. H., Vol-II: 295
Koyi, H., Vol-II: 545
Kozak, L. J., Vol-II: 520, 533
Kozee, H. B., Vol-II: 161
Koziej, J., Vol-I: 387
Kozma, A., Vol-II: 318
Kposowa, A. J., Vol-II: 485
Kraemer, H., Vol-I: 86
Kraemer, H. C., Vol-I: 86–87
Krafka, C., Vol-II: 589
Kraimer, M. L., Vol-II: 454
Krajewski, H. T., Vol-II: 498, 502–503, 510

Kral, M. J., Vol-I: 163
Kramarae, C., Vol-I: 381–382, 385, 387–388, 393, 401
Kramarow, E. A., Vol-II: 519
Kramer, B. S., Vol-II: 527
Kramer, D. A., Vol-I: 148–149
Kramer, G. A., Vol-I: 321
Kramer, L., Vol-II: 655
Kramer, S., Vol-II: 480
Krane, V., Vol-II: 569–570, 573–574, 577–578
Krantz, D. S., Vol-I: 456
Krassas, N. R., Vol-II: 171
Kraus, L. A., Vol-I: 438
Krauss, R. M., Vol-I: 438
Kraut, R., Vol-II: 282, 602
Kravetz, D., Vol-I: 30; Vol-II: 197–198
Kravitz, R. L., Vol-II: 522
Krekling, S., Vol-I: 319
Krestan, J. A., Vol-II: 94–95, 102, 104, 255
Krieger, N., Vol-I: 179; Vol-II: 120
Kril, J. J., Vol-I: 244
Kring, A. M., Vol-I: 242, 420, 432, 435, 442; Vol-II: 35
Krishnan, H. A., Vol-II: 351, 456
Krishnan, S. S., Vol-I: 347
Krishnayya, S., Vol-I: 392
Kroeber, A. L., Vol-I: 160
Kroger, J., Vol-I: 528, 562–565
Kroll, J. K., Vol-II: 95
Kroner, T., Vol-I: 198
Kroska, A., Vol-II: 68
Krueger, J. I., Vol-II: 24
Krug, E. G., Vol-II: 482
Kruger, A., Vol-I: 241
Kruger, D. J., Vol-II: 285–286
Krugman, S., Vol-I: 432
Kruijver, F., Vol-I: 116
Kruijver, F. P. M., Vol-I: 224
Krupa, M. H., Vol-I: 327
Krupat, E., Vol-II: 522
Krupp, D., Vol-I: 432
Krysik, J., Vol-II: 604
Ksansnak, K. R., Vol-I: 501
Ku, L. C., Vol-I: 52, 137; Vol-II: 299
Kubberød, E., Vol-I: 462–463
Kuebli, J., Vol-II: 141
Kuehl, T., Vol-I: 241
Kuehne, V. S., Vol-I: 564
Kufera, J., Vol-II: 483
Kuga, M., Vol-I: 246
Kuh, D., Vol-II: 165
Kuhlman, J. S., Vol-I: 326
Kuhn, A., Vol-I: 504
Kuhn, D., Vol-I: 516, 528
Kuhn, M., Vol-I: 218
Kuhn, S. L., Vol-I: 267
Kuhn, T., Vol-I: 82
Kühnen, U., Vol-II: 449
Kuijer, R. G., Vol-II: 546, 548

Kuiper, A. J., Vol-II: 119–120, 367
Kulik, L., Vol-I: 572; Vol-II: 625, 627, 633
Kulis, S., Vol-II: 625
Kulka, R., Vol-II: 43
Kulynych, J. J., Vol-I: 245
Kumanyika, S. K., Vol-II: 160
Kümmel, G., Vol-II: 691
Kung, H. C., Vol-II: 228, 526, 542
Kunter, M., Vol-II: 385
Kuntsche, S., Vol-II: 480
Kunz, K., Vol-I: 245
Kupanoff, K., Vol-I: 536
Kupersmidt, J., Vol-I: 397
Kupersmidt, J. B., Vol-I: 397
Kurdek, L., Vol-II: 411
Kurdek, L. A., Vol-I: 64, 66; Vol-II: 285, 412
Kuriansky, J. A., Vol-I: 571
Kurilla, V., Vol-II: 204
Kuring, J. K., Vol-II: 156–157, 172
Kurita, J. A., Vol-II: 340
Kurland, B., Vol-I: 307
Kurokawa, M., Vol-I: 441
Kuse, A. R., Vol-I: 221, 322
Kushner, M. A., Vol-II: 599
Küskü, F., Vol-II: 383, 391
Kutchins, H., Vol-II: 105
Kvale, S., Vol-I: 106
Kwan, V. S. Y., Vol-II: 352
Kwang, T., Vol-I: 92
Kyllonen, P. C., Vol-I: 321
Kyrejto, J. W., Vol-II: 576

L

L'Hirondelle, N., Vol-I: 321, 328
La Freniere, P., Vol-I: 511
Labella, A. G., Vol-I: 544
Laberge, S., Vol-II: 566
Labouvie-Vief, G., Vol-I: 442, 561, 568–569
LaBrecque, S. V., Vol-I: 537
Lachlan, K., Vol-II: 167
Lachman, M. E., Vol-I: 328
Lader, D., Vol-II: 478
Laessle, R. G., Vol-I: 456
LaFleur, S. J., Vol-II: 340
LaFrance, M., Vol-I: 84, 89, 194–195, 411, 419–420, 437–438; Vol-II: 21, 69, 71, 75–76, 338
Lagan, H. D., Vol-I: 53
Lagerspetz, K. M. J., Vol-II: 315
Lago, T., Vol-II: 313
Lagro-Janssen, A. L., Vol-II: 474
Lahey, B. B., Vol-I: 547
Lahiff, M., Vol-II: 619
Lai, L., Vol-II: 342, 347
Laird, J., Vol-I: 67; Vol-II: 255, 263
Laird, N., Vol-II: 363
Lajoie, S. P., Vol-I: 332
Lajtha, A., Vol-I: 365

Lakoff, R., Vol-I: 380–381, 383, 387
Lal, S., Vol-I: 25
Lalonde, R. N., Vol-II: 288
Lalta, V., Vol-II: 453
Lalumiere, M. L., Vol-II: 285
Lam, K. S. L., Vol-II: 543
Lam, L. T., Vol-II: 482
Lam, M., Vol-II: 504
Lamacz, M., Vol-II: 367
LaMar, L., Vol-II: 361
LaMay, M. L., Vol-II: 301
Lamb, M. E., Vol-I: 362; Vol-II: 225, 383, 385
Lamb, S., Vol-II: 95, 193
Lambdin, J., Vol-I: 195
Lambert, A. J., Vol-II: 340
Lambert, M. J., Vol-II: 234
Lambert, S. M., Vol-II: 568
Lambert, S., Vol-II: 272
Lambrey, S., Vol-I: 329
Lamke, L. K., Vol-II: 296
Lamon, S. J., Vol-I: 303, 531; Vol-II: 386
Lancee, W., Vol-II: 95
Landa, A., Vol-II: 347
Landis, K. R., Vol-II: 140, 498
Landrine, H., Vol-I: 105, 192; Vol-II: 95–96, 104, 195, 534
Lane, J. M., Vol-I: 50, 53
Lane, K. A., Vol-II: 265, 447
Laner, M. R., Vol-II: 289–290, 298
Lang, F. R., Vol-I: 566
Langabeer, K. A., Vol-I: 68
Lange, C., Vol-II: 325
Langeland, W., Vol-II: 100
Langer, E. J., Vol-II: 364
Langer, S. J., Vol-II: 114, 119, 121–122, 125
Langford, N. M., Vol-I: 328
Langhout, R., Vol-II: 634
Langhout, R. D., Vol-II: 429
Langley-Evans, A. J., Vol-I: 246
Langley-Evans, S. C., Vol-I: 246
Langlois, J. A., Vol-II: 483
Langlois, J. H., Vol-I: 143
Langrock, A., Vol-I: 318
Langton, R., Vol-I: 31–32
Lannon, P., Vol-II: 623
Lanphear, B. P., Vol-II: 482
Lansford, J. E., Vol-I: 397
Lanyon, L. J., Vol-I: 221
Lanyon, R. I., Vol-II: 522
Lanza, S., Vol-II: 389
Lapchick, R., Vol-II: 566–567, 572–573
Lapierre, L. M., Vol-II: 436
LaPorte, R. E., Vol-I: 187
Larkey, L. K., Vol-I: 185
Larkins, A. G., Vol-II: 385
Larose, S., Vol-II: 383
Larsen, R. J., Vol-I: 434; Vol-II: 511

Larsen, S., Vol-II: 474
Larson, J., Vol-I: 386; Vol-II: 137
Larson, L. M., Vol-II: 228, 235
Larson, M., Vol-II: 645, 649
Larson, R., Vol-II: 117
Larson, R. W., Vol-I: 436, 536–537, 539–540, 544–545; Vol-II: 384
Larsson, M., Vol-I: 248
Larue, J., Vol-I: 326
Laschever, S., Vol-I: 383–384
Lasco, M. S., Vol-I: 225
Lasky, B., Vol-II: 343
Laszlo, A. C., Vol-I: 24
Lather, P., Vol-I: 103, 106–107, 111, 403
Latour, B., Vol-I: 194, 202
Lau, B. H-B., Vol-I: 145–146
Lau, H., Vol-II: 139
Lau, S., Vol-I: 355
Lau, T., Vol-II: 502
Laub, J. H., Vol-I: 546
Laumann, E. O., Vol-I: 478, 480; Vol-II: 321
Launder, C., Vol-I: 53
Laungani, P., Vol-I: 163
Laurenceau, J. P., Vol-II: 294
Lauriello, J., Vol-II: 532
Laursen, B., Vol-I: 545
Lautenbacher, S., Vol-I: 241
Lautenschlager, G., Vol-I: 227
Lauterbach, K. W., Vol-II: 543
Laux, G., Vol-II: 519
Lauzen, M. M., Vol-II: 644
Lavezzary, E., Vol-II: 43
Lavine, H., Vol-II: 659
Lavish, L. A., Vol-I: 352
Law, D. J., Vol-I: 322
Lawless, P., Vol-II: 431
Lawrence, A. A., Vol-II: 367
Lawrence, M., Vol-II: 168
Lawrence, M. A., Vol-I: 114, 260, 317, 497
Lawrence-Lightfoot, S., Vol-I: 114
Lawrenz, F., Vol-I: 531
Lawson, D. M., Vol-II: 210
Lawson, R., Vol-II: 187
Lawton, C. A., Vol-I: 7, 317–332
Layton, H. S., Vol-II: 646
Lazar, M., Vol-I: 395, 403
Lazarus, R., Vol-I: 146
Lazarus, R. S., Vol-II: 432, 495–497, 499, 503–505, 511, 550
Le Resche, L., Vol-I: 241
Le, J., Vol-I: 238, 241
Le, V. N., Vol-II: 71
Leadbeater, B. J., Vol-II: 134, 139
Leader, D., Vol-II: 616
Leahy, T., Vol-II: 579
Leaper, C., Vol-I: 280–283, 397, 414, 512, 531, 536, 538; Vol-II: 338

Lear, M., Vol-II: 650
Leary, D. E., Vol-I: 200, 202
Lease, S., Vol-I: 67
Leavy, P. L., Vol-I: 103, 113
Leavy, P., Vol-I: 3; Vol-II: 3, 168
LeBeau, L. S., Vol-I: 416–417, 444
Leberman, S., Vol-II: 566
Lebesis, M., Vol-II: 343
LeBlanc, M. M., Vol-II: 431
Lebolt, A., Vol-II: 141
Leck, J. D., Vol-II: 436
Leder, G. C., Vol-II: 383, 385
Ledger, G., Vol-I: 354
Lee, B. B., Vol-I: 237
Lee, C. J., Vol-II: 485
Lee, D., Vol-II: 424
Lee, K., Vol-II: 436
Lee, N., Vol-I: 204
Lee, N. C., Vol-II: 541
Lee, N. S., Vol-II: 288
Lee, R. M., Vol-II: 194–195
Lee, S., Vol-I: 307
Lee, S. E., Vol-II: 362
Lee, T., Vol-I: 11, 13, 194, 549
Lee, Y., Vol-II: 165
Leeb, B. F., Vol-II: 545
LeeTiernan, S., Vol-II: 67
Legare, C. H., Vol-I: 501, 506
Lehavot, K., Vol-II: 340
Lehman, A., Vol-II: 507
Lehmann, W., Vol-I: 326
Lehrke, S., Vol-I: 456
Lehrner, J., Vol-I: 248
Leiblum, S., Vol-I: 480–481
Leichty, G., Vol-II: 171
Leinbach, M. D., Vol-I: 504–505, 510
Leisring, P. A., Vol-II: 230
Leit, R. A., Vol-I: 90, 535; Vol-II: 160, 166–167, 172
Leitenberg, H., Vol-I: 478
Lekas, H. M., Vol-II: 371
Lemieux, A., Vol-I: 203
Lemieux, S., Vol-I: 457
Lemmon, C. R., Vol-I: 458
Lengua, L. J., Vol-II: 24, 27
Lenney, E., Vol-I: 134
Lennon, M., Vol-II: 414
Lennon, R., Vol-I: 435
Lenroot, R. K., Vol-I: 280
Lensky, D. B., Vol-II: 50
Lenskyj, H., Vol-II: 579
Lensvelt-Mulders, G. J. L. M., Vol-II: 603
Lent, R. W., Vol-II: 380, 383
Lentz, E., Vol-II: 454
Leo, R. A., Vol-II: 591, 596
Leon, C., Vol-I: 329
Leon, D. A., Vol-II: 481
Leon, G. R., Vol-II: 161

Leonard, K., Vol-II: 314
Leonardelli, G. J., Vol-II: 352
Leong, F. T. L., Vol-II: 231, 269
Leong, H., Vol-I: 238
Lepore, S. J., Vol-II: 550
Leranth, C., Vol-I: 217
LeResche, L., Vol-I: 241
Lerman, H., Vol-II: 192
Lerner, C., Vol-II: 566
Lerner, H., Vol-I: 472
Lerner, N., Vol-I: 439; Vol-II: 454
Lerner, R. M., Vol-I: 326
Leschied, A. W., Vol-II: 548
Leslie, L. A., Vol-II: 8, 254–255, 260
Lester, R., Vol-II: 50
Lethbridge-Cejku, M., Vol-II: 525
Letherby, G., Vol-I: 573
Letourneau, K. J., Vol-I: 511
Leung, A. K., Vol-II: 460
Leung, K., Vol-I: 165, 167, 169–172
Leung, M. L., Vol-I: 108
Leupnitz, D. A., Vol-II: 191
Leuty, M., Vol-I: 445
Lev, A. I., Vol-II: 111, 114–115, 118–120, 122–123, 125, 367
Levant, R., Vol-I: 43, 46; Vol-II: 522
Levant, R. F., Vol-I: 45, 52, 137, 139, 150; Vol-II: 113, 123, 221–225, 228–229, 233–234, 238
LeVay, S., Vol-I: 217, 223, 225, 483
Levenson, R. W., Vol-I: 437, 440, 443; Vol-II: 265, 499
Lever, J., Vol-II: 157
Levi-Minzi, M., Vol-I: 53
Levin, J., Vol-I: 396–398
Levin, R., Vol-II: 527
Levine, E. A., Vol-II: 528
Levine, M. E., Vol-I: 245
Levine, M. P., Vol-I: 86–87, 97, 318; Vol-II: 156, 165–166, 168, 658
Levine, R., Vol-II: 289
Levine, S. C., Vol-I: 318, 326
Levine, T., Vol-II: 297
Levinson, D., Vol-I: 167
Levinson, M. H., Vol-I: 44
Levinson, W., Vol-II: 523
Levitt, S., Vol-II: 339
Levy, B., Vol-II: 285
Levy, G. D., Vol-I: 510, 515; Vol-II: 340
Levy, L. J., Vol-I: 321
Levy, S. R., Vol-I: 194; Vol-II: 370
Lewald, J., Vol-I: 244
Lewin, C., Vol-I: 323
Lewin, M., Vol-I: 149; Vol-I: 366
Lewins, A., Vol-I: 123
Lewinsohn, P., Vol-II: 142
Lewinsohn, P. M., Vol-I: 543–544
Lewis, C., Vol-I: 304
Lewis, C. D., Vol-I: 349

Lewis, I., Vol-I: 236
Lewis, K. N., Vol-II: 196
Lewis, L. L., Vol-II: 447–448
Lewis, M., Vol-II: 156
Lewis, R. J., Vol-II: 509
Lewis, S. I., Vol-II: 430
Lewis, S. M., Vol-I: 239
Lex, U., Vol-I: 245
Leymann, H., Vol-II: 424
Li, G., Vol-II: 482–483
Li, M. Y., Vol-II: 320
Li, Q., Vol-II: 320
Li, W. L., Vol-I: 10
Li, W., Vol-II: 553
Liben, L. S., Vol-I: 282, 318–320, 323–324, 500, 503, 508, 515–516; Vol-II: 385
Liburd, L. C., Vol-II: 549
Lichtenstein, M., Vol-I: 196
Lichter, D., Vol-II: 405, 407, 409
Liden, R. C., Vol-II: 454
Lieberman, M. A., Vol-II: 143
Liebert, R. S., Vol-I: 50
Liebler, A., Vol-I: 412–413
Lieblich, A., Vol-I: 116
Liebman, M., Vol-I: 457
Lievens, F., Vol-II: 71
Light, K. C., Vol-I: 235, 436
Lightdale, J. R., Vol-II: 312
Lightfoot, C., Vol-I: 114, 319
Lilienfeld, S. O., Vol-II: 96
Liller, K. D., Vol-II: 319
Lillis, J., Vol-II: 165
Lim, S., Vol-II: 429, 436–437
Lima, L., Vol-II: 454
Lin, C. A., Vol-II: 662
Lin, E. J., Vol-I: 170
Lin, J., Vol-II: 154, 659
Lin, K., Vol-II: 646
Lin, M. H., Vol-II: 352
Lincoln, A., Vol-II: 483
Lincoln, Y. S., Vol-I: 106, 122
Lind, A., Vol-II: 120
Lindberg, L., Vol-II: 599
Lindberg, S. M., Vol-I: 87, 262, 299, 531, 549; Vol-II: 142, 154, 386
Linder, M., Vol-II: 100
Lindgren, R., Vol-I: 246
Lindorff, M., Vol-II: 506, 512
Lindsay, J. J., Vol-I: 413
Lindsay, K., Vol-II: 77
Lindstedt, K., Vol-I: 515
Lindstrom, P., Vol-I: 225, 249
Linebarger, D. L., Vol-I: 505
Lingard, B., Vol-II: 379
Linimon, D., Vol-I: 383; Vol-II: 340
Link, B. G., Vol-II: 147

Linn, M. C., Vol-I: 262–263, 299–300, 305, 318–320, 331, 569; Vol-II: 386
Linney, J. A., Vol-II: 633
Linsenmeier, J. A. W., Vol-I: 512
Linville, D., Vol-II: 258
Linz, D. G., Vol-II: 660
Lipford-Sanders, J., Vol-II: 205
Lipinski, J. P., Vol-II: 155
Liposvsky, J. A., Vol-II: 195
Lippa, R., Vol-I: 134, 143, 150, 192
Lippa, R. A., Vol-I: 193, 309, 312; Vol-II: 21–22, 27, 323, 362
Lips, H., Vol-I: 34, 364–366
Lips, H. M., Vol-II: 91, 95, 104, 379, 388
Lipsey, M. W., Vol-I: 477
Lisak, D., Vol-I: 48; Vol-II: 230, 236
Lisoway, A., Vol-I: 264, 321
Litosseliti, L., Vol-I: 388, 402–403
Little, A. C., Vol-II: 286
Little, J. K., Vol-I: 503
Little, M., Vol-I: 328
Little, T. D., Vol-I: 546
Littlefield, M. B., Vol-I: 513
Litwiller, R. M., Vol-I: 323
Liu, F., Vol-I: 317, 327
Liu, L. L., Vol-I: 271
Liu, W. M., Vol-I: 53; Vol-II: 223, 226–227, 229, 232–234
Liu, Z., Vol-II: 646
Lively, K. J., Vol-I: 440
Livezey, A., Vol-II: 579
Livingston, N., Vol-I: 391
Livingston, R. W., Vol-II: 451
Lloyd, G., Vol-I: 32
Lo, V., Vol-II: 653
Loaiza, S., Vol-I: 459
Lobel, T. E., Vol-I: 512
Lobliner, D. B., Vol-I: 516
Löbmann, R., Vol-II: 484
LoCicero, A., Vol-I: 110
Lockard, J., Vol-II: 270
Lockford, L., Vol-I: 115
Lockheed, M. E., Vol-II: 339, 346
Lodhi, P. H., Vol-II: 26–27
Lodi-Smith, J., Vol-I: 571
Loeber, C. C., Vol-II: 340
Loevinger, J., Vol-I: 560
Logan, K., Vol-I: 289
Logue, A. W., Vol-I: 463
Lohaus, A., Vol-I: 503
Lohman, D. F., Vol-I: 321
Lohr, B. A., Vol-II: 371
Lomax, E., Vol-I: 21
Lombard, J., Vol-I: 248
Lombardi, E. L., Vol-II: 120
Lombardi, W. J., Vol-I: 196
Lombardo, J. P., Vol-I: 536

Lomskey-Feder, E., Vol-II: 674
Loney, B. R., Vol-II: 74
Long, B. C., Vol-II: 575
Long, R. G., Vol-I: 330
Longcope, C., Vol-I: 227
Longhurst, J. G., Vol-II: 137
Longino, H., Vol-I: 103
Longmore, M. A., Vol-II: 407
Longpré, S., Vol-I: 320
Lonner, W. J., Vol-I: 162, 164, 166, 170, 172
Loo, C., Vol-II: 616
Lopez, E., Vol-II: 160
Lopez, S., Vol-II: 269
López-Escámez, J. A., Vol-I: 243
Lopiano, D. A., Vol-I: 549
Lorant, V., Vol-I: 101
Lorber, J., Vol-II: 115, 123, 225, 406
Lorde, A., Vol-I: 35, 204; Vol-II: 214
Lorenz, F. O., Vol-I: 544; Vol-II: 139
Lorenz, J., Vol-I: 243
Loriaux, D. L., Vol-I: 226
Loring-Meier, S., Vol-I: 323
Lorion, R. P., Vol-II: 619, 635
Lorr, M., Vol-II: 324
Lott, B., Vol-I: 382, 401; Vol-II: 101
Lotz, A., Vol-II: 650
Louderback, L. A., Vol-II: 361
Loudermilk, S., Vol-II: 570
Louis, T., Vol-II: 543
Lounsbury, J., Vol-II: 229, 616
Lourenco, S. F., Vol-I: 326
Lourens, P. F., Vol-II: 483
Louse, G., Vol-I: 265
Lovas, G. S., Vol-II: 314
Lövdén, M., Vol-I: 248, 329
Love, L. R., Vol-I: 438
Lovejoy, M., Vol-II: 160
Lovelace, K., Vol-I: 328
Lövgren, M., Vol-II: 545
Lovrinic, J. H., Vol-I: 243
Lowe, P. A., Vol-I: 569–570
Lowell, E. L., Vol-II: 41
Lowenstein, R. J., Vol-II: 209
Lowery, B. S., Vol-I: 497; Vol-II: 77
Lowes, J., Vol-II: 159, 165
Lowinger, R., Vol-II: 230
Lowry, D. T., Vol-II: 644, 646
Loxton, D., Vol-II: 484
Lozano, R., Vol-II: 482
Lu, T. G. C., Vol-II: 32
Lubinski, D., Vol-I: 14, 135, 310, 317; Vol-II: 15, 386
Lubinski, D. S., Vol-I: 310
Lucas, J. W., Vol-II: 518
Lucas, K., Vol-II: 650–651, 657
Lucas, R. E., Vol-I: 431
Luce, C. B., Vol-II: 453
Lucey, A. B., Vol-II: 578

Luchetta, T., Vol-I: 195, 372
Luciano, L., Vol-II: 160, 166, 169–170, 172
Ludolph, P., Vol-II: 95
Ludwig, A. M., Vol-I: 345
Lueck, M., Vol-II: 95
Luecke-Aleksa, D., Vol-I: 511
Luhtanen, R., Vol-I: 496–497
Lumley, M. A., Vol-I: 442
Lund, M., Vol-II: 217
Lunde, C., Vol-II: 156, 165
Lundquist, L., Vol-I: 434, 438
Lundy, A., Vol-I: 44
Lunt, I., Vol-I: 541
Luo, L., Vol-II: 619
Lupton, M. J., Vol-II: 169
Lurie, N., Vol-II: 532
Lurye, L. E., Vol-I: 500–501, 509, 515
Lusterman, D. D., Vol-II: 256
Lutgendorf, S. K., Vol-II: 553
Luttrell, W., Vol-I: 115
Lutz, S. E., Vol-I: 513
Lybomirsky, S., Vol-II: 141
Lydon, J. E., Vol-II: 294
Lye, D., Vol-II: 410, 413
Lykes, M. B., Vol-I: 103, 108, 118
Lynam, D., Vol-I: 548
Lynch, C. I., Vol-II: 661
Lynch, J. E., Vol-I: 91
Lynch, L., Vol-I: 1; Vol-II: 1
Lynch, M., Vol-II: 414
Lynch, M. E., Vol-I: 530; Vol-II: 389
Lyness, K. S., Vol-II: 448, 455, 457
Lynn, J., Vol-II: 529
Lynn, R., Vol-I: 9, 301, 304, 306; Vol-II: 27
Lyons, A., Vol-I: 35
Lyons, A. C., Vol-II: 477
Lyons, J., Vol-II: 684–686
Lyons, N., Vol-I: 105
Lyons, P. C., Vol-II: 326
Lyons, P. M., Vol-I: 458–459
Lyons, T., Vol-II: 385
Lytton, H., Vol-II: 390
Lyubelsky, J., Vol-II: 235
Lyubomirsky, S., Vol-II: 144

M

Maas, C. J. M., Vol-II: 603
Maass, A., Vol-I: 433
Maberly, K. J., Vol-I: 328
Mac Iver, D., Vol-II: 388
Macafee, C., Vol-II: 327
Macari, S., Vol-I: 509
Maccoby, E., Vol-I: 193, 396
Maccoby, E. E., Vol-I: 28, 88, 260, 280, 496, 498, 500, 506, 511, 514–515, 527, 532, 536, 538–539, 541, 544; Vol-II: 282, 313, 322–323, 326
Maccoby, E. M., Vol-I: 193, 240, 298, 302, 317, 322

MacCorquodale, P., Vol-II: 290
MacDermid, S., Vol-I: 563, 570–571; Vol-II: 411
MacDermid, S. M., Vol-I: 571
MacDiarmid, J. I., Vol-I: 462
MacDonald, G., Vol-II: 288
Macefield, V. G., Vol-I: 243
Macera, C. A., Vol-II: 567
MacFadden, A., Vol-I: 328
MacGeorge, E. L., Vol-II: 253
MacGregor, M. W., Vol-I: 431
MacInnis, D., Vol-II: 46
Macintyre, S., Vol-I: 474–475
Macionis, J. J., Vol-I: 160
Mack, D. E., Vol-II: 574, 576
Mackay, J., Vol-II: 541–542
MacKenzie, E. J., Vol-II: 482
Mackey, W. C., Vol-I: 49
MacKinnon, C., Vol-I: 387
MacLean, A. B., Vol-I: 223
MacLeod, C. M., Vol-I: 238
Macleod, C., Vol-I: 109
MacLusky, N. J., Vol-II: 217
MacPherson, G. M., Vol-I: 318
MacPherson, J., Vol-I: 500
Macrae, C. N., Vol-II: 287
Madden, L., Vol-II: 652
Maddox, K. B., Vol-II: 650
Maddux, W. W., Vol-II: 460
Madon, S., Vol-I: 437; Vol-II: 231, 340, 360, 449
Madronio, C., Vol-I: 180
Madsen, K. M., Vol-II: 295, 297, 598
Madson, L., Vol-II: 294
Maess, B., Vol-I: 244
Maggs, J., Vol-II: 409
Magley, V. J., Vol-II: 11, 423–437, 685
Magnée, T., Vol-I: 239
Magnusson, D., Vol-I: 543
Magovcevic, M., Vol-II: 135, 137, 226
Mahadzir, M., Vol-I: 328
Mahaffey, A. L., Vol-II: 371
Mahalik, J. R., Vol-I: 15, 51–53, 55, 138–139, 150, 535; Vol-II: 15, 117, 135, 137, 203, 212, 224, 226, 228–229, 234–236, 241, 267, 340, 528, 545–546
Maher, L., Vol-II: 487
Maher, M. J., Vol-II: 371
Maier, G., Vol-II: 48
Maines, D. R., Vol-II: 393
Maing, D. M., Vol-II: 117
Maio, G. R., Vol-II: 656
Maixner, W., Vol-I: 241
Majerovitz, S. D., Vol-II: 501, 551
Majied, K., Vol-II: 104
Major, B., Vol-I: 84, 194, 197; Vol-II: 30, 67, 296, 631
Majors, R. G., Vol-II: 227
Majumdar, S. R., Vol-II: 530
Mak, T., Vol-II: 646
Makar, R. O., Vol-I: 329

Makhijani, M. G., Vol-II: 343–344, 351, 450, 457, 674, 678
Maki, P. M., Vol-I: 223–224
Makkar, J. K., Vol-II: 160
Makoul, G., Vol-II: 523
Malafi, T. N., Vol-II: 292
Malamuth, N. M., Vol-I: 201; Vol-II: 281, 660
Malanchuk, O., Vol-I: 497; Vol-II: 384
Malcolm, J. P., Vol-II: 362
Malenchuk, O., Vol-II: 573
Malin, E. L., Vol-I: 323
Malinowski, B., Vol-I: 159, 162, 167
Malinowski, J. C., Vol-I: 328–329
Malkin, A. R., Vol-II: 648
Malle, B. F., Vol-II: 362
Malley, J., Vol-I: 458
Malley-Morrison, K., Vol-II: 317–319
Mallucchi, L., Vol-I: 496
Malone, B. E., Vol-I: 413
Malone, K. R., Vol-II: 671
Maloney, N., Vol-II: 526
Malouf, D., Vol-II: 114, 368
Malouf, M. A., Vol-I: 219
Malson, H., Vol-I: 117
Malterud, K., Vol-II: 546, 549
Maltz, D., Vol-I: 385–386, 389
Mancl, L., Vol-I: 241
Mandel, H., Vol-II: 446
Mangalparsad, R., Vol-II: 160
Mangun, G. R., Vol-I: 222
Mani, L., Vol-II: 292
Manigart, P., Vol-II: 673, 691
Manke, B. A., Vol-I: 143
Mann, V. A., Vol-I: 222, 326
Manne, S., Vol-II: 501
Manning, J. T., Vol-I: 225, 324
Manning, V., Vol-II: 195
Mannix, L. M., Vol-II: 167
Mannon, S., Vol-II: 413
Mannon, S. E., Vol-II: 415
Manolio, A., Vol-II: 482
Mansfield, A. F., Vol-I: 501; Vol-I: 53
Mansfield, E. D., Vol-II: 50
Mansfield, P., Vol-I: 485
Mansfield, P. K., Vol-I: 362
Manstead, A., Vol-II: 21
Manstead, A. S. R., Vol-I: 430, 434–435, 441–442
Manthei, R. J., Vol-II: 242
Mantle, D., Vol-I: 393
Manuck, S. B., Vol-I: 442
Manuel, T., Vol-II: 453–454
Maple, S. A., Vol-II: 47, 390
Mar'i, S. K., Vol-I: 347
Maracek, J., Vol-I: 382–383
Marantz, S. A., Vol-I: 501
Marcia, J., Vol-I: 528
Marcia, J. E., Vol-I: 152, 562

Marcus, G., Vol-I: 115
Marcus, H., Vol-I: 503, 508
Marcus, S. C., Vol-II: 519
Marecek, J., Vol-I: 20, 29–33, 106, 193, 197–198, 381, 387; Vol-II: 64, 66–67, 83, 117, 197–198
Mares, M., Vol-II: 662
Margulis, S. T., Vol-II: 326
Marin, A. J., Vol-II: 684
Marin, B., Vol-II: 301
Marin, B. V., Vol-II: 145
Marin, T., Vol-II: 497
Marina, N., Vol-I: 6, 133–152
Markell, M., Vol-I: 516
Markman, H. J., Vol-II: 268
Markovic, N., Vol-I: 187
Markowitz, F., Vol-I: 63
Marks, A. C., Vol-I: 484
Marks, J. P. G., Vol-II: 407
Marks, L. I., Vol-II: 229
Marks, N. F., Vol-II: 326, 415
Marks, S. R., Vol-I: 571
Markstrom-Adams, C., Vol-I: 516, 531
Markula, P., Vol-II: 576
Markus, E. J., Vol-I: 328
Markus, H., Vol-II: 158, 643
Markus, H. R., Vol-I: 441; Vol-II: 26, 66
Marlowe, C. M., Vol-II: 648
Marlowe, D., Vol-II: 602
Marmot, M., Vol-II: 475, 482
Marotta, N., Vol-I: 243
Marquart, J., Vol-II: 594
Marra, M., Vol-I: 394, 395
Marrett, C. B., Vol-I: 284
Marsh, H. W., Vol-I: 288; Vol-II: 31–33, 389
Marshall, B. L., Vol-I: 567–568
Marshall, J., Vol-I: 10, 106; Vol-II: 679
Marshall, L. L., Vol-II: 312
Marshall, N. L., Vol-I: 539, 116
Marshall, P., Vol-II: 228
Marshall, T. C., Vol-II: 281–301
Marsiglia, F., Vol-II: 625
Marske, A. L., Vol-II: 167, 658
Martell, R. F., Vol-II: 346, 448
Martin, A. J., Vol-I: 219, 288; Vol-II: 379
Martin, C., Vol-II: 368
Martin, C. E., Vol-I: 66, 476
Martin, C. K., Vol-I: 456–457
Martin, C. L., Vol-I: 84, 495, 500–501, 503–504, 508, 510–511, 514–516, 531; Vol-II: 360, 387
Martin, C. M., Vol-II: 340
Martin, D., Vol-II: 588
Martin, D. J., Vol-I: 244
Martin, D. M., Vol-I: 223, 249
Martin, E., Vol-I: 117, 201–202, 362; Vol-II: 170
Martin, J., Vol-II: 452
Martin, J. I., Vol-II: 114, 119, 121–122, 125
Martin, L. L., Vol-I: 446

Martin, P. R., Vol-I: 237
Martin, P. Y., Vol-II: 340, 452
Martin, R., Vol-II: 347
Martin, R. R., Vol-II: 338–339
Martin, S. B., Vol-II: 229
Martin, T., Vol-II: 27
Martin, T. A., Vol-II: 26
Martin-Baro, I., Vol-I: 35
Martindale, C., Vol-I: 351
Martinez, D., Vol-I: 65, 160, 166, 170–171
Martinez, E., Vol-II: 155
Martinez, R., Vol-II: 97
Martinko, M. J., Vol-II: 427, 431
Martino, S. C., Vol-I: 547
Martino, W., Vol-I: 280, 286, 291; Vol-II: 379
Martins, Y., Vol-I: 98; Vol-II: 156–157, 172, 659
Martyna, W., Vol-I: 195
Marx, D. B., Vol-I: 93, 259
Marx, F., Vol-II: 576
Marx, R., Vol-II: 120–122
Masaki, S., Vol-I: 222, 326
Mashoodh, R., Vol-I: 226
Maslach, C., Vol-I: 172
Maslow, A., Vol-II: 56
Maslow, A. H., Vol-I: 346, 352
Mason, A., Vol-II: 50, 53
Mason, C., Vol-II: 620
Mason, J. L., Vol-II: 63–83
Mason, K. L., Vol-II: 320
Massa, L. J., Vol-I: 327
Massey, J., Vol-II: 137
Masson, P., Vol-I: 568
Mast, M. S., Vol-I: 8, 411–422, 438; Vol-II: 8, 324–325, 338
Masters, M. S., Vol-I: 318–319
Masters, W., Vol-II: 190
Masters, W. H., Vol-I: 474, 486
Mastro, D. E., Vol-II: 644, 646, 648
Mastropieri, M. A., Vol-II: 385
Masuda, A., Vol-I: 243
Matarazzo, S., Vol-I: 239
Mathason, L., Vol-I: 332
Matheson, G., Vol-II: 409
Mathews, C., Vol-I: 67
Mathews, V. P., Vol-I: 67
Mathy, R. M., Vol-II: 113
Matkin, G. S., Vol-I: 93
Maton, K. I., Vol-I: 531
Matschiner, M., Vol-II: 342
Matsuda, H., Vol-I: 330
Matsuda, S., Vol-II: 623
Matsumoto, D., Vol-I: 432, 440–441; Vol-II: 324
Matsunami, H., Vol-I: 248
Matthews, G., Vol-I: 439
Matthews, L., Vol-II: 619
Matthews, M. H., Vol-I: 307, 330
Matthews, R. A., Vol-II: 203, 429

Mattis, J. S., Vol-I: 150; Vol-II: 226
Mattison, A., Vol-I: 67
Mattson, S. L., Vol-I: 220
Matula, K. E., Vol-I: 562
Mau, W. C., Vol-I: 304, 306; Vol-II: 383
Maughan, B., Vol-I: 548
Maume, D., Vol-II: 406; Vol-II: 482
Maume, D. J. Jr., Vol-II: 337, 446
Maurer, B., Vol-I: 202
May, J. G., Vol-I: 8, 245, 345, 495–518
May, K. E., Vol-II: 348
Mayer, J. D., Vol-I: 439
Mayer, K. H., Vol-II: 136
Mayer, R. E., Vol-I: 327
Mayes, S., Vol-II: 133, 290
Maylor, E. A., Vol-I: 225
Maynard, A. E., Vol-I: 66
Mayring, P., Vol-I: 111
Mays, V., Vol-I: 69
Mays, V. M., Vol-I: 63, 65, 480; Vol-II: 103, 135, 138, 144, 224, 486
Mazerolle, P., Vol-II: 329
Mazure, C. M., Vol-II: 136–137
Mazzella, R., Vol-I: 567
Mazzeo, J., Vol-I: 220
McAdams, D., Vol-I: 116
McAdams, D. P., Vol-I: 563–564, 567; Vol-II: 42, 49–51, 54
McAlinden, F., Vol-I: 381
McAndrew, F., Vol-I: 398–399
McAnnally, L., Vol-II: 416
McAuley, E., Vol-II: 573
McAuliffe, T. L., Vol-I: 487
McAuslan, P., Vol-II: 284, 631
McBey, K., Vol-II: 338
McBurney, D. H., Vol-I: 323
McCabe, M., Vol-II: 161, 163, 165
McCabe, M. P., Vol-I: 542; Vol-II: 156, 165, 168, 173
McCaffree, K., Vol-II: 624
McCaffrey, D., Vol-I: 547
McCall, D. T., Vol-II: 531
McCallister, S. G., Vol-II: 574
McCann, C., Vol-II: 672, 674
McCann, T., Vol-I: 463
McCarthy, M., Vol-II: 619
McCarthy, P., Vol-II: 203
McCartney, K., Vol-I: 87–88
McCarty, M. J., Vol-I: 463
McCaughan, E., Vol-II: 545
McCaughy, M., Vol-I: 202
McCauley, C., Vol-II: 169
McCauley, C. D., Vol-II: 455
McClarty, K. L., Vol-II: 31
McClelland, D., Vol-II: 46
McClelland, D. C., Vol-I: 571; Vol-II: 41–42, 44–46, 49, 51, 54
McClennen, J. C., Vol-II: 631

McClintock, M. K., Vol-I: 248
McClive, T., Vol-I: 368
McClure, E. B., Vol-I: 411, 414, 419–420, 438
McConahay, J. B., Vol-I: 516
McConnell, A. R., Vol-I: 433
McConnell-Ginet, S., Vol-I: 390, 404
McCormick, C. M., Vol-I: 227
McCoy, N. L., Vol-I: 481
McCrae, R. M., Vol-II: 81
McCrae, R. R., Vol-I: 166, 170, 442, 560; Vol-II: 25–26, 81, 447
McCray, A. D., Vol-I: 284
McCreary, D. R., Vol-I: 1–15, 53, 59, 98, 121, 136, 143, 145, 220, 222, 535, 544, 567–568; Vol-II: 1–14, 99, 155, 157–161, 167, 170, 340, 360, 478, 522, 543, 659, 688
McDaniel, A. K., Vol-II: 286, 290
McDaniel, M. A., Vol-I: 270, 323
McDaniel, S. H., Vol-II: 255
McDaniels, J. S., Vol-I: 68
McDavis, R., Vol-II: 231
McDermott, C., Vol-I: 429, 447
McDermott, R. J., Vol-II: 319
Mcdonagh, D., Vol-II: 201
McDonald, K., Vol-I: 397; Vol-II: 627
McDonald, L. M., Vol-II: 503
McDonald, T. W., Vol-I: 148; Vol-II: 344
McDowell, M. A., Vol-II: 543
McDowell, T., Vol-II: 254, 269
McElroy, J. C., Vol-II: 452
McEnally, M., Vol-II: 340, 346
McEnery, T., Vol-I: 391
McEntee, D. J., Vol-II: 547
McEwen, B. S., Vol-I: 215, 222, 226–227
McFadden, D., Vol-I: 243
McFadyen, J., Vol-II: 686
McGarvey, S. T., Vol-II: 160
McGaughey, D., Vol-II: 111
McGee, J. S., Vol-I: 244
McGeorge, C. R., Vol-II: 271
McGeorge, P., Vol-I: 517
McGlone, F., Vol-I: 246
McGlone, J., Vol-I: 324, 327
McGoldrick, M., Vol-II: 255, 263
McGonagle, K. A., Vol-II: 134
McGowan, J. F., Vol-I: 224
McGrath, D., Vol-I: 380; Vol-II: 339
McGrath, E., Vol-II: 97
McGue, M., Vol-II: 431
McGuffog, I., Vol-II: 472
McGuinness, D., Vol-I: 236, 244
McGuire, C. V., Vol-I: 497
McHale, S. M., Vol-I: 143, 501, 511, 536–537, 544; Vol-II: 296, 411, 413
McHugh, M., Vol-I: 193–194; Vol-II: 100, 614, 633
McHugh, M. C., Vol-I: 8, 88, 361–374, 379–404, 568; Vol-II: 312

McHugh, P., Vol-II: 119
McHugh, T-L. F., Vol-I: 112, 120
McKay, M., Vol-I: 289
McKee, B., Vol-I: 44; Vol-II: 672, 674
McKeever, P., Vol-II: 95
McKeever, T. M., Vol-II: 530
McKeever, W. F., Vol-I: 239, 325
McKelley, R. A., Vol-I: 138; Vol-II: 229
McKenna, H., Vol-II: 545
McKenna, K. Y. A., Vol-II: 327, 662
McKenna, W., Vol-I: 112, 192, 260
McKenzie, K. J., Vol-I: 324
McKeown, R. E., Vol-II: 485
McKillop, E., Vol-I: 328
McKinlay, J. B., Vol-I: 227
McKinley, J. C., Vol-II: 78
McKinley, N. M., Vol-I: 91, 139; Vol-II: 154, 156, 171
McKinley, W. O., Vol-II: 165
McKinney, C. W., Vol-II: 385
McKinney, K., Vol-II: 299, 425
McKinnon, L., Vol-II: 75
McKown, C., Vol-I: 284
McLaren, L., Vol-II: 165
McLaughlin, K. A., Vol-II: 136, 141, 144–145
McLaughlin, M. L., Vol-I: 393; Vol-II: 295
McLaughlin-Volpe, T., Vol-I: 496
McLean, K., Vol-II: 365
McLeod, J. D., Vol-II: 140, 498, 501–502
McMahon, A. M., Vol-II: 339
McMahon, L. F. Jr., Vol-II: 529
McMahon, L. R., Vol-I: 25
McMahon, M. A., Vol-I: 324
McMaster, L. E., Vol-II: 320
McMillan, J., Vol-I: 380, 390
McMillan, J. R., Vol-II: 339
McMillan, K. K., Vol-I: 138; Vol-II: 522
McMillen, J., Vol-II: 621
McMullen, L. M., Vol-II: 338
McMullen, S., Vol-I: 486
McNair, R., Vol-II: 263
McNall, K., Vol-I: 431
McNally, J., Vol-II: 570
McNamara, A. M., Vol-II: 530
McNamara, W., Vol-II: 50
McNaughton-Cassill, M., Vol-II: 414
McNay, L., Vol-II: 169
McNulty, J. L., Vol-II: 76
McNutt, L., Vol-II: 195
McPherson, D., Vol-II: 411
McPherson, M., Vol-II: 480
McQueen, A., Vol-II: 544
McQueen, G., Vol-I: 203
McRitchie, D. A., Vol-I: 244
McWhirter, D., Vol-I: 67
McWhirter, E. H., Vol-II: 105, 383
McWilliams, J. M., Vol-II: 518
Mead, M., Vol-I: 159, 162, 167, 173, 259

Meade, A. C., Vol-I: 220
Meagher, M. W., Vol-I: 242
Meaney, M. J., Vol-I: 217
Meara, E., Vol-II: 518
Meares, E., Vol-II: 616
Mears, D., Vol-II: 607
Mease, A. L., Vol-II: 269
Meck, W. H., Vol-I: 221, 323
Medin, D. L., Vol-I: 199, 506
Medina-Mora, M. E. V., Vol-I: 165
Mednick, M. T., Vol-I: 193, 198
Mednick, M. T. S., Vol-I: 27
Meece, J. L., Vol-I: 283; Vol-II: 379–381, 385, 388
Meehan, A. M., Vol-I: 327
Meehl, P. E., Vol-II: 588
Meeker, B. F., Vol-II: 345
Meert, S. K., Vol-II: 460
Megens, J., Vol-I: 224
Megens, J. A., Vol-II: 113
Meginnis-Payne, K. L., Vol-II: 201–202
Meh, D., Vol-I: 240
Mehl, M., Vol-I: 391
Mehl, M. R., Vol-II: 20
Mehra, D., Vol-I: 347
Mehrabian, A., Vol-I: 412
Meier, J., Vol-II: 414
Meikle, D. B., Vol-I: 269
Meilman, P. W., Vol-I: 528
Meissen, G., Vol-II: 633
Meissner, H. I., Vol-II: 544
Meissner, K., Vol-I: 245
Mellinger, T., Vol-II: 223
Mellon, S., Vol-II: 551
Melnick, M. J., Vol-II: 576
Meltzer, A. L., Vol-II: 11, 13, 517–535
Menaged, M., Vol-II: 226
Menaghan, E. G., Vol-II: 143
Menard, L., Vol-II: 98
Menard, W., Vol-II: 162
Mendelson, M., Vol-II: 144
Mendoza-Denton, R., Vol-II: 67, 141
Meneely, J., Vol-I: 353
Mentzel, H. J., Vol-I: 243
Menvielle, E. J., Vol-II: 118
Menzie, C. R., Vol-I: 392, 402
Merighi, J. R., Vol-II: 522
Merlis, S. R., Vol-II: 258
Merluzzi, T. V., Vol-II: 290
Merrell, K. W., Vol-II: 32
Merriwether, A., Vol-II: 171, 660
Merten, J., Vol-I: 441, 544
Merton, S., Vol-I: 397
Mervis, G., Vol-I: 196
Meslé, F., Vol-II: 472
Mesquita, B., Vol-I: 440; Vol-II: 432
Messer, S. B., Vol-II: 234
Messerschmidt, J. W., Vol-I: 51; Vol-II: 225–227

Messineo, M., Vol-II: 647–648
Messman, S. J., Vol-II: 283
Messner, M., Vol-I: 112; Vol-II: 225
Messner, M. A., Vol-I: 112; Vol-II: 571–572, 577–578
Metalsky, G. I., Vol-II: 142
Metheny, E., Vol-II: 570
Metsapelto, R., Vol-II: 27
Metts, S., Vol-II: 297, 326
Metz, H., Vol-II: 230
Metz, L. M., Vol-II: 546
Metzl, J. M., Vol-II: 97
Metzler, J., Vol-I: 221, 238, 318; Vol-II: 48
Meyenburg, B., Vol-II: 112, 119
Meyenn, B., Vol-I: 280, 286, 291
Meyer, G. J., Vol-II: 63, 65
Meyer, I., Vol-I: 68, 69
Meyer, I. H., Vol-I: 186–187; Vol-II: 133, 135–136, 138, 360, 368, 486, 509
Meyer, K., Vol-II: 204
Meyer, S., Vol-I: 457
Meyer, S. L., Vol-II: 267
Meyer, W., Vol-II: 119
Meyer, W. J., Vol-I: 224
Meyer-Bahlburg, H. F., Vol-I: 140; Vol-II: 118
Meyer-Bahlberg, H. F. L., Vol-I: 140, 226
Meyerowitz, J., Vol-II: 114
Meyers, S. A., Vol-II: 285
Meyerson, D. E., Vol-II: 454, 461
Mezulis, A. H., Vol-I: 545; Vol-II: 136, 146
Michael, A., Vol-I: 138; Vol-II: 117, 384
Michael, R. T., Vol-I: 44, 112, 478, 483; Vol-II: 321
Michaelis, B., Vol-II: 140
Michaels, M. W., Vol-II: 647
Michaels, S., Vol-I: 478; Vol-II: 321
Michalenok, J., Vol-II: 574
Michaud, C. I., Vol-I: 459, 464
Michelson, K., Vol-I: 63
Middleton, K. R., Vol-II: 530
Midgley, C., Vol-II: 388–389
Mier, H. I., Vol-I: 240
Miethe, T. D., Vol-II: 607
Migdal, S., Vol-I: 563–564
Migeon, C. J. 115; Vol-I: 219
Mignot, P., Vol-II: 383
Mihalko, S., Vol-II: 573
Mikels, J. A., Vol-I: 567
Milar, K. S., Vol-I: 20
Miles, C., Vol-I: 224–225, 324
Miles, C. C., Vol-I: 134, 192, 204, 365
Miles, E., Vol-II: 415
Miles, L., Vol-I: 117; Vol-II: 287
Miletich, D., Vol-II: 589
Miley, A., Vol-II: 623
Milhausen, R. R., Vol-II: 286
Milich, R., Vol-I: 354
Milkie, M. A., Vol-II: 405, 407, 445
Millard, J. E., Vol-II: 648

Miller, A. D., Vol-I: 69
Miller, A. S., Vol-I: 112
Miller, C. R., Vol-I: 330
Miller, C. T., Vol-II: 138, 143
Miller, D. L., Vol-II: 338
Miller, D. T., Vol-I: 195–196, 199, 328, 500–502, 506–507, 509, 514; Vol-II: 448
Miller, I. J., Vol-I: 246
Miller, J., Vol-I: 194
Miller, J. B., Vol-I: 105; Vol-II: 117, 188, 191–192, 208, 213–214
Miller, J. G., Vol-I: 163
Miller, J. S., Vol-II: 449
Miller, K. E., Vol-II: 576
Miller, L. C., Vol-II: 33, 154, 326, 347
Miller, L. K., Vol-I: 328
Miller, M., Vol-II: 365
Miller, M. K., Vol-II: 645, 647
Miller, N., Vol-I: 440; Vol-II: 313, 315
Miller, P. J., Vol-I: 114
Miller, R. J., Vol-II: 21
Miller, R. S., Vol-II: 294, 323–324
Miller, S. L., Vol-II: 449
Miller, S. W., Vol-I: 568
Miller, T. R., Vol-II: 482
Miller, W., Vol-II: 544
Miller, W. R., Vol-II: 235
Millon, C., Vol-II: 70
Millon, T. M., Vol-II: 70, 81
Millot, J. L., Vol-I: 248
Mills, C. J., Vol-I: 304
Mills, J. A., Vol-II: 170
Mills, J. S., Vol-I: 98, 567, 571; Vol-II: 659
Mills, M., Vol-II: 379
Mills, S., Vol-I: 33
Millsap, R. E., Vol-II: 72
Milne, A., Vol-I: 517
Miltner, W. H., Vol-I: 243
Milton, L. P., Vol-II: 456
Milun, R., Vol-I: 328
Min, J., Vol-II: 33
Minamoto, F., Vol-I: 236
Miner, A. G., Vol-II: 685
Minkler, M., Vol-I: 186
Minnotte, K. L., Vol-II: 415
Minoshima, S., Vol-I: 242–243
Minter, S., Vol-II: 111, 119, 368
Minton, H. L., Vol-I: 21
Mintz, L., Vol-II: 155
Mintz, L. B., Vol-II: 237
Mira, M., Vol-I: 458
Mirabeau, O., Vol-I: 344–345
Miranda, J., Vol-II: 520
Mirande, A., Vol-II: 412
Mirgain, S. A., Vol-I: 437, 439
Miron, D., Vol-I: 240
Mischel, W., Vol-II: 65, 67–68, 83

Mishkin, M., Vol-I: 236
Mishkind, M. E., Vol-II: 156
Mishra, G., Vol-II: 484
Mishra, R. C., Vol-I: 326
Misle, B., Vol-II: 95
Mistretta, C. M., Vol-I: 246
Mistry, R., Vol-I: 502
Mitchell, A. A., Vol-II: 427
Mitchell, C., Vol-I: 319; Vol-II: 619
Mitchell, J., Vol-II: 188
Mitchell, J. N., Vol-I: 236
Mitchell, J. P., Vol-II: 155
Mitchell, M. B., Vol-I: 10, 20
Mitchell, P., Vol-I: 236
Mitchell, V., Vol-I: 564, 568, 571, 574
Mitra, A., Vol-I: 662
Mitrook, M., Vol-I: 661
Mitrushina, M., Vol-II: 605
Mittal, M., Vol-II: 263
Mittenberg, W., Vol-II: 603
Mize, L. K., Vol-II: 264
Moane, G., Vol-I: 35, 118, 571
Moebius, M. M., Vol-II: 117
Moelker, R., Vol-II: 673
Moen, P., Vol-I: 570–571; Vol-II: 401–402
Moffat, S. D., Vol-I: 84, 222–223, 227
Moffitt, T. E., Vol-I: 535, 543, 546–548
Moghaddam, F. M., Vol-I: 34
Mogil, J. S., Vol-I: 242
Mohan, R. N., Vol-II: 97
Mohanty, C. T., Vol-I: 105–106; Vol-II: 461
Mohr, J. J., Vol-II: 363–364
Moise-Titus, J., Vol-II: 645
Molde, H., Vol-II: 474
Molinaro, C., Vol-I: 326
Molinsky, A., Vol-II: 460
Moller, A. R., Vol-II: 113
Moller, C., Vol-I: 246, 511
Möller, C. G., Vol-I: 246, 511
Møller, M. B., Vol-I: 244
Möller-Leimkuehler, A., Vol-II: 228
Molloy, B. L., Vol-II: 160
Molnar, B. E., Vol-II: 631
Monaco, N. M., Vol-II: 383
Mondello, M., Vol-II: 572
Money, J., Vol-I: 194, 260, 367; Vol-II: 111, 115–116, 366–367
Mongeau, P. A., Vol-II: 290
Mongin, S. J., Vol-II: 483
Monroe, S. M., Vol-II: 137, 143, 146
Monsour, M., Vol-II: 284
Montano, D. E., Vol-II: 340
Monte, F., Vol-I: 262, 300
Montello, D. R., Vol-I: 328
Montepare, J. M., Vol-II: 451
Montero, M., Vol-II: 613, 635
Montgomery, K., Vol-II: 432

Montgomery, S., Vol-I: 285; Vol-II: 620
Montoro, R., Vol-II: 362
Mood, D., Vol-II: 551
Moody, M. S., Vol-I: 324
Mooney, K., Vol-II: 675
Mooney, K. M., Vol-I: 457, 462–463
Moore, A., Vol-II: 414
Moore, C., Vol-II: 429
Moore, D., Vol-I: 499
Moore, D. S., Vol-I: 318
Moore, H. A., Vol-II: 380
Moore, L., Vol-I: 547
Moore, L. J., Vol-I: 201
Moore, L. M., Vol-I: 246
Moore, R. J., Vol-I: 47, 52
Moore, R. L., Vol-II: 293
Moore, S. T., Vol-II: 228
Moos, R., Vol-II: 235, 633
Moradi, B., Vol-I: 98; Vol-II: 194–195, 200–201, 205–206, 211
Morales, A., Vol-I: 223
Moran, J. D., Vol-I: 350
Morawski, J., Vol-I: 26, 364, 366
Morawski, J. G., Vol-I: 31–32, 192
Moray, S. M., Vol-II: 122
Moretti, M. M., Vol-I: 549
Morey, L. C., Vol-II: 70, 73–75, 77, 81
Morey, L., Vol-II: 204
Morgan, B. L., Vol-II: 205
Morgan, C. D., Vol-II: 41
Morgan, E. E. Vol-I: 256
Morgan, E. M., Vol-I: 475; Vol-II: 291
Morgan, F., Vol-II: 347
Morgan, M., Vol-I: 117, 542; Vol-II: 167
Mori, D., Vol-I: 460–461
Mori, S., Vol-II: 233
Morin, P., Vol-I: 390
Morin, S., Vol-I: 17
Moriyama, H., Vol-I: 245
Morland, I., Vol-I: 194
Morling, B., Vol-II: 56
Morosan, P., Vol-I: 244
Morra, N. N., Vol-I: 393
Morrell, S., Vol-II: 485
Morrin, K. A., Vol-I: 329
Morris, A., Vol-II: 628
Morris, A. M., Vol-I: 572
Morris, A. S., Vol-I: 549
Morris, E. L., Vol-I: 456
Morris, L. M., Vol-II: 509
Morris, T. L., Vol-I: 66, 68
Morrison, D., Vol-II: 660
Morrison, E. W., Vol-II: 452
Morrison, J. A., Vol-I: 53
Morrison, K., Vol-II: 234, 317–319
Morrison, M. A., Vol-II: 156
Morrison, T., Vol-I: 196

Morrison, T. G., Vol-II: 156
Morrison-Beedy, D., Vol-I: 487
Morrongiello, B. A., Vol-II: 484
Morrow, A. L., Vol-I: 365
Morrow, J. E., Vol-II: 455
Morrow, P. C., Vol-II: 452
Morrow, R. G., Vol-II: 578
Morrow, T. J., Vol-I: 242
Morton, G., Vol-II: 254–255, 260
Morton, T. A., Vol-I: 193
Morton, T. L., Vol-II: 294
Mosca, L., Vol-II: 543
Moseley, W., Vol-II: 116
Moser, D. K., Vol-II: 487, 543
Mosewich, A. D., Vol-II: 576
Mosher, C., Vol-II: 550
Mosher, C. E., Vol-II: 550
Mosher, C. J., Vol-II: 607–609
Mosher, D. L., Vol-I: 52
Mosher, M., Vol-II: 319
Moskos, C., Vol-II: 673, 676–677, 682
Moskowitz, D. S., Vol-I: 421; Vol-II: 21
Mosquera, P. M. R., Vol-I: 435; Vol-II: 282
Mostert, I., Vol-II: 349
Motheral, B. R., Vol-II: 530
Motulsky, A. G., Vol-I: 237
Moulin, A., Vol-I: 243
Mountcastle, V. B., Vol-I: 240
Mowbray, C., Vol-II: 624
Moya, P. M. L., Vol-I: 32
Moyer, R., Vol-I: 195
Moynihan, R., Vol-II: 98
Mraz, W., Vol-I: 352
Msimang, S., Vol-II: 542
Müchele, A., Vol-II: 207
Muday, T., Vol-I: 431
Muderrisoglu, S., Vol-I: 440
Muehlenhard, C. L., Vol-II: 321
Muehlenkamp, J. J., Vol-II: 153
Mueller, J. M., Vol-I: 34
Mueller, S. C., Vol-I: 219, 329
Mueser, K. T., Vol-II: 266
Mugny, G., Vol-I: 194
Muhlenbruck, L., Vol-I: 413
Muir, S. L., Vol-II: 165, 168
Mukherjee, S., Vol-II: 484
Mulac, A., Vol-I: 380
Mulder, M., Vol-II: 285
Mulick, P. S., Vol-II: 363
Mullally, S., Vol-I: 500
Mullan, J. T., Vol-II: 143
Mullaney, H. A., Vol-II: 605
Mullany, L., Vol-I: 394, 395
Mullen, B., Vol-II: 459
Mullis, T., Vol-II: 318
Mulvey, A., Vol-II: 613–614, 622, 628
Munch, S., Vol-II: 523

Mundorf, J., Vol-II: 657
Mundorf, N., Vol-II: 657
Munnoch, D. A., Vol-II: 483
Muñoz-Laboy, M. A., Vol-II: 371
Munson, L. J., Vol-II: 685
Munson, M., Vol-II: 621
Muntaner, C., Vol-II: 478
Murdock, G. P., Vol-I: 167
Murgio, A., Vol-II: 482
Murnen, S. K., Vol-I: 6, 81–98, 479; Vol-II: 6, 156, 170, 174, 342, 658
Murphy, C. M., Vol-II: 267
Murphy, M., Vol-II: 482
Murphy, N. A., Vol-I: 413, 417
Murphy, R., Vol-II: 154
Murphy, S. A., Vol-II: 323
Murphy, S. E., Vol-II: 450
Murphy, S. L., Vol-II: 228, 526, 542
Murphy, T., Vol-II: 371
Murray, A. D., Vol-I: 244
Murray, H. A., Vol-II: 41
Murray, M., Vol-I: 116
Murray, S. H., Vol-II: 165
Murray, S. L., Vol-II: 294
Muscat, A. C., Vol-II: 575
Musen, G., Vol-II: 530
Musick, M. A., Vol-II: 228
Mussap, A. J., Vol-II: 169
Mussen, P. H., Vol-II: 386
Mustanski, B. S., Vol-I: 225
Musteen, M., Vol-II: 460
Muth, E. R., Vol-I: 245
Muth, J. L., Vol-I: 567; Vol-II: 156, 158
Muuss, R. E., Vol-I: 528
Myaskovsky, L., Vol-II: 338–339, 347

N
Naftolin, F., Vol-I: 218
Nagurney, A. J., Vol-II: 295
Nagy, G., Vol-II: 388–389
Naidoo, L., Vol-II: 294
Naigles, L. R., Vol-II: 341
Nakash-Eisikovits, O., Vol-I: 440
Namageyo-Funa, A., Vol-II: 549
Nanin, J. E., Vol-I: 64
Nankervis, B., Vol-II: 72
Napier, A. Y., Vol-II: 265–266
Naples, N. A., Vol-I: 105
Napoli, D. S., Vol-I: 24
Narayan, K. M. V., Vol-II: 531
Nardi, P., Vol-II: 281
Nash, H. C., Vol-II: 104
Nash, S. C., Vol-I: 516
Nass, R., Vol-I: 219
Nassif, A., Vol-II: 644
Nast, H., Vol-I: 107
Nath, L. E., Vol-I: 434, 435

Nathans, J., Vol-I: 237
Nathanson, C., Vol-II: 533
Naylor, K. E., Vol-II: 414
Neal, D. J., Vol-II: 347, 349
Neal, L. V. I., Vol-I: 284
Neale, M. A., Vol-II: 349
Neave, N., Vol-I: 226
Neckerman, H., Vol-I: 397
Neece, W. M., Vol-I: 573
Neff, D., Vol-II: 448
Neff, K. D., Vol-II: 35–36, 294, 298
Neff, L. A., Vol-II: 501, 504, 507–509, 511
Neff, N. L., Vol-I: 322
Nehls, N., Vol-II: 95
Neighbors, H. W., Vol-II: 228
Neilands, T., Vol-I: 33
Neilson, I., Vol-I: 222
Neitz, J., Vol-I: 237
Neitz, M., Vol-I: 237
Nelissen, M., Vol-I: 398
Nell, V. P., Vol-II: 545
Nellen, V. C., Vol-II: 576
Nelson, A., Vol-II: 672
Nelson, B. D., Vol-I: 330
Nelson, C. B., Vol-II: 134
Nelson, D. L., Vol-II: 502
Nelson, J. A., Vol-I: 147
Nelson, J. D., Vol-I: 320, 322
Nelson, S., Vol-I: 386
Neptune, D., Vol-II: 170–171, 647–648
Ness, T. J., Vol-I: 241
Nesse, R., Vol-II: 410
Neto, F., Vol-I: 649
Nettle, D., Vol-II: 19, 29
Nettleton, C., Vol-II: 486
Neuberg, S. L., Vol-I: 85, 418
Neufeld, K. J., Vol-II: 481
Neugarten, B., Vol-I: 570–571, 573
Neuhauser, H. K., Vol-I: 245
Neuman, J. H., Vol-II: 423, 427, 431
Neumann, C. S., Vol-II: 31
Neumann, S. A., Vol-I: 442
Nevers, C. C., Vol-I: 22
Newberry, A. M., Vol-II: 255
Newbrough, J. R., Vol-II: 635
Newcomb, M. D., Vol-I: 136, 140, 165; Vol-II: 7, 24
Newcombe, N., Vol-I: 7, 88, 239, 308
Newcombe, N. S., Vol-I: 259–272, 317, 325–328, 338
Newhouse, C., Vol-I: 329
Newman, D. L., Vol-I: 535
Newman, L. K., Vol-II: 123
Newman, L. S., Vol-I: 510, 515
Newman, M. L., Vol-I: 222
Newman, W. L., Vol-II: 592
Newport, F., Vol-II: 447, 449
Newson, J., Vol-I: 330
Newson, L., Vol-I: 456

Newton, T., Vol-I: 9; Vol-II: 9, 498–499, 507
Ng, S. H., Vol-I: 195
Ng-Mak, D., Vol-II: 621
Nguyen, D., Vol-II: 426
Nguyen, T., Vol-I: 247
Nguyen-Michel, S. T., Vol-I: 460
Nicholls, J. G., Vol-II: 388
Nicholls, T. L., Vol-II: 604
Nichols, D., Vol-II: 647
Nichols, T. E., Vol-I: 242
Nichols, T. R., Vol-I: 546
Nicholson, A., Vol-II: 482
Nicholson, G., Vol-I: 463
Nicolson, P., Vol-I: 117
Nielsen, C., Vol-I: 246
Niemann, Y. F., Vol-II: 449
Nieschlag, E., Vol-I: 348
Nightingale, D., Vol-I: 33
Nijssen, A., Vol-II: 502
Niklasson, M. K., Vol-I: 246
Nilsson, L. G., Vol-I: 248
Nilsson, T., Vol-II: 318
Nisbett, R. E., Vol-I: 171, 200
Nishii, L. H., Vol-II: 301
Nkomo, S. M., Vol-II: 451, 454, 458
Nobel, E., Vol-I: 247, 346, 354
Nobunaga, A. I., Vol-II: 483
Nock, S., Vol-II: 411
Nocon, M., Vol-II: 472
Noe, A. W., Vol-II: 349
Nolan, C., Vol-I: 326, 483
Noland, V. J., Vol-I: 319
Nolen-Hoeksema, S., Vol-I: 9, 298, 543; Vol-II: 9, 74, 133–147, 297
Noll, S. M., Vol-I: 91; Vol-II: 156–157, 659
Nonas, E., Vol-I: 217
Noon, M., Vol-I: 395, 397
Nora, A., Vol-I: 285
Norcross, J. C., Vol-II: 221, 234
Nordberg, P. B., Vol-II: 590
Nordin, S., Vol-I: 249
Norenzayan, A., Vol-I: 161
Noret, N., Vol-I: 290
Norman, L., Vol-II: 566–567
Norman, M. A., Vol-I: 106, 568
Norman, R. Z., Vol-II: 345
Norris, M., Vol-II: 674
Norris, P., Vol-II: 352
Norris, S. L., Vol-II: 531
North, F., Vol-II: 475
Northen, S., Vol-II: 553
Northouse, L. L., Vol-II: 551
Norton, G. N., Vol-I: 456
Norton, R. N., Vol-II: 482
Norwich, K. H., Vol-I: 244
Norwood, J. D., Vol-I: 462
Nosek, B., Vol-I: 281

Nosek, B. A., Vol-I: 35, 497; Vol-II: 447
Nowell, A., Vol-I: 299, 302, 304–305
Nowicki, S. Vol-I: 414
Nurius, P., Vol-II: 643
Nurnberg, H. G., Vol-II: 532
Nutt, R. L., Vol-II: 255–256
Nuttall, R. L., Vol-I: 317, 325; Vol-I: 317, 325
Nuttbrock, L., Vol-II: 145
Nylen, K., Vol-I: 222
Nylund, D., Vol-II: 225

O
O'Bannon, R., Vol-II: 626
O'Barr, W., Vol-I: 381, 387
O'Boyle, C., Vol-I: 504–505
O'Brien, E. J., Vol-I: 317
O'Brien, K. M., Vol-II: 228–229
O'Brien, M., Vol-I: 402
O'Brien, R., Vol-II: 228, 236
O'Brien, T., Vol-II: 496–497
O'Brien, T. B., Vol-II: 499
O'Connell, A. N., Vol-I: 20, 25
O'Connor, E., Vol-I: 67
O'Connor, E., Vol-I: 411
O'Connor, P., Vol-II: 171, 281–282
O'Connor, R. C., Vol-II: 510
O'Doherty, S., Vol-II: 380
O'Donnell, A., Vol-I: 227
O'Donnell, C., Vol-II: 620
O'Donnell, L., Vol-II: 620
O'Donohue, W., Vol-II: 360
O'Hanlan, K. A., Vol-II: 486
O'Heron, C. A., Vol-I: 143
O'Kane, G. M., Vol-II: 477
O'Kearney, R., Vol-I: 436
O'Keefe, J. A., Vol-I: 226, 345
O'Laughlin, E. M., Vol-I: 264
O'Leary, A., Vol-II: 161
O'Leary, K., Vol-I: 381
O'Leary, M. M., Vol-II: 74
O'Leary, V., Vol-II: 677
O'Loughlin, C., Vol-II: 284
O'Malley, M. S., Vol-II: 526
O'Malley, P. M., Vol-I: 224
O'Meara, J. D., Vol-II: 283
O'Meara, K. P., Vol-II: 98
O'Neal, E. C., Vol-II: 314
O'Neil, J., Vol-I: 47, 51–54, 144–145, 150
O'Neil, J. M., Vol-I: 123, 225; Vol-II: 123, 225, 255–256, 266
O'Reilly, C. A., Vol-II: 348, 350
O'Sullivan, L. F., Vol-I: 527, 531, 540; Vol-II: 299
Oakes, J., Vol-II: 388
Oathout, A., Vol-II: 295
Obbo, C., Vol-I: 116
Oberg, C., Vol-I: 248
Oberlander, S., Vol-I: 362

Oborn, K. L., Vol-II: 460
Ochs, R., Vol-II: 363–365
Ochse, R., Vol-I: 562
Ochsner, K. N., Vol-I: 432–443
Oddone, E. Z., Vol-II: 533
Odgers, C. L., Vol-I: 549
Ofotokun, I., Vol-II: 534
Ogilvie, D. T., Vol-II: 460
Ogletree, R. J., Vol-I: 53
Ogletree, S. M., Vol-I: 392; Vol-II: 650
Ogloff, J. R., Vol-II: 604
Oguz, C., Vol-II: 502
Oh, E., Vol-I: 392
Ohlott, P. J., Vol-II: 455
Ohnishi, T., Vol-I: 330
Ojeda, L., Vol-I: 150
Öjehagen, A., Vol-II: 476
Okazaki, S., Vol-II: 623
Okely, A. D., Vol-II: 480
Okimoto, T. G., Vol-II: 346, 447
Okonofua, F. E., Vol-II: 155
Oksenberg, A., Vol-II: 524
Okut, H., Vol-II: 622
Olafsson, R. F., Vol-II: 434
Olak, J., Vol-II: 529
Oldenburg, B., Vol-II: 472
Oldham, J. D., Vol-I: 194
Olfson, M., Vol-II: 519
Olivardia, R., Vol-II: 99, 158–159, 162, 166, 172, 575
Oliver, C., Vol-II: 318
Oliver, G., Vol-I: 141, 456–457, 459–460, 463–464
Oliver, K. K., Vol-II: 165
Oliver, M. B., Vol-I: 476–477, 479–480; Vol-II: 299, 656
Oliver, P., Vol-II: 614
Olkin, R., Vol-I: 193
Ollendick, T. H., Vol-II: 221
Ollie, M., Vol-II: 621
Olm-Shipman, C., Vol-II: 337
Olmstead, E. B., Vol-II: 343
Olofsson, J. K., Vol-I: 249
Olsen, M., Vol-II: 533
Olson, J. E., Vol-II: 326, 329, 648
Olsson, E. S., Vol-II: 113
Olsson, M. J., Vol-I: 248
Olweus, D., Vol-II: 328, 599
Ong, A. D., Vol-I: 161
Ong, K. L., Vol-II: 543
Ontai, L. L., Vol-I: 143
Onyx, J., Vol-I: 115
Opie, A., Vol-I: 108
Oquendo, M. A., Vol-II: 224
Orbach, S., Vol-II: 156
Orbuch, T., Vol-II: 412–413
Orduña, M., Vol-II: 618
Orford, J., Vol-II: 430
Organ, D. W., Vol-I: 452–453
Orlick, T., Vol-II: 570

Orlofsky, J. L., Vol-I: 142–143, 150
Ormerod, A. J., Vol-I: 282–283
Ormrod, R., Vol-II: 319
Orr, J. S., Vol-I: 456
Orsini, N., Vol-II: 476
Orthner, D. K., Vol-II: 686
Ortiz, M. L., Vol-I: 165, 221, 328
Ortiz-Torres, B., Vol-II: 627
Ortola, G., Vol-II: 620
Ortony, A., Vol-I: 506
Orwoll, E. S., Vol-I: 223
Oryol, V. E., Vol-II: 26
Osbaldiston, R., Vol-II: 45
Osborn, T. W., Vol-I: 223
Osgood, D. W., Vol-I: 501, 537; Vol-II: 389
Osherson, S., Vol-I: 432
Osipow, S. H., Vol-I: 29
Ost, J., Vol-I: 187
Ostchega, Y., Vol-II: 543
Osterman, K., Vol-II: 429
Ostrov, J. M., Vol-II: 320
Ostrove, J., Vol-I: 566–567
Ostrove, J. M., Vol-I: 563, 566
Ostrow, D., Vol-II: 135
Oswald, D. L., Vol-I: 285, 515
Otsuka, N., Vol-I: 245
Otsuka, R., Vol-I: 456
Ott, E. M., Vol-II: 341
Otto, S., Vol-I: 198
Otto, S. J., Vol-II: 526
Ouimette, P., Vol-II: 74
Outhwaite, W., Vol-I: 122
Overman, W. H., Vol-I: 224
Overton, W. F., Vol-I: 327–328, 503, 567
Ovesey, L., Vol-II: 118
Oviatt, S. K., Vol-I: 223
Owen, J., Vol-I: 383
Owen, J. W., Vol-II: 340
Owen-Anderson, A., Vol-I: 510
Owens, C. L., Vol-I: 571
Owens, L. K., Vol-II: 161
Owens, R. G., Vol-II: 474, 485
Owens, S. S., Vol-II: 576
Owen-Smith, A., Vol-II: 52
Owens-Nicholson, D., Vol-II: 161
Oyama, S., Vol-I: 200
Oyebode, J., Vol-II: 318
Ozanne-Smith, J., Vol-II: 482
Özbilgin, M., Vol-II: 382–383, 391
Ozel, S., Vol-I: 326
Özkale, L., Vol-II: 391
Ozonoff, A., Vol-I: 187

P

Paccaud, F., Vol-II: 476
Pace, R., Vol-II: 543
Pachankis, J. E., Vol-I: 63; Vol-II: 141, 145

Packard, M. G., Vol-I: 325
Padesky, C. A., Vol-II: 82
Paganini-Hill, A., Vol-II: 524
Page, R. M., Vol-I: 547
Page, S., Vol-II: 104
Page, S. E., Vol-II: 456
Paget, S. A., Vol-II: 550
Paglin, M., Vol-I: 311
Paik, I., Vol-II: 447
Paikoff, R. L., Vol-I: 534, 536
Pakkenberg, B., Vol-I: 217
Palella, F. J., Vol-II: 533
Pallesen, P., Vol-II: 474
Palmary, I., Vol-I: 105, 118
Palmer, C. T., Vol-I: 91
Palmieri, P. A., Vol-II: 433
Palomares, N., Vol-I: 434, 430
Pals, J., Vol-I: 564
Paluch, R., Vol-I: 456
Paluck, E. L., Vol-I: 89, 411, 437; Vol-II: 21, 338, 643
Pang, J., Vol-II: 42, 44, 48, 57
Pang, J. S., Vol-II: 44, 56–57
Pangalila, R. F., Vol-II: 483
Paniagua, F. A., Vol-II: 236
Pannu, M., Vol-II: 288
Pantoja, P., Vol-II: 301
Paolillo, J. G. P., Vol-II: 457
Papp, P., Vol-II: 255
Parada, R. H., Vol-II: 31
Paradie, L., Vol-I: 372
Parameswaran, G., Vol-I: 319, 328
Pardie, L., Vol-I: 195
Pardo, S. T., Vol-II: 10, 359–371
Pardo, T., Vol-II: 366
Parent, J. D., Vol-II: 448
Parent, M. B., Vol-I: 329
Parham, W. D., Vol-II: 580
Parikh-Patel, A., Vol-II: 528
Paris, J., Vol-II: 95
Park, B., Vol-I: 500
Park, D., Vol-II: 351, 456
Park, D. C., Vol-I: 568
Park, J., Vol-I: 330
Park, J. H., Vol-II: 288
Park, K., Vol-I: 483
Park, R. J., Vol-I: 565–566
Park, S., Vol-II: 234
Parke, R. D., Vol-II: 386, 406
Parker, F., Vol-II: 620
Parker, H., Vol-I: 513
Parker, L., Vol-II: 269
Parker, L. M., Vol-II: 532
Parker, P. S., Vol-II: 460
Parker, S., Vol-I: 513; Vol-II: 160
Parkes, M. A., Vol-II: 690
Parkhill, M. R., Vol-II: 284
Parkin, D. M., Vol-II: 541

Parks, M. R., Vol-II: 282
Parlee, M. B., Vol-I: 27–29, 194, 401
Parman, C. L., Vol-II: 520
Parrett, K. L., Vol-II: 551
Parsons, J. E., Vol-II: 330, 379, 383–385, 388
Parsons, J. T., Vol-I: 64; Vol-II: 371
Parsons, T., Vol-I: 134; Vol-II: 406
Parsons, T. D., Vol-I: 244, 319
Pascale, L., Vol-I: 383
Pascalis, P., Vol-I: 504
Pascarella, E. T., Vol-I: 285
Pascoe, C. J., Vol-II: 227
Pashler, H., Vol-I: 330
Paskett, E. D., Vol-I: 184
Pasloski, D. D., Vol-II: 338
Passero, R. N., Vol-I: 363
Pastò, L., Vol-II: 688
Pastore, A. L., Vol-II: 316, 321
Patai, D., Vol-I: 106
Patchin, J. W., Vol-II: 320
Patel, V., Vol-II: 51
Patrick, B. C., Vol-II: 385
Patrick, C. J., Vol-II: 74
Patsdaughter, C. A., Vol-II: 486
Patten, S. B., Vol-II: 546
Patterson, C. J., Vol-I: 67, 501, 565; Vol-II: 411
Patterson, D. W., Vol-I: 573
Patterson, J., Vol-I: 383
Patterson, M. M., Vol-I: 186, 512, 517
Patton, C., Vol-II: 603
Patton, G. C., Vol-I: 548
Patton, M. Q., Vol-I: 112
Paul, J., Vol-I: 66, 121
Pauling, M. L., Vol-II: 103
Paulson, P. E., Vol-I: 242
Pavalko, E. K., Vol-II: 410
Pavel, S., Vol-I: 184
Pavlidou, T. S., Vol-I: 388
Pawlowski, B., Vol-II: 286
Pawlowski, L. M., Vol-I: 62
Paxton, S. J., Vol-II: 155, 165, 168, 173
Peacock, D., Vol-II: 542
Peake, P. K., Vol-II: 67
Pearce, J. K., Vol-II: 255
Pearce, N. A., Vol-II: 451
Pearcey, S. M., Vol-I: 226
Pearlin, L. I., Vol-II: 143, 145
Pearson, C. M., Vol-II: 423–424, 429, 435
Pedersen, K. E., Vol-I: 244
Pedersen, S., Vol-II: 327, 576
Pederson, E., Vol-II: 228
Pederson, L., Vol-I: 187
Pederson, L. L., Vol-II: 477
Pedhazur, E. J., Vol-I: 135, 192
Peek, C., Vol-II: 588
Peekna, H. M., Vol-II: 521
Pegalis, L., Vol-II: 295

Peiro, J. M., Vol-II: 503
Pekrun, R., Vol-I: 444; Vol-II: 382, 385, 388
Peleg-Oren, N., Vol-II: 525, 548
Peletz, M. G., Vol-II: 114
Pelias, R. J., Vol-I: 118–119
Pelled, L. H., Vol-II: 350
Pellegrini, A. D., Vol-I: 263, 265
Pellegrino, J. W., Vol-I: 319, 322
Pelletier, J., Vol-I: 240, 320
Pelletier, L. C., Vol-II: 388
Pellis, V. C., Vol-I: 220
Peña, E. D., Vol-I: 171, 173, 322
Penhale, B., Vol-II: 318
Penn, P., Vol-II: 255
Pennebaker, J., Vol-I: 391
Penner, L. A., Vol-II: 326
Penrod, S., Vol-II: 660
Penton-Voak, I. S., Vol-II: 286
Pepitone-Arreola-Rockwell, F., Vol-I: 198
Peplau, L. A., Vol-I: 64–66, 72, 480; Vol-II: 68, 157, 282, 294, 297, 363–364, 411
Pepler, D., Vol-I: 540; Vol-II: 319–320
Perchellet, J. P., Vol-I: 217
Perdue, L., Vol-II: 166
Peregrine, P. N., Vol-I: 160
Perez-Albeniz, A., Vol-II: 329
Pergram, A. M., Vol-II: 21
Perkins, D. N. T., Vol-II: 633
Perkins, H., Vol-II: 409, 411
Perkins, R., Vol-II: 192
Perlesz, A., Vol-II: 263
Perlin, M. J., Vol-II: 553
Perlman, D., Vol-II: 282, 295, 323, 328
Perloff, R. M., Vol-II: 510
Perrin, E. C., Vol-I: 67
Perrone, D., Vol-II: 594–595
Perrot-Sinal, T. S., Vol-I: 226
Perrott, D. A., Vol-I: 200
Perry, C. L., Vol-II: 161
Perry, D. G., Vol-I: 142, 150, 192, 497–499, 512, 515, 531
Perry, J., Vol-II: 95
Perry, J. C., Vol-II: 195
Perry, L. A., Vol-I: 282
Perry, M., Vol-I: 283, 436
Perry, P., Vol-I: 484
Perry, Z. W., Vol-II: 647
Perry-Jenkins, M., Vol-I: 537, 529; Vol-II: 407, 411, 413
Person, E., Vol-II: 118
Person, S., Vol-II: 543
Péruch, P., Vol-II: 330
Perunovic, W. Q. E., Vol-II: 34
Perz, J., Vol-I: 440
Pestello, F., Vol-II: 407
Peter, J., Vol-I: 7, 8, 191–204, 244, 542; Vol-II: 171
Peters, D. H., Vol-II: 481
Peters, G. R., Vol-I: 463

Peters, J. F., Vol-I: 143
Peters, M., Vol-I: 222, 225, 318, 322, 324
Petersen, A., Vol-II: 473, 477
Petersen, A. C., Vol-I: 87, 147, 263, 300, 318–320, 530, 535–536, 544, 547; Vol-II: 386
Petersen, J., Vol-I: 8, 471–488
Peterson, A. C., Vol-I: 9, 142, 198, 325, 461, 529, 548, 564
Peterson, B., Vol-II: 166
Peterson, B. E., Vol-I: 564; Vol-II: 9, 41–58
Peterson, B. S., Vol-I: 325
Peterson, C., Vol-II: 146
Peterson, J. B., Vol-I: 461
Peterson, M., Vol-I: 548; Vol-II: 167
Peterson, R. E., Vol-I: 529
Peterson, S. B., Vol-I: 198
Peterson-Badali, M., Vol-I: 142
Petito, C. K., Vol-I: 225
Petri, M., Vol-II: 542
Petro, Z., Vol-I: 218
Petronio, S., Vol-II: 326
Petrucci, L., Vol-I: 219
Petty, E. M., Vol-I: 194
Pewewardy, N., Vol-II: 263
Pezaris, E., Vol-I: 317, 325
Pfaefflin, F., Vol-I: 368
Pfafflin, F., Vol-II: 112, 119, 368
Pfeffer, C. A., Vol-I: 194
Phares, V., Vol-II: 155
Pharmer, J. A., Vol-II: 347
Phelan, J., Vol-I: 285
Phelan, J. C., Vol-II: 145, 147
Phelan, J. E., Vol-II: 298–299
Phelan, S., Vol-I: 196
Philippot, P., Vol-I: 440
Philips, B., Vol-II: 204
Phillips, D. M., Vol-II: 607
Phillips, K. A., Vol-II: 158–159, 161–162, 575
Phillips, K., Vol-I: 222, 324, 326; Vol-II: 99, 352
Phillips, K. W., Vol-II: 344, 349
Phillips, M., Vol-I: 393
Phillips, M. D., Vol-I: 245
Phillips, S. L., Vol-II: 297
Philpot, C. L., Vol-II: 256
Phinney, J. S., Vol-I: 160–161
Phoenix, A., Vol-I: 110, 185; Vol-II: 475
Piaget, J., Vol-I: 319, 496, 503; Vol-II: 188
Piccolo, R. F., Vol-II: 351, 459
Pichado, M., Vol-I: 218
Pichler, S., Vol-II: 371
Pickering, A. S., Vol-II: 166
Pickering, D. I., Vol-II: 686
Pickren, W. E., Vol-I: 20
Pidada, S., Vol-II: 312
Pidgeon, N., Vol-I: 111
Pienta, A. M., Vol-I: 573
Pierce, P. F., Vol-II: 686

Pierce, T. W., Vol-II: 318
Pietromonaco, P. R., Vol-I: 436; Vol-II: 294
Pietrzak, J., Vol-II: 141
Pignone, M., Vol-II: 544
Piirto, J., Vol-I: 346, 348
Pike, K. L., Vol-I: 161
Pike, K. M., Vol-I: 438
Piliavin, J. A., Vol-II: 338–339
Pilkington, N., Vol-I: 68
Pilkington, N. W., Vol-II: 367–368
Pillard, R., Vol-I: 63
Pillard, R. C., Vol-II: 27
Pillay, Y., Vol-II: 194
Pilon, D. A., Vol-II: 56
Pina, D., Vol-II: 413–414
Pinch, P., Vol-II: 690
Pincus, A. L., Vol-II: 26
Pincus, H. A., Vol-II: 519
Pinderhughes, E., Vol-II: 255, 261–262
Pinker, S., Vol-I: 202, 259, 261
Pinto, K., Vol-II: 412
Piorkowski, R., Vol-II: 43
Piotrkowski, C. S., Vol-II: 502–503
Pipher, M., Vol-I: 345; Vol-II: 30, 117, 253
Piquero, A., Vol-II: 329
Piran, N., Vol-I: 118; Vol-II: 170
Pisecco, S., Vol-I: 145
Piskur, J., Vol-I: 194
Pita, J., Vol-I: 459
Pittinsky, T. L., Vol-I: 284, 353, 433
Pitts, M. K., Vol-I: 388
Pituch, K. A., Vol-II: 226, 229
Pjrek, E., Vol-I: 444
Plailly, J., Vol-I: 249
Plant, E. A., Vol-I: 193, 431; Vol-II: 97
Plante, R. F., Vol-II: 113
Plassman, B. L., Vol-II: 523
Pleak, R., Vol-II: 119, 125
Pleck, J. H., Vol-I: 44, 47, 49–50, 52–53, 134, 136–138, 145; Vol-II: 117, 256, 266, 281–282, 294, 297, 299, 402, 415
Pledger, M., Vol-II: 480
Pleis, J. R., Vol-II: 525
Pliner, P., Vol-I: 456–458, 460–461, 567
Plomin, R., Vol-I: 302
Plous, S., Vol-II: 170–171, 647–648
Plug, C., Vol-I: 562
Plugge-Foust, C., Vol-I: 68
Plumb, P., Vol-I: 510
Plummer, D. C., Vol-II: 227
Poag, J. R., Vol-I: 354
Podolski, C., Vol-II: 645
Podolsky, D. K., Vol-II: 529, 544
Pohar, S. L., Vol-II: 530
Polefrone, J. M., Vol-I: 442
Polivy, J., Vol-I: 455–466; Vol-II: 8, 167

Pollack, W. S., Vol-I: 45, 50, 538; Vol-II: 222, 224–225, 228–230, 236, 238
Polo, M., Vol-II: 43
Pols, H., Vol-I: 203
Polsky, N., Vol-II: 595
Polzer, J. T., Vol-II: 349, 456
Pomaki, G., Vol-II: 499
Pomerantz, A., Vol-I: 199
Pomerantz, W. J., Vol-II: 482
Pomerantz-Zorin, L., Vol-II: 460
Pomeroy, D., Vol-I: 329
Pomeroy, W., Vol-I: 486
Pomeroy, W. R., Vol-I: 66
Ponse, B., Vol-II: 363
Ponseti, J., Vol-I: 225
Ponterotto, J. G., Vol-I: 122; Vol-II: 228
Ponton, C. W., Vol-I: 243
Poole, D. A., Vol-I: 330
Pope, H. G. Jr., Vol-I: 53, 90, 535; Vol-II: 99, 155, 158–162, 166–167, 170, 172, 575
Pope, R. L., Vol-I: 34
Popiel, D., Vol-II: 98
Popovic, J. R., Vol-II: 533
Popp, D., Vol-I: 484
Porath, C. L., Vol-II: 429, 435
Porche, M. V., Vol-I: 15, 137–138, 150; Vol-II: 15
Portegijs, W., Vol-II: 453
Porter, J., Vol-II: 486
Porter, L. S., Vol-II: 508–509, 511
Porter, N., Vol-II: 192
Portillo, M., Vol-I: 353
Pöschl, S., Vol-II: 646
Post, E. M., Vol-I: 123, 137, 248
Post, M. W., Vol-II: 483
Post, R. M., Vol-II: 134, 195
Postmes, T., Vol-I: 193
Poteet, M. L., Vol-II: 454
Potosky, A. L., Vol-II: 527
Potter, B. K., Vol-II: 477
Potter, J., Vol-I: 111
Potuchek, J., Vol-II: 410
Poulin-Dubois, D., Vol-I: 500–501
Powell, B., Vol-I: 440
Powell, D. A., Vol-I: 442
Powell, G. N., Vol-II: 448
Powell, J. W., Vol-II: 483
Powell-Griner, E., Vol-II: 473
Power, C., Vol-II: 169
Powers, D., Vol-II: 114
Powers, J. L., Vol-II: 76
Powers, J. S., Vol-II: 575
Powlishta, K. K., Vol-I: 500–501; Vol-II: 23
Pratarelli, M. E., Vol-I: 194
Pratt, C., Vol-II: 484
Pratt, D., Vol-I: 507
Pratt, J., Vol-I: 307, 328; Vol-II: 568, 651
Pratt, M., Vol-II: 567

Prättälä, R., Vol-II: 473
Pratto, F., Vol-I: 7, 191–204; Vol-II: 7, 362, 662
Prentice, D. A., Vol-I: 195, 198–199, 456, 506–507; Vol-II: 312, 340, 448
Prepin, J., Vol-I: 217
Prescott, J., Vol-I: 247
Prescott, S., Vol-I: 197
Presnell, K., Vol-I: 86; Vol-II: 155
Presser, H. B., Vol-II: 402, 410
Pressly, P. K., Vol-II: 232
Preston-Schreck, C., Vol-II: 646–647, 649
Prestopnik, J. L., Vol-I: 329
Pretty, G., Vol-II: 579, 619
Pribor, E. F., Vol-II: 195
Price, B., Vol-I: 327, 330
Price, D. D., Vol-I: 241, 243
Price, R. H., Vol-II: 140
Priesing, D., Vol-II: 114, 368
Priest, R. F., Vol-II: 677
Prihoda, T., Vol-II: 622
Prilletensky, I., Vol-I: 31, 35; Vol-II: 272, 613, 635
Prince, H. T., Vol-II: 677
Prince, V., Vol-I: 486
Pringle, R., Vol-I: 285
Prkachin, K. M., Vol-I: 438
Proctor, B., Vol-II: 123
Propp, K. M., Vol-II: 339, 349
Protopopescu, X., Vol-I: 223, 225
Proulx, C. M., Vol-II: 296
Proulx, R., Vol-II: 361
Prouty, A. M., Vol-II: 255
Prouty-Lyness, A. M., Vol-II: 255
Provencher, V., Vol-I: 457
Proverbio, A. M., Vol-I: 239
Pruitt, B. H., Vol-II: 452
Pruzinsky, T., Vol-II: 153
Pryor, D., Vol-I: 66
Pryor, J. B., Vol-II: 290, 660
Pryzgoda, J., Vol-I: 2, 365, 373; Vol-II: 2
Psalti, A., Vol-II: 260
Puentes, J., Vol-II: 283
Pugh, M. D., Vol-II: 343, 350
Puhl, R., Vol-II: 167
Pulkkinen, L., Vol-II: 27, 322
Puolakka, K., Vol-II: 545
Purcell, D. W., Vol-I: 68
Purcell, P., Vol-I: 281
Purdie, V., Vol-II: 141
Purdie-Vaughns, V., Vol-I: 198
Putallaz, M., Vol-I: 397
Puterman, E., Vol-II: 499, 504
Putnam, F. W., Vol-II: 195
Putnam, L., Vol-I: 395, 397
Puts, D. A., Vol-I: 217, 270, 323–324
Pyke, K., Vol-II: 405, 409, 412
Pyszczynski, T., Vol-II: 169

Q
Qian, H., Vol-II: 327
Quaiser-Pohl, C., Vol-I: 326
Quas, J., Vol-I: 442
Quick, J. C., Vol-II: 502
Quigley, K. S., Vol-I: 457
Quine, L., Vol-II: 424
Quinlan, D. M., Vol-II: 139
Quinn, C. E., Vol-II: 168
Quinn, D. M., Vol-I: 85, 91, 306; Vol-II: 157, 659–660
Quinn, P. C., Vol-I: 318, 504
Quinsey, V. L., Vol-II: 285

R
Raag, T., Vol-I: 143
Rabinowitz, F. E., Vol-I: 45, 50, 54; Vol-II: 135, 137, 224–225, 229–230, 232, 234–236
Rabinowitz, V. C., Vol-II: 588
Raboy, B., Vol-II: 411
Rachlin, K., Vol-II: 119
Rackliff, C. L., Vol-I: 143
Rademacher, J., Vol-I: 244
Rader, J., Vol-II: 201–202, 205, 211–212
Radkowsky, M., Vol-II: 136, 140
Rado, S., Vol-I: 61
Radway, J., Vol-I: 399
Raffaelli, M., Vol-I: 143
Rafi, A., Vol-I: 328
Raghunathan, T. E., Vol-II: 476
Ragins, B. R., Vol-II: 449, 458
Ragsdale, J. D., Vol-II: 293
Rahav, M., Vol-II: 145
Rahman, Q., Vol-I: 225, 328
Raidt, T., Vol-II: 363
Raina, T. N., Vol-I: 347
Rainie, L., Vol-II: 653
Rainville, P., Vol-I: 243
Raitt, F. E., Vol-II: 64, 72
Raj, R., Vol-II: 125
Rajendran, P., Vol-I: 347
Rakowski, W., Vol-II: 544
Ram, N., Vol-II: 568
Ramage, K., Vol-II: 339
Ramazanoglu, C., Vol-II: 282
Ramirez-Valles, J., Vol-I: 187
Ramos, V., Vol-II: 31
Ramrattan, M. E., Vol-I: 63; Vol-II: 141
Ramsay, J. O., Vol-II: 82
Ramsden, M. W., Vol-I: 142–143
Ramsey, S. J., Vol-II: 325
Randall, E. P., Vol-I: 327
Randel, A. E., Vol-II: 341
Rane, A., Vol-II: 474
Raney, A. A., Vol-II: 647
Rani, M., Vol-II: 481
Rankin, S. R., Vol-II: 578
Raofi, S., Vol-II: 521

Rapagna, S. O., Vol-I: 349
Raphael, B., Vol-II: 477
Raphaeli, N., Vol-I: 242
Rapkin, B., Vol-II: 633
Rapoport, R., Vol-II: 452
Rappaport, J., Vol-II: 613, 619
Rappoport, L., Vol-I: 463
Rapson, R. L., Vol-I: 239
Raskin, M., Vol-II: 100
Rasky, E., Vol-II: 473
Rasmussen, K., Vol-I: 242
Rastogi, M., Vol-II: 260
Ratcliff, K., Vol-II: 414
Rauch, J., Vol-II: 650
Rauh, V., Vol-II: 620
Raven, B., Vol-I: 416
Raver, J. L., Vol-II: 301
Ravussin, E., Vol-II: 478
Rawlins, W. K., Vol-II: 284
Rawsthorne, L. J., Vol-II: 29
Ray, S., Vol-II: 652
Rayburn, T. M., Vol-II: 188, 193
Rayner, C., Vol-II: 423–424, 429–430
Rayyan, F., Vol-II: 625, 633
Razani, J., Vol-II: 605
Read, G., Vol-I: 56
Read, J. G., Vol-II: 553
Read, S. J., Vol-II: 33
Real, T., Vol-II: 229–230, 238
Realo, A., Vol-I: 441
Ream, G., Vol-I: 480
Reardon, P., Vol-I: 197
Reason, P., Vol-I: 118, 122
Reavey, P., Vol-I: 119
Rechtsteiner, E. A., Vol-II: 518
Redaelli, M., Vol-II: 543
Reddy, D. M., Vol-II: 350
Redman, L. M., Vol-II: 478
Reed, B. R., Vol-I: 115, 135, 487
Reed, V., Vol-II: 337
Reed-Danahay, D. E., Vol-I: 115
Reed-Sanders, D., Vol-I: 135
Reedy, C. S., Vol-I: 187; Vol-II: 114
Reel, J. J., Vol-II: 574–575
Reeves, J. B., Vol-I: 52
Regan, P. C., Vol-II: 286–287
Régner, I., Vol-I: 284, 289
Rehkopf, D. H., Vol-I: 179
Rehm, J., Vol-II: 481
Reich, S. M., Vol-II: 613, 635
Reichard, R. J., Vol-II: 450
Reichert, T., Vol-II: 170–171
Reid, C., Vol-II: 619
Reid, H., Vol-I: 330, 545
Reid, P. T., Vol-I: 35, 198, 290; Vol-II: 260
Reid-Griffin, A., Vol-I: 330
Reidy, E. B., Vol-II: 410

Reimer, M. A., Vol-II: 546
Reimers, S., Vol-I: 225, 324
Reinaart, R., Vol-I: 35
Reinharz, S., Vol-I: 33, 103, 106, 108, 111, 113
Reinking, R., Vol-I: 322
Reips, U., Vol-II: 602
Reis, H. T., Vol-II: 281–282, 294
Reis, L. A. G., Vol-II: 526
Reiter, E. O., Vol-I: 354, 533–534
Reiter-Palmon, R., Vol-I: 354
Rejskind, F. G., Vol-I: 349
Rekers, G. A., Vol-II: 118, 122
Remafedi, G., Vol-II: 156
Remer, P., Vol-I: 35; Vol-II: 92–94, 192
Rennie, H., Vol-II: 484
Renzetti, C. M., Vol-II: 632
Repetti, R. L., Vol-II: 143
Resnick, H. S., Vol-II: 316
Resnick, M. D., Vol-II: 140, 156
Resnick, S., Vol-I: 279
Resnick, S. M., Vol-I: 219
Restrepo, D., Vol-I: 246
Reuman, D., Vol-II: 43, 388
Reusch, J. E., Vol-II: 531
Reuter, M., Vol-I: 354, 567
Reuter-Lorenz, P. A., Vol-I: 567
Reuveni, H., Vol-II: 524
Revenson, T. A., Vol-II: 497, 501, 543, 546–547, 550–551, 554
Reyes, C., Vol-II: 200
Reyes, O., Vol-II: 623, 634
Reynolds, A. L., Vol-I: 34
Reynolds, C. R., Vol-I: 569; Vol-II: 602
Reynolds, J. R., Vol-II: 415
Reynolds, K. A., Vol-II: 547
Reznikoff, M., Vol-II: 295–296
Rguibi, M., Vol-II: 160
Rheman, U. S., Vol-II: 499–500, 509
Rhoads, K. V., Vol-II: 343
Rhode, D. L., Vol-II: 337
Rhodes, J. E., Vol-I: 103
Rhodes, J., Vol-II: 623
Rhodes, K., Vol-I: 195
Rhodes, L., Vol-II: 473
Rhodes, M., Vol-I: 502, 506–507
Rhodes, N. D., Vol-I: 143
Rhodes, S., Vol-II: 368
Rholes, W. S., Vol-I: 196
Rhudy, J. L., Vol-I: 242
Rhyne, D., Vol-II: 298
Riach, P. A., Vol-II: 447
Ribbens, J., Vol-I: 106
Ricciardelli, L. A., Vol-I: 542; Vol-II: 156, 161, 163, 165, 168, 173
Rice, J. K., Vol-II: 264
Rice, R. E., Vol-II: 653
Rice, R. W., Vol-II: 677–678

Rich, J. B., Vol-I: 223
Richards, H., Vol-II: 160, 168
Richards, J. L., Vol-II: 318
Richards, M. H., Vol-I: 172, 436, 535–536, 538–539, 544; Vol-II: 117, 384
Richards, M., Vol-I: 147; Vol-II: 424
Richardson, A. E., Vol-I: 328
Richardson, A. G., Vol-I: 347
Richardson, D. R., Vol-II: 312, 314
Richardson, D. S., Vol-II: 313–314, 631
Richardson, L., Vol-I: 111, 285
Richardson, P. W., Vol-II: 382
Richardson, R., Vol-II: 673–674
Richardson, S. S., Vol-II: 525
Richardson, V. E., Vol-I: 573
Richelme, C., Vol-I: 217
Richeson, J. A., Vol-I: 438
Richins, M. L., Vol-II: 166
Richman, E. L., Vol-II: 576
Richman, J. A., Vol-II: 436
Richman, R. A., Vol-I: 248
Richmond, C., Vol-II: 487
Richmond, K., Vol-I: 9, 137, 139; Vol-II: 9, 111–125
Rickard, K. A., Vol-I: 148
Rickard, K. M., Vol-II: 201
Ricketts, W. A., Vol-II: 360
Ridder, E. M., Vol-II: 135
Riddle, B., Vol-II: 94–95, 99
Rideout, V. J., Vol-II: 651
Rideout, V., Vol-I: 542
Ridge, D., Vol-I: 51; Vol-II: 168
Ridgeway, C., Vol-II: 346
Ridgeway, C. L., Vol-I: 90; Vol-II: 281, 283, 339, 341–342, 345
Ridley, C. A., Vol-II: 210
Riedel, M., Vol-II: 607
Rieger, G., Vol-I: 512
Rieke, M. L., Vol-II: 80
Riemer, B. A., Vol-II: 571
Riemer, M., Vol-II: 613, 635
Riepe, M. W., Vol-I: 330
Rierdan, J., Vol-I: 535, 544
Riessman, C. K., Vol-I: 116
Riessman, C. K., Vol-II: 297
Riger, S., Vol-I: 31–32
Riggio, R. E., Vol-I: 75
Riggle, E. D., Vol-I: 69, 187
Riggle, E. D. B., Vol-II: 114, 125
Rilea, S. L., Vol-I: 325
Riley, III, J. L., Vol-I: 241
Rimé, B., Vol-I: 440
Rimmer, J. H., Vol-II: 567
Rincón, C., Vol-I: 540; Vol-II: 141
Rinehart, R., Vol-I: 111
Ring, C., Vol-II: 258
Rink, F., Vol-II: 461
Riordan, C., Vol-I: 288

Riordan, C. A., Vol-II: 347
Riordan, C. M., Vol-II: 350
Risco, C., Vol-II: 194–195
Riseley, D., Vol-II: 368
Rissman, E. F., Vol-I: 218
Ristock, J., Vol-II: 626, 631
Ristock, J. L., Vol-II: 196, 258, 509–510
Risvik, E., Vol-I: 462–463
Ritsma, S., Vol-II: 228
Ritter, B. A., Vol-II: 449
Ritter, K. Y., Vol-I: 64
Rivadeneyra, R., Vol-I: 542
Rivas, D., Vol-I: 285
Rivera, M., Vol-II: 94
Rivers, B. M., Vol-II: 528
Rivers, C., Vol-II: 631
Rivers, I., Vol-I: 290
Rivers, S. E., Vol-I: 439; Vol-II: 454
Rizza, M. G., Vol-I: 280
Rizzo, A. R., Vol-I: 244
Roach, K. A., Vol-I: 307
Roades, L., Vol-II: 292
Robbins, A. S., Vol-II: 527–528
Robbins, D., Vol-I: 327
Roberson-Nay, R., Vol-I: 202
Robert, A., Vol-II: 10
Robert, M., Vol-I: 10, 240, 267, 269–270, 319–320, 322, 325–326, 330
Roberts, A., Vol-I: 150
Roberts, B. W., Vol-I: 571; Vol-II: 33–34
Roberts, D. F., Vol-I: 542
Roberts, H., Vol-I: 106
Roberts, J. E., Vol-II: 141
Roberts, M. C., Vol-II: 117
Roberts, R., Vol-II: 195
Roberts, R. A., Vol-I: 35
Roberts, R. D., Vol-I: 439
Roberts, S. J., Vol-II: 552
Roberts, S. K., Vol-I: 290
Roberts, T. A., Vol-II: 153–154, 157, 169–171; Vol-I: 91, 571
Roberts, W. L., Vol-II: 319
Robertson, A., Vol-II: 362
Robertson, C. W., Vol-II: 385
Robertson, J. M., Vol-II: 224–226, 228, 230
Robertson, M., Vol-II: 619
Robertson, R. M., Vol-II: 543
Robeson, W. W., Vol-I: 539
Robey, C. S., Vol-II: 295
Robin, L., Vol-I: 436
Robinson, B., Vol-I: 7, 68
Robinson, B. E., Vol-II: 206
Robinson, B. W., Vol-II: 672
Robinson, D. A., Vol-II: 201, 205
Robinson, E., Vol-I: 199
Robinson, J., Vol-II: 404–405, 407, 408–410
Robinson, J. P., Vol-II: 404–405, 407, 445

Robinson, L., Vol-II: 497
Robinson, M. D., Vol-I: 430, 434, 436
Robinson, M. E., Vol-I: 241
Robinson, S. L., Vol-II: 423, 428
Rocher, S., Vol-I: 134
Rochlen, A. B., Vol-I: 138; Vol-II: 226, 228–229, 363–364
Rochtchina, E., Vol-I: 236
Rodbotten, M., Vol-I: 462
Rodham, K., Vol-II: 478
Rodin, J., Vol-I: 246, 345; Vol-II: 156, 168
Rodriguez, G. M., Vol-II: 205
Rodriguez, I., Vol-II: 503
Rodríguez-Carmona, M., Vol-I: 237
Roe, C. M., Vol-II: 530
Roe, L. S., Vol-I: 456
Roe, M. T., Vol-I: 456
Roeder, M. R., Vol-I: 63
Roeltgen, D., Vol-I: 218
Roen, K., Vol-II: 113, 121
Roe-Sepowitz, D., Vol-II: 604
Roeser, R. W., Vol-II: 393–394
Roets, G., Vol-I: 35
Rogelberg, S. G., Vol-II: 349
Rogers, A., Vol-I: 105
Rogers, C. R., Vol-I: 352; Vol-II: 56
Rogers, H. J., Vol-I: 67
Rogers, P. L., Vol-I: 413, 441
Rogers, P. O., Vol-II: 296
Rogers, R., Vol-II: 72, 602
Rohde, W., Vol-I: 122; Vol-II: 51, 54
Rohlinger, D. A., Vol-II: 549
Rohrbaugh, M. J., Vol-II: 551
Roizman, S., Vol-I: 248
Roland, P., Vol-I: 249
Roll, C., Vol-II: 620
Rollman, G. B., Vol-I: 240
Rollnick, S., Vol-II: 235
Rollock, D., Vol-I: 442
Rolls, B. J., Vol-I: 456–457, 462
Romans, S. E., Vol-II: 73
Romatowski, J. A., Vol-II: 287
Romberger, B., Vol-II: 451, 453
Romero, A., Vol-II: 618
Romney, D. M., Vol-II: 390
Ronai, C. R., Vol-I: 115
Roof, R. L., Vol-I: 323
Roopnarine, J., Vol-II: 412
Roopnarine, J. L., Vol-I: 445
Root, M. P., Vol-II: 103, 195
Roper, E. A., Vol-II: 568
Rosabianca, A., Vol-I: 433
Rosario, M., Vol-I: 63–64, 545; Vol-II: 621
Rosch, E., Vol-I: 196, 361; Vol-II: 32
Roscoe, B., Vol-II: 319
Rose, A. J., Vol-I: 445, 539
Rose, H., Vol-I: 511

Rose, J. G., Vol-II: 521
Rose, N., Vol-I: 202
Rose, N. R., Vol-II: 542
Rose, R., Vol-II: 482
Rose, R. J., Vol-I: 322
Rose, S., Vol-II: 292, 509
Rose, S. E., Vol-II: 476
Rose, S. M., Vol-II: 289, 292
Rosemann, T., Vol-II: 519
Rosen, A. B., Vol-II: 529, 545
Rosen, R. C., Vol-I: 486
Rosenbaum, A., Vol-II: 230
Rosenbaum, R. S., Vol-I: 223
Rosenberg, B. G., Vol-I: 236
Rosenberg, D., Vol-I: 319
Rosenberg, M., Vol-II: 118, 389
Rosenberg, P. J., Vol-II: 363
Rosenberg, R., Vol-I: 20, 22
Rosener, J. B., Vol-II: 458
Rosenfeld, D., Vol-I: 105, 117
Rosenfeld, S., Vol-II: 414
Rosengard, D. S., Vol-II: 647
Rosenhall, U., Vol-I: 244
Rosenholtz, S. J., Vol-II: 352
Rosenkrantz, P. S., Vol-I: 28; Vol-II: 104, 188, 678
Rosenthal, N. B., Vol-I: 30
Rosenthal, R., Vol-I: 306, 318, 412–413, 441; Vol-II: 295, 386
Rosette, A. S., Vol-II: 351
Rosik, C. H., Vol-II: 361
Rosip, J. C., Vol-I: 438
Roskos-Ewoldsen, B., Vol-I: 325, 329
Rosoff, B., Vol-I: 36
Rospenda, K. M., Vol-II: 436
Ross, C. E., Vol-I: 463
Ross, F. I., Vol-II: 482
Ross, J., Vol-I: 218–219
Ross, J. M., Vol-II: 361–362, 365
Ross, L., Vol-I: 200
Ross, L. T., Vol-II: 20, 284
Ross, M., Vol-I: 63
Ross, N., Vol-II: 487
Ross, S. I., Vol-I: 284
Ross, S. P., Vol-I: 330
Rossano, L., Vol-I: 186
Rosser, B. R. S., Vol-II: 362, 365
Rosser, R. A., Vol-I: 220
Rosser, S. V., Vol-I: 285, 287
Rossi, A. S., Vol-I: 326
Rossiter, M. W., Vol-I: 20, 21
Rossouw, J. E., Vol-I: 185
Rostosky, S. S., Vol-I: 69, 187; Vol-II: 114
Rotella, S., Vol-II: 387
Roter, D. L., Vol-I: 436; Vol-II: 523
Roth, D. A., Vol-I: 461
Roth, S. A., Vol-II: 255
Roth, S., Vol-I: 354

Rothbart, M., Vol-I: 196; Vol-II: 94, 193
Rothblum, E., Vol-I: 63, 66, 71–72, 369; Vol-II: 193
Rothblum, E. D., Vol-I: 66; Vol-II: 138, 411
Rothenberg, A., Vol-I: 352
Rotheram-Borus, M. J., Vol-I: 63, 68, 545
Rothfield, P., Vol-I: 117
Rothgerber, H., Vol-I: 446; Vol-II: 168
Rothschild, L., Vol-I: 197
Rothstein, A., Vol-II: 203
Rottman, L., Vol-II: 287
Rotundo, M., Vol-II: 426
Roughgarden, J., Vol-II: 113
Rounsley, C. A., Vol-I: 60, 71
Roush, P. E., Vol-II: 675
Rousset, S., Vol-I: 463
Rovet, J. F., Vol-I: 220
Rowatt, W. C., Vol-II: 362
Rowe, J., Vol-I: 566–567
Rowe, J. W., Vol-I: 227
Rowe, M., Vol-II: 71
Rowe, R., Vol-I: 548
Rowen, C. J., Vol-II: 362
Rowley, S. A. J., Vol-I: 496
Royet, J. P., Vol-I: 249
Rozee-Koker, P., Vol-I: 198
Rozelle, R. M., Vol-II: 449
Rozenkrantz, P. S., Vol-II: 64
Rozin, P., Vol-II: 169, 649
Rubenfeld, K., Vol-II: 296
Rubenson, D. L., Vol-I: 344
Rubin, A. M., Vol-II: 660
Rubin, D. B., Vol-I: 318; Vol-II: 386
Rubin, L. B., Vol-II: 299
Rubin, L. R., Vol-II: 660
Rubin, R. M., Vol-I: 573
Rubin, Z., Vol-II: 297–298
Rubinow, D. R., Vol-I: 458
Rubinstein, G., Vol-I: 50; Vol-II: 26–27
Rubio, V. J., Vol-I: 322
Ruble, D., Vol-I: 8, 84, 465–518
Ruble, D. N., Vol-I: 219, 505, 509, 527, 529–532, 549; Vol-II: 8, 330, 368, 387, 521
Ruch, W., Vol-I: 172
Ruddick, S., Vol-I: 32
Rude, S. N., Vol-II: 452
Rude, S. S., Vol-I: 35
Ruderman, M. N., Vol-II: 455
Rudkin, J. K., Vol-II: 613
Rudman, L. A., Vol-I: 420; Vol-II: 290, 298–299, 347, 449–450, 647, 660–661
Rudolph, K. D., Vol-I: 445, 539, 545; Vol-II: 139
Ruebelt, S. G., Vol-II: 205
Ruehlman, L. S., Vol-II: 522
Ruffin, M. T., Vol-I: 182
Ruffine, S., Vol-II: 95
Rufolo, A. M., Vol-I: 311
Ruggiero, G., Vol-I: 321

Ruiz de Esparza, C. A., Vol-II: 237
Rukavishnikov, A. A., Vol-II: 26
Rule, N. O., Vol-II: 451
Rumery, S. M., Vol-II: 349
Runco, M. A., Vol-I: 7, 343–355
Runtz, M., Vol-II: 208
Rupp, L. J., Vol-I: 110
Rusbult, C. E., Vol-I: 64; Vol-II: 294–295
Russ, S. W., Vol-I: 351–352, 354
Russell, D., Vol-II: 103
Russell, G. M., Vol-I: 69, 72, 103, 118–119
Russell, J., Vol-II: 648
Russell, M., Vol-II: 69
Russell, S. T., Vol-II: 136, 138, 142
Russo, N. F., Vol-I: 20, 25, 27, 370–371; Vol-II: 97
Rust, P. C., Vol-I: 480; Vol-II: 363–365
Ruth, J. E., Vol-I: 25, 259, 348
Rutherford, A., Vol-I: 6, 19–36
Rutland, A., Vol-I: 517
Rutter, A., Vol-II: 322, 431
Rutter, M., Vol-I: 532, 543
Rutter, V., Vol-I: 64
Rüttiger, L., Vol-I: 237
Ruzek, S., Vol-II: 523
Ryalls, B., Vol-I: 263
Ryalls, B. O., Vol-I: 515
Ryan, A. D., Vol-II: 455–456, 461
Ryan, A. M., Vol-II: 633
Ryan, C., Vol-I: 66
Ryan, H., Vol-I: 187
Ryan, K. D., Vol-II: 265
Ryan, K., Vol-I: 218
Ryan, L., Vol-I: 547
Ryan, M. K., Vol-I: 193; Vol-II: 455–456, 461
Ryan, R. M., Vol-II: 29, 297, 386, 388
Ryan, S., Vol-I: 10, 243
Ryb, G. E., Vol-II: 483
Rydell, R. J., Vol-I: 433
Ryff, C. D., Vol-I: 563–564
Rysman, A., Vol-I: 395, 399

S

Saad, L., Vol-II: 369–370
Saal, F. E., Vol-II: 284
Sabalis, R. F., Vol-II: 116–117
Sabin, K., Vol-I: 187
Sabo, D. F., Vol-II: 576
Sachs-Ericsson, N., Vol-II: 224
Sackett, P. R., Vol-II: 349, 426
Sadalla, E. K., Vol-II: 285
Sadava, S. W., Vol-I: 136; Vol-II: 167
Sadetsky, N., Vol-II: 528
Sadker, D., Vol-I: 283, 285, 388
Sadker, M., Vol-I: 283, 285, 388
Saegert, S., Vol-II: 626
Safren, S. A., Vol-II: 136, 140, 142
Sagarin, B. J., Vol-I: 392

Sagas, M., Vol-II: 646
Sage, G. H., Vol-II: 570
Sager, C., Vol-II: 156
Sagi, E., Vol-I: 244
Sagrestano, L. M., Vol-II: 52
Sahm, W. B., Vol-I: 503
Saidel, T., Vol-I: 187
Sailer, C. A., Vol-II: 365
Saitta, M. B., Vol-I: 421
Sajjadi-Bafghi, S. H., Vol-I: 354
Sakuma, N., Vol-I: 222, 326
Salas, E., Vol-II: 340, 343, 347
Salem, D., Vol-II: 619
Sales, E., Vol-II: 330
Salguero, G., Vol-I: 243
Salili, F., Vol-II: 56
Salinero, J., Vol-I: 243
Salomone, R. C., Vol-I: 289, 291
Salovey, P., Vol-I: 397, 399, 418, 439; Vol-II: 454
Saltaris, C., Vol-I: 545
Salthouse, T. A., Vol-I: 567–568
Salvy, S-J., Vol-I: 456, 461
Salzinger, S., Vol-II: 621
Samad, A., Vol-I: 328
Samar, R., Vol-I: 390
Samelson, F., Vol-I: 23
Sameroff, A. J., Vol-II: 383–384
Sampson, E. E., Vol-I: 31
Sampson, R. J., Vol-I: 546
Samuel, L., Vol-I: 553
Samuels, C. A., Vol-II: 24
Sanbonmatsu, D. M., Vol-I: 198
Sanchez, B., Vol-II: 623
Sanchez, D. T., Vol-I: 92; Vol-II: 291, 299
Sanchez, L., Vol-II: 409–410, 412
Sanchez-Hucles, J., Vol-II: 460, 615
Sandberg, D. E., Vol-I: 140
Sanderman, R., Vol-II: 501, 548, 552
Sanders, B., Vol-I: 318
Sanders, G., Vol-I: 224, 226, 324
Sanders, C. E., Vol-II: 386
Sanders, S., Vol-I: 187
Sandfort, T. G. M., Vol-II: 135, 224, 369
Sandler, J. C., Vol-II: 604
Sandman, D., Vol-II: 228
Sando, I., Vol-I: 245; Vol-I: 243
Sandoval, C., Vol-I: 31
Sandstrom, M. J., Vol-I: 547
Sandstrom, N. J., Vol-I: 329
Sandvik, E., Vol-I: 434
Sani, F., Vol-I: 496, 500
Sanikhani, M., Vol-II: 367
Sankar, P., Vol-I: 179
Sansanwal, D. N., Vol-I: 347
Santacreu, J., Vol-I: 322
Santana, V., Vol-II: 195
Santoni, V., Vol-I: 328

Santor, D. A., Vol-II: 82
Santos de Barona, M., Vol-I: 198
Santosh, C., Vol-I: 330
Sapadin, L. A., Vol-II: 283
Sapienza, P., Vol-I: 262, 300
Saracho, O. N., Vol-I: 354
Saragovi, C., Vol-II: 23–25, 43
Sarah, E., Vol-II: 383, 385
Sargent, S. L., Vol-II: 656
Sarigiani, P. A., Vol-I: 547
Saris, R. N., Vol-I: 35
Sarlund-Heinrich, P., Vol-II: 209
Saron, C., Vol-II: 54
Sartore, M. L., Vol-II: 646
Sartucci, F., Vol-I: 239
Sarwer, D., Vol-II: 163
Sasanuma, S., Vol-I: 222, 326
Sasao, T., Vol-II: 620, 623–624, 634
Sasse, D. K., Vol-I: 13, 53, 535, 544, 567–568; Vol-II: 13, 99, 155, 157, 159–161
Sato, H., Vol-I: 243, 245
Sauaia, A., Vol-II: 531
Saucier, D. A., Vol-I: 323; Vol-II: 658
Saucier, D. M., Vol-I: 7, 53, 143, 215–227, 264, 321, 328–330, 535, 567–568; Vol-II: 158, 170
Saucier, G., Vol-II: 28
Saults, S. J., Vol-I: 317
Saunders, A., Vol-I: 548
Saunders, B. E., Vol-II: 195
Sausa, L. A., Vol-II: 367–368
Sava, S., Vol-I: 328
Savic, I., Vol-I: 225, 249
Savin-Williams, R., Vol-I: 10, 63, 480
Savin-Williams, R. C., Vol-I: 194, 540; Vol-II: 10, 140, 359–371
Sawalani, G. M., Vol-I: 546
Sawrey, D. K., Vol-I: 269
Sax, L., Vol-I: 236–237, 278–281, 284, 287–288
Saxberg, J. K .J., Vol-I: 220
Sayer, L. C., Vol-II: 405, 409, 446
Scalliet, P. G. M., Vol-II: 527
Scalora, M. J., Vol-II: 322
Scantlebury, K., Vol-I: 283; Vol-II: 385
Scarborough, E., Vol-I: 20–21, 26
Scarce, R., Vol-II: 591–592, 596
Scaringi, V., Vol-I: 138
Scarr, S., Vol-I: 193, 204
Schacher, S., Vol-II: 258
Schaefer, C., Vol-II: 505
Schaefer, K., Vol-I: 324
Schafer, A., Vol-I: 443
Schaffer, D. R., Vol-II: 295
Schaie, K. W., Vol-I: 569
Schalamon, J., Vol-II: 482
Schane, R. E., Vol-I: 546
Schank, J. C., Vol-I: 248
Schappert, S. M., Vol-II: 474, 521

Schare, M. L., Vol-II: 164
Scharrer, E., Vol-II: 645–646, 649
Scharrón-del-Río, M. R., Vol-II: 233
Schat, A. C. H., Vol-II: 431
Scheffer, I. E., Vol-II: 598
Scheffler, S., Vol-II: 207
Schei, B., Vol-II: 207
Scheier, M. F., Vol-II: 434
Schein, V. E., Vol-II: 342–344, 347, 677
Schellhase, A., Vol-II: 646
Schelling, T., Vol-I: 511
Schelp, L., Vol-II: 483
Schenk, E., Vol-II: 482
Schenk, F., Vol-I: 329
Scher, M., Vol-I: 45; Vol-II: 222–223, 230–231, 237
Scherer, C. R., Vol-I: 392
Scherer, K. R., Vol-I: 435, 441
Schermer, F., Vol-II: 165
Scheurich, J., Vol-I: 118
Schiaffino, A., Vol-II: 479
Schiappa, E., Vol-II: 656
Schiedel, D. G., Vol-I: 562–564
Schieman, S., Vol-I: 435
Schienle, A., Vol-I: 443
Schiffman, M., Vol-I: 226
Schillace, M., Vol-II: 113
Schiller, J. S., Vol-II: 519
Schilling, E. A., Vol-II: 497
Schippers, M. C., Vol-II: 348, 456
Schlaug, G., Vol-I: 244
Schlegel, A., Vol-I: 159, 161
Schlegel, R., Vol-I: 549
Schleicher, A., Vol-I: 244
Schleicher, T. L., Vol-II: 344, 346
Schlich, P., Vol-I: 463
Schmader, T., Vol-I: 97
Schmalz, D. L., Vol-II: 571
Schmidt, C. E., Vol-II: 548
Schmidt, F., Vol-II: 75
Schmidt, S., Vol-I: 243
Schmitt, D., Vol-II: 362
Schmitt, D. P., Vol-II: 285–287
Schmitt, J. P., Vol-II: 285
Schmitt, N., Vol-II: 652
Schmitz, J. A., Vol-II: 228
Schmitzer-Torbert, N., Vol-I: 265
Schmoll, F., Vol-II: 362
Schnabel, P., Vol-II: 135, 224
Schneider, B. W., Vol-II: 430
Schneider, E. C., Vol-II: 529, 545
Schneider, H., Vol-II: 553, 629
Schneider, J., Vol-I: 363; Vol-II: 339
Schneider, J. A., Vol-II: 161
Schneider, K. S., Vol-II: 685
Schneider, K. T., Vol-II: 433
Schneider, L. J., Vol-II: 196
Schneider, M., Vol-II: 629

Schneider, S., Vol-II: 290
Schneider, S. L., Vol-II: 648
Schnell, F. I., Vol-II: 579
Schnurr, S., Vol-I: 395
Schober, C., Vol-I: 69
Schofield, M., Vol-II: 484
Schoggen, P., Vol-II: 633
Scholtz, A. W., Vol-I: 245
Schoning, S., Vol-I: 221, 223
Schooler, D. L., Vol-II: 660
Schope, R., Vol-I: 68
Schope, R. D., Vol-I: 565; Vol-II: 340
Schork, M. A., Vol-I: 227
Schrimshaw, E. W., Vol-I: 64; Vol-II: 371
Schröder, H., Vol-II: 619
Schroeder, M., Vol-I: 7, 62
Schruijer, S. G. L., Vol-II: 349
Schteingart, D. E., Vol-I: 227
Schulenberg, J. E., Vol-II: 224, 384
Schuler, R., Vol-I: 544
Schulman, G. I., Vol-II: 339, 341
Schultheiss, O. C., Vol-II: 42–45, 48, 51–58
Schultz, A. M., Vol-II: 578
Schultz, H. K., Vol-II: 165, 168
Schultz, W. W., Vol-I: 483
Schupak-Neuberg, E., Vol-II: 658
Schuster, C. R., Vol-II: 529
Schwabacher, S., Vol-I: 193, 197
Schwartz, J. H., Vol-I: 64, 66, 236
Schwartz, P., Vol-I: 390; Vol-II: 291–292, 298, 363, 412
Schwartz, P. M., Vol-I: 548
Schwarz, N., Vol-II: 648
Schwarzer, R., Vol-II: 619
Schwarzwald, J., Vol-I: 242; Vol-II: 460
Schweingruber, H., Vol-I: 531
Schweinle, W., Vol-II: 329
Schwesinger, G. C., Vol-I: 23
Schwochau, S., Vol-II: 430
Schyns, B., Vol-II: 448
Scott, C. L., Vol-II: 654, 660
Scott, C. R., Vol-II: 327
Scott, J., Vol-II: 156
Scott, K., Vol-II: 620
Scott, K. A., Vol-II: 343, 451
Scott, L., Vol-II: 621
Scott, R. P. J., Vol-I: 11
Scruggs, T. E., Vol-II: 156
Sczesny, S., Vol-I: 8, 411–422; Vol-II: 8, 342, 448–449
Seals, D., Vol-II: 320
Sears, B., Vol-II: 139
Sears, D. O., Vol-I: 185
Sears, R. B., Vol-I: 187
Seashore, H. G., Vol-I: 320
Seccombe, K., Vol-II: 101
Sechler, E. S., Vol-I: 198
Sechzer, J. A., Vol-I: 371
Sedgwick, E. K., Vol-I: 193, 195; Vol-II: 228

Sedlacek, W. E., Vol-II: 228
Seeff, L. C., Vol-II: 544
Seeley, J., Vol-II: 142
Seeley, J. R., Vol-I: 543; Vol-I: 543
Seem, S. R., Vol-II: 104, 192–193
Seeman, T. E., Vol-I: 227; Vol-II: 143
Sefl, T., Vol-II: 624
Segal, D. L., Vol-II: 67, 690
Segal, M., Vol-II: 686–689, 692
Segall, A., Vol-II: 475
Segall, M. H., Vol-I: 164, 166; Vol-II: 311
Segebarth, C., Vol-I: 249
Segrist, D., Vol-I: 195
Segrist, K., Vol-I: 372
Seibert, S. E., Vol-II: 454
Seidlitz, L., Vol-I: 436
Seidman, E., Vol-II: 388–389, 576, 619–620, 633
Seil, D., Vol-II: 116–118, 121
Sekaquaptewa, D., Vol-I: 198; Vol-II: 447
Seligman, M., Vol-II: 232
Seligman, M. E. P., Vol-II: 146
Sell, I., Vol-I: 486
Sellers, A., Vol-I: 138; Vol-II: 522
Sellers, J. G., Vol-I: 222; Vol-II: 20
Sellers, R. M., Vol-I: 496–497
Sells, L. W., Vol-II: 379–380
Selnow, G. W., Vol-I: 392
Selwyn, N., Vol-II: 652
Selwyn, P. A., Vol-II: 534
Semyonov, M., Vol-II: 446
Sen, M. G., Vol-I: 500–501
Senchak, M., Vol-II: 282
Sengelaub, D. R., Vol-I: 323
Senin, I. G., Vol-II: 26
Senko, C., Vol-II: 48
Sensibaugh, C., Vol-II: 283
Sentis, K. P., Vol-II: 158
Sepekoff, B., Vol-I: 66
Seraphine, A. E., Vol-II: 319
Serbin, L. A., Vol-I: 500–501, 511, 514, 531
Serdula, M. K., Vol-I: 467; Vol-II: 153, 473
Serewicz, M. C. M., Vol-II: 290–291
Sergi, I., Vol-I: 321
Serrano-Garcia, I., Vol-II: 613, 627
Sershen, H., Vol-I: 365
Seto, M. C., Vol-I: 367; Vol-II: 285
Settle, A. G., Vol-II: 226
Settle, R. G., Vol-I: 248
Sever, L. M., Vol-II: 371
Seward, G. H., Vol-I: 25–26, 204
Sexton, T. L., Vol-II: 269
Sexton, V. S., Vol-I: 20
Seyfried, S., Vol-II: 622
Seymour, J. D., Vol-II: 473
Seymour-Smith, S., Vol-II: 475
Shabsigh, R., Vol-I: 568
Shackelford, S., Vol-II: 285–286

Shackelford, T. K., Vol-II: 343, 346–347, 350
Shadish, W. R., Vol-I: 81, 82–83, 89, 96
Shaefer, C., Vol-I: 146
Shafer, M. E., Vol-II: 31
Shaffer, D., Vol-I: 68
Shaffer, D. R., Vol-II: 576
Shaffer, M. A., Vol-II: 502, 504, 509
Shah, P., Vol-I: 202
Shanahan, M. J., Vol-I: 559, 574
Shanklin, E., Vol-I: 160
Shannon, C. A., Vol-II: 436
Shapiro, J. R., Vol-I: 85
Shapiro, M. F., Vol-II: 534
Shapiro, R. J., Vol-I: 346
Shapiro, R., Vol-II: 134
Shapka, J. D., Vol-II: 32
Sharma, D., Vol-I: 349
Sharma, G. K., Vol-II: 482
Sharma, V. P., Vol-I: 347, 354
Sharpe, L. T., Vol-I: 237
Sharpe, M. J., Vol-II: 24
Sharpe, S., Vol-II: 282
Sharps, M. J., Vol-I: 327
Shaul, M. P., Vol-II: 546
Shauman, K. A., Vol-I: 304, 308
Shavelson, R. J., Vol-II: 31
Shaver, P., Vol-II: 282, 294
Shaver, P. R., Vol-II: 281, 297
Shaw, H., Vol-I: 86
Shaw, H. E., Vol-II: 658
Shaw, L. H., Vol-II: 652
Shaw, M., Vol-II: 205
Shaw, S. M., Vol-II: 473, 478
Shea, D. L., Vol-I: 317
Shea, M. T., Vol-II: 195
Sheehe, P. R., Vol-I: 248
Sheffield, C. J., Vol-I: 91
Shefte, S., Vol-II: 453
Sheikh, C., Vol-I: 386
Sheinberg, M., Vol-II: 255
Sheldon, J. P., Vol-I: 194
Sheldon, K. M., Vol-II: 29, 45
Shellenbarger, S., Vol-II: 170
Shelton, B., Vol-II: 405, 407, 409–412
Shen, X., Vol-I: 238
Shen, Y.-C., Vol-II: 414
Shepard, D., Vol-II: 235
Shepard, D. S., Vol-II: 224–226, 236–237
Shepard, R. N., Vol-I: 221, 238, 318
Shepherd, M., Vol-II: 633
Sherer, M., Vol-II: 525, 548
Sheridan, P. M., Vol-II: 117
Sherif, C. W., Vol-I: 29, 108, 401; Vol-II: 341
Sherman, E. M. S., Vol-II: 605
Sherman, J. A., Vol-I: 27, 317
Sherman, J. J., Vol-I: 241
Sherman, J. W., Vol-II: 167

Sherman, S. J., Vol-I: 517
Sherr, L., Vol-II: 473
Sherrod, N., Vol-II: 229, 241
Sherrod, N. B., Vol-I: 49, 51
Sherry, D. F., Vol-I: 266
Sherry, J. L., Vol-II: 650–651, 657
Sherwin, B., Vol-I: 458
Sherwood, A., Vol-I: 436
Sherwood, D., Vol-II: 579
Sheu, H. B., Vol-II: 228
Shide, D. J., Vol-I: 457
Shidlo, A., Vol-I: 62, 69
Shields, C. G., Vol-II: 255
Shields, S. A., Vol-I: 22–23, 81, 200, 363, 381, 433, 436, 444; Vol-II: 443
Shiffman, K. S., Vol-II: 167, 647–648
Shiffman, S., Vol-I: 439; Vol-II: 454
Shih, M., Vol-I: 11, 284, 353, 433
Shih, P. C., Vol-I: 322
Shikany, J. M., Vol-II: 543
Shildrick, M., Vol-I: 31
Shilts, R., Vol-II: 453
Shimada, K., Vol-I: 245
Shin, J. K., Vol-II: 228
Shinn, M., Vol-II: 628, 633
Shinsako, S. A., Vol-II: 436
Shipman, K., Vol-I: 434
Shirley, L., Vol-I: 496
Shiverick, S. M., Vol-I: 506
Shkolnikov, V. M., Vol-II: 472
Shoda, Y., Vol-I: 65, 67
Shoham, V., Vol-II: 266
Sholl, M. J., Vol-I: 329
Shope, J. T., Vol-II: 476
Shore, L. M., Vol-II: 350
Short, S., Vol-II: 478
Shorter-Gooden, K., Vol-I: 512
Showers, C. J., Vol-I: 299; Vol-II: 30
Shrader, C. B., Vol-II: 351, 456
Shrestha, A. B., Vol-I: 326
Shroff, H., Vol-II: 154
Shroff, K., Vol-II: 164
Shryne, J. E., Vol-I: 483
Shugarman, L. R., Vol-II: 529
Shukla, J. P., Vol-I: 347, 354
Shullman, S. L., Vol-II: 424
Shulman, S. R., Vol-II: 204
Shultz, S. R., Vol-I: 221, 323
Shweder, R. A., Vol-I: 163
Siahpush, M., Vol-II: 479
Siann, G., Vol-II: 382, 391
Sibley, C. G., Vol-II: 362
Sidanius, J., Vol-I: 198; Vol-II: 362
Siebert, E. R., Vol-I: 220
Siefert, K., Vol-I: 570
Siegel, A. W., Vol-I: 329
Siegel, J. M., Vol-I: 544

Siegel, K., Vol-II: 371
Siegel, L. J., Vol-II: 136, 140
Siever, M. D., Vol-II: 172
Sigerson, K., Vol-II: 342–343
Sigle-Rushton, W., Vol-II: 297
Sigmon, S. T., Vol-II: 77
Sigmundson, H. K., Vol-I: 194
Sigmundson, K., Vol-II: 366
Signorella, M. L. 312, 385; Vol-I: 327, 500–502, 508, 514–516
Signorielli, N., Vol-II: 167, 644–647
Siladi, M., Vol-I: 508
Silakowski, T. D., Vol-I: 392
Silberman, E. K., Vol-II: 195
Silberstein, L., Vol-II: 168
Silberstein, L. R., Vol-II: 156
Silk, J., Vol-I: 536
Silva, P., Vol-I: 543
Silva, P. A., Vol-I: 548
Silver, C., Vol-I: 123
Silver, C. B., Vol-I: 567, 570
Silver, W. L., Vol-I: 246
Silverman, B. E., Vol-I: 438
Silverman, I., Vol-I: 221–222, 263, 265, 318, 438, 514
Silverstein, L. B., Vol-II: 10, 253–273
Silverstein, L. R., Vol-II: 166
Silverstein, L. S., Vol-II: 223–233
Silverstein, O., Vol-II: 255
Silverstein, S., Vol-II: 449
Silverthorn, P., Vol-I: 547
Silvestri, M., Vol-II: 453, 457
Simantov, E., Vol-II: 228
Simcock, G., Vol-I: 509
Simi, N. L., Vol-II: 203, 212
Siminerio, L., Vol-II: 550
Simkins, B. J., Vol-II: 351, 456
Simkins-Bullock, J., Vol-I: 381
Simmons, D., Vol-II: 95
Simmons, R. G., Vol-II: 389
Simner, J., Vol-I: 204
Simon, A., Vol-II: 650
Simon, R. V., Vol-II: 137
Simon, R. W., Vol-I: 302, 434–435, 540
Simon, T., Vol-II: 620
Simon, W., Vol-II: 289
Simone, D. H., Vol-II: 203
Simonelli, C. J., Vol-II: 318
Simonoska, R., Vol-I: 244
Simons, R. L., Vol-I: 544; Vol-II: 139
Simonton, D. K., Vol-I: 345–347
Simon-Tuval, T., Vol-II: 524
Simpson, J. A., Vol-II: 286, 293
Simpson, P. A., Vol-I: 433, 435
Simpson, R., Vol-I: 572
Simpson, W. G., Vol-II: 351, 456
Sinclair, S., Vol-I: 497; Vol-II: 77
Sinding, C., Vol-I: 108

Author Index

Sing, R., Vol-II: 576–577
Singer, B. H., Vol-I: 227
Singh, A. A., Vol-II: 205
Singh, D., Vol-I: 226
Singh, J., Vol-I: 172, 226
Singh, V., Vol-II: 456
Singleton, E., Vol-II: 242
Singleton, S. B., Vol-I: 91
Sinha, D., Vol-I: 166
Sirarenios, G., Vol-I: 220
Sirin, S. R., Vol-II: 340
Sirkin, M., Vol-I: 52
Sjölund, B., Vol-I: 241
Sjomeling, M., Vol-II: 661
Sjöqvist, F., Vol-II: 474
Skay, C. L., Vol-II: 203
Skeen, P., Vol-I: 68
Skelton, R. W., Vol-I: 328
Skidmore, J. R., Vol-I: 51–52, 145
Sklarsky, K. G., Vol-II: 521
Skodol, J. B., Vol-II: 103
Skogstad, A., Vol-II: 424, 429
Skouteris, H., Vol-II: 173
Skowronski, J. J., Vol-I: 497
Skrypnek, B. J., Vol-II: 69
Skrzypiec, G., Vol-I: 463
Skultety, K. M., Vol-I: 563, 571
Slabbekoorn, D., Vol-I: 222–225, 270, 324
Slaby, R. G., Vol-I: 496, 511
Slade, D., Vol-I: 396
Slap, G. B., Vol-II: 230
Slapion-Foote, M. J., Vol-II: 432
Slater, A., Vol-II: 156, 166, 168
Slater, A. M., Vol-I: 504
Slaytor, E., Vol-II: 485
Sledge, W. H., Vol-II: 272
Slevin, K. F., Vol-I: 108
Sloane, P. D., Vol-II: 523
Sloman, S. A., Vol-I: 199
Slone, M., Vol-I: 512
Slonje, R., Vol-II: 320
Slykhuis, D., Vol-I: 330
Small, D., Vol-I: 247, 384
Small, D. M., Vol-I: 247
Smalley, K. B., Vol-I: 138
Smalley, R., Vol-II: 24
Smart, R., Vol-II: 235
Smeets, P. A., Vol-I: 247
Smetana, J. G., Vol-I: 511; Vol-II: 340
Smiler, A. P., Vol-I: 6, 43, 53, 133–152; Vol-II: 6, 225
Smircich, L., Vol-II: 452
Smit, E., Vol-II: 567
Smith, A. G., Vol-II: 42
Smith, B. L., Vol-II: 541
Smith, C. A., Vol-I: 361–374; Vol-II: 8, 325
Smith, C. P., Vol-II: 43
Smith, C., Vol-I: 8, 20, 413; Vol-II: 330

Smith, D. A., Vol-II: 551
Smith, D. A. F., Vol-II: 496, 499–501
Smith, D. W. E., Vol-II: 482
Smith, D., Vol-I: 103, 105, 115; Vol-II: 620
Smith, E., Vol-I: 443
Smith, G. S., Vol-II: 482
Smith, J. L., Vol-I: 418, 438, 496, 512
Smith, J., Vol-I: 109, 559, 569–570; Vol-II: 123
Smith, L. D., Vol-I: 202
Smith, L. K., Vol-I: 220
Smith, M. D., Vol-I: 393; Vol-II: 434
Smith, M., Vol-I: 248
Smith, M. E., Vol-I: 238, 463
Smith, P., Vol-II: 272
Smith, P. H., Vol-II: 485
Smith, P. K., Vol-I: 418, 438; Vol-II: 320
Smith, R. A., Vol-II: 444
Smith, R. L., Vol-I: 147
Smith, R. M., Vol-I: 321
Smith, S., Vol-II: 166
Smith, T. E., Vol-I: 531, 536, 538
Smith, Y. S., Vol-II: 367
Smithies, C., Vol-I: 107, 111
Smith-Lovin, L., Vol-I: 390; Vol-II: 281, 283
Smith-Rosenberg, C., Vol-I: 20
Smithson, I., Vol-I: 285
Smolak, L., Vol-I: 6, 81–98; Vol-II: 6, 156, 164–165, 168, 170–171, 174
Smolen, J. S., Vol-II: 545
Smollar, J., Vol-II: 282
Snarey, J., Vol-I: 564
Sneed, J. R., Vol-I: 566
Snelbecker, G. E., Vol-I: 351
Snell, A. F., Vol-I: 136
Snell, W. E., Vol-I: 52; Vol-II: 550
Snihur, A. W. K., Vol-I: 221, 226
Snodgrass, S. E., Vol-II: 282
Snow, C. E., Vol-I: 307
Snowden, L., Vol-II: 622–623
Snyder, D. K., Vol-II: 210
Snyder, E., Vol-I: 140; Vol-II: 571
Snyder, H. N., Vol-I: 547
Snyder, K., Vol-II: 460
Snyder, L., Vol-II: 662
Snyder, M., Vol-II: 69
Snyder, P. J., Vol-I: 330
Socarides, C. W., Vol-I: 50
Socarides, C., Vol-I: 61
Soderstrom, C., Vol-II: 483
Soeters, J., Vol-II: 673, 676, 689
Sofaer, S., Vol-II: 544
Solberg, V. S., Vol-II: 228
Solimeo, S., Vol-II: 549
Sollie, D. L., Vol-II: 296
Solomon, B., Vol-II: 282
Solomon, C. R., Vol-II: 410
Solomon, L., Vol-I: 456

Solomon, M. R., Vol-II: 166
Solomon, N. G., Vol-I: 269
Solomon, S. E., Vol-II: 411
Solomon, S. G., Vol-I: 237
Somers, C. L., Vol-II: 165
Sommer, K. L., Vol-I: 499; Vol-II: 324
Sommers, C. H., Vol-I: 278, 286
Son, L., Vol-I: 61, 140, 144, 564
Sonenstein, F. L., Vol-I: 52, 137; Vol-II: 299
Song, J., Vol-II: 326
Sonnenberg, C. M., Vol-II: 296–297
Sontag, L. M., Vol-I: 543
SooHoo, S., Vol-II: 575
Sorby, S. A., Vol-I: 332
Sorter, R. G., Vol-II: 164
Soskolne, V., Vol-II: 525, 548
Soto, C. J., Vol-I: 570
South, S. J., Vol-II: 284, 405, 409–410
Southam, A. M., Vol-I: 483
Southworth, A., Vol-II: 370
Spacks, P., Vol-I: 399
Spain, R. D., Vol-II: 460
Spalding, L. R., Vol-II: 363–364, 411
Spangler, W., Vol-II: 44–45, 48
Spanswick, S. C., Vol-I: 226
Sparks, G. G., Vol-II: 657
Spasojevic, J., Vol-II: 144
Spataro, S. E., Vol-II: 340
Spaulding, L. R., Vol-I: 66
Speakmon, G., Vol-II: 155
Spears, B., Vol-II: 565
Spears, R., Vol-II: 348
Spector, P. E., Vol-I: 433; Vol-II: 436
Spector-Mercel, G., Vol-I: 117
Speed, H., Vol-II: 647
Speer, P., Vol-II: 616
Speer, P. W., Vol-II: 635
Spees, J. M. G., Vol-II: 648
Spelke, E. S., Vol-I: 220, 304, 306, 309
Spence, I., Vol-I: 307, 328; Vol-II: 70, 651
Spence, J. T., Vol-I: 14, 47, 50, 52, 134–136, 144, 146–147, 150–152, 192, 307, 460, 515; Vol-II: 14–15, 22–23, 295, 549, 569
Spencer, M. B., Vol-I: 516
Spencer, R., Vol-I: 113
Spencer, S. J., Vol-I: 85, 306; Vol-II: 450, 660
Spender, D., Vol-I: 195, 388; Vol-II: 383, 385
Sperry, S., Vol-II: 163, 166
Spetch, M. L., Vol-I: 329
Speziale, B., Vol-II: 258
Spicer, R. S., Vol-I: 482
Spidel, A., Vol-II: 604
Spitzberg, B. H., Vol-II: 283
Spitze, G., Vol-II: 405, 409–410
Spitzer, B. L., Vol-I: 90; Vol-II: 167
Spitzer, M., Vol-I: 330
Spitzer, R. L., Vol-II: 73, 103, 112

Sprague, J., Vol-I: 123
Sprangers, M., Vol-II: 545
Sprecher, S., Vol-I: 481; Vol-II: 289, 297, 299–300, 327
Spreen, O., Vol-II: 605
Spritzer, K., Vol-II: 552
Spritzer, M. D., Vol-I: 269
Spruijt-Metz, D., Vol-I: 460
Srull, T. K., Vol-I: 196
St. John, S. C., Vol-II: 365
St. Lawrence, J., Vol-II: 473, 626
Stacey, J., Vol-I: 107
Stack, L., Vol-II: 623
Stafford, J., Vol-II: 436
Stafford, L., Vol-II: 293, 296
Stage, F. K., Vol-II: 47, 390
Stainton-Rogers, W., Vol-I: 122
Stake, J. E., Vol-II: 9, 19–36
Stake, R. E., Vol-I: 9, 112
Staley, C. M., Vol-I: 392
Staller, K. M., Vol-I: 106
Stallworth, L. M., Vol-II: 362
Stam, H. J., Vol-I: 117
Standley, T. C., Vol-II: 645
Stanford, K., Vol-I: 282, 301–302
Stangor, C., Vol-I: 1, 495, 503, 510; Vol-II: 1
Stanley, J. C., Vol-I: 165, 304
Stanton, A. L., Vol-II: 434, 543, 546–547
Stanton, G. C., Vol-II: 31
Stanton, S. J., Vol-II: 52
Stapleton, J. T., Vol-II: 553
Stapleton, K., Vol-I: 392
Stapp, J., Vol-I: 14, 47, 135, 146, 192, 515; Vol-II: 14, 22, 295
Star, S. L., Vol-II: 112
Starek, J., Vol-II: 568
Stark, R., Vol-I: 443
Starkes, J. L., Vol-I: 322
Starkman, M. N., Vol-I: 227
Starks, R., Vol-I: 386
Starr, A., Vol-I: 249
Starr, J. M., Vol-I: 302
Staten, J. L., Vol-II: 528
Statham, A., Vol-I: 285
Stattin, H., Vol-I: 543
Staudinger, U. M., Vol-I: 567
Stayner, D. A., Vol-II: 272
Steadman, L., Vol-II: 173
Stechuchak, K. M., Vol-II: 519
Steeds, R. P., Vol-I: 242
Steel, P., Vol-II: 436
Steele, C., Vol-I: 194
Steele, C. M., Vol-I: 84–85, 284–285, 327, 353, 430, 569; Vol-II: 48, 66, 141, 387, 450, 660–661
Steele, J., Vol-II: 66
Steer, R. A., Vol-II: 70, 214
Steffen, V. J., Vol-I: 421; Vol-II: 313, 674
Steffens, M. C., Vol-II: 363, 369

Stefic, E. C., Vol-II: 324
Stein, J. A., Vol-II: 24
Stein, R. I., Vol-II: 658
Stein, R. T., Vol-II: 339
Stein, T. S., Vol-II: 103
Steinberg, A., Vol-II: 155
Steinberg, L., Vol-I: 536–537, 549; Vol-II: 76
Steinberg, M. B., Vol-II: 478
Steindl, R., Vol-I: 245
Steiner-Pappalardo, N. L., Vol-II: 296
Steinmetz, S. K., Vol-II: 318
Stelzner, S. P., Vol-II: 633
Stenberg, A. E., Vol-I: 244
Stephens, C., Vol-II: 486–487
Stephenson, N., Vol-I: 115
Stepper, S., Vol-I: 446
Stericker, A., Vol-I: 363
Sterling, B., Vol-I: 383
Sterling, B. S., Vol-II: 340
Stermer, S. P., Vol-I: 97
Stern, A., Vol-II: 340
Stern, E., Vol-I: 171
Stern, K., Vol-I: 248
Stern, R. L., Vol-II: 545
Stern, R. M., Vol-I: 245
Stern, S. R., Vol-II: 644, 646, 648–649
Sternberg, M. R., Vol-II: 533
Sternberg, R. J., Vol-I: 413, 417; Vol-II: 72, 168
Stets, J. E., Vol-I: 436
Stevens, D., Vol-II: 415
Stevens, D. P., Vol-II: 415
Stevens, J., Vol-II: 160
Stevens, K., Vol-I: 278–281, 287–288
Stevens, M. A., Vol-I: 45; Vol-II: 10, 221–243
Stevens-Miller, M., Vol-II: 367
Stevenson, H. W., Vol-I: 307
Stevenson, M. R., Vol-I: 195, 531; Vol-II: 631
Stewart, A. J., Vol-I: 9, 20, 36, 193, 429, 447, 559–575; Vol-II: 9, 42, 45–46, 49, 53–54, 58
Stewart, A., Vol-I: 103, 110
Stewart, D., Vol-I: 392; Vol-II: 346
Stewart, J. H., Vol-II: 528
Stewart, L., Vol-I: 281
Stibal, J., Vol-II: 430
Stice, E., Vol-I: 86, 544; Vol-II: 155, 658
Stickle, T. R., Vol-II: 266
Stier, D., Vol-II: 51
Stiles-Shipley, J., Vol-II: 574
Still, L., Vol-II: 505
Stiner, M. C., Vol-I: 267
Stinson, F. S., Vol-II: 133
Stiver, I., Vol-I: 105
Stiver, I. P., Vol-II: 192, 208, 214
Stock, S. A. K., Vol-II: 543
Stockard, J., Vol-II: 24, 30
Stockdale, M. S., Vol-II: 284, 430, 434, 436, 457
Stockman, A., Vol-I: 237

Stockton, M., Vol-I: 479
Stogdill, R. M., Vol-II: 678
Stollenwerk, B., Vol-II: 543
Stoller, R. J., Vol-I: 50; Vol-II: 117–118
Stone, J., Vol-I: 105, 353; Vol-II: 647, 661
Stone, K. J., Vol-II: 520
Stonecypher, J. F., Vol-II: 188, 193
Stoner, S. A., Vol-I: 92–93
St-Onge, R., Vol-I: 240, 320
Stoppard, J., Vol-I: 96
Stoppard, J. M., Vol-II: 69, 96
Stormer, S., Vol-II: 159
Stormshak, E. A., Vol-II: 24, 27
Story, M., Vol-II: 156
Stoverinck, M. J., Vol-II: 474
Strack, F., Vol-I: 240, 320
Strassberg, D. S., Vol-I: 72
Straub, R. O., Vol-I: 459–460
Straube, T., Vol-I: 243
Straus, M. A., Vol-II: 210
Strauss, A. L., Vol-I: 111
Strauss, E., Vol-II: 605
Strauss, J., Vol-I: 432; Vol-II: 176
Strayer, F. F., Vol-I: 511
Street, A. E., Vol-II: 436
Street, R. L. Jr., Vol-II: 522
Strelan, P., Vol-II: 172
Stricker, G., Vol-II: 221
Strickland, B. R., Vol-II: 97
Strickland, G., Vol-I: 68
Striegel-Moore, R., Vol-I: 246; Vol-II: 168
Striegel-Moore, R. H., Vol-II: 156, 171, 473
Striepe, M. I., Vol-II: 206, 284
Strobel, M. G., Vol-I: 350
Stroh, L. K., Vol-I: 433, 435; Vol-II: 452
Stronegger, W. J., Vol-II: 473
Strong, R. A., Vol-I: 328, 331
Stroop, J. R., Vol-I: 237–238
Strough, J., Vol-I: 539
Strouse, G. A., Vol-II: 651
Strube, M. J., Vol-II: 160
Struening, E. L., Vol-II: 145
Strul, S., Vol-II: 26–27
Strycker, L., Vol-II: 622
Stryker, S., Vol-II: 33
Stuart, A., Vol-I: 243, 363
Stuart, V., Vol-II: 242
Stuart-Smith, S., Vol-I: 363
Stubbe, M., Vol-I: 395
Stubbs, A. D., Vol-I: 202
Stubbs, M. L., Vol-I: 544
Stuck, B. A., Vol-I: 249
Stucky, B. D., Vol-I: 546
Stueve, A., Vol-II: 620
Stuhlmacher, A. F., Vol-I: 96
Stull, D. E., Vol-II: 295
Stumpf, H., Vol-I: 318–319

Stunkard, A. J., Vol-I: 457
Sturla, E., Vol-I: 529
Sturman, T. S., Vol-II: 43
Stürzebecher, E., Vol-I: 243
Styne, D. M., Vol-I: 534
Su, J., Vol-II: 473
Suarez-Orozco, C., Vol-II: 160
Suarez-Orozco, M. M., Vol-II: 160
Subotnik, R., Vol-I: 350–351
Subramaniam, P. R., Vol-II: 228
Subramanian, S. V., Vol-I: 179
Suchindran, C., Vol-I: 534; Vol-I: 534
Sue, D., Vol-II: 223, 227
Sue, D. S., Vol-II: 223
Sue, D. W., Vol-II: 231, 265, 268, 566
Sue, S., Vol-II: 554
Sugarman, D. B., Vol-II: 316
Sugimura, K., Vol-I: 574
Sugrue, P. A., Vol-II: 154
Suguru, S., Vol-II: 289
Suh, E. J., Vol-II: 21
Suitor, J., Vol-II: 413
Suizzo, M. A., Vol-II: 294, 198; Vol-I: 138
Sulak, P., Vol-I: 241
Sullivan, E., Vol-II: 449
Sullivan, G., Vol-II: 171
Sullivan, H. S., Vol-I: 560
Sullivan, J. G., Vol-II: 133
Sullivan, K., Vol-I: 317
Sullivan, M., Vol-II: 411
Sullivan, M. A., Vol-I: 163
Sullivan, O., Vol-II: 404–405, 408–409, 416
Sullivan, Q., Vol-I: 481
Sullivan, S., Vol-I: 65
Summerfield, A. B., Vol-I: 435
Summers, A., Vol-II: 645, 647
Sunday, S., Vol-I: 36
Supple, A. J., Vol-II: 602
Susman, E. J., Vol-I: 534, 543
Susskind, J. E., Vol-I: 517
Sussner, B. D., Vol-I: 159
Sutfin, E., Vol-II: 411
Sutherland, D., Vol-II: 477
Sutherland, R. J., Vol-I: 221, 226, 264, 328
Sutton, S. K., Vol-I: 236, 242, 351
Sutton-Smith, B., Vol-I: 236
Suyemoto, K. L., Vol-II: 68
Suzuki, K., Vol-I: 246
Svanstrom, L., Vol-II: 483
Swaab, D., Vol-II: 116
Swaab, D. F., Vol-I: 218, 224–225; Vol-II: 116
Swami, V., Vol-II: 160
Swaminathan, H., Vol-II: 67, 76, 81–82
Swan, S., Vol-II: 424, 433, 685
Swanberg, J. E., Vol-II: 402
Swann, J., Vol-I: 388
Swann, S., Vol-II: 367–368

Swann, W. B., Vol-II: 31
Swann, W. B. Jr., Vol-II: 456
Swanson, C., Vol-I: 437
Swanson, C. L., Vol-I: 437
Swanson, J., Vol-II: 102
Swarr, A., Vol-I: 539
Swartz, M., Vol-II: 134
Swearer, S. M., Vol-I: 538
Sweeney, D., Vol-II: 659
Sweet, S., Vol-I: 570
Sweeting, H., Vol-II: 475, 480
Swift, C., Vol-II: 613–614, 618, 628–629
Swim, J., Vol-I: 393
Swim, J. K., Vol-I: 144, 147–148, 151–152, 393; Vol-II: 170, 457
Swinburn, B. A., Vol-II: 160
Swiss, D. J., Vol-II: 453
Swody, C. A., Vol-II: 428
Sworowski, L. A., Vol-II: 546
Symons, D., Vol-II: 285
Syngal, S., Vol-II: 529
Szalacha, L., Vol-I: 290
Szasz, T., Vol-II: 125
Szecsenyi, J., Vol-II: 519
Szinovacz, M., Vol-II: 410
Szkrybalo, J., Vol-I: 495–496
Szymanski, D. M., Vol-I: 94; Vol-II: 205, 509

T
Tabachnick, B., Vol-I: 88
Tabar, L., Vol-I: 526
Taft, A. J., Vol-II: 484
Tagaris, G. A., Vol-I: 239
Tager, D., Vol-I: 53; Vol-II: 225
Tajfel, H., Vol-I: 496, 513; Vol-II: 348
Takahashi, H., Vol-I: 243, 245
Takahashi, M., Vol-I: 567
Takeuchi, S., Vol-I: 246, 432
Talbani, A., Vol-II: 288
Tamis-LeMonda, C. S., Vol-I: 496, 500, 505; Vol-II: 225
Tamkins, M. M., Vol-II: 346, 450
Tamres, L. K., Vol-II: 433
Tan, E. S. N., Vol-I: 62
Tan, U., Vol-I: 324
Tang, C. S., Vol-II: 320
Tang, C. S-K., Vol-I: 145–146
Tang, T. N., Vol-II: 301
Tanghe, A., Vol-I: 497
Tanidjojo, L., Vol-II: 646
Tanke, E. D., Vol-II: 69
Tannen, D., Vol-I: 379, 385–386, 388–391, 393–395, 398; Vol-II: 253
Tanner, J. L., Vol-II: 384
Tanner, L., Vol-II: 672, 676–677, 687
Tanner, L. M., Vol-II: 673, 676, 686–688
Tanner-Smith, E. E., Vol-II: 647

Tantleff, S., Vol-II: 159
Tantleff-Dunn, S., Vol-II: 153, 166–167, 658
Taps, J., Vol-II: 540–541
Taraban, C., Vol-II: 295
Tarasiuk, A., Vol-II: 524
Tarmina, M. S., Vol-II: 486
Tartre, L. A., Vol-II: 386
Tarule, J. M., Vol-I: 32, 105, 198
Tashiro, T., Vol-II: 297
Tasker, F., Vol-I: 67
Tasker, R., Vol-I: 224
Tassinary, L. G., Vol-I: 434
Tata, S. P., Vol-II: 228
Tatla, S., Vol-II: 288
Tatum, C., Vol-II: 532–533
Tatum, C. M., Vol-I: 184
Tauna, N., Vol-II: 169
Tavris, C., Vol-I: 403; Vol-II: 117
Taylor, A., Vol-I: 318
Taylor, B., Vol-I: 535–536
Taylor, D., Vol-II: 98
Taylor, D. G., Vol-I: 239, 266.
Taylor, D. L., Vol-II: 68, 98
Taylor, K., Vol-II: 501
Taylor, L., Vol-I: 187, 506; Vol-II: 368
Taylor, L. D., Vol-II: 167, 658
Taylor, M. G., Vol-I: 506, 544
Taylor, R., Vol-II: 485
Taylor, S., Vol-II: 314, 546
Taylor, S. E., Vol-II: 30, 70, 141, 143, 434, 498, 503–505, 507, 553
Taylor, T., Vol-II: 121, 125
Taylor, V., Vol-I: 107, 110, 118, 195
Tedeschi, J. T., Vol-II: 435
Tedeschi, R. G., Vol-II: 279
Tegano, D. W., Vol-I: 350
Teh, K., Vol-II: 115
Teillon, S. M., Vol-I: 227
Tellegen, A., Vol-I: 14, 135; Vol-II: 15, 70, 79–81
Templin, T., Vol-II: 551
ten Have, M., Vol-II: 369
Tenenbaum, G., Vol-II: 579
Tenenbaum, H. R., Vol-I: 307
Tennant, C., Vol-II: 502
Tennen, H., Vol-II: 434, 511, 546
Teo, T., Vol-I: 30, 34
Tepper, B. J., Vol-I: 242, 457; Vol-II: 346
Terenzini, P. T., Vol-I: 285
Terenzio, M., Vol-II: 614
Terlecki, M., Vol-I: 332
Terlecki, M. S., Vol-I: 271, 326
Terman, L. M., Vol-I: 134, 192, 204, 365
Terndrup, A. I., Vol-I: 64
Terracciano, A., Vol-I: 166, 442
Terracciano, A. Jr., Vol-II: 25, 447
Tessema, M. T., Vol-II: 677

Tetenbaum, T. J., Vol-I: 135, 192
Tetlock, P. E., Vol-I: 200
Tewksbury, R., Vol-II: 111
Thayer, J. F., Vol-I: 200
Thayer, S. E., Vol-II: 652
Theis, K. A., Vol-II: 542
Thelan, M. H., Vol-II: 165
Thelwall, M., Vol-I: 391
Theodore, P. S., Vol-II: 360–361
Thijs, J., Vol-I: 498, 516
Thill, K. P., Vol-II: 649
Thinus-Blanc, C., Vol-I: 330
Thissen, D., Vol-II: 76, 82
Thoennes, N., Vol-II: 631
Thoits, P. A., Vol-I: 496; Vol-II: 504
Thomas, D. A., Vol-II: 295–296, 554
Thomas, G., Vol-II: 21, 293, 325
Thomas, H., Vol-I: 320
Thomas, K., Vol-II: 165
Thomas, M. D., Vol-II: 675
Thomas, P. J., Vol-II: 675
Thomas, V., Vol-II: 686
Thomas-Hunt, M. C., Vol-II: 344, 349
Thompson, A., Vol-II: 289
Thompson, B. J., Vol-II: 203
Thompson, D. E., Vol-II: 455, 457
Thompson, E. H. Vol-I: 47, 52–53, 134, 136, 146, 150; Vol-II: 281–282, 294, 297
Thompson, H. B., Vol-I: 22
Thompson, J. K., Vol-I: 10, 20, 54, 88; Vol-II: 10, 153–174, 568
Thompson, J., Vol-II: 156
Thompson, L., Vol-II: 405, 407, 410
Thompson, M. M., Vol-II: 688
Thompson, N. L., Vol-I: 117
Thompson, S., Vol-II: 574
Thompson, S. K., Vol-I: 140, 504
Thompson, W. L., Vol-I: 22–23, 328
Thomsen, T., Vol-I: 239, 324
Thomson, D. A., Vol-II: 226
Thomson, E., Vol-II: 410, 412
Thomson, R., Vol-II: 282
Thorndike, R. M., Vol-I: 172
Thorne, B., Vol-I: 381, 401
Thornhill, R., Vol-I: 91, 191, 268; Vol-II: 285–286
Thornton, A. R., Vol-I: 243
Thornton, M., Vol-II: 288
Thorpe, G., Vol-I: 302
Thrash, T. M., Vol-II: 44, 48
Thunberg, M., Vol-I: 434
Thurau, D., Vol-I: 485
Thurstone, T. G., Vol-I: 318
Tichenor, V., Vol-II: 409
Tickle, J. J., Vol-I: 412
Tiedemann, J., Vol-I: 306
Tiedens, L. Z., Vol-II: 432

Tiefer, L., Vol-I: 27; Vol-II: 112
Tielsch, J. M., Vol-II: 483
Tiggemann, M., Vol-I: 91, 98; Vol-II: 155–157, 159, 161, 165–166, 168, 171–173, 477, 573, 659
Tillmann-Healy, L., Vol-I: 107
Tillmann-Healy, L. M., Vol-I: 119
Timberlake, S., Vol-II: 454, 458
Timlin-Scalera, R. M., Vol-II: 228
Timm, A., Vol-I: 187
Timm, R., Vol-II: 195
Timmerman, G., Vol-II: 425, 428
Timmers, M., Vol-I: 430, 434, 440
Tishelman, C., Vol-II: 545
Tither, J. M., Vol-II: 284
Tjaden, P., Vol-II: 631
Tjosvold, D., Vol-II: 338
Tlauka, M., Vol-I: 329, 330
Tobach, E., Vol-I: 36
Tobin, P., Vol-I: 318
Tobin, R. M., Vol-I: 434, 441, 445
Tobin-Richards, M. H., Vol-I: 535
Todd, Z., Vol-I: 374
Tokar, D. M., Vol-I: 136
Tolkien, J. R. R., Vol-I: 191
Toll, B. A., Vol-II: 477
Tolman, D., Vol-I: 105, 113
Tolman, D. L., Vol-I: 15, 137–138, 150; Vol-II: 15, 117, 284, 287, 290, 298–299
Tomczak, R., Vol-I: 330
Tomich, P. L., Vol-II: 547
Toner, B. B., Vol-II: 95, 213
Tong, S. T., Vol-II: 653
Tooby, J., Vol-I: 261, 267
Toohey, S., Vol-II: 633
Tooke, W., Vol-II: 285
Torgerson, D., Vol-II: 115
Torges, C. M., Vol-I: 573
Torgrud, L., Vol-II: 162
Toro, P., Vol-II: 289, 300, 412, 620
Toro-Morn, M., Vol-II: 289, 300, 412
Torrance, E. P., Vol-I: 346, 349–350
Torrance, H., Vol-I: 121
Torre, M. E., Vol-I: 108
Torres, S., Vol-II: 204, 627
Torres-Burgos, N., Vol-II: 627
Toth, E., Vol-I: 396; Vol-II: 169
Tottenham, L. S., Vol-I: 221
Tourish, D., Vol-II: 282
Touyz, S. W., Vol-II: 165
Tovar-Blank, Z. G., Vol-II: 226
Tovée, M. J., Vol-II: 160
Towle, E., Vol-I: 317
Townsend, A. L., Vol-II: 195
Townsend, D. W., Vol-I: 242
Townsend, N. W., Vol-II: 402
Toyokawa, T., Vol-II: 623

Tracey, T. J., Vol-II: 197, 212, 226
Tracy, A. J., Vol-I: 138; Vol-II: 117
Trager, K. D., Vol-II: 650
Trautner, H., Vol-I: 501
Trautner, H. M., Vol-I: 501, 503, 517
Travis, C. B., Vol-II: 11, 13, 81, 517–534
Trawalter, S., Vol-II: 661
Treasure, J., Vol-I: 247, 464
Treichler, P., Vol-I: 385
Treloar, C., Vol-II: 160
Tremblay, A., Vol-I: 457
Tremblay, L., Vol-I: 322
Tremblay, P., Vol-II: 645
Tremblay, S., Vol-I: 319
Trepanier, M. L., Vol-II: 287
Tresemer, D. W., Vol-I: 28
Trevathan, W. R., Vol-II: 287
Triandis, H. C., Vol-I: 160, 162–163, 169, 173
Trickett, E., Vol-II: 614
Tripp, T. M., Vol-II: 431
Trivers, R. L., Vol-I: 260–261, 473; Vol-II: 285
Troiden, R. R., Vol-I: 541
Tropp, J., Vol-I: 328
Trosch, S., Vol-II: 624
Trost, M. R., Vol-II: 285
Tröster, A. I., Vol-I: 330
Trudeau, K. J., Vol-II: 550
Truijen, S., Vol-I: 245
Trujillo, N., Vol-II: 571
Trusty, J., Vol-II: 384
Truswell, A. S., Vol-I: 458
Tsai, J. L., Vol-I: 435, 437, 442
Tsang, J., Vol-II: 347
Tschann, J. M., Vol-II: 301
Tseng, S., Vol-II: 677
Tso, A. W. K., Vol-II: 543
Tsui, A. S., Vol-II: 350
Tu, X., Vol-I: 487
Tuccillo, L., Vol-II: 290
Tucillo, J. A., Vol-II: 598
Tucker, C. J., Vol-I: 144
Tucker, K. L., Vol-II: 144, 577
Tuggle, C. A., Vol-II: 647
Tuinstra, J., Vol-II: 501, 552
Tuiten, A., Vol-I: 321
Tullmann, D. F., Vol-II: 543
Tuna, C., Vol-II: 424
Turgeon, L., Vol-II: 266
Turner, C. S., Vol-II: 460
Turner, C. W., Vol-I: 72; Vol-II: 255
Turner, D. L., Vol-I: 134
Turner, H., Vol-II: 319
Turner, J. A., Vol-II: 236
Turner, J. C., Vol-I: 513; Vol-II: 385
Turner, J. R., Vol-I: 496
Turner, K. L., Vol-I: 572
Turner, L., Vol-II: 368

Author Index

Turner, R. K., Vol-I: 538
Turner, R. N., Vol-I: 497–498
Turner, S. P., Vol-I: 122, 497–499
Turnley, W. H., Vol-II: 340
Turrell, G., Vol-II: 472
Tuttle, G., Vol-I: 63
Tutty, L. M., Vol-II: 208
Tversky, B., Vol-I: 202
Twenge, J. M., Vol-I: 91, 133, 135, 151, 298, 421, 480; Vol-II: 22, 134, 157, 329–330, 341, 659
Tyler, T. R., Vol-II: 327
Tylka, T. L., Vol-II: 156, 161, 173
Tyrka, A. R., Vol-I: 535, 544
Tyson, P., Vol-I: 50

U

Ugurbil, K., Vol-I: 239
Ubeda, C., Vol-II: 482
Uchida, A., Vol-I: 385–387
Udell, W., Vol-I: 528
Udry, J. R., Vol-I: 484, 530, 534
Ueland, O., Vol-I: 462–463
Ugawa, Y., Vol-I: 330
Uher, R., Vol-I: 247, 464
Uhlmann, E. L., Vol-I: 431; Vol-II: 342
Uitenbroek, D. G., Vol-II: 473
Ullrich, P. M., Vol-II: 553
Ulsh, H. M., Vol-II: 97
Umberson, D., Vol-II: 477, 498
Underwood, M. K., Vol-I: 546
Underwood, W., Vol-II: 327, 528
Ungar, S., Vol-I: 202
Unger, J. B., Vol-I: 460
Unger, R., Vol-II: 34, 64, 71, 73, 168, 615, 620, 631, 633, 672, 680, 682, 685, 691
Unger, R. K., Vol-I: 2, 27, 29, 33, 106, 133, 194, 364–365, 368, 381, 402, 460; Vol-II: 2
Ungerleider, L. G., Vol-I: 236
Unikel, E., Vol-II: 338
Unruh, A. M., Vol-I: 240
Upchurch, R., Vol-II: 501, 510–511
Updegraff, K., Vol-I: 536
Urbana, S., Vol-II: 66
Urbanski, L., Vol-I: 27
Urberg, K. A., Vol-I: 501
Urbina, S., Vol-II: 605
Urey, J. R., Vol-I: 389
Urland, G. R., Vol-II: 449
Urwin, C., Vol-I: 118
Ussher, J., Vol-II: 168–169
Ussher, J. M., Vol-I: 117, 367, 440
Utz, R. L., Vol-II: 410
UyBico, S. J., Vol-I: 184
Uzzo, R. G., Vol-I: 463

V

Vablais, C. M., Vol-II: 75
Vaccarino, F. J., Vol-I: 462
Vaillant, G., Vol-I: 564
Vaillant, G. E., Vol-I: 44, 562–563, 567; Vol-II: 51
Vaitl, D., Vol-I: 443
Valanis, B. G., Vol-II: 552
Valdez, E., Vol-II: 412
Valente, S. M., Vol-I: 223–224
Valentin, I., Vol-II: 187
Valentine, K., Vol-II: 290
Valkenberg, P. M., Vol-II: 171, 654; Vol-I: 542
Vallerand, R. J., Vol-II: 388
van Amerom, G., Vol-II: 478
van Asbeck, F. W., Vol-II: 483
van Beek, Y., Vol-I: 414
Van Cleave, E. F., Vol-II: 389
van Dam, K., Vol-II: 71
Van de Heyning, P., Vol-I: 245
van de Poll, N. E., Vol-I: 225, 324
van de Vijver, F., Vol-I: 165, 167, 169–172
Van de Vliert, E., Vol-II: 413
van den Berg, P., Vol-I: 88; Vol-II: 153
Van Den Bosch, W. J. H. M., Vol-II: 228
van den Brink, W., Vol-II: 100
Van Den Eeden, S. K., Vol-II: 527
Van Den Hoogen, H. J. M., Vol-II: 228
Van der Heide, B., Vol-II: 653
Van der Heijden, P. G. M., Vol-II: 603
van der Kolk, B., Vol-II: 95, 195
van der Meulen, J., Vol-II: 673, 676, 689
van der Zaag, C., Vol-I: 244
van Dolderen, M. S. M., Vol-I: 414
van Engen, M. L., Vol-II: 338, 454, 458, 677
Van Etten, M. L., Vol-I: 547
van Ginkel, W. P., Vol-II: 455
Van Goozen, S. H., Vol-II: 367
Van Goozen, S. H. M., Vol-I: 222, 224–225
Van Gundy, K., Vol-I: 435
van Hoeken, D., Vol-I: 247
van Honk, J., Vol-I: 223, 321
Van Houtte, M., Vol-I: 289–290
Van Hove, G., Vol-I: 35
Van Hulle, C. A., Vol-I: 445
van Jaarsveld, C. H., Vol-II: 547–548
van Kesteren, P. J., Vol-II: 113
Van Kleef, G. A., Vol-II: 350
van Knippenberg, D., Vol-II: 348, 350, 456
Van Langen, A., Vol-II: 390
Van Leuvan, P., Vol-II: 391
Van Maanen, J., Vol-II: 594
van Middendorp, H., Vol-II: 546
Van Strien, J. W., Vol-I: 239,
Van Strien, T., Vol-I: 457
Van Toller, C., Vol-I: 248
van Vianen, A. E. M., Vol-I: 435; Vol-II: 453, 455

van Well, S., Vol-I: 145–146
van Wijk, C. M. G., Vol-II: 474
Van Winkle, B., Vol-II: 595
Van Wuk, C. M. T. G., Vol-II: 228
Vance, C. M., Vol-II: 432
Vandell, D. L., Vol-II: 97
Vandenberg, S. G., Vol-I: 221, 318, 322
Vandevijvere, S., Vol-II: 473
Vandewater, E. A., Vol-I: 563–565, 571
Vanman, E. J., Vol-I: 434
Vanni, D., Vol-II: 297
Vanwesenbeeck, I., Vol-II: 655
Vargas, P., Vol-II: 447
Vartanian, L., Vol-I: 458
Vartanian, L. R., Vol-I: 458, 466; Vol-II: 167
Vartia, M., Vol-II: 429
Vasey, P. L., Vol-II: 122
Vasilyeva, M., Vol-I: 326
Vásquez, E., Vol-II: 554
Vasquez, H., Vol-II: 634–635
Vasta, R., Vol-I: 308, 319–320, 326, 328
Vaughter, R. M., Vol-I: 29
Vaz, K. M., Vol-I: 116
Vazquez, R., Vol-I: 187
Veach, P. M., Vol-I: 531
Vecchi, T., Vol-I: 323
Vecchio, R. P., Vol-II: 262, 269–271, 458, 677
Vederhus, L., Vol-I: 319
Velázquez, J. A., Vol-I: 165
Veldhuizen, S., Vol-II: 476
Velting, D. M., Vol-I: 68
Veniegas, R. C., Vol-II: 68
Venn, C., Vol-I: 118
Ventrone, N. A., Vol-II: 289–290, 298
Verbaten, M. N., Vol-I: 242
Verbrugge, L. M., Vol-II: 511, 519
Verdi, A. F., Vol-II: 338
Vereeck, L., Vol-I: 245
Verette, J., Vol-II: 294
Vergara, T., Vol-I: 368
Verhofstadt, L. L., Vol-II: 501–502, 507
Verini, I., Vol-I: 202
Verkuyten, M., Vol-I: 498, 516
Verma, J., Vol-II: 289
Vernon, L. J., Vol-II: 195
Vernon, M. K., Vol-II: 384
Vernon, M. L., Vol-II: 297
Vernon, S. W., Vol-II: 544
Veroff, J., Vol-II: 42–43, 46–47, 52, 55–56
Verstervelt, C. M., Vol-II: 204
Verwijmeren, T., Vol-II: 294
Vessey, J. T., Vol-II: 224
Vestergaard, M., Vol-II: 598
Viaud-Delmon, I., Vol-I: 329
Victor, R. G., Vol-II: 543
Vida, M., Vol-II: 388, 390, 573
Vidaurri, M., Vol-I: 226

Viera, A. J., Vol-II: 520
Vierikko, E., Vol-II: 322
Vigfusdottir, T. H., Vol-II: 165
Vigier, B., Vol-I: 217
Viken, R., Vol-II: 322
Villeponteaux, L. A., Vol-II: 195
Villimez, C., Vol-II: 174
Vincent, J., Vol-II: 572, 647
Vincent, M. A., Vol-II: 156
Vincent, T., Vol-II: 614
Vinnicombe, S., Vol-II: 456
Vinokur, A. D., Vol-II: 686
Virshup, L. K., Vol-I: 496
Visio, M., Vol-II: 430, 571
Visscher, B. R., Vol-II: 553
Vissers, J. A., Vol-II: 483
Visweswaran, K., Vol-I: 110
Vitale, A. M., Vol-II: 114, 119, 124–125
Vitale, S., Vol-I: 236
Vito, D., Vol-II: 204
Vizzard, J., Vol-I: 458
Vladar, K., Vol-I: 245
Voci, A., Vol-I: 497
Vogel, D. L., Vol-I: 194, 437; Vol-II: 228–229, 231–232, 235
Vogel, S. R., Vol-I: 28; Vol-II: 64, 104, 188, 678
Vohs, K. D., Vol-II: 24, 289
Volkwein, K. A. E., Vol-II: 579
Volle, F., Vol-II: 618
Von Brunschot, M., Vol-I: 548
von Cramon, D. Y., Vol-I: 245
von Hippel, W., Vol-II: 447
Von Korff, M., Vol-I: 241
Vondracek, F. W., Vol-II: 384
Voracek, M., Vol-I: 441
Vosshall, L. B., Vol-I: 248
Vounatsou, P., Vol-II: 486
Vowels, C. L., Vol-II: 658; Vol-I: 567
Voydanoff, P., Vol-II: 407
Voyer, D., Vol-I: 218, 300, 318–321, 325
Voyer, S., Vol-I: 221, 263, 326
Vrana, S. R., Vol-I: 442
Vrangalova, S., Vol-II: 10, 359–371
Vroom, V. H., Vol-II: 678
Vrugt, A., Vol-I: 411, 419–420

W
Wade, N. G., Vol-II: 228–229
Wager, T. D., Vol-I: 443
Wagner, B., Vol-II: 340
Wagner, B. M., Vol-I: 544–545
Wagner, C., Vol-II: 363, 369
Wagner, D. G., Vol-II: 339, 343
Wagner, G. A., Vol-II: 476
Wagner, S. H., Vol-II: 659
Wahrman, R., Vol-II: 343, 350
Wainwright, N., Vol-II: 171

Author Index

Waisberg, J., Vol-II: 104
Waismel-Manor, R., Vol-II: 448, 452–453, 455
Wajcman, J., Vol-II: 457
Wakitani, Y., Vol-I: 236
Walbourn, L., Vol-I: 457, 462–463
Waldegrave, C., Vol-II: 263, 269–270
Walden, H., Vol-I: 456
Waldman, D., Vol-II: 448
Waldo, C., Vol-II: 622, 685
Waldo, C. R., Vol-II: 195, 430, 433
Waldron, J., Vol-II: 574
Waldstein, S. R., Vol-I: 445
Walker, A., Vol-II: 405, 407, 410
Walker, A. J., Vol-II: 410
Walker, E., Vol-I: 542
Walker, G., Vol-I: 53; Vol-II: 255
Walker, H. A., Vol-II: 339, 341
Walker, K., Vol-II: 282–283
Walker, L., Vol-II: 73, 94
Walker, L. E. A., Vol-II: 72, 237
Walker, S. G., Vol-II: 42
Walkerdine, V., Vol-I: 117–118
Wallace, J. M., Vol-I: 547
Wallbott, H. G., Vol-I: 435
Wallen, A. S., Vol-II: 346, 450
Wallen, K., Vol-I: 220
Wallentin, M., Vol-I: 245
Waller, D., Vol-I: 329
Waller, G., Vol-II: 658
Waller, N. G., Vol-II: 82
Waller, P. F., Vol-II: 476
Wallerstein, N., Vol-I: 186
Walrath, C., Vol-II: 478
Walsh, F., Vol-II: 255
Walsh, J. L., Vol-I: 542
Walsh, M., Vol-I: 283
Walsh, M. R., Vol-I: 25
Walsh, N., Vol-II: 474
Walsh-Bowers, R., Vol-I: 369
Walster, E., Vol-II: 287
Walter, B., Vol-I: 260, 443
Walter, L. C., Vol-II: 546
Waltermaurer, E., Vol-II: 195
Walters, E. E., Vol-II: 473
Walters, L., Vol-I: 68
Walters, M., Vol-II: 255
Walther, J. B., Vol-II: 653
Walton, M., Vol-I: 201
Walworth, J., Vol-II: 119
Walzer, S., Vol-II: 293, 297
Wampold, B. E., Vol-I: 83; Vol-II: 221, 241–242
Wampold, E. B., Vol-II: 234
Wandersman, A., Vol-II: 613
Wang, B., Vol-II: 543
Wang, J., Vol-II: 486
Wang, P. S., Vol-II: 527
Wang, S., Vol-I: 114

Wang, V. O., Vol-II: 272
Wang, X. Y., Vol-I: 236
Wansink, B., Vol-I: 247, 463
Ward, L., Vol-I: 112, 144, 150, 542
Ward, L. M., Vol-I: 542; Vol-II: 171, 655
Ward, M., Vol-I: 328, 542; Vol-II: 660
Ward, R., Vol-I: 179, 542, 544; Vol-II: 410, 414
Ward, T., Vol-II: 242
Warden, D., Vol-II: 510
Wardlaw, D., Vol-II: 620
Wardle, J., Vol-I: 456, 462
Wardrop, J., Vol-II: 387
Warin, J., Vol-I: 510
Warner, M., Vol-I: 196
Warner, M. B., Vol-II: 73
Warner, S., Vol-II: 603
Warnke, M., Vol-II: 94
Warren, K., Vol-I: 283
Warren, M. P., Vol-I: 534–535, 543
Warren, W. H., Vol-I: 266
Warrington, M., Vol-I: 289, 291
Warshaw, M., Vol-II: 195
Wartell, M. S., Vol-I: 325
Wasco, S. M., Vol-II: 12, 613–636
Washington, N., Vol-I: 512
Wasserman, L. M., Vol-I: 237
Waterman, A. S., Vol-I: 566
Waterman, P. D., Vol-I: 179
Waters, H. S., Vol-I: 263
Waters, P. L., Vol-I: 532
Watson, C., 195
Watson, D., Vol-II: 33
Watson, D. R., Vol-I: 243
Watson, J., Vol-II: 607
Watson, K. R., Vol-II: 487
Watson, L. F., Vol-II: 484
Watson, N., Vol-II: 154
Watson, N. V., Vol-I: 222, 266
Watson, W. L., Vol-II: 482
Watt, H. M. G., Vol-II: 11, 379–394
Watts-Jones, D., Vol-II: 255
Watzlawick, P., Vol-II: 264
Waxman, S., Vol-I: 199
Way, N., Vol-I: 107
Wayne, J. H., Vol-II: 425
Weatherall, A., Vol-I: 201
Weatherall, R., Vol-II: 478
Weaver, J., Vol-I: 242; Vol-II: 656–657
Webb, R. M., Vol-I: 310
Webber, S. S., Vol-II: 348
Webb-Johnson, G., Vol-I: 284
Weber, G. N., Vol-II: 365
Weber, K., Vol-II: 545
Webley, P., Vol-I: 330
Webster, B., Vol-I: 369
Webster, L., Vol-I: 135
Webster, M., Vol-II: Jr., Vol-II: 345

Wechsler, D., Vol-I: 301–302, 320, 569; Vol-II: 70
Weden, M. M., Vol-II: 476
Weeks, L. E., Vol-I: 318
Weeks, R., Vol-II: 230
Weel, C. V., Vol-II: 474
Wegener, D. T., Vol-I: 151
Wegesin, D. J., Vol-I: 226
Wegner, D. M., Vol-I: 460
Wei, R., Vol-II: 653
Weiffenbach, J. M., Vol-I: 246
Weightman, D. R., Vol-I: 226
Weil, E., Vol-I: 288–289
Weimann, G., Vol-II: 342, 346
Weinberg, G., Vol-II: 359
Weinberg, M., Vol-I: 63, 66
Weinberg, M. K., Vol-I: 113
Weinberg, M. S., Vol-I: 475
Weinberg, R., Vol-II: 570
Weinberger, D. R., Vol-I: 245
Weinberger, J., Vol-II: 44
Weinblatt, M. E., Vol-II: 545
Weiner, B., Vol-I: 200
Weingarten, H. P., Vol-I: 462, 464
Weinraub, M., Vol-I: 504, 510
Weinrich, J. D., Vol-II: 365
Weinstein, M., Vol-II: 158
Weinstein, R. S., Vol-I: 284
Weinstein, S., Vol-II: 369
Weinstein, S. E., Vol-I: 457, 460
Weintraub, J. K., Vol-II: 42, 434
Weintraub, W., Vol-II: 42, 434
Weir, T., Vol-I: 437
Weis, L., Vol-I: 103, 106, 114
Weis, S., Vol-I: 245
Weisenberg, M., Vol-I: 242
Weiser, L., Vol-I: 396
Weiss, E. L., Vol-II: 137
Weiss, J. T., Vol-II: 364
Weiss, M. G., Vol-II: 486
Weiss, M. R., Vol-II: 570
Weiss, R. L., Vol-II: 268
Weiss, T., Vol-I: 243
Weissman, M. M., Vol-II: 134
Weisstein, N., Vol-I: 26–27, 366
Weitlauf, J. C., Vol-II: 74
Weitzel-O'Neill, P. A., Vol-II: 345
Weizenbaum, F. B., Vol-I: 456, 458
Welander, G., Vol-II: 483
Weller, A., Vol-I: 248
Weller, L., Vol-I: 248
Wellman, B., Vol-II: 281
Wells, A., Vol-I: 396
Wells, B., Vol-I: 480
Wells, S., Vol-II: 314–315
Welsh, G. S., Vol-II: 76
Welsh, K. M., Vol-II: 54, 483

Welshimer, K. J., Vol-I: 53
Welton, A. L., Vol-I: 327
Wendler, C., Vol-II: 379, 388
Wenk, N. M., Vol-II: 197, 202
Wennberg, P., Vol-II: 204
Wenzlaff, R. M., Vol-I: 460
Werbart, A., Vol-II: 204
Werbel, J. D., Vol-II: 351, 456
Werbs, M., Vol-I: 243
Werlen, E., Vol-II: 621
Werner, A., Vol-II: 546, 549
Werner, O., Vol-I: 171–173
Wert, S. R., Vol-I: 397, 399
Wertheim, E. H., Vol-II: 165, 168, 173
Weseen, S., Vol-I: 106
Wesman, A. G., Vol-I: 320
Wesselink, P., Vol-II: 170
West, A., Vol-I: 351–352, 354
West, C., Vol-I: 2, 120, 367, 389–390, 394, 401; Vol-II: 295, 406–407, 523
West, C. M., Vol-II: 258
West, P., Vol-II: 480
Westad, F., Vol-I: 462
Westbury, E., Vol-II: 208
Westen, D., Vol-I: 259; Vol-II: 95, 234
Wester, S., Vol-II: 228, 231–232, 235
Wester, S. R., Vol-I: 437
Westerman, D., Vol-II: 653
Westheimer, K., Vol-I: 290
Westling, E. W., Vol-I: 548
Westmoreland, T., Vol-II: 487
Weston, K., Vol-I: 67
Weston, P. J., Vol-II: 530
Westphal, W., Vol-I: 241
Wetherell, M., Vol-I: 117, 192; Vol-II: 475
Wetzel, R. D., Vol-II: 195
Wetzels, P., Vol-II: 484
Whalen, P. J., Vol-II: 285
Whaley, A. L., Vol-II: 233
Whallett, E. J., Vol-II: 483
Wheaton, B., Vol-I: 531
Wheelan, S. A., Vol-II: 338, 350
Wheeler, R. C., Vol-II: 546
Wheelwright, S., Vol-I: 309
Whelan-Berry, K. S., Vol-I: 570
Whetstone-Dion, R., Vol-II: 347
Whiffen, V. E., Vol-II: 96–97
Whissell-Buechy, D., Vol-I: 246
Whitbeck, L. B., Vol-II: 384, 619
Whitbourne, S. K., Vol-I: 563, 566, 571, 574
White, A. J., Vol-I: 237, 248, 515
White, D. R., Vol-I: 167; Vol-I: 501
White, H. R., Vol-I: 530–531
White, J., Vol-I: 442
White, J. B., Vol-II: 364
White, J. D., Vol-II: 365
White, J. L., Vol-II: 227, 236

White, J. W., Vol-I: 95; Vol-II: 315
White, K. J., Vol-II: 23
White, K. M., Vol-I: 560, 562
White, S. W., Vol-II: 297
Whitehead, A., Vol-II: 173
Whitehead, J., Vol-I: 97
Whiteman, S., Vol-I: 511
Whiteman, S. D., Vol-I: 501, 537
Whitesell, N. R., Vol-I: 532
Whitley, B. E. Vol-I: 194, 480
Whitley, B. E. Jr., Vol-II: 24, 360–362, 458, 652
Whitney, K., Vol-II: 348
Whitt, E. J., Vol-I: 285
Whittemore, A. S., Vol-II: 527
Whittle, S., Vol-II: 112, 368
Whorf, B., Vol-I: 400
Whorf, B. L., Vol-I: 361
Whorley, M. R., Vol-I: 54, 136, 145
Wichstrom, L., Vol-I: 95, 544
Wichstrøm, L., Vol-II: 369
Wick, D. P., Vol-II: 43
Wickens, C. D., Vol-I: 238
Widiger, T. A., Vol-II: 73, 77, 95
Widman, D., Vol-I: 223, 330
Widom, C. S., Vol-II: 137
Widrow, L., Vol-I: 49
Wiedenbauer, G., Vol-I: 329
Wiederman, M. W., Vol-II: 164
Wieling, E., Vol-II: 260, 263
Wiesenthal, D. L., Vol-II: 315
Wigboldus, D. H. J., Vol-I: 418
Wigfield, A., Vol-I: 510, 569; Vol-II: 379, 388–389
Wilchins, R., Vol-I: 364; Vol-II: 114, 121, 123, 125
Wilchins, R. A., Vol-II: 368
Wilczynski, C., Vol-I: 396
Wild, B., Vol-I: 239
Wild, W., Vol-II: 690
Wildman, B., Vol-I: 381
Wildman, H. E., Vol-I: 389
Wilgenbusch, T., Vol-II: 32
Wilhelm, J. A., Vol-I: 136
Wilkie, J., Vol-II: 414
Wilkinson, L., Vol-I: 4, 83; Vol-II: 4
Wilkinson, L. C., Vol-I: 284
Wilkinson, R. G., Vol-II: 272
Wilkinson, S., Vol-I: 31, 113, 117–118, 198
Wilkinson, W., Vol-II: 120
Wilkinson, W. W., Vol-II: 361
Willard, B., Vol-II: 93
Willems, P. P., Vol-II: 384
Willemsen, T. M., Vol-II: 338, 358
Williams, A. E., Vol-I: 242
Williams, C., Vol-I: 10, 63, 262, 299; Vol-II: 166
Williams, C. C., Vol-I: 262, 531; Vol-II: 386
Williams, C. L., Vol-I: 221, 323; Vol-II: 79, 341

Williams, D., Vol-I: 63
Williams, D. H., Vol-I: 221, 224
Williams, D. R., Vol-I: 228; Vol-II: 228
Williams, D. T., Vol-II: 647
Williams, J., Vol-I: 108; Vol-II: 402, 452
Williams, J. E., Vol-I: 133, 150, 169, 170, 221; Vol-II: 312, 343
Williams, J. H., Vol-II: 428–429
Williams, J. K., Vol-I: 327
Williams, J. M., Vol-II: 483
Williams, K., Vol-II: 297
Williams, K. Y., Vol-II: 348, 350, 413–414
Williams, M. B., Vol-II: 103
Williams, R. W., Vol-I: 63, 66, 236, 323, 540, 570
Williams, S. K., Vol-I: 536
Williams, S. L., Vol-I: 317
Williams, W. M., Vol-I: 283, 300, 480
Williamson, S., Vol-II: 573
Willig, C., Vol-I: 122
Willis, R., Vol-II: 486
Willis, S., Vol-I: 241; Vol-II: 384, 386
Willis, S. L., Vol-I: 569, 574
Willis, T., Vol-I: 96
Willness, C. R., Vol-II: 436
Willoughby, T., Vol-II: 652
Wills, C., Vol-I: 246
Wills, T. A., Vol-II: 501, 504–505
Wilson, B. D. M., Vol-II: 613
Wilson, C. J., Vol-II: 236, 242
Wilson, D. B., Vol-I: 89, 477; Vol-I: 396
Wilson, E. M., Vol-I: 216–217
Wilson, E. O., Vol-I: 36, 259
Wilson, G. D., Vol-I: 225–226
Wilson, H. C., Vol-I: 248
Wilson, I., Vol-II: 112–114, 122
Wilson, I. B., Vol-II: 553
Wilson, J., Vol-I: 289
Wilson, J. F., Vol-I: 329
Wilson, J. R., Vol-II: 383
Wilson, K., Vol-II: 122
Wilson, M. S., Vol-II: 362
Wilson, P. A., Vol-II: 383
Wilson, R. S., Vol-I: 568
Wilson, T., Vol-II: 626
Wilson, V., Vol-I: 302
Wilson-Glover, A., Vol-II: 527
Wilson-Smith, D. N., Vol-II: 340
Wimbush, J. C., Vol-II: 602
Winch, G., Vol-I: 512
Windle, M., Vol-I: 49
Windle, R. C., Vol-I: 49
Wing, R. R., Vol-I: 459
Wingard, D. L., Vol-II: 547
Wingood, G., Vol-II: 626
Wink, P., Vol-I: 567
Winkel, J., Vol-I: 321
Winkler, D., Vol-I: 444

Winner, E., Vol-I: 317
Winslow, D., Vol-II: 672, 680
Winstead, B. A., Vol-II: 295
Winter, D., Vol-II: 41–43, 45, 50, 52–55, 57–58
Winter, D. G., Vol-I: 562, 573
Winter, S., Vol-I: 369
Winters, K., Vol-II: 111, 122–125
Winters, K. K., Vol-II: 119
Wintrup, G., Vol-II: 579
Wirth, M. M., Vol-II: 52, 54
Wirth, R. J., Vol-I: 95
Wisco, B. E., Vol-II: 141
Wise, E. A., Vol-I: 241
Wisniewski, A. A., Vol-I: 219
Wisniewski, A. B., Vol-II: 115
Wisniewski, N., Vol-II: 137
Wissow, L., Vol-I: 69
Wissow, L. S., Vol-II: 138
Witelson, S. F., Vol-I: 225
Witkin, H. A., Vol-I: 319
Wittert, G., Vol-I: 223
Wittig, M. A., Vol-I: 319
Wituk, S., Vol-II: 633
Wobbes, T., Vol-II: 548
Woike, B., Vol-II: 43, 45
Wold, C., Vol-II: 552
Wolf, N., Vol-II: 153
Wolf, R., Vol-I: 69
Wolf, R. C., Vol-II: 138
Wolf, T., Vol-I: 66
Wolf, Y., Vol-I: 242
Wolfe, D., Vol-II: 405
Wolford, J. L., Vol-I: 328
Wolgers, G., Vol-I: 323
Wolke, D., Vol-I: 282
Wollett, A., Vol-I: 117
Woltz, D. J., Vol-I: 321
Wong, L. K., Vol-II: 460
Wong, A. C., Vol-I: 236
Wong, L., Vol-I: 106
Wong, M., Vol-I: 431
Wong, M. M., Vol-II: 282
Wong, P. T. P., Vol-II: 295
Wong, T. Y., Vol-II: 483
Wong, Y. J., Vol-II: 226, 238
Wood, C. H., Vol-I: 503
Wood, D., Vol-I: 571; Vol-II: 34
Wood, J. T., Vol-II: 283, 294
Wood, J. W., Vol-II: 286
Wood, K. R., Vol-I: 195
Wood, N., Vol-I: 248
Wood, P. K., Vol-II: 135, 137, 288
Wood, W., Vol-I: 35, 84, 167–168, 201, 203, 313, 389, 393, 415, 421, 434, 446, 475, 481; Vol-II: 168, 311, 324, 329, 339, 343, 345, 347–349, 387, 461, 677
Woodard, E. H., Vol-II: 662
Wood-Barcalow, N., Vol-II: 173

Woodcock, R., Vol-I: 301
Woodford, M. S., Vol-II: 224
Woodhill, B. M., Vol-II: 24
Woodruff, P. G., Vol-II: 546
Woods, D., Vol-II: 532
Woods, E., Vol-I: 69
Woods, E. R., Vol-II: 138
Woods, K. E., Vol-II: 320
Woods, S., Vol-I: 282
Woods, S. C., Vol-I: 247
Woods, W. J., Vol-I: 186
Woodson, J. C., Vol-II: 115
Woodwell, D. A., Vol-II: 518
Woodzicka, J. A., Vol-I: 438
Woolard, J. L., Vol-II: 651
Woolf, V., Vol-I: 345–347
Woolley, S. R., Vol-II: 255
Woolsey, L., Vol-I: 198
Worchel, S., Vol-II: 343
Worell, J., Vol-I: 35; Vol-II: 92–94, 117, 192, 201, 205, 211, 213
Wornian, K., Vol-II: 648
Worrell, T. R., Vol-II: 190, 644, 647
Worsley, A., Vol-I: 463
Worthman, C., Vol-I: 534
Worthman, C. M., Vol-I: 548; Vol-II: 133
Wortley, P. M., Vol-I: 187
Wortman, C., Vol-II: 410
Wortman, C. B., Vol-II: 140
Wosinska, W., Vol-II: 347
Wraga, M., Vol-I: 327
Wrase, J., Vol-I: 240, 243
Wren, B., Vol-II: 112
Wright, C., Vol-I: 96
Wright, C. I., Vol-I: 240
Wright, D. L., Vol-II: 602
Wright, H. N., Vol-I: 248
Wright, J. C., Vol-I: 226, 518
Wright, J. D., Vol-I: 383, 543; Vol-II: 383, 543
Wright, L. W. Jr., Vol-II: 360, 363, 371
Wright, M., Vol-I: 226
Wright, O., Vol-II: 650
Wright, P., Vol-II: 483
Wright, R., Vol-I: 328
Wright, T. M., Vol-I: 318
Wrightsman, L., Vol-I: 47
Wrightsman, L. S., Vol-I: 145
Wrisberg, C. A., Vol-II: 229
Wrosch, C., Vol-I: 573
Wu, T. Y., Vol-II: 476
Wu, X. C., Vol-II: 137
Wunderlich, A. P., Vol-I: 330
Wüstenberg, T., Vol-I: 324
Wuyts, F., Vol-I: 245
Wyke, S., Vol-II: 474
Wylie, R. C., Vol-II: 31
Wysocki, C. J., Vol-I: 248

Wysocki, V. H., Vol-I: 97

X
Xavier, J. M., Vol-II: 120
Xie, Y., Vol-I: 304, 308
Xin, K. R., Vol-II: 350
Xu, J., Vol-II: 352, 526, 530, 542

Y
Yablonsky, L., Vol-II: 591
Yager, T. J., Vol-I: 140
Yagil, D., Vol-II: 433
Yahr, J., Vol-I: 504
Yamada, E. M., Vol-II: 338
Yamauchi, Y., Vol-I: 246
Yamaura, A., Vol-I: 245
Yancey, A. K., Vol-I: 544
Yang, A. S., Vol-I: 549
Yang, E. Y., Vol-I: 243
Yang, K., Vol-I: 162
Yang, X., Vol-II: 76, 81–82
Yang, Y., Vol-II: 33
Yanico, B. J., Vol-I: 135; Vol-II: 32
Yarab, P., Vol-II: 283
Yardley, L., Vol-I: 103, 110
Yarhouse, M. A., Vol-I: 62
Yarnold, P. R., Vol-I: 135
Yassin, A. A., Vol-I: 483
Yates, A., Vol-I: 482
Yates, L., Vol-II: 388
Ybarra, O., Vol-II: 299
Yee, D. K., Vol-I: 457; Vol-II: 156, 384
Yee, M., Vol-I: 516
Yeh, M., Vol-II: 232
Yelland, C., Vol-II: 156, 161
Yellin, J., Vol-II: 655
Yeo, R. A., Vol-I: 227, 264
Yesavage, J. A., Vol-I: 49
Yetton, P. W., Vol-II: 678
Yik, M. S. M., Vol-II: 26
Yin, D., Vol-II: 528
Yip, P. S., Vol-II: 485
Yodandis, C. L., Vol-I: 91
Yoder, J. D., Vol-I: 31, 91, 148; Vol-II: 34, 55, 57, 341, 344, 346, 349, 449, 677, 679
Yoder, K., Vol-II: 619
Yoon, K. S., Vol-II: 384
Yopchick, J. E., Vol-I: 438
Yoshimura, I., Vol-I: 246
Yost, M. R., Vol-II: 53, 58
Young, J., Vol-II: 320
Young, J. M., Vol-II: 332
Young, K., Vol-I: 505; Vol-II: 623
Younger, M. R., Vol-I: 289, 291, 515
Youniss, J., Vol-II: 282, 324
Youniss, R. P., Vol-II: 282, 324
Yousem, D. M., Vol-I: 249

Yrope, Y., Vol-I: 418
Yu, J. H., Vol-I: 10, 186
Yu, K .K., Vol-II: 485
Yu, W., Vol-II: 525
Yuan, A. S. V., Vol-II: 169
Yuen, H. P., Vol-II: 485
Yunger, J. L., Vol-I: 142, 512
Yutzy, S. H., Vol-II: 195
Yzerbyt, V., Vol-I: 134
Yzerbyt, V. Y., Vol-I: 418

Z
Zabin, L. S., Vol-II: 476
Zachar, P., Vol-II: 231
Zacks, E., Vol-I: 64; Vol-II: 257
Zacks, R. T., Vol-I: 432
Zahn, J., Vol-II: 566
Zahn-Waxler, C., Vol-I: 435, 543
Zakrisson, I., Vol-II: 362
Zalk, S. R., Vol-I: 516–517
Zambarano, R. J., Vol-I: 226
Zamutt, A., Vol-I: 562
Zand, D., Vol-II: 24, 289, 292
Zane, N., Vol-II: 232
Zangari, M., Vol-II: 255
Zani, A., Vol-I: 239
Zanna, M. P., Vol-I: 195
Zapf, D., Vol-II: 424
Zaridze, D., Vol-II: 481
Zaslavsky, A. M., Vol-II: 518
Zawacki, T., Vol-II: 284
Zebrowitz, L. A., Vol-II: 451
Zeedyk, M. S., Vol-I: 105; Vol-II: 64, 72
Zeidner, M., Vol-I: 439
Zeinier, R., Vol-I: 236
Zeira, A., Vol-II: 628
Zelditch, M. Jr., Vol-II: 345, 352
Zelkowitz, P., Vol-I: 531
Zellman, G., Vol-II: 330
Zellner, D. A., Vol-I: 459
Zeman, J., Vol-I: 434
Zemitis, O., Vol-I: 393
Zera, D., Vol-I: 541
Zewdie, S., Vol-II: 450
Zhang, J., Vol-I: 173
Zhang, X., Vol-I: 167
Zhou, J., Vol-II: 116, 350
Zhou, J. N., Vol-I: 224
Zhuang, H., Vol-I: 248
Ziebland, S., Vol-I: 51
Zilbergeld, B., Vol-I: 485
Zilberman, M. L., Vol-II: 476
Zilles, K., Vol-I: 244
Zillmann, D., Vol-I: 242; Vol-II: 657, 661
Zimmerman, D. H., Vol-I: 2, 120, 367, 389–390, 401; Vol-II: 1, 115, 295, 406, 523
Zimmerman, H., Vol-I: 389, 394

Zimmerman, L. I., Vol-II: 686
Zimmerman, M., Vol-II: 633
Zimmerman, T. S., Vol-II: 648
Zingales, L., Vol-I: 262, 300
Zinn, A., Vol-I: 218
Zinser, O., Vol-I: 330
Zivian, M. T., Vol-I: 90; Vol-II: 167
Zlotnick, C., Vol-II: 195, 619
Zoino, J., Vol-II: 159
Zones, J. S., Vol-II: 159
Zormeier, M. M., Vol-II: 283
Zosuls, K., Vol-I: 496, 500–501, 504, 509–510
Zosuls, K. M., Vol-I: 509
Zou, S., Vol-I: 236
Zozulya, S., Vol-I: 247
Zubeck, J. P., Vol-I: 246
Zubek, J., Vol-II: 30
Zucker, A. N., Vol-I: 563, 567
Zucker, K. J., Vol-I: 139, 141–142, 495, 510–511; Vol-II: 112–118, 122, 340, 367–368
Zuckerman, A., Vol-II: 506
Zuckerman, D., Vol-II: 527
Zuckerman, H., Vol-I: 345–346, 348, 354
Zuckerman, M., Vol-II: 48
Zuidhoek, S., Vol-I: 240
Zuloaga, D. G., Vol-I: 217–218
Zumpe, D., Vol-I: 483
Zurbriggen, E. L., Vol-I: 475; Vol-II: 43, 50, 53, 58, 291
Zuriff, G. E., Vol-I: 193
Zurkovsky, L., Vol-I: 323
Zuroff, D., Vol-II: 43, 82
Zuroff, D. C., Vol-II: 43, 82
Zuschlag, M. K., Vol-I: 566
Zusho, H., Vol-I: 248
Zusman, M. E., Vol-II: 283
Zwicker, A., Vol-II: 11, 495–512
Zylan, K. D., Vol-I: 247

Subject Index

Note: Volumes followed by locators refer to locators of respective volume numbers.

A

AAMFT, see American Association of Marriage and Family Therapists (AAMFT)
AAS, see Anabolic-androgenic steroids (AAS)
AASP, see Association for Applied Sport Psychology (AASP)
AAUW, see American Association of University Women (AAUW)
Abilities, academic, Vol I: 7, 284, 297–313
  availability of intervention, Vol I: 312
  beyond girls and mathematical ability, Vol I: 311–312
  complexity of questions, Vol I: 300
  constellations of, Vol I: 313
  effect size vs. practical significance, Vol I: 311
  extend gender differences research cross-nationally, Vol I: 313
  and gender, Vol I: 300
    intelligence, Vol I: 300–302
    mathematical ability, Vol I: 302–305
    verbal ability, Vol I: 305
  gender and preferences, Vol I: 308–309
    differences, Vol I: 312–313
    explanations, Vol I: 309–310
  gender similarities/differences, Vol I: 297–298
    explanations, Vol I: 306–308
    implications, Vol I: 311
    methodologies, Vol I: 297–298
  intelligence, Vol I: 300–302
    gender similarities/differences in means, Vol I: 301
    gender similarities/differences in variance, Vol I: 301–302
  mathematical ability, Vol I: 302–305
    aptitude vs. grades, Vol I: 304–305
    gender similarities/differences in means, Vol I: 302–303
    gender similarities/differences in variance, Vol I: 303–304
  statistics, Vol I: 298–300
    meta-analyses, Vol I: 298
    variance ratio, Vol I: 299
  verbal ability, Vol I: 305
    gender similarities/differences in means, Vol I: 305
    gender similarities/differences in variance, Vol I: 305
Ability and occupational choice, Vol II: 386–387
  differential aptitude test, Vol II: 386
  mathematics achievement data, Vol II: 386
ABR, see Auditory brain stem responses (ABR)
Abuse, Vol I: 10, 13, 29–30, 67–68, 71, 92, 106–107, 165, 182, 261, 399, 545, 549; Vol II: 10, 13, 35, 50, 53, 76, 92–93, 95–96, 98, 100, 102–104, 119, 121–122, 125, 137–139, 143–144, 146, 162, 189–191, 194, 196, 199, 201, 205, 208–210, 222, 224, 226–227, 230, 235, 255, 258, 261, 311, 316–318, 329, 367, 369, 431, 473–476, 479–484, 486–487, 522, 574–575, 579, 589, 591–592, 594, 596, 614, 620–621, 625–626, 631–632, 673, 680–682, 684, 690
Abuse of authority, military, Vol II: 681–682, 690
Academic abilities, Vol I: 7, 284, 297–313; Vol II: 7, 384
Academic preferences, Vol I: 7, 297, 308–313; Vol II: 7
Accidental violence, Vol II: 311–312
Achievement
  behaviors, expectations and values, Vol II: 573
  motivation, Vol II: 2, 41, 45–49, 56, 57
    definition, Vol II: 41, 45
    implicit/explicit measures, Vol II: 48–49, 49
    motive to avoid success, Vol II: 47–48
Acquired Immunodeficiency Syndrome (AIDS), Vol II: 104, 121, 125, 533, 542, 553, 626–627, 690
Active aggression, Vol II: 427
Actual power, Vol I: 416–418
ADAM, see Androgen decline in the aging male (ADAM)
Adaptation to Life, Vol I: 44–45
ADF, see Australian Defence Force (ADF)
Adolescence
  future directions, Vol I: 548–550
  gender identity changes
    "configured gender identity," Vol I: 529
    "general gender identity," Vol I: 529

Adolescence (*cont.*)
    intensification hypothesis, Vol I: 530–532
    See also Gender intensification hypothesis
    global identity changes, Vol I: 528–529
        development of self, Vol I: 528
        stage theory of development, Vol I: 528
    person-in-context, *see* Person-in-context influences
    role of gender in development of psychopathology, Vol I: 543–548
    See also Psychopathology, role of gender in development of
Adolescent Femininity Ideology Scale (AFIS), Vol I: 15, 138, 150
Adolescent Masculinity in Relationships Scale (AMIRS), Vol I: 137
Adolescents
    body dissatisfaction
        Argentinean and Swedish, cross-cultural comparison, Vol II: 156
    development and physical activity, Vol II: 576–577
    instrumentality and expressiveness mediated gender differences
        internalizing/externalizing symptoms, Vol II: 23
    interpersonal stressors, impact on, Vol II: 139
    LGB, peer violence victims, Vol II: 138
    media influences
        boys, risk of muscle dysmorphia, Vol II: 99
    self-esteem, Vol II: 30–31
    sexual minority, Vol II: 136, 138, 142, 143
    suicidal ideation, Vol II: 153
        fashion, Vol II: 153
        fiction, Vol II: 153
        function, Vol II: 153
Adrenalectomy, Vol I: 226
Adrenocorticotropic hormone secretion, Vol II: 116
Adult development and aging, Vol I: 44, 559–575
    future directions, Vol I: 573–575
    gender and aging bodies, Vol I: 566–570
        ADAM, Vol I: 568
        age-related changes, Vol I: 567
        AMS, Vol I: 568
        increasing body image satisfaction, Vol I: 567
        menopause/andropause, Vol I: 568
        PADAM, Vol I: 568
    gender and aging minds, Vol I: 568–570
        CVLT, Vol I: 569
        mitigated stereotypes, Vol I: 569
        WAIS-R, Vol I: 569
    gender and changes in social roles across lifespan, Vol I: 570–573
        changing work and family roles, Vol I: 571–573
        concept of marriage, change in, Vol I: 572
        empty nest syndrome, Vol I: 571
        gender/roles/well-being, Vol I: 570–571
        parenting and grandparenting issues, Vol I: 572
        retirement, Vol I: 572

    gender and personality in adulthood, Vol I: 560–566
    See also Personality and gender in adulthood
Adulthood, after puberty, Vol I: 220–226
    activational effects, Vol I: 222
    andropause, Vol I: 222
    assumptions, Vol I: 221
    homosexual individuals, Vol I: 225
        commissural system, Vol I: 225
    MRT, Vol I: 221
    naming tasks, Vol I: 222
    navigational tasks, Vol I: 221
    object location memory, Vol I: 221
    recalling landmarks, Vol I: 221
    transgendered individuals
        FtM/MtF, Vol I: 224
    verbal ability/memory/fluency, Vol I: 222
Advanced Placement (AP), Vol I: 281
AERA, *see* American Educational Research Association (AERA)
Aesthetic Plastic Surgery, Vol I: 163
AFEOS, *see* Armed Forces Equal Opportunity Survey (AFEOS)
Affect Intensity Measure (AIM), Vol I: 434, 436
Affiliation–intimacy motivation, Vol II: 41, 49–52, 54, 57
    physiological correlates, Vol II: 51–52
    relationships, Vol II: 50–51
AFIS, *see* Adolescent Femininity Ideology Scale (AFIS)
"A game for every girl and every girl in a game," NAAF, Vol I: 565
Agency, Vol I: 9, 14, 47, 53, 90, 95, 135, 150, 201, 362, 367, 386, 415, 568, 570; Vol II: 9, 15, 23, 25, 27, 43, 100, 174, 190, 198, 290–291, 299, 343–348, 352, 448, 451, 549–550, 593–594, 608
Aggression
    accidental violence, Vol II: 311
    active, Vol II: 427
    in children, peer violence, Vol II: 319–321
        adolescence, Vol II: 320
        cyberbullying, Vol II: 320–321
        gender differences, Vol II: 320
        greater levels in boys, Vol II: 320
        preschoolers, Vol II: 319
    controlled laboratory study, Vol II: 314–315
        greater aggression in men, Vol II: 314
        lower levels of stranger aggression against women, Vol II: 314
        manipulation, Vol II: 315
    definition, Vol II: 311–312
    expressions of aggression in everyday life
        personal experiences of violence, Vol II: 315–316
    future directions
        aggression/prosocial behavior in other cultures, Vol II: 330
        aggression/prosocial behavior, interactions, Vol II: 328–329

Subject Index

    lack of social context in laboratory, Vol II: 329–330
    use of psychology student samples, effects, Vol II: 330
  gender and criminal behavior, Vol II: 316
  indirect aggression, Vol II: 312
  intimate partner violence and aggression, Vol II: 316–317
    "common couple violence," Vol II: 317
    Conflict Tactics Scale, Vol II: 316
    "intimate terrorist," Vol II: 317
    man on woman, Vol II: 316
    woman on man, Vol II: 317
  malicious rumors, Vol II: 312
  nonviolent aggression, Vol II: 312
  physical aggression, Vol II: 312
  rape, Vol II: 321–322
    sample of married battered women, Vol II: 321
  "relational aggression," Vol II: 312
  relationship manipulation, Vol II: 312
  sibling violence, Vol II: 318–319
    brother-to-brother, Vol II: 319
  social ostracism, Vol II: 312
  stereotypes of gender and aggression, Vol II: 312–314
    BSRI, Vol II: 313
    levels of provocation, Vol II: 313
    Richardson Conflict Response Questionnaire, Vol II: 313
  verbal aggression, Vol II: 312
  and violence towards children/elderly family members, Vol II: 317–318
    caretakers' stress and depression, Vol II: 317
    DHHS, Vol II: 317
    NCEA, Vol II: 318
    NEAIS, Vol II: 318
    parental stress, Vol II: 318
    physical child abuse, Vol II: 317
  workplace violence, Vol II: 322
    expressed hostility/obstructionism/overt aggression, Vol II: 322
    interpersonal violence, Vol II: 322
    organization violence, Vol II: 322
Aging bodies, Vol I: 9, 566–568
  ADAM, Vol I: 568
  age-related changes, Vol I: 567
  AMS, Vol I: 568
  increasing body image satisfaction, Vol I: 567
  menopause/andropause, Vol I: 568
  PADAM, Vol I: 568
  See also Adult development and aging
Aging male syndrome (AMS), Vol I: 568
Aging minds, Vol I: 559, 567–570
  CVLT, Vol I: 569
  mitigated stereotypes, Vol I: 569
  WAIS-R, Vol I: 569
  See also Adult development and aging

"Agoraphobia," Vol II: 99, 100
Agreeableness, Vol I: 434, 441, 445
AIDS, see Acquired Immunodeficiency Syndrome (AIDS)
AIM, see Affect Intensity Measure (AIM)
AIS, see Androgen-insensitivity syndrome (AIS)
AJCP, see American Journal of Community Psychology (AJCP)
Ally McBeal, Vol II: 655
Almeida's cultural context model, Vol II: 261
Alpha socializers (men), Vol II: 654
Alzheimer's disease and long-term care, Vol II: 523–525
Ambient stimuli, Vol II: 428
Ambiguous genitalia, Vol I: 218; Vol II: 116
Ambivalent Sexism Inventory, Vol I: 144, 147–148
American Association of Marriage and Family Therapists (AAMFT), Vol II: 260
American Association of University Women (AAUW), Vol I: 282
American Bar Association Commission on Women in the Profession, Vol II: 601
American College Personnel Association, Vol I: 45, 46
American Educational Research Association (AERA), Vol II: 601, 604
American Journal of Community Psychology (AJCP), Vol II: 614, 616–617, 628–629, 633
American Journal of Men's Health, Vol I: 48
American Psychological Association (APA), Vol I: 2–4, 8–9, 73–74, 91, 94–96, 98–100, 111–113, 118, 121–122, 162, 192–193, 221, 223, 233, 563–564, 568, 587, 590, 601, 604, 609; Vol II: 2–4, 8–9, 24–25, 27, 59, 69, 70–71, 121–122, 195, 197, 202, 367–373, 486
  diagnostic system, Vol II: 73
  guidance, Vol I: 367
  society, Vol II: 221
  style manual, Vol I: 369–371, 373
American Psychiatric Association Ethics Code, Vol II: 66
American psychological association division 35, Vol I: 2, 47; Vol II: 2
American psychological association division 44, Vol I: 70
American psychological association division 51, Vol II: 257
American Psychology-Law Society, Vol II: 587
American Woman and Politics, Vol II: 337
AMIRS, see Adolescent Masculinity in Relationships Scale (AMIRS)
AMS, see Aging male syndrome (AMS)
Anabolic-androgenic steroids (AAS), Vol II: 162, 474
"Androcentric ideology of contemporary science," Vol I: 36
Androcentrism, Vol I: 60, 373, 382
Androgen decline in the aging male (ADAM), Vol I: 568
Androgen-insensitivity syndrome (AIS), Vol I: 218
Androgen receptors (ARs), Vol I: 218

Androgens, Vol I: 83, 215–220, 222–224, 241–242, 249, 270, 323–324, 533, 568
Androgyny, Vol I: 14, 28, 50, 52, 134–135, 140, 192, 352–366, 530, 532, 570
  shift theory, Vol I: 354
Andropause, Vol I: 222, 223, 484, 568; Vol II: 99
Androstenone, Vol I: 248
Animal Liberation Front (1993), Vol II: 592
Antecedents of gender identity and stereotyping, Vol I: 499, 502–507
  cognitive development, Vol I: 502–504
    constancy, Vol I: 503
    level of classification skills, Vol I: 503
    conceptual distinctions of gender categories and labeling, Vol I: 504
  essentialism, Vol I: 506–507
    category-based reasoning, Vol I: 506
    presence of "andro" or "estro," Vol I: 506
  parent and sociocultural influences, Vol I: 504–505
    communication, Vol I: 505
    society at large, Vol I: 505
    under-representation in media, Vol I: 505
  perceptual distinctions of gender categories, Vol I: 504
Antidepressant medications, prescription of, Vol II: 520
Anti-Mullerian hormone, Vol I: 216–217
Anti-nepotism, Vol I: 21, 25
Antisocial and deviant behaviors, Vol II: 423–424
Antisocial personality disorder (APD), Vol II: 94–95, 193
Anxiety, Vol I: 9, 10, 13, 63, 85, 91, 146, 240–242, 287, 317, 330, 399, 420, 430, 432–433, 435, 437, 441, 444–445, 472, 485–488, 538, 545
AP, *see* Advanced Placement (AP)
APA, *see* American Psychological Association (APA)
APA Board of Social and Ethical Responsibility in Psychology, Vol I: 370
APA style, Vol I: 369–371, 373
APD, *see* Antisocial personality disorder (APD)
Appraisal processes
  appraisals of incivility, Vol II: 433
  primary appraisal, Vol II: 432
  sentimental stereotypes, Vol II: 432
  sexual harassment appraisals, Vol II: 433
APSE, *see* Associated Press Sports Editors (APSE)
APSE websites and newspapers, Vol II: 572
Aptitude *vs.* grades, Vol I: 304–305
Armed Forces Equal Opportunity Survey (AFEOS), Vol II: 682
Army Culture and Climate Survey, Vol II: 690
ARs, *see* Androgen receptors (ARs)
Arthritis, Vol II: 500, 507, 519, 552, 554
Assertiveness training, Vol I: 2, 382–383, 385
  critique of, Vol I: 382–383
    woman-blaming approach, Vol I: 383
  research on, Vol I: 383
    gender-based evaluations of speech style, Vol I: 383
    sex of model and participant, Vol I: 383
    sex of target actor and respondent, Vol I: 383
Associated Press Sports Editors (APSE), Vol II: 572–573
Association for Applied Sport Psychology (AASP), Vol II: 568
Association for women in psychology (AWP), Vol I: 27
Athletes and non-athletes, differences, Vol II: 569
Atlas of World Cultures, Vol I: 167
Attainment value, Vol I: 310
Attention seekers (women), Vol II: 654
Attention-seeking behavior, Vol II: 94
Attitudes toward gender roles, Vol II: 2, 404, 408, 410–411, 625, 627
Attitudes Toward the Male Role Scale, Vol I: 47, 52
Attitudes toward Women Scale (AWS), Vol I: 136, 144, 146–148, 151
Audition and vestibular perception
  ABR, Vol I: 243
  anatomical analyses, cytoarchitectonic methods, Vol I: 244
  electromotile properties, Vol I: 243
  loudness sensitivity, Vol I: 243–244
  OAE, Vol I: 243
  pitch perception, Vol I: 244
  sound detection mechanisms, Vol I: 243
  sound localization, Vol I: 244
  supramodal language network, Vol I: 245
  vestibular apparatus, Vol I: 245
    disorders in women, Vol I: 245
    estrogen therapy, Vol I: 246
    function/malfunction results, Vol I: 245
    morphometric analysis, Vol I: 245
Auditory brain stem responses (ABR), Vol I: 243
Australian Defence Force: Career and Family Study, Vol II: 681
Australian Institute for Health & Welfare, Vol II: 473
Australian Men's Health Forum, Vol I: 47
Australian Psychological Society, Vol I: 44
Autosomal DSD, Vol I: 218, 219
Availability of intervention, Vol I: 312
  visual–spatial ability, Vol I: 312
AWS, *see* Attitudes toward Women Scale (AWS)

B

BAB, *see* Beauty and the Beast (BAB)
Balancing work/family, military context, Vol II: 402, 686–688
Barna research group poll, Vol II: 370–371
Batterers, Vol I: 391
BDD, *see* Body dysmorphic disorder (BDD)
BDI, *see* Beck Depression Inventory (BDI)
Beauty ideal, Vol II: 157, 159–160, 166, 174
Beauty and the beast (BAB), Vol II: 656
Beck Depression Inventory (BDI), Vol II: 70, 80, 82, 214
Bed nucleus of stria terminalis (BSTc), Vol II: 116
Behavioral maintenance, Vol II: 293–294, 296
Behavioral risk factors, Vol II: 472–473, 476

Subject Index

Behavior setting theory, Vol II: 633
Bem Sex Role Inventory (BSRI), Vol I: 14, 47, 50, 134–139, 143, 145, 151, 352, 366, 499; Vol II: 14–15, 22–23, 287, 312, 323, 657
Benevolent sexism, forms, Vol II: 137, 290
Bent twig model, Vol I: 325
Berdache, Vol II: 114
Berdahl's sex-based harassment theory, Vol II: 430
BFI, *see* Big Five (BFI) personality factors
Bicultural stress, Vol II: 618
Big Five, Vol II: 9, 25, 26, 28, 29
  See also Five-factor model (FFM)
Big Five (BFI) personality factors, Vol I: 9, 143, 434, 441
  agreeableness, Vol I: 434, 441
  assertiveness, Vol I: 441
  conscientiousness, Vol I: 441
  extraversion, Vol I: 441
  neuroticism, Vol I: 441
Binet–Simon scale, Vol I: 301–302
Binge-eating disorder, Vol II: 162
Biopsychosocial determinants, Vol II: 1
Bisexuality, Vol I: 61–66, 69–70, 72, 367, 480; Vol II: 363–365, 371
Bissu of South Sulawesi, Vol II: 114
Black and White adolescent participants, Vol II: 339
Block Design tests, Vol I: 263, 265, 320
Blood oxygen level dependent functional magnetic resonance imaging (BOLD fMRI), Vol I: 237, 239
Blueprint for manhood (masculinity ideology), Vol II: 226
BMI, *see* Body mass index (BMI)
BMS, *see* Brannon Masculinity Scale (BMS)
Board of Ethnic Minority Affairs, Vol I: 370
Boas–Benedict–Mead approach, Vol I: 259
Body cognitions, Vol II: 158–161
  appearance-related information, Vol II: 158
  body-ideal internalization, Vol II: 159–161
  body schematicity, Vol II: 158–159
Body dysmorphic disorder (BDD), Vol II: 10, 99, 158, 161–162
Body feelings
  appearance anxiety, Vol II: 157–158
  body dissatisfaction, Vol II: 155–156
  body shame, Vol II: 156–157
Body image
  adolescent suicidal ideation, Vol II: 153
    fashion, Vol II: 153
    fiction, Vol II: 153
    function, Vol II: 153
    gender and body behaviors, Vol II: 161–164
    gender and body cognitions, Vol II: 158–161
    gender and body feelings, Vol II: 155–158
    gender and body perceptions, Vol II: 153–155
  differences in literature, Vol II: 153
  and muscularity, Vol II: 575–576
  and physical activity, Vol II: 575

  sport and eating disorders, Vol II: 574–575
  and sport participation, Vol II: 574
  tripartite model of social influence, Vol II: 166–168
  See also Body image, theory
Body image, theory
  gender socialization, Vol II: 168–170
  objectification theory, Vol II: 170–172
  tripartite model of social influence
    media, Vol II: 166–168
    parents, Vol II: 164–165
    peers, Vol II: 165–166
Body mass index (BMI), Vol II: 29, 155, 529
Body perceptions, Vol II: 153–155
  fragmented *vs.* functional, Vol II: 154
  overestimate *vs.* underestimate, Vol II: 155
  third person *vs.* first person, Vol II: 154
Body shape, Vol II: 161, 172–173, 473–474
Body weight, influence on screening practices, Vol II: 545
BOLD fMRI, *see* Blood oxygen level dependent functional magnetic resonance imaging (BOLD fMRI)
Borderline personality disorder (BPD), Vol II: 94–95
Bowen's systems theory, Vol II: 255
BPD, *see* Borderline personality disorder (BPD)
Brain development, Vol I: 279, 280, 289
  boys, Vol I: 289
  girls, Vol I: 280
Brain differences, Vol I: 84, 225
Brain imaging, Vol I: 7, 235, 239–240, 242, 244–245, 247, 249, 250
  gustation, Vol I: 246–247, 249
  techniques, Vol I: 250; Vol II: 7
    EEG, Vol I: 250
    fMRI, Vol I: 250
    PET, Vol I: 250
Brain parts, nasal epithelium, Vol I: 247
  amygdala, Vol I: 247
  hippocampus, Vol I: 248
  orbitofrontal cortex, Vol I: 247
Brannon Masculinity Scale (BMS), Vol I: 52, 136–137
Breadwinner/good provider, Vol I: 1, 227, 229, 402, 409
Breast cancer research, Vol II: 528
Breast Evaluation Clinic, Vol II: 526
British high school, survey, Vol II: 478
  substance and level of use, gender differences, Vol II: 478
British Medical Journal, Vol II: 169
British Time Use study, Vol II: 478
Brooks' mastery model, Vol II: 256
Brunswikian lens model, Vol I: 416
BSRI, *see* Bem Sex Role Inventory (BSRI)
BSTc, *see* Bed nucleus of stria terminalis (BSTc)
Building social capital, barriers, Vol II: 454–455
  old boys' networks, Vol II: 454

Bullying, Vol I: 11, 282, 290, 538; Vol II: 11, 31, 315, 319–320, 328–329, 367, 423–424, 427, 429–430, 433–434, 681
Buss' framework of aggression
  dichotomies of aggression, Vol II: 427
  social roles theory, Vol II: 427
  workplace bullying/aggression concerns, outcomes
    three-part model (Neuman and Baron), Vol II: 427

C

CAH, *see* Congenital adrenal hyperplasia (CAH)
California Achievement Tests (CAT), Vol I: 302
California Personality Inventory (CPI), Vol I: 566
California Psychological Inventory, Vol I: 351
California Q-Sort test, Vol I: 351
California Verbal Learning Test (CVLT), Vol I: 569
Canadian Forces Attrition Information Questionnaire (CFAIQ), Vol II: 686
Canadian Forces (CF), Vol II: 672
Canadian Research Institute for Advancement of Women (CIRAW), Vol II: 534
Cancer, Vol II: 525–529
  breast cancer, Vol II: 526–527
  colorectal cancer, Vol II: 529
  lung cancer, Vol II: 528–529
  prostate cancer, Vol II: 527–528
    health-care systems, Vol II: 527
Cancer Genetics Network (CGN), Vol I: 185–186
Cape Verdean community, Vol II: 627
CAPS, *see* Cognitive-affect personality system (CAPS)
Cardiac/cardiovascular reactivity, Vol I: 442–443
Cardiovascular agents, Vol II: 520
Cardiovascular disease, Vol II: 162–163, 542–543
Career aspirations, Vol I: 288; Vol II: 330, 388, 402, 660
Career success, Vol I: 310; Vol II: 46, 48
Career Incentive Act (1977), Vol I: 281
Career-oriented feminists, Vol II: 371
Career progression and leadership, Vol II: 677–679
Care work, Vol II: 346
Carol Gilligan's theory, Vol I: 32
CAT, *see* California Achievement Tests (CAT)
Catholics, teachings about homosexuality, Vol II: 370–371
CBAQ-F, *see* Child Behavior and Attitude Questionnaire for Females (CBAQ-F)
CBPR, *see* Community-based participatory research (CBPR)
CCM, *see* Cultural context model (CCM)
Cell biology and internal molecular processes, Vol II: 525
Center for Sex Offender Management, Vol II: 598
Centers for Disease Control and Prevention (CDC), Vol II: 480, 520, 523–525, 530, 531–533, 541, 576
Central nervous system agents, Vol II: 520
Centre for Gender Research, University of Oslo, Vol I: 44

CF, *see* Canadian Forces (CF)
CFAIQ, *see* Canadian Forces Attrition Information Questionnaire (CFAIQ)
CFNI, *see* Conformity to Feminine Norms Inventory (CFNI)
CGN, *see* Cancer Genetics Network (CGN)
Characteristics of group members
  descriptive beliefs, Vol II: 448
  prescriptive beliefs, Vol II: 448
Charter of Human Rights and Freedoms, Vol II: 690
Chemical senses, Vol I: 246–249
  nasal epithelium
    androstenone, Vol I: 248
    human pheromone, Vol I: 248
    main brain areas, Vol I: 247
    menstrual synchrony, Vol I: 248
    olfactory receptor, Vol I: 247
    tipof- the-nose phenomenon, Vol I: 248
    VNO, Vol I: 248
  tongue
    basic tastes, Vol I: 246
    glossopharyngeal, Vol I: 246
    gustation, Vol I: 247
    PROP, Vol I: 246
    PTC, Vol I: 246
    sex-specific patterns, Vol I: 247
    taste buds of tongue, Vol I: 246
    vagus, Vol I: 246
    visual food stimuli, Vol I: 247
  See also Brain parts, nasal epithelium
Chicago lesbian community's strategies, Vol II: 258
Child Behavior and Attitude Questionnaire for Females (CBAQ-F), Vol I: 140–141
Child Behavior and Attitude Questionnaire for Males (CBAQ-M), Vol I: 140–141
Childcare, Vol I: 11, 110, 312, 475, 485, 572; Vol II: 11, 137, 266, 282, 401, 403, 404, 407, 409, 411, 413, 445, 500, 647, 687, 689
Child Gender Socialization scale, Vol I: 144
Childhood, behavior in, Vol I: 219–220
  cognitive and motor skills, Vol I: 220
  fantasy play, Vol I: 219
  gonadal activity, Vol I: 219
Childhood, gender identity and stereotyping, Vol I: 495–496
Childhood sexual abuse (CSA), Vol II: 76, 138, 144, 201, 208
Cholesterol lowering (statins), Vol II: 520
Cholinesterase inhibitors, Vol II: 524
Chronic illness, diagnosis/treatment of
  adjustment to chronic illness
    absence of psychological disorders, research, Vol II: 546
    maintenance of adequate functional status, Vol II: 547
    quality of life, impact on, Vol II: 547

Subject Index

ways for (Stanton, Collins, and Sworowski), Vol II: 546
AIDS mortality rates in men/women, Vol II: 542
causes of death, US
    breast and cervical tumors in men, Vol II: 541
    cardiovascular/cerebrovascular diseases, cancers, Vol II: 541
    lung and prostate cancers in men, Vol II: 542
'chronic,' defined, Vol II: 543
differences in adjustment
    agency and communion, Vol II: 549–550
    dyadic coping and interpersonal context, Vol II: 550–552
    psychological adjustment, Vol II: 547–549
disease knowledge
    CVD, disease knowledge and risk perception, Vol II: 544
    Homko's findings, Vol II: 543–544
    mortality risks, findings, Vol II: 543
early disease diagnosis, Vol II: 545
future research
    cultural and religious implications, Vol II: 553–554
    sexual minority status, Vol II: 552–553
HIV/AIDS research, Vol II: 542
Promundo's challenges for AIDS prevention (Greig), Vol II: 542
reaction to diagnosis
    emotional functioning in men/women (Lövgren), Vol II: 545
    men's adaptive help-seeking strategies (Addis and Mahalik), Vol II: 545
screening practices
    body weight, influence in, Vol II: 545
    colorectal cancer screening, barriers/facilitators, Vol II: 544
    health insurance status, criteria for, Vol II: 544
    Medicare eligibility, US, Vol II: 544
Chronicle of Higher Education, Vol II: 337
Chronic Obstructive Pulmonary Disease (COPD), Vol II: 228, 548
Chronic strain in women, causes/effects, Vol II: 137
CIRAW, see Canadian Research Institute for Advancement of Women (CIRAW)
Civil Rights Act of 1964, Vol II: 187
Classroom, gendered, Vol I: 277–291, 279–286
    biological and learning differences, Vol I: 287
        hard-wired brains, Vol I: 279, 287
    disadvantage, Vol I: 279
    in educational attainment, explanations, Vol I: 286–290
        biological and learning differences, Vol I: 287
        cultural factors, Vol I: 289
        gender equity programs, Vol I: 287
        single-sex education *vs.* co-education, Vol I: 288
    educational benefits, Vol I: 291
    gendered classroom, Vol I: 279–286
        gendered curriculum, Vol I: 281
        peer interactions, Vol I: 281
        teacher behaviors, Vol I: 283
    gendered curriculum, Vol I: 281
    gendered structure of education, Vol I: 277–279
    peer interactions, Vol I: 281
        co-educational classroom, Vol I: 282
    race/ethnicity with gender, intersects, Vol I: 290
    teacher behaviors, Vol I: 283
        Black students, Vol I: 283–284
        drop-out rate, Vol I: 284
        Hispanic students, Vol I: 284
        White students, Vol I: 283
Client's *biological sex versus* the client's *gender presentation*, Vol II: 193
Client Therapy with Women Scale (CTWS), Vol II: 201
Clinical assessment, Vol II: 125, 238, 598, 603
Code of menstrual invalidism, Vol I: 26
Coeducation, Vol I: 26, 282, 288–289, 291
Co-educational school, Vol I: 288
Coercive femininity, Vol II: 117
Coercive power, Vol I: 416
Cognitive ability tests, Vol II: 68, 70
    Wechsler Adult Intelligence Scales, Vol II: 70
Cognitive-affect personality system (CAPS), Vol II: 67, 83
Cognitive appraisal theory (1984), Lazarus and Folkman, Vol II: 432
Cognitive maintenance, Vol II: 293
    unconscious inhibition of mimicry, Vol II: 294
Cognitive mechanisms
    bereaved gay men, study of, Vol II: 144
    community-based LGB/heterosexual adolescents, study, Vol II: 144–145
Cognitive processes, Vol I: 5, 7, 84, 223, 238, 307, 317, 322–323, 331, 517; Vol II: 5, 7, 142, 145, 460
    spatial memory processes, Vol I: 322–323
    spatial strategies, Vol I: 322
Cognitive social learning theory, Vol I: 474–475, 477
    media models, Vol I: 475
    sexual double standard, Vol I: 475
Cognitive style, Vol I: 352–354, 545
Colonialism, definition, Vol II: 270
Colonoscopy, screening method, Vol II: 529
Colorectal cancer screening, barriers/facilitators, Vol II: 544
Coming of Age in Samoa, Vol I: 159
Commissural system, Vol I: 225
Committee on Disability Issues in Psychology, Vol I: 370
Committee on Ethical Guidelines for Forensic Psychologists, Vol II: 587, 590
Committee on Lesbian and Gay Concerns, Vol I: 367, 370
Committee on Psychosocial Aspects of Child and Family Health, Vol I: 67

Committee on Women in the NATO Forces (CWINF), Vol II: 689
Communication, Vol I: 5, 8, 11, 13–14, 63, 113, 117–118, 160, 184, 192–193, 195, 197–198, 200, 202–204, 313, 359–425, 540; Vol II: 5, 8, 11, 14, 23, 200, 210, 253, 261, 264–268, 294–296, 300, 320, 323–324, 327, 346, 351, 432, 456, 499, 521–525, 543, 552–553, 589–592, 619, 645, 654, 663, 673–674
Community-based participatory research (CBPR), Vol I: 186
Community psychologists, Vol I: 613–618, 620–626, 628–629, 631–635; Vol II: 35
Community psychology, Vol II: 12, 613–635
    gender observations
        as contextual variable, Vol II: 625–628
        gender treatment over time, Vol II: 628–629
        as grouping variable, Vol II: 618–623
        as process variable, Vol II: 623–624
        reflections and future directions, Vol II: 629–635
    integration of theory, Vol II: 613
    research, gender treatment, Vol II: 613–635
        conceptualization of gender, Vol II: 615–616
        integration of theory, Vol II: 613
        method, Vol II: 616–617
    social ecological perspective, Vol II: 613
Community-residing men and women, Vol II: 497
Compassionate love, Vol II: 311, 323, 327–328
    care for intimates/strangers, Vol II: 328
Complementarity hypothesis, Vol I: 22
Conceptions, gender, Vol I: 366, 401–402
Confidentiality and anonymity, Vol II: 591–594, 602
Confirmatory factor analyses (CFA), Vol I: 137, 147, 148, 150–151
Conflict Tactics Scale, Vol II: 316
Conflict Tactics Scale 2 (CTS-2), Vol II: 210
Conformity to Feminine Norms Inventory (CFNI), Vol I: 139, 150
Conformity to Male Norms Inventory (CMNI), Vol I: 52, 138–139
Congenital adrenal hyperplasia (CAH), Vol I: 139, 141, 218–220, 307, 323–324, 366; Vol II: 112, 116
Congressionally Directed Medical Research Program, Vol II: 528
Construction, gender
    women/men task performance, role in
        doing housework is also "doing gender," Vol II: 407
        "feminine"/"masculine" duties categorization, Vol II: 407
    See also Gender theories
Contemporary psychotherapy practice, Vol II: 271
Contemporary trends in couples and family therapy, Vol II: 264–271
    cultural competence and EBT, Vol II: 268–269
    evidence-based treatment, Vol II: 264–265
    physiology/socialization/power, empirical research on, Vol II: 265–266
    problems with first-order change, Vol II: 266–268
    social justice perspective, Vol II: 269–271
Contextualization, future research, Vol II: 393
    individual-level predictors, Vol II: 393
Continuing problem of white, heterosexual privilege, Vol II: 254, 262–264
Controlled laboratory studies, aggression, Vol II: 314–315
    lower levels of stranger aggression against women, Vol II: 314
    manipulation, Vol II: 315
    men's greater aggression, Vol II: 314
Convenience sampling, Vol I: 181–182, 187
Conventional heterosexual relationships, Vol II: 293
Conventional/realistic personality, Vol II: 233
Conversation, Vol I: 28, 51, 107, 113–115, 117–118, 344, 363, 379–380, 385–399, 401, 404, 412, 434, 436, 440, 500, 505, 515; Vol II: 21, 165, 207, 236, 239–240, 282, 290, 295, 312, 677
Conversational control, Vol I: 388, 390, 397
Conway's calculations, Vol II: 113
"Cooperating with a mental illness," Vol II: 119
COPD, *see* Chronic obstructive pulmonary disease (COPD)
Coping, Vol II: 1, 11, 433–435, 495–511
    emotion-focused, Vol II: 499
    problem-focused, Vol II: 499
    relationship-focused, Vol II: 499
    sexual harassment
        "affirmative defense" to, Vol II: 434
        COPE, Vol II: 434
        non-assertive techniques, women's response to, Vol II: 434
    transactional model, Vol II: 496
Corticosterone, Vol I: 226
Cortina's multi-level theory, Vol II: 426
Counseling men, Vol I: 13, 45, 54; Vol II: 13, 233, 242, 326
Couples and family therapy, contemporary trends in, Vol II: 264–271
    cultural competence and EBT, Vol II: 268–269
    evidence-based treatment in couples therapy, Vol II: 264–265
    physiology/socialization/power, empirical research on, Vol II: 265–266
    problems with first-order change, Vol II: 266–268
    research, Vol II: 268
    social justice perspective, Vol II: 269–271
Covert sexism, *see* Selective incivility theory
CPI, *see* California Personality Inventory (CPI)
Creative performance, Vol I: 343–344, 347, 349, 351–354
Creative potential, Vol I: 343–344, 347, 349–355, 364
Creative women, cases, Vol I: 344–347, 351–353
    description of women, Vol II: 351

Subject Index

Creativity, Vol I: 2, 7, 103, 343–355, 561
   androgyny and cognitive styles, Vol I: 352–353
      stereotype threat, Vol I: 353
   androgyny shift theory, Vol I: 354
   creative women, cases, Vol I: 344–346
   culture and gender, Vol I: 347–349
      arguments, Vol I: 348
      range of reaction, Vol I: 349
   gender differences
      in divergent thinking, Vol I: 349–350
      in personality indicators, Vol I: 350–352
      issues, Vol I: 343
Creativity Styles Questionnaire-Revised (CSQ-R), Vol I: 352
Crime dramas *(Medium, The Closer)*, Vol II: 644
Criminal behavior, gender and, Vol II: 316
Critical consciousness, Vol II: 263, 269, 272, 631, 633–635
Cross-cultural communication, Vol I: 379, 385
Cross-cultural community based research, Vol II: 633
Cross-cultural comparison, Vol II: 156, 209, 311, 393
Cross-cultural data, sources, Vol I: 49, 167–169
   Atlas of World Cultures, Vol I: 167
   Cross-Cultural Research Methods, Vol I: 167
   Ethnographic Atlas, Vol I: 167
   fieldwork, Vol I: 167
   governmental and other statistics, Vol I: 167–168
   Human Relations Area Files, Vol I: 167
   Standard Cross-Cultural Sample, Vol I: 167
   study-specific data collections, Vol I: 168–169
   See also Cross-cultural research
Cross-cultural research, Vol I: 65, 159–173, 332, 366; Vol II: 343
   advantages of, Vol I: 163–164
      increased variance of processes and variables, Vol I: 164
      isolation of variables, Vol I: 164
      search for universals and expansion of theory, Vol I: 163–164
   describing cultural elements, Vol I: 161
   describing social groups, Vol I: 160–161
      culture, Vol I: 160
      ethnicity and race, Vol I: 160
      nationality, Vol I: 160–161
      society, Vol I: 160
   issues with translation, Vol I: 170–173
      back-translation, Vol I: 171
      decentering, Vol I: 172
      equivalence of translation, Vol I: 171–172
      management of problems, Vol I: 172–173
      response styles, Vol I: 172
   nature of measurement issues, Vol I: 169–170
      five-factor personality theory, Vol I: 170
      natives, Vol I: 169
      sojourners, Vol I: 169
   psychological universals, Vol I: 161–162
   sources of cross-cultural data
      Atlas of World Cultures, Vol I: 167
      Cross-Cultural Research Methods, Vol I: 167
      Ethnographic Atlas, Vol I: 167
      fieldwork, Vol I: 167
      governmental and other statistics, Vol I: 167–168
      Human Relations Area Files, Vol I: 167
      Standard Cross-Cultural Sample, Vol I: 167
      study-specific data collections, Vol I: 168–169
   study of culture, psychological approaches, Vol I: 162–163
      cross-cultural psychology, Vol I: 162
      cultural psychology, Vol I: 162–163
      indigenous psychology, two groups, Vol I: 163
   types of research designs, Vol I: 164–167
      context sampling exploratory studies, Vol I: 165–166
      generalizability studies, Vol I: 166
      psychological differences studies, Vol I: 165
      simply exploratory studies, Vol I: 165
      theory-driven studies, Vol I: 166–167
Cross-cultural research designs, types of, Vol I: 164–167
   context sampling exploratory studies, Vol I: 165–166
   generalizability studies, Vol I: 166
   psychological differences studies, Vol I: 165
   simply exploratory studies, Vol I: 165
   theory-driven studies, Vol I: 166–167
Cross-Cultural Research Methods, Vol I: 159–173
Cross dressing/Cross-dresser, Vol I: 369; Vol II: 114, 367
Cross-gender identification, Vol II: 112, 122–123
Cross-sex friendships
   degree of sexual interest of men/women, Abbey's research, Vol II: 283
   "friends with benefits" relationships, study, Vol II: 283
   misperception, contributing factor to sexual harassment, Vol II: 284
   sexual activity, impact, Vol II: 283
   sexual tension, cause of, Vol II: 283
Cross-sex interactions, Vol I: 10, 66, 187, 226, 362, 385–386, 390, 401, 507, 532; Vol II: 283, 295
CSA, *see* Childhood sexual abuse (CSA)
CSQ-R, *see* Creativity Styles Questionnaire-Revised (CSQ-R)
CTS-2, *see* Conflict Tactics Scale 2 (CTS-2)
CTWS, *see* Client Therapy with Women Scale (CTWS)
Cultivation theory, Vol II: 167
Cultural context model (CCM), Vol II: 261, 269
Cultural elements, Vol I: 161
Cultural factors, gendered classroom, Vol I: 5, 14, 289, 297, 308, 474, 484–486
   educational disadvantage, Vol I: 289
   LGBTQ students, Vol I: 290
Cultural specificity, emotions, Vol I: 441–442
   basic expressions, Vol I: 441
Culture of muscularity, Vol II: 160
Curriculum, Vol I: 7, 118, 198, 281; Vol II: 7, 260, 381, 565

CVLT, *see* California Verbal Learning Test (CVLT)
CWINF, *see* Committee onWomen in the NATO Forces (CWINF)
Cyberbullying, Vol II: 320
Cytoarchitectonic methods, Vol I: 244

D
Darwinian evolutionary theory, Vol I: 22, 260, 261, 271
DAT, *see* Differential Aptitude Tests (DAT)
DEBQ, *see* Dutch Eating Behavior Questionnaire (DEBQ)
Deepening Psychotherapy with Men, Vol I: 45
Demand/Withdraw pattern/Sequence, Vol II: 499–500
Department of Defense (DoD), Vol II: 528, 682
Department of Defense Sexual Harassment Survey, Vol II: 682
Department of Education, Science, and Training (DEST), Vol II: 380
Department of Immigration and Multicultural Affairs, Vol II: 487
Department of National Defence (DND), Vol II: 687, 690
Department of State v. Washington Post, Vol II: 593
Dependent personality disorder (DPD), Vol II: 94, 193
Dependent stressors, Vol II: 134–135
Depression
    BDI theory, Vol II: 80, 82, 214
    biased theories, construct of depression, Vol II: 73–74
    child abuse, cause, Vol II: 317
    cognitive factors
        hopelessness, Vol II: 142
        rumination, Vol II: 142–143
    depression scale, Vol II: 74
    diagnostic criteria, Vol II: 96
    division of labor, direct/indirect effects, Vol II: 414
    gender, sexual orientation, and vulnerability to, Vol II: 133–147
    HABDI, Vol II: 206
    internalizing symptoms, Vol II: 23
    label of depression for women, arguments, Vol II: 96–97
    maternal depression, GID cases, Vol II: 118
    negative spillover across work/family, outcomes, Vol II: 415
    neuroticism, mental health variable, Vol II: 25, 27, 29
    during the postpartum period, Vol II: 97
    Real Men, Real Depression public health campaign, Vol II: 241
    research in chronically ill populations, Vol II: 546
    stress-mediation model of vulnerability to depression, Vol II: 9
    undiagnosed condition in men, Vol II: 230
    women's vulnerability to
        lower body esteem (Hyde and colleagues), Vol II: 142
        negative attributional style, Vol II: 142
        rumination, Vol II: 141

DEST, *see* Department of Education, Science, and Training (DEST)
Developmental job experiences, Vol II: 455
DHHS, *see* US Department of Health and Human Services (DHHS)
DHT, *see* Dihydrotestosterone (DHT)
Diabetes and utilization of care, Vol II: 531
    health effects, Vol II: 530
    interventions and programs, Vol II: 531–532
Diabetes Intervention Reaching and Educating Communities Together (DIRECT), Vol II: 531
Diagnosis, Vol I: 9, 12, 29, 141, 186, 219, 241; Vol II: 9, 12, 71–72, 74–75, 81, 91–100, 102, 103, 105, 111–112, 118–119, 121–125, 135, 191–196, 236, 270, 434, 501, 520, 522–523, 525, 530–531, 533, 541–555
Diagnosis and intervention, psychological testing, Vol II: 72
Diagnostic and Statistical Manual, Vol II: 9, 91, 111, 192
Dichotomies of aggression
    active–passive, Vol II: 427
    direct–indirect, Vol II: 427
    physical–verbal, Vol II: 427
Diet of ideal media, Vol II: 167
Difference as deficit, Vol I: 380, 400; Vol II: 8
    critique of Lakoff's model, Vol I: 381–382
    research on Lakoff's model, Vol I: 380–381
    women's speaking style, Vol I: 380
Difference model of gender and language, Vol I: 380
    as deficit, *see* Difference as deficit
    as dominance, *see* Dominance approach, difference as
Differential Aptitude Tests (DAT), Vol I: 302; Vol II: 386
Differential social attention, Vol II: 118
Digital rectal examination (DRE), Vol II: 527
Dihydrotestosterone (DHT), Vol I: 216, 218
DIRECT, *see* Diabetes Intervention Reaching and Educating Communities Together (DIRECT)
Direct forms of aggression, Vol II: 427
Director of Military Gender Integration and Employment Equity (DMGIEE), Vol II: 676
Disclosure of potential conflict of interest, Vol II: 597–598
Discourse analysis, Vol I: 116–118, 362, 379, 389, 403
Discrepancy strain, Vol I: 50
Discrimination and prejudice, Vol II: 196, 362, 446–447
Disease Control and Prevention (CDC), Vol II: 480, 520, 523–525, 530–533, 541, 576
Disease-modifying antirheumatic drugs, Vol II: 545
Disorder of sex development (DSD), Vol I: 366; Vol II: 218–219
Distress, diagnosis, assessment, and sociocultural influences, Vol II: 192–196
    feminist therapy, Vol II: 196
    gender and sexism, Vol II: 192–193

Subject Index

"Isms," effects, Vol II: 193–195
traumatic experiences, Vol II: 195–196
Divergent thinking, Vol I: 349–350, 352
verbal and figural activities, Vol I: 349
Diverse recruitment, research projects, Vol I: 179–188
examples, Vol I: 184–187
capture–recapture method, Vol I: 187
CBPR, Vol I: 186
clinical trial/observational study, Vol I: 185
convenience or snowball recruitment methods, Vol I: 186
diversity in a large clinical trial, WHI, Vol I: 185
psychological phenomena study, Vol I: 184–185
recruitment strategies for SMW, Vol I: 186–188
strategies for enhancing diversity, Vol I: 185–186
model of recruitment
contact stage, Vol I: 183
enrollment stage, Vol I: 183–184
preparatory stage, Vol I: 182–183
self-selection bias, Vol I: 182
types of recruitment, Vol I: 180–182
choosing recruitment strategy, difficulties, Vol I: 181–182
convenience sampling, Vol I: 181
eligibility criteria, Vol I: 182
population-based recruitment, Vol I: 180–181
purposive recruitment, Vol I: 181
Diversity documents discriminatory treatment, Vol II: 632
Division of labor
household labor, outcomes of
emerging focus on fairness evaluations, Vol II: 413–414
marital happiness, satisfaction and quality, Vol II: 413
psychological adjustment, Vol II: 414
work–family and family–work spillover, Vol II: 415
men at work/women at home, cultural template of
asymmetrically permeable work/family roles, Vol II: 402
child care demands/family needs, women's role, Vol II: 402
dual-earner families, Vol II: 402
household labor, history/importance, Vol II: 402–404
impact of industrialization on labor, Vol II: 403
labor sphere before twentieth century, Vol II: 403–404
modern conveniences, impact on household labor, Vol II: 403–404
specific social/environmental conditions, influence of, Vol II: 403
US Census Bureau's recent American Community Surveys, Vol II: 402
methods of studying household labor, Vol II: 407–408

predictors of household labor, empirical findings
age and life course, Vol II: 410
attitudes toward gender roles, Vol II: 410–411
earnings, Vol II: 409
education, Vol II: 410
lesbian and gay couples and families, Vol II: 411–412
marital status and union type, Vol II: 411
race and ethnicity, Vol II: 412
women's/men's employment, Vol II: 408–409
theories of household labor
exchange/resource theories, Vol II: 404–406
gender theories, Vol II: 406–407
See also Household labor theories
work and family
influence of jobs on family life, example, Vol II: 401–402
Rosabeth Moss Kanter's perspective, Vol II: 401
DMGIEE, *see* Director of Military Gender Integration and Employment Equity (DMGIEE)
DND, *see* Department of National Defence (DND)
DoD, *see* Department of Defense (DoD)
DoD Sexual Harassment Survey, Vol II: 683
Domestic labor, Vol II: 404–405, 411, 416, 478, 646
Domestic violence, Vol I: 28, 30, 361; Vol II: 72, 137, 182, 191, 199, 258, 262, 484, 608, 631, 632
Dominance, Vol I: 34, 90, 138, 200–201, 203, 239, 244, 269–270, 287, 289, 324–325, 353, 385, 387–391, 393, 397, 400, 403–404, 412, 414–419, 438, 537, 539; Vol II: 23, 51, 57, 102, 169, 255, 258–259, 261, 263, 266, 269, 282, 294, 337, 339, 347, 362, 426, 430, 448, 542, 569, 601, 627, 649
Dominance approach, difference as, Vol I: 387
gender and inequality, Vol I: 387–388
dominant behavior, Vol I: 387
linguistic style, Vol I: 387
social status, Vol I: 387
interruptions, Vol I: 389–391
profanity, Vol I: 391–393
resisting and derogating women's requests, Vol I: 391
batterers, Vol I: 391
nagging, Vol I: 391
talking time, Vol I: 388–389
in classrooms, Vol I: 388
volume of words/power relationship, Vol I: 388–389
verbal harassment as dominance, Vol I: 393
Dominant behavior, Vol I: 387; Vol II: 346
of men, Vol I: 388
of women, Vol I: 387
Double bind, Vol I: 27, 198, 383–385, 404, 433; Vol II: 94, 345–347, 351–352, 433, 450–451, 458–459
Double jeopardy, Vol II: 135, 510
DPD, *see* Dependent personality disorder (DPD)

Dramedies *(Sex and the City, Desperate Housewives)*, Vol II: 644
DRE, *see* Digital rectal examination (DRE)
Drive for muscularity, Vol II: 10, 99, 154, 158, 161, 170, 576, 659
　See also Muscular-ideal internalization
Drive for Thinness subscale of the Eating Disorders Inventory-2, Vol I: 165
Drop-out rate, Vol I: 284, 290
Drug therapy (treatment), Vol II: 97
DSDs, *see* Disorders of sex development (DSDs)
DSM, *see* Diagnostic and statistical manual of mental disorders (DSM)
DSM-IV Casebook, Vol II: 103
DSM-IV diagnostic category, definition, Vol II: 73
DSM-IV disorder, Vol II: 231
Dual earner, Vol I: 537; Vol II: 402
Dust bowl empiricism, *see* MMPI/MMPI-2
Dutch Eating Behavior Questionnaire (DEBQ), Vol I: 457, 459
Dyadic relationships, Vol II: 506
Dynamic spatial ability, Vol I: 318, 322, 332
Dysfunction strain, Vol I: 50–51

E

Early women's sport and physical education
　"A game for every girl and every girl in a game," NAAF, Vol II: 565
　masculine model domination, Vol II: 565
　Roberta Park's historical analysis, Vol II: 565
　women's physical education programs, goals, Vol II: 565
EAT-26, Vol I: 165
Eating, amount of
　interactions, Vol I: 458–462
　　desirable male partner/familiarity of partner, Vol I: 461
　　disinhibited eating, Vol I: 459
　　male–female dyads, Vol I: 462
　　menstrual cycle, Vol I: 458–459
　　negative alliesthesia, Vol I: 458
　　partner sex/desirability/familiarity, Vol I: 460–461
　　PMS, Vol I: 458
　　rebound effects, Vol I: 460
　　social influence, Vol I: 461–462
　　stress and eating, Vol I: 459–460
　　thought suppression and expression, Vol I: 460
　main effects
　　caloric intake, Vol I: 457
　　DEBQ, Vol I: 457
　　difference in size, Vol I: 457
　　impression management, Vol I: 457–458
　　men eat more, reason, Vol I: 456
　　RMR, Vol I: 457
　　TFEQ, Vol I: 457
　　weight gain, negative utility, Vol I: 457
　　See also Eating behavior, sex and gender differences
Eating behavior, sex and gender differences
　amount eaten, Vol I: 456–462
　　See also Eating, amount of
　directions for future research, Vol I: 466
　food preferences, Vol I: 462–464
　　See also Food preferences
　hunger, Vol I: 464
　　fasting ghrelin levels, Vol I: 464
Eating disorders, Vol I: 10, 13
　attitudes, Vol I: 91–93, 97
　in men, Vol I: 54
　prevention, Vol I: 86, 87
　in women, Vol I: 247
Eating Disorders Inventory-2, Vol I: 165
EBP, *see* Evidence-based practice (EBP)
EBPP, *see* Evidence-based practice in psychology (EBPP)
EBT, *see* Evidence-based treatment (EBT) movement
Eccles' developmental model, Vol II: 573
ECJ, *see* European Court of Justice (ECJ)
Economists' traditional human capital theories, Vol II: 445
ECP, *see* Emergency Committee in Psychology (ECP)
Education, Vol I: 5, 7, 15, 22, 28, 57, 71, 77–78, 118–119, 125, 135, 160, 170, 187, 199, 205–207, 209, 221, 239, 263, 269, 284–285, 290, 300, 337, 344–345, 379–383, 390, 405, 408, 410, 413, 415, 445–446, 472–473, 480, 487, 496, 524, 526, 528, 531–533, 542, 563–566, 578–579, 596, 601, 606, 615, 662, 689; Vol II; 7, 22, 28, 57, 77–78, 118–119, 170, 187, 199, 205–207, 209–210, 221, 239, 263, 269, 284–285, 290, 300, 337, 344–345, 379–383, 390, 405, 408, 410, 413, 415, 445–446, 472–473, 480, 487, 496, 524, 526, 528, 531–533, 563–566, 578–579, 596, 601, 606, 615, 689
EEGs, *see* Electroencephalograms (EEGs)
Effect sizes, Vol I: 4, 5, 14, 83, 89, 96, 220, 224, 241, 263, 265, 298–301, 303–306, 309, 311, 318–321, 324, 414–415, 418, 477; Vol II: 4, 5, 14, 21, 26, 30, 35, 283, 360, 386, 504, 643
Effect size *vs.* practical significance, Vol I: 311
Egalitarianism, Vol I: 146
Egalitarian therapy relationship, promotion, Vol II: 203
Ego dystonic homosexuality, Vol II: 103
Electroencephalograms (EEGs), Vol I: 238–239, 250
Electroencephalography (EEG), Vol I: 238, 249
Electromyography, Vol I: 434
Elevation of traditionally feminine values (Seward), Vol I: 26
Elizabeth Cady Stanton, Vol II: 565
　man's claim to physical superiority, rejection, Vol II: 565

Subject Index

Embedded figures test, Vol I: 263, 265–267, 320, 326, 373, 503, 560
Emergency Committee in Psychology (ECP), Vol I: 23–24
Emergent leadership, Vol II: 341–342, 351
   social influence, advantage in, Vol II: 341
Emerging media
   cell phone use, gender differences, Vol II: 653
   computer use
      children's computer use, Calvert's survey, Vol II: 652
      frequency of internet use, age factor interaction with gender, Vol II: 652
      and internet, Vol II: 652
   fictionalized websites, use
      sexual double standard interaction effect, Vol II: 653
   male adolescents, heavy gamers, Vol II: 652
   Pew Internet and American Life project report, findings, Vol II: 652
   SNS by younger adults, use of, Vol II: 653
   See also Social networking sites (SNS)
   See also Media
Emotion(al), Vol I: 434
   competence, Vol I: 439
      MSCEIT, Vol I: 439
      overwhelmed/cerebral labeled, Vol I: 439
   expressed in behavioral contexts, Vol I: 436–437
      stonewalling, Vol I: 437
   and expression, self-report, Vol I: 434–436
      general emotional experience and expression, Vol I: 434
      measure, Vol I: 434
      specific emotions, Vol I: 435–436
      See also Expression/emotion, self-reported
   functioning, neural substrates of, Vol I: 443
      brain lateralization, Vol I: 443
      fMRI/PET scans, Vol I: 443
      limbic system activation, Vol I: 443
   regulation, Vol I: 432–434
      agreeableness, Vol I: 43
      anxiety, negative/self deprecating thoughts, Vol I: 433
      BFI personality factors, Vol I: 43
      double bind emotionality, Vol I: 433
      gender–emotion stereotypes, Vol I: 432
      overreaction, and lack of expression, Vol I: 433
      personality-related factors, Vol I: 432
      positive/negative emotions, Vol I: 433
      specific emotions stereotyped, control over, Vol I: 432
      stereotype threat, Vol I: 433
      surface acting, Vol I: 433
   stereotypes, nature of, Vol I: 430–432
Emotional contagion, Vol I: 239, 434, 446
Emotional stoicism, Vol II: 236, 237, 546
Emotion-centered couples therapy, Vol II: 264

Emotion-focused coping, Vol I: 499; Vol II: 497–498, 503–504, 511
Emotion/socialization, Vol I: 429–448
   cultural specificity, Vol I: 441–442
   emotion(al)
      competence, Vol I: 439
      expressed in behavioral contexts, Vol I: 436–437
      functioning, neural substrates of, Vol I: 443
      regulation, Vol I: 432–434
   facial expressions/nonverbal behaviors, Vol I: 437–438
   gender differences, etiology of, Vol I: 443–446
      developmental perspective, Vol I: 444–445
      distal/proximal cues, Vol I: 445–446
   nonverbal decoding skill, Vol I: 438–439
   physiological arousal, Vol I: 442–443
   relationship specificity, Vol I: 439–440
   self-reported emotion and expression, Vol I: 434–436
      general emotional experience and expression, Vol I: 434
      measure, Vol I: 434
      specific emotions, Vol I: 435–436
   stereotypes/display rules, Vol I: 430–432
      accuracy of, Vol I: 432
      emotional stereotypes, nature of, Vol I: 430–432
Empathizers, Vol I: 309
Empathy/nurturance and sensitivity to nonverbal cues, Vol II: 323–325
   degree of empathy, variation in, Vol II: 325
   interpersonal sensitivity, Vol II: 325
   thinking based on nonverbal behavior, Vol II: 324
Employer-based insurance programs, Vol II: 518
Employment
   protection, Vol II: 368
   women and men
      participation in housework, Vol II: 409
      time availability hypothesis, Vol II: 408–409
      See also Household labor
Empty nest syndrome, Vol I: 2, 571, 572
Endocrine disorders, Vol I: 218–219, 270, 483, 529; Vol II: 115
Endogenous behavioral problems, Vol II: 93
English-related skills, Vol II: 388
Enzyme 5-α reductase, Vol I: 216, 529
EP, *see* Evolutionary psychology (EP)
Epidemiology, Vol II: 133–136, 526, 542
Epidemiological studies, Vol II: 133–135, 224, 504
Epistemological debates and methodological developments (1980s and 1990s), Vol I: 30
   feminist empiricism, Vol I: 31–32, 35
   feminist methods, Vol I: 33–34
      principles (Gergen), Vol I: 33–34
   feminist postmodernism, Vol I: 32–33
      criticism, Vol I: 34
      principles (Gergen), Vol I: 33–34
   feminist standpoint epistemologies, Vol I: 32

Epistemological debates (*cont.*)
  influence of political/cultural activities of women's movement, Vol I: 31
  NOW, Vol I: 30
  second-wave feminism, Vol I: 30
EPLF, *see* Eritrean People's Liberation Front (EPLF)
Equal Treatment Directive, Vol II: 368
Erikson's theory, Vol I: 9, 560–566; Vol II: 9
  critiques of gender in
    Rochester Adult Longitudinal Study, Vol I: 563
  culture/sexual orientation/history in, Vol I: 565–566
    cohort influences on identity formation, Vol I: 566
    CPI, Vol I: 566
    ego integrity, Vol I: 561
    workable social identity, Vol I: 561
  developmental theory, critiques of, Vol I: 563–565
    additional stages, Vol I: 563
    cross-gender trade-off of qualities, Vol I: 565
    distal social roles, Vol I: 563
    ego integrity, Vol I: 565
    generativity, Vol I: 564–565
    intimacy and identity, Vol I: 564
    proximal family issues, Vol I: 563
  of personality development, Vol I: 560–561
Eritrean People's Liberation Front (EPLF), Vol II: 676
ERPs, *see* Event-related potentials (ERPs)
Estradiol, Vol I: 215, 245, 270, 323
Estrogen, Vol I: 83, 215, 218–219, 223, 241–242, 244, 246, 249, 323–324, 330, 459, 464, 480, 483–484, 487, 533, 534; Vol II: 115, 133, 524
  cyclic variations, Vol I: 241
  estradiol (E), Vol I: 215
  nociception/pro-nociceptive properties, Vol I: 242
  pain disorder effects, Vol I: 241
  in pain sensitivity, Vol I: 241
  therapy, Vol I: 246
Ethical issues, Vol II: 591–599
  confidentiality and anonymity, Vol II: 591–594
  disclosure of potential conflict of interest, Vol II: 597–598
  harm, Vol II: 594–596
  informed consent, Vol II: 596–597
  interstate research, Vol II: 598–599
Ethic of openness, Vol II: 295
Ethnic backgrounds, Vol II: 157, 173, 476, 576, 634
Ethnic or visible minorities, career progression of, Vol II: 677
Ethnocentrism, Vol I: 34; Vol II: 193
Ethnographic Atlas, Vol I: 167
Euclidean-based strategies, Vol I: 221, 330–331
European Court of Human Rights, Vol II: 368–369
European Court of Justice (ECJ), Vol II: 368
European Union's Committee, Vol II: 98
European Union trans persons, protections for, Vol II: 368
Evaluation of FFM research/directions, study of gender issues, Vol II: 28–30

Event-related potentials (ERPs), Vol I: 238–239, 243–244, 249
Evidence-based practice (EBP), Vol II: 221, 233–234, 271–272
Evidence-based practice in psychology (EBPP), Vol II: 221, 233
Evidence-based treatment (EBT) movement, Vol II: 10, 254
Evolutionary context, gender in, Vol I: 259–272
  advantageous trait, sex-specific, Vol I: 269–270
  empirical questions, Vol I: 271
  evolutionary explanations, Vol I: 265
    man the hunter, woman the gatherer, Vol I: 266–268
  hormonal variation in EP, Vol I: 270
  sex differences, causation of, Vol I: 271
  spatial cognition, sex differences, Vol I: 262
    classic literature, Vol I: 263
    navigation, Vol I: 264–265
    object location memory, Vol I: 263–264
Evolutionary explanations, Vol I: 36, 195, 201–202, 242, 265–270, 325; Vol II: 651
  man who gets around hypothesis, Vol I: 268–269
  men hunt, women gather rule, Vol I: 266–268
    adaptation environment, Vol I: 267
    aiming, Vol I: 266
    gathering, Vol I: 267
    tool making, Vol I: 267
    tracking, Vol I: 266
Evolutionary psychology (EP), Vol I: 7, 35, 49, 201–202, 259–263, 265, 271, 373, 471, 473–474
  biopsychosocial approach, Vol I: 262
  hypotheses, Vol I: 261
  sexual selection theory, Vol I: 473
  sexual strategies theory, Vol I: 474
Evolutionary theory of mate preferences
  parental investment, Vol II: 285–287
  reproduction, pivotal factor for women, Vol II: 285
  SST, Buss and Schmitt (1993)
    Bem Sex Role Inventory (Bem, 1974), Vol II: 287
    conventional mate preference research, Vol II: 287
    short/long-term mating strategies, Vol II: 285
    women across ovulatory cycle/natural menstrual cycles, Vol II: 286
    women at peak fertility, Vol II: 286
    women's description of men as "nice guys" and "jerks," Vol II: 286
Exchange/resource theories, approaches
  exchange and resource perspectives, critiques, Vol II: 405–406
  relative resources and economic dependency
    neoclassical economic theory, Vol II: 405
    relative resources hypothesis, Vol II: 405

time availability/constraints
  indicators, employment/marital/parental status/family composition, Vol II: 405
Exercise, Vol I: 108, 110, 185, 367, 389, 396, 402, 431, 444, 457, 486; Vol II: 29, 42, 44, 161, 166–167, 233, 240, 263, 340, 344, 349–350, 443, 476–478, 500, 524, 544, 550, 563–580
Expectancy-value model, Vol I: 297, 310; Vol II: 387–388
Expectation states theory, research on, Vol II: 345
Experiments of nature, Vol II: 115
Expert power, Vol I: 416
Explicit motives, Vol II: 42, 44, 49
Exploratory/confirmatory factor analytic techniques, Vol II: 32
Exploratory factor analysis (EFA), Vol I: 137–146, 148–149, 151–152
Expression/emotion, self-reported, Vol I: 434–436
  emotions, Vol I: 435–436
    feelings of dysphoric self-consciousness, Vol I: 435
    feelings of vulnerability, Vol I: 435
    men emotions, Vol I: 435
    negative emotions, Vol I: 435
    positive emotions, Vol I: 435
  general emotional experience/expression, Vol I: 434
    AIM, Vol I: 434
    electromyography, Vol I: 434
    emotional contagion, Vol I: 434
    GSS, Vol I: 434
    measure, Vol I: 434
Expressiveness/instrumentality/mental health, Vol II: 24–25
Externalizers, Vol I: 118, 442
Extra-pair copulation/flirtation, Vol II: 286
Extraversion, Vol I: 140, 413, 441
Extrinsic questionnaire measures of achievement, Vol II: 48

F

Facebook, Vol II: 653–654
Face-to-face talk, gossip, Vol I: 396
Facial expressions/nonverbal behaviors, Vol I: 412, 431–432, 437–438, 441
  non-Duchenne/Duchenne smiles, Vol I: 438
Family therapy and couples counseling, issues, Vol II: 253–273
  authors' social locations, Vol II: 254
  contemporary trends in, Vol II: 264–271
    cultural competence and EBT, Vol II: 268–269
    evidence-based treatment, Vol II: 264–265
    physiology/socialization/power, empirical research on, Vol II: 265–266
    problems with first-order change, Vol II: 266–268
    social justice perspective, Vol II: 269–271
  continuing problem of White, heterosexual privilege, Vol II: 262–264
  feminist revision of family therapy (1970–2000), Vol II: 254–255
  intersectionalities framework, Vol II: 261–262
  men from a feminist perspective, working with, Vol II: 256–257
  queering the discussion, Vol II: 257–259
    GLBT family studies, Vol II: 257
    tensions between race/ethnicity and gender/feminism, Vol II: 260–261
Fantasy play, *see* Childhood, behavior in
Fathering, Vol I: 2, 45, 269, 362; Vol II: 2, 272
FBI, *see* Federal Bureau of Investigation (FBI)
Fear
  about psychotherapy, Vol II: 223
  being controlled by others, Vol II: 56
  being in public, Vol II: 100
  in bisexual men, Vol I: 67; Vol II: 227, 230
  loss of respect and authority, Vol I: 121
  loss of control, Vol I: 444
  mental illness, Vol II: 100
  negative reprisals, Vol II: 368
  of behaving assertively, Vol I: 146
  of crime, Vol II: 620
  of drinking, Vol II: 240
  of femininity, Vol II: 237
  of generating anti-semitism, Vol II: 262
  of not being nurturing, Vol I: 146
  of physical unattractiveness, Vol I: 146
  of power, Vol II: 47, 56
  of rejection, Vol II: 49, 365
  of religious fundamentalism, Vol I: 67
  of safety, Vol I: 91
  of separation, Vol II: 73, 94
  of success, Vol I: 28; Vol II: 47–49
  of unemotional relationships, Vol I: 146
  of victimization, Vol I: 146
  weakness, Vol II: 52, 55
Fecal occult blood testing (FOBT), Vol II: 529
Federal Bureau of Investigation (FBI), Vol II: 608
Federal Communications Commission-mandated educational television, Vol II: 645
Federal Judicial Center's Research Division, Vol II: 601
Federal rules of evidence, Vol II: 590
Feel-good feminism, Vol II: 253
Female-to-male (FtM) sex reassignment, Vol I: 224
Female-to-male transsexuality, Vol II: 113
Feminine beauty ideals, unrealistic nature of, Vol II: 157
Feminine Gender Role Stress Scale (FGRS), Vol I: 146
The Feminine Mystique (Betty Friedan), Vol I: 27, 43
Feminine speech styles, Vol I: 387
Feminine-stereotype
  domains, Vol I: 414
  gender, Vol I: 443
    emotional, Vol I: 444
Femininity, Vol II: 22
Femininity, cultural models of, Vol II: 473
Femininity effect in relationships, Vol II: 296

Femininity Ideology Scale (FIS), Vol I: 139, 148–150
Feminism and the women's movement scale (FWM), Vol II: 205
Feminism in family therapy/tensions between race/ethnicity and gender, Vol II: 260–261
Feminism & Psychology, Vol I: 2, 27, 105, 107, 122; Vol II: 2
Feminist approaches to working with men, Vol II: 254, 256
Feminist empiricism, Vol I: 31–32, 35
    standpoint theory/postmodernism, Vol I: 31
Feminist Identity Composite (FIC), Vol I: 149
Feminist Identity Development Scale (FIDS), Vol I: 139, 149
Feminist Identity Scale (FIS), Vol I: 139, 148–150; Vol II: 201
Feminist family therapy, Vol II: 254, 256–257, 260, 262–263
Feminist methods, Vol I: 33–34
Feminist postmodernism, Vol I: 31–33, 403
    common to all feminist psychological approaches, Vol I: 32
    criticism, Vol I: 34
    feminist linguists concerns, Vol I: 403
    principles (Gergen), Vol I: 33–34
Feminist practice, emergence of, Vol I: 29–30, 109
Feminist praxis, Vol II: 211
Feminist psychologists, Vol I: 1, 26, 28–31, 35–36, 192–195, 369; Vol II: 1, 189, 190
Feminist psychology, Vol I: 20, 29, 35–36, 118, 201–202; Vol II: 64, 73, 190, 196
Feminist psychotherapies, theory/research/ practice, Vol II: 187–215
    distress, diagnosis/assessment/sociocultural influences, Vol II: 192–196
        feminist therapy, meaning of, Vol II: 196
        gender and sexism, Vol II: 192–193
        "Isms," effects, Vol II: 193–195
        traumatic experiences, Vol II: 195–196
    future research, Vol II: 211–214
        clients' perceptions and experiences of feminist therapy, Vol II: 212–213
        current and future practice, Vol II: 214–215
        efficacy, evaluation, and outcome research, Vol II: 213
        feminist/non-feminist practices, Vol II: 212
        feminist therapists, differentiation, Vol II: 211
        theoretical considerations, Vol II: 213–214
    outcome and evaluation research, Vol II: 205–211
        childhood sexual abuse, adult survivors of, Vol II: 208–209
        immigrant/international women, Vol II: 206–208
        men who abuse their partners, Vol II: 210
    perceptions, Vol II: 196–197
    praxis, Vol II: 198–205
        general practices, Vol II: 198–202
        therapeutic relationship, issues, Vol II: 202–205

Feminist revision of family therapy, Vol II: 254–255, 261
Feminist revolution in psychology, Vol I: 26–30
    emergence of a psychology for women, Vol I: 26–28
    emergence of feminist practice, Vol I: 29–30
    emergence of psychology for women, Vol I: 26–28
        The Feminine Mystique (Betty Friedan), Vol I: 27
        positivism's preferred method, limitations of, Vol I: 29
        Psychology Constructs the Female, Vol I: 26
        Psychology Constructs the Female; or, The Fantasy Life of the Male Psychologist, Vol I: 27
        sex differences research, Vol I: 28
        sex-typed behaviors, studies on, Vol I: 28
        Toward a Redefinition of Sex and Gender in Psychology, Vol I: 29
        Women and Madness (Phyllis Chesler), Vol I: 27
Feminist self-disclosure inventory (FSDI), Vol II: 203
Feminist standpoint position, Vol I: 105
Feminist standpoint theory, Vol I: 31–33
    Carol Gilligan's theory, Vol I: 32
    maternal thinking, Vol I: 32
Feminist Theories and Feminist Psychotherapies: Origins, Themes, and Variations, Vol II: 191
Feminist theorists, Vol II: 20, 22, 34, 65, 67, 83, 191, 256, 686
Feminist Therapists (perceptions of), Vol I: 10, 30; Vol II: 10, 195–205, 211–213
Feminist Therapy Behavior Checklist (FTB), Vol II: 200–202, 211
Feminist Therapy Institute, Vol I: 30; Vol II: 198
Feminist therapy, meaning, Vol II: 196
Fetus development, Vol I: 216–219
    abnormalities, Vol I: 218–219
        AIS, Vol I: 218
        ambiguous genitalia, Vol I: 218
        CAH, Vol I: 219
        DSD, Vol I: 219
        endocrine disorders, Vol I: 218
        masculinization, Vol I: 218
        TS, Vol I: 218
    brain, Vol I: 217–218
        ARs, Vol I: 218
        INAH1, INAH2, INAH4, INAH3, Vol I: 217
    reproductive organs, Vol I: 216–217
        FOXL 2/FIG X, proteins, Vol I: 217
        Mullerian tract, Vol I: 216
        sertoli cells, Vol I: 216
        SRY gene, Vol I: 216
        WNT 4 gene, Vol I: 217
        Wolffian tract, Vol I: 216
FFM, *see* Five-factor model (FFM)
FFM traits, difference in, Vol II: 26–29
FGRS, *see* Feminine Gender Role Stress Scale (FGRS)
FIC, *see* Feminist Identity Composite (FIC)
Fictionalized websites, Vol II: 653
    sexual double standard interaction effect, Vol II: 653

Subject Index

FIDS, *see* Feminist Identity Development Scale (FIDS)
First Change Sheet, Vol I: 370
First-generation literature, pathologizing homosexuality, Vol I: 61–62
    change-of-orientation therapy, Vol I: 62
    homosexuality, Vol I: 62
    LGB identity, Vol I: 62
    oedipal conflict, Vol I: 61
    reparative or conversion therapies, Vol I: 61
    sexual identity therapy, Vol I: 62
First onsets *vs.* duration of depression
    biological changes, impact, Vol II: 134
    factors associated (Nolen-Hoeksema and Hilt), Vol II: 134
First psychological test, Vol II: 21
FirstWave, Vol I: 21–23
    applied psychology after World War I, Vol I: 21
    attention to "woman problem," Vol I: 23
    community of ideas debate, Vol I: 22
    Laura Spelman Rockefeller Memorial Fund, Vol I: 21
    The Mental Traits of Sex, Vol I: 22
    of feminism, Vol I: 20, 81
    studies on mental and motor abilities during menstruation, Vol I: 23
    studies to debunk stereotypes about women, Vol I: 23
    variability hypothesis, test, Vol I: 22
    women in higher education, Vol I: 21
    young women of experimental psychology class, Vol I: 22
FIS, *see* Femininity Ideology Scale (FIS); Feminist Identity Scale (FIS)
Five-factor model (FFM), Vol II: 20, 25–30
    agreeableness, Vol II: 25
    conscientiousness, Vol II: 25
    extroversion, Vol II: 25
    neuroticism, Vol II: 25
    openness, Vol II: 25
    research evaluation/directions, study of gender issues, Vol II: 28–30
    traits, difference in, Vol II: 26–28
Flexibility, Vol I: 172, 186, 192, 349, 350, 352–353, 355, 480, 485, 501–502, 530, 531
Fluency, Vol I: 222, 224–225, 305, 312, 349, 350, 352
FMRI, *see* Functional magnetic resonance imaging (fMRI)
FOBT, *see* Fecal occult blood testing (FOBT)
FOIA, *see* Freedom of Information Act (FOIA)
Follicular phase, Vol I: 223, 241, 458, 465; Vol II: 286
Food and Drug Administration (FDA), Vol II: 98
Food preferences, Vol I: 455, 462–464
    appetite, definition, Vol I: 462
    interactions, Vol I: 463–464
        menstrual cycle, Vol I: 463–464
        stress, Vol I: 464
    main effects, Vol I: 463
        acceptance of red meat, Vol I: 463
        concern about appearance, Vol I: 463
        low-calorie food, Vol I: 463
        preference for chocolate, Vol I: 462
        vegetarianism, largely female phenomenon, Vol I: 463
    specific appetites, Vol I: 462
    See also Eating behavior, sex and gender differences
Forensic psychology, gender research in, Vol II: 12, 587–608
    defining gender, Vol II: 588
    ethical issues, Vol II: 591–599
        confidentiality and anonymity, Vol II: 591–594
        disclosure of potential conflict of interest, Vol II: 597–598
        harm, Vol II: 594–596
        informed consent, Vol II: 596–597
        interstate research, Vol II: 598–599
    goals and final disclaimer, Vol II: 588–589
    methodological and epistemological pluralism, Vol II: 588
    methodological issues, measurement, Vol II: 599–608
        archival data, Vol II: 607–608
        fairness and bias in measurement, Vol II: 604–606
        reliance on self-report, Vol II: 607
        reliance on simulation research, Vol II: 606–607
        response bias, Vol II: 602–604
        sampling, Vol II: 599–601
    research, Vol II: 589–590
        forensic *vs.* therapeutic roles, Vol II: 590
        standards research in other contexts, Vol II: 589–590
Formal task-oriented contexts, Vol I: 389
The Forty-nine Percent Majority: The Male Sex Role, Vol I: 44
FOXL 2/FIG X, proteins, Vol I: 217
Freedom of Information Act (FOIA), Vol II: 593
Friends, Vol II: 655
Friendster, Vol II: 653
From "Fair Sex" to Feminism, Vol II: 565
FSDI, *see* Feminist self-disclosure inventory (FSDI)
FTB, *see* Feminist Therapy Behavior Checklist (FTB)
FtM, *see* Female-to-male (FtM) reassignment
Functional magnetic resonance imaging (fMRI), Vol I: 237–239, 241–444, 247, 249–250, 443, 447, 487
FWM, *see* Feminism and the women's movement scale (FWM)

G

Games Inventory, Vol I: 140–141, 151
Gay and Lesbian Alliance Against Defamation (GLAAD), Vol II: 124
Gay and lesbian individuals, sexual prejudice against, Vol II: 359–362
    homophobia and its discontents, Vol II: 359–360
        etiological factors, environmental, Vol II: 360

Gay and lesbian individuals (*cont.*)
　in-group domination, Vol II: 362
　internalized biphobia, Vol II: 365
　internalized homophobia, Vol II: 362
　religion, Vol II: 361–362
　sex and gender, Vol II: 360–361
　sexual prejudice against bisexual individuals, Vol II: 363–365
　sources of prejudice
　　sex/gender/sexual orientation, Vol II: 363–365
Gay men/lesbians in the military, Vol II: 689–691
　policy comparisons, Vol II: 690–691
GDI, *see* Gender-Related Development Index (GDI)
GEDAD, *see* Gender expression deprivation anxiety disorder (GEDAD)
Gender
　attribution, Vol I: 364
　and body behaviors, Vol II: 161–164
　　anabolic steroid use, Vol II: 162–163
　　avoidance, Vol II: 164–168, 172
　　BDD, Vol II: 162
　　cosmetic surgery, Vol II: 163
　　eating disorders, Vol II: 162
　flexible, Vol I: 368
　fluid, Vol I: 368
　identity, Vol I: 364
　queer, Vol I: 368
　roles, Vol I: 364
Gender and gender collective, Vol I: 36
Gender-appropriate activities, Vol II: 383, 385, 573
Gender as contextual variable, Vol II: 618, 625–628
　cultural narratives, Vol II: 627–628
　individual gender-related attitudes, Vol II: 625–626
　relationships as context, Vol II: 626–627
Gender as grouping variable, Vol II: 618–623
　demographic variable, Vol II: 620
　descriptive variable, Vol II: 618–620
　individual-level within an ecological framework, Vol II: 622
　intersecting variable, Vol II: 622–623
　risk or protective factor, Vol II: 620–621
　in theoretical relationship, Vol II: 621
Gender aware therapy, Vol II: 237
Gender based strategy, Vol II: 69
Gender Behavior Inventory for Boys/CBAQ, Vol I: 140
Gender bias
　bias in structural issues and statistical assumptions, Vol II: 77–78
　differential item endorsement probability, Vol II: 75
　different item meaning, reference groups, Vol II: 75–76
　gendered correlates of item bias, Vol II: 76
　in media
　　analysis of *Monday Night Football*, Trujillo, Vol II: 571
　　Italian coverage of 2004 Olympics, Vol II: 572
　　Messner's research on gender stereotyping, Vol II: 571
　　themes of, Vol II: 572
　operationalization, biased test construction
　　differential item endorsement probability, Vol II: 75
　　different item meaning, reference groups, Vol II: 75–76
　　gender and social appropriateness of items, Vol II: 77
　　MMPI-2 scales for rape victims/molested children, Vol II: 76
　　PTSD assessment, Vol II: 74
　in personality assessment process
　　assessment bias/criterion bias, Vol II: 73
　personality/psychopathology tests
　　biased test construction, Vol II: 74–75
　social appropriateness of items, Vol II: 77
　theories
　　androcentric understanding of personhood, Vol II: 73
　　construct of depression, men/women, Vol II: 73–74
　　DSM-IV diagnostic category, Vol II: 73
Gender coevolution, Vol II: 256
Gender, combat, and warrior ethic, Vol II: 674–676
Gender convergence, Vol II: 480
Gender diagnosticity, Vol I: 143
Gender differences, etiology of, Vol I: 363–365, 443–446
　developmental perspective, Vol I: 444–445
　distal/proximal cues, Vol I: 445–446
　　feedback processes, Vol I: 446
　　smiling, Vol I: 446
　in divergent thinking, Vol I: 349–350
　in personality indicators, Vol I: 350–352
　　conceiving data, Vol I: 351
　　description of women, Vol I: 351
　　positive/negative side, Vol I: 350
Gender differences in sexuality, Vol I: 471–488
　explaining gender differences in sexuality
　　biological factors, Vol I: 482–484
　　other factors, Vol I: 485–486
　　self-reports, Vol I: 481–482
　　socio-cultural factors, Vol I: 484–485
　future direction, Vol I: 487
　research on gender differences in sexual behaviors
　　large surveys, Vol I: 478
　　meta-analytic findings, Vol I: 476–478
　　other sexual behaviors, Vol I: 478–479
　sexual attitudes
　　gender and mate selection and retention, Vol I: 481
　　gender differences in attitudes toward homosexuality, Vol I: 479–480
　　gender differences in sexual desire, Vol I: 480–481
　theories

Subject Index 795

cognitive social learning theory, Vol I: 474–475
evolutionary psychology, Vol I: 473–474
gender schema theory, Vol I: 476
neo-analytic theory, Vol I: 473
psychoanalytic theory, Vol I: 471–472
social structural theory, Vol I: 475
transgender, Vol I: 486–487
Gender differences/roles
athletes and non-athletes, differences, Vol II: 569
Duda, research by, Vol II: 570
gender roles and gender conflict, Vol II: 570
gender stereotypes, Vol II: 570–571
McNally and Orlick, research by, Vol II: 570
ultramarathoners, Vol II: 569
Weinberg and colleagues, research by, Vol II: 570
Gender dysphoria (GDI), Vol I: 71, 141–142, 369, 486–487
Gender dysphoric disorder (GID), Vol I: 486
Gendered behavior measures, Vol I: 139–143
CAH, Vol I: 139
CBAQ-F, Vol I: 140
CBAQ-M, Vol I: 140–141
Games Inventory, Vol I: 140
Gender Behavior Inventory for Boys/CBAQ, Vol I: 140
gender diagnosticity, Vol I: 143
gender dysphoria/GDI, Vol I: 141
gender identity, Vol I: 142
GID, Vol I: 139
GIDYQ-AA, Vol I: 141–142
Recalled Childhood Gender Identity/Gender Role Questionnaire, Vol I: 141
SRBS, Vol I: 142–143
Gendered curriculum, Vol I: 281
Gendered language, social roles, Vol I: 8, 402
Gendered nature of workplace mistreatment
concepts (Andersson and Pearson)
aggression, violence, and incivility, Vol II: 424
organizational deviance, definition, Vol II: 424
sexual harassment, Vol II: 424
workplace bullying, Vol II: 424
frameworks of antecedents
Buss' framework of aggression, Vol II: 427–428
contextual influences on mistreatment, Vol II: 428
incivility, Vol II: 426–427
sexual harassment, Vol II: 425–426
impact on men/women
psychological and physical consequences, Vol II: 436
work-related consequences, Vol II: 436–437
profiles of targets and perpetrators
bullying, Vol II: 429–430
incivility, Vol II: 429
sexual harassment, Vol II: 430–431
workplace aggression/violence, Vol II: 431

See also Profiles (gendered) of targets and perpetrators
reactions to
appraisal processes, Vol II: 432–433
coping processes, Vol II: 433–435
escalating aggression, Vol II: 435
Gender effects on group behavior, Vol II: 337–347, 351
communal and social behavior, Vol II: 337–339
Black and White adolescent participants, Vol II: 339
meta-analytic reviews, Vol II: 338
emergent leadership, Vol II: 341–342
gender stereotypes/effects, Vol II: 343
men's resistance to women's influence/leadership, Vol II: 342–343
social influence, Vol II: 339–341
Gender Empowerment Measure (GEM), Vol I: 167, 168
Gender equity programs, Vol I: 286, 287, 289
Gender expression deprivation anxiety disorder (GEDAD), Vol II: 124
Gender Gap Index (GGI), Vol I: 307
Gender harassment, Vol II: 424, 502, 680–682, 686, 692
Gender identity, Vol I: 8, 49–50, 60, 68, 70–72, 139, 141–142, 218, 260, 284, 364, 368–369, 440, 486, 495–518, 527–550
Gender identity disorder (GID), Vol I: 9, 139, 141, 498, 510–511; Vol II: 111–125
Gender identity disorder not otherwise specified (GIDNOS), Vol II: 112
Gender identity disorder of childhood (GIDC), Vol II: 111–112
Gender identity/GIDYQ-AA, Vol I: 141–142
Gender inclusive language, Vol I: 363
Gender-integrated executive teams, organizational effectiveness, Vol II: 456–457
Gender intensification hypothesis, Vol I: 87, 529–532
gender-typed activities and behaviors, Vol I: 531–532
self-perceptions and self-concept, Vol I: 530–531
Gender irrelevant strategy, Vol II: 69
Gender/leader stereotypes, Vol II: 447–449, 450
Gender marking, Vol II: 571–572
See also Gender bias
Gender/military psychology, Vol II: 671–691
gay men and lesbians, Vol II: 689–691
lesbians and gay men, policies comparisons, Vol II: 690–691
gender and harassment, Vol II: 679–686
harassment experiences, Vol II: 680–683
surveys, conclusions, Vol II: 684–686
segregation and progression
career progression of ethnic or visible minorities, Vol II: 677
gender and occupational segregation, Vol II: 672–674
gender, career progression, and leadership, Vol II: 677–679

Gender/military psychology (*cont.*)
 gender, combat, and the "warrior ethic," Vol II: 674–676
 gender differences in occupational stratification, Vol II: 676–677
 work–family issues, Vol II: 686–689
  balancing work and family, Vol II: 687–688
  work–family policies of various countries, Vol II: 688–689
Gender/motivation for achievement, affiliation–intimacy, and power
 achievement motivation, Vol II: 45–49
  implicit/explicit measures, Vol II: 44–45, 48–49
  motive to avoid success, Vol II: 47–48
 advice and promising areas for future research, Vol II: 57–58
 affiliation–intimacy motivation, Vol II: 49–52
  physiological correlates, Vol II: 51–52
  relationships, Vol II: 50–51
 power motivation, Vol II: 52–55
  physiological correlates of power, Vol II: 54–55
  profligacy and responsibility training, Vol II: 53–54
 social contextual factors/social motives, Vol II: 55–57
 social motives in women/men, measuring, Vol II: 43–44
 social motives, reemergence of interest, Vol II: 42–43
Gender neutral strategy, Vol II: 68
 pattern of performance, Vol II: 68
Gender policing, Vol II: 430
Gender, quantitative approaches, Vol I: 81–98
 research approaches in contemporary gender research, Vol I: 90–98
 scientific study, Vol I: 81–90
Gender-Related Development Index (GDI), Vol I: 141, 168
Gender-related personality theory, Vol II: 20
Gender research, contemporary approaches, Vol I: 90–98
 content analysis
  gender and power, Vol I: 97
  portrayal of male and female characters on video game covers, Vol I: 97
 experiments, Vol I: 91–93
  contingency manipulation, Vol I: 93
  relationship contingency, Vol I: 92
 longitudinal studies, Vol I: 94–95
 meta-analysis
  advantage of, Vol I: 96
  hypermasculine or hostile masculine beliefs, Vol I: 96
  virtual negotiation, Vol I: 96
 nonexperimental quantitative methods, Vol I: 93–94
  advantage of a correlational design, Vol I: 94
  HLM, Vol I: 94
  latent growth modeling (LGM), Vol I: 95

Gender Role Conflict Scale (GRCS), Vol I: 47, 52–53, 145
Gender Role – Feminine (GF) Scale, Vol II: 79
Gender role identity, Vol I; 48–50; Vol II: 236
Gender Role – Masculine Scale (GM), Vol II: 79
Gender-role socialization, Vol I: 6, 8, 11, 13, 15, 53, 64, 134, 143–144, 280–281, 287, 289, 326, 330, 429–448, 495, 535, 537; Vol II: 6, 8, 11, 13, 100, 230, 237, 256, 261, 265, 292, 546, 549, 554
Gender-role stereotypes, Vol II: 21, 94, 382, 655, 661
Gender role strain model (GRS), Vol II: 256
Gender role stress/conflict, measures of, Vol I: 144–146
 FGRS, Vol I: 146
 GRCS, Vol I: 47, 52–53, 145
 MGRS, Vol I: 52–53, 145–146
 RABBM, Vol I: 145
 restrictive emotionality, Vol I: 137, 145
Gender schema theory, Vol I: 476, 508
Gender, scientific study, Vol I: 81–90
 content analysis, Vol I: 89–90
 double blind, Vol I: 82
 experimental approaches, Vol I: 83–85
  aspects of biological sex, Vol I: 84
  evolutionary theory, Vol I: 84
  fixed factor, Vol I: 84
  gender polarization, Vol I: 84
  prenatal hormone exposure, Vol I: 84
  stereotype threat, Vol I: 84
  stereotype threat in women, Vol I: 85
 longitudinal designs and statistical control, Vol I: 86–88
  advantage of, Vol I: 87
  ANOVA, Vol I: 88
  bias associated with unmeasured variables, Vol I: 88
  controls into correlational–longitudinal research, Vol I: 87
  correlational–longitudinal data, Vol I: 88
  eating disorders prevention programs, Vol I: 86
  fixed and variable risk factors, Vol I: 86
  relationship between self-surveillance and depression, Vol I: 87
  SEM, Vol I: 88
 meta-analysis, Vol I: 89–89
  application/procedures, Vol I: 89–89
 nonexperimental research, Vol I: 85–86
  between-groups design, Vol I: 85
  causal modeling, Vol I: 86
  correlational design, Vol I: 85
  Pearson correlation coefficient, Vol I: 85
  SEM, Vol I: 86
 relationship between independent and the dependent variable, Vol I: 82
 theory, Vol I: 82
 validity issues, Vol I: 83
  construct validity, Vol I: 83

Subject Index

external validity, Vol I: 83
field experiments, Vol I: 83
hypothesis validity, Vol I: 83
internal validity, Vol I: 83
quasi-experimental design, Vol I: 83
statistical validity, Vol I: 83
Gender-segregated work adaptation, example
traditional/nontraditional gender theories, Vol II: 406
See also Gender theories
Gender sensitive approach, Vol II: 253
Gender sensitives couples therapy, Vol II: 253
Gender similarities/differences
explanations, Vol I: 306–308
implications, Vol I: 311
intelligence
means, Vol I: 301
variance, Vol I: 301–302
mathematical ability, Vol I: 302–305
aptitude *vs.* grades, Vol I: 304–305
means, Vol I: 302–303
variance, Vol I: 303–304
methodologies, Vol I: 297–298
expectancy-value model, Vol I: 297
narrative review approach, Vol I: 298
SEM, Vol I: 297
statistics used, Vol I: 298–300
meta-analyses, Vol I: 298
VR, Vol I: 299
summary, Vol I: 306
verbal ability, Vol I: 305
means, Vol I: 305
variance, Vol I: 305
Gender similarities hypothesis, Vol I: 262, 306, 487, 569, 643; Vol II: 569, 643
Gender socialization, Vol I: 134, 143–144, 281, 287, 289, 326, 330, 445, 495, 537; Vol II: 48, 153, 168–170, 174, 192, 213, 255–256, 496, 505, 509–510, 674
Gender socialization scale, Vol II: 213
Gender/socioeconomic status, Vol II: 480–482
Gender-stereotyped beliefs, Vol II: 573
Gender stereotypes, Vol I: 2–3, 8, 10–12, 14, 21, 84–85, 89–90, 97, 191, 193, 197–198, 222, 284, 286, 291, 297, 302, 306, 309–310, 318, 327, 362, 374, 381, 411, 421, 430–432, 436, 438, 471, 475–476, 499–502; Vol II: 91–105, 343, 521, 570, 660
agentic qualities, Vol II: 447
boys' sports/girls' sports, ratings, Vol II: 571
communal qualities, Vol II: 447
Eleanor Metheny, classic analysis
'*not socially appropriate*' sport for women, Vol II: 570
key masculine features (Kane and Snyder), Vol II: 571
and physician–patient communication, Vol II: 521–523

gender stereotypes, Vol II: 521
health beliefs and physician–patient communication, Vol II: 522–523
reporting style, Vol II: 522
Gender stereotypes in diagnostic criteria, Vol II: 91
diagnostic categories replete with gender stereotypes, Vol II: 93–101
anxiety disorders, Vol II: 99–101
mood disorders, Vol II: 96–99
personality disorders, Vol II: 93–96
fundamental assumptions, Vol II: 92–93
issues that cut across diagnostic categories, Vol II: 101–104
gender-role factors in seeking treatment, Vol II: 104
poverty, Vol II: 101–102
race and racial discrimination, Vol II: 102–103
stereotypes concerning sexual orientation and identity, Vol II: 103–104
violence and abuse, Vol II: 102
Gender/stress/coping, Vol II: 495
contextual model of stress and coping process, Vol II: 496f
gender differences:considered in context, Vol II: 497–498
models of, Vol II: 495–497
social support, gender differences in, Vol II: 504–509
perceived *vs.* received social support, Vol II: 506–507
social support networks, Vol II: 507–509
structural and functional aspects, Vol II: 505–506
stress, coping, and gender in diverse populations, Vol II: 509–510
stress/coping, gender differences, Vol II: 497–504
coping with chronic illness, Vol II: 500–502
coping with interpersonal stress, Vol II: 498–500
coping with work-related stress, Vol II: 502–504
in women and men, Vol II: 510–511
Gender-syntonic interests, Vol II: 118
Gender theories
gender construction
women/men task performance, role in, Vol II: 407
socialization and gender role
"expressive role," women, Vol II: 406
gender-segregated work adaptation, example, Vol II: 406
"instrumental role," men, Vol II: 406
major determinant of labor division, Vol II: 406
Gender-typed traits and behaviors, Vol II: 625
Gender variance, Vol I: 369; Vol II: 114, 120–121, 123, 125
Generalizers, Vol I: 442
General Social Survey (GSS), Vol I: 434
Genes and Gender Collective, Vol I: 36
Genital reassignment surgery (GRS), Vol I: 71
GGI, *see* Gender Gap Index (GGI)

GID, *see* Gender identity disorder (GID); Gender identity disorder (GID)
GIDC, *see* Gender identity disorder of childhood (GIDC)
GIDNOS, *see* Gender identity disorder not otherwise specified (GIDNOS)
GIDYQ-AA, *see* Gender identity/GIDYQ-AA
GLAAD, *see* Gay and Lesbian Alliance Against Defamation (GLAAD)
Glamour and *Cosmopolitan* approximates, Vol II: 172
Glamour magazine, Vol II: 166
Glascock's research
  physical, verbal, and indirect aggression, Vol II: 649
Glass ceiling, Vol I: 404; Vol II: 337, 382, 676–677, 691
Glass cliff, Vol II: 455–456, 461
Glass escalator, Vol II: 341
Glass slipper effect, Vol II: 661
GlaxoSmithKline, Vol II: 523
Global self-esteem
  definition, Vol II: 30–31
  extensive critical reviews, Vol II: 31
  model of self-evaluation, Vol II: 31
Glucocorticoids, Vol I: 215, 226–227
  Cushing's disease, Vol I: 227
Goal-oriented therapy process, Vol II: 235
God's eye perspective, Vol II: 588
Gonadal steroids, Vol II: 55, 115
Gossip, Vol I: 393–399
  feminist analysis, Vol I: 399
  functions, Vol I: 396
    face-to-face talk, Vol I: 396
    organizational gossip, Vol I: 397
    person talk, Vol I: 396
  and gender, Vol I: 397
    conceptions, Vol I: 398
    on romantic relations, Vol I: 398
Government-issued identification, Vol II: 368
Graduate Record Examination (GRE), Vol II: 71, 72
GRE, *see* Graduate Record Examination (GRE)
Group behavior, Vol II: 10, 337, 338, 339, 347, 351
  CEOs, women, Vol II: 337
  future directions, Vol II: 351–352
  gender effects on group behavior, Vol II: 337–342
    emergent leadership, Vol II: 341–342
    men's resistance to women's influence/leadership, Vol II: 342–343
    social influence, Vol II: 339–341
  gender effects on group performance, Vol II: 347–351
    mixed-gender groups, Vol II: 348–350
    same-gender groups, Vol II: 347–348
  gender stereotypes/effects, Vol II: 343–347
    agency and double standard, Vol II: 343–345
    communion and double bind, Vol II: 345–347
    medical treatments advertisements, Vol II: 343
    stereotypes, disadvantage lies in, Vol II: 343

Group differences in depression
  stress and sexual minorities' greater vulnerability to depression, Vol II: 137–139
  stress and women's greater vulnerability to depression, Vol II: 137
  stress factor, Vol II: 136
Group interaction, experimental research on, Vol II: 343
Group Membership by Chance, Vol II: 600
Group performance, effects on, Vol II: 347–351
  mixed-gender groups, Vol II: 348–350
  same-gender groups, Vol II: 347–348
GRS, *see* Gender role strain model (GRS)
GSS, *see* General Social Survey (GSS)
Guidelines for avoiding heterosexual bias in language, Vol I: 370
Guidelines for avoiding racial/ethnic bias in language, Vol I: 370
Guidelines for Avoiding Sexism in Psychological Research, Vol I: 371
Guidelines for Non-Handicapping Language in APA Journals, Vol I: 370
Guidelines for nonsexist language in APA journals, Vol I: 370
Guidelines for nonsexist use of language, Vol I: 370
Gustation, Vol I: 246, 247, 249

H

Ha'aretz (Newspaper), Vol II: 446
HAART, *see* Highly Active Antiretroviral Therapy (HAART)
HABDI, *see* Hmong adaptation of the beck depression inventory (HABDI)
Handbook of Counseling and Psychotherapy with Men, Vol I: 45
Handbook of Qualitative Methods, Vol I: 106
Harassment
  experiences of military personnel, Vol II: 680–683
  gender, Vol II: 424, 502, 656, 680–682, 692
  in military, Vol II: 679–686
    conclusions from surveys, Vol II: 684–686
    harassment experiences, Vol II: 680–683
Hard science, Vol II: 189
Hard-wired brain, Vol I: 279, 287
Harry Benjamin International Gender Dysphoria Association, Vol II: 119
Harvard Business School's MBA program, Vol II: 55
Hate crimes, Vol II: 139, 143, 146–147, 367–368, 369
Hazards of Being Male: Surviving the Myth of Male Privilege, Vol I: 44
Hazing, definition, Vol II: 681
Health behaviors, Vol II: 472–474
  anorexia nervosa, Vol II: 474
  behaviors, Vol II: 472–474
  convergence, Vol II: 480
  demographic/other social categories, Vol II: 478–479
  gender/ socioeconomic status, Vol II: 480–482
  health differences, gender, Vol II: 476–478

Subject Index

health service use and health-related symptoms, Vol II: 474–475
high-risk activities, Vol II: 480–485
life expectancy, Vol II: 471–472
patterns of risk, gendered, Vol II: 475–476
socioeconomic context, Vol II: 479–480
Health-care access and utilization, Vol II: 517–535
  Alzheimer's disease and long-term care, Vol II: 523–525
    long-term care, Vol II: 524–525
  ambulatory care, Vol II: 519
    preventive care and screening visits, Vol II: 519
  cancer, Vol II: 525–529
    breast cancer, Vol II: 526–527
    colorectal cancer, Vol II: 529
    lung cancer, Vol II: 528–529
    prostate cancer, Vol II: 527–528
  diabetes, Vol II: 530–532
    diabetes and utilization of care, Vol II: 531
    health effects, Vol II: 530
    interventions and programs, Vol II: 531–532
  gender stereotypes and physician–patient communication, Vol II: 521–523
    gender stereotypes, Vol II: 521
    health beliefs and physician–patient communication, Vol II: 522–523
    reporting style, Vol II: 522
  race and ethnicity, differences, Vol II: 519
Health-care coverage, Vol II: 518
Health differences, gender, Vol II: 476–478
Health promotion
  physical activity, key factor, Vol II: 567
Health Revitalization Act of 1993, Vol II: 534
Health service use and health-related symptoms, Vol II: 474–475
Hedge, Vol I: 380–381
Hegemonic masculinity, Vol II: 226–227, 571
Helping others, Vol II: 105, 325–326
  helping profession, Vol II: 326
  heroic actions/chivalry, Vol II: 326
  prosocial personality, Vol II: 326
Help seeking, Vol I: 53–54; Vol II: 25, 103–104, 226, 228–229, 232, 234, 241–243, 475, 545–546, 618, 622
Hemispherization, Vol I: 244
Herrmann Brain Dominance Instrument, Vol I: 353
He's Just Not That Into You (Behrendt & Tuccillo, 2004), Vol II: 290
Heterosexuality, Vol I: 61, 66, 103, 117, 196, 367, 385, 483, 499, 512
Heterosexual relationships, *see* Heterosexuality
Heterosexuals and sexual minorities
  developmental trends, Vol II: 136
  mood disorders in, Vol II: 135
  stress and vulnerability to depression
    adaptational effort, Vol II: 138
    discrimination, Vol II: 138–139

hate crimes, Vol II: 139
sexual minority stress, Vol II: 138
victimization, Vol II: 138
Hidden figures/patterns, *see* Embedded figures test
Hierarchical linear modeling (HLM), Vol I: 94
Higher arousal levels, *see* Fear
Highly Active Antiretroviral Therapy (HAART), Vol II: 534
High negative arousal, *see* Mild shock
High-risk activities, health/health behaviors, Vol II: 482–485
Hirja, transgendered social groups, Vol II: 115
Histrionic personality disorder (HPD), Vol II: 94, 95
HIV, *see* Human immunodeficiency virus (HIV)
HIV risk-reduction interventions, Vol II: 624
HLM, *see* Hierarchical linear modeling (HLM)
Hmong adaptation of the beck depression inventory (HABDI), Vol II: 206
Homonegativism, Vol II: 359, 360
Homophobia, Vol II: 359–360, 362
Homosexual individuals, *see* Homosexuality
Homosexuality, Vol I: 59–64, 66, 69–72, 108, 225, 282, 366–367, 479–480, 484, 541; Vol II, 79, 103, 111, 114–115, 118, 122, 191, 225–226, 291, 359, 361–365, 369–371, 430, 449, 458, 486, 553, 645, 690–691
Hopelessness, Vol II: 142
Hormonal and Surgical Sex Reassignment, Vol II: 119
Hormonal susceptibility, theories of, Vol II: 92
Hormones, Vol I: 60, 71, 83–84, 185, 215–219, 222–227, 241–242, 244, 246–249, 270, 279–280, 307, 318, 323–324, 330–331, 364–365, 459, 465, 482–484, 533–534, 543, 545, 568; Vol II: 23, 51–52, 54–55, 58, 96–97, 99, 111, 115–116, 120, 313, 505, 528
Hospital admissions and procedures, Vol II: 520
  National Hospital Discharge Survey records, Vol II: 520
Hostile sexism, Vol II: 137
Hostile working environment, *see* Harassment; Unwanted sexual attention
Household labor
  definition, Vol II: 407
  housework, Vol II: 407
  methods of study
    other household labor measured as total household labor, Vol II: 407
    research techniques, Vol II: 408
    time-consuming major household tasks, Vol II: 407
    time diary studies/survey, Vol II: 408
  outcomes of
    emerging focus on fairness evaluations, Vol II: 413–414
    marital happiness, satisfaction and quality, Vol II: 413

Household labor (cont.)
  psychological adjustment, Vol II: 414
  work–family and family–work spillover, Vol II: 415
  predictors, empirical findings
    age and life course, Vol II: 410
    attitudes toward gender roles, Vol II: 410–411
    earnings, Vol II: 409
    education, Vol II: 410
    lesbian and gay couples and families, Vol II: 411–412
    marital status and union type, Vol II: 411
    race and ethnicity, Vol II: 412
    women's and men's employment, Vol II: 408–409
Household labor, research techniques
  direct observations, Vol II: 408
  historical comparative methods, Vol II: 408
  in-depth interviews, Vol II: 408
Household labor theories
  exchange/resource theories, approaches
    critiques of exchange and resource perspectives, Vol II: 405–406
    relative resources and economic dependency, Vol II: 405
    time availability/constraints, Vol II: 404–405
  gender theories
    gender construction, Vol II: 406–407
    socialization and attitudes toward gender role, Vol II: 406
  methods of studying household labor, Vol II: 407–408
Housework, Vol II: 405, 408
HPA, *see* Hypothalamic-pituitary-adrenal (HPA) axis
HPD, *see* Histrionic personality disorder (HPD)
Human immunodeficiency virus (HIV), Vol II: 533
Human Relations Area Files, Vol I: 167
Hunger, Vol I: 247, 455, 458, 464, 466
Hyperlipidemia, Vol II: 519
Hypermasculinity, Vol II: 649
  callused attitude toward women or sex, Vol II: 649
Hypermesomorphy, Vol II: 172
Hypermuscular men parallels, Vol II: 162
Hypersexual masculine role, Vol II: 99
Hypertension, Vol II: 222, 519, 531, 543, 545
Hypervigilance, Vol II: 100
Hypothalamic-pituitary-adrenal (HPA) axis, Vol I: 226, 533

I

Identity and stereotyping in early/middle childhood, Vol I: 495–518
  antecedents of gender identity and stereotyping, Vol I: 502–507
    cognitive development, Vol I: 502–504
    conceptual distinctions of gender categories and labeling, Vol I: 504
    essentialism, Vol I: 506–507
    parent and sociocultural influences, Vol I: 504–505
    perceptual distinctions of gender categories, Vol I: 504
  Bem Sex-Role Inventory, Vol I: 499
  consequences
    gender identity, Vol I: 508–514
    self-socialization theories, Vol I: 508
    stereotyping, Vol I: 514–517
  definition, Vol I: 495–496
  future directions, Vol I: 517
  gender stereotyping, Vol I: 499–502
    definition, Vol I: 500
    developmental trajectory, Vol I: 500–502
    See also Stereotyping, gender
  individual differences and variation, Vol I: 498–499
  multidimensionality, Vol I: 496–498
  See also Identity, gender
Identity disorder, concerns/controversies, Vol II: 111–125
  current controversies, Vol II: 121–123
    GID qualify as mental disorder, Vol II: 121–123
    insurance debate, Vol II: 123–124
    recommendations for reform, Vol II: 124–125
    recommendations to ensure insurance coverage for SRS, Vol II: 124
  estimated prevalence, Vol II: 113–115
  etiology, Vol II: 115
    biological explanations, Vol II: 115–116
    psychodynamic explanations, Vol II: 118
    psychosocial explanations, Vol II: 116–117
  GID criterion, diagnosis of, Vol II: 112
  history and diagnostic criteria, Vol II: 111–112
  transgender health concerns, Vol II: 120–121
  treatment, Vol II: 118–120
Identity, gender
  consequences of, Vol I: 508–514
    emotional involvement, Vol I: 513
    gender category membership, Vol I: 513
    gender labeling, Vol I: 510
    identity and adjustment, Vol I: 511–513
    identity and behavior and preferences, Vol I: 508–511
    identity and intergroup relations, Vol I: 513–514
    identity and sex segregation, Vol I: 511
    identity, attention, and memory, Vol I: 511
  definition, Vol I: 495
    between 18 and 24 months, Vol I: 495
    constancy at 6–7, Vol I: 495
    three stages, Vol I: 495
  multidimensionality
    centrality or importance, implicit and explicit, Vol I: 496–497
    centrality or importance, stable or chronic form, Vol I: 497
    evaluation or regard, Vol I: 497
    felt pressure, Vol I: 498

Subject Index

felt typicality, Vol I: 498
other dimensions, Vol I: 497–498
private regard, Vol I: 497
See also Stereotyping, gender
Identity (global) changes in adolescence, Vol I: 528–529
development of the self, Vol I: 528
stage theory of development (Erikson), Vol I: 528
Ideology measures, Vol I: 136–139, 150
AFIS, Vol I: 138
AMIRS, Vol I: 137
BMS, Vol I: 136
CFNI, Vol I: 139
CMNI, Vol I: 138
FIS, Vol I: 139
MRAS, Vol I: 137
MRNI, Vol I: 137–138
MRNS, Vol I: 136–137
IDF, *see* Israeli Defence Forces (IDF)
IDVS, *see* International Dating Violence Study (IDVS)
Imagination games, Vol II: 651
Implicit/explicit measures, distinction between, Vol II: 44–45
Implicit inversion theory, Vol II: 449
Implicit motives, Vol II: 42–45, 51, 58
In a Different Voice, Vol I: 105
INAH3, *see* Third interstitial nucleus of the anterior hypothalamus (INAH3); Third interstitial nucleus of the anterior hypothalamus (INAH3)
Incivility, Vol I: 11; Vol II: 11, 423–424, 426–429, 432–433, 435–437
Incompatible leader/ gender roles, effects, Vol II: 449–451
In-depth interviews, Vol II: 408, 654
Indirect aggression, forms, Vol II: 312, 427
Individual male/female leaders, effectiveness of, Vol II: 457–458
Industrial-Organizational Psychology, Vol II: 671
Informal contexts, Vol I: 389
Information/decision-making approach, Vol II: 348
Informed consent, forensic research, Vol II: 596–597
Infrequency-Psychopathology (Fp) Scale, Vol II: 76
Inner Journeys, Public Stands, Vol I: 119
Insidious trauma, Vol II: 195, 214
Institute of Medicine Committee on Lesbian Health Research Priorities, Vol I: 186
Institutional Review Board (IRB), Vol II: 596
Instrumentality and expressiveness as mediators, Vol II: 23
Intellectual rejecters, Vol II: 654
Intelligence, Vol I: 7, 23, 84, 162, 191, 200–221, 300–302, 320, 345, 353, 413, 418, 439, 568–569
gender similarities/differences in mean/variance, Vol I: 301–302
Intelligence quotient (IQ), Vol I: 301–302, 349, 569

Intelligence tests, Vol I: 23, 162, 300–302, 413, 439; Vol II: 65, 70, 81
See also Cognitive ability tests
Intensifiers, Vol I: 380
Interaction, family, Vol I: 385
Internalizers, Vol I: 442
Internalizing/externalizing depressive symptoms, Vol II: 135
International Association for Studies of Men, Vol I: 44
International Conference on Community Psychology in 2006, Vol II: 635
International Dating Violence Study (IDVS), Vol I: 94
International Journal of Men's Health, Vol I: 48
International Society for Men's Health, Vol I: 44
International Society for Men's Health sponsors a biennial World Conference on Men's Health and Gender, Vol I: 47
International Test Commission, Vol II: 605
Interpersonal factors and sexual minorities' vulnerability to depression
rejection sensitivity, Vol II: 140–141
social support, Vol II: 140
Interpersonal judgement, Vol I: 413; Vol II: 234
Interpersonal mechanisms, Vol II: 145
Interpersonal sensitivity/accuracy, Vol I: 413–415, 417–419, 438
Interpersonal theories of depression, Vol II: 139
Interpersonal violence, Vol II: 322, 362, 617, 632
Interruptions, Vol I: 389–391, 393, 397, 415, 417, 419, 421, 574
turn-taking norms, Vol I: 390, 412
Intersectionalities framework, Vol II: 261–262, 272
Third interstitial nucleus of the anterior hypothalamus (INAH3), Vol I: 217
Inter-University Consortium for Political and Social Research, Vol II: 607
In the Game:Gay Athletes and the Cult of Masculinity (Eric Anderson), Vol II: 578
In the Room with Men, Vol I: 45
Intimacy, male inhibition to, Vol II: 282
self-disclosure and responsiveness, Vol II: 282
Intimacy motivation, Vol II: 41, 49–52, 54, 57
Intimate partner violence (IPV), Vol I: 94
Intimate romantic relationships
costs of gender-role traditionalism for
relational costs, Vol II: 298–299
sexual costs, Vol II: 299–300
phase I: coming together
desire for attractive mate, study, Vol II: 284
evolutionary theory, Vol II: 285–287
mate preferences, Vol II: 284–288
men's preference for attractive mates, fMRI study, Vol II: 284
in polygynous societies, Vol II: 284–285
relationship initiation and dating, Vol II: 288–293
socio-ecological theories, Vol II: 287–288

Intimate romantic (*cont.*)
    phase II: relational maintenance, Vol II: 293–296
    phase III: coming apart, Vol II: 296–297
Intimate terrorist, Vol II: 317
Intrinsic/interest value, Vol I: 310
IPV, *see* Intimate partner violence (IPV)
IQ, *see* Intelligence quotient (IQ)
IRB, *see* Institutional Review Board (IRB)
IRT, *see* Item response theory (IRT)
Israeli Defence Forces (IDF), Vol II: 673
Issues in psychological testing of personality and abilities
    construction of personality tests
        empirical tests, Vol II: 78–80
        IRT, Vol II: 81–82
        theoretically developed tests, Vol II: 80–81
    current practice of psychological testing
        test functions, Vol II: 71–72
        types of tests, Vol II: 70
    gender bias and tests of personality and psychopathology
        biased operationalization, Vol II: 74–77
        biased theories, Vol II: 73–74
        bias in structural issues and statistical assumptions, Vol II: 77–78
    psychological assessment and testing
        assumptions, Vol II: 65–68
        context and assessment experience, Vol II: 64–65
        gender and norms, Vol II: 68–69
        process, definition, Vol II: 63
        psychological testing, role in assessment, Vol II: 63–64
Issues, women as leaders, Vol II: 443
Item response theory (IRT), Vol II: 67, 76, 81–82

J
Jamaicans demographic differences, Vol II: 620
Jarheads, Girly Men, and the Pleasures of Violence, Vol I: 119
Jerks, Vol II: 286
Jewish religious communities, Vol II: 364
Joint Task Force (JTF), Vol II: 674
Journal of Applied Sport Psychology, Vol II: 568
Journal of Community and Applied Social Psychology, Vol II: 617
Journal of Feminist Family Therapy, Vol II: 254, 257, 260
Journal of GLBT Family Studies, Vol II: 257
Journal of Homosexuality (Silverstein, Charles), Vol I: 70
Journal of Marriage and Family Therapy, Vol II: 255, 257, 260
Journal of Men's Studies, Vol I: 48
Journal of Sport & Exercise Psychology, Vol II: 568
The Joy Luck Club, Vol II: 261
JTF, *see* Joint Task Force (JTF)
Just Sex? The Cultural Scaffolding of Rape, Vol I: 117

K
Kamphoff's dissertation research on female coaches, Vol II: 566
Key imagery, Vol II: 41, 45
Key masculine features (Kane and Snyder), Vol II: 571
Key socializers, Vol II: 383
Klein Sexual Orientation Grid (KSOG), Vol I: 66
Known-groups comparison technique, Vol II: 78
KSOG, *see* Klein Sexual Orientation Grid (KSOG)

L
Labyrinth, Vol II: 443–462
Lakoff's model, Vol I: 380–382
    critique of, Vol I: 381–382
        androcentrism, Vol I: 382
        neutral language, Vol I: 382
    research on, Vol I: 380–381
        courtroom testimony, Vol I: 381
        hedge, Vol I: 380
        intensifiers, Vol I: 380
        tag question usage, Vol I: 380
    speaking style of women, Vol I: 380
Language, and power (she said, he said), Vol I: 379–404
    difference as deficit, Vol I: 380
        critique of Lakoff's model, Vol I: 381–382
        research on Lakoff's model, Vol I: 380–381
        women's style of speaking, Vol I: 380
    difference as dominance, Vol I: 387
        gender and inequality, Vol I: 387–388
        interruptions, Vol I: 389–391
        profanity, Vol I: 391–393
        resisting and derogating women's requests, Vol I: 391
        talking time, Vol I: 388–389
        verbal harassment as dominance, Vol I: 393
    future research, Vol I: 400
        changing conceptions of gender, Vol I: 401–402
        directions for, Vol I: 404
        gendered language in relation to social roles, Vol I: 402
        importance of context, Vol I: 401
        toward a feminist postmodern approach to gender and language, Vol I: 403–404
        toward a postmodern perspective, Vol I: 402–403
    remediating women's deficits, Vol I: 382
        assertiveness training, Vol I: 382–383
        critique of negotiations deficit, Vol I: 384–385
        negotiation, deficit in women's communication, Vol I: 383–384
        research on assertiveness training, Vol I: 383
    two cultures approach, Vol I: 385–386
        critique of miscommunication models, Vol I: 386–387
        miscommunication, Vol I: 385
    women's talk as relational, Vol I: 393
        gossip, Vol I: 395–399
        men's deficiencies, Vol I: 399–400

Subject Index

minimal responses, Vol I: 394
placing value on women's talk, Vol I: 393–394
small talk, Vol I: 394–395
Language of gender, Vol I: 361–374
APA style manual on gender/sexuality/ethnicity, Vol I: 369
compliance evaluation with guidelines, Vol I: 372–373
guidelines to reduce bias, Vol I: 371–372
acknowledge participation, Vol I: 372
level of specificity, Vol I: 371
sensitive to labels, Vol I: 372
language and sexual minorities, Vol I: 367–369
APA, Vol I: 367
LGBTQ, Vol I: 368
queer theory, Vol I: 368
transgendered/transsexual, Vol I: 368
transpeople, Vol I: 369
masculinity and femininity (M-F tests), Vol I: 365–367
BSRI, Vol I: 366
sex/gender differences, Vol I: 363–365
gender attribution, identity, role, Vol I: 364
sexual dimorphism, Vol I: 364
Language to think, impotance of, Vol I: 171–172, 195, 382
Latent growth modeling (LGM), Vol I: 95
LatiNegras, dark-skinned Latinas, Vol II: 261
Laura Spelman Rockefeller Memorial Fund, Vol I: 21
Lavender ceiling, Vol II: 449
Lazarus and Folkman's cognitive appraisal theory (1984), Vol II: 432, 550
LBGT, *see* Lesbian, gay, bisexual, and transgender (LGBT)
Leadership
differences in women/men
managerial roles produces skilled female, Vol II: 460
spillover/internalization, gender-specific norms, Vol II: 460
transformational repertoire, Vol II: 460
effectiveness, Vol II: 455–461
gender-integrated executive teams, organizational effectiveness, Vol II: 456–457
individual male/ female leaders, effectiveness of, Vol II: 457–458
leadership style/ leaders' effectiveness, Vol II: 458–460
style/ leaders' effectiveness, Vol II: 458–460
transformational /transactional leadership styles, Vol II: 459
Learning styles, Vol I: 279, 287–288
Legitimate power, Vol I: 416
Lesbian and gay couples and families
biological and non-biological mothers, Vol II: 411
Carrington's study, Vol II: 411
household labor among, Vol II: 411

Lesbian couples therapy, Vol I: 10; Vol II: 10, 254
Lesbian, gay, and bisexual (LGB), Vol I: 62–63, 65, 65–72; Vol II: 121, 138, 144, 195, 257–259, 364, 367, 509, 511, 564, 622
families, Vol II: 257
Lesbian, gay, bisexual, and transgender (LGBT), Vol I: 6, 59–72, 181, 187–188, 290, 368, 466, 538–539, 541, 545, 549, 565
health issues, Vol II: 486
Lesbian, gay, bisexual, transgender, and questioning (LGBTQ), Vol I: 290, 368
Lesbianism, Vol I: 117, 367; Vol II: 361, 578
Lesbians and gay men in military
policy comparisons, Vol II: 690–691
Lexapro, Vol II: 520
Leydig cells, Vol I: 216
LFAIS, *see* Liberal feminist attitude and ideology scale (LFAIS)
LGB, *see* Lesbian, gay, and bisexual (LGB)
LGBT, *see* Lesbian, gay, bisexual, and transgender (LGBT)
LGBT issues, emergence/development of psychological study
APA, Vol I: 59
first-generation literature, pathologizing homosexuality, Vol I: 61–62
change-of-orientation therapy, Vol I: 62
homosexuality, Vol I: 62
LGB identity, Vol I: 62
oedipal conflict, Vol I: 61
reparative or conversion therapies, Vol I: 61
sexual identity therapy, Vol I: 62
second-generation literature, psychological adjustment research, Vol I: 62–63
homosexuality = psychopathology, Vol I: 63
terminology, Vol I: 59–60
androcentricism, Vol I: 60
gender, definition, Vol I: 59–60
gender identity, Vol I: 60
gender nonconforming, Vol I: 60
gender normative, Vol I: 60
sexual orientation, Vol I: 60
transgender, Vol I: 60
third-generation literature, identity/diversity
bisexuality, Vol I: 65–66
gender differences/gender-role socialization, Vol I: 64
lesbian, gay, and bisexual youths, Vol I: 67–68
race, ethnicity, and culture, Vol I: 64–65
relationships, families, and parenting, Vol I: 66–67
sexual prejudice and heterosexism, Vol I: 68–69
trends/directions, Vol I: 59–60
brief history, Vol I: 69–70
from categories to complexity, fourth generation, Vol I: 72

LGBT issues (*cont.*)
    fourth generation, from categories to complexity, Vol I: 72
    gender/transgender issues, Vol I: 70–71
    sexual orientation, Vol I: 72
LGBTQ, *see* Lesbian, gay, bisexual, transgender, and questioning (LGBTQ)
LH, *see* Luteinizing hormone (LH)
Liberal Feminist Attitude and Ideology Scale (LFAIS), Vol II: 205
Liberation psychologists, Vol I: 35
Life expectancy, Vol II: 11, 471–473, 479, 481–482, 487
    social and economic circumstances, Vol II: 471
Line-angle judgment task, spatial perception, Vol I: 320, 322, 324
Linguistic relativity, Vol I: 361
Linguistic style, Vol I: 382, 385, 387
Lipstick lesbians, Vol II: 371
Long hours/ relocation, demands for, Vol II: 452–453
Long-term mating strategy, Vol II: 285–286
Lord of the Rings (film), Vol I: 191
Loudness sensitivity, Vol I: 243–244
Lower face-to-body ratio (face-ism), Vol II: 647
Low negative arousal, *see* Anxiety
Low responders, Vol I: 442
Luteal phase, Vol II: 29, 223, 241, 324, 458–459, 464–465
    dysphoric disorder, Vol II: 98
Luteinizing hormone (LH), Vol II: 115

M

Machismo and marianismo, Vol II: 627
Macho Scale, Vol I: 52
Magnocellular RGCs (M cells), Vol I: 236
Major depressive disorder (MDD), Vol II: 96, 134
Mak Nyah, Vol II: 115
Maladaptive behaviors, Vol II: 550, 574
Male body and football, patriarchal images (Trujillo), Vol II: 571
Male-centered treatment methods, Vol II: 232
Male clients knowledge, Vol II: 223–230
    cultures of masculinity, Vol II: 225–227
Male-dominated, military workplace, Vol II: 680
The Male Machine, Vol I: 44
Male managerial model, Vol II: 678
Male Role Attitudes Scale, Vol I: 52
Male Role Norms Inventory (MRNI), Vol I: 52, 137–138
Male Role Norms Scale (MRNS), Vol I: 52, 136–137
Male Roles Attitudes Scale (MRAS), Vol I: 137–138
Male sponsors mentor, Vol II: 269
Male-to-female (MtF) sexual reassignment, Vol I: 224
Male-to-female transsexuality, Vol II: 113
Malicious rumors, Vol II: 312
Managers/management, Vol I: 65, 93, 116, 172, 194, 395, 404, 457–458, 460–462, 571
Manhood in the Making, Vol I: 45
Man-to man harassment, *see* Gender policing

Manual for Scoring Motive Imagery in Running Text, Vol II: 42
'Man who gets around' hypothesis, Vol I: 268–269
    issue, Vol I: 268
    polygamy, Vol I: 268
    signs
        difficulty of human birth, Vol I: 268
        pair bonding, Vol I: 268
        women's sexual receptivity, Vol I: 268
Marital distress, persons, Vol II: 266
Marital happiness, satisfaction and quality
    congruent/similar attitude spouses, impact, Vol II: 413
    couple's division of labor, impact, Vol II: 413
    emotion work performance, Vol II: 413
Marital Satisfaction Inventory-Revised (MSI-R), Vol II: 210
Marital status and union type, Vol II: 411
Marital structure hypothesis, Vol II: 500
Marlowe-Crowne Social Desirability Scale, Vol II: 602
Marriage, Vol I: 25, 61, 66–67, 69, 95, 144, 164, 345–346, 348, 436, 473, 486, 561, 564–566, 570–572; Vol II: 52, 119, 137, 222, 239–240, 254–255, 257, 260, 265, 267–270, 284, 286, 288–289, 292–293, 297–298, 301, 327, 369–370, 411, 413, 446, 498–500, 507, 511, 532, 677
Masculine Depression Scale (Magovcevic and Addis), Vol II: 135
Masculine Gender Role Stress Scale (MGRS), Vol I: 52–53, 145–146
Masculine generics, Vol I: 195, 362–363, 370, 372–373
Masculine ideal of lean muscularity, Vol II: 161
Masculine organizational culture, Vol II: 453–454
Masculine-sensitive psychotherapy, rationale for, Vol II: 223–225
    epidemiological studies, Vol II: 223
    multicultural counseling competency, Vol II: 223
Masculine speech styles, Vol I: 383, 387
Masculine sports activities, Vol II: 570
Masculine-stereotypic domains, Vol I: 414
Masculine-stereotypic gender, Vol I: 442
    rational, Vol II: 444
Masculinity
    concept of, Vol II: 477
    and femininity, history, Vol II: 21–23
        unmitigated agency/communion, Vol II: 23
    femininity, personality theory, Vol II: 21–25
        expressiveness/instrumentality/mental health, Vol II: 24–25
        history, Vol II: 21–23
        instrumentality and expressiveness as mediators, Vol II: 23
    and femininity, reconceptualization of, Vol II: 23
    measurement of
        Attitudes Toward the Male Role Scale, Vol I: 52
        Brannon Masculinity Scale, Vol I: 52

Subject Index

citations of instruments used in measurement of masculinity, Vol I: 52t
    Conformity to Masculine Norms Inventory, Vol I: 52
    Gender Role Conflict Scale, Vol I: 52–53
    Macho Scale, Vol I: 52
    Male Role Attitudes Scale, Vol I: 52
    Male Role Norms Inventory, Vol I: 52
    Masculine Gender Role Stress Scale, Vol I: 52–53
    Stereotypes About Male Sexuality Scale, Vol I: 52
over femininity, promotion, Vol II: 621

Masculinity and men, paradigms for psychological study
beyond essence, identity, and strain, Vol I: 51
essentialist, biological, and evolutionary paradigms, Vol I: 48–49
    aspects of men's psychology with biological processes, correlate, Vol I: 49
    man-to-child affiliative bond, Vol I: 49
    understanding men in several ways, Vol I: 49
gender role identity paradigms
    Bem Sex Role Inventory, Vol I: 50
    gender role strain analysis, Vol I: 50
    limitations, Vol I: 50
    Personal Attributes Questionnaire, Vol I: 50
gender role strain paradigms
    discrepancy/trauma/dysfunction, strain, Vol I: 50–51

Masculinity–Femininity (Mf) Scale, Vol II: 79
homosexuals category identification, Vol II: 79

Masculinization, Vol I: 218

Mathematical ability, Vol I: 302–305, 307, 310–312
aptitude *vs.* grades, Vol I: 304–305
gender similarities and differences
    in means, Vol I: 302–303
    in variance, Vol I: 303–304
moving beyond girls and, Vol I: 311–312
    greater variability, Vol I: 311
    little attention, Vol I: 312

Mating strategies
evolutionary benefits, types, Vol II: 285–286
See also Evolutionary theory of mate preferences

Mayer, Salovey, and Caruso Emotional Intelligence Test (MSCEIT), Vol I: 439

McClintock effect, *see* Menstrual synchrony

M cells, *see* Magnocellular RGCs (M cells)

McHugh's therapeutic goals, Vol II: 119

MD, *see* Muscle dysmorphia (MD)

MDD, *see* Major depressive disorder (MDD)

Measurement issues, cross culture, Vol I: 169–170
five-factor personality theory, Vol I: 170
natives, Vol I: 169
sojourners, Vol I: 169

Measuring gender, Vol I: 133–152
definitions of gender, masculinity, and femininity, Vol I: 150

measures of role conflict and role stress, Vol I: 144–146
measures of support for and adherence to cultural gender norms, Vol I: 134–144
    See also Support for and adherence to cultural gender norms, measures of
measures related to the relative position of men and women in society, Vol I: 146–149
    See also Position of men and women in society, measures related to
moving forward, Vol I: 151–152
psychometric and methodological concerns, Vol I: 150–151
scale age, Vol I: 151

Media
key areas of impact
    aggression, Vol II: 657–658
    self/sexual objectification, Vol II: 658–660
    stereotyping, media threats and solutions, Vol II: 660–661
media content, quantity/quality of gender representation
    Black/White women, media representation, Vol II: 648
    British/Saudi Arabian television commercials, content analyses, Vol II: 644
    children/adults as targets, comparisons, Vol II: 645
    entertainment media, gender differences in, Vol II: 644
    entertainment media, intersection of gender and age representation, Vol II: 645
    femininity and physical beauty, association, Vol II: 648
    femininity and thinness, equating, Vol II: 648–649
    hypermasculinity and physical aggression, correlation, Vol II: 649
    masculinity and muscularity, equating, Vol II: 649
    natural athletic ability, African American men, Vol II: 647
    nonheterosexual sitcom characters study (Fouts and Inch), Vol II: 645
    paid position of labor, men/women (US), Vol II: 646
    physical appearance, gender differences, Vol II: 647
    physical, verbal, and indirect aggression, Vol II: 649
    research on US media content, Vol II: 644
    traditional acceptance of men's/women's domains, Vol II: 647
pervasive cultural modeling of gender roles (Bussey and Bandura), Vol II: 643
phenomenon of possible selves, Vol II: 643

Media (*cont.*)
  social environment, influence of, Vol II: 643
  uses, *see* Media and gender, uses
Media and gender, uses
  film genres, Vol II: 656–657
  new media
    Calvert's survey of children's computer use, Vol II: 652
    cell phone use, gender differences, Vol II: 653
    frequency of internet use, age factor interaction with gender, Vol II: 652
    internet and computer use, Vol II: 652
    male adolescents, heavy gamers, Vol II: 652
    Pew Internet and American Life project report, findings, Vol II: 652
  sexually explicit content, Vol II: 654–656
  video games
    male/female ratio (3:1) engaged, Vol II: 650–651
    natural cognitive abilities, sex differences, Vol II: 651
    research in college population (Lucas and Sherry), Vol II: 651
    sensorimotor games, genre form, Vol II: 651
    traditional/physical/imagination games, women/men perspectives, Vol II: 651
Media, quantity/quality of gender representation
  Black/White women, media representation, Vol II: 648
  British/Saudi Arabian television commercials, content analyses, Vol II: 644
  children/adults as targets, comparisons, Vol II: 645
  crimes, men/women coverage, Vol II: 650
    men over/under-represented as criminals, Vol II: 650
    rape victims, "virgin" or "vamp" narrative, Vol II: 650
  entertainment media, gender differences in, Vol II: 644
  entertainment media, intersection of gender and age representation, Vol II: 645
  femininity and physical beauty, association, Vol II: 648
  femininity and thinness, equating, Vol II: 648–649
  hypermasculinity and physical aggression, correlation, Vol II: 649
  masculinity and muscularity, equating, Vol II: 649
  natural athletic ability, African American men, Vol II: 647
  nonheterosexual sitcom characters study (Fouts and Inch), Vol II: 645
  paid position of labor, men/women (US), Vol II: 646
  physical appearance, gender differences, Vol II: 647
  physical, verbal, and indirect aggression, Vol II: 649
  research on US media content, Vol II: 644
  traditional acceptance of men's/women's domains, Vol II: 647
Media Reference Guide, Vol II: 124
Medicaid system, Vol II: 272
Medicare, Vol II: 544
Medications, Vol II: 519–520
Medicines and Healthcare Products Regulatory Agency (MHRA), Vol I: 47
Meginnis-Payne's study, Vol II: 202
Menace II Society, Vol II: 658
Men and Masculinity conference, Vol I: 44–45
Men and masculinity, emergence and development of psychology
  conferences
    Australian Men's Health Forum sponsors an annual National Men's Health Conference, Vol I: 47
    International Society for Men's Health sponsors a biennial World Conference on Men's Health and Gender, Vol I: 47
    MHRA, Vol I: 47
    National Conference on Men and Masculinity, Vol I: 46
    National Organization of Men Against Sexism (1975), Vol I: 46
  journals, Vol I: 47–48
    American Journal of Men's Health, Vol I: 48
    International Journal of Men's Health, Vol I: 48
    Journal of Men's Studies, Vol I: 48
    Psychology of Men & Masculinity, Vol I: 48
    Psychology of Women Quarterly, Vol I: 47
    Sex Roles, Vol I: 47
  organizations, Vol I: 45–46
    American College Personnel Association, Vol I: 45
    Men and Masculinity conference, Vol I: 45
    Men Treating Men Network, Vol I: 46
    National Organization of Changing Men, Vol I: 45
    NOMAS, Vol I: 45
    Society for the Psychological Study of Men and Masculinity, Vol I: 46
    Standing Committee for Men, Vol I: 45
    Task Force on Men's Roles in Psychotherapy, Vol I: 46
  paradigms for psychological study of men and masculinity
    beyond essence, identity, and strain, Vol I: 51
    essentialist, biological, and evolutionary paradigms, Vol I: 48–49
    gender role identity paradigms, Vol I: 49–50
    gender role strain paradigms, Vol I: 50–51
  publications, Vol I: 44–45
    Adaptation to Life, Vol I: 44
    Deepening Psychotherapy with Men, Vol I: 45
    The Forty-nine Percent Majority: The Male Sex Role, Vol I: 44
    Handbook of Counseling and Psychotherapy with Men, Vol I: 45

Subject Index

Hazards of Being Male: Surviving the Myth of Male Privilege, Vol I: 44
The Male Machine, Vol I: 44
Manhood in the Making, Vol I: 45
Men and Masculinity, Vol I: 44
Men:Evolutionary and Life History, Vol I: 45
The New Handbook of Psychotherapy and Counseling with Men, Vol I: 45
A New Psychotherapy for Traditional Men, Vol I: 45
In the Room with Men, Vol I: 45
The Seasons of a Man's Life, Vol I: 44
Sentimental Men, Vol I: 45
   recommendations, Vol I: 54–55
   research trends on psychology of men/masculinity
      measurement of masculinity, Vol I: 52–53
      men and mental health, Vol I: 54
      men and physical health, Vol I: 53–54
Men are from Mars, Women are from Venus (Gray, 1992), Vol II: 290
Men:Evolutionary and Life History, Vol I: 45
Men from feminist perspective, working with, Vol II: 256–257
Men hunt, women gather rule, Vol I: 266–268
   adaptation environment, Vol I: 267
      Agricultural Revolution (12,000–10,000 BCE), Vol I: 268
   aiming, Vol I: 266
      mental rotation, Vol I: 266
      spatial tests, Vol I: 266
   exceptions, Vol I: 268
   gathering, Vol I: 267
      edible plants, Vol I: 267
      nomadic group, Vol I: 267
   tool making, Vol I: 267
   tracking, Vol I: 266
      hunting journey, Vol I: 266
Men in psychotherapy, skills for, Vol II: 233–238
   clients' gender-role identity, Vol II: 236
   engaging men in psychotherapy, Vol II: 234
   genuine and real, Vol II: 236
   goals match needs of male client, Vol II: 235
   male clients, educate, Vol II: 235
   masculine face, Vol II: 234–235
   men have in entering and being in psychotherapy, Vol II: 234
   patient, Vol II: 235
Menopause, Vol I: 84, 117, 222–224, 241, 483–484, 560, 567–568; Vol II: 99, 168, 521, 524
Men's adaptive help-seeking strategies (Addis and Mahalik)
   emotional stoicism/self-reliance, Vol II: 546
   sex differences research, Vol II: 545–546
The Men's Bibliography, Vol I: 44
Men's deficiencies, Vol I: 399–400
Men's Health Network, Vol I: 44

Men's resistance to women's influence and leadership, Vol II: 342–343
Menstrual cycle phases, Vol I: 223–224, 241, 247, 458, 466
   follicular phase, Vol I: 223
   luteal phase, Vol I: 223
   menstrual phase, Vol I: 223
Menstrual synchrony, Vol I: 248
Mental health
   service, Vol II: 229
   variables/expressiveness, relationships, Vol II: 24
Mental Rotation Task (MRT), Vol I: 221, 223, 225, 238–239, 263, 280, 318; Vol II: 651
Mental rotation test, Vol I: 318, 323, 327
   primary mental abilities test, Vol I: 318
The Mental Traits of Sex, Vol I: 22
Men the particular, not *man the generic*, Vol I: 48
Men Treating Men Network, Vol I: 46
Men/women position in society, measures related to, Vol I: 146–149
   Ambivalent Sexism Inventory, Vol I: 147–148
   AWS, Vol I: 146–147
   FIC, Vol I: 149
   FIDS, Vol I: 149
   FIS, Vol I: 148–149
   MS, Vol I: 147
   OFS, Vol I: 147
   SSE, Vol I: 148
Meredith and Brian, description for, Vol II: 268
Meredith's vulnerability, Vol II: 268
Meta-analysis, Vol I: 4, 88–90, 96, 98, 193, 241, 245, 263–265, 268, 271, 298, 303, 305, 311, 321, 324, 416, 438, 476–482, 500, 546, 569; Vol II: 4, 21, 32, 44, 135, 283, 296, 313, 316, 327, 329, 341–342, 344, 347–348, 350, 360, 383, 386, 423, 431, 433, 436, 450, 457–459, 472, 501, 552, 655
Meta-analytic reviews, Vol I: 298, 338, 414, 443, 481; Vol II: 338
Methodological issues, forensic research, Vol II: 599–608
   measurement, Vol II: 601–608
      archival data, Vol II: 607–608
      fairness and bias in measurement, Vol II: 604–606
      reliance on self-report, Vol II: 607
      reliance on simulation research, Vol II: 606–607
      response bias, Vol II: 602–604
   sampling, Vol II: 599–601
Metrosexual, Vol II: 163
M–F tests, Vol I: 365–367
   See also Language of gender
MI, *see* Myocardial infarction (MI)
Mild shock, Vol I: 242
Military, Vol I: 12, 24, 202, 327, 574; Vol II: 12, 42, 340, 369, 430, 436, 453, 457, 522, 671–692
Mineralocorticoids, Vol I: 215
Minimal responses, Vol I: 394

Minnesota Multiphasic Personality Inventory, Vol I: 351; Vol II: 70
Minority stress, concept of, Vol II: 509
Miscommunication models, Vol I: 385
    critique of, Vol I: 386–387
        impacts, Vol I: 386
        misinterpreted dominance, Vol I: 387
    problems, Vol I: 385
Misinterpreted dominance, Vol I: 387
Misinterpreted status effects, Vol I: 391
Mixed-gender context, Vol I: 385
MMPI-2 Fake-Bad-Scale, Vol II: 76
MMPI-2 Infrequency (F) Scale, Vol II: 76
MMPI/MMPI-2
    GM/GF Scale, Vol II: 79
    Masculinity-Femininity (Mf) Scale, Vol II: 79
    Revised Clinical (RC) Scales, Vol II: 79–80
    sexual inversion, Vol II: 79
Models of aggression, Vol II: 427
    See also Buss' framework of aggression
Moderate arousal level, *see* Anxiety
Modern Sexism (MS), Vol I: 147
Monday Night Football, Vol II: 571
Money's paradigm, Vol I: 194
Mood Disorders, Vol II: 96–99
Mothering, Vol I: 362
Motivation, Vol I: 2, 5, 8–9, 11, 15, 91, 136, 152, 271, 351–352, 392, 422, 427–488, 495, 507, 568; Vol II: 2, 5, 8–9, 11, 15, 41–58, 167, 171, 235, 241, 256, 325, 360–363, 370, 381–382, 385, 387–389, 391, 393, 406, 430, 435, 454, 479, 522, 573, 577, 598, 607, 651, 653–654, 658, 660, 678
Motivational factors, Vol I: 439
MRAS, *see* Male Roles Attitudes Scale (MRAS)
MRNI, *see* Male Role Norms Inventory (MRNI)
MRNS, *see* Male Role Norms Scale (MRNS)
MRT, *see* Mental Rotation Task (MRT)
MS, *see* Modern Sexism (MS)
MSCEIT, *see* Mayer, Salovey, and Caruso Emotional Intelligence Test (MSCEIT)
MSI-R, *see* Marital Satisfaction Inventory-Revised (MSI-R)
MtF, *see* Male-to-female (MtF) sexual reassignment
Mullerian tract, Vol I: 216
    anti-Mullerian hormone, Vol I: 216–217
Multiculturalism, Vol I: 6; Vol II: 6, 254, 260, 263, 269, 271
Multicultural psychology of women, building, Vol I: 34–35
    ethnocentrism, Vol I: 34
    globalization movement, Vol I: 34
    multicultural psychology, feminist psychology, and social activism, Vol I: 35
    postcolonial critique, Vol I: 34
Multicultural sensitivity of therapeutic approaches, Vol II: 272

Multidimensionality, Vol I: 496–498
Multi-dimensional process model of gender, Vol II: 68
Multi-dimensional self-concept, Vol II: 31–33
Multiple identities, Vol I: 65, 429; Vol II: 225, 254, 261
Multiple voicing, Vol I: 111
Muscle dysmorphia (MD), Vol II: 99, 158, 161–162, 575
The Muscular Ideal, Vol I: 54; Vol II: 13, 160–161, 165–166, 169
Muscular-ideal internalization, Vol II: 160–161
Myocardial infarction (MI), Vol II: 500
My Space, Vol II: 653

N
NAAF, *see* National Amateur Athletic Federation (NAAF)
Nagging, Vol I: 8, 391, 400
    batterers, Vol I: 391, 399–400
Naming, gendered hierarchy of, Vol II: 571–572
NASA lost on the moon paradigm, Vol II: 344
National Amateur Athletic Federation (NAAF), Vol II: 565
National Archive of Criminal Justice Data, Vol II: 607
National Center for Education Statistics (NCES), Vol I: 277–278, 284, 288, 307, 309–310, Vol II: 337, 379
National Center for Health Statistics, 2007, Vol II: 517–520, 524, 530, 533
National Center for State Courts, Vol II: 601
National Center on Elder Abuse (NCEA), Vol II: 318
National Coalition of Anti- Violence Programs (NCAVP), Vol II: 367–368
National Collegiate Athletic Association (NCAA), Vol II: 571–572, 575
National Committee for the Mathematical Sciences, Vol II: 380
National Comorbidity Study, mental health survey, Vol II: 134
National Conference on Men and Masculinity, Vol I: 46
National Council ofWomen Psychologists (NCWP), Vol I: 24, 26
National Council on Measurement in Education (NCME), Vol II: 601, 604, 609
National Defence Headquarters, Vol II: 676
National Diabetes Education Program (NDEP), Vol II: 531
National Elder Abuse Incidence Study (NEAIS), Vol II: 318
National Epidemiologic Survey on Alcohol and Related Disorders, Vol II: 134
National Geographic Smell Survey, Vol I: 248
National Health and Nutrition Examination Survey (NHANES), Vol II: 520
National Health and Social Life Survey (NHSLS), Vol I: 478, 533
National Hospital Discharge Survey records, Vol II: 520
National Incident Based Reporting System, Vol II: 608

Subject Index

National Institute for Occupational Safety and Health (NIOSH), Vol II: 431
National Institute of Mental Health (NIMH), Vol II: 228, 230
National Institutes of Health (NIH), Vol I: 185, 261, 524, 534, 542, 593
National Longitudinal Study of Adolescent Health, Vol I: 478
National Organization for Women (NOW), Vol I: 30, 149
National Organization of Changing Men, Vol I: 45
National Organization of Men Against Sexism (NOMAS), Vol I: 45–46
National Science Foundation (NSF), Vol I: 308–309; Vol II: 379–380
National Survey of Sexual Attitudes and Lifestyles (NATSAL II), Vol I: 478
Nat Kadaw, Vol II: 114
NATO, see North Atlantic Treaty Organization (NATO)
Natural athletic ability, African American men, Vol II: 647
Naval Equal Opportunity and Sexual Harassment Survey (NEOSH), Vol II: 683
NCAA, see National Collegiate Athletic Association (NCAA)
NCAVP, see National Coalition of Anti- Violence Programs (NCAVP)
NCEA, see National Center on Elder Abuse (NCEA)
NCES, see National Center for Education Statistics (NCES)
NCME, see National Council on Measurement in Education (NCME)
NCMs, see Non-commissioned members (NCMs)
NCO, see Non-commissioned officer (NCO)
NCWP, see National Council of Women Psychologists (NCWP)
NDEP, see National Diabetes Education Program (NDEP)
NEAIS, see National Elder Abuse Incidence Study (NEAIS)
Need for Affect scale, Vol II: 656
Negative emotions, Vol I: 240, 243, 431, 433, 435–437, 545
Negatively valenced emotions
  anxiety, Vol I: 242
  fear, Vol I: 242
Negotiating the labyrinth, gender and leadership, Vol II: 443
  discrimination/ prejudice, Vol II: 446–447
  gender and leader stereotypes, Vol II: 447–449
  incompatible leader and the gender roles, effects, Vol II: 449–451
  leadership effectiveness, Vol II: 455–461
    individual male and female leaders, effectiveness of, Vol II: 457–458
    leadership style and leaders' effectiveness, Vol II: 458–460
  organizational effectiveness of gender-integrated executive teams, Vol II: 456–457
  organizational barriers to women's leadership, Vol II: 451–455
    barriers to building social capital, Vol II: 454–455
    challenges of obtaining desirable assignments, Vol II: 455
    demands for long hours and relocation, Vol II: 452–453
    masculine organizational culture, Vol II: 453–454
  representation of women in leader roles, Vol II: 443–445
  seat of parliament held by women in selected nations, Vol II: 445f
  women among managers, legislators, and senior officials, Vol II: 444
  work–family issues, Vol II: 445–446
Negotiations, Vol I: 383–385, 430, 574
  critique of, Vol I: 384–385
    negotiation remediation training, Vol I: 385
  in women's communication, Vol I: 383–384
  observational learning, girls, Vol I: 384
Neo-analytic theory, Vol I: 473
  casual sex or extra-marital affairs, Vol I: 473
  relational need, woman, Vol I: 473
Neoclassical economic theory, Vol II: 405
NEO-FFI, see NEO five factor inventory (NEO-FFI)
NEO five factor inventory (NEO-FFI), Vol II: 26
NEO personality inventory-revised (NEO-PI-R), Vol II: 26
NEO-PI-R, see NEO personality inventory-revised (NEO-PI-R)
NEOSH, see Naval Equal Opportunity and Sexual Harassment Survey (NEOSH)
Neuroimaging techniques/technology, Vol I: 242
Neuroticism, Vol II: 25–26, 29
Neutral language, Vol I: 371, 380, 382
The New Handbook of Psychotherapy and Counseling with Men, Vol I: 45
A New Psychotherapy for Traditional Men, Vol I: 45
New Zealand Defence Force (NZDF), Vol II: 682
NHANES, see National Health and Nutrition Examination Survey (NHANES)
NHSLS, see National Health and Social Life Survey (NHSLS)
Nice guys, Vol II: 286
Nigerian students report (college-aged), Vol II: 155
NIH, see National Institutes of Health (NIH)
NIMH, see National Institute of Mental Health (NIMH)
NIOSH, see National Institute for Occupational Safety and Health (NIOSH)
Non-commissioned members (NCMs), Vol II: 673, 676–677, 679, 685, 688
Non-commissioned officer (NCO), Vol II: 691
Non-contextual rectangle task, spatial perception, Vol I: 320
Non-Duchenne/Duchenne smiles, Vol I: 438

Nonreproductive hormones, *see* Glucocorticoids
Nontraditional gender-role attitudes, Vol II: 197
Nonverbal behavior, Vol I: 8, 28, 324, 411–422, 414, 416, 432, 437–439, 441, 444, 447
    for accurate person perception, Vol I: 412–414
        domains, Vol I: 413
        interpersonal sensitivity/accuracy, Vol I: 413
    comprises of, Vol I: 412
    definition, Vol I: 412
    disentangling gender and power, Vol I: 418–419
    and gender, Vol I: 414–415
        meta-analytic reviews, Vol I: 414
    gender and power differences, Vol I: 415t
    personality traits criterion, Vol I: 413
    and power, Vol I: 411–422
        Brunswikian lens model, Vol I: 416
        disentangling gender/power with nonverbal behavior, Vol I: 418–419
        gender and nonverbal behavior, Vol I: 414–415
        gender as moderator, Vol I: 419–420
        interpersonal accuracy, Vol I: 417–418
        nonverbal behavior, definition, Vol I: 412
        nonverbal behavior for accurate person perception, Vol I: 412–414
        nonverbal expression of power, Vol I: 416
        perception of power, Vol I: 417
    roles of
        emotions expression, Vol I: 412
        equivocal, Vol I: 412
Nonverbal communication, Vol I: 400, 412, 419; Vol II: 323–324, 432
Nonverbal decoding skill, Vol I: 438–439
Nonviolent aggression, Vol II: 312, 315
Norms
    testing strategies, strengths/limitations
        gender based, Vol II: 69
        gender irrelevant, Vol II: 69
        gender neutral, Vol II: 68
Norm theory, Vol I: 196–198, 200
North American native tribes, Vol II: 144
North American society, Vol II: 362
North Atlantic Treaty Organization (NATO), Vol II: 672–673, 676, 689
North by Northwest (film), Vol I: 191, 195–196
Northside Center for Child Development in 1946, Vol I: 25
"Not man enough" harassment, Vol II: 431
'*Not socially appropriate*' sport for women (Metheny), Vol II: 570
NOW, *see* National Organization for Women (NOW)
6-n-propylthiouracil (PROP), Vol I: 246
NSF, *see* National Science Foundation (NSF)
NZDF, *see* New Zealand Defence Force (NZDF)

O

OAE, *see* Otoacoustic emissions (OAEs)
Objectification theory, Vol II: 170–172
Objective tests
    MMPI-2, Vol II: 70
    See also Personality tests, construction of
Object location memory, Vol I: 221, 223, 263–265, 267, 321, 323, 327, 329–330
Observations and gaps
    differences in doing gender research across fields, Vol II: 13–14
    measurement, Vol II: 14–15
    men and boys in gender research, Vol II: 13
    overstating the magnitude of differences, Vol II: 14
Obtaining desirable assignments, challenges, Vol II: 455
Occupational choice, Vol II: 379
    ability, Vol II: 386–387
        DAT, Vol II: 386
        mathematics achievement data, Vol II: 386
    barriers and supports, Vol II: 383
    explanations, Vol II: 382–383
    future research
        contextualization, Vol II: 393
        longitudinal designs, Vol II: 393–394
        world of work, changing, Vol II: 392
    gender stereotypes, Vol II: 383
    media, Vol II: 385
    parents, Vol II: 383–384
        productive technical careers, Vol II: 384
    peers, Vol II: 384–385
    perceived abilities and motivations, Vol II: 387–389
    seven women, study of, Vol II: 390
    stages of the STEM pipeline, Vol II: 381f
    STEM careers definition, Vol II: 381
    teachers, Vol II: 385
Occupational segregation, Vol II: 672–674
Occupational stratification, gender differences in, Vol II: 676–677
OECD, *see* Organization for Economic Co-operation and Development (OECD)
OFS, *see* Old-fashioned Sexism (OFS)
Old-fashioned Sexism (OFS), Vol I: 147–148, 151
Olfaction, Vol I: 248–249
Olympic motto
    Citius, Altius, Fortius ("swifter, higher, stronger"), Vol II: 564
One-way causal effect, Vol II: 20
On-line therapeutic interventions, Vol II: 229
Operation Desert Storm, Vol II: 675
Opposite-sex sexual harassment (OSSH), Vol II: 430–431
Orbitofrontal cortex, Vol II: 285
Organisation for Economic Cooperation and Development (OECD), Vol II: 380, 517
Organizational barriers to women's leadership, Vol II: 451–455
    barriers to building social capital, Vol II: 454–455
    challenges of obtaining desirable assignments, Vol II: 455

Subject Index

demands for long hours and relocation, Vol II: 452–453
masculine organizational culture, Vol II: 453–454
Organizational citizenship behavior, Vol II: 452
Organizational deviance, definition, Vol II: 424
Organizational gossip, Vol I: 397
Organization for Economic Co-operation and Development (OECD), Vol II: 380, 517
Organization violence, Vol II: 322
Originality, Vol I: 349–350, 352, 354
Orthogonal personality traits, Vol I: 192
OSSH, *see* Opposite-sex sexual harassment (OSSH)
Osteoarthritis, Vol II: 519
Ostracism, social, Vol II: 312
Otoacoustic emissions (OAEs), Vol I: 243
Outcome and evaluation research, therapeutics, Vol II: 205–211
  adult survivors of childhood sexual abuse, Vol II: 208–209
  immigrant/international women, Vol II: 206–208
    Hmong women living in US, Vol II: 206
    women in Bosnia–Herzegovina, Vol II: 207–208
  men who abuse their partners, Vol II: 210
Over narrative review, advantages, Vol I: 298
Overreaction, women, Vol I: 433

P

P300, Vol I: 238
PADAM, *see* Partial androgen deficiency in the aging male (PADAM)
Pain, Vol I: 240–243, 249, 412; Vol II: 22, 81, 97, 214, 224, 226, 229–230, 238–241, 256, 324, 484–485, 519–520, 522, 546, 549, 554
Panic and phobic disorders, Vol II: 99
Paper folding test, Vol I: 263, 266, 320, 328
PAQ, *see* Personal attributes questionnaire (PAQ)
PAR, *see* Participatory action research (PAR)
Parallelism, Vol I: 419, 421
Parent socialization model, Vol II: 383–384
Parents/parenting, Vol I: 8, 11, 61, 63, 66–68, 71, 113, 139, 143–144, 146, 220, 260, 280, 282–283, 288, 300, 306–307, 309–310, 330, 352–353, 373, 445, 475, 485, 498, 504–505, 509, 534–537, 544, 547, 561, 564, 570–575; Vol II: 8, 11, 56–57, 76, 113–114, 117–118, 125, 137–138, 164–165, 196, 222, 226, 233, 241, 258, 264, 267, 285, 288, 291–293, 297, 299, 317–318, 366, 380–384, 390, 401, 406, 414, 445–446, 518–519, 566, 572–573, 596, 598–600, 617, 643, 647–648, 652, 662
Partial androgen deficiency in the aging male (PADAM), Vol I: 568
Participatory action research (PAR), Vol I: 118; Vol II: 272
Partner (intimate) violence and aggression, Vol II: 316–317, 423, 431
  common couple violence, Vol II: 317

Conflict Tactics Scale, Vol II: 316
intimate terrorist, Vol II: 317
man on woman, Vol II: 316
woman on man, Vol II: 317
Parvocellular retinal ganglion cells (P cells), Vol I: 236–237
1972 passage of Title IX, Vol II: 565–566
Passive aggression, Vol II: 427
Pathognomonic symptoms, Vol II: 94
Pathologize women's biology, Vol II: 93
Patterns of risk, gendered, Vol II: 475–476
Paxil, Vol II: 520
P cells, *see* Parvocellular retinal ganglion cells (P cells)
Peer interactions, Vol I: 281, 430, 500; Vol II: 174, 367
Peer relations
  cross-sex friendships
    degree of sexual interest of men/women, Abbey's research, Vol II: 283
    friends with benefits relationships, study, Vol II: 283
    misperception, contributing factor to sexual harassment, Vol II: 284
    sexual activity in, impact, Vol II: 283
    sexual tension, cause of, Vol II: 283
  same-sex friendships
    Dindia and Allen's meta-analysis (1992), Vol II: 283
    gynocentric study, Vol II: 283
    intimacy findings in men/women, Vol II: 282
    men's competence with other men, Vol II: 282
    self-disclosure findings in adolescents, Vol II: 282
    social learning theories, findings (Maccoby), Vol II: 282
    women's expressive/sensitive behavior, impact, Vol II: 282
People-things dimension, Vol I: 309
Perceived abilities, Vol I: 11, 309; Vol II: 11, 387–390
Perceived power, Vol I: 416, 418
Perceptions of feminist therapy/therapists, Vol II: 196–197
Personal Attributes Questionnaire (PAQ), Vol I: 14, 47, 50, 134–138, 143, 145–147, 151–152, 366, 460; Vol II: 15, 22
Personal disclosure, Vol II: 10, 326–327
  blogs or web-logs, Vol II: 327
  true self/actual self, Vol II: 327
Personalismo, concept of, Vol II: 236
"The personal is political," Vol II: 263
Personality, Vol II: 19
  disorders, Vol I: 29; Vol II: 73, 81, 92–96, 118, 192–193, 195, 230–231
  five-factor model, Vol II: 25–30
    evaluation of FFM research/directions, study of gender issues, Vol II: 28–30
    FFM traits, difference in, Vol II: 26–28
    future research, direction, Vol II: 33–36

Personality (*cont.*)
- sense of coherence, Vol II: 35–36
- social/situational contexts, Vol II: 33–34
- wellness and transcendence, studying, Vol II: 34–35
- gender differences in personality, influences, Vol II: 20–21
- gender theory, Vol II: 19
- individual differences, study of, Vol II: 19
- masculinity/femininity, personality theory, Vol II: 21–25
    - expressiveness/instrumentality/mental health, Vol II: 24–25
    - history, Vol II: 21–23
    - instrumentality and expressiveness as mediators, Vol II: 23
- measurement, Vol II: 19
- self-evaluations, gender differences, Vol II: 30–33
    - global self-esteem, Vol II: 30–31
    - multi-dimensional self-concept, Vol II: 31–33

Personality and gender in adulthood
- critiques of Erikson's developmental theory, Vol I: 563–565
    - additional stages, Vol I: 563
    - cross-gender trade-off of qualities, Vol I: 565
    - distal social roles, Vol I: 563
    - ego integrity, Vol I: 565
    - generativity, Vol I: 564–565
    - intimacy and identity, Vol I: 564
    - proximal family issues, Vol I: 563
- critiques of gender in Erikson's theory
    - Rochester Adult Longitudinal Study, Vol I: 563
- culture, sexual orientation, and history in Erikson's theory, Vol I: 565–566
    - cohort influences on identity formation, Vol I: 566
    - CPI, Vol II: 566
    - ego integrity, Vol I: 561
    - workable social identity, Vol I: 561
- Erikson's theory of personality development, Vol I: 560–561
- *See also* Adult development and aging

Personality and psychopathology, objective/projective tests, Vol II: 70
Personality and role identity structural model (PRISM), Vol II: 34
Personality disorders
- de-contextualized diagnosis, Vol II: 95
- HPD, diagnostic criteria for, Vol II: 94

16 Personality Factor (16PF), Vol II: 69, 78
Personality influences, gender differences in, Vol II: 20–21
Personality models
- multi-dimensional process model of gender, Vol II: 68
- process model for personality (Mischel and Shoda), Vol II: 67

Personality tests, construction of
- empirical tests
    - factor analysis, Vol II: 78
    - known-groups comparison method, Vol II: 78
    - MMPI and MMPI-2, Vol II: 78–80
    - 16PF, Vol II: 80
    - IRT, Vol II: 81–82
    - theoretically developed tests, Vol II: 80–81

Personal progress scale, Vol II: 213
Person-environment fit, model of, Vol II: 389
Person-in-context influences, Vol I: 532–542
- cross-gender interactions, overcoming gender segregation and developing romantic relationships, Vol I: 539–541
    - group social activities, Vol I: 540
    - heterosexual dating activity, Vol I: 540
    - same-sex romantic relationships, Vol I: 541
- culture/media, Vol I: 541–542
    - media-saturated environment, Vol I: 541
    - portrayals of gender-stereotyped behavior, Vol I: 542
- family, Vol I: 536–537
    - parent's influence, Vol I: 536
- peers, Vol I: 537–539
    - peer acceptance of LGBT adolescents, Vol I: 538
    - "pressure," Vol I: 538
- puberty, Vol I: 533–536
    - DMS, Vol I: 535
    - early maturation hypothesis, Vol I: 535
    - FSH, Vol I: 533
    - hormonal changes, Vol I: 533
    - HPA, Vol I: 533
    - HPG, Vol I: 533
    - LH, Vol II: 533
    - physical changes of puberty, Vol I: 533–534
    - pubertal effects on identity and gender-typed behavior, Vol I: 534–536
    - pubertal timing models, Vol I: 535

Person talk, gossip, Vol I: 396, 416
PET, *see* Positron emission tomography (PET)
Phenylthiocarbamide (PTC), Vol I: 246
Physical activity, Vol I: 180; Vol II: 472–473, 476–477, 479–480, 550, 564–568, 570–571, 573–579
Physical Activity and Sport in the Lives of Girls, Vol II: 576
Physical enactment games, Vol II: 651
Physical forms of aggression, Vol II: 427
Physically disabled women, barriers to participation, Vol II: 574
Physician–patient relationship, Vol II: 523
Physiological arousal, Vol I: 429, 442–443; Vol II: 49, 52, 54, 264–266
- cardiac/cardiovascular reactivity, Vol I: 442
- emotional stimuli, Vol I: 442

Picture story exercise (PSE), Vol II: 42–45, 48–51, 53–55, 57–58
- PSE measures of achievement, Vol II: 48

Subject Index

Planning programs, Vol II: 517
Plumb-line task, *see* Spatial perception
Pluralism, methodological/epistemological, Vol II: 588
PMDD, *see* Premenstrual dysphoric disorder (PMDD)
PMS, *see* Premenstrual syndrome (PMS)
Political activism expressions, Vol II: 359
Political psychologists, Vol I: 35
Politics of exclusion, Vol II: 102
Politics of nature and nurture, Vol II: 633
Polygamy, Vol I: 268
Polygyny, Vol II: 285
Popular ideals of womanhood, Vol II: 403
Population-based recruitment, Vol I: 180–182, 185–186
Population-based survey, Vol II: 479
Population Reference Bureau, Vol II: 471, 481
Position of men and women in society, measures related to, Vol I: 146–149
    Ambivalent Sexism Inventory, Vol I: 147–148
    AWS, Vol I: 146–147
    FIC, Vol I: 149
    FIDS, Vol I: 149
    FIS, Vol I: 148–149
    MS, Vol I: 147
    OFS, Vol I: 147
    SSE, Vol I: 148
Positive emotions, Vol I: 242, 433, 435, 439–440, 479; Vol II: 25, 27, 297, 339, 434
Positive/negative affective tone, Vol II: 428
Positivism's preferred method, limitations of, Vol I: 29
Positron emission tomography (PET), Vol I: 225, 242–244, 249–250, 443, 447
Postmodernism, Vol I: 32, 400, 403
    discourse analysis, Vol I: 403
Postmodern perspective, Vol I: 400, 402–403
    power, Vol I: 402
Post-traumatic Stress Disorder (PTSD), Vol II: 74, 95, 100, 190, 436, 548–549, 685
    symptoms, Vol II: 94
Poverty, Vol I: 35, 290, 574; Vol II: 92, 97, 101–103, 121, 481, 485, 510, 518, 524, 542, 614, 635
Power
    coercive, Vol I: 416
    dynamics, Vol II: 196, 211, 268, 462, 624, 626, 635, 644, 647
    expert, Vol I: 416
    legitimate, Vol I: 416
    motivation, Vol II: 41, 52–55
        physiological correlates of power, Vol II: 54–55
        profligacy and responsibility training, Vol II: 53–54
    to name, Vol I: 361, 400
    nonverbal expression, Vol I: 416
    perceptions, Vol I: 417
    referent, Vol I: 416
    reward, Vol I: 416
    and status relationship, Vol I: 387
    and volume of words relationship, Vol I: 388–389

Praxis, Vol II: 198–205
    general practices, Vol II: 198–202
        qualitative research, Vol II: 198–199
        quantitative research, Vol II: 200–202
    therapeutic relationship, issues, Vol II: 202–205
        men as feminist therapists, Vol II: 204–205
        nature of relationship, Vol II: 202–203
        self-disclosure, Vol II: 203
        termination, Vol II: 204
Preferences, academic, Vol I: 308–309
    explanations, Vol I: 309–310
        empathizers, Vol I: 309
        expectancy-value model, Vol I: 310
        extensive model, Vol I: 310
        systemizers, Vol I: 309
    gender differences, Vol I: 312–313
    task values, Vol I: 310
        attainment value, Vol I: 310
        intrinsic/interest value, Vol I: 310
        utility value, Vol I: 310
Prejudice
    sources of
        sex/gender/sexual orientation, Vol II: 363–365
    against transgender individuals, Vol II: 366–369
        consequences of gender prejudice, Vol II: 368–369
        contextual origins, Vol II: 366–367
        prevalence of gender prejudice, Vol II: 367–368
Preliminary Scholastic Aptitude Test (PSAT), Vol I: 302
Premenstrual dysphoric disorder (PMDD), Vol II: 97–98
Premenstrual syndrome (PMS), Vol I: 108, 458
Prenatal hormone exposure, Vol I: 84, 280, 484
Primary appraisal, Vol II: 432, 495
Primary mental abilities test, *see* Mental rotation test
PRISM, *see* Personality and role identity structural model (PRISM)
Problem-focused coping, Vol I: 497–499, 503–504, 511
Process model for personality (Mischel and Shoda), Vol II: 67
    CAPS, Vol II: 67
    if–then situation–behavior profiles, Vol II: 67
Profanity, Vol I: 391–393, 402
    coarse language, Vol I: 391–392
Profiles (gendered) of targets and perpetrators
    bullying
        same-sex bullying rates of men/women, Vol II: 430
    incivility, Vol II: 429
    sexual harassment
        Berdahl's sex-based harassment theory, Vol II: 430
        gender policing, Vol II: 430
        "not man enough" harassment, Vol II: 431
        OSSH, Vol II: 430
        SSSH, Vol II: 430

Profiles (*cont.*)
   workplace aggression/violence
      homicides, cause of job-related deaths, Vol II: 431
Progesterone, Vol I: 216, 245; Vol II: 51–52
Progestins, Vol I: 216, 245
Projective tests
   the Rorschach, Vol II: 70
   See also Personality tests, construction of
Proliferation of Gay/Straight Alliances, Vol II: 370
Promundo, Vol II: 542
Pronounced gender roles, Vol II: 266
PROP, *see* 6-n-propylthiouracil (PROP)
Prosocial behavior
   compassionate love, Vol II: 327–328
      intimates/strangers, Vol II: 328
   empathy, nurturance, and sensitivity to nonverbal cues, Vol II: 324–325
      degree of empathy, variation in, Vol II: 325
      interpersonal sensitivity, Vol II: 325
      thinking based on nonverbal behavior, Vol II: 324
   helping others, Vol II: 325–326
      helping profession, Vol II: 326
      heroic actions/chivalry, Vol II: 326
      prosocial personality, Vol II: 326
   personal disclosure, Vol II: 326–327
      blogs or web-logs, Vol II: 327
      true self/actual self, Vol II: 327
Prostate cancer survivors, Vol II: 527
Prostate-specific antigen (PSA), Vol II: 527
Proximal factors, Vol I: 430, 440, 445
Prozac, Vol II: 97–98, 317, 520
Prozac on the Couch (book), Vol II: 97
PSA, *see* Prostate-specific antigen (PSA)
PSAT, *see* Preliminary Scholastic Aptitude Test (PSAT)
PSE, *see* Picture story exercise (PSE)
Psychiatric drug treatment research, Vol II: 96
Psychoanalytic/psychodynamic therapies, Vol II: 203
Psychoanalytic theory, Vol I: 20, 159, 471–472, 528
   castration anxiety, Vol I: 472
   Electra conflict, Vol I: 472
   homoseductive mother, Vol I: 472
   libidinal instinct, Vol I: 472
   oedipal conflict, Vol I: 472
   See also Gender differences in sexuality
Psychoeducational workshops, Vol II: 125, 229
Psychological adjustment, gender differences in
   distress in cancer patients, study of
      PTSD scores in men/women, Vol II: 548
      feminine/masculine identity, issues, Vol II: 548
      men and women with CVD, study of, Vol II: 548
      older adults with Parkinson's disease, Solimeo study, Vol II: 549
   patients with COPD, study of, Vol II: 548
Psychological androgyny, Vol II: 22, 296
Psychological approach to study of culture, Vol I: 33, 162–163
   cross-cultural psychology, Vol I: 162
   cultural psychology, Vol I: 162–163
   indigenous psychology, two groups, Vol I: 163
Psychological assessment and testing
   assumptions
      personality: traits or processes?, Vol II: 67–68
      psychometric theory, Vol II: 66
      universal human abilities, culture issues, Vol II: 66
   context and assessment experience, Vol II: 64–65
   gender and norms, Vol II: 68–69
   identity variable, components, Vol II: 64
   process, definition, Vol II: 63
   psychological testing, role in assessment, Vol II: 63–64
      extroversion/depression/gifted, Vol II: 64
      intelligence, Vol II: 64
      personality, Vol II: 64, 65
      psychopathology, Vol II: 64
      test scores, basis/norms, Vol II: 65
      transgendered people, Vol II: 65
Psychological Association Task Force, Vol II: 171
Psychological measurement theory or psychometrics, Vol II: 66
Psychological tests
   test functions
      diagnosis and intervention, Vol II: 72
      tests for selection, SAT/GRE, Vol II: 71–72
      tests of achievement, Vol II: 71
   types
      cognitive ability tests, Vol II: 70
      personality and psychopathology tests, Vol II: 70
Psychological universals, Vol I: 161–162, 164, 166
   problem of imposed etics, Vol I: 162
Psychology Constructs the Female, Vol I: 26
Psychology Constructs the Female; or, The Fantasy Life of the Male Psychologist, Vol I: 27
Psychology, gender study development in
   basic and experimental psychology, gender research in
      brain and behavior, Vol II: 7
      communication, Vol II: 8
      emotion and motivation, Vol II: 8
      history of psychology, Vol II: 6
      learning, education, and cognitive processes, Vol II: 7
      life span development, Vol II: 8–9
      research methods, Vol II: 6–7
   social and applied psychology, gender research in
      abnormal and clinical psychology, Vol II: 9–10
      health psychology, Vol II: 11–12
      industrial–organizational psychology, Vol II: 11
      personality psychology, Vol II: 9
      psychotherapy, Vol II: 10
      social psychology, Vol II: 10–11
      special topics, Vol II: 12
The Psychology of Men & Masculinity, Vol I: 48, 90, 257

Psychology of men/masculinity, research trends
- Attitudes Toward the Male Role Scale, Vol I: 52
- Brannon Masculinity Scale, Vol I: 52
- measurement of masculinity
  - attitudes Toward the Male Role scale, Vol I: 52
  - Brannon Masculinity Scale, Vol I: 52
  - citations of instruments used in the measurement of masculinity, Vol I: 52t
  - Conformity to Masculine Norms Inventory, Vol I: 52
  - Gender Role Conflict Scale, Vol I: 52–53
  - Macho Scale, Vol I: 52
  - Male Role Attitudes Scale, Vol I: 52
  - Male Role Norms Inventory, Vol I: 52
  - Masculine Gender Role Stress Scale, Vol I: 52–53
  - Stereotypes About Male Sexuality Scale, Vol I: 52
- men and mental health, Vol I: 54
- men and physical health, Vol I: 53–54
  - Drive for Muscularity Scale, Vol I: 53
  - *The Muscular Ideal*, Vol I: 54
  - Swansea Muscularity Attitudes Questionnaire, Vol I: 53

The Psychology of Sex Differences (Maccoby and Jacklin), Vol II: 88

Psychology of women, emergence and development
- building a multicultural psychology of women
  - multicultural psychology, feminist psychology, and social activism, Vol I: 35
- epistemological debates and methodological developments of the 1980s and 1990s
  - feminist empiricism, Vol I: 31
  - feminist methods, Vol I: 33–34
  - feminist postmodernism, Vol I: 32–33
  - feminist standpoint epistemologies, Vol I: 32
- feminist revolution in psychology
  - emergence of a psychology for women, Vol I: 26–28
  - emergence of feminist practice, Vol I: 29–30
- FirstWave, Vol I: 21–23
  - applied psychology after World War I, Vol I: 21
  - attention to "woman problem," Vol I: 23
  - community of ideas debate, Vol I: 22
  - Laura Spelman Rockefeller Memorial Fund, Vol I: 21
  - *The Mental Traits of Sex*, Vol I: 22
  - studies on mental and motor abilities during menstruation, Vol I 23
  - studies to debunk stereotypes about women, Vol I: 23
  - variability hypothesis, test, Vol I: 22
  - women in higher education, Vol I: 21
  - young women of the experimental psychology class, Vol I: 22
- persistent dilemmas and future directions
  - androcentric ideology of contemporary science, Vol I: 36
  - feminist empiricism, Vol I: 35
  - Genes and Gender Collective, Vol I: 36
  - *Sociobiology: The New Synthesis* (Wilson E. O.), Vol I: 36
- psychology and/of women at mid-century, Vol I: 23–26
  - APA, Vol I: 24
  - code of menstrual invalidism, Vol I: 26
  - elevation of the traditionally feminine values (Seward), Vol I: 26
  - ECP, Vol I: 23
  - intelligence test, development and use, Vol I: 23
  - NCWP, Vol I: 24
  - Northside Center for Child Development in 1946, Vol I: 25
  - racism and sexism, Vol I: 25
  - racism and sexism/anti-semitism and sexism, Vol I: 25
  - Society for the Psychological Study of Social Issues Committee on Roles of Men and Women in Postwar Society, Vol I: 26
  - women's proportionate lack of prestige, reason, Vol I: 25
- Seneca Falls Convention in 1848, Vol I: 20

Psychology of Women Quarterly (PWQ), Vol I: 47, 90, 197; Vol II: 2–3, 617

Psychopathology, role of gender in development of, Vol I: 59–63, 72, 543–548
- aggression and other externalizing behaviors, Vol I: 545–548
  - association with antisocial behavior, Vol I: 548
  - gender differences in the etiology of aggression, Vol I: 547
  - role of puberty in emergence of externalizing behaviors, Vol I: 548
  - role of puberty in the emergence of externalizing behaviors, Vol I: 548
  - unique patterns of gender differences in aggression, Vol I: 545–547
  - unique patterns of gender differences in substance use, Vol I: 547–548
- depression and other internalizing behaviors, Vol I: 543–545
  - media sources, Vol I: 544
  - pubertal timing, Vol I: 544
  - stress in important relationships, Vol I: 544

Psychotherapist's attitudes, Vol II: 230–233
- multicultural considerations paradigm to psychotherapy, Vol II: 231–232
- negative biases against male clients, Vol II: 231
- strength-based perspective, Vol II: 232–233

Psychotherapy with men, Vol II: 221
- addressing and assessing masculine socialization, Vol II: 238–239
- evidence-based practice, Vol II: 221
- finding strength in being vulnerable, case study, Vol II: 222–223

Psychotherapy (*cont.*)
  male clients knowledge, Vol II: 223–230
    presenting concerns, Vol II: 229–230
    psychological help, Vol II: 228–229
  men in psychotherapy, skills for, Vol II: 233–238
    be genuine and real, Vol II: 236
    be patient, Vol II: 235
    clients' gender-role identity, Vol II: 236
    engaging men in psychotherapy, Vol II: 234
    goals match needs of male client, Vol II: 235
    male clients, educate, Vol II: 235
    masculine face, Vol II: 234–235
    men have in entering and being in psychotherapy, Vol II: 234
  psychotherapist's attitudes, Vol II: 230–233
    multicultural considerations paradigm to psychotherapy, Vol II: 231–232
    negative biases against male clients, Vol II: 231
    strength-based perspective, Vol II: 232–233
  psychotherapy thoughts, Vol II: 243
  revisiting, case, Vol II: 239–243
    effective treatments and improving therapy outcome, Vol II: 242–243
    helping men to seek psychological help, Vol II: 241–242
    retaining men in psychotherapy, Vol II: 242
Psychotropic medications for women, Vol II: 521
PsycINFO database, Vol I: 43, 616
PTC, *see* Phenylthiocarbamide (PTC)
PTSD, *see* Post-traumatic stress disorder (PTSD)
Puberty, Vol I: 84, 219–226, 241, 246, 280, 282–283, 324, 331, 456, 527, 530, 533–536, 543–445, 548; Vol II: 118, 168–169
  DMS, Vol I: 535
  early maturation hypothesis, Vol I: 535
  FSH, Vol I: 533
  hormonal changes, Vol I: 533
  HPA, Vol I: 533
  HPG, Vol I: 533
  LH, Vol I: 533
Publications and Communications Board, Vol I: 370
Puerto Rican culture, Vol II: 627
Purposive recruitment, Vol I: 181
Pursuer/distancer pattern, Vol II: 265

Q

Qingfu (frivolous), Vol II: 293
Qualitative inquiry in gender studies
  contemporary forms, Vol I: 117–118
    conversation analysis, Vol I: 118
    discourse analysis, Vol I: 117–118
  developing forms, Vol I: 118–121
    action research, Vol I: 118
    Participatory action research (PAR), Vol I: 118
    performance-based research, Vol I: 119–121
  divergent paths, Vol I: 122–123
    handbooks, Vol I: 122

  ethnography, Vol I: 114–116
  future directions, Vol I: 121–122
    challenges for qualitative methods within gender studies, Vol I: 121
    evidence-based practices, Vol I: 121
    gender/women/feminism/ and qualitative methods, Vol I: 121–122
  major methods, Vol I: 111–117
    case study, Vol I: 111–112
    ethnography, Vol I: 114–116
    focus groups, Vol I: 113–114
    interviews, Vol I: 112–113
    narrative research, Vol I: 116–117
  major methods in the qualitative study of gender, Vol I: 111–117
  narrative research, Vol I: 114–116
  qualitative methods, Vol I: 104–111
Qualitative methods, Vol I: 6, 34, 104–111, 115, 121–123
  characteristics of qualitative inquiry in gender research that have challenged the mainstream
    'First World' or 'Third World' academies, Vol I: 109
    Foucaultian argument on representation, Vol I: 109
    reflexivity, Vol I: 109
    researcher/researched/reader relationship, Vol I: 106–108
    situated knowledge, Vol I: 105
    value-basis of research, Vol I: 105–106
  diverse approaches to qualitative methods
    constructionist perspective, Vol I: 110–111
    empiricist perspective, Vol I: 110
    grounded theory approach to doing qualitative research, Vol I: 111
Queer theory, Vol I: 368; Vol II: 215
Questioning, Vol I: 23, 63, 120, 290, 350, 368, 380, 499, 512, 518, 536; Vol II: 91, 111, 120, 189, 205, 364, 523, 635, 685
Quid pro quo, *see* Sexual coercion

R

RA, *see* Rheumatoid arthritis (RA)
Race and ethnicity, Vol II: 412
  differences, Vol II: 519
  Latino/families, study, Vol II: 412
  See also Household labor
Racial and Gender Report Cards, Lapchick, Vol II: 567
Racism/anti-semitism and sexism, Vol I: 25
RALS, *see* Rochester Adult Longitudinal study (RALS)
Randomized Response Techniques (RRT), Vol II: 603
Rape, Vol II: 321–322
  sample of married battered women, Vol II: 321
  victims, virgin or vamp narrative, Vol II: 650
Rapport talk, Vol I: 386
RAT, *see* Remote Associates Test (RAT)
rCBF, *see* Regional cerebral blood flow (rCBF)

Subject Index

Real man, Vol II: 101, 649
Recalled Childhood Gender Identity/Gender Role
    Questionnaire, Vol I: 141
Recruitment, Vol I: 7, 179–188
    examples, Vol I: 184–187
        capture–recapture method, Vol I: 187
        CBPR, Vol I: 186
        clinical trial/observational study, Vol I: 185
        convenience or snowball recruitment methods,
            Vol I: 186
        diversity in a large clinical trial, WHI, Vol I: 185
        recruitment strategies for SMW insuring
            diversity, Vol I: 186–188
        specific strategies for enhancing diversity in
            recruitment, Vol I: 185–186
        studies of psychological phenomena, psychology
            department subject pool, Vol I: 184–185
    model of
        contact stage, Vol I: 183
        enrollment stage, Vol I: 183–184
        preparatory stage, Vol I: 182–183
    types of, Vol I: 180–182
        choosing recruitment strategy, difficulties, Vol I:
            181–182
        convenience sampling, Vol I: 181
        eligibility criteria, Vol I: 182
        population-based recruitment, Vol I: 180–181
        purposive recruitment, Vol I: 181
Referent power, Vol I: 416
Reflections and future directions, Vol II: 629–635
    conceptualizing gender systemically, Vol II: 632–633
    critical consciousness as essential to quality research,
        Vol II: 633–635
    redefining dualisms, Vol II: 631–632
*Reflections on the Work of Feminist Theorist Jean Baker
    Miller*, Vol I: 105
Regional cerebral blood flow (rCBF), Vol I: 242
Reimbursement of medications, Vol II: 111
Rejection sensitivity, Vol II: 140–141, 143, 145–146
Relational aggression, Vol II: 312
Relational costs, Vol II: 298–299
Relational maintenance
    behavioral/cognitive, types, Vol II: 293
    commitment, Vol II: 294
    intimacy
        responsiveness, Vol II: 295–296
        self-disclosure, Vol II: 294–295
    relationship satisfaction, Vol II: 296
        stereotypic femininity and masculinity, Vol II:
            296
Relationship
    as context, theme, Vol II: 625
    initiation and dating
        social and dyadic contexts, role of peers and
            romantic partners, Vol II: 291
        sociocultural contexts, dating scripts, Vol II:
            289–290

manipulation, Vol II: 312
    quality, key components of
        commitment, Vol II: 294
        intimacy, Vol II: 294
Relationship-focused coping, Vol I: 496, 499
Remote Associates Test (RAT), Vol I: 350
Report talk, Vol I: 386
Research findings
    category norms, Vol I 196–197
        norm theory, Vol I: 196–197
    clients' perceptions and experiences of feminist
        therapy, Vol II: 212–213
        experience of diverse groups, Vol II: 213
    current and future practice, Vol II: 214–215
    description, Vol I: 193
    differentiation between feminist therapists, Vol II:
        211
        men as feminist therapists, Vol II: 211
        second and third waves, Vol II: 211
    effects of category norms, Vol I: 197–199
        category norms, Vol I: 198–199
        induction, Vol I: 199
        intersectional invisibility, Vol I: 198
        reasons for undoing, Vol I: 197–198
    efficacy/evaluation and outcome research, Vol II: 213
    feminist/non-feminist practices, Vol II: 212
        general practices, Vol II: 212
        particular phases and processes of therapy, Vol II:
            212
    language to thinking, impotance of, Vol I: 195
    scientific metaphors and analogies, Vol I: 199–203
        evolutionary analyses of gender-related findings,
            Vol I: 202
        gender-related metaphors, Vol I: 201
        visual metaphors, Vol I: 202
    'sex' or 'gender,' Vol I: 193–195
        Money's paradigm, Vol I: 194
        multiple meanings, Vol I: 194
        political climate, Vol I: 194
    theoretical considerations, Vol II: 213–214
    third wave of theorizing, Vol I: 192
    traits, behaviors, preferences, Vol I: 192
Responsiveness, Vol II: 282, 295–296
Resting metabolic rate (RMR), Vol I: 457, 466
Restrictive Affectionate Behavior between Men
    (RABBM), Vol I: 145
Restrictive Emotionality (RE), Vol I: 137, 145
Retinal ganglion cells (RGCs), Vol I: 236
Revisiting, case, Vol II: 239–243
    effective treatments and improving therapy outcome,
        Vol II: 242–243
    helping men to seek psychological help, Vol II:
        241–242
    retaining men in psychotherapy, Vol II: 242
Reviving Ophelia (Pipher), Vol II: 30
Reward power, Vol I: 416
RGCs, *see* Retinal ganglion cells (RGCs)

Rheumatoid arthritis (RA), Vol II: 500, 507, 542, 545–546, 550–551
Richardson Conflict Response Questionnaire, Vol II: 313
Risky (and healthy) behaviors, choice, Vol II: 476
RMR, *see* Resting metabolic rate (RMR)
Robotic surgery, Vol II: 528
Rochester Adult Longitudinal study (RALS), Vol I: 563, 566
Rod-and-frame test, *see* Spatial perception
Rogerian therapies, Vol II: 188
Rogue sexism, Vol II: 426
Role conflict/stress, measures of, Vol I: 144–146
Role congruity theory, Vol II: 678–679
Rorschach Inkblot Method, Vol II: 209
Routine maintenance behaviors, Vol II: 293, 296
RRT, *see* Randomized Response Techniques (RRT)
Rumination, Vol I: 95, 431–432, 545; Vol II: 141–144, 146, 154, 621
Rumination and depression, gender differences in, Vol II: 154

S

Sa-i-gu riots in Los Angeles, Vol II: 620
Same-sex conversations, Vol I: 390, 394; Vol II: 295
Same-sex friendships, Vol II: 281–284
  Dindia and Allen's meta-analysis (1992), Vol II: 283
  gynocentric study, Vol II: 283
  intimacy findings in men/women, Vol II: 282
  men's competence with other men, Vol II: 282
  self-disclosure findings in adolescents, Vol II: 282
  self-disclosure/responsiveness, male inhibition to, Vol II: 282
    social learning theories, findings (Maccoby), Vol II: 282
    women's expressive/sensitive behavior, impact, Vol II: 282
Same-sex sexual harassment (SSSH), Vol II: 430–431
  homosexuality, higher rate indication, Vol II: 430
Sampling, forensic research, Vol II: 599–601
SANDF, *see* South African National Defence Force (SANDF)
San Francisco assessment, Vol II: 120
Sarafem (Eli Lilly), Vol II: 98
SAT, *see* Scholastic Aptitude Test (SAT)
SAT-M, *see* Scholastic Aptitude Test-Math (SAT-M)
Schedule of Sexist Events (SSE), Vol I: 148
Scheffler and Müchele's program, Vol II: 207
Scholastic Aptitude Test-Math (SAT-M), Vol I: 304
Scholastic Aptitude Test (SAT), Vol II: 71–72, 302
Science, Engineering, and Technology (SET), Vol II: 380
Scottish Mental Survey, Vol I: 302
SCS, *see* Self-Compassion Scale (SCS)
SDO, *see* Social dominance orientation (SDO)
SDQ I, *see* Self-Description Questionnaires I(SDQ I)
SDQ II, *see* Self-Description Questionnaires II(SDQ II)

SDQ III, *see* Self-Description Questionnaires III(SDQ III)
The Seasons of a Man's Life, Vol I: 44
Second Change Sheet, Vol I: 370
Second-generation literature, psychological adjustment research, Vol I: 62–63
  homosexuality = psychopathology, Vol I: 63
Second-wave feminism, Vol I: 30, 193, 287
Secrecy and Silence in Research, Vol I: 107
Sedatives and tranquilizers, Vol II: 521
SEER, *see* Surveillance, Epidemiology, and End Results (SEER)
Segregation and progression, gender/military careers
  career progression of ethnic or visible minorities, Vol II: 677
  gender and occupational segregation, Vol II: 672–674
  gender, career progression, and leadership, Vol II: 677–679
  gender, combat, and the "warrior ethic," Vol II: 674–676
  gender differences in occupational stratification, Vol II: 676–677
Selected serotonin reuptake inhibitors (SSRIs), Vol II: 520
Selective incivility theory, Vol II: 426
Self-actualization, Vol I: 352, 512
Self-compassion, Vol II: 35–36
Self-Compassion Scale (SCS), Vol II: 35
Self-concept, Vol II: 9, 20, 31–33, 168, 361, 381, 576
Self-conscious, Vol II: 157
Self-Description Questionnaires III(SDQ III), Vol II: 31
Self-Description Questionnaires II(SDQ II), Vol II: 31
Self-Description Questionnaires I(SDQ I), Vol II: 31
Self-disclosure, Vol II: 282, 294–295
Self-esteem, Vol I: 14, 63, 67–68, 97, 165, 283, 288, 352, 422, 498, 512–513, 530, 535, 544, 563, 568; Vol II: 13, 15, 20, 24–25, 30–33, 36, 75, 97, 99, 117–118, 155, 160, 165, 190, 199–200, 207–208, 253, 348, 362, 431, 484, 506, 510, 512, 545, 573, 576, 685
Self-evaluations, gender differences, Vol II: 30–33
  global self-esteem, Vol II: 30–31
  multi-dimensional self-concept, Vol II: 31–33
Selfish gene hypothesis, Vol I: 260
  See also Evolutionary psychology (EP)
Self-objectification, Vol I: 91–92, 94, 97; Vol II: 171–172, 575, 659
Self-perceptions in sport
  gender, expectations, and participation
    achievement behaviors, Vol II: 573
    Eccles' developmental model, Vol II: 573
    exercise and self-perceptions, study (Tiggemann and Williamson), Vol II: 573–574
    parental influence and youth sport involvement, Vol II: 573
    women with physical disabilities, barriers, Vol II: 574

Subject Index

physical activity and adolescent development
    participation rates among race/ethnic groups, Vol II: 576
    physical/psychosocial benefits, Vol II: 576
    sport participation, impact on self-esteem of women (Richman and Shaffer), Vol II: 576
    Youth Risk Behavior Survey, Vol II: 576
physical activity, gender, and body image
    body image and muscularity, Vol II: 575–576
    body image and physical activity, Vol II: 575
    body image and sport participation, Vol II: 574
    body image, sport, and eating disorders, Vol II: 574–575
Self-promoting manner, achievements, Vol II: 347
Self-reliance, Vol II: 546
Self-socialization theories, Vol I: 508, 532
SEM, *see* Structural equation modeling (SEM)
Seneca Falls Convention in 1848, Vol I: 20
Sense of coherence (SOC), Vol II: 35–36
    comprehensibility, Vol II: 35
    manageability, Vol II: 35
    meaningfulness, Vol II: 35
Sensorimotor games, Vol II: 651
Sentimental Men, Vol I: 45
Sentimental stereotypes, Vol II: 432
Sentinel lymph node (SLN) biopsies, Vol II: 526
SEQ, *see* Sexual Experiences Questionnaire (SEQ)
Sertoli cells, Vol I: 216
SES, *see* Socioeconomic status (SES)
SET, *see* Science, Engineering, and Technology (SET)
Sex and gender, sensation and perception, Vol I: 235–250
    audition and vestibular perception, Vol I: 243–246
        OAE, Vol I: 243
        sound detection mechanisms, Vol I: 243
    chemical senses, Vol I: 246–249
    somatosensation, Vol I: 240–243
    vision, Vol I: 235–240
        optical coherence tomography, Vol I: 236
        photoreceptor cells, Vol I: 235
        types of photopigments, Vol I: 236
Sex and Temperament in Three Primitive Societies, Vol I: 159
Sex and the Social Order., Vol I: 26
Sex differences, physiology of, Vol I: 215–227, 363–365
    adulthood, after puberty, Vol I: 220–226
    glucocorticoids, role of nonreproductive hormones, Vol I: 226–227
    steroid hormones, classification and synthesis of, Vol I: 215–216
        behavior in childhood, Vol I: 219–220
        fetus, development of sex, Vol I: 216
Sex differences research, Vol I: 28, 35, 193; Vol: 546
Sex-dimorphic behavioral patterns, Vol II: 115
Sex-Fair Research, Vol I: 371
Sex reassignment
    FtM, Vol I: 224
    MtF, Vol I: 224

Sex reassignment surgery (SRS), Vol II: 111, 114, 119, 123, 366–367
Sex Role Behavior Scale (SRBS), Vol I: 142–143, 150
Sex Roles (SR), Vol I: 47, 90; Vol II: 2
Sex-specific patterns, brain
    hypothalamus, Vol I: 247
    prefrontal cortex, Vol I: 247
    ventral striatum, Vol I: 247
Sex-typed behaviors, studies on, Vol I: 28
Sexual and gender prejudice, Vol II: 359
    Catholics, study of young, Vol II: 371
    future research directions, Vol II: 370–371
    gender prejudice against transgender individuals, Vol II: 366–369
        consequences of gender prejudice, Vol II: 368–369
        contextual origins, Vol II: 366–367
        prevalence of gender prejudice, Vol II: 367–368
    positive attitudes toward sexual minorities, Vol II: 369–370
    sexual prejudice against gay and lesbian individuals, Vol II: 359–362
        bisexual individuals, against, Vol II: 363–365
        homophobia and its discontents, Vol II: 359–360
        in-group domination, Vol II: 362
        internalized biphobia, Vol II: 365
        internalized homophobia, Vol II: 362
        religion, Vol II: 361–362
        sex and gender, Vol II: 360–361
        sources of prejudice, Vol II: 363–365
Sexual and reproductive health, Vol II: 532–535
    future directions, Vol II: 534–535
    HIV/AIDS, Vol II: 533–534
    sexual health issues, Vol II: 532
Sexual attitudes, differences in, Vol I: 471, 473, 477–481, 485–488, 542
    attitudes toward homosexuality, Vol I: 479–480
    gender and mate selection and retention, Vol I: 481
        mate retention tactics, Vol I: 481
        women's economic and social dependency on men, Vol I: 481
    sexual desire, Vol I: 480–481
    See also Gender differences in sexuality
Sexual behaviors, differences in
    large surveys, Vol I: 478
    meta-analytic findings, Vol I: 476–478
        magnitude of gender differences, calculations, Vol I: 477
        product of cultural differences, Vol I: 478
    other sexual behaviors, Vol I: 478–479
        exposure to sexually explicit material, Vol I: 479
        fantasies, Vol I: 478
        orgasm consistency, Vol I: 478
    See also Gender differences in sexuality
Sexual coercion, Vol II: 424
Sexual costs, Vol II: 299–300
Sexual dimorphism, Vol I: 217, 224, 364

Sexual dysfunction, Vol I: 69, 91, 223
Sexual Experiences Questionnaire (SEQ), Vol II: 681
Sexual harassment, Vol II: 11, 87, 91, 282–283, 288, 290–291, 361, 545, 574
   power, leading cause, Vol II: 425
   power of "maleness," Vol II: 425
   sex-based social status, Vol II: 425
   sexual expression, forms of (Berdahl), Vol II: 426
   societal/organizational disparities, men/women, Vol II: 425
   types
      gender harassment, Vol II: 424
      sexual coercion, Vol II: 424
      unwanted sexual attention, Vol II: 424
Sexual inequality, Vol I: 379, 387, 403
Sexual inversion, Vol II: 79
Sexuality, differences in
   biological factors, Vol I: 482–484
      anatomical differences, Vol I: 482
      brain differences, Vol I: 482–483
      hormones, Vol I: 483
      menopause, Vol I: 484
      prenatal factors, Vol I: 483–484
      pubertal development, Vol I: 484
      testosterone replacement therapy, Vol I: 483
      vasopressin, Vol I: 483
   other factors, Vol I: 485–486
      body esteem, Vol I: 485
      disproportionate role in family, Vol I: 485
      sex education, Vol I: 486
      sexual inhibition, performance/consequences, Vol I: 485
      structured masturbation exercises, Vol I: 486
   self-reports, Vol I: 481–482
   socio-cultural factors, Vol I: 484–485
      cultural gender roles, Vol I: 484–485
   See also Gender differences in sexuality
Sexuality in sport and physical activity
   homophobia and professional sport, Vol II: 577–578
   sexual harassment in sport and exercise, Vol II: 579
   sexual prejudice in non-professional sport and physical activity, Vol II: 578–579
Sexually explicit content, media
   exposure and recreational attitudes towards sex, Vol II: 654–655
   sexual media targets/imapct, men and women, Vol II: 655
   stereotyped attitudes toward sex, Ward's study, Vol II: 655
      sports intelligence, Vol II: 661
Sexually transmitted diseases (STDs), Vol II: 533
Sexual minorities and heterosexuals
   developmental trends, Vol II: 136
   mood disorders in, Vol II: 135
   stress and vulnerability to depression
      adaptational effort, Vol II: 138
      discrimination, Vol II: 138–139
      hate crimes, Vol II: 139
      sexual minority stress, Vol II: 138
      victimization, Vol II: 138
Sexual minority, Vol I: 5, 186–188, 290, 368, 447, 538, 540–541, 549; Vol II: 33
   gender/sexual identity, Vol I: 368
   positive attitudes toward, Vol II: 369–370
   stress, Vol II: 137–138, 144
Sexual minority women (SMW), Vol I: 186–188
Sexual orientation and vulnerability to depression
   bisexual, Vol I: 367
   cognitive factors
      and sexual minorities' vulnerability to depression, Vol II: 142–143
      and women's vulnerability to depression, Vol II: 141–142
   epidemiology, men/women
      developmental trends, Vol II: 134
      first onsets *vs.* duration of depression, Vol II: 134–135
      National Comorbidity Study, mental health survey, Vol II: 134
      National Epidemiologic Survey on Alcohol and Related Disorders, Vol II: 134
      symptom differences and treatment seeking, Vol II: 135
   group differences in depression
      stress and sexual minorities' greater vulnerability to depression, Vol II: 137–139
      stress and women's greater vulnerability to depression, Vol II: 137
      stress factor, Vol II: 136
   heterosexual, Vol I: 367
   homosexual, Vol I: 367
   interpersonal factors
      and sexual minorities' vulnerability to depression, Vol II: 140–141
      and women's greater vulnerability to depression, Vol II: 139–140
   lesbian, Vol I: 367
   sexual minorities and heterosexuals
      developmental trends, Vol II: 136
   sexual orientation, definition of, Vol II: 364
   stress-mediation model of vulnerability to depression
      cognitive mechanisms, Vol II: 144–145
      interpersonal mechanisms, Vol II: 145
Sexual preference, Vol I: 367, 486, 538, 541
Sexual prejudice, Vol II: 577
Sexual script theory, Vol II: 289
Sexual Socialization Scale, Vol I: 144
Sexual strategies theory (SST), Vol II: 285
Sexual tension, *see* Cross-sex friendships
SFSCS, *see* Six factor self-concept scale (SFSCS)
Shavelson's model, Vol II: 31
Short-term mating strategy, Vol II: 285
Sibling violence, Vol II: 318–319
   brother-to-brother, Vol II: 319

Subject Index

SIM, *see* Standard Interactionist Model (SIM)
Simi/Mahalik study, Vol II: 203
Single/collaborative floors, talking time, Vol I: 389
Single-sex education, Vol I: 288, 289, 291
Single-sex education *vs.* co-education, Vol I: 288–289, 291
Single-sex group, Vol I: 385
Single-sex school, Vol I: 288
    effects, Vol I: 288
Sissy, Vol II: 578
Six factor self-concept scale (SFSCS), Vol II: 32
SLE, *see* Systemic lupus erythematosus (SLE)
SLN, *see* Sentinel lymph node (SLN) biopsies
Small talk, Vol I: 379, 386, 393–395, 404
Smile, Vol I: 89, 412, 414–415, 419, 430, 437, 445–446, 531
Smoking-Related Cancers and Breast Cancer in US, Vol II: 529
SMPY, *see* Study of Mathematically Precocious Youth (SMPY)
SMW, *see* Sexual minority women (SMW)
SNS, *see* Social networking sites (SNS)
SOC, *see* Sense of coherence (SOC)
Social age, Vol II: 645
Social categorization/social identity theory, Vol II: 348
Social construction, Vol I: 9, 29, 51, 116, 167, 192–193, 204, 260, 367, 401; Vol II: 9, 66, 72, 83, 122, 168–169, 174, 189, 191–192, 226, 255, 281, 615, 620, 671
Social context, importance of, Vol II: 21, 624
Social contextual factors/social motives, Vol II: 55–57
Social dominance orientation (SDO), Vol II: 362
Social ecological perspective, Vol II: 613
Social groups, Vol I: 1, 6, 160–161, 197, 269, 347, 371, 498, 513, 539
    culture, Vol I: 160
    ethnicity and race, Vol I: 160
    nationality, Vol I: 160–161
    society, Vol I: 160
Social–historical context, sport/exercise psychology
    biological/physical and competitive/hierarchical, highlights, Vol II: 564
    early women's sport and physical education, Vol II: 565
    gender and physical activity/exercise participation
        inactivity, risk factor for diseases, Vol II: 567
        Kimm, adolescent girl's activity tracking, Vol II: 567
    Olympic motto, Vol II: 564
    from 1970s to today's gendered sport
        female coaches, Kamphoff's dissertation research on, Vol II: 566
        Leanne Norman, arguments on UK coaching system, Vol II: 567
        1972 passage of Title IX, Vol II: 565–566
        Whites and Blacks, leadership roles, Vol II: 567
        WNBA data in USA, example, Vol II: 566
        women coaching men at Division I level, Vol II: 566
Social influence, advantage in, Vol II: 341
Socialization, practices, Vol II: 168
Social learning theories, Vol II: 282
Socially transmitted diseases/ disorders (STD), Vol II: 191
Social motives
    achievement, Vol II: 41
    affiliation–intimacy, Vol II: 41
    power, Vol II: 41
    reemergence of interest, Vol II: 42–43
    in women and men, measuring, Vol II: 43–44
Social networking sites (SNS), Vol II: 653–654
    alpha socializers and attention seekers, Vol II: 654
    Facebook, Vol II: 653
    Friendster, Vol II: 653
    functional users, men/boys, Vol II: 654
    MySpace, Vol II: 653
    non-users/intellectual rejecters, no gender differences, Vol II: 654
    qualitative investigation, effects, Vol II: 654
Social perception, Vol II: 580
Social rejection, Vol I: 431
Social roles across lifespan, changes in, Vol I: 570–573
    changing work and family roles, Vol I: 571–573
    concept of marriage, change in, Vol I: 572
    gender, roles, and well-being, Vol I: 570–571
        empty nest syndrome, Vol I: 571
    issues of parenting/grandparenting, Vol I: 572
    retirement, Vol I: 572
Social roles theory, Vol II: 20–21, 343, 427
Social/situational contexts, Vol II: 33–34
Social status, Vol I: 20, 31, 180, 384, 387, 443
Social structural theory, Vol I: 168, 475, 478, 484; Vol II: 288
Social support
    gender differences in, Vol II: 504–509
        direct effect and buffering models, Vol II: 505
        perceived *vs.* received social support, Vol II: 506–507
        social support networks, Vol II: 507–509
        structural and functional aspects, Vol II: 505–506
    and interpersonal stress, Vol II: 139–140
Social threshold hypothesis, Vol II: 113
Society for the Psychological Study of Men and Masculinity, Vol I: 46–48
Society for the Psychological Study of Social Issues Committee on Roles of Men and Women in Postwar Society, Vol I: 26
Society for the Psychological Study of Social Issues (SPSSI), Vol I: 26, 70
Sociobiology, Vol I: 36, 259–260
Sociobiology: The New Synthesis (Wilson E. O.), Vol I: 36
Sociocultural gender-based ideologies, Vol II: 625

Socio-ecological theories of mate preferences
    Buss's study (1989), Vol II: 288
    cultural variability in mate preferences, Vol II: 288
    girls' healthy sexuality (Tolman's view), Vol II: 287
    social structural theory (Eagly and Wood), Vol II: 288
Socioeconomic context, Vol II: 479–480
Socioeconomic gradient, Vol II: 479
Socioeconomic status (SES), Vol II: 528
Soft butches, Vol II: 371
Somatosensation, Vol I: 240–243
    analgesic effects, Vol I: 242
    emotions, Vol I: 242
        negatively valenced, Vol I: 242
        positively valenced, Vol I: 242
    estrogen–cytokine interaction, Vol I: 241
    higher arousal level (fear), Vol I: 242
    moderate arousal level (anxiety), Vol I: 242
    neuroimaging techniques, Vol I: 242
    pain disorders, Vol I: 241
        irritable bowel syndrome, Vol I: 241
    pain perception, Vol I: 240
    pain sensation, Vol I: 240
        chronic pain, Vol I: 241
        cold-pressure pain, Vol I: 241
        heat stimuli, Vol I: 240
    PET, Vol I: 242
    sex hormone changes, Vol I: 241
SOQ, *see* Sport Orientation Questionnaire (SOQ)
Sound perception, *see* Audition and vestibular perception
South African National Defence Force (SANDF), Vol II: 673
Spatial abilities, Vol I: 317–332
    biological factors, Vol I: 323–326
        brain organization, Vol I: 324–325
        evolutionary explanations, Vol I: 325–326
        hormonal influences, Vol I: 323–324
    cognitive processes, Vol I: 322–323
        spatial memory processes, Vol I: 322–323
        spatial strategies, Vol I: 322
    experiential and sociocultural factors, Vol I: 326–331
        sociocultural differences, Vol I: 326–327
        spatial experience, Vol I: 326
        stereotype threat, Vol I: 327
        training effects, Vol I: 327–328
        wayfinding, Vol I: 328–331
    gender and spatial abilities relationship, Vol I: 317
    relationship between
        androgen and spatial ability, Vol I: 324
        testosterone and spatial abilities, Vol I: 324
    and testosterone, androgen relationship, Vol I: 324
    types of, Vol I: 318–322
        dynamic spatial ability, Vol I: 322
        mental rotation, Vol I: 318
        object location memory, Vol I: 321
        spatial perception, Vol I: 319–320
        spatial visualization, Vol I: 320–321
    types of spatial abilities, Vol I: 318–322
        dynamic spatial ability, Vol I: 322
        mental rotation, Vol I: 318
        object location memory, Vol I: 321
        spatial perception, Vol I: 319–320
        spatial visualization, Vol I: 320–321
Spatial cognition, sex differences, Vol I: 7, 218, 262–265, 317, 331–332
    classic literature, Vol I: 263
    navigation, Vol I: 264–265
    object location memory
        reason, Vol I: 263–264
Spatial perception, Vol I: 318–320, 322, 325, 327–328, 331
    line-angle judgment task, Vol I: 320
    non-contextual rectangle task, Vol I: 320
    plumb-line task, Vol I: 319
    rod-and-frame test, Vol I: 319
    water-level task, Vol I: 319
Spatial visualization, Vol I: 302, 318, 320–321, 323, 326–327, 332
    block design, Vol I: 320
    embedded figures test, Vol I: 320
    paper folding, Vol I: 320
Speaking style
    of men, Vol I: 285, 379, 387–388, 404, 414–415
    of women, Vol I: 380, 383, 386, 404
Speaking time, Vol I: 412, 414–419, 421
Spontaneous talk, Vol I: 401
Sport and exercise psychology
    advancing gender research and social action, Vol II: 579–580
    framework for gender
        cultural sport studies, Vol II: 564
        gender issues, Vol II: 564
        gender psychology, Vol II: 564
        multicultural psychology, Vol II: 564
    gender and self-perceptions in sport
        gender, expectations, and participation, Vol II: 573–574
        physical activity and adolescent development, Vol II: 576–577
        physical activity, gender, and body image, Vol II: 574–576
    gender and sexuality in sport and physical activity
        homophobia and professional sport, Vol II: 577–578
        sexual harassment in sport and exercise, Vol II: 579
        sexual prejudice in non-professional sport and physical activity, Vol II: 578–579
    gender issues, Vol II: 564
    gender scholarship
        AASP conference programs, Vol II: 568
        cultural study perspectives (Fisher, Butryn, and Roper), Vol II: 568
        gender bias in media, Vol II: 571–573

Subject Index

gender differences and gender roles, Vol II: 569–571
race/ethnicity research, Duda and Allison, Vol II: 568
social–historical context
  biological/physical and competitive/hierarchical, highlights, Vol II: 564
  early women's sport and physical education, Vol II: 565
  gender and physical activity/exercise participation, Vol II: 567–568
  Olympic motto, Vol II: 564
  from 1970s to today's gendered sport, Vol II: 565–567
Sport competence, gender differences in (Eccles), Vol II: 573
Sport Orientation Questionnaire (SOQ), Vol II: 569
SRBS, see Sex Role Behavior Scale (SRBS)
SRS, see Sex reassignment surgery (SRS)
SRY gene, Vol I: 216–217
SSE, see Schedule of Sexist Events (SSE)
SSM, see Standard sociobiological model (SSM)
SSRIs, see Selected serotonin reuptake inhibitors (SSRIs)
SSSH, see Same-sex sexual harassment (SSSH)
SSSM, see Standard Social Science Model (SSSM)
SST, see Sexual strategies theory (SST)
Standard Cross-Cultural Sample, Vol I: 167
Standard Interactionist Model (SIM), Vol I: 261, 271–272
Standards for Educational and Psychological Testing, Vol II: 601, 604, 609
Standard Social Science Model (SSSM), Vol I: 259–261
  claims, Vol II: 259–260
Standard sociobiological model (SSM), Vol I: 260–262, 264–266, 268–271
Standing Committee for Men, Vol I: 45–46
Standing Ovation: Performing Social Science Research about Cancer, Vol I: 108
Stanford–Binet Intelligence Test, Vol I: 301–302
Status-based stressors, Vol II: 144–147
STDs, see Sexually transmitted diseases/disorders (STDs)
STEM, Vol II: 379
  engineering, Vol II: 379
  mathematics, Vol II: 379
  science, Vol II: 379
  technology, Vol II: 379
Stereotypes
  disadvantage, Vol II: 343
  and effects on group behavior, Vol II: 343–347
    agency and double standard, Vol II: 343–345
    communion and double bind, Vol II: 345–347
    medical treatments advertisements, Vol II: 343
    stereotypes, disadvantage, Vol II: 343

feminine gender role, Vol II: 94
of gender and aggression, Vol II: 312–314
  Bem Sex Role Inventory (BSRI)
  masculine task, Vol II: 344
  threat, Vol II: 48
Stereotypes/display rules, Vol I: 430–432
  accuracy of, Vol I: 432
    emotional regulation styles, Vol I: 432
    gender differences expression over experience, advantage, Vol I: 432
    self-reports or actual behavior, Vol I: 432
  emotional stereotypes, nature of, Vol I: 430–432
    Americans (intense/expressive/ruminated/less distracted), Vol I: 430–431
    counterstereotypic man/woman, Vol I: 431
    emotional expression over experience, advantage, Vol I: 431
    emotion-specific for womens/girls and mens/boys, Vol I: 431
    ethnic groups, comparison, Vol I: 431
    European Americans' beliefs over ethnic groups, advantage, Vol I: 431
    face expressions, Vol I: 431
    gender stereotypes, Vol I: 431
    negative social consequences, Vol I: 432
    social rejection, Vol I: 431
    stereotypic expectations/actual expressions, Vol I: 431
Stereotype threat, Vol I: 84–85, 284–285, 289, 306, 327, 353, 430, 433–434, 444, 447, 569
Stereotyping, gender, Vol I: 499–502
  definition
    action-based activities, Vol I: 500
  developmental trajectory
    dual process model, Vol I: 501
    possible consequences, Vol I: 514–517
    stereotype knowledge, attention, and memory, Vol I: 515
    stereotype knowledge, behaviors, and preferences, Vol I: 514–515
    stereotype use and adjustment, Vol I: 515–516
    stereotype use and intergroup relations, Vol I: 516–517
  See also Identity, gender
Steroid hormones, classification and synthesis of, Vol I: 215–220, 222–224, 226–227
  activational effects, Vol I: 215
  adrenal glands secretion, Vol I: 215
    androgens, Vol I: 215
    glucocorticoids, Vol I: 215
    mineralocorticoids, Vol I: 215
  behavior in childhood, Vol I: 219–220
    cognitive and motor skills, Vol I: 220
    gonadal activity, Vol I: 219
    play, Vol I: 219
  fetus, development of sex, Vol I: 216
  gonadal function, Vol I: 215

Steroid hormones (*cont.*)
    gonads secretion
        androgens, Vol I: 215
        estrogens, Vol I: 215
        progestins, Vol I: 215
    organizational effects, Vol I: 215
Stonewalling, Vol II: 265, 437
Street harassment, Vol I: 393
    See also Verbal harassment as dominance
STEM (science, technology, engineering, mathematics), Vol I: 11; Vol II: 379–382, 386–387, 389–391, 393–394
Strengths-based approach, Vol II: 613, 619
Strength-based counseling/therapy, Vol II: 232
Stress
    appraisals, types of, Vol II: 495
        appraisal process, Vol II: 496
        primary, Vol II: 495
        secondary, Vol II: 495
    coping and gender in diverse populations, Vol II: 509–510
    and coping, contextual model of, Vol II: 496
    and coping, gender differences, Vol II: 497–504
        chronic illness, Vol II: 500–502
        interpersonal stress, Vol II: 498–500
        work-related stress, Vol II: 502–504
    and coping in women and men, Vol II: 510–511
        social support, Vol II: 504
    and women's greater vulnerability to depression
        chronic strain of gender role, Vol II: 137
        lower social status and power, cause, Vol II: 137
        victimization
            child sexual abuse, Vol II: 137
            domestic violence, Vol II: 137
            rape victims, Vol II: 137
Stress-mediation model of vulnerability to depression
    acute/chronic stressors, impact on women and sexual minorities, Vol II: 143
    cognitive mechanisms
        bereaved gay men, study of, Vol II: 144
        community-based LGB/heterosexual adolescents, study of, Vol II: 144–145
        gender and sexual orientation disparities, factors, Vol II: 143
    interpersonal mechanisms, Vol II: 145
Stroop effect, Vol I: 237–238
Structural equation modeling (SEM), Vol I: 86, 88, 90, 92, 95, 97, 297
Study of dominance, Vol I: 387
Study of Mathematically Precocious Youth (SMPY), Vol I: 310
Support for and adherence to cultural gender norms, measures of, Vol I: 134–144
    Child Gender Socialization scale, Vol I: 144
    gendered behavior measures, Vol I: 139–143
        CAH, Vol I: 139
        CBAQ, Vol I: 140
        CBAQ-F, Vol I: 140
        CBAQ-M, Vol I: 140–141
        Games Inventory, Vol I: 140
        gender diagnosticity, Vol I: 143
        gender dysphoria (GDI), Vol I: 141
        gender identity, Vol I: 142
        GID, Vol I: 139
        GIDYQ-AA, Vol I: 141–142
        recalled childhood gender identity/gender role questionnaire, Vol I: 141
        SRBS, Vol I: 142–143
    gender socialization, Vol I: 143–144
    ideology measures, Vol I: 136–139
        AFIS, Vol I: 138
        AMIRS, Vol I: 137
        BMS, Vol I: 136
        CFNI, Vol I: 139
        CMNI, Vol I: 138
        FIS, Vol I: 139
        MRAS, Vol I: 137
        MRNI, Vol I: 137–138
        MRNS, Vol I: 136–137
    Sexual Socialization Scale, Vol I: 144
    trait measures, Vol I: 134–136
        BSRI, Vol I: 134–135
        PAQ, Vol I: 134–136
Support gap theory, Vol II: 507
Surveillance, Epidemiology, and End Results (SEER), Vol II: 526
Swearing, Vol I: 146, 392; Vol II: 315, 427
Swimsuit study, Vol II: 659
Symptom differences and treatment seeking, depression, Vol II: 135
Systemic lupus erythematosus (SLE), Vol II: 542
Systemizers, Vol I: 309

T

Tag question formations, Vol I: 380–381, 385, 404
Talking time, Vol I: 388–389
    and power relationship, Vol I: 388–389
    single/collaborative floors, Vol I: 389
Task Force on Men's Roles in Psychotherapy, Vol I: 46
TAT, *see* Thematic apperception test (TAT)
Teacher behaviors, Vol I: 279, 283
Teachers' preferential treatment of boys, Vol II: 385
Teaching styles, Vol I: 285, 287, 291
Tearoom Trade, Vol II: 597
Teenage mutant ninja turtles (TMNT), Vol II: 656
Temporal experience of pleasure scale (TEPS), Vol II: 35
Tend-and-befriend theory, Vol II: 505
TEPS, *see* Temporal experience of pleasure scale (TEPS)
Terminology, Vol I: 2, 8, 13, 59–60, 62, 171, 362, 367–368, 471
    androcentricism, Vol I: 60
    gender, definition, Vol I: 59–60
    gender identity, Vol I: 60
    gender nonconforming, Vol I: 60

Subject Index

gender normative, Vol I: 60
sexual orientation, Vol I: 60
transgender, Vol I: 60
Testicular examinations, Vol II: 532
Testosterone, Vol I: 49, 83, 216, 226, 239, 241, 270–271, 323–324, 330–331, 483–484, 486–487, 533–534, 568; Vol II: 286
    treatment, Vol II: 99
Tests for selection, SAT/GRE
    gender bias complexity, example, Vol II: 72
    psychological tests, Vol II: 71–72
Texas A&M University Corps of Cadets, Vol II: 678
TFEQ, *see* Three-Factor Eating Questionnaire (TFEQ)
The Institute for Diversity and Ethics in Sport, Vol II: 572
The L Word, Vol II: 645
Thematic apperception test (TAT), Vol II: 41
Themes of gender bias
    First football, then men's basketball, and then everything else, Vol II: 572
    He was always on my mind, Vol II: 572
    Parents are noteworthy, especially athletic fathers, Vol II: 572
    Race only matters for men, Vol II: 572
    She must have played with the boys to get that good, Vol II: 572
    Straight is great, but gay is nowhere, Vol II: 572
Theories of gender and sexuality
    cognitive social learning theory, Vol I: 474–475
    evolutionary psychology, Vol I: 473–474
    gender schema theory, Vol I: 476
    neo-analytic theory, Vol I: 473
    psychoanalytic theory, Vol I: 471–472
    social structural theory, Vol I: 475
    See also Individual
Theory of Mental Tests (Gulliksen), Vol II: 66
Theory & Psychology, Vol I: 117
Therapy retention rates, Vol II: 242
Therapy with women scale (TWS), Vol II: 201
The Rules (Fein & Schneider, 2005), Vol II: 290
The Sport Psychologist, Vol II: 568
The Tucker Center (2007), Vol II: 577
Thin ideal, Vol I: 13, 97; Vol II: 13, 159–161, 164, 166, 169
Third gender, Vol I: 486; Vol II: 114, 631
Third-generation literature, identity/diversity/descriptive research
    bisexuality, Vol I: 65–66
        American Institute of Bisexuality, Vol I: 66
        The Bisexual Option (Fritz Klein), Vol I: 66
        Journal of Bisexuality, Vol I: 66
        KSOG, Vol I: 66
    gender differences
        gender-role socialization, Vol I: 64
        lesbian, gay, and bisexual youths, Vol I: 67–68
            risk of HIV infection, Vol I: 68
            victimization of LGB youths, Vol I: 68

race, ethnicity, and culture, Vol I: 64–65
    effects of multiple marginalized identities, Vol I: 65
    experiences of racial and ethnic LGBT individuals, Vol I: 65
    studies on White individuals/White gay men, Vol I: 64
relationships/families and parenting, Vol I: 66–67
    Committee on Psychosocial Aspects of Child and Family Health, Vol I: 67
    families headed by LGB people, Vol I: 67
    families of choice, Vol I: 67
    family issues of LGB people, Vol I: 67
    gay baby boom, Vol I: 67
    LGB and heterosexual couples, major differences, Vol I: 66
sexual prejudice and heterosexism, Vol I: 68–69
    depression/alcoholism and other substance-related problems, Vol I: 69
    heterosexism, definition, Vol I: 68
    impact of, Vol I: 68–69
Third interstitial nucleus of the anterior hypothalamus (INAH3), Vol I: 217
Three-Factor Eating Questionnaire (TFEQ), Vol I: 457
Time-consuming major household tasks, Vol II: 407
Time use, Vol II: 404, 407–408, 416, 478
Tip-of-the-nose phenomenon, Vol I: 248
Title IX of the Education Amendments (1972), Vol I: 281; Vol II: 187
TMNT, *see* Teenage mutant ninja turtles (TMNT)
Torrance tests, creative thinking, Vol I: 349–350
    elaboration, Vol I: 349
    flexibility, Vol I: 349
    fluency, Vol I: 349
    originality, Vol I: 349
Total household labor, Vol II: 407
Toward a New Psychology of Women, Vol I: 105
Toward a Redefinition of Sex and Gender in Psychology, Vol I: 29
Traditional cultural models, Vol II: 473
Traditional games, Vol II: 651
Trait measures, Vol I: 134–136, 435
    BSRI, Vol I: 134–135
    PAQ, Vol I: 134–136
Transgender
    countless self-labels, Vol II: 114
    female to male transsexual (FtM), Vol I: 487
    gender dysphoric disorder, Vol I: 486–487
    gender reassignment, Vol I: 487
    male to female transsexual (MtF), Vol I: 487
    See also Gender differences in sexuality
Transgendered individuals, *see* Transgenderism
Transgendered persons, Vol I: 9, 71, 368; Vol II: 631
Transgenderism, Vol I: 368–369, 486
Transitioning, Vol II: 119–120, 240, 301, 368

Translation, issues with, Vol I: 170–173
  back-translation, Vol I: 171
  decentering, Vol I: 172
  equivalence of translation, Vol I: 171–172
  management of problems with translation, Vol I: 172–173
  response styles, Vol I: 172
Transpeople, Vol I: 369
Transsexualism, Vol I: 368–369
Trauma and Recovery (Herman), Vol II: 208
Trauma Content Index, Vol II: 209
Trauma strain, Vol I: 50–51
Trauma Symptom Inventory (TSI), Vol II: 209
Trends/directions, LGBT
  brief history, Vol I: 69–70
  from categories to complexity, fourth generation, Vol I: 72
  creation of journals, Vol I: 59–60
  gender/transgender issues, Vol I: 70–71
  sexual orientation, Vol I: 72
Trichromatic theory, Vol I: 236
Tripartite model of social influence, Vol II: 164–168
  media, Vol II: 166–168
  parents, Vol II: 164–165
  peers, Vol II: 165–166
Triple jeopardy, Vol II: 259
TS, *see* Turner's syndrome (TS)
TSI, *see* Trauma Symptom Inventory (TSI)
Turner's syndrome (TS), Vol I: 218–219
Turn-taking norms, Vol I: 390, 412
Two cultures approach, Vol I: 65, 164–166, 385, 399
  miscommunication models, Vol I: 385
    critique of, Vol I: 386–387
Two-Spirit People, Vol II: 144
TWS, *see* Therapy with women scale (TWS)

U
UCR, *see* Uniform Crime Reporting program (UCR)
Ultra-masculine in man-to-man harassment, *see* "Not man enough" harassment
Umami, Vol II: 246
UNFPA, *see* United Nations Population Fund (UNFPA)
Uniform Crime Reporting program (UCR), Vol II: 608
United Nations Development Programme, Vol II: 443, 445
United Nations Population Fund (UNFPA), Vol I: 277–278
Universal human abilities, culture issues
  American Psychological Association Ethics Code, test standards by, Vol II: 66
  classical testing theories/psychometrics, challenges IRT, Vol II: 67
    social constructionist and postmodern theorists, Vol II: 66
Unmatched Count Technique, Vol II: 602
Unmitigated agency, gender-role traits, Vol II: 23
Unmitigated communion, Vol II: 23, 295

Unwanted sexual attention, Vol II: 424, 430, 681
US Bureau of Labor Statistics, Vol II: 337, 351, 431, 444
US Department of Education (USDOE), Vol I: 288, 291
US Department of Health and Human Services (DHHS), Vol II: 317
US Department of Health and Human Services (USDHHS), Vol II: 567
USDHHS, *see* US Department of Health and Human Services (USDHHS)
USDOE, *see* US Department of Education (USDOE)
US Marine Corps colonel, Vol II: 675
  organization for a common goal, Vol II: 675
  presence of or potential for danger, Vol II: 675
  willingness to sacrifice, Vol II: 675
US National Center for Educational Statistics, Vol II: 445
US personality research, Vol II: 27
Utility value, Vol I: 310

V
Variance ratio (VR), Vol I: 299, 304–305
Vassar College, Vol II: 565
Verbal ability, Vol I: 89, 222, 225, 299–302, 305–306, 308, 310, 350, 415, 496
  gender similarities and differences
    in means, Vol I: 305
    in variance, Vol I: 305
Verbal aggression, Vol II: 312
  forms of, Vol II: 427
Verbal behavior, Vol I: 382, 387, 413, 416, 420
Verbal communication, Vol I: 400, 412
Verbal harassment as dominance, Vol I: 393
Vestibular perception, Vol I: 243–246
Verticality, Vol I: 266, 270, 319, 416
Video games
  male/female ratio (3:1) engaged, Vol II: 650–651
  natural cognitive abilities, sex differences, Vol II: 651
  research in college population (Lucas and Sherry), Vol II: 651
  sensorimotor games, genre form, Vol II: 651
  traditional/physical/imagination games, women/men perspectives, Vol II: 651
Vietnam War veterans, Vol II: 100
Violence
  and aggression toward children and elderly family members, Vol II: 317–318
    caretakers' stress and depression, Vol II: 317
    NCEA, Vol II: 318
    NEAIS, Vol II: 318
    parental stress, Vol II: 318
    physical child abuse, Vol II: 317
    US Department of Health and Human Services (DHHS), Vol II: 317
    See also Aggression
  and aggression toward children/elderly family members, Vol II: 317–318

Subject Index

in everyday life/personal experiences of, Vol II: 315–316
Virtual negotiations, Vol I: 96
Visceral pain disorders, Vol I: 241–242
Vision, sex differences in, Vol I: 235–240
    BOLD fMRI, Vol I: 237
    EEGs, Vol I: 238
    M cells, Vol I: 236
    men's and women's vision, differences in, Vol I: 236
    MRT, Vol I: 238
    optical coherence tomography, Vol I: 236
    P300, Vol I: 238
    P cells, Vol I: 236
    PCR genetic analysis
        four-pigment heterozygotes, Vol I: 237
    photopigments, Vol I: 236
    photoreceptor cells, Vol I: 235
        cone cells, Vol I: 235
        rod cells, Vol I: 235
    RGCs, Vol I: 236
    stroop effect, Vol I: 237–238
    trichromatic theory, Vol I: 236
    types of photopigments, Vol I: 236
Visual–spatial ability, Vol I: 240, 279–280, 301, 311–312
VNO, see Vomeronasal organ (VNO)
Vocational Educational Act (1976), Vol I: 281
Volume of words, see Talking time
Vomeronasal organ (VNO), Vol I: 248
VR, see Variance ratio (VR)

W

WAIS, see Wechsler Adult Intelligence Scale (WAIS)
Wait and see disease, see Rheumatoid arthritis (RA)
Water-level task, see Spatial perception
Wayfinding, Vol I: 7, 317–332
    Euclidean-based strategies, Vol I: 330
WCQ, see Women and Counselling Questionnaire (WCQ)
Wechsler Adult Intelligence Scale (WAIS), Vol I: 301–302, 569
Wechsler Intelligence Scale for Children (WISC), Vol I: 301
The Wedding Banquet, Vol II: 261
Weight concerns, women
    motivation for smoking, Vol II: 479
Wellness and transcendence, studying, Vol II: 34–35
Western medical institutions, Vol II: 366
WHI, see Women's Health Initiative (WHI)
White-collar jobs, Vol II: 227
Whorfian hypothesis, Vol I: 361
WHO, see World Health Organization (WHO)
WISC, see Wechsler Intelligence Scale for Children (WISC)
WNBA, see Women's National Basketball Association (WNBA)
WNT 4 gene, Vol I: 217
Wolffian tract, Vol I: 216–217

enzyme 5-α reductase, Vol I: 216
Leydig cells, Vol I: 216
Woman-blaming approach, see Assertiveness training
Woman to woman harassment, Vol II: 431
Women and Counselling Questionnaire (WCQ), Vol II: 202
Women and Madness, Vol I: 27; Vol II: 188
Women at mid-century, psychology and/of, Vol I: 23–26
    APA, Vol I: 24
    code of menstrual invalidism, Vol I: 26
    elevation of the traditionally feminine values (Seward), Vol I: 26
    ECP, Vol I: 23
    intelligence test, development and use, Vol I: 23
    NCWP, Vol I: 24
    Northside Center for Child Development in 1946, Vol I: 25
    racism and sexism/anti-semitism and sexism, Vol I: 25
    Society for the Psychological Study of Social Issues Committee on Roles of Men and Women in Postwar Society, Vol I: 26
    women's proportionate lack of prestige, reason, Vol I: 25
Women in leader roles, representation of, Vol II: 443–445
Women in the Community, issue on, Vol II: 627
Women, role of
    decision-making authority, Vol II: 444
    domestic responsibilities, Vol II: 445
    as entrepreneurs, Vol II: 445
    in managerial roles, Vol II: 443
    as political leaders, Vol II: 444
Women's and men's employment
    participation in housework, Vol II: 409
    time availability hypothesis, Vol II: 408–409
    See also Household labor
Women's Counseling Services, Vol II: 190
Women's deficits remediation, Vol I: 382–385
    assertiveness training, Vol I: 382–383
        research on, Vol I: 383
    negotiations deficit
        critique of, Vol I: 384–385
        in women's communication, Vol I: 383–384
Women's Educational Equity Act (1974), Vol I: 281
Women's gender-role socialization, Vol II: 100
Women's Health Book Collective, Vol II: 523
Women's Health Initiative (WHI), Vol I: 185
    clinical trial (CT) and an observational study (OS), Vol I: 185
Women's Language, Vol I: 381–382, 387, 399, 402
Women's Liberation Movement, Vol I: 1, 6, 10, 20, 26, 361; Vol II: 565
Women's Movement, Vol II: 46, 113
    influence of political/ cultural activities of, Vol II: 31
Women's National Basketball Association (WNBA), Vol II: 566

Women's proportionate lack of prestige, reason, Vol I: 25
Women's talk, Vol I: 385–386, 393–400
   gossip, Vol I: 395–399
   men's deficiencies, Vol I: 399–400
   minimal responses, Vol I: 394
   placing value on, Vol I: 393–394
   small talk, Vol I: 394–395
Women's Ways of Knowing, Vol I: 31, 105
Work–family issues, Vol II: 445–446
   in military, Vol II: 686–689
      balancing work and family, Vol II: 687–688
      work–family policies of various countries, Vol II: 688–689
Work-life balance, Vol I: 11–12; Vol II: 11–12, 382, 687–688
Workplace bullying, Vol II: 424
Workplace mistreatment
   concepts (Andersson and Pearson)
      aggression, violence, and incivility, Vol II: 424
      organizational deviance, definition, Vol II: 424
      sexual harassment, Vol II: 424
      workplace bullying, Vol II: 424
   gendered frameworks of antecedents
      Buss' framework of aggression, Vol II: 427–428
      contextual influences on mistreatment, Vol II: 428
      incivility, Vol II: 426–427
      sexual harassment, Vol II: 425–426
   gendered frameworks of antecedents of
      Buss' framework of aggression, Vol II: 427–428
      Cortina's multi-level theory, Vol II: 426
      Cortina's (2008) selective incivility theory, Vol II: 426
      Cortina's (2008) theory of selective incivility, Vol II: 426
      organizational climate, impact, Vol II: 428
      rogue sexism, Vol II: 426
      selective incivility, Vol II: 426
   gendered profiles of targets and perpetrators
      bullying, Vol II: 429–430
      incivility, Vol II: 429
      sexual harassment, Vol II: 430–431
      workplace aggression/violence, Vol II: 431
   impact on men/women
      psychological and physical consequences, Vol II: 436
      work-related consequences, Vol II: 436–437
   reactions to
      appraisal processes, Vol II: 432–433
      coping processes, Vol II: 433–435
      escalating aggression, Vol II: 435
   sexual harassment
      power, leading cause, Vol II: 425
      sex-based social status, Vol II: 425
      sexual expression, forms of (Berdahl), Vol II: 426
      societal/organizational disparities, men/women, Vol II: 425
      tolerance–sexual harassment relationship, Vol II: 428
Workplace violence, Vol II: 322
   expressed hostility/obstructionism/overt aggression, Vol II: 322
   interpersonal violence, Vol II: 322
   organization violence, Vol II: 322
   See also Aggression
World Health Organization (WHO), Vol II: 133, 481
World Professional Association for Transgender Health (WPATH), Vol II: 125
Worldviews of women and men, Vol I: 386
World War II (WWII), Vol I: 6, 23, 26
WPATH, *see* World Professional Association for Transgender Health (WPATH)
Wundt's laboratory (1879), Vol II: 1

Y
Youth Risk Behavior Survey, Vol II: 576

Z
Zoloft, Vol II: 520

Printed in the United States of America